A Dictionary
of
Surnames

A DICTIONARY
—OF—
SURNAMES

Mark Antony Lower

Wordsworth Editions

First published as *A Dictionary of the Family Names of the United Kingdom*
by John Russell Smith, London, and G.P. Bacon, Lewes, 1860.

This edition published 1988 by Wordsworth Editions Ltd,
8b East Street, Ware, Hertfordshire.

ISBN 1-85326-916-6

Printed and bound in Great Britain by Mackays of Chatham.

PRELIMINARY DISSERTATION.

I.

𝕿𝔥𝔢 𝕺𝔯𝔦𝔤𝔦𝔫 𝔞𝔫𝔡 𝕻𝔯𝔬𝔤𝔯𝔢𝔰𝔰 𝔬𝔣 𝕾𝔲𝔯𝔫𝔞𝔪𝔢 𝕷𝔦𝔱𝔢𝔯𝔞𝔱𝔲𝔯𝔢.

THE illustrious Camden, " Nourice of Antiquitie," has been happily termed the common fire whereat all after-coming British antiquaries "have kindled their little torches." The *Britannia*, one of the finest literary projects ever carried into execution, is the basis of all British topography, and needs no commendation; but there is another of his works which, though trivial in bulk, and held in much less consideration than the " Chorographical Description," is of greater positive value, as containing the germ of all modern antiquarianism. I allude to the " *Remaines concerning Britain.*" This comparatively small volume consists of some fourteen essays on various branches of archæology, which are not only highly curious and original in themselves, but most suggestive of more elaborate enquiries and illustrations; in fact each essay is a brief upon which large pleadings may be based—the foundation whereon a spacious structure may be reared. For example, the essay on " Money" is the first attempt that was made to illustrate the coinage of these realms, long before such a science as numismatics was dreamed of. Again, the dissertation on " Apparell " is the groundwork of subsequent treatises on British costume. The chapter on " Languages" is a curious piece of philology; and the rest all serve more or less as themes upon which many volumes have since been written. One of the best of these prolusions is that on " SURNAMES," extending in the ' sixth impression,' 1657, to more than fifty pages. It shows great and original research, and it has been extensively made use of by all subsequent writers on the subject. The great antiquary, after a sketch of the history of second or *sur*-names in different ages and countries, traces the first appearance of settled family names in England about the time of the Norman Conquest. He next treats of Local names in the two classes of which they consist; namely, first, those which are derived from the *names* of specific localities, towns, villages, manors, &c.; and, secondly, those which allude to the *situation* of the residences of the original bearers, such as Field, Cliffe, Wood, &c. Then follow remarks on surnames derived from Occupations and Professions; from Offices and Functions, civil and ecclesiastical;

from "Qualities of the Minde;" from "Habitudes of Body;" from Ages and Times; from the Weapons of War borne by the first of the name; from Parts of the Body; from Costume; from the Colours of complexion and clothing; from Flowers and Fruits; from Animals, whether Beasts, Birds, or Fishes; from Christian Names; from Nicknames or 'Nursenames;' from By-names (sobriquets); and from Signs of Houses. All these are illustrated by examples and curious anecdotes; and the dissertation is wound up with remarks on Changed and Corrupted surnames, Latinizations of surnames in ancient charters, and references to analogies in classical nomenclature. As a whole, there are few essays of the period more readable or instructive than this of Camden on Surnames.

The next illustrator of the subject is Verstegan, who, in his *Restitution of Decayed Intelligence in Antiquities concerning our Nation*, published in 1605, devotes a Chapter to the enquiry " How by the Surnames of the families in England, it may be discerned from whence they take their Originals, to wit, whether from the ancient English Saxons, or from the Danes and Normans." This Chapter is mostly based upon Camden, and has little value, either historical or philological. A few of his definitions will sufficiently demonstrate this :—

" Bolt, of the straightness of his body.
" Cole, of his blackness.
" Dod, of that thing anciently so called which groweth in the sides of waters among flags, and is of boys called a fox-tail.
" Gower, of a certain kind of cake.
" Rows, of his making a noise !
" Russel, of his fatness.
" Stone, *of some cause concerning it !*
" Yong, of his fewness of years."

After Verstegan, I am not aware of any British writer who undertook to illustrate this curious subject, except in the most desultory manner, until a comparatively recent date. N. Bailey, in his *English Dictionary*, gives definitions of many surnames, and there are detached articles in many of the Magazines of the last century. The best of these are the Essays which appeared in the *Gentleman's Magazine* for 1772. These were written by the Rev. Dr. Pegge, F.S.A., under the pseudonym of T. Row. Some time in the last century was printed Buchanan *On Ancient Scottish Surnames* (re-printed 1820): but the title misleads, as the subject of the book is the history of some Scottish clans. In 1804 the Rev. Mark Noble, F.S.A., published *A History of the College of Arms*, in the preliminary dissertation of which, there are some good incidental remarks on family names.

In *Archæologia*, vol. XVIII. pp. 105, 111, James H. Markland, Esq., D.C.L., F.S.A., printed a valuable paper, entitled " Remarks on the Antiquity and Introduction of Surnames into England." This appeared in 1813.

In 1822, Mr. J. H. Brady published a small duodecimo volume called *A Dissertation on the Names of Persons*, which, among much amusing, though irrelevant matter, contains several ingenious remarks on English surnames ; and the Rev. Edward Duke's *Halle of John Halle*, furnishes some illustrations of the subject.

Such were the materials at the command of the student of our family nomenclature when, about the year 1836, my attention was first directed to its investigation, though at that time my residence in a village, remote from libraries, rendered these materials all to me as if they had not existed; and, indeed, my own researches were conducted in total ignorance of there having been any labourer in this field before me.

Some years before that, in my early boyhood, I had accidentally met with Horne Tooke's *Diversions of Purley*. Attracted by the title, which seemed to promise some stories of " fun and frolic," I opened the book, read, and was arrested by the wonderful genius of the author, though there was much upon his pages that transcended my boyish range of thought. That book, then, directed my mind—always desirous *causas rerum cognoscere*—into a channel of investigation, which while it has entailed upon me no small amount of toil, has also been the consolation of a too anxious and too laborious existence.

The result of my desultory studies of Surnames first appeared in the columns of a provincial newspaper—the *Sussex Express*—at irregular intervals during the year 1838. In the following year these scraps were published in a pamphlet of 68 pages, bearing the title of " The Book of English Surnames, being a short Essay on their Origin and Signification." The impression, like the book itself, was very small, but some copies of it having fallen into the hands of gentlemen interested in the subject, I was encouraged to enlarge my plan. Accordingly in 1842, I published " English Surnames, Essays on Family Nomenclature, Historical, Etymological, and Humorous," London, post 8vo. pp. 240. Of this a considerable edition was sold in about nine months; and in 1843 a second and enlarged edition (pp. 292) appeared. This was followed in 1849, by a third and still augmented edition in two volumes post octavo, (pp. xxiv. and 264, and pp. vi. and 244), my last publication on the subject.

Encouraged by such a measure of success, I began to make notes for the present work, feeling persuaded that I had not over-estimated the interest of the subject as a curious, but as yet an imperfectly developed branch of archæology and philology. In this design I was urged on by numerous communications from almost every part of the world where the English language is spoken, and where British Surnames are borne. Hundreds, nay, thousands, of letters, a few conveying—but the great majority seeking—information as to the names of the writers, reached me, and the process is still going on. So much, at present, for the procuring causes of the *Patronymica Britannica*.

I shall now give a brief account of the various contributions to this department of English literature since my earliest treatise on the subject, whether as independent works or as communications to periodical publications.

Mr. John, now Dr., O'Donovan, whose antiquarian learning requires no commendation from me, printed in the " Irish Penny Journal " (Dublin, 1841), a series of six able articles on the Origin and Meaning of Irish Family Names. Of his labours I have freely availed myself.

In 1842, the Rev. C. W. Bradley, M.A., Rector of Christ Church, Connecticut, published a small brochure entitled " Patronomatology, an Essay on the Philosophy of Surnames." 8vo. Baltimore, U.S. To the author of this essay, which evinces considerable ability and research, I owe many thanks.

In 1846, the late eminent scholar, John M. Kemble, Esq., M.A., published a small pamphlet on the Names, Surnames and Nicknames of the Anglo-Saxons; but this, relating as it does to a period antecedent to the adoption of hereditary or family names, possesses little in common with my specific object.

The Edinburgh Review for April, 1855, contains a considerable article on English Surnames. The classification adopted is : " 1st. Norman names dating from the Conquest. 2nd. Local English Names. 3rd. Names of Occupation. 4th. Derivatives from the Christian Names of father or mother. 5th. Names given on account of personal peculiarities. 6th. Names derived from the animal, mineral, and vegetable kingdoms. 7th. Names derived from the Celestial Hierarchy. 8th. Irish, Scotch,

French, Flemish, Dutch, German, Spanish and other continental names, mainly imported within the last two centuries." Of the able and scholarly writer of this article I have to complain that, although he has based his remarks chiefly upon my "English Surnames," the title of which he has adopted, and although he would not apparently have written his essay without the assistance of my previous researches, he has but slightly acknowledged me, and has mis-spelt my name on each occasion of its being mentioned, though he has paraded at the head of his article the titles of a French and a German publication,* both of which, though excellent in their kind, touch but incidentally, and then not always correctly, upon the subject of English family names! I trust that there are not many public critics in our land to whom the *insidentes humeris non sine supercilio* would so justly apply as to this Edinburgh Reviewer.†

The first attempt at a *Dictionary* of Surnames, at least in our language, that I have seen, is that by B. H. Dixon, Esq., K.N.L., formerly of Boston in the United States, now of Toronto in Canada. It was first privately printed at Boston in 1855 ; 8vo. pp. xviii. 80. This was suppressed by the author, who issued a second edition in 1857; 8vo. xxvi. 86. The work illustrates a few hundreds only of surnames, many of which are German, Dutch, French, &c. The Introduction is very interesting and amusing, and has afforded me some assistance.

In 1857 also appeared at Boston, a work entitled *Suffolk Surnames*,‡ by N. J. Bowditch, Esq., 8vo. pp. 108. This was followed in 1858 by a greatly enlarged edition—a handsome octavo of 384 pages. Mr. Bowditch has arranged, in a most humorous and amusing manner, such names as had occurred to his professional notice as a conveyancer, in deeds, &c., as well as those which he had met with in various directories, subscription-lists, and similar collections of names. He observes that his volume might bear the title of " Directories Digested; or the Romance of the Registry."

I am sure that my reader will excuse, while the author will pardon, my making a few extracts from this singular and entertaining *melange* of Surnames. It is right to bear in mind that the author has "sometimes regarded their apparent, rather than their actual, derivations and original meanings." Mr. Bowditch acknowledges the assistance he received from the article in the *Edinburgh Review* above mentioned, and from Mr. Dixon's publication, as well as from what he is pleased to call my "elaborate essay." He adds : " Had I seen these publications at an earlier period, the great extent of the subject would have deterred me altogether." I am sure that many, in common with myself, will feel glad that Mr. Bowditch's reading in this direction was originally thus limited.

I shall make, quite at random, an inroad into Mr. Bowditch's pleasant pages, as the very best method that I could adopt of exhibiting the vast and odd variety of family nomenclature. At the same time I must remind the reader, that many of the names borne on the other side of the Atlantic are from sources unconnected with England, Scotland, Wales, and Ireland, to which the present volume is devoted. The American nation comprises the greatest admixture of races yet experienced in the history of the world; and family names of every imaginable origin are, therefore, to be found in that country. I cannot perhaps more forcibly illustrate this, than by

---

* Essai Historique et Philosophique sur les Noms d'Hommes, de Peuples, et de Lieux. Par Eusèbe Salverte. 2 vols. 8vo. Paris, 1824.

Die Personennamen insbesondere die Familiennamen und ihre Entstehungsarten auch unter Berücksichtigung der Ortsnamen. Von August Friedrich Pott. Leipzig, 1853.

† The Quarterly Review, for April, 1860, has treated my labours much more handsomely.

‡ Suffolk County consists of the city of Boston, and its suburb, Chelsea.

giving the following singular list of names of three letters, as extracted from the *New York Directory*. It will be seen that very few of them are English:

Abt	Ast	Ber	Daw	Etz	Kab	Mas	Nix	Rad	See	Utz
Ach	Atz	Bli	Dax	Erb	Kas	Max	Olt	Rau	Sim	Vey
Adt	Aug	Boe	Dod	Erk	Kip	Mon	Ort	Ree	Syz	Voy
Aey	Aul	Boh	Don	Ery	Kos	Naf	Ott	Rek	Uch	Wex
Ahl	Aur	Bom	Dun	Igo	Len	Nam	Otz	Roh	Ulm	Wey
Ahm	Bal	Bos	Ege	Ihl	Loy	Nee	Pia	Ruc	Unz	Wie
Alt	Bek	Bow	Elz	Ing	Lus	Neu	Pim	Sam	Ure	Yhn
Arl	Bem	Bub	Epp	Jex	Luz	Ney	Qua	Sax	Utt	Yoe

Bowditch. p. 10.

"Mr. Augur has a case now pending, which his opponent doubtless feels to be a bore: he is of an old family. A Mr. Augur appears in 1658; and Mr. Augurs received the notice of our forefathers in 1671. Both Sibel and Sibell are found in New York. Mr. Soldem has ventured to bring a suit. Our Messrs. Parson, Parsons, Shriever, Friar, Friary, Priest, Divine, Deacon, Creed, Quaker, Church, Pray, and Revere, are probably not more pious than our Mr. Pagan or Mr. Turk. Both Mr. Churchman and Mr. Mussalman live in New York; also Messrs. Bigot, Munk, and Nunns. Mr. Rosery lives at Lockport, C. W.; Dr. Kirkbride at Philadelphia; also Messrs. Bigot, Bapst, and Musselman. Mr. Layman, in 1857, committed a murder at the South, and will doubtless be hung without benefit of clergy. Mr. Praed, one of England's sweetest poets, has by no means confined his muse to sacred themes. Dr. Verity lives at Haysville, C.W. An English clergyman, the Rev. Arundel Verity, falsely and fraudulently converted to his own use, funds designed for conversion of the heathen. Mr. Newgate (1651) was not an escaped convict; nor does it appear that Mr. Selman (1674) was a slaveholder. Mr. Mothersell lives at Kingston, C.W. No clerical associations surround the name of Rev. William Youngblood of New York. A Dr. Youngblood lives at Sandwich, C.W. Pleasant M. Mask of Holly Springs, Miss., treacherously murdered a young lady in 1857. We have both the Bible and the Coran in our directory. Mr. Pastor makes casks instead of converts, and can operate better upon hoops than upon heathens; but though our Pastor is a cooper, our Cooper was the best of pastors."—Pp. 23, 24.

"We have Angel, (what a misnomer for a lawyer! unless derived from the *coin*, when it becomes appropriate); Bogle, a spectre; Geist, the German for spirit; Soul, Fay, and Mabb; also Warloch. We have also Engal and Engals, from the German for "angel." Mr. Puck lives in New York. Mr. Wand, of that city, deals in *spirits*. Our Mr. Paradise did not venture on the Eden of matrimony without making a marriage settlement, duly recorded (L.653, f. 284). We have also Soll (Latin for *sun*); Mond (German for *moon*); Moon, Moone, Starr, Starrs, and Star. Mr. Solis prefers the genitive case. We have also Cloud. The attorney-general of Iowa is named Cloud. Mr. Cloudman lives at Levant. I find but one Sky. Sky, indeed, has been extensively used up in ending off names in Poland! Skey lives in Philadelphia. Elsewhere there are families of Heaven, Devil, and Hell. In the New York Directory there are ten families of Hellman. Mr. Helhouse was an English author in 1819. Among the graduates of Yale, are three named Dibble. Mr. Dibble lives at Brookfield, Connecticut; Mr. Teufel (German for *devil*) at Bridgeport; and this last is common in New York. Indeed, our name of Holl is, I believe, pronounced as if spelt with an *e*. And we have Deuell, Diehl, Devlin, and Debell. Himmel (German for *heaven*) was a well-known German composer. Eden is the name of a distinguished English family. Both Eden and Edenborn are found in Philadelphia. * * * The heathen deities, Odin, Backus, and Mars, dwell with us. Rev. Mr. Mars is a clergyman at Worcester. The goddess Flora keeps house in Boston. An edition of Pallas's Travels appeared in 1812. * * * Mr. Jupiter lives at Wateringbury, Conn.; Mr. Jove in New York; Mr. Soul at Lagrange. Mr. Plannet is found in our directory, and sells beer! Mr. Planert lives in New York; Mr. Comet in Montreal.

"Columbus discovered a world; and so have I. Mr. World lives at Orilla, C. W." —Pp. 47, 48, 49.

"Nations are represented by Greek, Gretian, Switzer, Sabine, Britton, English, French, Dutch, German, Hollander, Irish, Russ, Dane, Fleming, Malay, Norman, Lombard, Scott, Welsh, Picard, Finn, Wallach, Wallack, Turk, Amerigo, &c. Our Thomas Gipsey is, in name, a citizen of the world. There was an English author named Welchman in 1767. Mr. Hunn was a clergyman in Hadley in 1839. Mr. Neil Etheopean died in 1727. John Bohemion made a deed in L.10, f. 269. George Sirian was a gunner in our navy in 1849. Mr. Vandal lives at St. John's, C. E.; and in Philadelphia, I find families of Algier and Algiers.

"Countries are represented by Poland, Gaul, Spain, Spane, Flanders, Holland, Hague, Greenland, Finland, Brittain, Scotland, Savoy, Wales, Ireland, Guernsey, Garnsey, Lorain, Virginia, Maine, Domingo, Rhodes, Barbadoes. Mr. England lately died at Newburyport. In L. 169, Mr. Canada is party to a deed. Mr. Iceland lives at Sandhill, C.W. Mrs. Norway lives at Brewster, Mass. Greece is found at Chatham, C. E. Mr. Brazil lately died in Suffolk county. Mr. France appears in our directory for 1857. The firm of Bates and France failed in New York in 1857. Mr. Illius is, perhaps, of Trojan descent. Mr. Clime and Mr. Countraman of New York seem to have no fixed residence. Our Mr. Freeland's name is but an *alias* for America. Mr. Acie, who appears in our colony records 1677, may perhaps claim his name from another continent."—Pp. 95, 96.

"Mr. Hopper was a well-known American philanthropist. One of the present judges of Maryland (1857) bears that name. Mr. Budge lives at Lee, Me.; Mr. Stubbs at Wellfleet; Mr. Shove at Uxbridge; Mr. Toward at Augusta, Me.; and Mr. Presson at Lynn. Frederick Jump of Ashland, N. Y., failed in 1857. Dr. De Camp was a graduate of Yale. In the New York Directory I find nineteen families of Quick; also Mr. Rusher, Mr. Racer, Mr. Start, Mr. Leap, Mr. Leaper, Mr. Stivers, Mr. Springman, Mr. Spry, Mr. Stalker, Mr. Stamper, Mr. Wran, Mr. Went, Mr. Passmore, Mr. Hopp, Mr. Hopps, Mr. Jerker, Mr. Stramm, Mr. Walk, Mr. Wellstood, Mr. Ambleman, Mr. Stanback, Mr. Slow, Mr. Slowey, Mr. Hobbler, Mr. Fagg, Mr. Tag, Mr. Dally, Mr. Tarry, Mr. Rest, Mr. Stops. Mr. *Fugit*, the Kansas murderer, though acquitted, has been obliged to *fly* from the territory.

"Mr. Rushout is a British M.P., and that name is found in Roxbury. Mr. Climb lives at Selby, C. W. We have Climic. Mr. Clymer is a graduate of Harvard. [He will, doubtless, eventually take the highest degree.] Mr. Clymer of Philadelphia signed the Declaration of Independence. Mr. Creeper lives at Hampton. Mr. Diver was witness as to a late fire in North-Street: and that name is found in Philadelphia; as are also Divin and Stemmer. Mrs. Slider appears in our directory for 1857, and Francis Flyer in our Colony Records, 1629. Mr. Flew lives in Philadelphia; and Mr. Reising lives at Elmeira, C. W.

"Mr. Puller is a Member of Parliament. Rev. George Tugwell published a work on sea-anemones in London, 1857. Wrigley's Mathematical Collections appeared in London in 1845. Sir R. B. Crowder is one of the judges of the English court of Common Pleas; and in Illinois is a firm of Crowder and Co. Mr. Haule became a colonist here in 1638, as did Mr. Twitchwell in 1633, and Mr. Lug in 1647. Mr. Prest was admitted a freeman in 1643. In the New York Directory I find seven families of Stucke, Mr. Pulling, and Mr. Pullman; also Mr. Tugwell and Mr. Tug*not.* Mr. Tuggy lives at Montreal."—Pp. 77, 78.

"Mr. Fabel lives at Chatham, C. W.; and in Philadelphia there are four families of Fable: also Messrs. Muse and Paradee. Mr. Versey lives at Canfield; Mr. Penphraise at Cobourg; Mr. Learn at Ridgeway; Mr. Lingo at Westport; Mr. Spellin at Toronto. Mr. Tuype, of that city, goes for printing: Mr. Nibbet seems to prefer manuscript. Both Quire and Ream are found in Philadelphia, and furnish writing materials. In that city I find, also, a Mr. Wrighter, nineteen families of Righter, and eight families of Roat; also eight families of Book, Mr. Bookman, Mr. Spell, Mr· Spellbink, Mr. Spellinbuch, and two families of Word. Quil appears in the Buffalo Directory for 1855."—P. 185.

As I am dealing (although not scientifically) with the Surnames of the great Transatlantic nation—our brothers or near kinsmen for the most part—I trust that I shall not be deemed guilty of impropriety in continuing these quotations from Mr. Bowditch's really curious volume, to an extent somewhat out of proportion to the other notices which I am giving of surname literature.

For they shew, better than any original observations of my own could do, the vast variety of the subject which I have undertaken to elucidate. They prove, too, the force of verbal corruption in a new and only partially established nation, in which, until of late, literature has been comparatively little cultivated. Like plants translated to a new soil, the family names of the old world are modifying themselves in their new *habitat* in a manner unprecedented in the history of language. The family nomenclature of America is a philological curiosity and phenomenon.

"Law," says Mr. Bowditch, "has furnished many names of families; as Brass, *(its raw material)*, Wyles, Law, Laws, Lawless, Coad, Court, Leet, Roll, Record, Docket, Case, Traverse, Levy, Chancellor, Mace, Judge, Justice, Foreman, Sheriff, Sheriffs, Constable, Marshall, Beadle, Crier, Sumner, Warning, Warner, Warn, Sessions, Dunn, Dunham, Dunning, Jewett, Sewall, Fee, Fines, Bail, Lien, Search, Ferriter, Nabb, Ketchum! Mr. Getum lives at Toronto, C.W. Mr. Fetchum appears in the Middlesex Records . . . . I do not add Lyes to this collection; though it is justified by the conundrum: 'Why is a lawyer like a person who cannot sleep at night?'—'Because he first *lies* on one side, and then he *lies* on the other.' . . . . . Messrs. Doe and Roe are not fictitious personages. Mr. Warrant, Mr Argue, and Mr. Countsell, all live in New York; as does Mr. Writmire—a most suggestive name. J. G. Fee, of Madison, Ky., is a clergyman, having apparently mistaken his profession. Pulling and Pynchon was an old law firm in Salem, colloquially called *Pullem and Pinchem.* Mr. Sheard, of Toronto, has a name appropriate to a patron of the law. Dane cites the law-cases of Legal, Title, Fairtitle, Goodtitle, Fetter, &c. . . . . In New York I find families of Dun, Dunner, Detter, Duely, Ittem *(item)*, Legal, &c.; also Satchell, which seems to belong here, as a green bag was formerly a lawyer's badge. Pp. 186, 187. Mr. Sparrow was a member of our bar in 1839. Mr. Sparhawk, i.e. sparrowhawk, has a more appropriate name; as have also Mr. Shears, Mr. Shearer, Mr. Skinner, Mr. Keen, and Mr. Scaley. Mr. Trick was permitted to serve on the grand jury (1674). Mr. Blacklaw lives in New York. Mr. Carlaw, of the same city, can give only travelling advice. Mr. Greenlaw would seem to be equally untrustworthy. If the law be viewed as one of the black

b

arts, as was once suggested by the late Douglas Jerrold, it is a curious coincidence that its chief ministers are Coke and Blackstone !

" We have two names which seem amenable to the law—Mr. Swindle and Mr. Robb ; and unless Mr. Sharper and Mr. Trickey are careful, their names will bring them into trouble. P. 189.

" The late European belligerents ought to have employed as umpire our fellow-citizen, Mr. Royal Makepeace. Mr. Jobs lived in New York—a name in the plural rather suggestive of city-contracts. Our Mr. Job is a family man, and probably owns railroad stock. Messrs. Tittle, Blank, and Cyfer, have insignificant names. Mr. Blankman and Mr. Aught live in New York. At Philadelphia I find families of Blanck, Blank and Blankman, two families of Dito, and six families of Null. . . . Mr. Farless was sued in 1857. Mr. Mear made a deed in December, 1856. *More* is very *common*. Mr. Most appears in the Directory. Mr. Overmore was admitted a freeman in 1671 ; and Mr. Climax himself lives in New York. Messrs. Very and Welcombe appear extremely cordial ; while, on the other hand, Messrs. Nay, Nott, Nevers, Nerey, Naromore, Denio, and Miss Repell, seem quite the reverse. Mr. Denyer lives at Toronto, C.W. . . . In New York are found the names of Doolady, Duduit, and Ducom —all implying a pressing request. . . . Alexander Garden was a distinguished botanist of the last century. . . . Mr. Cars is a carman ; and Mr. Carty a driver. Pp. 42, 43.

" Mr. Coache lives at St. John's, C.E. ; Mr. Van at Strathroy, C.W. ; Mr. Still-wagon at Toronto." P. 213.

Mr. Bowditch has a curious chapter on misapprehended, translated, and changed surnames ; e.g. :—

" In 1844, one Joseph Galliano died in Boston, and in our probate records he has the *alias* of Joseph Gallon —that having been his popular name. Plamboeck, in some of our conveyances, became Plumback. These are names in a transition state. A foundling named Personne (i. e. *nobody*) became Mr. Pearson. Jacques Beguin of Texas, as we learn from Olmstead, became John Bacon ! Mr. Cisco is sub-treasurer of New York. The family originated in a foreigner named John Francisco, who, for brevity, voluntarily changed his signature to John F. Cisco. A German named Rübsum, who emigrated to Charleston, S.C., became by translation Mr. Turnipseed. The Blague family of this country became Blake ; Everedd was altered to Webb ; Fitzpen became Phippen. Crowninshield was formerly popularly called Groundsell. . . . . A distinguished lawyer of Middlesex county, named Burnside, disliking his Christian name, applied for leave to change it ; and, as he wrote a very bad hand, it was supposed that he wished to change his surname also into Bumside ! The change was made accordingly ; and after suffering a year's penance, it became again necessary to ask legislative aid." Pp. 241, &c.

In the United Kingdom, when we change a name for another, it is ordinarily at the mandate of some testator who has made it a condition of acquiring property, but in America the change is often made for the sake of euphony ; thus, a Mr. Samuel Quince Whitefoot, disliking the metre of his name, deprived it of its final foot, and now, under legislative sanction, he writes himself S. Q. White. "An entire family of Corporal in 1847 laid aside that rank ; and a very numerous family of Vest *divested* themselves in 1848. Mr. Thomas Jest, in 1850, decided that it was no joke to retain such a name any longer." In these last cases the change was for something totally different ; not the mere adding of a letter, or the omission of a disliked syllable. As the example has now been fairly set, it is probable that in time the Americans will have the purest family nomenclature in the world—all such coarse and indelicate names as those alluded to by Hood being for ever laid aside, since the American " party " *has a* voice and a veto :—

> "A name—if the party had a *voice,*
> What mortal would be a Bugg by choice,
> As a Hogg, a Grubb, or a Chubb rejoice,
> Or any such nauseous blazon ?
> Not to mention many a vulgar name,
> That would make a door-plate blush for shame,
> If door-plates were not so *brazen!* "

One more extract, exhibiting some harmony between the name and the calling of the bearers, must bring these humorous passages to a close.

" Rev. Mr. Service reads the Methodist-Episcopal service at Lynden, C.W.; and Rev. Mr. Rally, of Haysville, C.W., manifestly belongs to the church-militant. Mr. Lappe, of New-Hamburg, C.W., is a shoemaker ; Miss Vest, of Toronto, a dress-maker ; Mr. Vizard, of Peterborough, an attorney ; and Mr. Supple, of Pembroke, a member of the provincial Parliament, 1857. Messrs. Carveth, of Port Hope, C.W., and Mr. Gash, of Dunville, C.E., are butchers. Mrs. Lone is a widow at Oriquois, C.E. Mrs. Cinnamon, of Kingston, C.W., keeps a grocery. The Messrs. Broadwater, of Philadelphia, are fishermen. Mr. Brick, of that city, is a mason; and Mr. Cart-man, a labourer. Mr. Bricklayer, of Montreal, is a labourer ; Mr. Rumble, of Clinton, C.W., a wagon-maker; and Mr. Saddler, of Adelaide, C.W., a harness-maker. Mr. Builder, of Caledonia, C.W., is merely a cabinet-maker. [On the other hand] Mr. Spurgeon, of Toronto, C.W., has cure of soles, not of souls ; and Mr. Hatter, of Ottawa, C.W., is a shoemaker. Mrs. Bloomy is a school-mistress at St. Zepherine, C.E.—an employment decidedly unfavourable to the complexion."

Mr. Bowditch's Index Nominum of 114 pages is a philological curiosity.

In 1857 appeared a small work, entitled *The Family Names of the Folks of Shields traced to their Origin.* By William Brockie. South Shields, 8vo., pp. 113. In this ingenious little essay, the author classifies the names of the people of North and South Shields, two rising towns, situated respectively in the counties of Northumberland and Durham, in the following manner :—

LOCAL—

I.—ANGLO-NORTHUMBRIANS. From Northumberland, Durham, York, Cumberland, Westmoreland, Lancashire.

II.—SCOTO-NORTHUMBRIANS. From cos. Linlithgow, Edinburgh, Haddington, Berwick, Roxburgh, Selkirk, Dumfries.

III.—OLD ENGLISH. From ' England Proper,' that is " south of the Humber and east of the Dee and Wye."

IV.—BRITONS OF STRATHCLUYD. From cos. Peebles, Lanark, Renfrew, Ayr, Wigton, Dumbarton.

V.—SCOTS, PICTS, AND SAXONS. From beyond the FORTH.

VI.—ORCADIANS. From Orkney and Shetland.

VII.—SOUTH BRITONS. From Wales, Cornwall, and the Isle of Man.

VIII.—IRISH.

IX.—FRENCH.

X.—LOCAL NAMES NOT IDENTIFIED.

XI.—GENTILE OR NATIONAL NAMES, as English, Fleming, Scott, &c.

XII.—GENERIC LOCAL NAMES, as Burn, Craggs, Croft, Holm.

XIII.—NATURAL OBJECTS. Names expressive of these, from the Anglo-Saxon, Scottish, French, Irish, Welsh, Gaelic, Danish, Dutch, Italian, and Greek languages. Some of the etymologies are of a very doubtful kind.

XIV.—FROM OBJECTS, such as tools, weapons, costume, parts of ships and houses.

XV.—FROM OCCUPATIONS AND PROFESSIONS.

XVI. XVII. XVIII. XIX.—FOREIGN NAMES.

XX.—Patronymics, or names derived from those of parents or ancestors. These are estimated at 263.

XXI.—Descriptive. (From personal, moral, and other qualities.)

This brochure is interesting and amusing, though some of its statements are open to animadversion. I have obtained several useful hints from it.

In the same year appeared, from the American press, *An Etymological Dictionary of Family and Christian Names; with an Essay on their Derivation and Import.* By William Arthur, M.A. New York, small 8vo., pp. 300. This is apparently the production of a young writer, from whom better things may be expected.

By far the most important of these recent works on Family Nomenclature appeared in 1858, under the title of *English Surnames, and their Place in the Teutonic Family.* By Robert Ferguson. London, f.-cap. 8vo., pp. 430. I forgive the author his small trespass in having plagiarized, in part, the title of my former work, in consideration of the pleasure and advantage I have derived from his pages, numerous quotations from which will be found in this volume. The following Table of Contents will convey some idea of the nature of Mr. Ferguson's labours.

Chapter—
I.—Introduction.
II.—Names signifying Man and Woman.
III.—Names derived from, or connected with, Teutonic Mythology.
IV.—Names derived from, or connected with, Hero Worship.
V.—Names taken from Animals.
VI.—Names taken from Trees, Plants, Metals, &c.
VII.—Names taken from War, Arms, and Warlike Occupations.
VIII.—Names expressive of Peace, Friendship, and Affection.
IX.—Names derived from Relationship.
X.—Names derived from Nationality.
XI.—Old Saxon and Anglo-Saxon names.
XII.—Scandinavian Names.
XIII.—Patronymics and Diminutives.
XIV.—Names derived from Physical Characteristics.
XV.—Names derived from Mental and Moral Qualities.
XVI.—Names derived from Office or Occupation.
XVII.—Names from the Sea and the Sea Life.
XVIII.—Local Surnames.
XIX.—General Observations.
XX.—Conclusion.
&c., &c.

So many references to these prolusions will be found throughout my pages that my estimate of them will be inferred from such frequent notice. Like the rest of us who explore the mazes of *nominal* etymology, the author sometimes falls into a bog or quagmire, visible enough to all eyes but his own; and he might perhaps be justly charged with giving too great a prominence to the Scandinavian element in our Nomenclature, an error in which he is evidently a disciple of Worsaae; while his researches into the history of " the Northmen in Cumberland and Westmoreland " have naturally given his mind a further bias in that direction. But as he justly observes in the preface—" The field is a wide one, and there will be much to add—it is a difficult one, and there will be much to correct." " I hope to have the credit," he continues, " of having fairly grappled with the subject, and of having done something to lift up the veil which hangs over our English names."

Last, and least in bulk, not the least in amusing interest, of recent publications on this subject, is a brochure of 72 pages published in 1859, entitled *Surnames*

Metrically Arranged and Classified. By Thomas Clark, Esq. Mr. Clark's arrangement of the names is into forty-six groups, each representing a certain set of objects or ideas, with little reference to etymology. Several quotations from the work will be found in this volume.

Here I close my cursory review of what has been done in the English language in the way of classifying and illustrating Family Nomenclature. More elaborate productions are spoken of as forthcoming, and there are grounds for predicting, that at no distant period this department of philology will assume proportions, and achieve an importance, which twenty years ago were not even dreamed of. As I have ever, throughout my literary career, endeavoured to observe the maxim *Suum Cuique*, so I hope that all after-coming cultivators of this curious and extensive field, will be willing to admit my claim to having been the first, since the days of the illustrious Camden, who attempted to reduce to a method the *farrago* of terms by which the men and women of our happy country are distinguished among the nations of the world.

II.

𝕺𝖋 𝖙𝖍𝖊 𝕾𝖚𝖇𝖏𝖊𝖈𝖙 𝖆𝖙 𝖑𝖆𝖗𝖌𝖊.

N my Essay on English Surnames, I have entered somewhat fully into the history and classification of our family nomenclature; and it is unnecessary here to go over the same ground. I shall therefore content myself with some new illustrations of the subject, in the same order as was pursued in the former work.

1. ANTIQUITY OF SURNAMES.—I see no reason for departing from the year 1000, as the proximate date for the assumption of family names. The practice commenced in Normandy, and gradually extended itself into England, Scotland, and Ireland. I have assumed, that although the use of surnames may, on the whole, be regarded as one of the importations of the Norman Conquest, yet they were occasionally hereditary among the Anglo-Saxons at a date anterior to that event, and many generations before the general adoption of family designations. This is pretty satisfactorily proved by a document in the Cottonian MSS. quoted in Sharon Turner's History of the Anglo-Saxons. This document (No. 1356 in Cod. Dipl.) has no date, but there can be no doubt of its being earlier than 1066. It states that—" Hwita *Hatte* was a keeper of bees in Hæthfelda ; and Tate *Hatte*, his daughter, was the mother of Wulsige, the shooter ; and Lulle *Hatte*, the sister of Wulsige, Hehstan had for his wife in Wealadene. Wifus, and Dunne, and Seoloce were born in Hæthfelda. Duding *Hatte*, the son of Wifus, is settled at Wealadene ; and Ceolmund *Hatte*, the son of Dunne, is also settled there ; and Ætheleah *Hatte*, the son of Seoloce, is also there ;

and Tate *Hatte*, the sister of Cenwald, Mæg hath for his wife at Weligan; and Ealdelm, the son of Herethrythe, married the daughter of Tate. Werlaff *Hatte*, the father of Werstan, was the rightful possessor of Hæthfelda." Hence Mr. Ferguson remarks, that the existing *Hatt* is probably the "oldest hereditary surname we have on record."

2. LOCAL SURNAMES.—To be named after one's own landed possessions seems to have been an inevitable result of the feudal system. The Norman Conquerors, who had in many instances used the territorial *De*, introduced the fashion into England. Camden's remark that there is no "village in Normandy that gave not denomination to some family in England" is justly followed by another, that "every town, village, or hamlet in England and Scotland hath afforded names to families."

This is a large subject, and demands a separate essay : but I can only touch upon one or two of its more prominent points.

While comparatively few existing British families can indicate the very manor in Normandy, in England, or in Scotland, from whence their founders, in the eleventh, twelfth, thirteenth, or fourteenth century, borrowed their names, there are multitudes who have no direct proof of being territorially associated with the places whose names they bear, even though there is strong probability in many cases that such was the fact. In numberless instances the founder of a surname was merely a resident at the place from which it was borrowed, and not its feudal proprietor. This is especially the case in names derived from considerable towns.

Though local surnames, as above intimated, have been borrowed from every part of England, the practice was probably most rife in Cornwall, where the Tre, Pol, Pen, &c., seem to have been used almost to the exclusion of the other species of names. This is remarkable, as in the other Celtic portions of these realms—Wales, Ireland, the Highlands of Scotland, &c.—the patronymical surname was almost always preferred, and the Ap, the O', and the Mac were the prefixes instead of the Anglo-Norman De. In the Cumbrian province territorial surnames appear, however, as in Cornwall, to have been in favour. Out of a list of 55 Cumberland families extinct before A.D. 1500, thirty-nine took their designations from the places where they were settled.*

My original intention was, to exclude from this work all British local surnames. The design being chiefly etymological, I thought I should forward that object very little in informing the reader that 'York' was derived from the city, and 'Essex' from the county, so called. But on mature consideration I came to the conclusion, that though the meaning of names was my main object of research, a natural curiosity might exist on the part of the reader to know when a particular surname first appeared in ancient records, and that I might thus usefully combine its *history* with its etymology. Besides, it is not always easy, without a considerable acquaintance with gazetteers, and other topographical books, to determine what are, or what are not, local names. Who for example, not having heard of some ten obscure localities which hardly find a place upon any map, would take the well-known surnames Hartshorne, Blenkinsopp, Farewell, Inkpen, Ellerker, Blencowe, Clewer, Antrobus, Inskip, and Charley, to be territorial designations; yet this is undoubtedly the case.

The number of local surnames is immense; but while a large proportion of them can be identified with their localities, an equal, if not a larger, one cannot be so identified by means of the ordinary topographical dictionaries. A careful examination of the *indices locorum* of our best county histories would shew the origin of many of these from extinct manors and petty territorial possessions; and no inconsiderable num-

---

* Ferguson's Northmen in Cumberland, &c.

ber of them have either lost their designations or corrupted them almost beyond identification. And it may be observed as a rule, that the more trivial the locality which has given rise to a surname—a poor hamlet, perhaps, or a farm of small dimensions—the more likely the first assumer of the designation is to have been the owner of such locality. Every topographical inquirer must have remarked the number of surnames that have originated from these humble possessions; and how many have either become utterly extinct or have been transferred to other, and often remote, districts. The proportion of English families who still enjoy possession of the lands from which their surnames are derived, as Ashburnham of Ashburnham, Wombwell of Wombwell, Polwhele of Polwhele, is infinitessimally small. The same remark applies to the Scottish families who properly write themselves 'of that Ilk.'

Besides these more regular local names, there are two other classes which are derived from places; namely—1. Those which indicate the country or district from which the family came, as Ireland, Maine, Cornwall (with the adjective forms, Irish, Maunsel, Cornwallis) &c.; and 2. Those which are borrowed from the *situation*, rather than the name, of the original bearer's residence; as Hill, Wood, Tree, originally At-Hill, At-Wood, At-Tree, &c. See this class of names largely treated of in English Surnames, vol. i. pp. 59—91.

I may observe here, that in a few of the many cases in which I have failed to identify local surnames with localities, I have proved them to belong to this class by giving the etymology of the word.

3. SURNAMES DERIVED FROM TRADES, OCCUPATIONS, AND OFFICES.—I have little to remark here, beyond what has been said in *English Surnames*. Several names of this class occur in Domesday Book, shewing their early use among the Normans. Some of these, as Carpentarius, Faber, Barbitonsor, may be regarded as *descriptions*, rather than names, though Carpenter, Smith, and Barber afterwards became hereditary names. The official names Pincerna, Dapifer, &c., usually *aliased* other and more regular names, and were not in a strict sense of the word hereditary, though the corresponding designations Botiler, Steward, and the like, afterwards became so. But, as I have sufficiently shewn elsewhere, surnames were in a very unfixed condition in the early generations after the Conquest. Sometimes one and the same individual would bear three surnames—one territorial, another patronymical, and the third official. The powerful Richard, son of Gilbert Crispin, Earl of Brionne, in Normandy, and Earl of Clare, in England, bears *five* names in Domesday, viz. :—

1. Richard *de Tonebridge*, from his lordship of that name in Kent.
2. Richard *Benfeld*.
3. Richard *de Benefacta*.
4. Richard *de Clare*, from the Suffolk lordship.
5. Richard *Fitz-Gilbert*, from his father's baptismal name.[*]

It would seem that, among the Anglo-Saxons, words designating employments were sometimes used as we now employ baptismal or Christian names. For example, a Coleman (or Colemannus) and a Wodeman are found among the under-tenants of Domesday. Whether these persons had been baptized by those names, or whether they were, by occupation, respectively a charcoal-burner and a woodman, does not appear.

While surnames remained irregular and unfixed, as they did among the common people, throughout a great part of the middle ages, it is often difficult to determine whether the affix is a surname, or whether it is simply a descriptive epithet. It was sometimes both, especially as a particular vocation was frequently pursued hereditarily.

[*] Dugdale's Baronage. Kelham's Domesday.

In the reign of Edward I., we find a dancing girl called Maude Makejoy, which evidently refers to her occupation. Much later, temp. Henry VI., I have seen the name Renneawaie (Run-away) applied to a *perfuga;* but the most curious instance of this sort is to be found so late as 15 Edward IV., in an extract from a record book of the manor of Hatfield Broad-Oak, co. Essex, which shows how a poacher upon the manor, who bore the name of 'Partridge-taker,' from his illicit occupation, was fined twelve pence for his offence :—

"Item dicit, quod Robertus Partrychetaker intravit gareniam hujus manerii, et in eadem *cepit perdrices,* et illas asportavit, sine licentiâ Domini."*

4. SURNAMES DERIVED FROM CHARACTERISTICS OF MIND AND BODY.—The rationale of this class of names has been discussed in Eng. Surn., vol. i. pp. 139—148; and my remarks there, and in various articles in the present work, are sufficient on this division of our subject.

5. SURNAMES DERIVED FROM BAPTISMAL OR PERSONAL NAMES.—This most fertile source of family names has received due attention in my former work; and I have only one or two further illustrations to offer.

To any one who will examine this dictionary, few things will be more obvious than that a large number of modern surnames are identical with Anglo-Saxon personal names before the Conquest. This may appear to be no more remarkable than that the Celtic names of Ireland and Scotland deprived of *O'* or *Mac*, or the Anglo-Norman names despoiled of *Fitz*, or the Welsh names destitute of *Ap*, should have remained in our family nomenclature—yet I think there is a difference between these really patronymical forms and those old Teutonic designations; because the latter would more naturally have assumed the desinence ING (more rarely SUNU), which would have adhered, and become permanent. My theory is this :—

For several generations after the in-coming of the Normans, the Anglo-Saxon race, down-trodden by their imperious conquerors, had (with few notable exceptions) small consideration as to their names—little more, it would appear, than their fellow burthen-bearers, the horse and the bullock. But when some of them, by force of character, emerged from what might with truth be called the common herd, they would assert for themselves the distinction of a *nom de famille*, and emulate the Norman example. It is not difficult to imagine one of these adopting an argument like the following : "Well, though I have been a serf, I have purchased my freedom, and, as a free man, I am determined to resume as much as I can of the social position which my family, under the Norman sway, have lost. My great-great-grandfather, who possessed the lands upon which I have till lately been a mere chattel, fell at Hastings, bravely defending his country's liberties. He was called Wulsi, that being his only name. Now, my name is Edward; but, as many Edwards still remain in servitude, I am anxious to distinguish myself as a free Englishman from those unhappy individuals, and I will therefore adopt the additional name of Wulsi, and call myself Edward Wulsi ; and all my posterity shall be known after our common forefather as Wulsis." By this kind of ancestor-worship, it is highly probable that the old pre-Norman nomenclature has in numerous cases been handed down to the present day.

Mr. Ferguson observes, that it may be a question whether the epithets of Teutonic antiquity—the "surnames of illustrious men may not sometimes, on the principle of hero-worship, have been adopted by other men in after times as surnames, or even in some cases as baptismal names. We have a few names which correspond with the surnames borne by distinguished personages, long before the time when surnames

* Inf. W. Clayton, Esq.

became hereditary." The instances cited by Mr. F. are Ironside, Barfoot, Lightfoot, Ludbrock, and Barnacle. In this connection see the articles Robynhod and Littlejohn in the present volume.

Although I cannot agree with M. Salverte * that a moiety of family names are derived from baptismal appellations—at least in the British Islands—this is indisputably one of the largest sources of these appellatives. This will be apparent if we reflect that not only has nearly every " font-name " become a surname *per se*, but also in its various patronymical, or rather *filial* forms and its nicked, or abbreviated modifications. A reference to the article *William* in this work, and to what I have already said in English Surnames, vol. i. p. 166, will show how copious a source of nomenclature this has been. The Irish, Gaelic, and Welsh surnames, as will be seen elsewhere, are almost exclusively of this kind.

Under the head *Patronymics and Diminutives*, Mr. Ferguson has the following judicious observations :—" Of the two Teutonic patronymics, *ing* and *son*, common in English names, the former is more properly Germanic, the latter Scandinavian. 1. *Ing* or *inger* signifies son, offspring, being cognate with the English *young*. It was discontinued about the time of the Conquest, and consequently all the names in which it appears are carried back to Anglo-Saxon times. In some few cases, however, the termination *ing* in proper names may not be from this origin, but rather local, from *ing*, a meadow.† 2. The termination *son* is a characteristic feature of all the Scandinavian countries, while in Germany, on the other hand, it is of comparatively rare occurrence. So well is this distinction understood, that a writer on the ' Nationality and Language in the Duchy of Sleswick and South Jutland,' advances the frequency of names ending in *son* as an argument for the Danish character of the population." Too much stress ought not, however, to be laid upon this termination to prove the nationality of the bearer, since in England it is affixed to Christian names of every origin, as I have stated under the article Son in this dictionary.

Mr. Dixon remarks that the equivalent of our English *son* is in Germany *sohn*, often corrupted to *son* and *sen*, and in Holland *zoon*, also generally changed to *son, sen*, and *se*, or abbreviated to *z*.

6. THE ANIMAL AND VEGETABLE KINGDOMS have supplied a rich variety of family names. See the articles Birds, Quadrupeds, Fishes, Trees and Plants, &c. In English Surnames, vol. 1, p. 186, I have given a list of names identical with the designations of MINERALS. Mr. Clark, with his usual ingenuity, adduces a more copious one :—

> ———" We've Agate, Allum, Brass,
> Chalk, Copper, Crystal, Flint, and Glass ;
> Slate, Iron, Freestone, Sand, Clay, Mould,
> Lime, Lias, Pewter, Silver, Gold ;
> Stone, Garnett, Emery, Argent, Nickel,
> *Talk*, Jewell, Jasper, Brick, and Brickell ;
> Salt, Ruby, Winstone, Ore, and Nodes,
> Gravel and Coal—by wagon loads ;
> And lastly, Diamond, Tinn, and Zincke."

But the curiosity of this catalogue is, that scarcely a single name "means what it says." They are principally derived from localities, and several are known modifications of baptismal names.

7. To what I have said respecting the small class of surnames derived from SYMBOLS, such as the charges of the Armorial Shield, the Signs of Innkeepers and

---

* Essai sur les Noms, &c.

† I believe that in *many*, if not most cases, the termination *ing* denotes a local origin, and ranks with HAM, LEY, TON, &c. It signifies a meadow. But when the *ing* occurs in the middle of the name of a place, as in Bedd*ing*ham, Will*ing*ton, Poss*ing*worth, it is the Saxon filial : thus Beddingham, or rather Bedingham, signifies the *ham*, or home, of the *inga*, or sons, of *Beda*, or Bede.

Tradesmen, &c., I have nothing to add, except that I should be disposed rather to limit than to extend it. Compare, for instance, what, following Mr. Montagu's "Study of Heraldry," I have said in English Surnames, i. 195-6., respecting the name SEPTVANS with what is stated in the present volume.

8. Several new illustrations of surnames, supposed to be derived from the SOCIAL RELATIONS, PERIODS OF TIME, AGE, &c., will be found scattered through this volume ; but in the article TIMES AND SEASONS it will be seen that many names apparently from this source belong to other categories.

9. Touching surnames indicative of RIDICULE AND CONTEMPT, I have only to remark here, that this kind of nomenclature was largely imported into England in Norman times. Among early designations which were anything but complimentary, but which adhered to descendants, and were borne in the XII. and succeeding centuries—some even remaining to our own times—the following three classes may be adduced ; viz., those derived,—

a. From dangerous or ill-reputed beasts, such as Urso, Purcell, Machell, (Malchien), Lupus (Lovel), Maulovel, Asinus (L'Asne); *Anglicè*, Bear, Pig, Evil-dog, Wolf, Bad-wolf, Ass, &c.
b. From personal deformities, such as Malemains, Malebranche, Foljambe, Tortesmains, Maureward, Vis-de-Leu, Front-de-Bœuf ; *Anglicè*, Bad-hands, Bad-arm, Bad-leg, Twisted-hands, Squinter, Wolf's-face, and Bullock's-head.
c. From moral defects, such as Malvoisin, Mauduit, Mautenant; *Anglicè*, Bad-neighbour, Ill-conducted, Faithless (?), &c.

Analogous surnames of indigenous growth, and later date, are widely scattered over the pages of this volume.

10. With regard to surnames apparently relating to the VIRTUES AND OTHER ABSTRACT IDEAS, I have found occasion to modify some of the statements which I formerly advanced.

11. Surnames identical in form with OATHS AND EXCLAMATIONS, though a very limited class, are more numerous than I formerly considered them to be, as will be seen on perusal of the dictionary.

12. On the family names said to have been borrowed from HISTORICAL INCIDENTS, and to which I have devoted the first chapter of Vol. II. of English Surnames, I have bestowed a considerable amount of criticism, and the result is, that they are, at least in numerous instances, derived from much more probable, though less romantic, sources. See, for example, Lockhart, Dalziel, Napier, Tyrwhitt, Skene, Erskine, and many other articles in the present volume.

13. FOREIGN SURNAMES NATURALIZED in these islands have caused me much trouble, from the difficulty which exists of determining when an immigrating family may be truly said to have become denizens of the United Kingdom. This by no means depends upon length of residence; for while there are many (especially those connected with merchandise), who, though long *among* us, are not *of* us, there are, on the other hand, still more who, albeit their settlement is recent, may be reckoned among the truest-hearted of Britons. I have endeavoured to follow the middle course, of neither hastily admitting, nor of unfairly rejecting, surnames of foreign origin, according to the means of judging which I possessed. Without a range of enquiries far wider than was within my power, it has been impossible to decide accurately on this subject. You cannot pass through the streets of any great town—of London especially—without remarking the large number of foreign names which are seen on every hand, though whether those names belong to recent settlers, or to families of several generations' standing, nothing short of elaborate investigation could

decide. In the London Directory for the year 1852, page 839, no less than *fifty-one* traders, in consecutive order, bear foreign names! These are principally Germans.

Whatever my sins of omission on this score may have been (those of *commission* are not to be found), I trust that few of those naturalized names which have adorned our annals in literature, science, arts, politics, or war, have been overlooked.

14. The CORRUPTIONS which hundreds of our family names have undergone tend to baffle alike the genealogical and the etymological inquirer. These mainly proceed from two causes—first, the unfixed orthography of ancient times; and secondly, the desire which seems inherent in most minds of attaching a signification to names. In addition to many other instances occurring in these pages, I may mention that Shire-cliffe has become *Shirtley*; Ollerenshaw, *Wrench*; Molineux, *Mull*; Debenham, *Deadman*; Wainhouse, *Venus*; Sibthorpe, *Tharp*; MacLeod, *Ellicott*; Lenthall, *Lentern*; Delamond, *Dollymount*; Pasley, *Parsley*; Gillingham, *Gillicum*; Satherley, *Saturday*; Pickford, *Pickfat*; Clavesley, *Classey*; Thurgod, *Thoroughgood*; Talbois, *Tallboys*. Mr. Ferguson well observes that "the tendency of corruption is almost invariably *towards* a meaning, and not away from one"—because people like to know what they are talking about, and hence our uneducated folk call asparagus "sparrow-grass," and the passiflora a "passion-flower."*

The inexact orthography of the middle ages has led to much error and misapprehension, as might be expected when the name of Shirecliffe is found spelt in fifty-five, and that of Mainwaring in one hundred and thirty-one, different ways. But another cause of uncertainty has arisen from what may be called the *variations* rather than corruptions of names, as when in deeds executed by the same person, he is called indifferently Chapman and Mercator, or Smith and Faber. In deeds of one and the same person, whose name would now be written John Church, or John Kirke, and who flourished in Derbyshire in the reign of Edward III., the following variations occur:—

> John atte Schirche,
> John at Chyrch,
> John del Kyrke,
> Johannes de Kyrke,
> John Othekyrke,
> John at Kyrke.†

In Scotland still greater irregularities prevailed, and do still prevail, as when kinsmen write themselves Ballantyne, Bannatyne, Ballenden, and Belenden. The following extract of a letter, addressed to me by Mr. Alexander Gardyne, will sufficiently attest this want of uniformity in the orthography of family names:—

"I have always prided myself upon bearing a very uncommon *black-letter looking surname*, which in our part of the country—say Forfarshire—is clipped down in common parlance to *Gairn*. During the greater part of a somewhat advanced life I have been content to call myself *Gardyne*, and to receive the aforesaid equivalent for it; but having recently made a pilgrimage to Fatherland, after many years absence from Europe, it has, unhappily, resulted in placing me somewhat in the position of Jacob Faithful, with this difference, however, in my favour, that whereas Maryatt's hero was in search of a Father, with me it was only a Grandfather; the imperfect registration of the parish authorities of Glammis having so mystified that interesting relative to me, as to baffle my endeavours to fix his identity, to say nothing of the suspicion it has awakened in my mind that as regards the name I have so long borne, I have, in nautical phrase, been sailing 'under false colours.' I may here state that my worthy parent was gathered to his fathers long before I felt any great curiosity about the Gardynes of the Nether Middleton, in the Glen of Ogilvie, and that, moreover, having no relatives of my own name beyond an aged mother and a maiden sister—being, in fact, the last of my race and a bachelor to boot, my sources of information as to the history of my family were so few in number, and so scant in detail, that I considered it would be advisable, before seeking the immediate locality of my ancestors, to check off the genealogical scraps in my possession, principally of an oral and legendary character, with that never-to-be-doubted record, the Parish Register.

"In carrying out this resolution I realized 'the pursuit of knowledge under difficulties,' for,

---

* An old sailor once told me, almost in the same breath, that he had "sarved" on board the *Billy-Rough-un* (Bellerophon); and that he had seen *Muster Abraham Packer* (Ibrahim Pacha).

† Inf. Rev. J. Eastwood.

on making known my wants to the functionary of Glammis, and furnishing my name, he drew forth a shabby volume, and therefrom responses of such a startling character, as to leave me in considerable doubt between my belief in the oracular quality usually ascribed to such records, and my own identity. The first entry turned up by the worthy interpreter, and assigned to my family, was the birth, Feb. 6, 1767, of

'*Margaret Gairden, lawful daughter of Alex. Gairden, Nether Middleton.*'

The date of this event and everything else but the orthography of the name agreeing, I was obliged to accept it for what it undoubtedly was—the registry of my father's elder sister. Muttering to myself that here was, at all events, something like an approach to a reconciliation of my written name of Gardyne with the pronounced one of Gairn, the next turned up by the old gentleman and presented to me, as one of the said family, was thus recorded:—

'*Born Oct. 30, 1768, David Dalgairns, lawful son of Alex. Dalgairns, Nether Middleton.*'

'Beheading' this, I got my pronounced name at once; but what is more surprising is, that on referring to my own memoranda I was satisfied that the said David Dalgairns was *my own father*, the brother of Margaret Gairden, and both the children of the worthy farmer at Nether Middleton, calling himself, or rather being called by the sessions clerk of the day both *Gairden* and *Dalgairns*; and, as if this confusion were not enough, the said David Dalgairns bearing himself in later life, and handing down to the next generation, the name of *Gardyne!*"

My correspondent goes on to inform me that he has discovered the additional forms of *Garden, Garn, Gardin, Gardne, Garne, Dalgarn, Dalgarner, Dalgardns, Dalgardyne, and Dalgarna*, all springing of course from GARDEN, with or without its medieval prefix DEL. And I may add, from the information of Mr. William *Jerdan* M.R.S.L., &c., that his family and that of *Jardine* were identical, both names being additional products of the fertile Garden!

15. In my former work will be found a chapter on CHANGED SURNAMES. To what is there said, I would add a few words on the practice prevalent in the middle ages, of ecclesiastics, especially the regulars, forsaking their ancestral names, and adopting either the name of the place in which they were born, or that of some distinguished angel, saint, or father of the church. Being *civiliter mortui*, dead to the world, they assumed, with their spiritual life, a new name.* The following is a remarkable set of instances :—

On October 17, 1537, the religious fraternity of Winchcombe, co. Gloucester, consisted of the abbot and seventeen monks, who, as parties to a document of small importance executed that day, sign themselves by their assumed or spiritual names. On December 3, 1539, little more than two years later, when they executed their deed of surrender to Henry VIII., laying aside these designations, they sign in their secular or civil names, as shown below :—

Bond of Oct. 17, 1537.	*Surrender, Dec.* 3, 1539.
Ricardus Ancelmus, *Abbas*	Richard Mounslow, *last Abbot*
Johannes Augustinus, *Prior*	John Hancock, *Prior*
Willelmus Omersley	William Craker
Johannes Gabriel	John Whalley
Ricardus Angelus	Richard Freeman
Willelmus Maurus	William Blossom
Willelmus Overbury	William Bradley
Hugo Egwinus	Hugh Cowper
Ricardus Barnardus	Richard Boidon
Ricardus Martinus	Richard Parker
Georgius Leonardus	George Foo
Johannes Anthonius	
Gulielmus Hieronymus	William Trentham
Christoferus Benedictus	Christopher Chawnfut
Walterus Aldelmus	Walter Cowper
Richardus Michahel	Richard Williams
Willelmus Kenelmus	William Howard
Ricardus Ambrosius	Richard Banister.†

* Alban Butler remarks that this is done, "partly to express their obligation to become new men, and partly to put themselves under the special patronage of certain saints, whose examples they propose to themselves for their models."—*Lives of the Saints*, June 29.

† Communicated to the Archæological Journal, by Albert Way, Esq., M.A., F.S.A.

My former researches were devoted almost exclusively to English family names. The present volume includes those of the other 'nationalities,' which with England make up the United Kingdom. A few remarks on Scotch, Welsh, and Irish surnames therefore seem necessary here.

SCOTCH SURNAMES.

These range themselves under two classes; those of the Highlands, and those of the Lowland Counties. The surnames of the Celtic, or Highland, population are chiefly of the patronymical class, and known by the prefix *Mac*. A large number of these, through the courtesy of gentlemen who had taken the trouble to collect them, I have been enabled to print in the dictionary. With these names I have etymologically little to do. They are simply Christian names with the patronymical prefix, and it is no part of my plan to explain those designations, which belong to a more recondite branch of etymology than I have yet investigated, and about which even Gaelic philologists are frequently " wide as the poles asunder."* Had I followed the advice of some of my esteemed friends and correspondents beyond the Tweed, I should have omitted Scottish surnames altogether from this work. However profane the act of a Southron's meddling with the northern nomenclature may be considered, with me it was a matter of all but absolute necessity that I should bring in as many as I could collect of Scottish surnames, for the simple reason that they are borne by many thousands of English families whose ancestors, at a period more or less remote, crossed the Cheviots and the Tweed, and became *de facto* Englishmen. What, I ask, would be thought of a Dictionary of English Surnames that did not admit within its covers the names of Stuart, Campbell, Murray, Macpherson, Bruce, Douglas, and Erskine !

Scottish surnames are doubtless a difficult subject to deal with, and this principally by reason of the system of clanship so long prevalent in that kingdom. In Scotland whoever joined a particular clan, no matter what his position or descent, assumed the surname of his chief, and this was accepted as an act of loyalty. In England, had any retainer of a feudal baron presumed to do such a thing, he would soon have found himself at the bottom of the deepest dungeon of the castle !

A *clan*, therefore, is a very different thing from a *family*. When the system of Clanship originated is unknown. Nothing certain is known of it by documentary evidence before the year 1450, although the genealogies of many who were then chiefs of clans may be traced to much earlier periods. See Skene, *passim*. It is probable that no two enumerations of clans would correspond with each other, and the whole subject is involved in considerable obscurity, as their historian himself frankly confesses. The following list of clans is quoted as one of the latest that have appeared in print :—

LIST OF HIGHLAND CLANS.

Buchanan	Forbes	Mac Donnell	Mac Lean
Cameron	Fraser	Mac Farlane	Mac Leod
Campbell	Gordon	Mac Dougal	Mac Nab
Chisholm	Graham	Mac Gregor	Mac Neil
Colquhoun	Grant	Mac Intosh	Mac Pherson
Cumming	Gunn	Mac Kay	Mac Quarrie
Drummond	Lamont	Mac Kenzie	Mac Rae
Farquharson	Macalister	Mac Kinnon	Munro
Ferguson	Mac Donald	Mac Lachlan	Menzies

* In a few instances I have given the etymons of Gaelic names as supplied to me by the courtesy of correspondents. If they should be found incorrect, the fault belongs to Celtic rather than to South-Saxon ignorance.

Murray	Oliphant	Rose	Sinclair
Ogilvie	Robertson	Ross	Stewart
		Sutherland *	

Some of these bear undoubted evidence of being, at least as to their names, any-thing but of Celtic origin, as Mr. Skene has sufficiently shown.

The Lowland and Border clans were formed in imitation of the Gaelic, but the family names of these districts are in principle and classification precisely analogous to those of England.

The introduction of surnames into Lowland Scotland seems, as in England, to have been chiefly brought about by Norman influence and example. No precise period can be assigned for it. As in the case of most fashions, the adoption was gradual. Many of the Norman noblesse who had brought family names across the Channel not long after the Conquest, transferred themselves to North Britain, and of course did not drop those designations into the river Tweed. It is asserted in Father Augustin Hay's "Genealogie of the Sainteclairs," that King Malcolm Canmore called a general council at Forfar, in 1061, in which he directed his chief subjects, after the custom of other nations, to adopt names from their territorial possessions. (Volens ut Primores, quod antea non fuerat, aliarum more gentium, a prædiis suis cognomina caperent).† I can-not say, however, that I have seen any proof of territorial surnames in Scotland before the XII. century, and they are certainly unusual before the XIII.

WELSH SURNAMES.

THE Welsh, like most of the other Celtic nations, adopted Patronymics by way of sur-names. The prefix *Ap*, applied to the father's baptismal designation, showed the filial relation, and was continued through every link of the longest pedigree. Henry VIII. discountenanced this unfixed nomenclature, and, during his and the succeeding reigns, the name of the father or of some earlier ancestor began to be adopted by gentle families. Hence, nearly the whole of the family names of the Principality are derived from Christian names; and hence the great frequency of Jones, Williams, Evans, Thomas, Morgan, Davis, &c.

But, until within quite recent times, say about the beginning of the present cen-tury, the practice of using simple patronymics prevailed in the southern counties of the principality; in other words the baptismal name of the father was the surname of the son.

Thus, if Morgan Richards had three sons; John, William, and Griffith, they would be John Morgan, William Morgan, and Griffith Morgan.

John Morgan's two sons, Peter and James, would be Peter Jones and James Jones.

William Morgan's two sons, Job and Abel, would be Job Williams and Abel Wil-liams.

And Griffith Morgan's two sons, Howel and Cadwallader, would be Howell Grif-fiths and Cadwallader Griffiths.

About the year 1825, at the Hereford assizes, a witness in a Welsh cause was ex-amined before Mr. Justice Allan Park. His name was John Jones. He was asked if he had always gone by that name, and he said he had. He was then asked whether at the time when he lived at Carmarthen, he did not go by the name of Evan Evans, and

---

* Folks of Shields, p. 96.
† Gen. Sainteclaire, p. 3. See also art. Seton in this Dict.

to this he replied in the affirmative. This apparent discrepancy was explained to the court by Mr. Taunton (afterwards Sir William Taunton, and a Judge of the Court of King's Bench), who stated that Evan is the Welsh synonym of John, and Evans that of Jones; and that John Jones might be called indifferently Evan Jones, John Evans, or Evan Evans, without any real change of name.*

IRISH SURNAMES.

These are formed after the Celtic method by the prefixes *O'* and *Mac*, the former being, however, by far the most usual. See *O*, in the body of the work.

The word *O'*, signifying grandfather, or more loosely any ancestor, appears to have been in use in times of remote antiquity. In some instances the name of the progenitor became fixed and stationary as a family name by the addition of this prefix so early as the XI. century. This was chiefly in noble and distinguished families; and O'Brien, O'Mahony, O'Donohoe, O'Donovan, O'Dugan may be mentioned as examples of surnames adopted at that early period, at the instance of King Brian Boru. See Eng. Surn. ii. 67. In some few cases the prefix *Mac* can be traced to a like antiquity.

These patronymics formed the staple of Irish family nomenclature until the conquest of Ireland by the Anglo-Normans in the reign of Henry II. At that epoch many non-Celtic surnames were introduced by the followers of Strongbow, and some of their descendants adopting the Irish manners, costumes, and language, became more Irish than Irishmen—*Hibernis ipsis Hiberniores*, and went so far, especially in the province of Connaught, as to translate their names; while on the other hand many of the Irishmen in more immediate contact with their Conquerors adopted English names. The FitzGeralds, the Butlers, the Costellos, the Nangles, the Gibbons, the Burkes, the Carews, the D'Altons, the De Courcys, the Graces, the Husseys, and scores of other families, many of whom exhibited a strong Irish nationality, sprang from England at and after the period alluded to.

In 1465 (5. Edward IV.) a legislative enactment took place, commanding the Irish who dwelt in the counties of Dublin, Meath, Uriell, and Kildare, to adopt "English Surname," either that of a town, as Sutton, Chester, Trym, Corke, Kinsale, —that of colour, as White, Blacke, Browne—that of arte or science, as Smith or Carpenter—that of office, as Cooke, Butler, and the like. How far this mandate was obeyed we know not. Such English Surnames are of course abundant in Ireland, but whether many of them can be attributed to legislation is extremely doubtful, since there has always been a considerable immigration of English and Scotchmen into the sister island, to say nothing of the voluntary adoption of English names in different ages.

A correspondent (Wm. J. O'Donnavan, Esq.) has furnished me with a list of surnames apparently derived from places in Ireland. The indigenous Irish were prouder of the ancestral patronymic than of territorial names, and therefore the number of this class is extremely small. And even from that small number deductions must be made : First—of those names which are taken from peerage titles, such as Desmond, Galtrym, Howthe, Naas, and Swordes, which were but aliases for FitzGerald, Hussey, St. Lawrence, FitzGerald, and Croly. Also Kildare, Kilkenny, Ormond, and Deasy : Secondly—of those which, though identical with names of places in Ireland, have really

* Inf. F. A. Carrington, Esq. See some curious anecdotes on this subject in English Surnames, vol. i., p. 18.

imposed those names on, instead of taking them from, the localities, such as Archdall, (Castle-Archdall) and Devenish (Court-Devenish) both English names and families : Thirdly—of those that are corruptions of indigenous patronymics, and have no connection with the places whose designations they resemble, as Carbery, Ennis, and Shannon. Thus expurgated, Mr. O'Donnavan's list stands as under, and it is quite probable that it is susceptible of still further pruning :—

"*Names before* 1600. Adare, Attry, Cashell, Callan, Derpatrick, Dromgoole or Drumgould, Finglas, Galway, Galbally, Malofant, Oriell or Uriell, Pallis.

"*Names in present use.* Antrim, Annaly, Ardagh, Augrhim, Banaher, Corballis, Corbally, Cork, Corrigans, Derry, Durrow, Dangan, Fingal, Fernes, Gorey, Gowran, Golden, Kerry, Killery, Kenlis, Kells, Killarney, Killeen, Kyle, Limerick, Lusk, Longford, Meath, Monaghan, Meelick, Prehen, Sligo, Slane, Skryne, Tuyan, Tyrone.

"*Names of doubtful origin.* Clare, Down, Den, Holywood, Louth, Mayo, Moyne, Money, Rush, Ross, Slaney, Sutton, Shaen. These are as likely to have been assumed from English as from Irish localities."

Dr. O'Donovan's researches, referred to at page v. *ante*, leave little to be desired as to the history and classification of Surnames in Ireland ; while Mr. D'Alton's " King James's Irish Army List "—of which, I learn, a new edition has lately appeared—will afford much valuable information on the subject of Irish families, their fortunes, and their misfortunes.

III.

Statistics of Surnames.

SOME Statistics relative to the subject of this volume naturally find a place here.

First—as to the *Number* of these vocables. It will possibly astonish most readers, to be told that this is as great as that of the words composing our language. According to the best authorities, the number of words in the English tongue (if we reject the obsolete on the one hand, and the technical and the unauthorized on the other) amounts to about thirty-five thousand. Now there is good reason for accepting the calculation of the Rev. Mark Noble, based upon a proximately ascertained enumeration of the surnames of which A is the initial letter (1500), and the proportion which that letter is found to bear to the other letters of the alphabet, that the number of *English* surnames must amount to between thirty and forty thousand.* And if we add in the Irish, Scottish, and other non-English family names which come within the scope of the present undertaking, we may safely assume that Mr. Noble's estimate rather falls short of than exceeds the truth.

This calculation, roughly made many years since, has recently received singular

---

* Hist. Coll. Arms. Prelim. Dissert.

corroboration in a most trustworthy quarter—the sixteenth Annual Report of Her Majesty's Registrar-General, printed in 1856. By the courtesy of that gentleman I am allowed to reproduce the following statements, the result of a careful official analysis.

" The probable number of surnames in England and Wales has been the subject of conjectural estimates based on a small collection of facts. By the careful collation of all the registration indexes it could be approximately ascertained; for during a period of more than seventeen years it is probable that almost every resident family contributed to the registers an entry of birth, death, or marriage. The task of collating upwards of two hundred immense quarterly indexes would, however, involve a vast amount of labour without any commensurate result; moreover the number of names is constantly varying, owing, on the one hand, to emigration, or to the extinction of families by death, and on the other, to the introduction of fresh names by foreigners and immigrants, to the corruption of existing names always going on amongst the illiterate, and to various other circumstances. I have ascertained the number of different surnames contained in one quarterly index of births, and in another of deaths ; the former selected with reference to the period of the last census, and the latter without premeditation. The following are the results :—

		Persons registered.	Different surnames.
BIRTHS.	Quarter ending 31st March, 1851	157,286	25,028
DEATHS.	Quarter ending 31st March, 1853	118,119	20,991

" According to these numbers, there were for every 100 of the births registered about 16 different surnames, and for every 100 of the deaths about 18, reckoning every surname with a distinctive spelling, however slightly it may differ from others, as a separate surname. Taking the two indexes together, and by a careful collation eliminating all duplicates, the numbers stand thus :—

Persons registered.	Different surnames.	Different surnames to every 100 persons.	Persons to one surname.
275,405	32,818	11·9	8·4

" An alphabetical list of 32,818 surnames, the largest collection yet made, is thus obtained ; and as this result is furnished by two quarterly indexes only, it may be assumed as a rough estimate that the whole number in England and Wales is between *thirty-five* and *forty thousand*. It is important, however, to remember that the list includes a large number derived from the same roots as others, commonly agreeing in sound, but differing in orthography often only to the extent of a single added or substituted letter. By these trifling variations the number is immensely increased. The name of *Clerk*, for instance, is also commonly spelt *Clark* and *Clarke*, one and the same primary name (from *clericus*) being implied in the three forms ; but three separate items necessarily appear in the list, for practically as *surnames* they represent different and distinct persons and families. Again, the widely spread name of *Smith* appears in family nomenclature also as *Smyth*, *Smythe*, and even as *Smijth*. It is not usual, however, to regard these diverse forms as representing one name only, nor would their bearers probably all concur in admitting the common origin of the several variations. Until a comparatively recent period, an entire disregard of uniformity and precision in the mode of spelling family names prevailed, even amongst the educated classes, and many family Bibles and writings might be adduced as evidence that this was apparently less the result of carelessness than of affectation or design. While the *sound* was in a great measure preserved, the number of different surnames became greatly multiplied by these slight orthographical variations, as well as by other corruptions; and if, in reckoning the number, each original patronymic with its modifications were counted as one, the list of 32,818 would be considerably reduced.*

" The contribution of Wales to the number of surnames, as may be inferred from what has been already stated, is very small in proportion to its population. Perhaps nine-tenths of our countrymen in the Principality could be mustered under less than 100 different surnames† ; and while in England there is no redundancy of surnames, there is obviously a paucity of distinctive appellatives in Wales, where the frequency of such names as *Jones*, *Williams*, *Davies*, *Evans*, and others, almost defeats the primary object of a name, which is to distinguish an individual from the mass. It is only by adding his occupation, place of abode, or some other special designation, that a particular person can be identified when spoken of, and confusion avoided in the ordinary affairs of life. The name of *John Jones* is a perpetual incognito in Wales, and being proclaimed at the cross of a market town would indicate no one in particular. A partial remedy for this state of things would perhaps be found in the adoption of a more extended range of Christian names, if the

---

* The reader will bear in mind that the Registrar-General's functions are limited to England and Wales only.

† " Of the 328 Registration Officers and their deputies acting in the districts of Wales 207 are comprised under 17 surnames, in the following proportions; viz: *Jones* 46, *Williams* 26, *Davies* 16, *Evans* 16, *Thomas* 15, *Roberts* 14, *Lewis* 11, *Hughes* 10, *Edwards* 8, *Lloyd* 8, *James* 6, *Griffith* 6, *Morgan* 6, *Rees* 6, *Owen* 5, *Morris* 4, *Ellis* 4. There is only one officer of the name of Smith (!)"

Welsh people could be induced to overcome their unwillingness to depart from ancient customs, so far as to forego the use of the scriptural and other common names usually given to their children at baptism."

I am authorised to state, that in some early Report the Registrar-General will print a list of all the Surnames of England and Wales occurring in the official indexes of a single year. This will necessarily be a document of great curiosity and interest.

The reader, seeing that we possess certainly more than 30,000 surnames, will naturally ask why this volume should contain less than one half of that number. This I shall hereafter have occasion to apologise for and to explain.

Secondly—as to the comparative commonness of our most frequently occurring surnames, the Registrar-General furnishes the following information :—

" The subjoined Table of 50 of the most common surnames in England and Wales is derived from 9 quarterly indexes of births, 8 of deaths, and 8 of marriages; and although the inquiry might have been extended over a more lengthened period, it was found that the results were in general so constant as to render a further investigation unnecessary. When arranged according to the numbers in each index, the names appeared almost always in the same order, and the variations, when they occurred, rarely affected the position of a name beyond one or two places. These 50 names embraced nearly 18 in every 100 persons registered. The three names at the head of the list, *Smith, Jones,* and *Williams,* are, it will be observed, greatly in advance of the others; and if the numbers may be taken as an index of the whole population, it would appear that on an average one person in every 28 would answer to one or other of these three names."

TABLE XVI.—FIFTY of the most common Surnames in England and Wales, with the aggregate Number of each entered in the Indexes of Births, Deaths, and Marriages in the Year ending 30th June 1838, of Births in the Quarter ending 31st March, 1851, and of Births, Deaths, and Marriages in the Year 1853.

	SURNAMES.	Number of Entries of each Surname.		SURNAMES.	Number of Entries of each Surname.
1	SMITH	33,557	26	HARRIS	7,042
2	JONES	33,341	27	CLARK	6,920
3	WILLIAMS	21,936	28	COOPER	6,742
4	TAYLOR	16,775	29	HARRISON	6,399
5	DAVIES	14,983	30	DAVIS	6,205
6	BROWN	14,346	31	WARD	6,084
7	THOMAS	13,017	32	BAKER	6,013
8	EVANS	12,555	33	MARTIN	5,898
9	ROBERTS	10,617	34	MORRIS	5,888
10	JOHNSON	9,468	35	JAMES	5,755
11	ROBINSON	9,045	36	MORGAN	5,691
12	WILSON	8,917	37	KING	5,661
13	WRIGHT	8,476	38	ALLEN	5,468
14	WOOD	8,238	39	CLARKE	5,309
15	HALL	8,188	40	COOK	5,300
16	WALKER	8,088	41	MOORE	5,269
17	HUGHES	8,010	42	PARKER	5,230
18	GREEN	7,996	43	PRICE	5,219
19	LEWIS	7,959	44	PHILLIPS	5,124
20	EDWARDS	7,916	45	WATSON	4,771
21	THOMPSON	7,839	46	SHAW	4,759
22	WHITE	7,808	47	LEE	4,731
23	JACKSON	7,659	48	BENNETT	4,671
24	TURNER	7,549	49	CARTER	4,648
25	HILL	7,192	50	GRIFFITHS	4,639
				TOTAL	440,911

The Registrar General makes some pertinent remarks on the grouping of these familiar surnames. "It seems," he says, "that of the 50 most common names more than half are derived from the Christian or fore-name of the father, and they are literally *sire*-names or *sirnames*." Thirteen are derived from employments and occupations; seven from locality; two from peculiarities of colour—Brown and White. King, the thirty-seventh in point of commonness, stands the sole representative of its class.

TABLE XVII.—FIFTY of the most COMMON SURNAMES in England and Wales, arranged with reference to their Origin.

SURNAMES.	Numbers (from the foregoing Table).	SURNAMES.	Numbers (from the foregoing Table).	SURNAMES.	Numbers (from the foregoing Table).
Derived from CHRISTIAN or FORENAMES.		*Derived from* CHRISTIAN or FORENAMES—*cont.*		*Derived from* LOCALITY.	
				Wood - -	8,238
Jones - -	33,341	Phillips - -	5,124	Hall - - -	8,188
Williams - -	21,936	Watson - -	4,771	Green - -	7,996
Davies - -	14,983	Bennett - -	4,671	Hill - - -	7,192
Thomas - -	13,017	Griffiths - -	4,639	Moore - -	5,269
Evans - -	12,555				
		(27 Names) -	246,032	Shaw - -	4,759
Roberts - -	10,617			Lee - - -	4,731
Johnson - -	9,468	*Derived from* OCCUPA-			
Robinson - -	9,045	TIONS.		(7 Names) -	46,373
Wilson - -	8,917				
Hughes - -	8,010	Smith - -	33,557		
		Taylor - -	16,775	*Derived from* PERSONAL	
Lewis - -	7,959	Wright - -	8,476	PECULIARITIES.	
Edwards - -	7,916	Walker - -	8,088		
Thompson - -	7,839	Turner - -	7,549	Brown - -	14,346
Jackson - -	7,659			White - -	7,808
Harris - -	7,042	Clark - -	6,920		
		Cooper - -	6,742	(2 Names) -	22,154
Harrison - -	6,399	Ward - -	6,084		
Davis - -	6,205	Baker - -	6,013		
Martin - -	5,898	Clarke - -	5,309	*From other Circum-*	
Morris - -	5,888			*stances.*	
James - -	5,755	Cook - -	5,300		
		Parker - -	5,230	King - -	5,661
Morgan - -	5,691	Carter - -	4,648		
Allen - -	5,468				
Price - -	5,219	(13 Names) -	120,691	TOTAL -	440,911

Under the article SMITH in this dictionary, I have given the Registrar-General's statistics of the two great names Smith and Jones. I shall here add his table which shows first, the estimated number of persons bearing each of the 50 names, and secondly, the proportion which they bear to the population of England and Wales. It will be seen that one person in every 73 is a Smith; one in every 76 a Jones; and one in every 148 a Taylor. The most striking feature, perhaps, of this table, is, the exceedingly limited monarchy possessed by our Kings; for it clearly appears that if all the Kings in England and Wales should come to an understanding to divide these realms in a fair and equitable manner, each monarch could claim but 434 subjects. In other words, every four hundred and thirty-fifth man amongst us is a King!

It is observed in this very interesting Report, that the class of surnames derived from occupations is peculiarly instructive, " as illustrating the pursuits and customs of our forefathers; many of them furnish evidence of a state of society impressed with the characteristics of feudal times; and not a few are derived from terms connected with the amusements of the chase and other field sports to which our ancestors were so ardently attached. Widely different would be a national nomenclature derived from the leading occupations of the present day. The thousands employed in connection with the great textile manufactures would take precedence even of the *Smiths*; while the *Taylors* would give place to the shoemakers (now scarcely recognisable under the not common surname of *Suter*, with its variations Soutter, Sowter, &c.) as well as to the *Colliers*, the *Carpenters*, the *Farmers*, and others."

I must remark, however, what appears to have escaped the notice of the Registrar-

General, that the *Hosiers* go to swell the number of artizans in leather (see Hosier in this dictionary); that the Colliers of old times were not pitmen, but were makers of charcoal; and that Farmer as applied to the husbandman is a word that has come into use in times long subsequent to the introduction of surnames.

"The *Hawkers, Falconers, Bowyers, Fletchers, Arrowsmiths, Palmers, Pilgrims, Friars,* and *Freres,* and a host of other family names, derived from various callings which have become obsolete in this country, would be wanting."

TABLE XIX.—ESTIMATED NUMBER of PERSONS in ENGLAND and WALES bearing the under-mentioned Fifty most common SURNAMES. (Deduced from the Indexes of the Registers of Births, Deaths, and Marriages, and the estimated Population in the Year 1853.)

SURNAMES.	Estimated Number of Persons in 1853.	Of the entire Population One in	SURNAMES.	Estimated Number of Persons in 1853.	Of the entire Population One in
ALLEN	40,500	454	LEE	35,200	523
			LEWIS	58,000	318
BAKER	43,600	422			
BENNETT	35,800	514	MARTIN	43,900	420
BROWN	105,600	174	MOORE	39,300	468
			MORGAN	41,000	449
CARTER	33,400	551	MORRIS	43,400	424
CLARK	50,700	363			
CLARKE	38,100	483	PARKER	39,100	471
COOK	38,100	483	PHILLIPS	37,900	486
COOPER	48,400	380	PRICE	37,900	486
DAVIES	113,600	162	ROBERTS	78,400	235
DAVIS	43,700	421	ROBINSON	66,700	276
EDWARDS	58,100	316	SHAW	36,500	504
EVANS	93,000	198	SMITH	253,600	73
GREEN	59,400	310	TAYLOR	124,400	148
GRIFFITHS	34,800	529	THOMAS	94,000	196
			THOMPSON	60,600	304
HALL	60,400	305	TURNER	56,300	327
HARRIS	51,900	355			
HARRISON	47,200	390	WALKER	59,300	310
HILL	52,200	352	WARD	45,700	402
HUGHES	59,000	312	WATSON	34,800	529
			WHITE	56,900	323
JACKSON	55,800	330	WILLIAMS	159,900	115
JAMES	43,100	427	WILSON	66,800	275
JOHNSON	69,500	265	WOOD	61,200	301
JONES	242,100	76	WRIGHT	62,700	293
KING	42,300	435	TOTAL OF 50 SURNAMES	3,253,800	5·7

The subject of the local distribution of surnames is one that deserves more attention than it has received. While some names are scattered broad-cast over the kingdom, others are almost peculiar to some county or lesser district. Not to mention the famous example of Tre, Pol, and Pen in Cornwall, we may almost localize the termination *hurst* to Sussex and Kent, *combe* to Devonshire, and *thwaite* to Lancashire and the adjacent counties, because in those districts respectively most of the *places* with those terminations are found. But this is not always confined to surnames derived from places. Some other names seem to adhere to the district which gave them birth with a fond tenacity, as I have elsewhere had occasion to observe.* The locomotive character of the present age is, however, doing much to alter this, and to fuse all provincial peculiarities and distinctions. It would be well, therefore, for competent observers in various parts of the kingdom to record the *habitats* of particular names ere the opportunity now existing shall have passed away.

* Contrib. to Literature, p. 166.

IV.

Principal Collections of Surnames.

THE main sources for the history of *English* Surnames may be briefly enumerated.

Many personal or baptismal names in use in Anglo-Saxon times, such as are scattered everywhere up and down in the Saxon Chronicle, and the Codex Diplomaticus, became in course of time, hereditary or family appellations; but sufficient allusions to these will be found in the body of this work, and I shall therefore limit my observations on this subject to Domesday Book and subsequent records.

The document called Domesday, by common consent allowed to be the finest national record in Europe, was compiled by commissioners appointed by William the Conqueror, and finished about the 1086. It is a faithful summary of all the lands of his realm (three or four northern counties excepted), and contains the names of their proprietors. Sir Henry Ellis's General Introduction to Domesday, published in 1833, contains lists of all the tenants, from which it is evident that surnames of the heritable kind were very unusual, many even of the great Norman proprietors being entered simply by their Christian name, or by that accompanied by some description, and sometimes, as we have before seen, one and the same tenant is called by different names in different places. The common people (except in a few isolated cases already noticed) did not aspire to the dignity of a family name. As a specimen of the descriptions rather than surnames found in this noble Survey, I subjoin an extract from the Introduction, of under-tenants bearing the baptismal name of Ulf.

Vlf quidam homo, *Buck.* 149 b.
Vlf et frater ejus, *Yorksh.* 374.
Vlf cilt, *Linc.* 366.
Vlf diaconus, *Yorksh.* 373, 374.
Vlf fenisc, *Hunt.* 203, *Derb.* 277 b., *Nottingh.* 280 b., *Linc.* 354 b. bis. v. Vlfenisc, Vlffenisc.
Vlf fil. Azor, *Northampt.* 220 bis.
Vlf fil Borgerete, *Buck.* 146 b.
Vlf filius Suertebrand, *Linc.* 336.
Vlf homo Asgari stalre, *Buck.* 149 b.
Vlf homo Heraldi Comitis, *Buck.* 146.
Vlf homo Wallaf Comitis, *Northampt.* 228.
Vlf huscarle Regis E. *Midd.* 129, *Buck.* 149.
Vlf pater Sortebrand, *Clam. in Chetst.* 377.
Vlf tope sune,* *Clam. in Chetst.* 376 b.
Vlf teignus R. E. *Midd.* 129, *Buck.* 148 b. bis. 149, 149 b., *Camb.* 196 b. 197, 197 b. bis., *Essex* 27.

The Winton Domesday, a survey of the lands which had belonged to King Edward the Confessor, made on the oath of eighty-six burgesses of Winchester in the time of Henry I. is remarkable for the number of surnames which it comprises.†

---

* Vlf filius Topi was one of the witnesses to William the Conqueror's Charter to the Abbey of Peterborough. See Mon. Ang., last edition, vol. i. p. 383.

† Sims's Manual for the Genealogist, &c.

The Monastic Records, such as chartularies, leiger-books, registers, chronicles, &c., contain many early family names, as also do a great number of Ancient Charters in the public offices, and in private possession. A vast number of these have in the lapse of succeeding centuries, become extinct. The Public Records of the kingdom, published by the Record Commission, either *in extenso*, or in calendars, such as the Liber Niger, or Black Book of the Exchequer, temp. Henry II.; the Patent Rolls, commencing temp. King John; the Charter and Plea Rolls, and many others, abound in early surnames, and throw much light on the rise and progress of these appellations.

The most valuable of these authentic documents, for our purpose, are the two folio volumes known as the Rotuli Hundredorum, or Hundred Rolls, of the date of 1273. King Edward I., on his return from Palestine, after the death of his father, Henry III., caused inquiries to be made into the state of the demesnes, and of the right and revenues of the crown, many of which, during the previous turbulent reign had been usurped both by the clergy and the laity. The inquisitions being made upon the oath of a jury of each hundred throughout the realm, this mass of documents is appropriately called Rotuli Hundredorum, or the Hundred Rolls.

Of the Indices Nominum of these volumes, which contain references to about 70,000 persons, I have made extensive use. The period at which the Rolls were drawn up, was one when family names, which had been gradually coming into use for nearly two centuries, had become general among all classes of persons; not indeed with the regularity which prevailed in later centuries, though almost every individual mentioned in the record bears a surname of some kind. Some of the surnames are in Latin, some in French, and some in English. The prefixes of the local names are *De*, *At (ate* or *aten)*, *In the*, &c. Most of the names derived from occupations, offices, &c., retain the *Le*, though this is sometimes omitted. Not unfrequently the same person's name is written in two or three languages, with twice that number of varying orthographies. I have gone through the whole of these copious indices for the purpose of collating the family names of the thirteenth century with those of the nineteenth, and it cannot fail to strike the curious reader how great a general similarity exists between the nomenclature of the liegemen of King Edward I. and that of the subjects of Queen Victoria. The letters H.R. throughout this dictionary refer to these ancient surnames.

The other publications of the Record Commission, and various chronicles, &c., down to the XVI. century contain useful illustrations of our family nomenclature.

With regard to the existing nomenclature of the people of England and Wales, the returns deposited in the office of the Registrar General may be considered to contain every name; and when that official shall have carried out his intention of printing all the names registered in a whole year, we may expect to have an approximately complete list of the designations not only of the English and Welsh people, but also of settlers from Scotland and Ireland, and of the strangers for the time being within our gates.

As yet, the greatest repertorium of printed surnames is the London Directory—that wonderful book which not only supplies us with the designations of literally millions of Englishmen, but also shews us how and where they "live and move, and have their being." Every district of the United Kingdom is more or less represented there, for the simple reason that there is no district that does not, in our enterprizing age, send some or many of its denizens to the capital. Two hundred years ago old Fuller foresaw the concentrating force of this great city, and predicted that in time all England would 'Londonize,'—"*et tota Anglia Londonizabit;*" and even so it is; London in this, as in many other respects, is England, or rather the United Kingdom. You may trace from Caithness to Cornwall, and from the mouth of the Thames to that of the Shannon, and few, comparatively, will the names be, borne by Englishman, Welshman, Cornishman, Scotchman, Gael, or Irishman, that have not a place in that great *nominal* treasure-house. In fact it is commonly remarked of an unusual name, that "it is not to be found in the London Directory." Of that bulky tome, as well as of the local directories of several great provincial cities and towns, I have largely availed myself.

It will be observed that very often in the ensuing pages I have spoken with distrust and disparagement of what is called the Roll of Battel Abbey. In my English Surnames I printed three considerable lists of Norman surnames going under this general designation, not however without duly cautioning the reader against accepting them as genuine documents of the period to which they are ascribed.

Fuller investigation convinces me that the Roll of Battel Abbey is a nonentity. But like many other mythic things, we may safely say that it *ought* to have existed. For, the Conqueror on the field of Hastings made a famous vow that if God would grant him the victory over the English, he would found upon the spot a great Abbey, wherein masses should be said for all those who should be slain in the battle. Now, when the Victor carried his intention into effect, there *ought* to have been a bede-roll or list of those whose souls were thus to be cared for; (and this, as Mr. Hunter has well observed, would have been "in the highest and best sense, the Battel Abbey Roll;") but if we consider the utter improbability of his having had a muster-roll of the vast army who embarked with him on this expedition, and at the same time reflect upon the impossibility of the monks performing the Church's rite individually for the souls of the thirty thousand warriors who are said to have fallen on that dreadful day, we shall at once see that, however theoretically accordant with the vow such an arrangement may have been, it could not be practically carried out.

It may be urged, however, that a Roll containing the names of the leaders and grandees of the expedition was preserved. But to this it may be replied that, although Battel Abbey was unusually rich in every kind of monastic chronicle, record, and other muniment, most of which are preserved to the present day, no mention whatever is found of such list or Roll, either during the existence of the Monastery or at its Dissolution.

But while the existence of any such record as an authoritative roll of the Norman invaders is denied, there can be no doubt that the various lists which purport to be *the* Roll of Battel Abbey are of considerable antiquity—much earlier probably than the date of the Reformation, though certainly much later than the year 1066. Mr. Hunter mentions no less than ten such lists, but in no case is there an attribution of them either to Battel Abbey or to any authority nearly contemporary with the Conquest. It is not necessary to accept the censure of Camden and of Dugdale as to the falsifications of one or any of these lists by the monks of Battel in order to gratify the vanity of benefactors. They were doubtless drawn up, as a matter of curiosity, by private individuals, and without any sinister design. Perhaps the greatest proof of their being non-official, and of a date long subsequent to the Conquest is, that many of the names of distinguished followers of William which are found in Domesday Book have no place in any copy of the so-called Battel Abbey Roll. The whole question has been fully and most ably treated by the Rev. Joseph Hunter, F.S.A., in vol. VI. of the Sussex Archæological Collections, and it is therefore unnecessary to enter further into the subject.

V.

Miscellaneous Observations.

IN dealing with the surnames of my fellow subjects and countrymen, the principal object I have had in view has always been to shew from what sources those multitudinous and various words are derived, and to give a rationale of the means by which they have become the distinguishing marks of kindreds and families. It is but just to enter into some details on this subject, for the twofold purpose of guarding the reader against misapprehensions as to my real intentions, and of defending myself from the possible accusation of not having fully discharged the labour I have undertaken to perform. For this purpose it will be necessary to state in general terms my own views of the whole subject, so that there may be no mistake as to whether ' performance ' on my part falls short of ' promise,' in the laborious pages now offered to public notice, or not.

My design throughout has been chiefly etymological—using that word in its most popular, and least technical sense. I wish to convey to the inquirer information as to the immediate origin of each particular surname. Thus if a man is known among his neighbours by a word which is identical with the name of a place, an occupation, or an office—by a word which is expressive of a physical or mental quality—by a word which is identical with some object natural or artificial—my duty is simply to state that that man's surname is derived from such place, occupation, office, quality, or object, and to show, as well as I can, how that surname came to be adopted six or seven hundred years ago, more or less, as the distinctive mark of the original bearer's posterity in all time to come. It is no more a part of my design to enter into the history of the word which has become a surname, than it is the duty of the man who puts bricks and stones into a wall to make himself acquainted with the chemical ingredients of the brick or the geological formation to which he is indebted for the stone. I wish to be clearly understood upon this point, because I infer from the remarks of many of my correspondents, that they imagine that I am to trace every name to the radical meaning of the word which it represents, than which nothing has ever been further from my intention.

But while thousands of surnames of the kinds above referred to may be said to explain themselves, there are multitudes of others of which the meaning is, to most persons, entirely hidden. Words obsolete for centuries in our spoken and written language are still retained in our family nomenclature, fossilized, as it were, alongside of words still current and known to all.

And here lies the principal charm of this pursuit. It is interesting enough to know that the Mortimers came from a place so called in Normandy; that the Stuarts sprang from a personage who was in old times the High Steward of Scotland; that the Rouses sprang from a certain Norman, who, like his countryman and sovereign, was called Rufus by reason of his red hair; that the Longs descended from a tall, and the Shorts from a diminutive specimen of human kind—that our Ashes and our

Elmeses, in the old unsophisticated times, were content to bear designations borrowed from some great tree, near which they dwelt—all this, I say, is very pleasant knowledge; but it is among names derived from less obvious sources, from obsolete words, from forgotten employments, customs, offices, and dignities, from old and disused personal appellations, and from a host of other such-like things, that the curious enquirer finds his chief enjoyment; and to examine and place in their proper ranks and orders these fossils of earlier stratifications is the object of every one who enters with zeal and judgment into this wide but hitherto little known field of inquiry.

At the present time, a taste seems to prevail for fanciful etymology; but I have little sympathy with those philologists, to whom "the deduction of Jeremiah King from a cucumber is child's (not to say *childish*) play." I am not one of those

> ————"learn'd philologists who chase
> A panting syllable through time and space,
> Start it at home, and hunt it, in the dark,
> To Gaul, to Greece—and into Noah's Ark!"

If I can find a reasonable etymon for a name upon the surface, I do not consider it worth while "to dig and delve ten fathoms deep" for one. Of course there are many exceptions to this as to most other rules, and it will be seen in numerous instances in these pages, that surnames very often signify something entirely different from what at first sight they seem to represent.

Of speculative etymology we have already more than enough. Much time, paper, and ink would be saved if men would look a little more at the *obvious*, and a little less at the *recondite*, in these investigations. In support of this remark, in respect of Surnames, let me adduce a single instance : The name *Affleck* is explained in the little publication "The Folks of Shields," as a derivation from the Gaelic '*abhleag*, a burning coal,' and in a far more important work, as '*a*, negative, and *fleck*, a SPOT ; *spotless*.' These are the opinions of two gentlemen bearing respectively the Scottish names of Brockie and Ferguson, who, if they had taken the trouble to look into a gazetteer of their fatherland, would have found that *Affleck* is simply a local corruption of Auchinleck, a well-known place in Ayrshire. It would be easy to multiply instances, but I hope that this one is quite sufficient to illustrate the present argument.

To prevent misapprehension of another kind, let me say that it was never intended to give a genealogical character to this work. This would have involved interminable labour to little purpose. Next to the derivation of a name, its history and origin have claimed my attention. In the case of territorial and of foreign surnames, I have endeavoured, as often as possible, to mention the epoch at which it first appears in our records. Occasionally, when the history of a name requires it, some genealogical details are given, but these are as few and slight as possible.

And now I come to another point requiring explanation—the numerous omissions of surnames from this work. Thousands of names have been passed over *sub silentio*, and for this a variety of reasons can be assigned. In the first place, it has never been any part of my plan to hunt after names, but only to record and to illustrate such as have crossed my path. Secondly : Thousands of local surnames which I have met with, I have been unable to identify with the places from which they were derived. I had some thoughts of making a list of these unidentified names, but this would have been of little practical utility. Thirdly : Hundreds of names have been so corrupted as to baffle the most ingenious guess-work that I could bring to bear upon them. Fourthly : Many foreign names naturalized here have not appeared of sufficient standing to claim a place. These and other minor reasons must be my apology for the numerous omissions that every reader will be able to discover. I trust, however, that

e

the number of well-known and widely-spread names that have been overlooked is comparatively small. I believe, moreover, that the names to be found in the Patronymica Britannica represent nine-tenths of the numerical strength of the United Kingdom, the omissions being principally of those names which are limited either to remote districts, or to an exceedingly small number of individuals.* On the whole, the surnames that do not appear at all have cost me more trouble than those that do.

One more duty remains for me to perform, and that is the very agreeable one of returning my sincere thanks to the numerous friends who have assisted my labours by their kind and interesting communications. The list of these would more than occupy this page, but I cannot refrain from mentioning the names of a few to whom I have been specially indebted.

My best thanks are due to the Right Honourable the Earl of Stair, for the list of Scottish Surnames commencing with *Mac*, printed at pp. 205 et seq., and to Patrick Boyle, Esq., of Shewalton, N.B,, for a supplementary list, also printed at p. 208. To Charles Dalrymple, Esq., F.S.A., Scotl., of West Hall, in Aberdeenshire, I am under great obligations for many useful criticisms and suggestions. David Mackinlay, Esq., of Pollokshields, Glasgow, placed at my disposal a copious list of surnames with many useful elucidations, the result of his own researches on the subject. From Sir Erasmus Dixon Borrowes, Bart. ; from William Smith Ellis, Esq. ; from James T. Hammack, Esq.; from Wm. J. O'Donnavan, Esq.; and from J. Bertrand Payne, Esq., I have received valuable aid; nor must I omit to record my obligations to George Graham, Esq., Her Majesty's Registrar-General, for his permission to make use of much of the matter on " Family Nomenclature," contained in his XVI. Annual Report.

SURNAMES USED AS CHRISTIAN NAMES.—" Reader, I am confident an instance can hardly be produced of a surname made Christian in England, save since the Reformation; before which time the priests were scrupulous to admit any at the font except they were baptised with the name of a Scripture or legendary saint. Since, it hath been common ; and although the Lord Coke was pleased to say he had noted many of them prove unfortunate, yet the good success in others confutes the general truth of the observation."—Fuller's Worthies, vol. i. p. 160.

The following observations from Dean Trench's *Study of Words*, are well worthy of transcription here :—

" I am sure there is much to be learned from knowing that the Surname, as distinguished from the Christian name, is the name over and above, not the 'sire'-name or name received from the father, but 'sur'-name (super nomen)—that while there never was a time when every baptised man had not a Christian name, inasmuch as his personality before God was recognised, yet the Surname, the name expressing a man's relation, not to the kingdom of God, but to the worldly society in which he lives, is only of a much later growth, an addition to the other, as the word itself declares. And what a lesson at once in the upgrowth of human society, and in the contrast between it and the heavenly society, might be appended to this explanation. There was a period when only a few had Surnames—only a few, that is, had any significance or importance in the order of things temporal ; while the Christian name from the first was common to every man."

I would say a few words as to the title I have chosen for this work—*Patronymica Britannica*—since an objection may be raised to such a use of the former word. A

* The name Brushfield is limited to ten persons, and that of Fairholt to a single individual.

patronymic, in its true and original sense, is a modification of the father's name borne by the son, as Tydides, the son of Tydeus. The ancients formed their patronymics by an addition at the end of the father's name, and modern nations have done the same in several instances, as, for example, in such names as John*son*, Paulo*witz*, Peter*kins*. In others, the filial relation is shown by a prefix, as in *O'*Brien, *Mac* Intosh, *Fitz*-Herbert, *Ap* John. These may be correctly called *patronymical surnames;* while those that are derived from places, occupations, physical characteristics, and the rest, have no claim to be so considered.

But there is a secondary sense in which the word *patronymic* applies to every surname. It is the "father name," and shows the relation of the individual to a particular family descended from a common parent. Just as the Christian name should designate the individual as a member of the visible church of God, so the surname identifies him with his Father and his Father's Fathers, up to the very *fons et origo* of the name.

ADDITIONAL NOTES RECEIVED DURING THE PRINTING OF

THE SUPPLEMENT.

AUNGIER. AUNGER. This name is found in England temp. Edward I. and II., when flourished Hervey of Staunton, a Judge, and the founder of Michael House (now merged in Trinity College, Cambridge), who was of this family. The name is derived from the province of Anjou, and is found in charters in the Latinized form of Angevinus.

BRYAN. The signification of this name is given in the dictionary. The family were seated, from a very early period, at Tor-Bryan, co. Devon; as also at Langherne, in South Wales, and Woodford Castle, co. Dorset. Of this family was the chivalrous Sir Guy Bryan, Lord Bryan, K.G., temp. Edward III., and standard-bearer at the celebrated battle of Calais. He is called Sir Guy Bryan by contemporary writers. See Scrope and Grosvenor Roll, Beltz's Order of the Garter, &c. But in an inscription formerly at Seale, co. Kent, his second son, William, was called "Dominus Willelmus *de* Bryene" (ob. 1395). This territorial prefix was doubtless a clerical blunder. Other spellings of the name are Brian, Brien, Brianne, &c. The Christian name Guy was frequent in the family.

BUTLIN.* "In Northamptonshire Boutevillaine is now corrupted to Butlin. I have had documents of the time of Elizabeth in my hands, in which it has been given 'Butlin, alias Boutevillaine,' and in Bridges' Northamptonshire it occurs in an inscription." Communicated by Edward Pretty, Esq., F.S.A.

CITOLIN. See under Sitterling in these Notes.

CROWDY. In the West of England a violin is called a "crowdy-kit;" in Scotland "crowdie" means porridge, or something of a similar kind. These are both extremely unlikely etymons, and the name is probably local.

DICKEY. This name might well be taken as one of the "nursenames" of Richard, but against this a correspondent strongly protests. Another, but rather

fanciful derivation, is from the "Clan of the Dike," or Roman Wall. (See, however, Dykes in the dictionary.) A family pedigree deduces them from a Celtic clan called the Clanna Diagha, founded by a chieftain called Diagha and Dega. The family went from Scotland into Ireland about the year 1666, and settled in co. Derry. Inf. A. M'Naghten Dickey, Esq.

DICKIE. An older form of Dickey, above.

DRAKEFORD. The name is clearly local, though the place is not to be found. The family have long been connected with Staffordshire, and there is a tradition of their having been anciently called De Drakensford.

DUDENEY.* In Hogg's Picturesque Views, published in 1786, there is a view of a building called Dudeney chapel, which is said to have stood in Ashdown Forest, co. Sussex. No such building is now remembered in the district; but as the surname seems to be localized to Sussex, it is probably indigenous to that county, and not of French origin as I have suggested in the body of the dictionary.

FELL.* We must not overlook the adjective meaning of this word, which is sharp, keen, biting, cruel, from the A.-Sax. *felle.*

FOURACRE. This name, sometimes written Foweraker, has been for some centuries connected with Exeter. It is doubtless local, the termination signifying a field. The arms of the family, "on a saltire five escallop-shells," have been thus expounded by an advertising "herald":—

"*This* arms *is* a reward for valour in mounting an enemy's wall; for which the saltire was used as a ladder; and the scallops show the founder of this family to have been *five times* on pilgrimage to the Holy Land!"

A facetious correspondent remarks that the name was most likely borrowed by the crusading hero (never before heard of by the family) from the fact of his having been present with Cœur de Lion, in 1190, *afore Acre!*

HENSMAN. " Hensman, alias Hench-man." Bridges' Northamptonshire.

HERVEY.* According to Collins, "the surname of Hervey or Harvey, written anciently with Fitz (i.e., son of Hervey), is derived from Robert Fitz-Hervey, a younger son of Hervey, Duke of Orleans, who is recorded among those valiant commanders who accompanied William the Conqueror in his expedition into this kingdom in 1066." Although this statement does not appear to be well supported, there is no doubt of the early Norman origin of the noble family. *De* Hervey is evidently a misnomer, as the name is derived from the baptismal Hervé, which was by no means unusual in Norman and later times. See under Harvey.

HORSENAIL.* It has been discovered that this Kentish name is a corruption of Arsenal. Mr. C. Roach Smith has seen a seal inscribed with the name (D') Arsenel.

KINNINMONTH. A corruption of the Scottish local name, Kynninmond.

LYNAM. There are places called Lyneham in cos. Oxford and Wilts. The family occur in Cornwall as Lynham at any early period, and the Irish branch are said to have sprung from that county.

LYNOM. See Lynam.

MEDLAND * The H.R. De Medelands occur in Cambridgeshire, but the existing family spring from Devonshire, and in that county there is a manor called Medland.

NORWAY. Possibly from the country, but far more likely a corruption of some English local name—Northway for instance.

PECKOVER. This surname is local, though the place is not ascertained. The termination *over* (A-Sax. *ofer*) signifies a margin, brink, bank, or shore. Halliwell quotes from a medieval poem the following lines :—

> " She came out of Sexlonde
> And rived here at Dovere,
> That stondes upon the sees *overe*."

PERCEVAL,* not Percival, is the ancient and recognised orthography.

SHAKSPEARE.* The earliest person of this name discovered by the Poet's best and most recent illustrator, Mr. Halliwell, is Thomas Shakspeare, who was officially connected with the port of Youghal, in Ireland, in 1375; but recent research has adduced an earlier possessor of the name, in the person of one Henry *Shakespere*, who was holder of a ploughland in the parish of Kirkland, co. Cumberland, in the year 1350. Notes and Queries, Aug. 18, 1860. Hence it is probable that the name originated on the Border, and had its rise in those feuds from which the Armstrongs, the Bowmans, the Spearmans, and other belligerent families also derived theirs.

SHENSTONE. A parish in Staffordshire.

SITTERLING. In the parish register of St. John, Lewes, a certain surname undergoes various changes from " Citoline " to " Sitterling." This is about the year 1640, and no doubt refers to the family of one of John Evelyn's instructors. " It was not till the yeare 1628," says that admirable diarist, " that I was put to learne my Latine rudiments, and to write, of one Citolin, a Frenchman in Lewes." Diary i. 8.

STREATFEILD.* I think there is no doubt of the derivation of this name from the locality which I have indicated, notwithstanding the occasional forms Stratvile, Stretvile, &c. The latinization *De Strata Villa* has been supposed to imply "the paved town." Among some papers preserved in the family, it is noted that an ancestor, travelling about a century since in Saxony, met with a family named Streightveldt, who bore the arms and crest of the Kentish Streatfeilds. Inf. W. C. Streatfeild, Esq.

TRAYTON. This family, originally written Treton, and springing from Cheshire, settled at Lewes, co. Sussex, in the XVI. century. The family became extinct in the XVIII. century, but not the *name*, for, singularly enough, at Lewes, and in a great many of the surrounding parishes, Trayton is extremely common as a baptismal name, among families totally unconnected by blood. Many who bear it would be astonished to learn that it is not as regular a Christian name as Henry, or George, or Philip.

VIDGEN. Said to be a corruption of Fitz-John.

⁎ In the Ulster Journal of Archæology, vols. v. and vi., there are two very curious and interesting papers, on the names prevalent in the counties of Down and Antrim, with *maps* showing their localization, by the Rev. A. Hume, LL.D. This mode of illustration, if applied to the British islands at large, would be of great importance and value.

Family Characteristics.

Many English families, especially in the northern counties, are characterised by some epithet, complimentary or otherwise, which usually begins with the same letter as the surname. A few of these will be found scattered through the dictionary. The following were sent me by the late Mr. M. A. Denham, of Pierse Bridge :—

DURHAM.

The beggarly Baliols.
The base Bellasis.
The bloody Brackenburies.
The bold Bertrams
The bauld Blakestones.
The brave Bowes.
The bare-boned Bulmers.
The bacchanalian Burdons.
The clacking Claxtons.
The confident Conyers.
The crafty Cradocks.
The cozening Croziers.
The eventful Evers.
The friendly Forsters.
The filthy Foulthorpes.
The generous Garths.
The handsome Hansards.

The hoary Hyltons.
The jealous Jennisons.
The lamb-like Lambtons.
The light Lilburnes.
The lofty Lumleys.
The mad Maddisons.
The manly Mairs.
The noble Nevilles.
The politic Pollards.
The placid Places.
The ruthless Ruths.
The salvable Salvins.
The shrewd Shadforths.
The sure Surtees.
The testy Tailboys.
The wily Wilkinsons.
The wrathful Wrens.

NORTHUMBERLAND

The princely Percys.
The potent Percys.
The peerless Percys.
The proud Percys.
The thrifty Thorntons.
The fierce Fenwicks.

The heartless Halls.
The greedy Greys.
The warlike Widdringtons.
The courteous Collingwoods.
The royal Roddams.

YORKSHIRE.

The grave Gascoynes.
The proud Pickerings.
The trusty Tunstalls.
The undefiled Tunstalls.
The lofty Cliffords.

The grave Griffiths.
The stern Stapletons.
The manly Mauleverers.
The tall Tilneys.*

* Of what a *lofty* disposition must one branch of this eminent family be, who not content to pass through the world as Tall Tilneys, must needs add a Long Pole to their name!

Explanation of Abbreviations, &c.

Arthur.—Etymological Dictionary of Family and Christian names, by William Arthur, M.A.

Bowditch.—Suffolk Surnames, by N. J. Bowditch. (See p. vi).

B. L. G.—The Landed Gentry of Great Britain and Ireland, by Sir Bernard Burke, Ulster.

Collins.—The Peerage of England, by Arthur Collins, Esq.

Cod. Dipl.—Codex Diplomaticus Saxonici Ævi. Saxon Charters, collected by J. M. Kemble, Esq., M.A.

Cotgrave.—A Dictionarie of the French and English Tongues, compiled by Randle Cotgrave. 1632.

D'Alton.—Illustrations, Historical and Genealogical, of King James's Irish Army List, 1689. By John D'Alton, Esq., Barrister. Dublin, 1855.

Dixon.—Surnames, by B. H. Dixon, Esq. (See p. vi).

Domesd.—Domesday Book.

Encycl. Herald.—Encyclopædia Heraldica, or a complete Dictionary of Heraldry, by W. Berry. Four vols. quarto.

Ferguson.—English Surnames, and their place in the Teutonic Family. (See p. xii).

To prevent misapprehension, it is as well to remark, that Eng. Surn. throughout means my own former work; while the volume of Mr. Ferguson is always referred to as here indicated.

Halliwell.—A Dictionary of Archaic and Provincial Words, &c., from the Fourteenth Century, by J. O. Halliwell, Esq., F.R.S. 2 vols. 8vo.

H. R.—Rotuli Hundredorum—the Hundred Rolls. (See p. xxx).

Jacob.—Jacob's Law Dictionary.

Kelham.—1. Domesday Book Illustrated, 1788. 2. Anglo-Norman Dictionary, 1779.

Landnamabok.—Islands Landnamabok, hoc est, Liber Originum Islandiæ. Copenhagen, 1847.

For most of the references to this work I am indebted to Mr. Ferguson's volume.

Nisbet.—System of Heraldry, by A. Nisbet, Esq. 2 vols. fol. Edinburgh, 1722.

N. and Q.—Notes and Queries.

R. G. 16.—The Sixteenth Annual Report of the Registrar General. Published by authority, 1856.

Richardson.—Dictionary of the English Language, by Chas. Richardson, L.L.D.

Shirley.—The Noble and Gentle Men of England, by Evelyn Philip Shirley, Esq., M.A. 1859.

ERRATA.

P. 13. ASSENDER. Pronounciation.
39. BRAYBROOK should be BRAYBROOK.
62. CLIVE—*from* the time, &c.
88. DEWEY. *Read*, Walter de Douuai, not Dounai.
103. ELLIS. The quotation beginning "Elles or Ellis—ends at husband.
166. HUNTER. *Read*, "The Hunters of Polmood, ... in the V. cent."
173. JOHN. For *Mickejohn* read *Micklejohn.*
180. KINLOCK should be Kinloch.
192. LEIGHTON. Read *vicecomes.*
192. 'LEMPRIERE. *For* Ex. inf. *read* Ex inf.
205. MAC. *For* Lord Stair, *read* the Earl of Stair.
220. MAULEVERER. *Read* Norroy, king of arms.

In a volume containing so many thousands of proper names, errors of orthography will doubtless be found, though it is hoped that they are comparatively few and trifling.

LIST OF SUBSCRIBERS.

The Earl of ABERGAVENNY, Eridge Castle.

R. T. Abraham, Esq., Heavitree, Exeter.

Sir R. Shafto Adair, Bart., Adair House, St. James's Square, London.

Thomas T. Adams, Esq., Ballinlanders, Tipperary.

George Ade, Esq., 12, Manchester Square, London.

Mrs. George Allfree, Linton, Staplehurst, Kent.

Richard Almack, Esq., F.S.A., Long Melford, Sudbury.

Thomas Francis Anderson, Esq., Liverpool.

Thomas Arkcoll, Esq., Langney.

The Earl of Ashburnham, Ashburnham Place.

Arthur Ashpitel, Esq., F.S.A., Poets' Corner, Westminster.

William Wakeford Attree, Esq., Recorder of Hastings, Fig-tree Court, Temple.

Thomas Attwood, Esq.

The Lord Auckland, Lord Bishop of Bath and Wells.

John Tattersal Auckland, Esq., F.S.A., Bourbel Villa, Eastbourne.

The Rev. CHARLES C. BABINGTON, M.A., F.R.S.. F.S.A., St. John's College, Cambridge.

G. P. Bacon, Esq., Lewes.

John Bacon, Esq., F.S.A., 35, Bathwick Hill, Bath.

John N. Bagnall, Esq., Charlemont Hall, Wednesbury.

John Baker Baker, Esq., Buxted.

Edward H. S. Banks, Esq., Rye.

Francis Barchard, Esq., Horsted Place, near Uckfield.

Richard Barratt, Esq., Lewes.

The Rev. M. W. Barton, M.A., Brandon Hill Bristol.

Thomas Barton, Esq., Threxton, near Watton, Norfolk.

Brian B. Barttelot, Esq., Stopham, Petworth.

Thomas Bateman, Esq., F.S.A., Youlgrave, co. Derby.

W. E. Baxter, Esq., Lewes.

William Baxter, Esq.

Lieut.-Col. North Ludlow Beamish, K.H., F.R.S., Lota Park, Cork.

Miss Beard, Rottingdean.

Charles Beard, Esq., Rottingdean.

Charles Beard, Esq., Lewes.

The Rev. Jas. Beck, Parham, Steyning.

William Beckwith, Esq., Seacox Heath, Hurstgreen.

Charles Beke, Esq., Ph.D., F.S.A., F.R.G.S., &c., &c., Belvedere, Mauritius.

James Bell, Esq., Cranbrook.

Mr. Thomas Berry, Brighton.

The Rev. G. C. Bethune, M.A., Chulmleigh, Devon.

Miss Bishop, Wargroves, Herstmonceux.

William Henry Blaauw, Esq., M.A., F.S.A., F.R.G.S., Beechland.

William Madox Blackwood, Esq., F.S.A., 1, Queen's Villas, Windsor.

Robert Blair, Esq., 42, Union Street, Greenock.

John Blaker, Esq., The Priory, Lewes.

Edgar Blaker, Esq., Lewes.

Robert Willis Blencowe, Esq., M.A., The Hooke, Sussex.

John George Blencowe, Esq., M.P., Bine Ham, Lewes.

Sir Charles R. Blunt, Bart., M.A., Heathfield Park.

Miss Julia R. Bockett, Brading, Burghfield, Reading.

Sir John P. Boileau, Bart., V.P.S.A., F.R.S., &c., 20, Upper Brook Street, and Ketteringham Park.

Colonel Boldero, Lowbeding, Horsham.

Henry Boldero, Esq., St. Leonard's Forest, Horsham.

His Imperial Highness the Prince Louis Lucien Bonaparte, 8, Westbourne Grove, West.

Joseph Boord, Esq., Verulam House, St. John's Wood. 2 copies.

The Rev. Carey H. Borrer, M.A., Rector of Hurst-Pierpoint.

William Borrer, Esq., F.L.S., &c., Henfield, Hurst-Pierpoint.

John Borrer, Esq., Portslade.

Sir E. Dixon Borrowes, Bart., Barretstown Castle, Ballymore-Eustace.

Beriah Botfield, Esq., M.P., M.A., F.R.S., F.S.A., &c., &c., Norton Hall, Daventry.

N. I. Bowditch, Esq., 9, Pemberton Square, Boston, Mass.

Patrick Boyle, Esq., M.A., Shewalton, Irvine, N.B.

The Honble. Henry Brand, M.P., Glynde.

The Lord Braybrooke, F.S.A., &c., Audley End. 2 copies.

His Excellency Henry H. Breen, Esq., Government House, St. Lucia.

The Marquis of Bristol, 6, St. James's Square, London. 2 copies.

William Henry Brockett, Esq., Gateshead.

Alexander Brown, Esq., Cowdray, Petworth.

The Rev. Henry Browne, M.A., Pevensey.

George Browning, Esq., F.S.S., Lewes.

John Collingwood Bruce, Esq., L.L.D., F.S.A., Newcastle-upon-Tyne. 2 copies.

W. Downing Bruce, Esq., F.S.A. Lond. and Scotl., &c., &c., Kilbagie House, Clackmannan.

Geo. B. Bruce, Esq., M. Inst.C.E., 24, Gt. George St., Westminster.

T. N. Brushfield, Esq., Medical Superintendent, County Asylum, Chester.

The Rev. Guy Bryan, M.A., F.S.A., Woodham Walter, Malden, Essex.

George Burgess, Esq., 18, Lincoln Street, Mile End Road, London.

Sir Bernard Burke, Ulster King of Arms, Dublin.

The Venerable Charles Parr Burney, D.D., F.R.S., F.S.A., &c., &c., Archdeacon of Colchester, Wickham-Bishop's Rectory, Witham, Essex.

Sir Charles Merrik Burrell, Bart., M.P., Knepp Castle.

Henry Mathews Burt, Esq., 34, Compton Terrace, Islington.

George Bushby, Esq., Lewes.

The Rev. Charles Henry Butcher, 1, Sussex Villas, Bridge Road, Hammersmith.

Mr. James Butland, Bookseller, Lewes.

George Slade Butler, Esq., Cler. Pacis, Rye.

John Rose Butlin, Esq., F.S.A., 37, Gordon Square, London.

The Rev. Archdall Buttemer, M.A., Stoke Park Villas, Guildford.

THOMAS DOWNIE CALTHROP, Esq., 7, Whitehall Place, Westminster.

John Campbell, Esq., M.D., R.N., Woking, Surrey.

William John Campion, Esq., Danny, Hurst-Pierpoint.

Henry Campkin, Esq., Reform Club, London.

George A. Carthew, Esq., F.S.A., East Dereham.

Saint Catherine's College, Cambridge. Per Rev. Henry Philpott, D.D., Master, Vice-Chancellor of Cambridge, and Chaplain to H.R.H. Prince Albert.

Richard Redmond Caton, Esq., F.S.A., Park, Oswestry.

Henry Catt, Esq., Arnold House, Brighton. 2 copies.

William Catt, Esq., Portland Place, Brighton.

Charles Catt, Esq., Brighton.

George Catt, Esq., Bishopston Mills.

Miss Helen Cattell, Westerham.

John Young Caw, Esq., F.S.A., F.R.S.L., Fountain Villa, Cheetham Hill, Manchester.

John Nurse Chadwick, Esq., King's Lynn.

William Chaffers, Esq., F.S.A., 66, Jermyn Street, London.

David N. Chambers, Esq., F.S.A., 47, Paternoster Row.

Richard S. Charnock, Esq., F.S.A., 8, Gray's Inn Square, London.

The Lord Bishop of Chichester, Palace, Chichester.

The Literary Society, Chichester.

Thomas Clark, Esq., Godalming.

Hyde Clarke, Esq., 42, Basinghall Street, London.

John Clayton, Esq., F.S.A., &c., Newcastle-upon-Tyne. 2 copies.

William Clayton, Esq., Dover.

Edward Cobb, Esq., Haverstock Hill.

Thomas Cobbe, Esq., Longcroft, Devizes.

John Colbatch, Esq., Sylvan Lodge, Brighton.

Charles A. Cole, Esq., Public Record Office, London.

Carlos Coleman, Esq., Chitcombe, Brede, Sussex.

J. H. Campion Coles, Esq., Eastbourne.

Boyce Harvey Combe, Esq., Oaklands, Sedlescombe, Sussex.

Alfred Compigné, Esq., Queensberry Lodge, Elstree, Herts, N.W.

George Cooke, Esq., Lewes.

Charles Cooper, Esq., 2, Florence Place, New Cross Road, S.E.

Charles Henry Cooper, Esq., F.S.A., Town Clerk of Cambridge.

Frederick Cooper, Esq., 40, Norfolk Square, Brighton.

William Durrant Cooper, Esq., F.S.A., Hon. Mem. Mass. Hist. Soc., 81, Guilford Street, Russell Square.

Joseph Cooper, Esq., Lewes.

The Rev. George Elwes Corrie, D.D., Master of Jesus College, Cambridge.

Richard W. Cotton, Esq., Barnstaple, Devon.

John Ross Coulthart, Esq., F.S.A., Scotl., Croft House, Ashton-under-Lyne. 2 copies.

William Courthope, Esq., Somerset Herald, Barrister-at-Law.

The Rev. Charles J. Crawford, D.D., Woodmansterne Rectory, Epsom.

Sir Edward Sheppard Creasy, Judge Advocate of Ceylon.

Robert Crosskey, Esq., Lewes.

James Crowdy, Esq., F.S.A., 17, Serjeant's Inn, Fleet Street.

H. Cunliffe, Esq., F.S.A., Albany, Piccadilly.

J. Brendon Curgenven, Esq., 11, Craven Hill Gardens, Hyde Park.

Captain G. C. D'Albiac, Brighton.

The Rev. Joseph Dale, M.A., Bolney (deceased).

Charles Dalrymple, Esq., F.S.A., Scotl., West Hall, Inch, co. Aberdeen.

J. Stuart Dalton, Esq., Liverpool Free Public Library, Duke St., Liverpool.

The Rev. George Henry Dashwood, M.A., F.S.A., Stow-Bardolph, Downham.

Henry D'Aveney, Esq., Blofield, Norwich.

Major-Gen. F. Davies, Danehurst, Uckfield.

Joseph Barnard Davis, Esq., F.S.A., Shelton, Staffordshire.

The Rev. W. H. Davey, M.A., Theological College, Chichester.

Mr. Thos. Davey, 195, High Street, Lewes.

The Rev. Charles Day, L.L.B., Vicar of Mucking, Romford, Essex.

Miss Dealtry, Bolnore, Cuckfield.

James Dearden, Esq., F.S.A., &c., Rochdale Manor.

Messrs. Deighton, Bell, & Co., Agents to the University of Cambridge.

The Earl De La Warr, Buckhurst.

Edward S. Dendy, Esq., Rouge-Dragon, Arundel.

The Rev. Pierre De Putron, M.A., Rodmell Rectory, Sussex.

H.G. The Duke of Devonshire, Devonshire House, London.

Hugh Welch Diamond, Esq., M.D., F.S.A., Twickenham House.

Thomas Dicker, Esq., Warminster.

Charles Scrase Dickins, Esq., Coolhurst.

C. Wentworth Dilke, Esq., F.S.A., 76, Sloane Street.

B. Homer Dixon, Esq., K.N.L., Toronto, Canada West.

Robert William Dixon, Esq., Seaton Carew, co. Durham.

Henry William Dobell, Esq., Eltham, Kent.

John George Dodson, Esq., M.P.

Robert Thomas Dolan, Esq., Newhaven.

Andrew J. Doyle, Esq., Lewes.

Sir William Domville, Bart., Southfield Lodge, Eastbourne (deceased).

William J. O'Donnavan, Esq., Barrister-at-Law, 2, Cloisters, Temple.

D. Drakeford, Esq., Dillions, Crawley.

Mr. Dudeney, Milton House, Lewes.

Sir James Duke, Bart., Portland Place.

Mr. R. A. Durrant, Wellingham.

Frecheville L. Ballantine Dykes, Esq., Ingwell, Whitehaven. 2 copies.

Arthur Eden, Esq., Ticehurst.

Richard Edmunds, Esq., Worthing.

The Rev. H. T. Ellacombe, M.A., F.S.A., Rectory, Clyst St. George.

The Earl of Ellesmere, Bridgewater House.

Sir Henry Ellis, K.H., B.C.L., F.S.A., &c., &c., 24, Bedford Square.

Joseph Ellis, Esq., Brighton.

William Smith Ellis, Esq., Barrister-at-Law, Hydecroft, Crawley.

Colonel Elwood, Clayton Priory, Hurst-Pierpoint (deceased).

Mrs. Elwood, Clayton Priory, Hurst-Pierpoint.

The Right Hon. T. Erskine, The Grove, Eversley, Winchfield.

John Evans, Esq., F.S.A., Nash Mills, Hemel Hempsted.

George Farncombe, Esq., Bishopston.

John P. Fearon, Esq., Ockenden, Cuckfield.

John Fenwick, Esq., F.S.A., Newcastle-upon-Tyne.

Robert Ferguson, Esq., Morton, Carlisle.

William Figg, Esq., F.S.A., Lewes.

John Purcell Fitz-Gerald, Esq., Boulge Hall, Suffolk.

M. N. R. Purcell Fitz-Gerald, Esq.

The Rev. William Anthony Fitz-Hugh, M.A., Streat Rectory.

The Right Honble. Henry Fitz-Roy, M.P., 42, Upper Grosvenor Street (deceased).

J. B. Fletcher, Esq., Bersted Lodge, Bognor.

Sir William Browne Folkes, Bart., M.A., F.R.S., F.S.A., Hillington Hall, King's Lynn.

Edward Foss, Esq., Churchill House, Dover.

The Rev. Philip Freeman, M.A., Thorverton Vicarage, (for Cullompton Clerical Book Club).

Gilbert J. French, Esq., F.S.A. London and Scotl., Bolton, Lancashire.

Thomas Frewen, Esq., Brickwall, Northiam.

The Lord Viscount GAGE, Firle Park.

Sir Thomas Rokewode-Gage, Bart., F.S.A., Hengrave Hall, Bury St. Edmunds.

John Gainsford, Esq., 4, London Road, Brighton.

Joseph Gardner, Esq., Architect, Folkestone.

John Garland, Esq., F.L.S., Dorchester.

The Rev. Charles Gaunt, M.A., Isfield Parsonage.

Francis Harding Gell, Esq., Coroner for East Sussex, Lewes.

George Gent, Esq., Moyns Park, Steeple Bumpstead, Essex.

John Gibbs, Esq., Maze-Hill Cottage, St. Leonards-on-Sea.

George Carew Gibson, Esq., F.S.A., Sandgate Lodge, Steyning (deceased).

William Ginner, Esq., J.P., Hastings.

J. Wyllie Giuld, Esq., 3, Park Circus, Glasgow.

J. H. Glover, Esq., F.S.A., Buckingham Palace.

Burwood Godlee, Esq., J.P., Leighside, Lewes.

Mr. Henry Goldsmith.

C. E. Goodhart, Esq., M.A., Langley Lodge, Beckenham.

John Robert Gooding, Esq., Southwold, Suffolk.

Mrs. Gorring, Seaford.

John Gosden, Esq., Eastbourne.

The Rev. J. Gould, M.A., Burwash Rectory.

J. Grandidge, Esq., Bury Road, Rochdale.

The Rev. Thomas Grantham, M.A., Bramber Rectory, Steyning.

William Grantham, Esq., Hove, Brighton.

Richard Gravely, Esq., Newick.

The Rev. C. S. Green, M.A., St. Anne's Rectory, Lewes.

The Rev. H. T. Griffith, Alby Hill, Hanworth, Norwich.

The Rev. John Griffith, M.A., Principal of Brighton College.

The Rev. Robert Scarlett Grignon, Rector of St. John's, Lewes.

The Rev. Edmund W. Grinfield, M.A., &c., &c., 6, Lower Brunswick Place, Brighton.

John Grover, Esq., Lewes.

Miss E. Grover.

Robert Growse, Esq., 9, Wellington Square, Hastings.

Edmund Grundy, Esq., 26, High Street, Manchester.

Daniel Gurney, Esq., F.S.A., North Runcton, King's Lynn.

JAMES HACON, Esq., Long Dale Villa, Oxton, Cheshire.

William D. Haggard, Esq., F.S.A., 50, Brunswick Road, Brighton.

Edward Hailstone, Esq., F.S.A., &c., Horton Hall, Bradford.

The Venerable W. H. Hale, M.A., Archdeacon of London, Charterhouse.

William Hallett, Esq., Alderman, Brighton.

Mr. James Hammond, Lewes.

John Alexander Hankey, Esq., Balcombe Place.

Mrs. S. Hannington, Hurst-Pierpoint.

The Rev. L. Vernon Harcourt, M.A., 29, Portland Place.

John Harris, Esq., Lesney Park, Erith, S.E.

Mrs. Harrison, Brighton.

William Harrison, Esq., F.G.S., &c., Galligreaves House, nr. Blackburn, Lancashire.

William Harvey, Esq., F.S.A., Lewes.

Charles Harwood, Esq., F.S.A., Recorder of Shrewsbury, Folkestone.

The Hastings Mechanics' Institution.

J. M. Head, Esq.

Charles Hill, Esq., F.S.A., West Hoathly, Sussex.

John Hillman, Esq., Lewes.

Robert Hillman, Esq., St. Anne's, Lewes.

John Hodgson Hinde, Esq., M.P., F.S.A., &c., Acton House, Northumberland.

The Rev. William Henry Hoare, M.A., Oakfield, Crawley.

John Hodgkin, Esq., Barrister-at-Law, Shelley's, Lewes.

Nathaniel Hollingsworth, Esq., F.S.A., 22, Gower Street, London.

Henry Holman, Esq., Gate House, East Hothly.

Mrs. W. Sancroft Holmes, Eastbourne.

A. J. Beresford Hope, Esq., M.P., M.A., F.S.A., &c., Bedgbury, Kent.

Richard Hoper, Esq., Barrister-at-Law, Temple.

John Hoper, Esq., Shermanbury (deceased).

Henry Hoper, Esq.

D. D. Hopkyns, Esq., F.S.A., Weycliffe, St. Catherine's, Guildford.

Thomas Horton, Esq., 6, Green Street, Grosvenor Square

Philip Henry Howard, Esq., F.S.A., Corby Castle, Carlisle.

James Howell, Esq., Westfield House, Brighton.

William Egerton Hubbard, Esq., Lower Beeding.

Wm. Henry Huffam, Esq., Dock Office, Hull.

B. Husey-Hunt, Esq., Lewes.

Thomas Huson, Esq.

Edward Hussey, Esq., Scotney Castle.

P. E. Hyde, Esq., Engineer and Surveyor's Office, Town Hall, Worthing.

HENRY INGLEDEW, Esq., Newcastle-on-Tyne.

The Rev. Henry M. Ingram, M.A., Highgate, London.

E. T. Inskip, Esq., Bristol.

HENRY JACKSON, Esq., St. James's Row, Sheffield.

J. Livingston Jay, Esq., Royal Hospital, Greenwich.

Mr. Jeffery, Lewes.

WILLIAM KELL, Esq., F.S.A., Gateshead.

William Polhill Kell, Esq., Lewes.

Samuel Kemp, Esq., 37, Canonbury Square, Islington. 2 copies.

C. E. Kempe, Esq., Pembroke Coll., Oxon.

James Kidder, Esq., Lewes.

W. King, Esq., M.D., 23, Montpellier Road, Brighton.

Thomas King, Esq., 33, Richmond Place, Brighton.

Sir Norton Knatchbull, Bart., F.S.A., Mersham Hatch, Ashford.

J. Knight, Esq., East Lavant.

George Knott, Esq., Woodcroft, Cuckfield.

The Rev. John Knowles, Ph.D., F.S.A., F.G.S., Grantham.

The Historic Society of LANCASHIRE and Cheshire. By J. H. Genn, Esq., 3, Orient Street, Everton, Liverpool.

R. G. Latham, Esq., M.D., &c., &c., &c., Greenford, Middlesex.

Robert Laurie, Esq., Clarencieux King of Arms, College of Arms, London.

Major Egerton Leigh, High Leigh, Warrington.

Thomas C. Leslie, Esq., Westhall, co. Aberdeen. 2 copies.

The Lewes Library Society.

John Lewis, Esq., Lewes.

The Liverpool Library, Bold Street, Liverpool.

Lieut.-Colonel G. Carr Lloyd, Lancing.

Charles Edward Long, Esq., M.A., 8, Chapel Street, Grosvenor Square, London.

R. W. Lower, Esq., Folkestone.

John Lucas, Esq., Lewes.

The Rev. W. Collings Lukis, M.A., F.S.A., The Rectory, Collingbourne Ducis, Marlborough.

The Rev. G. C. Luxford, M.A., Felpham, Bognor.

Mrs. MABBOTT, Southover Priory, Lewes (deceased). 2 copies.

Major W. E. A. Mac-Donnell, New Hall, Ennis, Ireland.

Lieut.-Colonel Mackay, Lewes.

W. B. Mackeson, Esq., F.G.S., &c., Hythe.

David Mackinlay, Esq , Pollokshields, Glasgow. 5 copies.

Colonel McQueen, Canterbury.

John Macrae, Esq., Lewes.

W. E. Mallet, Esq., Westhill, Jersey.

W. E. Mallet, Esq., Chalkwell Hall, Essex.

Manchester Free Library. R. W. Smiles, Esq., Librarian.

The "Lassie of Mannameade."

Mr. Thomas Martin, Cliffe, Lewes.

Mr. Alderman Martin, Brighton.

Joseph Mayer, Esq., F.S.A., F.R.A.S., Liverpool.

The Rev. Thomas Medland, The Vicarage, Steyning.

The Rev. T. R. Medwin, Stratford-on-Avon.

William Mence, Esq., 7, Clayton Square, Liverpool.

Robert Mercer, Esq., Sedlescombe.

The Rev. Fredk. Mounteney Dirs Mertens, M.A., New Shoreham.

Francis Mewburn, Esq., Larchfield, Darlington.

Thomas J. Monk, Esq., Lewes.

Sir Francis Graham Moon, Bart., F.S.A., London.

Henry Moon, Esq., M.D., Brighton.

The Rev. Louis Henry Mordacque, M.A., Haslingden Parsonage, Lancashire.

Frederick Morgan, Esq., Henfield.

The Rev. F. O. Morris, Nunburnholme Priory, Hayton, York.

E. Morris, Esq., Lewes.

Charles James Muggeridge, Esq., Berstead Lodge, Twickenham.

John R. Mummery, Esq., 38, Mortimer Street, West, Cavendish Square.

W. Augustus Munn, Esq., Throwley House, Feversham.

James Barclay Murdoch, Esq., 223, St. Vincent Street, Glasgow.

Sir George Musgrave, Bart., F.S.A., Edenhall, Penrith.

Sheridan Muspratt, Esq,, M.D., F.R.S., &c., College of Chemistry, Liverpool.

HENRY FREDERICK NAPPER, Esq., Guildford.

John Neal, Esq., Liverpool.

John Nealds, Esq., Wellesley Cottage, Guildford.

John Nicholl, Esq., F.S.A., 8, Canonbury Place, London.

John Gough Nichols, Esq., F.S.A., &c., &c., Parliament Street.

Edward Nicholson, Esq., Lewes.

J. E. Nightingale, Esq., The Mount, Wilton.

Mr. James Noakes, Chiddingly.

H.G. The Duke of Norfolk, E.M., Arundel Castle.

John Manship Norman, Esq., Dencombe, Crawley, Sussex.

Mr. George Norman, Cooksbridge Brewery, Lewes.

T. Herbert Noyes, Esq., Jun., B.A., The Home Office.

Mr. Nye, 35, London Road, Brighton.

J. T. ODAM, Esq., St. Neot's, Huntingdonshire.

Lady Ogle, Withdeane, Brighton.

The Rev. John Olive, M.A., Vicarage, Hellingly.

Mrs. W. Olliver, Eastbourne.

Henry Onderdonk, Esq., Junior, Jamaica, Long Island, New York.

Sir John Orde, Bart., Kilmory, Loch Gilp Head.

The Rev. Augustus Orlebar, M.A., Farndish, Wellingborough.

George Ormerod, Esq., D.C.L., F.S.A., &c., Sedbury Park, Chepstow.

The Ven. W. B. Otter, Archdeacon of Lewes, Cowfold.

Frederic Ouvry, Esq., F.S.A., 66, Lincoln's Inn Fields.

Lt.-Colonel PAINE, Patcham Place.

Cornelius Paine, Esq., Jun., Surbiton Hill, Surrey.

Mr. A. Pam, Lewes.

J. P. Parkinson, Esq., D.C.L., Ravendale, Grimsby.

John Henry Parker, Esq., F.S.A., Oxford.

The Rev. Augustus Parsons, M.A., Southover, Lewes.

Messrs. John Latter, and Charles, Parsons, Lewes.

J. Bertrand Payne, Esq., &c., &c., Holmesdale, Jersey.

Edward Peacock, Esq., F.S.A., The Manor, Bottesford, near Brigg.

Richard Wilde Pearson, Esq., 31, Stockwell Park Road, Brixton, Surrey.

The Rev. John Peat, M.A., Rector of Hangleton, 4, Albany Villas, Cliftonville, Brighton.

William Peckover, Esq., F.S.A., Wisbech.

Apsley Pellatt, Esq., Staines.

Charles Spencer Perceval, Esq., LL.D., F.S.A., 24, Old Square, Lincoln's Inn.

Frederick Perkins, Esq., F.S.A., Chipstead Place, Kent, and 14, Royal Crescent, Brighton.

The Rev. John Louis Petit, M.A., F.S.A., 9, New Street, Lincoln's Inn.

John Pavin Phillips, Esq., High Street, Haverfordwest.

John Phillips, Esq., Hastings.

J. H. Pickford, Esq., J.P., M.D., M.R.I.A., Brighton.

Mr. F. Pickton, Perry's Place, Oxford Street.

J. A. Picton, Esq., F.S.A., 19, Clayton Square, Liverpool.

William H. Pilcher, Esq., 18, New Broad Street, London.

William Pinkerton, Esq., Jersey Villas, Hounslow.

Lewis Pocock, Esq., F.S.A., Southover Priory, Lewes.

Edward Polhill, Esq., 17, Brunswick Square, Brighton.

The Rev. Richmond Powell, M.A., South Stoke Rectory, Arundel.

The Rev. Thomas Baden Powell, M.A., Newick Rectory.

The Rev. John Peckleton Power, M.A., Huncote Grange, Enderby, co. Leicester.

Edward Pretty, Esq., F.S.A., Chillington House, Maidstone.

John Edward Price, Esq., London.

Sir James Prior, R.N., F.S.A., F.R.A.S., 20, Norfolk Crescent, Hyde Park.

The Rev. J. R. Pursell, B.A., Park Crescent, Brighton.

THOMAS QUAIFE, Esq., Inland Revenue, Somerset House.

JAMES RAMSBOTHAM, Esq., Crowborough Warren, Tunbridge Wells.

William Ranger, Esq., Local Government Office, Whitehall, London.

The Rev. Henry Wm. G'h Meade Ray, The Elms, Derby.

John Chandos Reade, Esq., Shipton Court, Chipping Norton.

Mrs. William Rees, Spring Gardens, Haverfordwest. 2 copies.

Robert Reeves, Esq., Stream, Chiddingly.

Messrs. Relfe, Brothers, 150, Aldersgate St.

A. Henry Rhind, Esq., F.S.A., Sibster, Wick, N.B., and Down House, Durdham Down, Bristol.

Mr. J. Richards, Bookseller, Lewes.

H.G. The Duke of Richmond, Goodwood.

John Rickman, Esq., Jun., Lewes.

John Rickman, Esq., Wellingham (deceased).

George Charles Rigden, Esq., Lewes. 2 copies.

P. F. Robertson, Esq., Halton, Hastings.

The Rev. Divie Robertson, M.A., Beeding Priory, Hurst-Pierpoint.

E. W. Robins, Esq., Brighton.

E. G. Robinson, Esq.

James Rock, Esq., Jun., J.P., Hastings.

William Roots, Esq., M.D., F.S.A., Surbiton, Kingston-on-Thames.

G. Roots, Esq., F.S.A., 3, Tanfield Court, Temple.

Thomas Ross, Esq., Claremont, Hastings.

Richard Rowland, Esq., Creslow House, Buckinghamshire.

Captain J. S. Rundle, R.N., Carlisle.

The Rev. Henry John Rush, M.A., Rustington Vicarage, Littlehampton.

J. Watts Russell, Esq., D.C.L., F.R.S., F.S.A., &c., Ilam Hall, Ashbourne, Derby.

WILLIAM SALT, Esq., F.S.A., &c., 23, Park Square, Regent's Park.

John Sanders, Esq., Governor of County Prison, Lewes.

Mr. James Sanders, Jun., Hailsham.

T. F. Sanger, Esq. (for the Alfriston Reading Room).

John Sansom, Esq., Buslingthorpe, Market Rasen.

John Saxby, Esq., Northease.

The Honourable P. Campbell Scarlett, C.B., Abinger Hall, Dorking. 2 copies.

John Charles Schreiber, Esq., Henhurst, Woodchurch, Kent.

The Rev. John Scobell, M.A., Southover Rectory.

Thos. Scott, Esq., 2, Gloucester Road, Peckham Grove, Camberwell.

Sir Sibbald D. Scott, Bart., F.S.A., Southwick Crescent, Hyde Park.

George Scrase, Esq., Lewes.

Captain Henry Thomas Settle, Royal Sussex Artillery, Lewes.

The Rev. H. D. Sewell, M.A., Headcorn Vicarage, Kent.

C. F. Shand, Esq., Advocate, Edinburgh.

W. E. C. Shaw, Esq., 7th Hussars, Umballah.

The Earl of Sheffield, Sheffield Park.

Rear-Admiral Sir Henry Shiffner, Bart., Coombe (deceased).

The Rev. George C. Shiffner, M.A., Hamsey Rectory, Lewes.

Evelyn Philip Shirley, Esq., M.P., M.A., F.S.A., &c., Lower Eatington Park, Stratford-on-Avon.

J. A. Sibthorpe, Esq., Brighton.

Henry Simmons, Esq., J.P., Seaford.

The Rev. Edw. H. M. Sladen, M.A., Alton Barnes, near Pewsey, Wilts. 2 copies.

Joseph Sladen, Esq., Hartsbourne Manor, Bushey Heath, Hertfordshire.

George Smith, Esq., LL.D., F.S.A., &c., Trevu, Camborne, Cornwall.

Wm. Tyler Smith, Esq., M.D., Upper Grosvenor Street.

John Alex. Smith, Esq., M.D., 7, W. Maitland Street, Edinburgh.

Charles Roach Smith, Esq., M.R.S.L., F.S.A., &c., &c., Strood, Kent.

Mr. John Smith, High Constable of the Borough of Lewes.

Lewis Smythe, Esq., M.D., Lewes.

The Rev. Joseph Sortain, B.A., 43, Norfolk Square, Brighton (deceased).

The Dowager Lady Stanley of Alderley, Holmwood, Reading.

Professor Arthur Penrhyn Stanley, D.D., F.S.A., &c., &c., Ch. Ch., Oxford.

Henry Stevens, Esq. (of America), 4, Trafalgar Square, London. 3 copies.

Thos. Stone, Esq., Newhaven (deceased).

The Rev. George D. St. Quintin, 20, Eversfield Place, St. Leonards-on-Sea.

J. Fremlyn Streatfeild, Esq., 15, Upper Brook Street, Park Lane.

W. Champion Streatfeild, Esq., Chart's Edge, Westerham.

The Sussex Archæological Society, Lewes.

The Rev. Edward C. Swainson, M.A., Wistanstow, Shrewsbury.

Professor Campbell Swinton, University of Edinburgh.

John Sykes, Esq., M.D., Doncaster.

Lord TALBOT DE MALAHIDE, F.R.S., F.S.A., Malahide Castle, Dublin.

H. Fox Talbot, Esq., F.R.S., Lacock Abbey. 2 copies.

John Tanswell, Esq., Inner Temple, and Temple House, Nunhead, Surrey.

H. A. Thompson, Esq.

William Thorn, Esq., M.D., 87, Harrow Road.

Mr. B. H. Thorpe, Battle.

The Rev. Canon Tierney, F.R.S., F.S.A., Arundel.

John Timbs, Esq., F.S.A., 88, Sloane Street.

W. H. Tinney, Esq., Q.C., 31, Montague Place, Russell Square.

W. H. W. Titheridge, Esq., General Register Office, Somerset House.

Sir Thos. Tobin, F.S.A., Ballincollig, near Cork.

William Tooke, Esq., F.R.S., V.P.Soc.Arts, Treas. R.S.L., 12, Russell Square. 2 copies.

Charles Tooke, Esq., Hurston Clays, East Grinstead.

F. R. Tothill, Esq., J.P., Seaford.

The Very Rev. R. C. Trench, D.D., Dean of Westminster.

Sir Walter Calverley Trevelyan, Bart., M.A., F.S.A., F.G.S., Wallington, Newcastle-on-Tyne.

The Rev. Thomas Trocke, M.A., Brighton.

The Rev. Edward Trollope, B.A., F.S.A., Leasingham, Sleaford.

N. Trübner, Esq., Paternoster Row. 6 *copies*.

Martin Farquhar Tupper, Esq., Albury, Guildford.

The Rev. Edward Turner, M.A., Maresfield Rectory.

James Singer Turner, Esq., J.P., Chyngton, Seaford.

Richard Turner, Esq., Howard Lodge, Tunbridge Wells.

N. Tyacke, Esq., M.D., Chichester.

Colonel Charles John Kemeys Tynte, M.P., F.S.A., Halswell House, Bridgewater.

J. R. Daniel Tyssen, Esq., F.S.A., 9, Lower Rock Gardens, Brighton.

THOMAS B. UTTERMARE, Esq., Langport, Somerset.

The Rev. EDMUND VENABLES, M.A., Bonchurch, I.W.

The Rev. Edward Ventris, M.A., Incumbent of Stow-cum-Quy, and Chaplain to Lord St. Leonards, 4, Causeway, Cambridge.

The Rev. Geo. Verrall, Bromley, Kent.

William Verrall, Esq., Manor House, Southover.

The Rev. James H. Vidal, M.A., Chiddingly Vicarage.

The Rev. J. REYNELL WREFORD, D.D., F.S.A., 24, St. Michael's Hill, Bristol.

Weston Styleman Walford, Esq., F.S.A., Barrister-at-Law, 2, Plowden Buildings, Temple.

W. H. Wall, Esq., The Larches, Tunbridge Wells.

W. Wansey, Esq., F.S.A., Bognor.

The Rev. John Ward, Wath Rectory, Ripon.

Edward Waugh, Esq., Cuckfield.

Albert Way, Esq., M.A., F.S.A., &c., Wonham Manor, Reigate.

Charlotte, Lady Webster, St. Leonards-on-Sea.

Richard Weekes, Esq., Hampton Lodge, Hurst-Pierpoint.

Harrison Weir, Esq., Peckham.

John Jenner Weir, Esq., 6, Haddo Villas, Blackheath.

The Hon. and Rev. Reginald W. Sackville West, M.A., Withyham Rectory.

R. Whitbourn, Esq., F.S.A., Godalming.

Robert White, Esq., 8, Claremont Place, Newcastle-on-Tyne.

H. W. White, Esq., London.

Thomas Whitfeld, Esq., Hamsey House.

George Whitfeld, Esq., J.P., Lewes.

Henry Whitfeld, Esq., M.R.C.S., Ashford.

Mrs. Colonel Willard, Eastbourne. 2 *copies*.

Thomas Willement, Esq., F.S.A., Davington Priory, Faversham.

G. T. Williamson, Esq., Brighton.

James Williamson, Esq., M.D., Southwold, Suffolk.

Stephen Williamson, Esq., 13, Virginia St., Glasgow.

Sir Thomas Maryon Wilson, Bart., Searles.

Joshua Wilson, Esq., Tunbridge Wells.

William Winkley, Esq., Jun., Harrow.

Thos. Wright, Esq., M.A., F.S.A., Sydney Street, Brompton.

Richard Woodman, Esq., Glynde.

The Rev. G. H. Woods, M.A., Shopwyke House, Chichester.

Miss Woodward, Uckfield.

The Lord Bishop of Worcester, 24, Grosvenor Place.

Hugh P. Wyatt, L.L.D., 18, Oxford Square, Hyde Park.

The Honourable Percy Wyndham, M.P., Petworth.

The Earl of YARBOROUGH, 17, Arlington Street, London.

Richard Yates, Esq., F.S.A., Beddington, Croydon.

Sir Charles George Young, Garter King of Arms, D.C.L., F.S.A., College of Arms.

Arthur John Young, Esq., Bradfield Hall, Bury St. Edmunds.

PATRONYMICA BRITANNICA.

A.

A, as the initial syllable of many surnames, has at least three distinct origins,
namely : I. A contraction of 'at,' formerly
a very common prefix to local names ; thus
John at the Green became John à Green ;
John at the Gate, John à Gate or Agate ;
John at the Court, John à Court, &c. II.
A corruption of 'of,' as John à Dover, Adam
à Kirby. III. It implies descent, and is
derived either from the Latin preposition
'a,' or more probably from the vernacular
'of,' the word 'son' being understood. For
example, John à Walter is precisely the
same kind of designation as John ap Thomas among the Welsh, John Mac-Donald
among the Scotch, or John Fitz-Hugh of
the Anglo-Norman period.

"It was late in the XVII. cent. (observes the Rev.
M. Noble) that many families in Yorkshire, even of
the more opulent sort, took stationary names. Still
later, about Halifax, surnames became in their dialect
genealogical, as William a Bills a Toms a Luke," that
is, William the son of Bill, the son of Tom, the son of
Luke. Hist. Coll. Arms, 22. This sort of nomenclature is said still to prevail in remote parts of Cumberland and Westmoreland.

This prefix was gradually dropped for the
most part during the XVI. and XVII.
centuries, except in those instances where,
by force of euphony, it had been made to
coalesce with the name itself, as in Abank,
Attree, Abarrow, Abridge, Abrook, &c.

AARON. AARONS. A common Jewish surname.

ABADAM. A recent resumption of the
old baronial name of Ap- or Ab- Adam.
See B. L. G.

ABANK. See Banks.

ABARROW. ABAROUGH. At or near
a barrow or tumulus See ATTE.

ABBEY. Perhaps originally given to
some menial attached to a monastery, as
'John of the Abbey;' more probably, however, from Abbé, the ecclesiastical title,
since we find it written in the H. R. le
Abbe. The Scottish form is Abbay.

ABBISS. Probably Abby's (that is
Abraham's) son. Ferguson, however,
thinks it is the A-Sax. Abbissa, a name
borne by one of the sons of Hengist.

ABBOT. See Ecclesiastical Surnames.
A sobriquet most likely applied to such
leaders of medieval pastimes as acted the
Abbot of Unreason, the Abbot of Misrule,
&c. Abet in Domesd. is a baptismal name.

ABBS. Probably a nickname of Abraham ; so Tibbs from Theobald, and Watts
from Walter. To the similar name *Abbes*
are assigned the arms, "a lady abbess,
proper !"

ABDY. An estate in Yorkshire, where
the family anciently resided.

A'BECKETT. A name of doubtful etymology. Mr. Ferguson derives it from the
A-Sax. *becca*, an axe, of which he considers
it a diminutive. The O. Fr. *bequet* is applied to a species of apple, a fish, and a
bird, and the arms attributed to Thomas à
Becket contain three *beckits*, or birds like
Cornish choughs. The A by which the
name is prefixed is, however, the customary
abbreviation of *at*, and shows it to be of
the local class. The A-Sax. *becc*, a brook,
whence we have many local and family
names, may have had a diminutive *becket*,
or "the little brook," but I confess that I
find no such word.

ABEL. ABELL. From the personal
name. It frequently occurs temp. Edwd. I.
in the same forms.

☞ **ABER.** A Celtic prefix to many names
of places, signifying "any locality of
marked character, either knolly or
marshy, near the mouth of a stream,
whether the stream falls into a lake or
sea, or runs into confluence with another
stream." Gazetteer of Scotland. Several
such localities have given rise to surnames, as Abercrombie, Aberdwell,
Aberkerdour, Abernethey.

ABERCORN. A parish in co. Linlithgow.

ABERCROMBIE. A parish in Fifeshire, the original residence of the Barons Abercromby, temp. Jas. II. of Scotl.

ABERDEEN. A well-known Scottish city.

ABERDOUR. A parish of Aberdeenshire.

ABERNETHEY. A town in the shires of Perth and Fife.

ABETHELL. (Welsh.) Ab Ithel, the son of Ithel.

ABETOT. See Abitot.

ABILON. Probably from Ablon, in the canton of Honfleur, in Lower Normandy.

ABITOT. Now Abbetot, in the arrondissement of Havre, in Normandy. The founder of this family in England was Urso de Abetot or Abetoth, brother to Hugh de Montgomery, Earl of Arundel. He was sometimes called Urso Vicecomes, and Urso de Worcester, because he was made hereditary sheriff of the county of Worcester. He was one of the Conqueror's great councillors. Kelham.

ABLE. See Abell.

ABLEWHITE. A curious corruption of Applethwaite, in the parish of Windermere, co. Westmoreland.

ABNEY. An estate near the Peak, in co. Derby, possessed by a family of the same name in very early times.

ABRAHAMS. 1. The personal name. It occurs in the H.R., as Abraam, Abbraham, and fils Abrahee. Some Jewish families have in recent times modified it to Braham. 2. The township of Abram, co. Lancaster.

ABRAM. ABRAMS. ABRAMSON. See under Abraham.

ABRINCIS DE. From Avranches, in Normandy. "Rualo de Abrincis, or Averenches, a valiant and skilful soldier, marrying Maud, daughter and heir of Nigel de Mandevil, lord of Folkestone, had all her lands and honours given to him in marriage by King Henry I." Banks. The town of Avranches is the capital of an arrondissement in the department of La Manche, in Lower Normandy.

ABRISCOURT. A known corruption of Dabridgcourt.

ABROOK. See under Brook.

ABSELL. A contraction of Absolom?

ABSOLOM. ABSOLON. The personal name.

It is strange that any parent should give his son a baptismal appellation like this, associated as it is with all that is vile and unfilial; yet an instance has occurred within my own observation. As a surname it was not unusual in the middle ages. In the H.R. it occurs as *Abselon* and *Absolon*. The latter is Chaucer's orthography:

"Now was ther of that chirche a parish clerke,
The which that was ycleped *Absolon*."
Millere's Tale.

ABURNE. Contraction of at-the-Burn, or brook; also an old orthography of auburn, and may relate to the colour of the hair:

"Her black, browne, *aburne*, or her yellow hayre,
Naturally lovely she doth scorn to weare."
Drayton.

ABVILE. H.R. Abbeville, the well-known town in Picardy. The family came in with William the Conqueror, and Wace mentions Wiestace or Eustace d'Abevile among those who rendered their commander great aid. Taylor's Chron. of Norm. Conq. p. 214.

AC or **ACK.** The initial syllable of many local surnames, signifying oak (A.-Sax. *ac*), as, Ackfield, Ackworth, Akehurst or Ackhurst, Ackham, Acked, or Aked, &c.

ACH or **AUCH.** A prefix in many topographical names of Gaelic origin. It signifies simply "a field" in a loose or general sense of that word. From it proceed the surnames Achmuty, Achany, &c.

ACHARD. An early personal name. As a surname it is found in the H.R.

ACHILLES. An ancient family of this name bore two lions rampant endorsed, probably with reference to the lion-like acts of the classical hero. Encyc. Herald. In the H.R. the name is written A Chillis.

ACHYM. "Signifies in British (Cornish) a descendant, issue, offspring, or progeny." The family were of great antiquity in Cornwall. D. Gilbert's Cornw. IV. 23. Acham appears from heraldic evidence to be the same name.

ACKERMANN. Germ. See under Akerman.

ACKER. ACKERS. See under Akerman.

ACLAND. "From the situation of their ancient seat in Lankey, near Barnstaple, co. Devon, which being in the midst of a large grove of oaks (in Saxon *ac*), obtained the name of Ac or Oakland. . . They were settled in this place as early as the reign of Henry II." Kimber's Barts.

ACKROYD. See under Royd.

ACLE. A parish in Norfolk, where the family resided temp. Edw. I.

ACLOME. From Acklam, the name of two parishes (East and West) in the North Riding of Yorkshire.

ACOURT. A'COURT. See Court.

ACTON. The Gazetteer mentions fifteen parishes or townships so called, and there are many other minor localities. The Actons of Acton, in Ombersley, co. Worcester, are said to have been settled there in Saxon times. They were certainly there temp. Henry III.

ADAIR. A branch of the great Anglo-Hibernian family of Fitz-Gerald settled at Adare, a village in co. Limerick, and thus acquired the local surname. In the XV.

century Robert Fitz-Gerald de Adair, in consequence of family feuds, removed to Galloway, in Scotland, and dropping his patronymical designation, wrote himself Adair, a name which has since ramified largely on both sides of the Irish Channel. In temp. Chas. I., the senior branch transferred themselves from Galloway to co. Antrim, where they resided for some generations, until on the acquisition of English estates they again settled in Britain.

The migrations of the family may be thus stated: 1. England before the Conquest. 2. Ireland. 3. Scotland. 4. Scotland cum Ireland. 5. Ireland. 6. Ireland cum England. 7. England cum Ireland. Inf. Rev. Wm. Reeves.

ADAM. ADAMS. ADAMSON. The personal name, much more used as a baptismal appellation in the middle ages than at present. In the H.R. it is written, Adam, Adams, fil' Ad, and ab Adam. There are various modifications of this name which have also become surnames. See Eng. Surn. ii., 166, and subsequent articles in this work, all under AD.

ADAMTHWAITE. See Thwaite.

ADCOCK. A diminutive of Adam. See termination Cock.

ADCOT. Sometimes the same as Adcock, which see; sometimes local.

ADDECOTT. Addy is a "nurse-name" of Adam, and *cot* a further diminutive; "little Adam." See termination Cott.

ADDENBROOK. From residence near a brook, originally Atten-broke. See prefix Atte and Atten.

ADDERLEY. A parish in Shropshire.

ADDY. A "nursename" of Adam; "little Adam." Hence Addis or Addy's, Addiscott, Addiscock, and Addison.

ADEY. ADIE. ADY. See Addy.

ADDICE. ADDIS. Addy's son, the son of Adam.

ADDICOT. A diminutive of Addy or Adam.

ADDINGTON. Parishes in Surrey, Bucks, Kent, and Northampton.

ADDISCOCK. See Addy.

ADDISCOT. See Addy.

ADDISON. See Addy.

ADE. A curt form or diminutive of Adam. In the archives of Edinburgh we find "Ade, alias Adamson." In Sussex and Kent it has been varied to Ayde, Adé, Adey, and Adye. In medieval records Ade is the usual contraction of Adam.

ADEANE. The same as Dean with the prefix *a* for *at*.

ADKIN. ADKINS. ADKINSON. A diminutive of Adam. See termination Kin.

ADLARD. ADLER. See Alard. Adelard, H. R. Adelardus, Domesd.

ADLINGTON. Townships in Cheshire and Lancashire.

ADNAM. A corruption of Addingham, parishes in Yorkshire and Cumberland. It is sometimes written Adnum.

ADOKES. Probably the old Welsh personal name Adoc, from whence also Ap Adoc, now Paddock.

ADOLPH. ADOLPHUS. The personal name. As a surname it is of recent introduction.

ADRIAN. A personal name, the Lat. Hadrianus.

ADRECY. See Darcy.

AFFLECK. A singular contraction of the surname Auchinleck, borne by an ancient family 'of that ilk' in Ayrshire. Sir Edmund Affleck created baronet in 1782, was sixth in descent from Sir John Auchinleck, son of Gilbert A. of Auchinleck. Baronetage.

AGAR. Aucher, a Norman personal name, whence Fitz-Aucher.

AGATE. At-the-Gate, of some town or forest; less probably, a sobriquet 'applied to a diminutive person, in allusion to the small figures cut in agate for rings.' Nares and Halliw. in voc.
"In shape no bigger than an agate stone On the forefinger of an alderman,"
Romeo and Juliet, i., 4.

AGENT. The occupation.

AGER. See Aucher.

AGG. See Female Christian Names.

AGGAS. Probably the son of Agatha, since such forms as Fil'Agath' and Fil'Agacie are found in the H.R. See Female Christian Names.

AGLIONBY. The family "trace their descent from Walter de Aguilon, who came into England with William the Conqueror, and into Cumberland with Randolph de Meschines. He gave name to the place of his dwelling, and called his seat or capital messuage Aguilon, or Aglion's building." Such is the statement of Hutchinson (Cumberland i, 195), and there is no doubt that a person called Aglion or some similar name, in early times, imposed the name on the manor of Aglion-by, but whether that personage came from Normandy as here asserted may well be doubted. See Aguillon.

AGNEW. Possibly from the French *agneau*, a lamb; but more likely from Agneaux, a village in the arrondissement of St. Lo, in Normandy. Co. Wigton, XIV. cent.

AGUE. Fr. *aigu*, corresponding with our Sharpe.

AGUILAR. Span. 'Of the eagle.' Comp. Aquila, Eagles, &c.

AGUILLIAMS. Another form of Guilliam or Ap William.

AGUILLON. Banks says that Manser de Aguillon, the first of this family mentioned, lived temp. Richard I. They were a Norman race, and as the name is frequently spelt Aquilon it is probably a mere variation of Aquila, q.v.

AIGUILLON. Fr. a spur. This name was probably conferred on the original bearer to denote his impetuosity, and may therefore be classed with our own *Hotspur*, as borne by the celebrated Henry Percy, temp. Henry IV. The family had possessions in West Sussex in the reigns of the Norman kings. See preceding article.

AIKIN. A Scottish Christian name, as "Aikin Drum."

AIKMAN. *Ac* is the A-Sax and *Aik* the Scottish for oak, and the families of this name bear *inter alia* an oak-tree in their arms. The surname however is probably a modification of Akerman, or of the Domesd. Agemund.

AINULPH. An ancient personal name.

AINSLEY. AINSLIE. A place in Scotland, but I cannot ascertain the county. Thomas de Ainslie, the baronet's ancestor, was "of that ilk" in 1214.

AINSWORTH. A chapelry in the parish of Middleton, near Manchester.

AIR. From Ayr, a town of Scotland, capital of Ayrshire. The family had doubtless lost sight of their having been originally "of that ilk" when they assumed for arms, Argent, a *cameleon* proper, in allusion to the unsubstantial food of that animal.

AIRD. Defined as "any isolated height of an abrupt or hummocky character, either on the coast or in the interior" of Scotland. Imp. Gaz. Scot. The word occurs in composition in many Scottish names of towns and parishes, as well as separately.

AIREY. This Cumberland family consider the name to have been borrowed from some elevated dwelling among the mountains called an Eyrie, such designations for residences not being uncommon. The "Eagle's Nest" would be a much more eligible name for an abode than Rook's-nest, Goose-nest, or Stoat's-nest, which are still to be found. See Aquila. An *aery* also signifies a place for the breeding or training of hawks. Ellis, Introd. Domesd. I, 341.

AIRTH. A barony in Stirlingshire.

AISKELL. Probably the same as Askew and Ayscough.

AISLABIE. One of the oldest names in the county of Durham, from Aislaby, a parish on the river Tees, on the banks of which the family still reside. In old documents it is written Asklackby, Ayzalibie, and in about fifty other modes.

AISTROP. Probably a corruption of Aisthorpe or East Thorpe, a parish of Lincolnshire.

AITCHISON. Qu. if this common Scot. name be not a corruption of Archie's son, the son of Archibald?

AITKEN. Probably the Scot. form of Atkin.

☞ AKE, as a prefix, is the same as Ac, which see. Examples occur in Akeland, Akehurst, Akeley, Akeris, &c.

AKERISE. Probably from Acrise, a parish in Kent. De Acrise, H.R.

AKERMAN. A-Sax. *Æcer-mon*, a fieldman, farmer, ploughman, clown. Bosworth. The German *Ackermann*, naturalized amongst us, has precisely the same signification. The forms in the H.R. are Akerman, le Akermon, le Akermannes, Acherman, and le Acreman. Sometimes the Akermanni were a peculiar class of feudal tenants, the tenure of whose lands is uncertain, as it is stated that the lord could take them into his own hands when he would, yet without injury to the hereditary succession. These holdings were very small, consisting in some instances of five acres only. Hale's St. Paul's Domesd., p. xxiv. "Agricola, *œcer-man*." Wright's Vocab. p. 74.

AKINHEAD. AKINSIDE. Doubtless local; from Aikin, an early proprietor.

ALABASTER. O. Eng *alblastere*, a cross-bowman. In Latin, *Albalestarius*, under which form it occurs in the H.R. See Arblaster.

ALARD. ALLARD. A corruption, it is said, of the A-Sax. personal name Æthelwald, but Ælard occurs in Domesd. as a tenant of Earl Godwin in the time of the Confessor. "The name flourished in Winchelsea from the Conqueror's days." Collins. Cooper's Winchelsea.

ALASTER. ALISTER. Celtic form of Alexander.

ALBANY. Originally the same as Albion —Britain; but after the Roman invasion the name was restricted to Scotland. Ultimately the appellation was still further limited to the somewhat extensive district of the Highlands, which includes Breadalbane, Athole, part of Lochaber, Appin, and Glenorchy. This district has frequently given the title of Duke to a younger son of the king, both before and since the union of the two crowns. As a surname it has been borne by several respectable families.

ALBEMARLE. Odo, Count of Champagne, married Adelidis, niece of William the Conqueror, and in her right became Lord of Albemarle, Albamale, or Aumale, in Normandy. At the Conquest of England he received large possessions in Holderness. Wace mentions his presence at the battle of Hastings as the "Sire d'Aubemare." This was more properly a title than a surname, although it occurs as the latter in the H.R. The title has also been borne by the families of De Fortibus, Plantagenet, Monk, and Keppel. Albemarle is a small ancient town, chef-lieu of a canton in the arrondissement of Neufchatel. It is now called Aumale, and it gave title of duke to a branch of the royal house of Bourbon.

ALBERT. A well-known Teutonic baptismal name. Albrecht and Albrett are modifications.

ALBIN. Alban.

ALBINI, DE. William de Albini attended William the Conqueror at the Conquest. Wace mentions him as "the butler d'Aubignie." Rom. de Rou. Taylor, p. 221, where some genealogical notes will be found. But Wace is in error in calling the Hastings warrior, "*botcillers*," since the official surname, Pincerna, or the butler, was borne not by him but by his descendant of the same names, who received the manor of Buckenham from Henry I., by the tenure of being butler at the King's coronation, an office now discharged by his descendants, the Dukes of Norfolk. He had also another name, *Strongimanus*, or the "stronghanded," from his having slain a lion under very extraordinary circumstances. See Eng. Surn. His son was created Earl of Arundel. Aubigny, the original residence of the family in Normandy, is in the Cotentin. Taylor, p. 220. Nigel de Albini occurs in Domesd. as a tenant in capite in co. Bucks. He slew Robert, Duke of Normandy's horse at Tenerchebrai, and brought Robert himself prisoner to his brother, King Henry I. His descendants assumed the name of Mowbray. Kelham.

ALBOMINSTER. An ancient Cornish family. A corruption of the latinization de Albo Monasterio, "of the white monastery," the designation of more than one religious house. See under Blackmonster. Albimonast. H.R.

ALBON. Alban, a personal name, borne by the proto-martyr of England.

ALCHIN. ALLCHIN. A known corruption of Alchorne.

ALCHORNE. A manor in the parish of Rotherfield, Sussex, where the family lived in the XIV cent. Some of their descendants, still resident in that parish, have, within a generation or two, corrupted their name to Allcorn.

ALCOCK. (See termination Cock). A diminutive of Hal, or Henry. In the H.R. it is written Alcoc and Alcock.

☞ ALD. A prefix of local names, the A-Sax. *eald*, old, ancient; as in Aldridge, Aldwinckle, Aldworth, Aldham, Aldwark, &c.

ALDBOROUGH. A Suffolk seaport, a Yorkshire market-town, and a Norfolk village.

ALDE. O. Eng., old. A Domesd. personal name.

"Princes and people *ald* and yong,
All that spac with Duche tung."
Minot's Poems (Halliw.)

Aldman (i. e., old man) occurs as a surname in the H.R.

ALDEN. Perhaps Halden, co. Kent.

☞ ALDER. Enters into the composition of many local names, and consequently of surnames. It indicates places favourable for the growth of the tree in some instances, but much oftener it is no doubt a corruption of the A-Sax. personal name Aldred, as in Alderford,

Alderby, Aldernham, Aldersey, Alderton—the ford, the dwelling, the home, the island, and the enclosure, of Aldred.

ALDERMAN. The Eolderman of Saxon times was a person of great distinction. In Domesd. Aldreman occurs without a prefix, so that it appears to have become first a baptismal, and then a family name.

ALDERSEY. An estate in co Chester, possessed by the family temp. Henry III., and still owned by them.

ALDERSON. The son of Alder or Aldred. The H.R. have, however, "fil' Aldith," Aldith's son.

ALDINGTON, A par. in Kent, and a hamlet in Worcestershire.

ALDIS. See Aldous.

ALDOUS. ALDHOUS. A local name; "the old house."

ALDRED. An A-Sax. personal name.

ALDRICH. An ancient personal name. As a surname it is found in the H.R.

ALDRIDGE. Places in Staffordshire and elsewhere.

ALDUS. Local. "The old house."

ALDWINCKLE. Two parishes in co. Northampton are so called.

ALDWORTH. A parish in Berkshire, which the family originally possessed.

ALE. Apparently an ancient Christian name, as we find in the H.R. the form fil' Ale, the son of Ale. In the south of England the surname Earle is often pronounced Ale.

It is an odd fact that we have in English family nomenclature all the terms ordinarily applied to malt liquors; Ale, Beer, Porter, and Stout; yet not one of these appellations is in the remotest degree related to Sir John Barleycorn; for Beer is the name of a place, and Porter that of an occupation, while Stout refers to the moral quality of courage or bravery, and, as we see above, Ale seems to have been a personal name.

ALEFOUNDER. In most places the official whose duty it is to inspect the malt liquor of a hundred or franchise is called the ale-taster or ale-conner. The origin of "founder" is uncertain.

"At a Court Leet or Law Day, and Court of the Portmen of the Borough of New Buckenham, the sub-bailiff, affiers, searchers and sealers of leather, examiners of fish and flesh, *alefounders*, inspectors of weights and measures, and a pinder were appointed." (*Norfolk Chron.*, Aug. 19, 1854).

In the records of the manor of Hale in the XV cent., one Thomas Layet is mentioned as being fined for having brewed once, 2d., and for having concealed the "founding-pot" (quia concelavit le fowundynge pot), 3d. *Three Early Metr. Rom., Camd. Soc.* p. xxxviii.

ALEGH. 'At the Lee' or meadow. See Leigh or Lee. Its form in the H.R. is A la Legh. Attlee is another existing form of the same name.

ALEHOUSE. From residence at one; an innkeeper.

ALEMAN. 1. See Alman. 2. A dealer in ale.

ALESBURY. Aylesbury, co. Buckingham.

ALEX. A nickname of Alexander; or perhaps Allic or Alick, a Domesd. name.

ALEXANDER The personal name. In the H.R. it is variously written, as Alexandre, fil' Alex, Alexandri, &c. A common name itself, it has become, by the abbreviating process, the parent of others still more so. From its last two syllables we have Sander, Sanders, Sanderson, Saunder, Saunders, Saunderson, Sandie, Sandison, Sandercock; from its first two syllables we get in like manner, Alex, Allix, Alley, and Alken; and besides these forms we have the corruptions Elshender, Elshie, and probably Assender.

ALFORD. Parishes in cos. Lincoln and Somerset.

ALFRED. The personal name. Very common in Domesd. and later, as Alured.

ALFREY. Probably a corruption of Alfred; or it may be local, though I cannot discover any place so designated. The name belongs, I think, almost exclusively to Sussex. The forms Ælfer, Alfere, and Alferus occur before 1086 in that county. Domesd.

ALGAR. See Elgar. In the H.R. the forms are Algar and Algor.

ALGERNON. The personal name.

ALICOCK. A diminutive of Alick, the nickname of Alexander.

ALINGTON. The Alingtons of Horseheath, co. Camb., claimed descent from Hildebrand de Alington, "under-marshal to the Conqueror at Hastings," though their pedigree was not traceable beyond temp. Edw. IV.

ALISON. William Alis occurs in Domesday as a chief tenant in Hampshire under the Conqueror, and he was probably the patriarch of the large tribe of the Ellises, as well as of the Ellisons, Alisons, Fitz-Ellises, &c. See under Ellis. It may be remarked that the vulgar pronunciation of Ellis in the South is exactly the same as that of the female personal name Alice. The prevalence of the Christian name Archibald, and the use of the fleur-de-lis by the Alisons support this conjecture.

ALKINS. Probably the same as Hawkins.

ALLAINE. See Allen.

ALLAN. See Allen. Also Gael. *allean*, grim, fierce.

ALLANSON. See Fitz-Alan.

ALLARDYCE. An estate in the parish of Arbuthnot, co. Kincardine.

ALLAWAY. Alloway, a parish in Ayrshire.

ALLBLASTER. O. Eng. *alblastere*, a cross-bowman.

ALLBONES. Perhaps a corruption of Aldbourne. So Hollowbone from Holybourne. The personal name Alban may, however, be the source.

ALLBRIGHT. A personal name (Albert). Ailbriht occurs in Domesd. anterior to 1086.

ALLCARD. An A-Sax. personal name, Alcheard. Codex Dipl. 520.

ALLCOCK. See Alcock.

ALLCROFT. See Croft.

ALLEN. From the personal name Alan, common in Norman times. Edw. Allen or Alleyne, when he founded Dulwich College, 1619, directed that the master and the warden of his establishment should bear the name of Alleyne or Allen, a regulation which has always been adhered to without much inconvenience, on account of the numerousness of the families bearing it. There are more than fifty coats-armorial assigned to the surname.

Scaliger, who reckoned among his ancestry some who bore the name of Alan, deduces the word from a Sclavonic term, signifying "a hound." Chaucer applies this name to a breed of large dogs:
"Abouten his char ther wenten white *alauns*,"
for deer or lion hunting; and the Lords Dacre used for their supporter an *alaun* or wolf-dog; but Camden dissents from this derivation, and thinks as the name was introduced here in the Conqueror's time by Alan, Earl of Brittany, that it was from an Armorican source, and equivalent to the Roman "Ælianus, that is, sun-bright."

ALLENBY. Allonby, a parish in Cumberland.

ALLENDER. A small river in the shires of Dumbarton and Stirling.

ALLENSON. The son of Allen or Alan. Perhaps in some cases from Alençon, in Normandy.

ALLERTON. There are parishes and chapelries so called in cos. Lancaster, York, Somerset, &c.

ALLEY. A small passage or lane between houses. Perhaps, however, a diminutive or nursename of Alfred, Allen, or some other Christian name.

ALLEYNE. See Allen.

ALLFREE. See Alfrey.

ALLGOOD. Algod occurs before Domesd. as a personal name.

ALLIBONE. A corruption probably of Hallibourne, i.e., Holy-bourne.

ALLICK. A common nickname of Alexander; but Allic and Alich occur in Domesd. as baptismal.

ALLINGHAM. A parish in Kent.

ALLNUTT. The A-Sax. Ælnod or Alnod. Domesd. ante 1086.

ALLOM. See Hallam.

ALLOTT. Probably the same as Hallett.

ALLTREW or **ALTREE.** A-Sax. *ald*, old, and *treow*, tree—a local surname.

ALLWORK. Aldwark, a hamlet in co. Derby.

ALLWRIGHT. Perhaps a maker of awls. See Wright.

ALMACK. The family have a tradition that the first Almack was a Mac-All, of Argyleshire, who transposed the syllables of his name on coming to the South.

Most if not all the existing bearers of this singular patronymic descend from a Richard *Almoke*, of Yorkshire, whose curious will, with that of his son John, is printed in Arch. Journ. v. 316. In 34 and 35, Hen. VIII., this Richard is written Awmoke, and still later Hawmoke. It is worth recording that "Almack Place," in Hong Kong, was named after William A., one of the founders of the city of Victoria in that Colony, who died on his voyage from China in 1846. The founder of the celebrated Almack's Rooms was of a Yorkshire *Quaker* family. The Almack motto, based upon the supposed Scottish extraction of the race, is MACK AL SICKER.

ALMAINE. Not from the Fr. Allemagne, Germany, as might be supposed; but from Allemagne, a place near Caen, famous for its quarries of Caen stone. From this identity of name, that stone is often misunderstood to have been brought from Germany.

ALMAN. From the Fr. *l'Allemand*—the German. See however, Almaine. The family were in E. Sussex in the XIV cent.

ALMER. See Aylmer.

ALMIGER. Probably a corruption of Alnager, "an officer, who by himself or his deputy, looks to the assize of all cloth made of wool throughout the land, and puts a seal for that purpose ordained unto them. Stat. 35 Edw. III." Termes de la Ley. See Aulnager in Jamieson.

ALMON. ALMOND. See Alman and Ellman.

ALMONT. A corruption of the latinization "de Alto Monte," and therefore synonymous with Monthaut and Mountain.

ALPHÉ. ALPHEN. ALPHEW. AL-PHEGH. See under Elphick.

ALPHRAMAN. *Alfarez*, Span., an ensign. According to Halliwell, this term is used by Ben Jonson and Beaumont and Fletcher; and Nares, on the authority of Harl. M.S. 6804, affirms that it was in use in our army during the civil wars of Charles I. It is therefore possible that Alphraman may be equivalent to the old corrupt "ancient," or ensign. The reader will doubtless call to mind the "Ancient Pistol" of Shakspeare.

ALPINE. MacAlpin, a Scottish name.

ALPRAM. Alpraham, a parish in Cheshire.

ALS. A place in Burian, co. Cornwall.

ALSAGER. A chapelry in Cheshire.

ALSCHUNDER. Supposed to be a corruption of Alexander, which in Scotland is, in common parlance, pronounced Elshiner.

ALSFORD. Two parishes in Hampshire, and one in Essex bear the name of Alresford.

ALSOP. ALLSOP. This ancient race were seated at Alsop-in-the-Dale, in Derbyshire, about the time of the Conquest, and there continued in an uninterrupted descent for 19 or 20 generations.

ALSTON. Places in cos. Lancaster, Worcester, &c.

ALTARIPA DE. See Hawtrey and Dealtry.

ALTERIPE. See Altaripa de.

ALTHORPE. Places in cos. Northampt., Lincoln, and Norfolk.

ALTON. A town in Hampshire, and parishes or places in cos. Wilts, Dorset, Stafford, &c.

ALUM. ALLUM. See Hallam.

ALVERD. This name is sometimes written Alured, i.e., Alvred or Alfred, but it may occasionally be a corruption of Alford. Another variation is Alvert.

ALWYN. An A-Sax. personal name. It has taken the various forms of Aylwin, Elwin, Alwine, Aylen, &c., &c. Fitz Alwyn was the first Lord Mayor of London, from 1189 to 1212.

ALWORTHY. Most likely a corruption of Aldworth. See ALD and WORTH.

AMAND. A Saint Amand was venerated in Normandy, and there are several places in that province which bear his name. Fil' Amand, i.e., Fitz-Amand, occurs in the H.R.

AMBER. An A-Sax. personal name, whence Amberley, Ambersham, Amberhill, &c.

AMBLER. *Le Ambleur*, Fr., an officer of the king's stable. Ambuler means an ambling horse.

"Soo was Epynogrys and his lady horsed, and his lady behynde hym upon a softe *ambuler*." *Morte d'Arthur*, ii., 148.

AMBROSE. The Greek personal name. Divine, immortal.

AMCOTTS. A township in co. Lincoln.

AMER. See Amour.

AMEREDITH. The same arms are assigned to this name as to that of Meredith; the initial "A" may therefore be regarded as the equivalent of "Ap."

AMERVILLE. Probably the same as Amfreville. Eight places of this latter name are given in Itin. de la Normandie, and are said to have received their designation from the personal name Anfred. "Ces Amfreville devraient être écrits Anfreville, puis que leur nom latin est Anfredivilla." Itin. p. 373.

AMES. A corrupt spelling, though still retaining the sound, of *Exmes*, a town in the department of Orne, in Normandy.

AMESBURY. A town in Wiltshire.

AMHERST. The pedigree is traced to A.D. 1400, at Pembury, co. Kent, and the locality of Amherst is in that parish.

AMIAS. Camden treats this as a personal name, deducing it from the Lat. *amatus*. "The earls and dukes of Savoy, which be commonly called Aimé, were in Latin called Amadeus, that is, 'loving God,' as Theophilus. We do now use Amias for this, in difference from Amic, the woman's name. Some deduce Amias from Æmilius, the Roman name." It may be added, however, that the town of Amiens, in Picardy, is spelt Amias by our old chroniclers. In R.G. 16 it is written wrongly—or, at all events, *Amiss!*

AMIES. Probably another form of Amias, which see.

AMMON. Either Amand or Hammond

AMOORE. See Amour.

AMOR. The same as Amour, which see.

AMORY. AMERY. From the personal name Emeric or Almericus, equivalent to the Italian Amerigo, latinized Americus, whence the name of the great western continent. It seems to have undergone the following changes: Emeric, Emery, Amery, Amory, Ammory, and in Domesd. Haimericus. It is asserted, however (B.L.G.), that "the family of D'Amery came to Engl. with the Conqueror from Tours."

AMOS. The personal name.

AMOUR. A-Moor, that is, at or of the moor, from residence upon one.

AMPHLETT. "Amflete, *Amfleot* et aliis *Ampleot* [Sax.], a haven in France (as I gesse) near Boloigne." Lambarde's Dict.

AMSON. Probably a corruption of Adamson.

AMYAND. The first baronet of this name (1764) was grandson of M. Amyand, a native of France, who quitted that country on the Rev. of the Edict of Nantes, 1685. Baronetage.

AMYE. Fr. *ami.* A friend. L'Amye occurs temp. Eliz. as a Frenchman in Sussex.

AMYOT. A derivative of the personal name Amias. Amiot. H.R.

ANCELL ANSELL. Anselm, a well-known Norman Christian name.

ANCHOR. 1. An inn sign. 2. An anchorite or hermit.

"An *anchor's* cheer in prison be my hope."
Hamlet.

AND. A family of this name bore as arms a Roman "&." Encycl. Herald. "And" would appear to have been either a qualifying epithet or an ancient personal designation, since it often occurs in composition with topographical terms; e. g., Andborough, And-by, And-over, An-croft.

ANDERS. Probably a corruption of Andrews.

ANDERSON. The son of Andrew.

ANDERTON. A township and estate in co. Lancaster, formerly possessed by the family.

ANDREW. The personal name.

ANDREWS. The son of Andrew.

ANDROS. A corruption of Andrews. This orthography is in use in the Channel Islands.

ANGELL. A common inn sign. More probably, however, from Anegole or Angold, a personal name, as we find it occasionally with the suffix *son.* Sometimes there may be a direct allusion to the celestial hierarchy, as in the cognate foreign surnames Angelo, Angellis, Angellico.

ANGELSON. The son of Anegold, a personal name.

ANGER. Perhaps from one who personated this vice in some miracle play; more probably, however, from *hanger*, a word descriptive of locality. A hanger is a wooded declivity.

"The high part to the south-west consists of a vast hill of chalk, rising three hundred feet above the village; and is divided into a sheep-down, the high wood, and a long hanging wood called the Hanger." *White's Selborne.*

ANGEVINE. A native of Anjou. In the H.R. the name is written with the prefix "le."

ANGOS. See Angus.

ANGOVE. "In this parish (Illogan) liveth Reginald Angove, Gent., i. e., Reginald the Smith, a sirname assumed in memory of his first ancestor, who was by trade and occupation a smith. And of this sort of sirname in England thus speaks Verstigan:

"From whence came Smith, all be it knight or squire, But from the smith that forgeth in the fire."
Hals MSS. D. Gilbert's Cornwall.

ANGUISH. ANGWISHE. Probably local, from its termination in *wish*; or perhaps a corruption of Angus.

ANGUS. The ancient name of Forfarshire, in Scotland.

ANHAULT. Probably a corruption of Hainault, a territory or province of the Netherlands.

ANKETELL. Anchitel, a personal name of Scandinavian origin, occurring in Domesd. and other early records.

ANN. ANNS. See Anne.

ANNADALE. See Annan.

ANNAN. A parish in co. Dumfries, on the river of the same name, whence Annandale.

ANNANDALE. Sometimes written Annadale. See Annan.

ANNE. Anna is a Scandinavian male personal name of high antiquity, and hence, perhaps, Anne, Anson, Anns, Annett, Anning.

ANNESLEY. A parish in co. Nottingham, which was possessed by the family from the reign of the Conqueror, 1079.

ANNEVILLE. There are several villages in Normandy bearing this name. The English family, according to De Gerville, originated from Anneville-en-Saine, a parish in the arrondissement of Valognes. One of the family was lord of that place in 1066; his brother joined the Conqueror's army, and became progenitor of the d'Anvilles of this country. Mem. Soc. Ant. Normandie, 1825.

ANNIS. See Female Christian Names.

ANSELME. Anselm, a well-known personal name. It is sometimes corrupted to Ancell and Ansell.

ANSLOW. A township in co. Stafford.

ANSON. Such names as An-son, Nelson, Bet-son, &c., have been regarded as a sort of metronymics, and therefore considered indicative of illegitimacy; but I think there is little doubt of the former part of these names being in many cases corruptions of masculine appellations. Anson is probably a contraction of Alanson.

ANSTEY. Parishes and places in cos. Herts, Leicester, Warwick, Wilts, and Devon.

ANSTIS. Probably a contraction of Anastasius.

ANSTRUTHER. William de Candela held the barony of Anstruther, in co. Fife, about 1153. His grandson Henry appears to have assumed the surname in or before 1221. Baronetage.

ANTHON. ANTON. 1. An abbreviation of Anthony. 2. A river of Hampshire.

ANTHONY. The personal name; also a parish in Cornwall. Places called St. Antoine and Antoigni occur in Normandy.

ANTILL. Ampthill, a parish in co. Bedford.

ANTROBUS. A township in Cheshire, the original residence of the family, sold by them temp. Hen. VI., but repurchased in 1808, by Sir Edm. Antrobus.

ANTRON. A place in the parish of Sithney, co. Cornwall.

ANVERS. The city of Antwerp, in Belgium. Danvers is another form of the same name.

ANVIL. See Anneville.

☞ **AP.** A Welsh prefix, signifying "the son of." It was sometimes written AB and VAP. See Eng. Surn., i., 17., for anecdotes and remarks. Andrew Borde, in his Boke of Knowledge, makes a Welshman say :

"I am a gentylman and come of Brutus blood,
My name is ap Ryce, ap Davy, ap Flood.

*   *   *   *

My kyndred is ap Hoby, ap Jenkin, ap Goffe,
Because I do go barelegged I do cache the coffe."

Sometimes the letter P or B (in *ab*) coalesced with the following syllable, and thus Ap Ryhs became Price; Ap Howell, Powell; Ap Robyn, Probyn; Ab Ithell, Bithell; Ab Enyon, Benyon.

ANWYL. (Welsh.) Dear, beloved.

AP ADAM. (Welsh.) The son of Adam, Adamson.

APE. *John le Ape.* H.R. This "Jackanapes" appears to have been an inhabitant of the parish of St. Frideswide's, Oxford. Prof. Leo. thinks that the ape *(simius)*

gave name to some English localities, which seems incredible. It is true, however, that we have some names of places, of which this word is a component syllable, as Apethorpe, Apeton, Apewood, Apenholt, Apedale, &c.

APEDAILE. See Ape.

APEELE. At-the-Peel. See Peel.

AP GRIFFYN. (Welsh) The son of Griffin or Griffith.

AP GWENWEY. (Welsh.) The son of Gwenwey.

AP HARRY. (Welsh.) The son of Harry, Harrison. Hence Parry.

AP HOWELL. (Welsh.) The son of Howell. Hence Powell.

APJOHN. (Welsh.) The son of John, Johnson. It is sometimes strangely corrupted into Upjohn and Applejohn.

AP MADOC. (Welsh.) The son of Madoc.

AP MERICK. (Welsh.) The son of Meirric.

AP MEURICE. (Welsh.) The son of Meurice or Morris.

APOSTLES. Probably a religious inn sign.

APOWELL. (Welsh.) Ap Howel, the son of Howel.

APPELBY. APPLEBY. APPLEBEE. The co. town of Westmoreland ; also parishes in cos. Leicester and Lincoln.

APPENRICK. (Welsh.) Ap Henrick, the son of Henrich or Henry.

☞ **APPLE,** a prefix to many local surnames, is the A-Sax. *æpl*, and denotes a place where apples abounded, as Appleby, Applesbury, Apledrefield, Apelton, or Appleton, &c.

APPLEFORD. A chapelry in Berks.

APPLEGARTH. (Apple and garth.) An enclosure for apple trees, an orchard. It has been corrupted to Applegath, Applegate, &c.

APPLEJOHN. Most probably a corruption of the Welsh Ap-John. There was, however, a species of apple which bore this name. "Do I not bate? Do I not dwindle?" says Falstaff; "Why my skin hangs about me like an old lady's loose gown; I am withered like an old *Apple-John*." Hen. IV., act iii. An apple grown in the eastern counties is still known by this *appell*ation.

APPLEMAN. A grower of, or dealer in apples. The trade of a costermonger derives its name from costard, a large kind of apple, the commodity in which he principally dealt. The original Mr. Appleman must then have been a medieval costermonger.

APPLETON. Parishes and places in cos. Berks, Chester, Lancaster, Norfolk, York, &c.

APPLETREE. (A-Sax. *æpl* and *treow*). Our Saxon forefathers named many localities—which have since given rise to surnames—from trees. Appledore, Kent, Appledore, Devon; Appledram, Sussex, and other places are well-known to have derived their designations thus. The Saxon Chronicle describes the battle of Hastings as having taken place *æt thære háran apuldran*, "at the hoary apple-tree," probably from same venerable tree of that species growing near at hand. Contrib. to Lit. 71. The "hoar apple tree" was a common landmark in Saxon times. Mr. Hamper has collected no less than 14 instances in different counties. Archæologia XXV, 35.

APPLEYARD. APPULYARD. APILIARD. An orchard. The word is employed by Hulvet in his Abecedarium, 1552. Halliw.

APPS. Apparently a genitive form of Ape or Appe; a personal name, ante 1066. Domesd.

APREECE. APREES. AP RICE. AP RYCE. (Welsh). Ap Rhys, the son of Rhys. The baronet's family (Apreece) claim descent from Gruffyth ap Rees, prince of South Wales. Hence Price.

AP ROBERT. (Welsh). The son of Robert. Hence Probert. The name sometimes took the form of Robin, and hence Ap Robyn, Probyn.

APSLEY. A manor in Thakeham, co. Sussex, where the family were resident in 1347.

AP THOMAS. (Welsh.) The son of Thomas.

APWENWYN. (Welsh.) The son of Enyon or Wenwyn. This name has also taken the form of Benyon.

AQUILA DE. "The surname of this family was originally assumed from Aquila, in Normandy; so denominated by reason an eagle had made her nest in an oak growing there when the castle was first building. Eugenulf de Aquila accompanied Duke William into England." Banks. The family were banished by Henry III., and probably never returned, as their name does not occur in more recent times, unless, indeed, the modern *Egles* be a translation of it. See *Michell*. The manor of Pevensey, co. Sussex, of which the De Aquilas were anciently lords, is still called the "honour of the Eagle," from that circumstance. Eugenulf, who is called by Master Wace Engerran de l'Aigle, fell at Hastings. Ord. Vit. "And Engerran de l'Aigle came also, with a shield slung at his neck, and, gallantly handling his spear, struck down many English. He strove hard to serve the Duke well for the sake of the lands he had promised him." Taylor's Roman de Rou, p. 21.

ARABIN. I am informed that the founder of this family came over with William III., and fought at the battle of the Boyne.

ARAGAND or ARAGUNE. Probably from Arragon, the Spanish province.

ARBER. See Harbour.

ARBLASTER. An arbalistarius or cross-bowman.

> "And in the kernils* here and there,
> Of *arblastirs* great plenty were."
> *Rom. of the Rose*, 4198.

It was sometimes applied to the cross-bow itself:

> "With *alblastres* and with stones,
> They slowé men and braken bones."
> *Kyng Alisaunder*, 1211. (*Halliw.*)

Several of the distinguished archers at the battle of Hastings became tenants in chief under the Conqueror, and are entered in Domesd. with the surname Arbalistarius or Balistarius. Hence the names Alabaster, Blast, and others.

ARBUCKLE. A possible corruption of Harbottle.

ARBURY. ARBERY. A township in Lancashire.

ARBUTHNOT. A parish in Kincardineshire. The first of the family was Hugh de Aburbothenoth, who assumed his surname from the lands which he acquired in 1105 with the daughter of Osbert Olifard, and on which his descendants have resided for more than twenty generations. Peerage.

ARBUTT. Probably a corruption of Herbert.

ARCEDECKNE. See Archdeacon.

ARCH. From residence near one. A bridge is often provincially called an arch.

ARCHARD. A provincial pronunciation of orchard.

ARCHBELL. A corruption of Archibald.

ARCHBISHOP. See Ecclesiastical Surnames.

ARCHBOLD. A corruption of Archibald.

ARCHBUTT. A corruption of Archibald.

ARCHDEACON. An eminent Cornish family in the XIV. cent. wrote themselves Archdekne. The cognate name Archidiacre occurs in France, from which country the English family would appear to have migrated, since three cheverons form the main feature of the arms of both families, as well as of another English family named Archidecknie.

ARCHER. The progenitor of the Barons Archer is said to have been Fulbert L'Archer, who came in with the Conqueror. Ext. Peerage. But this name must have had many distinct origins. See ARCHERY.

☞ ARCHERY. In old English warfare the long bow was the favourite weapon, and it was also the chief instrument of the national pastime. Our family nomenclature abounds in names relating to archery; thus we have Archer and Bowman, Bowyer and Bowmaker, Arrow-

---

* Embrasures of a wall.

smith and Fletcher, Stringer and Butts, besides many others whose reference to the pursuit is less obvious.

ARCHIBALD. The baptismal name.

ARCHIE. In Scotland, a diminutive or nurse-name of Archibald.

ARKCOLL. Perhaps from the parish of of Ercall Magna, or High Ercall, in Shropshire. A more likely derivation, however, is from the Dutch Van Arkel, a noble family renowned for their courage.

According to an ancient proverb, of all the nobles of Holland, the Brederodes were the noblest, the Wassenaars the oldest, the Egmonts the richest, and the Arkels the stoutest in conflict :

"Brederode de edelste, Wassenaars de outste, Egmont de rijkste, en Arkel de stoutste."

The locality from which the Arkels derived their title was so called from the remains of a temple dedicated in Roman times to Hercules. It is worthy of notice that the A-Sax. form of Hercules is *Ercol*. Dixon's Surnames. Arkil was also a Saxon name. Arkil, a great baron of Northumbria, who fled before William the Conqueror, settled in Scotland, and became the founder of the Earls of Lennox.

ARDEN. The Ardens of Arden, co. Warwick, claimed direct descent from Sivard de Arden, son of Turchil de Warwick, who, though of Saxon origin, held under the Conqueror as a tenant in chief. See Arderne.

ARDERNE. "The traditionary account of the origin of this family is from Turchetil, son of Alwyn, officiary earl of Warwick, in the time of Edward the Confessor; which Turchetil succeeded his father, but being afterwards deprived of his earldom by William the Conqueror, retired to the woody part of the county, and assumed the name of Arderne or Arden." Banks.

ARDES. ARDIS. ARDYS. ARDERES. May be various forms of the same name. There are two small parishes in Kent called Upper and Lower Hardres. See Hardres and Hards. In Scot. Allardyce is so corrupted.

ARDLEY. A parish in co. Oxford.

ARESKIN. A sufficiently obvious corruption of the Scottish name Erskine, which, indeed, is so pronounced in the North.

AREY. See Airey.

ARGALL. Possibly from Ercall, a parish in Shropshire.

ARGENTE. ARGENT. A contraction of Argenton.

ARGENTON. ARGENTINE. Argentan, a considerable town in the south of Normandy, formerly written Argentomagus. David de Argentomago was a tenant in chief under the Conqueror, in cos. Bedford and Camb. His descendants were ennobled as barons Argentine.

ARGEVILLE. Perhaps from Argueil, near Neufchatel, in Normandy.

ARGLES. Possibly a corruption of Argyle, the Scottish county.

ARGUMENT. This strange name occurs in the R.G. 16. It is probably a corruption of the French *aigu mont*, mont-agu, mons acutus, the sharp-pointed hill. There is a

hamlet bearing the name of Aigumont, in the arrondissement of Dieppe, in Normandy.

ARIELL. Ariel, the name of an angel, cognate with Michael, Gabriel, &c.

ARIES. Probably a Latinization of the name Ram. Aris, Areas, and Arés seem to be mere variations in the orthography.

ARKELL. See Arkcoll.

ARKWRIGHT. An "ark," in the north, signifies a meal or flour-chest, which is usually made of oak, and sometimes elaborately carved. Halliw. The maker of such chests was an Arkwright. The strong boxes in which the Jews kept their valuables, were anciently called their arks (*archas*). Hunter's Hallamshire Glossary. *Arca* is used in this latter sense by the classical writers :

Quantùm quisque suâ nummorum servat in arcâ, Tantum habet et fidei.

Juv. Sat. iii., 143.

The word occurs in Fœdera 45, Hen. III. In the H.R. the surname occurs as *le Coffrer*, coffer-maker.

ARKYBUS. The *harquebus* or hand-cannon, and probably also the man who wielded it. See a cognate example of this double application under Arblaster.

ARLE. Possibly from Arles, in Provence.

ARM. Appears to have been an ancient personal name. It is found in composition with the local surnames, Armfield, Armstead, Armsby, Armsworth, &c.

ARMENY. ARMONY. Old spellings of Armenia. This name originated, perhaps, in the days of pilgrimages and crusades.

"Shewe me the ryght path To the hills of Armony."—*Skelton.*

ARMIGER. ARMINGER. Lat. *armiger*, an esquire, the next in degree to a knight. The upper servants of an abbey were also called Armigeri.

"Concessimus etiam Alano per annum unam robam cum furura de eodem panno quo vestiuntur armigeri nostri." A.D. 1300. *Regist. of Battel Abbey.*

ARMINE. Dutch for a beggar ; but a more probable derivation is from Armine, a chapelry in the parish of Snaith, in the W. Riding of Yorkshire.

ARMITAGE. A provincial pronunciation of hermitage; also a parish in Staffordshire. The Armytages of Kirklees, co. York, trace their patronymic back to the reign of King Stephen. Baronetage.

ARMORER. The occupation.

ARMOUR. A corruption of Armourer.

ARMSTRONG. Doubtless from strength of limb, as displayed in war and athletic sports. Armstrang is the same, and Strongi'th'arm, a cognate surname. The well-known border clan of Armstrong were of old a truly armipotent race, and Johnnie A., their chief, the great freebooter, lived in Eskdale; while Liddesdale was another *habitat* of the family.

"Ye need not go to Liddisdale, For when they see the blazing bale Elliots and Armstrongs never fail."

Lay of Last Minstr.

The influential family of this name in Ireland, of Scottish origin, settled there on the attainder of Sir Thomas A. for the Rye House Plot, and they still enjoy large estates in King's co., and in cos. Limerick, Tipperary, &c. The A's, of Fermanagh, who claim descent from a brother of the celebrated Johnnie, settled in that co. about the commencement of the XVII. cent.

Tradition asserts that the original name of this renowned race was Fairbairn, and that an ancestor who was armour-bearer to one of the Scottish Kings, once saved his royal master's life on the battle field by lifting him on horseback after he had been dismounted. The crest of the family, "an armed hand and arm; in the hand a leg and foot in rich armour, couped at the thigh," is said to allude to the manner in which Fairbairn raised the King to the saddle. For this service the monarch gave his follower broad lands in the S. of Scotland, together with the appellation Armstrong.

☞ ARN. The initial syllable of many local names, as Arncliffe, Arnwood, Arney, Arnholt, meaning respectively the cliff, the wood, the island, and the grove of eagles, from the A-Sax. *erne*, an eagle. Occasionally, however, it may be derived from *arn*, the Scottish for an alder tree.

ARNE. A parish in Dorsetshire; also a Norse personal name. See Heimskringla, i, 201.

ARNEY. A nick-name for Arnold, whence Arnison.

ARNISON. See Arney.

ARNOLD. The personal name; also a parish in the county of Wilts.

ARNOLL. ARNELL. ARNALL. ARNULL. ARNOULD. Corruptions of Arnold.

ARNOTT. ARNETT. Corruptions of Arnold.

ARNULFE. The same as Arnold, which in medieval records is sometimes latinized Ernulphus.

ARRAS. From the French city, the capital of the ci-devant province of Artois, once famous for its manufacture of tapestry, and the source of the "arras hangings," with which the chambers of our ancestors were erewhile adorned.

ARRINGTON. A parish in co. Cambridge.

ARROW. A parish co. Warwick; a township co. Chester; also two western rivers.

ARROWSMITH. A maker of arrows, or rather arrow-heads. This, in the days of archery, was a distinct trade. In the curious burlesque poem, Cock Lorelles Bote, these artizans are called "arowe-heders."

ART. A nickname for Arthur.

ARTER. A vulgar pronunciation of Arthur.

ARTHUR. The Christian name. Other surnames from it are Atty, Atts, Atkin, Atkins, Atkinson, Atcock. Aikin and Aitkin may be northern varieties.

ARTIS. Artois, the French province.

ARTOIS. The French province.

ARUNDELL. Roger de A., who took his name from the Sussex town, was a tenant-in-chief at the making of Domesd., and ancestor of the Lords A., of Wardour. Dudg. Bar. ii, 422. Kelham, 157.

☞ AS, as a termination, is generally a corruption of Hurst, e. g., Byas should be Byhurst; Tyas, Tyhurst; Haslas, Hazelhurst; Boggas (and Boggis?), Boghurst.

ASBONE. A corruption of Asborne or Ashborne.

ASCOT. ASCOTT. Parishes and places in cos. Berks, Warwick, and Oxon.

ASCOUGH. See Askew.

ASCUE. See Askew.

ASDALL. A modern Irish corruption of Archdall, a local name.

☞ ASH. The premier syllable of many names of places, and of surnames derived from them, as Ashdown, Ashton, Ashley, Ashwell, Ashurst, Ashford, Ashburne, &c. It denotes a place where this species of tree flourished.

ASH. ASHE. There are places so called in Derbyshire, Surrey, Hampshire, and elsewhere. It seems probable, however, that the name was sometimes adopted from residence near a remarkable ash tree. We find the *Atten-Ashe* of the XIV. cent. contracted into *Nashe* soon after. In the H.R. it is latinized *ad Fraxinam* and *de Fraxino*. The French *Dufresne* is its synonym.

ASH — CRAFT — CROFT — MEAD — MORE. Localities unknown.

ASHBEE. A corruption of Ashby.

ASHBURNER. A maker of potash or some such article. Latinized in charters, *Cinerarius*. Sussex Arch. Coll. viii., 152.

ASHBURNHAM. The noble earls of this surname and title claim to have possessed Ashburnham, co. Sussex, from before the Norman Conquest. In 1066 Bertram de Ashburnham, son of Anchitel, son of Piers, was constable of Dover, and held out against William. Peerage.

ASHBY. A local name occurring 18 times in the Gazetteer, mostly in the cos. of Lincoln, Leicester, and Northampton.

ASHCOMBE. Places in Devonshire, Sussex, &c.

ASHCONNER. An old method of divination by ashes is mentioned by Herrick, i., 176.

"Of ash-heapes by the which ye use,
Husbands and wives by streaks to chuse,
Of crackling laurell, which fore-sounds
A plenteous harvest to your grounds."

An "ash-conner" was therefore probably a

man well skilled in this mode of foretelling events—a cunning man. An ale-conner in a corporate town is the person appointed to superintend the assize of malt liquors.

ASHDOWN. A great district, formerly a forest, in Sussex.

ASHENBOTTOM. See Bottom.

ASHENDEN. Ashendon, co. Bucks.

ASHER. Perhaps the same as Ashman.

ASHES. From residence near a grove of ash trees.

ASHFIELD. Places in Suffolk and elsewhere.

ASHFORD. AISHFORD. Parishes in Kent, Derby, and other counties.

ASHLEY. Parishes in Staffordshire, Wilts, Cambridge, &c.

ASHLIN. Ashling, a parish in Sussex.

ASHMAN. In A-Sax. poetry *æsc* or ash is constantly used in the sense of spear, because the staff of a spear was usually made of that wood. So the Latin *ferrum* signifies both iron and sword. Ashman is therefore the equivalent of spearman. Its forms in the H.R. are Asscheman, Aschman, and Ashman; and in Domesd. Assemannus.

ASHPLANT. A corruption of the local Aspland, as the cognate Ashpole appears to be of Ash-pool, a pool near which ash trees grow.

ASHTON. The Gazetteer mentions eighteen parishes and townships so called, in various counties, and there are many minor localities of the same name.

ASHURST. A parish in Kent, another in Sussex.

ASHWELL. Parishes in cos. Herts, Rutland, and Norfolk.

ASHWOOD. Villages in Staffordshire and other counties.

ASHWORTH. A chapelry in Lancashire.

☞ **ASK.** As a prefix in such local surnames as Askeby, Askham, Askley, Askerby, Askwith, &c., is probably the A-Sax. *æsc*, an ash tree.

ASKE. A township in the N.R. of Yorkshire, the ancient abode of the family.

ASKER. A corruption of Askew.

ASKEW. Aiskew, a township in the parish of Bedale, N.R. Yorkshire; Ascue, Ayscue, Ascough, and Ayscough, are various spellings of this patronymic.

ASKIN. A modern Irish corruption of Arcedekne.

ASKHAM. ASCHAM. Parishes in Yorkshire, Notts, and Westmoreland. Roger Ascham, toxophilite and schoolmaster, was a Yorkshireman.

ASPALL. A parish in Suffolk. In Ireland Archbold or Archibald is so corrupted.

ASPDEN. A parish in Herts.

ASPIN. Aspen, a species of poplar tree.

ASS. The animal; a sobriquet.

ASSER. An ancient personal name, as Asserius Menevensis, the preceptor of King Alfred. Two tenants called Azor are found in Domesd.

ASSENDER. Perhaps from Assendon a township, co. Oxford : 'r' and 'n,' in vulgar pronounciation are often used interchangeably; thus Hickman and Hickmer, Heasman and Heasmar, Harmer and Harman, all English family names. It may however be a corruption of Alexander.

ASSMAN. (H.R. *Asseman*.) A donkey-driver. A book printed by Wynkyn de Worde, entitled "Informacyon for Pylgrymes," has the following direction:—

"Also whan ye take your asse at porte Jaffe (Joppa) be not too longe behynde your felowes, for and ye come betyme, ye may chuse the best mule or asse that ye can, for ye shall pay no more for the best than the worst. Also ye must gyve your *Asseman* there of curtesy a grote of Venyse." *Retrosp. Rev.* ii., 326.

ASTLEY. Astley, co. Warwick, was possessed by Thos. Lord A. (killed at Evesham, 49, Hen. III.), the ancestor of the Baronet's family.

ASTON. The Gazetteer of England contains nearly fifty Astons, and above twenty armorial coats are assigned to the name. Lord Aston's family descend from Aston, co. Stafford in the XIII. cent.

☞ **AT. ATE. ATTE. ATTEN.** A common prefix to early surnames, to designate the locality of the bearer's residence, as Atte-Wood, by or near a wood; Att-Tree, at the tree; Atten-Oke, near or at the oak, &c. The N in *Atten* was added for euphony before a vowel. These were common forms in the fourteenth century. Subsequently At or Atte was softened to A, as A'Gate for At-Gate, A-Broke for At-Brook, &c. Many names are so written down to the time of Elizabeth and later. In some instances the At or Att is still retained, as in Attwood, Atwells, Atwater, Attree, &c. Sometimes the final N of Atten is made to coalesce with the name, though the Atte is dropped, and hence we get such names as Noakes (Atten-Oke), Nash (Atten-Ash), &c.

The following names with these prefixes are met with in medieval documents. Several of them are now extinct, but the others remain in forms variously modified. I shall add explanatory words where necessary, but most of the names will be found in their proper places in the Dictionary.

Ate or *Atte*—barre—berne (barn)—brigge (bridge)—brok (brook)—brug (bridge) —brugeende (at the bridge end)—bury —burn—chirche—chyrchene (at the church end, i.e., of the village)—churche-haye (churchyard)—cleyf (clift)—croch (See Crouch)—crundle—cumbe (See Combe)—dam (weir or river dam)—dene (SeeDean)—dich (ditch)—drove (drove-way for cattle)—dune (a down or hill)— elme (tree)—felde (field)—fen, fenne (marshy spot)—flod (an expanse of water) ford—forth—forge—grange—gappe (in a wall or hedge)—gardin—gate—grave (grove)—grene—hache (a forest gate)—hale (a hall)—harne (?)—hegge and haye (a hedge)—hide—hil—hulle—and hyl (a hill) hok (See Hooke)—howe (an eminence)—lak (a lake)—lee (a meadow)—lane—line (a lime tree)—londe (a heath)—lownde (a lawn)—lowe (a hill)—med or mede (a meadow)—melneway (road to a mill)—mere—mershe (a marshe)—more (a moor)—nasse (ash tree, the N coalescing)—Atenelme (an elm tree)—Atenesse (ash or nesse, doubtful)—Atenock (an oak tree)—Atenorchard (an orchard)—Atenotebeme (a common medieval name—*nut-beam*, hazel)—pilere (pillar)—pleystowe (a recreation ground)—pol (a pool)—pond—porte—punfald (poundfold)—putte (a pit)—pyrie (pear orchard?)—sete (seat) stiele (stile)—stone—streme (a stream), streteshend (at the end of the street)—tunishend (at the town's end)—wal—water—welle—welde (weald, wood)—wence (?)—westende (at the west end)—wey (a road?)—wich (a salt spring)—wod or wode (a wood)—wolf hongles (a place where wolves were hung *in terrorem*. A-Sax, *hongian*, to hang; comp. *hangles* in Halliw.)—wurth (See Worth).

ATCHESON. Probably the same as Hutchison.

ATCOCK. See Arthur.

ATHERTON. A chapelry in Lancashire.

ATTHILL. See Hill.

ATKEY. At the key or quay.

ATKIN. ATKINS. ATKINSON. See Arthur.

ATLEE. ATLEY. See Lee.

ATMORE. See Moore.

ATTENBOROUGH. A parish in co. Northampton.

ATTLOWE. See Lowe.

ATTY. ATTYE. See Tye and Arthur.

ATWATER. See Waters.

ATWELL. See Wells.

ATWICK. See Wick.

ATWOOD. ATTWOOD. See Wood.

ATWORTH. See Worth.

AUBERVILLE. Roger de Auberville came in with the Conqueror and is mentioned in Domesd. as holder of 18 manors in Essex and Suffolk. Baronetage. De Abreville. H.R.

AUBREY. A Norman personal name, as Aubrey or Albericus de Vere. A pedigree of this family drawn up by Vincent, Windsor Herald, temp. Elizabeth, commences with "Saint Aubrey, of the blood royal of

France, came into England with William the Conqueror, anno 1066, as the Chronicles of All Souls College testify, which are there to be seen tyed to a chaine of iron." Courthope's Debrett. What the Chronicle here referred to may be, I know not, but there is no doubt of the Norman origin of the family.

AUCHINCRAW. A village in Berwickshire.

AUCHINLECK. A parish in Ayrshire. The surname is sometimes corrupted to Affleck, and is always so pronounced.

AUCKLAND. AUKLAND. Bishop Auckland, and three other places in co. Durham.

AUDLEY. Formerly Alditheley, a parish and estate in co. Stafford, from which a branch of the noble family of Verdon assumed the surname, temp. King John. Dugdale.

AUGER. AUCHER. A Norman name, whence Fitz-Aucher. Also a corruption of Alsager, a place in Cheshire. Archæologia vol. xix. p. 17.

AUGUR. See Auger.

AUGUST. Auguste, the Fr. form of Augustus.

AUKWARD. See Ward. The keeper of the hawks.

AULD. The Scotch form of Eld—old.

AUREL. The Fr. form of Aurelius.

AUSENDER. See Assender.

AUST. A chapelry in co. Gloucester.

AUSTEN. AUSTIN. Augustine, the well-known baptismal name, so abbreviated in O. Fr. and Eng. The Lond. Direct. presents us with a Mr. Austing.

AUSTWICK. A township in W. R. of Yorkshire.

AVANT. Probably from Havant, a town in Hampshire; or it may be from the old war-cry, *Avant!* "Forward!"

AVENEL. The sire des Biars, who was at the battle of Hastings (Taylor's Roman de Rou., pp. 219, 227), bore the name of Avenals, without prefix. William Avennel probably the "sire" referred to, was lord of Biars, in the canton d'Isigny, and seneschal to the Count of Mortain. (De Gerville, Mem. Soc. Ant. Norm.) It does not appear whether the surname was originally derived from Avenelles, in the department of Eure.

AVENON. The city of Avignon in France.

AVERANCE. Avranches. See Abrincis.

AVERY. This is a name which may claim its origin with nearly equal probability from several distinct sources, which I shall briefly enumerate. I. *Aviarius*, a keeper of the birds. The Forest Charter (s. 14,) enacts that freemen may have in their woods "*avyries* of sparhawkes, falcons, eagles, and herons." II. *Avery*, the place where forage for the king's horses was kept; either from the Lat. *avena*, Anglo-Norm. *haver*, oats, or from *aver*, a northern provincialism for a working horse. III. *Alberic*, a German personal name, latinized Albericus, and softened in Norman times to Aubrey.

AVIS. AVES. The personal name Avice, latinized Avitius, is found before 1086. Domesd.

AXE. Two western rivers are so called,

AXFORD. A tything in Ramsbury, co. Wilts.

AXON. Axton, a hundred in Kent.

AXUP. Axehope, local. See Axe and Hope.

AYER. See Eyre.

AYLETT. See Aylott.

AYLIFFE. See Ayloff.

AYLMER. Ailmarus, Æilmar, or Ailmar, occurs several times in Domesd. as a personal name.

AYLOFF. A baptismal name ante 1086. Ailof. Domesd.

AYLOTT. A personal name ante 1086. Ailet. Domesd.

AYLWARD. Ælward and Ailward were personal names before 1086.

AYLWIN. Alwinus, Alwin, and other forms occur in Domesday as personal names.

AYNSWORTH. See Ainsworth.

AYRTON. A township in Yorkshire.

AYSCOUGH. See Askew.

AYTON. Parishes and places in cos. York and Berwick.

AYTOUN. A parish in Berwickshire.

B.

BABB. See Female Christian Names.

BABER. Probably from the hundred of Babergh, in Suffolk, though some of the name affect a descent from the Sultan Baber or Babour, the founder of the Mogul dynasty in Hindostan, A.D. 1525!

BABINGTON. The family traditions point to Normandy as the source of the race. The *name*, however, is derived from Great and Little Babington, near Hexham, co. Northumberland, where the family were located in the XIII. and XIV. centuries, and there are reasons for believing that they resided there "from the period of the Conquest or before it." Topog. and Geneal, i., 135. Some of the name may spring from Babington, co. Somerset.

BABY. From its termination probably local.

BACCHUS. Certainly not from the God of Wine, but a corruption of Bakehouse, which see.

BACHELOR. See Batchelor.

BACK. (Pluralized to Backs, whence Bax.) Sometimes synonymous with Beck, but more generally either a wharf or a ferry. Hence Backman and Backer.

BACKER. The same as Backman.

BACKHOUSE. See Bakehouse.

BACKMAN. One who had the care of a back or ferry. See Back, Baxman, H.R.

BACON. A seigniory in Normandy. According to the genealogy of the great Suffolk family of Bacon, one Grimbald, a relative of the Norman chieftain William de Warenne, came into England at the Conquest, and settled near Holt. His greatgrandson is stated to have taken the name of Bacon. This was only a resumption of an ancient Norman surname, which is still existing in the North of France. William Bacon, in 1082, endowed the abbey of the Holy Trinity at Caen. Taylor's Roman de Rou. The name is in the Battel Roll, and in the H.R. it is written variously Bachun, Bacun, and Bacon. In some instances the surname may be a corruption of Beacon. From their connection with Bayeux, the Bacons were sometimes latinized De Bajocis.

BADCOCK. See Bartholomew.

BADD. *Bad* in the Coventry Mysteries means bold.

BADDELEY. A parish in Cheshire.

BADDER. A bather. Ferguson.

BADGER. 1. A huxter or hawker. "If any person shall act as a *badger* without license, he is to forfeit five pounds." Jacob's Law Dict. The etymon seems to be the Fr. *bagagier*, or baggage-carrier. "Badger is as much to say as Bagger, of the Fr. word baggage, i. e., sarcina; and it is used with us for one that is licensed to buy corn or other victuals in one place, and carry them to another." Termes de la Ley. 2. A parish in Shropshire.

BADKIN See Bartholomew.

BADLESMERE. A parish in Kent, where the family were resident in the XIII. cent.

BADMAN. Bead-man, O. E., from A-Sax. *biddan.* One who prays for another. The word is more commonly written "beadsman."

BAGGALLAY See Baguly.

BAGGE. (Of Norfolk.) Said to be of Swedish extraction.

BAGNALL. A chapelry in the parish of Stoke-upon-Trent, co. Stafford.

BAGOT. BAGOD. Domesd. The family have possessed Blythefield and Bagot's Bromley, co. Stafford, from the time of the Conquest.

BAGSTER. The same as Baxter.

BAGULY. A township in Cheshire, formerly owned by a family of the same name.

BAGWELL. Bakewell, co. Derby?

BAILEY. BAILY. 1. From Bailli, in the arrondissement of Neufchatel; Bailli in that of Dieppe, in Normandy; Bailey, a township in Lancashire; or Bailie, a township in Cumberland. 2. Another form of bailiff, a title of office applied in many ways under our feudal and municipal laws. 3. A name given to the courts of a castle formed by the spaces between the circuits of walls or defences which surround the keep. Gloss. Arch.

BAILLIE. The Scottish form of Bailiff or Bailey. See Bailey.

BAINBRIDGE. A township in Yorkshire.

BAINES. BAYNES. A village near Bayeux, in Normandy, probably so called from Fr. *bain,* a bath.

BAIRD. Said to be the Scottish form of *bard,* or poet. Jamieson. This, however, is doubtful as to the surname, which in North Britain is widely spread. Its principal modes of spelling have been Bard, Byrd, Bayard. The last supports the tradition of a derivation from the south of France, the country of the Chevalier Bayard, the knight *sans peur, sans reproche.*

That the family are numerous is not to be wondered at, if even a few of them have been as prolific as was Gilbert Baird of Auchmedden, who by his wife Lilias had 32 children; this was in the XVI. cent. That great prophet, Thomas the Rymer, is said to have predicted that "there shall be an eagle in the craig while there is a Baird in Auchmedden." And it is asserted that, when the estate changed hands in the last century the eagles deserted their eyrie—only to return, however, when the lands reverted to a Baird. Account of name of Baird, Edinburgh, 1857.

BAIRNSFATHER. The father of the bairn or child—a sobriquet.

BAKE. An estate in St German's, Cornwall.

BAKEHOUSE. From residence at one or employment in it. It has been cor-

rupted to Backhouse, and still further to Bacchus. Thus the provider of bread has assimilated himself to the tutelar divinity of wine!

BAKEPUZ. BAKEPUCE. In the H. R. Bagepuz. From Bacquepuis, in the arrondissement of Evreux, in Normandy.

BAKER. The occupation. In old documents, Pistor, Le Bakere, &c.

BAKEWELL. A market town and great parish in Derbyshire.

☞ **BAL.** A Gaelic local prefix which, like Bally, in Ireland, implies a town, or rather a central seat of population on a single estate—the homestead; in short an equivalent of the A-Sax. *tun,* which means anything from an enclosure containing a single habitation, up to a veritable *town.* Several places in the Celtic portions of Scotland, with this prefix, have given surnames to families, as Balcasky, Balcanquall, Balmain, &c.

BALAAM. Doubtless local. Bale-ham.

BALBIRNIE. An estate in Fifeshire.

BALCH. An abbreviation of Balchin.

BALCHIN. A very old Teutonic personal name, in old German Baldechin. In Domesd. a Balchi is mentioned as living before the compilation of that record. Baldachini is an Italian, and Baldechin a German family name.

BALCOCK. A diminutive of Baldwin.

BALCOMBE. A parish in Sussex.

BALDERSON. A northern deity, the son of Odin (and the wisest, most eloquent, and most amiable of the northern Gods) bore the name of Balder, which also became a name of men, whence the places designated Baldersby, Balderston, and Balderton, in what are called the Danish counties. The A-Sax. *balder* signifies prince, hero.

BALDERSTON. A chapelry in co. Lancaster.

BALDHEAD. Probably local; or, perhaps, from loss of hair.

BALDOCK. A town in co. Herts.

BALDRIC. Hugh fil' Baldri was sheriff of Northumberland. Domesd. In other counties he is styled fil' Baldrici. A baptismal name.

BALDWIN. The baptismal name. Several chief tenants in Domesd. are called Baldwinius and Baldvinus. H. R. Baudewyne.

BALDY. Perhaps from Baldwin.

BALE. A parish in co. Norfolk.

BALES. A pluralization of Bale.

BALFOUR. A castle and fief in Fifeshire of which county the chiefs were hereditary sheriffs. The family sprang from Siward, a Northumbrian, who settled in Scotland temp. Duncan I.

BALGUY. This singular name borne by an ancient Peak family is apparently a corruption of Baguly. The arms are identical with those of Baguly of B., co. Chester. Lysons' Derbyshire.

BALIOL. Guy de Baliol entered England at the Conquest, and was lord of Biweld, co. Northumberland. His lineal descendant, John de B., was, on the award of Edward I., made King of Scotland. There are several localities in Normandy called Bailleul: that which claims to be the birthplace of this noble and royal race is Bailleul-en-Gouffern, in the arrondissement of Argentan, called in charters Balliolum. "On prétend, sans beaucoup de fondement, que c'est de cette commune que sont originaires les Bailleul, rois d'Ecosse." Itin. de la Normandie.

BALL. A nickname of Baldwin. A West of England provincialism for *bald*.

"As BAD AS BALL'S BULL—who had so little ear for musick that he kicked the fiddler over the bridge!"— An eastern-counties proverb. (Halliw.)

BALLANTYNE. This Scottish name has undergone remarkable changes. "Sir Richard of Bannochtine of the Corhous," who flourished circ. 1460, sometimes wrote himself Bannachty', and his son is called Sir John Bannatyne. This spelling continued till temp. Chas. II., when the proprietor of Corhouse was called indifferently John Bannatyne and Johne Ballentyne, and his son is described as the son of John Ballenden. In fact, down to a recent period, the forms Bannatyne and Ballantyne have been used indifferently by brothers of one house, and even by the same individual at different times. Inf. F. L. B. Dykes, Esq.

BALLARD. An ancient baptismal name. Balard, H. R.

BALLINGER. A corruption of Fr. *boulanger*, a baker. Also a small sailing vessel. See Halliw.

BALLOCK. Gael. Spotted in the face.

BALMER. Qu. O. Fr. *baulmier*. A dealer in fragrant herbs.

BALSAM. From Balsham in Cambridgeshire, which Fuller characterizes as "an eminent village," and the only one in England bearing the name. The place was anciently called Bals-ham, not Balsh-am.

The corruptions made by the "genteel" in names of places within the last 50 years are very much to be reprobated. I allude especially to names with two consonants in the middle. These consonants which should, according to etymology, be kept distinct, are made to coalesce in a most improper manner, and Walt-ham becomes Walth-am, Felp-ham Felph-am, Bent-ham Ben-tham, and Hails-ham Hail-sham!

BALSTON. Ballesdon, co. Berks.

BALY. See Bailey, &c.

BAMBER. A village in Lancashire.

BAMFIELD. See Bampfylde.

BAMFORD. Places in cos. Derby and Lancaster.

BAMPFYLDE. At Weston, co. Somerset, XIII century, whence Weston Bampfylde. The ancient orthography is Baumfilde.

BAMPTON. Towns, places, and parishes in cos. Oxon, Devon, Westmoreland, and Cumberland.

BANBURY. A town in Oxfordshire.

BANCE. Probably of French Protestant-refugee origin. Bance occurs at Paris, and De Bance in Guienne.

BANCOCK. A second diminutive of Ban or Banny, Barnabas.

BANCKER. A corrupt spelling of Banker.

BANDINEL. From Ranuncio Bandinelli of Sienna, in Italy, whose descendant, David B., renounced the Roman Catholic faith, was the intimate friend of Archbishops Abbott and Laud, and of James I., and finally Dean of Jersey. Baccio Bandinelli, the famous sculptor and rival of Michàel Angelo, and also Pope Alexander III. were of this family. They claimed descent from one Band-Scinel, a renowned warrior of Aix-en-Provence, circ. 846, who was sent as military governor to Sienna. Inf. J. B. Payne, Esq., F.S.A.

BANE. BAYN. Scotland. Gaelic, *bane*, white or fair, as Donald Bane, "the fair Donald;" often confused with Baines, which see.

BANES. See Baines.

BANGER. A provincialism for a large person, see Halliw. Or, possibly, from one of the Bangors in Wales.

BANGHAM. Banningham, a parish in Norfolk.

BANKS, BANKES. Anciently written Atte-bank, A-Bank, &c. The A-Sax. implies a bench, bank, or hillock—a place whereon to sit, whether indoors or out.

"As KNOWING AS BANKS'S HORSE." Banks was a well-known vintner in Cheapside, temp. Elizabeth, and his horse "Morocco" was remarkable for his sagacity. See more of both in Halliw.

BANN. BANS. BANSON. Banny is a known nickname of Barnabas, and this group of names is probably from the same source. Ferguson says A-Sax. *bana*, a slayer.

BANNATYNE. See Ballantyne.

BANNER. May have had an origin similar to that of Bannerman.

BANNERMAN. As early as the days of Malcolm IV. and William the Lion, the office of king's standard-bearer was hereditary in Scotland, and gave name to the family. The armorial coat refers to the name and office, being "a banner displayed arg.; on a canton azure, St. Andrew's Cross."

BANNISTER. BANISTER. Banastre occurs in Holinshed's Roll of Battel Abbey. Camden derives it from *balneator*, the keeper of a bath. 2. A term used in the parish accounts of Chudleigh, co. Devon, and supposed to mean a traveller in distress.

BANWELL. A parish in co. Somerset.

D

BANNY. A provincial nickname of Barnabas.

BANNYERS. Said to be Fr. *De-la-Banniere*, 'of the banner'—a standard-bearer.

BAPTIST. An O. Fr. personal name.

BARBAULD. In the Life of Mrs. Barbauld it is said, that the grandfather of her husband, the Rev. Rochemont Barbauld, (to whom she was married in 1774,) was, when a boy, carried on board ship, enclosed in a cask, and conveyed to England, where he settled, and had a son, who was chaplain to a daughter of king George II., wife of the Elector of Hesse. He attended her to Cassel, where Rochemont was born. About the year 1699, the Rev. Ezekiel and the Rev. Peter Barbauld were among the French Protestant ministers settled in London after the Revocation of the Edict of Nantes.

BARBER. BARBOR. BARBOUR. The occupation. Le Barbur. Barbator, H. R.

BARBERIE. Barberi, famous of old for its abbey (1170), is a parish near Falaise, in Normandy.

BARCHARD is apparently identical with the Burchard or Burchardus of Domesd., where it is used as a baptismal name.

BARCLAY. We find a Theobald de Berkeley, probably an offshoot of the English family, settled in Scotland, so early as temp. David I. Fourth in descent from him was Alex. de B., who married the heiress of Mathers, and wrote himself De Berkeley of Mathers. His great grandson Alex. changed the spelling to Barclay in the XV. century. Geneal. Acc. of Barclays of Ury.

BARDELL. Corruption of Bardolf.

BARDOLPH—F. Hugh Bardolph, (called by Wace, Hue Bardous,) who was contemporary with William the Conqueror, was ancestor of the great baronial house of Bardolf, alike celebrated in the annals of England and of Normandy.

BARDON. A place in co. Leicester.

BARDSEA. A township in co. Lancaster; the name was assumed by an early possessor, who was a cadet of the barons of Malpas. Eng. Surn. ii., 49.

BARE. A township, co. Lancaster.

BAREBONES. (See in Godwin's Commonwealth an explanation of the error concerning this name.) Barbone, the ancient and existing name, has been defined as "the good or handsome beard."

BAREFOOT. Probably local. A Norwegian king, however, bore this sobriquet.

BARENTINE. A place in the arrondissement of Rouen in Normandy, near the Rouen and Havre Railway.

BARENTON. A town in the arrondissement of Mortain, in Normandy.

BARFF. *Barf* or *Bargh* means in the North, a horseway up a hill.

BARFORD. Parishes and other places in cos. Bedford, Norfolk, Warwick, Oxon, &c.

BARGE. Perhaps an inn sign.

BARHAM. The family were lords of Barham, in Kent, at an early period, and according to Philipot, the Kentish genealogist, descendants of Robert de Berham, son of Richard Fitz-Urse, and brother of one of the assassins of Thomas à Beckett.

BARING. The peer and the baronet descend from John Baring of Devonshire, Esq., (XVIII. cent.) son of John Baring, minister of the Lutheran church at Bremen, in Saxony, whose ancestors had been either municipal officers or Lutheran ministers of that city from the time of the Reformation. Courthope's Debrett. The name is possibly identical with that of Behring, the eminent navigator.

BARKER. A tanner, from his using bark of trees in his trade. In the old ballad of the King and the Tanner in Percy's Reliques, the latter calls himself "a *barker*, Sir, by my trade." Eng. Surn. Barcarius and Le Barkere. H.R.

BARKLEY. See Barclay.

BARLEY. Parishes and places in cos. Hertford and York.

BARLEYMAN. In Scotland, one who assists at the Burlaw or Barley courts, assemblies held in rural districts to determine on local concerns. Jamieson.

BARLICORN. Sir John Barleycorn, it seems, was no mythical personage, but a living person. 'Joh'es Barlicorn' was, in the time of Edw. I. one of the tenants of Berclawe, co. Cambridge. H.R. See Graindorge.

BARLING. A parish in Essex.

BARLOW. Townships in cos. York and Derby.

BARLTROP. A corruption of Barleythorpe, co. Rutland.

BARMBY. Two parishes and a chapelry in Yorkshire.

BARMORE. Barmoor, a township in Northumberland.

BARN. A pre-Domesd. name; Barne, Bern. For Siward Barn, the patriot rebel against William Conq. see Sax. Chron. Ingram, 276.

BARNABY. A nickname of Barnabas.

BARNACK. A parish in co. Northampton.

BARNACLE. A hamlet in co. Warwick.

BARNARD. A well-known Teutonic personal name.

BANARDISTON. A parish in Suffolk, said to have been the residence of the family temp. Will. I. B.L.G.

BARNEBY. Barnby in the E.R. of Yorkshire, anciently possessed by the family.

BARNES. BARNS. 1. The same as Berners, which see. Dame Juliana Berners, the author of the well-known treatise on sporting and heraldry called the Boke of St. Albans, wrote herself Berns and Barnes. 2. From residence near a barn; say a monastic or manorial barn. Atte Berne is the XIV. cent. orthography. 3. Barnes, a parish in co. Surrey. See however Barn.

BARNETT. A town in Hertfordshire, and parishes in that co. and in Middlesex and Lincoln. In many instances the name Barnard is so corrupted. It is—why I know not—a common name among the Jews.

BARNEWALL. Lord Trimlestown's ancestor, De Bernvale, accompanied William the Conqueror to England in 1066. He came from Lower Brittany, and was allied to the dukes of that province. The family settled in Ireland temp. Hen. II. Peerage.

BARNEY. 1. A parish in Norfolk. 2. A contracted form of Barnabas and of Barnard.

BARNFATHER. See Bairnsfather.

BARNFIELD. A hundred in Kent, and places in other counties.

BARNHAM. Parishes in Sussex, Suffolk, and Norfolk. Barnum is a corruption of it.

BARNSTON. A curt pronunciation of Barnardiston.

BARNWELL. Parishes in cos. Cambridge and Northampton. See Barnewall.

BARON. BARRON. Does not imply any dignity. In Norm. Fr. it means only a husband; and in O. Eng. it is simply *barn*, or *bairn*—a child. Halliw. Sometimes it may have been given as a sobriquet. 2. Baron, a village near Caen, in Normandy. Le Baron, Le Barun. H.R.

BAROUGH. See Barrow. Two townships co. York are called Barugh.

BARR. 1. A parish and a hamlet in co. Stafford; also a parish in Ayrshire. 2. The gateway of a fortified town. 3. A pre-Domesd. name Bar, meaning probably either A-Sax. *bar*, bear, or *bár*, boar—a sobriquet. De la Bare. H.R.

BARRATT. The same as Barrett, which see. One family so called settled in England on the persecution of the Fr. Protestants, consequent upon the Revocation of the Edict of Nantes.

BARRELL. A corruption of Barwell.

BARRETT. BARRITT, &c. Baret, a personal name of Teutonic origin, is found here in Saxon times. See Domesd. In various forms it has always been very common in France and England.

BARRINGER. The old Teutonic personal name Berengarius, whence also the Fr. Beranger.

BARRINGTON. Some of the families of this name claim a Norman descent, and derive their name from Barenton (which see). The Irish baronet deduces himself from a Saxon progenitor, keeper of the Forest of Hatfield in the days of the Conqueror. Le Neve derives the name from an imaginary Saxon called Barentine, but according to Sir Jonas Barrington's Memoirs, the family's Norman origin is unquestionable. The surname was variously written Barentin, Barentyn, Barenton, Barentine, and at length took the English form of Barrington. There are parishes bearing this name in four English counties.

BARRISTER. The occupation.

BARROW. Parishes and places in cos. Derby, Gloucester, Northumb., Rutland, Salop, Suffolk, Chester, Somerset, Lincoln, Leicester, &c. See Borrowes.

BARRY. In some instances from the Welsh ab Harry, the son of Henry; but the Barrys of Roclaveston, co. Notts., claim to be descended from Godfridus, who flourished at Teversal, in that shire, temp. Will. I. In the H.R. the surname appears without a prefix. There is a parish of Barry in co. Forfar.

BARSHAM. Parishes in Norfolk and Suffolk.

BARTELL. A contraction of Bartholomew. In the N. of England, the Feast of St. B. is called Bartle.

BARTER. Probably the O. Eng. *barrator*, one who stirs up strife between the king's subjects, either at law or otherwise.

BARTH. See Bartholomew.

BARTHELEMY. See Bartholomew.

BARTHOLOMEW. A well-known Christian name, which, besides having itself become a surname, has given rise to many others, viz.: Barthelemy, Barth, Bartlett, Barttelot, Bartle, and Bartie; also, through its *nicked* form, to Batt, Batts, Bate, Bates, Batson, Bateson, Batey, Batty, Battye, Battcock, Badcock, Badkin, and Batkin.

BARTIE. See Bartholomew.

BARTLE. See Bartholomew.

BARTLETT. See Barttelot.

BARTLETT. See Bartholomew.

BARTON. The Gazetteer gives thirty-seven parishes, towns, and places so called in various counties of England. In the W. of England the demesnes of a manor or any considerable homestead are called *bartons*.

BARTRUM. A corruption of Bertram.

BARTTELOT. The Barttelots of Stopham have a tradition that they came into England at the Conquest, and settled at a place called La Ford, in that parish, in which they still reside. They are of undoubted antiquity, and the church of Stopham contains a long series of their monuments. The name is probably, like the modern Fr. Berthelet, a diminutive of Bartholomew.

BARWELL. A parish in co. Leicester.

BARWICK. Parishes and places in cos. Essex, Somerset, Norfolk, York, &c. Also an old spelling of Berwick.

BARWIS. BARWISE. An ancient name, at Ilekirk, co. Cumberland, and doubtless local.

BASE. See Bass.

BASHFORD. Basford, places in cos. Notts, Stafford, and Chester.

BASIL. The personal name. Basil, Basile, Basille. H.R.

BASIRE. A modification of Basile. So in Normandy Cecire from Cecile, and Mabire from Mabile. Mem. Soc. Ant. Norm. 1844.

BASKERVILLE. The head of this family was at the battle of Hastings, (Taylor's Roman de Rou, p. 229.) He is styled Martels de Basqueville (Ibid). The parish of Baskerville, now Bacqueville, is in the arrondissement of Dieppe. One of his descendants, who was butler to king Stephen, resumed the name of (William) Martel.

BASKETT. Probably Fr. Basquet, a diminutive of Basque, a native of Biscay; a page or footboy, because the natives of that province were often so employed.

BASS. Fr. *bas*, short, low of stature. Le Bas is a very well-known Fr. surname, and has been naturalized here since the Revocation of the Edict of Nantes.

BASSETT. O. Fr. *basset*, ' a dwarf or very low man." Cotgrave. This family, who became great barons and gave their name as a suffix to Drayton Basset, Winterbourne Basset, &c., are said to have been of humble origin. One of the family appears in Domesd. as an undertenant. Ordericus Vitalis speaks of Ralph B. as having been raised by Henry II. from an ignoble stock, and from the very dust—" de ignobili stirpe ac de pulvere." The B.'s of Beaupré, however, claim descent from Turstin B., the Conqueror's grand falconer. B.L.G.

BASSINGHAM. Places in cos. Norfolk and Lincoln.

BASSINGTHWAITE. Bassenthwaite, a parish in co. Cumberland.

BASSINGTON. A township in Northumberland.

BASTABLE. A corruption of Barnstaple, co. Devon.

BASTARD. In Norman times illegitimacy was not regarded with the same contempt as now. The Conqueror himself, though illegitimate, not only succeeded to his father's duchy, but frankly avowed himself a bastard in official writings. Robert Bastard appears in the Domesd.

survey as an important tenant in capite in Devonshire, in which county the family have ever since flourished as great proprietors. Bastardus, le Bastard, and *de* Bastard. H.R.

BASTICK. Bastwick, a chapelry, co. Norfolk.

BATCHELOR. The word bachelor has long been a sore puzzle to etymologists. Whatever its origin, it seems to imply something inchoate—the partial achievement of a desired object; thus a bachelor of arts, laws, &c., is one who having attained a certain scholastic honour, aspires after the higher degree of master or doctor; so a knight-bachelor is one who in the exercise of chivalry has won his spurs, but hopes to be elected into some order ; while the bachelor of common life is one, who having attained the age of manhood, has not yet taken a position necessary to the proper fulfilment of the social relation—that of marriage. The surname may have been applied originally to persons in this *imperfect* condition, either in the scholastic, the chivalric, or the social sense.

BATCOCK. (See Cock.) A sub-diminutive of Bartholomew. Badecok and Batecok, H.R. The form Batecok is suggestive of ' fighting cock' which may be the true source of the name, from ' bate,' conflict, combat ; a sobriquet given to a boxer, or metaphorically to a quarrelsome person.

BATE. BATES. BATSON. See Bartholomew.

BATEMAN. A-Sax. *bát*, a boat. A boatman. A less likely derivation is from the O. E. *bate*, strife—one who contends, which is rather supported by the analogous surname Bater. It is probable that the Derbyshire family came from Norfolk (Lysons) and so they may have been descendants of the old Norse *vikingr*. Like many other names terminating in *man*, this appears to have been originally a baptismal appellation. A Bateman de Apletrewyk occurs in the H.R. in co. York.

BATER. See Bateman.

BATEY. See Bartholomew.

BATH. BATHE. A city in Somersetshire.

BATHER. The keeper of a bath.

BATHGATE. A town in co. Linlithgow.

BATHURST. An ancient manor near Battel Abbey, co. Sussex, which was possessed by the family in the XIV. cent.

BATKIN. See Bartholomew.

BATLEY. A parish in Yorkshire.

BATSFORD. An estate at Warbleton, co. Sussex, which had owners of its own name in the XIV. cent. It was variously written Battesford, Batisford, &c.

BATSON. See Bartholomew.

BATT. BATTS. BATTSON. See Bartholomew.

BATTLE. BATTAILE. Battel, a town in Sussex, so named from the battle, commonly called, of Hastings. The surname is latinized De Bello.

BATTEN. The family of B. of Somerset have been seated there for nearly six centuries. They are considered of Flemish origin. Among eminent merchants of the staple (wool-trade) temp. Edw. I., were several De Beteyns and Batyns. B. L. G. 2. An estate in the parish of North Hill, co. Cornwall, "from which place was denominated an old family of gentlemen surnamed Battin." Hals, in D. Gilbert's Cornwall, ii., 227.

BATTERSBY. An estate and township in co. York, long possessed by the family.

BATTY. BATTYE. See Bartholomew.

BAUCOCK. BAWCOCK. A diminutive of Baldwin.

BAUD. A-Norm. baude. Joyous.

BAUER. Germ. Boor, husbandman.

BAUERMAN. Germ. bauer-mann.

BAUGH. An old Scottish word signifying bad or indifferent; but the name is probably local.

BAVENT. The lords B., who gave the suffix to Eston-Bavent, co. Suffolk, were a Norm. family, and came from a place still so called, four leagues N.E. of Caen.

BAVERSTOCK. A parish in Wilts.

BAVIN. A corruption of Bavent.

BAWN. Celtic. Fair-haired.

BAWSON. Son of Ball, or Baldwin.

BAWTREE. Bawtry, a town in Yorkshire. The family resided there temp. Edw. I. H.R.

BAX. See Back.

BAXTER. The O Eng. and Scot. form of Baker. See termination STER. See also Eng. Surn. i., 114, &c. John le Bakestere. H.R.

BAYFIELD. A parish in Norfolk.

BAYFORD. A parish in Herts, in which co. the family resided temp. Edw. I. H.R.

BAYLES. Descendants of a refugee family, who fled from a persecution of the Protestants in the Low Countries, and settled at Colchester.

BAYLEY—LIE—LIFF—LIS—LISS, &c. See Bailey.

BAYLY. "The Bailies or Baylys derived their name from their ancestors having anciently been bailiffs of the districts of Carrick, Kyle, and Cunningham, in Scotland." See Bayly of Ballyarthen, co. Wicklow, in B.L.G. See Bailey, &c.

BAYNARD. Ralph Baignard, or Baniardus, was a tenant in chief at the making of Domesd. in Essex and Suffolk. The head of his barony was Baynard's Castle, in Thames Street, London, which was lost by his grandson Henry's taking part against Hen. I. Kelham.

BAYNE. In Scotland this name is probably in some instances a corruption of the Gaelic word "Baan," or "Bhaan" white— but as the arms are bones (Scotticé banes) placed saltier-wise, it is possibly equivalent to Bane or Bone.

BAYNTUN. Bainton, parishes and places in cos. York, Northampton, and Oxford.

Perhaps the vilest pun ever uttered was that on the name of a late M.P. "Why is the member for York not a member?" "Because he baint un !" (Bayntun).

BEACHAM. A vile mispronunciation of Beauchamp.

BEACON. Elevated spots in many districts, where beacon fires were formerly lighted to announce the approach of the enemy, are still called beacons. Residence on such a place probably originated the name. See Hobler.

BEADLE. BEADELL. A well-known office. In Domesd. we have, among the greater tenants, Godwin Bedellus, and "Bedellus quidam Regis," a certain beadle, apparitor, or messenger of the King. Le Bedel is very common in H.R.

BEADON. Probably local; and of considerable antiquity in co. Devon, as Beaudin, Beadyn, &c.

BEAK. See Beke.

BEALE. BEAL. 1. A hamlet in the detached portion of Durham. 2. An opening between hills; a narrow pass. Jamieson. Ferguson thinks it an ancient personal name. Beli, the Scandinavian giant, was slain by Freyr. But Le Beale is found in H.R.

BEALES. See Beale.

BEAMISH. The Beamishes of co. Cork have been settled there nearly three centuries, but nothing is known of the earlier history of the name, which would appear to be derived either from the Germ. Bohmisch, a Bohemian, or from Beamish, a township in Durham.

BEAN. BEANE. A Scotch abbreviation of Benjamin.

BEANBULK. This name, as well as Beanshop, Beanship, and Beanskin, baffles my etymological skill. They may possibly be connected with the vegetable, like the Roman family of Fabii, whose name originated in their being great cultivators of the bean (faba), as were the Cicerones of the cicer, or chick pease, and the Pisones, of the pisum, or pea. A hamlet in co. Leicester is called Barton-in-Fabis, or Barton-in-the-Beans.

BEAR. A gentleman in Kent, some years since, rejoiced in the christian and sur-(or rather un-christian and sur-ly)-names of Savage Bear. Eng. Surn. Although I do not recollect any other instance of this name in modern English, the nomenclature of many European countries, both personal and local, abounds with it in various forms.

A writer in Edinb. Rev. April, 1855, observes that "a proper name obtained from the bear, is still preserved in Bernard, while Ursus and Urso are names of great antiquity. St. Ursus belongs to the V. cent. Ursus, Ursinus, De Ursinis, are found in England after the Conquest as names of clergymen, not unfrequently foreigners. But the Bear had ceased to exist in England so long before hereditary surnames were adopted, that traces of the old king of the northern forest are mainly to be found in such surnames as are derived from the names of places. Urswick, in Lancashire, is a source of such a surname." [This is a misapprehension. Urswick is more likely from *eofer*, A-Sax. for wild-boar, and *wic*. I have no faith in the derivation of one word from two languages]. "Some of the names Berens, Berridge, Berworth, Berney, Berenham, Beresford, Berford, Berewick, Baring, Bearcroft, Bearsley, may be derived from the bear; but *bere*, the A-Sax. for barley, which was much cultivated in early times, is a more probable etymology for most of them. On the continent, Berlin derives its name from the bear, which is the city's armorial bearing, as it is of the canton and city of Berne. The bear has been highly honoured in the Scandinavian peninsula, where many surnames compounded with Björn, indicate a derivation from him. He gave his name to Albert the Bear, Margrave of Brandenburg, who flourished early in the XII. cent. At Rome, he produced the Orsini, in France, St. Ursus, and in Britain, St. Ursula, who is said to have headed the 11,000 virgins in achieving the honours of martyrdom at Cologne, and who in more recent times has been patroness of the Ursuline sisters, and of the celebrated Princess Des Ursins."

BEARD. When the unnatural process of shaving was unknown, as it was during a great part of the middle ages, many persons were known by sobriquets having reference to this appendage to the manly chin. Besides Beard, we have, or have had, Blackbeard, Fairbeard, Longbeard, Heavybeard, and Beardman. A common form in H.R. is *cum Barba*, as Hugo cum-Barba, Johannes cum Barba. In Domesd. the powerful Hugh de Montfort is sometimes described as Hugo Barbatus. The name may, however, be local, from Beard, a township in Derbyshire.

BEARMAN. Probably the same as Berward.

BEATH. A parish in Fifeshire.

BEATON. This great Scottish name is a corruption of Bethune. On the occasion of the marriage between James II of Scotland and Mary of Gueldres in 1448, a member of the distinguished family of Bethune, coming into Scotland in the train of the princess, was solicited by James to remain at the Scottish court, where he married the heiress of the great house of Balfour. His name was corrupted by the Scots to Bethun, Beton, and Beaton. See L'Histoire Genealogique de la Maison de Bethune, par André du Chesne. Paris, 1639.

BEATSON. The son of Beattie, which see.

BEATTIE. An "abbreviation of the female name Beatrix." Jamieson. See Female Christian Names which have become Surnames.

BEAU. Fr. Fine, handsome.

BEAUCHAMP. This illustrious name is found in many countries of Europe—e. g. in France as Beauchamp, in Scotland as Campbell, in England as Fairfield, in Germany as Schönau, and in Italy as Campobello. It was introduced into England at the Norman Conquest by Hugh de Belchamp, Beauchamp, or de Bello Campo, to whom William gave 43 lordships, chiefly in the county of Bedford. Between forty and fifty coats are assigned in the armorial dictionaries to this name, which, in vulgar parlance, is vilely corrupted to *Beecham*. The Itin. de la Normandie mentions a Beauchamp near Avranches, and a Beaucamp near Havre.

BEAUCLERK. Fr. *beau clerc;* "Fine scholar"—an honourable appellation bestowed on men versed in letters; among others upon our Henry I. The present surname was imposed by Charles II. on his natural son Charles, first duke of St. Albans. The opposite name *Mauclerc*—the bad scholar—is found in ancient records.

BEAUFOY. Not 'fair faith,' as it might appear from the Fr.; but *bella fagus*, "fair beech," the name of a locality now called Beau-Fai, in the arrondissement of Mortagne, in Normandy. Ralph de Bella Fago, or Beaufoy, accompanied the Conqueror, and became a tenant in chief in Norfolk and Suffolk. He was a near relative of William de Beaufoe, the Conqueror's chancellor and chaplain. Kelham's Domesd. Dixon mentions that the latinization is sometimes Bella Fide, equivalent to Truman and Trusty.

BEAUMAN. Originally Bauman. The family were expelled from Bohemia for their Lutheran opinions, and a branch settled in Holland, from whence, after the accession of William III., they transferred themselves to co. Wexford. B.L.G.

BEAUMONT. Roger de Belmont appears in Domesd. as a chief tenant in cos. Dorset and Gloucester. According to Sir H. Ellis, he was a near kinsman of the Conqueror, being a lineal descendant of that king's great grandfather. Some trace the noble English families from the Viscounts Beaumont of Normandy, and others from the blood-royal of France. The Itin. de la Normandie gives five places in that province called Beaumont, i. e., 'the fair or beautiful hill,' and there are English parishes, &c., so called in cos. Cumberland, Essex, and Leicester. In charters the name is written De Bello Monte.

BEAUSIRE. A Huguenot family in Ireland. Fr. *beau-sire*, "fair sir." Belsire is found in the H.R.

BEAUVESYN. O. Fr. *bel voisin*, fair or good neighbour, the opposite of Malvoisin or Mauvesyn.

BEAUVOIR. DE BEAUVOIR. Derived from a follower of the Conqueror, called Beauvois, who by some genealogists is made father of the Sir Bevis of Hamptoun, of medieval romance (which, however, represents him as a pre-Norman). The family afterwards settled in Guernsey, then in cos. Suffolk and Middlesex. The De Beavoirs of Berks, the De Beauvoirs of

Ireland, and the various families of Beaver, Beever, Bevor, &c., claim descent from a common stock. See Life of Capt. P. Beaver, R.N., by Admiral Smyth.

BEAVAN. BEAVEN. The same as Bevan.

BEAVER. See Beauvoir.

BEAVIS. See Bevis.

BECCLES. A town in Suffolk. De Beckles, H.R.

BECK. BECKE. Teutonic *becc*. A rivulet or small stream, in various dialects of England. Bec in Normandy gave name to a baronial race, and a Flemish family of Bec, wholly unconnected with them, held Eresby and other manors at the time of the Domesd. survey. Gent. Mag., Jan., 1832.

BECKET. BECKETT. See A'Beckett. There is a tything in co. Berks so called.

BECKFORD. A parish in Gloucestershire, in which county the family first appear, in connection with the Abbey of Gloucester, in the XII. cent. De Beckford. H.R.

BECKINGHAM. Parishes in cos. Lincoln and Notts. De Bekingham occurs in the former co. H.R.

BECKLEY. Parishes in cos. Sussex and Bucks.

BECKMAN. Beck, a stream, and man. See termination Man.

BECKWITH. The last syllable is a corruption of *worth*. Most of the armigerous families of the name spring from Yorkshire, and Beckwith, a hamlet in the parish of Pannal, in that county, is probably the cradle of the race. It is said (see B.L.G.) that the original name of the family was Malbie, or Malbysse, and that it was changed to B. temp. Hen. III.

BECON. See Beacon.

BEDALE. A parish in Yorkshire.

BEDDING. From Bede. The descendants of Beda. See Ing.

BEDDOE. Perhaps a modification of Bede. Ferguson.

BEDE. A personal name of great antiquity, borne by the "venerable" A-Sax. historian.

BEDFORD. Godwidere and Osgar de Bedeford were tenants in capite in Bedfordshire, 1086. Domesd. The former had held the same lands before the Conquest.

BEDHAMPTON. A parish in Hants. De Bedampton, H.R.

BEDINGFIELD. Orgerus de Pugeys (or Longueville) came hither at the Conquest, and was one of the four knights of the Lord Malet, lord of the manor of Eye, co. Suffolk, who gave him the manor of Bedingfield in that vicinity, *unde nomen*. Courthope's Debrett.

BEDINGHAM. A parish in Norfolk.

BEDINGTON. A parish in Surrey.

BEDWELL. A hamlet, co. Bedford. De Bedewell, H.R.

BEDWIN. Two parishes, in Wilts. Bedewine. H.R.

BEE. Probably allusive to the industry of the original bearer, or the sign of his shop.

☞BEE, as a termination, is a corruption of 'by.' Examples: Holmbee, Battersbee, Bradbee, Boltbee.

BEEBY. A parish in co. Leicester.

BEECH. From residence near a tree of this species. Atte-Beche. Also a place in co. Stafford. See, however, Beke.

BEECHER. Becher is found in the H.R, without any prefix. Le Becher, Le Becchur, and Le Beechur, also occur there.

BEEDHAM. See Beetham.

BEEMAN. BEMAN. In former times, when mead or methlegn was a favourite beverage, the number of bees kept in England must have been much larger than now. *Bee-parks*, or enclosures, exist in several parts of the country, though now appropriated to other uses. The keeper of such a park was called *Custos Apium*— "keeper of the bees"—whence Beeman. His duties are defined in the Gloss, of Services, Cott. M.S. Titus. A. XXVII. fol. 150. Ellis, Introd. Domesd. Among the Domesd. tenants of Herefordshire is a Custos Apium. In one instance, however, this surname is a known corruption of Beaumont.

BEER. BEERE. BEARE. Two places on the banks of the Tamar, in co. Devon, are called Beer-Alston and Beer-Ferris, while two others in Dorsetshire bear the names of Beer-Hacket and Beer-Regis.

BEESON. A corruption of Beeston.

BEESTON. Parishes, &c. in cos. Bedford, Chester, Norfolk, Notts and York.

BEET. Perhaps the same as Beath.

BEETHAM. A parish in Westmoreland.

BEETLE. A corruption of Bedel or Beadle—the office.

BEEVOR. BEEVERS. See Beauvoir.

BEGG. A personal name. An A-Sax. saint was so called.

BEHARREL. Three brothers of this name from Holland came over with Sir C. Vermuyden to assist in draining Hatfield Chase, co. York, temp. Chas. I.

BEIGHTON. Parishes in cos. Norfolk and Suffolk.

BEKE. This family has no connection with that of Bee or Beck; nor is it of Norman origin. It was founded in England by the Goisfred de Beche, of Domesd. De Beche and De la Beche were the Norman-Fr. modes of writing the Flemish Van der Beke, which was, doubtless, the real name borne by this Godisfred in his native country, where he had a good estate. There can be no doubt that the *ch* was sounded hard, for in East Kent, where the family acquired the estate of Lyving's-Bourne, they altered the prefix to Bekes, and the parish still bears the designation of Beakesbourne, while, in some Kentish records, the name is written De la Beke. The barons Beke of Eresby were of this family.

At the present day there are Van der Beekes in Holland, Vander Beckes in Germany, and Del Becques in Belgium and Fr. Flanders. Inf. C. Beke, Esq.

Beek or Beke is Dutch for brook or rivulet, and therefore etymologically identical with Brook and Beck.

BELASYSE. The genealogists of this family assert, that the great ancestor of the Earls Fauconberg was one Belasius, who came over with the Conqueror in 1066, and became general against the forces of Edwin and Morcar in the Isle of Ely. His son, Roland, married the heiress of Ralph de Belasyse, of that Ilk, in the bishoprick of Durham, and thereupon assumed her surname. Collins. De Belasyse is doubtless found in early Norman times, though Belasius is probably a figment. Bellasis is a hamlet near Morpeth.

BELCHER. O Fr. *bel chere*, good company. So Boncompagnon, and our own Goodfellow, &c.

BELCOMBE. A recent refinement upon Bulcock, properly Boulcott, a local name.

BELCUMBER. Belencombre in the arrondissement of Dieppe in Normandy. De Belecumbr', De Belencumbr', &c. H.R.

BELDAM. "A woman who lives to see a sixth generation descended from her." Kennett. The surname, however, is doubtless local. See Eng. Surn. i. 213.

BELESME. In the Battel Roll Belemis. The second son of Roger de Montgomery was so named. Kelham. Bellême is a town, once of great strength, in the arrondissement of Mortagne, and it gave name to a powerful race of counts.

BELFORD. A parish in Northumberland.

BELGRAVE. A parish in co. Leicester, long possessed by the family.

BELKE. Probably Belgh, a hamlet in co. Nottingham.

BELL. This common surname is doubtless *le Bel*, O. Fr. for fine, handsome; and in this form it is found in the H.R. The chief habitation of the Bells has long been on the Scottish border. In a MS. of 1590, relating to the defences of that district, we find in Cumberland, under Bridekirk, this entry: "About them is a great surname of Bells and Carlisles, who have been long in feud with the Irwyns." Again: "In Gilsland is no great surname: the Belles is the most." Archæolog. XXII. p. 169—70.

BELLAIRS. Hamon, one of the sons of Nigel de Albini by Maud de Aquila, niece of Hugh Lupus, assumed the name of De Beler, subsequently corrupted to Bellars and Bellairs. B.L.G.

BELLAMY. Dr. Giles regards this as a corruption of the Norman surname Belesme; but there is abundance of evidence to shew that it is the old or Norman-French *bel-amy*, "fair friend," used much in the depreciatory way in which we now employ "good fellow." When William Rufus had scolded his chamberlain for offering him a a pair of silk hose that had cost only three shillings, and the official had procured a worse pair for a mark, Robert of Gloucester makes the monarch say—

"Aye *bel-amy*, quoth the King, these were well bought ;
In this manner serve me, other ne serve me not."
Camd. Rem.

The Promptorium defines the word, "Amicus pulcher, et est Gallicum, et Anglice dicitur, fayre frynde."

BELLARNEYS. A probable corruption of the Fr. name Beauharnais, "fine armour."

BELLASISE. (See Belasyse). A hamlet in the parish of Stannington, co. Northumberland. This ancient family afterwards removed, unfavourably for themselves, to Henknoull, whence the old northern distich :

"Bellasis, Bellasis, daft was thy knoll,
When exchanged Bellasis for Henknoull."
Sharpe's Chronicon Mirabile.

BELLCHAMBERS 1. A name appropriate enough for church tower. 2. "Bellus Camerarius" may have been the sobriquet of a "handsome chamberlain." See Chamberlain, Chambers, &c.

BELLENDEN. See Ballantyne. That it is a distinct name, however, is proved by the existence of De Bellenedene in the H.R.

BELLET. William Belet, steward of William the Conqueror, was a tenant-in-chief in cos. Hants and Dorset. Domesd. As the name is not prefixed by De, it is doubtless a descriptive sobriquet, perhaps signifying a "handsome little fellow." His descendants were barons by tenure till temp. Hen. III. Nicolas' Synopsis.

BELLEW. Probably of Norman origin, meaning *bel-eau*, in Lat. *bella-aqua*, the fair water ; the designation of some locality. Belleau is a parish in Lincolnshire. John de B. was a baron of Parliament temp. Edw. I.

BELLHOUSE. A-Sax. *bel-hús*, a mansion. It was a mark of dignity to be possessed of a bell. In the reign of Athelstan every ceorle or freeman who owned five hides of land, a church, a kitchen, and a *bell-house* took rank as a Thane. De Belhus and De la Belhuse are in H.R.

BELLINGHAM. The pedigree is deduced from Alan de B., of Bellingham, in Northumberland, temp. William the Conqueror. In the XV. and XVI. cent. a younger branch became widely extended in Sussex, and in that county there existed contemporaneously with it, a distinct family of B., who seem to have borrowed their name from Belingeham, a manor near Hastings, mentioned in Domesday.

BELLMAN. An officer in corporate towns, who rings his bell and proclaims the hour of the night.

BELLOW and **BELLOWS** bear arms similar to those of Bellew.

BELLRINGER. From very early ages England has been famous for its bells; so much so, that Britain was known even in Saxon times as "the ringing island." A skilful ringer of the medieval period would readily acquire this surname.

BELLY. A curious corruption of Bel-eau. See Bellew.

BELSHAM Balsham, a parish in co. Cambridge.

BELTON. Parishes in cos. Leicester, Lincoln, Rutland, and Suffolk.

BELWARD. "One Beluard" occurs as a Domesd. tenant, co. Gloucester, and William Belward, lord of Malpas, co. Chester, founded many great Northern families. See Eng. Surn. ii. 49.

BENCHE. Benche and Bence occur in the H. R., without the prefix *de* or *le*. The A-Sax. *bene* and Fr. *banc* signify, like the modern *bench*, a long seat affording accommodation for more than one person; hence the Queen's bench, the bench of Bishops, a bench of magistrates, or any plurality of dignified persons. The surname probably originated in some ancient legal court.

BENCOCK. See Benjamin.

BENDISH. See Bennett and Bendyshe.

BENDYSHE. A manor in Radwinter, co. Essex, acquired in the XIII. cent. by one of the De Westley family, who thereupon assumed his surname from it.

BENE. See Bean. See also Eng. Surn. i. 222.

BENETFINK. The name of a parish in London.

BENFIELD. Places in cos. Northampt. and Durham.

BENGE. A curt or nicked form of Benjamin.

BENHACOCK. See Benjamin.

BENHAM. A tything in co. Berks.

BENJAMIN. The personal name. As a surname it is chiefly, but not altogether, confined to the Jewish families. The derivative surnames are Benn, Bean, Benns, Benson, Benhacock, Bencock, Benkin, Benny, Bense.

BENKIN. See Benjamin.

BENN. BENNS. See Benjamin.

BENNELL. Benwell, co. Northumb.

BENNETT. From the personal name Benedict. In the reigns of Edwards II. and

III. the name is found thus modified: Fitz Benedict, Benediscite, Bendiste, Bendish, Bennett. This was in the city of Norwich. N. and Q. v. 291. The derivation from *benet*, a minor order of priests, is improbable.

BENNICK. Benwick, a chapelry, co. Cambridge.

BENNINGTON. Parishes in cos. Lincoln and Herts.

BENNISON. The son of Bennet or Benedict, or of Benjamin.

BENNY. BENEY. See Benjamin. Perhaps local.

BENSE, i.e. Ben's. See Benjamin.

BENSLEY. Most persons of the name trace back to Norfolk and Suffolk, and there is a tradition of Danish descent. The name is certainly found in Sweden. The celebrated Benzelius, Archbishop of Upsal, derived his surname from the village of Benzely near that city. (V. Gorton and Watkins). In Domesd. we have a Benzelinus, apparently a follower of the Conqueror, and as the forms Benesle, Bensleyn, &c., are used indiscriminately, there is little doubt of these names coming from a common Scandinavian source. The name is found in 28 forms of spelling. Inf. T. Bensley, Esq.

BENSON. See Benjamin. But De Benson is found in H.R.

BENSTED. Binsted, places in Hants and Sussex.

BENT. An open plain, common, or moor. See Eng. Surn. i. 64.

BENTHALL. A parish in Shropshire.

BENTHAM. There is not much reason to doubt that this name is derived from the parish of Bentham, in the West Riding of Yorkshire. Jeremy Bentham, however, fancied himself descended from the German Counts of Bentheim, and, utilitarian and democrat though he was, at one time actually meditated the purchase of some property which had formed part of their territories. Westminster Rev., July, 1853.

BENTINCK. William B. (first duke of Portland) accompanied William III. to this country from Holland in 1688.

BENTLEY. Parishes and places in cos. Hants, Stafford, Suffolk, Warwick, York, Essex, Derby, Sussex, &c.

BENTON. A parish in Northumb.

BENWELL. A township in Northumberland. The Benwells were descended from the Shaftos of that county.

BENYON. Ab Enion, "the son of Enion," a Welsh personal name. See remarks under Bunyan, Pinion, and Onion.

BERE. See Beer. De Bere, H.R.

BEREBREWER. See Brewer.

BERESFORD. A manor and township in Astonfield, co. Stafford, possessed by the ancestors of the several noble families of

E

this surname for centuries. In the XVII. it passed by marriage to the family of Cotton, the Angler, and the fishing-house which he built for Isaac Walton still exists. In 1823 Lord Beresford repurchased the estate of his ancestors, and it now belongs to A. J. Beresford Hope, Esq., M.P. &c.

BERGER. Fr. A shepherd.

BERKELEY. This noble race descend from Thos. de B., lord of Berkeley castle, co. Gloucester, temp. Edw. I., and fifth in lineal succession from Harding, a Dane of royal blood, and one of the companions of William the Conqueror. Hence the name and title Fitz-Hardinge in connection with the family. Such is the statement of the Peerages, "though it is well ascertained," says a correspondent of Gent. Mag., June 1846, that the founders of the house, "Harding of Bristol, and his son Robert Fitz-Harding, were only burghers of that city." Sayers' Hist. Bristol.

BERKS. Possibly from the county.

BERMINGHAM. A baronial family, who derived their name from their manor and castle of Birmingham, co. Warwick, where they were settled temp. Hen. I.

BERNAL. Probably the same as the O. Frankish personal name Bernald. Ferguson. It may, however, be the same as Burnell.

BERNARD. BERNARDSON. A well-known personal name.

BERNAYS. See under Berney.

BERNERS. According to Domesd., Hugh de Berners, as a tenant in chief, held Evresdon, co. Cambridge. The Itin. Norm. mentions six localities called Bernières, in different parts of Normandy, but which of them is the cradle of this noble race is unknown. A very different origin is assigned in Arch. Journ. vii., 322, viz.: O. Fr. *bernier*, a vassal who paid *berenage*, a feudal due for the support of the lord's hounds. Berner, Bernerus, &c., are found in Domesd. as baptismal names.

BERNEY. The baronet's family are asserted to have been seated at Berney, near Walsingham, co. Norfolk, *at the time* of the Norman Conquest—a great improbability, although their very early settlement there cannot be questioned. Bernays is of distinct origin, being a recent importation from Germany; it is supposed that the latter family were originally French, and that they derived their designation from the town of Bernay, in the department of the Eure, in Normandy.

BERNOLD. An A-Sax. personal name.

BERNONVILLE. A Fr. refugee family after the Rev. of the Edict of Nantes.

BERRALL. See Burrell.

BERRINGTON. Places in cos. Durham, Gloucester, Salop, Worcest., Hereford, &c.

BERRY. A parish in Devon; but from the commonness of the name it must be regarded as another form of Bury, which see. See also Burgh.

BERTIE. A very pretty tradition brings the Berties, at the time of the Saxon invasion, from Berti*land*, in Prussia, to Bertie-*stad*, now Bersted, in Kent, where "one of our Saxon monarchs gave him a castle and town !" A Cottonian MS. makes one Leopold *de* Bertie (!) constable of Dover Castle in the time of King Ethelred, but his son of the same name, being out of favour at court, retired to France. From that country in the year 1154 his descendant came to England with Henry II., who restored to him his ancestral estate at Bersted. See Burke's Ext. Peerage.

BERTRAM. A well-known baptismal name. The family is Norm., dating from temp. Hen. I., when William B. founded the Priory of Brinkburne, co. Northumb. Also local, as William de B. occurs in Domesd. as a tenant in chief, co. Hants. Two baronies by tenure were held in the name of Bertram down to the XIII. cent.

BERTRAND. The same as Bertram.

BERWARD. Bear-ward, the keeper of a bear.
"Here is Jenkyne Berwarde of Barwycke."
Cocke Lorelle's Bote.

BERWICK. In Domesd. a *berewica* generally means an outlying portion of a manor. Of places so called we have, besides the great northern town, parishes, &c., in cos. Sussex, York, Northumb., Wilts, Haddington, &c.

BESFORD. A parish in co. Worcester.

BEST. BESTE. This name has probably no connection with the adjective. In the H. R. it occurs as Le Beste, 'the beast,' a sobriquet; but there is one well-authenticated instance, in which it is a corruption of the Norman Basset. Inf. Stacey Grimaldi, Esq., F.S.A.

BESWICK. Places in cos. York and Lancaster. The B.'s of Gristhorpe have been seated there for upwards of four centuries. B.L.G.

BETHAM. See Beetham.

BETHELL. See Bithell.

BETHUNE. This illustrious name is traceable, beyond question, to Robert, surnamed Faisseus, seigneur of the town of Bethune, in Artois, in the year 1000, and there is good reason to suppose that he was a descendant of the ancient Counts of Artois. His descendants, who were ennobled in every grade and in various countries, reckon among their number many princes of Hainault in Flanders, Cardinal Beaton in Scotland, and the great Duc de Sully in France. See L'Histoire Genealogique de la maison De Bethune par André du Chesne, Paris, 1639. (See Beaton).

BETTELEY. Betley, co. Stafford.

BETTS. See Betty.

BETTY. BETTYES. See Female Christian Names become Surnames. Bede mentions a priest called Betti, A.D. 653.

BEUTYMAN. BEAUTYMAN. More likely from the 'booty' than from the good looks which the first of the name was possessed of. The Scotch orthography is Bootiman, and a correspondent suggests that "boothie"-man, or cottager, is the meaning.

BEVAN. Welsh. Ab Evan, the son of Evan.

BEVER. See Beauvoir.

BEVERIDGE. Beferige, i. e. "the Beaver's edge," occurs in Cod. Dipl. Several other local names in Befer, in that collection, show that the beaver was an inhabitant of this island in Saxon times.

BEVERLEY. Can be traced as residents at Beverley, co. York, to temp. King John, B.L.G.

BEVIS. Camden treats of this among Christian names, and thinks it may be corrupted from " the famous Celtique king, Bellovesus." The town of Beauvais, in France, is however a more likely source for the surname. The Sir Bevys of medieval romance seems to have no place in veritable history, though Heylin claims him as a real Earl of Southampton. The first instance of the surname that I can call to mind is in Sir John Bevis, or Befs, who took Richard, brother of King Henry III., prisoner in a windmill at the battle of Lewes, in 1264. See Beauvoir. A Goisbert de Belvaco occurs in Domesday.

BEW. Ab Hugh, the son of Hugh. Welsh.

BEWICK. Old and New Bewicke are in Northumb., where the family, (well known as a border clan, and still better for having produced the restorer of the art of wood-engraving,) flourished immemorially.

BEWLEY. See Bowley.

BEYER. Dutch Beyers—" of Bavaria."

BIBB. BIBBENS. BIBBY. Fancifully derived from O. Norse bif, movement. Ferguson.

BIBER. Perhaps the same as " bibber," one too much addicted to potations. The name is found in H.R., without any prefix.

BIBLE. Probably an Irish corruption of some other name.

BICK. An A-Sax. personal name, Bicca. Cod. Dipl. 994.

BICKER. BICKERS. A parish in co. Lincoln.

BICKERSTAFF. The O. Eng. bicker means to skirmish or contend, and a bicker-staff, therefore, probably signifies a weapon analogous to a quarter-staff, or single stick. The name belongs to the same class as Longsword, Broadspear, &c.

BICKERSTETH. A name of uncertain origin; perhaps the same as Bickerstaff.

BICKERTON. Townships in Chester and Northumb.

BICKLEY. A township in Chester.

BICKNELL. Bickenhall, co. Somerset, or Bickenhill, co. Warwick.

BICKTON. A manor in St. Eve, co. Cornwall, held by the family in Norman times. D. Gilb. Cornw. i. 412.

BIDDEL. Perhaps Biddulph; perhaps beadle.

BIDDER. A-Sax. biddere, a petitioner— " petitor, vel petax." Wright's Vocab. p. 60. equivalent to ' beadsman.' Piers Plowman views the bidderes with small favour ; he calls them ' Roberdes knaves,' and classes them with vagabonds :—

> "Bidderes and beggeres
> Fast about yede,
> With hire belies and hire bagges
> Of breed ful y-crammed."
> *Vision, l.* 79.

BIDDLE. 1. A modification of Biddulph. 2. A-Sax. bydel, a beadle, messenger, herald, or proclaimer. Biddle, without a prefix, is found in the H.R.

BIDDULPH. A parish in co. Stafford, very anciently possessed by the family, who descended from Ricardus Forestarius, a great Domesd. tenant. Erdeswick's Staffordshire.

BIFFEN. Qu. Bevan ?

BIGG. BIGGE. BIGGS. A præ-Domesd. personal name, Biga. The officer who provided carriages for the king was called a Biga—probably with some reference to the Lat. biga, a two-horse chariot. Ellis, Introd. Domesd. i. 91.

BIGGAR. A parish in co. Lanark. Also Scot., a builder.

☞ BIGGIN. A common termination of local names, especially in the North. It means a building of considerable size— a house, as opposed to a cottage. A-Sax. byggan to build.

BIGLAND. Bigland Hall, co. Lancaster, where the family are said to have been seated from the time of the Conquest.

BIGNALL-NELL-NOLD. A township in co. Stafford.

BIGOD, BIGOT. " When Rollo had Normandy made over to him by Carolus Stultus, with his daughter Gisla, he would not submit to kiss Charles's foot. And when his friends urged him by all means to kiss the king's foot, in gratitude for so great a favour, he made answer in the English tongue, Ne se by God ; that is, Not so by God. Upon which the king and his courtiers deriding him, and corruptly repeating his answer, called him Bigod; from whence the Normans are to this day termed Bigodi." Camd. Britannia, Ed. 1722, Vol i. p. ccix. It was said of that people that at every other word they would swear " By God," and thus Bigod, (whence our word bigot,) became synonymous with Norman. The equivalent French oath ' Par Dieu,' has in like manner become an English surname. See Pardew.

Why one particular baronial family of Normandy should have assumed a name attributed to Normans in general is not very obvious. That the name was understood to be derived from the source indicated above, even long after the Conquest, appears from a speech made by Ralph, Earl of Chester, an opponent of King Stephen, before the great battle of 1141. "Next comes," says he, "Hugh *By-God*, his name merely sounding his perjury, who thought it not sufficient to break his oath with the Empress (Maud), but that he must be once again foresworn, as all the world doth know that Henry at his death bequeathed the crown to Stephen, to the prejudice of his daughter;—a man, in a word, who accounts treachery a virtue, and perjury a courtly quality." *Speed's Chronicle.*

BIKER. A village near Newcastle-upon-Tyne.

BILKE. Ferguson deduces Bill, Bilson, Bilke, &c., from Bil, a small *goddess* among the Scandinavians, but I much question the legitimacy of such parentage.

BILL. A nickname of William.

BILLET. Probably a corruption of the great baronial name Belet.

BILLIARD. Ferguson ranks this name with Bill, Bilke, &c.

BILLING. BILLINGE. Parishes, &c., in cos. Northampt. and Lancaster (two in each).

BILLINGHURST. A parish in Sussex.

BILLINGS. A pluralization of Billing?

BILLINGSLEY. A parish in co. Salop.

BILLINGTON. Chapelries in cos. Bedford and Lancaster.

BILLITER. Apparently a bell-founder. The Promptorium has *bellezeter* (Halliw.), which Mr. Way derives from the A-Sax. *zeotere, fusor.* "*Zetynge* of metelle, as bellys, *fusio*." The old name of Billiter Lane, in London, was originally "Belzettar's Lane" (Stowe), doubtless from the bell-founding trade there carried on.

BILLMAN. A soldier who carries a war-bill or battle-axe. Cotgrave has "Bouscheron, a bill-man, a faggot-maker," from the wood-bill used in that employment.

BILLS. BILLSON. See Bill and Bilke above.

BILLY. Not from William, but from a place in the arrondissement of Caen, in Normandy. Also a comrade, companion. Jamieson.

BILNEY. Parishes in Norfolk.

BILTON. Places in cos. York and Warwick.

BINDLOOSE. This contradictory-looking name, formerly written Byndlos, is probably local.

BINFIELD. A parish in Berks.

BING. See Byng.

BINGHAM. Seated temp. Henry I., at Sutton-Bingham, co. Somerset, and afterwards now at Melcombe-Bingham. Said to be of Saxon antiquity.

BINGLEY. A parish in Yorkshire.

BINNEY. Binnie, in the parish of Uphale, Linlithgowshire.

BINNIE. See Binney.

BINNINGTON. A township in Yorkshire.

BINNS. A place in Abercon, co. Linlithgow.

BIRBECK. A district of Westmoreland.

BIRCH. Parishes and chapelries in cos. Essex, Hereford, and Lancaster.

BIRCHAM. Three parishes in Norfolk.

BIRCHENSTY. An estate in Sussex, contracted to Birsty.

BIRD. See Birds.

☞ **BIRDS,** *Names of, which have become Surnames.* The names of animals have in all ages, and among nearly all nations, been applied as sobriquets to individuals, and these in modern times have acquired the force of surnames, and thus been handed down hereditarily. How common such names are in our family nomenclature, has often been made the subject of remark. See anecdotes in Eng. Surn., i., 178, et seq. A writer in Edinb. Rev., April, 1855, says—"We once knew Hawkes, a Hare, a Peacock, and a Partridge, all quietly dwelling in the same staircase at Trinity College, Cambridge, where a Coote was at the same time an occasional visitor; and we have been honoured by the friendship of a distinguished Whig, whose mother was a Crow, whose nieces were Sparrows, whose housekeeper was a Partridge, and whose cook was a Raven."

For a list of surnames from Birds, see Eng. Surn. *ut supra.* But as usual when generalising, we are apt to attribute to this source many names which do not belong to it; for example, Bunting, Buzzard, Barnacle, Drake, Gosling, Corbett, Parrott, Starling, Wrenn, and Pye, have proven etymologies which take them out of this category, and probably many others have no reference to the "winged nation."

BIRDSEYE. Local: "the island of birds."

BIRDWHISTLE. Birdoswald, on the Roman Wall in Cumberland, the station Amboglanna, is so pronounced locally.

BIRKBECK. See Birbeck.

BIRKETT. A corruption of Birkenhead, co. Chester.

BIRLEY. The cradle of this family is the township of Balderston, co. Lancaster, where the lands of Birclogh or Byrlogh belonged to them, in or before temp. Edw. II. B.L.G.

BIRNIE. A parish in Morayshire.

BIRT. See Burt.

BISH. See Byshe.

BISHOP. See Ecclesiastical Surnames.

BISHOPRICK. The co. of Durham is

frequently called, in old writings, *par excellence*, the Bishoprick, and hence this surname.

BISLEY. A town in co. Gloucester, and a parish in Surrey.

BISS. Perhaps Bish, formerly written Bysse. Ferguson, however, says that Bis is an old Teutonic personal name, and thinks Bissell and Bissett may be its diminutives; but Bissell is found prefixed by De, showing its local origin, and Bisset is said by Camden to mean a dove.

BISSELL. See Biss.

BISSETT. See Biss. The Bisets were barons by tenure in 1153.

BITHELL. Ab-Ithel, the son of Ithel, a Welsh personal name.

BLAAUW. This name, a somewhat recent introduction from Holland, signifies 'blue,' probably from the favourite colour of the costume of the primitive bearer of it. It occurs in various forms among the magistrates of Amsterdam, and is identical with *Bleau*, borne by the eminent printer, the friend of Tycho Brahe, and the well-known author of some of the earliest maps. This is perhaps the only name *now* borne by an English family that can boast of five consecutive vowels, (Bl a^2u^3), although a thirteenth-century orthography of Newman gives six—Nieuw*e*man.

BLABER. Probably some occupation. In Scotland it means a kind of French cloth. Jamieson. Blaber without prefix is found in H.R.

BLACK. Blac and Blache are præ-Domesday names, and doubtless refer in general to the dark complexion and black hair of the original owners. Mr. Wright tells us that Wulric the Black, the ally of the famous Hereward the Saxon, was "so named because on one occasion he had blackened his face with charcoal, and thus disguised, had penetrated unobserved among his enemies, and killed ten of them with his spear before he made his retreat. Essays, ii., 102.

BLACKADDER. A probable corruption of Blackater, a river in the south of Scotland.

BLACKAMORE. R.G. 16. See Blackmore.

BLACKBEARD. See Beard.

BLACKBIRD. Probably "black-beard."

BLACKBURN. A great town in Lancashire.

BLACKE. See Black.

BLACKER. See Blaker.

BLACKETT. Dan. *blakket*, greyish. Ferguson. But the B.'s of Northumb. trace to Richard de Black-heved, or Blackhead, forester of Stanhope, 1350; and the name is consequently local.

BLACKFORD. Parishes in cos. Perth

and Somerset, and minor localities in many others.

BLACKHALL. Or Blackwell. A township in Cumberland.

BLACKHEAD. Either from black hair or local. See Blackett.

BLACKIE. Probably a diminutive of Black—applied to a man of dark complexion.

BLACKLEY. A chapelry in co. Lancaster.

BLACKLOCK. From the colour of the hair. So Whitelock, Silverlock, &c.

BLACKMAN. A baptismal name originally derived from the personal quality of a dark complexion. It is common in A-Sax. charters, and several persons called Blacheman and Blachemannus occur in Domesd. as holders antecedently to the making of that survey. One of these is in Kent, where there is a parish called Blackmanstone, which may have been named after him.

BLACKMONSTER. This repulsive name is a corruption of Blanchminster, the White Monastery, the designation of more than one religious house. *Blancmuster* is an ancient alias for the town of Oswestry. The name was commonly latinized *De Albo Monasterio*.

BLACKMORE. A parish in co. Essex. Blachemer is a præ-Domesd. baptismal name.

BLACKSHAW. A village in co. Dumfries.

BLACKSTONE. A ridge of hills in Lancashire.

BLACKSTOCK. Places in Sussex and other counties.

BLACKWELL. Parishes, &c., in cos. Derby, Durham, Worcester, and Cumberland.

BLACKWOOD. Lord Dufferin descends from a Scottish family. Adam B. was one of the privy-council to Mary, Queen of Scots. I find no locality of this name in North Britain, except the Blackwood Hills, co. Dumfries.

BLADE. Ferguson thinks from O. Norse *bleydi*, implying bashfulness.

BLADON. A parish in co. Oxon.

BLAGDEN. Blagdon, places in Somerset, Northumb., &c.

BLAGROVE. Blagrave, a tything in Berkshire.

BLAIN. See Blane.

BLAIR. The Blairs "of that ilk" in Ayrshire, have been seated in that co. for more than 600 years. They claim the chiefship of all the Blairs in the S. and W. of Scotl., though that honour is challenged by the B.'s of Balthayock, co. Perth, who date back to the beginning of the XIII. cent. B.L.G. Blair, in Scottish topography, signifies a moss or heath, and as there are many localities so called, there may be several distinct families. Imp. Gaz. Scotl. Some etymologists make the word signify a battle-field.

The existing Blairs of Blair spring from a cadet of Scott, who married the heiress, and adopted her surname, but have none of the blood of that race.

BLAKE. "*Bleke*, wan of colour," Palsgr. A-Sax. *blœĕ, blác*, pallidus—a person of pale complexion. The Blakes of Ireland descend from Richard B., who accompanied Prince John to that country in 1185, and settled in co. Galway.

BLAKELEY. Another form of Blackley.

BLAKENEY. A parish of Norfolk, in which co. the family had great possessions. The B.'s of Ireland, settled there temp. Eliz., were a younger line.

BLAKER. BLACKER. Cotgrave defines a blacker as *noircisseur*. The latter word he Englishes by " blacker, blackener, *bleacher*," &c., thus confounding two opposite ideas, and literally "making white black." The truth is, that the A-Sax. *blac*, unaccented, means black, while *blác* signifies pale or white, and the derivative verb, *blácian*, to bleach, or make pale. The Promptorium makes ' bleykester' and ' whytster' synonymous, and explains them by *candidarius*, a whitener or bleacher of linen, which is doubtless the meaning of this surname. *Blacre*, apparently used as a baptismal name, is found in Domesd. The Blackers of co. Armagh, derive themselves traditionally from Blacar, a Northman chief who settled at Dublin early in the X. cent. Burke's Commoners, ii. 48.

BLAKESLEY. A parish in Northampt.

BLANCH. Fr. *blanc*. White—of light complexion. Blanche. H.R.

BLANCHARD. BLANSHARD. Cotgrave says, "an order of Friers, who goe ordinarily in *white* sheets." It had most likely a wider application, to any person who affected white raiment. See Jamieson.

BLANCHETT. Perhaps a diminutive of Blanch, white.

BLANCHFLOWER. *Blanch fleur*, Fr. white flower. I have seen this name in Sussex documents of XVII. cent. Blancheflor occurs in an old Fr. romance as the name of a lady. See Wright's Essays, i. 88.

It is not unworthy of remark in connection with this name, which looks like an awkward mixture of French and English, that, at the period at which it originated, the French word *fleur* was giving birth to two English words between which there *now* seems to be little relation, except similarity of sound; viz. ' flower' and ' flour.' The truth is that *flour*, (which more immediately resembles the parent word,) simply means by metaphor *flos* farinae, fleur de farine, the finest part of ground corn, as we say ' the flower of the family'—of the nobility,' &c. Indeed there is a phrase in which even now the words are convertible, namely ' flour of sulphur' and ' flowers of sulphur.'

BLANCHMAINS. Fr. *blanches mains* " white hands." From this peculiarity Robert de Beaumont, 3rd earl of Leicester,

received his sobriquet; it also became the hereditary surname of a family. The cognate name Blanchfront, or rather Blaunkfront likewise occurs.

BLANKFRONT. An A-Norm. surname, *blanc-front*, "white forehead."

BLANCPAIN. BLAUNCHPAYN. Literally translated in Whitebread, which see. There was a species of bread so called in the XIII. cent. Hugh de Elsfield, circ. 1220, gave one virgate of land in Elsfield, co. Oxon, to the prioress of Studley, and further directed one hundred white loaves of the sort called in Oxford *blanpeyn* to be given to the nuns for ever on the feast of the assumption. " Dedi et concessi prædictis monialibus centum panes albos, de panibus illis qui vocantur *blanpeyn* apud Oxon." Dunkin's Oxfordshire, i. 135.

BLAND. The adjective *bland*, mild, gentle, is, I think, of insufficient antiquity to be the etymon. It is probably one of the many forms of Blundus, Blondus, Blond, &c., meaning fair or light-haired. The Blands of Kippax, at a very early period, resided at and gave name to Bland's Gill, co. York.

BLANDFORD. A town in co. Dorset.

BLANEY. From one of the two places called Blagni, near Bayeux, in Normandy.

BLANK. BLANKS. See Blanch.

BLANKETT. See Blanchett.

BLATCHLEY. A parish in Bucks. (Bletchley.)

BLATHERWYCK. A parish in co. Northampton.

BLATHWAYT. Said to be the same as Braithwaite. See Thwaite.

BLAUNCFRONT. Fr. *blancfront;* having a white forehead. It is sometimes written Blaunchfront.

BLAYNEY. Of Welsh extraction, claiming descent from Cadwallader, king of Britain. The first Lord B. created by James I., and settled in Monaghan, was Edward, son of Thomas-ap-Evan-Lloyd-Blayney.

BLAZE. An ancient personal name, borne by St. Blase or Blaise, the patron of the wool-combers of England. See Brady's Clavis Calend. i. 201.

BLEADEN. Bleadon, co. Somerset.

☞ **BLEN.** A syllable occurring in several Cumbrian local surnames, as Blencowe, Blennerhasset, Blenkinsopp, &c. It seems identical with the *blan* in Blantyre, Dumblane, &c., and probably like the Cambro-Brit. *blaen* signifies a point or top.

BLENCOWE. There are two townships of this name in Cumberland; one in the parish of Dacre, the other in that of Greystoke. The family name is derived from the latter, where temp. Edw. III. resided Adam de Blencowe, standard-bearer to

William, 'the Good Baron of Greystoke', at the battle of Poictiers. Hutchinson's Cumberland. Other forms of the name are Blinko, Blinkowe, &c.

BLENKARNE. An estate in Cumberland.

BLENKINSOPP. A township in the parish of Haltwhistle, co. Northumb. The castle there was the seat of the family, a race well remembered for their border feuds in olden times, and designated by Camden as "a right ancient and generous family."

BLENNERHASSET. A township in the parish of Torpenhow, co. Cumberland. By a mistake of N for U, this name is often found mis-spelt Bleuerhasset and Bleverhasset. Members of this ancient race represented Carlisle during almost every reign from Richard II. to James I.

BLESSED. Probably a translation of the Latin name Benedictus, and thus synonymous with Bennett.

BLETHYN. An ancient Welsh personal name. Meredith ap Blethyn was prince of North Wales in the XI. cent.

BLEW. Probably the same as Bellew.

BLEWITT. See Bluet.

BLIGH. Perhaps the same as Blythe.

BLISS. A John Bliss occurs in the H.R. without any prefix of De or Le. The name seems to be connected with the A-Sax. verb *blissian*, lætificare, to make glad or joyous. The singular name Alicia Blissewenche in the H.R. appears to be nearly synonymous with that of Maud Makejoy, whose dancing afforded Edward, prince of Wales, so much pleasure in 1297. See Eng. Surn. ii. 15.

BLOCKLEY. A parish in co. Worcester. *now 'glos,*

BLODLETER. (Bloodletter, a phlebotomist.) Gold le Blodleter occurs in the records of Yarmouth in the XIV. cent., and one Blodletere still earlier in the H.R.

BLOFIELD. A parish in Norfolk, in which co. the family were seated at an early date.

BLOIS. From the city of Blois in France. The family were settled in Suffolk, temp. Rich. I. or John. Courthope's Debrett.

BLOMFIELD. See Bloomfield.

BLONDEVILLE. Blonville, a place near Pont l'Eveque, in Normandy.

BLONG. Fr. *Le Blanc*, white. A Huguenot family in Ireland.

BLOOD. O. Norse *blaudr*, bashful, timid. Ferguson.

BLOOMER. A 'bloom' is a mass of iron that has gone a second time through the fire—A-Sax. *bloma*; and a 'bloomary' was a refining house; hence probably a Bloomer was a person employed in the manufacture of iron.

BLOOMFIELD. A village in co. Worcester, and probably other localities. Norfolk has long been the greatest *habitat* of the name.

BLORE. A parish in Staffordshire, comprising the district called Blorcheath, memorable for the great battle between the Yorkists and Lancastrians in 1459.

BLOSSEVILLE. A village near Rouen, now called Bon-Secours, a great resort for devotees to the Virgin Mary.

BLOUNT. French *blond*, fair-haired, light-complexioned. The great baronial house of Blount, lords Mountjoy, deduced themselves from William, son of Blound, earl of Guisnes, one of the companions of the Conqueror, who was traditionally derived from the *Biondi* of Italy and the *Flavii* of classical Rome ! It is probable that there are several families so designated from the personal peculiarity of the original assumers, without any consanguinity. It has taken various forms; as for example in the H.R. *le Blond, le Blont, Blunt, le Blunte, le Blound*, &c. It may be regarded as the Anglo-Norman synonym of our indigenous White; and some of the Irish Blunts have in recent times translated it into White. The Norwegian royal surname, *Harfager*, means 'fair-haired,' and in the H.R. we have a Flaxennehed.

BLOW. A contraction of Bellew, Bellow, which see. The parish in Norfolk popularly called Blo'-Norton is really Norton-Belleau.

BLOWER. Probably the same as Blore, q. v. There is however a Le Blower in H.R. denoting some occupation.

BLOXAM. BLOXSOME. Bloxham, a parish in Oxfordshire; Bloxholme, a parish in co. Lincoln.

BLUE occurs in Scotland, but I have not met with it in England. It is probably derived from the favourite colour of the costume of the original bearer.
In a church in Berkshire the following epitaph is *said* to exist :—
    " Underneath this ancient pew,
      Lieth the body of Jonathan Blue.
N.B. His name was Black, but that wouldn't do !"

BLUETT. The family of Bluet is said by Camden to have come from Brittany. The name is spelt in the Battel Roll Bluet, and Bluat, and elsewhere Bloet.

BLUMPAY. An American corruption of Blancpied, or Whitefoot. Eng. Surn.

BLUNDELL. Blondel well-known in France, in both ancient and modern times, and rendered romantic by the fidelity of Blondel de Nesle, the minstrel of Cœur de Lion, is a personal name—a diminutive of Blond, fair-haired or light-complexioned. As an Eng. surname it dates beyond the XIV. cent.

BLUNDEN. See Den.

BLUNDER. BLUNDRED. Probably an ancient personal name. Ferguson makes the former signify drowsy, stupid, from O. Norse *blunda*, to sleep.

BLUNDERFIELD. A corruption of Blondeville. This awkward and unpromising name was borne some years ago by a farming bailiff at Bayfield Hall, co. Norfolk.

BLUNSUM. Bluntisham, a parish in co. Hunts, so pronounced.

BLUNT. See Blount. Robert and William Blundus were tenants in chief under the Conqueror. Domesd.

BLYTH. BLYTHE. 1. Towns in Yorkshire and Northumberland, and rivers in several counties. 2. The adjective *blithe*, merry, gay ; whence Blythman.

BLYTHMAN. See Blyth.

BLYTON. A parish in co. Lincoln.

BOAG. See Bogue.

BOAKS. See under Noakes.

BOAR. Though not a common surname itself, this is one which forms the centre of a considerable group of family names, of which the principal are Wildbore, Hogg, Wetherhogg, Clevehogg, Pigg, Purcell, Gryce and Grisell. Porcus occurs temp. King John. Hoggett and Hoggins, as well as Piggins, may be diminutives. Hogsflesh is clearly connected, but Gammon and Bacon belong to other classes. These names correspond with the Aper, Suillus, Scrofa, Porcius, and Verres of the Romans.

When in A-Sax. times wild boars ranged the primeval forests of our island, many localities were designated from them, and in Domesday Book a very considerable portion of the property on most manors consisted of woods which supported an estimated number of hogs, and the swineherd's duty was even more important than that of the shepherd. The principal prefixes of local surnames from this source are—

1. EVER, as in Everton, Everley, Evers, Ebers. A-Sax. *eofer*, a wild boar.
2. BAR, as in Barwood, Barham, Barlow, though in some instances the Bear may have a better claim, for *bar* is the A-Sax. for *ursus*, as *bár*, for *aper*. In the rude Zoology of our ancestors such a slight distinction as a simple accent gave would be sufficient for discrimination between two savage denizens of the woods. (See Bear).
3. SWIN, as in Swindale, Swinton, Swinburne. A-Sax. *swin*.
4. Sow, as in Sowdon, Sowerby, Sowton.
5. PIG, as in Pigdon, Pighills.
6. HOG, as in Hogben, Hogwood, though the Teutonic *hog* (high) may assert in these instances an equal claim.

BOARDER. A cottager. See Borde.

BOARDMAN. A cottager. See Borde.

BOASE. Perhaps the same as Bowes.

BOAST. Perhaps a corruption of some local name like Bowhurst.

Some thirty years ago, a worthy possessor of this name, while dressing one winter morning, wrote it with his finger nail upon a frosted pane of his window—"*Boast*"—and then added—"not thyself of to-morrow, for thou knowest not what a day may bring forth." True and prophetic words—for in one short hour (having been crushed by the fall of a building) he was brought into that chamber—dead!

BOAT. See Bott.

BOATBUILDER. The occupation.

BOATMAN. The occupation.

BOATWRIGHT. See Wright.

BOBBIN. A surname of Robert. Vide old nursery song of "Robin and Bobbin."

BOBBY. A nickname of Robert.

BOBKIN. A double diminutive of Robert.

BOCHER. An archaic form of Butcher.

BOCHYM. A manor in Cury, co. Cornwall, held by the family, temp. Henry VIII.

BOCKING. A parish in Essex. De Boking is found in H.R. in association with co. Gloucester.

BOCKETT. The ancient surname variously written Boket, Bocket, Buckwit, Bucket, &c., is probably of Norman origin, as it occurs in the form of Buket in Scriven's list in Fuller's Church History, in that of Buquet of Caumont, in Milleville's Armorial de France, 1845, and in that of De Bocquet in the Nobiliare Normand., 1666. Froissart also mentions a Bucquet, a fellow-general with the renowned Sir John Hawkwood, temp. Edw. III, at the battle of Brignais. But it may possibly be of English origin, as there was a considerable family of Bokeyt or Bokeyt, in the parish of Little Hempston, co. Devon. Westcote's Devon. Inf. Miss Julia R. Bockett.

BOCOCK. See Bawcock.

BODDINGTON. Parishes in cos. Gloucest. and Northampton.

BODDY. See Body.

BODEN. BOADEN, Bodin or Boding, a præ-Domesd. name.

BODFISH. BOTFISH. R.G. 16. Possibly Fr. *beau-fils*, son-in-law.

BODILY. BODILLY. A Cornwall name, and probably local there.

BODGER. Probably the same as Badger.

BODICOTE. Bodicote Grange, near Banbury, co. Oxon., which had owners so called in the XIII. cent.

BODINEL. An estate in Bodmin, co. Cornwall, anciently possessed by the family.

BODKIN. A younger son of the Fitzgeralds of Desmond and Kildare settled in Connaught in the XIII. cent., and obtained, as was not then uncommon, a sobriquet which usurped the place of a surname, and so was handed down. This was Bawdekin, probably from his having affected to dress in the costly material of silk and tissue of gold, so popular in that age under the name of *baudkin*. (See Halliw.) The Bodkins still use the "Crom-a-boo" motto of the Fitzgeralds. The Bokekin of the H.R. is probably from a different source.

BODLE. This name occurs in the Nonæ return of 1341 at Herstmonceux, co. Sussex, under the form of *le Bothel*, and a place in that parish named after the family is still called Bodle-street. There is a manor of Bodyll in Northumberland. The old Scottish coin called a 'bodle' is said to have received its designation from the celebrated Bothwell. Again A-Sax. *botl*, and Angle *bodl*, signify a dwelling.

BODRIGAN. An estate in Gorran, co. Cornwall, where the family resided temp. Edw. I. C. S. Gilbert's Cornwall, and H.R.

BODY. Boda, (latinized Bodus,) occurs in Domesd. as a previous tenant, and therefore probably a Saxon. Now *boda* is A-Sax., and *bodi* O.-Norse, for a messenger, and, in a subordinate sense, a preacher. It follows, therefore, that Truebody is equivalent to 'faithful messenger,' Lightbody to 'active messenger,' and Freebody to 'ambassador of peace.' (A-Sax. *frith*, peace.) Again Handsomebody (the original meaning of handsome being handy, active) is a 'useful messenger,' while Goodbody, originally written Godebodi, may be no other than God's messenger—a preacher of the Gospel. The Gr. ἄγγελος is used in the double sense of messenger and preacher in Mark, i. 2. See Ferguson for further conjectures.

BOEVY. The family is of Dutch origin.

BOFFEY. Probably same as Boughey, a local name.

BOGIE. A river of Aberdeenshire.

BOGE. BOGUE. Boge occurs on Sax. coins, as the name of a moneyer.

BOHUN. Humphrey de Bohun came hither with the Conqueror, and was a tenant in capite in Norfolk and elsewhere. Domesd. From him sprang a great baronial race. The Norman *habitat* of the family appears to have been the village of Bohon in the arrondissement of St. Lo.

BOILEAU. On a tablet in Ketteringham church, Norfolk, to the memory of John Peter Boileau, Esq., it is stated that "he was the son of Simeon B., Esq., merchant, of Dublin, whose father, Charles Boileau, baron of Castlenau and Sainte Croix, in the province of Languedoc, in France, fled to England in 1691, on the persecution of the Protestant religion." The family descend in an unbroken line from Etienne Boileau, first grand provost of Paris in 1250; and they were early professors and zealous defenders of the reformed faith. Another branch of the family fled from France into Italy to avoid persecution, and subsequently wrote themselves Bevelaqua. The Duke of Bevelaqua bears the same arms as the English baronet, and both names are of course equivalent to our indigenous Drinkwater.

BOILS. A corruption of Boyle ?

BOLD. A-Sax., a house or dwelling. It may 'sometimes refer to a courageous disposition.

BOLDEN. From Bolden, an estate in Ellel, co. Lancaster. B.L.G.

BOLDERO. The family pedigree is clearly traced back to the XV. cent., in co. Suffolk. Similar armorials are assigned to the name of Boldrowe in the same

county, and also to that of Boldron. Both these latter forms are purely *local*, and Boldron is a township in the parish of Bowes, in Yorkshire. The motto of this family is a happy pun—"Audax *ero !*"

BOLE. BOLES. See Bowles.

BOLEBECK. Hugh de Bolebeck, so surnamed from his fief near Havre, came in with the Conqueror, and was a tenant in capite in co. Bucks, where his descendants remained for several generations.

BOLEYNE. The genealogy of the unfortunate Queen goes no further back than 1451, when Sir Geoffrey B. was lord-mayor of London. The surname is doubtless derived from the Fr. town Boulogne.

BOLITHO. A Cornish name, probably local in that county.

BOLLARD. See Bullard.

BOLLEN. See Boleyne.

BOLNEY. A manor and parish in Sussex, possessed by the family in XIV. cent.

BOLT. A-Sax. See Bold.

BOLTER. A maker of bolts or blunt-headed arrows, much in use among medieval fowlers. Randle Holme, however, defines a bolt as an arrow with a round knob, with a sharp point proceeding from it.

BOLTON. Towns, parishes, and places in cos. Lancaster, Cumberl., Northumb., York, Westmorel., Haddington, &c. The first-mentioned gave name to an important family.

BOMGARSON. According to Gent. Mag., Oct. 1820, this is the Germ. *baum-garten*, tree-garden, orchard. The Fr. *bon-garçon* is a far likelier etymon. Ferguson thinks it a patronymic of "A-Sax. *bongar*, a fatal spear," but there is no proof of such a name having existed.

BOMPAS. See Bumpus.

BONAFONS. Fr. *bon enfant*, "good child." A Huguenot family in Ireland.

BONAR. A village of Sutherlandshire, and a feudal barony of which the family were possessed temp. William the Lion, *ante* 1200.

BONAVUE. Fr. *bon neveu*, "good nephew." French Protestant refugees in Ireland.

BOND. A-Sax. *bonda*, a householder, proprietor, husbandman. Latinized Paterfamilias, according to Mag. Brit. i. 61, "and rightly enough as it should seem, because much in the same sense in composition we use hus*bond* or husband." Le Bond. H.R. There are several persons called Bonde in Domesd., one of whom is somewhat contradictorily called "*liber homo*."

BONE. A probable corruption of Bohun. See Bowne.

BONES. A corruption of Bone.

F

BONFELLOW. Perhaps a partial translation of either Goodfellow or Boncompagnon.

BONHAM. Although no place so called appears in the topographical dictionaries, this would appear to be, like Bonby, Bonchurch, &c., the name of some locality. There was, however, a religious order called *bonhommes*, or friars minors, from whom the name may have originated. Bonhomme occurs in the H.R. as a stationary surname.

BONIFACE. A well-known personal name, borne by several popes, &c.

BONIFANT. See Bonyfant.

BONITHON. An estate in the parish of Cury, co. Cornwall, where the family flourished till temp. Queen Anne.

BONNER. O. Fr. *boner* and Fr. *bonaire*. Gracious, kind. Bishop Bonner was an excellent illustration of Horace Smith's dictum, that surnames " ever go by contraries."

BONNELL. The family came from Ypres. Thos. B. settled at Norwich on the Duke of Alva's persecution. His great-grandson was accomptant-general of Ireland.

BONNET. Fr. a Cap. Probably allusive to some fashion adopted by the first bearer.

BONNICK. Bon(w)ick, a township in Yorkshire.

BONNY. BONNEY. " Bonny ; good in any respect; having good features, good complexion, good form, good and manly dispositions." Richardson. Fr. *bon*, good. An enviable surname. In the S. of England the name Boniface is thus contracted.

BONNYCASTLE. I do not discover this ' fair fortress' in any book of topographical reference.

BONNIMAN. See Bonny.

BONSALL. A parish in co. Derby.

BONTYNE. See Bunting.

BONVILLE. In Holinshed's list Bondevile. An ancient Norman family, ennobled as barons in 1449. The Itin. de la Norm. shows three places so called—two near Rouen, and the other near Yvetot.

BONYFANT. Fr. *bon enfant*, literally translated in our Goodchild.

BOODLE. See Bootle.

BOOG. See Boge.

BOOGLE. Probably *bugle*, O. E., a bullock. See Bugler.

BOOKER. 1. See Bowker. 2. *Bócere*, (*c* hard,) A-Sax. A writer, doctor, interpreter.

BOOKLESS. " Not so called from the scantiness of his library, but rather from the good use he made of what he had—Old Norse *boklæs*, book-learned, or, perhaps rather, able to read—a much more notable fact in his day than that of being without books." Ferguson.

BOONE. Probably a corruption of Bohun, as Moon is of Mohun. Boon is, however, an adjective referring to natural disposition; gay, merry. It is now only retained in the phrase " boon companion." Fr. *bon compagnon*.

BOORD. See Borde.

BOORE. A farmer, a rustic. So the Lat. Rusticus, Germ. Bauer, &c.

BOORMAN. See Borrer.

BOOSEY. A place covered with bushes or wood. See Jamieson.

BOOT. BOOTE. Perhaps a trader's sign.

BOOTHMAN. See Beutyman.

BOOTH. " An house made of *bowes*." Tyndall. A temporary building or shed, in Low Lat. *botha*. The form in the H.R. is De la Boothe. But the great family of B. of Lancashire and Cheshire take their designation from their lordship of Booths in the former county, where they resided in the XIII. cent.

BOOTHBY. Two parishes in co. Lincoln ; but the baronet springs from co. Stafford.

BOOTLE. Places in cos. Cumberland and Lancaster.

BOOTY. A præ-Domesday name, Boti. A Gilbert de Budi was a tenant in chief in co. Warwick.

BORDE. BOORD. BOARD. O. Fr. *borde*, " a little house, lodging, or cottage of timber, standing alone in the fields . . . and in some parts of France any messuage, farme, or farme house." Cotgr. In Domesd. the occupants of cottages are called *bordarii*, and amount to 82,119 in number. See Ellis, Introd. Domesd. The Fr. form of the surname is De la Borde.

BOREHAM. Places in cos. Essex and Sussex.

BOREMAN. See Borrer.

BORLASE. A descendant of Taillefer, the celebrated follower of William the Conqueror, is said to have settled at Borlase in the parish of St. Wenn, co. Cornwall, from which manor he assumed the surname, since variously written Burlas, Burlace, Borlas and Borlase. C. S. Gilbert's Cornw.

BORLEY. A parish in Essex.

BORN. The same as Bourn.

BOROUGH. BOROUGHS. See Burgh.

BORRADAILE. Borrowdale, a chapelry in Cumberland.

BORRELL. See Burrell.

BORRER. This name appears in Sussex from the XV. cent. under the forms of

Bourer, Boorer, Borer and Borrer, the extra 'R' being a somewhat recent addition. These, together with the Atte-Bore, Atte-Bowre, de la Bore, Boreman, and other modifications, are probably derivable from the A-Sax. *búr*, a bower, inner room, or bed-chamber. Every baronial residence had its 'Ladye's Bower,' and the original Atte Bore, or De la Bore, (subsequently modified to Borer,) was probably the chamberlain of a great feudal household. This supposition is strongly supported by the A-Sax. name for chamberlain, which is '*bur-thegn*' bower-thane—one who was admitted to the private apartments and councils of the lord.

BORROW. See under Burgh.

BORROWES. See the art. Burgh, De Burgh, &c.

In addition to what is said under Burgh and Burke, I may here remark that the first departure from the form De Burgh appears temp. Edw. I., when the name was sometimes written Atte Burgh, Atte Buregh, &c. This orthography became very common temp. Edw. III. The Lords Burgh of Gainsborough, descendants of Hubert de Burgh, Earl of Kent, were written A'Burgh, Aborough, and Barow, and the Irish Lord Deputy in 1599, Lord Burroughes. The late Sir Wm. Betham, Ulster king of arms, deduced the pedigree of the Irish baronet family of Borrowes from the great Hubert, through the Atte Boroughs or De Burghs of Hants, and the Barrowes and Aboroughs of Calais. Henry Borrowes, the first settler in Ireland, was the son of Erasmus Aborough. Inf. Sir Erasmus D. Borrowes, Bart.

BORSTALL. A winding road up a steep hill—common to many places on the South Downs in Sussex. See Suss. Arch. Coll. ii. 292. A-Sax. *beorh stigele*, "the hill or mountain path." Also a parish in co. Bucks.

BORTHWICK, Lands near Borthwick Water in co. Selkirk appear to have given this surname. B.L.G. There is also a parish in Edinburghshire so designated.

BORWICK. A chapelry in Lancashire.

☞**BOS.** A Cornish word said to mean a house or dwelling. It is found in Boscawen, as well as in Bosmetherick, Bospidnick, Bosistow, Bosaverne, Bossowsack, and other names of Cornish origin.

BOSANQUET. Pierre Bosanquet of Lunel in Languedoc, at the period of the Rev. of the Edict of Nantes, had seven children, two of whom, John and David, sought refuge in England, and from the latter the various English branches are descended. The name is local, and it was formerly prefixed with 'De.'

BOSBURY. A parish in co. Hereford.

BOSCAWEN. The earl of Falmouth's family were possessors of the estate of Boscawen-Ros, in Burian, co. Cornwall, temp. King John. Hals asserts that an Irish gentleman settled there temp. Edw. IV., and assumed the name. D. Gilbert's Cornwall.

BOSHER. Perhaps the same as Bourchier.

BOSLEY. A parish in Cheshire.

BOSS Probably local. De Boss. H.R. co. Norfolk.

BOSTOCK. A township in co. Chester.

BOSTON. A town in co. Lincoln, and a hamlet in co. York.

BOSVILLE. In the H.R. De Bosevil. Bosville is a village of 1400 inhabitants, near Yvetot in Normandy. The family were in England in 1126, and probably from the period of the Conquest.

BOSWELL. Originally De Bosevil, (H.R.) — of Norman extraction. They migrated from England to Scotland in the reign of David I.

The change from Ville to Well as a termination is also seen in the alteration of Rosseville to Roswell, La Ville to Larwell or Larwill, Frecheville to Fretwell, &c.

BOSWORTH. Parishes in co. Leicester, one of which is historical for its famous battle.

BOTFIELD. According to Mat. Paris, Geoffrey and Oliver de Bouteville, brothers, came from Poitou to assist King John, and from the former of these the heralds deduce John de l'Inne, otherwise John of-th'Ynne of Botefield, near Church-Stretton. From 'the Inn,' the seat of the Botefeldes at that place, was formed the surname of Thynne, (Marquis of Bath.) Others of the same stock retained Boteville or Botfield, and it is a moot point whether the name was imported from France or derived from the locality in Shropshire, to which a Saxon etymology would readily apply. The principal variations are Boteville, Botvile, Bottefeld, and Botfield. The last form is found as far back as 1549. Inf. Beriah Botfield, Esq., M.A., F.S.A., &c.

BOTHAM. See Bottom.

BOTILER. In ordinary life a wine-merchant or butler. The king's botiler, or 'Pincerna regis,' was an officer of considerable importance, answering to the collectors of customs in modern ports. In virtue of his office he was empowered to seize for the king's use, from every ship laden with wine, one cask from the prow and one from the poop, paying for each twenty shillings. Jacob's Law Dict. Le Boteler, le Botiller, H.R.

BOTLEY. Places in cos. Hants, Hereford, &c.

BOTONER. Le Botoner, H.R. The button-maker.

BOTREUX. BOTTREAUX. William de B. held great possessions in Cornwall temp. Henry I., the chief of which was Botreux's-castle, by contraction Boscastle. The family were Norman, and doubtless came from Les Bottereaux, near Evreux.

BOTT. Local—in the H.R. De Botte, co. Norfolk. Perhaps, sometimes the Germ. *bote*, a messenger. Ferguson thinks Botton, Botten, Botting, &c., modifications of the same word.

BOTTEN. BOTTING. Local. A Peter de Botine occurs in the H.R., co. Dorset, temp. Edw. I.

BOTTERILL. Probably the same as Bottreaux. In Ayrshire, however, a thickset, dwarfish person is so designated. Jamieson.

BOTTLE. A-Sax. *bótl*, a dwelling, mansion, or hall. Hence Harbottle, Newbottle, and other names.

☞ **BOTTOM.** A termination of many local surnames, as Oakenbottom, Othenbottom, Owlerbottom, Longbottom, Sidebottom, Shoebottom, Ramsbottom, Shufflebottom, &c. It has been explained by the O-Eng. *bothna* or *buthna*, an enclosure for cattle; but in the S. of England it means simply a valley or depressed ground.

BOTTON. Local. De Botton, H.R.

BOTVILLE. See under Botfield. There is a place near Valognes in Normandy, called Boutteville.

BOUCHER. See Butcher, and Bourchier.

BOUCHERETT. Matthew Boucheret, a descendant of the ancient French family of De Boucherat, settled at Willingham, co. Lincoln, and was naturalized in 1644. B.L.G.

BOUGHTON. Parishes, &c., in cos. Kent, Norf., Northampt., Notts, Chester, &c. The baronet's family, then called De Boveton, were of co. Warwick in XIV. cent.

BOUIL. Camden mentions this among Norman surnames introduced here in the XI. cent. It is of course identical with Bovill, and probably also with Boyle.

BOULTER. One who sifts meal—an occupation formerly distinct from that of the miller. See Richardson and Halliwell.

BOULTON. See Bolton.

BOUND. See Bowne. Also O.E. *boun*, Prepared, ready. See interesting remarks in Richardson's Dict.

BOUQUET. Probably from Bouquetot, near Pont-Audemer in Normandy. It is now scarcely known except by its corruption Buckett.

BOURCHIER. A Norman name of uncertain origin. Holinshed's list gives a Bourcher, but the family do not appear to have been ennobled until 1292, in the person of Sir William B., third son of William B., earl of Eu, in Normandy. The name is written so variously as to render its etymology very doubtful. Burser is one of its numerous forms. The latinization De Burgo Charo, "of the dear borough," affords us no clue. It is sometimes confounded with Boucher, O. Fr. for butcher.

BOURDILLON. Descendants of the Rev. Jacob Bourdillon, minister of a refugee congregation in London, who left France in consequence of the Rev. of the Edict of Nantes in 1685.

BOURKE. The same as Burke.

BOURN. BOURNE. Parishes and places in cos. Cambr., Durham, Lincoln, Hants, Sussex, &c. Many trivial localities are so called, and Atte Burne is a common medieval surname. As a topographical term it means sometimes a bound or limit, (Fr. *borne*,) and sometimes a running stream, (A-Sax. *byrna*.) See Eng. Surn. i. 64.

BOURNER. The modern form of At-Bourne. See prefix ATTE.

BOURTON. Parishes, &c. in cos. Berks, Bucks, Dorset, Warwick, Oxon, Gloucest., &c.

BOUTCHER. See Bourchier.

BOUTELL. BOWTELL. Perhaps from Bouteilles, a village near Dieppe in Normandy.

BOUTEVILEIN. A great family of Norman origin. The name has undergone the following degradations: Butvelin, Butwilliam, Butlin!

BOUVERIE. Fr. an ox-stall. Lawrence des Bouveries, a native of Sainghien, near Lisle in Flanders, fled to England on account of his religion, and settled at Canterbury in 1568. From him descends the Earl of Radnor. Courthope's Debrett.

BOVEY. Two parishes in co. Devon.

BOVINGDON. A chapelry in co. Herts.

BOVILLE. Bouville (Bovis villa) a parish in the arrondissement of Rouen. De Boville, De Boyvile, &c. H. R.

BOW. Parishes in Devon and Essex.

BOWCHER. See Bourchier and Butcher.

BOWDEN. BOWDON. The B.'s. were of Bowdon Hall, co. Derby, in the XV. cent. Yet they have a tradition that they are of Norman descent, and that the name was originally Bodin. In 1572 two protestant Walloons, Nich. and John Bowden, settled at Rye. Lansd. MS. 15. 70.

BOWDITCH. BOWDIDGE. An estate in Dorsetshire, possessed by the family at an early period.

BOWDLER. Probably the name of some ancient employment, as Le Boudler occurs in H. R. "To buddle" signifies to cleanse ore. North.

BOWELL. Probably the same as Boville and Boyle, which see. De Bowell. H.R.

BOWEN. Welsh, Ab-Owen, Owen's son. Pembrokeshire is the greatest *habitat* of this name.

BOWER. A Scotticism for Bowyer. Also a room in a feudal mansion. See under Borrer.

BOWERMAN. A Chamberlain. See under Borrer.

BOWERS. See Bower.

BOWES. A parish in Yorkshire.

BOWKER. The A-Sax. *buc* is a water-vessel, and 'to bouke' in P. Plowman means to wash. We still call a great washing of linen a 'bucking.' Hence the original Bowker must have been a washerman. See Lavender.

BOWLAND. A township in Lancashire.

BOWLER. In Fifeshire, 'to bowl' is to boil. One who cooks. Or perhaps a maker of bowls.

BOWLES. Domesd. presents us with two tenants in chief called Bolie and Bollo, the former in Hants, and the latter in Dorset. Bouelles is the name of a place near Neufchâtel in Normandy. Ferguson derives it, and several similar names, from the O. Norse *bauli*, a bull, but it is probably local, as De Bolle is found in H.R.

BOWLEY. Probably a corruption of the Fr. *beau-lieu*, a "beautiful situation." Several places in England and Normandy were so called.

BOWLING. A township in Yorkshire.

BOWMAKER. A common employment in the days when archery was in vogue.

BOWMAN. An archer. A common name on the English border under the Percys, and derived from their weapon—the long bow.

> "Come Spearman ; come Bowman ;
> Come bold-hearted Truewicke :
> Repel the proud foe-man,
> Join lion-like Bewick'"
> *Richardson's Gathering Ode.*

See, however, Bulman.

BOWMER. The same as Bulwer.

BOWNE. In a document of the XVI. cent. the name of Bohun is thus spelt. Sussex Arch. Coll, iii., 187. It also means ready, prepared. Jamieson.

BOWNESS. A parish in Cumberland.

BOWSHER. BOWSER. The same as Bowcher.

BOWYER. A maker of bows for archery. A Bowyer's Company still exists in London.

BOX. A place in co. Wilts, remarkable in modern times for its long railway tunnel.

BOXALL. BOXELL. This name is clearly traced to Boxhulle, an ancient manor in Salehurst, co. Sussex, among whose lords was Alan de B., one of the earliest Knights of the Garter. In this same county the name has been queerly varied to Boxall, Boxsell, Buckshell, Baxhall, &c.

BOXER. A pugilist.

BOY, See Boys.

BOYALL. A corruption of Boyle?

BOYCE. The name of the Scottish historian Boethius, spelt Boece and Boyce, may be derived from the Fr. *bois*—wood.

BOYCOTT. An estate in co. Salop, still possessed by the family.

BOYD. Gael. *boidh.* Fair or yellowhaired. A nephew of Walter, first high-steward of Scotland, circ. 1160, was known by this appellation, and was ancestor of the lords Boyd, earls of Arran, and lords Kilmarnoch—a family conspicuous in Scottish history, and now represented by the earl of Errol.

BOYER. See Bowyer. But this is also Fr. A family so called settled in Ireland after the Rev. of the Edict of Nantes.

BOYES. See Boys.

BOYKETT. A corruption of Boycott.

BOYLE. Sir Richard B., father of Sir Robert B., one of the barons of Scotland who swore fealty to Edw. I. in 1296, was of Kelburne in N.B. It is probable that he was of Norman descent, and that the surname is a modification of Boville, as it was written Boyvill or Boyvile in the XIII. and XIV. cent. See Boville.

BOYMAN. Perhaps a person who looked to the *buoys* near some port or dangerous sea passage.

BOYNE. An ancient thanedom of Scotland, which included Banff. Gaz. Scotl.

BOYNTON. A parish in the E. R. of co. York, where the baronet's family resided temp. Hen. III.

BOYS. Fr. *bois*, a wood. The latinized form De Bosco, 'of the wood,' is retained in the Fr. Dubois, Dubosq, &c., while Attwood is the precise Eng. equivalent.

BOYSE. See Boys.

BOYSON. Perhaps boatswain, vulgo *boson*; or more probably a Fr. local name compounded with *bois*, a wood.

BOYTON. Parishes in Devon, Wilts, and Suffolk.

BRABAN. From the duchy of Brabant. The name occurs in the present orthography in the H.R. ; otherwise we might with equal probability derive it from the parish of Braborne, co. Kent.

BRABANT. See Braban.

BRABAZON. The English and Irish Brabazons claim from Jacques le Brabazon, who is said to have come into England with the Conqueror and to have borne the honourable distinction of "The Great Warrior." His posterity settled, during the early Norman reigns, at Betchworth, co. Surrey, and from them descended in an unbroken line the B.'s, earls of Meath, and baronets in Ireland. The name, variously written Barbauzon, Barbanzon, Brabazon, &c., is traditionally derived from the town or castle of Brabazon, in Normandy, but as no such locality can be found, its true source appears to be Brabant in Flanders, as stated in Lodge's Peerage of Ireland. In that duchy the village and castle of Brabançon had lords of the same name, one of whom espoused a grand-niece of Godfrey of Bouillon, King of Jerusalem, circ. 1100. See Geneal. Hist. of Fam. of Brabazon. Paris, 1825.

A Brabançon was a native of Brabant.

The mercenary soldiers employed by William Rufus, Stephen, Henry II., and John, were so called from their having principally come from that district. See Grose, Military Antiq. Edit. 1786, i. 56. Like the Genoese and Swiss of later times, they were soldiers by trade, and lent their services to any monarch who would pay them best.

BRACE. A parish in co. Salop.

BRACEBRIDGE. A parish near Lincoln, possessed by the family in XIII. and XIV. cent.

BRACEY. Perhaps from Bréci, or from Brecei in Normandy.

BRACKENBURY. Apparently from Brackenborough, co. Lincoln, in which shire the family are still seated. They claim to be of Norman descent. See B.L.G.

☞ **BRAD.** A-Sax. *brád*, broad or large. A component syllable of numerous local surnames, as Bradfield, Bradley, Braddon, Braddock, &c.

BRADBEE. Bradby, a chapelry in co. Derby.

BRADBROOK. Local — ' the broad brook.'

BRADBURY. A township in Durham.

BRADDON. Bradden, co. Northampt. in which co. the family were originally seated.

BRADEN. Bradon, a parish in co. Somerset.

BRADFIELD. Parishes, &c., in cos. Berks, Essex, Norfolk, York, and Suffolk.

BRADFORD. A great town of Yorkshire, and places in cos. Devon, Lancaster, Northumb., Stafford, Somerset, &c.

BRADFUTE. The Scottish form of Broadfoot.

BRADING. A parish in the Isle of Wight.

BRADLEY. Parishes, &c., in cos. Berks, Chester, Derby, Leicester, Lincoln, Hants, Stafford, &c.

BRADNEY. A place in co. Somerset, belonging to Sir Simon de Bredenie in 1346. Bardney or Bradney, co. Lincoln, may also have a claim. There is a tradition of Norman descent.

BRADSHAW. A chapelry, co. Lancaster, "where the Bradshaws have flourished from the time of the Saxons, the present owner thereof being Thomas Bradshaw Isherwood, Esq." B.L.G. Bradshaw, near the Peak of Derbyshire, gave name to another ancient family. Lysons.

BRAGG. BRAGGER. Skelton uses *brag* in the sense of proud, insolent; it also signifies brisk, full of spirits. Halliw. The Scandinavian Apollo was so called.

BRAHAM. Among the Jews, a modified form of Abraham.

BRAID. The northern form of Broad.

BRAIDWOOD. A village in Lanarkshire.

BRAILSFORD. A parish in co. Derby, possessed by the family from Nicholas de B. temp. Henry II., till temp. Richard II. Lysons.

BRAINE. See Brayne.

BRAITHWAITE. A township in Cumberland. De Bratwayt occurs in H.R. in co. York.

BRAKE. A word of various significations, as a large barrow, an enclosure for cattle, &c.; but the name is probably derived from a *brake* according to Kennett's definition — " a small plat or parcel of bushes growing by themselves." The word is familiar to Shakspereans : " Through bog, through bush, through *brake*, through briar." See Halliwell in voc.

BRAMLEY. Parishes, &c., in cos. Hants, Surrey, and York.

BRAMPTON. Parishes, &c., in cos. Cumberl., Derby, Hunts, Lincoln, Norfolk, Suffolk, Northampt., York, &c.

BRAMSTON. The B's of Skreens trace lineally to temp. Rich. II., but I cannot find the locality from whence the name was assumed.

BRANCH. A hundred in co. Wilts. Branche, Braunche, H. R.

BRANCHFLOWER. See Blanchflower.

BRAND. O. Norse *brandr*, a sword, whence the O. Eng. *brand*, with the same meaning. As a personal name it occurs in the genealogy of the Northumbrian kings from Woden. It was a very common old Scandinavian name, and it is still used in Iceland. Brand is found in Domesd. as a previous tenant. Mr. Denham observes, that it is rather singular that the ordinary synonym for a sword should be *brand*. The name of the weapon taken from King Bucar by the Cid was *Tizona*, or the fire-brand. And he adds that " many swords were flamboyant; hence the word *brand*." Slogans of N. of Eng. p. xvii.

BRANDARD. The same as Brander.

BRANDER. 1. Perhaps synonymous with Sworder. See Brand. 2. An officer belonging to a manor. His duties are not exactly known ; it has been conjectured that he was the petty executioner who *branded* criminals, and had charge of the pillory and cuckingstool. See Archæologia XXXIII. 277.

BRANDON. Places in cos. Northumb. Suffolk, Norfolk, and Warwick.

BRANDRAM. From the Scand. *brand*, a sword, and *ram*, strong—'strongsword.' Ferguson.

BRANDY. A Scandinavian name, *Brandi*, " one having a brand or sword." Ferguson.

BRANDRETH. Probably the same as Brandard. See Brand.

BRANFILL. There is armorial evidence of the identity of this family with that of Bamfield. B.L.G.

BRANKSTON. Branxton, a parish in Northumb.

BRANSCOMBE. A parish in Devon.

BRANSFORD. A hamlet in co. Worcester.

BRANSTON. A parish in co. Lincoln.

BRANTON. A township in Northumberland.

BRAOSE. The castle of Braose, now Brieuse, is two leagues from Falaise in Normandy. It was built by Robert de Braose, who had two sons: 1. Alan, who with his posterity remained in Normandy, and 2. Robert, who came to England with the Conqueror, but died soon after. He left, however, two sons: 1. William, who founded the baronial house of Braose of Bramber, Gower, &c., and 2. Adam, ancestor of the *Bruces* of Skelton, Annandale, &c., and of King Robert Bruce. Dr. Johnston's Hist. of Fam. of Bruce. See Bruce.

BRASS. Perhaps a synonym of Strong. The A-Sax. *braesen* signifies both made of brass, and strong, powerful. Ferguson.

BRASSINGTON. A chapelry in co. Derby.

BRASTED. A parish in Kent.

BRATHWAYTE. See Braithwaite.

BRATT. O. Norse *brattr*, impetuous; the name of a Northman in the Landnamabok. Ferguson.

BRAUND. See Brand.

BRAY. This name occurs in all the copies of the so-called Roll of Battel Abbey, and that a great family so designated migrated from Normandy at the period of the Conquest seems pretty certain. Three places in that province are still called Brai; two in the arrondissement of Falaise, and one in that of Bernai. But we have also at least two places called Bray in England; one a parish in Berkshire, well known for its time-serving ecclesiastic, who amidst all the fluctuations of creeds in the XVI. century, made it his ruling principle " to live and die vicar of Bray;" the other, an estate in the parish of St. Just, near Penzance, co. Cornwall. This latter, according to Hals, " gave name and origin to an old family of gentlemen surnamed De Bray, who held in this place two parts of a knight's fee of land 3. Hen. IV. I take the Lord Bray of Hampshire to be descended from this family." D. Gilbert's Cornwall, ii. 282. As a proof of the wide diffusion of the name, it may be mentioned that the dictionaries of Heraldry assign more than twenty different coats of arms to it.

BBAYBROOK. A parish in Northampt. Robert de Braibroc was a baron by tenure temp. King John.

BRAYNE. BRAIN. BRAINE. Mad, furious, from A-Sax. *brinnan*, to burn. Jamieson.

BRAZIER. The occupation. Sometimes varied to Brasier, Brashier, and Brasher. Le Brazur, H.R.

BREADCUTT. Most likely a corruption of Bradcote; so Notcutt from Northcote. De Bredecote, H.R.

BREADS. BREEDS. Brid, an A-Sax. name.

BREADY. Parishes in co. Dorset.

BREAKSPEARE. According to Camden, Nicholas Breakspeare, the monk of St. Albans, afterwards Adrian the Fourth, (the only English Pope,) derived his name from a place in Middlesex, bearing that designation. I cannot, however, find any locality in that county which is so called. Most of his biographers fix his birth-place either in Hertfordshire or in Buckinghamshire. It is a curious circumstance that about half a century ago there resided at Brill on the Hill, in the latter county, one of the reputed birth-places of the pope, a man in humble life who bore his identical Christian and surnames of Nicholas Breakspeare. N. and Q. May 3, 1856. The surname clearly belongs to the same category as Shakspeare, Broadspear, Langstaffe, &c.

BREAM. BREEM. 1. A chapelry in co. Gloucester. 2. O. Eng. *brim*, renowned, famous, from A-Sax. *breman*, to celebrate. 3. A baptismal name. Breme, a freeman of Edw. the Confessor, was slain at Hastings. Domesd.

BREDE. A parish in Sussex.

BREDEL. A French refugee family who settled in London after the Rev. of the Edict of Nantes in 1685.

BREDON. A parish in co. Worcester.

BREE. A northern word signifying a brow or declivity, apparently the same as the " brae" of Scottish song. See Brae in Jamieson.

BREEN. When in 1607 Hugh O'Neill, earl of Tyrone, went into voluntary exile, the government of James I. wished to displace his adherents from Ulster, in order to introduce an English colony there. One of the seven native septs thus dispossessed were banished to the distant county of Kerry, where, to avoid persecution, they dropped the unpopular name of O'Neill, and adopted instead that of Breen, from Braon O'Neill, the head of their branch. Inf. H. H. Breen, Esq.

BRENAN. BRENNAN. BRENNAND. O. Norse *brennandi*, fervidus, vehement, earnest. Ferguson.

BREEZE. Corresponds with Bresi, a Northman name in the Landnamabok, by metathesis for *bersi*, O. Norse, a bear. Ferguson.

BRENDON. An estate in St. Dominick, co. Cornwall, possessed by the family in early times.

BRENT. Small rivers in Middlesex and Somerset, and parishes in Suffolk, Somerset, and Devon.

BRERETON. One of the great Cheshire families who can be proved to have existed at or near the time of the Conquest, and are yet unnoticed in Domesd. Ormerod. They came over with the Conqueror, in the train of Hugh Lupus, with Gilbert de Venables, to whom they were apparently related, and settled at Brereton, from which place the name was assumed as early as temp. William Rufus.

BRETON. Le Breton in the H.R. A Breton, a native of Brittany. The name is common in France. See Brett.

BRETT. Brito, a native of Brittany. The parish of Samford Brett, co. Somerset, was the lordship of Hugh Brito, one of the assassins of Thomas á Becket. Domesday Book abounds with Brito as a surname. No less than seven persons bearing it were tenants in chief in many counties. They had probably served in the Conqueror's army under his great ally, Alan, earl of Brittany. Morant's Essex. Kelham's Domesd. In Scotland, *Brets* was a name given to the Welsh or ancient Britons in general: also to those of Strath-Clyde, to distinguish them from the Scots and Picts. Jamieson.

BRETTENHAM. Parishes in Norfolk and Suffolk.

BREWER. 1. *Bruyere*, Fr., a heath. This was a frequent name in Norman times. The principal English family were settled in Devonshire at the time of the Domesd. survey, and founded Tor Abbey. In after times they impressed their name upon Teign Brewer and Buckland Brewer in that county, as also upon Temple Brewer, co. Lincoln. Among those of the name in France, Thibaut de la Bruyere, the crusader, stands conspicuous. The orthography is much varied, the principal forms in the H.R. being Brewer, Brewere, de Bruario, de la Bruere, Brywer, de Brueris. 2. The occupation. In the H.R. it occurs in the Latin and Norman-French forms of Braciator and Le Bracer. The business of brewing was formerly carried on by women, and hence the A-Sax. feminine termination *stre*, in Brewster. In the H.R. we find the name of one Clarissa la Braceresse. In the XV. cent. the name as well as the occupation was often written Berebrewer.

Fuller, speaking of William Brewer, a man famous in our early annals, says: "His mother, unable to maintain him, cast him in *brewers*, (whence he was so named,) or in a bed of brakes in the New Forest. . . . King Henry II., riding to rouse a stag, found this child, and caused him to be nursed and well brought up." Worthies, i. 431. He afterwards created him baron of Odcomb.

BREWHOUSE. A known corruption of Braose.

BREWIN. See Bruin.

BREWSTER. A brewer. See termination STER, and Eng. Surn. in voc.

BRIAR. See Bryer.

BRICE. A personal name. The feast of St. Brice, bishop and confessor, is on the 13th of November. There are three places in Normandy denominated from him.

☞ BRICK. A common syllable in local surnames, signifying bridge, from A-Sax. *bricg*, a bridge; as Shubrick, Brickhill, Bricklande, Brickdale, Brickwood.

BRICKDALE. An estate in co. Lancaster, possessed by the family temp. Edw. I.

BRICKMAN. A brickmaker; or more probably Briggman, i.e. Bridgeman.

BRIDE. May be the A-Sax. *brid*, a bird; but is more probably the Gael. Mac-Bride, by the suppression of Mac. Brideson is an anglicized form of that name.

St. Bride or Bridget was a celebrated saint of Celtic stock, and was much venerated in Ireland, Scotland, and Wales, where many places take their names from her. A well-known church in Fleet Street is dedicated to her, and from a sacred well under her invocation, in the same parish, the *arx palatina* of our early kings took the name of Bridewell. The palace afterwards became a prison, and hence Bridewell has become a generic term for small or minor prisons.

BRIDESON. See Bride.

BRIDGE. From residence at one. The medieval forms are Ate-Bruge, Atte Brigge, &c. It has been pluralized in the forms of Bridges, Brydges, &c.; and has given rise to Bridger and Bridgman. The A-Sax. is *bricg*; whence Brigg and Briggs. In the H.R. we have Ate Brugeende, i.e. 'at the bridge-end.'

BRIDGEBUILDER. See Bridgman.

BRIDGER. See Bridge, and the termination ER.

BRIDGES. See Bridge.

BRIDGETT. See Female Christian Names.

BRIDGEWATER. A town in Somerset.

BRIDGMAN. From the remotest antiquity, the building of bridges was considered a pious and charitable deed, and hence the erection and custody of them was confided to the priesthood. The Roman pontifices or higher order of priests were so styled *a ponte faciendo*. In the middle ages chapels were commonly built either upon or at the approaches of bridges. In some places the reparations of a parish church and those of a bridge were paid for out of a common fund.

The conjunction of the duties of superintending the church and the bridge of a town, which is not unusual in similar situations, may be distinctly traced at Henley-upon-Thames as early as the reign of Edw. II. There are numerous instances in early times of grants and bequests to the "church and bridge;" and up to the present day the bridge-masters for the time being have, by prescription, been churchwardens of the parish of Henley. Parl. Gaz. The charter granted by Queen Elizabeth to the corporation, styles that body "the warden, bridgemen, burgesses, and commonalty of Henley." This was dated 1568; but at a much earlier period the words "bridgeman" and "churchman" were used indiscriminately to denote the same official; and this was doubtless the case in other places. Our nomenclature affords several analogous names, as Briggs (from *brig*, an archaic form of bridge), Bridger, Pontifex, a latinization yet retained, and (in America) Bridgebuilder, which, I am told, is a translation in very modern times of the German Brückenbauer.

BRIDLE. Possibly from Bridell, co. Cardigan.

BRIEN. See Bryan and O'Brien.

BRIERLEY. A township in Yorkshire.

BRIGG. Glanford-Brigg, co. Lincoln.

BRIGGS. See Bridge.

BRIGHAM. A township and estate in Yorkshire, possessed by the family for several centuries.

BRIGHT. A-Sax. *beort*, brilliant, illustrious. It is this ancient Teutonic root that is found in numerous personal names like Albert, Cuthbert, Lambert, &c. Brighting seems to be a patronymical derivative.

BRIGHTING. See Bright.

BRIGHTMAN. A man of sprightly character.

BRIGHTON. A name of recent assumption; since that town—the modern Baiæ—has only been so called since the middle of the XVII. cent.

BRIGHTWELL. Parishes in cos. Berks, Suffolk, Oxon, &c.

BRIGNALL. A parish in Yorkshire.

BRIGSTOCKE. A parish in co. Northampton.

BRILL. A parish in co. Bucks.

BRIM. See Bream.

BRIMBLE. O. Norse *brimell*, a seal; a Scandinavian personal name. Ferguson.

BRIMFIELD. A parish in co. Hereford.

BRINCKMAN. From Hanover with George I.

BRIND. A township in the parish of Wressel, co. York.

BRINDLE. A parish in Lancashire.

BRINDLEY. A township in Cheshire.

BRINE. An Irish corruption of O'Brien.

BRINGLOW. Brinklow, co. Warwick.

BRINKLEY. A parish in co. Cambridge.

BRINKWORTH. A parish in Wilts.

BRINTON. A parish in Norfolk.

BRISCO. "They were called De Birkskeugh, because their first ancestors dwelt at Birkskeugh, or Birchwood, a place by Newbiggin, in a lordship belonging to the priory of Carlisle," in the XIII. cent., or earlier. Denton's Cumberland MSS. They were, however, lords, not tenants, of that fee. Hutchinson's Cumb. ii, 458.

BRISK. From character and disposition.

BRISLEY. A parish in co. Norfolk.

BRISTER. A corruption of Bristowe, which see.

BRISTOLL. Bristol, the city.

BRISTOWE. An old orthography of Bristol—also of Burstow, co. Surrey. The

G

Bristows of Broxmore derive from a John de Burstow of the latter place, 1294. Stephen de Burstow, temp. Richard I. was styled De B. alias Fitzhamon, of which distinguished family he was probably a cadet. See Brayley's Surrey.

BRITTAINE. Breton; a native of Brittany.

BRITTON. My late friend, Mr. John Britton, F.S.A., the oldest antiquary of England, writing in his eighty-sixth year, says: "Britton, Britain, Briten, Bretten, Brittain, &c.—not common in England. I find that they abounded in parishes between Bath and Bristol. I have names from ten different registers. They rarely emigrated to Bath, Bristol, or London." A branch however did settle at Bristol about a century ago, and thence removed to Jamaica. The respectable family of Breton, of Kent and Sussex, usually pronounce their name as if spelt Britton, and there is no doubt of its original identity with it. See Breton.

BRIXEY. Apparently a personal name. Brixi occurs in the Domesd. of Nottinghamshire.

BROADRIBB. Probably a corruption of Broderip.

BROAD. This name which might at first sight appear to relate to *breadth* of back and shoulders—the "vidth" which Mr. Tony Weller associates with "visdom"—really refers to that part of a river which expands into a mere or lake. Le Brode, or The Broad, is a name which was given in ancient times to many such localities.

"*Broad* is a provincial term used in Suffolk and Norfolk, to designate that part of a river where the stream expands to a great width on either side."
                     Southey's Hist. of Brazil.

Brode is also a personal name occurring in Domesday.

☞BROAD. See Brad. Hence Broadbent, Broadbridge, Broadhead, Broadstock, Broadmead, Broadwell, &c.

BROADFOOT. Perhaps from the personal peculiarity; but more likely local.

BROADHEAD. Perhaps local, or perhaps from a personal peculiarity. Brodheved, H.R.

BROADSPEAR. From the weapon of the original assumer. So Langstaffe, Longsword, &c.

BROADWATER. A parish in Sussex.

BROADWAY. Parishes in cos. Worcester, Dorset, and Somerset. A common Gipsy surname.

BROADWOOD. Two parishes in Devon.

BROCK. A-Sax. *broc.*—A badger. (See however Brockman). Also a medieval form of Brook. From one or other of these sources come the local surnames Brockbank, Brocksopp, Brockwell, Brockhurst, Brocklehurst, Brockway, &c.

BROCKETT. According to Harrison's Descr. of Engl. p. 226, a *brocket* is a stag in his second year, but other authorities apply the term to one in his third year. Hence the adoption by the family of a stag for their crest. Leland uses the word as a diminutive of brook—"A *broket* to the sea." Itin. iii. 132. But the true derivation of the surname appears to be from A-Sax. Brochesheved—"the head of the brook," the form in which it appears in the Pipe Rolls, 3. King John, (co. Essex.) There is evidence, principally heraldric, that the Brockheveds, Brockheads, Brockets or Bracketts, were of a common stock with the Brokes, Brookes, &c.

BROCKELL. Brockhall, a parish in Northamptonshire.

BROCKHOLES. The B.'s of Claughton, where they have been seated from the XIV. cent., formerly possessed Brockholls, co. Lancaster.

BROCKLEBANK. A parish in Cumberland.

BROCKLESBY. A parish in co. Lincoln.

BROCKLEY. Parishes in cos. Somerset, Suffolk, and Kent.

BROCKMAN. The Kent family occur as Brokeman, in the XIV. cent. It may be synonymous with Brookman and Brooker; but *brock* is O. Eng. both for a draught horse and a badger, and the primitive Brockman may have been either a horseman, as Kennett suggests, or a hunter of badgers. See Eng. Surn. i. 176.

BRODERIP. The manor of Bowdrip near Bridgewater is said to have been given to this family by Henry II. As if this were not sufficient to account for the name, there is a ridiculous tradition that the first person who bore it was "sauce-bearer" to that monarch, and that from his undue fondness for the contents of the sauce-bowls, the king gave him the sobriquet of "Bag-o'-drip," since refined to Broderip!

BRODIE. Lands in the shire of Nairn. The Brodies of that Ilk date from the XIII. cent., and are still in possession.

BRODRICK. Came from Normandy temp. William Rufus, and settled in co. York. Peerage.

BROKE. An archaism of Brook. The baronet springs from William de Doyto del Broke, circ. temp. King John.

BROKER. See Brooker.

BROMAGE. A corruption of Bromwich.

BROMBY. A parish in co. Lincoln.

BROME. Tradition derives the B.'s of W. Malling from Broome, co. Salop, their residence from the XIII. to the XVI. cent. B.L.G.

BROMFIELD. Parishes in cos. Cumberland and Salop.

BROMHEAD. An estate in Hallamshire, co. York, which passed from the family through an heiress so early as temp. Richard II. Courthope's Debrett.

BROMLEY. Parishes and places in cos. Kent, Stafford, Northumb., Essex, Middlesex, &c. The word is pure A-Sax., and equivalent to "broom-field."

BROMWICH. A town in co. Stafford, and places in co. Warwick.

BROND. See Brand.

BROOK. BROOKE. From residence near a stream. Its medieval forms are Ate-Broc, Atte-Broc, Attenbroke, &c., afterwards softened to A-Broke, and pluralised to Brooks and Brookes. Brooker and Brookman are simple variations of the same name.

BROOKER. See Brook, and the termination ER.

BROOKMAN. See Brook, and the termination MAN.

BROOKS. BROOKES. See Brook.

BROOM. BROOME. Some families claim to be of Plantagenet origin with an anglicised name; but the name is more likely to be local, from one of the parishes so called in cos. Norfolk, Suffolk, Stafford, Bedford, and Durham.

BROOMAN. In Domesd. Bruman. Fr. "a sonne-in-law." Cotgr.

BROOMFIELD. Parishes in cos. Essex, Kent, Somerset, &c.

BROOMHALL. Bromhall, co. Berks, or Broomhaugh, co. Northumb.

BROSTER. An old form of Brewster.

BROTHER. Apparently not from the relation of kindred, but from a baptismal name. There was a Danish king so called, as also one of the Scandinavian kings of Dublin. In Germany the corresponding name of Bruder is found. Two Danish nobles at the Court of Canute also bore the name. Ferguson. The forms in Domesd. are Broder, Brodre, &c., and in the H.R. Brother and Le Brother. Hence Brothers, Brotherson, and the local Brotherton.

BROTHERS. See Brother.

BROTHERSON. See Brother. Also like the O. Norse, *brodurson*, a nephew.

BROTHERTON. A parish in Yorkshire. See Brother.

BROUGH. Parishes, &c., in cos. Westmoreland, Derby, York, &c.

BROUGHAM. From Brougham castle, co. Westmoreland, the Roman station Brocovum of Antoninus. The De Burghams held it temp. Edw. Confessor, and their successors, varying the name to Bruham, Broham, Browham, &c., have been, with a temporary interruption, possessors ever since. See Hutchinson's Cumberland, i. 299.

BROUGHTON. From Broughton, co. Stafford, and first assumed by a descendant of Hugh de Vernon (Baron of Shipbrook, temp. Will. I.) in or about the reign of Edw. I.

BROUNE. The Scottish form of Brown.

BROWKER. See Brooker.

BROWN. BROWNE. One of the commonest of our family names, entering into the proverb, "Smith, Jones, Brown, and Robinson," to designate the *ignobile vulgus*. According to the Reg. General's XVI. Report, it stands sixth among the surnames of England and Wales in point of numbers, Williams, Taylor, and Davies intervening between Jones and this. Within a given period the Smiths were 33,557, and the Browns, 14,346. Its etymology is obvious, and like the Roman Fuscus, the Fr. Le Brun, the Germ. and Dutch Bruin, the name refers to the dark complexion of its original bearers. It is difficult to discriminate between the Browns of Saxon and those of Norman descent, the old orthography being in both instances *brun*. Domesd. has several Bruns, apparently Saxon, but the Battel Abbey Roll has its Le Brun from Normandy, and subsequently we have Le Bruns in plenty, in England, Scotland, and (at Henry II.'s invasion) in Ireland, and ultimately in every rank of society. The Scottish form is Broun, a retained medievalism. A family of Fr. refugees who settled in Norfolk after the Rev. of the Edict of Nantes, 1685, under the name of Brunet, now write themselves Browne.

BROWNBILL. A well-known weapon in medieval warfare.

BROWNING. An A-Sax. baptismal name, usually written Bruning. The appellation originally referred to complexion.

BROWNJOHN. See under the termination JOHN.

BROWNLIE. BROWNLY. A place in co. Kincardine.

BROWNSMITH. See Smith.

BROWNSWORD. See Sword.

BROWSTER. See Brewster.

BROXHOLM. A parish in co. Lincoln.

BRUCE. I always conjectured that the Bruces of Scotland were of a common stock with the great baronial house of Braose of Bramber, in Sussex, Gower, in Wales, &c. A passage in Drummond's British Families seems conclusive on this point:—"Nathaniel Johnstone, M.D., wrote a history of the family of Bruce; he affirms the identity of the Bruces and Braoses. The assertion is supported by many probabilities.

"1. The Baron of Bramber was not a mere upstart who had signalised himself for the first time in the ranks of the Conqueror's army, for he held lands and churches in Normandy, as is asserted by writings still extant. 2. The alliances first recorded of his descendants are of the first families of the country. 3. The spelling of the name in one of the oldest records, (6 John, Claus. Rot.) The name of the Baron of Bramber is spelt Breus, and one of the latest ways of spelling by his posterity is Brewes; the spelling of another is Bruys and Brehus, whilst Pagan, one of the sons of Robert de Brus, writes his name Brausa, and in another charter Braiosa, the very spelling supposed to be peculiar to the Barons of Bramber, and which name is written identically the same in both families. What is really extraordinary is, that in more than

one instance the father signs his name Robert *de Brus*, and the son Pagan de *Brehuse*. The difference in orthography arises from the different way in which the people of Sussex and Herefordshire would pronounce the same name from the people of Yorkshire and Scotland." There is a general resemblance, also, between the arms of the Braoses of Normandy and England and those of the Bruces of Scotland. M. de Gerville, however, deduces the royal Bruces of Scotland from a perfectly distinct source, namely, from the Château d'Adam, in the great parish of *Brix*, a few miles south-east of Cherbourg. This château was built in the time of the dukes of Normandy, by Adam, a lord of Brix, whom M. de Gerville presumes to have been an ancestor of the Bruce who accompanied the Conqueror into England. The name of the parish has frequently been written *Bruis*. Mem. Soc. Antiq. Normandie, 1825. See *Braose*.

The following passage, from Boswell's Tour in the Hebrides with Dr. Johnson, is of some interest:—"We proceeded to Fort George. When we came into the square, I sent a soldier with the letter to a Mr. Ferne. He came to us immediately, and along with him came Major Brewse, of the Engineers, pronounced Bruce. He said he believed it was originally the same Norman name with Bruce, and that he had dined at a house in London where were three Bruces, one of the Irish line, one of the Scottish line, and himself of the English line. He said he was shown it in the Heralds' Office spelt in fourteen different ways." I think it would be easy to produce double that number of spellings.

BRUDENELL. The name is probably local. As to its origin, we learn only from Collins, that it was of good and chivalrous repute, temp. Hen. III., and that it was diversely written Bredenhill, Bretenill, Britnill, Bricknill, Bredenhull, Brutenelle, and Brudenell. Peerage, 1768.

BRUFF. Hearty, jolly, healthy, proud. Halliw.

BRUIN. 1. A nickname of the bear. 2. *Bruin*, Du. brown, dark complexioned.

A small shopkeeper in Surrey had a board, announcing the sale of "Tabel Bear," affixed to his wall, and under it a waggish neighbour wrote, "His own Bruin!"

BRUISE. One of the many forms of Braose or Bruce. R.G. 16.

BRUNNE. See Bourne and Brown.

BRUNROBYN. This name occurs in the archives of Yarmouth. A certain litigious fellow named Robert, a tailor, thence called Robert Tailor, frequently figures as "Brown Robin the Tailor," or more curtly as "Brunrobyn." Papers of Norfolk Archæol. Soc. iv., 253.

BRUNSWICK. Some traders so called appear in the Lond. Direct., and seem to be of German origin.

BRUNT. Probably a corruption of Brent, places so called in cos. Somerset, Devon, Suffolk, &c.

BRUNTON. Two townships in Northumberland.

BRUSH. Perhaps from Germ. *brusch*, broom. See Broome.

BRUSHFIELD. A small village and manor in the parish of Bakewell, co. Derby, anciently written Brightrithfield and Brithrithtfield (quasi, "the field of Brihtéric"— an A-Sax. personal name). The family have long been located about Eyam, a few miles distant, and they have ever been remarkable for their paucity of numbers. At present not above ten persons in England,

and those all related to each other, bear the name. Inf. T. W. Brushfield, Esq.

BRUTON. Parishes, &c., in Northumb. and Somerset.

BRYAN. BRYANT. Bryan is a Celtic personal name of great antiquity, implying originally, regulus, or chieftain.

BRYCESON. BRYSON. The son of Brice, which see.

BRYDGES. Originally written Bruges, and assumed to be of Flemish origin, from the famous city of that name.

BRYDSON. 1. The son of Bryd, an A-Sax. personal name. 2. See Bride.

BRYER. The same as Brewer, in the local sense.

BRYON. See Brian.

BUBB. BUBBS. From Bubba, an ancient Teutonic name. Ferguson.

BUCHAN. A district of Aberdeenshire, which gave title of earl to the families of Cummins and Erskine. The first of the Buchans is stated to have been a son of the last Earl of Buchan of the Comyn family.

BUCHANAN. A parish in co. Stirling, possessed by the family in early times.

BUCK. The animal, famed in the chase, and familiar as an armorial ensign and as a trader's sign. Le Buc. H.R.

☞ BUCK. Many local surnames have been borrowed from this animal, some of which are not readily explainable, as Buckmill, Buckthought, Buckner, and Bucktooth. Buckoke, Buckthorpe, and others, are quite intelligible, though the localities are unknown to me.

BUCKENHAM. Four parishes in Norfolk, anciently Bokenham.

BUCKETT. See Bouquet.

BUCKINGHAM. The town from which the shire is named.

BUCKLAND. Parishes and places in cos. Berks, Bucks, Gloucest., Herts, Kent, Surrey, Somerset, Devon, Dorset, &c.

BUCKLE. Probably corrupted from the local name Buckwell.

BUCKLER. Doubtless from the trade of making buckles. Le Bokeler, H.R. See under Smith. The name has, however, been thought to be a corruption of Beauclerk.

BUCKLEY. A township in Cheshire.

BUCKMAN. One who had the care of bucks.

BUCKMASTER. One who had the care of deer, or who superintended the sport of stag-hunting.

BUCKNALL,—NELL,—NILL. Parishes, &c., in cos. Lincoln, Stafford, Oxon, and Hereford.

BUCKSTON. The same as Buxton (the Derbyshire family).

BUCKTON. A township in Yorkshire.

BUCKWORTH. A parish in co. Hunts.

BUDD. A præ-Domesd. personal name. Boda, Bodus, &c.

BUDDEL. Le Budel and Budellus. H.R. Halliwell has budel, a beadle.

BUDDEN. BUDDING. See Boden.

BUDDEN. BUDDLE. BUDGE. Ferguson derives these names from the Teut. bote, a messenger.

BUGG. Tom Hood has said—

"A name! if the party had a voice,
What mortal would be a Bugg by choice?"

But though it is not as the old phrase is, " a pretty name to go to bed with," yet, as Mr. Ferguson says, there are several "crumbs of etymological comfort for the Buggs. I think (he adds) a good case may be made out, to show that it is a name of reverence rather than of contempt." At all events it is a name that an A-Sax. lady, Hothwaru Bucge, was not ashamed of, albeit she was a holy woman and an abbess. Kemble. Ferguson thinks it is derived from a root implying bowed or bent. However that may be, it is evidently of the same origin as Bogue.

BUGLEHORN. R. G. 16. See Bugler.

BUGLER. BUGLAR. (The bugle-horn was originally the horn of a bull, anciently in some dialects so called. Sir John Maundeville tells of " griffounes" with talons as large as " hornes of grete oxen, or of bugles, or of kyzn !") A player on the bugle-horn.

BUIST. Thick and gross. "He is a buist of a fellow—he is a gross man." Jamieson.

BULFINCH. See Birds.

BULFORD. A parish in Wilts.

BULHEAD. May be either local, or the heraldric sign of an inn, or a sobriquet derived from baldness—A-Sax. bold, bald, and heved, head. It most probably comes from the last-mentioned source, as Boleheved is found in the H.R.

BULKELEY. A township in Cheshire, now Buckley.

BULL. A very natural sobriquet, as well as a common inn-sign, and a frequent heraldric charge. It may, however, be a personal name, as the forms Bole, Bolle, &c., are found in Domesd. The corresponding names Taureau, Torel, Tyrel, Torelli, Bulle, &c., are plentiful on the continent. Let no Frenchman, however, think that "John Bull" is the commonest of designations in England, for in the Lond. Direct. of 1852, I find only four people so called.

BULLARD. Bull-ward—either the man who presided over the sport of bull-baiting, or the one who had the care of the "townbull."

BULLCOCK. See Belcombe.

BULLEN. See Boleyne.

BULLER. A-Norm. A deceiver. Halliwell quotes from an ancient poem :—

"The sexte case es of fals *bullers*,
Both that tham makes and that tham wers."
MS. Cot. Vesp, A. iii., f. 161.

Several Le Bolurs appear in H.R.

BULLEY. A parish in co. Gloucester.

BULLICK. Bullwick, co. Northampt.?

BULLOCK. Doubtless from the animal. Le Bœuf occurs as an early A-Norm. surname, as also does Front-de-Bœuf, "bullock's forehead."

BULLMAN. Bollman in the Orkneys means a cottager. It is always pronounced *bowman*. Jamieson.

BULLPIT. Probably such a place as that described by Hentzner. "There is a place built in the form of a theatre, which serves for baiting of bulls and bears."— Travels in England.

BULMER. Parishes in cos. Essex and York. A distinguished family derived from the latter, and flourished temp. Henry I. See Baronage.

BULSTRODE. An estate in co. Bucks, long possessed by the family. This origin of the name is tolerably satisfactory, but tradition accounts otherwise for it. It is asserted that—

"When William conquered English ground,
Bulstrode had per annum three hundred pound."

At all events he seems to have been a substantial personage and a sturdy; for when the Conqueror gave away his estate to a Norman follower, he and his adherents, *mounted upon Bulls*, resisted the invaders, and retained possession. Afterwards, accompanied by his seven sons, mounted in the same fashion, he went under safe conduct to William's court, and the Conqueror was so much amused with the strangeness of the scene, that he permitted the stalwart Saxon to hold his lands under the ancient tenure, and conferred upon him and his heirs for ever the surname of *Bullstrode!* See Hist. and Allusive Arms.

BUMPSTEAD. Two parishes in Essex.

BUMPUS. Fr. *bon pas*, good pace, or good passage. It may therefore either be local, or have reference to the pedestrian powers of the assumer. Conf. Malpas.

BUNBURY. A cadet of the Norman house of St. Pierre accompanied Hugh Lupus, earl of Chester, at the Conquest, and obtaining the manor of B. in Cheshire, assumed his surname from it.

BUNGAY. A town in Suffolk.

BUNKER. Fr. *bon cœur*, "good heart," from the moral quality of the original bearer.

BUNKLE. A parish in Berwickshire. Also a Scottish term for a stranger.

BUNN. Probably the Fr. *bon*, and equivalent to Good.

BUNNY. Probably from Bunny, co. Notts. The B.'s of Ibdrope were said to have held that Hampshire estate from temp. King John. B.L.G.

BUNTING. Probably local; *buntin* is however a Scottish word meaning short and thick, as "a *buntin* brat," a plump child. Jamieson. The Bunteins were of Ardoch in the middle ages. A Thomas Bunting swore allegiance to Edward I. of England, in 1296. Bunting without a prefix occurs in H.R.

BUNYAN. Nomen venerabile! Although associated in sound with that pedal excrescence, a *bunnion*,—so calculated to hinder the Progress of a Pilgrim!—this surname is in reality derived from the Welsh Ab Enion, the son of Enion, a personal name. So Bevan from Ab Evan, Bithell from Ab Ithell, &c. From Benyon to Bunyan, the transition is easy and natural. The Bunyans were a Gipsy race.

BURBAGE. Places in cos. Wilts and Leicester.

BURBIDGE. See Burbage.

BURCH. See Birch.

BURCHARD. Burchard, Burchardus, &c., a personal name in Domesday.

BURCHATT. BURCHETT. See Burchard.

BURDEN. See Burdon.

BURDER. A bird-catcher, formerly written Byrder. See a quaint anecdote in Eng. Surn. i. 119.

BURDETT. Hugh Burdet, and Robert Burdet, occur as tenants in Domesd. The former, who was ancestor of the baronets of Bramcote, was settled in co. Leicester. The baronets of Burthwaite seem to be of another family, and bear different arms. The origin of the name is unknown; that it is not local is shown by the non-existence of the territorial *De* in the earliest records.

BURDON. Two townships in co. Durham.

BURFIELD. A parish in Berks. De Burfield, co. Oxon. H.R.

BURFORD. Places in cos. Oxon and Salop.

BURGER. Burgher; in Scotland the same as Burgess in England.

BURGESS. BURGES. A freeman of a corporate town or borough.

☞BURGH. A component syllable in many local surnames. It also stands alone, and may be derived from one or more of the various places so called in Cumberland, Suffolk, Norfolk, and Lincoln. It is the A-Sax. *burh, bureh, byrig*, a word common to most German dialects, and somewhat resembling the Gr. πύργος, turris. This is subject matter for a lengthened dissertation, had we space for it, but it will be sufficient for the present purpose to observe, that its meaning appears to be that which Richardson assigns, viz.—"a place of defence or security," whether that place be a walled town, a mountain, or the place in which the "conies," though "but a feeble folk," fortify themselves. Imperial Petersburgh, royal Edinboro', and a rabbit's Burrow, have therefore a community of origin and of name. The word occurs very largely in local nomenclature, sometimes as a prefix or termination, and sometimes in the middle of a name, and in variously modified forms, as *burg*, *bur*, *ber*, *berk*, *borough*, *brough*, *berry*, *barrow*, *bury*, &c.

BURGHERSH. Burwash, co. Sussex, was anciently so called, and thence the Barons from 1303 to 1369.

BURGON. See Burgoyne.

BURGOYNE. A native of Burgundy. The date of this family's settlement in England is uncertain. They have a tradition of having been in co. Bedford from temp. John, (Courthope's Debrett's Baronetage); but Lysons asserts that they did not possess lands in that shire till about 1465, having resided at a more remote date in co. Cambridge. If this be so, we must not accept as genuine a certain rhyming grant, by which John of Gaunt assigns to a member of the family the lands of Sutton and Potton in the former county :—

"I, John of Gaunt, | And the heirs of his loin,
Do give and do grant, | Both Sutton and Potton,
Unto Roger Burgoyne, | Until the world's rotten."

BURKE. A hardened pronunciation of Burgh, and equivalent to Borrowes, &c. See Burgh. The great Irish family are traced to the Anglo-Norm. De Burghs, one of whom settled in Ireland soon after the acquisition of that country by the English monarchs. The name Alfric de *Burc*, apparently of Saxon origin, appears in the Domesd. of Suffolk. In the H.R. the name of the famous Hubert de Burgh, temp. King John, is sometimes written De Burk.

BURKIT. BURKITT. BURKETT. See Birket.

BURLACE. See Borlase.

BURLAND. A township in co. Chester.

BURLEIGH. BURLEY. (Often interchangeably used.) Places in cos. Northampt., Rutland, Hants, York, &c.

BURLINGHAM. Three parishes in Norfolk.

BURLINGTON. An older and more correct orthography of Bridlington, co. York.

BURLS. A corruption of Borel, Burrell.

BURMAN. The same as Boreman.

BURMISTER. A mayor, or chief officer of a borough (*burgi magister*), a corruption either of the German *burgemeister*, the Dutch *burgomaster*, the Russian *bourmister*, or the Danish *borgemester*.

BURN. BURNS. BURNE. BURNES. BURNESS. Known variations of the same name, which however may have several origins. Sometimes it appears to be equivalent to Bourne, and in the North a small stream is still called a *burn*. In Saxon times, however, it seems to have been a personal name, whence Burneston, Burnesdale, and such-like local names. In the time of Edward the Confessor, Godric de Burnes was a great landholder in Kent, and his posterity continued in that co. for several centuries. In Scotland the name appears in early records, under such various forms as to baffle the most astute genealogist in any attempt to deduce a clear pedigree. It is, however, within recent generations that the near kinsmen of Robert Burns have varied that name to Burnes and Burness. See, for an elaborate account of this surname, "Notes on his Name and Family, by James Burnes, K.H., F.R.S." Edinburgh, 1851.

BURNARD. A corruption of Bernard.

BURNBY. A parish in Yorkshire.

BURNELL. The etymon is uncertain, unless it be a diminutive of Brun. The family, who gave the suffix to Acton Burnell, co. Salop, are found in England so early as 1087. Dugdale.

BURNETT. Probably a corruption of Bernard; or it may be, by a transposition of letters not uncommon, the Fr. *brunet*, brownish, tawny, and so a diminutive of Browne. 2. A parish in Somersetshire.

BURNEY. Probably the same as Bernay, which see. A Ralph de Bernai occurs in the Domesd. of Worcester and Hereford.

BURNHAM. Parishes in cos. Bucks, Essex, Somerset, Norfolk, &c.

BURNINGHAM. Briningham, co. Norfolk.

BURNMAN. See BOURN and MAN.

BURNSIDE. Villages in the shires of Fife, Nairn, and Kincardine.

BURNUP. Probably Burnhope, a local name.

BURR. Said to be of Dutch extraction.

BURRELL. Plain, rude, unpolished. 'Borel-clerks,' lay clerks; 'borel-folks,' laymen. The Franklin in Chaucer says in his prologue—

"But, sires, because I am a *borel* man,
At my beginning first I you beseche
Have me excused of my rude speche.
I lerned never rhetorike certain ;
Things that I speke, it mote be bare and plain ;
I slept never on the mount of Pernaso,
No lerned Marcus Tullius Cicero."

The following quaint passage, written temp. Elizabeth, is put into the mouth of a 'plowman,' and illustrates a feature in the arrangements of our churches—the rood-loft—interesting to ecclesiologists :—

"When Master Paradin began his speech of the crosse he wakened me. I remember well when it stood at the upper end of our church body (nave) and had a trim loft for it, with a curten drawne before it to keepe it warme ; yea, zur, zutch was the time then, that we *borrell folke* were taught there was a God upon it, and we must creepe many a time, and make many offerings of eggs to it for our sinnes."—Ferne's Blazon of Gentrie.—Lacie's Nobilitie, page 99.

There are however other, and perhaps more probable, etymons for the name. Borel occurs in Domesd. as a baptismal name, and a township in Yorkshire is called Burrel. The Baronet's family were seated in Northumberland, but removed into Devon in the XIV. and into Sussex in the XV. century.

BURRISH. From Burwash, co. Sussex, still locally so pronounced.

BURROUGHS. See Burgh.

BURROWES. See Burgh.

BURROWS. See Burgh.

BURSLEM. A town in Staffordshire.

BURSTALL. Parishes in cos. York and Suffolk.

BURSTER. A corruption of Burstow, co. Surrey.

BURT. The trivial name of a fish ; but the surname is no doubt derived from the A-Sax. *beorht*, bright, clear, splendid. The founder of the family was probably a "shining character." Berte, however, is found as a personal name in H.R.

BURTENSHAW. Anciently written Byrchenshaw, i. e., the shaw or grove of birch trees.

BURTON. A fortified enclosure. (A-Sax.). Hence the names of no less than forty parishes and places in England, and hence the commonness of this surname. The B.'s of Longner are deduced from Boerton or Burton, in Condover, co. Salop, B.L.G.

BURTWELL. A corruption of Brightwell.

BURWASH. A parish in Sussex, formerly Burghersh, whence the barons of that title.

BURY. Towns and places in cos. Lancaster, Suffolk, Sussex, &c. See also Burgh.

BUSBRIDGE. An ancient Sussex family. Locality unknown.

BUSBY. A village in co. Renfrew.

BUSH. See Bysh. This word, now applied to a low thick tree, formerly meant a whole wood or grove (sylva, nemus), and this proper sense is retained in America and Australia. Atte-Busche therefore, in medieval writings, is equivalent to De Bosco, while the singular name Cutbush is simply a translation of Tailgebosch, Tallebosc, (Taille-bois) so common in Domesd. There is nothing clearer in the etymology of surnames than that the dissimilar appellations Cutbush and Talboys mean one and the same thing, or that Bush and Boys are identical.

BUSHBY. A hamlet and estate at Thornby, co. Leicester.

BUSHELL. BUSSELL. A Norman family who supplied the affix of Newton-Bushell, co. Devon.

BUSK. Busch, an ancient Swedish family settled at Leeds early in the XVIII. cent. B.L.G.

BUSS. Ferguson says a " stout man." A Sivard Buss occurs in Domesd. and there were Norsemen and Norsewomen called respectively Buss and Bussa. Hence would come the O. Norse *bùstinn*, burly—our name Bustin. Ferguson. In the S. of Engl. Buss is a common nickname of Barnabas.

BUSTARD. See Birds.

BUSTIN. See Buss.

BUSSEY. Anciently written Buci, Bussi, &c., probably from Boussei, a place in the arrondissement of Evreux, in Normandy. Robert de Boci was a tenant in chief in co. Northampt. Domesd. One of the same family gave the suffix to Kingston-Buci or Bowsey, co. Sussex.

BUSTER. The local pronunciation of Burstow, in Surrey.

BUSWELL. See Boswell.

BUTCHER. The occupation. Le Bocher, H.R. Some of the older forms are easily confounded with Bourchier. In ancient times this was a title of honour bestowed by the French on great warriors ! See Eng. Surn. i. 121.

BUTE. A great island of Scotland.

BUTLAND. This common Devonshire name is probably a corruption of one of the many places called Buckland in that county.

BUTLER. See under Botiler. The origin of the great Irish family of Butler is a vexed question. They have been variously deduced—from Herveius, a companion of William the Conqueror—from the illustrious De Clares—and from a brother of Thomas à Becket. Certain it is that they went over to Ireland, temp. Henry II., and that the name is derived from the office of King's Butler, which was conferred upon Theobald surnamed *le Boteler* by that monarch in 1177, and remained hereditary in his descendants for many generations. The head of the family claimed prisage and butlerage for all wines imported into Ireland, and it was not until 1810 that the claim was finally surrendered, for the valuable consideration of £216,000.

BUTLIN. See Boutevilein.

BUTT. But—the name of several places in the arrondissement of Falaise.

BUTTEMER. Two or three generations since was written Buttermer, and it is presumed to have been derived from a famous northern Lake.

BUTTER. Boterus and Botorus are found as personal names in Domesday.

BUTTERICK. See Butterwick.

BUTTERWICK. Places in cos. Durham, Lincoln, York, &c.

BUTTERWORTH. A township in Lancashire.

BUTTERY. Probably analogous to Kitchen, Chamber, &c. It may however be a corruption of Botreaux.

BUTTON. The pedigree of the Hampshire family was traced to the XIII. cent. as De Button; and as it was sometimes spelt Bitton it may have been derived from the parish of Bitton, co. Gloucester. In Sussex, Burton is often pronounced Button.

BUTTRESS. A corruption of Botreux.

BUTTS. The marks for archery. In old times all corporate towns, and most parishes, had a provision for this sport, and numerous fields and closes where the long bow was exercised are still called " The Butts."

BUTVELIN. See Boutevilein.

BUTWILLIAM. See Boutevilein.

BUXTED. A parish in Sussex.

BUXTON. Places in cos. Derby, Hereford, and Norfolk. The baronet traces to the XV. cent. in the last-named county. The Buxtons of Derby, in the XIII. cent., wrote themselves De Bawkestone. Lysons.

BUZZACOT. Probably Buscot, co. Berks.

BUZZARD. An A-Norm. family, named Bosard or Bossard, were influential in Bedfordshire in the XIV. cent., and ·gave the suffix to Leighton-Buzzard. Lysons.

BUZZY. See Bussey.

☞ **BY.** A very common termination of names of places in the north of England, many of which have, of course, given names to families. It is an old Scandinavian word signifying primarily a farm-house or dwelling, and afterwards a village or town. It is found only in what are called the Danish counties, and particularly in Lincolnshire, in which there are no less than 212 places with this desinence. See Worsaae's Danes in England, which contains some curious notes respecting it. Several names of places are adduced which seem to have reference to the particular nation or tribe by whom those places were first colonized, viz :—

Romanby,	by the	Romans.
Saxby,	„	Saxons.
Flemingsby	„	Flemings.
Frisby	„	Frisians.
Scotsby	„	Scots.
Normanby	„	Normans.
Danby	„	Danes, &c.

Other places with this termination are more satisfactorily attributed to individuals; thus, a Northman or Dane called

Rollo, or Rolf, gave name to Rollesby.		
Hacon	„	„	Haconby.
Sweyn	„	„	Swainby.
Thirkel	„	„	Thirkelsby.
Brand	„	„	Brandsby.
Osgod	„	„	Osgodby, &c., &c.

And these compounds have in turn given name to as many families.

As a surname, *By* is probably the shortest we possess.

BYASS. Bias was one of the seven sages of Greece; but we must probably look for the origin of this name in an unclassical corruption from Byhurst, a local designation; or it may be the De Byus of the H.R.

BYE. See **BY.** But it seems also to have been a personal name, as Fil.' Bye occurs in H.R.

BYERS. The chateau of Biars in the canton of Isigni, La Manche, Normandy, had lords of its own name, temp. Conq. De Gerville. Mem. Soc. Ant. Norm. 1825.

BYFIELD. A parish in co. Northampton.

BYFORD. A parish in Herts.

BYGATE. See under Gates.

BYGRAVE. A parish in Herts.

BYGROVE. See Groves.

BYNG. From the occurrence of such compounds as Bingley, Bingham, Bingfield, in names of places, it is highly probable that Bing, or Byng, was an ancient personal name.

BYRNE. In Scotland, a topographical expression, implying the high part of a farm where young sheep are summered—or dry heathy pasture for weanlings. Celt. *bryn*, a hill. Jamieson. The Irish family of O'Byrne claim from Hermon, the youngest son of Milesius. B.L.G.

BYRON. The poet's ancestors were of unquestioned Norman origin. Ernisius de Burun held 32 lordships in Yorkshire, and Ralph de Burun, 13 in Notts and Derby, at the compilation of Domesday. Kelham. Others derive the name and family from the town of Biron in Guienne.

BYSH. BYSSHE. Aluric Busch (? de Bosco) was a Domesd. tenant in co. Herts. See Cutbush and Bush. In some medieval writings "bishop" is thus abbreviated.

BYSSHOP. See Bishop.

BYTHESEA. The gentry family of this name have a tradition that their ancestor was a foundling, and that he obtained his surname from the place where he was discovered—"by the Sea." It is far likelier to have been derived from residence in such locality. At-Sea is a common medieval name, and both correspond with the continental De la Mer, Delmar, De Meer, &c., as well as with the Pelagius, Pontius, &c. of antiquity.

BYTHEWAY. See Way.

BYTHEWOOD. From residence near a wood.

BYWATER. See Waters.

BYWOOD. See Wood.

BYWORTH. A manor in Petworth, co. Sussex.

C.

CABBELL. Probably descended from "Jean Cabibel cy devant ministre de Brassac," one of the seventy-seven French Protestant refugee ministers who signed the Declaration of Faith in 1691 ; penes J. S. Burn, Esq. There is, however, a Ri'cus Cabel in H.R.

CABBURN. Cabourn, a parish in Lincolnshire.

CABLE. Probably the same as Caple or Capel.

CABOT. See Chabot.

CADBURY. Two parishes in co. Somerset.

CADBY. Cadeby, places in cos. Leicester and York.

CADE. See illustrations of this name in Eng. Surn. i. 112. 202. Notwithstanding Shakspeare's allusion, it may be doubted whether the name is derived from cade, a barrel. Several Cades are mentioned in H.R. without prefix.

In addition to what I have said (ut supra) respecting the probable residence of Jack Cade, the arch-rebel, at Heathfield, co. Sussex, I may mention that I have seen the will of another John Cade of Heathfield, which was proved at Lewes so lately as the year 1600.

CADELL. CADDELL. 1. (Welsh.) Warlike, stout. 2. Probably a corruption of Caldwell. An ancient family, Caldwell of that Ilk, flourished in co. Renfrew, down to the end of the XVII. century.

CADGER. A packman, or itinerant huckster. According to Kennett "a cadger is a butcher, miller, or carrier of any load." Halliw.

CADMAN. A maker of cades, or barrels. Cademan, H.R.

CADNEY. A place in Lincolnshire.

CADOGAN. Earl Cadogan's family deduce from the princes of Powys in Wales, some of whom bore the baptismal name of Cadwgan or Kydwgan, which, by the suppression of the patronymical ap, became an hereditary surname.

☞ CAER. CAR. The initial syllable of many local names, which have become surnames, especially in Scotland and Cornwall. It is a Celtic word signifying "an artificial military strength, whether fort or castle."

CAESAR The celebrated Sir Julius Cæsar, master of the rolls, temp. James I., was son of one of Queen Elizabeth's physicians, who according to Fuller's Worthies, (ii. 326) was descended from the ancient family of the Dalmarii in Italy. In the epitaph on Sir Julius Cæsar, written by himself, and formerly existing at Great St. Helen's, in London, he is styled "Julius

Dalmare, alias Cæsar." But according to a more recent authority the original family name was Adelmare. Peter Maria Adelmare of Treviso, near Venice, L.L.D., had a son, Cæsar Adelmare, M.D., who settled in England in 1550. This gentleman had several sons, one of whom received the baptismal name of Julius ; this was the celebrated Sir Julius, who adopted his father's prænomen as a fixed surname for his family. Lodge's Life of Sir Julius Cæsar. The name still exists in the county of Surrey, principally in humble life. See anecdotes in Eng. Surn., vol. i., page 209. A correspondent at Godalming writes : "We have here more than one Julius Cæsar ; in fact, we have twelve Cæsars, all of one family. Julius Cæsar, the younger, is a noted cricketer, and one of the Eleven of All England."

CAFE. Perhaps from Scot. caif, tame, familiar.

CAFFIN. Fr. chauve, from Latin calvus, bald. Hence the name of the great Protestant reformer, Calvin. The forms in the H.R. are Le Cauf, Chauf, Chaufyn. An eminent example of the application of this sobriquet is in Charles the Bald, King of France.

CAGER. See Cadger.

CAILEY. CAILAY. See Cayley.

CAIN. Gael. Beloved.

CAINE. See Cane.

CAINS. See Keynes.

CAIRD. A Gipsy ; a travelling tinker ; a sturdy beggar. Jamieson.

CAIRN. "Any locality, stream, or mountain, designated from a cairn or ancient sepulchral tumulus." Gaz. Scotl.

CAISTOR. CAISTER. A town in Lincolnshire and two parishes in Norfolk are so called.

CAKEBREAD. Seems to belong to the same category as Whitbread, Wastel, &c.

CAKEPEN. One Wm. C., a baker, appears in the early records of Lewes Priory.

CALCOTE. CALCUTT. Contractions of Caldecott, q. v.

CALCOTT. A contraction of Caldecott.

CALDECOTT. There are many localities in England bearing this name, and there is also a Caude-Côte in Normandy. Like Cold-Harbour, about which so much has been written, the Caldecots are said to lie principally in the vicinity of Roman roads. "It is a singular fact," says the Rev. John Taddy, "that wherever we have traces of a Roman road, we find hamlets in the near neighbourhood of it of the

H

name of Caldecott. I could quote abundance of such." Papers of the Architect. Soc. of Northampton, York, Lincoln, and Bedford, Vol. II., page 429. The Caldecotts of Rugby claim from Calcot or Caldecote, co. Chester, of which place their ancestors were mesne lords in the time of the Conqueror. B.L.G.

CALDELOUERD. This singular name of *Le Caldelouerd* is found in the H.R. Qu: 'the called Lord,' a sobriquet.

CALDER, signifying a wooded stream, is a name borne by several small rivers and streams, and by places on their banks in Scotland.

CALDERWOOD. See Calder.

CALDWELL. "The cold well." Several localities in various counties are so designated.

CALE. CAIL. CALLIN. CALKIN. Apparently derivatives of some personal name—possibly Charles.

CALEY. See Cayley. The H.R. however show us Le Caly and Le Calye—apparently denoting some employment.

CALF. CALFE. An island of Argyleshire.

CALHOUN. A contraction of Colquhoun.

CALISHER. A correspondent suggests 'Calaiser,' a man of Calais.

CALL. 1. Probably Macall, by the suppression of the first two letters. See Art. MAC. 2. A-Sax. *calla*, the same as *carl* or *ceorl*, a man. Ferguson. Calle. H.R.

CALLAGHAN. CALLAHAN. The Irish O'Callaghan.

CALLANDER. CALLENDER. A kind of lark was so called ; but a likelier derivation is from *calenderer*, a presser of cloth —a trade still existing.

> "I am a linen-draper bold,
>   As all the world doth know,
> And my good friend, the Calender,
>   Will lend his horse to go."
>   *John Gilpin.*

The name is also local, from places in the shires of Perth, Stirling, &c.

CALLAWAY. A corruption of Galloway?

CALLER. One who drives oxen or horses under the yoke. Jamieson.

CALLEY. The Calleys of Wilts deduce from Norfolk. I find no locality so denominated, and the family may possibly spring from the Scottish M'Caulays.

CALLOW. Places in cos. Hereford and Derby.

CALMADY. The family are said to be lineally descended from John C. of Calmady, 1460. The name is therefore local.

CALMAN. Identical with the old Scandinavian Kalman, and the Frankish Carloman. Ferguson. Caleman. H.R.

CALTHORPE. The ancestors of Lord C. assumed the name from Calthorpe, co. Norfolk, temp. Hen. III., and they are said to have been resident there from the time of the Conquest. Courthope's Debrett.

CALTHROP. See Calthorpe. The C.'s of Gosberton claim descent, (collateral it is to be presumed,) from Walter de C., bishop of Norwich, in the XIII. cent.

CALTON. Places in cos. Stafford and York, and suburbs of Edinburgh and Glasgow.

CALVARY. Many monastic establishments had within their ambit an elevated mound representing the supposed 'mount' Calvary, the scene of our Lord's Passion. A spiral path leading to its summit was called "the way of the cross," *(via crucis,)* and hither on Good Fridays a large crucifix was borne in procession by the monks, and fixed upon the summit. A fine example of a *calvary* exists at Lewes Priory. The surname was probably derived from residence near such a spot.

CALVER. A hamlet in Derbyshire.

CALVERLEY. John Scott came into England in the suite of the Princess Maud of Scotland, on her marriage with King Henry I., and acquired the estate of Calverley, co. York, whence he adopted the surname, and where he was resident in 1136. From him descended a right knightly progeny.

CALVERT. The baronet's family trace to a Mr. C., who was minister of Andover, co. Hants, in the XVI. cent., and probably of French extraction.

CALWAY. See Callaway.

CAM. Rivers in cos. Cambridge and Gloucester. Del Cam, and De Cam. H.R.

CAMBER. 1. A place in E. Sussex. 2. An ancient form of Comber. 3. A-Norm., a brewer. Kelham.

CAMBRAY. The well-known city of the Netherlands. De Cambreye. H.R.

CAMDEN. The great antiquary, "the Nourice of Antiquitie," was descended from a plebeian family in Staffordshire. Noble's Coll. of Arms. The name may have been originally taken from Campden, co. Gloucester. The house in which William Camden lived, at Chiselhurst co. Kent, is called Camden Place, and from it the Marquis Camden derives his title.

CAMERON. In an ancient manuscript history of this valorous Highland clan, it is said : "The Camerons have a tradition among them, that they are originally descended of a younger son of the royal family of Denmark, who assisted at the restoration of king Fergus II., anno 404. He was called Cameron from his *crooked nose*, which that word imports. But it is more probable that they are of the ancient Scots or Caledonians that first planted the country." Skene, in his Highlanders of Scotland, (ii. 193,) agrees to the Celtic derivation; but it must be remembered that in the Lowland county of Fife there is a considerable parish so called, which would discountenance this opinion. Robertus de Cambrun, dominus de Balegrenach swore fealty to Edw. I. at Perth in 1296.

CAMMEL. Two parishes in co. Somerset. Sometimes a corruption of Campbell.

CAMMIS. The same as Camoys.

CAMOYS. The fair daughter of Chaucer's Miller of Trompington is described as having a "camoys nose," by which it appears we are to understand an organ of the "snub" or retroussé species. Halliwell says, "CAMOISE, crooked, flat, (A-Norm.) Also spelt camuse. The word is generally applied to a nose." But the baronial family used the territorial "De," as early as temp. Henry III., and they were most probably surnamed from some locality in Normandy.

CAMP. Aluric Camp or Campa was a Domesd. tenant in the eastern counties. Kelham supposes that he was a champion; but he had held under Edward the Confessor, and, as Ellis observes, the office of champion does not occur so early. It is doubtless connected with Kemp, which see. In Selkirkshire, camp still means "brisk, active, spirited." Jamieson.

CAMPBELL. The Campbells' claim to a Norman origin is said to be unfounded. It is based upon the presumed existence of a Norman family called De Campo Bello. Skene says that no such name is found, though the Beauchamps did most certainly so latinize themselves. The oldest spelling (that in Ragman Roll, A.D. 1296) is Cambel or Kambel. The two great branches of the family were distinguished as Mac-Arthur and Mac-Cailinmor. Skene, Scott. High. ii. 280. If the De Campo Bello theory were true, the name would be a synonym of Beauchamp and Fairfield. The name is deduced by Gaelic etymologists from cambeul (pronounced cam-pal) which means "crooked mouth." Whether the family be of Norman or of Gaelic origin, the clan bearing their name are the most numerous and powerful in the Highlands, and formerly, under their chiefs, the earls, marquises, and dukes of Argyle, they could muster 5000 fighting men, who were generally arrayed against the Stuart family. It is to their superior influence and power, and the dread of them by other clans, that we probably owe the disparaging proverb, "LIKE A CAMPBELL, EVER FAIR AND FALSE." By the Highlanders the clan Campbell are called "Clan Duine," and their chiefs have always been styled Mac-Calean-Mohr (not Mac-Callum More as Sir Walter Scott has it,) i. e. "the son of Colin the Great," in memory of their distinguished ancestor, Sir Colin Campbell of Lochow, who in the XIII. cent. laid the foundation of the greatness of his family. This name

is abundant in the province of Ulster. "It is somewhere recorded, that a Scotch regiment, quartered at Carrickfergus in the XVII. century, contained no less than 110 John Campbells." Ulster Journ. of Archæology. No. 20.

CAMPER. A-Sax. cempa, a combatant.

CAMPIN. The same as Campion.

CAMPION. A champion. Ital. campione. O. Eng. and Scot. campioun. See Kemp. The C.'s of Danny were of Campion's Hall, co. Essex, temp. Edw. II. The forms of orthography in H.R. are Campion, Le Campioun, Campiown, Le Campiun, Campyun, &c.

CAMPKIN. CAMKIN. Probably a diminutive of Camp or Kemp—a combatant or fighting man.

CAMPS. Many localities where Roman, Saxon, or other ancient earthworks exist are so called.

CANCELLOR. The same as Chancellor, Lat. cancellarius. Le Canceler. H.R.

CANDLEMAKER. The trade.

CANDLER. See Chandler.

CANDY. An island in Essex.

CANE. Cane, Cana, or Canus, appears in the Domesd. of Sussex, as a baptismal name, and as a surname it is still found in that county. See Eng. Surn., i. 29.

CANEY. Probably the same as Cheyney.

CANN. A parish of Dorset.

CANNING. Probably from Cannings, co. Wilts, (Bishop's Cannings). The two viscounts, Canning and Stratford de Redcliffe, are descended from W. Cannynges, the pious founder of St. Mary Redcliffe, Bristol, in the XV. cent.

CANNON. A canon, a member of an ecclesiastical order. See Ecclesiastical Surnames. In the H.R. Le Cannon, Le Canon, Canoun. There is a place called Canon, near Lisieux in Normandy.

CANOCHSON. Canock is the Gaelic Corimich or Kenneth, and hence Canochson is a translation of Mac Corimich, which is the same as Mac Kengyie—the old form of Mac Kenzie.

CANON. CANNAN. See Cannon.

CANT. 1. Germ. kante, a corner, edge, coast—a local name radically equivalent to Kent. 2. Strong; hearty; lusty. Halliw.

CANTALUPE. This ancient Norman family, renowned for having produced a Saint (Thomas C., bishop of Hereford 1275) was seated in early times at Hempston-Cantilupe, co. Devon. The heiress married Sir Thomas de West, ancestor of the Earl de le Warr, whose second title is Viscount Cantalupe. There are several places in Normandy called Canteloup, Canteleu, &c., but from which of them the surname is derived is not positively certain, though M. de Gerville says, it is the parish of Chanteloup, in the canton of Brehal, in Lower Normandie. Mem. Soc. Ant. Normandie. The surname has been spelt in a variety of modes, as Cantelo, Cantelou, Cantelhope, Canteloy, Chantelo, Cantalupe, Cantelupe, Cantilupe, Cantulupe, &c.

CANTELO. See Cantalupe.

CANTER. Lat. *cantor.* A precentor or chanter.

CANTLE. Probably the same as Cant, or its diminutive.

CANTON. Fr. A territorial division or district.

CANTOR. Lat. a singer; a precentor in a church, still so styled in cathedral churches.

CANTRELL. CANTRILL. Probably Low Lat. *canterellus*—"the little singer."

CANUTE. The Danish personal name.

CAPEL. The Earl of Essex descends from a lord-mayor of London, 1503. The surname is probably derived from one of the parishes so called in Surrey, Kent, and Suffolk. The Capels of Gloucestershire claim from How Capel, co. Hereford. In charters it is latinized De Capella.

CAPELIN. Synonymous with Chaplin, which see.

CAPERN. CAPEROUN. See Quaife. In H.R. Caperun.

CAPLIN. See Chaplin.

CAPP. CAPPS. Probably borrowed from that article of costume. See under Quaife, Mantell, Freemantle, &c. &c.

CAPPELL. See Capel.

CAPPER. 1. A maker of caps. 2. Apparently, says Jamieson, a cup-bearer—a person in the list of the king's household servants. Le Cappere. H.R.

CAPPUR. See Capper.

CAPRON. See Caperoun.

☞ **CAR.** See under CORNISH SURNAMES.

☞ **CAR.** See CAER.

CARADOC. Lord Howden claims descent from Caradoc and the princes of Wales. Peerage. See Cradock.

CARD. The same as Caird, which see.

CARDEN. CARDON. William Cardon or Cardun appears in the Domesd. of Essex, as one of the homines of Geoffrey de Magnaville. A township in Cheshire bears the name of Carden.

CARDER. One who dresses wool, so called from the *card* or comb which he uses.

CARDINALL. See Ecclesiastical Surnames. There is a family of Cardinali in Italy.

CARDMAKER. A maker of *cards*, instruments with wire teeth, with which wool is 'teased' or worked.

CARE. CARES. Probably the same as Carr or Kerr.

CARELESS. A well-known corruption of Carlos.

CAREW. The Carews of Wales, Cornwall, &c., are descended from Gerald de Carrio, called by Giraldus Cambrensis (his relative) Gerald de Windsor and Fitz-Walter, who was castellan of Pembroke castle under Arnulf de Montgomery. He married Nest, a concubine of King Henry I., and had two sons; William Fitzgerald, the progenitor of the Carews, and Maurice who accompanied Strongbow into Ireland, and founded the FitzGeralds, Geraldines, and Geralds of that country. Gent. Mag., May, 1829. Carew castle is near Milford Haven. Carey is said to be another form of this name, which circ. 1300 was spelt De Carru.

CAREY. The Carews of the West of England pronounce their name as if written Carey, and hence the surnames have been accounted identical. See Anecdote in Eng. Surn. ii. 39. See, however, Cary.

CARGILL. A parish in Perthshire.

CARL. CARRAL. CARLIN. Foreign modifications of Carolus, Charles.

CARLE. A-Sax. *ceorl*, a man, a rustic, a stout man. Carl is used in all these senses in Scotland. Also see under Caryll.

CARLEILL. See Carlisle.

CARLEY. Scot. *carlie*, a little man—a diminutive of *carl*. Jamieson. Perhaps however local.

CARLISLE. CARLYLE. The city in Cumberland.

CARLOS. CARLOSS. A corruption of Carolus, Charles.

CARLTON. CARLETON. The English gazetteer shows twenty-two parishes, townships, &c. so called, and there are many others. Lord Dorchester's family deduce from Carleton, co. Cumberland.

CARLYON. An estate near Truro, Cornwall, in which co. the family have long been eminent.

CARMAN. Not so likely from the occupation, as from residence at a Carr. See Carr and Man. More probable than either, is its derivation from the personal name Carman, mentioned in Domesd.

CARMICHAEL. CARMICHEL. An ancient barony and parish in co. Lanark, possessed by the family in the XII. cent., and probably even earlier. From thence the family of C. of Carspherne, in the stewartry of Kircudbright, are presumed to have sprung. For the genealogy of the latter family, see Knowles's Gen. of Coulthart.

CARMINOW. A manor and barton in the parish of St. Mawgan, co. Cornwall. In the XIV. century there was a remarkable controversy in the Court of Chivalry, or Earl Marshal's Court, touching the right of bearing the coat-armorial, "Azure, a bend Or," which was claimed by the three families of Scrope, Grosvenor, and Carminow. In the course of the pleadings, Carminow averred that these had been the ensigns of the Carminows ever since the days of King Arthur! and moreover that one of his ancestors bearing these arms had been ambassador from king Edward the Confessor to either the French king or the duke of Normandy. To this it was replied on the part of Scrope, that in case the ancestor alluded to "lived at Carmenow before the Norman Conquest, those arms could not be appropriated to him by the name of De Carmenow, *for it was not the custom of the Britons till about a hundred years after to style themselves from local places, with the Latin preposition or particle De, after the manner of the French; but before were generally distinguished by the names John-Mac-Richard, Richard-Mac-Thomas, Robert-Ap-Ralph, &c., that is to say, the son of Richard, Thomas, and Ralph, according to their lineal descents.*" Hals, in D. Gilbert's Cornwall, iii., pp. 130, 131. I may add, that Carminow was nonsuited, and compelled to make the addition of a "Label of three points Gules" to his previous coat, "and was so distasted therewith that he chose for the motto of this new bearing arms, a Cornish sentence, which abundantly expressed his dislike thereof: CALA RAG GER DA—id est, "A Straw for Fame!" Ibid.

CARNABY. A parish in Yorkshire.

CARNACHAN. Said to be derived from the Gael. *carnach*, a heathen priest.

CARNE. The Carnes of Nash, co. Glamorgan, "descend in an unbroken line from Ynyr, king of Gwent, brother of Ithel, who was slain in 846. His great-grandson, Thomas *o'r* Carne, was brought up at Pen-carne, whence he was named Carne." Such is the statement, which may pass *quant. val.*, in B.L.G.

CARNEGIE. The first of the earl of Northesk's family on record, is Duthac de C. 1410. The locality does not appear in the Gaz. of Scotland.

CARNELL. May be a local name ending in WELL, with the W suppressed. There was however a bird so called, (see Eng. Surn.)—apparently a kind of lark. See Halliw. in voc. Calander.

CARNSEW. See under Carveth.

CARPENTER. The well-known trade. Domesd. mentions several tenants in chief under the name of Carpentarii.

CARR. Collins (Peerage, edit. 1768, v. 83.) remarks that "the Cars or Kers are undoubtedly a very ancient people in this island, but it is uncertain whether they be of French or English extraction. Those who contend for the former, allege that the baron Ker and other families of his name now existing in France, trace their origin higher than the time of William,

duke of Normandy, who, being attended by a considerable commander of their name in 1066, rewarded him for his bravery and conduct with divers possessions in the north of England. . . . The Cars of England and France have the same armorial bearings, viz., Gules, on a cheveron Argent, 3 mullets of the First. Others are of opinion that the surname is local, and was at first assumed by the owners of the lands and baronies of Car and Carshall in Lancashire." The Scottish Kers bear their arms of different tinctures from those of England and France; and Collins adds, that some are of opinion that they are "Aborigines, and endeavour to support their conjecture by affirming the surname to be Gaelic or Celtic." They were numerous and flourishing temp. Alexander III. A.D. 1249. I think it highly probable that this monosyllabic name may be traced to several local sources. A *car* in various dialects signifies "a wood or grove on a moist soil, generally of alders. Any hollow place or marsh is also called a car." In Anglo-Saxon, on the contrary, it means a lock. Again in Lincolnshire it signifies a gutter. Halliwell. Once more, the Celtic *caer* means a fortification, and 'carr' is applied in various districts to a place where some castle or earthwork has existed.

CARRIAGE. Probably a corruption of Carr-Edge, or some similar local name.

CARRERE. O. Fr. and Eng. a quarry.

CARRICK. 1. In Scotl. a crag or craig—any rocky locality. 2. The southern district of Ayrshire is so called.

CARRIER. Originally a messenger.

CARRINGTON. Places in cos. Chester and Lincoln.

CARROLL. 1. Possibly from the romantic rock so called in co. Sutherland. 2. A modification of Carolus, Charles.

CARRUTHERS. A hamlet in the parish of Middlebie, co. Dumfries.

CARSE. A Scot. topographical expression, probably meaning a low alluvial tract near a river, as the Carse of Gowrie, of Forth, of Falkirk, &c.

CARSON. Probably Charles's son.

CARSTAIRS. A parish in Lanarkshire.

CARSWELL. A parish united with Buckland, co. Berks.

CARTER. The occupation—a driver of carts. In medieval documents Carectarius and Le Carectar.

CARTERET. A parish adjoining Barneville, in the arrondissement of Valognes, in Normandy, immediately opposite to Jersey. Its seigneur took part in the Conquest of England, 1066. The Jersey family left the parent stock in the reign of Philip Augustus, and another descendant was created Lord Carteret in England. De Gerville, in Mem. Soc. Antiq. Normandie. 1825.

CARTHEW. "The name is local, compounded of Car-dew, or Car-thew, i.e. Rock Black in this parish." (St. Issey.) Hals, in D. Gilbert's Cornwall. ii 255. 'Caerdhu' would rather signify in Celtic, the black castle or fortification. The family were eminent in Cornwall temp. Edw. II.

CARTIER. Fr. *chartier*. A carter.

CARTMAN. The same as Carter.

CARTMEL. A town in Lancashire.

CARTTAR. A whimsical orthography of Carter.

CARTWRIGHT. See under Wright.

CARTY. The Irish M'Carthy.

CARVER. The occupation.

CARVETH. Carverth or Carveth, an estate in the parish of Mabe, co. Cornwall. The family originally bore the name of Thoms. "Those gentlemen, from living at Carveth or Carverth in Mabe, were transnominated from Thoms to Carverth; as another family of those Thomses, from living at Carnsew in the said parish, were transnominated to Carnsew; and there are some deeds yet extant, dated temp. Henry VIII. which will evidence the truth of this fact, as Mr. Carverth told me." Hals, in D. Gilbert's Cornw. ii. 94.

CARWOOD. A parish in Salop.

CARY. See Carey. "The ancient family of Cary derives its surname from the manor of Cary or Kari, as it is called in Doomsday Book, lying in the parish of St. Giles-on-the Heath, near Launceston." B.L.G. See Carew.

CARYLL. CARELL. Carle was an under-tenant in Sussex before Domesday, and about the XV. century the name begins to appear among the gentry of that county. A more likely derivation, however, is from Carel in the arrondissement of Lisieux in Normandy.

CASE. This name is found in the H.R. and may be the Anglo-Norman *cas*, chance, hazard—probably with reference to the character, or some incident in the life, of the first person who bore it. So Hazard has become a family name. A family in Devonshire thus designated account for it by a tradition that, about two hundred years since, a foundling was laid at the door of a certain gentleman, to whom popular scandal attributed its paternity; the gentleman denied the allegation, but from motives of humanity had the infant taken care of, and, from the circumstance of its having been enclosed in a packing-case, imposed upon the poor foundling this curious appellation. The Fr. *case*, from Latin *casa*, a mean house, cottage, or hut, is, however, a more likely etymon.

CASELEY. See Castley.

CASH. A place in Strathmiglo, co. Fife.

CASHMERE. R.G. 16. Does not refer to the "far-off East," but to some English locality unknown to me. *Mere* is not unfrequent as a termination.

CASSAN. The family of Cassan, or De Cassagne, derive from Stephen Cassan, a native of Montpellier, who fled into Holland at the Rev. of the Edict of Nantes, and afterwards accompanied Schomberg into Ireland. B.L.G.

CASSELL. A shortened pronunciation of Castle?

CASTELL. See Castle.

CASTELLAN. The guardian of a castle. O. Fr. *chastellan*.

CASTELMAN. A castellan; constable of a castle; "keipar of the Kingis Castell." Jamieson.

CASTLE. From residence in one. De Castello. H.R.

CASTLEGATE. From residence near the gate of a fortress.

CASTLEMAN. One who had the care of a castle—a castellan.

CASTLEY. A township in Yorkshire.

CASTON. A parish in Norfolk.

CASWELL. See Carswell. Perhaps, however, from Caswell Bay in the Bristol Channel.

CATCHASIDE. CATCHESIDES. R.G. 16. Doubtless corruptions of some local name.

CATCHPOOLE. In Low Latin *cachepollus*, a catchpole, or petty constable. In Piers Plowman, the executioner who broke the legs of the thieves at the Crucifixion is so designated:
> "A *cachepol* cam forth,
> And cracked both hire legges."

Le Cacher in the H.R. is probably synonymous. In those documents we meet likewise with the names Le Cacherel and Cacherellus, which, according to Jacob and Halliwell, also signify a catchpole or inferior bailiff. "In stipendiis Ballivi xIIIs. IVd: in stipendiis unius *cachepolli* IXs. VIIId. Consuet. Farendon. Thorn mentions "cacherellos vicecomitis," the sheriff's under bailiffs. This last form of the name seems to have become extinct.

CATER. CATOR. Formerly *acater*, a caterer or purveyor. Halliw. Le Catour, Le Catur. H.R. The place allotted to the keeping of provisions purchased for the court was called the *acatry*, and the purchaser himself bore the name of the Achatour. Le Achatur is another form in the H.R.
> "A gentil manciple was ther of the temple,
> Of which *achatours* mighten take ensemple."
> *Chaucer, Cant. T.* 570.

CATERER See Cator.

CATESBY. A parish in co. Northampton, in which county the family chiefly resided.

CATHARINE. See Female Christian Names.

CATHCART. The earl of this title derives his name from the lands and town of Cathcart, co. Renfrew, and from Reynald de C. in the XI. cent.

CATHERICK. Catterick, a parish in Yorkshire.

CATLIN. CATELIN. CATLING. This name reminds one of that of the Roman incendiary Cataline, as Fuller suggests. Worthies ii. 234. It may possibly belong to the same class as Cato, Cæsar, Virgil, &c. Its forms in the H.R. are Catelyn and Catoline.

CATMORE. CATMUR. Catmere, co. Berks.

CATNACH. The surname Cattanach is found in the Highlands of Scotland. Gael. *catanach*, a warrior.

CATO. An old Germ. name. Ferguson.

CATON. Until the close of the XVI. cent., Catton and De Catton; from the manor of Catton near Norwich, which in Domesday is spelt Catun and Catuna. The family were located in Norfolk from time immemorial till the middle of the last century. The latinizations Catonus, Gathonus, and Chattodunus occur in old records.

The annexed illustration, representing the seal of Bartholomew de Catton, has been kindly presented by R. R. Caton, Esq. F.S.A. The matrix was found in Norfolk.

CATT. From the animal—like Lion, Bear, Wolf, &c. The family are probably of Norman origin, and the name was written Le Chat. Ilbert de Chaz, whose tombstone is at Lacock Abbey, came from Chaz or Cats in the neigbourhood of Bohun. A family of Le Cat were lords of Berreuil, near Gournay, in the XV. cent. The records of Norfolk show that the name of Le Chat, Le Cat, or Catt, existed at or about Heveningham from temp. King John till the XV. cent. The Ketts of Wymondham are said to have been a branch of the family. See Pedigree, &c., in Records of House of Gournay. There was also an ancient Teutonic personal name, Cato or Cat, whence perhaps the local names Cateby, Catton, Catcott, &c. An old family in Kent wrote themselves De Cat, implying a local origin. Philipott's Vill. Cant. 75.

CATTELL. The Welsh Annals (Annales Cambriæ, Mon. Hist. Brit.) mention a Catell, king of Powys, in A.D. 808, and other eminent personages of the same Christian name. Cattal is, however, the name of a township in the W. R. of Yorkshire. The forms in the H.R. are De Catallo and Catel. A French Protestant refugee family of Catel settled in England temp. Elizabeth.

CATTERNS. Probably from one of the places called St. Catherine's, in cos. Somerset, Dorset, Surrey, &c.

CATTON. See Caton.

CAUDLE. A corruption of Cauldwell, a hamlet in Derbyshire.

CAUDWELL. Cauldwell, co. Derby.

CAUGHT. R.G. 16. Possibly a Cockney pronunciation of Court.

CAUL. A dam-head. Jamieson.

CAULCUTT. The same as Caldecott.

CAULTON. See Calton.

CAUSEY. A causeway, or raised path, latinized De Calceto. A priory in Sussex bore this designation from its having stood at the end of a causeway.

CAVALIER. A horseman, knight.

CAVALL. "Caval signifieth a horse." Camd. Fr. *cheval*, from Lat. *caballus*.

CAVE. Two parishes in Yorkshire, called North and South Cave, were the residence of the ancestors of the Caves now of Stretton, co. Derby, soon after the Conquest. Shirley.

CAVELL. CAVILL. Cavill, a township in Yorkshire.

CAVENDISH. Roger de Gernon, a cadet of the great Norman family, temp. Edw. II., acquiring with the heiress of John Potton, the lands of Cavendish, co. Suffolk, adopted De Cavendish for his surname. Peerage.

CAW. Probably the same as Call.

CAWDREY. See Cowdery.

CAWLEY. See Calley.

CAWOOD. A parish in Yorkshire.

CAWSTON. CAUSTON. A parish in Norfolk.

CAWTHORN. A parish in Yorkshire.

CAXTON. The illustrious printer was born in Kent about the year 1412. The name occurs in Sussex in 1341, (Nonæ,) and in Cambridgesh. and Hunts temp. Edw. I. (H.R.) as De Caxton, doubtless from Caxton a parish in co. Cambridge.

CAY. Formerly spelt Key. B.L.G.

CAYLEY. CAYLY. Cailli in the arrondissement of Rouen gave title in 1661 to a marquisate. Some six centuries earlier, it had probably given name to the A-Norm. family, whose representative, temp. Edw. I., was Hugh de Cailly of Orby, co. Norfolk, ancestor of the baronetic and other existing branches of the surname.

CAYSER. In the H.R. *Le Cayser* is nothing more nor less than Cæsar. This illustrious patronymic is borne at the present day, (teste London Directory) by a smith-in-general, a tailor, and a bird-cage maker.

CEASE. R.G. 16. Possibly from Seèz or Seès, a town of Normandy.

CECIL. The name of this noble family was written in ancient times, Sitsilt, Sicelt, Seycil, Seisil, Cyssell, &c., until William Cecil, Lord Burghley, Queen Elizabeth's famous minister, from a whimsical notion that he was descended from the Roman Cæcilii, adopted the present orthography. The family, doubtless of Norman origin, can be traced to Robert Sitsilt, who in 1091 assisted Robt. Fitz-Hamon in the conquest of Glamorganshire. Collins.

CERNE. Parishes in cos. Dorset, &c.

CHABOT. CABOT. A common French surname. In the latter form it is of frequent occurrence in Jersey. It appears to be derived from the little fish known by us as the "bullhead," but on the shores of Normandy and the Channel Islands, where it abounds, as the *chabot* or *cabot*. Sebastian Cabot, the discoverer of Newfoundland (born at Bristol in 1477) is generally asserted to have been of Venetian extraction, but there is much reason to believe that his father was a native of Jersey, between which island and the port of Bristol there was commercial intercourse from an early period.

CHAD. CHADS. The A-Sax. personal name, rendered illustrious in England by St. Chad or Cedde, third bishop of Lichfield, in the VII. century.

CHADWELL. A parish in Essex.

CHADWICK. Chadwyke, a hamlet in the parish of Rochdale, the property of the family in the XIV. cent.

CHADWIN. An ancient personal name.

CHAFF. Probably from Fr. *chauve*, bald.

CHAFFER. See Chaffers.

CHAFFERS. This name is believed by a family bearing it, to be a rather recent corruption of the German *schafer*, shepherd.

CHAFFIN. See Caffin.

CHAFFINCH. The bird.

CHAIGNEAU. A Fr. Protestant refugee family, settled in Ireland.

CHALDECOTT. See Caldecott.

CHALFONT. Two neighbouring parishes in co. Bucks.

CHALK. In the county of Kent, where this name is principally found, there are a parish and a hundred so designated, and there is also in co. Wilts, a parish called Broad-Chalk.

CHALKER. A digger of Chalk. Le Chalker. H.R.

CHALLACOMBE. A place in co. Devon.

CHALLEN. The family have sometimes borne the arms of Challenor, but query, if the name be not derived from Chalons in Champagne or Chalons in Burgundy?

CHALLENGER. CHALLENGE. Probably identical with Champion.

CHALLENOR. See Chaloner.

CHALLIS. CHALLICE. Probably from Chalus in Guienne, memorable for the death of Cœur de Lion. De Chales. H.R.

CHALLON. See Challen.

CHALMERS. Scot. *chalmer*, a chamber. A name taken from the office of chamberlain, dating as far back as the XII. cent. in the household of the Scottish kings. It is latinized De Camera, and corresponds with Chambers and De la Chambre. The family of C. of Gadgirth, co. Ayr, who seem to have been chiefs of the name, sprang from Reginald of the Chalmer, who flourished circ. 1160. They fell into decay in the XVII. cent. Other families in various parts of Scotland bore the same arms and were probably cadets. In the H.R. we find Le Chalmer, which may be synonymous with Thatcher, from the O. Fr. *chalme* or *chaume*, thatch.

CHALONER. Cole admits this name into his Dictionary as that of an ancient family. It means in old French either a boatman, from *chalun*, a boat ; or a fisherman, from *chalon*, a kind of net. N. & Q., v. 592. It occurs in the H.R. in the forms of Le Chalouner, Le Chaluner, Le Chalunner.

CHALON. See Challen. De Chalouns, Chaluns, H.R.

CHAMBERLAIN. CHAMBERLAYNE. A well-known officer of state, in royal and noble houses and courts. There are several distinct families bearing the surname. Aiulfus Camerarius (the latinized form) was a tenant in chief in co. Dorset, and probably the Conqueror's own chamberlain. One of his possessions in that county is still called Hampreston-Chamberlaine. Ellis, Introd. Domesd. The Chamberlaynes of Maugersbury claim from John, count of Tancarville, whose descendants were hereditary chamberlains to kings Henry I., Stephen, and Henry II. The office of the *camerarius* was to take charge of the king's camera or treasury, and answered to the treasurer of the household at present. Kelham. Besides Aiulfus above mentioned, at least five other tenants in capite so designated occur in Domesday.

CHAMBERS. See Chambre de la.

CHAMBRE DE LA. Literally, 'of the Chamber.' Certain royal courts were anciently styled cameræ or chambers ; e.g., the Painted chamber, the Star chamber, &c. See the Law Dictionaries. Hence the title of chamberlain. Subordinate officers were styled Trésorier, &c.,—de la Chambre: hence the surname. See Chamberlain.

CHAMIER. Fr. Protestant refugees. See Deschamps. Perhaps Fr. *chaumière*, a cottage. This name was introduced into

England at the Revocation of the Edict of Nantes, 1685. The Chamiers of France had been distinguished Protestants of long standing.

CHAMOND. In Charters, De Calvo Monte. Chaumont, in the arrondissement of Argentan in Normandy. The name in this orthography occurs in the Battel Roll.

CHAMP. Fr. A field.

CHAMPAGNE. From the French province.

CHAMPERNOWNE. CHAMPERNON. The parish of Cambernun, in the canton of Coutances in Normandy, gave name to this family, who in their turn gave designation to Clist-Champernowne, co. Devon. De Gerville in Mem. Soc. Ant. Normandie, 1825. In the XIII. cent. the name was latinized 'De Campo Arnulphi.'

CHAMPION. One that fights a public combat in his own or another man's quarrel. Cotgrave. The well-known office of King's Champion has been hereditary in the families of Marmion and Dymoke for centuries. Le Champion, Le Champiun, &c. H.R.

CHAMPNEYS. Fr. *Champagnois.* A native of Champagne. Berry attributes four coats to this name, and twenty-one to that of Champney. It is sometimes varied to Champness. The family claim to have been seated at Orchardley, co. Somerset, from the period of the Conquest. Sir Amian C. lived there temp. Henry II. Courthope's Debrett. The latinization is De Campania.

CHANCE. Originally Chancé. The same as Chancey.

CHANCELLOR. A name applied to various offices, civil and ecclesiastical. Richardson.

CHANCEY. Scot. *chancy,* Fr. *chanceux,* fortunate, happy. Jamieson. See however Chauncy.

CHANDLER. Originally a maker of candles, though now erroneously applied to a dealer in small wares. In the H.R. Le Chaundeler, Le Candeler, and Candelarius.

CHANDLESS. Perhaps a corruption of Chandler.

CHANDOS. Robert de C., ancestor of the barons of that name, came from Normandy with William the Conqueror, and obtained by arms large possessions in Wales.

CHANNING. Apparently an ancient personal name. Chening. Domesd. in Hants.

CHANTER. A singer.

CHANTRY. CHANTREY. An appendage to a church, in which prayers for the dead were chanted. Also the residence of the precentor (cantor) of a collegiate church. In many places lands set apart for the endowment of a chantry are so called.

CHAPEL. From residence near one. In the H.R. we find it written Capello, De Capella, Chaple, and Chapel; and elsewhere De la Chapel and Chapelle.

CHAPLIN. A chaplain; a priest who did the duty of a chapel. Latin *capellanus.* See under 'Ecclesiastical Surnames,' in this Dictionary. Albert Chapelain, a Domesd. tenant in chief, was the king's chaplain. "The word *capellanus* may likewise be interpreted both secretary and chancellor, for these officers were in early times one and the same, being always an ecclesiastic, and one who had the care of the king's chapel." Spelman. Kelham. Other Chaplains occur in Domesd. In the H.R. the name is found under the forms of Capellanus, Chapelein, &c.; we also find Capelyn, now Capelin.

CHAPMAN. A-Sax. *ceápman.* Any one who traffics, buys, or sells. Richardson. In medieval deeds one and the same person is described as Chapman and Mercator. Le Chapman, H.R. About 150 traders in London very appropriately bear this name.

CHAPPELL. CHAPPLE. See Chapel.

CHARD. A town in co. Somerset.

CHARKER, 'To chark' is to make charcoal; a Charker is therefore a charcoal burner.

CHARLES. 1. The baptismal name. 2. A parish in co. Devon. In H.R. it is found as a surname without prefix.

CHARLESWORTH. A hamlet in Derbyshire.

CHARLEY. 1. A diminutive of Charles. 2. A liberty in co. Leicester.

CHARLTON. CHARLETON. Parishes and places in cos. Berks, Gloucester, Kent, Sussex, Wilts, Worcester, Somerset, Northumb., Dorset, &c. &c. The Charltons of Hesleyside descend from Adam, lord of the manor of Charlton in Tynedale, co. Northumb., 1303. B.L.G.

CHARLWOOD. A parish in Surrey, and places in other counties.

CHARMAN. Probably a charcoalburner, from 'char.' It may however be the masculine of char-woman—a man who works by the day in trivial occupations. The H.R. form is Le Charrer.

CHARNOCK. A township and estate in the parish of Standish, co. Lancaster, anciently the possession of the family. The name has been written Chernoke, Charnoke, &c.

CHARPENTIER. Fr. A carpenter. The family bearing the name are obliged to submit to the Anglo-French pronunciation *Sharpenteer!*

CHART. Parishes, &c. in cos. Kent and Surrey.

CHARTER. Probably from the town of Chartres, in France.

CHARTERIS. CHARTERS. (Scotl.) Corruptions of Charterhouse—from resi-

I

dence at or near a Carthusian monastery. Comp. Temple.

CHARTIER. Fr. A wagoner, carter.

CHARTRES. CHARTRESS. A large town in the department of Eure et Loire, in France.

CHASE. A *chase* "is a privileged place for the receipt of deer, &c., being of a middle nature betwixt a forest and a park." Nelson's Laws of Game.

CHATAWAY. From its termination, doubtless local.

CHATER. A river of Rutlandshire is so called. See Chaytor.

CHATFIELD. A locality which is not identified, but apparently near Lewes, Sussex.

CHATLEY. A hamlet in Essex.

CHATT. A celebrated district in Lancashire is called Chat Moss.

CHATTERIS. A parish in the Isle of Ely, co. Cambridge.

CHATTERLEY. A township in co. Stafford.

CHATTERTON. Chadderton, a chapelry in Lancashire.

CHATTO. There is, I believe, a place so called in the S. of Scotland. It may however be the Fr. *château*.

CHATWIN. The same as Chetwynd.

CHAUCER. See under Hosier.

CHAUNCY. Cauncy occurs in Holinshed's so-called Roll of Battel Abbey, and Chauncy in that of Leland, and the progenitor of the family is said to have come into England with the Conqueror, from a place of that name near Amiens.

CHAUNDLER. See Chandler.

CHAUNTLER. See Chandler.

CHAWORTH. Patrick de Cadurcis, or Chaworth, a native of Brittany, accompanied William the Conqueror, and was a baron by tenure under that monarch. The name was sometimes latinized De Chauris.

CHAYTOR. See Chater; but, qu. if both these names may not be derived from the office of king's *escheator*—the person appointed to inquire into escheats, or property lapsing to the crown through want of heirs and other causes.

CHEALE. CHEELE. 1. Perhaps the same as the Scottish *chiel*, which has the several meanings of child, servant, or fellow, in either a good or bad sense, although, according to Jamieson, more commonly expressive of disrespect; it also implies a stripling, or young man, and is sometimes an appellation expressive of fondness. Perhaps its best synonym is "fellow."

> "A chiel's amang us takin' notes,
> And faith he'll prent it."
> *Burns.*

2. A local name. De Chele is found in H.R. co. Lincoln.

CHEAPE. A-Sax. *ceápan* to buy. A market; whence Eastcheap and Cheapside in London, and many other local names.

CHECKLEY. A parish co. Stafford, and a township co. Chester.

CHEEK. CHEKE. See Chick.

CHEER. CHEERS. Fr. *cher*—like the English Dear.

CHEESE. Ferguson ranks this with the A-Sax. Cissa, the Frisian Tsjisse, &c. Chese. H.R.

CHEESMAN. A maker of, or dealer in cheese. Le Cheseman, Le Chesemaker. H.R. Analogous to the modern 'butterman.'

CHEESEMONGER. The trade.

CHEESEWRIGHT. See under Wright.

CHEEVER. Fr. *chèvre.* A goat. In the Domesd. of Devonshire is a tenant in capite called William Chievre, otherwise Capra. In B.L.G. it is stated, that "the family was established in England by a Norman knight in the army of the Conqueror, and in Ireland by Sir William Chevre, one of the companions of Strongbow."

CHEFFIN. See Caffin.

CHENEVIX. A Huguenot family, settled in Ireland. One of that name was consecrated bishop of Waterford, 1745.

CHENEY. From Quesnay in the canton of Montmartin, department of La Manche, Normandy. De Gerville, Mem. Soc. Antiq. Normandie, 1825; but Mr. Walford with more probability derives the family from Cahagnes in the department of Calvados, a village of 2000 inhabitants, lying S.W. of Caen. They held a fief of the Count of Mortain, and attended him to the Conquest of England; and the feudal relation was retained long afterwards in the rape of Pevensey, co. Sussex, where their estate was called Horsted Keynes. They also denominated Milton Keynes, co. Bucks, Winkley Keynes, co. Devon, Combe Keynes, co. Dorset, and Keynes Court, co. Wilts. Sussex Arch. Coll. i. 133. The orthography has taken numerous forms, particularly De Chaaignes de Caisneto, Keynes, de Cahaysnes, and more recently Caney and Cheney. It has also been variously latinized De Caneto, De Casineto, and De Querceto—the last under an erroneous impression that the name had its origin in *chesnaie*, a grove of oaks.

CHEPMAN. See Chapman.

CHEQUER. An inn sign.

CHERITON. Parishes in cos. Warwick, Kent, Hants, Devon, and Somerset.

CHERRINGTON. Places in cos. Gloucester and Salop.

CHERRY. Of Fr. Huguenot origin, and said to be descended from the family of De Cheries, seigneurs of Brauvel, Beauval, &c., in Normandy. B.L.G. Chéris is a place near Avranches. The name is latinized De Ceraso.

CHERRYMAN. A grower of cherries or a dealer in that fruit. So Appleman, Pearman, Notman (i.e. Nut-man), &c.

CHESHIRE. CHESSHYRE. The palatine county.

CHESNEY. Probably O.F. *chesné*—the oak tree.

CHESNUT. The tree—from residence near a remarkable one.

CHESSALL. Perhaps from Chesil Bank, co. Dorset.

CHESSMAN. See Cheesman.

CHESTER. The palatine city; also places in Durham, Northumb., and Derby. It was probably from Little Chester, in the last-named co., that the Chesters of Cocken-hatch assumed the name.

CHESTERMAN. 1. A native of Chester, just as we say a Cornishman, a Kentish-man. 2. Many places where Roman and other military stations (*castra*) existed are called *chesters*, and residence at such a spot may have conferred the surname.

CHESTERTON. Parishes, &c. in cos. Cambridge, Hunts, Oxford, Stafford, and Warwick.

CHESTON. The same as Chesterton.

CHETHAM. CHEETHAM. A chapelry in the parish of Manchester, formerly possessed by the family. In America the name is corrupted to Chetum.

CHETUM. An American corruption of Chetham. See Anecdote in Eng. Surn.

CHETWODE. Seated at Chetwode, co. Bucks, as early as the Conquest. There soon after, Robert de C. founded a priory. The family resided at C. for more than twenty generations. Courthope's Debrett.

CHETWYND. A parish in Shropshire, where the family were seated in or before the reign of Henry III.

CHEVALIER. Fr., a knight or horse-man. *Chivaler* was the medieval equivalent of *miles*. Le Chevaler. H.R.

CHEVELEY. Parishes in cos. Berks and Cambridge.

CHEVERON. Possibly from Fr. *chevrier*, a goat-herd.

CHEW. A parish of Somerset. Cheux, a village near Caen in Normandy.

CHEYNE. CHEYNEY. CHEYNELL. Modifications of Cheney, which see.

CHICH. A parish in Essex. St. Osyth —Chich.

CHICHELEY. A parish in co. Bucks.

CHICHESTER. The family were ancient in Devonshire before their connection with Ireland, and the name is doubtless derived from Chichester, co. Sussex, though some genealogists assert that it is from Cirencester, co. Gloucester.

CHICK. See Chich.

CHIDELL. Cheadle, towns in cos. Chester and Stafford.

CHIDLOW. A township in Cheshire.

CHIFFINCH. A provincial pronunciation of Chaffinch.

CHILCOTT. Chilcote, a chapelry in co. Derby.

CHILD. The son and heir in noble and royal families. The word was employed by Spenser, and in the old ballads, as the "Childe of Elle," "Child Waters," &c. See Eng. Surn. i. 214. In Domesd. the epithet Cild or Cilt is applied to several persons of distinction. Le Child. H.R.

CHILDE. CHILDS. See Child.

CHILDREN. Corresponds, as Ferguson thinks, with the O. Germ. personal name Childeruna or Hilderuna.

CHILLMAN. Perhaps from A-Sax. *cille*, a wooden tankard, or leather bottle, and *man*. Childman and Childmannius are found in the H.R.

CHILTON. Parishes in cos. Berks, Bucks, Somerset, Suffolk, Durham, Wilts, &c.

CHILVERS. A parish in co. Warwick.

CHIMBLEY. Probably a corruption of Cholmondeley.

CHIMNEY. Probably local.

CHIN. Perhaps a diminutive of Chinbald, but more likely local. A De Chene occurs in H.R. co. Bedford, and there is also a Le Chene.

CHINBALD. An A-Sax. personal name.

CHINNOCK. Three parishes in Somerset.

CHIPCHASE. A place in Northumberland.

CHIPMAN. See Chapman.

CHIPP. See Cheape.

CHISEL. Chishall, two parishes in Essex.

CHISHOLM. The right of the C's to be considered a Gaelic clan has been strongly asserted, but Skene thinks their Lowland origin evident, and he deems them a Norman race from Roxburghshire. Scot. Highl. ii. 313. The name however is Saxon enough, from *cisil*, gravel, and *holm*, a river island. The Highland estate in Inverness-shire has been so named from the family in recent times. The chief is always distinguished as *The* Chisholm. There is a proverb to the effect that, "there are only four *The's* in the Highlands; *The* Chisholm, *The* Macintosh, *The* Devil, and *The* Pope"!

CHISLETT. A parish in Kent.

CHISM. An Ulster corruption of the Scottish Chisholm.

CHISMAN. See Cheeseman.

CHITTY. Freckled. "Every lover admires his mistress, tho' she be very deformed, ill-favoured, wrinkled, pimpled, pale, red, yellow, tanned, yellow-faced; have a swollen juggler's platter-face, or a thin, lean, *chitty* face . . . . ; be crooked, dry, bald, goggle-eyed; [though] she looks like a squiz'd cat," &c. &c. Burton's Anatomy of Melancholy.

CHIVERS. See Cheever.

CHOAT. Probably the same as Chute.

CHOICE. See Joyce.

CHOLMLEY. See Cholmondeley.

CHOLMONDELEY. From the lordship of that name in Cheshire, which was possessed by the family under the Norman earls palatine of Chester. The family sprang, in common with many others, from the celebrated William Belward, lord of Malpas.

I cannot refrain from reprobating the curt and absurd pronunciation of this name—*Chulmley* or *Chumley*. Strange that some of our most aristocratic families, who would not willingly concede one jot of their dignity in other respects, should be willing to have their ancient names thus nicked and mutilated. Why should the St. Johns submit to be Sinjen'd, the Majoribanks to be Marchbank'd, the Fitz-Johns to be Fidgen'd, or the Cholmondeleys to be Chumley'd? Why should the contractions of illiterate "flunkeys" be accepted in the places of fine old chivalrous sounds like those? I would fain have this practice reformed altogether.

CHORLEY. Parishes in cos. Lancaster and Chester.

CHOWNE. Castle Chiowne, Chioune, Chun, or Choon, in Cornwall, is a very ancient ruin. See Archæologia, XXII. 300. Davies Gilbert says that this appellation "is well known to mean a house in a croft." Hist. Cornw. iii. 244. Chun, a Welsh family name, is probably identical in signification. Chone. H.R. The Chownes of Kent and Sussex were said to be descended from a follower of the Conqueror, who came from La Vendée. B.L.G.

CHRIPPES. The same as Cripps.

CHRISP. See Crisp.

CHRISTIAN. Very common in some parts of Scotland. Sir Walter Scott tells a story of an unsuccessful *gaberlunzie* woman who in the bitterness of her disappointment exclaimed: "Are there no Christians here?" and was answered: "*Christians!* nae, we be a' Elliots and Armstrangs!" When leprosy was the scourge of Europe, the disease was sometimes personal, and the patient was called *lazarius* or *ladre*; sometimes hereditary, and then the sufferers were termed Giezites and Les Gezits, from Gehazi, the false servant of Elisha, from whom they were believed to be descended. Sometimes they were called Cagots de Chanaan, lepers of Canaan, from this belief; but "their most curious title, *Crestiaas* or Christians, was not given them in direct affirmation, but in denial of a negative, '*not non-Christian*,' because being considered of Gehazi's lineage,—not only Jews, but Jews under a curse,—many would be disposed to repel them from communion." N. and Q. v. 494.

CHRISTIE. CHRISTY. CHRISTEY. See Christopher.

CHRISTMAS. CHRISMAS. Originally imposed, Camden thinks, as a baptismal name, in consequence of the individual having been born on the day of the festival. In like manner in France, Noel was first a Christian, afterwards a family name.

CHRISTOPHER. The Christian name, whence Christoffers, Christopher, Christopherson, Christie, Christy, Christey, and probably Chrystall. Also Kitt and Kitson.

CHRISTOPHERSON. See Christopher.

CHRYSTALL. Probably a corruption of Christie for Christopher.

CHUMLEY. A contraction of Cholmondeley.

CHURCH. From residence near one. In the H.R. this name is found under various forms, as Atte Chirche, De la Chirke, Ecclesia, De Ecclesia, and Ad Ecclesiam.

CHURCHER. From residence near some church; or it may be the same as Churchman.

CHURCHILL. Kelham makes Roger de Corcelles, a great Domesd. tenant in the western counties, the ancestor of the Dukes of Marlborough. See Courcelle. Churchill has, however, a sufficiently English aspect, and as we find four parishes in different counties so called, we need hardly seek for a Norman origin.

CHURCHMAN. One who had the care of a church—a churchwarden. See Bridgman. Le Chercheman occurs in the H.R.

CHURCHYARD. From residence near one. The forms in the H.R. are Ate Churchehaye (the enclosure of the church), and *De* and *In* Cimeterio, the cemetery.

CHURTON. Places in cos. Chester and Wilts.

CHUTE. A parish in Wilts, from which county the Chutes of Kent and Somerset probably sprang.

CIBBER. Caius Gabriel Cibber, the father of Colley Cibber the dramatist, was a native of Flensburg in Holstein, and settled in London a short time before the restoration of the Stuarts.

CITIZEN. A member of the commonwealth. The French have the same family name in Citoyen.

CLACHAN. Gael. A druidical circle.

CLACK. A hamlet in Wiltshire.

CLAGGETT. See Cleggett.

CLAPCOTE. A liberty in the parish of All-Hallows, Berkshire.

CLAPHAM. Parishes, &c., in Surrey, Bedford, Sussex, Yorkshire, &c.

CLAPP. An early Danish surname. Osgod Clapa was a Danish noble at the court of Canute. From him it is supposed that Clapham, co. Surrey, where he had a country house, derives its name. Ferguson. Hence Clapson, and the local surnames Clapton, Clapham, Clapcote, Clapperton, Clapshaw, Clapshoe, &c.

CLAPPERTON. I do not find the locality ; but see Clapp.

CLAPPS. The son of Clapa, an A-Sax. personal name.

CLAPSHAW. Local—" the shaw or wood of Clapa." See Clapp.

CLAPSHOE. A corruption of Clapshaw.

CLAPSON. See Clapp.

CLAPTON. Parishes, &c., in cos. Gloucester, Northampton, Somerset, and Cambridge.

CLARE DE. "The whole of the southern district eventually fell under the feudal control of the great De Clare or Clarence family, who have given their name to an English town, an Irish county, a royal dukedom, and a Cambridge college." Dr. Donaldson, in Cambridge Essays, 1856, page 60. The name was first assumed from the barony of Clare, co. Suffolk, by Richard Fitz-Gilbert, a companion of the Conqueror, son of Gilbert Crispin, Earl of Brione in Normandy, who was son of Geoffrey, a natural son of Richard I., duke of Normandy.

CLARENCE. CLARANCE. See Clare.

CLARK. CLARKE. Lat. *clericus.* Fr. Le Clerc. A learned person—that is, one who could in old times read and write—accomplishments not so rare, after all, as we are sometimes induced to think, since this is among the commonest of surnames. Clark stands 27th and Clarke 39th in the Registrar General's comparative list: and for 33,557 Smiths registered within a given period, there were 12,229 Clarks and Clarkes. Thus for every three hammermen we have at least one ' ready writer.' If the Reg. General had reckoned Clark and Clarke as one name, it would have stood *ninth* in point of numerousness. As a surname, Clarke appears frequently to have *aliased* some other appellative; for instance the baronet family, C. of Salford, originally Woodchurch, from the parish of that name in Kent, soon after the Conquest became Clarkes (Le Clerc) in consequence of a marriage with an heiress, and the family for some generations wrote themselves "Woodchurch alias Le Clerc," and vice versa, until at length the territorial appellation succumbed to the professional one, which was right, for

" When house and land be gone and spente,
    Then learning is most excellent."

Several other instances might be quoted to show that medieval bearers of the name were very proud of it, and hence, doubtless, its present numerousness. The word has several compounds in our family nomenclature, as Beauclerk, Mauclerk, Kenclarke, Petyclerk—the good, the bad, the knowing,

and the little clerks, Several Domesday tenants are designated Clericus.

CLARKSON. The son of a clerk.

CLARY. Possibly from Cléri, near Alençon in Normandy.

CLAVERING. The family spring from Eustace, a noble Norman, who had two sons ; Serlo de Burgo, who built Knaresborough castle, and John the One-eyed, (Monoculus). The latter had a son Pagan, (" the One-eyed Pagan !"—qu. Cyclops ?) and another son Eustace, the progenitor of this line, who derive their name from Clavering, co. Essex. See Kimber's Baronetage.

CLAVILE. Walter de C. was a tenant in chief in Dorset and Devon. Domesd. His male descendants continued to possess lands in the former county till 1774. Lysons. Two Clévilles occur in the Itin. Norm. ; one near Pont l'Evêque, the other near Yvetot.

CLAXTON. Parishes, &c. in cos. Norfolk, Durham, Leicester, and York.

CLAY. Several localities bear this name, but the surname must sometimes have been adopted from residence in a clayey district. The forms in the H.R. are Cley, Clai, in le Clay, del Clay, and de la Cleye. Le Clayere may be synonymous, although a Cleymanne was, according to the Promptorium Parvulorum, a dauber or plasterer.

CLAYDON. Parishes, &c., in Suffolk, Oxon, and Bucks.

CLAYPOLE. A parish in Lincolnshire.

CLAYTON. Parishes and places in cos. Stafford, Sussex, York, and Lancaster. The Claytons of the last-named shire claim descent from one Robert, who came into England with the Conqueror, and received Clayton in reward of his services. B.L.G.

CLAYWORTH. A parish in co. Notts.

CLEARE. See Clare.

CLEARY. See Clary.

CLEASBY. A parish in Yorkshire.

CLEAVE. See Cleeve.

CLEAVER. One who cleaves wood. In forest districts, lath-cleaving is still a distinct occupation.

CLEE. Parishes in cos. Lincoln and Salop.

CLEEVE. Parishes, &c., in Gloucester, Somerset, and Worcester.

CLEGG. " O. Norse, *kleggi*, a compact mass. There was a Northman with this surname in the Landnamabok." Ferguson.

CLEGGETT. Perhaps Cleygate, a manor in Surrey.

CLEGHORN. A place in co. Lanark.

CLELAND. The family were " of that Ilk," in co. Lanark, temp. Alexander III.

and connected by marriage with Sir William Wallace. B.L.G.

CLEMENCE. See Clement.

CLEMENT. The personal name, whence the modifications Clements, Clemence, Clementson, Clemitson, Clemmans, Clemmit, Climpson.

CLEMENTS. CLEMENTSON. See Clement.

CLEMITSON. See Clement.

CLEMMANS. See Clement.

CLEMMIT. See Clement.

CLENCH. A parish in Norfolk.

CLENDON. Perhaps Clandon, co. Surrey.

CLENNELL. A township in Northumberland.

CLERK. CLERKE. See Clarke.

CLEVE. CLEEVE. Parishes in cos. Gloucester, Somerset, and Worcester.

CLEVEHOG. This name is found in the H.R. several times, and in one instance is borne by a lady, 'Sibilla Clevehog.' Cleve-gris (gris A-Norm., a pig) occurs in the same records. Whether from some hazardous encounter with a wild boar, or from the occupation of the hog-butcher, I leave others to decide.

CLEVELAND. A hamlet in the parish of Ormesby, co. York.

CLEVERLY. A corruption of Claverley, co. Salop.

CLEVLAND. The C.'s of Devonshire are a branch of the Cleulands or Clelands of co. Lanark.

CLEWER. A parish in Berkshire, formerly called Cleworth.

CLIBURN. A parish in Westmoreland.

CLIFF. Parishes, &c., in cos. Kent, York, Sussex, Northampton, and Wilts.

CLIFFORD. The noble family, surnamed from Clifford (their castle and lands in co. Hereford, which they acquired in marriage in the XII. cent.), came from Normandy with the Conqueror, and then bore the name of Fitz Pons. They claimed lineal descent from Richard, Duke of Normandy, the grandfather of William I. In charters, the name is latinized De Clivo Forte.

CLIFT. See Cliff.

CLIFTON. Parishes, &c., in many counties. The Cliftons of Clifton, co. Lancaster, have possessed that estate for more than six centuries.

CLIMMIE. A Scottish diminutive of Clement.

CLIMPSON. See Clement.

CLINCH. A township in Northumberland.

CLINKER. A-Norm. clink, to ring. A ringer of bells.

CLINKSCALES. As skell signifies a well, (see Skell) the second syllable may be a corruption of it, and thus the name would be local. A capital surname for a shopkeeper.

CLINTON. The duke of Newcastle derives from Reinbaldus, who came hither at the Conquest, and assumed his surname from Glimpton, (anciently written Clinton) co. Oxford, part of the possessions granted to him for his services. Peerage. Some authorities make Reinbald a De Tancarville.

CLISBY. See Cleasby.

CLIST. At least seven places in co. Devon are so denominated.

CLITHEROE. A town in Lancashire.

CLIVE. The earl of Powis's ancestors derived their name from Clive, co. Salop, in which county the family have been seated the time of Henry II.

CLIXBY. A parish in co. Lincoln.

CLOAKE. CLOKE. Probably from the costume of the first bearer. So from Mantell, &c.

CLODD. Perhaps the same as Clode.

CLODE. Fr. Claude, from Lat. Claudius.

CLOGG. Ferguson derives it from the Danish klog, prudent.

CLOKE. See Cloake.

CLOSE. Any piece of ground that is enclosed with hedge, wall, or water.

CLOTHIER. CLOTHMAN. A maker of cloth, or a dealer in that article.

CLOUD. In Scotland, M'Cloud is the corruption of Mac Leod.

CLOUGH. A ravine, glen, or deep descent between hills. N. of Eng. Cloff, Scotl. The Cloughs of Plas-Clough claim a Norman origin, from the Seigneurs de Rohan, and appeal to their name and arms for proof. B.L.G. To my eye, both arms and name are as English as need be.

CLOUTER. Clut, A-Sax., signifies in a secondary use a seam or sewing, and hence to clout in various provincial dialects means to patch or mend, especially shoes. "Old shoes and clouted," O. Test. The Promptorium Parvulorum gives—"Clowter, or coblere, sartorius," and also "Clowter of clothys, sartorius, sartor." Hence a Clouter was a man who either improved the 'understanding,' or mended the 'habits' of his customers; i.e. either a cobbler or a tailor; probably the former.

CLOUTMAN. See Clouter.

CLOVE. Probably a variation of Clough.

CLOW. A rock. A-Sax. Halliw. 'Clows,' in Dugdale's Hist. of Imbanking, signify floodgates.

CLOWES. Probably the same as Clow.

CLOWSER. The Scotch clouse is a sluice or mill-dam. Hence Clowser may be "sluice-man"—probably a miller.

CLUFF. See Clough.

CLUNIE. Cluny, places in cos. Aberdeen and Inverness.

CLUNN. Clun, a town in Shropshire.

CLUTTERBUCK. The family settled in England from the Low Countries, at the time of the Duke of Alva's persecution of the Protestants. In 1586 Thomas Cloerterbooke was sheriff of Gloucester, and from that co. the existing gentry families of C. spring.

CLUTTON. A township in Chester, in which co. the elder line of the family still reside.

CLYBURN. Cliburn, a parish in Westmoreland.

CLYDE. The great and beautiful Scottish river.

CLYDESDALE. The dale or valley of the Clyde in Scotland.

COACHMAN. The menial servant.

COAD. COADE. A wood or forest. A Breton name, from the Celtic *coit*, sylva, nemus.

COALES. See Cole.

COAT. See Cott.

COATES. Parishes, &c., in cos. Gloucester, Leicester, Lincoln, Sussex, York, &c.

COBB. There is perhaps no monosyllable in any language that has so many distinct meanings as *cob*. It may be thought curious to enumerate them. As a VERB, it signifies, 1, to strike; 2, to pull the ear or hair; 3, to throw; and 4, to outdo. As a NOUN, it stands for—5, a seed-basket; 6, the material of mud walls; 7, a hay-stack of small dimensions; 8, clover seed; 9, an Hiberno-Spanish coin; 10, a lump or piece; 11, a sea-gull; 12, the fish called the miller's thumb; 13, a harbour, as the Cobb of Lyme-Regis; 14, a young herring; 15, a leader or chief; 16, a wealthy or influential person; 17, a small horse; 18, a spider (whence cob-web); 19, the bird called a shoveller. It has also many compounds, as—cob-castle, a prison; cob-coals, large pit-coals; cob-irons, andirons; cob-joe, a nut at the end of a string; cob-key, a bastinado used among sailors; cob-loaf, a loaf of peculiar form; cob-nut, a well known dessert fruit—also a game played with it; cob-poke, a bag carried by gleaners; cob-stones, large stones; cob-swan, a very large swan; cob-wall, a wall composed of clay and straw. The heralds in devising arms for the various families of Cobbe and Cobb, have as usual alluded to some of these objects; thus Cobb of Bedfordshire has fish (be they herrings or miller's thumbs), and shovellers in his coat; Cobb of Peterbridge, co. Norfolk, displays two swans (cob-swans) and a fish; another Cobb of Norfolk carries two teals (? shovellers) and one fish; while Cobb of Oxfordshire gives two shovellers and a (cob-) fish. This however by the way. As to the sur-

name, it may be derived either from—1, Cobb, a port or haven: we have besides the names Port and Harbour in our family nomenclature; 2, from the fish or the bird, in the same way that we have Pike, Salmon, Hawk, Sparrow; 3, a chief or leader: in Cheshire, *to cob* signifies to outdo or excel another in any effort; or 4, a wealthy or influential person, as in the following lines from Occleve:—

"Susteynid is not by personis lowe,
But *cobbis* grete this riote sustene."
(See Halliwell, Johnson, Eng. Surn.)

This is a very ancient surname. One Leuricus Cobbe occurs in the Domesd. of Suffolk, doubtless as a Saxon.

COBBETT. A corruption of Corbett or Corbet.

COBBIN. Local. De Cobbin. H.R. co. Lincoln.

COBBLEDICK. Local. De Cupeldik. H.R.

COBBLER. The occupation. Le Cobeler, H.R.

COBBOLD. "From the Kobold of Germany, a harmless and often kindly sprite, something like the Scotch brownie, may perhaps come our name Cobbold; but this is doubtful, for we have the name of Cobb, answering to a Germ. and Dan. name Kobbe, and 'bald' or 'bold' is one of the most common Teutonic composites." Ferguson. Cubold, an A-Sax. personal name, is found in Domesday.

COBBY. Brisk, lively, proud, tyrannical, headstrong. Halliwell—who quotes a northern proverb: "Cobby and crous, as a new-washed louse."

COBDEN. See DEN.

COBHAM. Parishes in Surrey and Kent.

COBURN. A 'fashionable' pronunciation of Cockburn.

COCHRANE. COCHRAN. The family were resident in co. Renfrew for many centuries. See Peerage, Earl of Dundonald. The name is probably local, from a place in the district of Paisley.

COCK. The bird—corresponding to the Lat. Gallus, the Fr. Le Coq, Cochet, Coquerel, the Germ. Hahn, &c. Sometimes it was as probably a sobriquet applied to a diminutive person. See COCK, below.

☞**COCK.** A termination common to many surnames. Several theories have been advanced as to its meaning, which I have discussed at large in Eng. Surn. i. 160—165. After mature consideration I still adhere to the opinions there expressed; namely, that though it may in some instances be a corruption of COTT, a local termination, and in others may relate to the male of birds, it is, in a great majority of cases, a diminutive of ordinary baptismal names, like -*kin*, or -*ott*, or -*ett*. I shall not, therefore, go over the old ground, but content myself with giving as full a list as I have been able to collect, of names with this desinence, for with names beginning with the syllable I have here nothing to do. I do not pretend to account for every name, but elucidations of most of them will be found in their proper places in this book.

Acock, Adcock, Addiscock, Alcock, Atcock.

Badcock, Bancock, Benhacock, Beacock, Barcock, Batcock, Bawcock, Bullcock.

Drocock.

Elcock.

Grocock. Glasscock.

Hancock, Hitchcock, Haycock, and Heycock, Hillcock, Heacock, Hedgcock. Hiscock.

Johncock, Jeffcock.

Locock, Luccock, Leacock, Laycock, Lovecock.

Marcock, Meacock, Maycock, Mulcock.

Ocock.

Pocock, Pidcock, Peacock, Pencock, Palcock.

Ranecock, or Raincock.

Sandercock, Slocock, Straycock, Simcock, Stercock, Silcock, Salcock.

Tancock, Tillcock.

Watcock, Woolcock, Wilcocke.

☞ COCK. This syllable in many local names refers probably to the woodcock rather than to the *gallus*, especially in such names as Cocksedge, Cockshaw, Cockshote, Cockshut, Cocksworth.

COCKAIGNE. COKAINE. COKAYN. 'Cokaygne' seems to have been a sort of medieval Utopia. Perhaps the earliest specimen of English poetry which we possess, and which Warton places earlier than the reign of Henry II., is the humorous description of it, beginning—

"Fur in see, bi west Spaygne
Is a lond ihote Cockaygne."

Whatever may be the origin of the word, it is evidently connected with the much-debated *cockney*, which probably implied an undue regard for luxury and refinement in the persons to whom it was applied—generally to Londoners as contrasted with "persons rusticall." See Way's Prompt. Parv. Halliwell's Dict.

COCKBURN. Probably from either Cockburnlaw, co. Berwick, or from Cockburnspath in the same county. There is a mountain in Berwickshire which is so called.

COCKELL. See Cockle and Cockerell.

COCKER. In various English dialects means a cock-fighter. Halliwell. See however Coker.

ACCORDING TO COCKER—

is a common phrase as to the correctness of an arithmetical calculation. Edward Cocker was a celebrated arithmetician who flourished in the time of the Commonwealth. Le Cockere, H.R.

COCKERELL. O. Eng. *cokerelle.* A young cock, "gallulus." Prompt. Parv.

COCKERTON. A township in Durham.

COCKESBRAYN. This surname occurs in the H.R. 'Cockbrained' is an epithet of much more recent use, implying, according to Halliwell, fool-hardy or wanton.

COCKETT. A diminutive of cock, *gallus,* like the Fr. Cochet from Coq.

COCKFIELD. Parishes in Durham and Suffolk.

COCKIN. A-Norm. *cokin*—a rascal.

COCKING. A parish in Sussex.

COCKLE. Perhaps applied as a term of contempt to the followers of Wickliffe, who were regarded as cockle, tares, or *zizania* among the true Catholic wheat. More probably the second syllable may be a corruption of *hill.* Or it may be like Cockett, a diminutive of cock, *gallus.*

COCKMAN. A cockfighter.

COCKRAM. Cockerham, a parish in Lancashire.

COCKRELL. See Cockerell.

COCKS. See Cox.

COCKSHUT. A chapelry in co. Salop, and many minor localities.

CODDINGTON. Parishes in cos. Chester, Hereford, and Notts. The Irish family migrated to Ireland from Cheshire in 1656. B.L.G.

CODMAN. Doubtless the same as Cotman, though a correspondent suggests that it means pedlar, from the *cod* or bag in which he carries his wares.

CODNOR. Places in Derbyshire.

CODRINGTON. A parish united with Wapley, co. Gloucester, where the family were seated in the XV. century, and probably much earlier.

COE. 1. In Norfolk, an eccentric old man. 2. A Scottish rivulet giving name to Glencoe. There is a Beatrix le Coe in H.R.

COFFEE. COAFFEE. COFFEY. May be local, or may be of common origin with Coffin, Caffin, &c., the root being *calvus,* bald. "Coffee," says Ferguson, "I take to be the same as Coifi, the name of a converted heathen priest, who, on the reception of Christianity by the people of Northumbria, undertook the demolition of the ancient fanes. It has been asserted that this is not an A-Sax. but a Cymric name, and that it denotes in Welsh a Druid, but Mr. Kemble has shown that it is an adjective formed from *cóf,* strenuous, and means "the bold or active one."

COFFIN. This family possessed Alwington manor, co. Devon, temp. William Conq.. and they still reside at Portledge in that manor. B.L.G. Colvin or Colvinus held lands in chief (probably the same) under Edward the Confessor.

COGAN. Local. H.R. co. Devon.

COGHILL. The baronet descends from John Cockhill of Cockhill, gent., who lived at Knaresborough, co. York, temp. Richard II.

COHAM. An estate near Torrington, co. Devon, still in possession of the family, who trace their pedigree only to 1547, though they were doubtless proprietors at a much earlier date. B.L.G.

COHEN. A common Jewish surname, —the Hebrew for Priest. Nearly sixty traders of this name occur in Lond. Direct.

COKE. Lat. *coquus, cocus*, a cook. In the rude old ages when family surnames began, the chief officers of the kitchens of kings and great men were persons of importance. For example, in Domesday we find several Coci, some of whom were tenants in capite, and one is expressly named " Coquus quidam Regis." The orthography *coke*, for cook, is retained by Chaucer ; and in the family of the Earl of Leicester, illustrious for its great lawyer and its great agriculturist, it still exists. In most cases, however, it has taken the form of Cook.

COKER. 1. The original meaning of *coke* is charcoal, prepared or 'cooked' by a Coker, or charcoal-burner. 2. Two parishes in co. Somerset, with which one family were associated as early at least as 1272. B.L.G.

COKEYNE. See Cockaigne.

COLBOURNE. A township in Yorkshire.

COLBRAN. COLBRAND. A personal name of great antiquity. It occurs in Cod. Dipl. charter 925,and it is probably of Scandinavian origin. According to Ferguson it may either mean *kolbrandr*, a burning coal, or be a compound of *kollr*, 'helmeted,' and the proper name Brand. Both Colbrand and Colebrand are found as under tenants in Domesday.

COLBURN. See Colbourn.

COLBY. A parish in Norfolk, and a township in Westmoreland.

COLCHESTER. The town in Essex.

COLCLOUGH. An estate in Staffordshire, in which county the family resided temp. Edw. III. The Irish branch settled at Tintern, co. Wexford, about the middle of the XVI. cent.

COLD. A corruption of Cole.

COLDMAN. A corruption of Coleman.

COLDRED. An A-Sax. personal name.

COLDSTREAM. A parish in Berwickshire.

COLE. Places in cos. Wilts and Somerset. Also a very ancient Teutonic personal name. In Domesd. it appears as a baptismal—in the H.R. as a family name.

K

COLEBROOKE. Places in Salop and Devon.

COLEBY. A parish in co. Lincoln.

COLEGATE. COLGATE. A place in St. Leonard's Forest, near Horsham, Sussex.

COLEMAN. COLMAN. An ancient A-Sax. personal name mentioned by Bede. Coleman and Colemannus in Domesd. Probably derived from the occupation of charcoal burning, and synonymous with Collier.

COLENSO. R.G. 16. makes this a Cornish name.

COLENUTT. See Colnett.

COLERIDGE. A hundred and a parish in co. Devon.

COLES. A genitive form of Cole.

COLET. COLLETT. " Acolyth, *acolythus*, in our old English called a *colet*, was an inferior church servant, who next under the sub-deacon waited on the priests and deacons, and performed the meaner offices of lighting the candles, carrying the bread and wine, and paying other servile attendance." Kennet's Parochial Antiq. Burn's Eccles. Law. See Collett below.

COLEY. The same as Cowley, Cooley, &c.

COLFOX. The same as the Colvox of the H.R., whatever that may be.

COLIN. In Scotl. probably different from the Eng. Collins. Gaelic etymologists derive it from *cailean* or *coilean*, " the man of the wood," or forester. It is still in use as a Christian name.

COLLARBONE. A presumed corruption of Collingbourne, co. Wilts. So Hollowbone from Hollybourne.

COLLARD. Mr. Ferguson fancifully derives it from A-Sax. *col*, a helmet, and *heard*, hard. But I find no such hard-headed gentleman in any early record.

COLLARMAKER. The occupation.

COLLEDGE. Probably local, and with no reference to any seat of learning, or abode of charity.

COLLEGE. In the west of England any court or group of cottages having a common entrance from the street is called a *college*, and residence at such a place rather than in a university probably originated the name.

COLLEN. See Collin, and Colin.

COLLER. An idler. See Eng. Surn.

COLLETT. Has been derived from *colet*, an acolyte, the fourth of the minor sacerdotal orders ; but its true meaning is " little Nicholas." Thus the parents of St. Colette, who held St. Nicholas in great veneration, gave their child in baptism the name of " *Colette*, c'est à dire *Petit Nichole*." Edinb. Rev. April, 1855.

COLLEY. The original surname of the Marquis Wellesley, the Duke of Wellington, &c., was written Cowley, temp. Hen. VIII.

COLLICK. Probably Colwick, co. Nottingham.

COLLIER. A maker of charcoal, formerly a much more important and common occupation than now. In medieval documents it is written Le Coliere, Carbonarius, &c.

COLLIN. COLLINS. COLLIS. Colin is one of the diminutives of Nicholas, and Collins may be its genitive, and Collis a corruption thereof. There are, however, other assigned etymons, as Fr. *colline*, a hill, and Gael. *cuilein*, a term of endearment. But Collinc is also an ancient baptismal name, which existed before the compilation of Domesday. According to B.L.G. the Collinses of Walford existed, *eo nomine*, in the time of the Conqueror, in cos. Hereford and Salop.

COLLING. COLLINGS. See under Collin.

COLLINGHAM. Parishes in cos. York and Nottingham. Like Collingridge, Collington, Collingwood, Collingbourne, &c., this local name seems to be derived from some early proprietor called Colling.

COLLINGWOOD. I cannnot discover the locality. It is probably in Northumb., where the family have flourished for several centuries.

COLLINSON. COLLISON. See Colin.

COLLISON. Colin's son—the son of Nicholas. Coly, Colys, and fil'Colini are found in the H.R.

COLLMAN. See Coleman.

COLLYER. See Collier.

COLNETT. The Hampshire family are said to be descended from a French Protestant refugee who settled at Gosport, and introduced glass-making. Colenutt appears to be the same name.

COLPITTS. I have observed this name about Newcastle-upon-Tyne. It was probably assumed in the first instance by a person resident near a *coal-pit*.

COLPUS. A Surrey surname. Calpus, probably a Saxon, is found in Domesday.

COLQUHOUN (pron. Cohoon). An ancient clan seated near Loch Lomond. The name was taken from the lands of Colquhoun in Dumbartonshire. Umfridus of Kilpatrick, who had a grant of them from Maldowen Earl of Lennox about 1250, was founder of the family.

COLSON. The son of Cole. This was the name of one of the Danish invaders of Northumbria, where Coulson is still a common family name.

COLSTON. A parish in co. Notts.

COLT. Ferguson thinks this a corruption of the name Gold; but it appears in the XIII. cent. in its present form, and I see no reason why it should not be derived from the animal, especially as Le Colt is found in H.R. The Colts of co. Lanark derive from Blaise Coult, a French Huguenot refugee in the XVI. cent.

COLTMAN. A trainer of colts.

COLTON. Parishes, &c. in cos. Norfolk, Stafford, and York.

COLVILLE. There are three places in Normandy called Colleville, situated in the respective neighbourhoods of Caen, Bayeux, and Yvetot. From which of these came William de Colvile of Yorkshire, and Gilbert de Colavilla of Suffolk, mentioned in Domesd., is not ascertained. The Scottish peer descends from Philip de C., a scion of the A-Norm. family who settled beyond the border in the XII. cent. Colevil, Colevile, Coleville, Colwile, Colewille. H.R.

COLVIN. Colvin or Colvinus was a Devonshire tenant in chief, and held his lands in the reign of Edw. the Confessor, and at the making of Domesd. See Coffin.

COLWELL. A corruption of Colville. H.R.

COLYER. See Collier.

COMBE. COMBES. From A-Sax. *comb*, Celt. *cwm*, a hollow in a hill, a valley. In medieval writings, At-Comb, At-Cumb, &c. There are places called Comb or Combe in Sussex, Devon, Somerset, &c.—Combs in Suffolk—Coombe in Wilts, Dorset, and Hants,—and Coombs in Sussex, Derby, and Dorset. Several of these have conferred their names on families.

☞COMBE, *as a termination.* See preceding article. A correspondent has sent me a list of surnames with this desinence. Some of these will be found identified with the localities which gave them birth in their proper places in this work. Of others the situation is unknown to me.

Ashcombe, Aynscombe.

Barnscombe, Brimblecombe, Burcombe, Bronescombe, Brownscombe, Buncombe, Bascombe, Belcombe, Brimacombe, Branscombe, Bidecombe, Battiscombe, Buddicombe, Biddlecombe, Balcombe.

Corscombe, Challacombe.

Doddescombe, Dimscombe, Discombe, Duncombe, Dacombe, Delacombe, Dunscombe, Dascombe, Dorkcombe.

Ellacombe or Ellicombe, Encombe, Escombe, Edgecombe.

Farncombe, Fearncombe.

Goscombe, Gatcombe.

Hanscombe, Halcombe, Harcombe, Hollicombe, Holcombe, Haccombe, Harcombe.

Jacombe.

Kingcombe.

Larcombe, Loscombe, Liscombe, Lipscombe, Luscombe, Luccombe, Levercombe. Morcombe.

Norcombe, Newcombe, Nutcombe.

Puddlecombe, Puddicombe, Pincombe, Prattiscombe.

Ranscombe, Rascombe.

Stincombe, Sercombe, Smallcombe, Smallacombe, Slocombe, Stancombe, Seecombe, Southcombe, Syndercombe, Salcombe.

Tingcombe, Tincombe, Tidcombe, Tuddicombe, Totscombe.

Withecombe, Woolcombe, Winchcombe, Wescombe, Wollocombe, Whitcombe, Warnecombe, Widecombe, Winscombe, Wiscombe, Welcombe.

Vinecombe.

Yarcombe, Yescombe.

Professor Leo asserts that *cumb* means a mass of water—it originally signified a trough or bowl, and subsequently, not a valley—as Bosworth wrongly asserts—but an extensive though running sheet of water. The Professor's ground for this statement appears to be the occurrence of a *hedfod* and an *œwylm*,—a head and a spring—in connection with a *cumb*; (Cod. Dipl. II. 28, 29.) but surely this is very slender evidence for so sweeping an assertion. The upper end of a valley is called its *head*, and that there should be a *spring* in a valley is nothing extraordinary. I maintain, therefore, with Dr. Bosworth, that COMBE *is* a valley, either with or without water. Within the compass of a morning's walk from the spot where I write this, there are a score or two of COMBES without a drop of water. In fact, the South Downs are full of these depressions, which, from their geological position, can no more 'hold water' than can this notion of the learned philologist of Halle.

COMBER. 1. One who combs or prepares wool. 2. A modification of At-Combe. See termination ER.

COMBERBACH. A township in Cheshire.

COMER. Perhaps the same as Comber.

COMFORT. Perhaps a corruption of the local surname Comerford.

COMIN. See under Cumming.

COMLEY. Doubtless local, rather than personal.

COMMANDER. R.G. 16. A leader in some enterprise. Le Comandur, H.R.

COMMERELL. 1. From Heilbronn in Suabia in 1732, and naturalized in 1752. 2. Comberwell near Bradford, co. Wilts, gave name to a family called De Comerwelle, whence probably this surname, in some cases. Vide Jackson's Account of Kingston House, Bradford, reprinted from the Wiltshire Archæological Magazine.

COMMINS. See under Cumming.

COMMON. Local—from residence at one.

COMMONER. 1. Local—from residence at a common. See termination ER. 2. A member of a university.

COMMONS. A pluralization of Common.

COMPTON. The Marquis of Northampton derives from Turchil, possessor of Arden, co. Warwick, before the Conquest. His descendant Osbert, in 1169, assumed the name of Compton from his estate in the same county. The Gazetteer mentions thirty other places of this name in various counties.

COMRIE. A parish in Perthshire.

COMYN. See Cumming.

CONAN. An ancient personal name occurring in the poems of Ossian. It is sometimes corrupted to Cannon and Canning.

CONCANON. CONCANNEN. The O'Concanons derive from Dermot, brother of Murias, 29th king of Connaught, who flourished in the IX. cent. B.L.G. The surname seems to have been established prior to the XI. cent.

CONDER. "*Conders* (in Fishery) are those who stand upon high places near the sea-coasts, with boughs, &c., in their hands, to make signs to the men in fishing-boats, which way the shoal of herrings passes, which they discover by a kind of blue colour the fish make in the water." Bailey's Dict. See Eng. Surn.

CONDUIT. Local—from residence near one.

CONGERTON. Perhaps either Congerston, co. Leicester, or Congleton, co. Chester.

CONGREVE. An estate in co. Stafford, which has been held by the family almost from the time of the Conquest. B.L.G.

CONINGSBY. A parish in Lincolnshire. The peers of this name are descended from a family who formerly possessed Coningsby, a town in co. Salop. Burke's Ext. P. But qu: 1. Can such descent be shown? 2. Is there a town so called in Shropshire?

CONNELL. The Irish¯ O'Connell, sans O.

CONNELLAN. The family O'Connellan is Milesian and deduced from the great family of O'Neill. B.L.G.

CONNINGTON. Conington, parishes in cos. Cambridge and Hunts.

CONNOCK. Cornish. Rich, prosperous, thriving, successful. Davies Gilbert's Cornwall, i. 176.

CONNOP. Probably Conhope, a township in co. Hereford.

CONNOR. See O'Connor.

CONQUEROR. A victor—probably in some rustic game. Conquestor is found in the H.R. The singular name Conquergood is not easily explained.

CONQUEST. Probably a contraction of Conquestor. "Willelm' *Conquestor*" is the name of a private person mentioned in the H.R., and Robert *Conqueraunt* is found in the same documents. Houghton-Conquest, co. Bedford, derives its suffix from the family, who were possessors of it before 1298. Esch. 26. Edw. I. Lysons.

CONRATH. Probably Conrad, a personal name.

CONSTABLE. An office formerly of high dignity in royal courts. The great Yorkshire family descend from Robert de Laci, whose ancestors had been constables of

Chester under the celebrated Hugh Lupus, temp. Will. Conq.

CONSTANCE. Probably Coutances in Normandy, which is latinized Constantia.

CONSTANT. 1. A contraction of Constantine. 2. An honourable appellation denoting the constancy of the bearer. 3. A sobriquet applied to one who was regular and pertinacious in some habit or custom. I knew a person whose real name was Hastings, who was better known among his neighbours as 'Old Constant,' from the regularity with which he appeared at a certain time in a certain place.

CONWAY. One of the few local surnames adopted from places in Wales. The extinct noble family was traced to 5 Richard II. Conway or Aberconway is in co. Caernarvon.

CONY. Of common origin with the Ducs de Coigni in France. The ancestor was chamberlain to Isabella of France, and accompanied her to England on her marriage with king Edw. II. The Eng. family's armorial coat is identical with that of the present Duc de Coigni. Gent. Mag. May, 1859.

CONYERS. "Of this ancient family, originally wrote Coigniers, denominated from a place of that name in France, was Roger de Coigniers, that came into England about the end of the reign of Will. the Conqueror, to whom the bishop of Durham gave the constableship of Durham." Kimber. The family gave the suffix to Howton Coigniers, co. York.

CONYNGHAM. The family of the Marquis C. and of Lord Londesborough descend from the Scottish house of Cunyngham and from the Earls of Glencairne.

COODE. Code was a tenant before the compilation of Domesd. An ancient family long settled at Morval, co. Cornwall, have at various periods written themselves Code, Coad, and Coode. C. S. Gilbert's Cornw. ii. 72.

COOK. COOKE. The occupation. In Domesd. there are several tenants styled Cocus, and one, 'quidam Coquus Regis.' Coke is an archaic form of the name. The Lond. Direct. has more than 250 traders of this surname.

COOKES. Cook pluralized.

COOKSON. One of the few instances of the addition of the termination *son* to a profession or employment. So Smithson, Stewardson, Shepherdson. Fil'Coci is its form in the H.R.

COOKWORTHY. Doubtless local, the Y being an unnecessary addition.

COOLEY. Probably a corruption of Cowley. The ancestors of the Duke of Wellington, prior to their assumption of the name of Wesley or Wellesley, wrote their name indifferently Colley, Cowley, and Cooley. *Times*, 15 Sept., 1852. So Cooper was anciently Cowper.

COOLING. A parish in Kent.

COOMBER. See Comber.

COOMES. See Coombe.

COOPER. The occupation—a maker of barrels, tubs, &c.; originally from *coop*, to keep or contain anything, whether wine in a cask, or a hen in her prison. A-Sax. *kepan, cepan*. See Cowper. Le Coupere, Coupare, Cuparius, &c., H.R.

COPE. In Domesd. signifies a hill. Bailey's Dict.

COPEMAN. 1. A chapman or merchant. Halliwell. 2. Bailey says that *cope* was a tribute paid to the king out of the lead mines in Wicksworth, co. Derby. Perhaps the collector of this tax was the original Copeman. 3. Cope is also the name of a priest's vestment; and the Copeman may have been the maker of that article. 4. It may be equivalent to Hillman. See Cope.

COPLESTONE. A hamlet in the parish of Colebrook, co. Devon, said to have been possessed by the family before the Conquest. Polwhele's Devon. ii. 35. See Croker.

COPLEY. Very ancient in Yorkshire. Local—but I do not find the place.

COPNER. A-Sax. *copenere*, a lover.

COPP. The top of a hill, or any eminence.

COPPEN. COPPIN. Elevated—as "*coppin* in hevin," elevated to heaven. Jamieson. The root appears to be A-Sax. *cop*, the summit. Probably from the lofty residence of the first bearer.

COPPER. A cup bearer. "Palice of Honour," quoted by Jamieson. A-Sax. *cop*, a cup.

COPPERWHEAT. A corruption of Copperthwaite. See Thwaite.

COPPERWRIGHT. See under Wright.

COPPINGER. '*Copenere*' is the A-Sax. for lover; but a more probable derivation is from *coppin*, which Halliwell defines as 'a piece of yarn taken from the spindle.' A Coppinger was then perhaps in medieval times one who had the care of yarn or who produced it. To LIVE LIKE A COPPINGER is a Suffolk proverb, which points to the wealth and hospitality of a family of this name who flourished in the XVI. and XVII. cent. at Buxhall in that county. Gent. Mag. Jan. 1831. The name is found in the archives of Cork so early as temp. Edw. II. B.L.G.

COPPOCK. From the termination, probably local. See OCK.

COQUERELL. See Cockerell.

CORBET. Corbet, a noble Norman, came into England with the Conqueror, and from his son Roger Corbet descended the baronial house, as well as the families of the name now existing. Courthope's Debrett.

CORBY. Parishes, &c. in cos. Lincoln, Northampton, and Cumberland.

CORDER. Perhaps a maker of cord—analogous to Roper. Le Corder. H.R.

CORDEROY. Fr. *Cœur de Roi*, king-hearted; metaphorically applied to a man of noble and generous disposition. Perhaps, however, the same as Cowdray.

CORDINER. Fr. *cordonnier*. A shoe-maker. In the H.R. Le Cordewener, Le Cordewaner, Corduanarius, &c.

CORDREY. See Corderoy.

CORDUKES. In Ireland, said to be a corruption of the Fr. surname Cordeaux, which means literally small cords or lines.

CORDY. Ferguson derives it from O. Norse *kordi*, a sword, but it is more probably local.

CORFE. Parishes in cos. Dorset and Somerset.

CORK. Not from the Irish city, as has been conjectured, but from Corc, an ancient Celtic personal name.

CORKER. Perhaps a maker of corks.

CORLEY. A parish in co. Warwick.

CORMACK. A personal name. Gael. M'Cormac.

CORNS. CORNU. R.G. 16. See under Cowhorn.

CORNELIUS. The personal name.

CORNELL. A local pronunciation of Cornwall?

CORNER. From residence at the corner of a street or highway. In the H.R., De la Cornere. It was latinized by *in Angulo*. In the second vol. of the Rolls it occurs as *in Agglo* five times (all with different Christian names,) as *in Anglo* 17, and as *in Anglo* 19 times. A less likely derivation is from Le Coruner and Coronator, a coroner. De Corner and Le Corner are also found in the H.R. See Nangle.

CORNEWALL. Richard, second son of King John, titular King of the Romans and Earl of Cornwall, had according to Sandford's Geneal. Hist. two natural sons, Richard de Cornewall, and Walter de C. From the former sprang the barons of Burford, now represented by Geo. Cornewall Legh, of High Legh, co. Chester, Esq., the Cornewalls of Delbury, co. Salop, &c.

CORNEY. A parish in Cumberland. Also a nickname of Cornelius.

CORNFORD. Perhaps Cornforth, co. Durham.

CORNISH. Belonging to Cornwall—applied originally to one who had removed from that to another county. A family so called at St. Issey in Cornwall, "originally descended from one William Cornish, who settled here temp. Queen Mary, a *Welshman*." D. Gilbert's Cornw., ii. 255.

☞ CORNISH SURNAMES. The local surnames of Cornwall present some marked peculiarities, which render it convenient to treat of a large body of them in one article. In most of the countries and districts where the Celtic dialects prevail, or have prevailed, the family names are principally of the *patronymical* class—the son or descendant having assumed the name of the father or ancestor with some prefix. For instance, most of the Gaelic sur-names were personal names compounded with *Mac*; the Irish with *O*'; the Welsh with *Ap* or *Ab*. In Cornwall, however, the names are principally of the *local* sort, and as the names of places in that county are generally derived from Celtic roots, possessing, as to the first syllable at least, a generic meaning, it has become proverbial that—

> "By Tre, Pol, and Pen,
> Ye shall know the Cornish-men."

while a less known and more comprehensive distich with more truth affirms that—

> "By Tre, Ros, Pol, Lan, Caer, and Pen,
> You may know the most of Cornishmen."

TRE is equivalent to the A-Sax *tun*, a town, or enclosure; Ros to heath, or unenclosed ground; POL, to pool; LAN, to church; CAER or CAR, to a fortified place; and PEN, to a headland. In Breton local names and surnames, the same prefixes occur, though "pol" is written *poul*, and "car," or "caer," *ker*. In Wales there are likewise many place-names with these syllables, with modified orthographies and modified significations—Tre, Rhos, Pwll, Llan, Caer, and Pen; but these with rare exceptions have not given names to families. In Scotland, Ros, Caer, and perhaps some of the others, occur in the same sense; and also in Ireland, but as these are but rarely, if at all, found as surnames, they belong rather to topographical than to family nomenclature. In the following lists I have arranged such Cornish surnames as have occurred to me *en masse*, reserving such elucidations as seem necessary for their particular and proper places in the alphabetical order of the work.

SURNAMES IN TRE.—Trebarfoot, Trebersey, Trebilliock, Trebilcock, Treby, Trecarrell, Tredenham, Tredidon, Tredinham, Tredinick, Tredrea, Trefelens, Treffrey, Trefusis, Tregaga, Treagagle, Treagago, Treganyan, Tregarick, Tregarthen, Tregea, Tregeagle, Tregean, Tregeare, Tregedick, Tregenna, Tregian, Tregillas, Tregion, Treglisson, Tregonnell, Tregors, Tregose, Tretgohnan, Tregoweth, Tregoze, Tregury, Tregyon, Trehane, Trehavarike, Trehawke, Treiagn, Treice, Trejago, Trekynin, Trelander, Trelawney, Tremaine, Tremanheer, Trembraze, Tremearne, Tremanheere, Tremere, Tremle, Tremogh, Trenance, Trencreek, Trengone, Trengore, Trenhayle, Trenheale, Trenouth, Trenoweth, Trenwith, Trerize, Tresahar, Tresilian, Tresithney, Treskewis, Trethake, Trethinick, Trethurfe, Trevanion, Trevannion, Treveale, Treveally, Trevellans, Trevelles, Trevener, Trevenor,

Treverlyn, Trevethen, Trevilian, Treville, Trevingy, Trevisa, Trevithick, Trevorva, Treweeke, Trewenethick, Trewerne, Trewhella, Trewhythenick, Trewin, Trewinard, Trewolla, Trewoofe, Trewoolla, Trework, Treworthen, Trewren.

SURNAMES IN ROS.—Roscarrack, Roscarrock, Roscorla, Roscrow, Roscruge, Rosecossa, Roskymer, Rosogan, Roswarne, Roseveal, Roskilly.

SURNAMES IN POL.—Polamonter, Polkinghorne, Polwhele (modified in Sussex to Polhill), Polley, Polwin, Pollexfen (?), Polglaze, Polwarth, Polyblank (?).

SURNAMES IN LAN.—Lanbaddern, Lance, Lander, Langhairne, Langherne, Lanhadern, Lanhedrar, Lannar, Lanwordaby, Lanyon.

SURNAMES IN CAR.—Cardew, Cardinham, Carew, Carlyon, Carminowe, Carne, Carnesew, Carrow, Carthew, Carverth, Carveth.

SURNAMES IN PEN.—Penalmick, Penaluna, Penarth, Pencarow, Pencoil, Pendarves, Pender, Pendrea, Peneligan, Penferm, Penforme, Penhallow, Penhalluwick, Penhellick, Penkevil, Penlee, Penlyer, Pennalyky, Pennant, Penneck, Penpons, Penrin, Penrose, Pentine, Pentire, Penularick, Penwarne.

For another group of Cornish surnames see the article NAN.

CORNOCK. The family settled in Ireland temp. Cromwell. B.L.G. The name may be from Carnock, a parish in Fifeshire.

CORNWALL. See Cornewall.

CORNWELL. A parish in Oxfordshire.

CORNWALLIS. Originally applied to a native of Cornwall; so Wallis to a Welshman, Londonoys to a Londoner, &c. Le Cornwaleys, Cornvaleis, &c. H.R.

CORRIE. CURRIE. Sir Walter Scott has introduced this ancient word into the beautiful funeral song of the Clansman, in his Lady of the Lake:—

"Fleet foot in the *corrie*,
 Sage counsel in cumber,
 Red hand in the foray,
 How sound is thy slumber."

An explanatory note to the word says:— "Corrie or Cori; the *hollow* side of the hill where game usually lies."

CORRY. See Corrie.

CORSBIE. CORSBY. Perhaps Cosby, co. Leicester. See Cosby.

CORSCOMBE. A parish in co. Dorset.

CORSELLIS. Refugees from the Low Countries, who settled in Essex or Norfolk. A descendant became lord of the manor of Layer-Marney, in Essex.

CORSHAM. A parish in Wiltshire.

CORSTON. Places in cos. Somerset, Wilts, and Worcester.

CORT. Probably the O. Norse *kortr*, short. Ferguson.

CORTIS. Courteous. See Curtis and Curteis.

CORY. The same as Corrie.

CORYTON. An estate in Lifton, co. Devon, possessed by the family as early at least as 1242. C. S. Gilbert's Cornwall.

COSBY. A parish and estate co. Leicester, said to have been the property of the family before the Conquest.

COSCAR. See Mac Oscar.

COSGROVE. COSGRAVE. A parish in Northamptonshire.

COSHAM. Probably the same as Corsham.

COSSENS. COSSINS. See Cousins.

COSSENTINE. A correspondent of N. & Q., x. 409, states, that more than thirty years ago he knew a small farmer of this name in Cornwall, as illiterate as men of his class usually are, and in straightened circumstances, who notwithstanding was the "high lord" of a considerable estate in or near to the parish of St. Veep, and exercised manorial rights over certain woodlands there. This man's statement was, that his family "were formerly Emperors of Constantinople, that their name was Constantine, and that it had been softened into *Cossentine* by vulgar pronunciation. When the Turks took the city, his family made their escape, and came to England, bringing with them great wealth, with a portion of which they bought the property of which he was still the 'high lord;' and a large sum was also deposited in the Tower of London." The honest man doubtless believed himself to be a descendant of the Eastern Emperors, and thought the possession of the ancestral right referred to a sufficient confirmation of his lofty claim. The probability however is, that his forefathers were a gentry family whose surname had been borrowed from the parish of Constantine in Cornwall, and that he had confounded them with another family who settled in the XVII. cent. at Landulph, in that county, and who were veritable descendants of the imperial house. See Paleologus. In the reign of Queen Elizabeth, a family of Costentyne resided in the West Riding of Yorkshire.

COSSINGTON. Parishes in cos. Leicester and Somerset.

COSSOM. See Cosham.

COSTEKER. Of a common origin with the O. Germ. name Custica. Ferguson.

COSTELLO. Among the many A-Norm. settlers in Ireland, temp. Henry II., was Hostilio de Angulo. His descendants were called Mac-Ostello (son of Hostilio) which by still further corruption became Costello.

COSTER. COSTAR. Du. "*Koster*, deurwaarder van een Catholyke kerk." Marin's Dict. A sacristan.

COSTIDEL. Costedhall, a manor in Essex. Hist. Lewes, ii. App. i.

COSTOMER. A collector of royal customs was called a *customer* so lately as the XVII. cent.

COSTON. Parishes in cos. Leicester and Norfolk.

COTE. See Cott.

COTGRAVE. A parish in co. Nottingham. De Cotegrave occurs in that county in H.R. There was also a Cheshire family of this name. Thomas, one of the grandsons of the great William Belward, Lord of Malpas, held the lands of Cotgrave, and from them assumed the surname De Cotgrave.

COTHAM. Places in cos. Nottingham and Lincoln.

COTHER. A corruption of the name of several places and rivers in Scotland called Calder.

COTHERBONG. "I know," says a Lancashire correspondent, "a man whose name was Calderbank, from the river Calder; his grandson on entering the militia persisted that it was Cotherbong, under which corrupt spelling it was enrolled. I was only satisfied by a reference to the grandfather."

The same correspondent pertinently adds: "Names which are unaccountable are generally mere corruptions of names of places or other words. The ignorant do not know how to spell; the curate, the registrar, and the relieving-officer just do it *phonetically*, and take no interest, and no trouble: and thus a perpetual corruption is going on.

COTMAN. The *cotmannus*, i.e., the cottarius, cotter, or cottager, of Domesd. was one who held by free socage tenure, and paid rent in provisions or money. Ellis, Introd. Domesd. In H.R. Cotman is used as a baptismal name.

COTON. See Cotton.

COTSFORD. Cottesford, a parish in co. Oxon.

☞ **COTT. COT. COTE.** A common termination of local surnames, as in Walcott, Caldecott, Norcot, Northcote, Southcote, &c. It appears to be the A-Sax *côte*. Professor Leo observes that, " if *selë* be the dwelling of the wealthy— of landowners, *côte* on the other hand indicates the abode of the poorer classes. Cote is the house of an indigent dependent countryman, who, without any personal estate, holds a transferable tenement in fief. It was originally a house of mud, or of earth, with loam walls." The prefixed word sometimes indicates the owner's name, and is sometimes descriptive of the situation.

COTTAGE. From residence in one.

COTTAM. See Cotham.

COTTER. COTTAR. Scotch. A cottager. See Cotman.

COTTERELL. COTTRELL. In feudal times, " the *coterellus* held in absolute villenage and had his person and goods disposed at the pleasure of the lord." Kennet's Paroch. Antiq. He was probably so called,

like the Cotmanni, or Cottarii of Domesd. from residing in a cottage. Another origin may be from the *cotarelli, costeraux, coteraux,* mercenary soldiers and freebooters whose trade was war and pillage, (Conf. Brabazon) and who were so called from the *coterel,* a large knife they carried. Cotgrave defines *cotereaux* as " a certaine crue of peasantly outlawes who in old time did much mischiefe unto the nobilitie and clergie."

COTTINGHAM. Parishes in cos. York and Northampton.

COTTLE. Perhaps from the district now called Cottles in Wiltshire.

COTTON. Cottun, a place in the department of Calvados in Normandy; also several parishes in the counties of York, Chester, Stafford, &c. Both forms, viz. De Cottun, and De Cotton, are found in the H.R. The Eng. Gazetteer gives many places called Cotton. Lord Combermere's family trace unbrokenly to the days of King John, and there is some evidence of their having been seated at Cotton or Coton, co. Salop, prior to the Conquest.

A correspondent sends me the following note from a family pedigree. "Cotwn is an ancient British word, and signifies in the Welsh language 'an enclosure.' The very great antiquity of the family in Cheshire, as well as the name of their seat, shows them to be of British extraction." The successive steps of the orthography seem to have been Cotun, Coton, Cotton.

COTTRELL. See Cotterell.

COUCHMAN. Probably the same as *coucher,* which Bailey defines as, "an old word signifying a factor residing in some foreign country for traffic."

COULES. See Coles.

COULMAN. See Colman.

COULSON. See Colson.

COULTER. A lake at St. Nynians, co. Lanark, is so called.

COULTHART. According to Tradition and a most elaborate Pedigree, the Coultharts of Coulthart, co. Wigtown, are descended from Coulthartus, a Roman lieutenant who fought under Julius Agricola, and who gave his name to certain lands near Whithorn, which in much later times were erected into a barony, and returned to the family its generic appellation, when surnames became common. The genealogy in question associates the heads of the family with many great national events in connection with the Romans, Picts, Scots, Danes, Irish, Normans, &c., and may pass *quantum valeat.* It is sufficient to observe, that few families in Britain can claim a more respectable origin than the Coultharts of Coulthart and Collyn, as attested by documentary evidence. There can be no doubt of the name having originated from the place, as it is written, in the XIII. and XIV. centuries, with the territorial prefix DE. The name of the Scottish locality is probably synonymous with that of Coudhard, a village in the department of Orne, a few miles N.E. of Argentan in Normandy. It is deserving of mention, that the head of this family (in whom now centres the blood of Coulthart " of that Ilk," Ross of Renfrew, Macknyghte, Glendonyn of Glendonyn, Carmichael of Carspherne, Forbes of Pitscottie, Mackenzie of Craighall, and Gordon of Sorbie) has immemorially borne supporters to his coat-armour, allusive to the name, and perhaps this may be considered a unique instance of *canting supporters.* A COLT and a HART uphold the ancestral escocheon, and I am enabled to give an engraving of a seal appended to a charter of Sir Roger de Coulthart, dated 1443. The surrounding legend is " Sigillum Coultharti."

COULTON. A parish in co. Lancaster.

COUMBE. See Combe.

COUNCILMAN. The office.

COUND. A parish in Salop.

☞ COUNTIES, NAMES OF, WHICH HAVE ORIGINATED SURNAMES. — Berkshire and Barkshire; Cheshire and Chesshyre; Cornwall with Cornish; Cumberland; Derbyshire and Darbishire; Devonshire and Devon, with Devenish; Dorsett and Dorset; Durham; Essex; Hampshire; Kent with Kentish: Lancashire and Lankshear; Rutland; Somerset; Suffolk; Surrey; Sussex; Westmoreland; Wiltshire, Willshire, and Willsher.

These surnames must have been originally given, for the most part, to persons emigrating from one county to another. Thus a person from Derbyshire settling in Sussex, would naturally get from his rustic neighbours the appellation of " the Darbishire man," and at length by the dropping of unnecessary words, he would be called simply " Darbishire," and that in course of time would become his acknowledged surname. Analogous to this is the origin of such names as French, Scott, Welsh, Fleming, bestowed on foreigners who had settled in England. In some cases, however, these names

have a much more dignified origin. See for example, Cornwall, and Essex.

In Wales and Ireland names thus formed will hardly be looked for, and in Scotland those which appear to be of the same class have probably other origins.

COUPAR. COUPER. Parishes in Fifeshire and Perthshire. Sometimes a corruption of Cooper.

COUPER. See Cowper and Coupar.

COURAGE. 1. Perhaps from Currage, a manor in the parish of Cheveley, co. Bucks. 2. A family of this name settled here after the Rev. of the Edict of Nantes.

COURCELLE. A place near Bernay— another near Andeli in Normandy.

COURCY DE. According to De Gerville this Norman family did not originate from the parish of Courcy near Coutances, but came from the arrondissement of Falaise, Calvados. Mem. Soc. Antiq. Normandie, 1825. Richard de Curci was a Domesd. tenant in chief in co. Oxford. The latinization in charters is De Curceo.

COURT. From residence at a court or manor-house. At-Court, A'Court, Court. A branch of the great Sussex family of Covert corrupted their name to Couert and Court. Inf. W. D. Cooper, Esq., F.S.A.

COURTENAY. COURTNEY. Though the pedigree of this family is carried up to Pharamond, the founder of the French monarchy in the year 420, Gibbon only traces the residence of the race at Courtenay, in the Isle of France, to the year 1020. Indeed it would be useless to attempt to carry the origin of the surname beyond that point, notwithstanding the extremely curious and ingenious suggestion which follows: In the history of France we find, that "Charlemagne avait donné l'Aquitaine, avec le titre de roi, à son fils Louis, sous la tutelle de Guillaume au *Court-Nez,* duc de Toulouse." Now who knows but the great French family of the Courtenays, and the illustrious Courtenays of Devonshire, may owe their name to this deficiency of nose in William of Toulouse? Though he does not pretend to get at the root, Gibbon only traces the family to 1020, when they were established at Courtenay; but the sobriquet was given about the year 790, and might have conferred a name upon the castle which William inhabited, and the country round it." N. & Q. vi. 106.

COURTHOPE. First occurs in a Subsidy Roll at Wadhurst, co. Sussex, in exactly its present form, temp. Edw. I. Philipot, Somerset-herald, derives it from the hamlet of Court-at-Street, co. Kent, which is improbable, and the real source of the name appears to be the lands of Curthope, in Lamberhurst, in that co., which Theobald, archbishop of Canterbury, in the XII. cent. gave to the abbey of Leeds. Hasted, v. 308.

COURTIER. Fr. A ship-broker ; probably a recent importation from France.

COUSENS. COUSINS. From the Fr. *cousin*, consanguineous, kinsman, relation by blood. Cosin, Cosyn. H.R.

COUZENS. COZENS. See Cousens.

COVE. Places in cos. Hants, Suffolk, &c.

COVENTRY. The city in co. Warwick.

COVER. 1. A place where game is preserved. 2. *Couver*, a domestic connected with a court kitchen. Halliw.

COVERDALE. Perhaps from Cuerdale, a township in Lancashire.

COVERT. "Coverts," says Nelson, "are those woods which are thickets, and full of trees touching one another .... a covering or hiding-place for deer." Laws of Game. The great Surrey and Sussex family of Covert, whose contiguous manors are said to have extended from Southwark to the English Channel, traced their pedigree to temp. Henry II.

COVINGTON. COVENTON. A parish in co. Huntingdon.

COW. Apparently local. There is a place called Cow-Honeybourne in Gloucestershire, and a John de Cowe occurs in the H.R., co. Bedford. It may however be a sobriquet, for both De Cu and Le Cu are found in the same records, and *cu* is an ancient orthography of cow.

COWAN. Probably a corruption of Colban, an ancient Celtic name, since Colbanstoun in the S. of Scotl. was corrupted to Cowanstoun.

COWARD. Although the popular derivation of this opprobrious word from "cow-herd" (whose occupation would be regarded with some disdain by the chivalrous in the middle ages) is untenable, I think it quite probable that the *surname* may be from that source, like Shepherd, Hayward, and other similar names.

COWBRAIN. A known corruption of Colbran !

COWCHER. See under Couchman.

COWDRAY. COWDERY. COWDEROY. The map of Normandy exhibits many localities called ' Le Coudray,' meaning a wood or grove of hazels. There is also an estate called Cowdray, near Midhurst, co. Sussex. De Coudray. H.R.

COWELL. Possibly from Cowal, a considerable district of Argyleshire.

COWHORN. R.G. 16. The H.R. have the similar name, Corndeboef (*corn-de-bœuf*) and Corns and Cornu still exist as surnames. Perhaps applied originally to one who blew a cow's horn. See Bugler.

COWHUS. (*Cowhouse.*) Occurs in the H.R. It may perhaps be a translation of the French *Bouverie*.

COWIE. A village in co. Kincardine.

COWL. Probably of similar origin with Quaife, which see.

COWLEY. Parishes, &c. in cos. Gloucester, Middlesex, Oxford, and Salop.

COWLING. Places in Suffolk, Kent, and Yorkshire.

COWLSTOCK. Probably Calstock, co. Cornwall. See however Eng. Surn. i. 203.

COWNDON. Coundon, places in Durham and Warwick.

COWNE. Probably Cound, a parish in co. Salop.

COWPER. The old spelling of Cooper. The pronunciation of the poet's name, an unnecessarily vexed question, is settled by this identity. Both the earl and the poet sprang from a Sussex family, who in 1495 wrote themselves Cooper.

COWSTICK. COSTICK. See Cowlstock.

COWTON. A parish and two townships in Yorkshire.

COX. COXE. See Eng. Surn. under Cock, i. 165. Probably a synonym of Little. It may, however, be the same as Cook, from its latinized form, thus : Cocus, Cocks, Cox.

COXELL. Either Coxall, co. Hereford, or Coxwell, co. Berks.

COXON. Coxswain ?

COY. M'Coy, sans Mac.

COYFE. See Quaife, which in Kent and Sussex was so spelt until within the last century.

COYNE. See Coyney.

COYNEY. The manor of Weston-Coyney, in the parish of Caverswall, co. Stafford, seems to have been in possession of the family from temp. Hen. III. B.L.G. The family probably came from Coigni, near Coutances, in Normandy.

CRABBE. Probably a sobriquet allusive to the awkward gait of the bearer. It occurs in H.R. in the same orthography and without prefix.

CRABTREE. Probably belongs to the same category as Appletree, which see.

CRACE. Fr. *gras*, from Lat. *crassus*, O. Eng. *crasse*. Fat.

CRACKANTHORPE. See Crakenthorpe.

CRACROFT. The family were lords of the manor of Cracroft, co. Lincoln, in 1284, B.L.G.

CRADDOCK. See Cradock.

CRADOCK. Welsh, Cradoc, latinized Caractacus—illustrious in British history from the patriotic opposition of the Silurian leader, Caractacus, to the forces of the Roman emperor Claudius.

AS CUNNING AS A CRAFTY CRADOCK.

This proverb in Ray's collection is supposed to apply to an astute, and not over conscientious, ecclesiastic, John Cradock, of

L

Durham, at the end of the sixteenth century.

CRAFFORD. See Crawford.

☞ **CRAFT.** A corruption of Croft, as in Horscraft, Calcraft, &c. See Croft.

CRAFT. A northern pronunciation of Croft.

CRAFTER. The occupant of a craft (croft), or small piece of land. Jamieson.

CRAGG. CRAGGS. See Craig.

CRAGGY. Probably Craigie.

CRAIG. A parish in Forfarshire, and an estate in Perthshire. As a topographical expression, *Craig* has the same meaning as Carrick, which see.

CRAIGHEAD. A place in the parish of Dailly, co. Ayr.

CRAIGIE. Parishes in cos. Ayr, Perth, and Linlithgow.

CRAIGMYLE. Probably Craigmill, a village in the Clackmannan division of the parish of Logie.

CRAKE. CRAIKE. A parish in co. York.

CRAKENTHORPE. A manor in co. Westmoreland, which had owners of its own name in XII. cent.

CRALLAN. Perhaps from Crollon, a village in the department of La Manche, in Normandy. It is sometimes written Crellin.

CRAMBROOK. Cranbrook, co. Kent.

CRAMER. Germ. *krämer*, a mercer or general dealer in a small way of business. *Creamer* is, according to Halliwell, a provincial name for "one who has a stall in a market or fair," which is evidently of the same origin. Again, to *crame* means in the North to join or mend, and a tinker is called a *cramer*. Halliwell.

CRAMOND. A parish in the shires of Linlithgow and Edinburgh.

CRAMP. Possibly from Crambe, a parish in Yorkshire.

☞ **CRAN.** The first syllable of several local surnames, signifying crane. This was formerly a common bird in England, and its designation was borrowed by numerous localities. Among surnames we have—Craney (the isle of cranes), Cranfield, Cranston, Cranmer (crane's lake), Cranswick, Cranwell, &c.

CRANBERRY. Doubtless local—Cranbury.

CRANE. The bird—probably first applied to a tall, meagre person. Cran, Crane. H.R.

CRANFIELD. CRANEFIELD. A parish in Bedfordshire.

CRANK. Brisk, jolly, merry. Halliwell.

CRANLEY. A parish in Surrey.

CRANMER. Anciently Crane-mere—the hill side of a low swampy country at Long Melford, co. Suffolk.

CRANSTON. A parish in Edinburghshire, sometimes written Cranstoun.

CRANSTOUN. See Cranston. The Cranstouns were old borderers ,and their motto, "Thou shalt want ere I want," probably refers to any Englishman in general. This charitable sentiment has its parallel in the *grace* after meat of an old lady in Sussex: "Thank God, I've had a good dinner, and I don't care who ha'n't !"

CRANWELL. A parish in Lincolnshire.

CRASHAW. CRAWSHAW. CRAWSHAY. Local—'the shaw or coppice frequented by crows.'

CRASKE. O. Fr. *cras*. Fat. Prompt. Parv.

CRA'STER. The manor of Cra'ster, *olim* Crawcestre, near Alnwick, was held by the family temp. Henry I., and still belongs to Cra'ster of Cra'ster Tower. B.L.G.

CRASWELLER. See Crosweller.

CRAUFUIRD. CRAUFURD. See Crawford.

CRAVEN. In the days of chivalry this word meant a coward—one who 'craved' mercy from an antagonist, and it was also applied to a fighting-cock that failed in combat.

"No cock of mine, you crow too like a *craven*."
Taming of the Shrew.

But the surname is probably derived from Craven, a district of Yorkshire.

☞ **CRAW.** The Anglo-Saxon word *craw* or *crawe* signifies, not only crow, but also the jackdaw, chough, and other congeners of that bird. Several localities bear names commencing with this syllable, and surnames have been borrowed from them, as Crawford, Crawley, Crawshaw, Crawthorne, Crawcombe, &c. In H.R. we have a John Crawenest, i.e. Crow's-nest.

CRAWCOUR. This name, which is found in the London Directory, is apparently a corruption of the baronial Crevecœur.

CRAWFORD. A parish of Lanarkshire, and several other places in North Britain. Sir Reginald de Craufurd, sheriff of Ayrshire in 1296, seems to have been the common ancestor of many branches of the family. The name was anciently written Craufuird.

Tradition says that the first bearer of this name was one Mackornock, who signalized himself at an engagement by "the water of Cree in Galloway, by discovering of a Foord, which gave a signal advantage to his party." Hence he got the name of Cree-Foord or Craufurd!! See Crawfurd's Description of Renfrewshire.

CRAWLEY. Parishes, &c., in Northumb., Oxon, Hants, Sussex, and Bedford.

CRAY. A mutilation of Macray.

CRAZE. Halliwell has "Crayze, a wild fellow." Conf. Craze in Jamieson.

CREAGH. This ancient Irish family claim descent from the famous Niall of the Nine Hostages, and they bore his name until, in a campaign against the Danes, the head of this section having come off victorious, the citizens of Limerick placed green boughs in the headstalls of their deliverer's horses, and the chief himself received the complimentary title of O'Niall *na Creavh*, or "O'Niall of the Green Branch." The crest of the Creaghs of Ballyandrew, co. Cork, is a horse's head with a laurel branch in the headstall of the bridle. B.L.G.

CREAKE. Two parishes in Norfolk.

CREAM. A merchant's booth; a stall in a market. Teut. *kraem*, taberna rerum venalium. Jamieson.

CREAMER. See Cramer. In Scotland a pedlar, or one who keeps a booth.

CREAN. Formerly O'Crean, a very ancient family in Sligo.

CREASE. (A Lancashire word.) Loving, fond.

CREASEY. See Creasy.

CREASY. Doubtless from Crecy in Picardy, so memorable in English history for the battle between Edw. III. and the French. The family are said to have come hither at the Conquest. Cressy appears in Holinshed's list. The name has undergone many changes in orthography. Among the tenants of the manor of Robertsbridge, temp. Eliz. was an Edward Crescye, and Crescye was at that period the mode of spelling the French town.

CREATON. Two places in co. Northampton.

CREE. Probably from McCrie or Macrae.

CREED. A parish in Cornwall.

CREEDY. A river in Devonshire.

CREELMAN. One who carries a wicker basket, called in the North a *creel*.

CREGOE. An estate in the parish of Tregony, co. Cornwall.

CREIGHTON. See Crichton.

CRESEY. See Creasy.

CRESPIN. See Crispin.

CRESSET. A fire-cage borne on a lofty pole by way of beacon or guiding light. See one figured and described in Eng. Surn. i. 203, 204. The soldier or watchman who carried such a light might in the XIII. or XIV. cent. naturally acquire the surname.

CRESSWELL. CRESWELL. A township and estate in Northumberland, possessed by the family temp. Rich. I., and still belonging to them.

CRESSY. See Creasy.

CREVEQUER. Hamo, the head of this celebrated race, came into England with the Conqueror, from Crevecœur, his estate in the arrondissement of Lisieux. The name was latinized 'de Crepito Corde,' that is, says Lambarde, Peramb. of Kent, 'Crackt-Heart.' By others it is interpreted "of the trembling heart." Hamo, who was sheriff of Kent for life, was otherwise called Sheriff, alias Dapifer. Hasted.

CREWE. The ancestors of Lord C. were lords of Crewe, co. Chester, 13 Edward I.

CREWES. See Crewys.

CREWYS. A West of England family, so ancient that an old distich asserts that—

"Croker, Crewys, and Coplestone,
When the Conqueror came were at home."

CREYKE. Probably from Craike in the N. Riding of Yorkshire. De Creyke occurs in that co. in the XIV. cent.

CRICHTON. An ancient castle and estate in Edinburghshire, well known in history, and long the seat of the family.

"Crichton! though now thy miry court
But pens the lazy steer and sheep;
Thy turrets rude and tottered keep
Have been the minstrel's loved resort."
Marmion.

Here also was born the "Admirable Crichton."

CRICK. Places in cos. Northampt. and Monmouth. Camden derives the surname from the Welsh "krick, that is curl-pate."

CRICKETT. CRICKITT. Cricket, two parishes in co. Somerset.

CRIMP. A dealer in coals. Norfolk. Halliw.

CRIOL. A great Norman family, (in Domesd. Cruel,) who appear to have come from Criel near Dieppe.

CRIPPS. The same as Crisp. Such transposition of consonants is not uncommon.

CRISP. The curt or abbreviated form of Crispin.

CRISPIN. Grimaldus I., prince of Monaco, married Crispina, daughter of Rollo, duke of Normandy, and had, besides other children, Crispinus, baron of Bec, who flourished about the year 1000. The next in succession assumed the paternal name by way of surname, and was called Gilbert Crispin, baron of Bec. He had three sons William, Gilbert, and Milo. William and Gilbert fought at the battle of Hastings, and Milo, whether present or not on that memorable field, received a large share in the spoil, namely the honour of Wallingford and eighty-eight lordships. See Gent. Mag., Jan. 1832.

CROAK. The same as Croke. Ferguson says O. Norse, *krokr*, bent or crooked.

CROCKER. 1. A maker of earthen jars, provincially called *crocks*. Le Crockere. H.R. 2. A corruption of Croker.

CROCKFORD. Possibly Crocketford, a village in co. Kirkcudbright.

CROFT. Places in cos. Leicester, Lincoln, York, Durham, and Hereford. Croft castle, in the first-named county, was the seat of an ancient family to which it gave name.

☞ CROFT. "Croft is a little close or pightle adjoining to an house, either used for pasture or arable, as the owner pleases; and it seems to be derived from the old word *creaft*, that is handicraft, because the lands are for the most part manured with the best skill of the owner." Termes de la Ley. The word is, however, pure A-Sax., and is defined by Bosworth as a small enclosed field. This is a very common termination for surnames; as Cockcroft, a poultry yard; Haycroft, a rickyard; Ashcroft, a close where ash-trees grow; Horsecroft, a yard for horses, Allcroft (for Hallcroft) an enclosure by the hall, &c.

CROFTON. Places in cos. Salop, Kent, York, and Lancaster. The noble family descend from the Croftons of C. in the last-named county.

CROFTS. Probably a pluralization of Croft.

CROKE. Apparently the same as Crooke, which see. Leswin Croc, however, occurs in Domesd. as a tenant prior to the Survey, in cos. Suffolk and Essex.

CROKER. The Crokers of Lineham are said to be of Saxon origin and to have been settled in Devon before the Conquest, on the authority of an ancient alliterative rhyme:—

"Croker, Crewys, and Coplestone
When the Conqueror came were at home."

CROLY. See Crowley.

CROMARTIE. A town and parish in the shire of the same name in Scotland.

CROMMELIN. Samuel C., of a respectable family at Armancour in Picardy, on the Rev. of the Edict of Nantes took refuge in Holland. His sons settled at Lisburn, in co. Antrim, as linen manufacturers under the auspices of William III. B.L.G.

CROMPTON. A township in Lancashire.

CROMWELL. The family of the Protector were of Welsh origin, and bore the name of Williams. Though of ancient descent they abandoned that surname at the instigation of King Henry VIII., and Sir Richard Williams, the Protector's lineal ancestor, being sister's son to Thomas C., the noted vicar-general, adopted his uncle's family name. That person was of humble origin, and there is no proof of any connection with the Lords Cromwell of Tateshall castle, co. Lincoln, whose pedigree goes back to the days of King John. Cromwell, the place from which the name is derived, is a parish in Nottinghamshire.

CROOK. CROOKE. CROOKES. Places in Westmoreland, Durham, and Moray, are called Crook, but the name is probably identical with Croke.

CROOM. 1. A parish in Yorkshire. 2. Gael. A circle of stones.

CROSBIE. See Crosby.

CROSBY. Parishes, &c. in cos. Ayr, Cumberland, Lincoln, York, Westmoreland, and Lancaster, and an ancient chapelry in Ayrshire.

CROSCOMBE. A parish in co. Somerset.

CROSHAW. See Crashaw.

CROSIER. A crosier is a bishop's staff, fashioned like a shepherd's crook, symbolical of his spiritual pastorate—but this is an unlikely origin for the name, which is more probably derived from the old Fr. *croiseur*, one who stamps or marks anything with a cross, or perhaps from *croisé*, one who has designated himself with the Christian symbol—a Crusader.

CROSS. This name is sufficiently explained under the article Crouch.

CROSSE. "The family of De la Croyz, De Cruce, Del Crosse, Crosse, as the name is variously spelt in ancient deeds, were seated at Wigan, co. Lancaster, in the reign of Edw. I., and about the year 1350 were seated at Crosse Hall in Liverpool, and afterwards at Crosse Hall in Chorley." B.L.G.

CROSSFIELD. A place at Uist in the Hebrides.

CROSSKEY. Doubtless an ancient trader's sign—"the Crossed-keys," perhaps originally borrowed from the arms of some bishopric. The Catholic dogma of the "power of the keys" led to the frequent adoption of this symbol, as seen in the arms of the sees of York, Peterborough, St. Asaph, Gloucester, Exeter, Ripon, Cashell, Ferns, Dromore, Down and Connor, Limerick, &c.

CROSSLAND. A township in Yorkshire.

CROSSLEY. The Crossleys of Scaitcliffe, co. Lancaster, anciently Del Croslegh, are of unknown antiquity. B.L.G. I find no locality so called.

CROSSMAN. Probably from residence near a cross. See Cross and Crouch.

CROSSWELL. CROSSWELLER. In the middle ages, when many wells were deemed sacred, crosses were often erected near them, to denote their sanctity. A resident near such a spot would readily acquire the surname of Atte Cross-well, which would afterwards modify itself to Crossweller. See Eng. Surn. i. 90.

CROSTHWAITE. A parish in co. Cumberland, and a chapelry in co. Westmoreland.

CROSWELLER. See under Crosswell.

CROTON. Crowton, a parish in Cheshire.

CROUCH. O. Eng. from Lat. *crux*—a cross. The word was applied in general to such crosses as stood at the intersection of two roads. These crosses were frequently dedicated to some saint and served also as direction posts—and although they have long disappeared, they have left the name of 'cross' and 'crouch' upon many localities, especially in the South of England. In Sussex, where the name is one of the oldest indigenous designations (especially in the Cinque Ports) it is found in the forms of Crouch and De Cruce, 20 Edw. I. Cooper's Winchelsea. In the H.R. it is written Ad Crucem, and elsewhere At Crouch. Croucher and Crouchman are also derived from the same source.

CROUCHER. See Crouch.

CROUCHMAN. See Crouch. Croche-man. H.R.

CROUGHTON. A parish in Northampt. and a township in Cheshire.

☞ CROW. This initial syllable of several local names is borrowed from the bird. See CRAW. Among other surnames from this source are Crowhurst, Crowley, Cromer, Croham, Crowshaw, and perhaps Crowfoot.

CROW. CROWE. From the bird, like Raven, Rook, &c. We find it written Craw in the H.R., where also we meet with Crawenest or Crow's-nest.

CROWDER. A player on the *crowd*, an ancient species of violin with six strings. (Irish *cruit*, Welsh *crwth*). In the West of England a small fiddle is still called a "crowdy-kit." It appears to have been a favourite instrument in Britain so early as the VI. cent. In Wickliffe's translation of the Bible, in Judges xi. 34, Jephthah's daughter is described as coming to meet her father "with tympans and *croudis*," i. e. with drums and fiddles. Way's Prompt. Parv.

CROWDON. Croydon, co. Cambridge, was formerly so written.

CROWER. In the H.R. *Le Crower*. Among the religious puerilities of the middle ages was the office of "King's Cock-crower." I have seen in some old wardrobe accounts of (I think) the time of Edward I. entries for the payment of a person for crowing like a cock at the door of the king's bedchamber at Easter. Hence probably the surname.

This absurd custom, which was intended to typify Peter's fall and repentance, was continued at our court even at the commencement of the last century. A rather laughable occurrence led to its discontinuance. It had been the practice during Lent for an official designated the *king's cock-crower* to usurp the office of watchman and to *crow*, instead of crying, the hour of the night. "On the first Ash-Wednesday after the accession of the House of Hanover, as the Prince of Wales, afterwards George II., sat down to supper, this officer abruptly entered the apartment, and according to established usage proclaimed, in a sound resembling the shrill pipe of a cock, that it was 'past ten o'clock.' Taken by surprise and imperfectly acquainted with the English language, the astonished prince naturally mistook the tremulation of the assumed crow as some mockery intended to insult him : nor was it without difficulty that the interpreter explained the nature of the custom, and satisfied him that a compliment was designed, according to the court etiquette of the time. From that period we find no further account of this important officer." Brady's Clavis Calendaria.

CROWFOOT. This name may be local. See Crow, and the termination FOOT; but it is more probably derived from some peculiarity of gait on the part of the original bearer. 'To strut like a crow in a gutter,' is a proverbial phrase.

CROWHURST. Parishes in Sussex and Surrey, the former of which had land-owners of its own name temp. Edw. I. Crowherst. H.R.

CROWLEY. A township in co. Chester.

CROWN. A popular inn sign.

CROWTHER. See Crowder.

CROXTON. Parishes and places in cos. Cambridge, Lincoln, Chester, Norfolk, Leicester, Stafford, &c.

CROYDEN. Probably the same as Croydon.

CROYDON. Parishes in Surrey and Cambridge.

CROZIER. See Crosier.

CRUCEFIX. Possibly a religious sign.

CRUDEN. A parish in Aberdeenshire.

CRUIKSHANK. Scotch. "Crooked legs"—a sobriquet.

CRUISE. See Crewys.

CRUM. See Croom.

CRUMP. Belgic *crom*, uncus. Crooked, in relation to personal deformity. "Crumpt or crookt." Nomenclator, p. 44. Halliwell.

CRUNDEL. There is a parish called Crundal, in Kent, and another called Crondall, in Hampshire; but from the occurrence of '*Ate Crundle*' in the H.R. some of the families bearing the name probably derive it from the A-Sax. *crundel* or *crundryll*, a designation frequently occurring in charters. "I find," says Dr. Leo, "no explanation of the word *crund* in any of the Gothic dialects, except in the Old High German. According to the regular transposition of the Anglo-Saxon consonants in words derived from that dialect, the primitive word should be *chrunt* or *chrunti*, and this word is found in the Gloss. Junii, where it is explained by the middle Latin word *cerula*, or, as it is also written, *coerola*, i.e. *arca*, *arcula*, *pyxis*. A Crundel or Crundwell is therefore a spring or well, with its cistern, trough, or reservoir, to receive the water, such as are still found in the banks by the side of great roads, sometimes furnished with an iron ladle secured by a chain." Leo's Local Nomenclature of the A-Saxons, translated by Williams, p. 95.

CRUNDEN. A contraction of Cruttenden.

CRUSE. See Crews.

CRUTCH. A district in Halfshire, co. Worcester.

CRUTCHER. The same as Croucher.

CRUTTENDEN, vulgo CRITTEN-DEN. A place in West Kent. In 1481 the name was written Crotynden.

CRUTTWELL. Probably Crudwell, co. Wilts.

CRUX. A latinization of Cross.

CRYER. The officer in corporate towns, &c., who makes public announcements.

CRYTON. See Crichton.

CUBISON. See Cubitt.

CUBITT. I cannot explain this some-what common and well-known surname, unless it be a diminutive or corruption of a personal name, which seems to be supported by the existence of the patronymical Cubison. Jamieson has "Cube, Cubie, probably the abbreviation of Cuthbert." If this con-jecture be correct, Cubitt and Cuthbert are most likely identical.

CUBLEY. A parish in Derbyshire.

CUCKNEY. A parish in co. Notts.

CUCKOLD. According to Camden, a corruption of the local name Cockswold.

CUCKOO. The bird. In the XIV. cent. it was written Le Cucko, Cuckuk, Cucku, &c.

CUDDIE. A Scottish nurse-name for Cuthbert.

CUDWORTH. A parish in Somerset, and a township in Yorkshire.

CUERTON. Cuerden, a township in Lancashire.

CUILLEAN, whence O'CUILLEAN. This name, which is often corrupted to Cullen, and anglicized to Collins, signifies catullus, whelp. Ulster Journ. of Archæo-logy, No. 2. The tribe or clan of Cullen took their name from Cuilean, an Irish chief of the VIII. cent. O'Donovan.

☞ CUL. For several names with this syllable, see COL.

CULCHETH. A township in Lancashire possessed by the family at an early date.

CULHAM. A parish in Oxfordshire.

CULL. Silly, simple. North. Halliw.

CULLEN. 1. Irish. See Cuillean. 2. An old spelling of Cologne.

CULLIFORD. A hundred in co. Dorset.

CULLING. See Cullen.

CULLOCH. Macculloch, sans Mac.

CULPECK. Probably Kilpeck, co. Here-ford.

CULVER. A pigeon. See Dove.

Among the marvels of the East, Sir J. Maundeville mentions that people besieged in a town, so as to be cut off from succour "maken letters, and bynden hem to the nekke of a colver, and letten the colver flee." p. 118. A-Sax. culfre.

CULVERHOUSE. A dove-cot. See Culver.

CUMBER. 1. The same as Comber. 2. "One of the A-Sax. words for an ensign or standard was cumbor, whence probably Cumbra, the name of an A-Sax. chief, A.D. 756. (Roger of Wendover). One having or bearing a standard. Ferguson.

CUMBERLAND. The county.

CUMIN. See Cumming.

CUMING. CUMINGS. See Cum-ming.

CUMMIN. CUMMINS. See Cum-ming.

CUMMING. This ancient family claim descent from the great house of Comines in France. They seem to have come into Britain at the Conquest, though they do not appear eo nomine in Domesd. Holinshed's list shows the name of Comin, and Leland's that of Comyn. According to the Scotch genealogists, Robert Cumine was earl of Northumberland by gift of the Conqueror, and acted vigorously against the Saxon insurgents. His descendant, William C. was lord-chancellor of Scotland temp. king David I., who ascended the throne in 1124, and he laid the foundation of what became one of the most influential and wealthy houses in Scotland. Courthope's Debrett. Other authorities claim for the family a Celtic original, chiefly, it would appear, on the strength of there having been an abbot of Icolmkill in the VI. cent. called Cum-mine, and another in the VII. named Comineas Albus. Dixon.

CUMMINGS. See Cumming.

CUMNOR. A parish in co. Berks.

CUMPER. Supposed by Ferguson to be the same as Cumber.

CUNDALL. CUNDELL. A parish in Yorkshire.

CUNNIGAN. In Ireland often con-founded with Cunningham, though it is a distinct name.

CUNNING. Wise, skilful. In this sense the word is employed in the authorized ver-sion of the O. Test.

CUNNINGHAM. The northern district of Ayrshire, containing many parishes, whence the old earls of Glencairn. Conyng-ham and Cunynghame are varieties of this name.

CUNYNGHAME. See Cunningham.

CUPAR. Cupar-Angus, Cupar-Fife, Cupar Grange, &c., well-known places in Scotland.

CUPIL. H.R. Probably from the old French, Goupil, a fox, a surname still in use in the vicinity of Havre.

CUPPLEDITCH. The same as Cobble-dick.

CURETON. Perhaps Cuerden, co. Lancaster.

CURLEOPLE. Gilbert White, in his Natural History of Selborne, mentions two tribes of Gipseys, who in his time were in the habit of visiting that village. One was called Stanley, "but the other is distinguished by an appellation somewhat remarkable. As far as their harsh gibberish can be understood, they seem to say that the name of their clan is *Curleople*. Now the termination of this word is apparently Grecian: and as Mezeray and the gravest historians all agree that these vagrants did certainly migrate from Egypt or the East, two or three centuries ago, may not this family name, a little corrupted, be the very name they brought with them from the Levant?"

CURLL. CURL. Probably the same as the Scottish *carl*, which is connected with the Germ. *kerl*, fortis, corpore robusto praeditus. See Jamieson.

CURR. Doubtless a mis-spelling of Ker.

CURRANT. R.G. 16. Has probably some connection with the Lat. *curro*, and the Fr. *courant*.

CURRER. O. Eng. *currour*, from Lat. *curro* ; a runner, running footman, messenger, *courier*. Curur XIII. cent., Currer XIV. cent. Battel Abbey Deeds.

CURREY. CURRY. Three parishes in Somerset are called Curry. See, however, Currie and Corrie.

CURRIE. 1. The same as Corrie. 2. A parish near Edinburgh.

CURRYER. The occupation.

CURSON. See Curzon.

CURTEPIE. H.R. Apparently anglicised from the A-Norm. *Curtespée*, 'shortsword,' from the fashion of the original bearer's weapon. So that famous son of Fair Rosamond, William, Earl of Salisbury, bore the name of Longuespee, or Longsword.

CURTIS. CURTEIS. CURTOYS. Norm. Fr. *curteis, curtois*. Civil, courteous. See Eng. Surn. i. 143.

CURWEN. The Curwens of Workington claim descent from the famous Gospatric, earl of Northumberland. They "took that name by covenant from Culwen, a family of Galloway, the heir whereof they

had married." Camden. De Culwen was changed to Curwen temp. Henry VI. B.L.G.

CURZON. Geraldine de Curzon came into England with the Conqueror. His descendants were in Derbyshire temp. Hen. I., and Curzon, Lord Scarsdale, is 'of Scarsdale' in that county.

CUSACK. There are two distinct origins assigned to this name. On one side it is asserted that the family spring from an illustrious race, the Sieurs de Cusac of Guienne in the IX. cent.; and on the other that they are of ancient Irish extraction, from Isog, founder of the Clan Isog or Clan Cusack, and eleventh in descent from Olioll Olium, king of Munster in 234. B.L.G.

CUSDEN. CUSDIN. Cutsdean, a chapelry, co. Worcester.

CUSHION. Co. Limerick and elsewhere. A corruption of Mac Ossian. It is otherwise written Cushin and Cussen, and anglicised to Cousins, but pronounced Cuzzeen. Ulster Journ. of Archæol. No. 2.

CUSHIN. CUSHING. See Cushion.

CUSSEN. See Cushion.

CUTBEARD. See Cuthbert.

CUTBUSH. See Bush.

CUTCHEY. A supposed corruption of Culcheth.

CUTHBERT. An A-Sax. baptismal name, whence also Cuthbertson, the corruption Cutbeard, the diminutive Cutts, and perhaps Cuxon.

CUTHBERTSON. See Cuthbert.

CUTLER (in Scotland often CUTLAR). The trade, from *couteau*, Fr. a knife, *coutelier*, a knife-maker. In the H.R. we find it written Le Coteler and Le Cotiler.

CUTTER. A northern provincialism for engraver. Halliw.

CUTTLE. Cuthill or Cuttle is a suburb of Prestonpans, co. Haddington. In several surnames the final LE represents HILL in a shortened pronunciation. This remark may be of use to the reader, to whom I would say in the words of an illustrious possessor of this name—"When found make a Note of."

CUTTS. CUTS. Camden thinks this is a nickname of Cuthbert.

D.

DABB. DABBS. DABSON. Dab is, I think, a trivial or nurse-name of David.

DABNEY. A corruption of D'Aubigné.

DACE. Not so likely from the fish so called as from some continental locality named Ace or Aes with the prefix D'.

DACRE. Early genealogists pretend that this name was borrowed during the Crusades from Acre in Palestine, (quasi D'Acre). "The d'Acres took their name from Acres in the Holy Land, where one of their ancestors fought. Mr. Gale would derive the name from the Cohors Dacorum stationed here,"—viz. at Dacre, co Cumberland. Hutchinson's Cumb. i. 468. Whatever may have been the origin of the name of the place, there is no doubt that the family derive their surname from it, as we find them in possession temp. Edw. I., and from them at a subsequent period sprang the two noble houses of Lord Dacre of Gilsland, called Dacre of the North, and Lord Dacre of Herstmonceux, called Dacre of the South. The latter title came however through a female into the family of Fynes, from whom through other female lines it has descended to the present peer.

DADD. DADE. Probably an ancient personal name, since we find the derivative Dadson.

DADSWELL. Probably from Dowdeswell, a parish in Gloucestershire.

D'AETH. An old Kent family, said to have come originally from the town of Aeth in Flanders. The name has been corrupted to Death.

DAFFY. A diminutive of David.

DAGG. Ferguson thinks it may be derived from the Teut. dæg, day.

DAGGER. Probably from the implement, like Sword, Brownbill, &c.

DAILY. DAILLEY. Dailly, a parish in Ayrshire.

DAIN. DAINES. See Dane.

DAINTRY. Daventry, co. Northampton.

DAISY. Possibly from the ancient barony of Aisié (D'Aisié) in the arrondissement of Pont Audemer in Normandy—now written Aisier.

DAKIN. DAKEYNE. See David. The motto of this widely-spread family, STRYKE DAKEYNE, THE DEVIL'S IN THE HEMPE, is said to have originated from an incident in a sea-fight. It was used temp. Edw. VI., and probably much earlier.

D'ALBIAC. There are three towns in Languedoc bearing the name of Albiac. The family derive from Albiac del Conté in the department of Aveyron. They were early and devoted adherents to the reformed faith. At the massacre of St. Bartholomew (24 Aug., 1572,) four out of seven brothers of this name, who were then residing at Paris, fell beneath the knife of the assassin. The surviving three escaped into Languedoc, where their descendants remained in comparative security until after the Revocation of the Edict of Nantes in 1685, when some of the descendants, abandoning all considerations of fortune, kindred, and country, fled from a land where they could not exercise the religion of their adoption, and settled in England. These were James D'Albiac of Nismes. and his three sons, James, Simon, and Pierre, who left France in 1693. The last however embraced Roman Catholicism, returned to his native country, and regained a portion of the confiscated estates. The present representative of this ancient and noble family in England, is Her Grace the Duchess of Roxburghe, daughter of the late Lieut. Gen. Sir Charles D'Albiac, K.C.H., who was third in descent from James D'Albiac of Nismes.

DALBY. Parishes in cos. Lincoln, York, Leicester, &c.

☞ DALE. A termination of local surnames. It signifies, generally, a valley, and in the North more particularly a river valley, as Tyndal from the Tyne, Annandale, from the Annan, Tisdale from the Tees, Esdaile from the Esk, Redesdale from the Rede, &c.

DALE. A valley. The medieval form was At Dale, softened afterwards to A'Dale, as often found in parish registers of the XVI. cent., and widely renowned through the ballad of Robin Hood and Allin a'Dale. In the H.R. we find De Dale, and De la Dale.

DALGETY. A parish in co. Fife.

DALGLEISH. Local in Scotland?

DALISON. A supposed corruption of D'Alençon, from the town in Normandy, and said to have been introduced at the Conquest. Its older forms are Dalyson and Dallison.

DALLAS. A parish in co. Moray. The name is traced by Douglas to the year 1298, as De Dallas. Other ancient orthographies are De Doleys and Dollas.

DALLAWAY. Daliwey occurs without prefix, in H.R. co. Lincoln.

DALLING. A parish in Norfolk.

DALLINGTON. A parish in Sussex.

DALLISON. The extinct baronet's family are said to have descended from William d'Alanzon (Alençon) who came into England with the Conqueror. Burke's Ext. Baronetage. See Dalison.

DALLMAN. 1. Possibly Dale-man, an inhabitant of a valley. In Scotl. a "dale's-man." 2. The same as D'Almaine.

DALMAHOY. An estate in the shire of Edinburgh, whose owners of the same name were great barons in the XIII. cent.

D'ALMAINE. See Almaine.

DALMAN. See Dallman.

DALRY. A town and parish in Ayrshire.

DALRYMPLE. About the end of the thirteenth century the lands of Dalrumpill or Dalrumpyl in Ayrshire belonged to the ancestors of the Earl of Stair, who assumed their surname from them. Gaelic etymologists derive the name of the place from *Dal-chrom-puil*, "the meadow of, or by, the crooked pool." This renowned family, which has probably produced more eminent men than any other in Scotland, was not ennobled until the XVII. century, by the title of Viscount (afterwards Earl) of Stair.

DALSTON. Ranulph de Meschines, earl of Chester, temp. Will. Conq., gave Dalston in Cumberland to Robert, second brother of Hubert de Vaux, who derived his name from that manor, and founded the family.

DALTON. Parishes and places in cos. Lancaster, Northumberland, Durham, York, Dumfries, Lanark, &c. Dalton Hall, in the first named co., had owners of its own name temp. Edw. III. From them sprang the Daltons of Thurnham.

DALTREY. De Alta Ripa. See Hawtrey.

DALWAY The Irish family migrated from Devonshire in 1573, under Walter, earl of Essex, B.L.G.

DALYELL. The same as Dalzell and Dalziel, which see.

DALYNGRUGE. Sir Edward Dalyngruge, the builder of Bodiam Castle, co. Sussex, in the XIV. cent., was descended from a family who possessed Dalyngruge, a manor near East Grinstead, now called Dallingridge. The name was variously written Dalyngrigg, Dalegrigg, Dalyngregge, &c.

DALZIEL. DALZELL. Anciently written Dallyell, Daleel, Dalyiel, &c. From the barony of Dal-yeel (i.e. 'the beautiful meadow') on the river Clyde. The Earls of Carnwath are the chiefs of the family. The often-quoted romantic story which assigns another origin for the name (See Eng. Surn. ii. 8.) has neither history, etymology, nor common sense to support it.

DAMARELL. The family descended from Robert de Albemarle, a great tenant in chief under William the Conqueror in Devonshire. Stoke Damarell and Milton

M

Damarell have hence their suffixes. Lysons' Devon.

DAMER. This name, as well as Damory, is said to have been derived from the Norman fief of De la Mer, near the mouth of the Seine.

DAMES. 1. Perhaps the same as Ames with the local prefix D'. 2. Perhaps an old personal name. Dame without prefix is found in H.R.

DAMORY. Said to be synonymous with Damer.

DAMPIER. Dampierre, a place near Dieppe, and another in the department of Orne, both in Normandy.

DAMPRECOURT and DAMPRETICOURT occur in Norman times, but of their origin I am ignorant, except that they are French and *local*.

DAMSON. "Dame's son," but whether the son of Dame, apparently an old Christian name, or "filius dominæ," I know not.

DANBY, (i.e. the Dane's dwelling.) Parishes in Yorkshire.

DANCASTER. A corruption of Doncaster.

DANCE. Perhaps from A.-Sax. *Densc*, Danish.

DANCER. One skilled in the saltatory art. One Hervius le Dansur is found in the H.R.

DANCEY. 1. A corruption of Dantsey, or Dauntsey, a parish in Wiltshire. 2. Dancé, a place in the department of Orne, in Normandy.

DAND. DANDY. Familiarly used in Scotland for Andrew. Pitcairn's Trials, Index.

DANDELYON. Fr. *Dent de lion*, "lion's tooth;" probably from the formidable character of the first who bore it. So Cœur de Lion, Front de Bœuf, &c. This family, of Norman origin, were great proprietors in the Isle of Thanet, and became extinct about the beginning of Edw. IV. See Lewis's Isle of Tenet, 1723.

DANDO. 1. A corruption of D'Anlo. Ashton Dando, a tything in the parish of Ashton, was formerly called Ashton D'Anlo. Curios. of Bristol. 2. An O.-Germ. personal name. Several persons of this surname occur in H.R.

DANDY. See Dendy. One Dandi occurs in the H.R. of Lincolnshire as an under bailiff, but whether that was his surname or his Christian appellation does not appear.

DANE occurs singly in Domesd., in the counties of Notts and Lincoln, as a personal name, like Norman, Frank, &c.; and Danus as a distinctive epithet or surname is added to the personal names Osmund, Simond, Strang, and Turchil to indicate their Danish birth or extraction. But

Dane is also a topographical expression, the meaning of which is not clear. In the H.R. we find both Atte Dane, and De la Dane.

DANGER. D'Angers—from Angers, the capital of Anjou in France.

DANGERFIELD. See Dangerville.

D'ANGERVILLE. Five places in Normandy still bear the name of Angerville.

DANIEL. The baptismal name, very common as a surname, and the parent of Daniels, Dann, &c.

DANIELS. See Daniel.

DANN. See Daniel.

DANSAYS. French Protestant refugees who settled at Rye, co. Sussex, in 1685, immediately after the Revocation of the Edict of Nantes. Holloway's Rye, 582.

DANSEY. William Dauntesey held lands in Wiltshire temp. Henry III., and his son Richard D. held lands in that co. and in Hereford. Camden. See Dancey.

DANTZIGER. A native of Dantzig, the capital of West Prussia, according to the German mode of adding ER to denote residence in a town.

DANVERS. William Denvers, evidently one of the Conqueror's adherents, occurs in the Norfolk Domesd.; and genealogists assert that a Roland D'Anvers assisted at the Conquest. The name may be derived from the city of Antwerp, continentally written Anvers.

DAPIFER. Qui dapes fert. Qui cibos mensæ imponit. Literally, a bearer of dainties—a sewer; in old times a principal officer in the households of kings and magnates. This was borne as a second or official surname by several distinguished persons under the Norman kings, especially by the celebrated Eudo Dapifer of Domesd. He was fourth son of Hubert de Rie, and steward of the Conqueror's household. Kelham.

DARBEY. See Darby.

DARBISHIRE. See Counties.

DARBY. A corruption of Derby. So Darbishire from Derbyshire.

D'ARCY. DARCEY. Under William the Conqueror, Norman de Adreci, or Areci, was a tenant in chief in Lincolnshire, which was the principal seat of the family during many generations, whence the earl of Holderness. Collins' Peerage. The name was gradually corrupted to its present form. The name Audresset, apparently the same, still exists in the Norman town of Louviers.

DARELL. "William de Orrell, a gentleman of the north parts of Normandie, soe called of a castle and family of that countrie, (and soe by contraction the vowels E and O are changed to A, by which *Darell* is pronounced for De Orell,) the which

came in with the Conqueror, being for his good services done in the North. . . . endowed with the possessions of a Saxon called Etheldred of Broadsworth, an ancient seat twelve miles west of Yorke." Such is the statement attached to an old pedigree quoted in Burke's Commoners. The family were undoubtedly ancient at Sesay in Yorkshire, but there appears to be no documentary evidence for the above assertion; neither does any place in the north of Normandy bear the name of Orrell. The Norman origin of the family, is, however, probable.

DARKE or DARK. This name, which is not uncommon in the West of England, is probably identical with the De Arcis, of Domesday book. William d'Arques, or de Arcis, was lord of Folkestone, co. Kent, temp. William I., having settled in England after the Norman Conquest. His ancestors were *vicomtes* of Arques, now a bourg and castle, four or five miles from Dieppe in Normandy. Stapleton on the barony of William of Arques, in Canterbury Report of Brit. Archæological Association, p. 166.

DARKIN. A corruption of Dorking, a town in Surrey, still so pronounced by the uneducated of the locality.

DARKMAN. From complexion.

DARLEY. A parish and a township in co. Derby.

DARLING Ælfmar Dyrling, a noble youth, is mentioned in the Saxon Chronicle. Mr. Kemble says, "*dyrling* and *cild*, (darling and child) are terms used to denote the young nobles of a house, perhaps exclusively the eldest son, in whom all expectation rests." The difficulty is, to account for such designations having become hereditary surnames.

DARLINGTON. A town in co. Durham.

DARNALL. DARNELL. A chapelry in co. York.

DARNTON. The local pronunciation of Darlington.

DARRINGTON. A parish in Yorkshire.

DART. A river of Devonshire.

DARTMOUTH. A town in Devonshire.

DARTON. A parish in Yorkshire.

DARVELL. DARVILL. An estate near Battel, co. Sussex.

DARWIN. Deorwyn was an A-Sax. female name. Ferguson, p. 198.

DASENT. See Decent.

DASH. Possibly from De Ash, a local name.

DASHWOOD. I cannot find any locality so called, but the name may have been originally De Ashwood, then D'Ashwood, and finally Dashwood. This would answer to the old latinization, De Fraxineto, a twelfth century surname, with which it is doubtless identical.

DAUBENEY. The same as D'Albini. See Albini De.

D'AUBERNON. The Abernon of Domesday sprang from the fief in Normandy of that name, and was tenant in chief in co. Surrey, giving name to Stoke Daubernon.

DAUBUZ. The first immigrant of this family into England was the Rev. Charles Daubuz. " He was a native of Guienne, but at twelve years of age was driven from his native country, with his only surviving parent, Julia Daubuz, by the religious persecution of 1686.... He died in 1717." Hunter's Hallamshire, page 175.

DAUKES. Like Dawkes, a diminutive of David.

DAUNE. Probably from Fr. *aune*, an alder tree.

DAUNT. Said to be the same as the Dauntre of the so-called Battel Abbey Roll. B.L.G.

DAVENEY. The town and castle of Avené, near Louvaine in Flanders, were occupied by our King Edward I., and from that place the family probably migrated to England. In 1279 we find John and Hugh de Aveney resident at Lakenheath and Wongford, co. Suffolk. At a later period the name in different forms is found in the neighbouring counties of Norfolk and Cambridge. In the fifteenth century it underwent various corruptions, and was written Daubeney, Daubeny, Deweney, &c. Still later it got twisted out of all identity of form as Dybnye, Debney, Dibney, and even Obney. At length these different spellings came to distinguish different branches, until towards the middle of the last century, when the orthography prevalent in each was fixed and handed down, the knowledge of any former identity between such differing names having been lost, except to such genealogical enquirers as Mr. H. Daveney, of Norwich, who has courteously supplied these particulars. The Catton branch of the family appear to have preserved the old and correct orthography for more than three centuries back.

DAVENPORT. A township and estate in Cheshire, which gave name to a family remarkable for their fecundity, as witness the proverb, AS MANY DAVENPORTS AS DOGS' TAILS. They claim descent in an unbroken line from one Ormus de Davenport, who flourished in the time of the Conqueror.

DAVES. See David.

DAVEY. DAVIE. DAVY. Three forms of David, which see. The first is the English, the second the Scottish, and the third the more prevalent Welsh orthography.

DAVID. Though of ancient standing in Wales, this Christian name scarcely appears in England before the Conquest. Modified in various forms it has since produced many family names, some of which are among the commonest in use, as Davids, Davidson, Davidge—Davey, Davy, Davie—Davies, Davis, Daviss, Daves, Davison. From Daw, the nickname, come Dawe, Dawes, Daws, Dawson, Dawkes, Dawkins, Dawkinson, and from another form of the nickname, according to Camden, we get Day, Dayes, Dayson, and Dakin.

DAVIDGE. See David.

DAVIDS. DAVIDSON. See David.

DAVIES. See David. Owing to the commonness of the Welsh patronymical use of Davies, this name stands fifth in point of numerousness in England and Wales, yielding priority only to Smith, Jones, Williams, and Taylor. In the XVI. Ann. Rep. of the Registrar Gen., the number of Williamses registered within a given period was 21,936, Taylors 16,775, and Davises 14,983; but as Davis is to all intents and purposes identical with Davies, by adding in 6206 Davises, this name numbers 21,188 individuals, beating the Taylors out of the field, and well-nigh vanquishing the Williamses. In fact by taking in the Davisses and the Daveses, I believe the aggregate of the name would stand next after Smith and Jones for numerousness.

DAVIS. DAVISS. See Davies and David.

DAVISON. See David.

DAWBER. The medieval name of a plasterer. Le Daubere. H.R.

DAWE. DAWES. DAWS. See David. In some cases the derivation may be from the O.-Fr. *awe*, which Roquefort defines as a water, river, fountain, or pond; and this notion is supported by the former mode of writing the name—D'Awes, which makes it the equivalent of De Aquis.

DAWKES. DAWKINS. See David.

DAWNAY. The genealogists of Viscount Downe's family set out with a statement that " Sir Paine Dawnay, of Dawnay Castle in Normandy, came in with the Conqueror;" but this off-hand account requires a little examination. In the first place, I do not see the surname in Domesday, and secondly, though somewhat versed in the topography of Normandy, I cannot find ' Dawnay Castle' where the respectable knight had his residence. Yet substantial truth is probably conveyed in this sparkling sentence. Daunay is doubtless D'Aunai, and there are at least seven places called Aunai in Normandy; one of which, Aunai l'Abbaye, in the arrondissement of Vire, was an ancient barony, and from thence probably the family came. At all events the D'Aunays were eminent in Cornwall in the fourteenth century. As a

"Curiosity of Heraldry," I may note that the crest of the family is a Demi-Saracen, holding in one hand a lion's paw, and in the other a gold ring set with a sapphire. This cognizance originated, it is said, in manner following. Sir William D. was made a 'general' at Acre by King Cœur-de-Lion in 1192, for having killed, first a chief prince of the Saracens, and afterwards a mighty lion, whose paws he cut off and presented to Richard. The king, delighted with the 'general's' exploit, took a ring from his royal finger and presented it to him; and that sapphire ring is still in the possession of Lord Downe—tangible evidence of the truth of this circumstantial narration.

DAWSON. See David. The late earl of Portarlington averred that it ought to be D'Ossoune! Arthur says there is a town in Normandy called Ossone, but the Itin. Norm. does not give it.

DAY. 1. See David. 2. A tradition states that a follower of the Conqueror settled at Eye in Suffolk, and assumed therefrom the name of D'Eye or Deye.

DAYES. See David.

DAYLABOURER. From the occupation.

DAYMAN A known corruption of Dinan. B.L.G.

DAYRELL. This family who gave the suffix to Lillingston Dayrell, co. Bucks, which they have possessed from temp. Richard I., are of a common stock with the the Darells of Sesay, Calehill, &c. See Darell.

DAYSON. See David.

☞**DE.** A French preposition prefixed to a surname to show that the bearer is owner of a certain estate or territory, as Jourdain de Saqueville, William de Warren. This practice which originated in France, and which still continues to some extent in that country, was one of the many importations of the Norman Conquest. Such followers of William as had been noble before the Conquest, generally retained their ancestral denominations after they acquired their lands in England, but their younger sons and others applied the DE to those estates which had been awarded to them as their portion of the conquered country, and styled themselves De Hastings, De Winton, De Bodiam, &c. This prefix continued in use till the fifteenth century when it was gradually laid aside. During the present century a few instances of the resumption of the DE have occurred, with the sanction of the royal sign-manual. In France at the present day it is regarded as a distinctive mark of nobility, and though one not belonging to the "noblesse" should bear it by courtesy, it would not be conceded to him in any legal instrument. He would be disparagingly described as "Bernardin Sauville, com-

munement appellé Bernardin de Sauville," or the like. Many families have borrowed surnames from places of which they were never proprietors, but in medieval documents the DE is generally pretty good evidence that either the person himself or some ancestor owned the lands from which his name was derived.

The French DE must not be confounded with the Dutch DE, which is an article equivalent to our the and the French le. The latter occurs in a few family names naturalized here and in America.

DEACON. The ecclesiastical office. Walter the Deacon was at the compilation of Domesday a tenant in chief in the counties of Gloucester and Essex.

DEADLY. See Deadman.

DEADMAN. A known corruption of Debenham. In Sussex it is further corrupted to Deadly!

DEAKIN. The same as Dakin.

DEAL. The town in Kent. Sometimes a corruption of Dale.

DEALCHAMBER. A corruption of De la Chambre.

DEALTRY. See Hawtrey.

DEAN. DEANE. A-Sax. *denu*, a vale or plain. Atte Dene is the common form in old times, implying residence at such a place. There are, however, eighteen parishes or places called Dean in the Gazetteer of Engl., and Dene occurs in Domesd. as a personal appellation.

DEANS. A village district of Lanarkshire.

DEAR. 1. Appears to be synonymous with the Fr. family name Cher, the Latin Carus, &c. 2. Deor occurs in the Codex Exoniensis as a personal name. It is doubtless derived from the deer, so spelt in A-Sax.

DEARDEN. Evidently local, perhaps from a place so called near Edenfield in Bury, co. Lancaster. "The ancient and modern pronunciation of the name by the natives of Lancashire is Du-er-den," which Cowell, with fanciful ingenuity, interprets "a thicket of wood in a valley." See B.L.G. The Deardens of Rochdale Manor claim descent from Elias de Duerden, temp. Hen. VI., but so early as the thirteenth century the name of Durden, Durdent, or Duredent is variously applied to a certain knight who may have been a progenitor of the family.

DEARING. See Dering.

DEARLING. See Darling.

DEARLOVE. 1. Possibly local—from *deer*, the animal, and *low*, a hill. 2. The old Germanic personal name Deorlaf.

DEARMAN. 1. An A. Sax. personal name. In Domesday Dereman and Derman. 2. A keeper of deer.

DEARY. "There was a Diora, bishop of Rochester, whose name must have been an epithet of affection." Ferguson.

DEASE. "Of Milesian origin." B.L.G. But as the oldest individual of the family of Dees or Dease adduced, lived no longer since than the days of Henry VII., we must take this statement at its fair value.

DEATH. "Death" was a common character in the medieval mysteries or miracle plays: but this surname is probably derived from a local source. Aeth is a place in Flanders, and the family of Death or D'Aeth of Knowlton, baronets, are asserted to have come from that locality. See Burke's Ext. Baronetage.

DE BATHE. Hugo de Bathe is said to have accompanied Strongbow into Ireland in 1176. The surname was probably derived from the city of Bath.

DEBENHAM. DEBNAM. A town in Suffolk.

DE BLAQUIERE. John Blaquiere, Esq., settled in England after the Revocation of the Edict of Nantes, 1685, and his son, Sir John B., was created Baron de Blaquiere in the peerage of Ireland. The chief branch of the family had been long seated at Sorraye, in Limousin, and had ranked among the noblesse of France for more than five hundred years. Previously to the expatriation, the immediate ancestry of Mr. John B. resided at Loreze in Languedoc. Courthope's Debrett.

DEBONNAIRE. Fr. Meek, gentle, good-natured. Settled in England after the Rev. of the Edict. of Nantes ; descendants of John Debonnaire, of St. Quentin—now represented by Wm. Debonnaire Haggard, Esq., F.S.A. There was, however, a much earlier importation of the name into England, for I find in the H.R. the name of one Philip Debeneyre.

DE BURGH. The Marquis Clanricarde deduces his descent from Charles, 5th son of the Emperor Charlemagne, who was the common ancestor of the counts of Blois, the kings of Jerusalem, the great baronial De Burghs of England, the Burkes of Ireland, and a number of other ancient families. The surname is said to have been assumed by John, earl of Comyn, in the XI. cent.

DECENT. Probably from the becoming demeanour of the first owner of the surname. Dasent may be a corruption.

DECKER. Dutch, *dekker*, one who covers roofs with tile, slate, or thatch.

DE CRESPIGNY. "This family is originally of Normandy, where Maheus Champion was lord of Crespigny about 1350." Courthope's Debrett.

DEE. Well-known rivers in Cheshire and Aberdeenshire.

DEEBLE. Perhaps one of the numerous corruptions of Theobald.

DEEKER. Perhaps a corruption of Dacre.

DEER. DEERE. Sometimes, doubtless, from the animal, like Buck, Hart, Stagg, &c. ; but it is also a local name from two parishes, Old and New Deer, in Aberdeenshire.

DEGORY. See Digory.

DE HORNE. The ancestors of the De Hornes, of Stanway Hall, were exiled from Holland for their Protestantism temp. Elizabeth. Oliver De Horne, of Nieuw-Kirke, near Ipres, settled at Norwich temp. James I. B.L.G.

DEIGHTON. A parish and places in co. York.

☞ **DEL.** A Norm. Fr. prefix to many medieval surnames, signifying "of the" as Del Dykes, Del Claye, Del Ho, &c.

☞ **DE LA.** Fr. "of the." This prefix is found with many medieval surnames. It does not necessarily imply the French extraction of the bearer, for many of the names are purely English; e. g. De la Broke, De la Bury, De la Cumbe, De la Dale, De la Field, De la Forde, De la Fenne, De la Grene, De la Halle, De la Hoke, De laLane, De la Pleystowe, De la Stone, and very many others occurring in medieval records.

DE LA BECHE. (Probably Beke—see that name.) Nicholas De la Beche, of Aldworth, co. Bucks, was a baron by writ summoned to parliament 16. Edw. III., 1342.

DELACHAMBRE. See Chambre, de la.

DE LA CHEROIS. At the Rev. of the Edict of Nantes, 1685, three brothers of this ancient and noble French family fled into Holland, and were received into one of the Huguenot regiments raised by the Prince of Orange. They accompanied that personage to England at the Revolution, and eventually settled in Ireland. The family came originally from Cheroz or Cherois, in the province of Champagne. B.L.G.

DE LA CONDAMINE. This ancient and noble family, distinguished through many generations for their military and literary abilities, were long settled in Languedoc, and a branch were recently resident at Metz. The English branch derive from André de la Condamine, co-seigneur de Serves, born in 1665. This gentleman, who was the head of the family, professed the Protestant faith and took refuge from persecution in this country about the year 1714, with his lady, Jeanne Agerre, 'fille de noble Pierre Agerre de Fons,' and six of their children. The eldest son, Pierre, returned to his native country and to the ancient faith. Heavy misfortunes befel him ; he lost a portion of his property by the great earthquake of Lisbon, and the remainder by a fire at Paris. The De la Condamines of Guernsey and England are descended from Jean Jacques, the fourth son of André. About the period of the

Revolution of 1789, the family conceiving a horror of every thing French disused the *De la*, which however they have of late years resumed. The origin of this surname is very curious. The family were, as we have seen, co-seigneurs of Serves and as such the head of the house wrote himself *Condominus* (or "joint lord") which by a slight orthographical change became De la Condamine, and settled down into an hereditary surname. It is right however to add, that a junior branch have always maintained " que son nom venait de *Campus Domini*, le champ du maitre, ou le champ seigneurial, et dans l' ancien lanquedocien, on apellait du nom de Condamine, le champ ou l'enclos attenant au château du seigneur." (the field or enclosure belonging to the lord's castle.) Nobiliare Universel de France, Paris, 1819, vol. xvi. p. 447.

DE LA MER. See Damory.

DELAMOTTE. See Motte.

DELANY. The Irish patronymical O'Dulainé has been thus gallicised.

DELAP. A known corruption of Dunlop, which see.

DE LA POLE. See Pole.

DELARUE. Fr. "Of the street."

DELAUNE. Fr. *de l aune*, "Of the elder tree," congenerous with Oak, Ash, &c.

☞DE LE. This prefix is found with a few medieval surnames, as De le Berne, De le Hil, De le Clif. It is, of course, the equivalent of the modern Fr. *du*, "of the." See De la.

DELFOSSE. Fr. *De la Fosse.* "Of the Ditch." See Foss.

DE L'ISLE. See Lisle.

DELL. A little dale or valley. From residence in one.

DELLER. One who resided in a dell. See termination ER.

DELLOW. Fr. *De l'Eau.* The same as Waters.

DELMAR. Fr. *De la Mer.* "Of the Sea."

DELORME. Fr. *De l'Orme.* The same as Elms.

DELVE. DELVES. De Delve occurs in H.R. indicating the local origin of the name. I do not find the A-Sax. *delf*, *dælf*, means a digging, and the name may be cognate with Ditch, Foss, &c.

DEMON. This name is found in the 16th Report of the Registrar-General. I have not met with it elsewhere. It may, perhaps, have descended from medieval times, and from some one who played the devil in a miracle play. A more probable origin, however, is from the northern *dee*, day, and *mon*, man; day-man, a man who works by the day; or from the Fr. Du Mont.

DE MONTMORENCY. The family derive from Geoffrey of Montmorenci, a younger son of Hervé de Montmorenci, grand butler of France, whose elder son was ancestor of the great Dukes de Montmorency, of Luxembourg, of Beaumont, and Laval. Geoffrey's descendants had large possessions in England and Ireland, in which latter country they eventually settled. In the XV. century they assumed the name of Morres, but the ancient and distinguished patronymic was resumed by the third Viscount Montmorency, who succeeded to the title in 1756.

DEMPSTER. A judge; the officer of a court who pronounces doom. A-Sax. *deman*, to judge. Jamieson. The Isle of Man is divided into two districts, over each of which a *deemster* still presides. Before the Union, there was an officer in the Scottish senate called the Dempster of Parliament, probably corresponding with the English "Speaker." This office was hereditary in the ancient family of Dempster of Auchterless, and hence their surname. In the old M.S. poem called Cursor Mundi, quoted by Halliwell, we read:—

" Ayoth was thenne *demester*
Of Israel foure-score yeer."

☞DEN. A local termination, frequently occurring in the Weald of Kent and Sussex. It is synonymous with *dean*, a valley; but in this district it has the peculiar signification of "a woody valley, or place yielding both covert and feeding for cattle, especially swine." Somner's Roman Ports in Kent, p. 108. The right of pannage, or hog-feeding, in this woody tract —the Sylva Anderida of anterior times —is called in Saxon charters *Denbera.* Somner. Dr. Bosworth defines *denbære* as "wood-bearing, woody, yielding mast." In a charter of the year 804, Kenwulf, King of Mercia, and Cuthred, King of Kent, gave to the Monks of St. Augustine " xiij denberende on Andred," which a chronicler subsequently rendered, "xiij *dennas* glandes portantes—13 *Dens* yielding acorns or mast in the forest of Andred." The following list contains such surnames with this termination as appear to me to belong exclusively to the Wealden district of Kent, Sussex, and Surrey.

Ashenden.

Ballden, Barnden, Blechenden, Boddenden, Brickenden, Blunden, Boulden, Brigden, Brissenden, Barden, Brogden.

Conden, Cobden, Chittenden, Couden, Cruttenden, Crunden, Chapden, Carden.

Evernden.

Fishenden, Fowden, Farnden.

Gosden, Godden, Gadsden, Goulden.

Hepden, Haffenden, Horsmonden, Hasden, Harenden, Henden, Hensden, Haiselden, Hearnden, Hesden, Hosden, Holden, Hoverden, Hovenden, Holmden, Hayden, Hobden, Harden, Horden.

Igglesden, Iden, Iddenden.

Jenden.

Lumsden, Lechenden, Lovenden, Lowden.

Maplesden, Mayden, Marsden.

Newenden, Norden.

Ockenden, Oxenden, Ovenden, Ogden, Oden (?)

Plurenden, Polesden, Pagden, Pittlesden, Pattenden, Picklesden.

Quittenden.

Rigden, Ramsden, Rayden.

Singden, Sinden, Surrenden, Shatterden, Standen, Sladden, Southerden, Sugden.

Tappenden, Twissenden, Tenterden, Tilden, Twysden.

Uden.

Varden.

Whelden, Witherden, Wickenden, Wisden, Wetherden.

Yalden.

DENBIGH. Probably from Denby, a parish in co. Derby, rather than from the Welsh town.

DENCE. See Dench.

DENCH. Denshe and Dench are medieval forms of Danish. A-Sax. *Denisc.*

DENDY. The family tradition is, that the name was originally D'Awnay, or Dawndy. In the sixteenth century it was written Dendye, and from that time the chief habitat of the family has been the borders of Surrey and Sussex. In the parish register of Newdigate, co. Surrey, I have observed the spellings Dandie, Dandy, Dendy. See Dawnay.

DENHAM. Parishes in cos. Suffolk and Bucks.

DENIAL. "Martha Denial, widow, æt. 75, was buried in Ecclesfield churchyard, 3rd Feb. 1851. Her husband, Joseph Denial, told the parish clerk that his grandfather was found when an infant deserted in a church-porch, and that he was surnamed Denial as one whom *all deny*, and was christened Daniel, which is composed of the same letters. This is the tradition of the origin of a surname now common in this parish." Notes and Queries, III., p. 323.

DENIS. See Dennis.

DENISON. DENNISON. The son of Denis. See, however, Dennistoun.

DENMAN. See the termination, DEN and MAN. The form in H.R. is Ate Dene. A dweller in a dene or 'den' would be called a Denman or a Denyer. The writer of the article on Surnames in Edinb. Rev. April, 1855, thinks the original Denman was a swineherd.

DENMARK. From the country.

DENNE. An ancient Kentish family deduced from Robert de Dene, butler (*pincerna*) to Edw. the Confessor. He is said to have been a Norman, though the surname is English, and is doubtless derived from West Dean, co. Sussex. Sussex Arch. Coll. v. 157.

DENNETT. 1. A diminutive of Denis. 2. There is an unsupported tradition in the Sussex family that the name was originally At Denne, or Dean, and that by a syllabic transposition it became Den-At or Dennett.

DENNINGTON. A parish in Suffolk.

DENNIS. DENIS. A baptismal name: the patron saint of France. Sometimes, however, as Ferguson observes, it may be from the A.-Sax. *Denisca*, Danish, and this is confirmed by the Le Deneys of the H.R.

DENNISTOUN. The Dennistouns "of that Ilk," have an extraordinary way of accounting for their surname. One Danziel, or Daniel, (say they) probably of Norman extraction, settled in Renfrewshire, and calling the estate Danzielstoun, assumed therefrom his surname! The family are unquestionably ancient, the name appearing in a charter of king Malcolm IV., who died in 1165, but the Norman Danziel is probably a genealogical figment. The English Denisons are said to have sprung from a cadet of this ancient house, who went from Scotland temp. Charles I., and fought at Marston Moor. B.L.G.

DENNY. DENNEY. Denis—the baptismal name. Some families so called are known to have settled here from France after the Rev. of the Edict of Nantes, 1685.

DENSILL. DENZIL. An estate in Mawgan, co. Cornwall, which was possessed by the family down to the sixteenth cent., when one of the heirs female married Hollis.

DENSTON. Places in cos. Stafford and Suffolk.

DENT. A township and chapelry in Yorkshire, and a place in Northumberland.

DENTON. Parishes in cos. Durham, Hunts, Kent, Lancaster, Lincoln, Norfolk, Oxon, Northampt., Sussex, York, and Northumberland.

DENYER. See Denman.

DE PUTRON. The village or contrée de Putron, of which the family were anciently lords, is in Guernsey, but there is good authority in the heraldic archives of Paris for the De Putrons having ranked among the nobility of Normandy in the thirteenth century. They seem to have been resident near Falaise. De Puytren, well known as the name of the eminent French surgeon, has been supposed to be identical.

DERBY. The town.

DERICK. DERRICK. A contraction of Theodoric. Ainsworth.

DERING. The source of this ancient family, (whence the affix of Surenden-Dering, co. Kent,) appears to be from that of De Morinis, who probably originated in the territory of the Morini in the N.E. of France. One of the early members, Deringus de M., seems to have stamped his baptismal appellative upon his descendants as a surname in the twelfth century. See Hasted's Kent; but it is to be remarked that there was in that county prior to Domesday a tenant who bore the name of Derinc filius Sired.

DE RINZY. The estate of Clobemon, co. Wexford, was granted by Charles I. to Sir Matthew de Renzy, a native of Cullen in Germany, and a descendant of George Castriota, the famous Scanderbeg. The family still possess Clobemon Hall. B.L.G.

DERMOTT. See Diarmuid.

DERN. DERNE. A solitary place. A.-Sax. *dierna.*

DERRICK. A Flemish Christian name. See Derick.

DESCHAMPS. (Now Chamier). Fr. Protestant refugees from Bergerac in Perigord.

DESPAIR. "Richard Despair, a poor man buried." Par. Reg., East Grinstead, Sussex, 1726. Probably a corruption of the French family name Despard.

DESPENCER. DESPENSER. See Spencer or Spenser.

DE ST. CROIX. Many places in France and particularly in Normandy are dedicated to the Holy Cross. The English family left Normandy at the Rev. of the Edict of Nantes, and settled in the island of Jersey from whence they have subsequently transferred themselves to this country.
Since their settlement in England, the family have uniformly omitted the E final of *Sainte,* contrary to grammar—apparently for the purpose of making the name more intelligible to the English eye.

DE TEISSIER. A member of the noble Italian family Teisseri of Nice, settled in Languedoc, and his descendants became Barons of France. Lewis, Baron de Teissier, settled in England in the last century, but the title of baron was disused until 1819, when, at the desire of Louis XVIII. and with the consent of the Prince Regent, it was resumed by James de Teissier, the representative of the family.

DETHICK. An estate in Derbyshire, now Dethwick, which was possessed by the family temp. Hen. III.

DEUCE. In various dialects this is one of the many aliases of the Devil. The name (which may be found in the 16th Report of the Registrar General) is more probably a corruption of D'Ewes, which see.

DEUCHAR. An ancient parish in co. Selkirk.

DEVALL. See Devoll.

DEVENISH. The family first appear as gentry in co. Sussex about the year 1399. The name, clearly indicative of a Devonshire origin, is cognate with Kentish, Cornish, &c. The Irish branch, who transferred themselves to the sister island in the reign of Henry VIII., have a tradition

that it is corrupted from a Saxon root signifying "deep waters," and that their original patronymic was Sutton; but there is no evidence of the truth of either statement. Le Deveneys, Deveneys, and Devenist are found in H.R., and there is an Isabella *la* Deveneis.

DEVERELL. In most cases the same as Devereux. There are, however, English localities called Deverell and Deverhill in cos. Dorset and Wilts.

DEVEREUX. "Of this family, which had its surname from Evreux, a town in Normandy, and came into England with the Conqueror, there were divers generations in England before they became barons of the realm." Banks. Bar. i. 287.

DEVEY. I have no doubt of the local origin of this name, though Ferguson considers it a diminutive of "dove."

DEVIL. This surname occurs in many languages; but the only instance of it which I recollect in England is that of the monk, Willelmus cognomento Diabolus. See Eng. Surn. i., 223. The French De Ville, naturalized amongst us, has often been misunderstood to be the synonym of Satan, and various vowel changes have been made by the bearers of it to avoid this very objectionable notion. Hence it is commonly written Divall, Divoll, Devall, &c., while in records Devol, Devile, Deyvil, &c., are found.

DEVOLL. Notwithstanding my explanation of Devil by De Ville, Mr. Ferguson deduces the pedigree of Devoll, Devall, &c., direct from Satan, which is, methinks, giving the devil *more* than his due. By way of salvo, however, Mr. Ferguson admits that they may possibly be diminutives of "dove!"

DEVON. Perhaps from Devonshire; but it may be from the river Devon in the cos. of Perth, Kinross, and Clackmannan.

DEVONPORT. Must be a corruption of Davenport, for the large suburb of Plymouth now so called has only borne that designation a few years.

DEVONSHIRE. From the county.

DEW. Probably from Eu in Normandy, commonly called la Ville *d'Eu.*

DEWAR. A hamlet in the parish of Heriot, Edinburghshire. The patriarch of the family is said to have received the lands of Dewar in reward for his having slain a formidable wolf. Gaz. of Scotland.

DEWDNEY. See Doudney.

D'EWES. "Sir Simonds was grandchild unto Adrian D'ewes, descended of the ancient stem of Des Ewes [des Eaux, the synonym of our English *Waters*] dynasts or lords of the dition of Kessel in the duchy of Gelderland, who came first thence when that province was wasted with civil war, in the beginning of king Henry the Eighth." Fuller's Worthies iii. 195.

DEWEY. Walter de Dounai was a great

baron and lord of Bampton and Were, under William the Conqueror. In Domesd. he occurs as a tenant in capite in the counties of Devon, Wilts, Dorset, and Somerset. He is sometimes called Walscinus. It is probable that he came from Douay in France.

DE WINTON. Robert de Wintona, or de Wincestria, (doubtless a native of Winchester) went into Glamorganshire with Robert Fitzhamon, soon after the Conquest, and built the castle of Lanquian, near Cowbridge. His descendants continued to use those names for many generations, but at length their place was usurped by the byename (for it can hardly be a corruption) Wylcolyna or Wylklyn, and this was at length further degraded into Wilkins. Thus it remains with many of the existing branches, though others have by royal authority resumed the ancient designation of De Winton.

DEWSBURY A town in Yorkshire.

DEXTER. Possibly from Lat. *dexter*, in the sense of lucky, fortunate—the antithesis of *sinister ;* but more likely a contraction of De Exeter, from the chief town of Devonshire.

D'EYNCOURT. Walter de Aincurth or D'Eyncourt came over with William the Conqueror, and received from him several lordships in the shires of Northampton, Derby, Nottingham, York, and Lincoln, in which last Blankney became his caput baroniæ. Kelham's Domesd.

DIAL. A corruption of Doyle.

DIAMOND. In the parish register of Brenchley, co. Kent, there is an entry to the effect that, in 1612—'John Diamond, son of John du Mont the Frenchman, was baptized.' The elder Du Mont was a Kentish iron-master, who had settled in that county from France. Inf. H.W. Diamond, M.D., F.S.A.

DIARMUID. An ancient Irish personal name, anglicized to Dermott, Darby, and even to Jeremiah. Ulst. Journ. Archæol., No. 2.

DIBBLE. Perhaps the same as Tipple, Theobald.

DIBDIN. Dibden, a parish in Hampshire.

DICEY. Probably local—though Ferguson thinks it may be O. Germ., Disi or Disa, from Goth. *deis*, wise.

DICK. See Richard.

DICKENS. The same as Digons, which see.

DICKER. A district in Sussex, formerly an extensive waste. Ate Dykere occurs temp. Edw. III. among the Barons of the Cinque Ports, and *le* Dykere some years earlier, in the same county.

DICKESON. See Richard.

DICKINS. See Digons and Richard.

N

DICKISON. See Richard.

DICKMAN. 1. From residence near a dyke, or possibly a constructor of dykes, locally called *dicks*. 2. The same as Dykeman.

DICKS. See Richard.

DICKSEE. The same as Dixie.

DICKSON. See Richard.

DIDSBURY. A chapelry of Manchester.

DIGBY. A parish in Lincolnshire. The noble family are of great antiquity in co. Warwick.

DIGG. See Digory.

DIGGENS. See Digons.

DIGGERY. Degory, a personal name.

DIGGES. The same as Dicks. See Richard.

DIGGINS. DIGGINSON. See Digons.

DIGHTON. See Deighton.

DIGONS. Diquon or Digon is an early 'nursename' of Richard. One of the messengers of Eleanor, countess of Montfort, in 1265, was called Diquon. Blaauw's Barons' War. In the "Hundred Merry Tales" there is an anecdote of a rustic from the North of England, who, as Richard III. was reviewing some troops near London, stepped out of the ranks and clapping the monarch upon the shoulder, said : "Diccon, Diccon ! by the mis ays blith that thaust kyng !" (Dick, Dick ! by the mass I'm glad you are king!) Nor must we forget the Shakspearean—

> "Jocky of Norfolk be not too bold ;
> For *Dickon* thy master is bought and sold."
> *King Richard III., Act. 5, Sc. 3.*

Dickens is the more usual form of this name. It may be remarked that the word "Dickins" used as a nickname of Satan has a different origin, being a contraction of the diminutive *Devilkins*.

DIGORY. DEGORY. The personal name, whence probably the modifications Digg, Digges, Diggins. Digginson ; though these may perhaps be from Dick and Richard.

DIKE. See Dyke.

DILGER. See Dilke. Dilker. H.R.

DILKE. Presumed to be Danish, as it is chiefly found in the Danish counties from temp. Edw. I. According to Förstemann, the root of Dill, Dilley, Dillow, *Dilke*, Dilger (*ger*, spear), and Dillimore (*mar*, illustrious) is the old High Germ. *tilen*, to overthrow. Corresponding Old German names are Dilli, Tilli, Tillemlr, and modern German Dill and Till. Ferguson, p. 380. A Nicolaus Dilkes occurs in the H.R. of Cambridgeshire.

DILL. See Dilke. There is, however, a hundred so called in Sussex. Dill without prefix is found in H.R.

DILLER. "To dill" is a Northernism meaning to finish, and both this name and

Dillman may have been derived from some handicraft.

DILLEY. See Dilke.

DILLIMORE. See Dilke.

DILLMAN. See Diller.

DILLON. The common ancestor of the noble Dillons of Ireland was Henry Dillon, who settled in that country in the year 1185. King John, while Earl of Mortain, gave him immense tracts of land about Drumrany, which were afterwards collectively known as Dillon's country. See Geneal. Hist. of the Fam. of Brabazon, p. 17. Nothing seems to be known of the ancestors of this personage or of the origin of the name.

DILLOW. See Dilke.

DILLWYN. A parish in Herefordshire.

DIMBLEBY. A corruption of Thimbleby, places in cos. York and Lincoln.

DIMMACK. See Dymock.

DIMMOCK. See Dymock.

DIMOND. See Diamond.

DIMSDALE. Probably Dinsdale, a parish in Durham, and a township in Yorkshire.

DINAN. A town in Brittany, whose viscounts, dating from the end of the tenth century, became ancestors of several noble houses in France, and of Foulke de Dinan, a baron by tenure under the Conqueror. His posterity were barons by writ from 1295 to 1509. The name has been wonderfully corrupted, having gone through the following changes: Dinan, Dinant, Dynaunt, Dynham, Dymant, Deimond, Dyamond, Deyman, and Dayman.

DINE. DINES. See Dyne.

DINGLE. "A narrow valley between two hills." Bailey.

DINGLEY. A parish in Northamptonshire.

DINGWALL. A parish and royal burgh in Ross-shire.

DINHAM. A hamlet in Monmouthshire.

DINMORE. A district connected with the parish of Clun-Gunford, co. Salop.

DINSDALE. A parish co. Durham, and a township co. York.

DIPLOCK. A corruption of Duplock.

DIPNALL. Dippenhall, a tything in the parish of Crondale in Hampshire.

DIPPERY. Fr. Du Pré, 'Of the Meadow.' D'Ypres—from Ypres in Flanders, has however been suggested to me.

DIPPLE. An ancient parish now comprehended by that of Speymouth, in Morayshire.

DIPROSE. A corruption of De Préaux. There are in Normandy seven places called

Préaux, two of which are St. Michel de Préaux and Notre-Dame de Préaux.

DIRK. DIRCKS. Corruptions of Derick.

DISHER. A maker of bowls or dishes. It is used in a feminine form as Dyssheres in Piers Plowman.

DISNEY. "Disney, alias De Iseney, he dwelleth at Diseney, and of his name and line be gentilmen of Fraunce," says Leland, speaking of Norton-Disney, co. Lincoln. The surname appears in the various lists called the Roll of Battel Abbey, and the family came, it would appear, from Isigni, near Bayeux, a small town, famous at present for its butter.

DITCH. From residence in or near the ditch of a fortified town, like the French De la Fosse. Its forms in the H.R. are De Fossa, De la Fosse, &c., and there is one unlucky wight called "Absolon in le Dyche."

DITCHBURN. A township in Northumberland.

DITCHER. The occupation. Fossator. H.R.

DITCHLING. A parish in Sussex.

DITCHMAN. Probably the same as Dickman.

DITTON. Parishes in cos. Kent, Lancaster, Cambridge, Surrey, Salop, &c.

DIVENNY. DIVIN. See O'Divny.

DIVER. 1. Possibly from expertness in diving. 2. A river in Wiltshire.

DIVERS. Apparently a French local name, the D of De coalescing.

DIVES. Probably a corruption of Dive. Uxor Boselini de Dive was a tenant in capite under William the Conqueror, co. Cambridge. Kelham's Domesd. There is a village so called in the department of Calvados in Normandy. De Dyve, Le Dyve. H.R.

DIVIE. A romantic river in Morayshire.

DIVINE. Probably formed like Divers above.

DIVOLL. See Devil and Devoll.

DIX. See Richard.

DIXEY. See Dixie.

DIXIE. According to Wootton's Baronetage the family are descended from Wolstan, earl of Ellenden (now called Wilton) who married the sister of Egbert, the first monarch of all England; and there are other traditions of their immense antiquity. The name is probably not very ancient, and the heralds' Visitations only commence the pedigree with Wolstan Dixie who flourished about the time of Edw. III.

DIXON is Dick's son, that is Richard's son. "In Scotland it has been variously written at different periods, as Dicson, Dykson, Dikson, Diksoun, Diksoune, Dixson, and Dickson. They are descended from one Richard Keith, said to be a son of the family of Keith, earls-marshal of Scotland, and in proof thereof they carry in their arms the chief of Keith Mareschal. This Richard was commonly called Dick, and his sons, with the carelessness of that age, were styled "Dickson." It is probable that he was the son of the great Marshal, Hervey de Keth, (ob. 1249,) by his wife Margaret, daughter of William, third lord Douglas." Dixon on Surnames. Boston, U. S., 1857. The Irish Dixons came from Scotland, in a clan, in the reign of Henry VIII. In 1617, if not earlier, they bore the arms of the English Dixons, which goes far to prove community of origin for the Dixons, Dicksons, &c., of the three kingdoms. The oldest spelling in Ireland is Dykesone. Inf. Sir Erasmus Dixon Borrowes, Bart. The great baron of Malpas, co. Chester, William Belward, had two sons, David and Richard. The latter's third son, Richard, surnamed Little, on account of his diminutive size, had two sons, the younger of whom was John, who received the surname of Richardson (Filius Ricardi) from his father's Christian name. It has been conjectured that some of the Dixons of the North of England, who trace their pedigree to the county of Chester, may be descendants of that John Richardson, alias Dick's son.

DOBB. DOBBS. See Robert.

DOBBIN. DOBBINS. See Robert.

DOBBY. DOBBIE. See Robert.

DOBELL. Perhaps originally from the Roman personal name, Dolabella. The French have always been fond of adopting classical names, and this occurs as a surname in Normandy in the twelfth and thirteenth centuries in the form of Dolbell. In 1296, however, it is found in Sussex as De Dobel, implying a *local* origin, and in the sixteenth century the family ranked with the gentry of that county, bearing the canting arms of a Doe between three Bells.

DOBINSON. The son of Dobin or Robert.

DOBLE. The same as Dobell, which is commonly pronounced Double.

DOBREE. Probably D'Aubri. The Itin. Norm. shows two places so called, viz. Aubri-en-Exmes, and Aubri-le-Panthon, both in the arrondissement of Argentan in Normandy.

DOBSON. See Robert.

DOCKER. A township in Westmoreland.

DOCKING. A parish in Norfolk.

DOD. The Dods of Edge claim from Hova, son of Cadwgan Dot. He about the time of Henry II. married the heiress of the lord of Edge, co. Chester, who is presumed to have been the son of Edwin, a Saxon thane, who was allowed to retain his lands after the Conquest. Ormerod,

(Hist. Cheshire), adduces arguments in favour of Cadwgan Dot's having been descended from a Saxon called Dot, who, at the Conquest, had been expelled from the lands in Cheshire which he had held jointly with that very thane Edwin. Dod of Edge, and their cadet Dod, of Cloverley, rank amongst the most ancient territorial families in the kingdom.

DODD. DODDS. Doda, an A.-Sax. personal name, whence Dodds, Dodson, &c. Its forms in the H.R. are Dod and Dodde, and in Domesd. Doda, Dode, and Dodo.

DODDRIDGE. Evidently local, but I know not the place. De Doderig, H.R., co. Devon.

DODGE. A corruption of Dodds, the genitive of Doda. See Dodd.

DODGSON. The same as Dodson.

DODMAN. A class of men called Dodomanni appear in the Exon Domesday, and afterwards as Dodeman and Deudeman. The word awaits explanation. See Dudman. Several De Dodmanstones occur in H.R.

DODSON. The son of Doda. Alwinus Dodesone occurs in Domesday as a tenant in chief, Hertfordshire, 142. He was doubtless of Saxon blood.

DODSWORTH. Dodworth, a township in Yorkshire.

DOE. From the animal, like Hart, Buck, Roe, &c. Those mythical 'parties' to so many legal proceedings, "JOHN DOE and RICHARD ROE," are evidently of forest extraction, and point to the days when forest laws prevailed and venison was a sacred thing. In H.R. there is a John le Doe.

DOGGETT. An old London name, probably corrupted from Dowgate, one of the Roman gateways of the city. Ferguson makes it a diminutive of the Icelandic *doggr*, and the English *dog*, but no such diminutive is found.

DOHERTY or **O'DOHERTY.** "The surname is derived from Dochartach, lord and prince of Inishowen, co. Donegal," a direct descendant of "Cean Faola, prince of Tire Connell, now the county of Donegal, and 12th in descent from Conal Gulban, 7th son of Niall of the Nine Hostages," from whom so many of the ancient Irish families are descended. B.L.G.

DOLAMORE. The termination shows its local origin, though I find no place so designated. Ferguson, however, deduces it from O. Norse *döll*, a woman, and *mar*, illustrious.

DOLBEN. "The name is presumed to be taken from *Dol-Ben*-Maen, a place between Caernarvon and Pemnorfa." Courthope's Debrett's Baronetage. If it be so, this is one of the extremely few local surnames that have originated in Wales.

DOLBY. See Dalby.

DOLE. 1. *Dole* or *doole* is an eastern and southern provincialism for a boundary mark, whether an earthen mound or a post of stone or wood. In the western counties it means a low, flat, place. Halliw. 2. Dol, a well known town in Brittany. Doll, Dolle, De Doll. H.R.

DOLLAR. A town and parish in Clackmannanshire.

DOLLING. About the year 1580, a younger son of the Count Dolling, of Dolling, near Toulouse, having embraced Huguenot opinions, is said to have fled into England, and settled in the Isle of Purbeck.

DOLMAN. DOLLMAN. The verb "to dole" signifies to share or divide; to set out in portions or lots, whether of land, goods, or money. A.-Sax. *dœlan*. Perhaps the original *Doleman* may have been a distributor either of alms, or of lands under the "tenantry" arrangements of feudal times. Or he may have been such a "judge or divider"—that is arbitrator—as the one mentioned in Luke XII. 14. A less desirable derivation is from the A.-Sax *dol*, foolish, erring, heretical, and *man*. Doleman. De la Dole. H.R.

DOLPHIN. An ancient personal name. One Dolfin was a tenant-in-chief in cos. Derby and York at the making of Domesd. The family were in Ireland before the year 1307. B.L.G.

DOMESDAY. Not from the famous national record so often referred to in these pages, nor from the Day of Doom; but from one of the many religious establishments to which the name of Maison-Dieu, *Domus Dei*, or "God's House," was given.

DOMMINNEY. This singular name occurs in Lond. Direct. It may be a corruption of Domine—a sobriquet.

DOMVILLE. Donville in the arrondissement of Lisieux, in Normandy, was anciently written Dumoville, as in a papal bull of 1210. Itin. de la Normandie. The family, who probably entered England at the Conquest, were resident in co. Chester from the time of Henry III. till the beginning of the XVIII. cent.

DONAHOO. A corruption of the Irish name O'Donohogue.

DONALD. A well-known northern personal name, whence Donalds, Mac Donald, Donaldson, Donnison, Donkin. Gaelic etymologists derive the name from "Donhuil," *i.e.*, "brown-eyed."

DONALDS. See Donald.

DONALDSON. See Donald.

DONCASTER. A town in Yorkshire.

DONE. A great Cheshire family, whom Ormerod designates as "a race of Warriors who held Utkinton (supposed to be the 'Done' of Domesday), as military tenants of Venables, from the time of King John. . . . . The chiefs of this house will be

found in the battle rolls of Agincourt, Bloreheath, and Flodden." Miscell. Palat. p. 90. The name is pronounced Dōne, as is seen in Drayton's description of the bloody battle between Henry IV. and Hotspur Percy:

"There Dutton, Dutton kills; a Done doth kill
    a *Done;*
A Booth, a Booth; and Leigh by Leigh is over-
    thrown;
A Venables against a Venables doth stand;
And Troutbeck fighteth with a Troutbeck hand to
    hand;
There Molineux doth make a Molineux to die,
And Egerton the strength of Egerton doth try;
O Cheshire, wert thou mad, of thine own native
    gore,
So much until this day thou never shed'st before."
            Polyolbion, Song 22.

This family, or at least the female members thereof, seem to have been remarkable for their beauty, if we may trust the proverb, quoted by Ray.

"AS FAIR AS LADY DONE."

DONELAN. One of the most ancient families in Ireland, deriving from Cahal, 2nd son of Morough Molathan, King of Connaught, who died A.D. 701. One of his descendants built the castle of Bally-Donelan, co. Galway. B.L.G.

DONHUE. See Donahoo.

DONKIN. See Donald and Duncan.

DONNAVAN. See Donovan.

DONNE. Izaak Walton, in his Life of Dr. Donne, says that "his father was masculinely and lineally descended from a very ancient family in Wales." The etymon is probably *don*, black or dark complexioned. It must not be forgotten, however, that one Donne, a tenant in chief, held land in Devon, temp. Edw. Conf. Domesd.

DONNISON. See Donald.

DONOVAN or O'DONOVAN. This great Irish family spring from a chieftain of the X. cent., who was killed in 977, by the famous Brian Boru. By old writers the name is written Dondubhan, which signifies "brown-haired-chief." O'Donovan in Irish Pen. Journ. p. 331.

DOO. The Scottish for Dove? Le Do. H.R.

DOOGOOD. Has probably no allusion to practical benevolence, but, like many other surnames terminating in *good*, is the corruption of a local name with the desinence *wood*. Or it may possibly be a corruption of the Scottish Dugald.

DOOLITTLE. I fear that the original owner of this name was a lazy fellow, though some of his descendants have been distinguished for zeal and industry.

DOON. 1. A-Sax. *dún*, a hill. 2. A 'bonny' river with 'banks and braes,' in Ayrshire.

DOORS. Dores, a castle said to have been the abode of Macbeth, in the parish of Kettins, co. Forfar.

DORE. A chapelry in Derbyshire, and a parish in co. Hereford—Abbey Dore.

DORLING. Probably the same as Darling. A.S. *deórling.*

DORMAN. A-Sax. *dór*, a gate or large door, and *man*. A door-keeper, porter.

DORMAR. See Dormer.

DORMER. Collins traces Lord Dormer's family no higher than the XV. cent. With the origin of the name I am unacquainted.

DORRELL. Probably the same as Darell.

DORRINGTON. A parish in Lincolnshire, and a township in Shropshire.

DORTON. A parish in Buckinghamshire.

DORVELL. See Dorville.

DORVILLE. Probably from one of the two places in Normandy now called Douville, situated respectively in the arrondissements of Andeli and Pont-l'Evêque.

DORWARD. See Durward.

DOSSELL. A richly ornamented cloak worn by persons of high rank. Lat. *dorsale.* Analogous to Mantell.

DOSSETOR. DOSSETTER. Corrupted from Uttoxeter, co. Stafford. So Rossiter from Wroxeter.

DOSSON. The same as Dowson.

DOTTRIDGE. Mr. Ferguson ingeniously derives this name from the Low German Deotric, Theoderic; but it is more probably identical with Doddridge.

DOUBBLE. DOUBELL. See Dobell.

DOUBLE. A sobriquet relating to extraordinary size—or to duplicity of character? The name Dobell is often so pronounced.

DOUBLEDAY. This name and its companion, Singleday, baffle my ingenuity.

DOUBLEMAN. The same as Double.

DOUBLETT. " An old fashion'd garment for men; much the same as a waistcoat." Bailey. Also a military garment covering the person as low as the waist. The corresponding French surname is Pourpoint. The name was first given on the same principle as Cloake, Mantell, &c.

DOUCH. An old orthography of ' Dutch,' by which however we must understand, not a Hollander, but a German : the latter word being of rather recent importation into English. The first translation of the whole Bible into our language, by Miles Coverdale, is stated on the title page to have been rendered " out of the Douche (meaning German) and Latyn into Englyshe, 1535." Even so lately as 1660, Howell, in the preface of his Lexicon says, " the root of most of the English language is *Dutch*," by which of course he means the Teutonic or old German.

DOUDNEY. As the name Oudney occurs, it is very probable that Doudney (with its variations, Dewdney, Dudeney, &c.) is the same designation with the prefix D', although I have not been successful in finding any place in Normandy, or elsewhere in France, called Oudeney or Oudenai.

DOUGALL. (Generally Mac-Dougall). Gael. *dhu*, black, and *gall*, a stranger—an expression used by the Celtic inhabitants of Scotland to denote a Lowlander, or any one not of their own race. It is still in use as a baptismal name.

DOUGHTON. A parish united with Dunton. co. Norfolk.

DOUGHTY. A.-Sax. *dohtig*, valiant, hardy, manly.

DOUGLAS. The most powerful and widely celebrated family that Scotland ever produced. The name was assumed from lands on the small river Douglas, in Lanarkshire, (Gael. *duf-glas, du-glas,* i.e., dark grey, from the colour of its waters), where William of Dufglas was established as early as 1175. This illustrious race, renowned throughout western Europe for its romantic career, may well be accounted an " historical " family, for as Hume, the annalist of the House, has it—

" SO MANY, SO GOOD, AS OF THE DOUGLASES HAVE BEEN, OF ONE SURNAME WAS NE'ER IN SCOTLAND SEEN."

The family rose into power under King Robert Bruce, of whom " the good Lord James of Douglas " was the most distinguished adherent, but suffered a partial eclipse when the ninth earl, James, rebelled against King James II. The earls of Angus, however, partly restored the ancestral glory of the house, which has always continued to be one of the most important in Scotland.

DOULTON. Probably Dolton, a parish in Devonshire.

DOUSBERY. Probably Dewsbury, co. York.

DOUTHWAITE. See Thwaite.

DOVE. The bird. Also a beautiful river of Derbyshire.

DOVER. The Kentish town.

DOVEREN. Doveran, a river in the shires of Banff and Aberdeen.

DOVAY. Possibly D'Auffai, "of Auffai," a small town near Dieppe, in Normandy.

DOW. Probably a corruption of the Gaelic, *Dhu*, i.e. black ; but *dow* or *doo*, the Scottish for dove or pigeon, may be the origin. Dow, without prefix, is found in H.R. It also appears to have been a personal name, and to have given rise to Dowson, Dowse, Dowsing, and Dowsett, and also to the local name Dowsby in Lincolnshire.

DOWDESWELL. A parish in Gloucestershire.

DOWER. A rabbit's burrow, *cuniculus.* Prompt. Parv.

DOWLAND. A parish in Devonshire.

DOWNE. DOWN. A-Sax. *dún*, a hill, as the South Downs, Marlborough Downs, &c. From residence in such a locality have come the surnames Downe, Downer, Downman, Downes, &c. The H.R. form is Ate-Dune, i.e. 'At the Down.'

DOWNER. See Downe.

DOWNES. See Downe.

DOWNEY. Perhaps the same as Downie.

DOWNHAM. Parishes, &c., in cos. Norfolk, Cambridge, Essex, and Lancaster.

DOWNIE. A range of hills in Forfarshire, and a headland in Kincardineshire.

DOWNING. This common surname is doubtless local, but I cannot ascertain the place.

DOWNMAN. See Downe.

DOWNTON. Parishes in Wiltshire and Herefordshire.

DOWNWARDS. Mr. Ferguson ingeniously derives it from A-Sax. *dún*, a down or hill, and *weard*, a watchman—"a lookout man on the Downs."

DOWSE. DOWSETT. DOWSING. DOWSON. See Dow.

DOXEY. DOXSEY. Corruptions of *De Dockesey*, H.R. Dockesey may probably be *insula anatum*, the island of ducks.

DOYLE. One of the commonest of Irish surnames, and presumed to be of Anglo-Norman origin. See D'Oyley. It is found as Doyl and Doil in England, temp. Edward I. H.R.

D'OYLEY. Robert de Oilgi was a tenant-in-chief in many counties, and Wido de O. in co. Oxford. Domesd. The former is mentioned in the chartulary of Oseney Abbey as a sworn companion of Roger de Ivery (fratres jurati et per sacramentum confœderati) in assisting at the invasion of England. Ellis, Introd. According to genealogists the ancestors of these persons were lords of Olgii or Oyly in Normandy long before the Conquest. The map of modern Normandy shows no such locality as Oilgi, or Oyly, but there are three places in the neighbourhood of Falaise, called Ouilli. It was probably to Ouilli-le-Basset in the canton of Falaise, written in the XI. cent. Oillei (and latinized Olleium) that the family originated.

DOYNE. Originally O'Doyne of Castle-bracke in Ireland. B.L.G.

DRAGE. Perhaps one of the modifications of Drogo, the personal name.

DRAKE. Not from the waterfowl, but from A-Sax. *draca* (Latin *draco*,) a dragon. *Le Dragun*, the Anglo-Norman form, occurs in the H.R., but the nearest approach to this that I have seen in modern times is Drago, a name which existed at Ely about a century since. Several families of Drake bear as arms the wyvern, or two-legged dragon; and it is worthy of remark that in giving to various pieces of cannon the names of monsters and animals of prey, that of 'drake' was assigned to a peculiar species of gun, as those of caliver, basilisk, culverin, fawconet, saker—all appellations of serpents and rapacious birds—were to others. The compounds, "fire-drake," and "hell-drake," become intelligible when the latter syllable is understood to mean, not the harmless and familiar denizen of the pool, but the 'fell dragoun' of medieval romance. Sir Thomas Smith, in his treatise "De Republica Anglicana," speaking of his contemporary, the celebrated Elizabethan admiral, Sir Francis Drake, (contrary to the generally received notion that he was born in Devonshire,) asserts that he was the son of a fisherman in the Isle of Wight, and that the name of Drake was not his family appellation but an assumption: "*Draconis nomen ipse sibi sumpsit, quod est serpentum quoddam genus.*" He adds that the Dunkirkers fitted out a fine ship called the Dog, for the purpose of hunting and perhaps catching this *sea-serpent*: "*Dunkercani insignem navem instruxerunt, Doggam (id est Canem) a se appellatam, innuentes eâ se Draconem hunc venaturos et forte capturos.*" Le Drac is an ancient form of the name.

DRAPER. A draper—a dealer in cloth. Fr. *drap*. Le Draper. H.R.

DRAWBRIDGE. First imposed upon a retainer in a fortified house whose duty it was to superintend the drawbridge. Harry o' the Drawbridge would be a very likely appellation for such a guardsman.

DRAWSWORD. A name analogous to Shakspeare. Draweswerd. H.R.

DRAWWATER. A drawer of water; or perhaps local. Drawater. H.R.

DRAX. A parish in Yorkshire.

DRAY. A diminutive of Drogo. Dreye. H.R.

DRAYCOTT. Parishes and places in cos. Derby, Wilts, Berks, and Stafford.

DRAYNER. A drainer, or conductor of water. See Leader.

DRAYSON. The son of Drogo or Dray.

DRAYTON. Towns, parishes, &c., in cos. Berks, Leicester, Norfolk, Oxon, Somerset, Stafford, Buckingham, Cambridge, Nottingham, &c.

DRESDEN. From the metropolis of Saxony.

DRESSER. Probably some handicraft.

DREW. DREWE. 1. Drogo, an early Norman personal name, was so anglicised. 2. It is a common nickname for Andrew. 3. Dreux, a town of Brittany. At the time of the Norman survey, Herman de Dreuues was a tenant-in-chief in Herefordshire. There is a *Le Dreu* in H.R.

According to the preamble of the pedigree of the Drews of Youghal, arranged by

Sir Wm. Betham, Ulster, the family descend " from Drogo or Dru, a noble Norman, son of Walter de Ponz, and brother of Richard, ancestor of the Cliffords who accompanied William the Conqueror into England." There are apparently several tenants-in-chief called Drogo in Domesd., and one of them who had great possessions at Drewscliffe and elsewhere in co. Devon, is now represented by E. S. Drewe, Esq., of The Grange, in that shire. B.L G.

DREWETT. Probably a diminutive of Drogo or Drew, q. v.

DREWRY. See Drury.

DRIFFIELD. A parish and market-town in Yorkshire.

DRING. *Drengage* was a feudal tenure said to be peculiar, or nearly so, to the northern counties. Sir Henry Ellis, in his Introduction to Domesday, says:—"The *drenchs* or *drenghs* were of the description of allodial tenants, and from the few entries in which they occur, it certainly appears that the allotments of territory which they possessed were held as manors." But there are proofs of drengage having been far from a free tenure, which both Spelman and Coke consider it; for it appears from the Boldon Book that the services of the *drengh* were to plough, sow, and harrow a portion of the bishop of Durham's land; to keep a dog and horse for the bishop's use, and a cart to convey his wine; to attend the chase with dogs and ropes, and perform certain harvest works. Spelman says the *drengs* were such as, being at the Conquest put out af their estate, were afterwards restored. In Lye's Saxon Dict. *dreng* is defined as " miles," vir fortis. See Notes and Queries, VII. p. 137-8. Halliwell gives a different definition ; he says " *Drenges*, a class of men who held a rank between the baron and thayn. *Havelok*." The ordinary interpretation would be Soldiers.

DRINKDREGS.   DRINKMILK. DRINKSOP. I have authority for the existence of these names, which appear to belong to the same category as Drinkwater. I cannot account for them.

DRINKWATER is said in Magna Britannia, vol. i. p. 60, to be a corruption of Derwentwater. Camden also places it among local surnames, without specifying the place ; but Drinkewater is found in H.R., and the occurrence of Boileau among French, and Bevelacqua among Italian family names, seems rather to indicate that it was originally imposed upon some early ' teetotaller.'

DRISCOLL. The Irish O'Driscoll, sans O.

DRIVER. A carter or wagoner. Alic' la Driveres (a female wagoner!) occurs in H.R.

DROOP. Ferguson says, O. Norse, *driúpr*, sad.

DRON. A parish in Fifeshire.

DROVER. A driver of cattle.

DRUCE. Drew's, that is, the son of Drew or Drogo.

DRUITT. See Drewett.

DRUMMER. I suppose Mr. Arthur's roundabout definition is the right one : " One who, in military exercises, beats the drum."

DRUMMOND. " The noble house of Drummond," says Collins, " derived from Malcolm Beg (i.e. ' low ' or ' short '), who flourished under Alex. II., and being possessed of the lands of Drymen, co. Stirling, took that surname, which in after times varied to Drummond." Peerage, edit. 1768. v. 77. The name is found spelt in eighteen different ways. Ulster Journ. Arch. No. 20. Of these Drumyn, Drummane, and Dromond are the principal.

DRURY. The founder of the family in England is mentioned in the Battel-Abbey Roll. He settled first at Thurston and subsequently at Rougham, co. Suffolk, and his descendants continued in possession of that estate for about six hundred years. B.L.G.

DRYBOROUGH. Dryburgh, co. Berwick, famous for its romantic abbey, where—

> "——— in solemn solitude,
> In most sequestered spot,
> Lies mingling with its kindred clay,
> The dust of Walter Scott."

DRYDEN. As in the oldest records the name is spelt Dreyden, Driden, &c., it is fair to presume that it is of local origin, although the place itself is not ascertained. Mr. Arthur, however, gives quite another etymology, namely: " Welsh, *drrydwn*, BROKEN NOSE (!) According to Evans, Jonreth surnamed Drwydwn, the father of Llewelyn, was the eldest son of Owain Groynedd, but was not suffered to enjoy his right on account of that blemish !" Who Jonreth was, or when he lived, Mr. Arthur does not inform us, though we cannot but regret that in a two-fold sense his nose was thus " put out of joint."

DRYSDALE. Dryfesdale, a parish in Dumfrieshire.

DU. The initial syllable of many surnames of Fr. origin naturalized amongst us. It is of course the preposition *de* conjoined with the article *le*, and answers a purpose similar to that of *atte* in O. Eng. surnames ; for instance Dubois is ' of the wood,' (our Wood or Attwood) ; Dubosc, ' of the thicket,' (our Shaw) ; Dubourg, ' of the burg,' (our Burrowes) ; Duchesne and Ducane, ' of the oak,' (our Noakes) ; Dufour ' of the oven ;' Dufort ' of the fort ;' Dupree, Duprey, (*pré*) ' of the meadow,' (our Mead) ; Dupuy ' of the well,' (our Wells) ; Duvall, Duval, ' of the valley,' (our Dale) ; and many others.

DUBB. Dubbe, an A-Sax. personal name.

DUBBER. A word of uncertain meaning. It may signify either a trimmer or binder of books, (See Halliwell,) or a maker of tubs. (See Eng. Surn.)

DU CANE. O. Fr. *Du Quesne*, "of the Oak." Gabriel, Marquis du Quesne, grandson of the celebrated Admiral Abraham du Quesne of Dieppe, fled to this country at the Rev. of the Edict of Nantes. At an earlier period another branch of the family being Huguenots, settled in Holland, from whence they were driven by the persecution of the Duke of Alva, and settled here temp. Elizabeth. The orthography was altered to its present form in the XVII. cent. The existing family are descended from this branch.

DUCAREL. The family were French Protestant refugees after the Rev. of the Edict of Nantes.

DUCIE. Two places in Normandy are called Duci; one near Bayeux, the other near Caen. The first of this family who settled in England came from Normandy with an armed force to support Isabel, consort of Edw. II. against the Spencers. Atkin's Gloucest. Collins' Peerage.

DUCK. Most likely Le Duc, 'the duke,' as written in H.R.

DUCKETT. DUCKITT. Possibly from the Scot. *dukate*, dow-cate, dove-cot, or pigeon-house. See Jamieson. The Ducketts of Fillingham, co. Lincoln, were resident there in 1205. B.L.G.

DUCKRELL. Duckerel is the old diminutive of duck, as is 'cockerel' of cock, and hence this surname, probably with reference to the gait of the first person to whom it was applied.

DUCKWORTH. Before the time of Henry VIII. it was written Dykewarde. B.L.G. An officer who had the care of dykes.

DUDENEY. See Doudney.

DUDLEY. A town and castle in co. Worcester. In Norman times it was the fief of the De Someries, whose descendants were barons by tenure, though, as Sir H. Nicolas observes, it is questionable whether their title was that of "Dudley." So far as I see, no noble family called Dudley was ever possessor of that barony. Dudley, one of the notorious extortioners of Henry VII., claimed to be a descendant of the Suttons, barons Dudley, and his father is said to have assumed the name of Dudley, though a more probable account makes him a travelling carpenter. Monasticon, v. 5.

DUDMAN. Apparently an ancient personal name implying some quality or some employment. In Domesd. Dodeman and Dudeman. See Dodman.

DUFF. "This noble family is derived from Fife Mac-Duff, who was a man of considerable wealth and power in Scotland temp. king Kenneth II., and gave that prince great assistance in his wars with the Picts about the year 834." Kenneth made him a *maormor* or kinglet, and gave him the lands which he called after his Christian name, Fife, now the shire or county of that designation. Courthope's Debrett. His descendants, from their great dignity, were sometimes called kings of Fife, and they were entitled to place the king of Scotland on the inaugural stone, to lead the van of the royal army, and to enjoy the privilege of a sanctuary for the clan Mac-Duff, of which he was the founder. Gaz. Scotl. The Earl of Fife is a descendant of a junior branch of this ancient line.

DUFFELL. See Duffield.

DUFFEY. Probably D'Auffay, a small town in Normandy, on the Dieppe and Rouen railway. In H.R. Dofi.

DUFFIE. Scotch. A soft, silly fellow. Jamieson.

DUFFIELD. A parish in co. Derby, and two townships in Yorkshire.

DUFFUS. A parish on the coast of Morayshire, Scotland. The name may, however, be a corruption of Dovehouse, like Bacchus from Backhouse, or Malthus from Malthouse. In support of the latter derivation, we may cite the de Duffus, del Duffus, Dufhus, Columbiers, and de Columbariis of the H.R. Residence near one of the great monastic or manorial pigeon-houses of the middle ages would readily confer such a surname.

DUFTON. A parish in Westmoreland.

DUGALD. The same as Dougall.

DUGDALE. From the termination manifestly local, but I cannot discover the place. The family were long resident in Lancashire. Noble's Hist. Coll. Arms.

DUGDELL. See Dugdale.

DUKE. 1. Lydgate and other old writers employ this word in its etymological sense of *leader*. In Capgrave's Chronicle, under the year 1381, we read: "In this yere, in the month of May, the Comones risen ageyn the King.... Her *duke* was Wat Tyler, a proud knave and malapert." 2. Camden makes it a nickname of Marmaduke.

DUKES. See Duke.

DUKESON. This name was probably applied in the first instance to the illegitimate son of a Duke. It is analogous to Fitzroy.

DUKINFIELD. The ancestors of the baronet were seated at Dukinfield in Cheshire as early at least as the reign of Edward I.

DULHUMPHREY. Of the origin of this singular name nothing is known, though it has certainly no reference to the want of vivacity in any particular Humphrey. It may be a corruption of some French local name with the prefix De, Du, or De la.

DULMAN. See Dolman.

DUMBRELL. Qu. *dummerel*, a silent person? Halliwell.

DUMMER. A parish in Hampshire.

DUMONT. Fr. 'Of the hill.'

DUMSDAY. See Domesday.

DUNBAR. A parish and town in Haddingtonshire, anciently the fief of the famous historical earls of Dunbar, immediate descendants of Gospatric, earl of Northumberland, who fled into Scotland with Edgar Atheling at the Norman Conquest, and to whom Malcolm Canmore gave the manor soon afterwards.

DUNCAN. The Gael. Donn-cann (pronounced Doun-kean,) signifying "Brownhead." Originally and still a Christian name.

DUNCANSON. See Duncan.

DUNCH. Deaf; dull.

"I waz amozt blind and *dunch* in mine eyez."
Halliwell.

DUNDAGEL. A castle in Cornwall, now written Tintagel.

DUNDAS. The family of Dundas "are generally believed to have sprung from the Dunbars, earls of March, who derived themselves from the Saxon princes of England;" (B.L.G.) not however from the resemblance of names, as might be thought, for the two localities are unconnected. Uthred, second son of the first Earl of March, temp. David I., obtained the barony of Dundas in West Lothian.

DUNDEE. The Scottish town.

DUNFORD. A known corruption of Durnford.

DUNHAM. Parishes and places in cos. Chester, Nottingham, Norfolk, &c.

DUNK. A Dutch surname, rather common both here and in America. It is probably an epithet implying dark or obscure. Du. *donker.*

DUNKIN. An Eng. corruption of the Scottish Duncan. The Duncans 'came south' at an early date, for one Donecan had got as far as Somersetshire at the making of Domesd. In the XIV. cent. it was often written Dunkan and Duncon in English records.

DUNLOP. (Often corrupted in Scotland to Dunlap and Delap.) Traced to the year 1260, when Dom. Gulielmus de Dunlop was lord of Dunlop in Ayrshire, an estate still in possession of the family.

DUNMAN. The same as Downman.

DUNMOLL. Qu. Dunmow, co. Essex, famous for its bacon-flitch, the reward of connubial fidelity?

DUNN. Dun, Dunne, Dunna, were A-Sax. personal names, and Done, Donne, &c. are in Domesd. Kemble considers them "adjectives relating to the dark colour of the persons," but Mr. Ferguson rather fancifully connects them with thunder, and with Thor, the god of thunder. But that the surname is sometimes local is shown by its H.R. forms, De Dun, De la Dune, &c. A-Sax., *dún*, a hill.

DUNNAGE. Dunwich, co. Suffolk.

DUNNELL. Perhaps a corruption of Donald.

DUNNING. Dunning, proprietor of Latham, co. Chester, and ancestor of the family of Lathom, or Latham, of that place, was contemporary with the making of Domesday Book. Whether he was a continued possessor, of the Saxon race, or a Norman grantee, is, Dr. Ormerod thinks, doubtful. His son was called Siward Fitz-Dunning. Miscellanea Palatina, p. 60. The contemporary lord of Kingsley, co. Chester, also bore the personal name of Dunning, as did several other persons in Norman times.

DUNSBY. A parish in co. Lincoln.

DUNSFORD. A parish in the county of Devon.

DUNSTALL. A township in the parish of Tatenhill, co. Stafford.

DUNSTANVILLE. Reginald de Dunstanville was a baron by tenure in the western counties, temp. Henry I. The family were doubtless Norman, but I do not find the locality from which they assumed their name.

DUNSTER. A town and parish in co. Somerset. De Dunsterre. H.R.

DUNSTONE. DUNSTAN. More probably from one of the places so called in cos. Lincoln, Norfolk, Northumberland, and Stafford, than from the well-known A-Sax. personal name.

DUNTON. Parishes in cos. Bedford, Bucks, Essex, Norfolk, and Leicester.

DUPLEX. DUPLEIX. Probably refers neither to duplicity of character nor to a corporeal bulk of double proportions. It is most likely a Fr. local name with the prefix *Du.*

DUPLOCK. This name appears in old parish registers in East Sussex as Du Plac, and is therefore probably of French origin. It may have been introduced in the sixteenth century, when many Frenchmen settled in that county to carry on the iron-works then flourishing there. Its etymology is obscure.

DUPONT. Fr. 'Of the Bridge.'

DUPPA. Said to be a corruption of D'Uphaugh, 'of the upper *haugh,*'—haugh being a low flat ground on the borders of a river (Jamieson); but of this I have strong doubts.

DUPRE. Fr. *Du Pré.* 'Of the Meadow.'

DURANT. DURAND. See Durrant.

DURBIN. DURBAN. Local—from Urbin or Urbino, the Italian city, the birth-place of Raphael.

DURDEN. 1. See Dearden. 2. An A.-Norm. sobriquet — *Duredent*, "hard tooth." See H.R.

DURHAM. The northern city, anciently written Duresme.

DURHAMWEIR. Apparently from a dam or weir in co. Durham. This singular name is found in Scotland.

DURIE. An estate in the parish of Scoonie, co. Fife.

DURLEY. Parishes in Hants and Somerset.

DURNFORD. A parish in Wiltshire.

DURRANT. An ancient personal name, in Latin Durandus, under which form it occurs in Domesday. An early Norman proprietor of this name founded Duran-ville (called in charters *Durandi villa*) near Bernai, in or before the eleventh century. The name of the immortal author of the *Inferno* was by baptism Durante—afterwards shortened by his familiar friends into Dante.

DURRELL. Probably the same as Darell.

DURSTON. DURSTAN. See Thurston. Also a parish co. Somerset.

DURWARD. A-Sax. *duru-weard*, a door-keeper, a porter. "A Porter, which we have received from the French, they (the Anglo-Saxons) could in their own tongue as significatively call a *Doreward*." Camden's Remaines.

DURY. The 'braes of Dury' are in the parish of Fowlis-Wester in the centre of Perthshire.

DUTTON. A very ancient Cheshire family surnamed from Dutton in that county, but of Norman descent, having sprung from Rollo, the conqueror of Neustria, through William, earl of Eu, who married a niece of William the Conqueror. Their founder was Odard, nephew of the far-famed Hugh Lupus, who gave him the barony of Dutton.

DUX. Lat. A leader; the same as Duke.

DWIGHT. Possibly a corruption of Thwaite.

DWYER. Said to be the Gaelic *do-ire*, a woody uncultivated place. Arthur.

DYCE. 1. Anciently De Dyce or Diss, co. Norfolk. 2. A parish in Aberdeenshire.

DYCHE. Probably the same as Ditch, though it is sometimes pronounced like Dyke. The words *dyke* and *ditch*, indeed, appear to be etymologically identical, and primarily to mean a barrier or defence; and to this day in some provincial dialects a water-course is called a *dyke* or *dick*.

The A.-Sax. *díc* means both a mound or bank, and a ditch, trench, or moat.

DYER. The occupation; *tinctor*. Teinturier, its equivalent, is a Fr. surname, and the famous Italian painter Tintoretto, whose family name was Robusti, was so called because his father had been a *tintore* or dyer.

DYKE. See Dykes. The baronets of Sussex and Kent sprang from the family of Dykes of Cumberland.

DYKEMAN. A maker of dykes. See Dyke.

DYKES. There is every reason to believe that this name is derived from no less an object than Hadrian's Roman Wall —the "Barrier of the Lower Isthmus." The family originated at Dykesfield, co. Cumberland, on the line of that celebrated defence. There is no doubt that the popular appellation of Hadrian's work was "the Dyke," or "the Dykes," just as "Graham's Dyke" was that of the more northern defence of Lollius Urbicus. See much interesting information on this subject in Dr. Bruce's "Roman Wall," edit. 1853, pp. 279, et seq., and Preface, p. ix. Dykesfield may have been so named either from the family, or immediately from the fact of the barrier's passing over the place. However this may be, the surname Dykes was borrowed from the wall itself, as appears from its earliest known form, which is not De Dykesfield, but Del Dykes, i. e. "of the Dykes." Robert Del Dykes, the first recorded individual of the family, is mentioned in a deed (without date, but known from internal evidence to be) of temp. Henry III., penes F. L. B. Dykes, Esq. Another ancient northern family of the same district—that of Thirlwall—also derive their appellation from the Roman Wall. See Thirlwall.

DYMOCK. This ancient family, in which the office of KING'S CHAMPION has long been hereditary, claim descent from Tudor Trevor, lord of Whittington in Shropshire, (ancestor of the Pennants,) from whom sprang David ap Madoc, commonly called Dai, whence the gradual corruptions, Dai-Madoc, Damoc, Dymoc, Dymock. Such is the statement in B.L.G., but having no faith in such twisted derivations, I shall take the liberty of deducing the name from the parish of Dymock in Gloucestershire, the birth-place of the "Man of Ross," and also, it is said, of the celebrated breed of sheep now called Merino, exported from thence to Spain in the fourteenth century.

DYMOND. See Diamond.

DYNE. Anciently Dine. Might come from the Fr. *digne*, worthy. There is a statement, however, I know not of what authority, that the family were identical with the Dyves, who came into England from Normandy with the Conqueror. De Dine. H.R.

DYVE. See Dives.

E.

EACHARD. ECHARD. An ancient personal name. Achard. Domesd.

EADE. EADES. Probably the same as Eady. A Joh'es fil'Ede occurs in H.R.

EADY. EADIE. Ædi occurs as a personal name in Domesday. In Scotland Edie is the 'nurse-name' of Adam.

EAGER. EAGAR. A trait of character; or, perhaps, a corruption of Edgar (spelt in A-Sax. Eâdgar) by the suppression of the letter D.

EAGLE. EAGLES. EGLES. Metaphorically applied to a person of ambitious or soaring disposition. There are several legendary stories of eagles which may have originated the name; e. g. that of De Aquila mentioned in this Dictionary, and the well-known Stanley tradition. See Curiosities of Heraldry, page 187. The Eagle is also a familiar heraldric bearing and a common inn sign.

EAGLETON. Eggleton, co. Hereford, or Egleton. co. Rutland.

EALAND. Probably Elland, co. York.

EAMES. Probably the same as Ames.

EARDLEY. A township in Staffordshire.

EARITH. Erith, a parish in Kent.

EARL. EARLE. EARLES. A-Sax. eorl. Primarily a man—a man of valour or consideration—vir; afterwards a head, ruler, leader, or hero; and finally a nobleman of the highest rank, equivalent to an " ealdor-man ;" an Earl. See Bosworth.

EARLY. A liberty in the parish of Sonning, co. Berks.

EARNES. Perhaps from the A-Sax. earn, an eagle.

EARNSHAW. Local—from A-Sax. earn, an eagle, and sceaga, a wilderness, (Leo) grove, or shaw.

EARTHROWL. This remarkable name, which occurs twice in London Direct., 1852, would appear to be derived from A-Sax. ear, the ear, and thyrl, an aperture, hole, or perforation—" the ear-hole." The word nostril is a compound of nase, the nose, and thyrl—a cognate expression. How " ear-hole " became a surname I do not venture even to guess.

EARWAKER. This apparently absurd name may, with great probability, be derived from the Germ. Herr-wacker, "gallant lord," or " noble sir." Domesday, however, shows us a previous tenant in Devon, who rejoiced in the appellation of Eureuuacre.

EARWHISPER. Qu. ear-whisperer— a conveyer of scandals ?

EASEL. Perhaps the A-Sax. esol, an ass.

EASLEY. Eastley, a place in Hampshire.

EASON. EASSON. A corruption of Easton.

EAST. See under North. Del Est, " of the East." H.R.

EASTBURY. Places in Berks, Dorset, &c.

EASTER. This name may be derived with nearly equal probability from several distinct sources, as : 1. From the parishes called Easter in Essex. 2. From the Christian festival, like Christmas, Noel, Pentecost, &c. : we have also Pask from Lat. Pascha, O. Fr. Pasche. 3. From the old Teutonic divinity, Ostre or Eastre. 4. It may be synonymous with Eastman and Easterling. The last derivation is supported by the form Le Ester of the H.R.

EASTERLING. A native of the Hanse Towns, or of the East of Germany. Merchants trading with us from those parts are called in medieval writings " Mercatores Estrenses."

EASTGATE. From residence near the eastern gate of a town. The medieval form would be " Atte, de, or in, Estgate." Northgate, Westgate, and Southgate, well-known surnames, originated in like manner from the contiguity of the bearers' residences to the respective gates.

EASTHAM. Parishes in cos. Chester and Worcester.

EASTHOPE. A parish in Shropshire.

EASTICK. Eastwick, by the suppression of w, the same as in Greenwich, Woolwich, &c.

EASTMAN. Probably synonymous with Easterling, which see.

EASTO. Perhaps a corruption of East-hope.

EASTON. Like Norton, Sutton, Weston, in its origin, meaning an enclosure or homestead, lying relatively towards the east. Besides minor districts and farms, there are seventeen parishes, hamlets, tythings, &c., in England so designated.

EASTWICK. A parish in Hertfordshire.

EASTWOOD. Parishes in Essex and Nottinghamshire.

EASUM. A provincial pronunciation of Evesham, co. Worcester.

EASY. EASEY. 1. From indolence of character. 2. The name of some locality ?

3. By transposition of letters from Esay, the old form of Isaiah.

EATON. Parishes and places in cos. Leicester, Chester, Berks, Nottingham, Salop, Derby, Hereford, Bedford, &c.

EATWELL. Probably from Etwall, a parish in Derbyshire.

EAVES. A township in Staffordshire.

EAVESTAFF. Most likely a corruption of Heave-staff, analogous to Hurlbat, Shakeshaft, Wagstaff, and Shakspeare.

EBBETS. Ferguson derives it from an O. German name—Ibbet.

EBBLEWHITE. A corruption of Applethwaite, a township in Westmoreland.

EBBS. From an old Frisian name Ebbe. Ferguson.

EBELING. See Evelyn.

EBELTHITE. The same as Ebblewhite.

EBERS. Perhaps from A-Sax. *eofer*, a boar. See Boar.

☞ **ECCLES**— as a component part of many local names—is not, as has been erroneously conjectured, derived from the Lat. *ecclesia*, implying the existence of a church in early times; neither can it be a corruption of *eagle's*. It is probably a modification of some A-Sax. personal name. Among surnames with this word as a root, we have Eccleshall, Ecclesbourn, Ecclesfield, Eccleston, Icklesham, Igglesden, &c.

ECCLES. 1. A parish in Lancashire; another in Norfolk. 2. "Assumed by the proprietors of the lands and barony of Eccles in Dumfries-shire, as early as the period when surnames first became hereditary in Scotland. John de Eccles was a personage of rank in the reign of Alexander III." B.L.G.

ECCLESFIELD. A parish in Yorkshire.

☞ **ECCLESIASTICAL SURNAMES.**— While it is easy to understand why names of civil offices and occupations should have become transmissible or hereditary surnames, it is not so obvious how such names as Pope, Cardinal, Bishop, Abbott, Prior, Archdeacon, Rector, Parsons, Vicar, Priest, Deacon, Clerk, Friar, Monk, Saxton, Pontifex, Novice, &c., have found their way into our family nomenclature. A writer in the Edinb. Rev., April, 1855, says : "Most probably such names were given by mothers, or nurses, or playfellows, and, adhering to individuals, when surnames began to be hereditary, were handed down to posterity." There were Roman families called Flaminius and Pontifex, who were neither flamens nor priests, though Sigonius reckons them amongst those whose ancestors had held such offices. This explanation, however, will not apply to modern surnames, which have originated long subsequently to the enforced celibacy of the Roman Catholic priesthood. Noble (Hist. Coll. Arms) thinks that the bearers of these sacerdotal names originally held lands under those who really were entitled to them from office. Another theory is, that the names were assumed by the children of persons who on becoming widowers had entered into holy orders. Florence of Worcester, under A.D. 653, mentions one Benedictus Biscop (bishop) who certainly never enjoyed episcopal authority. According to Kemble, the last true-born king of Kent, was surnamed 'Pren,' or the Priest, because, before his advancement to regal honours, he had received ordination. Similar was the case of Hugh de Lusignan, a French archbishop, who by the death of elder brothers unexpectedly became a great seigneur, and who, by Papal dispensation, resigned his ecclesiastical dignity on the condition that he and his posterity should use the name of *Archevesque*, and bear a mitre over their arms for ever. Camden. In the reign of king John we find a *Jew* bearing the surname of 'Bishop'—'Deulecres *le Eveske*.' Ed. Rev. ut supr. About the same time a manorial tenant of St. Paul's is described as "Gulielmum aurifabrum, cognomento *Monachum*," which, as he was a married goldsmith, was of course a sobriquet. Hale's Domesday of St. Paul's. In many instances the surname was probably imposed by way of scandal, when the putative father of an illegitimate child was of the ecclesiastical order.

ECCLESTON. Parishes and townships in cos. Lancaster and Chester. An ancient family were seated at Eccleston in the latter shire, temp. Henry III., and continued in possession until the last generation when it was sold, and the estate of Scarisbrick, with the name acquired by marriage about the same period. Shirley's Noble and Gentle Men of England, p. 117.

ECHINGHAM. A parish in Sussex, possessed by the family from temp. Henry II. till 1482. See Hall's Echyngham of Echyngham, Lond. 1850.

ECHLIN. Crawford the genealogist in a MS., dated 1747, deduces the family from Philip le Brun, who flourished in Fifeshire temp. Robert I., and was enfeoffed with lands called Echlin in that county by Roger de Mowbray. The family were transplanted to Ireland by Dr. Robert Echlin, bishop of Down, temp. James I. B.L.G.

ECK. Probably an old personal name. Ecke, a well-known character in the German poems of the middle ages, seems to have been a sort of Teutonic demigod. See Ferguson.

ECKERSALL. Supposed to be a corruption of Eccleshall, a parish in Staffordshire.

ECKINGTON. Parishes in cos. Derby, and Worcester ; also the parish in Sussex now known as Ripe.

ECKROYD. The same as Ackroyd.

EDDELS. Mr. Ferguson ingeniously derives this name from a common source with that of Attila, the renowned leader of the Huns. It appears to signify "grandfather." Mr. F. remarks that " it is difficult to conceive how such a name could in the first instance be baptismal, and how an infant could be called Father or Grandfather. But it is not difficult to conceive how the name might be given as a title of honour and respect to the head of a family or of a people, and how, once established as a name, it might afterwards become baptismal."

EDDIKER. The singular name Earwaker (q. v.) is thus corruptly called and written in Lancashire.

EDDIS. See Edis.

EDDIS. EDDISON. May be derivatives either of Edie (see Eady), or of Edward through Eddy.

EDDY. See Eady and Eddis ; perhaps a nickname of Edward.

EDE. See Eade.

EDEN. Though the pedigree is not traced higher than the year 1413, there is no reason to doubt that the name is local and derived from either Castle Eden or Little Eden in the county of Durham, where, as Mr. Courthope asserts, the family were resident for several generations prior to the close of the XIV. cent.

EDENBOROUGH. Probably Edinburgh.

EDES. EEDES. See Eades.

EDEY. EDAY. See Eady.

EDGAR. Eâdgar, a well-known and royal personal name among the A-Saxons. There are probably several distinct families of this designation. The Scottish family deduce themselves from Gospatrick, earl of Northumberland, temp. William I., who was a kinsman of Eâdgar Atheling, and a descendant of king Eâdgar, great grandson of Alfred the Great. The Edgars of Suffolk claim from a John Edgar of Dunwich, living in 1237. B.L.G.

☞ **EDGE.** The side of a hill ; a ridge— whence Wolledge, Titheredge, Erredge, Muggridge, Edgeworth, Edgecombe, Egerton, Edgerley, Edgington, Edgley, &c.

EDGECOMBE. See Edgecumbe.

EDGECUMBE. The earl of Mount-Edgecumbe's family were in possession of Eggcombe or Edgcumbe, an estate in the parish of Milton-Abbot, co. Devon, as early as the XIII. century. C. S. Gilbert's Cornwall, i. 444, note.

EDGELER. See Hedgeler.

EDGELL. A corruption of Edgehill.

EDGER. Probably a corruption of Hedger, the occupation.

EDGERLEY. A township in Cheshire.

EDGEWORTH. 1. A parish in Gloucestershire. 2. The family of Miss Maria Edgeworth, the novelist, claim from Edward Edgeworth, bishop of Down and Connor, who settled in Ireland temp. Elizabeth. His ancestors were originally of Edgeworth, now called Edgeware, in the county of Middlesex. B.L.G.

EDGHILL. Edgehill, a chapelry in co. Lancaster, and a hilly ridge in Warwickshire, famous for a battle between Charles I. and the Parliamentarians.

EDGLEY. See Edgerley.

EDGWORTH. A township in Lancashire.

EDIKER. See Eddiker.

EDINBURGH. The Scottish metropolis.

EDINGTON. A parish in Wiltshire, and places in cos. Somerset and Northumberland.

EDIS. EDISON. May be from the same source as Eady; but see Eddis.

EDKINS. A diminutive of Edward.

EDLIN. Probably a corruption of the A-Sax. Atheling.

EDMESTON. EDMISTON. A corruption of Edmonstone.

EDMETT. Probably the same as the Etemete of the H.R.; perhaps originally imposed as a sobriquet upon some great carnivorist.

EDMONDS. EDMUNDS. EDMONDSON. EDMUNDSON. The son of Edmund.

EDMONSTONE. An estate in Newton, co. Edinburgh.

EDMONDSTOUNE. Edmundus, said to have been a younger son of Count Egmont of Flanders, who attended Margaret, daughter of Edgar Atheling into Scotland, in 1070, rose to great eminence, and became the progenitor of the E.'s of cos. Roxburgh and Lanark. B.L.G. He is said to have imparted his name to Edmonstone in Edinburghshire, from which estate his successors subsequently derived their distinctive appellation. Courthope's Debrett.

EDOLPH. An ancient personal name, written in the Saxon Chronicle Eâdulph. The same as Adolphus.

EDRIDGE. May be local, though I do not find the place; it is, however, more probably the well known A-Sax. name Eâdric, with a softened termination.

EDSAW. The same as Edsor?

EDSOR. EDSER. Perhaps corruptions of Edensor, co. Derby. See Ensor.

EDWARD. The personal name, which has given rise as surnames to Edwards, Ethards, Edwardson, Tedd, and perhaps to Edes, Edkins, &c.

EDWARDES. (Bart.) "Descended in the male line from the ancient kings or princes of Powysland in Wales. They became seated at Kilhendre, in the parish of Ellesmere, Shropshire, as early as the reign of Henry I. The surname of Edwardes was first assumed by John ap David ap Madre of Kilhendre, temp. Hen. VII., and he was great-grandfather of Sir Thomas Edwardes, the first baronet." Courthope's Debrett. Shirley. Edwardes of Rhyd-y-gors claims from Ethelstan Glodrydd, through Cadwgan, lord of Radnor, and Edwardes of Sealy Ham claims from the celebrated Tudor Trevor. B.L.G.

EDWARDS. This name is so common that more than two hundred and fifty London traders bear it. In the Registrar-General's List it occupies the twentieth place for frequency, there being for every four Smiths or Joneses about one Edwards, or 25 per cent. Many families of Edwards and Edwardes are of Welsh patrician origin. For example, Edwards of Nanhoron descends from one of the royal tribes of Wales through Sir Griffith Lloyd and Sir Howell y Fwyallt; Edwards of Ness Strange descends from Einion Effel, lord of Cynllaeth, co. Montgomery, 1182; Edwards of Old-Court, co. Wicklow, claims from Roderick the Great, king of all Wales in 843, through his younger son, Tudwall *Gloff* or "the lame," whose descendants settled in Ireland in the XVII. century. It may seem remarkable that such a thoroughly Saxon name should occur so frequently in Welsh families of ancient blood, but it must be remembered that settled surnames do not appear among the Welsh till within the last two or three centuries, long after the prejudices against our early Edwards had passed away. See Edwardes.

EDWARDSON. See Edward.

EDWARDSTON. A local surname mentioned by Camden. Place unknown.

EDY. EDYE. See Eady.

EEDLE. Edolph, an A-Sax. personal name.

EEL. EELES. Most likely some A-Sax. personal name softened from Æl, Æthel.

EGAN. 1. The *cineal Eoghain*, were the 'genus' or progeny of Eoghan, a great Irish chief contemporary with St. Patrick. The name is anglicised to Owen and Eugene. O'Donovan in Irish Penny Journ. p. 327. Gaelic, *eigin*, force, violence; hence strong-handed, active. Arthur.

EGERTON. The Egertons have a common descent with the Cholmondeleys from the celebrated William Belward, baron of Malpas, under the Norman earls-palatine of Chester. David de Malpas, son of Belward, was grandfather of David de Egerton, so named from a township and estate in the parish of Malpas, of which he was possessor.

EGG. Probably a hardened pronunciation of the A-Sax. *ecg*, an edge. See Edge. De Egge, H.R., co. Salop.

EGGAR. Mr. Ferguson thinks it "signifies an inciter, stimulator," as we say "to egg on," but it is far more likely to be a corruption of Edgar.

EGGS. A corruption of Exe, the Devonshire river? But see Egg.

EGLETON. A parish in Rutlandshire.

EGMON. EGMOND. The Van Egmonds were one of the most eminent families of Holland, and derived their surname from their residence at the mouth (*mond*) of the river Hegge, in North Holland. There is an old Dutch proverb, which makes Brederode the noblest, Wassenaar the oldest, Egmont the richest, and Arkel the boldest, of the aristocracy of Holland. Dixon.

EGREMONT. An ancient barony in Cumberland, from which the Wyndhams in more recent times took the title of earl.

EIGHTEEN. From the number—though it is difficult to account for its adoption as a name. We have, however, several analogous surnames.

ELAM. Eleham, or Elham, a parish in Kent.

ELD. ELDE. ELDER. I think these names must be taken literally as relating to the advanced age of the original bearer, (A-Sax. *eald*) especially as we have the correlatives Young and Younger.

ELDRED. The extinct baronet family of Saxham, co. Suffolk, claimed a Saxon origin. The *name* is an A-Sax. personal appellation.

ELDRIDGE. Perhaps local. *Eldridge*, *elriche*, or *elritch*, is, however, a medieval word signifying "wild, hideous, ghastly, lonesome, uninhabited except by spectres." Gloss. to Percy's Reliques, edit. 1839. In the ballad of Sir Cauline is a description of an "eldridge knight." The fair Christabelle sends her lover on a perilous errand, but forewarns him—

> "The Eldridge knight, so mickle of might
> Will examine you beforne ;
> And never man bare life awaye,
> But he did him scath and scorne.
> That knighte he is a fond paynim,
> And large of limb and bone ;
> And but if heaven may be thy speede,
> Thy life it is but gone."

ELEMENT. Possibly a corruption of Alihermont, a district containing several parishes in the arrondissement of Dieppe in Normandy. Alihermont would readily become Alermont, Alémont, Element.

ELEN. A parish in Hampshire.

ELERS. "Peter Elers, of the ancient baronial family of that name, migrated from Germany, and came over to this country at the time when George I. was called to the throne." Burke's Commoners, IV. 418.

ELEY. See Ely.

ELFORD. A parish in Staffordshire, and a village in Northumberland.

ELGAR. An ancient personal name, still often used in the South as a baptismal appellation. Its forms in Domesd. are Algar and Ælgar.

ELIAS. Elias or Helyas was a very common A-Norm. baptismal name, and became the parent of the surnames Ellis, Ellison, and perhaps of Elliot, Elliotson, Els or Ells, Elson, Elley, Ellet, and Lelliot.

ELIOT. See Elliott.

ELKIN. ELKINS. ELKINSON. The derivation in Eng. Surn. i. 166, is probably incorrect. Mr. Ferguson has the following observations. "Allkins and Elkin may possibly mean 'Englishman.' So common was Alla or Ella as an early Saxon name, that the Northern Scalds familiarly termed Englishmen in general Ello-Kyn, the race of Ella. Wheaton's Hist. of the Northmen. Allkins and Elkin may, however, simply be diminutives of Alla or Ella."

ELKINGTON. Parishes in cos. Lincoln and Northampton.

ELLACOMBE. A place under the Haldon hills, co. Devon, where the De Ellacombes were resident in 1306.

ELLARD. Elard, an A-Sax. personal name.

ELLERKER. A township in the parish of Brantingham, Yorkshire.

ELLERY. A corruption of Hilary.

ELLES. ELLET. See Elias.

ELLESMERE. ELSMERE. A town and parish in cos. Salop and Flint.

ELLIOTT. A name of doubtful origin. A William Aliot came into England with the Conqueror, and the name seems to be connected with Alis and Ellis. But Hals, speaking of the Eliots (Lord St. Germain's family), says: "These gentlemen I take to be of Scots original and so denominated from the local place of Eliot, near Dundee." D. Gilbert's Cornwall. ii. 66. The name, though very widely spread, certainly seems in most instances to have come from N. Britain, where a great clan so called existed.

ELLIS. In the whole range of family nomenclature there is perhaps no name which admits of more variety of origin, or a greater number of differing forms. "Elles or Ellis in British," says Hals, in D. Gilbert's Cornwall, iii. 429, "is a son-in-law by the wife, and Els or Ells, a son-in-law by the husband. Ella or Ælla is a well-known regal name of A-Sax. times, and its genitive form would in later days become Ellis. From these two sources some of our very numerous families may have sprung, but there is little doubt that the surname

Ellis has for the most part been formed from the scripture name Elias, which does not occur as an A-Sax. name, but which was in use in France as early as the days of Charlemagne, as a baptismal designation, and afterwards gave name to several families of Elie. Elias, though uncommon now as a Christian name, was not so in the early Norman reigns, and indeed it had become hereditary at the time of the Norm. Conq., in the form of Alis. William Alis, mentioned in Domesd. and by Ordericus Vitalis, was progenitor of the Ellises of Kiddal, co. York, and Stoneacre, co. Kent, from whom sprang Sir Archibald Ellys, a crusader temp. Richard I., who is said to have originated the cross and crescents so common to the Ellis coat-armour. Ellis in later times, both in Wales and England, became a common personal name, and consequently there are in both countries many families of distinct origin. See 'Notices of the Ellises,' Lond. 1857. and Peds. of Ellis and Fitz-Ellis in 'Topographer and Genealogist,' vol. iii. The principal forms of this name in the H.R. are Eleys, Elice, Elies, Elis, Elys ; and other proven variations are Alis, Halis, Elias, Helias, Ellys, Elles, Hellis, Hellys, Hilles, Helles, Hollys, Holys, Holles, Iles, Ilys, Eyles, and Eales. Of course several of these forms are *etymologically* traceable to other and very different sources. Ellison, Alison, and Fitz-Ellis are also well-known surnames. Inf. W. S. Ellis, Esq.

ELLISON. See Ellis.

ELLMAN. Doubtless the Elmund, Almund, Ælmund, or Æilmundus of Domesd. —a baptismal name.

ELLWOOD. See Elwood.

ELMER. An A-Sax. personal name. An individual so designated was a tenant in chief in co. Hereford, temp. Domesd. The same as Aylmer.

John Elmer, bishop of London, temp. Eliz., once called Mr. Maddox " as mad a beast as he ever saw ;" but Mr. Maddox replied, " By your favour, Sir, your deeds answer your name righter than mine, for your name is Elmar, and you have *marred* all the *elms* in Fulham by lopping them."

ELMES. ELMS. This surname is congenerous with Ash, Oakes, &c., and there are many localities so designated in England.

ELMHIRST. An estate near Doncaster, co. York, which was owned by Robert de Elmehirst, temp. Edw. I., and still belongs to the family. Hunter's Doncaster.

ELMORE. See Elmer.

ELPHEE. See Elphick.

ELPHICK. There is a group of names which may fairly be placed around this as a common centre ; viz. Alphé, Alphen, Alphew, Alpheg, Elphee, Elfeck, Alphegh, &c. Ælfech occurs in Domesd. as having been a sub-tenant in Sussex, temp. Edw. Confessor, and not long previously, viz. A.D. 1006, St. Elphegus or Alphage was Archbishop of Canterbury. The personal name is evidently of A-Sax. origin, and it has been derived from two words in that language—*al*, all, and *fegan*, to fix or join, and interpreted to signify "a man who can do anything; a Jack of all Trades." Encycl. Perthensis.

ELPHINSTONE. The ancestor of Lord Elphinstone was, according to a family tradition, a German, who, marrying a relative of king Robert I., settled in Lothian, and gave his lands there the designation of Elvington, after his own name. Burke's Peerage. I do not find the slightest evidence in support of this statement, but there is abundant proof that the surname De Elphinstone was of good consideration from the XIII. century, when it occurs in charters dated 1250, 1252, &c. It was doubtless derived from the estate and village of Elphinstone co. Haddington.

ELS. ELLS. See Elias.

ELSHENDER. A northern corruption of Alexander.

ELSHIE. 1. Now Elshie-*shields*, a division of the parish of Lochmaben, co. Dumfries. 2. A Scottish nickname for Alexander.

ELSOM. Elsham, a parish in Lincolnshire.

ELSON. A corruption of Elston.

ELSTOB. A township in Stainton, co. Durham.

ELSTON. ELLSTON. Parishes, &c, in cos. Nottingham, Lancaster, &c.

ELSTOW. A parish in Bedfordshire, the birthplace of the "illustrious dreamer," John Bunyan.

ELSWORTH. ELSWORTHY. A parish in Cambridgeshire.

ELTHAM. A parish in Kent.

ELTON. Parishes and places in cos. Chester, Derby, Durham, Hereford, Huntingdon, Lancaster, Nottingham, &c.

ELVES. A corruption of Elwes.

ELWES. Not improbably from Alwi, an ancient personal name. Several of this name occur in Domesday Book as capital tenants, and at least two of them were of Saxon origin. Ellis's Introd. i. 372.

ELWYN. The same as Aylwin.

ELWOOD. Several tenants in chief in Domesd. are called Alwoldus or Aldwold, a contraction of the A-Sax. Æthelwald. Ellis, Introd. i. 373. A border clan of Elwood existed temp. Elizabeth. In a MS. tract copied in Archæologia, XXII., 168, it is stated in reference to Liddesdale, that "the strength of this country consisteth in two surnames of Armestronges and Elwoodes."

ELWORTHY. A parish in co. Somerset.

ELY. A city in Cambridgeshire.

EMANUEL. A well-known Jewish surname.

EMARY. See Amory.

EMBERSON. A corruption of Emerson.

EMBLETON. Parishes, &c., in cos. Northumberland, Cumberland, and Durham.

EMERICK. See Amory.

EMERSON. The son of Emeric or Almericus. See Amory.

EMERTON. See Emmerton.

EMERY. The ancient personal name Almericus. See Amory.

EMES. See Ames.

EMMENS. See Emmett.

EMMERSON. See Emerson.

EMMERTON. A parish in co. Bucks, more usually written Emberton.

EMMETT. Ferguson derives the group Emms, Emmens, Emmet, Emms, Emson, &c., from the A-Sax. *eám*, an uncle.

EMMOTSON. See Emmett.

EMMS. See Emmett.

EMPEROR. Probably a modern translation of Lempriere, which see.

EMSON. EMPSON. See Emmett.

ENGAINE. "The first mentioned of this name is Richard Engaine, in the time of the Conqueror, to whom he held the office of chief engineer. Hence the name D'Engaine from De Ingeniis." This very unlikely derivation is given without authority in Banks's Baronage, i. 292.

ENGALL. The same as Ingold.

ENGLAND. Engelond occurs several times in H.R. as a surname, without any prefix. It seems quite absurd to have adopted the name of one's country while still residing in it, as a family name; but I am inclined to think that it was first given to an Englishman when living in a foreign country, and that he, on his return, continued to use it. Or, England may possibly be the name of some obscure locality of which the family were anciently possessed, just as the Hollands take their name, not from the land of Dutchmen, but from a district of Lincolnshire.

ENGLEBURTT. The O. and Mod. Germ. personal name Englebert.

ENGLEDOW. See Ingledew.

ENGLEFIELD. A parish in Berkshire. The family continued in possession of the estate when Lambarde wrote, temp. Queen Elizabeth. "It is at this day part of the possessions of a man of that name, whearby it may appeare that the place som tyme gyveth name to the parson" (person). The Englefields are said to have been proprietors of the lands in the time of Egbert, some years before he became king of all England. This must of course be doubtful, though there seems to be evidence of their residence there before the Conquest.

ENGLEHEART. A recent importation from Germany. It is doubtless from the O. and Mod. Germ. personal name Engelhart.

ENGLISH. An additional name applied for distinction's sake, in early Norman times, to such persons as were permitted to retain their lands. Thus in Domesd. we find "quatuor Angli"—Four English, mentioned as holding in capite in Hampshire.

ENNESS. See Ennis.

ENNIS. A contraction of the Irish Mac Gennis.

ENSIGN. Probably a corruption of Enson, Henson, Henryson.

ENSOLL. See Insoll.

ENSOM. ENSUM. Ensham, co. Oxford.

ENSOR. The Ensors of Rollesby Hall, co. Norfolk, are descended from the Edensors of Staffordshire, who doubtless borrowed their surname from the parish of Edensor in the neighbouring county of Derby.

ENTWISLE. A township and estate in Lancashire, which was possessed by the family temp. Henry V. and VI., and doubtless much earlier.

ENYS. An estate in Cornwall, still possessed by the family, to whom it belonged temp. Edward III.

EOCHAGAN. EOGHAN. See Mageoghegan.

EPPS. The genitive form of an old personal name. A Roger Eppe is found in H.R.

☞**ER**, as a termination. In the XIII. and XIV. centuries, many small proprietors and cottagers assumed a stationary name, as we have seen, rather from the *situation* than from the *name* of their residences, generally prefixing 'At.' Thus one who dwelt by a brook was called At Broke, or for softness A'Broke, one who resided near the church was called AtChurch. In course of time the At was dropped, and the termination -ER, or very frequently -MAN, affixed; thus the one old name "At Brook' became the common parent of three modern ones—Brook, Brooker, and Brookman; so At-Church of Church, Churcher, and Churchman. Bourner, Croucher, Fenner, Fielder, Furlonger, Grover, Heather, Hother, Holter, Hoper, Knapper, Laker, Plainer, Ponder, Rayner, Slader, Streeter, Stocker, Stoner, Towner, Witcher, and numerous others, belong to this class.

In Germany, Belgium, &c., the suffix ER denotes the town from which the person came, as Rusbridger, Dantziger, Hamburgher. These and several other surnames similarly formed have been naturalized in England. Such names have generally been assumed by Jewish families.

ERBY. The same as Irby.

ERICKSON. From Eric, a Teutonic personal name.

ERIDGE. ERREDGE. An estate in the parish of Frant, co. Sussex.

ERITH. A parish in Kent.

ERLAM. A corruption of Earlham, co. Surrey.

ERLE. See Earle.

ERLING. An ancient Norse appellation. Magnus Erlingsson was king of Norway from 1162 to 1184.

ERNLEY. A parish in Sussex.

ERREY. Perhaps from the Teutonic personal name Eric.

ERRINGTON. Perhaps Erringden, co. York.

ERROL. A parish in Perthshire, from which the noble family of Hay take their title of earl.

ERSKINE. The name of this ancient and noble Scottish family is derived from the barony of Erskine on the Clyde, in Renfrewshire, and it was first assumed by Henry of Erskine, about the year 1220.

ESAM. Perhaps from Evesham, co. Worcester.

ESCOMBE. A chapelry in co. Durham.

ESAU. The personal name. It is strange that the maxim, "Bonum nomen bonum omen," could ever have been so disregarded as in the imposition of this designation as a family name. Stranger still is it that any parent in modern times should give it at the font! Yet I have known an Esau, as well as an Ananias and an Absolom.

ESDAILE. "At the Revocation of the Edict of Nantes, 1685, the ancestor of this family, descended from an honourable house, then represented by the Baron D'Estaile, being a Protestant, fled from France, and lived and died in obscurity in England." Such is the account in B.L.G., which, however, shows no connection between the existing family and the refugee. The name appears to be derived either from Eskdale in Cumberland, or from Eskdaleside, co. York.

ESGILL. A river in Herefordshire, now called the Eskle.

ESPINASSE. The founder of this family in England, was a French Protestant, who settled here under the sanction of Charles II., by his order in council, 28 July, 1681, authorizing the denization of foreign Protestants without fee.

ESPINETTE. The family bearing this name were French Protestants, who left their native place, Port Danvau, on the river Charente, near Rochelle, at the Rev. of the Edict of Nantes in 1685, and settled at Rye in Sussex. Holloway's Rye, p. 582.

ESQUIRE. See Armiger.

ESSELL. Probably the same as Hassell.

ESSEX. The county. One Swain of Essex was a tenant in chief in co. Huntingdon at the making of Domesday. Henry de Essexia, probably his descendant, was a powerful, but at length an unfortunate baron, temp. Henry II. See Chronicle of Battel Abbey, p. 95.

ESTAMPES. Now Etampes, a large town of France, department of Seine and Oise, twenty-eight miles S. by W. of Paris. Camden places this among French names introduced at the Conquest.

ESTARLING. See Easterling.

ESTCOURT. An estate at Shipton-Moign, co. Gloucester, which was the property of the family 14 Edw. IV. and doubtless much earlier. Shirley's Noble and Gentle Men, p. 87.

ESTWICK. See Eastwick.

ETHARDS. A common corruption of Edwards.

ETHELSTON. The Ethelstons of Wicksted Hall, co. Chester, claim descent from King Athelstan, and their pretensions are set forth in a certain Harleian MS. (No. 2042) entitled *Ethelestophylax!* B.L.G. Without conceding this lofty claim from the grandson of Alfred, we may fairly derive the *name* from its Anglo-Saxon prototype.

ETTRICK. The family of E. of High Barnes, co. Durham, trace to Dorsetshire, temp. Henry VIII. The name, however it got so far south, is in all probability derived from Ettrick, parish, river, and forest in Selkirkshire, where a certain well-known 'shepherd' wooed the Muses.

EU. EW. EWE. A town of Normandy, well known in ancient times for its powerful earls, and in the present century for the château of King Louis Philippe.

EUSTACE. From the proper name Eustachius. The family, settled in Ireland under Henry II., were of Norman descent.

EVANS. The genitive of Evan, a common Welsh baptismal name, equivalent to John.

EVANSON. The son of Evan.

EVE. Apparently an obsolete personal name—perhaps the same as Ivo; whence Eveson and Eves. A London perfumer (1852) bears the queer epicene appellation of Adam Eve! In the H.R. we have Adam, son of Eve—Ad fil' Eve!

EVELYN. Probably an ancient personal name corresponding with the German Ebeling or Abeling, the ING being patronymical. Burke, however, derives it from a place in Shropshire "now called Evelyn, but formerly written Avelyn and Ivelyn." B.L.G.

EVENDEN. See —DEN.

EVENING. See Times and Seasons.

EVERARD. A well-known Teutonic baptismal name. The family were ancient in the county of Essex. In Domesd. Ebrardus: in H.R. Eborard.

EVERETT. An evident corruption of Everard.

EVERINGHAM. A parish in Yorkshire.

EVERMUE. H.R. A small town in the arrondissement of Dieppe, hodie Envermeu.

EVERSFIELD. An old local surname in Sussex—locality unknown.

EVERSHED. Probably from Eversholt, a parish in Bedfordshire, or from Evershot, a parish in Dorsetshire.

EVERTON. Parishes, &c. in cos. Bedford, Notts, and Lancaster.

EVERY. See Avery.

EVES. See Eve.

EVESON. From Eve, which see.

EVIL. See Eyvile.

EVORS. EVERS. Probably the same as Mac Ivor, though Ferguson derives them from the A-Sax. *efor* or *efyr*, a boar.

EWART. A township in Northumberland.

EWELL. 1. A town in Surrey. 2. Ewald, an A-Sax. personal name.

EWEN. EWENS. See Ewing.

EWER. See Ure.

EWING. Euing, probably a Saxon, occurs in Domesday.

EXALL. Two parishes in co. Warwick. (Exhall.)

EXCELL. See Exall.

EXETER. The chief town of Devonshire. A Baldwin de Exeter was a tenant in chief in that county at the compilation of Domesday.

EXPENCE. In Clewer church "some very indifferent verses on a brass plate commemorate Martin Expence, a famous archer who shot a match against a hundred men near Bray, co. Berks." Lysons' Berks.

EXTON. Parishes in cos. Rutland, Somerset, and Hants.

EYLES. One of the many forms of Ellis.

EYRE. For the traditional origin of this name in the circumstance of a Norman knight having, at the battle of Hastings, succoured duke William of Normandy and given him *air* when he was in danger of suffocation—see Eng. Surn. ii. 3. The true meaning of the name seems to be *heir* (hæres) since the H.R. give us the forms of Le Eyr, and Le Eyre; in fact the O. Eng. orthography usually rejects the initial *h* in this word. Brother, Cousin, Friend, and various other words expressive of consanguineous and social relations, are also found in our family nomenclature.

EYRES. See Eyre.

EYTON. The family were certainly resident at Eyton, co. Salop, as early as the reigns of Henry I. and II. Shirley's Noble and Gentle Men, p. 190.

EYVILE. EYVILL. The name with the prefix *de* occurs in the H.R. It is doubtless derived from Normandy or France. A crasis of the preposition and the noun produce Devil!

F.

FABER. The latinization of Wright, which see.

FABIAN. FABYAN. An ancient personal name—the Latin Fabianus.

FACER. An impudent person ; a boaster. Halliwell. More probably a workman who puts the 'face' or finish upon some article of manufacture.

FADDY. A west of England provincialism, meaning frivolous.

FAED. Gael. *faidh*, a prophet?

FAGAN. A corruption of the patronymical O'Hagan. The Fagans of Feltrim, co. Cork, deduce themselves from Patrick O'Hagan, who opposed the invasion of Ireland by the Anglo-Normans in the XII. cent. See B.L.G.

FAGG. Feg occurs in Domesday, and Fag in the H.R. The Kentish family were long connected with the parish of Rye, co. Sussex, and perhaps derived their name from lands there, still called Fagg farm.

FAGGETTER. Fr. *fagoteur*, a fagotmaker. Cotgr.

FAIL. A corruption of the Gaelic Mac-Phail.

FAIR. FAYRE. Allusive to complexion. So the Latin Flavus, the French Blond, Blondel, &c., and the Italian Biondi, &c.

It is often found in composition with other words, in English family names, as will be seen below. Sometimes the epithet alludes to a personal peculiarity, as in Fairhead, Fairbeard, and sometimes to a local one, as in Fairford, Fairholm, Fairbank, Fairbridge, Fairburn.

FAIRBAIRN. *Bairn*, Scot., a child. A fair or beautiful child. It may, however, mean, like the French *beau-fils*, a step-son.

FAIRBEARD. See Beard.

FAIRBROTHER. See Farebrother.

FAIRCHILD. The same as Fairbairn, which see. In the H.R. we have Farchild and Fayrchild.

FAIRCLOTH. A corruption of Fairclough, (pronounced Faircluff). A 'clough' is a narrow ravine or glen.

FAIREST. Probably a local name.

FAIRFAX. A-Sax. *fœgr* and *feax*, fair-haired. The same as the Latin Flavus, the Fr. Blond, &c. "*Fax* and *vex* are the same, signifying hair. Hence Matthew of Westminster calleth a comet, which is *stella crinita*, a *vexed* star [A-Sax. *feaxed steorra*;] and this family had their name from beautiful bushy hair. I confess I find in Florilegus, writing of the Holy War, " Primum bellum Christianorum fuit apud pontem *Pharfax* fluminis; but cannot concur with them who hence derive the name of this family." Fuller, (Worthies of England, iii, 414,) who adds, that in his time (two hundred years ago) twenty generations of Fairfaxes had resided on one spot, at Walton, co. York—a rare instance of long territorial possession by one name and family. The existing representative of this ancient race is Lord Fairfax, an American by birth and parentage, who, with the same republican principles which actuated his great ancestor, prefers a quiet life at Woodburne in Maryland, to a seat in the House of Peers.

FAIRFOOT. Perhaps from *pedal* beauty, since the cognate Belejambe (fair leg) is found in H.R. ; more likely from the name of some locality. See the termination FOOT.

FAIRFOUL. FAIRFOWLE. A beautiful bird. Qu. a provincialism for peacock ?

FAIRFULL. Fearful, timid. Or perhaps the same as Fairfoul.

FAIRHAIR. See Fairfax.

FAIRHALL. Perhaps Fairhaugh, a place in Northumberland.

FAIRHEAD. From the light colour of one's hair, or perhaps a local name. See termination HEAD. Fairhevid, the Saxon, and Belteste, the Fr. forms of it, occur in H.R.

FAIRHOLT. The father of Mr. F. W. Fairholt, F. S. A., a well-known living author, came from Germany about the end of the last century, and translated his German appellative into Fairholt, which he bequeathed to his son, who is the only person now bearing it.

FAIRLAMB. Most likely a corruption of some local name terminating in *ham*.

FAIRLES. This northern surname, which originated near Durham, is of doubtful etymology, as it has been variously written Fairlie, Faderless, Farrales, and Fairless. Whether it is local, or whether it relates to the orphanhood of its first bearer, is uncertain, though the family consider it to be derived from a place now called Fawlees, or Fawnlease, near Wolsingham. Folks of Shields.

FAIRMAN. 1. A huckster, or attender at fairs. 2. (A-Sax. *faran*, to go). A messenger. The H.R. present the variations Fareman, Feirman, Fayrman.

FAIRMANNERS. This name has probably nothing to do with the *boni mores*, or deportment of the first bearer, but is most likely a translation of the French *Beaumanoir*, the 'fair manor,' or beautiful mansion or dwelling-place—a local name not uncommon in France.

FAIRN. Parishes in cos. Ross and Forfar.

FAIRPLAY. From fairness in sport or combat. So Playfair.

FAIRWEATHER. Fayrweder, H.R. See the cognate name Merryweather.

FAIRY. FAIREY. A-Sax. *fægr* and *ig*. 'Fair-island,' a local name. This surname which occurs in the Registrar-General's list has therefore no connection with Queen Mab, Puck, Robin Goodfellow, or any of their family.

FAITH. From one who personated this Christian virtue in some medieval miracle play. The anniversary of St. Faith, virgin and martyr, occurs in the Roman calendar on the 6th of October; perhaps the original owner of this surname was born on that day. See Christmas, Noel, Pentecost, &c.

FAITHFUL. Loyal, trustworthy.

FALCON. 1. The bird, from some fancied resemblance. 2. A trader's sign. The 'falcon and fetterlock' was a favourite badge of the house of York.

FALCONER. FALCONAR. One who pursued the sport of falconry, so much admired in the middle ages, when a patrician was recognised by "his horse, his hawk, and his greyhound." Kings and great men kept a state falconer, and in such estimation was the office held in Norman times that Domesday Book shews us four different tenants-in-chief besides others who are described each as *Accipitrarius*—hawker, or falconer. Even at the present time the Duke of St. Albans holds the office of Hereditary Grand Falconer of England; and a late possessor of the title made an unsuccessful attempt to reinstate the sport, which, however picturesque, is not exactly adapted to these days of *minie*-rifles and long-shots.

FALDO. F. and W. being interchangeable letters, this may be the same as Waldo.

FALKE. *Falk*, Danish, a Falcon.

FALKINER. See Falconer.

FALKNER. See Falconer.

FALKOUS. A North of England surname which has the variations Faucus, Fawcus, Farcus, and is sometimes confounded with Fawke, Fawkes, &c. It probably means *falco, faucon*, a hawk.

FALL. 1. See Times and Seasons. 2. In the North of England the name is frequently of Gipsy origin. See Faw. 3. The De Fall of the H.R. shows a local origin.

FALLOW. The Scottish form of Fellow, which see.

FALSTOLFE. FASTOLFE. A great Norfolk family, one of whose members Shakspeare is supposed to have caricatured in his immortal Sir John Falstaff. The name seems to be Scandinavian, and personal. It appears from Domesd., that a Fastolf held one church in the borough of Stamford, co. Lincoln, freely from the king.

FALVESLEY. An eminent family took their surname from Falvesley, co. Northampton, and one of the family was created a baron by this title 7 Richard II.

FANCOURT. Falencourt, a place near Neufchâtel in Normandy. De Fanecourt. H.R.

FANCY. Probably local. Vanchi, near Neufchâtel in Normandy, has been suggested.

FANE. Welsh, 'slender,'—an ancient personal name. The ancestors of the earls of Westmoreland, "wrote their name Vane, and descended," says Collins, "from Howel ap Vane of Monmouthshire, living before the time of William the Conqueror." Peerage, Edit. 1768. iii. 173. The Vanes (Duke of Cleveland) are of the same lineage. Coll. vi. 118.

FANNEL. An article of dress, a maniple or scarf-like ornament; *fanon*. Cotgrave.

FANNER. Perhaps the O. Fr. *veneur*, a hunter. Or it may be O. Eng. *faner*, a winnower, a word used by Lydgate. Fannere. H.R.

FANNY. Probably local—the nurse-name for Frances being of too recent a date.

FANSH and FONSH. Derbyshire corruptions of Fanshawe.

FANSHAWE. The family were resident at Fanshawe-Gate in the parish of Dronfield, co. Derby, at the middle of the XVI. cent., and doubtless much earlier. Lysons.

FARADAY. This, like other compounds of *day*, is not very easily explained. Mr. Ferguson derives it from A-Sax. *fara*, a traveller, with *dag* as a suffix; this, however, assists us but little.

FARAMOND. Pharamond, an ancient Teutonic personal name.

FARAND. See Farrant. In Lincolnshire *farrand* means deep, cunning.

FARCUS. See Falkous.

FARDEN. One Fardan occurs as an undertenant in Domesday.

FAREBROTHER. In Scotland, 'fatherbrother' is a phrase employed to designate an uncle; but we may with more than equal probability derive this name from *Fair*-brother, the equivalent of the French *beau-frère*, brother-in-law.

FAREWELL. Cannot be interpreted as 'good bye'; it is derived from a little parish in Staffordshire, known by the curious designation of Farewell-with Charley!

FAREY. See Fairy.

FARGUSON. See Ferguson or Farquharson.

FARLEY. FARLEIGH. Parishes and places in cos. Hants, Wilts, Surrey, Stafford, Somerset, Bedford, and Kent.

FARLOW. A chapelry in Staffordshire.

FARM. From residence at one.

FARMAN. See Fairman. Farman or Farmannus is however personal in Domesd.

FARMAR. FARMER. See Fermor.

FARMING appears in the Reg. Gen.'s list of odd names. It is doubtless local: perhaps a contraction of Farmington, co. Gloucester.

☞ **FARN**—the first syllable of several local surnames—is the A-Sax. *fearn*, fern, from the abundant growth of that plant. Hence Farnaby, Farnfold, Farnham, Farnwell, Farncombe, Farnsworth, Farndell, Farnden, Fernwold, Fernland.

FARN. An island on the Northumberland coast.

FARNALL. 1. A parish in Forfarshire. 2. Farnhill, a township in Yorkshire.

FARNCOMBE. An estate at West Blatchington, near Brighton, co. Sussex, where the family were resident in the XIII. century, and the neighbourhood of which is still their principal *habitat*.

FARNES. A-Sax. *fernes*; a desert or wilderness.

FARNFOLD. An ancient local name in Sussex; place unknown.

FARNSWORTH. Farnworth, two chapelries in Lancashire.

FARNHAM. Parishes, &c., in cos. Surrey, Dorset, Essex, Northumberland, Suffolk, Yorkshire, Bucks, &c. The surname occurs in co. Leicester, before the reign of Edw. I. B.L.G.

FARQUHAR. A common Scottish surname—the same as the Irish Ferchard, an ancient personal name in both countries. The London Farquhars spring from Aberdeenshire.

FARQUHARSON. The son of Farquhar. Shaw Fercharson was chief of the Macphersons in 1450. He was the great-grandson of Ferchar, from whom he derived his surname. See Skene's Highlanders, ii. 177.

FARR. FARRE. A parish in Sutherlandshire; a place in Inverness-shire.

FARRANCE. See Farrant.

FARRAND. Mr. Ferguson derives it from the O-Norse *farandi*, signifying a traveller; but see Farrant, with which it is no doubt identical.

FARRANT. The English form of Ferdinandus, Spanish Fernandez, Italian Ferando, O. French Ferant. Camden says that these forms are corruptions of Bertran or Bertram, which I doubt.

FARRAR. FARRER. Probably a corruption of Fair-hair, answering to Le Blond, Harfager, &c. In the H.R. we have Fayrher. In a document of the year 1555, a Norfolk incumbent is called John Fayrhawr, alias Farrar. Blomefield's Norfolk, vii. 286. 2. Perhaps another form of Ferrers.

FARRELL. The Farrells, now of Dalyston, spring from the O'Ferrals of Mornyng and Bawn, co. Langford, who were of the clan Boy. B.L.G.

FARRER. See Ferrers.

FARRIER. See under Shoesmith and Marshall.

FARRINGDON. Alsi de Farendone was a tenant in capite in the county of Bucks at the making of Domesday. He probably derived his surname from Farringdon in Berkshire.

FARRINGTON. The Baronet's family came from Lancashire, in which co. there is a township so called.

FARRIS. See Ferris or Ferrers.

FARSYDE. The Farsydes, *olim* Fawside, derive their name from the castle, lands, and villages of Easter and Wester Fawsyde, near Tranent in East Lothian, where they were seated as early as 1253. B.L.G.

FARTHING. See Money, denominations of.

FARWIG. A place at Bromley, co. Kent.

FATHER. In old records Fader. Probably to distinguish a person from his son bearing the same Christian name; just as in France they still say Pourpoint *père* (senior) in contradistinction to Pourpoint *fils* (junior).

FATT. Stout, large as to person. So the Fr. Le Gros, and the Germ. Feist, both naturalized as surnames in England.

FAUCUS. FAWCUS. See Falkous.

FAULCONER. See Falconer.

FAULD. A Scotticism for Fold.

FAULKNER. See Falconer.

FAULTLESS. Two London traders bear this unobjectionable name.

FAUNCE. Perhaps from A-Norm. *faun*, a flood-gate or water-gate.

FAUNTLEROY. FANTLEROY. As several armigerous families—apparently unconnected with each other—have borne this name, it is presumed to be of considerable antiquity in England. It is perhaps a corruption of an ancient Fr. war-cry—DE-FENDEZ LE ROI—'Defend the King!' In course of time, the meaning of the name being forgotten, the *De* would be dropped, and the remaining syllables would easily glide into Fauntleroy. For examples of other surnames derived from war-cries, see Hay and Halliday.

FAUSSETT. See Fawcett.

FAUX. See Vaux.

FAVELL. Fauville-la-Campagne is near Evreux, and Fauville-en-Caux, near Yvetot. The name is found as a suffix in Weston-Favell, co. Northampton.

FAW or FAA. A celebrated Gipsy family or clan in Scotland. King James V. issued an edict on behalf of Johnnie Faw, "lord and erle of Little Egypt." *Faw* or *fa'* is a Scottish verb for 'to obtain,' which, considering the acquisitive habits of this wandering race, is appropriate enough.

FAWCETT. Probably from Forcett, a township in the wapentake of Gillingwest, N. R. of Yorkshire. Forsyth and Faussett seem to be mere varieties of the same name.

FAWCON. See Falcon.

FAWCONBERGE. FAWCON-BRIDGE. The great barons by writ, De Fauconberg, were summoned to Parliament from 1295 till about 1376. The heiress married William, younger son of Ralph, 1st Earl of Westmoreland, who thereupon wrote himself W. Neville de Fauconberge. The name seems to be derived from an estate in Yorkshire, perhaps the same as that called in H.R. Fulkebrigge.

FAWKENER. See Falconer.

FAWKES. FAWKE. 1. The same as Vaux. 2. A modification of Fulke or Fulco.

FAWN. The young of a deer.

FAWSIDE. FAWCID. Older and more correct forms of Farsyde, which see.

FAZAKERLY. A township in the parish of Walton, co. Lancaster.

FEAR. Gaelic, a man, a hero—the Latin *vir*.

FEARN. A parish in Ross-shire, and another in Forfarshire.

FEARNHEAD. A township in Lancashire.

FEARNLEY. Two chapelries in Yorkshire are called Farnley.

FEARON. Feron, anciently Le Feron. Le Feyron, (H.R.) A name still well known in Normandy: derived by M. de Gerville from the same source as Ferrier—viz., from *fer, ferrum*—a worker in iron. Mem. Soc. Ant. Norm., 1844. There are horse-shoes in the arms of one family of this name.

FEARS. Probably the same as Ferris. E. Surn. ii. 95. *Fear* is, however, Gaelic for a man or hero.

FEAST. See Feist.

FEATHER. Probably a sobriquet applied to a person who wore a remarkable one in his cap.

FEE. A feudal possession. Sometimes certain lands obtained this name, e. g. Bassett's Fee, Neville's Fee.

FEETUM. A corruption of Feetham, a local name.

FEIST. German; fat. Feste. H.R.

FELBRIGGE. A parish in Norfolk, where the family resided temp. Edward I. De Felbrigg, H.R.

FELD. An old form of Field.

FELIX. Happy: a latinization, or the personal name.

☞ FELL. A component syllable in many local surnames, (see Fell below), such as Felbridge, Fellgate, Feltham, Felton, Grenfell, &c.

FELL. FELLS. "*By frith and by fell*," a common medievalism; equivalent to the classical "*per sylvam, per campum*." "Also there is difference between the fryth and the fel; the *fels* are understood the mountains, vallyes, and pastures, with corn and such like; [open ground] the *frythes* betoken the springs and coppyses" [woodlands.]—Noble Art of Venerie, quoted by Halliw.

FELLMONGER. A-Sax. *fell*, a skin. A dresser of sheepskins—a word still in use in the South, though not recognized by Richardson.

FELLOWES. FELLOWS. Besides its more proper meaning of 'companion,' the word Fellow is used in some dialects to signify a young unmarried man, or a servant engaged in husbandry.—Halliw. Chaucer uses the phrase "a proper felawe" to denote a well-formed young man. The H.R. spellings of the name are Le Felawe, Le Felawes, and Fellawe.

FELSTED. A parish in Essex.

FELTHAM. A parish in Middlesex.

FELTON. Parishes and places in cos. Hereford, Northumberland, Somerset, and Shropshire.

☞FEMALE CHRISTIAN-NAMES *which have become Surnames.*—Several family names have the appearance of being derived from the baptismal names of females, and this has been thought to imply illegitimacy, though it is not necessarily the case. King Henry II., though legitimate, was surnamed after his mother, Fitz-Empress. Recent research has convinced me that Alison, Anson, and some others are traceable to *male* names, though at first sight they appear to be derived from female ones. The following, however, seem clearly to be *metronymics*: Ann, Anns, Agg, and Aggas, from Agatha; Bridgett, Betts, Betty, Bettyes, from Elizabeth; Cath-arine, Susan, and Susans, Babb, from Barbara; Marjory, Margerison, Margetts, Margetson, Margison, Maggs, Magson, and perhaps Pegg, from Margaret; Moll, Molson, and perhaps Malkin, from Mary; with others. Beattie is the Scottish for Beatrix, whence that name, as also Beat-son. In the H.R. are found the forms Fil' Alice, Fil' Elene, Fil' Emme, and in one case the metronymic had be-come a regular surname, the "filius" hav-ing been dropped—Robertus Elyanore.

On this subject Camden observes: "Some also have had names from their mothers, as Fitz-Parnell, Fitz-Isabel, Fitz-Mary, Fitz-Emme, Maudlens, (Mag-dalen,) Susans, Mawds, Grace, Emson, &c.; as Vespasian, the emperour, from Vespasia Polla, his mother, and Popœa Sabina, the empress, from her grand-mother."

☞ FEN, a syllable of frequent occurrence in local surnames (see Fenn) as Fenwick, Fenton, Fensham, Swynfen, Fenrother, Fenning.

FENCOTT. Fencot, a hamlet in Oxford-shire.

FENDER. The O. E. *fend* signifies to defend, (see Halliwell *in voc.*); a 'Fender' may therefore mean a defender, and this indeed is almost proved by the Le Fendur of the H. R.—An appellation given in com-memoration of some remarkable exploit.

FENN. A-Sax. *fenn,* a marsh or bog. From residence near one. In old docu-ments the forms are Atte Fenne, Del Fen, De Fen, De Fenne, &c., sometimes modified to Fenner.

FENNELL. See Vennell.

FENNER. Fenn Place in the parish of Worth, co. Sussex, had owners for several generations, called from it Atte Fenne, but in the time of Henry VI. the name was changed to Fenner, while a Kentish branch wrote themselves Fenour. Camden con-siders the name a corruption of *Veneur,* Fr., a huntsman.

FENNING. May be local, but I do not find the place. I think it may possibly be a Scandinavian personal name, and the genitive form, Fennings, rather confirms this view.

FENROTHER. A township in Nor-thumberland.

FENTON. Parishes and places in cos. York, Lincoln, and Stafford. The neigh-bourhood of Leeds was the principal *habitat* of the name in the XIV. cent.

FENWICK. "The Fenwykes of Nor-thumberland, ["insignis et illustris Fen-wickorum progenies."] are of Saxon origin, and take their cognomen from their ancient fastness in the fenny lands in the vicinity of Stamfordham." Slogans of the North, p. 11. In 'border' times they formed a powerful clan, and were the constant allies of the Percies.

> "We saw come marching ower the knowes,
> Five hundred Fenwicks in a flock—
> With jack and speir, and bowes all bent,
> And warlike weapons at their will."
> 　　　　　*The Raid of the Reidswire.*

The family were characterized as " THE FIERCE FENWICKS," and " THE FEARLESS FENWICKS," and their slogan or war-cry was—

A Fenwyke! A Fenwyke!! A Fenwyke!!!

FERDINAND. The personal name.

FEREDAY. See Faraday.

FERGUS. FEARGUS. A Scottish saint (whence St. Fergus in Aberdeenshire)— Gaelic etymologists deduce the name from *fear,* a man, and *eas,* hardiness—energy—a man of hardy, energetic character.

FERGUSSON. FERGUSON. The son of Fergus, which see. This ancient family, characterized as—

" A line that has struggled for freedom with Bruce,"

trace themselves uninterruptedly from Jon-kine Fergusson, lord of Craigdarrock in 1298. B.L.G.

FERMOR. Low Lat. *firmarius.* Fr. *fer-mier,* a farmer. This word is in modern times used as the equivalent of agriculturist, whether a tenant or not. Originally it meant, one who held of another anything for a profitable use, and paid him a red-ditus or rent. Thus taxes, customs, &c. were *farmed* as well as lands. Le Farmer, and *de la* Fermer, are found in H.R. The family of Fermor (Baronet, 1725), came into England from France temp. Edward III., and settled in Sussex.

FERNE. Perhaps from the Farne is-lands on the Durham coast, anciently written Ferne.

FERNIE. FERNEE. An estate in the parish of Monimail, co. Fife.

FERRABY. FERRIBY. Parishes in cos. York and Lincoln.

FERRAND. FERRANT. "Imported at a very early period into the deanery of Craven, in Yorkshire, from Normandy, where it is still to be met with. From William de Fortibus, earl of Albemarle, Hugh Ferrand, in the XIII. cent. had a deed of grant to himself and his heirs of the office of Warder of Skipton castle." B.L.G.

FERRER. See Ferrers.

FERRERS. FARRARS. The Itin. de la Norm. gives nine places called Ferrière, and four called Ferrières, in Normandy. M. de Gerville considers the name to have some relation to the ancient iron-trade of that province, which is probable. Mem. Soc. Ant. Norm., 1844; but that this very ancient and noble family were farriers is an absurd notion, originating probably in some heraldric and feudal allusions. Many of the numerous coat-armours assigned to the name contain horse-shoes, and at Oakham, the chief town of Rutlandshire, an ancient barony of the family, a custom prevails to this day of demanding a horse-shoe of every peer of the realm who passes through the town, or a composition in money. See Wright's Rutland. Lewis' Topog. Dict., &c. Henry de Ferieres, ancestor of the old Earls of Derby, was a tenant in capite under the Conqueror, and held enormous estates in many counties, his caput baroniæ being Tutbury, in Staffordshire. Collins. Kelham. A tradition makes the original Ferrers Master of the Horse to the Conqueror. The following account is given in B.L.G., though no authority is cited. The family derive from Walchelin, a Norman, whose son Henry assumed the name of Ferriers, a small town of Gastinors in France, otherwise called Ferrières, from the *iron-mines* with which that country abounded.

FERREY. See Ferry.

FERRIER. A more correct orthography of Farrier, which see.

FERRIS. FERRIES. See Ferrers.

FERRY. 1. From residence near one. 2. Possibly however from *fer ey*, the remote or distant island. 3. Camden says, "For Frederick th' English have commonly used Frery and Fery, which hath been now a long time a Christian name in the ancient family of Tilney, and lucky to their house as they report."—Remaines, edit. 1674, p. 92.

FERRYMAN. The occupation—a very important one in old times when bridges were few.

FESANT. O. Eng., *fesaunt*, a pheasant.

FETHERSTONHAUGH. An estate in Northumberland. The founder of this ancient family is said to have been a Saxon commander named Frithestan, who, settling in that county at an early period, gave to the place of his abode the name of Frithestan's Haugh, which, when local surnames began to be used after the Conquest, was adopted by his descendants. Some genealogists distinguish between the Fetherston-haughs of Northumberland and the Fetherston-halges of Durham, but there seems to be no ground for such distinction. See Kimber. Other authorities deduce the family from a William de Monte, temp. King Stephen, through the Stanhopes. Courthope's Debrett.

FETTIPLACE. A tradition makes the founder of this family a "gentleman-usher" of William the Conqueror!—but the pedigree ascends only to John Feteplace, temp. Henry VI., grandfather of William F., a benefactor to Queen's College, Oxon. ob. 1516. Feteplace, Feteplece, &c., are found, however, in H.R.

FEVER. FEVERS. O. Fr. *Le fevre*, the smith.

FEW. Under the feudal system a *feu* was a dependency, or something held by tenure. The holder was sometimes called a *feuar*.

FEWSTER. 1. Halliwell has *fusterer*, a maker of pack-saddles. 2. *Feuster*, a female feoffee. See Few.

☞ FF. The double-f is used in some surnames, quite needlessly, in affectation of antiquity; e. g., Ffrench, Ffarington, Ffoulkes, Ffooks, Ffolliott. Now as double-f never did and never will begin an English word, this is ridiculous, and originates in a foolish mistake respecting the ff of old manuscripts, which is no duplication, but simply a capital f.

FFARINGTON. Farington, an estate in the parish of Penwortham, co. Lancaster. Farington or Ffarington Hall (see ☞ FF) was the residence of the family from temp. Henry III. till the year 1549. B.L.G.

FFOULKES. The pedigree is deduced from Marchudd ap Cynan, lord of Brynfenigi, who flourished in the ninth century. The name appears to have been borrowed from Ffoulk ap Thomas, who lived early in the sixteenth century, and whose descendants have ever since borne it.

FFRENCH. The ancestors of Lord Ffrench are said to have been seated at Castle Ffrench, co. Galway, for many centuries. Courthope's Debrett. The name was anciently written De Frignes, De ffreygne, Frynshe, &c. B.L.G.

FIDDLER. A violinist.

FIDLER. A mis-spelling of fiddler. The name is common about Ewell, co. Surrey.

☞ FIELD. A component syllable in a great number of family names. It has been said:—

"In *Field*, in Ham, in Ley, in Ton,
The most of English surnames run."

The A-Sax *feld* is applied to open localities, and is nearly equivalent to *campus*. Sometimes, however, it signifies "places detached but not entirely open, *loca sylvatica*, or swine-walks, which might at least be partially overgrown with brushwood." Williams's Trans. of Dr. Leo's

Local Nomencl., p. 101. This termination is found in many counties, but particularly in the three south-eastern ones of Sussex, Kent, and Surrey, and there it almost invariably pertains to spots cleared out of the great primeval forest of Andred, just as the 'woods' and the 'hursts' even to this day give proof of the original densely-wooded character of the country. The number of surnames with this termination must amount to hundreds; I shall cite but a sample: Aberfield, Bedingfield, Bousfield, Bayfield, Cranfield, Duffield, Eglesfield, Fairfield, Greenfield, Heathfield, Hartfield, Ifield, Lindfield, Mayfield, Mansfield, Stansfield, Sheffield, Tanfield, Tofield, Wingfield, Westfield.

FIELDER. A person who had the care of a common field.

FIELDING. In a document dated 9 Edw. II., mentioned by Collins, Geoffrey de Fielding calls himself "Filius Galfridi filii Galfridi, comitis de Hapsburg et domini in Laufenburg et Rin FILDING in Germania." It appears from the same authority that Geoffrey, earl of Hapsburg, by the oppression of Rodolph, emperor of Germany, being reduced to extreme poverty, Geoffrey, one of his sons, "served Henry III. in his wars in England, and because his father, Earl Geoffrey, had pretensions to the dominions of Laufenburg and Rin*filding*, he took the name of Filding."

FIENNES. FIENES. This noble family derive from Conon de Fiennes, who in 1112 was earl of Boulogne, taking his name from a village in the Boulonnais territory. John de Fiennes, a collateral ancestor, had accompanied William the Conqueror to England in 1066, and he and his descendants for five generations were constables of Dover castle and lord-wardens of the Cinque Ports. The name has been varied to Fenes, Fenys, Fynes, and Fines.

FIFE. The Scottish county.

FIFEHEAD. The easternmost point of Fifeshire, generally called Fifeness.

FIGG. A Feg occurs in Yorkshire ante 1086. Domesd., and a Figge in Kent 31. Edwd. III. In the latter co. at a later period the Figgs, Faggs, and Foggs flourished contemporaneously, and may have had a common origin. Other kindred forms are Fig, Figes, Figgs, &c.

FILBERT. Philibert, a French personal name. St. Philibert was abbot of Jumièges in the VII. cent., and several villages in Normandy and Picardy bear his name. From some one of these the filbert-nuts—*nuces de Sancto Philiberto*—are presumed to have been imported into England. This nut has been a particularly hard one for the teeth of etymologists. See Richardson. See also Mr. Blaauw, in Sussex Arch. Coll. vi. 46.

FILBY. A parish in Norfolk.

FILDER. See Fielder.

FILER. See Fyler.

FILIOL. In mod. Fr. *filleul*, a godson. 'Filiolus regis' occurs in the laws of Ina and of Henry I., and the Confessor makes grants 'filiolo suo'—to his godson or adopted son. Ellis, Introd. Domesd.

FILKIN. A diminutive of Philip.

FILLAN. A Scotch personal name; also a rivulet in Perthshire.

FILLINGHAM. A parish in Lincolnshire.

FILLMER. See Filmer.

FILLPOTTS. See Filpot.

FILMER. "This family formerly wrote their name Finmere, Fylmere, Filmour, and Filmor, temp. Edw. III., but of late, Filmer, and were seated at Otterinden in Kent, at a place called Finmore." Kimber's Baronetage.

FILMORE. An old German personal name (Filimer) signifying "full-famous." Ferguson.

FILPOT. A corruption of Philipot, from Philip.

FILTNESS. Local; place unknown. The name is common and ancient in East Sussex.

FINAL. See Vinall.

FINCH. Perhaps a corruption of Vincent. Vincent Herbert of Winchelsea, 20 Edw. I. bore the alias of Finch. The early pedigree of the Earl of Winchelsea's family is very obscure. Their former surname was Herbert, and one of the earliest if not the first who was known as Finch was this very Vincent. In support of this notion I may add, from Collins, that the family had previously borne their father's name, as Herbertus filius Herberti, &c. In the H.R. the spelling is Fynch; in 13 Edw. III., Vynche. In Sussex the baptismal name Vincent is often corrupted to Winch or Vinch.

FINCHAM. A parish in Norfolk.

FINCK. Germ. the bird, or rather class of birds, known by the general name of *finch*.

FINDEN. The same as Findon.

FINDLATER. A district in the parish of Fordyce in Banffshire.

FINDLAY. FINDLEY. See Finlay.

FINDON. A parish in Sussex.

FINER. A refiner of metals. "Fyners," with this meaning, are mentioned in the old poem called Cocke Lorelle's Bote.

FINES. See Fynes.

FINEUX. "The Frenchman which craftily and cleanly conveyed himself, and his prisoner T. Cryoll, a great Lord in Kent, about the time of king Edw. II., out of France, and had therefore Swinfield given him by Crioll, as I have read, for his fine conveyance was then called Fineux, and left that name to his posterity." Camd. Remaines, edit. 1674, p. 170.

Q

FINEWEATHER. See Merryweather.

FINGAL. Finegal appears as a tenant in Yorkshire before Domesd. He was probably of Gaelic descent.

FINGHIN. An ancient Irish surname, now anglicized to Florence, means ' fair offspring.' O'Donovan in Irish Penny Journ. p. 327.

FINGLASS. Probably Finlass, a river of Dumbartonshire.

FINK. A provincialism for Finch. See Finck.

FINLAY. An ancient Scottish personal name, said to be the same as Kinlay.

FINLAYSON. The son of Finlay, and equivalent to Mackinlay.

FINN. A native of Finland. A-Sax. plur. Finnas. Fin. H.R.

FINNINGLEY. A parish in the cos. of York and Nottingham.

FINNIS. A native of Finland; a Fin. Ulf Fenisc occurs as a previous tenant in Domesd. in cos. Derby, Nottingham, Lincoln, and Huntingdon, and Fin Danus (a Dane) in co. Bucks.

FIRBY. A township in Yorkshire.

FIREBRACE. The extinct baronet family, whose pedigree ascends only to the XVII. cent., seem to have had a tradition of a Norman origin (Burke's Ext. Barts.), and the name is said to signify *fier-bras*, "bold or stout arm," like our indigenous Armstrong and Strong i' th' arm. The H.R. form, *Ferbras*, is suggestive of " Iron-arm."

FIREMAN. The occupation.

FIRKIN. Perhaps the diminutive of some Christian name—perhaps an ancient trader's sign; but certainly not what Mr. Ferguson would have us think, viz: *fir-cyn*, ' race of man,' an impossible appellation.

FIRMAN. Either fireman, or *ferd-mon*, A-Sax., a soldier.

FIRMINGER. FURMINGER. Probably O. French, *fromageur*, a cheese-maker. In O. Scotch the word *furmage* is used for cheese.

FIRTH. A parish in Orkney; also a Scottish topographical word, signifying, 1. An æstuary or bay; 2. A sheltered place or enclosure. The etymon in both cases seems to be the A-Sax. *frithian*, to protect or shelter.

FISH. See FISHES, below.

FISHBOURNE. A parish in Sussex.

FISHPOND. From residence near one. Ad Fispond, H.R.

FISHER. This seems to be a sufficiently obvious derivation from the calling of a fisherman, especially since ' fisher' occurs in our version of the New Testament in this sense; and Leland in his Itinerary usually describes the smaller sea-coast places as " fischar tounes." In Domesd.

and other early records, we meet with the forms Piscator, Le Pecheur, &c. There is, however, curious evidence that some families bearing this name are descendants of Fitz-Urse, one of the assassins of Thomas à Becket. Fitz-Urse is said to have gone over to Ireland, and there to have become ancestor of the Mac Mahon family—Mac Mahon being the Celtic equivalent of 'Bear's son;' but other branches of the family remained in England, and gradually corrupted the family name thus; Fitzour, Fishour, Fisher. The great Kentish family of Berham, or Barham, is also deduced by Philipot, Harris, and other Kentish historians from the same source—apparently upon the strength of the first syllable of that name resembling the word *bear*, (Ourse—Ursus). See Quarterly Review, September, 1858, p. 379.

☞ **FISHES.** *Names of, which have become Surnames.*

The following catalogue of these has been arranged by Mr. Clark:

———— " Barnacle and Brill,
Crabbe, Cockle, Salmon, Trout, and Eel;
Bream, Dolphin, Haddock, Carp, and Loach,
Chubb, Winkles, Codd, Smelt, Pike, and Roach;
Base, Burt, Whale, Herring, Shark and Dace,
Tench, Gudgeon, Flounders, Roe, and Plaice;
Ray, Mackrell, Whiting, Grayling, Skate,
Perch, Mullett, Gurnard, Mussell, Spratt;
With Sturgeon, Lamprey, Pickerel, Sole,
And these perhaps include the whole,
Unless, indeed, we add thereto
The names of Fish and Fisher too."

Of these names, perhaps the majority are derived from sources unconnected with the inhabitants of the waters; for example, Barnacle, Brill, Bream, Roach, Perch, Mussell, and Winkles are local; Roe and Ray (Rae) belong to quadrupeds rather than fishes; and Burt, Mackrell, Salmon, Whiting, with several others, are shewn in their proper places to have no place in this category.

It is difficult to account for the adoption of the designations of fishes as proper names for persons and families. A few, such as Dolphin, Pike, and Crabbe, may have been borrowed from Heraldry; and others, such as Whale, Shark, and Herring, were perhaps sobriquets which having been applied to an individual afterwards adhered to his descendants.

FISK. A-Sax. *fisc*, a fish.

FIST. The same as Feist.

FITCH. A polecat—perhaps the sign adopted by some medieval furrier. It may however be a corruption of Fitz. H.R. Fitche.

FITCHETT. A polecat: formerly a term of contempt. It may have a much more respectable origin, from *Mont*fichett, which see. Fichet, without prefix, is found in H.R.

FITCHEW. 1. A corruption of Fitz-Hugh. 2. A kind of polecat—a word of contempt.

FITKIN. See Fitt.

FITNESS. See Filtness.

FITT. Apparently an ancient personal name, whence the diminutive Fitkin.

FITTER. A person who vends and loads coals, fitting ships with cargoes. Halliwell.

FITTIS. Said to be the Gael. *feadha*, forward, fierce, surly. Folks of Shields.

FITZ. Occurs at the present day as a surname without any addition. This is probably local, from the parish of Fitz in Shropshire; or it may be the Norman-Fr., Le Fitz, "the Son"—like Cousin, Frère, Brother, &c. Fiz. H.R.

☞ **FITZ.** A Norman-French prefix, signifying son, being a corruption of the Latin *filius*. Many of the names which occur in Domesday Book with *filius* and the father's name in the genitive case, become Fitz in later records. Like AP among the Welsh, and MAC among the Scotch, the Fitz prefixed to the father's name was the only surname in use in many noble families, thus: 1. Bardolf; 2. Akaris Fitz-Bardolf; 3. Hervey Fitz-Akaris; 4. Henry Fitz-Hervey; 5. Randolph Fitz-Henry, and so on, down to the time of Edw. III. This succession is found in the family known as Fitz-Hugh, which then became their permanent surname. In general, however, this patronymical method was disused at an earlier period. Camden informs us that "King Edward the First, disliking the iteration of *Fitz*, commanded the Lord John Fitz-Robert, an ancient baron (whose ancestours had continued their surnames by their fathers' Christian names) to leave that manner, and be called John of Clavering, which was the capital seat of his Barony. And in this time many that had followed this course of naming by Fitz, took them one settled name and retained it." Remains, p. 185. The origin of the word FITZ, which has so much puzzled some Antiquaries, is this: in contracting the word *filius*, our old scribes drew a stroke across the 'l,' to denote the omission of the following 'i,' and thus assimilated it in form to the letter 't.' The character 'z' is the usual contraction of 'us.' Thus the word looked like "*fitz*," and came to be so pronounced.

FITZ-CLARENCE. This surname was given to the natural children of the late Duke of Clarence, afterwards King William IV.

FITZ-ELLIS. The knightly family so named, who flourished at Waterpyrie near Oxford, sprang from Sir William Alis mentioned in Domesd. The forms are Fitz-Elys, Fitz-Elias, Fitz-Ellis, &c. See Ellis.

FITZ-GERALD. The *Geraldines*, as this great family are sometimes called, claim to be descended from the same stock as the Gherardini, a noble Florentine family, whose progenitor, Rainerio, flourished A.D. 910; but it is doubtful whether this is not a fiction of the XV. cent., invented as a compliment from the Italian family.

(Gent. Mag. Aug. 1858). It is however sufficient for the antiquity of this distinguished race to state, that their pedigree is perfect up to Otho, Other, or more properly Ohtere, who passed into England before the Conquest. The name itself is probaby derived from that chieftain's descendant, Maurice, the son of Gerald, (filius Geroldi) great-grandson of Otho, companion of William I. at the Conquest, who married Nesta the famous Welsh princess, temp. Henry I. Maurice Fitz-Gerald accompanied Strongbow in his invasion of Ireland, temp. Henry II., and thus built up in that country the fortunes of the family, which under the title of Leinster has yielded Ireland her only duke. The original Other, castellan of Windsor under the Confessor, is said to have sprung from a Norse vi-king Ohtere, whose descendants settled in Normandy, and to have been the common ancestor of the Windsor, Carew, Fitz-Maurice, Gerard, Otter, and many other families, as well as of that amusing and credulous historian, Giraldus Cambrensis.

FITZ-GIBBON. The earl of Clare's family, the chief of whom was styled THE WHITE KNIGHT, otherwise Clan-Gibbon, are a branch of the great Anglo-Irish Fitzgeralds, being descended from Gilbert, otherwise Gibbon, son of John Fitzgerald, ancestor of the houses of Kildare and Desmond. From the same stock spring the knights of Kerry, called THE BLACK KNIGHTS.

FITZ-HARRIS. See Harris.

FITZ-HERBERT. Herbert Fitz-Herbert is said to have come into England with the Conqueror. His descendants settled at Norbury, co. Derby, in 1125, and are still, I believe, possessors of the estate. Lysons' Derbyshire.

FITZ-HUGH. See under ☞Fitz. The great baronial race of this name descended from a feudal chief named Bardolph, who was lord of Ravensworth, co. York, at the period of the Conquest. The surname was not fixed until the time of Edw. III., when Henry Fitz-Hugh was summoned to Parliament as Baron Fitz-Hugh.

FITZ-JAMES. James, illegitimate son of king James II., by Arabella Churchill, sister of the great Duke of Marlborough, received the surname of Fitz-James, and was created Duke of Berwick. Being attainted after the Revolution of 1688, he was created Duke Fitz-James by the king of France, and the title is still enjoyed in that country by his descendant, the present Duc Fitz-James.

FITZ-MAURICE. The Marquis of Lansdowne's family are of common origin with the Fitz-Geralds, being descended from the famous Otho of Windsor, temp. Edw. Confessor. The surname is derived from an early ancestor, named Maurice Fitz-Gerald.

FITZ-PATRICK. The anglicized form of Giolla-Phadruic, an ancient Irish chief of the X. cent. Its literal meaning is, The Servant of St. Patrick. Such names were common in Ireland soon after the introduction of Christianity. O'Donovan, in Irish Penny Journal, p. 330. Comp. Gilchrist, Gillespie, &c. John Fitz-Patrick, descended from the ancient monarchs of Ireland, was ancestor of the Earls of Ossory, who became extinct in 1818.

FITZ-ROY. Filius Regis—"Son of a King." This surname has frequently been given to the illegitimate offspring of our monarchs, e. g. to Robert, natural son of Henry I.; to Geoffrey, bishop of Lincoln, natural son of Henry II.; to Henry, natural son of Henry VIII., by Elizabeth Blount; and to Charles, Henry, and George, natural sons of Charles II., by Barbara Villiers, Duchess of Cleveland. From Henry, the second of these, are descended the Duke of Grafton, and Lord Southampton.

FITZ-SWAIN. See Swainson.

FITZ-WILLIAM. The Earl of this title and surname is lineally descended from William Fitz-Goderic, a cousin of king Edward the Confessor. His son, William Fitz-William, is said to have been ambassador from England to the Norman court, and to have accompanied Duke William in the invasion of this country. He was at the battle of Hastings, and tradition asserts that in reward for his prowess, the Conqueror gave him a scarf from his own arm. Collins.

FITZ-WYGRAM. See Wigram.

FIVEASH. The name of a locality. There are two places in E. Sussex called respectively, Five-Ashes and Five-Ash Down.

FLACK. Possibly from Flagg, a township in co. Derby.

FLADGATE. Probably a corruption of Floodgate.

FLAGG. A township in the parish of Bakewell, co. Derby.

FLAMANT. O. Fr. *Flamand*, a Fleming. Le Flamant, H.R.

FLANDERS. From the country. See Fleming.

FLASH. See under Flashman. The Prompt. Parv. defines *flasshe* as 'watyr,' and under *plasche* we have "flasche, where rayne watyr stondythe." Mr. Way says, "a shallow pool, in low Latin *flachia, flasca*, O. Fr. *flache* or *flesque*." Camden, in his Britannia, applies the term to those artificial reservoirs in Sussex which had been formed for the driving of iron-mills.

FLASHMAN. *Flashes* is a word provincially applied to flood-gates. The Flashman probably had the care of such gates. See, however, Flash.

FLATMAN. A baptismal name One Floteman was an undertenant in Yorkshire before the compilation of Domesday. The name appears to have been originally the A-Sax. *flótmann*, a sailor.

FLAVEL. FLAVELL. An ancient family presumed to be of Norman extraction, who gave the affix to Flavel Flyford, co. Worcester. The name may be derived from the Low Lat. *flavellus*, a diminutive of *flavus*, yellow, or golden—perhaps with reference to the hair.

FLAXMAN. A dresser of flax, or a spinner. In old authors "flax-wife" signifies a female spinner who is married, probably to distinguish her from the *spinster*, or maiden of the distaff. The records of Castle Combe shew the existence in that district of a family who in the reign of Edw. III. were called Spondel, most probably a provincialism for "spindle," in allusion to the spinning trade carried on by them. One of the family is described as "Johannem Spoundel dictum Flexmangere," or flax-monger, and twenty years later this person, or a descendant, is simply described as "Johannes Flexman." See Scrope's Hist. of Castle Combe, reviewed in Quarterly Rev., vol. xcii., p. 291.

FLEET. A-Sax. *fleot.* A harbour for vessels, an arm of the sea, a haven; hence Northfleet, Southfleet, and the Fleet, a tributary of the Thames, which gave name to Fleet Street. The celebrated jurist, Fleta, is said to have adopted that name, about temp. Edw. II., from his having been a prisoner in the Fleet at the time when he wrote his treatise on the common law. Fuller's Wor. ii. 366. There are parishes in cos. Dorset and Lincoln so called.

FLEETWOOD. The place from which the name was derived is probably in Lancashire, where the family resided in the XV. cent., and in that county a new town bearing this designation has recently sprung into existence under the auspices of Sir Hesketh Fleetwood.

FLEGG. East and West Flegg are two hundreds in Norfolk.

FLEMEN. See Fleming.

FLEMING. FLEMMING. A native of Flanders. Many natives of that country joined William the Conqueror in the invasion of England. Several persons designated Flandrensis occur in Domesday Book; thus Winemar F. was a tenant in chief in co. Bucks, and Hugo F. in Bedfordshire. Walterus Flandrensis was a tenant in chief in Herts, Bucks, Bedford, &c. He "assumed this surname in regard he came from Flanders, and assisted William at the battle of Hastings. Walter Bek, who came over with the Conqueror, had a large inheritance in Flanders, and had several lordships given him in England; but whether Walter F. and Walter Bek were one and the same person does not sufficiently appear." Kelham's Domesday.

There have been numerous settlements of Flemings at subsequent periods, and Le Fleming was a very common surname throughout the middle ages.

FLESHER. A butcher; a word still in use in the North. In the H.R. the name is sometimes written Le Flesmongere, the *fleshmonger*. In Old Scotch, a *fleschour* was a hangman or executioner—carnifex.

FLETCHER. Fr. *flèche*, an arrow. A maker of arrows—a common and most necessary trade in the middle ages. Le Flecher, Le Flecchir, Le Fletcher. H.R.

FLEWELLEN. (Lond. Direct.) A corruption of Llewellyn, the Welsh baptismal and family name.

FLEXMAN. See Flaxman.

FLIGG. See Flegg.

FLINT. Our Anglo-Saxon ancestors had a subordinate deity whom they named Flint, and whose idol was an actual flint-stone of large size. The name of the god would readily become the appellation of a man, and that would in time become hereditary as a surname. Such it had become, without any prefix, at the date of the H.R., and even in Domesday we have in Suffolk an Alwin Flint. The town of Flint, in North Wales, may however have a claim to its origin.

FLITTON. A parish in co. Bedford.

FLOAT. 1. A-Sax *flóta*, a sailor. 2. Local; an ancient Hampshire family wrote themselves De Flote.

FLOCK. Probably from Floques, near Eu, in Normandy.

FLOCKHART. A guttural pronunciation of Lockhart.

FLOCKTON. A chapelry in Yorkshire.

FLOOD. The English corruption of Lloyd, which is too guttural for our organs of pronunciation. Andrew Borde in his Boke of Knowledge makes a Welchman say—

"I am a gentylman and come of Brutus' blood ;
  My name is Ap Ryce, Ap Davy, Ap *Flood*."

FLORENCE. The capital of Tuscany. It is sometimes written Florance. See also Finghin.

FLOUNDERS. Perhaps a corruption of Flanders.

FLOWER. The London Directory exhibits more than a quarter of a hundred of traders bearing this beautiful surname, which probably had its origin in some peculiar manly beauty or excellence, such as that implied in the phrases 'Flower of Chivalry,' Flower of the Family, &c. Le Floer. H.R.

FLOWERDAY. See Flowerdew, of which it is probably a corruption.

FLOWERDEW. Probably from '*fleur*' and '*Dieu*,' Fr. "God's flower," from some peculiar sanctity attached to the original bearer.

FLOWERS. See Flower.

FLOYD. The same as Flood, which see.

FLOYER. Burke says, that the pedigree of the Floyers of co. Dorset is "authentically deduced from Floierus, who settled soon after the Norman Conquest on the lands beyond the river Exe, co. Devon, whence the name of Floiers-Lands and Floiers-Hayes."

FLUDE. See Flood.

FLY. A place near Gournay, in Normandy, once famous for its great abbey. It was anciently called Flagi. Chron. of Battel Abbey, p. 49.

FOAKES. The same as Folkes.

FOARD. See Ford.

FOE. Probably *inimicus*, an enemy—the antithesis of the surname Friend; or it may be the Fr. *faux*, false, unfaithful. I believe the territorial De of De Foe was assumed by the author of Robinson Crusoe.

FOGGE. An ancient Kentish family, possibly identical with that of Fagge. Ferguson says "*fiog*," Danish, a simpleton.

FOLD. An enclosure for sheep or cattle.

FOLEY. Collins says that the family have been of ancient standing in co. Worcester, and some adjoining counties. Local: place unknown.

FOLGER. See Foulger.

FOLJAMBE. *Jambe* is Fr. for leg, and *fol, folle* is often employed in O. Fr. for something useless or of little value, as 'farine folle,' mill-dust, 'figue folle,' a good-for-nothing fig. Hence Foljambe was probably a sobriquet allusive to a useless or defective Leg. We find in the H.R. the antithetical *Bele-jambe*, or "handsome leg," as a surname, and indeed the *jambe*, or leg, gave rise to other sobriquets and family names in the middle ages. As a remarkable instance, in the far-famed Scrope and Grosvenor controversy, temp. Rich. II., one of the witnesses calls Edward I. "the good king Edward with the long legs,"—*ovez les long jaumbes.* This family were doubtless of Norman origin, and the pedigree is traced to Sir Thomas Foljambe, who was bailiff of the High Peak, co. Derby, in 1272.

FOLK. FOLKES. A corruption of the Norman personal name Fulco, from whence also Fulke.

FOLKARD. FOLKERD. Fulcher or Fulcherus, a Domesd. name, is doubtless the same as Folchard or Folcard, borne by an eminent Flemish scholar, who settled in England about the time of the Conquest and became abbot of Thorney.

FOLKER. See Folkard.

FOLLENFANT. Fr. "Foolish child" —probably a term of endearment.

FOLLETT. Fr. *follet*, "somewhat fond, pretty and foppish, a little foolish." Cotgr. Probably used by way of endearment. 'Feu follet' is an exact rendering of *ignis fatuus.* In the Domesday of Kent there is a William Folet.

FOLLIOT. FOLIOT. FFOLLIOTT. An old Fr. epithet formed from the extinct verb *foller*, to play the fool, to be merry or frolicsome. Comp. Follett. The family came into England at or soon after the Conquest. The surname has become historical from Gilbert Foliot, bishop of Hereford, the staunch defender of Henry II. against the demands of Thomas à Becket. One night as he lay ruminating on the quarrel of the king and the archbishop, a terrible and unknown voice sounded in his ears the words:—

Voice. "Folioth! Folioth! thy God is the Goddess Azaroth." (Venus.)
Foliot. Thou lyest, foule fiend; my God is the God of Sabaoth!"

FOLLY. "Any ridiculous building, not answering its intended purpose." Halliwell. Most counties have many spots so called; but I do not find Mr. Halliwell's definition always correct. I should prefer calling a "folly," a temporary or fragile building, and that seems to have been the sense of the Norman-French *foillie*. In the Roman de Rou of Master Wace, line 12,136 we read—

"Mult veient loges è *foillies*,"

which M. Pluquet explains as "baraques faites avec des branches d'arbre;"—temporary buildings made of branches of trees. See Notes and Queries, Nov. 1856. De la Folye. H.R.

FOLTHORPE. FOULTHORPE. A local name of northern origin. One of the principal *habitats* of the family was in the county of Durham, where they acquired (probably for no better reason than a play upon the first syllable) the undesirable appellation of the "THE FILTHY FOULTHORPES."

FONNEREAU. This family were founded in England by M. Zacharie F. who fled from La Rochelle at the Rev. of the Edict of Nantes, and settled in London. He is said to have been of noble descent, and a branch of the Earls of Ivry in Normandy. B.L.G.

FONT. Lat. *fons*, a spring. De Fonte, Ad Fontem. H.R.

FOOKES. FOOKS. See Folk, Folkes. Perhaps, however, the High German *fuchs*, a fox.

FOORD. See Ford.

FOOT. FOOTE. Probably from residence near the 'foot' of a mountain. This surname was hereditary from the time of the Conqueror. Among the undertenants of Domesday we have an Ernui Fot in Cheshire, and a Godwin Fot in Kent. The descendants of the latter gave the prefix to Foot's Cray. Fot is the common spelling in H.R.

FOOTMAN. Not a domestic servant, but a foot-soldier, an infantry man. It is used in this sense in Hall's Chronicle.

FORBES. A town and barony in Aberdeenshire. The family possessed that lordship as early as temp. William the Lion,

and were seated at Pitscottie in the same shire in 1476. Debrett. See Art. Coulthart.

FORCE. In the North, a waterfall, a cascade. Worsaae considers it of Danish origin, and finds fifteen localities with the termination in the northern counties. Danes in England, p. 71.

☞ **FORD.** A shallow place in a river, which may be crossed without bridge or boat—a common termination of local surnames.

"In *Ford*, in Ham, in Ley, in Ton
The most of English Surnames run."
Verstegan.

FORD. Parishes and places in cos. Durham, Sussex, Bucks, Northumberland, Salop, Wilts, Devon, &c.

FORDER. 1. A village near Trematon in Cornwall. 2. A modification of At Ford. See termination ER.

FORDHAM. Parishes in cos. Cambridge, Essex, and Norfolk.

FORDRED. An ancient personal name.

FORDYCE. A parish in Banffshire.

FORECAST. Quasi *forth-cast*; one cast forth; a foundling?

FORECASTLE. Probably local, and having no connection with a ship.

FOREHEAD. Local. See Head.

FORES. Probably Forres in Morayshire.

FOREST. FORREST. From residence in one. Forest is, however, the specific name of places in cos. Durham, Brecon, &c.

FORESTER. FORRESTER. "An officer made by letters patent under the great seal, and sworn to preserve vert and venison in the forest; and to attend upon the wild beasts within his bailiwick; to attach offenders there either in Vert or Venison, and to present the same at the courts of the Forest, that they may be punished according to the quantity and quality of their offences and trespasses. Some Foresters have their office in fee, paying to the king a fee-farm rent." Manwode, cited in Nelson's Laws of Game. In allusion to the origin of the name, many families of Forester bear bugle-horns in their arms. Several Forestarii are found in Domesday.

FORGE. From residence at one; a local synonym of Smith.

FORMAN. FOREMAN. (A-Sax.) The president or chief man of a company. Bailey. Still applied to the spokesman of a jury, and to the chief of a body of workmen.

FORMBY. A chapelry in Lancashire.

FORRETT. Possibly from Fr. *forêt*—a forest.

FORSAITH. See Forsyth.

FORSCUTT. See Foskett.

FORSTER. A curt pronunciation of Forester. There are many families of this name of separate origins. The Durham family were characterized as THE FRIENDLY FORSTERS.

FORSYTH. Probably from Forcett (whence also Fawcett) a township in the wapentake of Gillingwest, N.R. of Yorkshire.

FORT. Fr. *Le Fort.* Strong, powerful.

FORTESCUE. Doubtless from O. Fr. *forte escu,* "strong shield," referring probably to such a weapon carried by the primary bearer of the name. This, together with the punning motto of the family, "*Forte Scutum* salus *ducum,*" 'a strong shield is the safety of commanders,' doubtless led to the fabrication of the legend that the founder of the family, one Sir Richard le Fort, at the battle of Hastings was the safety of his commander, by bearing a *strong shield* in front of him. If we may trust genealogists of the old school, the field of Hastings witnessed many wonderful scenes and exploits; but as the Norman Duke was quite able to carry his own shield we may dismiss this story to the regions of romance. The Norman origin of the family is, however, pretty certain, and their residence at Winston in Devonshire, temp. King John, seems fully proved. Shirley's Noble and Gentle Men. If the name originated in any military incident, it is more likely to have taken place in the Holy Land, where two members of the family are said to have fought under Cœur de Lion.

FORTH. A well-known river of Scotland; also a village in Lancashire.

FORTNER. A combatant in a tilting match. See Eng. Surn. i. 109.

FORTUNE. A place in Haddingtonshire.

FORTY. FORTYMAN. *Forty* is used by the Scot. poet Douglas, in the sense of brave. Fr. *fort.* Hence these names probably refer to the courage of their original owners.

FORWARD. May refer to disposition, but is more probably the *fore-ward,* or guard —an advanced sentinel.

FOSBROKE. A township in Staffordshire, hodie Forsbroke. The family were settled in Northamptonshire temp. Rich. II.

FOSCUE. A corruption of Fortescue. Camden.

FOSDICK. FORSDIKE. Fosdyke, a parish in Lincolnshire. John de Focedik occurs in that shire temp. Edw. I. H.R.

FOSKETT. Probably from the ancient manor of Foscott, co. Bucks, or from Forscote, a parish co. Somerset.

FOSS. FOSSE. The ditch of a fortified place. Conf. De la Fosse, and Ditch.

FOSSETT. The same as Fawcett and Forsyth, which see.

FOSSEY. A Fosse-way, or ancient fortification of earth.

FOSTER. Sometimes a contraction of Forester: but there is an origin at least equally probable, viz: *fosterer,* one who feeds and has the charge of children instead of their parents. "When a gesithcundman left his land, he was at liberty to take away his Reeve, his Smith, and his child's Fosterer. Laws of Ina, King of Wessex. Thorpe, i. 145. Archæologia, xxxiii. 277.

FOTHER. Apparently an ancient Scandinavian personal name, to which probably we owe the local names and surnames, Fotherby, Fothergill, Fotheringham, Fotherley, &c.

FOTHERBY. A parish in Lincolnshire.

FOTHERINGHAM. A place in the parish of Inverarity, co. Forfar.

FOULGER. A-Sax. *folgere,* a follower, an attendant, a servant, a free-man who had not a house of his own, but who was the retainer of some "heorth-fæst," or house-keeper. Bosworth.

FOULIS. The ancestor of the baronet was in great favour with king James VI. of Scotland, whom he accompanied into England. The name is probably derived from one of the two parishes of Perthshire now called Fowlis-Easter and Fowlis-Wester. In charters it is latinized De Foliis.

FOULKES. The personal name, Fulco or Fulke, through the Fr. Foulques.

FOULSHAM. A town in Norfolk.

FOUND. This name was given to a foundling at Doncaster not many generations since. Eng. Surn. ii. 18. The corresponding name *Inventus* formerly existed there. Ibid.

FOUNTAIN. From residence near one —like the Fr. De la Fontaine.

FOURDRINIER. O. Fr. "The blacke thorne that beareth sloes; also the wild or mountain plumme tree." Cotgrave. The surname is analogous to our indigenous Thorne, Hawthorne, &c.

FOURMY. Fr. *fourmi*—an ant; probably allusive to industry.

FOURNIER. Fr. A baker or furnaceman.

FOURNISS. Furness, co. Lancaster.

FOWELL. The same as Fowle.

FOWKE. FOWKES. See Foulkes.

FOWLE. A bird of any species. Le Fowle. H.R.

FOWLER. A bird-catcher; a destroyer of birds by any method, whether with net, bird-bolt, or "fowling-piece." Le Fowelere. H.R.

FOWLES. FOWLS. See Foulis.

FOX. FOXE. 1. From the animal, like Wolf, Bear, Boar, &c. Le Fox. H.R.

2. In some cases it may be connected with the Yorkshire family of Fawkes, and if so with the Norman Vaux or De Vallibus.

FOXALL. FOXELL. See Foxhall.

FOXHALL. A parish in Suffolk.

FOXLEY. FOXLEE. Parishes, &c., in cos. Norfolk, Northampton, and Wilts.

FOXTON. Parishes, &c., in cos. Cambridge, Durham, and Leicester.

FOY. A parish in co. Hereford.

FOYSTER. An evident corruption of Forester, resulting from mispronunciation of the letter R.

FRAIN. See Freyne.

FRAMPTON. Parishes, &c., in cos. Dorset, Gloucester, Lincoln, &c. The Framptons of the first-named county have resided at Moreton from 1385. Shirley's Noble and Gentle Men.

FRANCE. From the country.

FRANCIS. Not from the personal name, which is of too recent introduction; but as in the H.R., Le Franceys, Le Franseys, Le Fraunceys, "the Frenchman."

FRANEY. See Freyne.

FRANK. FRANKS. FRANKES. The nursename Frank stands for Francis, Franciscus, and this may be in some instances the origin of the surname. *Le* Frank, however, appears in H.R., and may mean either "the free," an enfranchised man; or a "Franc," by nation.

FRANKHAM. I find no such place as Frankham, and the name seems not to be local, but the old Fr. Fraunchumme (homo liber) "a free man." The name is so written in H.R. See under Freeman.

FRANKLAND. Sometimes a corruption of Franklin.

FRANKLIN. In the H.R. Franckleyn, Frankelain (with and without the prefix Le), Franklanus, &c. Halliwell's definition is "a large freeholder." Properly the son or descendant of a *vilein*, who had become rich; but the term was also applied to farmers and country gentlemen of inconsiderable property. Chaucer's description, however, makes the Franklin a much more important personage. See Eng. Surn., i. 127-8.

FRANKOK. H.R. The personal name *Frane* occurs in Domesd., and this seems to be its diminutive.

FRANKS. See Frank.

FRANKTON. A parish in co. Warwick.

FRASER. "Of the Norman origin of the Frasers it is impossible for a moment to entertain any doubt." Skene's Highlanders, ii. 311. Down to the reign of Robert Bruce they appear to have remained in the southern counties of Scotland, though afterwards they removed to the North, and assumed the dignity of a clan. The advocates of their Celtic origin derive the name from *Frith-siol,* "forest race." Dixon. In the Ragman Roll it is spelt Fresar, Frizel, Freshele, Frisele, and Frisle. Ibid. *Frisell* occurs in the so-called Battel Roll, and an ancient fief near Neufchâtel, in Normandy, was called Fresles.

A perpetuity of Frasers is promised to Philorth (the estate of Fraser, Lord Saltoun), by the following rhyme :—

"As lang as there's a cock in the North,
There'll be a Fraser in Philorth."
Chambers' Popular Rhymes of Scotland.

The following anecdote is given by Mr. Dixon. *Surnames,* preface, p. xviii. :—

"An Irish gentleman once told me that in his youth the Fraser Fencibles were quartered near his father's residence, and that he had many times heard the roll called. It commenced Donald Fraser, senior ; Donald Fraser, junior ; Donald Fraser, Baine *(White)*; Donald Fraser, Ruadh *(Red)*; Donald Fraser, Buidhe *(Yellow-haired)*; Donald Fraser, Dubh *(Black)* ; Donald Fraser, No. 1 ; Donald Fraser, No. 2 ; and so on to Donald Fraser, No. 18., before a new baptismal name appeared."

FRATER. A latinization of Brother.

FREARSON. Perhaps "Friar's son," the son of a friar, anciently written *frere.*

FRECHEVILLE. The family descended from Ralph Fitz-Herbert, a tenant in capite in Derbyshire and the neighbouring counties. Lysons' Derb. The name, which is latinized De Frisca-villa, may have been derived from Francheville, near Argentan in Normandy. Camden considers Fretwell a corruption of it.

FREDERICK. The personal name. Frederic was a tenant in Kent prior to the making of Domesday.

FREE. Under the feudal system, one who was not in servile condition ; the same as Freeman, which see. Le Free. H.R.

FREEBODY. See under Body.

FREEBORN. Under the feudal law, one whose parents were not in a state of villenage. Freeburn is, however, the name of a parish in Scotland. The Friebernus of Domesd. and the Frebern of the H.R. point rather to an ancient baptismal name.

FREELAND. Perhaps local, though the place does not occur. In the H.R. it is Frelond, without prefix.

FREELOVE. In all probability the same as the A-Sax. name Frealaf. (Ferguson.) Frelove. H.R.

FREEMAN. *Fremond* is an A-Sax. personal name; but this surname is more probably derived from the social condition. "A Freeman *(liber homo),* is one distinguished from a slave; that is, born or made free." Jacob, Law Dict. In the early days of feudalism two neighbours bearing some common Christian name would be distinguished by epithets denoting their respective conditions, as John le Freeman and John le Bonde, and these epithets would often become family names. In the H.R. we have not only many Le Fremans, but also one Matilda Frewoman, and an Agnes Frewif, or free wife, probably the wife of a bondman. The name also occurs there in the forms of Franchome and Fraunchomme. Also one who has received the freedom of any corporation.

FREEMANTLE is latinized Frigidum-Mantellum, "cold cloak," which is sufficiently absurd. It should be Frieze-mantle, a cloak of *frieze* or Friesland cloth; as we now say, a Flushing coat, a Guernsey shirt, Nankin trowsers, &c. (Dixon).

FREERE. Fr. *frère*, a brother; also a friar, which Chaucer writes *frere*. In the H.R., Le Frere.

FREEZE. Possibly a native of Friesland.

FREESTONE. Perhaps local, from Frieston, a Lincolnshire parish; or perhaps a modification of Frithestan, the A-Sax. personal name.

FREETH. See Frith.

FREKE. FRECK. 1. O.-Eng., a man, a fellow. Halliwell. Also an epithet; quick, eager, hasty; firm, powerful, brave.

"*Ffrek* as a fuyre in the flynt."
    Thornton Romances, p. 234.
"We have foughten in faithe by yone fresche strandez, With the *frekkeste* folke that to thi foo langez."
    Morte Arthure (quoted by Halliwell).
"This day a man is fresche and *fryke*."
    MS. Cantab. Ff. ii. (Ibid).

2. An O. Germ. personal name; perhaps the same in origin as Fricker.

FRENCH. From the country. Le Frensch. H.R. See Francis. The Frenches of Frenchgrove, co. Mayo, are said to have sprung from Robert Fitz-Stephen de France, who accompanied Strongbow into Ireland temp. Henry II., and he is said to have been a descendant of one Theophilus de France, a follower of William I. at the Conquest. B.L.G.

FRERE. Fr. A brother.

FRERRY. A 'nurse-name' of Frederick. Camden.

FRESHVILLE. See Frecheville.

FRESHWATER. A parish in the Isle of Wight.

FRETWELL. Said by Camden to be a corruption of the Norman De Frecheville, but is more probably derived from Fritwell, a parish in Oxfordshire.

FREVILLE. A place between Ste. Mére Eglise and Valognes, in Normandy. It gave its name to a family celebrated both in that duchy and in England. Mem. Soc. Ant. Normandie, 1825. De Frivile. H.R.

FREW. A-Sax. *freo*, free — having liberty or authority.

FREWEN. FREWIN. "Is manifestly as old as the worship of Frea," the Teutonic Venus. Edinb, Rev., April, 1855. It occurs as the fourth from Woden in the genealogy of the Northumbrian kings. Its A-Sax. form is Freawin, signifying "dear

or devoted to Frea." Ferguson. Several tenants prior to the Domesd. survey bore it, as Frauuin, in Sussex, Frauuinus, in Devonshire, and Freowinus, in Suffolk.

FREWER. A free-man. See Frew, and the termination ER.

FREYNE. O. Fr. *fresne*, an ash-tree, from residence near one. So the modern Fr. surname Dufresne and our own Ash. In Norman times this name had the variations Fresnel, Fresnay, Frenne, &c.

FRIAR. See Ecclesiastical Surnames.

FRICKER. A-Sax. *fricca*, a crier or preacher—one who proclaims.

FRIDAY. From the day of the week; from some event which occurred to the original bearer on that day. So Munday, Christmas, Pentecost. This name is found in the H.R. in its modern orthography.

FRIEND. FREND. Probably characteristic of the original bearer. Le Frend. H.R.

FRIENDSHIP. This Devonshire name is probably local, the termination being a corruption of *hope*.

FRIER. 1. See Fryer. 2. "Many friars at the Reformation renounced their vows of chastity, married, and became fathers of families; from one of them descend the Friers of Melrose parish, Roxburghshire." Folks of Shields.

FRISBY. FRISBEE. A parish and a chapelry, co. Leicester.

FRISELL. Probably a native of Friesland.

FRISTON. A parish in Sussex.

FRITH. See under Fell.

FROBISHER. A furbisher or polisher of metals. Fr. *fourbisseur*, an artizan who polishes and mounts swords; a sword cutler. Boyer. In the Promptorium we read, "Foorbyschowre, eruginator," one who removes rust. The transposition of the *o* and the *r* has many analogies. The name Le Furbur in the H.R. is probably synonymous.

FROCKE. Analogous to Mantell, Cloake, &c.

FRODSHAM. A parish in Cheshire.

FROG. One *John Frog* flourished, appropriately enough, under King Edward Longshanks, in the green pastures of Newington, co. Oxford. H.R. ii. 761; and Burke's Armory gives the ensigns armorial of *Frogg;* but whether the name has descended, or rather leaped down, to modern times, I am unable to determine.

FROGGAT. A township in Derbyshire.

FROGMORTON. A corruption of Throckmorton.

FROISSART. The surname of the worthy old chronicler was borne much

R

earlier by Willelmus Froissart, a Domesd. tenant in co. Bedford. It is evidently connected with the Fr. *froisser*, and means a crasher or bruiser—no improper name either for a follower of the Conqueror, or for the historian of Cresci and Poictiers.

FROST. Frost is the name of a dwarf in the Scandinavian mythology, and our nursery hero, "Jack Frost," as Mr. Ferguson suggests, may be derived from that source. One Alwin Forst was a tenant in co. Hants before Domesd., and his name by a slight and common transposition would become Frost. The H.R. have many Frosts without prefix.

FROUDE. FROWD. The epithet *Frode*, wise, or much-knowing, was applied to more than one eminent Northman. See Laing's Chronicle of the Sea-Kings of Norway, i. 26 and 29. In Domesd. we find a Frodo, described as "frater Abbatis" (i.e., of St. Edmundsbury), and he had a son Gilbert, called " filius Frodonis," or Fitz-Froude.

FROYLE. A parish in Hampshire, which had owners of the same name in 1166. Lib. Nig. Scac.

FRY. Old English for *free*; in the H.R. Le Frye and Le Frie; the same as Free and Freeman, which see. Also with regard to disposition—free, noble.

> "The child that was so *fry*."
> *Rembrun, quoted by Halliwell.*

FRYER. A-Norm. Brother. Kelham.

FUBBS. A corruption of Forbes?

FUGGLE. FUGGLES. A-Sax. *fugel*, a fowl. In some instances the name has taken the more modern form of Fowle.

FULBROOK. FULBROKE, &c. Parishes in cos. Warwick, Oxon, &c.

FULFORD. The family assert a Saxon origin, and are said to have held Folefort, now Great Fulford, co. Devon, temp. William I. William de F., who held the estate temp. Richard I. is the first ascertained ancestor. His lineal descendant, Baldwin Fulford, Esq., still possesses it. Shirley's Noble and Gentle Men. There are also places called Fulford in cos. York and Stafford.

FULHAM. A town in Surrey.

FULKE. The A-Norm. personal name Fulco.

FULLALOVE. FULLILOVE. Qu. An amorous person—"full of love"?

FULLER. One who thickens and whitens cloth. The H.R. forms of the name are Le Fuller and Le Fullere, and the latinization Fullo.

FULLERTON. FULLARTON. Fullarton is a burgh and estate at Irvine in Ayrshire, to which place the family is traced in 1371. B.L.G.

FULLJAMES. A corruption of Foljambe.

FULLWAY. Fullaway, a tything in Wiltshire.

FULMER. A parish in Bucks.

FULTON. An extinct border village in co. Roxburgh.

FULWELL. A township in Durham.

FULWOOD. A township in co. Lancaster, for many generations the seat of the family.

FUNNELL. This name, though very common in Sussex, is, I think, rarely met with beyond the limits of that county. I will hazard a conjecture that it is a corruption of Fontenelle, now St. Wandrille-sur-Seine, in Normandy, an ancient barony, and the site of a famous monastery, near Caudebec. The corruption may have taken place thus:—Fontenelle, Fonnell, Funnell.

FUNNS. See Eng. Surn. i. 66.

FUNTNER. "Fontainier or Fontenier (celui qui a soin des eaux et des fontaines), water bailiff; he that has the charge of springs." Boyer's Dict. The Le Fontur of the H.R. is probably identical.

FURBER. See Frobisher.

FURBISHER. See Frobisher.

FURLONG. See Furlonger.

FURLONGER. A furlong, A-Sax. *furlang*, is a division of a common or tenantry field. It may have been the duty of the "Furlonger" to attend to the boundaries of such divisions.

FURMINGER. A cheese-maker. See Firminger. A Rob. Formagier, an Anselm le Formgir, and a Godfrey le Furmager are found in H.R.

FURNACE. Probably from Furness, co. Lancaster, celebrated for its fine monastery; perhaps, however, from residence near some great iron-furnace, before the existing method of smelting that metal was introduced.

FURNEAUX. A Norman family who came either from Fourneau-sur-Baise, near Falaise, or from Fourneaux-sur-Vire, near St. Lo. They gave the suffix to Pelham-Furneux, co. Herts.

FURNELL. See Furneaux.

FURNER. Fr. *fournier*, a baker or furnace man. Fournier, Dufour, &c., are common Fr. surnames.

FURNESS. FURNISS. Furness, co. Lancaster; but see Furnace.

FURNIVALL. Gerard de Furnival came from Normandy into England temp. Richard I., and accompanied that monarch to the Holy Land. His successors were barons by tenure and writ for several descents. Fourneville, the place in Normandy from which the name appears to have been derived, is in the neighbourhood of Honfleur.

FURSDON. An estate in the parish of

Cadbury, co. Devon. From the days of Henry III., if not from an earlier period, the family have resided at the place from whence the name is derived. Shirley's Noble and Gentle Men.

FURSE. An estate in the parish of Spreyton was possessed by a family of the same name, temp. Richard I. They claimed descent from the Ferse of Domesd., but the local origin is sufficient. See B.L.G.

FURZE. Furse, Ferse, an ancient personal surname. Domesd.

FUSMAN. Perhaps foot-man. Germ. *fusz*, foot.

FUSSELL. Said to be the Italian Fuseli. Fussel. H.R.

FUST. This name appears in the archives of Switzerland, Germany, &c., in early times, in the various forms of Faustus, Faust, Vaust, First, Furst, Futz, &c. Faust or Fust, the eminent printer of

Metz, was about contemporary with the first appearance of the name in Sussex, but whether there was any connection between the English and the continental name there is no evidence to show. See Kimber's Baronetage, ii. 255.

FYFE. FYFFE. See Fife.

FYLER. Probably a file-maker; or perhaps a spinner, from the Fr. *fil*, a thread.

FYNES. See Fiennes.

FYNHAGH. See Vinall.

FYNN. See Finn.

FYREBRAND. Possibly refers to a man of "incendiary" character, but is more likely an ancient inn sign.

FYSSHE. An O. Eng. orthography of fish.

FYTHELER. A fiddler. Le Fytheler. Non. Inq.

FYVIE. A parish in co. Aberdeen.

G.

GABB. The Lond. Direct. shews us several traders gifted with this patronymic, which Ferguson thinks derivable from the O. High German *geban*, to give. It is more probably a nick-name of Gabriel. Or it may relate to loquacity, for the A-Norm. *gabber* means to jest or talk idly. Wickliffe uses *gabbing* in the sense of lying and jesting; and in the H.R. we have Le Gabber as a surname.

GABBETT. The Gabbetts of Cahirline, co. Limerick, trace an English lineage to the year 1487. The name is probably identical with Garbett and Garbutt.

GABLE. Possibly a corruption of Gabriel.

GABRIEL. A personal name borrowed from the celestial hierarchy.

GABY. In many dialects a silly fellow. More probably a nick-name of Gabriel.

GAD. GADD. A-Sax. *gád*, a goad or spear. Halliwell quotes from an old MS. :
" And hys axes also smeten,
With *gaddes* of stele that made them to betyn."

GADSBY. Gaddesby, a parish in co. Leicester.

GADSDEN. GADESDEN. Gaddesden, two parishes in co. Herts.

GAEL. The Gaels of Charlton-Kings co. Gloucester, have written themselves, at various periods, "Galle, Gale, Gael, and originally De Gales." B.L.G. If this be correct, the family may have been of Welsh origin in Anglo-Norman times, when that country was known as Galles or Gales.

GAFFER. A provincialism for Grandfather.

GAGE. The oldest copy of the so-called Battel Abbey Roll mentions a De Gaugy or Gage as having come into England at the time of the Conquest. He settled in the forest of Dean, and his descendants were ennobled. Banks, i. 89. " Modern Heralds trace the genealogy of the family of Gage, now flourishing in the rank of the peerage, from this ancient stock." Ibid. p. 87.

GAICOTE. The first of this name was probably a medieval fop.

GAIN. GAINES. Gain. H.R.

GAINER. Probably a corruption of Gaymer.

GAINSFORD. GAYNESFORD. This ancient Surrey family are alleged, I know not on what authority, to have originated at *Gainford*, a great parish in co. Durham.

If so, their migration southward must have been early, as they were in their southern *habitat* temp. Edwd. II.

GAIRDNER. A local pronunciation of Gardener.

GAIRNS. The Gairn is a small river of Aberdeenshire.

GAISFORD. The same as Gainsford.

GAIT. See Gate.

GALABIN. Perhaps the same as Galpin.

GALBRAITH. A Celtic family of remote antiquity, formerly settled at Baldernoch in Stirlingshire. "The Galbraiths are called in the Celtic language Breatanuich or Clann a Breatanuich, i.e. Britons, or the children of the Briton. They were once a great name in Scotland, according to the following lines:—

"Bhreatanuich, o'n Talla dhearg
  Hailse sir Alba do shloinneadh."

That is:—

"Galbraiths from the Red Tower,
  Noblest of Scottish surnames."
            Fraser's Statist. Account.

GALE. A Scottish Highlander. Gale. H.R. See, however, Gael.

GALER. Perhaps the same as Gaylord.

GALL. An ancient personal name. Two saints Galle occur in the Roman Calendar, one of whom was a Scotch abbot.

GALLAND. The name of a locality unknown to me, whence belike Gallon.

GALLANT. R.G. 16. Brave in war. Galaunt, H.R.

GALLARD. See Gaylord. H.R. Gallard.

GALLAWAY. See Galloway.

GALLON. O. Norse *gallin*, crazy. Ferguson. The H.R. forms are Galien, Galiun, Galion, Galun, and Galeyn.

GALLOP. Probably local—the last syllable being a corruption of HOPE—Galhope.

GALLOWAY. An extensive district forming the S.W. corner of Scotland. The surname is written in the H.R., Galaway and Galewey.

GALLOWS. From residence near a place of public execution; or perhaps the hangman himself.

GALEY. GALLEY. Scandinavian surnames, which Ferguson deduces from *gáli*, crazy.

GALPIN. A corruption of Mac Alpin, thus Mac Calpin, Calpin, Galpin. See under *Mac.*

GALT. O. Norse *galti*; O. Eng. *galt*; a boar pig, like the Roman Verres. The word is still retained in the North of England. See Halliwell.

GALTON. A small hamlet in Dorsetshire, which was held by the De Galtons at an early period.

GALWEY. GALLWEY. From the town of Galway in Ireland—one of the very few local surnames that have originated in that country. The family are a branch of De Burgh. John de B., younger brother of Ulick de B., ancestor of the Marquis of Clanricarde, having accredited the bills of the citizens of Galway, was commonly known as Sir John de Galway. From this personage descended the extinct baronets Gallwey, and the existing Galweys of Lota, co. Cork.

GAMBLE. Gamel occurs both in Domesday and in the H.R. In the latter 'Fils Gamel' is also found. A.S. *gamol* or *gamel*, old, aged. It is compounded with some Domesd. names, as Gamel-bar, 'old bear'—Gamel-carle, 'old male,'—both in co. York. Gamblesby in Cumberland, probably derived its name from a Danish proprietor.

GAMBLING. H.R. Gamelin and De Gameling.

GAME. Gam was a Yorkshire tenant prior to Domesday.

☞ **GAME.** A corruption of the termination HAM, when a G precedes; thus, Walkingham becomes Walkingame (well known to school-boys), and Allingham, Allengame.

GAMMON. Apparently an old personal name. Gamen, Gamon, &c., are found in H.R. without prefix.

GAND. A corruption of Ghent or Gaunt.

GANDEE. See Gandy.

GANDER. The bird. The name of the celebrated Genseric, the Vandal chief, is believed to be Teutonic, and to signify like the modern Germ. *ganserich*, a gander. Why (as Prof. Donaldson remarks) a great warrior should bear such a name is not very obvious; "but, if anyone feels disposed to smile at such a title, he may correct the impression by recollecting that names of birds are not always imposed on the principles suggested by our modern associations." Cambridge Essays, 1856, p. 42. The professor proceeds to exemplify his observation in Attila's chief opponent, Aëtius, 'the aquiline,' synonymous with Orloff, the name of the Russian plenipotentiary at the Congress of Paris. In like manner Woronzow, a name equally well known in recent history, means "raven like;" and the classical as well as the modern nomenclature of families supplies us with numerous analogies. It must not be forgotten, however, that *gandr* in O. Norse means a wolf.

GANDY. Ferguson says, O. Norse *gandr*, a wolf.

GANT. See Gaunt. Le Gant and De Gant. H.R.

GANTLETT. See Gauntlett.

GAPP. From residence near some *gap* or pass. In the chalky cliffs of Sussex many places are so called, as Birling Gap,

Crowlink Gap, Cow Gap—some of which were defended by iron portcullises. The original Mr. Gapp was probably stationed near one of these. Gappe and Del Gap. H.R.

GARBETT. See Garbutt.

GARBUTT. From the Flemish personal name Gherbode. Georbodus, a Fleming, was created earl of Chester by the Conqueror, and a Gerbodo, probably of that nation, occurs in the Domesd. of Yorkshire.

GARD. Fr. A guard. See Ward. Le Gard and Le Garder. H.R.

GARDEN. From residence in or near one. See Gardener.

GARDENER. The occupation. Its forms in the H.R. are Le Gardener and Le Gardiner; also De Gardino and De Gardinis. Its principal modern forms are Gardiner, which according to Camden's joke denotes the gentleman! (E. Surn. i. 118) and the more plebeian Gardner: Gardener itself is rare.

GARDINER. See Gardener.

GARDNER. See Gardener.

GARDYNE. The O. Scottish form of Garden. It is asserted that the Gardynes, Jardynes, Gardens, and Jerdans are one and the same family. The Gairdynes of that Ilk, co. Forfar, are described by a writer of 1660 or 1670, as a very ancient race. B.L.G.

GARFORD. A chapelry in Berkshire.

GARLAND. A local surname, but I cannot find the place. John de Garlande, author of the Dictionarius, flourished in the XII. and XIII. cent. Though a professor at Paris, he was an Englishman by birth. See Wright's Vocab. p. 120. Gerland, the first mathematical writer in England after the Conquest, was living in 1086, but whether he was of English birth is uncertain. Garlond, Garland, and Gerlaundes occur in the H. R., without prefix.

The family have long possessed lands in Essex, Surrey, Lincolnshire, and Sussex. James Garland, Esq., who was born in 1768, gave to his daughter and heiress "a property at Penhurst, in the last-named county, which was granted to the family by King John, and of which the original grant is the only title deed." B.L.G.

GARLICK. In the H.R., Garlec, which looks like a sobriquet: otherwise it might be a contraction of Garlwick, the name of a place.

GARMAN. A-Sax. *gár*, a spear, and *man*. A spearman.

GARMENT. A corruption of the A-Sax. personal name Garmund. Cod. Dipl. 978.

GARNAULT. A French Protestant family, who settled in England at the Revocation of the Edict of Nantes.

GARNER. 1. A granary or storehouse. From residence at one. 2. A small river tributary to the Wye.

GARNET. GARNETT. Said to be a corruption of Gernet.

GARNHAM. A contraction of Gardenham, "The garden homestead."

GARRARD. GARRAD. Gerard, Gerald.

GARRETT. GARRATT. It has been decided legally (!) that Garrett and Gerald are but one name. Jacob, Law Dict., title *Misnomer*. But Garrett is a hamlet in Surrey, famous for its mock-mayor.

GARRICK. A parish united with Heckington, co. Lincoln. David Garrick is said to have been of French refugee extraction.

GARRISON. A corruption of Garriston, a township of Yorkshire.

GARROD. GARROOD. See Garrett.

GARROW. Probably local; but Arthur derives it from the British *garo*, fierce, keen, rough.

GARSTANG. A town in Lancashire.

GARSTIN. The O. Norse personal name, Geirsteinn, which is found in the Landnamabok. Ferg.

GARTH. A yard, or any small enclosure. Also places in cos. Montgomery and Glamorgan. It is a prefix to several names of places.

GARTON. Two parishes in co. York.

GARTSHORE. An estate in co. Perth, which has still owners of the same name.

GARVEY. The Irish family deduce themselves from the ancient monarchs of that island, through Garbhe or Garvey, that is "The Warlike," Prince of Morisk, co. Mayo, in the XV. cent. B.L.G.

GARVIE. See Garvey.

GARWAY. GARRAWAY. A parish in co. Hereford.

GASCOIGNE. GASCOYNE. A native of Gascony, the French province, which being in the possession of England, during a portion of the XIV. cent., supplied this country with many new families and names. See Ducatus Leodiensis, p. 181, for the twenty spellings of this name. The heads of the family were all Williams, the courageous Chief-Justice who sent Prince Henry to prison being one.

GASELEE. See Gazeley.

GASKELL. Arthur says, Gael. *gaisgeil*, valorous.

GASKIN. GASKOIN. See Gascoigne.

GASSON. Fr. *garçon*, a boy, or attendant.

GASTON. 1. A grassy enclosure. A-Sax., *gœrs*, grass, and *tun*, an enclosure. De la Garston. H.R. 2. A baptismal name, as Gaston de Foix.

GATACRE. A family of great antiquity, said to have been established at Gatacre, co. Salop (where they still reside) by Edward the Confessor. The pedigree, however, is not traced beyond the time of Henry III. Shirley's Noble and Gentle Men.

GATE. From residence near either the gate of a fortified town, or of a chase, forest, or the like. Its medieval forms are Ate Gate and Atte Gate, which have since the XV. cent. modified to Agate, Gater, and especially to Gates, now one of the commonest of surnames. In North Britain *gate* is equivalent to way; as in the phrase, "Gang your Gate" for "Go your way." See also Northgate, Southgate, &c. De la Gate, de Gate, and Le Gater, occur in the H.R.

GATEHOUSE. From residence at the gatehouse of a monastery, castle, or town.

GATER. See Gate, and the termination ER.

GATES. See Gate.

GATH. A corruption of Garth.

GATHERCOLE. GATHERCOAL. A gatherer or collector of coals? or of coles (cabbage)?

GATHERGOOD. As the opposite name Scattergood exists, I suppose this must be taken literally for a person of acquisitive and thrifty habits. Thomas Gadregod occurs in the Deeds of Battel Abbey, XIII. cent.

GATUS. A corruption of Gatehouse.

GATWARD. Gate-ward, a porter or gatekeeper.

GAUDY. May relate to foppery in attire, but is more likely to be of local origin. See Gawdy.

GAUNT. Like John, fourth son of Edward III., some families of this surname evidently derive it from the town of Gaunt, now Ghent, in Flanders. *De Gaunt* and *Le Gaunt* are both found in the H.R.; the latter form is probably from the personal peculiarity of the first bearer. Shakspeare makes John of Gaunt play upon his own name in Richard II. in this sense:—

"Oh, how my name befits my composition!
Old *Gaunt*, indeed, and *gaunt* in being old ;
Within me grief has kept a tedious fast ;
And who abstains from meat that is not gaunt ?
For sleeping England long time have I watched ;
Watching breeds leanness ; leanness is all *gaunt*."

Gilbert de Gand or Gant, a great Domesd. tenant, was son of Baldwin, Earl of Flanders, whose sister William the Conqueror married. Dugdale, i. 400.

GAUNTLETT. An iron glove. Perhaps adopted from some incident of war.

GAUSSEN. The family migrated to England at the Rev. of the Edict of Nantes. The last survivor of the French line, the Chevalier de Gaussen, long ambassador at the court of Berlin, died at Paris about the year 1851. Another branch is resident at Geneva. B.L.G.

GAVIN. See Gawen.

GAWDY. Local. Gawdy Hall, co. Norfolk.

GAWEN. GAWAN. A Welsh and O. Scotch personal name. "The Gawens of Norrington, in the parish of Alvideston, continued in that place four hundred fifty and odd yeares. On the south downe of the farme of Broad Chalke is a little barrow called Gawen's Barrow, which must bee before ecclesiastical lawes were established." Aubrey's Nat. Hist. Wiltshire, edit. Britton, p. 121. Sir Gawayn is one of the fabulous heroes of ancient chivalry, and nephew of King Arthur.

GAY. O. Fr. *gai*, cheerful, merry. A *De* Gay is found in H.R. (co. Oxon); but *Le* Gai and *Le* Gey are more common.

GAYER. Perhaps the Gare of the Wiltshire Domesday.

GAYLER. A jailor. In the H.R. Le Gayeler, Gaylur, and Gayolir.

GAYLORD. "Has no reference to aristocratical gaieties, but means simply jovial or jolly." E. Surn. i. 145. See Wright's Chaucer, 4364 :—

"A prentys dwelled whilom in our citee,
And of the craft of vitaillers was he ;
Gaylard he was as goldfynche in a schawe,
Brown as a bery, and a proper felawe."

Gaillard, as a family name, is well known in Normandy, and is borne as an affix by the Château-Gaillard, and by Gaillard-Bois, two communes in the arrondissement of Andeli.

GAYMER. Apparently a personal or baptismal name, which at an early period became a surname. Geoffrey Gaimar, the well-known Ang.-Norm. *trouvère*, or romantic poet, bore it about the middle of the XII. cent. See Wright's Edit. of his Metr. Chron. London, 1850.

GAYTON. Parishes and places in cos. Chester, Norfolk, Northampton, Stafford, Lincoln, &c.

GAYWOOD. A parish in Norfolk.

GAZE. Mr. Ferguson refers it to an Old German personal name, Gaiso, which Förstmann derives from *gais*, *ger*, a spear.

GAZELEY. GAZELEE. A parish in Suffolk.

GEAR. The origin assigned in Eng. Surn. i. 133, is hardly tenable. There is an estate so called in the parish of St. Earth, co. Cornwall.

GEARING. See Geering.

GEARY. An old personal name. Uxor Geri was a tenant-in-chief in co. Gloucester. Domesd. Gery, Geri. Domesd.

GEDDES. Several places in Scotland are called Geddes-hill, Geddeston, Geddeswell, &c. Hence Gedde is probably a personal name. According to the Statistical Account of Scotland, the family of Geddes, of Rachan in Peeblesshire, have possessed that estate for 1,300 years!

GEE. The Celtic Mac Gee, sans Mac.

GEELE. Dutch. Yellow—probably with reference to the bearer's hair or costume.

GEERE. GEER. See Gear.

GEERING. The A-Sax. personal name. The Domesd. of Hants gives us a Gerin, and that of Warwick, a Gerinus.

GEESON. The anglicised form of Mac Gee.

GELL. The classical name Gellius, through the French.

GENESE. A Genoese?

GENN. This name, which is Cornish, and rare, is believed to be the Celtic form (or rather root) of Planta-*gen*-ista, broom. The G is sounded hard.

GENOURE. The same as Jenner.

GENOWER. Seems about half way between Genoure and Genoa, but is probably neither.

GENT. Anglo-Norman. Neat; pretty; gallant; courteous; noble. Halliwell. *Gent* H.R. Perhaps, however, from the city of Ghent in Flanders. The Gents of Moyns Park, co. Essex, were of Wymbush in that co. in 1328, but obtained their present settlement by marriage with the heiress of Moyne, or Moyns, in the following century. Morant's Essex, ii. 353. Shirley's Noble and Gentle Men.

GENTLE. From disposition.

GENTLEMAN. Joh. Gentilman, and Nichs. Gentilman occur in H.R.

GENTRY. Probably local.

GEOFFREY. See Jeffery.

GEORGE. The personal name. Unlike most names of its class, it seems not to have given rise to any diminutive or derivative.

GERARD. A Norman personal name, probably identical with Gerald. In the H.R. it is written Fil' Gerardi. The baronet's family derive their origin from the same ancestor as the Dukes of Leinster and many other noble houses, viz., from Other, Castellan of Windsor, temp. Edw. Confessor, whose grandson Gerard, or Gerald, had a son William Fitz-Gerard, who founded the Cheshire and Lancashire Gerards. The family have possessed Bryn, in the latter county, uninterruptedly from temp. Edw. III. Courthope's Debrett.

GERISON. Is used for Margerison at Eckington, co. Derby. It is curious that at the same place there have been Megsons and Moxons—perhaps all descended from one and the same Margery. See Female Names, &c.

GERMAN. GERMAINE. Lat. *germanus;* of the same stock; a near kinsman; thus we say cousin-german for first-cousin. As a personal name it is of great antiquity in Britain, dating from St. German, the successful opponent of the Pelagian heresy in the fifth century. Possibly in some instances it is derived from the country, like French, Irish, &c.

GERNET. The house of G. of Lanca-shire were descended from Sir Roger G., hereditary forester of Lancashire, temp. Hen. III—the male representative of a great Norman family. Omerod, Misc. Pal.

GERNON. Robert de Gernon came into England with the Conqueror, and his descendant, Ralph de Gernon, temp. Hen. II., had two sons: 1.—Ralph, ancestor of the Gernons and Cavendishes of England; and 2.—Roger, who accompanied Strongbow into Ireland, and became progenitor of the Irish Gernons still subsisting at Athcarne Castle, co. Meath. Of the locality of Gernon, whence at the Conquest the family came, I am ignorant; but it appears not to be in Normandy. Gernun, Gernoun. H.R.

GERRANS. A parish in Cornwall.

GERRARD. See Gerard.

GERRETT. See Gerard.

GERVAIS. The French form of the personal name Gervasius, which we have corrupted to Jarvis. The family of Gervais of Cecil, co. Tyrone, descend from Jean G. of Tournon in Guienne, whose two sons, at the Rev. of the Edict of Nantes, fled into England.

GERVIS. See Gervais, Jervis, &c.

GEST. An old spelling of Guest.

GIBB. GIBBE. GIBBES. GIBBS. Diminutives of the Norman personal name Gislebertus, or Gilbert. According to B.L.G. several of the gentry families of this name, viz., those of Belmont, co. Somerset; Aldenham, co. Herts; Tyntesfield, co. Somerset; and apparently those of Derry, co. Cork, are descended from two brothers, Gibbe or Gibbes, temp. Richard II., one of whom was settled at Honington, co. Warwick, and the other at Fenton, co. Devon. Jenkin Gibbes, temp. Henry VII., a scion of the house of Fenton, whose descendants were of Elmerstone, co. Kent, possessed an ancient roll deducing the family from Normandy, where they were resident long before the Conquest of England. B.L.G. The identity of this name with the Fr. De Guibes has not been established, nor is it at all probable.

GIBBARD. GIBBERD. See Gilbert.

GIBBINGS. See Gilbert.

GIBBON. GIBBONS. GIBBENS. See Gilbert.

GIBBONSON. See Gilbert.

GIBSON. See Gilbert.

GIDDEN. A corruption of Gideon.

GIDDING. GIDDINGS. Gidding, parishes in cos. Huntingdon and Suffolk.

GIDDY. An ancient Cornish family, formerly written Gedy, Geddey, Gidey, &c. Possibly a nurse-name of Gideon.

GIDEON. The personal name.

GIDLEY. A parish in Devonshire. Gidley Castle, a fragmentary ruin, still belongs to the family.

GIFFORD. GIFFARD. The old historical Giffards of Normandy and England descended from the De Bollebecs, who were connected by marriage with Richard I., Duke of Normandy. Walter, son of Osborne de Bollebec, though surnamed "Giffard," or "the Liberal," seems also to have been *conservative* in the acquisition and retention of lands; for he got not only the fair domain of Longueville, near Dieppe, from Richard II. of Normandy, who created him Count de Longueville, but also the Earldom of Buckingham, with above a hundred manors in various counties of England, from William I., whom he had accompanied to the Conquest of this country. In Leland's time there were four "notable houses" of Gifford remaining in England, in the cos. of Devon, Southampton, Stafford, and Buckingham. At the present time the only one of these existing is the Staffordshire family, whose ancestor married the heiress of Corbosone, temp. King Stephen, and thus became Lord of Chillington, which has ever since been the abode of his posterity. Shirley's Noble and Gentle Men of England.

GILBART. GILBURD. Corruptions of Gilbert.

GILBERT. A personal name, largely introduced at the Norman Conquest, in the form of Gislebertus. See Domesd. *passim.* It is not only a very common surname, but has given birth to Gibb, Gibbs, Gybbes, Gibbard, Gibbings, Gibbonson, Gibson, Gill, Gilks, Gilpin, and many others.

GILDER. The occupation.

GILDERSLEEVES. This queer name is found in the Registrar General's cabinet of oddities, and is doubtless identical with that which was borne by the Roger Gyldenesleve of the H.R. Did he, or some ancestor, wear sleeves largely embroidered with gold?

GILES. The baptismal name.

GILKS. See Gilbert. This name was so common in the northern part of Oxfordshire in the last century, that, on the enclosure, in 1774, of some lands in the parish of Swalcliffe, it was necessary to describe six claimants thus :—

1. Thomas Adderbury Gilks (probably from some connection with the parish of Adderbury).

2. Thomas Gilks, of the Slat-house (a house covered with slate).

3. Thomas Gilks, at the Vine (a vine covered the front of his residence).

4. Thomas Shoemaker Gilks (from his business).

5. Thomas Gilks, at the Well (from contiguity to the village well?).

6. Thomas Sweetbriar Gilks (from a sweet-briar or eglantine with which his cottage was overgrown).

At a somewhat earlier period (1754) five Thomas Gilks voted at a contested election in respect of property in the same parish. Inf. D. D. Hopkyns, Esq.

GILL. 1. See Gilbert. 2. This word occurs singly as a surname, and also with many compounds, as Asgill, Pickersgill, Dowgill, Gilham, Gilby, &c. It either signifies a narrow pebbly rivulet in a ravine, or is a diminutive of Gilbert. According to B.L.G. the Gills of Devonshire have pos-

sessed lands in that county ever since the reign of King Stephen.

Of the barony of Gilsland in Cumberland, Camden thus speaks :—"A tract so cut or mangled with brooks, or so full of rivulets, that I should suppose it to have taken its name from those *gills*, had I not read in the register of Lanercost church, that one Gill, son of Bueth, who in the charter of Henry II. is also called Gilbert, anciently held it, and probably left his name to it." To this Gough adds :—"Gilsland might also take its name from Hubert de Vaux, since De Vallibus and Gills mean the same." But this is an inversion of the proper order of things, for the name De Vallibus or Vaux was borrowed from these *gills*. See Vaux.

GILLARD. Probably one of the many modifications of William, which see.

GILLBANKS. In old family records Ghylbanke. Gilbank, a small hamlet in co. Cumberland, in which county the family still reside.

GILLEANRIAS. Gael. The servant of St. Andrew. See Gill.

GILLEBRIDE. Gael. The servant of St. Bridget. See Gill.

GILLEMORE. The bearer of the broadsword to a Scottish chief.

GILLER. See Gill, and the termination ER.

GILLESPIE. A corruption of *Gille-Espuaig*, Gaelic, "the Servant of the Bishop." It was originally spelt Gillespic, and frequently employed in the Highlands as a Christian name.

GILLET. (In pronunciation *Jillet.*) The name is supposed to be derived from Gilleste, a town on the borders of France and Piedmont. Inf. Rev. Edw. Gillet. When the G is hard, the name is probably a derivation of Guillaume, William.

GILLETT. See Gillet.

GILLIAM. See William.

GILLIATT. See William.

GILLIE. A menial servant. Jamieson.

GILLIES. Gael. *Gille Jesa*, the Servant or Follower of Jesus ; "a youth under the protection of Jesus." Johnstone's Anecd. of Olave the Black. 1780.

GILLING. Two wapentakes and a parish in Yorkshire. De Gilling. H.R.

GILLINGHAM. Parishes in cos. Dorset, Kent, and Norfolk.

GILLMAN. Probably derived from Gill, in its topographical meaning, like Milman from Mill, and Hillman from Hill. The Irish family (originally from England in 1690) have a tradition of their descent from a Crusader who cut off the right leg of a Saracen—an event supposed to be commemorated in the family arms. B.L.G.

GILMAN. I should have said—from residence near a Gill, q. v.; but both Dixon and Arthur are against me. Mr. D. derives it from the Fr. surname, *Villemain*, which latter he (incorrectly) makes a diminutive of Guillaume, William.   Mr. A. states that "the Gillmans are said to have come from the province of Maine, with William the Conqueror, and to have settled in Essex." See preceding article.

GILLMORE. Gael. *Gille-mohr*, "great servant."   The armour-bearer of a Highland chief was so called, and was probably selected for his size and strength.

GILLON.   The Gillons of Linlithgow-shire consider themselves of Norman origin, but some derive the name from the clan Gille-eon.

GILLOTT.   See William.   Gillot, Gillote.   H.R.

GILLRAY.   See Gilroy.

GILMER.   See Gillmore.

GILMOUR.   GILMORE. See Gillmore.

GILPATRIC.   Gael.   The Servant of St. Patrick.

GILPIN.   See Gilbert.   An eminent family seated at Kentmere Hall, co. Westmoreland, temp. King John. B.L.G.

GILROY.   GILRAY.   Gael. *Gille ruadh* or *roy*, i. e. "the red lad." The celebrated Highland freebooter of the XVI. cent., Gilderoy, derived his designation from this source.   Arthur says, "*Gille-roimh*, a running footman attendant on a Highland chieftain ; or *Gille-righ*, the servant of the king."   Others make it equivalent to Fitz-Roy—the son of a king.   Thus do Gaelic etymologists differ.

GILRUTH.   The same as Gilroy.

GILSON.   The son of Gill or Gilbert.

GINKELL.   Godart de Ginkell, baron de Reede, came with William, Prince of Orange, into England.   He accompanied him to Ireland, where he besieged and took Athlone, for which service he was created Earl of Athlone.

GINMAN.   See Ginner.

GINN.   GIN.   Perhaps the same as Genn, with the G softened.

GINNER.   Now more usually spelt *Jenner*.   Old English *ginour*, an engineer, a craftsman.   Le Engynur, Le Ginnur, H.R. The word 'gin' is retained in our version of the Old Testament, and occurs in many old writers, in the bad sense of a trap, snare, or crafty device.   Pott derives Jenner from Januarius.

GIPP.   GIPPS.   GIPSON.   See Gilbert.

GIPSY.   Must be a surname of comparatively recent date, if borrowed from the wandering tribe so called.   See next article.

☞ **GIPSY SURNAMES.** Whatever may be the true origin of this remarkable nomadic race, it is pretty certain that they did not arrive here until late in the XV. century, and equally so that they did not possess when they came, any hereditary surnames.   *Faw* and *Curleople* (see those articles) are the only patronymics that I have met with that are not borrowed from well-known English family names.   For example, Smith is no uncommon appellation amongst them. I know a Gipsy Smith who, although possessed of several messuages and tenements, chooses to travel the country in his 'wan.' Again,   our   "illustrious   dreamer,", John Bunyan, an undoubted Gipsy, bore   a   name   of   Welsh   origin. There are plenty of Bakers, Coopers, Barnetts, Buckleys, Broadways, Drapers, Allens, Joneses, Glovers, Lights, Taylors, Williamses, Martins, Smalls, Blewitts, Carters, Bucklands, and Drapers. There are also Ballachys, Loversedges, Corries, Eyreses, Lees in plenty, and *Scamps* more than enough!   It is not wonderful that Carew is a favourite surname, when we know the career of the celebrated Bampfylde Moore Carew ; but where these wanderers picked up Bosville, Lovell, Mansfield, Plunkett, Stanley, and other aristocratic designations is not so easily explained.

A writer in N. and Q., April 17, 1858, says, that there are a quarter of a million of Gipsies of all kinds in the British Isles ; and he adds that in Scotland "there are Gipsies in every sphere of life —even barristers, clergymen, and gentlemen."

GIRARDOT.   From France, after the Rev. of the Edict of Nantes.

GIRDLER.   A maker of girdles—an ancient occupation.   The Girdlers' Company in London was incorporated in 1449.

GIRTH.   Gyrth, an A-Sax. baptismal name.

GISBORNE.   Gisburn, a great parish in Yorkshire, well-known for its priory, its wild cattle, and its forest outlaw, Guy of Gisborne.

GISSING.   A parish in Norfolk.

GITTINGS.   Gittin, a Welsh and Armorican personal name.

GLADDIN.   See Gladwin.

GLADDING.   GLADING.   An old word employed by Gower, in the sense of pleasant, cheerful.

GLADMAN.   The definitions in Eng. Surn. are not satisfactory to me.   That which I am now to assign will hardly be so to the bearers of the name.   Jamieson gives us *glad* or *glaid* as smooth, slippery ; and he adds, that it is also applied to one who is not to be trusted—"a slippery fellow."

GLADSTONE.   Local : place unknown.

GLADSON.   A corruption of Gladstone.

GLADWIN.   An A-Sax. personal name.

Gladewinus, Gladuin, &c. occur as ante-Domesd. tenants.

GLAISHER. GLAYSHER. A corruption of Glazier.

GLAISTER. Probably the same as Glenister, a local name, though *glaister* in Scotland signifies a thin covering of snow or ice. Jamieson. Again, Glasterer means a boaster. Ibid.

GLAIVE. GLAVE. A long cutting blade at the end of a lance. Halliwell. The name was assumed in the same way as Sword, Lance, and many others.

GLANFIELD. See Glanville.

GLANVILLE. A place in the arrondissement of Pont-l'Evêque, in Normandy. It is latinized 'De Glanvilla,' and anglicized Glanfield. Robert de Glanville, a tenant in Suffolk, temp. Domesd. was ancestor of the earls of Suffolk of that name.

The Glanvilles of Catchfrench, co. Cornwall, are descended from the G.'s of Halwell, co. Devon. circ. 1400, (Shirley's Noble and Gentle Men) and they, according to tradition, from Ranulf de Glanville, lord of Glanville, near Pont l'Evêque, who entered England with the Conqueror. C. S. Gilbert's Cornwall, ii. 171.

GLASGOW. The great northern city.

GLASIER. A glazier.

GLASS. A parish in cos. Aberdeen and Banff; also an island, a lake, and a river in Scotland.

GLASSBROOK. See Glazebrook.

GLASSCOCK. See Nicholas. The Glascocks of High Estre, co. Essex, traced their pedigree to temp. Edw. III.

GLASSCOTT. Glascote, a township co. Warwick. The Glascotts, who went into Ireland in 1649, claim, however, from the Glascocks of High Estre.

GLASSON. Glaston, parishes, &c., in cos. Rutland, Lancaster, and Somerset.

GLASSWRIGHT. A glass maker. Andrew le Glasswright occurs in the records of Great Yarmouth in the XIV. century. Papers of Norfolk Archæol. Soc., iv. 253. Little is known of the history of the glass manufacture in this country in the middle ages. In Sussex there are some traditions, but very little can be positively ascertained respecting it, notwithstanding Fuller's assertion that " plenty hereof is made in this county." In Thomas Charnock's Breviary of Philosophy we read:—

" As for glass makers, they be scant in this land,
    Yet one there is, as I do understand ;
    And in Sussex is now his habitation,
    At Chiddingfold he works of his occupation."

This was written in 1557. Chiddingfold is in Surrey, not Sussex.

GLAZEBROOK. A recent southern corruption of Grazebrook, which see.

GLAZIER. The trade.

GLEGG. Scottish, *gleg.* Quick of perception, keen, clever, expeditious. Scott in the *Antiquary* makes his old "bluegown" say:—" I was aye *gleg* at my duty —naebody ever catched Edie sleeping."

☞ **GLEN.** A common syllable in Celtic names of places, as Glendinning, Glendor, Gleneaglis, Glenister, Glenfield, Glenham, Glennie, Glenny, and Glenton.

It signifies a vale, or rather a narrow valley, formed by two acclivities bounding a stream or river, which gives rise to the local name. Thus Glenalmond is the glen or valley of the river Almond, Glenapp, that of the App, &c.

GLENDINNING. An ancient estate at Westerkirk, co. Dumfries.

GLENDONWYN. Probably the same as Glendinning or Glendonyn.

GLENDONYN. The exact spot from which the surname was adopted cannot be ascertained, but it was near the coast of Ayrshire. Robert de Glendonyn obtained a confirmation grant of the lands of Glendonyn from Alexander III. for his services at the battle of Largs. The heiress married Macknyghte in the XIV. century, and the representation now vests in Coulthart.

GLENISTER. GLINISTER. A locality in Scotland; but I do not find the place.

GLENNY. A place at Abernyte, in Perthshire.

GLENTON. Probably Glinton, co. Northampton.

GLIDE. See Glyde.

GLISTER. As Glaister.

GLITHEROW. See Clitheroe.

GLOVER. The occupation. Le Ganter. H.R.

GLYDE. GLIDE. A sort of road, or more properly speaking an opening. Aberdeenshire. Jamieson. 2. *Gleid*, squinting. Ibid.

GLYNDE. A parish in Sussex.

GLYNN. A place in the parish of Cardinham, co. Cornwall, the abode of " an ancient family of gentlemen of this name, who for many generations flourished there." Hals, in D. Gilbert's Cornwall, i. 171.

GLYNNE. The baronet derives his descent from Cilmin Droed-tu, one of the fifteen tribes of North Wales who were flourishing in A.D. 843. The local name was assumed in the XVI. cent.

GOAD. Probably Good. A-Sax. *gód.*

GOAT. A narrow cavern or inlet into which the sea enters. Jamieson.

GOATER. GOTER. A goat-herd ?

GOATMAN. A keeper of goats ; a goat-herd.

GOBLET. Perhaps a trader's sign.

GODBEHERE. R.G. 16. I have met

with it as a surname in Sussex, temp Hen. III. See under Goodbeer.

GODBID. A-Sax. *biddian*, to pray. See 'Gotobed.' Perhaps, however, a corruption of Godbert, a personal name also used in the XIII. cent. as a surname.

GODBODY. Probably a medieval oath —" By God's body."

GODBOLD. 1. Occurs in Domesd. as a previous A-Sax. tenant. 2. A-Sax. *gód* and *bold*—" the good dwelling."

GODDAME. (Parish-register of Charlton, co. Kent.) Probably 'good-dame,' a mother-in-law; so 'good-brother,' in some dialects, signifies brother-in-law; and there are several analogies in the French language: as *beaupere*,' step-father; ' *bellemere*,' mother-in-law. Perhaps it may be synonymous with godmother, which is found in the H.R., under the orthography of Godmoder, and borne by an individual named William, proving that at that time it had passed into a transmissible or family name.

GODDARD. Godardus appears in Domesd. as a personal name. The ancestor of the Goddards of Cliffe and Swindon are said to have been seated in Wiltshire before temp. Rich. II. B.L.G.

GODDEN. Often a corruption of Godwin.

GODDIN. See Godwin.

GODDING. Francis Goddinge, merchant, and his wife, Protestant refugees, left Dieppe and settled at Rye, co. Sussex, in 1572. Lansd. M.S., 15-70. But the name is also indigenous, for Goding, Godingus, &c., occur in A-Sax. times.

GODFREY. GODFREE. An ancient Teutonic personal name—the same as Geoffrey. The form Goisfridus is very common in Domesd. The Godfreys of Brook-Street House, Kent, are supposed to be descended from Godfrey le Fauconer, lord of the manor of Hurst in that county, in the reign of Henry II. B.L.G.

GODHELPE. 1. An exclamation : the name was probably given to a person who habitually used it. See 'Helpusgod.' 2. The A-Sax. name Godulph.

GODKIN. Perhaps a diminutive oath ; or it may be a nickname of Godfrey or Godwin.

GODLEE. See Godley.

GODLEY. A township in Cheshire, where the family of De Godlee were resident temp. Edward I. *Godelé* is an archaism for goodly, well favoured.

> " Feyre and longe was he thore,
> A *godelyar* man was none bore."
> *M.S. Cantab. Ff. ii.* 38 (Halliw.)

GODLIMAN. May have relation to the assumed sanctity of the first bearer, but is more likely to be a corruption of Godalming, the Surrey town, formerly so pronounced by the vulgar.

GODLOVEMILADY. This remarkable name really existed not many years since. The similar designation Rogerus *Deussalvet-dominas* (Roger God-save-the-Ladies) occurs in the Domesd. of Essex. It was probably the sobriquet of some admirer of the fair sex, who frequently employed the phrase.

GODMAN. (A-Sax. *gód*). The same as Goodman.

GODMEFETCH. " God-me-fetch"— " God take me"—a profane exclamation. See Godhelpe.

GODMUND. An A-Sax. baptismal name.

GODOLPHIN. A manor in the parish of Breage, near Helston, co. Cornwall, anciently written Godolghan, a word which is said to mean in the Cornish tongue "the White Eagle," whence the 'eagle displayed with two necks argent,' in the armorial shield. John de Godolphin is said to have possessed the manor at the time of the Conquest. C. S. Gilbert's Cornwall, i. 520.

GODRICH. GODERICH. See Goodrich.

GODSALL. See Godsell.

GODSALVE. Probably an exclamation—" God save you!"

GODSELL. Perhaps from Godshill, in the Isle of Wight. 2. The same as Godesilus, the name of an early Burgundian King. Ferguson.

GODSHALL. In charters, De Casa Dei. I do not find the locality.

GODSMARK. Appears to be of similar import to Godspenny, which see. It was formerly common in E. Sussex.

GODSON. The spiritual relation—identical with the Fr. *Filleul*. The name in its modern form is found in the H.R., as is also the singular surname Godmoder (Godmother).

GODSPENNY. This word in the N. of England means a deposit, or earnest-money. How it became a name is not clear.

GODWIN. A well-known personal name of Teutonic origin. In Domesd. it is very common.

GOFF. GOFFE. See Gough. When not a corruption of Gough, it is said to signify in the Armorican dialect "the smith." In the Cornish, Angove has the same meaning, while Trengrove is "strong smith." Queingoff is another Armorican surname meaning "whitesmith," according to the conjecture of Mr. Dixon. These are all, of course, allied to Gow.

GOLD. A personal or baptismal name. Golde and Goldus occur in Domesd., and Gold, in the H.R., had become a surname. As a baptismal name it was in use in the XIV. cent., when Gold le Blodleter is found as the designation of an inhabitant of Yarmouth. Papers Norf. Arch. Soc. iv. 253.

Mr. Ferguson observes that "there are several names which appear to express metaphorically the material of which a man is made. Such are the names of metals, at the head of which is Gold. This seems to have been a term of endearment, and to denote love, value, affection. An A-Saxon, ' Dudda, was a husbandman in Hæthfelda, and he had three daughters; one was called Deorwyn; the other Deorswythe; and the third Golde,' "—all terms significant of parental love. As a man's name, Gold must have been somewhat common in England, as many local names, since become surnames, are compounded with it; e.g., Goldby, Goldham, Goldney, Goldsbury, Goldsby, Goldsworthy, Goldthorpe. It also appears to have given rise to the names of Golden and Goulden, Golding and Goulding. The latter are probably patronymical.

GOLDBEATER. The trade. A Rob. le Goldbeter is found in H.R.

GOLDEN. See Gold.

GOLDFINCH. From the bird. Goldfinche. H.R. Sobriquets derived from names of birds are numerous. See Sparrow, Hawk, &c. Lavater found resemblances between human faces and those of oxen, goats, &c. So a friend of mine discovered in a neighbour of hers, not remarkable either for brilliancy of dress or sweetness of song, something which reminded her of a goldfinch. From similar caprices and notions many surnames doubtless arose.

GOLDING. See Gold.

GOLDRIDGE. Goldericus occurs in Germany in the IX. cent. as a personal name.

GOLDSBURY. Goldsborough, a parish in Yorkshire.

GOLDSBY. GOULDSBY. A parish in Lincolnshire, sometimes corrupted to Golceby.

GOLDSMIDT. Germ. *Goldschmid.* A goldsmith.

GOLDSMITH. The great value of the commodity in which the medieval goldsmith dealt rendered him a person of consequence. No less than three tenants-in-chief under the Conqueror are entered in Domesday under the name of Aurifaber. One of these, Otto Aurifaber, held in Essex, and his descendants, under the surname of Fitz-Otho, appear to have been hereditary mint-masters to the crown for two centuries, becoming extinct in 1282. Kelham. Ellis, Introd. The equivalent Fr. Orfévre, and the Germ. Goldschmid, are well-known surnames.

GOLDSPINK. A northern provincialism for Goldfinch.

GOLDWIN. An A-Sax. personal name.

GOLIGHTLY. Has nothing to do, I think, with lightness of foot. The name has many forms, to none of which a mean-

ing can well be attached; but from the termination it is probably local.

GOLLEDGE. Gulledge, an estate near E. Grinstead, co. Sussex.

GOLLOP. Probably the same as Gallop. The Gollops of Strode, co. Dorset, have a tradition of Danish or Swedish descent from a soldier of fortune who was living in 1465. B.L.G.

GOMERSALL. Gomersal, a township in Yorkshire.

GONVILLE. There are two places named Gonneville in the department of Seine Inferieure in Normandy, but from which of them the family came I am unable to determine.

GOOCH. GOOGE. GOODGE. Of uncertain origin; but Mr. Ferguson thinks the last form a derivation from the O. Norse *gud,* war. Goche without prefix is found in the H.R.

GOOD. From excellence of character, like the Fr. Le Bon.

GOODACRE. Probably Germ. *gottesaker,* a burying ground (literally God's Field).— Analogous to our Churchyard, and the medieval In Cemeterio.

GOODAIR. The same as Goodere.

GOODALE. Is probably local, being not Good-ale, but Goo-*dale.*

GOODAY. GOODDAY. GOODEY. GOODY. The third form rather countenances the supposition of a local origin. But it may be from the salutation "Goodday !" especially if GOODEVE may be considered correlatively.

GOODBAIRN. See Goodchild.

GOODBAN. Probably Good-bairn—Goodchild.

GOODBEER. A corruption of Godbehere—*Deus adsit!*—a name occurring in Sussex records of the XIII. century. It was probably applied as a sobriquet to some person who used this adjuration, the more recent form of which is " 'fore God."

GOODBEHERE. See Godbehere.

GOODBODY. A portly person—like the Fr. *Beaucorps*; perhaps, however, an oath: ' By God's body,'—not unusual in the middle ages. The orthography in the H.R. is Godbodi, which rather confirms the latter derivation. Under the name Pardew will be found some remarks on surnames derived from Oaths. See however the remarks under Body.

GOODBORN. See Goodbairn.

GOODBOYS. Doubtless a corruption of some French local name ending in *bois,* wood.

GOODCHAP. See Goodcheap.

GOODCHEAP. "Very cheap"—a common expression in old times, equivalent to the existing French phrase, *bon marché.* Perhaps a sobriquet applied to an early trader. The H.R. orthography is *Godchep*. The corresponding family name Goedkoop is found in Holland.

GOODCHILD. As 'good-brother' in some dialects means brother-in-law, so this name may mean a step-child. It may, however, refer to the natural disposition of the first bearer, as we find its opposite, *Evilchild*, in the H.R.

GOODDEN. A corruption of Goodwin, or Godwin. The Gooddens of Over Compton, co. Dorset, are descended from John Goodwyn, who flourished temp. Edward VI.

GOODE. See Good.

GOODEN. GOODING. GOODINGE. Corruptions of Godwin.

GOODENOUGH. The original bearer was perhaps a sufficiently worthy fellow, but I think his name had no reference to his moral qualities. Knowe is a Scotticism, equivalent to the southern *knoll*, a little round hill, and the prefix 'good' probably indicated the nature of the soil of the hill at or upon which he resided.

GOODERE. Whence Gooderson. Most likely an old personal name.

GOODEVE. Possibly from the salutation, "Good eve!" See Goodday. More probably, however, from the A-Sax. female name, Godiva, famous at Coventry.

GOODFELLOW. A man of sociable and friendly character. The Fr. have their Boncompagnon. Godfelawe. H.R.

GOODGER. See Goodyear. Halliwell tells us that in Devonshire Goodger means both Good-man, or husband, and the Devil. Let us hope that the *Damnonian* wives are not responsible for so evil an association of ideas !

GOODGROOM. *Grome* originally meant simply a servant. Among the Domesd. tenants-in-chief in co. Warwick was a Willelmus Bonvalest, of which William Goodgroom would be a literal translation. A Bonvalêt occurs in the H.R., as also a Gode Grum and several Le Godegrums. Or, taking the prior syllable as the name of the Divine Being, it may mean 'God's servant,' for we find, in the same records, Godeknave, and Godknave. 'Knave,' it must be remembered, was anciently no disgraceful epithet, but meant simply child or servant. See Gilchrist, &c.

GOODHAND. R.G. 16. A dexterous person.

GOODHIND. "The good farm-servant." See Hind.

GOODHUGH. GOODHEW. The latter syllable appears to be a mis-spelling of *hue*. Of good colour or complexion. Temp. Edwd. III. it was written Godeheue.

GOODHUSBAND. To contradistinguish the first bearer from another person of the same Christian name, who was not remarkable for fidelity towards his wife. In the

H.R. we find an Agnes Godhosbonde, which shows that it had become (temp. Edw. I.) a permanent surname. Younghusband is also a well-known family name.

GOODIER. See Goodyer.

GOODJER. The same as Goodyear.

GOODLAD. Apparently the English form of *Bon-garçon*, a Fr. surname.

GOODLAKE. The A-Sax. baptismal name Guthlac. It has been variously written Godelac, Godlac, &c.

GOODLUCK. The A-Sax. personal name Guthlac. Goodluck's Close at Norwich was formerly Guthlac's Close. Ferg.

GOODMADAM. Dixon says a patroness.

GOODMAN. 1. Gudmund, a very common Teutonic and A-Sax. baptismal name. 2. A common form of address in old times. Also a complimentary sobriquet. Thus a great-grandson of the famous William Belward was called Goodman. Eng. Surn. ii. 49.

GOODRAM. As Goodrum.

GOODRICH. 1. A parish in co. Hereford. 2. See Goodrick.

GOODRICK. An ancient Teutonic personal name, usually written Godric and Godericus. Very common in Domesday.

GOODRUM. A probable corruption of the Scandinavian name Guthrum.

GOODSON. 1. Another form of Godson. 2. The parish of Gooderstone, co. Norfolk, is so called. 3. It corresponds with the French *Beaufils*, son-in-law.

GOODSPEED. The sobriquet of a good runner ?

GOODWILL. GOODWILLIE. These singular names have no reference to the character, good or bad, of any of the vast Gulielmian tribe, but, according to Pittscottie, a good-willer and a well-wisher are synonymous. Jamieson.

GOODWIN. The same as Godwin.

GOODWRIGHT. See Wright. A maker of gads, goads, or spears.

GOODYEAR. In Domesd. Godere and Goderus ; in the H.R. Godyer. Goodman, or husband ; still used in this sense in Devonshire.

GOODYER. See Goodyear.

GOOK. GOWK. Ferguson says *gowk*, a northern name for the cuckoo. Gaukr, the O. Norse for this bird, appears in the Landnamabok as a baptismal name.

GOOLD. See Gold. . The Goolds of co. Cork, went thither from England in or about the reign of Henry VI. Courthope's Debrett.

GOOLE. A township in Yorkshire.

GOOSE. "The nobility of the goose is not so obvious as that of the swan. Yet it was in ancient and honourable use as a man's name. Genseric, the name of the great Vandal chief, is referred by Grimm to *gänserich*, a gander. But it was no doubt the wild goose that gave the name; and if we consider, we shall see that this bird has some qualities calculated to command the respect of those early roving tribes. A powerful bird, strong on the wing, taking long flights to distant lands, marshalled with the most beautiful discipline of instinct, it formed no inapt emblem of those migratory plunderers who renewed their unwelcome visitations with each succeeding spring." Ferguson. The name Goose is not unusual in East Anglia, and Gosland, Gosnell, Goslee, local surnames, appear to be from this source, as well, perhaps, as Goss, A-Sax. Le Gos is the H.R. form.

GOOSEMAN. A breeder of Geese.

GOOSEY. A tything in Berkshire.

GOODSHEEP. See Goodcheap.

GORBELL. See Gorbold.

GORBOLD. The O. Germ. Garibald (i.e. "spear-bold") has been thus anglicized, while in Italy it has taken the form of Garibaldi (Ferguson), where it is now appropriately borne by a patriotic hero.

GORDON. According to some genealogists this name is derived from Gordonia, a town in Macedonia; according to others from a manor in Normandy—origins literally too "far-fetched," since the parish of Gordon, in Berwickshire, where we find the family located at an early date, is its true source. "There is a nice little romance to the tune of making the founder of the family a certain Bertrand de Gourdon, who shot Richard the Lion-Hearted at Chaluz. According to history, this Gourdon was a common archer, who having been brought before the dying monarch was forgiven by him, and ordered to be liberated with a handsome present; but the Flemish general, who had no notion of such generosity, very coolly ordered him to be flayed alive. How, after such an operation, he could get into Scotland we are not told." N. and Q., Nov. 1, 1856. The cheerfulness of this family is exhibited in the proverb, THE GAY GORDONS.

An anonymous correspondent sends me the following—

"*Dialogue between the first Marquis of Huntley and his Gentleman-in-waiting.* MARQ.—Send me Sandy Gordon. GENT.—Wfat Sandy Gordon? MARQ.—Fite Sandy Gordon. GENT.—Wfat fite Sandy Gordon? MARQ.—Fite *fat* Sandy Gordon." And the White, Fat, Sandy Gordon was doubtless forthcoming. My correspondent asks: "How many Sandy Gordons must there have been in his lordship's service?"

GOREN. A corruption of Goring.

GORGES. The château de Gorges, one of whose lords was at the battle of Hastings, stands in the parish of the same name, in the canton of Periers, department of La Manche, Normandy. His descendant, Raoulde Gorges, married an heiress of Morville, and had the manors of Wraxall and Bradpole, cos. Dorset and Somerset, and was sheriff of Devonshire. M. de Gerville, in Mem. Soc. Antiq. Normandie, 1825.

GORMAN. *Gormand* is an old Scotticism for the Fr. *gourmand*, an enormous eater, a glutton.

GORME. Three lakes in Scotland are so called.

GORRING. GORRINGE. Sussex surnames, and doubtless modifications of the ancient local name Goring in that county. As in the case of Hardinge, the G in the latter of these two forms has been improperly softened, and the pronunciation is *Gorrinje*.

GORTON. A chapelry in the parish of Manchester.

GOSDEN. See under Den.

GOSHAWK. The bird.

GOSLAND. See Goose.

GOSLEE. See Goose.

GOSLIN. See Gosling.

GOSLING. GOSTLING. From the Anglo-Norman Christian name Joscelyn, or Goceline. Fil' Gocelini, Goscelin, Gosselin, and several other forms are found in the H.R. The assimilation of the name to that of a young goose by the addition of the *g* final is of modern date. Similar instances of the hardening of the soft *g* or *j* are observable in the Norman dialect. Thus *jambe* and *gerbe* are made *gambe* and *guerbe*.

GOSNELL. Anciently Gosnold, and therefore probably from some locality called Gosenwold, a wold or plain whereon geese were numerous.

GOSPATRICK. Originally a personal name, and stated in a rare tract by the Rev. Jas. Johnstone, entitled "Anecdotes of Olave the Black, King of Man," (1780) to signify the 'Boy of St. Patrick.'

GOSPELL. Gosbell, an ancient Teutonic personal name.

GOSSE. In Scotland, a sponsor for a child; but more probably the A-Sax. *gos*, a goose.

GOSSELIN. A family of Norman origin who have long resided in Guernsey. They claim descent from Robert Gosselin, who for eminent services in the rescue of Mont Orgueil from the French in 1339, is said to have been made governor of that fortress, and to have received from Edward III. a grant of the arms now borne by his descendants. B.L.G. The name is identical with Joscelyn.

GOSWICK. A hamlet in Northumberland.

GOTT. Apparently an old baptismal name. Will fil' Gotte. H.R.

GOTHARD. 1. Either Godard, the personal name, or Goat-herd. 2. A foolish fellow. North. Halliwell. Probably because the occupation of keeping goats required little skill. Conf. Coward.

GOTOBED. O. Germ. *Gott-bet*, 'Pray to God.' Talbot's Engl. Etymol. Robert Gotobed, Winchelsea, 20. Edw. I. Juliana Gotebedde, ibid. (Cooper). Notwithstanding Mr. Talbot's conjecture, we may as well, perhaps, take this name *au pied de la lettre*, and assume that it was given as a sobriquet to people more than ordinarily attached to their couch. A similar collocation of words forming a surname occurs in the H.R., viz.: Serlo *Go-to-kirke*, which was borne by one of the cottars of the hundred of Trippelowe, co. Cambridge, temp. Edw. I.—most probably in allusion to his constant attention to his public devotions.

GOUGH. Welsh. Red—from complexion.

GOULBORN. Golborn, townships in Cheshire and Lancashire. From the former, David, grandson of the patriarchal William Belward, baron of Malpas, originally assumed the name, in Norman times.

GOULD. See Gold. The Goulds are traceable in the municipal records of Exeter to the time of Edward III. Lysons.

GOULDEN. See Gold.

GOULDING. See Gold.

GOULDSMITH. See Goldsmith.

GOULTY. Probably the French *Gualtier*, (Walter) to which in sound it closely approximates.

GOURD. The A-Sax. personal name Gyrth or Gyrd.

GOURNAY (Now **GURNEY**). This ancient race accompanied Rollo into Neustria and became lords of Gournay, whence their name. Gournai-en-Brai is a town in the arrondissement of Neufchâtel. There were two Hugh de Gournays at the battle of Hastings, the father, an old man, leading on his vassals of Bray—

"———— li viel Hue de Gornai,
Ensemble o li sa gent de Brai."
Roman de Rou.

Both Hughs had grants from William, the *caput baroniæ* being in Norfolk, still the stronghold of the name, and their blood became mingled with that of the Conqueror himself, by the marriage of Gerard de Gournay with Edith, daughter of Wm. de Warenne, by Gundrada, daughter of William the Conqueror. He joined the first Crusade, 1096, and subsequently died on a pilgrimage to Jerusalem. From Walter de G. who flourished under Stephen, and whose son William still held a portion of the fief of Bray, " came a long line of country gentlemen in Norfolk, who seem never to have risen above or fallen below that honourable old status." *Athenæum*, Sept. 18, 1858.

GORE. A "narrow slip of ground," as Kensington Gore. See Faulkner's Kensington, p. 617.

GORING. A parish in Sussex where the ancestors of the baronet's family were resident at an early period. John de Goring was lord before temp. Edw. II.

GOW. Gael. A smith.

GOWAN. Scotch, a 'Daisy,' which is also (but why, it is difficult to guess) an English surname.

GOWARD. GOWAR. Corruptions of Gower.

GOWER. "All our Antiquaries agree that this family is one of the oldest in the county of York, and of Anglo-Saxon origin, though they differ as to its patriarch, whom some will have to be Sir Alan Gower, said to be sheriff of that county at the time of the Norman Conquest, A.D. 1066, and lord of Stittenham in the same county, [now possessed by the Duke of Sutherland, the chief of the house] while others with greater probability assert that it descended from one Guhyer, whose son, called William Fitz-Guhyer of Stittenham, was charged with a mark for his lands in the sheriff's account, 1167, 13 Henry II., and that Alan was very likely his son." Collins' Peerage 1768, v. 340. The poet Gower is said to have been of the Stittenham stock, though he did not bear the same arms. Leland says: "The house of Gower the poet yet remaineth at Switenham (Stittenham), in Yorkshire, and divers of them syns have been knightes." The noble Gowers pronounce their name as if written Gore, but a yeomanry family in the south of England make it rhyme with 'power,' or 'shower.'

GOWERS. See Gower.

GOY. A place on the river Seine in Lower Normandy.

GOYMER. See Gaimar.

GRABBY. A corruption of Groby, or some similar local name.

GRACE. Raymond Fitz-William de Carew, surnamed 'Crassus,' 'Le Gros,' and 'Le Gras,' accompanied Strongbow, Earl of Pembroke, in his celebrated expedition into Ireland in 1169, and he may be regarded "as the Achilles of the enterprise." He married Basilia de Clare, Strongbow's sister, with whom he acquired an enormous estate in Killarney, subsequently known as "the Cantred of Grace's country;" for "his cognomen Gros, given him on account of his prowess, gradually became first Gras, and then by English pronunciation Grace." Many of the English families of this name deduce their descent from Ireland. See Memoirs of the Fam. of Grace, by Sheffield Grace, Esq., F.S.A.

GRADDON. See Gratton.

GRADY. The Irish patronymical O'Grady, sans O.

GRAEME. According to the Scottish genealogists, who, as Camden tells us, "think surnames as ancient as the moon," this illustrious patronymic is derived from Greme, who was regent of Scotland during the minority of Eugene II. (commencing A.D. 419), and had many "engagements with the Britons, and by forcing that mighty rampart they had reared up between the rivers of Forth and Clyde, immortalized his name so much, as that to this day that entrenchment is called Graham's Dyke." Collins, who gravely states this, finds, however, no record of the family earlier than the time of King David I., A.D. 1125, when the name was written Greme. Somewhat later it was written De Graeme, which shows its *local* origin; and indeed it is simply a Scottish pronunciation of Graham, which see.

GRAFTER. Of trees?

GRAFTON. Parishes and places in cos. Chester, Gloucester, Hereford, Oxford, Worcester, Warwick, and Northampton. It is from Grafton-Regis in the last-named co. that the Duke of Grafton takes his title.

GRANTHAM. A town in Lincolnshire.

GRAPES. An innkeeper's sign.

GRAHAM. The name has always been written interchangeably with Græme—the Scottish orthography. The earliest traceable ancestor, (for we reject of course the fifth-century hero Greme—See Græme,) is William de GRAHAM, who settled in Scotland early in the XII. century. The surname therefore is clearly local, and from its termination undoubtedly English. The only place in S. Britain of the name which we find is Graham, near Kesteven in Lincolnshire. H.R., vol. i., page 288.

GRAIN. GRAINE. An island-parish of Kent.

GRAINGER. See Granger.

GRAMMER. O. Norse. *gramr*, a king. Ferg.

GRANCESTER. Grantchester, a parish in Cambridgeshire.

GRANDISON. Camden places this among the great families who came hither at the Conquest from the Netherlands. The name was eminent in the XIII. cent., and at the siege of Carlaverock (A.D. 1300) "William de Grandison (*Grant son*) bore paly, silver and azure, surcharged with a red bend, and thereon three beautiful eaglets of fine gold." Nicolas' Siege of Carlav.

GRANDORGE. The family of De Graind'orge existed in Normandy at an early period. In the reign of Louis XI. they were ennobled by the title of Vicomte de Graindorge of Falaise. In the reign of king Stephen, a branch came into England and assisted in the endowment of Furness Abbey. The family flourished in knightly degree until the XV. century, principally in Craven, co. York. A William G. fought at Agincourt, and a Nicholas G. was master-forester to Roger de Clifford. See Armorial General of France, Nicolas' Agincourt, and Whittaker's Craven. Our old English name of Barlicorn, (see H.R.) may be a translation. The arms of the family (three ears of barley) allude to the name.

GRANGE. Fr. A barn; applied in monastic times to the homestead of an outlying manor belonging to an abbey or priory. Mr. Chas. Knight says, "a lone farm-house."

"What tell'st thou me of robbing? this is Venice;
My house is not a *grange*."
Othello, i. 1.

Several hamlets in various cos. are so called.

GRANGER. See Grange. The bailiff who presided over one, was called Ate Grange, (H.R.) and afterwards Granger.

GRANT. "Nothing certain is known regarding the origin of the Grants. They have been said to be of Danish, English, French, Norman, and of Gaelic extraction, but each of these suppositions depends for support on conjecture alone." Skene's Highlanders, ii. 254. The advocates of a Gaelic source adduce a tradition which makes them McGregors. Those who consider the name French, derive it from *grand*. On the first appearance of the family in Scotland, it is written "dictus Grant," afterwards "le Grant," and sometimes ridiculously " de Grant," for there was no ancient property so called. As to "le," that particle was prefixed by clerks to most Highland epithets, as well as to Norman. The name first occurs in charters in 1258. Ibid. p. 256. Other accounts of the name are given by Dixon, edit. 1855, where we meet with the following anecdote. "A wag contrived to alter in the family Bible of a former laird of Grant, the words in Genesis, 'There were *giants* in those days,' into 'There were *Grants* in those days;' and the good old chief believed it!"

GRANVILLE. See Grenville.

GRASS. Fr. *gras*. Fat, stout.

GRASSBY. A parish in Lincolnshire.

GRATTON. A hamlet in Derbyshire.

GRAVE. 1. A northern pronunciation of Grove. 2. A bailiff or reeve. 3. A cave. 4. A personal name, whence Graves and Graveson.

GRAVELEY. Parishes in the counties of Herts and Cambridge. A Ralph de Gravele occurs in the hundred of Edwinstree, in the former shire, temp. Edward I. H.R.

GRAVELL. If not from Gravelle near Lisieux in Normandy, may be derived from the soil upon which the first proprietor of the name dwelt, like Clay, Sands, &c.

GRAVENOR. See Grosvenor.

GRAVER. Perhaps the same as Grover. See Grave.

GRAVES. See Grave, 4.

GRAVETT. A little Grove.

GRAY. See Grey.

GRAYGOOSE. A sobriquet. The name Greengoose is also found. It is probable that the two appellations originated in the same locality and were somewhat antithetical of each other—the Gray being the old, and the Green, the young, *goose*.

GRAYHURST. Perhaps from Gravenhurst, co. Bedford.

GRAYLING. See Fishes.

GRAYSON. See Greyson.

GRAZEBROOK. The G.'s of cos. Stafford and Gloucester descend from Gerseburg, Gersebroc, or Greysbrook, co. York, which manor they held with others in fee from the Conquest. B.L.G.

GRAZIER. The occupation.

GREAM. The same as Graham and Graeme, which see.

GREAR. See Gregory.

GREAT. From size, like the Fr. Le Grand, the Dutch De Groot, &c.

GREATA. A river of Cumberland.

GREATHEAD. Apparently from the personal peculiarity. Robt. Grosteste, the celebrated bishop of Lincoln, sometimes so wrote his name.

GREATHEART. A man of courage.

GREAVES. See Grieve.

GREEDY. From disposition.

GREELY. Local: probably in co. Rutland, as De Greley and De Greyley are found there in H.R. temp. Edw. I.

☞ **GREEN.** A common prefix to local surnames, many of which cannot be traced to their sources in the ordinary gazetteer, such as Greengrass, Greenhaigh, Greenhale, Greenhorne (!), Greening, Greenland, Greenleaf, Greentree, Greenslade, Greenway, Greenwell, Greenberry, Greengrow, (-grove,) Greenhalf, (-haugh,) Greensides, Greenacre, Greenhead, (-promontory.) The prefix is the A-Sax. *gréne*, and the compounds mostly explain themselves.

GREEN. From residence near an unenclosed space, or common ground. H.R. Ate-Grene, Del Grene, De-la-Grene, and A la Grene. As every village had its green, the commonness of the name is easily accounted for. The Lond. Direct. for 1852 mentions 222 traders so called, besides a few Greenes. Grene is also a personal name occurring in Domesday.

GREENE. See Green.

GREENER. From residence at a green.

GREENFIELD. A Lincolnshire hamlet. Also a corruption of Grenville or Granville.

GREENGOOSE See Graygoose.

GREENHILL. A liberty in co. Lincoln.

GREENHORNE. This undesirable surname appears to be of the local kind, and the place from which it is derived is probably in Scotland.

GREENHOW. A township co. York.

T

GREENISH. Has no reference to greenness, either physical or mental. It is doubtless a corruption either of Greenwich, co. Kent, or of ' Greenwish,' a local name.

GREENLEAF. A character in the pageants of Robin Hood. See Eng. Surn. i. 184, *note*.

GREENMAN. Perhaps the same as Greener; or it may be a keeper of game, from the colour of his costume in the old times of " vert and venison." A keeper of Broyle park, at Ringmer, co. Sussex, on retiring from his duties opened an inn, to which he gave the name of the Green Man, the sign being his own portrait.

The name was also given to the 'salvage' or ' man of the wood,' in old shows. See Woodhouse.

GREENWELL. "The wide-spreading and ancient family of Greenwell are descended from Gulielmus Presbyter, who in 1183, as appears from 'Boldon Buke,' held the lands of Greenwell in the parish of Walsingham, co. Durham, and whose son James assumed the name of the place of his inheritance." B.L.G.

GREENWOOD. I find no specific locality called by this name; but it is quite probable that in old times many a sylvan district gave a name of distinction to lovers of " vert and venison," whose abode was " the merrie green-wood."

GREER. See Gregory.

GREG. See Gregory. Gregg of Norcliffe Hall, co. Chester, claims from the clan Macgregor of Scotland. Kings James VI. (I) and Charles I. issued edicts against the clan Gregor, denouncing the whole clan, and forbad the use of the name; in consequence of which many of the race became Campbells, Gregorys, Greigs, and Gregs. B.L.G.

GREGORSON. See Gregory.

GREGORY. The well-known personal name has not only become a surname, but has given rise to various others, especially Gregorson, Gregg, Gregson, Griggs, Grigson, Greig, Grix, and possibly Grocock. These forms are mostly Scotch, and Grier and Grierson, not to mention Mac-Gregor, are entirely so.

The family of Gregory of Warwickshire is traced to John G., lord of the manors of Freseley and Asfordby, co. Leicester, in the XIII. cent. Shirley's Noble and Gentle Men.

GREGSON. See Gregory.

GREIG. See Gregory.

GREIVE. See Grieve.

GRENE. See Green.

GRENTMESNIL. Literally 'the great manor,' a place in Normandy. According to Ordericus Vitalis, Hugo de Grentmesnil was made governor of the county of Hants,

3 Will. Conq., and was high steward to that monarch's son Rufus. Kelham.

GRENVILLE. The Grenvilles of Wootton, co. Bucks, descend from Richard de Grenville, who came in with the Conqueror in the train of Walter Giffard, earl of Longueville and Buckingham, whose son in law he was. The name, which has been variously written, Greynevile, Greinville, Granville, &c., and latinized De Granavilla, was doubtless borrowed from Granville, the well-known seaport of Lower Normandy. The Grenvilles of the West are of the same stock. George G. of Stowe, in Cornwall, the poetical Lord Lansdowne, writing in 1711 to his nephew, Wm. Henry, Earl of Bath, says : " Your ancestors for at least five hundred years never made any alliances, male or female, out of the western counties : thus there is hardly a gentleman either in Cornwall or Devon, but has some of your blood, as you of theirs." Quart. Rev. v. CII. p. 297. The G.'s of the Buckinghamshire Stowe could boast of a still longer territorial stability.

The more correct form of the name is Granville, the spelling now and anciently used for the town. George Grenville, in his letter to his kinsman Charles, Lord Lansdowne, on the bombardment of the town of Granville, in Normandy, by the English fleet, alludes to the arms of Granville as till then preserved over one of the gates of that town :—

" Those arms which for nine centuries (?) have braved
The wrath of time, on antique stone engraved,
Now torn by mortars, stand yet undefaced
On nobler trophies, by thy valour raised.
Safe on thy eagle's wings they soar above
The rage of war or thunder to remove ;
Borne by the bird of Cæsar and of Jove."

The allusion here is to his lordship's creation as a Count of the Empire, the family arms to be thenceforth borne on the breast of the imperial eagle. It seems singular that the noble family should have tolerated the spelling Grenville, though Clarendon goes even further, and writes Greenvil, *passim.* A still grosser corruption brings the great town (*grande ville*) to the level of a *Green-field.* There is, however, a locality in Normandy which appears really to have experienced this metamorphosis, for of another Granville there runs a proverb :—

" Granville, grand vilain !
Une église et un moulin,
On voit Granville tout à plein."
Wright's Essays, i. 134.

GRESHAM. A parish in Norfolk.

GRESLEY. Did no such place as Gresley, co. Derby, exist, I should be disposed to assign, as the ancestor of the family, that Domesd. tenant, Albertus *Greslet,* who held " inter Ripam et Mersam ;" but the Gresley pedigree is clearly traced to the Conquest, and even to an earlier date, as cadets of the great house of Toni, hereditary standard-bearers of Normandy. Lysons' Derb. " Descended from Nigel, called De Stafford, mentioned in Domesd. and said to have been a younger son of Roger de Toni, and very soon after the Conquest established

in Derbyshire, first at Gresley (*unde nomen*) and afterwards at Drakelow in the same parish," where they still remain. Shirley's Noble and Gentle Men.

GRETTON. Places in cos. Northampton and Gloucester.

GREVILLE. Greville, a parish at the extremity of the isthmus of La Hogue in Normandy, is supposed to have given name to the Lord of Greville, who accompanied William I. to the Conquest of England ; but this is uncertain, as there were three distinct fiefs which gave to their possessors the title of Sire de Grevile. M. De Gerville in Mem. Soc. Antiq. Norm. 1825.

" This family was founded [re-founded] by the wool-trade in the XIV. cent., by William Grevel, 'the flower of the wool-merchants in the whole realm of England,' who died and was buried at Campden, in Gloucestershire, in 1401." Shirley's Noble and Gentle Men.

GREW. 1. A greyhound. North. (Old people in Sussex say *grewhound.*) 2. An old Scotticism for grove is *greue.* Jamieson.

GREY. Most genealogists derive this ancient and noble family from Fulbert, chamberlain to Robert, duke of Normandy, who held by his gift the castle of Croy, in Picardy, from whence the name is assumed to have been borrowed. There is however no evidence for this ; for the pedigree is only traced to Henry de Grey, to whom Richard Cœur-de-Lion gave the manor of Thurrock, co. Essex, which manor was subsequently known as Grey's Thurrock. From the "Recherches sur le Domesd." of D'Anisy, it appears probable that the family came from Grai or Gray, a village near Caen. However this may be, the first settler of the name in England, was clearly Anchitillus Grai, a Domesd. tenant in Oxfordshire.

GREYSON. Probably Gregorson, the son of Gregory.

GRICE. O. Fr. A pig. See Purcell.

GRIEF. See Grieve.

GRIER. See Gregory.

GRIERSON. The son of Gregor ; descended from the clan Gregor. B.L.G. under Macadam.

GRIEVE. A-Sax. *gerefa,* præses, like the Germ. *graf.* In Scotland the manager of a farm, or superintendent of any work— a reeve. It has been variously corrupted to Greive, Greaves, Greeves, &c.

GRIFFIN. A common baptismal name in Wales. Domesday shews us a Grifin in Cornwall, and in Cheshire a Grifin *Rex,* first a favourite of Edw. the Confessor, and afterwards a rebel against him. He was probably a Welsh border prince. The same old record presents us with a " Grifin puer" and a " Grifin filius Mariadoc," most likely identical, as a tenant in chief in co. Hereford.

GRIFFINHOOFE. This Germ. name was introduced into England by one of the physicians of Geo. I. Mr. Fox Talbot observes that, "one might suppose this to be from the Germ. *grafen-hof*, implying some person attached to the court of a count," if there had not existed a Germ. family name Greifenklau, or the Griffin's Claw. Eng. Etym. 302. In medieval poems &c. many references to griffins' claws are found. In "Ruodlieb," the hero wears, apparently, a hunting horn made of such a talon.

"Pendet et á niveo sibimet *gripis ungula* collo."

The so-called griffins' claws were doubtless the horns of some species of the genus *bos*, or, as Dr. Grew thinks, of the *ibex mas*. See some curious details in Curios. of Heraldry, pp. 97, 98.

GRIFFITH. GRIFFITHS. A well-known Welsh baptismal name.

GRIGGS. See Gregory.

GRIGNON. "Chagrin, et de mauvaise humeur," generally applied to children. Decorde's Dict. du Patois du Pays de Bray.

GRIGSON. GREGSON. See Gregory.

GRIMBELL. The old personal name Grimbald.

GRIMBLEBY. Apparently from Grimoldly, a parish in co. Lincoln.

GRIMES. Grym, an ancient personal name, apparently Scandinavian, whence Grimson and the local names Grimwood, Grimshaw, Grimsdale, Grimwade, and several others to be found in their proper places.

GRIMLEY. A parish in co. Worcester.

GRIMM. See Grimes. The etymon seems to be the O. Norse *grimr*, grim, fierce.

GRIMSBY. A town in Lincolnshire.

GRIMSON. See Grimes.

GRIMSTON. Several places bear this designation, four of them in Yorkshire, the ancient and present abode of the family. The pedigree is traced to Sylvester, who is traditionally said to have attended the Conqueror from Normandy in the capacity of standard-bearer: He settled at Grimston, and held his lands of the Lord Rosse, and he or his immediate descendants took the name of De Grymeston. B.L.G. His posterity have been resident there from the period of the Conquest. Shirley's Noble and Gentle Men.

GRINDALL. A chapelry in Yorkshire.

GRINDER. A journeyman miller—still so called in the S. of England. Le Grindar. H.R.

GRINDLEY. GRINDLAY. A township united with Tushingham, co. Chester.

GRINDON. Parishes in cos. Stafford and Durham.

GRINSTED. E. and W., parishes in Sussex.

GRINTER. One who has the care of a granary. Scotch *grainter*, from Fr. *grenetier*. In Aberdeenshire this person is called *grintalman*. Jamieson.

GRISELL. GRISSELL. A Saint Grizelda or Grizel occurs in Scotland, though omitted by Camerarius in his list of Scottish saints. Chambers' Pop. Rhymes of Scotland. A less complimentary derivation would be from *grisel*, the diminutive of the A-Norm. *gris*, a pig. So we have the vernacular Pigg, Wildbore, and other analogous surnames. See Purcell.

GRIX. See Gregory.

GROAT. See Money—or perhaps the same as Grote.

GROCER. The occupation.

GROCOCK. Possibly a diminutive of Gregory.

GRONOW. An ancient Welsh personal name. King Henry VII. was grand-maternally descended from Sir Tudor ap Gronow, who lived temp. Edw. III.

GROOM. GROOME. "One who attends, observes, takes or has the care or custody of anything, whether of horses, chambers, garment, bride, &c." Richardson. Dutch *grom*, an attendant.

GROOMBRIDGE. A chapelry in Kent.

GROOT. Originally De Groot, (that is the great or big) from Holland. The real surname of the illustrious Grotius. The connection between the Dutch and English Groots is sufficiently shewn in one of Dr. Johnson's letters to his friend, Dr. Vyse, of Lambeth. "I doubt not but you will readily forgive me for taking the liberty of requesting your assistance in recommending an old friend to his Grace the Archbishop, as Governor of the Charter-House. His name is De Groot; he was born in Gloucester; I have known him many years. He has all the common claims to charity, being old, poor, and infirm in a great degree. He has likewise another claim, to which no scholar can refuse attention; he is by several descents the nephew of Hugo Grotius—of him from whom perhaps every man of learning has learnt something. Let it not be said in any lettered country that a nephew of Grotius asked a charity and was refused. I am, reverend sir, your most humble servant, SAM. JOHNSON. July 9, 1777."

GROSE. See Gross.

GROSER. See Grocer.

GROSJEAN. See JOHN.

GROSS. GROSSE. Fr. *gros*. Great, big, as to stature.

GROSSMITH. See under Smith.

GROTESTE. See Greathead.

GROSVENOR. *Le Gros Veneur*—"the

great or chief hunter"—that office having been hereditary in the family under the dukes of Normandy. The family descend from an uncle of Rollo the founder of Normandy; and the first settler in England was Gilbert le Grosvenor, nephew of Hugh Lupus, earl of Chester, who was nephew of the Conqueror. This illustrious name is properly latinized Magnus Venator, but sometimes, absurdly, De Grosso Venatore.

GROTE. Perhaps Dutch *groot*, big of stature. See Groot. Grote without prefix is in H.R.

GROUCOCK. See Gregory.

GROUSE. "Is certainly not from the bird, but from an old Germ. name Grauso, VI. cent., which Förstmann refers to A-Sax. *greosan*, horrere." Ferguson.

GROUT. The same as Groot.

GROVE. From the original bearer's residence near one. Hence also the common names Groves and Grover. The Groves of Fern, co. Wilts, claim descent from John de Grove of Chalfont St. Giles, who died 26 Edward III.

GROVER. See Grove.

GROVES. See Grove.

GROWSE See Grouse.

GRUBBE. "The family of Grubbe, spelt in the old registers Grübe or Groube, migrated from Germany about the year 1430, after the Hussite persecutions, and subsequently settled at Eastwell in the parish of Potterne, co. Wilts, where they have ever since remained. B.L.G. The name is analogous in signification to our Pitt.

GRUMBLE. A corruption of the personal name Grimbald.

GRUMBRIDGE. See Groombridge.

GRUND. See Grundy.

GRUNDY. Apparently the old Teutonic personal name Grund, whence Grundisborough, a parish in Suffolk.

GRYLLS. An old Cornish family. The manor of Grylls (commonly mispronounced Garles), from which they probably derive their name, is in the parish of Lesnewth in that county.

GUBBINS. GUBBINGS. May be derived from the old Norman family name of Gobion; or more probably from the French *gobin*, a hunchback or ill-formed man. This name was borne by a singular tribe or horde of barbarians, who from the XV. to the XVII. century infested the borders of Dartmoor. Fuller, writing of them in 1662, says:—

"Hitherto have I met with none who could render a reason of their name. We call the shavings of fish which are little worth, gubbings; and sure it is they are sensible that the word importeth shame and disgrace. As for the suggestion of my worthy and learned friend, Mr. Joseph Maynard, borrowed from Buxtorfius that such who did 'inhabitare montes gibberosos' were called Gubbings, such will smile at the ingenuity, who dissent from the truth of the etymology.

"I have read of an England beyond Wales; but the Gubbings land is a Scythia within England, and they are pure heathens therein. It lieth nigh Brent-Tor, on the edge of Dartmoor. It is reported that some two hundred years since, two strumpets being with child, fled hither to hide themselves, to whom certain lewd fellows resorted, and this was their first original."

"They are a *peculiar* of their own making, exempt from bishop, archdeacon, and all authority, either ecclesiastical or civil. They live in cots (rather holes than houses) like swine, having all in common, multiplied without marriage into many hundreds. Their language is the dross of the dregs of the vulgar Devonian; and the more learned a man is, the worse he can understand them. During our civil wars, no soldiers *were quartered* amongst them for fear of *being quartered* amongst them. Their wealth consisteth in other men's goods, and they live by stealing the sheep on the moor; and vain it is for any to search their houses, being a work beneath the pains of a sheriff and above the power of any constable. Such their fleetness, they will outrun many horses; vivaciousness, they outlive most men, living in the ignorance of luxury, the extinguisher of life. They hold together like burrs; offend one, and all will revenge his quarrel.

"But now I am informed that they begin to be civilized, and tender their children to baptism and return to be men, yea, Christians again. I hope no civil people amongst us will turn barbarians, now these barbarians begin to be civilized."
Fuller's Worthies, i. 398.

GUDE. The Scottish form of Good.

GUDGEN. GUDGIN. See Fishes.

GUERIN. The family of this name in England derive from "a noble French family, established in Champagne, the Isle of France, and Auvergne." Burke's Armory.

GUERRIER. Fr. A warrior, soldier.

GUESS. A corruption of Guest.

GUEST. Gest, an A-Sax. name occurring in Domesd. and before, and signifying *hospes*.

GUESTLING. A parish in Sussex.

GUILLE. See under Mauger. The Jersey family sent some branches to England, where they altered the orthography to Gill.

GUILLIAM. See William.

GUILLIM. See William.

GUINNESS. A modern corruption of the old Irish Magennis.

GUISE. A district in the east of France.

GULL. Is susceptible of various interpretations, as: 1. The bird; 2. A dupe or fool, very common in the old dramatists, and still in use; 3. One of the numerous modifications of Guillaume, William; 4. See Guille.

GULLIVER. This name occurs in Lond. Direct., in juxta-position with Gulli*ford*, suggesting the local origin.

GUMBOIL. This "most villanous of all corruptions is the same no doubt as an old German name Gumpold or Gundbold." Ferguson.

GUMM. A-Sax. *guma*, a man.

GUMMERSALL. See Gomersal.

GUNN. GUN. An ancient personal name, or rather a contraction of one, such as Gundebert, Gundric, or Gundbald.

GUNNER. An ancient baptismal name borne by various persons who held lands prior to Domesd. It is variously spelt Gunner, Gunnerus, Gunnere, Gunnor, and Gonnar. Gunnora is probably its feminine.

GUNNING. An O. Norse personal name.

GUNSON. The son of Gun. See *Gunn.* Sackford Gunson, Esq., was one of the commissioners for Surrey, in 1649. Brayley's Surrey, i. 68.

GUNTER. GUNTHER. A tradition in the family says, from *gaunt d'or*, allusive to the golden gauntlets in their arms; but this is very improbable. Guntaric was an old Teutonic personal name, and Gonther and Gunter appear as tenants in Domesd.

GUNTON. Parishes in cos. Norfolk and Suffolk.

GUPPY. Perhaps O. Fr. *goupil*, a fox.

GURD. Gurth or Gyrth, an A-Sax. personal name, which was borne by one of the brothers of Harold, who fell with him at Hastings.

GURDON. "This family came into England with the Conqueror, from Gourdon on the borders of Perigord." B.L.G. But the earliest member of the family there mentioned is Sir Adam de G., who was keeper of Wolmer Forest, co. Hants, temp. Edward I.

GURNALL. GURNELL. Scott makes The Antiquary say of his residence: "I live here as much a Cœnobite as my predecessor, John o' the Girnell;" and the Scottish Dictionaries give "*girnall, girnell,* a large chest for holding meal." The novelist probably had in his eye a brother who presided over the garner or granary rather than over the meal-chest of "Monkbarns."

GURNARD. See Fishes.

GURNETT. A known corruption of Gernet.

GURNEY. See Gournay.

GURR. Probably from Gueures, a village in Normandy, near Dieppe. One Peter Gyrre, apothecary, from Dieppe, a Protestant refugee, arrived at Rye, co. Sussex, 1572. Lansd. M.S. 15-70.

GURRIER. Perhaps a corruption of the Fr. *guerrier*, a warrior.

GUTHRIE. An estate in Forfarshire, Scotland. This might be considered a tolerably satisfactory origin for the name, especially as the family continue to write themselves 'of that Ilk,' to the present day. Tradition, however, has invented another, which is amusingly absurd; I give it as I find it in Chambers' Popular Rhymes of Scotland:—
"One of the kings of Scotland, when on an aquatic excursion to the northern part of his dominions, was overtaken by a storm,

and driven ashore on the east coast, somewhere between Arbroath and Montrose. Getting in safety to land, the king, like the pious Æneas, under similar circumstances, turned his thoughts upon the means of acquiring food wherewith to satisfy his own hunger and that of his attendants, both considerably sharpened by the sea breeze. He had not, however, the good fortune of the Trojan hero in seeing—

—— "tres littore cervos
errantes;"

—nothing appeared on the bare Scottish coast but a poor fisherwoman, who was cleansing some small fishes she had just caught. "Will you gut one to me, good-wife?" said the monarch. "I'll gut three!" being her immediate answer, the king exclaimed in rapture at her heartiness and hospitality—

THEN GUT THREE
YOUR NAME SHALL BE!

and immediately put his family in possession of the adjoining lands, which yet continue to be the property of her descendant, the present Guthrie of Guthrie!"

GUTSELL. This elegant surname is chiefly found in Sussex, and may be that which, in the XIV. century was written De Guttreshole. Godsol and Godsouele, however, occur in the H.R., favouring the idea that as in the case of *Godbody*, an oath is intended. To swear by the body and soul of the Almighty was a prevalent vice of old times. King Edward III., at a tournament, had his trappings embroidered with this profane couplet:—

"HAY, HAY, THE WYTE SWAN;
BY GODE'S SOUL I AM THY MAN."

GUTTER. A drain for water. One Joh'es of the Gutter is found in the Nonæ returns, 1341.

GUY. The old personal name Guido, probably from Caius, and the Celtic Kei, as Baxter thinks. Glossary, p. 58.

GUYATT. See Wyatt.

GUYENNETTE. A native of Guienne?

GUYER. Old English *guyour*, a guider or leader. Piers Ploughman.

GUYMAR. GUYMER. See Gaymer.

GWATKIN. The Welsh form of Watkin, as Guillim is of William.

GWILT. Celtic *gwylt*, an inhabitant of the woods. Thompson's Etymons, p. 3.

GWINNETT. Welsh—and apparently a modification of Gwynne.

GWYN. GWYNNE. (Welsh) White.

GYDE. Possibly a nursename of Gideon.

GYLES. As Giles.

GYLL. See Gill.

GYPP. GYPSON. Probably the same as Gibb and Gibson.

H.

HABERDINE. Said to be identical with Hawardine, which is clearly the same as the local Hawarden. If so, Herberden is a still further departure from the true orthography.

HACK. A-Sax. *hege.* A hedge. The word *hack* is still used in this sense in co. Lincoln.

HACKBLOCK. Probably from some manual feat. Wagstaff, Hurlbat, Shakeshaft, &c., are of analogous derivation. See under Shakspeare.

HACKER. See Hackman. But Mr. Arthur derives it from a Dutch word signifying "a chopper, cleaver, or hewer, and figuratively, a brave soldier."

HACKETT. A known corruption of Harcourt, 1669. See Burn's Tradesmen's Tokens, p. 73. But Hacket, a non-prefixed surname, is found in H.R.

HACKFORTH. A township in Yorkshire.

HACKMAN. *Hack* is a provincial word for a pick-axe or mattock, and also for a hedge; hence Hackman and Hacker may imply either a maker of axes, or a mender of hedges.

HACKNEY. A parish in Middlesex. In H.R. the surname is written Hakeneie, Hakeneye, Hakenie, &c.

HACKSTAFF. See under Shakspeare.

HACKWELL. A parish in Essex.

HACKWITH. A corruption of Ackworth, a local name.

HACKWOOD. A corruption of *Ac-wood,* ".the wood of oaks."

HACON. A family so surnamed reside at Swaffham, co. Norfolk, and are doubtless of Norse extraction. Hacon the Good and Hacon the Broad-Shouldered occur among the Kings of Norway; and their deeds, with those of others of the name, are recorded in the Heimskringla. In the H.R. for Suffolk (i. 181), we find mentioned one Semannus Hacon, "Hacon the Sailor," which looks sufficiently Norwegian.

HADAWAY. See Hathaway.

HADDAN. HADDEN. See Haddon.

HADDOCK. Not so likely from the fish as from some place terminating in *ock.*

HADDON. Parishes and places in cos. Hunts and Northampton, as well as the famous Haddon Hall, in Derbyshire.

HADEN. See Haydon.

HADFIELD. A parish in Derbyshire.

HADGLEY. Probably Haddesley, a township and a chapelry in Yorkshire.

HADKISS. A corruption of Adkins.

HADLEIGH. HADLEY. Parishes in Suffolk, Essex, Berks, and Middlesex.

HADLOW. A parish in Kent, which "gave both seat and surname to a family ancient and conspicuous," temp. Edw. III. Philipott's Vill. Cantianum.

HADNUTT. Probably Hodnet, a parish in Shropshire.

HAFFENDEN. The locality does not seem to be known. The gentry family derive from Lawrence Haffen*den*, of Buggles-*den,* bailiff of Tenter*den,* temp. Richard III. This is sufficient proof of the origin of the race among the *dens* of Kent, even if we did not know that they formerly had lands at Smar*den* and Hal*den.* See DEN. It is worth recording, that a younger and decayed branch of this family, the representative of which branch was lately the keeper of a small country inn at Heathfield, co. Sussex, have, for a series of generations, had right of sepulture in Heathfield church, where numerous gravestones mark their claim to ancient gentry.

HAGAN. One of the heroes of the Nibelungen Lied bore this name. Hagen also occurs as an A-Sax. personal name in a charter of Ceadwalla, King of Wessex.

HAGG. Broken ground in a bog. Halliw.

HAGGARD. 1. According to B.L.G. the family are supposed to be derived from the Ogards of co. Herts. 2. Haggard is a corruption of "hay-garth," a rick yard, and is so employed in Hall and Holinshed, as well as in several provincial dialects. See Garth. 3, and most probably, an ancient baptismal name which occurs in Domesday as Acard and Acardus, and in the H.R. as Hacgard.

HAGGER. See Haggard.

HAGGERSTON. The pedigree is not regularly traced beyond Robert de Hagreston, lord of Hagreston in 1399, although a Robert de Hagardeston occurs in 1312. The name is derived from Haggerston Castle, co. Northumberland. Shirley's Noble and Gentle Men, p. 161. Some genealogists derive the name from Halkerston, in Scotland. William and Richard de H. are witnesses to a donation anno 1190. The settlement of the family in England seems to have taken place on the marriage of Thomas de H. with a coheir of Umfreville of Northumberland. Kimber's Baronetage.

HAGON. See Hacon.

HAGUE. Perhaps the same as Haig or Haigh.

HAGWORTHINGHAM. A place near Grimsby, co. Lincoln.

HAIG. From Sir R. Douglas' Baronage of Scotland it appears that this family claim a Pictish, or an ancient British extraction; but as in many similar cases the *name* is only traceable to the XI. century, and the reign of Malcolm IV. and William the Lion, when Petrus *de Haga* was lord of Bemerside, in Berwickshire. Twenty generations of Haigs have held that estate, and upon the authority of a distich, attributed to Thomas the Rhymer, the family is perennial:

TIDE, TIDE, WHATE'ER BETIDE,
THERE'LL AYE BE HAIGS IN BEMERSIDE.

The family motto, "Tide what may," seems to have reference to this flattering prediction. An anecdote is related of a no very remote ancestor of the family, Zorobabel Haig, Esq., with whose life the truth of it appeared likely to become extinct. The lady of Bemerside had blessed her loving lord with twelve daughters in succession, but a son by whom the name should be perpetuated was wanting. The worthy gentleman's faith was sorely tried, and the place is still pointed out whither he was wont daily to retire to pray that God would vouchsafe him an heir. At length the much-desired boon was sent, and the Rhymer's prophecy came into higher credit than ever. Scott's Minst. Scott. Border, iii. 209. Jerdan's Autobiography, vol. i. Chambers' Popular Rhymes, p. 24.

HAIGH. A township in Lancashire.

HAIL. See Hale.

HAILES. See Hales.

HAILEY. A chapelry in Oxfordshire.

HAILSTONE. Alestan is Athelstan, the ancient personal name. An Alestan was a tenant in chief in co. Hants at the making of Domesday. The surname may, however, be local, either from Hailston, a burn in co. Stirling, famous for its blocks of jasper, or from Ailston-hill near Hereford.

HAINES. Perhaps a corruption of Ainulph. Camden.

HAINSON. The son of Haine or Ainulph.

HAIR. A corruption of heir, the eldest son.

HAIRE. This Irish surname, previously to the year 1770, was written O'Hehir. The traditions of the family deduce them from the race of Fingal in the third cent., but historical evidence carries them back no further than the reign of Edw. III., 1365, when the representation of the family vested in the O'Haitchir or O'Hehir, chiefs of Hy Flancha and Hy Cormac, in the barony of Islands, co. Clare. In O'Connor's map of Ireland published about 1640, a large portion of that county still bore the name of "the O'Hehir country." Inf. Tho. Haire, Esq., M.D.

HAKE. Doubtless a contraction of Hacon.

HAKEWILL. Probably Hackwell, a parish in Essex.

HALDANE. Halfdene, a name occurring in the Saxon annals, is considered by Ferguson to imply a Danish extraction on one side only—"half Dane." Hence perhaps the surname of the Scottish family. Among the tenants in chief in Norfolk, appears a Godwinus Haldein. Haldanus, Haldane, and other forms also occur in Domesd.. principally in the eastern counties.

HALDEN. High Halden, a parish in Kent.

HALE. 1. Healthy, stout. A-Sax. *hæle*, a brave man, chief, or hero. 2. The name of many localities in various parts of England, particularly in cos. Chester, Cumberland, Kent, Lancaster, Northampton, Hants, and Lincoln. 3. A hall. The forms in the H.R. generally relate to this meaning, as De la Hale, En la Hale, In the Hale, &c.

HALES. A town in Norfolk. Roger de Halys in 19 Henry II. gave a tenement which he possessed in that place to the Abbey of Baungey. From him the Haleses of Woodchurch and Bekesbourne, co. Kent, and of Coventry, baronets, are presumed to have sprung. See Burke's Ext. Barts.

HALESWORTH. A town in Suffolk.

HALEY. HALY. See Hayley.

HALFACRE. A local name; or perhaps A-Sax. *hær-fægr*, fair or beautiful-haired.

HALFENAKED. Walter de Halfenaked lived in Sussex in 1314. The manorial estate from which he derived his name is now called Halnaker. It is near Goodwood.

HALFHEAD. Perhaps a corruption of Halford or some such local name.

HALFHIDE. Possibly the feudal holder of half a hide of land.

HALFKNIGHT. Might appear to refer to one who was only half a knight—an occasional servitor or follower; but from the occurrence of one Robertus *de* Halveknycht in the H.R. it should be of local origin. The DE however may have been an error of the scribe. Other H.R. forms are Halveknit and Halve Knycht.

HALFORD. Parishes, &c., in cos. Warwick and Salop.

HALFPENNY. See Money, denominations of. In H.R. we have Halpeni and Halpeny without prefix.

HALIFAX. HALLIFAX. The Yorkshire town.

HALKETT. Probably a diminutive of Hal, Henry. The Halketts of Hale Hill, co. Edinburgh, claim descent from the Halketts, who were "free barons in Fifeshire six hundred years ago." David de H. was a "powerful warrior" in the reign of King Robert Bruce. B.L.G.

HALKINS. See Hawkins, of which it is a more correct form.

HALL. A manor house. In medieval documents, Atte Halle, Del Hall, De Aula, &c. The principal apartment in all old mansions was the hall, and in feudal times it was a petty court of justice as well as the scene of entertainment. The chief servitor when the lord was resident, or the tenant when he was non-resident, would naturally acquire such a surname; and hence its frequency. Nearly 300 traders so called appear in the Lond. Direct.

The Halls of Cheshire are a cadet of the Kingsleys of that county. The elder branch of the family temp. Henry III. assumed the name of De Aula, or Del Hall, from the hall or mansion in which they resided.

HALLAM. There are parishes so called in Derbyshire and Yorkshire, and that part of the West Riding of the latter county which contains the parishes of Sheffield and Ecclesfield is known as Hallamshire.

HALLEKNAVE. A servant (*cnapa*, knave) who waits in the Hall. This name is found in the records of Leicester.

HALLER. 1. See Hall, and the termination ER. 2. More probably a native of Halle, in Germany.

HALLETT. 1. A-Sax. *haletta*, one who is hailed or greeted—a hero, an eminent man. 2. A diminutive of Hal or Henry.

HALLEY. Local; but I do not find the place.

HALLIDAY. A well-known Scottish border clan, who from their great animosity against the Southron are said to have adopted the war-cry or *slogan* of A HOLY DAY, (Scottice, "a *Haly* Day"), because the chiefs and people of Annandale, whenever they made a *raid* or foray upon the Saxon border, accounted the day spent in rapine and slaughter a *holy* one. Burke's Commoners, ii. 127. In the XIII. century the name began to be common on the south of the Tweed. There were English Hallidays in our Scottish and French wars under Edw. III. and Hen. V. The Hallidays of the western counties descend from Walter Halliday, called the *Minstrel*, who was master of the revels to King Edward IV., and acquired lands at Rodborough, co. Gloucester. B.L.G.

HALLIFAX. Halifax, a town in Yorkshire.

HALLING. A parish in Kent.

HALLIWELL. "The Holy Well"—a name given to many sacred fountains in the middle ages; but specifically applied to parishes and places in Lancashire, Middlesex, &c.

HALLOWAY. See Holloway.

HALLOWELL. The same as Halliwell.

HALLOWS. Hallow, a parish in co. Worcester.

HALLS. Either Hawes, which see, or a pluralization of Hall.

HALLWARD. The keeper of a hall. See WARD.

HALSE. 1. The son of Hal. See Henry. 2. A parish in co. Somerset.

HALSEY. The founder of this family was William Hawse *alias* Chamber, to whom Henry VIII. granted the rectory and patronage of Great Gaddesden, co. Hertford, where, under the name of Halsey, the family have ever since resided. B.L.G.

HALSHAM. Hailsham, a town in Sussex, where the family were flourishing in the XIV. cent.

HALSON. 1. The son of Hal or Henry. 2. The same as Alison.

HALSTEAD. A town in Essex.

HALTON. Parishes and places in cos. Lancaster, Chester, Buckingham, Northumberland, Lincoln, York, Sussex, &c.

HALY. See Hailey.

HAM. A-Sax. *hám*, a homestead, whence—

☞ HAM, as a component syllable in many local family names:

"In Ford, in *Ham*, in Ley, in Ton,
The most of English surnames run."

Professor Leo finds 96 out of 1,200 place-names in the Codex Dipl., vols. i. & ii., (or nearly one-twelfth of all the names of places in England mentioned in that collection of Charters) terminating in *hám*. Leo's Local Nomenclature, by Williams, p. 34.

HAMBLEDON. Parishes, &c., in cos. Rutland, Lancaster, Buckingham, and York.

HAMBROOK. A hamlet in co. Gloucester.

HAMBROUGH. Of Hanoverian descent. The epitaph on Henry Hambrough at ——, co. Huntingdon, records that he was of honourable ancestry. He was born in 1574. B.L.G.

HAMER. An O. Germ. personal name of the VIII. cent. whence probably also Hammer.

HAMES. See Ames.

HAMERTON. Descended from Richard de Hamerton, who was living in 1170, at Hamerton, co. York. In the reign of Edw. III. the family acquired Hellifield in the same county, where they still reside. Shirley's Noble and Gentle Men.

HAMILTON. A corruption of Hambledon, a manor in Buckinghamshire. William de Hambledon, a younger son of Robert de Beaumont, third earl of Leicester, "is said to have gone about the year 1215 into Scotland, where he was well received by Alexander II. From him sprang all the noble and other Scottish lines of Hamilton.

A foolish tradition places the emigration of Hambledon from England to Scotland a century later, temp. Edw. II., and connects it with his having taken part with the murderers of that King's favourite, Spenser. Compelled by the monarch's resentment to leave England, and being closely pursued into a forest, Hambledon and his squire changed clothes with a couple of woodmen, whom they accidentally met, and the better to sustain their assumed character, seized a saw and began to cut down a tree. While engaged in this act their pursuers passed by, and De Hambledon finding his attendant's gaze directed towards them, hastily cried out *"Through!"* and thus diverted him from the imprudence of revealing his features to their view. From this circumstance, continues the legend, the Hamiltons borrowed their crest—'an oak tree penetrated transversely in the main stem by a frame saw,' and their motto ' THROUGH!' "

The Hamiltons are a migratory race, and are to be found in almost every region of the world. In the kingdom of Sweden alone, there are three noble houses of this name, descended from officers who served Gustavus Adolphus in the 30 years' war. Grant's Memoirs of Sir John Hepburn, p. 33.

HAMLETT. Hamlet or Hamleth appears to have been an old Scandinavian personal name, whether the hero of Shakspeare's tragedy was a real character or only an imaginary one. If this derivation is incorrect, we can hardly fall back upon *hamlet*, a small village, for the origin of the surname. Grose says that it is a provincialism for a high constable.

HAMLIN. HAMLING. See Hamlyn.

HAMLYN. The ancient personal name, as Hameline Plantagenet, brother of Henry II.

HAMM. See Ham.

HAMMACK. HAMMICK. Devonshire surnames, believed to be derived from the Teutonic personal name Almaric or Almeric. In the Domesd. of Devonshire Haimericus holds Poltimore and other lands in capite, and he was probably the founder of the family. The usual orthography prior to the beginning of the XVIII. century was Halmarick, but it has been subsequently still further corrupted by some of its bearers by the substitution of the letter M for the liquid L—the obvious result of a rapid pronunciation of the word. At length it was contracted to a dissyllable. The older spelling is still preserved by a Staffordshire branch of the family. The baronet (created 1834) is of the Devonshire stock. The variation from Hammick to Hammack in another branch is said to have originated in a misspelling of the name in a royal commission. Inf. J. T. Hammack, Esq.

HAMMANT. See Hammond.

HAMMER. According to Grimm and Förstemann, Hammer or Hamer is " a name under which traces of Thor are still to be found in the popular speech of Germany, and it is derived, no doubt, from the celebrated hammer or mallet which he wielded." Ferguson. This is rather indirect and inconclusive etymology. In like manner Kemble derives the "hammerponds " of the Weald of Sussex from the cultus of Thor, *(Saxons in England),* though it is well known that the majority of those ponds were formed within the last three centuries for the purpose of driving the machinery of the vast hammers which were used in the manufacture of iron, formerly carried on to a large extent in that district. See Hamer.

HAMMERTON. See Hamerton.

HAMMICK. See Hammack.

HAMMON. See Hammond.

HAMMOND. Hamo is a well-known Domesd. personal name, which in later times assumed the form of Hamon, Hamond, Hammond.

HAMOND. See Hammond.

HAMP. As we have the local names Hampstead, Hampden, Hampsthwaite, &c., as well as the patronymical Hampson, this was probably an ancient personal name.

HAMPDEN. Great Hampden, co. Buckingham, where the patriotic John Hampden dwelt, in the ancient seat of his ancestors.

HAMPER. Apparently from the large coarse basket called in old times a *hanaper.* The Hanaper Office is a place where writs were formerly deposited in baskets, and the original Mr. Hanaper or Hamper may have been connected with that establishment. A Galfridus le Hanaper, occurs in H.R.— probably a sobriquet.

HAMPSHIRE. From the county.

HAMPSON. See Hamp.

HAMPSTEAD. Parishes, &c. in cos. Middlesex and Berks.

HAMPTON. Parishes and places in cos. Middlesex, Chester, Warwick, Hereford, Oxford, Worcester, Devon, Salop, Wilts, &c.

HAMSHAR. This Sussex family derive their name, not from the adjoining county, Hampshire, but from an estate called Hammesherne in the parish of Slaugham. Inq. Non. 1341.

HANBURY. A parish in co. Worcester, which in very early times was the seat of the family.

HANCOCK. See John.

HAND. HANDS. An ancient personal name. Hand and Hande are, however, surnames without prefix in H.R. Mr. Ferguson says: "Walking through Handsworth in Staffordshire, and seeing the name of Hand upon the shops, I said to myself, ' Handsworth is the *worth* or estate of a man called Hand, and these may be descendants of that man.' "

U

HAN

HANDFORD. A chapelry in co. Stafford.

HANDLEY. There are parishes so called in Cheshire and Dorset; but the name may with equal probability spring from Andeli, in Normandy, famous as the residence of Cœur de Lion, as the birth-place of Poussin, the painter, and for the tomb of Corneille, the dramatist. Richer de Andeli was a capital tenant in Hampshire at the making of Domesday.

HANDOVER. Probably a Cockney corruption of Andover.

HANDSOMEBODY. See under Body. It may however refer to personal beauty, like the Fr. *Beaucorps,* which is also a family name.

HANDSWORTH. A parish in Staffordshire.

HANDY. Expert, clever—the characteristic of the first bearer.

HANDYSIDE. As the orthography in the XVII. cent. was Handasyd, this name was perhaps originally given to a person who had a badly formed or ill-set hand. It may however be local—*side* being a very usual termination.

HANFORD. From Hanford or Honford, co. Chester, the original residence and estate of the family. See Ormerod's Cheshire, iii. 327.

HANGER. A wooded declivity. "The high part to the south-west consists of a vast hill of chalk, rising three hundred feet above the village; and it is divided into a sheep down, the high wood, and a long hanging wood called the HANGER." White's Selborne, Letter i.

HANHAM. A chapelry in co. Gloucester, which was in the XIII. cent. the fee of Peter de Hanham, the first of the name on record.

HANKEY. A modification of Hankin, the nickname or diminutive of Randolph, prevalent in some of the oldest families of Cheshire. The existing families of this surname derive from that county, and the name was borne there in the rank of gentry in the XV. century.

HANKIN. HANKINS. A Cheshire nickname for Randolph, as in the ancient family of Manwaring and many others. Hanks, Hankin, and Hankinson are modifications of it.

HANKINSON. See Hankin.

HANKS. See Hankin.

HANMER. A parish in Flintshire. The name was assumed from that place by its owner, Sir John Hanmer, temp. Edw. I. The original name of the family is said to have been Mackfel. See Burke's Ext. Baronetage. The estate is still in the family.

HANN. Germ. *hahn,* a cock.

HANNAH. See Female Christian Names.

HANNAY. Anciently Ahannay or Hannay, of Sorbie, in Wigtonshire. A Gilbert de Anneth or Hannethe is found in Ragman Roll, A.D. 1296. Nisbet's Heraldry.

HANNEY. A parish in Berkshire.

HANNINGTON. Parishes in cos. Hants, Northampton, and Wilts.

HANSARD. An ancient personal name, which Mr. Ferguson derives from the Gothic *ans,* semi-deus, a hero, with the termination *heard,* hard. The Hansards of Evenwood, co. Durham, formerly had a seat in the palatinate parliament convened by the bishop of Durham. Folks of Shields, p. 18. Hansard is also a provincialism for a bill-hook or hedge-bill. The Hansards of Durham were commonly characterized as the HANDSOME HANSARDS.

HANSELL. A corruption of Anselm, the personal name.

HANSHAW. The more common, but less correct, form is Henshaw. It is doubtless a compound of A-Sax. *hana* and *sceaga;* "the shaw frequented by woodcocks."

HANSLIP. Ferguson derives the former syllable from the Gothic *ans,* a demi-god or hero.

HANSON. See John.

HANWAY. A native of Hainault. That country was so called until temp. Henry VIII.

HANWELL. A parish in Middlesex, and another in Oxfordshire.

HANWORTH. Parishes in Middlesex, Norfolk, and Lincoln.

HAPPY. R.G. 16. From natural disposition.

HARALD. See Harold.

HARBARD. HARBERD. A modification of the personal name Herbert, which in its older and truer form, is Hárbárd, a common Scandinavian designation, which Mr. Ferguson considers to mean "hairy-beard;" but since a beard not hairy would be a great anomaly, I prefer "*hoary*-beard" as the truer rendering.

HARBORD See Harbard.

HARBOROW. Harborough, a parish in co. Warwick, and Market-Harborough, a town in Leicestershire.

HARBOTTLE. A small town in Northumberland.

HARBOUR. Any place of refuge, whether for ships, travellers, beasts of the chase, &c.

HARBUD. See Harbard.

HARBY. Places in cos. Leicester and Nottingham.

HARCOURT. A town and ancient

château, now in ruins, near Brionne in Normandy, which gave title to the Fr. Ducs de Harcourt. The ancient earls of Harcourt played a distinguished part in the history of Normandy. They were descended from Bernard, of the blood-royal of Saxony, who having been born in Denmark was surnamed the Dane. He was chief counsellor and second in command to Rollo at the invasion of Neustria in A.D. 876, and acquired Harcourt and other fiefs for his eminent services. Collins. Robert de Harcourt attended William I. to the Conquest of England, and his descendants possessed Stanton-Harcourt, co. Oxon, from 1166 to 1830, when the elder line became extinct. Shirley's Noble and Gentle Men. It is rather remarkable that this illustrious and widely-spread name should have preserved itself within the strict limits of patrician life. The London Direct. (1852) shows us only one tradesman so named, while Howards, Nevilles, Mortimers, Percys, Sinclairs, and Pierpoints are superabundant. I have known a Seymour who was a miller; a Pelham who was a rat-catcher; a Gage who was a mendicant; and a Fitz-Gerald who was a strolling player; there are Gipseys who are Stanleys; butchers who are Fortescues; huxters who are Hastingses; tailors who are Montagues; and bakers who are Warrens; but Harcourt, with the solitary exception I have named, seems exclusively to belong to high life.

HARDBOTTLE. See Harbottle.

HARD. A quay or landing place; a *hard*, that is a safe place for debarkation. The word occurs in several dialects, and a well-known instance of it as a topographical term is the 'Common Hard,' at Portsmouth.

HARDCASTLE. Must be, I think, a contraction of Harden Castle, the ancient residence of the Scotts of Harden, and a fine specimen to this day of a border fortress, in Roxburghshire.

HARDEN. A parish in Wiltshire.

HARDIE. A northern spelling of Hardy.

HARDIMAN. A man of courage and bravery.

HARDING. HARDINGE. "The Hardings—in A-Sax. Heardingas, in Old Norse Haddingjar—were celebrated as an illustrious and heroic race. Grimm supposes them to have been an Eastlying people of the Danes and Swedes. (Deutsch Myth.)" Ferguson. The late Lord Hardinge claimed to be descended from a Danish family settled near Derby. The Domesday forms are Harding, Hardingus, Hardinc and Filius Harding. The soft sound given to the G, when the E final is employed, seems to be a modern affectation, quite unworthy of this sturdy old race.

HARDINGHAM. A parish in Norfolk.

HARDMAN. According to an old superstition, a man "who by eating a certain herb became impervious to shot, except the shot was made of silver." Halliwell.

HARDMEAT. A curious corruption of Hardmead, a parish in Buckinghamshire.

HARDRES. Robert de Hardres is mentioned in Domesd. under Lyminge, co. Kent. There are two parishes in that county so called, and Hardres Court was the family seat down to the extinction of the baronetcy in 1764. An undisputed tradition says that the family came from Ardres in Picardy, and conferred their name upon the Kentish localities—a circumstance of rare but not of unique occurrence. In Heraldic Visitations and in records, the name is sometimes corrupted to Hards.

HARDS. The Sussex family so designated originally wrote themselves Hardres, and they are known to have been of that family.

HARDSTAFF. This name is found in Sherwood Forest, and looks like an appellation as old as the days of Robin Hood and Little John.

HARDWICK. Parishes, &c., in cos. Cambridge, Gloucester, Norfolk, Oxon, Suffolk, Worcester, York, Derby, Warwick, Bucks, Northampton, &c.

HARDY. Fr. *hardi*, brave, courageous, hardy. H.R. Hardi.

HARE. From swiftness of foot. "The family of Hare (of Stow-Bardolph, Barts.) claimed to be a scion of the house of Harecourt or Harcourt in Lorraine, who were counts of Normandy." Burke's Ext. Barts.

HAREBY. A parish in Lincolnshire.

HAREFIELD. A parish in Middlesex.

HAREFOOT. Many names of places have 'Hare' for their initial syllable, and many others, 'foot,' as their termination. I think, however, that this surname had a figurative reference to swiftness of foot. We have an instance of this application in king Harold Harefoot; and at the present day the family name *Pié-de-lièvre* exists in France.

HARFORD. The town and county of Hertford are vulgarly so pronounced, but there is a parish of Harford in Devonshire with which however the family do not appear to have been connected. According to Burke, "the *cunabula gentis* was Bosbury, co. Hereford, in the church of which parish there are several ancient monuments of the family." B.L.G.

HARGRAVE. HARGRAVES. Parishes, &c. in cos. Chester, Northampton, and Suffolk.

HARGREAVES. See Hargraves.

HARINGTON. HARRINGTON. A place in Cumberland, where Robert H. lived temp. Henry III. Shirley's Noble and Gentle Men. It is elsewhere asserted that the baronet springs from Osulphus, who held the manor of Flemingley in Cumberland temp. Richard I., and that his son took the name of Harington from a manor in co. Durham. Courthope's Debrett.

HARKER. A corruption of Harcourt.

HARLAND. I do not find any place so called. Herland occurs as one of the characters in the well-known romance of "Horn," as a personal name. See Wright's Essays, i. 104.

HARLEY. A parish in Shropshire, which, according to the genealogists of the noble family, was their residence before the Norman Conquest. " In an ancient leiger book of the abbey of Pershore, in Worcestershire," says Collins, " is a commemoration of a noble warrior of this name, who commanding an army under Ethelred, king of England, in his wars against Sweyn, king of Denmark, gave the Danes a great defeat near that town, about the year 1013. Before the Conquest, Sir John de Harley was possessed of Harley castle and lordship." The same, or another, Sir John de Harley accompanied the expedition to the Holy Land in 1098. By some genealogists, both French and English, the great house of Harlai in France are deduced from this stock, " though others maintain that they are denominated from the town of Arlai in the Franche-Compte of Burgundy." Collins. This ancient race is now represented by the Harleys of Down Rossal.

"Scaliger had a most ridiculous aversion to the name of Harlai, and he thus expresses himself in Latin-Gallic jargon. "Omnes Harlai sunt bizarres. Sunt quinque familiæ, et omnes avari." (All the Harlais are queer. There are five different families of them, and all of them miserly.) He proceeds to specify instances of their avarice, and closes his sarcasms with the character of "Dominus de Saint Aubin, qui est unus ex Harlais, gubernator de Saint Maixent. Semper vivit in hospitio, ne cogatur amicos excipere. Plus consumo in uno anno quam ille." (The sieur de St. Aubin, who is one of the Harlais, and governor of St. Maixent, always lives at an inn, that he may have an excuse for not entertaining his friends. Even I spend more in a year than he does). M. de Mouglas, one of the Harlai family, who had a particular esteem for Scaliger, happened to light one day upon this ill-tempered, weak paragraph. Very naturally he flung the book into the fire, and discarded its writer from his friendship." Andrews' Anecdotes, 1790.

HARLING. E. and W., parishes in Norfolk.

HARLOT. 1. A scoundrel. 2. A boor; synonymous with *carle*. Su-Gothic *haer*, exercitus, and *lude*, mancipium vile, a boor or villain. Jamieson.

HARLOWE. A hundred and a parish in Essex, and a township in Northumberland.

HARMAN. Hermann was the marching Mercury of the old Germans. " Irman, Armin, Eorman, Hermann," says Professor Donaldson, " is the oldest deity of our race. He combines the functions of the two later deities, Tiv, or Ziv, or Ziu, corresponding to Mars, and Wodan, corresponding to Mercury ; and therefore claims as his own both the third and the fourth days of the week. He is the Er or Eor of the Scythic tribes, and the Ares of the Greeks. He appears equally in the heroic Arminius of the Low Germans, and in the heroic Herminius of Roman fable." Cambridge Essays, 1856, p. 68. As an English surname, Herman or Harman is of great antiquity. Hermann, Hermannus, as a personal name, is found in Domesday.

HARMER. An ancient personal name, occurring in the Domesd. of Norfolk among the tenants in chief as Hermerus.

HARMSWORTH. A corruption of Harmondsworth, a parish in Middlesex.

HARNESS. The old word for body-armour. Hence Lightharness, and the Fr. Beauharnois, or " fair harness."

HAROLD. The well-known Scandinavian personal name, borne by Norwegian, Danish, and English kings.

HARPER. A performer on the harp.

HARPHAM. A parish in Yorkshire.

HARPUR. The family is traced to Chesterton, co. Warwick, temp. Henry I. and II. Shirley's Noble and Gentle Men, p. 47. The name is synonymous with Harper, since it occurs indifferently in H.R. as Le Harpur and Le Harpere.

HARRAD. A corruption of Harold.

HARRADINE. HARRADENCE. Probably corruptions of Harrowden, places in cos. Northampton and Bedford.

HARRAP. Probably a corruption of Hareup or Harehope, a township in Northumberland.

HARRIDGE. Harwich, co. Essex.

HARRIE. A Scottish pronunciation of Harry.

HARRIES. The pedigree is traced to Cruchton, co. Salop, A.D. 1463. It has been supposed that the Harries's are of the old race of " Fitz-Henry," mentioned in deeds of that county, and who were seated at Little Sutton prior to the reign of Edward III. Shirley's Noble and Gentle Men, p. 204.

HARRILD. The same as Harold.

HARRIMAN. HARRYMAN. To *harrie* is an old northernism for to pillage, and a Harriman is therefore a freebooter or ravager.

HARRINGTON. Parishes in cos. Lincoln and Northampton.

HARRIS. From Henry, through Harry, and thence Harrison. "It is in recent times only, that a Saxon Harris, equivalent to Harry's son, has been converted into the etymological mongrel of *Fitz-Harris*, which is almost as startling as Fitz-Harrison or Fitz-Thompson would be." Edinb. Rev., April, 1855.

HARRISON. See Henry.

HARROD. 1. Harold. 2. Harewood.

HARROP. See Harrap.

HARROW. A town in Middlesex.

HARROWER. The occupation. A tiller of land.

HARRY. See Henry. Harry was familiarly applied even to royal Henries. See Shakspeare, passim.

HARSTON. A parish in co. Cambridge.

HART. A male deer—a common charge of heraldry. Its medieval form as a surname is 'Le Hart.' We have a large importation of Harts from Germany, where the word implies hard, stiff, inflexible, rude, or severe. Many Jewish families bear this name.

HARTCUP. Of German extraction. B.L.G.

HARTFIELD. A parish in Sussex.

HARTING. A parish in Sussex.

HARTLAND. A town in Devonshire.

HARTLEY. Places in cos. Kent, Northumb., Westmoreland, Hants, Berks, &c.

HARTON. Townships in cos. Chester and York.

HARTOPP. Local: from *hart*, the animal, and HOPE, which see. The first of the family on record is Ralph Hartopp who was living in 1377. Burke's Ext. Barts.

HARTRIDGE. Local: "the hill or ridge frequented by deer."

HARTSHORN. HARTSHORNE. A parish in co. Derby.

HARTWELL. Parishes in cos. Buckingham and Northampton.

HARVARD. A Scandinavian personal name.

HARVERSON. The son of Harvard, which see.

HARVEY. HERVEY. An ancient Norman personal name—*Hervé.* M. de Gerville in Mem. Soc. Ant. Norm., 1844, observes: "We sometimes call it Hervot . . La Hervurie signifies the habitation of Hervé." As a family designation it appears in England in the XII. cent. Osbert *de* Hervey is styled, in the register of St. Edmundsbury, the son of Hervey. From him according to the Peerage sprang the Herveys, ennobled in England and Ireland, and also (in all probability, from the resemblance of their arms) the De Hervi's and Hervies of Aberdeenshire and other parts of Scotland.

HARVIE. A northern form of Harvey.

HARWOOD. Prior to the latter half of the XIV. cent. the name was written Harward and Hereward, and tradition derives the family from the celebrated Hereward, the patriot Saxon, who a few years after the Conquest headed his oppressed countrymen against the forces of William. He was the younger son of Leofric, earl of Mercia. See Ellis' Domesd. i. 308 and ii. 146. See also Wright's Essays, ii. 91, &c. It may however be of the *local* class, there being many places in England called Harwood.

HASELDEN. More commonly written Hesledon; a place in Gloucestershire, well-known for its abbey. It is often corrupted to Hazeldine, Haseltine, &c. See DEN.

HASELER. See Hasler.

HASELGROVE. Local: "the grove of hazel trees."

HASELL. HAZELL. Hasle, a township in Yorkshire.

HASELTINE. See Hazelden.

HASELTREE. From residence near a remarkable hazel. Conf. Oak, Ash, &c.

HASELWOOD. HAZELWOOD. Haslewood, a parish in Suffolk.

HASKER. A Spenserean word for a fish-basket is *hask.* Hence, perhaps, a maker of such baskets.

HASKINS. From Haw or Hal, Henry, with the diminutive KIN.

HASLEFOOT. Local: from the hazel tree and FOOT, which see.

HASLEHURST. The *hurst* or wood where hazel-trees abound.

HASLEMORE. Haslemere, a town in Surrey.

HASLER. The Dutch *hasselaer*, a hazel tree, has been suggested; but there are places in cos. Dorset, Warwick, and Stafford called Haselor.

HASSALL. A township in Cheshire gave name to a great family.

HASSARD. Of Norman extraction. The orthography was originally Hassart, and the extinct dukes of Charante were of the same family. Soon after the Conquest a branch settled in co. Gloucester, and afterwards removed into Dorsetshire. The Irish Hassards settled in that country from England, temp. Charles II. B.L.G.

HASSELL. 1. From the Christian name Asceline; so Ansell from Anselm. In the H. R., Fil'Acelini, Acellin, Acelyn. 2. Local: De Hassell, co. Oxon. H.R.

HASSETT. A common name in co. Kerry. It is believed to be a contraction of the surname Blenerhassett, just as Shanks is of Cruikshanks, Cott of Cottingham, and Mull of Molineux.

HASTIE. Probably alludes to temperament—quick, impulsive.

HASTINGS. That the town of Hastings, co. Sussex, the chief of the Cinque-Ports, derived its name from one Hasting, is evident from the Bayeux Tapestry, where it is styled *Hestenga-ceastra*, "the fortification of Hasting." Whether he was the well-known Northman pirate is, however, but matter of conjecture. The noble families of this surname are descended from Robert de Hastings, portreeve of that town, and steward to king William the Conqueror, (Collins' Peerage,) but it is possible that others may be of different origin, and that their name is a direct derivation or patronymic of Hasting, the personal name.

HASWELL. A township in Durham.

HATCH. In forest districts, a gate across the highway to prevent the escape of deer. At-Hache and De la Hacche are found in the H.R. Hache in Domesday appears as a personal name.

HATCHARD. The Achard of Domesday—a personal name. In H.R. it occurs as a surname.

HATCHER. From residence near a Hatch, which see, and also ER.

HATCHETT. Voltaire mentions a grand vizier of Turkey called Alep Baltagi, so named from *balta* which signifies a *hatchet*—that being the Turkish designation of the slaves who cut wood for the princes of Ottoman blood. " Ce vizir avait été baltagi dans sa jeunesse, et en avait toujours retenu le nom, selon la coutume des Turcs, que prennent sans rougir le nom de leur première profession, ou celle de leur père, ou du lieu de leur naissance." Voltaire, Charles XII. Our English family may also have derived their name from the use of the instrument. Hachet without prefix is found in H.R.

HATCHMAN. The same as Hatcher.

HATFEILD Parishes, &c., in cos. Hereford, Hertford, Essex, &c., bear the name of Hatfield. Several places so called are in Yorkshire, and in that county an ancient family, Hatfeild of Thorp-Arch, still exists.

HATFIELD. See Hatfeild.

HATFULL. A corruption of Hatfield.

HATHAWAY. HATHWAY. HADAWAY. Correspond with the Old Germ. names Hathuwi, Hathwi, Hadewi. Ferguson.

HATHERLEY. Two parishes in co. Gloucester.

HATHORNE. See Hawthorne.

HATLEY. HATELY. Parishes in Cambridgeshire.

HATRED. Mr. Ferguson derives this name from the O. Germ. one, Hadarat.

HATT. See Preliminary Dissertation.

HATTEMORE. The medieval Atte-More, with H prefixed.

HATTEN. A mis-spelling of Hatton.

HATTER. The occupation. Le Hatter and Le Hattere. H.R.

HATTERSLEY. A village and township in Cheshire.

HATTON. Several parishes, &c., bear this name in different counties. The noble family were descended from Sir Adam Hatton, of Hatton, co. Cheshire, grandson of Wulfrid, brother of Nigel, who was lord of Halton in the same county, by the gift of Hugh Lupus, Earl of Chester, soon after the Conquest.

HAUCOCK. The same as Alcock.

HAUGHTON. Parishes, &c., in cos. Durham, Chester, Northumberland, Stafford, Nottingham, &c.

HAVELL. See Havill.

HAVELOCK. A well-known Danish personal name. Geoffrey Gaimar's metrical romance, called " Le Lai d'Havelok le Danois," records the valorous doings of a great Danish chieftain. The family of the greatest hero of his age, the late Gen. Sir Henry Havelock, claimed to be of Danish extraction, having been, according to tradition, a scion of an ancient race descended from Guthrun, the historical viking of the days of Alfred, and settled at Great Grimsby from his time! There is indeed a tradition that that town was so named from a merchant called Grime, who obtained great wealth and honour in consequence of his having brought up an exposed child called Haveloc, who, after having been scullion in the king's kitchen, turned out to be a Danish prince. The curious corporate seal of the town seems to have some allusion to the circumstance, as it bears the names of ' Grym' and ' Habloc ; ' and one of the boundary marks of the corporation is known as ' Haveloc's Stone.'

HAVEN. HAVENS. 1. From residence near a port or haven. In Scotland the hollow or sheltered part of a hill is called the *haaf* or *haven*.

HAVILAND. A member of the ancient Norman family of De Havilland of Guernsey settled in Somersetshire temp. Henry VII., and founded this surname in England. Gent. Mag., June, 1852. The family originated in the Cotentin in Normandy, and settled in Guernsey before 1176. B.L.G. De Havilland, of Havilland Hall in that island, is still the representative of this ancient race.

HAVILL and HOVELL. Are said to be almost proven corruptions of Auberville.

HAWARD. See Hayward.

HAWARDEN. A town in Flintshire,

on the English border, seven miles from Chester.

HAWARDINE. Doubtless the same as Hawarden.

HAWES. Sometimes from Henry, through Hal, and so the parent of the surname Hawkins; but probably oftener from the O. Eng. and Scot. *haugh*, low-lying ground near a river—sometimes confounded with *hough*, a hillock. In le Hawe is a H.R. surname, as is also Del Hawes.

HAWGOOD. A corruption of Hawkwood.

HAWKE. The bird: allusive to keenness of disposition.

HAWKER. The remarks under Falconer apply to this name—this being the A-Sax., the other the A-Norm. form. The H.R. have Le Haukere, Le Hauckere, &c.

HAWKES. A diminutive of Harry or Henry, connected with Hal and Hawkins, as Wilkes is with Will and Wilkins.

HAWKHURST. A parish in Kent.

HAWKIN. HAWKINS. The diminutive of Hal or Haw, from Henry. The Hawkinses of The Gaer, co. Monmouth, and those of Cantlowes, co. Middlesex, claim a local origin from the parish of Hawking, near Folkestone, in Kent, of which Osbert de Hawking was possessor temp. Henry II. The family removed to Nash Court in the parish of Boughton-under-Bleane in the same county, and there remained until the year 1800. B.L.G.

HAWKINSON. The son of Hawkin, which see.

HAWKRIDGE. A parish in co. Somerset, and many minor localities.

☞ **HAWKS**—The first syllable of several surnames, from localities frequented by the bird, as Hawkshaw, Hawksby, Hawksley.

HAWKS. See Hawkes.

HAWKSWORTH. Places in cos. York, Notts, &c.

HAWKWOOD. Local: "the wood frequented by hawks." For the anecdote of the celebrated warrior of the XIV. cent., Sir John Hawkwood, being latinized Johannes Acutus, and re-translated into *Sharp*, see Verstegan's Restitution, as quoted in Eng. Surn. ii. 191.

HAWLEY. Places in Hampshire and other counties.

HAWTAINE. HAWTYN. O. Fr. *haultain*, "hautie, loftie, statelie, proud, highminded, surlie, disdainfull, arrogant." Cotgr.

HAWTHORNE. Hawthorn, a township in the parish of Easington, co. Durham, memorable for the fifty shipwrecks which happened there on Nov. 5, 1824. The New England family of this name left this country in or before 1634, and until recently wrote themselves Hathorne.

HAWTON. A parish in co. Notts.

HAWTREY. HAULTREY. The family were in Sussex in Norman times, and founded Heringham Priory, temp. Henry II. The name was derived from their residence on a high bank or shore— Norman-Fr. *haulte-rive*—and hence the latinization De Alta Ripa, often modified to Dealtry and Dawtrey, while Hawtrey and Haultrey are closer adhesions to the primitive form. "The chiefest house of these DAWTEREIS," says Leland, "is in Petworth paroche called the Morehalfe, a mile from Petworth toune. There is another house longing to them in Petworth by the chirch." The elder line subsisted at Moorhouse till 1758. Hauterive in the arrondissement of Alençon, in Normandy, was latinized Alta Ripa in the XI. cent. Itin. de la Norm.

HAY. A-Sax. *haeg*, Fr. *haie*, a hedge, and that which it encloses—a field or park. The map of Normandy shows many localities called La Haie, and from one of these, doubtless, came, in early Norman times, if not actually at the Conquest, the family once eminent in England and still so in Scotland. The name was written De Haia and De la Hay. King Henry I. gave to Robert de Haia the lordship of Halnaker, co. Sussex, and so early as the close of the XII. cent. William de H. passed into Scotland and held the office of *pincerna regis* or king's butler, temp. William the Lion. From his two sons descend Hay, marquis of Tweeddale, and Hay, earl of Errol, hereditary lord high constable of Scotland. These are well-ascertained facts, but tradition assigns a different origin both to name and family. It asserts that in 980 a yeoman called John de Luz and his two sons by their prowess reinvigorated the army of Kenneth III., when they were on the point of succumbing to the Danes. They took the yokes from the oxen with which they were ploughing, and so belaboured the invaders as to drive them from the field, amidst shouts of *Hay! Hay!* The king in reward for these services gave the yeoman as much land as a falcon could fly round (the lands of Loncarty near Fife), and in memory of the event the family adopted a falcon for their crest, two husbandmen with ox-yokes for their supporters, and Hay for their surname!

HAYBITTEL or **HAYBIDDEL.** A well-known name near Reigate in Surrey, written in XVI. cent. Heybetylle. Mr. Way (Sussex. Arch. Coll. v. 261) suggests that it is derived from *haia*, Fr. an enclosure, and *bedel* A-Sax., bydel, beadle, or bailiff. See Hayward.

HAYCOCK. Said to have been given to a foundling exposed in a hay field.

HAYCRAFT. See Haycroft.

HAYCROFT. From hay, and croft, a small enclosure: a place for hay-ricks.

HAYDAY. Corresponds with the O. Germ. name Haida of the VIII. cent. Ferguson.

HAYDEN. See Haydon.

HAYDIGGER. *Haydegines*, an archaism for a certain round or country dance. Perhaps a skilful performer in that dance may have first received this name.

HAYDON. Places in Essex, Dorset, and Northumberland.

HAYER. See under Hayman.

HAYES. Parishes in Middlesex and Kent.

HAYLEY. Hailey, a chapelry in co. Oxford.

HAYLING. HAILING. An island near the coast of Hampshire and Sussex.

HAYLORD. Probably "high-lord," or lord paramount. In the western counties this phrase is sometimes applied to the lord of a manor, however unimportant.

HAYMAN. Hay signifies both a hedge and what it encloses; hence Hayman and Hayer probably sometimes mean the same as Hayward, which see. But the Irish family of Hayman or Heyman deduce their pedigree from Rollo, the founder of Normandy, through the Crevecœurs, one of whom, Haimon de C., had a son Robert, who assumed his father's baptismal name as a surname, which he transmitted to his posterity. B.L.G.

HAYNE. HAYNES. See Haines.

HAYNOKE. A corruption of A'Noke. See Noakes.

HAYS. Hayes, parishes in Kent and Middlesex.

HAYSTACK. Said to have originated from a foundling.

HAYTER. The personal name Haitar, which occurs in Germany in the IX. cent. Ferg. It may however be local, from the hundred of Haytor in Devonshire.

HAYTON. Parishes, &c., in cos. Cumberland, Nottingham, York, &c.

HAYWARD. Fr. *haie*, a hedge, and *ward*, O. Eng. a guardian or keeper. Inclosures as well as the fences which encircled them were called *hays;* hence a Hayward was a person employed to watch enclosed fields.

> "I have an home and be a *Hayward*
> And liggen out a nyghtes,
> And kepe my corn and my croft
> From pykers and theves."
> *Piers Plowman.*

Jacob defines it as "one that keeps the common herd of cattle of a town;" and adds: "the reason of his being called a hayward may be because one part of his office is to see that they neither break nor crop the *hedges* of enclosed grounds, or for that he keeps the *grass* from hurt and destruction. He is an officer appointed in the lord's court for the due execution of his office." Law Dict. *in voc.* See *Hedgeler* in this Dict. The orthography in the H.R. is Hayward, Le Heyward, Le Heiward, Le Hayward.

HAWORTH. A chapelry in Yorkshire.

HAYWOOD. See Heywood. Also a liberty in co. Hereford, and a hamlet in co. Stafford.

HAZARD. See Hassard.

HAZELDEN. An ancient manor, in or near Dallington, co. Sussex. The name appears to have been corrupted to Haseldine, Haseltine, Hazeldine, Hesseltine, &c.

HAZLEDINE. See Hazleden.

HAZELGROVE. From residence near one.

HAZLERIGG. An estate in Northumberland, which belonged to the family temp. Edward I. Leland speaking of the head of the family, then living in Leicestershire, says: "Hazelrigg hath about 50li lande in Northumberland, where is a pratie pile of Hasilriggs, and one of the Collingwooddes dwelleth now in it, and hath the over-site of his landes." Shirley's Noble and Gentle Men.

☞ **HEAD.** A component syllable of many surnames derived from places, as Headford, Heading, Headland, Headley &c. See next article.

HEAD. A promontory or foreland, as Beachy Head, Spurn Head. Also the source of a river. Head or Hed, was a baptismal name in Scotland, in the XII. century. Hedde, without prefix, is found in H.R., as is also the A-Sax. form Heved.

HEADACHE. Mr. Ferguson says, "properly Headick, a diminutive of Head."

HEADEN. A parish in co. Nottingham.

HEADLAM. A township in co. Durham.

HEADWORTH. A township in co. Durham.

HEADY. 1. Self-willed. "Heady, high-minded." 2. Edie, Eddy, a diminutive of Edward.

HEAL. See Hele.

HEALEY. Places in Yorkshire and elsewhere.

HEALING. Probably Ealing, co. Middlesex.

HEANE. HEENE. A parish in Sussex.

HEAPS. HEAP. Probably the same as Monceux, which see.

HEARD. O.Eng. *herd*, a herdsman or keeper of cattle.

HEARDER. May either mean *herd*, a keeper of cattle, &c.; or *hurder*, a northern provincialism for a heap of stones, thus coming under the same category as Heap, Monceux, &c.

HEARDSON. The son of a herd or herdsman.

HEARN. HEARNE. A modification of the Irish O'Ahern.

HEARON. See Heron.

HEARSEY. See Hercy.

HEARTLY. The same as Hartley.

HEARTMAN. The same as Hartman.

HEARTWELL. The same as Hartwell.

HEASMAN. Qu. a headsman, executioner?

HEATH. From residence at a heath or common. In the H.R. Atte-Hethe, Apud Hethe, De la Hethe, &c.—in after times modified to Heather.

HEATHCOTE. The baronets trace to the XVI. century in Derbyshire. The name is local, though the place is unknown. —"The heath-cottage," or "The cot on the heath."

HEATHER. See Heath, and the termination ER.

HEATHFIELD. A parish in Sussex, where the family in plebeian condition still reside. Also places in several other counties.

HEATHWAITE. A chapelry in Lancashire.

HEATON. A parish in co. York, and townships in cos. Lancaster, Chester, Northumberland, &c. Heaton, co. Lancaster, gave name to a family in very early times, and from them sprang the Heatons of North Wales.

HEAVEN. HEAVENS. Cockney corruptions of Evan and Evans?

HEAVER. Hever, a parish and castle in co. Kent, memorable as the birth-place of Queen Anne Boleyn.

HEAVISIDE. More likely a local name than characteristic of what Dr. Johnson might call 'lateral ponderosity.' It may, however, have been a sobriquet, like that applied by the Norwegians to Magnus, king of Sweden, who had threatened them with invasion :—

> "The fat-hipped king with *heavy-sides*
> Finds he must mount before he rides."
> *Laing's Heimskringla,* III. 134.

HEBBERD. HEBBERT. The same as Hubert.

HEBBLEWHITE. See Ebblewhite.

HEBDEN. Two villages in Yorkshire.

HEBER. The Hebers take their name from a place in Craven, co. York, called Haybergh. Ernulphus de Haybergh lived at Milnethorpe in that co. towards the end of the XII. century. The name has passed through the changes Hayburgh, Heibire, Heiber, to Heber. B.L.G.

HEBERDEN. 1. See Haberdine. 2. A field formerly belonging to the Abbey of St. Edmund's Bury was called Heberden.

HECKIN. A Cheshire provincialism for Richard, and hence possibly the origin of Higgin, Higgins, and Higginson, though

Hugh (Hugo) may perhaps have the prior claim.

HECTOR. The personal name, derived from classical antiquity.

HEDDLE. A local name of Scandinavian origin. It was variously written Haidale, Hedal, and Heddell. The family held lands in Orkney prior to 1503. B.L.G.

HEDGE. See Hedges.

HEDGELER. Probably the *agillarius* of feudal times ; a "*hayward,*" or keeper of cattle in a field fed in common by many tenants. "Towns and villages had their *heywards* to supervise the greater cattle, or common herd of kine and oxen, and keep them within due bounds ; and if they were servile tenants, they were privileged from all customary services to the lord, because they were presumed to be always attending their duty, as a shepherd on his flock ; and lords of manors had likewise their heywards to take care of the tillage, harvest work, &c., and see there were no encroachments made on their lordships : but this is now the business of bailiffs." Kennet's Paroch. Antiq. Jacob's Law Dict. See HAYWARD.

HEDGELEY. A township in Northumberland.

HEDGER. A maker of hedges.

HEDGES. The modern form of At-Hedge—first derived from residence near one.

HEDGMAN. The same as Hedger or Hedges.

HEDLEY. Townships in Northumberland, Durham, and Yorkshire.

HEELE. See Hele.

HEEPS. HEAPS. Like the Norman name Monceux, heaps, *monticuli.* This may be a translation of Monceux.

HEIGHAM. A hamlet in the parish of Gaseley, co. Suffolk, which belonged to the family in 1340. Shirley's Noble and Gentle Men, p. 233. Also a hamlet in Norfolk.

HEIGHINGTON. Places in cos. Durham and Lincoln.

HEIGHTON. A parish in Sussex.

HELE. Hele, Heale, or Heal, is a manor in the parish of Bradninch, co. Devon. The pedigree commences with Sir Roger De la Heale, who was lord of Heale, temp. Henry III.

Matthew Hele, of Holwell, co. Devon, was high sheriff of the county the year of Charles the Second's Restoration, 1660, and so numerous and influential were the family that he was enabled to assemble a grand jury *all of his own name and blood,* gentlemen of estate and quality, which made the Judge observe, when he heard Hele of Wisdom, Esq. called—a gentill seat in the parish of Cornwood—' that he thought they must be all descended from Wisdom, in that they had acquired such considerable fortunes.' Burke's Ext. Barts.

v

HELLEWELL. See Halliwell.

HELLIER. The A-Sax. *helan*, like the southern provincialism, to *heal*, signifies to cover; and in the West of England a *hellier* is a thatcher or tiler, equivalent to the French *couvreur*, one who covers buildings with any material whatever. It was a kind of generic appellative, including the Thatchers, Tylers, Slaters, Shinglers, and Reeders, all of whom are also separately represented in our family nomenclature. In Walsingham's History, the arch-traitor, Wat Tyler, is designated "Walterus Helier."

HELLINGLY. A parish in Sussex.

HELLIS. See Ellis.

HELM. HELME. Teutonic, a helmet; a name borrowed from military associations. "*Helm* as a termination entered into a great number of regular Anglo-Saxon names, such as Eadhelm, Brighthelm, Alfhelm, &c. Wilhelm (William) is an earlier name, occurring in the genealogy of the East-Anglian kings from Woden."—Ferguson.

HELMS. See Helme.

HELPUSGOD. This name, probably derived from the frequent use of a profane adjuration by the original bearer of it, and cognate with Godhelp, Godmefetch, Godbehere, &c., is found in the Sussex Subsidy Roll of 1296. Sussex Arch. Coll., vol. ii.

HELSDON. Hellesden, a parish near Norwich.

HELSHAM. Hailsham, co. Sussex, is so pronounced, and a gentry family of De Halsham, existed in that co. in the XIV. cent.

HELY. An old form of Elias, the personal name.

HELYAR. See Hellier.

HEMBURY. Broad Hembury, a parish in co. Devon.

HEMINGFORD. Two parishes in co. Huntingdon. De Hemingford. H.R.

HEMMING. HEMMINGS. A Danish personal name.

HEMS. See under Emmett.

HEMPSTEAD. A manor in Framfield, co. Sussex, which had owners of the same name in the XIII cent.

HEMSWORTH. A parish in Yorkshire.

HENBERY. Parishes, &c., in cos. Gloucester and Chester are called Henbury.

HENCHMAN. A follower; an attendant upon a nobleman or personage of high distinction. A Chaucerian word.

"The said Duke was in hys yong age, after he had been a sufficient season at the gramer schole, *Hencheman* to Kyng Edward the iiii., and was then called Thomas Howard."

Weever's Funerall Mon. p. 834.

HENDER. See Hendower.

HENDERSON. Either from the personal name Hendric, or from Andrew—probably the latter.

HENDOWER. A distinguished Cornish family, who are said to have originated in Wales. The elder line became extinct about temp. Henry VIII., but younger branches who had abbreviated the name to Hender, were living near Camelford a few years since.

HENDRICK. HENDRICKS. HENDRIE. HENDRY. Hendric, an ancient personal name.

HENDY. Gentle, polite. Halliwell.

HENE. See Henn.

HENEAGE. Sir Robert de Heneage was in Lincolnshire, temp. William Rufus. I find no locality so called.

HENFREY. An ancient personal name, corresponding with the O. Germ. Enfrid.

HENLEY. Towns and places in cos. Warwick, Suffolk, Hants, and Oxford.

HENMAN. An ancient personal name, like the O. Germ. Enman.

HENN. The Irish family derive from an English one written Henne, but anciently Hene, and the name seems to have been originally derived from Hene now Heene, a hamlet or extinct parish, near Worthing, co. Sussex. A William de Hene is mentioned in Domesd., as holding of William de Braose in the immediate vicinity. There are Le Hens and Fil' Hens in H.R.

HENNIKER. The ancestors of Lord Henniker were a mercantile family from Germany, who settled in London early in the XVIII. century. Of the origin of the name I know nothing, but it is suspiciously like the German Henker, a hangman or executioner. That the executioner's employ, like other occupations, occasionally became a surname, is shown in the following anecdote:—

"Resolute, of late years, was the answer of Verdugo, a Spaniard, commander in Friseland to certain of the Spanish nobility, who murmured, at a great feast, that the sonne of a Hang-man should take place above them (for so he was, as his name importeth). Gentlemen (quoth he) question not my birth, or who my father was; I am the sonne of mine own Desert and Fortune ; if any man dares as much as I have done, let him come and take the table's end with all my heart."

Peacham's Compleat Gentleman.

HENNINGHAM. Heveningham (now Haveningham) a parish in Suffolk.

HENNIS. See Ennis.

HENRISON. See Henry.

HENRY. A personal name of Norman importation, which has given birth in a modified form to many surnames, including Henrison, Henson, Penry (ap-Henry),

Harry, Parry (ap-Harry), Harris, Harrison, Hall (from Hal), Hallett, Halkett, Halse, Hawes, Hawkins, Hawkinson, Allkins, Haskins, and perhaps Alcock. Thus as Henry has given name to the most numerous group of English monarchs, so it has furnished surnames for a very great number of their subjects.

HENSALL. A township in Yorkshire.

HENSHALL. Either Henshaw or Hensall.

HENSHAW. See Hanshaw. A township in Northumberland.

HENSMAN. A page; the confidant and principal attendant of a Highland chief; a *henchman*. Jamieson.

HENSON. See Henry.

HENTON. A district near Chinnor, co. Oxon.

HENWOOD. 1. A tithing in the parish of Cumnor, co. Berks. 2. Perhaps another form of Honywood. See that name.

HENZEY. See under Tyttery.

HEPBURN. From the lands of Hebburne, Hayborne, or Hepburne, co. Durham, near the mouth of the Tyne. Tradition derives the noble family seated in E. Lothian, from the XIV. cent., from an English gentleman taken prisoner by the Earl of March, who generously gave him lands, upon which he settled. From him descended the Earls of Bothwell, whose line ended with the notorious James H., Earl of Bothwell, Marquis of Fife, and Duke of Orkney, the husband of Mary, Queen of Scots, 1567. The battle-cry of this warlike race was—"A HEPBURN ; BIDE ME FAIR !"—(*i.e.*, Meet my onset fairly.)

HEPDEN. See under Den.

HEPTONSTALL. A chapelry in the parish of Halifax, co. York.

HEPPELL. HEPPLE. Two townships in Northumberland.

HEPWORTH. A township in the W.R. of Yorkshire; also a parish in Suffolk.

HERAPATH. See Herepath.

HERAUD. Might be either the personal name Harold; a herald-at-arms; or a derivation from the O. Norse *heradr*, the leader of an army.

HERBERT. An ancient personal name. The noble Herberts descend from Herbert, Count of Vermandois, who came hither with the Conqueror, and was chamberlain to William Rufus. B.L.G. Collins says : "the genealogists deduce the family from Herbert, a natural son of King Henry I., but I think it more evident that Henry Fitz-Herbert, chamberlain to the said king, was ancestor to all of the name of Herbert."

HERCY. The pedigree is traced to temp. Henry III., when Malveysin de Hercy was constable of the honour of Tykhill, co. York. The locality of Hercy does not appear either in the English Gazetteer or in the Itin. de la Normandie.

HERD. A-Sax. *hyrd*, a keeper of cattle, sheep, swine, &c.

HERDINGSON. The same as Fitz-Harding.

HERDMAN. A-Sax. *hirdman*, an attendant.

HERDSMAN. The occupation.

HEREFORD. From the city. The Herefords of Sufton Court, co. Hereford, claim from Roger de Hereford, a famous philosopher of the XII. century. B.L.G.

HEREPATH. "Might be from the A-Sax. *herepæd*, an army-path, in which case, it would be, I presume, local. But I think more probably from *herepád*, a coat of mail." Ferguson.

HERING. See Herring.

HERINGAUD. Norm. Fr. *herigaud*, an upper cloak. See Mantell, &c.

HERINGTON. Herrington, two townships in co. Durham.

HERIOTT. Heriot, a parish in Edinburghshire.

HERITAGE. Most probably the name of some lands or possessions, analagous to "the Franchise," "the Purchase," &c., frequently applied to estates. Heritag'. H.R.

HERLE. The Herles of Prideaux Castle, co. Cornwall, whose name has been occasionally written Earle and Hearle, are "descended from the house of West Hearle in Northumberland, of which Sir William Herle was made, by Edward III., chief justice of the Bench." C. S. Gilbert's Cornwall, ii. 145. De Herl, co. Northumberland. H.R.

HERMITAGE. The surname was probably first acquired by some person who dwelt near the abode of a solitary ascetic.

HERMON. See Harman.

HERNE A contraction of the Celtic O'Ahern.

HEROD. See Heraud.

HERON. Taken *au pied de la lettre* this name would appear to be derived from the bird; but Heron is a comparatively modern orthography, it having been formerly written Hairun, Heyrun, Heirun, &c. "Sir John Hairun entered England with the Conqueror, and was possessed of Ford Castle, and a very good estate." Kimber's Baronetage. There is a commune in the arrondissement of Rouen called Le Heron, but it does not appear whether this was the cradle of the race.

This family is thus spoken of in Denham's Slogans of the North of England:

"HASTINGS !" was evidently the slogan (or war cry)

of the ancient lords of Ford and Chipchase Castles. The Herons had also a stronghold at Twisell.

> "Sir Hugh the Heron bold,
> Baron of Twisell and of Ford,
> And captain of the Hold."
> *Marmion.*

Swinburn Castle also belonged to this family, as also did Bohenfield ; and Haddeston, the *caput baroniæ* of Heron or Heroune, was their ancient residence. Sir George Heron had the misfortune to be slain at the skirmish of the *Raid of the Reidswire*, to the great regret of both parties, being a man greatly respected by our Scottish neighbours, as well as the English. When the English prisoners were brought to Morton, at Dalkeith, and among other presents received from him some Scottish falcons, one of his train observed, that the English were nobly treated, since they got live Hawks for dead Herons." *Godscroft.*

HERRICK. This name was formerly spelt Eyryk, Eyrik, Eyrick, and Heyricke. Dean Swift, whose father married a lady of this family, informs us that "there is a tradition that the most ancient family of the Ericks derive lineage from Erick the Forester, a great commander, who raised an army to oppose the invasion of William the Conqueror, by whom he was vanquished, but afterwards employed to command that prince's forces, and in his old age retired to his house in Leicestershire, where his family hath continued ever since." Quoted in B.L.G.

HERRIES. A Norman race, probably from Heries in the arrondissement of Bayeux. They were settled in the S. of Scotl. from the XII. cent. and were, it is pretty certain, deduced from the A-Norm. family of Heriz, lords of Wiverton or Worton, co. Northampton. The elder line of Heriz or Herries ended in heirs female, in the XVI. cent., and the title of Lord H. was carried by the eldest co-heiress to the Lords Maxwell.

HERRING. Possibly from the fish, and originally applied by way of sobriquet, since in the XIV. cent. we find some compounds of it, now apparently extinct ; viz. Castherring, Schottenheryng, and Rotenheryng ! It is more likely however to be an ancient Scandinavian personal name, whence the names of the parishes, &c., of Herringby, Herringfleet, Herringstone, Herringswell, and Herrington.

HERRON See Heron.

HERSEY. See Hercy.

HERTFORD. The town.

HERVEY. See Harvey.

HERWARD. The well-known A-Sax. name Hereward.

HESKETH. Musard Ascuit, Hascoit, or Hasculfus, appears in Domesday as a capital tenant in the counties of Derby, Bucks, Oxford, Warwick, &c. Camden, speaking of the name Askew, erroneously says, that it comes from Ascouth, and that "from the old Christian name Aiscuith, which in Latin was Hasculphus and Hastulphus, that is, Speedy-Help." The baronet's family claim to have been possessed of Hesketh, co. Lancaster, from the Conquest, and the pedigree is deduced without hiatus from Rich. de Haskayth in the XIII. cent.

HESS. HESSE A native of Hesse ; a Hessian.

HESSELL. A narrowed pronunciation of Hassell.

HESSELTINE. See Hazelden.

HESTER. A spelling of Esther. See FEMALE CHRISTIAN NAMES.

HETT. A township in Durham.

HETTON. Townships in cos. Durham, Northumberland, and York.

HEVYBERD. "Heavy-beard." See Beard.

HEWARD. Possibly a corruption of Howard, but more likely of Hayward. Hayward's Heath, co. Sussex, was formerly with rustics Heward's Hoth.

HEWER. Of wood or stone ? See Cleaver and Stonehewer.

HEWES. A mis-spelling of Hughes. In the great Scottish family of Dalrymple the Christian name Hugh has generally been spelt *Hew.*

HEWETSON. See Hewett.

HEWETT. A diminutive of Hugh, and hence Hewitt, Hewetson, and Hewitson.

HEWGILL. Probably Howgill, a chapelry in Yorkshire.

HEWISH. A parish in Wiltshire.

HEWITT. See Hewett.

HEWLETT. Perhaps a diminutive of Hugh.

HEWSON. The son of Hugh.

HEXAMER. Of this singular name I can make nothing, unless it means a native of Hexham, co. Northumberland.

HEXT. A-Sax. *hexta*, O. Eng. *hext*, highest. Halliwell quotes from an ancient MS. :—

> "The Erchbischop of Canturberi,
> In Engelond that is *hext*."

The surname may relate either to physical height or to social eminence.

HEXTER. Possibly a corruption of Exeter.

HEY. The same as Hay.

HEYDEN. See Haydon.

HEYLIN. An old baptismal name. Filius Heilin is found in H.R.

HEYWARD. An old and more correct form of Hayward.

HEYWOOD. A town and chapelry in co. Lancaster. Heywood Hall was long the residence of the ancestors of the baronet's family.

HIBBARD. HIBBERD. See Hibbert.

HIBBERT. The Hibberts of Marple, Birtles, &c., co. Chester, claim descent from Paganus *Hubert*, who accompanied Richard Cœur-de-Lion in the Crusade of 1190. See Ormerod's Cheshire. An A-Sax. bishop of Lichfield was called Hygbert.

HIBBITT. A corruption of Hibbert, from Hubert.

HIBBS. From Hibb, the "nurse-name" of Hubert.

HICK. See Isaac; but it may be local, from Heck or Hick, a Yorkshire township.

HICKES. See Isaac.

HICKEY. See Isaac.

HICKIE. See Isaac.

HICKINBOTHAM. See Higginbottom.

HICKLING. HICKLIN. Parishes in cos. Nottingham and Norfolk.

HICKMAN. The pedigree of the extinct baronet family, Hickman of Gainsborough, is traced to Robert Fitz-Hickman, lord of the manors of Bloxham and Wickham, co. Oxford, 56 Henry III. Hence the name must originally have been a baptismal appellation. In the next reign we find both a Hykeman and a Walter Hikeman, in the same county, the former being apparently a Christian name. H.R.

HICKMOTT. Anciently Hicquemot—probably a derivative of Isaac.

HICKOCK. Said to be the same name as Hiscock, which see.

HICKOT. HICKOX. Diminutives of Hick, Hyke, or Isaac.

HICKS. The village so called in Gloucestershire can hardly have been the source of this numerous surname, which is generally derived, doubtless, from Hicque, or Hick, a nick-name of Isaac.

HICKSON. See Isaac.

HIDE. A feudal portion of land of uncertain extent, according to its quality. A hide appears generally to have been so much land as "with its house and toft, right of common, and other appurtenances, was considered to be sufficient for the necessities of a family." Archæologia, vol. xxxv. p. 470. There are specific localities called Hide, in Warwickshire, Bedfordshire, Herefordshire, and many other counties.

HIDER. See Hyder.

HIDES. See Hide.

HIGGINBOTTOM. Following a writer in Gent. Mag. Oct., 1820, I have elsewhere suggested that this strange word might be *Ickenbaum*, O. Germ. for oak tree. Another etymology assigned was *hickin*, a Lancashire provincialism for the mountain ash, and *bottom*, a low ground or valley. A correspondent suggests its identity with the Dutch family name Hoogenboom, which signifies "high tree," either from the first bearer's residence near one, or a sobriquet allusive to stature.

HIGGIN. HIGGINS. A diminutive of Hugh, through its Latin form Hugo. Hugonis the genitive case of that name (equivalent to Hugh's or Hughes') would easily become in rapid pronunciation Huggins, and Higgins. See however Heckin.

HIGGINS. See Isaac.

HIGGINSON. See Isaac.

HIGGS. See Isaac.

HIGHAM. Parishes and places in cos. Northampton, Kent, Derby, Suffolk, Bedford, Leicester, Sussex, &c., &c.

HIGHLEY. A parish in Shropshire.

HIGHWORTH. A town in Wiltshire, which has given birth to a surname spelt indifferently Earth, Worth, and Yerworth.

HIGSON. The same as Hickson.

HILDEBRAND. The personal name.

HILDER. 'The elder'—a word still used in Norfolk. This form also occurs in MS. Arundel, 220. Halliwell. But the Supp. to Alfric's Vocab. says "*hyldere*, lictor, vel virgifer," i.e., an usher or mace-bearer. Wright's Vocab., 60.

HILDERSLEY. Hildesley, a tything in Gloucestershire.

HILDROP. An obscure hamlet near Marlborough, co. Wilts.

HILDYARD. Formerly Hildheard, an ancient personal name. The family are said to have sprung from Robert Hildheard, who was of Normanby, co. York, in the year 1109. B.L.G.

HILEY. Highley, a parish in Shropshire.

HILGERS. An old personal name, corresponding with the Germ. Hilger, and the O. High Germ. Hildegar.

HILL. From residence upon one. Its medieval form is Atte-Hill. The Lond. Direct. has more than two hundred traders of this name, besides about one-eighth of that number in the pluralized form of Hills. The most distinguished family of this name, the Hills of Hawkstone (Viscount Hill), deduce themselves from Hugh de la Hulle ('of the Hill'), who held the estate of Court of Hill in the parish of Burford, co. Salop, temp. Richard I. Shirley's Noble and Gentle Men, p. 197. The Hills of Stallington, co. Stafford, are descended from the family of De Monte, of Castle Morton, co. Worcester, and they bore that name till the XV. cent., when it was anglicized to Hyll. See Nash's Worcestershire.

HILLEARY. Hilary, an ancient personal name.

HILLER. See Hellier.

HILLIARD. See Hildyard.

HILLIER. See Hillyer.

HILLMAN. From residence upon some hill. Its ancient forms are Atte-Hill, Ate Hull, &c.

HILLS. See Hill.

HILLYER. See Hellier.

HILTON. There are parishes and places so called in many counties, and probably several distinct families. The great baronial race who flourished in the XIV. cent. derived their name from the Castle of Hylton or Hilton, co. Durham, their ancient seat.

"The origin of the family of Hilton is lost in the clouds of remote antiquity. It has been stated that in the reign of King Athelstan, one of the family, presented a crucifix to the monastery of Hartlepool. A legendary tale states, that a raven flew from the North, and perching on the turrets of a tower seated on the Wear, received the embraces of a Saxon lady, whom her father, a powerful Abthane, had there confined, to protect her from the approaches of a Danish nobleman; by which may possibly be adumbrated, the origin of the family springing from a mixture of Danish and Saxon blood. . . . It is at least certain, that the house of Hilton existed in great splendour at the time of the Conquest, and had, long before its members were summoned to Parliament under Edward II., enjoyed the rank and reputation of barons by tenure, a title which, after the declension of the family, was constantly attributed to the chief of the name by popular courtesy." *Sharp's Hartlepool*, p. 167.
The characteristic of the family was, "THE HOARY HILTONS."

HIMBURY. See Hembury.

HINCE. See Ince.

HINCKLEY. A town in Leicestershire.

HINCKS. HINKS. HYNCKES. A diminutive of Henry, just as Wilkes is of William, Pirkes or Perkes of Peter, &c. A Chester family of this name were written Hinckes, temp. James I., and the word appears to have been pronounced as a dissyllable—Hinck-es. A century later, in order to prevent a crasis of the two syllables, an apostrophe replaced the disused E, and the name for two generations was actually written *Hinck's*. Inf. Edward Hincks, Esq.
Mr. Ferguson has a much more dignified origin for this surname. "Hinks," he says, "is no doubt a corruption of HENGIST or HINGEST, which signifies a stallion. Some traditions make Hengist a Frisian, in which language the word is *hingst*, which approaches nearer to Hincks. In the names of places, Hengist has become changed into Hinks, as in Hinksey, co. Berks," which, according to the Codex Diplomaticus, was in Saxon times written Hengestesige.

HIND. HINDE. A. S. *hine*. A domestic servant. Chaucer employs it rather of a man employed in husbandry. In an ancient poem we read:—

> "I am an *hine*;
> And I do use to go to plough,
> And earn my meat ere that I dine."
> *Percy's Rel.*

"A hind is one who looks after the rest of the servants, the grounds, cattle, corn, &c., of his master." C. S. Gilbert's Cornwall, i. 108.
In Devonshire it is synonymous with farm-bailiff.

HINDERWELL. A parish in York-shire.

HINDLEY. HINDLE. A chapelry in Lancashire.

HINDMAN. Analagous to Hartman, Buckman, &c., in relation to the care of deer. It may, however, be a pleonasm for Hind, which see.

HINDMARCH. See Hindmarsh.

HINDMARSH. Local: "The hinder or more remote marsh."

HINDSON. The son of a hind or farm bailiff. See Hind.

HINE. The same as Hind, and a more correct spelling of that word. The form in H.R. is Le Hine.

HINKLEY. See Hinckley.

HINKS. Properly Henks, from Henry; so Jenks from John, and Wilks from William. See however Hincks.

HINKSMAN. HINXMAN. Corruptions of Henchman.

HINTON. Parishes and places in cos. Salop, Hants, Somerset, Wilts, Gloucester, Northampton, Dorset, Berks, &c.

HIPKIN. See Hipp.

HIPP. An old Scandinavian name, whence Hipson, Hipkin, and the local Hippisley, Hipswell, &c.

HIPPER. The Hypper or Ibber is a river of Derbyshire, a tributary of the Rother.

HIPPISLEY. Local: but I do not find the place. In an ancient parchment pedigree, in the possession of the Hippisleys of Stoneaston, co. Somerset, is the following copy of a rhyming grant, said to have been made by John of Gaunt to an ancestor of the house. [N. B. "Time-honoured Lancaster" would appear to have been much addicted to versification of this kind, and several similar grants of his have been preserved. Pity it is that he did not get a little assistance from his contemporaries Gower and Chaucer, his verses being certainly amongst the roughest productions of the English muse.]

"I, John a-Gaunt do give and grant unto Richard Hippisley,
All the manors herein named, as I think in number seven;
To be as firm to be thine, as ever they were mine, from Heaven above to Hell below:
And to confirm the truth, I seal it with my great tooth, the wax in doe! !
"Stone-Easton, Carnley, Wakam, Tuddlhouse, Brasket, Charde, Hinton-Bluet."

HIPSON. See Hipp. Ipsen as a surname is still found in Denmark.

HIPWELL. Probably Hipswell, a chapelry in co. York.

HIRD. See Herd.

HIRST. See Hurst.

HISCOCK. A diminutive of Isaac.

HISCOCKS. See Isaac.

HITCHCOCK. Hitch is an old "nurse-name" of Richard, and COCK is the ordinary diminutive.

HITCHCOX. See Richard.

HITCHIN. A town in co. Hertford. Also a "nurse-name" of Richard.

HITCHINS. See Richard.

HITHE. A haven. A-Sax. Or specifically from the town of Hythe, co. Kent.

HITCHINSON. See Richard.

HIXON. The same as Hickson.

HOAD. A *hoad* in the South means a heathy or rough ground. In Sussex many names of places which comprise the syllable *hoth* or *heath* have had it corrupted by the peasantry to *hoad*, and thus Hothly and Roeheath become Hoadly and Roehoad. See HOTHER.

HOADLY. HOADLEY. The parishes of East and West Hothly, or Hoathly, are pronounced in the dialect of Sussex as Hoad-lie; and from one of these the surname has probably been derived.

HOAR. HOARE. Doubtless from A-Sax. *hár*, hoary, grey; applied to a person having a grey or hoary head. The common medieval form is Le Hore.

HOBART. Probably another form of Hubert.

HOBB. HOBBES. HOBBS. See Robert. Hobbe, Hobbis. H.R.

HOBBINS. See Robert.

HOBDAY. *Hob* is a country clown, (Halliwell), and *day* or *deye* one of the humblest class of husbandry servants, or as we now call them day-labourers. Eng. Surn. Hence a Hobday means an agricultural labourer.

HOBKINS. See Robert.

HOBLER. "As well *hobellers* as archers." Paston Letters, edit. 1841, ii. 154. "Hoblers or hobilers, so called from the hobbies or diminutive horses on which they rode, or more probably from *hobilles*, the short jackets which they wore. They were light horsemen, and proved of considerable service to Edward III. in his French expeditions. By the tenure of their lands they were obliged to maintain their nags, and were expected to be in readiness, when sudden invasions happened, to spread immediate intelligence of the same throughout the land." Ibid. Note. Lambarde writing in 1570, concerning beacons and their management in case of invasion, says: "But as no doubt the necessitie of them is apparent, so it were good that for the more speedie spreading of the knowledge of the enimies comming, they were assisted with some horsemen (anciently called of their hobies or nags, *Hobeliers*) that besides the fire, which in a bright shining day is not so well descried, might also run from beacon to beacon, and supply that notice of the danger at hande." Perambulation of Kent, edit. 1826., p. 65.

HOBMAN. In some local dialects this word signifies a clown, a rustic.

HOBSON. Hob is a known diminutive of Robert, and in some cases this surname is probably from that source; but it would seem that there was anciently some baptismal name like Ob, or Hob, as we find in the Domesd. of Suffolk one Leuric Hobbesune or Obbesune—probably a Saxon.

HOBY. 1. Robert, through Hob. Borde, in his Boke of Knowledge (1542) makes a Welshman say :—

> "I am a gentylman, and come of Brutus' blood,
> My name is ap Ryce, ap Davy, ap Flood;
> My kindred is *ap Hoby*, ap Jenkin, ap Goffe,
> Bycause that I go barlegged I do cach the coffe."

2. A parish in co. Leicester.

HOCKDAY. HOCKADAY. An ancient festival, which commenced the fifteenth day after Easter, was called indifferently Hokeday or Hocktide. There is much uncertainty as to the origin of the customs attending it, as well as to the etymology of the word. For what is known of both, see Brand's Popular Antiquities, edit. Ellis, i. 81, 109, &c. The surname must have been originally imposed on the same principle as that which gave rise to Christmas, Pentecost, Easter, &c. See TIMES AND SEASONS.

HOCKEN. HOCKIN. Corruptions of Hawkin, Hawkins, or of Hocking.

HOCKING. The Hokings, according to Ferguson, were a Frisian people, and derived their name from one Hoce, mentioned in the poem of Beowulf. Mr. Kemble (Archæolog. Journ.) observes that Hoce is a "mythical personage, probably the *heros eponymus* of the Frisian tribe, the founder of the Hocings, and a progenitor of the imperial race of Charlemagne."

HOCKLEY. A parish in Essex.

HOCKNELL. Hockenhull, a township in Cheshire.

HODD. 1. See Roger. Hod, Hodd, Hodde, H.R. 2. A personal name of great antiquity, which may be derived from Hodr, the blind son of Odin. See Ferguson.

HODE. See Hoad or Hood.

HODDER. A river of Yorkshire tributary to the Ribble. But there is a Le Hoder in H.R. denoting some occupation.

HODGE. HODGES. See Roger.

HODGKIN. See Roger. I have before me a document of the XV. cent. in which the same landed proprietor is called indifferently Roger and Hodgkyn.

HODGKINSON. See Roger.

HODGSON. The son of Hodge or Roger. This name in the North of England is pronounced Hodgin, while in the South it has taken not only the pronunciation, but the spelling, of Hodson or Hudson. The name of Hodgson is ancient at Newcastle-upon-Tyne, being found in records of temp. Edward I., and the Hodgsons of Stella and Acton, co. Northumberland, trace a clear pedigree to 1424.

HODNET. A town in Shropshire. De Hodenet. H.R.

HODSON. See Roger. The son of Hodge or Roger. It is curious that Hodgeson becomes in the North of England Hodgin—in the South, Hodson.

HOE. A-Sax. *hou*, a hill—as the Hoe at Plymouth.

HOESE. The same as Husee or Hussey.

HOEY. Originally MacHoey, a corruption of MacKay, but retaining a similar pronunciation.

HOFFMAN. Germ. *hofmann*, a courtier.

HOG. See Hogg.

HOGARTH. A place in Westmoreland.

HOGBEN. HOGBIN. Probably a pigstye; from *hog*, and *bin*, a crib or hutch. A-Sax. This Kentish surname was probably applied in the first instance to a swineherd.

HOGG. HOGGE. The animal—analogous to Wildbore, Purcell, &c. Those who object to be classed with the swinish multitude may prefer a derivation from the A-Sax. *hog*, which means prudent, careful, thoughtful. The northern Hoggs, however, claim descent from Hougo, a Norwegian baron, who is said to have settled in Ettrick Forest. Folks of Shields. p. 43. Who would have guessed at the baronial descent of our great Shepherd!

HOGGART. May be the same as Hogarth, though *hog-herd*, swine-herd, has been suggested.

HOGGER. See Hoggart.

HOGGETT. The same as Hugget.

HOGGINS. The same as Huggins.

HOGHTON. Adam de Hocton, held one carucate of land in Hocton (now Hoghton Tower), co. Lancaster, temp. Henry II. The present Sir Henry Bold Hoghton, who stands second on the roll of Baronets (1611) is the existing representative.

HOGSFLESH. A sobriquet, perhaps originally applied to a pork-butcher. Various shifts have been adopted to modify or change this uncomfortable surname. I have known instances of its being written Hoflesh, Hoxley, and even Oxley.

HOGWOOD. Local: a "wood abounding in swine."

HOILE. See Hoyle.

HOLBECHE. Holbeach, a town in Lincolnshire. The latinization in charters implies "the holy beech;"—De Sacra Fago.

HOLBECK. Townships in cos. York and Nottingham.

HOLBORN. A portion of London.

HOLBROOK. A parish in Suffolk, and a chapelry in Derbyshire.

HOLCOMBE. Parishes, &c., in cos. Somerset, Lancaster, Oxon, and Devon.

HOLD. A fortress, or any thing held out.

HOLDEN. May be local. See Den; but from the occurrence of such local names as Holden-by, Holden-hurst, Holding-ham, it looks like an ancient personal appellation.

HOLDER. Thin. Camden.

HOLDERNESS. A great district or wapentake of Yorkshire.

HOLDGATE. A parish in Shropshire.

HOLDING. Probably the same as Holden.

HOLFORD. A parish in Somersetshire.

HOLE. This word is in many dialects applied to a locality which lies much lower than the surrounding lands; and a resident at such a place would acquire the surname Atte Hole. Hoole and Hoyle are other forms of the same name.

HOLGATE. Holdgate, a parish in Shropshire. Also a township in co. York.

HOLIDAY. HOLLADAY. See Halliday.

HOLKER. Two townships in Lancashire.

HOLL. Holle, without prefix, is found in H.R.

HOLLAND. It has been stated on the authority of George of Croyland, who wrote an account of the family in 1550, that the noble and knightly race of this name could trace themselves backwards thirteen generations beyond the Norman Conquest! For 13 we should probably read 3; and there is a more credible genealogy which makes the *fundator gentis* one Otho, whose son Stephen flourished under Edw. the Confessor, as lord of Stevington, co. Lincoln, and his son, Ralph de Holand, it is said, continued to hold his lands by the permission of William the Conqueror. These lands were in the district of Lincolnshire still known as Holland, but there is also a Holland in Lancashire which belonged to the family. They were ennobled by Edward I., and their blood mingled with that of royalty itself by the marriage of Thomas de Holland with the lovely Joane Plantagenet, the *Fair Maid of Kent*, and granddaughter of King Edward III.

HOLLANDS. See Holland.

HOLLEBONE. Sometimes corrupted to *Hollowbone!* It is doubtless equivalent to 'holy bourne,' that is, a stream issuing from a holy spring or well. It is pronounced as a trisyllable.

HOLLET. Probably Holleth, a hamlet in the parish of Garstang, co. Lancaster.

HOLLEY. Probably local.

HOLLICK. Doubtless Holwick, a township in Yorkshire, by the suppression of W.

HOLLIDAY. See Halliday.

HOLLIER. A mispronunciation of Hellyer.

HOLLINGBURY. A conspicuous hill near Brighton, Sussex.

HOLLINGSWORTH. A manor in Mottram, co. Chester.

HOLLINGTON. A parish in Sussex.

HOLLOND. A variation of Holland, which see.

HOLLOWAY. A part of the parish of Islington, co. Middlesex.

HOLLYGROVE. From residence near a grove of holly.

HOLLYMAN. See Holyman.

HOLLYWELL. See Halliwell.

HOLMAN. May be a contraction of Holyman; but is more likely to be "*whole* man," a man of sterling mettle. It must be recollected that in medieval English *whole* was spelt without the w, and the commonest form of this name in the XIV. and XV. cent. is Holeman.

HOLMER. A dweller by a holm or low ground. See termination ER.

HOLMES. A holme is defined by Halliwell as 'flat land; a small island; a deposit of soil at the confluence of two waters. Flat grounds near water are called holms.'
"Some call them the *holmes*, because they lie low, and are good for nothing but grasse."
Harrison.
In Scotland a *holm* means both a small uninhabited island, and a detached or insulated rock in the sea.

HOLMS. See Holmes.

HOLNEY. Local: probably from Olney, co. Buckingham.

HOLROYD. A local name. (See ROYD.) The place is probably in the W. Riding of Yorkshire, where William de Howroyde or Holroyd, the Earl of Sheffield's ancestor, flourished temp. Edw. I.

HOLSTEN. From the province of Holstein.

HOLT. Halliwell says a grove, or small forest. On the South Downs generally, if not always, it is a small hanging wood. See other definitions in Eng. Surn. i. 75.* Leo says copse or wood, corresponding with the Germ. *holz.* The H.R. forms are De, De la, Del, and Le Holt. There are towns and places specifically named Holt in Norfolk, Wiltshire, Worcestershire, and Leicestershire.

HOLTER. A man who resided near a Holt. See termination ER.

HOLTMAN. See HOLT and MAN.

HOLTON, Parishes, &c., in cos. Lincoln, Oxon, Somerset, Suffolk, &c.

HOLYBROOK. Local: "the sacred stream"—in charters, De Sacro Fonte.

HOLYHEAD. The Welsh town.

HOLYMAN. In the Landnamabok, according to Mr. Ferguson, there are "forty-two men having Helgi (holy) for their baptismal name, while only three had acquired it as a surname." "Holyman," he adds, "corresponds with the German name Heiligmann." In Germany the name was formerly translated into the Greek *Osiander.*

HOLYOAK. From residence near an oak to which some sanctity was attached. The latinization in charters is, De Sacra Quercu.

HOMAN. The same as Holman.

HOME. See Hume, of which it is an older orthography.

HOMER. A medieval personal name. A saint bearing it gave name to St. Omer in Picardy, from whence the founder of the family may have come to England—not necessarily, however, since Homerton, Homersham, Homersfield, &c., point distinctly to some Anglo-Saxon proprietor who rejoiced in this poetical designation. The first of the family on record, according to Mr. Dixon, is Thomas *de* Homere, 1338, who had lands in co. Dorset. A family of Homer have been settled in Staffordshire for centuries. Surnames, p. 37.

HOMES. See Holmes.

HOMEWOOD. Local: "the wood of holm or holly."

HONDESDICK. Houndsditch in London gave name to a citizen, one Geoffrey de Hondesdick, temp. Edw. I. H.R.

HONE. Probably Holne, a parish in Devonshire. There is, however, a Hone without prefix in H.R.

HONEY. In Sussex this name has been corrupted from the local Holney; but Honey unprefixed is found in H.R.

HONEYBONE. HONEYBUM. Probably corruptions of Honeybourne or Cow-Honeybourne, co. Gloucester.

HONEYCHURCH. A parish in Devonshire.

HONEYMAN. In old times when mead or metheglin was a favourite beverage, and when sugar was unknown in England, the propagation of bees, and the production of honey, furnished employment for many persons; and hence the surnames Beeman and Honeyman. Honeman, Honiman, H.R. See Beeman.

HONEYSETT. Possibly from the A-Sax, *hunig,* honey, and *setl,* a seat or a setting—a *bee-park.* See under Beeman.

HONEYWELL. HONYWELL. HONYWILL. Probably local, from the termination WELL. It might "be given to a well from the sweetness of its waters." Ferguson.

HONNOR. See Honor.

HONOR. HONOUR. Probably the Lat. Honorius, through the French Honoré.

HONYWOOD. " The name is derived from Henewood near Postling in Kent, where the ancestors of this family resided as early as the reign of Henry III." Shirley's Noble and Gentle Men, p. 97.

HOO. HOOE. Parishes and places in cos. Hertfordshire, Sussex, Kent, &c.

HOOD. 1. From some peculiarity in the head-dress of the original possessor of the name. 2. But more probably Odo is the source.

HOOFE. If of English origin (which I doubt) may be connected with the A-Sax. Uffa or Offa, a well-known personal name.

HOOK. HOOKE. Many localities in England bear the name of "the Hook," an expression which is doubtless topographical, though its precise derivation is not known. It is probably allied to the Teutonic *hoe, hoh, hoch,* &c., all meaning a hill or elevated place. The surname was written in the XIV. cent. Atte Hooke, and this by crasis sometimes became Tooke. It may be mentioned that Hoke, as a personal name, occurs in Saxon times. See Beowulf, l. 2146, where we find the daughter of Hoke bewailing the death of her sons.

HOOKER. 1. See Hook, and the termination ER. 2. A maker of hooks.

HOOKEY. HOOKEYE. Probably local. The latter orthography makes a curious compound, and reminds us of one of Douglas Jerrold's witticisms. When asked if he knew Theodore Hook, he replied: " Oh yes, Hook and I are very intimate !"

HOOKMAN. See Hook, and the termination MAN. Hokeman without prefix is found in H.R.

HOOLE. Places in cos. Chester, Lancaster, and York.

HOOPER. The same as Hoper. John Hooper, bishop of Gloucester, a victim of the Marian persecution, wrote his name indifferently Hoper and Hooper. Perhaps in some cases a maker of hoops. The form of the name temp. Edward I. was Le Hopere. H.R.
A distinguished family of this name are of Dutch origin.

HOOTTON. Parishes, &c., in cos. York and Chester.

HOPE. 1. Parishes, &c., in cos. Derby, York, Flint, Kent, Salop, Hereford, &c. 2. A topographical expression, meaning a sloping hollow between two hills, "petite vallée entre des montagnes." Jamieson. " The side of an hill." Camden. Hence the surnames Hope, Hoper, and Hooper, as well as Hopekirk, Hopewell, &c. The H.R. form, De Hope, belongs to the first, and De la Hope to the second definition.

HOPER. From residence near a *hope* or valley. See Hope, and the termination ER. The Protestant bishop of Gloucester, temp. Queen Mary, wrote his name indifferently Hoper and Hooper.

HOPEWELL. Hopwell, co. Derby.

HOPGOOD. A corruption of Hopwood.

HOPKINS. HOPKYNS. From Robert, through Hob, with the diminutive *kin.* The H.R. form is Hobekyn. A family of this name have possessed a farm at Swalcliffe, co. Oxon, from the XIII. cent., and nineteen successive proprietors bore the Christian name of John. They believe themselves to be descended from a younger son of one of the three Sir *Robert* de Wykehams who were in succession owners of Swalcliffe, temp. John and Henry III. The arms too of Hopkyns appear to have been partly borrowed from those of Wykeham. Information of D. D. Hopkyns, Esq.

HOPKINSON. See Robert.

HOPPE. Probably the same as Hope.

HOPPER. A-Sax. *hoppere,* a dancer. Le Hoppar, Le Hopper, Le Hoppere. H.R.

HOPPING. Perhaps Hoppen, a township in Northumberland.

HOPPRINGLE. From the estate so called in the S. of Scotl. (Roxburghshire ?) The first syllable was dropped in the XVII. cent., and the name has since been known as Pringle. So says a northern correspondent—but see Pringle.

HOPPUS. The derivation from "hophouse" will hardly do, hops being of too recent introduction, unless indeed the name be very modern. It is more likely " Hopehouse," from residence near a *hope.* See Hope, 2.

HOPTON. Parishes and places in cos. Derby, Stafford, Suffolk, Salop, &c.

HOPWOOD. A township in Lancashire.

HORACE. I do not see why this name should not have been derived, through the French, from the Roman Horatius; but Mr. Ferguson deduces it from the O. Saxon, Friesic, and Norse, *hros, horaz, hross,* a horse.

HORD. Has been considered a corruption of Howard. Hord is however a Swedish surname, and it was borne by a distinguished general of Charles XII.

HORDE. Probably the same as Howard, or as Hord.

HORDEN. Dispensator, steward. Camd. From A-Sax. *hórd,* a hoard, or treasury.

HORE. See Hoare.

HORLEY. Parishes in cos. Surrey and Oxford.

HORLOCK. *Hoar* and *lock.* Having hoary locks; grey-headed. Similar names are Blacklock, Silverlock, Whitelock, &c.

HORNBLOWER. Cornage is a law term (Lat. *cornagium*) for a species of tenure in grand serjeanty, " the service of which was to blow a horn when any invasion of the Scots was perceived ; and by this tenure many persons held their lands northward, about the wall, commonly called the Pict's

Wall." Jacob, who cites Camden. The person who performed this duty for the lord, probably acquired the surname. At Ripon there prevails a peculiar custom, "which according to some is of a date prior to the Conquest, viz., to blow a horn every night at nine o'clock ; and formerly if any house or shop was robbed between that hour and sunrise the loss was made good to the sufferer, by a yearly tax of fourpence, imposed on every house-keeper. The tax is now discontinued, but the custom is still kept up of blowing the horn every night, three times at the mayor's door, and three times at the market-cross. The officer who performs this duty is called the *Horn-blower.*" Parl. Gazetteer. Blouhorn is met with in the H.R. ; and Blower and Horniblow still exist. " Cornicen, horn-blawere." Wright's Vocab. 73.

HORNBY. Parishes, &c., in cos. Lancaster and York.

HORNCASTLE. A town in Lincolnshire.

HORNE. One Alwin Horne held lands in Middlesex and Herts before the making of Domesday. Horn is a personal name of great antiquity, and is borne by the hero of a celebrated O. Eng. and Fr. romance. For his history, see Wright's Essays, vol i., Ess. iii.

HORNER. A manufacturer of horn. In London the horners and bottle-makers form one Company. Horn was anciently applied to many uses for which glass and other materials are at present employed. "Horns," says Fuller, "are a commodity not to be slighted, seeing I cannot call to mind any other substance so hard that it will not break ; so solid that it will hold liquor within it ; and yet so clear that light will pass through it. No mechanical trade but hath some utensils made thereof ; and even now I recruit my pen with ink from a vessel of the same. Yea, it is useful *cap-a-pie,* from combs to shoeing-horns. What shall I speak of many gardens made of horns to garnish houses ? I mean artificial flowers of all colours. And besides what is spent in England, many thousand weight are shaven down into leaves for lanthorns, and sent over daily into France . . . . . . No wonder then that the Horners are an ancient corporation, though why they and the bottle-makers were formerly united into one company passeth my skill to conjecture." Worthies of England, Lancashire. The union between the two trades was probably formed, because vessels for holding liquors were the staple commodity of both.

HORNIBLOW. Possibly a corruption of Hornblower.

HORNING. A parish in Norfolk.

HORNSEY. A parish in Middlesex.

HORNYOLD. The first recorded ancestor is John de H., temp. Edw. III. Local —place unknown.

HORSECRAFT. The horse-croft, an enclosure for horses.

HORSELL. A parish in Surrey.

HORSEY. A parish in Norfolk, and places in Sussex and Essex.

HORSFORD. A parish in Norfolk,

HORSLEY. Parishes and townships in cos. Northumberland and Derby.

HORSEMAN. HORSMAN. Either a chevalier as distinguished from a foot-soldier, or a keeper of horses. In H.R. we have one *Agnes* le Horseman—doubtless a clever *Amazon.*

HORSEMONGER. A horse-dealer ; whence Horsemonger Lane in London. In H.R. Le Horsemongere.

HORSNAILE. HORSNELL. Ferguson says, it may "refer to one who was as swift-footed as a horse." A-Sax. *snel,* quick, active. A Kentish farrier, with great propriety, lately bore this name in the former orthography.

HORTON. (A-Sax. *ort,* or wort, herbs, or vegetables, and *tún,* an enclosure—a garden). Parishes and places in cos. Bucks, Chester, Dorset, Gloucest., Kent, Northampt., Northumb., Salop, York, Stafford, &c.

HORWOOD. Parishes in cos. Buckingham and Devon.

HOSÉ. The same as Hussey.

HOSE. The garment. See Hosier.

HOSEY. Hosatus or Hussey, which latter see.

HOSIER. Camden explains Chaucer by Hosier. The hosier of modern times sells stockings and other soft 'under clothing.' Two hundred years ago, the hosiers of London were those tailors who sold ready-made clothes (*qui vendent des habits d'hommes tous faits.* Cotgr.) ; but the original hosier was he who encased the "nether man" in leather : " The *chaussure* commonly used in England, when surnames were first adopted by the commonalty, was of leather, covered both the foot and leg, and was called *hose.* Hosier, therefore, is the same with *Chaucier,* which comes from the Lat. *calcearius,* and differs but little in meaning from another word used to denote the man who followed this employment, viz., Sutor, Sowter, or Souter, which was in use in English from the time of Chaucer to that of Beaumont and Fletcher. It is still preserved in Scotland, and has become a surname in both countries." Edinburgh Review, April, 1855.

HOSKIN. See Roger.

HOSKING. See Hoskins.

HOSKINS. A softened pronunciation of Hodgkins.

HOSMER. Osmer was a Domesday tenant in chief, co. Dorset, who had held his lands temp. Edw. Confessor.

HOSTE. The ancestor of the baronet was Jacques Hoste, who was driven out of the Netherlands in 1569, by the persecutions under the Duke of Alva, and settled in England. His ancestors were influential in the city of Bruges in the XIV. cent. Courthope's Debrett.

HOTCHKINS. See Roger.

HOTCHKISS. A corruption of Hodgkins.

HOTHAM. A parish in Yorkshire. The name was assumed by Peter de Trehouse, who was living there in 1118. Shirley's Noble and Gentle Men.

HOTHER. *Hoth* in Sussex, where this surname occurs, signifies furze or gorse, and also an unenclosed ground where it grows. Atte Hoth is found in the XIV. cent. This probably became Hother. It may have sprung however from Other, a personal name of early date.

HOTTEN. HOTTON. Probably Hoton, co. Leicester, or Hoton-Pagnel, co. York.

HOUGH. A township in Cheshire.

HOUGHTON. Parishes and places in cos. Lancaster, Cumberland, Hunts, Hants, York, Northampton, Northumb., Norfolk, Bedford, Durham, Dorset, Leicester, &c.

HOULE. See Howell and Hoole.

HOUND. 1. A-Sax. *hund*, a hunting dog. A Gilbert le Hund is found in H.R. 2. The designation of a parish in Hampshire, which includes within its boundaries the far-famed Netley Abbey.

HOUNSELL. Possibly a corruption of Hounslow, co. Middlesex.

☞ **HOUSE.** A common termination of local surnames, as Woodhouse, Newhouse, Mirehouse, Whitehouse, Oldhouse, Hobhouse.

HOUSE. See remarks in Eng. Surn. i. 75. 1. It is probably the A-Sax. *husa*, a domestic servant. 2. Or, perhaps, Su. Goth. *hus*, arx, a castle.

HOUSEGO. Apparently the old Germ. personal name Husicho. Ferguson.

HOUSEHOLD. A *hold* is a fortress, or any thing held out. Hence Household may signify a fortified house.

HOUSELESS. Perhaps the sobriquet of a mendicant.

HOUSEMAN. HOUSMAN. 1. A domestic servant in contradistinction from one employed in husbandry abroad. 2. Like the A-Sax. *hús-weard*, a housekeeper; a man who has a house of his own.

HOUSLEY. The same as Ouseley.

HOUSTON. HOUSTOUN. The ancient knightly family so called originally bore the name of Paduinan from a place in co. Lanark. In the XII. cent. Hugh de P. acquired the lands of Kilpeter, and built a residence there, to which he gave the name of Hugh's Town, now Houston, co. Renfrew. His descendants of that Ilk borrowed their surname from it.

HOVELL. See Havill.

HOW. HOWE. HOWES. In the South, a small round hill; in the North, a hollow place or plain. The medieval form is At How, generally synonymous with Hill. A-Sax. *hou*—a mountain.

HOWARD. This noble historical name has been a sore puzzle to etymologists. See Eng. Surn. i. 133. A writer in the Quarterly Rev. vol. CII. says, the family "may be Saxon, may be Danish." They are more probably of Norwegian origin. Havard or Haavard was a common personal name among the Northmen. "It appears," says Laing, "to be the English name Howard, and left by them in Northumberland and East Anglia." Heimskringla. vol. i. p. 410. The seventeenth-century genealogists laboured hard to prove a Norman origin for this illustrious race, but authentic records extend back no farther than the XIII. cent., when the Howards rose into eminence in Norfolk; (See Peerage,) though Houardus, the Essex under-tenant of Domesday may be cited on that side.

HOWDEN. A large parish in Yorkshire, and a township in Northumberland.

HOWELL. 1. A very common Welsh baptismal name (Huel). 2. A Lincolnshire parish.

HOWETT. HOWITT. The same as Hewett, a diminutive of Hugh.

HOWGRAVE. A township in Yorkshire.

HOWIE. Supposed to be a corruption of the Fr. surname Hauy: another derivation is from the Scot. *howe*, a hollow.

HOWISON. The son of Hugh, Hughie, or Hewie. The old Scot. mode of spelling Hugh was Hew, as especially in the family of Dalrymple. In Renfrewshire, where the surname abounds, it is pronounced Hewie's-son.

HOWIS. A genitive form of Hugh. Also local: De Howys, H.R., co. Kent.

HOWKE. See Hooke, of which it is an earlier form.

HOWLAND. Probably Hoyland: three places in Yorkshire are so called.

HOWLE. A mis-spelling of Howell.

HOWLEY. A river in Cheshire.

HOWLYN. Supposed to be the Irish equivalent of the Welsh Llewellyn. Fitz-Howlyn became strangely modified to Mac Quillan. Ulster Journ. of Archæol., No. 2.

HOWORTH. The same as Haworth.

HOWROYD. The same as Holroyd. See ROYD.

HOWSE. See How.

HOY. The same as Hoey.

HOYLE. A Yorkshire topographer thus speaks of the *cunabula* of this family: "Hoile House, so called from being situate in a *hole* or *bottom*, gave name to a family who resided there as late as the beginning of the last century (1600), if not later. It is reckoned a very ancient situation, but has nothing remarkable about it now." Watson's Halifax, 1775. A respectable family of the name still existing deduce their pedigree from Edw. Hoyle of Hoyle House in 1528; but there are other local sources which may in some instances have originated the name, as Hoile House, co. Dumfries, Hoyle, a hamlet in West Sussex, &c. The "Hoele of Flyntshire" mentioned by Leland was probably a gentleman of the numerous race of the Howells. There is, or was, in Kent a family of Hoile, but from Hasted it would appear that their name was originally Hild. Hole and Hoole frequently interchange with Hoyle, and are doubtless synonymous.

HUBBARD. A corruption of Hubert.

HUBE. A contraction or "nurse-name" of Hubert.

HUBER. See Hubert.

HUBERT. The personal name. Among its derivatives in English family nomenclature we have Hubbard, Hibbert, Hibbins, Hibbs, Hibson, or Ibson, and probably Ibbotson.

HUCKETT. See Huggett.

HUCKIN. Probably Hughkin, a diminutive of Hugh, like Huggin.

HUCKSTEPP. Local: "of the high steep." In the XIII. cent. it is found in Sussex as De Hoghstepe.

HUDSON. See Roger and Hodgson.

HUDDLESTONE. A small parish in Yorkshire, which the family erewhile possessed, though they deduce their name from king Athelstan!

HUE. HUETT. HUETSON. Orthographical variations of the names Hugh, Hewet, Hewetson.

HUER. The same as Conder—which see.

HUFFAM. From Hougham, a parish in Kent. Robert de H. was constable of Rochester Castle in 1189, and was at Askalon with Cœur-de-Lion. Hougham Court remained in the family for many generations. The corruption of Hougham to the phonetic Huffam is not of recent date. Both forms are used indifferently in Hasted's Kent.

HUGGARD. See Hogarth.

HUGGETT. 1. A diminutive of Hugh — the same as Hewett. 2. Huggate, a parish in the E. Riding of Yorkshire.

HUGGINS. From Hugo, the Latin form of Hugh. The name Willelmus fil' Hugonis would as readily subside into William Huggins as into W. Fitzhugh, W. Ap-Hugh, or W. Hughson.

HUGH. This Norman Christian name, though of rare occurrence in its simple form, has furnished a host of derivatives, some of which would hardly be supposed to be of such origin. Who at first sight would take the five surnames, Fitzhugh, Pugh, Mackay, Hoey, and Huson, to be identical in meaning? Yet this is the case; for Fitzhugh is the A.-Norman rendering of 'Filius Hugonis,' *the son of Hugh;* Pugh is a contraction of the Welsh Ap-Hugh, *the son of Hugh;* Mackay, of the Gaelic Mac-Aiodh, *the son of Hugh;* Hoey is the same name deprived of its Mac; and Huson is clearly Hughson, *the son of Hugh.* Huggins, Higgins, Hutchins, Hitchins, Hutchinson, Hugginson, Hewet, Hewetson, Howitt, Howis, Howison, Huggett, Hoggins, as well as Hughes, Hughson, Hewson, and probably many other names, are diminutives and patronymics of Hugh, the soft, and of Hugo, the hard, form. See more, where necessary, under the respective names.

HUGHES. From Hugh, the personal name. See Hugo.

HUGHMAN. See Human.

HUGHSON. The son of Hugh.

HUGO. The A.-Norm. Christian name, whence Huggins, Higgins, Huggett, &c. It is very common in Domesday. See Hugh.

HUISH. Parishes in cos. Devon and Somerset.

HULL. O. Eng. A hill; but perhaps specifically from Hull, co. York.

HULLS. See Hulse.

HULME. Places in cos. Lancaster, Northumberland, and Cheshire.

HULSE. A township in Cheshire.

HULTON. "Hulton is in the parish of Dean (co. Lancaster) and it gave name to Bleythen, called de Hulton, in the reign of Henry II., and from him this ancient family, still seated at their ancestral and original manor, are regularly descended." Baines's Lancashire. Shirley's Noble and Gentle Men, p. 116.

HUM. A mispronunciation of Home.

HUMAN. A man who had the care of ewes—Ewe-man. Analogous to Tupman, one who took charge of rams.

HUMBERSTON. Parishes in cos. Lincoln and Leicester.

HUMBLE. Though looking like a moral characteristic, this appellation is doubtless derived from the manor of West Humble in the parish of Mickleham, co. Surrey.

HUMBLESTONE. Humbleton, a parish in Yorkshire, or perhaps Humberston, which see.

HUMBY. Places in Lincolnshire.

HUME. An ancient village and fortress in Berwickshire. The Homes or Humes were descended from the famous earls of Dunbar, and through them from Gospatrick, earl of Northumberland, and the Saxon monarchs of England.

HUMPHREY. HUMPHREYS. HUMPHRIES. The personal name.

HUNCHBACK. From the personal deformity of the first bearer.

HUNGER. Perhaps Ongar, co. Essex.

HUNKES. A diminutive of Humphrey; so we derive Wilkes from William, Jenks from John, &c.

HUNN. Grimm traces the name from the Huns of antiquity. The name Huna appears as that of a liberated serf in a charter of manumission, Cod. Dipl. 971. Ferguson. Le Hunne. H.R., co. Kent.

HUNNARD. Probably A-Sax. *hund*, a hound, and *weard*, a keeper—a huntsman or dog-keeper.

HUNNISETT. See Honeysett.

HUNNYBUM. A ludicrous corruption of the local Honeybourne.

HUNT. *Hunta*, A-Sax., a hunter; connected with *hund*, a hound or dog. See Hunter. Le Hunt is very common in H.R. and Hunteman is also found there.

HUNTER. Obviously derived from the chase, in old times a necessary art, as well as a favourite diversion. The Normans were great preservers and mighty hunters of game, and though the name is A-Sax. *(hunta)* it is generally considered that the families bearing it are chiefly of Norman origin. Under the Norman and early Scottish kings the office of king's hunter *(Venator Regis)* was one of considerable dignity. "The hunters of Polmood in Tweedsmuir pretend to have had a charter of their lands from Graeme, who broke through the Wall of Antoninus in the V. cent! Folks of Shields.

HUNTINGDON. The chief town of Huntingdonshire.

HUNTINGTON. Parishes and places in cos. Hereford, Cheshire, Stafford, and York. The late William Huntington (who wore a collar of SS of his own fabrication, See *Punch*, Sept. 17, 1859.,) was *Hunt*, by birth, and adopted the final and penult syllables on arriving at manhood.

HUNTLEY. A parish in co. Gloucester.

HUNTSMAN. See Hunter.

HUNWICK. A township in Durham.

HURDIS. In the Promptorium Parvulorum we find *Hurdyce* defined as 'utensile,' and 'supellex,' and *hustylment* given as its synonym. Now hustylment or hustelment is used in Wickliffe's version of the Bible as a rendering of the Vulgate *utensilia*, and Mr. Way proves from several medieval authorities that it ordinarily meant moveables, household-furniture, or implements; but in "Coer-de-Lion" and other works, *hurdys* clearly signify barricades, palisades,

or large shields called *pavises*. See Way's Prompt. Parv. The low-Latin *hurditius* or *hurditium* means the hurdles *(crates)* employed in ancient warfare—the hurdles or mat-work which covered the walls of towns ("crates quæ obducunt urbium muris"— Vossius) during a siege, to resist the battering-ram, as seen in ancient pictures. The surname may have been metaphorically applied to some gallant defender of a town or fortress.

HURLBAT. Halliwell, citing Howell, defines *hurlebat* as a kind of dart, which is clearly a misapprehension. I find the word in Boyer's Eng.-French, and Ainsworth's Latin Dictionaries. The latter gives it as the equivalent of the classical *cæstus*, and describes it as "a kind of club, or rather thong of leather, having plummets of lead fastened to it, used in boxing." But there was another implement of sport used in the time of Elizabeth for the game of 'hurling' which was called the "clubbe or hurlebatte." For a description of hurling, see Hone's Strutt's Sports and Pastimes, pp. 98-99. This surname, like Shakespeare, Wagstaffe, &c., comes from some feat of strength on the part of the original bearer.

Johnson gives "Whirlbat, anything moved rapidly round to give a blow," and adds, "It is frequently used by the poets for the ancient cæstus." He cites L'Estrange, Creech, and Dryden, for the use of the word.

The names Rob. Hurlebat, and Thos. Hurle-batte occur in documents 15 Ric. III. Notes and Queries, Jan. 24, 1857.

HURLER. A man practised in the game of hurling the ball, which is almost, if not quite, peculiar to the county of Cornwall. For a particular account of this game, which Strutt derives from the Roman play with the *harpastum*, see Carew's Survey of Cornwall, Book i. p. 73.

"In the month of August, 1657, a strange apparition of innumerable persons in white apparel, and in the act of *hurling*, was seen in that county, by many, in a field of standing corn, near Boscastle, which after some time vanished into the sea. Some of the spectators going afterwards into the field, found, contrary to their expectation, that the corn was no ways injured." *C. S. Gilbert's Cornwall*, i. 18.

HURLEY. A parish in Berkshire.

HURLOCK. The same as Horlock.

HURLSTONE. Hurlston, a township in Cheshire.

HURRER. A dealer in hats and caps. Notes and Queries, v. 137. The Hurrers' Company in London formerly comprised the cappers, hatmakers, and haberdashers.

HURST. Parishes and places in Sussex, Berks, Kent, Hampshire, Northumberland, York, and many other counties.

☞ **HURST.** A-Sax. *hyrst*, a wood or forest--whence numerous names of places which have become surnames, as Akehurst, Brinkhurst, Crowhurst, Dighurst, Elmhurst. The termination is principally found in the South-eastern counties, where it indicates the former existence of the great Sylva Anderida, or Forest of Andred.

HUSBAND. Not simply a married man (*maritus*), but anyone entrusted with the higher domestic duties or functions. In medieval documents the surname is written Le Husbande.

HUSEY. See Hussey.

HUSHER. Fr. *huissier*, an usher, or subordinate official of a court.

HUSKISSON. A corruption of Hodgkinson, the son of Hodgkin or Hugh.

HUSON. A contraction of Hughson—the son of Hugh.

HUSSEY. According to Stapleton's Rotuli Scaccarii Normanniæ, Osbert de H., who was living in 1180, was so named from *le Hozu*, a fief in the parish of Grand Quevilly near Rouen. And one Henry de la Hossé or Heuzé held, inter alias, the lands of Hossé. Ibid. Will. de Hosa occurs as witness to a deed of King Stephen soon after his accession. Ibid. In an old account of the Hussey family, the name is said to be "quasi de Hosa—from a boot or buskin," and the crest borne was a boot. Inf. Edw. Hussey, Esq., M.A. The ordinary latinization is Hosatus, 'hosed or booted,' but this is merely a pun, for the head of the family, who in the XII. cent. founded the abbey of Durford, co. Sussex, was otherwise written *De Hoese*—a plain proof that the name was of *local* origin.

There is another locality now spelt Heussé in the department of La Manche.

HUSSON. The same as Huson—the son of Hugh.

HUSTLER. Perhaps a corruption of *hosteler*, an innkeeper.

HUSTWITT. A parish in Yorkshire called Husthwaite is locally so pronounced.

HUTCHESON. See Hutchison.

HUTCHINS. HUTCHINGS. Northern diminutives of Hugh.

HUTCHINSON. See Hutchison. In England and Ireland this is the more frequent orthography. In the N. of England the name appears (but erroneously) to be regarded as a corruption of Richardson. Folks of Shields, p. 37.

HUTCHISON. Said to be Gaelic with an English termination. The son of Hugh.

HUTHWAITE. Probably Husthwaite, a parish in Yorkshire.

HUTSON. As Hudson.

HUTT. From residence in a hut—analogous to Cote.

HUTTON. Twenty-six parishes and townships in different counties bear this name.

HUXHAM. A place in Devonshire.

HUXLEY. A township in Cheshire.

HYDE. See Hide. "A hide (A-Sax. *hyd*) of land was about 120 acres ; also as much land as could be tilled with one plough, or would support one family ; a family possession." Bosworth. Sometimes a specific locality bears this name. Atte Hide. H.R.

HYDER. Under the feudal system, the tenant of a hide of land (see Hyde) was called a *hidarius*—whence Hyder. See Hale's St. Paul's Domesday, p. xxv. Sometimes it may be equivalent to Skinner.

HYKE. The same as Hick.

HYLTON. See Hilton.

HYNDMAN. See Hindman.

I.

IBBET. See Ilbert.

IBBETSON. The son of Ibbet or Ilbert. An ancient family in Yorkshire.

IBBOTSON. See Ilbert.

IBBS. See Ilbert.

IBERSON. See Ilbert.

IBISON. See Ilbert.

IBITT. See Ilbert.

IBSON. See Ilbert.

ICEMONGER. An ironmonger—from A-Sax. *isen*, iron, and monger.

IDDENDEN. See DEN.

IDE. Possibly Hide, with the initial letter suppressed. *Ide* was however an A-Sax., and is to this day a Frisian, proper name.

IDEN. A parish in Sussex.

IDESON. The son of Ide, which see.

IDLE. A chapelry in the parish of Calverley, co. York; also a river of Nottinghamshire.

IFE. The same as Ive.

IFILL. Perhaps a corruption of Ifield, co. Sussex.

IGGULDEN. IGGLESDEN. See DEN. In XIV. cent. documents it is spelt Iggulenden.

ILBERT. Though this baptismal appellation rarely appears as a surname in its proper form, it has given rise to the following:—Ibbet, Ibbitt, Iberson, Ibbetson, Ibbotson, Ibbs, Ibison, Ibson, &c.

ILBERY. Hilbury, a place in the hundred of Worrall, co. Chester.

ILDERTON. A parish in Northumberland.

ILES. Probably the same as L'Isle.

ILIFF. ILIFFE. Probably the same as Ayloff.

ILLINGWORTH. A chapelry in Yorkshire.

ILLMAN. The same as Hillman.

ILLYARD. The same as Hilliard.

ILOTT. The same as Aylott.

IMPEY. This name is, or has been, numerous in cos. Bucks, Surrey, and Essex, in which last county stands Impey Hall. See Morant's Essex.

INCE. Places in cos. Chester and Lancaster.

INCH. Several parishes and places in Scotland. *Inch* is a topographical expression signifying island. It has been derived from the British *ynys*, and the Gaelic *inis* —insula. "The word is said to occur with the same signification in some of the aboriginal languages of North America." Gaz. Scotl. But it sometimes denotes level ground contiguous to a river.

INCHBALD. The same as Inchbold.

INCHBOLD. Local; from *inch*, island, and *bold*, a dwelling: "the island home."

☞ **ING.** A very common termination of local surnames, for an explanation of which see Preliminary Dissertation. In Mr. Clark's "Surnames metrically Arranged and Classified," we have the following curious list with this termination, nearly every one of which, though of local origin, *looks* like the active participle of some well-known verb.

"Thus, then, we've Standing, Rising, Falling, Curling, Cupping, Cumming, Calling; Budding, Browning, Bedding, Baring, Watering, Weeding, Whiting, Waring; Codling, Culling, Ayling, Catching, Peeling, Paring, Painting, Patching; Stradling, Suckling, Swadling, Spending, Living, Loving, Larking, Lending; Fielding, Farming, Harrowing, Tilling, Bidding, Bending, Banning, Billing; Bowling, Ridding, Ranking, Running, Going, Laming, Keeping, Dunning;

Making, Marking, Manning, Moulding, Spilling, Sprawling, Schooling, Scolding; Heading, Harding, Hawking, Hopping, Shearing, Spearing, Chipping, Chopping; Riding, Walking, Fanning, Reading, Conning, Spiking, Shipping, Speeding; Hemming, Pulling, Holding, Cutting, Seeking, Tapping, Goring, Nutting; Twining, Pinching, Gambling, Hitching, Heeding, Learning, Picking, Twitching; Angling, Josling, Rounding, Skipping, Twilling, Topping, Tapping, Tipping."

INGE. Has been derived from the A-Sax. *ing*, a meadow. It is however far more probably a Scandinavian personal name. Inge, the son of Harald, was a distinguished king of Norway, in the XII. cent. Hence probably the local designation Ingham.

INGHAM. Parishes in cos. Lincoln, Norfolk, and Suffolk. See Inge.

INGILBY. There are several places in Yorkshire called Ingleby, and in that co., at Ripley Castle, the baronet's ancestors have been resident from the XIV. century. Courthope's Debrett.

INGLEDEW. The name of Angeltheow occurs in the genealogies of the Anglo-Saxon kings, as fourth in descent from Woden. See Sax. Chron. A.D. 626 and 755. "A Wodeno originem ducebat Angeltheawus." But I have not met with it elsewhere in Anglo-Saxon history. It is probable however that Ingledew, Engledue, and Engledow, as family names, are modern forms of it.

INGLIS. The old Scottish form of 'English,' formerly applied to the descendants of Englishmen settled in Scotland, especially of prisoners taken by Malcolm III. from the northern counties in 1070. For years after that date, we are told, English servants or slaves were to be found in every village, and almost in every house. Singularly enough, the baronet family, though of Scottish origin, deduce from William Inglis, who had, in 1395, a grant of lands and this surname from Robert III., for killing an Englishman on the borders— *Anglus ab Anglum occidendo;* truly as odd an origin as surname ever had !

INGOLD. INGALL. INGLE. A Scandinavian personal name, retained in the designations of Ingleby, Inglesham, Ingleton, Ingoldsthorpe, Ingoldsby, and other parishes and places, lying chiefly in what are called the Danish counties. The Domesday form is Ingaldus.

INGOLDBY. See Ingoldsby.

INGOLDSBY. A parish in Lincolnshire, of which, in 1230, Sir Roger de Ingoldsby, the founder of the family, was lord. Courthope's Debrett.

INGPEN. The same as Inkpen.

INGRAM. Latinized Ingelramus—an ancient personal name. It occurs in the various forms of Ingelram, Ingerham, &c.

There is also a parish in Northumberland called Ingram.

INGREY. Probably Ingrave, co. Essex.

INKPEN. A parish near Hungerford, co. Berks. "The manor was held at an early period, under the baronial family of Somery, by the Inkpens, who took their name from the village." Escheats Edw. I. and II. Lysons's Berkshire, p. 304.

INKSON. Ferguson derives it from a very early Teutonic name, Ingo, or Inge. See Inge.

INMAN. Inn-man, inn-keeper. Not perhaps equivalent to Taverner, but the person who had the charge of the "inn" or town-house of a nobleman.

INNES. An estate in the parish of Urquhart, co. Moray. The first possessor who assumed the name was Walter de Innes, who died in the reign of king Alexander II.

INNOCENT. A personal name, which has been borne by several Popes.

☞ **INSECTS and REPTILES.** Several surnames are identical in orthography with the names of Insects and Reptiles. We must again invoke the aid of Mr. Clark.

"The Beetle, Butterfly, and Bee,
The Emmet, Crickett, and the Flea;
The Moth, Mite, Maggot, and the Slugg,
The Grubb, Wasp, Spider, and the Bugg;
The Turtle, Frog, Blackadder, Leech,
With Newte and Worms—these all and each,
Together with the Summerbee,
Give many of the names we see."
Surnames Metrically Arranged, p. 30.

Of these, Butterfly, Wasp, Frog, and perhaps one or two others, may have been imposed as sobriquets; the rest are mostly traceable to other sources; for example, Beetle is Beadle or Bedel; Crickett is a place in Somersetshire; Maggott is a 'nursename' or diminutive of Margaret; Blackadder is corrupted from the name of a river; Leech is the Old English for surgeon; Bee is *by*, the Danish for a habitation, and Summerbee has relation neither to the season of flowers nor to the insect that gathers its stores from them, but is a corruption of Somerby, a local name.

INSKIP. A township in the parish of St. Michael, co. Lancaster, seven or eight miles from Preston.

INSOLL. May possibly be derived from the German *insel*, an island.

INVERARITY. A parish in Forfarshire.

INWARD. Qy.: inn-ward, the keeper of an inn? 'Inward' is however an archaism implying familiar, intimate; and to this day in Suffolk 'inward-maid' means a house-maid. Halliwell.

INWOOD. Intwood, a parish in Norfolk.

IPRES. Ypres, a town in Flanders. De Ipre. H.R.

IRBY. Places in cos. Cumberland Lincoln, and Chester.

IRELAND. A native of that country—an Irishman.

IREMONGER. Not a dealer in wrath, but a corruption of Ironmonger. Le Irmongere. H.R.

IRETON. A parish in Derbyshire, which belonged to the family temp. Richard Cœur-de-Lion. Henry, brother of Sewallis, lord of Eatington, co. Warwick, ancestor of the noble family of Shirley, had a son Fulcher de Ireton, lord of Ireton, direct ancestor of Henry Ireton, the son-in-law of Oliver Cromwell, whose father alienated Ireton in the reign of Elizabeth.

IRISH. A native of Ireland.

IRON. IRONS. Possibly from Airan, a village near Caen in Normandy.

IRONMAN. The name Isanman, which has the same meaning, is found in Germany in the IX. cent. Ferguson. See Isnard.

IRONMONGER. The trade. It is sometimes written Iremonger, and Isemonger or Icemonger. The latter form is from A-Sax. *isen*, iron.

IRONPURSE. Several individuals bore this surname in the reign of Edward I. Irenpurs, Irenpurse, &c. H.R.

IRONSIDE. A title of valour, well-known amongst us, from the days of the Saxon Edward, to those of Cromwell's 'Ironsides,' and since, whenever we speak of a robust person. Berry attributes five coats to this surname.

IRTON. "A family of very great antiquity, and resident at Irton, on the river Irt (co. Cumberland), from whence the name is derived, as early as the reign of Henry I." Shirley's Noble and Gentle Men. Samuel Irton, Esq., of Irton, still possesses the manor which was the fief of his ancestor more than seven centuries ago.

IRVINE. A parish and a river of Ayrshire. The family were of long standing in the S. and S.W. of Scotland, but the descendants of William de I., of Drum, co. Aberdeen, have been seated upon that estate ever since the days of king Robert Bruce, whose armour-bearer he was, and who gave him the lands. The name has been written Irwin, Irwyn, Irvin, &c., but Irving is a distinct name.

IRVING. An ancient parish in Dumfriesshire.

IRWIN. The Irish form of Irvine. The singular Christian name Crinus, which prevails in the family of I. of Tanragoe, co. Sligo, is traditionally derived from Krynin Abethnæ, the second husband of the mother of Duncan, King of Scotland.

ISAAC. This, as a baptismal name, was introduced about the time of the Conquest. One Isac appears as a chief tenant in Domesd. A few centuries later it was commonly 'nicked' to Hyke, Hicque, &c. Ultimately it gave rise to the various surnames of Isaacs, Isacke, Isaacson, Hike, Hick, Hicks, Hickes, Higgs, Higgins, Higginson, Hickson, Higson, Hixon, Hiscock, Hiscocks, Hickox, Hickie, and Hickey.

ISAACS. See Isaac.

ISAACSON. See Isaac.

ISACKE. See Isaac.

ISBELL. In H.R. Isabel. See Female Christian Names.

ISELTON. Properly Iseldon, the ancient name of Islington, near London.

ISHAM. A place in the hundred of Orlingbury, co. Northampton, where an elder branch of the existing family, Isham of Lamport, were seated soon after the Conquest. Shirley's Noble and Gentle Men.

ISLIP. Parishes in cos. Oxford and Northampton.

ISNARD. The name Isanhard occurs in the O. German of the VIII. cent. and means "iron-hard," or, as we should say, "as tough as iron."

ISON. See Ive.

ISRAEL. A common Jewish surname, from the personal designation.

ISTED. Probably of local English origin —Highstead, "the lofty situation." The family have, however, a tradition of a derivation "from Eysted, a large maritime town in the province of Schonen, in the kingdom of Sweden." It is conjectured that they settled at Framfield, co. Sussex, temp. Edward III. B.L.G.

ITCHINGFIELD. A parish in Sussex.

IVATTS. See Ive. A Joh. fil'Ivette is found in H.R.

IVE. This name with some variations of orthography seems to have existed in several countries. The town of St. Ives in Cornwall was designated after Iva, an Irish saint, and that of St. Ives in Huntingdonshire after St. Ivo, a Persian archbishop. Ive was also an A.-Sax. personal name, and Ivo was the Norman form. The surnames Ives, Iveson, Ivison, Ison, and perhaps Ivett and Ivatts, are derivatives.

IVERSON. The same as Iveson.

IVES. IVESON. See Ive. According to the 'Folks of Shields,' Ives or Iveson means Filius Judæi, son of the Jew. Filius Ivonis. H.R.

IVETT. See Ive and Ivatts.

IVIMEY. See under Ivy.

IVINS. IVENS. Corruptions of Evans.

IVISON. See Ive.

IVORY. "The family De Ivery were descended from Rodolph, half-brother to Richard the first, duke of Normandy, who for killing a monstrous boar, while hunting with the Duke, was rewarded with the castle of Ivery, on the river l'Evre, and

from thence entitled Comes de Iberio." Dunkin's Oxfordshire, i. 22. John de Ivery obtained the manor of Ambrosden, co. Oxon, in 1077, and Hugh de Ivri occurs as its lord in Domesday Book.

IVY. May be the same as Ive, or a derivative of it; but there was a favourite character in the old Christmas games called Ivy, whose antagonist was Holly; and the frolics of the *Holly-Boy* and the *Ivy-Girl* were maintained in Kent (but on St. Valentine's day) till towards the close of the eighteenth cent. Gent. Mag. 1779. See the song of the "Holly and Ivy" quoted in Hone's Mysteries, p. 94, where Ivy is made to be of the feminine gender:

"HOLY and his mery men, they dawnsyn and they syng;
 IVY and hur maydyns, they wepen and they wryng."

The singular name Ivymey, Ivimey, signifying *ivy-maiden*, Mr. Ferguson thinks may be from this source. The only difficulty is to account for such designations having become transmissible; but see Art. Female Christian Names, in this Dictionary. Ivyleaf may also belong to this class.

IVYLEAF. See under Ivy.

IVYMEY. See under Ivy.

IZARD. IZATT. IZOD. IZZARD. Of these names, probably of common origin, I can give no account. Burke, speaking of Izod of Chapel-Izod, says: "The name appears to be an old Irish one." B.L.G.

IZATSON. A corruption of Isaacson. See Eng. Surn., ii., 42.

JACK. A nickname which has, like many others, become a surname. With respect to this appellation, it is curious that meaning, as it originally did, *James*, from the French Jacques, and Latin Jacobus, it should have come to be considered as a synonym of *John*. It was usually applied in a contemptuous way, as in Jackanapes, Jackpudding, Jack-a-dandy, Jack-at-a-pinch, Jack-in-office, &c.

After writing the above, I met with the following passage, which rather militates against, though it does not disprove, my assertion, that Jack was originally Jacques or James, and not John. "I know not how it has happened, that in the principal modern languages, *John*, or its equivalent, is a name of contempt, or at least of slight. So the Italians use *Gianni*, from whence *Zani*; the Spaniards *Juan*, as *Bobo-Juan* or *foolish John*; the French *Jean*, with various additions; and in English when we call a man *a John*, we do not mean it as a title of honour. Chaucer uses *Jacke fool*, as the Spaniards do *Bobo Juan*; and I suppose *Jack-ass* has the same etymology." Tyrwhitt's Chaucer, note on v. 14,816. See in Thomson's Etymons, and Halliwell's Dict. a great number of uses to which the word Jack is applied.

JACKLIN. Fr. *Jacquelin*, a diminutive of James.

JACKMAN. A *jack* was a coat of mail, or rather a stout leather jerkin worn by soldiers, whence our diminutive, *jacket*. The wearer of such a garment would naturally be called a Jackman.

JACKS. The genitive form of Jack.

JACKSON. The son of John, or more properly of James (Jacques). See Jack. The Lond. Direct. has nearly 200 traders of this name.

JACOB. JACOBS. The first occurrence of this baptismal name in England, is I think in Domesday. It is now very common as a surname, especially in Jewish families.

JACOBSON. See Jacob.

JAFFRAY. The same as Geoffrey or Jeffery.

JAGGER. JAGGERS. A north-country word for a man who works draught horses for hire. Halliw.

JAGO. " As for the name Jago, whether it be derived from the Celtish-British Iago, and signifies James, or from *gago* or *jago*, a spear, or military tuck, I determine not, or from gages and pledges for battle ; however, this name was of ancient use in Britain ; for Galfridus Monmuthensis tells us of a king named Jago, before Julius Cæsar landed in Britain, that reigned twenty-five years, and lies buried at York." Hals, in Davies Gilbert's Cornwall, i., 397. The derivation from Iago, James (rather Spanish, however, than Celtic), is probably the correct one.

JAKEMAN. See Jackman.

JAMES. The first appearance of this Christian name in our annals is in Domesday. It afterwards became a common surname, besides giving rise to Jameson, Jamieson, Jempson, Jemmett. and probably through its French form, Jacques, to Jeakes, Jacklin, and the widely-spread Jackson ; though John, through its accepted nickname Jack, may have an equal claim to that familiar patronymic.

The baronets of this family, extinct in 1741, originally bore the name of Hæstrecht, the designation of their ancient lordship near Utrecht, in Holland. Roger son of Jacob van Hæstrecht came hither in the reign of Henry VIII., and being known after the Dutch manner by the name of Roger *Jacob*, that name finally settled into its equivalent *James*, and he and his posterity were afterwards always so called. See Burke's Ext. Barts.

A very ancient family of James of Pantsaison, co. Pembroke, have a tradition that that estate was owned by thirteen William Jameses in succession. B.L.G.

JAMESON. See James.

JAMIESON. The Scottish form of Jameson.

JANE. See FEMALE CHRISTIAN NAMES. It may, however, be a corruption of the Fr. Jean, John.

JANES. See John.

JANEWAY. JANNAWAY. A Genoese. See curious anecdote in Eng. Surn., i., 53.

JANNINGS. A more correct spelling than Jennings. See John.

JANSON. See John, and Janssen.

JANSSEN. Originally from Guelderland. The head of the family was the Baron de Heez, one of the Protestant leaders against the Inquisition and the tyranny of the Duke of Alva ; he unfortunately fell into the hands of the Duke of Parma, and lost his estate and his life. On the dispersion of his family, his youngest son took refuge in France, and settled at Angoulême, where he lived to a very advanced age, leaving "a great estate and a numerous issue." His grandson, Theodore Janssen, removed into England in 1680, and was subsequently created a baronet by George I.

JARDYNE. See Gardyne.

JARMAN. 1. Possibly a broad pronunciation of German. 2. A maker of jars and large coarse pottery.

JARRARD. A broad mispronunciation of Gerard.

JARRATT. JARRETT. JARRITT. Corruptions of Gerard or Gerald.

JARROLD. A mispronunciation of Gerald.

JARVIE. The same as Jervis or Jarvis.

JARVIS. A broad pronunciation of Gervase.

JASON. Albeit the baronet family of this name (extinct in 1738) bore in their arms " a golden fleece," I do not think they ever proved their pedigree from the leader of the Argonautæ. It is far more probable that they were only Jamesons with the omission of a couple of letters.

JAY. JAYE. A township united with Heath, in the parish of Leintwardine, co. Hereford.

JAYNE. See Jane.

JEACOCK. Probably a diminutive of James. Jeakins seems to be of the same origin, and both proceed from " Jeams," the rustic pronunciation of the name.

JEAFFRESON. See Jeffery.

JEAKE. JEAKES. See James.

JEANES. JEANS. Probably from the Fr. *Jean*, John.

JEARRAD. A corruption of Gerard.

JEBB. Apparently an old personal name, whence the patronymic Jebson.

JEBSON. See Jebb.

JEFF. JEFFS. See Jeffery.

JEFFCOCK. See Jeffery.

JEFFERIES. See Jeffery.

JEFFRIES. See Jeffery.

JEFFERSON. See Jeffery.

JEFFERY. JEFFERAY. The Teutonic personal name Godfridus, whence also Godfrey. In Domesday the ordinary form is Goisfridus. From it we get the modifications and derivatives, Jefferson, Jeaffreson, Jeffries, Jefferies, Jefferiss, Jeff, Jeffs, Jephson, Jepson, Jeffcock, Jefkins, with minor variations of spelling too numerous for insertion.

JEFFRISS. See Jeffery.

JEFKINS. See Jeffery.

JEGGINS. A corruption of Jenkins.

JELL. The same as Gell.

JELLICOE. Förstmann finds the personal name Geliko, Jeliko, in the O. German of the X. cent. Ferguson.

JELLIFF. The same as Joliffe.

JELLY. In the Scottish dialect *jelly* means worthy, upright. Jamieson.

JEMMETT. A diminutive of Jem or James.

JEMPSON. See James.

JENDEN. See termination DEN.

JENKINS. See John.

JENKINSON. See John.

JENKS. See John.

JENNER. Pott, in his "Die Personennamen insbesondere die Familiennamen," (Leipzig, 1853), considers this name a corruption of the classical Januarius; but I think the medieval *ginour*, a craftsman, engineer, or clever workman, a much likelier origin—a man of genius (*ingenii*) in any mechanical business. Waldinus Ingeniator (the engineer) occurs in the Domesday of Lincolnshire, as a tenant in chief.

JENNEY. The family of Jenney of Bredfield, co. Suffolk, "are supposed to be of French extraction, and the name to be derived from Guisnes near Calais. The first in the pedigree is Edward Jenney, grandfather of John Jenney, who died in 1460." Shirley's Noble and Gentle Men. "The name of this family was originally spelt Gyney." B.L.G.

JENNINGS. See John.

JENNISON. The son of Jane? See FEMALE CHRISTIAN NAMES. This family have acquired, in co. Durham, the character of the JEALOUS JENNISONS. Denham.

JENOURE. The same as Jenner.

JENSON. See John.

JEPHSON. From Geoffrey or Jeffery.

JEPSON. See Jeffery.

JERDAN. JERDEIN. See Gardyne.

JEREMY. The O. Eng. form of Jeremiah.

JERKIN. A diminutive of Jeremiah.

JERMAIN. The same as Germain and German.

JERMAN. A mis-spelling of German.

JERMY. Jeremy, Jeremiah.

JERMYN. JERMIN. The same as Germaine.

JERNEGAN. An old personal name of Norman introduction.

JERNINGHAM. Lord Stafford's ancestors wrote themselves Jernegan till the XVI. cent., when the name was corrupted to Jerningham. "The first that I meet with of this family was called Hugh, without any other addition, whose son was named Jernegan Fitz-Hugh, or the son of Hugh; he is mentioned in the Castle-Acre priory register, and he died about 1182." Kimber's Baronetage. His successors took the baptismal name Jernegan as their surname, and continued to use it until the period above-named.

JEROME. JEROM. The personal name.

JERRAD. See Gerard.

JERRAM. A corruption of Jerome.

JERRARD. The same as Gerard.

JERISON. May be either the same as Gerison, or the son of Jerry, that is Jeremiah.

JERROLD. A mis-spelling of Gerald.

JERVIS. The personal name Gervase, Gervasius.

JERVOISE. The same as Jervis.

JESSE. JESSEY. The personal name.

JESSON. Jesse's son.

JESSOP. From the Italian Giuseppe, Joseph?

JEUNE. Fr. "The young."

JEVINGTON. A parish in Sussex.

JEW. Doubtless from the nation of the primitive bearer.

JEWELL. Probably a corruption of the Fr. Jules, Julius.

JEWSBURY. Perhaps a corruption of Dewsbury.

JEWSON. The son of a Jew.

JEWSTER. *Jouster* has two widely different meanings: 1. One who takes part in a tournament; and 2. A retailer of fish. Cornwall.

JEX. Probably from Jacques, Fr. James.

JIFKINS. Probably a diminutive of Geoffrey, or of Joseph.

JINKINS. See Jenkins.

JINKS. An abbreviation of Jenkins, which see.

JOACHIM. The personal name.

JOANES. See John.

JOB. The personal name, whence also Jobson.

JOBBINS. Perhaps a diminutive of Job.

JOBLINGS. Probably a corruption of Jublains, a town in the department of Mayenne in France.

JOBSON. See Job.

JOCELYN. Lord Roden's family are "of Norman origin, said to have come into England with William the Conqueror, and to have been seated at Sempringham, co. Lincoln, by the grant of that monarch." Shirley's Noble and Gentle Men.

JODRELL. The family are traced to the Peak of Derbyshire in the year 1286, and there till the latter end of the XVIII. cent. the elder line continued. William Jauderell, the head of the family, temp. Edward III., served under the Black Prince in the wars with France.

JOEL. The personal name, common among the Jews.

JOHN. This baptismal name, which is of Norman introduction, has rarely passed into a surname. The Lond. Direct. for 1852 affords but one instance. It has been, however, the source, in various modified forms, of a considerable number of names, some of which are amongst the most common in the whole circle of our nomenclature. Its immediate derivative, Johnson, and its Welsh genitive form, Jones, substantiate this assertion; but we have besides Johns, Johnes, Joanes, Johncock, Janson, Jannings, Jennings, Jenks, Jenkyn, Jenkins, and Jinkins, Jenkinson, and perhaps Janes and Jenson. The Flemish nickname Hans from Johannes, seems to be the root of Hanson, Hancock, &c. Jack and Jackson might seem to claim the same parentage, but I think there is more reason for affiliating them upon James (See Jack).

☞ **JOHN.** A termination of several surnames, as

     Littlejohn,
     Micklejohn,
     Upjohn,
     Prettyjohn,
     Applejohn,
     Properjohn, and
     Brownjohn.

Some of these, as Upjohn and Applejohn, may be corruptions—the rest seem to be significant and descriptive. (Eng. Surn. i. 174.) John is a personal name so common throughout Christendom that some prefix by way of epithet seems occasionally to have been necessary, in order to distinguish between two or more persons bearing it; thus the French have their *Grosjeans,* 'big or fat Johns;' the Dutch their *Grootjans,* or 'bulky Johns;' the Italians their *Giovanizzi,* or 'handsome large Johns;' the Highlanders their *Mac-Fadyeans,* the sons of 'long John,'

as also their *Mac-Ivors* or sons of 'big John';' and the Lowland Scotch their *Mickejohns* or 'large stout Johns.'

In the H.R. we have one Duraund *le Bon Johan*—' Durrant the Good-John!'

JOHNCOCK. See John.

JOHNES. See John.

JOHNS. See John.

JOHNSON. See John. The Johnsons of Ayscough-Fee, co. Lincoln, claim from the house of Fitz-John of Normandy. Guillim's Display of Heraldry.

JOHNSTON. JOHNSTONE. Post-towns and parishes in Dumfriesshire and Renfrewshire. For a local surname this is exceedingly common, there being between sixty and seventy traders bearing it in Lond. Direct. It is often confounded with Johnson.

JOICE. See Joyce.

JOLIFFE. O. Eng. *jolif,* Fr. *joli,* which Cotgrave defines as "jollie, gay, trim, fine, gallant, neat, handsome, well-fashioned—also livelie, merrie, buxome, jocund."

JOLL. A nicked form of Jolland. Camd.

JOLLAND. JOLLANDS. Camden says that Jollan is a corruption of Julian. In the H.R. the forms of the name are Fil'-Jolani, Fil'Jollani, Jollayn, and Jolleyn.

JOLLEY. See Jolliffe.

JOLLY. JOLLIE. The same as Joliffe.

JONAS. The personal name.

JONES. A genitive form of John, through Johnes, common everywhere in England, but superabundant in Wales. Next to John Smith, John Jones is probably the most common combination of names in Britain. As the Registrar-general well observes, "the name of John Jones is in Wales a perpetual incognito, and being proclaimed at the cross of a market-town would indicate no one in particular." From the able Report of the same functionary (XVI. 1856) we learn that Jones is, for numerousness, second only to Smith; for while within a given period the number of Smiths registered throughout England, as born, married, or dead, amounted to 33,557, the Joneses in like circumstances were 33,341—a singularly close approximation. Old Daniel Fenning, the author of the immortal phrase, "Smith, Jones, Brown, and Robinson," was therefore quite right as to the order of precedence of the first two names, though the Reg. Gen. puts Brown sixth, and Robinson eleventh, on the roll of common surnames. The existing number of Joneses is estimated at 51,000 families, or about a quarter of a million of individuals. XVI. Report, p. xxii.

The commonness of some surnames, especially the Welsh, renders the bearers of them, though of good family, undistinguishable from the *ignobile vulgus.* Mr.

Edwards may be of as ancient blood as Mr. Neville, and high-sounding Mr. St. John is after all inferior in antiquity to plain Mr. Jones. For example—

JONES of Llanerchrugog Hall, Denbighshire, descends in a direct line from Gwaithvoed, lord of Cardigan and Gwent, A.D. 921, and represents one of the Fifteen Noble Tribes of North Wales.

JONES of Trewythen, co. Montgomery, derives from Cadwgan, lord of Nannau, son of Bleddyn ap Cynfyn, King of Powys.

JONES of Hartsheath, co. Flint, claims from Cowryd ap Cadvan, a chieftain of Dyffryn Clwyd in Denbighland. B.L.G.

JONSON. The same as Johnson.

JORDAN. JORDEN. Not, as has been fancifully conjectured, from the river Jordan, in Crusading times, but from Jourdain, an early Norman baptismal name, probably corrupted from the Lat. Hodiernus, which was a not uncommon personal name of the same period. It may be remarked that the names Jourdain and Hodierna, the feminine form, occur almost contemporaneously in the pedigree of Sackville. Marin's Dutch Dict. defines Jorden as Gregory, "een man's naam, Gregoire, nom d' homme."

"The family of Jordan is of Anglo-Norman origin. The first settler in Wales was Jordan de Cantington, one of the companions of Martin de Tours, in his conquest of Kemmes, temp. William I." B.L.G.

JORDESON. The son of Jordan, which see.

JOSELIN. See Joslin.

JOSEPH. JOSEPHS. The personal name. A common surname among the Jews, but not confined to that nation.

JOSKYN. A diminutive of Joseph.

JOSLIN. JOSLING. JOSLAND. Corruptions of the personal name Joscelyne.

JOURDAN. JOURDAIN. See Jordan.

JOY. Probably from one of the several places in Normandy called Jouy; or perhaps a contraction of Joyce.

JOYCE. O. Fr. joyeux, cheerful, hilarious; answering to Gay, Merry, Lively, &c.

JOYNSON. A corruption of Johnson.

JUBB. Perhaps a corruption of Job.

JUDD. Possibly Jude, the Christian name. The Dutch Jode, a Jew, also suggests itself; and if this be so, Judson must be equivalent to "Jew's son," Judkin to "the little Jew," &c.

JUDE. This now unusual Christian name was more common in old times, and possibly gave rise to Judd, Judkin, and Judson.

JUDGE. This surname can hardly have been borrowed from the office, because in this country judges have always been persons of dignity and consideration. It may

have been either a sobriquet, or a name given to an umpire in some medieval game.

JUDKINS. See Judd.

JUDSON. 1. See Jude. 2. See Judd. Most of the Judsons, both in England and America, trace their origin to the neighbourhood of Leeds, and the surname is still common in Yorkshire.

JUGG. Perhaps the sign of an inn.

JUGLER. Does not imply either a shuffling, dishonest person, or one skilled in the arts of legerdemain. It is the medieval jougelour, a minstrel, one who could play or sing, or both. It is true, however, that this person often combined both professions, namely, legerdemain and music. Hence Chaucer's expression—"Minstrales and eke jougelours that well to sing did her paine."

JULER. Perhaps a jeweller.

JULEUS. A mis-spelling of Julius.

JULIAN. JULIANS. The personal name.

JULIUS. The personal name.

JUMPER. The first Mr. Jumper would appear to have derived his name not from his saltatory skill, but from his having been a maker of jumps, a kind of short leather coat or boddice, formerly worn by women. See Bailey and Halliwell. Jumper is also a northern provincialism for a miner's boring tool, and may have been metaphorically applied to the miner himself.

JUPP. A nurse-name of Joseph.

JURDAN. See Jordan.

JURY. In the middle ages, when the Jews were a much-persecuted race, they resided partly by compulsion, partly by choice, in a particular quarter of our old towns and cities. Such a locality was usually called the Jewry, as the Old Jewry, in London. "Jewerie, a district inhabited by Jews." Halliw.

JUST. From probity of character; or more probably from an ancient personal name. Saint Just gives name to a Cornish parish.

JUSTICE. A magistrate; probably applied as a sobriquet. Justice was, however, personified in the old miracle plays. See particularly Hone's Anc. Mysteries, p. 38. et seq. It is remarkable that while we have several Le Justices in the H.R. we find one lady called Iva la Justice. Qu. was she a "miracle" actress?

JUSTINS. A genitive form of Justin, the personal name.

JUTSOM. JUTSUM. See Jutson.

JUTSON. Probably a corruption of Judson; though Ferguson thinks that, together with Jutting and Jutsom, it relates to a Jutish extraction.

JUTTING. See Jutson.

K.

KAIMES. 1. The same as Camoys. 2. Scot. *kaim*, a low ridge, an earthwork or camp, like the *Antiquary's* "kaims of Kinprunes."

KAIN. The same as Kane. The town of Caen in Normandy was sometimes so written in English records.

KAINES. The same as Keynes.

KAIRNS. See Cairn.

KALLANDER. The same as Callander.

KALLOWAY. The same as Callaway.

KANE. See O'Cahan.

KARBY. A corruption of Kirby.

KARR. The same as Carr.

KAVANAGH. The family claim descent from ancestors who were of old monarchs of all Ireland, and who at the invasion of Henry II. were kings of Leinster. They bore the surname of Mac-Murrough; but in 1171 Donell, son of Dermot Mac-Murrough, acquired that of Caomhanach or Cavanagh, which became hereditary. Donell's sister Eva married Strongbow, Earl of Pembroke, the leader of the English expedition.

KAYE. KAY. "The family of Kaye," says an old statement, "is of great antiquity in the county of York, being descended from *Sir Kaye, an ancient Briton, and one of the Knights of the warlike Table of that noble Prince Arthur, flower of chivalry ! !*" It is added that his descendant at the period of the "Norman Duke that made Conquest of England, was Sir John Kaye, Knight, who married the daughter and heir of Sir John Woodesham, of Woodesham, Knight, AN ANCIENT BRITON ! !" Not to speculate upon the age in round centuries that Miss Woodesham must have been at the time of her nuptials, we may ask, where is the proof of a De Woodesham or a De *anything* in England "before the time of the Conquest," when this match is alleged to have taken place? The truth seems to be, that at Woodsome in Yorkshire there resided in very early times a family of Kay, Keay, or Kaye, the head of which, some centuries later was created a baronet by Charles I. The patent expired in 1810, but was revived shortly afterwards in favour of the reputed son of the fifth baronet. The name may be a modification of Caius or some other personal designation.

Dr. John Caius or Kaye advanced Gonville Hall, Cambridge, to the dignity of a college in 1557, and that house is still called indifferently Caius' or Key's. He had a contemporary, Dr. Thomas Kay or Caius, who was master of University Coll. Oxon.

KEAL. East and West Keele, parishes in Lincolnshire.

KEALY. The same as Keeley.

KEAN. 1. See Keen. In the H.R. it is Kene, without prefix. 2. Keyne, a parish in Cornwall.

KEARSLEY. A township in Lancashire.

KEASLEY. Probably the same as Kearsley.

KEATE. KEATS. An old Cornish family bore the former name, as also did the extinct baronets of the Hoo in Hertfordshire. Hals, the Cornish topographer, gives this very uncomplimentary derivation of the name: "*Keate, ceate*, in British is fallacy, cheat, or delusion."

KEAY. See Kay.

KEBBLE. See Kibble.

KEBLE. See Kibble.

KEEBLE. See Kibble.

KEEL. Keele, a parish in co. Stafford.

KEELEY. Probably Keighley, co. York.

KEELTY. KIELTY. From the ancient personal name Caoilte, borne by one of the heroes of Ossian. Ulster. Journ. of Archæol. No. 2.

KEEN. KEENE. Perhaps sometimes from sharpness of disposition; but sometimes probably the Irish O'Kean, sans O'. Both Kene and Le Kene occur in H.R.

KEEP. Perhaps from residence at the "keep," or domestic department of a castle. If I may be allowed a little self-plagiarism here, I will extract from my "Contributions to Literature" (Lond. 1854. p. 279), the following passage :—

"Why is the strongest part of a castle called a *Keep?* This question has often suggested itself to me when viewing old baronial fortresses. The common notion seems to be, that the name originated in the fact that prisoners were *kept* there. The French equivalent is *Donjon*, whence may come our word "dungeon," and this may have suggested that etymology. I do not doubt that the baron who had a prisoner of mark would place him within the strongest walls which his feudal abode could supply. But for obvious reasons he would locate himself and his family there also. Now in our eastern and several other provincial dialects, the more usual sitting-room of a family is still called the "keeping-room." I think, therefore, the keep, or principal part of a castle was so called because the lord and his domestic circle *kept*, abode, or lived there. Shakspeare uses the word "keep" in the sense of to dwell, or reside :—

"And sometimes where earth-delving conies *keep*."
Venus and Adonis.

And again:
"And held in idle price to haunt assemblies,
Where youth, and cost, and witless bravery *keeps*."
Measure for Measure.

KEER. See Keir.

KEETE. See Keate.

KEEVIL. A parish in Wiltshire.

KEIGHLEY. A town and parish in Yorkshire.

KEIGWIN. An ancient Cornish family. Mr. Dixon derives the surname from Welsh and Cornish roots signifying White Dog, and the three greyhounds argent in the arms seem to allude to this derivation.

KEIR. A parish in Dumfriesshire.

KEITH. Several parishes and places in Scotland bear this name, which seems to be a Celtic descriptive term (*Caeth*) signifying 'confined or narrow.' The place from which the ancient family of Keith, hereditary Earls-Marshal of Scotland from 1010, derive their surname, is in the parish of Humbie, at the south-western extremity of Haddingtonshire. The district is still known as Keith-Marshall, though the estate has long passed away from the family. This is a sufficient origin of both name and family to satisfy ordinary curiosity, but the inventive genius of Scottish genealogists goes much further.

We have Camden's testimony that "some Scottish men think their surnames as ancient as the moone;" but the Earl-Marshal of Scotland, who from the nature of his office should be well-acquainted with these matters, was far more modest, and went back no further than just beyond the Christian era, a thousand years or so earlier than the commencement of any authenticated royal pedigree in Europe. The whole genealogy must be rich beyond expression, since the mere skeleton of it informs us—
1. That the Chatti, or Catti, a tribe of Germans, occupied the district now known as Hesse-Cassel from times of remote antiquity.
2. That about a century before the Christian era a part of this German tribe descended the Rhine and settled in Batavia, now Holland, where many places beginning with *Cat* mark their colonization.
3. That during the reign of Corbred II. of Scotland (a mythic king) about A.D. 76, a detachment of the Germano-Hollandic Catti emigrated to Britain, and landed at *Catness*, now corrupted (!) to *Caith*ness, that is to say, "the promontory of the Catti."
4. That about eight hundred years later, these immigrants turn up as the Clan Chattan, A.D. 831—834.
5. That, later still, these Catti called themselves Kethi, Keths, or Keiths, and that Robert, chief of the Clan Chattan, was created Hereditary Grand-Marshal of Scotland by King Malcolm II. A.D. 1010. This monarch gave him lands in the South of Scotland, *which he called after his own name!*
Risum teneatis amici?

KEKEWICH. This family, long resident in Cornwall and Devonshire, are said to have been of Lancashire origin. There is a township in Cheshire called Kekwick, from which the name was probably borrowed.

KELHAM. A Norman family, who derive their name from Kelham, near Newark-upon-Trent, co. Nottingham, where they were seated at an early period. They still bear in their arms three covered cups, in allusion to the office of cup-bearer to Alan, earl of Richmond, the Conqueror's son-in-law, which was held by their ancestor. B.L.G.

KELKE. The estate of Kelke, co. Lincoln, was owned by a family so designated from it. Berry's Encyc. Herald. There are also two townships in Yorkshire called Kelk.

KELL. 1. Formerly written Cail, and said by the family to be derived from Cailly in Normandy. See Cailey. In modern times some Christianized Jews have changed their names from Ezekiel to Kell.

2. A nickname of Charles—Carl, Karl, Kell. Hence the derivatives Kelson, and Kellie.

KELLAWAY. KELLEWAY. A parish in Wiltshire.

KELLETT. Kellet, two townships in Lancashire.

KELLY. KELLEY. The Kelleys were in old times resident in the parish of that name in Devonshire, and the Irish Kellys, now very numerous, bear the same arms. According to the genealogy in B.L.G., the Kellys of Kelly "may look back beyond the Conquest and derive themselves from the ancient Britons!" Mr. Shirley says: "Kelly is a manor in the hundred of Lifton, about six miles from Tavistock. The manor and advowson have been in the family at least from the time of Henry II. and here they have uninterruptedly resided since that very early period." Noble and Gentle Men, p. 59. The similar name Kellie is a diminutive of Charles. See Kell.

KELLOW. Kelloe, a parish in co. Durham.

KELSEY. North and South Kelsey are parishes in co. Lincoln.

KELSO. A town and parish in Roxburghshire. The family were in Ayrshire at an early period. Hugh de Kelso is mentioned in Ragman Roll, 1296. B.L.G.

KELSON. The son of Kell, i.e. Charles.

KEMBALL. The same as Kemble.

KEMBER. Identical with either Kemper or Kimber.

KEMBLE. A parish in co. Wilts. It has been erroneously considered a narrowed pronunciation of Campbell.

KEMEYS. The baronets, created 1642, extinct 1735, claimed to be of the old

Norman baronial house of Camois, which claim if not proven is highly probable. The family were early settlers in Wales, where "as lords of *Camaes* and St. Dogmaels in Pembrokeshire they exercised authority little short of regal." Burke's Ext. Barts.

KEMMISH. A corruption of Kemyss.

KEMP. KEMPE. Jamieson's definition is—"1. A champion. *Douglas.* 2. Sometimes it includes the idea of strength and uncommon size. *Bannatyne Poems.* 3. The champion of a party in controversy. *Winyet.*—A-Sax. *cempa,* miles ; Suedo-Gothic *kœmpe,* athleta; Danish, *kempe,* a giant; Islandic, miles robustus." In Scotland, the verb *to kemp* means to strive in whatever way, especially in the harvest-field ; a *kemper* is a reaper who tries to outdo another in the amount of his labour; and such a contest is known as a *kempin.* In the A-Sax. translation of the Gospels made about the year 1000, the word which in the Vulgate is *miles,* and in our version "soldier," is rendered *cempa.* *Kempes,* *kemperye-men* are words employed for fighting men, in the ballad of King Estmere in Percy's Reliques. Hence it appears that Kemp and Campion are closely allied, if not identical.

KEMPER. 1. A combatant. See Kemp. 2. A wool-comber.

KEMPSON. The son of a Kemp. See Kemp. This is one of the few surnames in which "son" is affixed to names of occupation, profession, or dignity. Smithson, Wrightson, Clarkson, and Dukeson are other examples.

KEMSTER. A wool comber. See termination STER.

KEMPTHORNE. The family name (which was originally Ley) was derived from an estate so called in the parish of Beer-Ferris, co. Devon. C. S. Gilbert's Cornwall.

KEMPTON. Perhaps Kempston, parishes in Norfolk and Bedfordshire.

KEMYSS. See Kemeys.

KENCLARKE. See Clarke.

KENDALL. Kent-dale, the valley of the Kent, a river of Westmoreland. The true name of the town known as Kendal is Kirkby-in-Kendale.

The Kendalls of Cornwall, long and still resident at Pelyn, were formerly of Treworgy in that county, but there does not seem to be any proof of their derivation from Westmoreland. It has been remarked of this family, that they have perhaps sent more representatives to the British Senate than any other in the United Kingdom. C. S. Gilbert's Cornwall. Shirley's Noble and Gentle Men.

KENDLE. See Kendall.

KENDRICK. See Kenrick.

KENEL. KENELL. Probably the

French surname Quesnel, an archaism for the oak-tree.

KENISTON. The same as Kynaston.

KENN. Parishes in cos. Devon and Somerset.

KENNARD. The same as Kenward, which is usually so pronounced.

KENNAWAY. 1. Probably the same as Kenewi or Kenewy, which occurs in H.R. both as a personal appellation and as a surname. 2. Kennoway, a parish in Fifeshire.

KENNAY. See Kenny.

KENNEDY. Celtic. *Cean-na-tighe,* meaning, it is said, the head of a sept or clan. The family descend from the ancient earls of Carrick in Ayrshire, and seem to have changed their name from Carrick to Kennedy in the XIV. cent. The chief was K. of Dunure, afterwards Earl of Cassilis (now Marquis of Ailsa). In the XVI. cent. the power of this great house in the shires of Ayr and Galloway was set forth in a popular rhyme :—

> " By Wigton and the town of Ayr,
> Port Patrick and the Cruives o'Cree,
> Nae man need think for to bide there,
> Unless he court wi' Kennedie."

KENNET. 1. The river Kennet in Berkshire. 2. The Scottish baptismal name Keneth. Its latinization is Cunetius.

KENNEY. The Kenneys, who settled in Ireland temp. Edw. IV. A.D. 1472, were of high antiquity in Somersetshire, deriving their name from Kenne in that county. So early as 12 Henry II., John de Kenne held two knight's fees in Kenne. The name has been variously spelt Kenne, Kenei, Kenny, and Kenney. B.L.G. (Kenny of Kilclogher.) But another family, Kenny of Ballinrobe, claim to be of Huguenot extraction, and to have gone from France into Ireland about the year 1660.

KENNINGTON. Parishes and places in Surrey, Kent, and Berkshire.

KENNY. Ferguson thinks that this corresponds with the Old Friesic *kenig,* a king. But see Kenney.

KENRICK. The family of Kenrick of Nantclwyd Woore, co. Denbigh, claim from David Kenrick who fought under the Black Prince at Creci and Poictiers. The name is clearly the A-Sax. baptismal Cynric, or as it is written in Domesd. Kenricus and Kenric.

KENSELL. Probably from Kensal Green, a hamlet in Middlesex.

KENSETT. KENSIT. A modification of Mackenzie.

KENSINGTON. A parish in Middlesex.

KENT. See Counties, Names of.

KENTISH. A native of Kent—cognate with Cornish, Devenish, &c.

KENTON. Parishes, &c., in cos. Somerset, Suffolk, Northumberland, and Devon.

KENWARD. An ancient personal name. One Kenewardus, or Keneward, mentioned in Domesd., was a Thane of Edward the Confessor, co. Gloucester. The name may have been originally derived from A-Sax. *cuna*, cows, and *weard*, a keeper.

KENYON. Lord Kenyon's family are descended from the Kenyons of Peele, co. Lancaster, and their surname is doubtless derived from the township of Kenyon in that shire.

KEOGH. A contraction of the Irish surname Mac Eochy, or Eochaid. The family claim descent from Fergus, king of Ulster, and from Roderick the Great, king of all Ireland.

KEPP. A hamlet in Perthshire.

KEPPELL. The ancestor of Lord Albemarle was Arnold-Joost van Keppel, lord of Voerst, a descendant of one of the most ancient houses in Guelderland, who accompanied King William III. to England in 1688, and was by him advanced to the title still enjoyed by the family. According to "Folks of Shields," the name is equivalent to De Capella.

KEPPOCH. An estate in Dumbartonshire.

KERBY. See Kirby.

KERDESTON. Kerdiston, a parish in Norfolk, which gave name to the Barons Kerdeston. The family is traced to Roger de K., temp. King John. Ext. Peerage.

KERN. 1. Scot. *kerne*, a foot-soldier armed with a dart or a dagger. 2. A beggar. Jamieson.

KERNOT. This name is found in Brittany, from whence it was probably imported into England after the Rev. of the Edict of Nantes.

KERR. KER. See Carr.

KERRELL. See Kyrle and Caryll.

KERRICH. This name occurs in the records of Dunwich, co. Suffolk, in 1299. B.L.G.

KERRY. KERREY. A parish in co. Montgomery.

KERSEY. A parish in Suffolk.

KERSWELL. "Kerswell of Kerswell is noticed by Norden, as being one of the principal houses of his day, but we have not been able to ascertain in what part of the county Kerswell was situated." C. S. Gilbert's Cornwall.

KERWIN. The same as Curwen, which see.

KESTELL. This family are known to have been resident at Kestell, in the parish of Egloshayle, co. Cornwall, from the time of King John till about the year 1737. C. S. Gilbert's Cornwall.

KESTEN. A contraction of Kesteven, co. Lincoln, or a mis-spelling of Keston, co. Kent.

KESTEVEN. A division of Lincolnshire.

KETLEY. A township in Shropshire.

KETT. See Catt.

KETTLE. 1. A parish in Fifeshire. 2. The personal name Chetell occurring in Domesday; in H.R. Ketel, Ketyl.

KETTLEWELL. A parish in Yorkshire.

KEVIN. Irish *cœmhgin*, "the beautiful offspring." O'Donovan, in Irish Penny Journ., p. 327.

KEY. KEYES. KEYS. The same as Kay, which see.

KEYMER. A parish in Sussex.

KEYNES. See under Cheney.

KEYNTON. Perhaps Keynston, a parish in co. Dorset.

KEYSER. German, *kaiser*, an emperor, a Cæsar. This name must be an importation from Germany, where it was probably first applied as a sobriquet. See Lempriere.

KEYT. The same as Keate.

KEYWORTH. A parish in Nottinghamshire.

KIBBLE. KIBBEL. Evidently an old personal name, whence the names of the localities Kibblestone, Kibblesworth, Kibblethwaite, &c.

KIBBLER. In the West of England *kibbles* is a name given to pieces of firewood, and a *kibbling-axe* is an axe used for cutting them; hence a Kibbler is a preparer of firewood, still a common trade in many places. In Bedfordshire, however, *to kibble* means to walk lamely (Halliwell), and so the surname may signify a cripple.

KIBBLEWHITE. A corruption of Kibblethwaite, a local name.

KIDD. KID. The young of a goat—analogous to Lamb, Colt, &c.

KIDDELL. KIDDLE. Kiddel, a township co. York.

KIDDER. One who travels with goods for sale. "A huckster who carries corn, victuals, &c., up and down to sell." Bailey. The Gothic *kyta* signifies to deal or hawk. Most if not all the Kidders of England spring from Maresfield, co. Sussex, where they may be traced back as far as the reign of Edward II. Sussex Archæolog. Collections. IX. 127.

KIDDERMINSTER. The town in Worcestershire.

KIDMAN. Probably the same as Kidder.

KIFFIN. See Kyffin.

☞ **KIL**—a syllable occurring in many Scottish local names, is the Celtic equivalent of *cell*—'cella religionis,' indicating the abode of some saint in the early days of British Christianity. Hence several family names, which taken in a secondary sense—*au pied de la lettre*—have a very curious, not to say startling, appearance. What a murderous climax, for instance, appears in the five names : Kilboy, Kilman, Kilmaster, Kilbride, Kilmany !

The O. E. *culle* signifying kill, necare, is found in several medieval but now extinct surnames, as Cullebulloc, Cullehare, Cullehog, &c.   H.R.

KILBURN. A hamlet in the parish of St. John, Hampstead, co. Middlesex, and a parish in Yorkshire.

KILBY. KILLBY. A parish in co. Leicester.

KILHAM. KILLHAM. A township in Northumberland, and a parish in Yorkshire.

KILLBEE. KILBEY. See Kilby. I may remark that many local names terminating in BY, are corrupted in the North to BEE.

KILLBOURN. See Kilburn.

KILLICK. Perhaps Kilnwick, co. York. Many provincial dialects drop the final N of Kiln; and the W in the termination '-wick ' and '-wich ' is usually suppressed, as in War(w)ick, Nor(w)ich. The northeastern border of East Sussex has long been a great habitat of the name.

2. The personal name Calixt or Calixtus. The saint in the Roman calendar so called is commemorated on Oct. 14.

KILLIGARTH. An estate in Talland, co. Cornwall, which belonged to the family till temp. Hen. VI. C. S. Gilbert's Cornw.

KILLIGREW, in charters, *Cheligrevus.* A manor in the parish of St. Erme, co. Cornwall, where this celebrated family resided from an early date down to the reign of Richard II.

KILLINGBECK Probably the name of some northern rivulet.

KILMANY. A parish in Fifeshire.

KILLMASTER. KILLMISTER. Near Wick, in Scotland, is a place called Kilminster, of which this name is a corruption. The word is easily referred to its etymon, but there is a legend which accounts for it in a different way. During the time of William the Lion, a number of persons, chiefly of the name of Harrold, having some ground of quarrel against the bishop of the diocese, waylaid him at this place, captured him, and *boiled him !* Hence the name Kill-minster, or, curtly, Kilminster.

KILNER. One who works at a furnace or kiln.

KILPACK. Kilpeck, a parish in Herefordshire.

KILPATRICK. A parish in Stirlingshire and Dumbartonshire.

KILPIN. Perhaps a corruption of Gilpin.

KILVINGTON. Parishes, &c., in cos. York and Nottingham.

KILWICK. See Killick.

KIMBER. A place in Cornwall is called South Kimber.

KIMBLE. See Kemble.

KIME. See Kyme.

KIMPTON. Parishes in Hertfordshire and Hampshire.

☞ **KIN.** In old Teutonic, a child ; hence the diminutives found in so many of our family names, as Wilkin, " Little William," Tompkin, " little Thomas," Perkin, " little Peter," &c. Very few if any names in this form are found in the H.R., and I believe that they are not seen very commonly before the fourteenth century. I have attempted in vain to ascertain the exact period of their introduction, and the precise source from which they sprang.

KINCAID. A place in the parish of Campsie, Stirlingshire.

KINCHANT. John Quinchant, a native of France, became a captain in Gen. Harry Pulteney's regiment of foot, and fell at the battle of Fontenoy, 1745. His son and successor, the direct ancestor of the Kinchants, now of Park Hall, co. Salop, adopted the present orthography.

KINCHIN. Mr. Ferguson says : " Kinchin seems to be A-Sax. *cynekin*, royal offspring." I should assign a much lower and later origin, for if I do not mistake, this word is London ' slang ' for a young thief.

KINDER. A hamlet in Derbyshire.

KINE. Kin, Kinne, and Kyne are found as surnames in H.R., probably implying the same as Cousin.

KING. A very common sobriquet in all ages and countries. Classical antiquity affords us the names of Basilius, Archias, Regulus, Cæsarius, &c., borne by people who, as Camden quaintly remarks, " were neither kings, dukes, nor Cæsars." There are plenty of Lerois in France, and Kœnigs in Germany, who are of no royal descent, and it is only within a few generations that the ' Kings ' of England have emerged from a plebeian grade. The name may very probably have originated in those popular medieval pastimes in which Kings of the Bean—of May—of Cockneys—of Misrule held temporary sway. For their functions see Brand's Pop. Antiq. edit., 1842.

It must not be forgotten, however, that the epithet *King* was sometimes applied to functionaries more regularly appointed, and recognized by the state. For example the author of the *Cléomadès* (from which Chaucer is supposed to have drawn his " Squire's Tale "), Adénès *le Roy*, was so named from his having been chief, or king, of the minstrels in the service of Henry III., duke of Brabant, in the thirteenth century. Nor need we go so far a-field, or so far back, to find such monarchs, for have we not at this moment, and much nearer home than either Brabant or Cologne, *Three Kings*—and *armipotent* kings too, in the right worshipful GARTER, CLARENCEUX, and NORROY, who sway their sceptres at the Heralds' College?

KINGCOMBE. A tything in Dorsetshire.

KINGDON. The family have flourished in Cornwall and Devon for some centuries. The name would appear to have been borrowed from Kingdon, an estate near Sharrow in the former county.

KINGHAM. A parish in Oxfordshire.

KINGHORN. A parish in Fifeshire.

KINGSBURY. Parishes in Middlesex, Warwick, and Somerset.

KINGSCOTE. Ansgerus or Arthur, owner of lands in Combe, in the parish of Wotton-under-Edge, co. Gloucester, the gift of the Empress Maude, is the patriarch of this venerable family. The surname was acquired by marriage with the heiress of Kingscote of Kingscote, soon after the reign of Henry II., and that estate is still possessed by the family. Shirley's Noble and Gentle Men.
    "Nigel Fitz-Arthur, grandson of Ansgerus the Saxon, in A. D. 1085, married Adeva, daughter of Robert Fitz-Harding, grandson of Sueno, 3rd King of Denmark, by Eva, niece of William the Conqueror. With this lady he received in dower the manor of Kingscote, called in Domesday Book, Chingescote." B.L.G.

KINGSFORD. Hamlets in cos. Warwick and Worcester.

KINGSLEY. A township and estate in co. Chester, the property of Sir Ranulph de Kingsley before 1128. In the XIII. cent. the family divided into two branches, the younger continuing the name of Kingsley, and the elder adopting that of De Aula or Hale. See Hale.

KINGSMILL. I find no such locality in the Gazetteers. The name appears to have been borne by an individual who farmed or resided at a royal mill. From the Hundred Rolls, 3. Edw. I., we learn that an inquisition was held touching the manors belonging to that monarch in Hampshire, when one of the jurors who gave evidence bore the name of Hugo de la Kingesmille— "Hugh of the King's Mill." The baronet family, extinct in 1823, traced their pedigree to Richard Kingsmill of the neighbouring county of Berkshire in the XV. cent.

KINGSTON. Twenty-four towns, parishes, &c., of this name are given in the English Gazetteer.

KINGTON. Parishes, &c. in cos. Huntingdon, Gloucester, Worcester, Dorset, and Wilts.

KINLESIDE. A local name apparently of Northern origin, though I cannot find the place. It may be a corruption of Kinneyside, a township in the parish of St.

Bees, co. Cumberland. It is also written Keenliside. At Stockton, co. Durham, it is corrupted to Kittliside, and at Newcastle to *Kittlehimside!*

KINLOCK. Many parishes, &c., in Scotland are so called.

KINNAIRD. Radulphus, surnamed Rufus, had a charter from King William the Lion, of the barony of Kinnaird in Perthshire, from whence the family assumed their surname. Hence Lord Kinnaird.

KINNELL. A parish in Forfarshire.

KINNERSLEY. Parishes in cos. Hereford and Salop.

KINSEY. Probably Kilnsey, co. York, by the suppression of L.

KINSLEY. Probably a contraction of Kinnersley.

KINSMAN. Analogous to Cousin.

KINTREA. Kintra, a village in Argyleshire.

KIPLING. A township in the N. Riding of Yorkshire.

KIRBY. (In charters, Cherchebeius, and originally written Kirkby). Parishes, &c., in cos. Essex, York, Warwick, and Norfolk. Places in cos. Lancaster, York, Nottingham, Lincoln, Leicester, and Westmoreland, still retain the form Kirkby, which is also a surname.

KIRCALDY. See Kirkcaldy.

KIRK. KIRKE. The northern pronunciation of Church. Many parishes in the northern counties have this prefix, as Kirk-Heaton, Kirk-Newton, Kirk-Malew, Kirk-Linton, Kirk-Oswald, Kirk-Sandal, &c. There are probably several distinct families of this name.

KIRKBRIDE. A parish in Cumberland.

KIRKBY. See Kirby.

KIRKCALDY. A royal burgh and parish in Fifeshire.

KIRKHAM. A town in Lancashire, and a liberty in Yorkshire.

KIRKLAND. Villages in the shires of Fife, Dumfries, Lanark, &c.

KIRKMAN. A northern form of Churchman, which see.

KIRKNESS. A headland in Shetland.

KIRKPATRICK. Parishes in the shires of Kircudbright and Dumfries.

KIRKTON. The Kirketons, ennobled by the title of baron by Edward III., derived their name and title from Kirkton, now Kirton, parts of Holland, co. Lincoln.

KIRKWOOD. Local : "the churchwood."

KIRTLAND. A corruption of Kirkland.

KIRWIN. This family, of ancient Irish extraction, have been seated at Blindwell, co. Galway from time immemorial. Until the time of Elizabeth the name was written O'Quirivane. "In a confirmatory grant of Charles II., reference is made to their recognition by Henry VII. and King John." B.L.G.

KISSICK. A corruption of Keswick, co. Cumberland.

KISTER. An abbreviation of Christopher.

KITCHEN. KITCHENER. Probably a name given to a servitor in the kitchen of some medieval nobleman.

KITCHIN. KITCHING. See Kitchen.

KITE. The bird—like Eagle, Falcon, Hawk, &c.

KITSON. The son of Kitt, i.e. Christopher.

KITT. A 'nurse-name' of Christopher.

KITTERMASTER. An obvious corruption of Kidderminster, the town in Worcestershire. The pedigree of K. of Meriden co. Warwick, given in B.L.G., shews the following phases: — Kydermister, 1543; Kydermaster, 1568; Kittermaster, 1649.

KITTLE. See Kettle.

KITTO. The late Dr. Kitto, the celebrated biblical illustrator, gives the following amusing, if not very convincing, account of the origin of his name:—

"I find myself much in the habit of endeavouring to make out the etymology of most of the proper names which come across me ; and it rarely happens that any name which has been the subject of this exercise, subsequently escapes my recollection. I will illustrate this point by my own. Few readers will be able to attach any signification to it. It long baffled my own enquiries, and I was disposed to refer its etymology to the unknown tongue. In this classical country a disposition exists to confound it with Cato, and in the Mediterranean, Spaniards would have it to be Quito, while my Italian friends vowed that it was Chetto, and claimed me for a countryman on the strength of it, triumphantly adducing my complexion as an undeniable proof of their position. This I had good reason for disputing, but had nothing better to propose, till I found that the very word, letter for letter—KITTO, is that which Dioscorides uses for a species of Cassia. This again, is called in Hebrew, *Kiddah*, which as well as the Greek probably represents the Phœnician name of the aromatic. Now the Phœnicians had much intercourse with the remote part of Cornwall, from which my grandfather brought his family ; and the probability is, that it was at least a Phœnician name, if it does not imply a Phœnician origin to those that bear it. The Lost Senses, page 166.

KITTS. See Kitt.

KLEIN. German. Little ; small in person.

KLYNE. A corruption of Klein.

KNAPMAN. A dweller upon a knap or hill.

KNAPTON. Places in cos. Norfolk and York.

KNAPP. 1. *Cnæp.* A-Sax. A top or knop. Bosworth. A hillock or *knap* of a hill. Cotgrave. In Sussex, the brow of a hill is called a *nab.*
2. *Cnapa.* A-Sax. A son, a boy, a youth, a *page,* equivalent to the Fr. *garçon.*

KNAPPER. See Knapp, and the termination ER.

KNATCHBULL. The first recorded ancestor of the family is John Knatchbull, who had lands in the parish of Lymne, co. Kent, in the reign of Edward III., and there some of the name remained down to the time of Charles I. The main branch were at Mersham-Hatch, in the same county, by purchase, temp. Henry VII., and there the present baronet yet resides. Shirley's Noble and Gentle Men. The etymology of this singular surname is not very obvious, but, in the absence of a better, I will suggest—*knatch,* a northern provincialism, meaning to strike or knock, and *bull* (taurus)—perhaps from some courageous adventure with an animal of that species. See Turnbull.

KNELL. See Kneller.

KNELLER. Sir Godfrey K. was a native of Lubeck ; but the name is also indigenous to England. Knelle is a topographical word of uncertain import, and a person residing at such a spot would be called At-Knelle or Kneller. The name was formerly very common in E. Sussex, and may have been derived from Great Knell, in the parish of Beckley. See Thorpe's Catalogue of Battel Abbey Charters.

KNEVETT. KNYVETT. See under Knife.

KNIFE. Ferguson says from Cniva, an early Gothic name, of which he considers Knevett a diminutive. Knif. H.R.

KNIGHT. 1. Applied, not to a person who actually possessed knighthood, but by way of sobriquet. See Lord, &c. See also Eng. Surn. i. 134. 2. Perhaps a more probable derivation is immediately from the A-Sax. *cniht,* a servant, youth, military follower. The A-Sax. *cniht-hád* implies, not the modern idea of knighthood, but the period between childhood and manhood. See Bosworth. The H.R. forms are Le Knigt, Kniht, Le Knit, Le Knyt.

KNIGHTLEY. The first known ancestor is Rainald, mesne Lord of Knightley, co. Stafford, under Earl Roger, temp. William the Conqueror. Domesd. Fawsley Hall, co. Northampton, the seat of the present baronet, was acquired by purchase, temp. Henry V. Baker's Northamptonshire. Shirley's Noble and Gentle Men.

KNIGHTON. Parishes and places in cos. Dorset, Leicester, Stafford, Worcester, &c.

KNILL. Sir John, a younger son of the unfortunate William de Braose, temp. King John, having received from his father the manor of Knylle or Knill, in the marches of Wales (co. Hereford), adopted De Knill as his surname. Knill of Knill became extinct in the XVII. cent.

KNIPE. A mountain in Ayrshire—parish of New Crunnock.

KNIVETON. KNYVETON. A parish in Derbyshire. The extinct baronet family descended from Sir Matthew de Kniveton, who flourished in that county temp. Edward I. Lysons' Derbyshire.

KNOCK. A hill; a knoll. Celtic and Gaelic, *cnoc*, collis. De la Knocke. H.R. See Knox.

KNOCKNAILE. Probably a sobriquet applied to a hammer-man of some description. A family of this name in Wiltshire were enriched by the spoliation of the monasteries by Henry VIII., and an old traditional rhyme thus records them and some of their neighbours:—

"HOPTON, HORNER, SMYTH, KNOCKNAILE, and THYNNE;
When Abbats went out, they came in."
Aubrey's Lives, vol. ii. p. 362.

KNOLL. See Knowles.

KNOLLYS. For the etymology see Knowles. The founder of the family, a person of humble origin, was the famous Sir Robert Knollys, who, after the battle of Poictiers had established the supremacy of the English in France, greatly enriched himself by incursions into that country, where he was known as "the very Devil for fighting" (*le veritable Demon de la Guerre*). The following distich by a contemporary poet records his prowess.

"O ROBERTE KNOLLIS, PER TE FIT
    FRANCIA MOLLIS;
ENSE TUO TOLLIS PRÆDAS, DANS
    VULNERA COLLIS."

O Robert Knowles, the stubborn souls
Of Frenchmen well you check;
Your mighty blade has largely preyed,
And wounded many a neck.
Bodiam and its Lords, p. 17.

KNOTT. The Scandinavian Cnut or Canute, a personal name. Camden says that the sandpiper or *knot*-bird, derives its name from King Canute. Britannia, 971. And Drayton in his Polyolbion sings—

"The Knot that callèd was Canutus' bird of old,
Of that great King of Danes his name that still
    doth hold;
His appetite to please that far and near was sought,
For him, as some have said, from Denmark hither
    brought."

A Cnut appears in the Domesd. of Derby, Nottingham, and York, and he was evidently either a Dane or of Danish extraction.

"Our surname of Knot, being so made by abbreviation, some say should more rightly be Kanut." Verstegan.

KNOWLER. A resident at a *knoll* or hill. See termination ER.

KNOWSLEY. A township in Lancashire, anciently Knouselegh. The family possessed the estate temp. Edward II., if not earlier.

KNOWLE. KNOWLES. Localities in many counties are so called, from A-Sax. *cnoll* a knoll, hill, or summit; a little round hill. See Knollys.

KNOWLTON. A parish in Kent.

KNOX. From the lands of Knocks or Knox, co. Renfrew. *Knock*, Gael., a round-topped hill. The Knoxes were of that Ilk at an early period, and sometimes wrote themselves of Ranfurly, whence the family of Knox, Earls of Ranfurly in Ireland. The great Reformer was of this family.

KNYFESMITH. See Smith.

KNYVETT. According to Camden this name is a corruption of *Dunevit*, and Leland derives it from Dunnevit, that is Dunneheved, the original name of Launceston, in Cornwall. It is said that Othomarus, lord of the castle and town of Launceston, took up arms against William the Conqueror, and was deprived of his possessions, which were afterwards restored to him on his marriage with a daughter of William Dammartin, a Norman. His descendants took the name of De Knyvet or De Knevet. See Burke's Ext. Barts. Knivet, Knivat, and Knyvet, as well as De Knyvet, are found in H.R.

KOE. This surname may be the O-Sax., North Frisian, and Danish *ko*, a cow. Mr. Ferguson, after alluding to surnames derived from the bear, the wolf, the boar, the horse, and the dog, and giving a rationale of their origin, says: "But the cow—the innocent and ungainly cow—what is there in her useful and homely life that could inspire sentiments of reverence in a fierce and warlike people? The honour which was paid to her was from a more ancient and a more deeply-seated source. From the time when Israel, tainted with Egyptian superstition, set up a golden calf, and said, 'These be thy gods which brought thee out of the land of Egypt'—and from who can tell how many ages before that time, the cow as the type of the teeming mother earth, has been an object of human idolatry. In the Northern system of mythology she is not, like the bear, the wolf, or the boar, sacred to any particular divinity, but appears—in what seems to be a fragment of a more ancient myth—as mysteriously connected with the first cause and origin of all things. Grimm has remarked (*Deutsch Myth.* p. 631), that the Sanscrit and Persian words for a cow correspond with a word signifying the earth. And he further observes upon the connection between Rinda, a name for the earth in Northern mythology, and the Germ. *rind*, an ox. I am unable, in the absence of proof derived from corresponding ancient names, to say whether any of our names derived from the cow are to be referred to this remote origin."

KYAN. A corruption of O'Cahan. The ancestors of the family were anciently princes of Derry, and a younger branch of the royal O'Neills. The Irish annals mention a Kian, king of Desmond, in 1014.

KYDD. See Kidd.

KYFFIN. A Welsh name. *Cyffin* in that language, implies a limit or abutment. The surname is therefore probably local.

KYLE. A topographical term implying a sound or strait. Jamieson.

KYME. The founder of this family founded also the Priory of Bolinton, co. Lincoln, temp. King Stephen. The Kymes "assumed the surname from a fair lordship, the principal place of their residence, in Kesteven, in the county of Lincoln." Burke's Ext. Peerage. The barony of Kyme is in abeyance.

KYMYEL. A place in the parish of Paul, co. Cornwall, anciently the residence of the family. C. S. Gilbert's Cornwall.

KYNASTON. "The Kynastons," says Mr. Shirley, "are lineal descendants of the ancient British princes of Powys, sprung from Griffith, son of Jorweth Goch, who took refuge in Shropshire" temp. Henry II., who gave him lands in that county, "to be held in capite by the service of being *latimer* (that is interpreter) between the English and the Welsh. He married Matilda, youngest sister and coheir of Ralph le Strange, and in her right became possessed of the manor of Kinnerley and other estates in Shropshire. Madoc, the eldest son of Griffith, seated himself at Sutton, from him called to this day Sutton-Madoc. Griffith Vychan, the younger son, had Kinnerley, a portion of his mother's inheritance, and in that manor he resided, at Tre-gynvarth, *Anglice* 'Kynvarth's Town,' usually written and spoken of as *Kynaston;* and hence the name of this family." Noble and Gentle Men, p. 183.

L.

LABORER. Fr. *laboreur*, a ploughman, or perhaps more generally a husbandman of any kind.

LABOUCHERE. This family left France at the Revocation of the Edict of Nantes, and became established in Holland. The first settler in England was Peter Cæsar Labouchere, Esq., who purchased estates in Essex and Somerset, and died in 1839.

LACER. A lace-maker.

LACESTER. A corruption of Lanchester, a parish in Cheshire.

LAC. Perhaps the Fr. *Du Lac*, "of the lake."

LACKEY. A personal attendant, a footman.

LACKINGTON. A parish in co. Somerset.

LACOCK or LAYCOCK. A parish in Wiltshire, famous for its abbey.

LACON. A township in the parish of Wem, co. Salop.

LACEY. See Lacy.

LACY. Roger de Laci, eldest son of Walter de L., came over with William the Conqueror, and was rewarded with the tenure in capite of 116 lordships. To Ilbert de Laci the Conqueror gave the castle and town of Pontefract, co. York, with 164 lordships. Kelham's Domesday. The two were probably related, though the degree of kindred is unknown. The Itinéraire de la Normandie mentions a place called Lassi, in the department of Calvados, which, as Ordericus Vitalis latinizes it *Lacceium*, is probaby the cradle of this renowned and noble surname, to which no less than 35 coats of arms are ascribed in the Encyc. Herald.

LADBROKE. The Warwickshire parish so called is a tolerably satisfactory origin; but it may be a personal name. It was the daughter of Lodbrok the Dane who wove the famous Raven Standard, which always announced victory to the Scandinavian marauders by fluttering like a living bird. Asser's King Alfred. Mon. Hist. Brit. p. 481.

LADBROOK. See Ladbroke.

LADD. A low common person—a plebeian. "To make lordes of *laddes*." Piers Ploughman.

LADDS. See Lade.

LADE. See Lathe. In Norfolk it means also a watercourse or drain. The old family of this name in Kent and Sussex, though retaining the true orthography, pronounce it corruptly Ladds. In O. English and Scotch, a *lade* means a canal or duct for water. The forms in H.R. are De Lade and De la Lade.

☞ **LADY.** There are several surnames of which this word forms part, and for which I cannot account, except upon the supposition that they are derived from some oath or invocation involving the name of "Our Lady," the Virgin Mary. They are Ladyman, Tiplady, Taplady, Toplady, and, strangest of all, Godlovemilady! Shakelady is a known corruption of Shackerley. In the H.R. we have a Roger Ducedame or Sweetlady, and the Registrar General's cabinet of curiosities shows us a recent or existing Lovelady.

LADYMAN. See Lady.

LAFOREY. La Forêt—Forest. John Laforey, only son and heir of Louis Laforey, and nephew of the Marquis de la Forêt of the province of Poitou, came into England with King William III. and was made governor of Pendennis Castle, co. Cornwall. His son was created a baronet.

LAGGAN. A parish in Inverness-shire.

LAHEY. LAHEE. Gael. *leighiche*, a physician. Arthur.

LAIDENHEAD. Danish *lodinhofd*, "shaggy head."

LAIDLER. Probably a corruption of Laidlaw, a local name.

LAIDMAN (or Lademan). 1. "A man who has the charge of a horse-load or of a pack horse. *The Bruce*. 2. The servant belonging to a miln, who has the charge of driving the loads to the owners, as well as of lifting them up. S." Jamieson. 3. Dan. *lade*, a barn. A barn-man, equivalent perhaps to Granger, which see.

LAING. A-Sax. *lang*, long; applied to a tall person.

LAINSON. The son of Alain or Alan.

LAIRD. The Scottish form of Lord.

☞ **LAKE.** A termination of many names of places and families, as Kerslake, Shiplake, Aslake, Timberlake, Westlake, Eastlake. Probably not from *lacus*, a lake, as no considerable body of water exists in some of the localities so called; but either from *lake* as applied to any small rivulet in the western counties, or from a hard pronunciation of the A-Sax. *leag*, territory or district.

LAKE. In the West, any small rivulet; also a parish in Wiltshire, united with Wilsford. De Lacu, De Lake, De la Lake, Atte Lake. H.R.

LAKEMAN. See Lake and MAN.

LAKER. See Lake and ER.

LAKIN. Perhaps Lacon, a township in Salop.

LALOR Formerly O'Lalor. Of ancient Irish extraction. They migrated from Ulster to the district of Leix in the Queen's Co. with the O'Mores, under whom they became influential chieftains. B.L.G.

LAMACRAFT. Probably Lamcroft, a hamlet in Lincolnshire.

LAMB. LAMBE. Charles Lamb asks, "Who first imposed thee, gentle name?" and jumps, or rather skips, to the conclusion that his ancestors were shepherds; but there is little doubt that the surname was derived from a common sign of houses. The Second Person in the Trinity, in allusion to the passage of scripture, "Behold the Lamb of God, &c.," is often in medieval art pourtrayed as a lamb bearing a small banner ensigned with a cross. This device usually known as the 'Holy Lamb' was frequently adopted as a sign, and, although its sacred origin is forgotten, many a country public-house is still known by it. Lamb and Le Lamb. H.R.

LAMBARD. LOMBARD. A native of Lombardy in Italy. In the middle ages the Lombards were great traffickers in money and the precious metals, and Lombard Street in London derives its name from them. This name is sometimes confounded with Lambert.

LAMBERT. 1. From the A-Sax. personal name. 2. From Lambert-sur-Dive, or Lambert-sur-Orne in Normandy. The former is the more probable, as we have other family names apparently derived from it, as Lampson, Lampkin, &c. Some of the Lamberts of Ireland seem, however, to have used the local prefix DE; and they are said to have settled in that country temp. Henry II.

LAMBETH A parish in Surrey.

LAMBKIN. A diminutive of Lambert.

LAMBLEY. Parishes in cos. Nottingham and Northumberland.

LAMBOLL. A corruption of the O. Germ. name Lambold.

LAMBOURNE. An estate in the parish of Perran Zabuloe, co. Cornwall, which was possessed by the family in the reign of Edward II. C. S. Gilbert's Cornwall. Also parishes, &c., in Berkshire and Essex.

LAMBSHEAD. A Scottish local surname.

LAMBTON. According to Surtees, this noble family (Earls of Durham) spring from Robert de L., lord of Lambton, in 1314. There was a John de Lambton who flourished before 1200, but descent from him is not proved. Hist. Durham, ii. 174. The family have been characterized as the "LAMB-LIKE LAMBTONS."

LAMBURN. See Lambourne.

LAMELIN. An estate in the parish of Lantegloss near Fowey, anciently the seat of the family. C. S. Gilbert's Cornwall.

LAMMAS. 1. From the season, like Christmas, &c. 2. A parish in Norfolk so called. Lammasse occurs without prefix in H.R.

LAMOND. The Highland clan, originally called Mac Laman, descended from

Laumanus filius Malcolmi in the XIII. cent.

LAMONT. 1. Possibly from Laumont, in the arrondissement of Vire in Lower Normandy. 2. The family of Lamont of Lamont, co. Argyle, date from the XI. cent. Interesting details of them are given in Skene's *Highland Clans.* B.L.G.

LAMOTT. See Delamotte.

LAMPEN. A Cornish surname, probably the same as Lampenc.

LAMPENC. A manor in Cornwall.

LAMPKIN. See Lambert, and the termination KIN.

LAMPLAW. A corruption of Lamplugh, a parish in Cumberland.

LAMPLOE. See Lamplugh.

LAMPLUGH. A parish in Cumberland, the residence of the family, "a race of valourous gentlemen successively for their worthyness knyghted in the field, all or most of them." Old account quoted in Hutchinson's Cumberland. The family were in possession temp. Henry II. Ibid.

LAMPORT. A parish in Northamptonshire. An estate now called Landport at Lewes, Sussex, had owners called Lamport temp. Edw. III.

LAMPRELL. Cotgrave has "*Lamprillon,* a lamprill or little lamprey"—the fish so fatal to Henry I.

LAMPREY. The fish.

LAMSON. See Lambert.

L'AMY. Fr. *L'Ami,* "the friend." The family of this name at Dunkenny, co. Forfar, is of considerable antiquity, and the surname is traced back in the Scotch Exchequer Records to 1329. B.L.G. Lamye was the name of a Frenchman settled in Sussex temp. Elizabeth.

☞ **LAN. LLAN.** Very common prefixes to names of localities in Cornwall and Wales. It signifies church, as in Llanthony, Llanstephan, Lanherne, Lanhidrock, &c.

LANCASTER. The chief town of Lancashire.

LANCE. A soldier armed with that weapon. In early times there was a regular force of light horsemen called from their offensive arms demi-lances. Some compounds occur as surnames; e.g. Shakelance, Bruselance, &c.

LANCELIN. An A.-Norm. personal name.

LANCHENICK. There are so many places in Cornwall beginning with *Lan-* and terminating with *-ck* (e. g. Landawidnick, Lanhidrock, Lanock, &c.), that I had arrived at the conclusion that this name was derived from some manor or *barton* in that county. The family however assert a German origin for their name, which they affirm should rightly be *Lanz-knecht,* lance-

2 B

knight, lancer, analogous to our indigenous Spearman, Billman, &c. Their crest favours this derivation, being a lion rampant, holding a broken lance. Inform. W. B. Paul, Esq. Lance-Knight is used by old authors in the sense of a foot-soldier, "Lasquenet, a lance-knight, or German footman." Cotgrave. "Our Lansquenight of Lowe-Germanie." Dekker's Knight's Conjuring. Blount however makes the lance-knight of the equestrian order. "Lance-knights" says he, "were anciently such *horsemen* in war as were armed with lances." See Halliwell.

LANDE. LAND. Fr. *lande,* a heath or moor. La Lande is a very common designation of localities in Normandy.

LANDELLS. Landelles, a place in the arrondissement of Vire, in Lower Normandy.

LANDER. In Cornwall and Devon the man who is stationed at the mouth of the shaft of a mine to receive the kibble or bucket. The Landers, well-known as African explorers, were natives of Cornwall. But see Landor.

LANDLORD. This name is found in H.R., in the orthography now employed.

LANDON. A township in Northumberland.

LANDOR. The family of the poet, whose ancestors wrote themselves Launde and Launder, claim to derive from the ancient family of De la Launde. The suppression of the prefix and the addition of the final R, has many analogies. See termination ER.

LANDSEER. One who over-looks or superintends land for another; a bailiff.

LANE. "In the Lane" and "By the Lane," as well as "In Lana," "Ad Lanam," "De la Lane," occur in medieval documents, and the name might therefore be reasonably considered as derived from residence in such a situation; but the Lanes of King's-Bromley, according to B.L.G., claim a Norman original from a Sir Reginald de Lone, who flourished in the XII. cent.

LANER. From residence in a lane. See ER. Le Laner. H.R.

LANFEAR. See Lanphear.

☞ **LANG.** A common prefix to names of places which have become surnames, as in Langbourne, Langshaw, Langton, Langridge, Langford, Langdale, i.e., respectively, the long stream,- wood, -enclosure, -ridge, -ford, -dale.

LANG. LANGE. A-Sax and O. Eng Long, tall. Also local. De Lang. H.R.

LANGBEARD. The peculiarities of fashion in beards have given rise to several surnames. In this instance the original bearer affected a long or patriarchal adornment of his face.

LANGDALE. Two or three places in Westmoreland, are so called. The family of the Lords Langdale (1658) held the manor of Langdale in the hundred of Pickering before the time of King John.

LANGDON. Parishes in Kent, Essex, &c. The Langdons of Cornwall derive from Langdon in the parish of Jacobstow, their ancient patrimony. C. S. Gilbert's Cornwall.

LANGFORD. Parishes, &c., in cos. Bedford, Berks, Norfolk, Essex, Somerset, Nottingham, Wilts, &c. The Cornish family derive from Roger de Langford, sheriff of Cornwall in 1225, who took his surname from his estate of Langford in the parish of Marham Church. C. S. Gilbert's Cornwall.

LANGHAM. There are places called Langham in cos. Essex, Suffolk, Norfolk, and Rutland. The baronet's family originated in the last-mentioned county. In 10. Edward I. Henry de Langham held three carucates of land in Langham, and from him the pedigree is regularly deduced.

LANGHERNE. A Cornish family, doubtless of the same origin as Lanherne, which see. To this family belonged the gigantic Cromwellian soldier, John Langherne, who is said to have been seven feet six inches in height, and proportionably active and strong. C. S. Gilbert's Cornwall.

LANGLEY. Parishes and places in cos. Durham, Essex, Kent, Leicester, Norfolk, Oxford, Salop, Warwick, Wilts, Derby, Buckingham, &c.

LANGLOIS. Fr. *l'Anglois*, "the Englishman." An importation from France, where it is as common a surname as 'French' is with ourselves.

LANGMAN. See Lang and Longman; a person of great stature.

LANGMEAD. Occurs in H.R. temp. Edw. I. as De Longo Prato, 'of the long meadow,' and a hamlet of that name is mentioned in the same record. In the XIV. cent. it is found in co. Devon, where it has since flourished in fourteen different modes of spelling, the principal of which are Langemede, Langmade, Langmaid, and Longmead. Inf. T. P. Langmead, Esq.

LANGRIDGE. A parish in Somersetshire. The Langridges of Sussex appear to be indigenous to that county, and the name De Langrigg is found there in the XIV. cent.

LANGRISH. A place in the parish of East Meon, co. Hants.

LANGSTAFF. "Long staff." The first bearer carried such a weapon. John o'the Lang-Staffe—a medieval sobriquet. There is a Will. Longstaf in H.R.

LANGSTON. A parish in Hampshire.

LANGTOFT. A parish in Lincolnshire.

LANGTON. Parishes and places in cos. Durham, Westmoreland, Lincoln, York, Leicester, Dorset, &c.

LANGWITH. A parish in Derbyshire, and townships in cos. York and Nottingham.

LANGWORTH. A hamlet in Lincolnshire.

LANHAM. Lavenham co. Suffolk is sometimes so written.

LANHERNE. A manor in the parish of St. Mawgan in Cornwall, where a family called Pincerna settled, and adopted the local name as their surname. They became extinct in the elder line temp. Edward I. C. S. Gilbert's Cornwall.

LANINE. A well-known corruption of Lanyon, which see.

LANKESTER. See Lancaster.

LANKIN. A diminutive of Leonard, which see, as also the termination KIN.

LANPHEAR. Gael. *lann-fear*, a pikeman. Arthur.

LANSDALE. The same as Lonsdale.

LANSDELL. Probably the same as Lansdale or Lonsdale.

LANSDOWNE. A plain near Bath, famous for a great battle between the forces of Charles I. and the Parliamentary army, 1643.

LANSELATT. A corruption of Launcelot.

LANYON. From the town of Lannion in Brittany. The family settled in Cornwall temp. Edw. II. Their estate in that county also bore the name of Lanyon, and their arms are almost identical with those of the French town. As the estate, which lies in the parish of Gwinnear, bore that name previously to their ownership, the coincidence is curious. There are however many other instances of identity in Breton and Cornish local names. See C. S. Gilbert's Cornwall, i. 120. "The Cornish and Armoric dialects," says Dr. Price, "are the most nearly allied in character, orthography, and sound of any two of the British (Celtic) dialects." Ibid. Hals, in Davies Gilbert's Cornwall, ii. 142, says "the first propagators of this family in Cornwall, came with many other French gentlemen into England with Isabella, wife of King Edw. II., and settled themselves in these parts," and adds that they "still give the arms of that town (Lanyon in Brittany) for their paternal coat-armour, viz.: in a field *Sable, a castle Argent standing on waves of the sea Azure; over the same a falcon hovering with bells.*" Whitaker believes that the town of Lannion bears only a castle for its cognizance, and that the falcon was added on account of similarity of sound to Lanner, the favourite bird in falconry. Mr. D. Gilbert observes, however, that the surname is always in Cornwall pronounced Lanine. Ut sup. 143.

LAPHAM. Probably Lopham, co. Norfolk.

LA POER. See Power.

LA PRIMAUDAYE. This family, previously renowned in France, settled in this country as Protestant refugees after the Revocation of the Edict of Nantes, 1685. In 1699, Gabriel de la Primaudaye, seigneur de la Goyere near Montagne in Poitou, was resident in London.

LAPWORTH. A parish in co. Warwick.

LARDER. Probably the same as Lardner, which see.

LARDNER. A swineherd, or rather the person who superintended the pannage of hogs in a forest. Eng. Surn. But Kelham (Norm. Fr. Dict.) says, "the officer in the king's household who presided over the larder." Whichever alternative the etymological reader may choose, he is certain to 'save his bacon,' since the word larder, as applied to the victualling department of a house, is derived from the Fr. *lard*, because bacon was the principal article therein deposited.

LARGE. Stout, big; the antithesis of Small.

LARKE. The bird; perhaps, however, a nickname of Lawrence, whence Larkin and Larkins.

LARKIN. LARKING. LARKINS. See Lawrence.

LARMOUTH. See Learmouth.

LARNED. Learned—a man of scholarship. (America.)

LARNER. Not *discipulus*, but a keeper of bacon. See Lardner.

LAROCHE. Fr. *la roche*, the rock. See Rock. "Peter Crothaire, of the province of Bordeaux, came into England in the train of George, Prince of Denmark, and at the desire of his master assumed the name of Laroche." His grandson, James Laroche, was created a baronet in 1776. Burke's Ext. Barts.

LARPENT Fr. *arpent*, an acre of land. L'arpent, "the acre." It is not very easy to account for its adoption as a surname, though there are analogies in Halfacre, Fouracre, and other family names.

LARRANCE. A vulgar pronunciation of Lawrence.

LARRY. 1. A nickname of Lawrence. 2. A place in the arrondissement of Alençon in Normandy.

LARWILL. Said to be a corruption of La Ville, which is probable—far more so than the tradition which states that the patriarch of the family came over with the Conqueror. It is said that when the latter, in landing at Pevensey, fell upon his hands on the sand, the former who was by, uttered the exclamation " La Will !" which thenceforth became his cognomen !

LASBURY. Lasborough, a parish united with Weston-Birt, co. Gloucester.

LASCELLES. The family ennobled as Earls of Harewood adopt this spelling, though Lassells appears to be the more ordinary orthography. In the Encyc. Herald. only three coats are ascribed to Lascelles, but nine to Lassells. La Lacelle is a place in the arrondissement of Alençon in Normandy. Some genealogists consider them of Breton extraction. Mr. Shirley says that the family trace to John de Lascelles, of Hinderskelfe, now called Castle-Howard, 9, Edward II. For seven generations immediately following, they were called "*Lascelles alias Jackson.*" Noble and Gentle Men of England. Dns. Rog's de Laceles. H.R.

LASHMAR. Traditionally said to be a corruption of Lechmere.

LATCHFORD. A hamlet in Oxfordshire.

LATE. Probably a sobriquet given on account of want of punctuality. Its opposite, Early, is also a surname, but that is otherwise accounted for, both in the body of this Dictionary, and in the Appendix.

LATER. See Latter.

LATEWARD. A *lathe* is a great division or part of a county, as the five lathes of Kent. See Lambarde's Peramb. of Kent. Bailey defines Lathreeve as an officer who had authority over a lathe; and reeve and ward are nearly synonymous; e.g. wood-reeve, wood-ward. See Ward.

LATHAM. Of this great family, whose name is derived from the chapelry of Lathom in the parish of Ormskirk, Mr. Ormerod observes, that they have "for six centuries presided, with little interruption, over the civil government of Lancashire," and that after the succession of the house of Stanley to the representation of the family, they long exercised a corresponding influence over Cheshire." The pedigree usually commences with Robert Fitz-Henry, Lord of Lathom, who between 1189 and 1199 founded Burscough Priory; but Mr. Ormerod has successfully proved it to a period almost, if not quite coeval with the Conquest, thus :—I. Dunning—whether a continued possessor, or a Norman grantee, does not appear; II. Siward Fitz-Dunning; III. Henry Fitz-Siward; IV. Robert Fitz-Henry, above mentioned. The patronymical *Fitz* was continued until about the middle of the XIII. century, when the fixed surname of De Lathom was adopted. See Ormerod's Miscellanea Palatina, pp. 60, 61, 62. The orthography Latham is comparatively modern.

LATHBURY. A parish in Buckinghamshire.

LATHE. Danish *lade*, a barn or granary. It was retained in medieval English, and it is still used in the northern counties in this sense. Gregory atte Lathe occurs in 21 Richard II.

LATHOM. See Latham.

LATIMER. A corruption of the A. Norm, *latinier*, a speaker of Latin, or more loosely, an interpreter—the term Latin having been formerly applied, as Halliwell observes, to languages in general. Sir John Maundeville, speaking of the route from Babylon to Sinai, says: "And men alle weys fynden *Latyneres* to go with hem in the contrees, and ferthere bezonde in to tyme that men conne the language." The noble families of this surname are descended according to the Peerages, from Wrenock, the son of Meirric, who held certain lands on the Welsh border, under the A. Norman kings, by the service of being *latimer*, or interpreter between the Welsh and the English. See also the article Kynaston. The name was prefixed by *Le* for several generations after its adoption.

LATOUCHE. David-Digues de la Touche, a Huguenot, settled in Ireland after the Revocation of the Edict of Nantes. He was a scion of the noble house of Blesois, who held considerable lands between Blois and Orleans. B.L.G.

LATTER. A *lat* in many dialects signifies a lath, from the A-Sax. *latta*, asseres; and hence it has been conjectured that a Latter means a lath-cleaver or splitter.

LATTIN. A branch of the family of De Latton, of Wiltshire, settled in Ireland, temp. King John, and thus corrupted the name. B.L.G. The De Lattons were an offset of the great Norman family of Stuteville.

LATUS. A mistaken latinization of Broad, which see. It is still in use.

LAUCHLAN. A Gaelic personal name, better known with the prefix Mac.

LAUD. See St. Lo.

LAUDER. A royal burgh in Berwickshire, which gives name to the district of Lauderdale.

LAUGHER. A likely sobriquet for a person addicted to much or frequent laughter. So Singer, Whistler, &c.

LAUGHTON. Parishes in cos. Sussex, Leicester, Lincoln, and York.

LAUNCE. See Lance.

LAUNCELOT. Though attributed to an ancient British hero, this name is apparently of no very high antiquity. It is probably a derivative of Lawrence.

LAUNDE. A plain place in a wood; an unploughed plain; a park, a lawn.

"For to hunt at the harts in thas hye *laundes*.
In Glamorgane with glee, thare gladchipe was ever,"—

says the alliterative poem of Morte Arthure. Halliwell.

LAUNDER. 1. A corruption of Lavender. 2. One whose residence was near a *laund*. See Launde and Landor.

LAUREL. One can hardly deduce this name from the beautiful tree which furnishes forth the victor's crown; a much likelier derivation is from the A.-Norm. *lorel*, a bad, worthless fellow. 'Cocke Lorel' was for-

merly a generic title for very great rascals —whence the celebrated satirical poem, "Cock Lorel's Bote," printed by Wynkyn de Worde. See Halliwell.

LAURENT. A French modification of Laurence.

LAURIE. A northern abbreviation of Lawrence.

LAUTOUR. The founder of the family in England was Jos. François Louis de Lautour, born in 1730, the descendant of an ancient Alsacian family, who claimed from a certain "Sire de la Tour," who is said to have flourished about A.D. 900. B.L.G.

LAVACHE. Fr. "the Cow"—either a sobriquet or an inn sign. *Lavash* is another form of the name, which seems to have been an early importation from France. See also Levache and Koe.

LAVENDER. This is one of the numerous instances occurring in our family nomenclature of a name's 'not meaning what it says.' As we have many surnames derived from the vegetable kingdom, this might well be associated with the well-known garden herb; but it comes from an entirely different source. The obsolete French word *lavandier*, a washer-*man*, is its real parent; and as *lavanderie*, wash-house, has become laundry, so has this surname become further corrupted to Launder and Lander.

In the Rotuli Hundredorum of co. Bedford, we find one Alicia la Lavendar holding a messuage and a rood of land (doubtless her "drying ground") at the annual rent of sixpence. H.R. temp. Edw. I.

LAVER. Three parishes in Essex are so called.

LAVERICK. 1. Laveroch is a place in the parish of Coldingham, co. Berwick. 2. Perhaps O. Eng. *laverock*, a lark. 3. But most probably from the A-Sax. personal name Leofric.

LAVEROCK. O. Eng. and modern Scotch, a lark. A natural sobriquet, imposed upon a person either for vocal powers or for a habit of early rising. The birds borne in the arms of this family are doubtless larks, though blazoned as martlets. The name may however be the same as the preceding

LAVERS. A pluralization of Laver.

LAVEY. LAVY. LAVIE. LAVIES. This set of names is so exactly parallel to Davey, Davy, Davie, Davies, that I think it must be derived, in like manner, from the familiar or 'nursery' form of some Christian name—possibly from Lawrence.

LAVILLE. Fr. "the Town."

LAW. (A-Sax, *hlaéw, hláw.*) 1. What covers, as a grave, a heap, a barrow, a small hill. 2. A tract of ground gently rising—a low. (Bosworth.) Still used in the North for an eminence.

☞ **LAW.** A termination common to many surnames derived from such localities, as Greenlaw, Fairlaw, Whitelaw. For several names beginning with this syllable, see under LAU.

LAWDAY. The more usual orthography of 'Loveday,' which see.

LAWDER. A parish in Berwickshire, *hodie* Lauder.

LAWER. *Lawere* is given in the Prompt. Parv. as the equivalent of a legist, jurist, lawyer, or scribe.

LAWES. LAWS. See Lawrence.

LAWFORD. A parish in Essex.

LAWFULL. Perhaps assumed in vindication of legitimacy of birth.

LAWKIN. A diminutive of Lawrence, which see—also the termination KIN.

LAWLESS. Perhaps referring to natural disposition; more probably however a corruption of Lovelace, the element of a chief indented occurring in the arms of several families of both these names.
Sir Hugh de Lawless of Hoddesdon, co. Herts, settled in Ireland temp. Henry II. and obtained a grant of Shangenagh, co. Dublin, where he built a castle. From him descends Lawless, Baron Cloncurry. I do not find the locality of Lawless.

LAWLEY. The family descend from Thos. Lawley, cousin and heir of John Lord Wenlock, K.G., temp. Edw. IV. Shirley's Noble and Gentle Men. The name is clearly local, but the place is unknown.

LAWLER. An Irish Surname, probably the same as Lalor.

LAWMAN. See Law and MAN. The H.R. forms are Lawman and Laweman.

LAWN. 1. Launde, a liberty in co. Leicester, and Laund, two townships in co. Lancaster. 2. See Launde.

LAWRENCE. The personal name, from the Lat. Laurentius. The following are its diminutives and derivatives; Lawrie, Larry, Larkin, Larking, Larkins, Lawes, Lawson, Lawkin.

LAWRIE. See Lawrence.

LAWSON. The son of Lawrence. According to Burke's Ext. Baronets, the patriarch of the family was John Lawson, who temp. Henry III. was lord of Fawlesgrave, co. York. From him the existing baronet is lineally descended.

LAWTON. "It is not improbable that the family are descended from Robert, a younger son of Vivian de Davenport, who settled at Lawton, co. Chester, in the 50th of Henry III., and assumed the local name: this assertion is borne out by the arms, which are evidently founded on those of Davenport." Shirley's Noble and Gentle Men.

LAWYER. The profession.

LAX. O. Norse. *lax*, A-Sax. *leax*, *lax*, a salmon; Ferguson thinks the name was originally applied to a salmon fisher.

LAXTON. Parishes, &c., in cos. Northampton, Nottingham, and York.

LAY. 1. Fr. *laie*, a lane through a forest. 2. Lay, not clerical; unlearned. In the latter sense the word is used by B. Jonson. H.R. Le Lay, Du Lay, and De Lay.

LAYARD. Probably Laird, the Scottish form of Lord.

LAYBOURNE. Leybourne, a parish in Kent.

LAYER. 1. Fr. *layeur*, a forest surveyor; one who makes roads through forests. 2. Three parishes in Essex are so called.

LAYMAN. Not in distinction from a clerk or learned person, but a personal name. Layamon, translator of the 'Roman de Brut' into semi-Saxon, flourished about the end of the reign of Henry II.

LAYTON. Townships in Lancashire and Yorkshire.

LAZARD. A *lazar* or leper. See Leper.

LAZARUS. A Jewish surname.

LAZENBY. LAZONBY. Lasenby, a locality in the parish of Kirk-Leatham, co. York, or more probably Lazonby, a parish in Cumberland.

☞ **LE.** A common prefix to medieval surnames, being the French definite article, equivalent to our *the*. It was dropped from English surnames after the XIV. cent., but it has been retained to the present day in France, though it generally coalesces with the noun to which it belongs, as Lemaire for Le Maire, Lemaitre for Le Maitre.

LEA. See LEE.

LEACH. A parish united with Marlston, co. Chester. Not in all cases to be confounded with Leech.

LEADBEATER. This name—variously corrupted to Leadbetter, Leadbitter, Lidbetter, and still further, in vulgar pronunciation, to Libbetter—signifies a beater of lead. In old times, before the process of rolling that metal into sheets by machinery was employed, it was laminated by the laborious manual operation of hammering; and as most churches and other large buildings were roofed with this material, the occupation of the *lead-beater* was a very common and necessary one. Le Ledbetre. H.R.

LEADBETTER. LEADBITTER. See Leadbeater.

LEADER. Probably the same as Waterleder (which occurs as a surname in the Nonæ) whatever that may mean. Halliwell says, 'a water-carrier,' but I am disposed to think a *leader* of water, i.e., a drainer, or an irrigator of land, or perhaps a conduit-maker.

LEAKE. East and West Leake are two parishes in co. Notts.

LEAL. LEALL. 1. O. Fr. and Scot., loyal, trustworthy. 2. A corruption of Lisle.

LEAN. The Gaelic Mac-Lean, sans Mac.

LEANEY. LENEY. *Leeny*, according to Grose, is active, alert.

☞ LEAP or LIP. A termination to several local names, originating in some feat at saltation connected with the chase, as Hindleap, Hartlip, &c.

LEAPINGWELL. See Well.

LEAR. Not from the personal name rendered illustrious by the great dramatist, but from Lire, in the arrondissement of Evreux in Normandy. Mr. Ferguson thinks it may have come originally from Hlér (Hleer) one of the names of the Neptune of Northern mythology.

LEARMOUTH. Evidently local, but I cannot find the place.

LEARNED. Primarily applied to a scholar.

LEASHMAN. See Leechman.

LEATH. A ward or division of Cumberland.

LEATHAM. Villages in Fife and Forfarshire are called Letham.

LEATHER. LEATHERS. An ancient personal name. One *Lethar* was a bishop in the days of Æthelbert. Cod. Dipl. 981. Hence the local surnames, Leatherby, Leatherdale, Leatherhead, and Leatherbarrow.

LEATHERBARROW. A hill near Windermere. Ferguson, p. 204.

LEATHERBY. See Leather.

LEATHERDALE. See Leather.

LEATHERHEAD. A town in Surrey, anciently Lederede.

LEAVER. LEAVERS. See Lever.

LE BLANC. Fr. "the White." Arms granted 1753.

LE BLOND. Fr. "the Fair-Haired." See Blount. The family settled in England after the Rev. of the Edict of Nantes, 1685.

LE BON. Fr. "the Good." Probably of the period of the Rev. Ed. Nantes, 1685.

LE BRETT. See Brett.

LECHE. The Leches of Carden, co. Chester, are said to be a branch of Leech of Chatsworth. (See Leech.) John has been the Christian name in this family, with one exception, for thirteen generations. Shirley's Noble and Gentle Men.

LECHMERE. A family of great antiquity, said to have migrated from the Low Countries, and to have received a grant of land called Lechmere's Field in Hanley, co.

Worcester, from William the Conqueror. Shirley's Noble and Gentle Men.

LECKY. The Leckys of Ireland are of Scotch extraction, and descend from a family so called in Stirlingshire, where in the parish of Gargunnock an estate called Leckie is still to be found.

LEDGER. "The very business-like name of Ledger may not improbably be a corruption of Ludegar, the name of a warlike king of the Saxons in the Nibelungen Lied." Ferguson. 2. A more probable derivation is from the Fr. *leger*, light, swift, nimble. 3. The most probable of all is from the Norman St. Leger, with the omission of the prefix.

LEDSHAM. A parish in Yorkshire.

☞ LEE. Itself a surname, with the various modifications Atte-Legh (now Atlee) Lea, Ley, Lighe, Lye, &c., is undeniably the A-Sax. *leáh*. It is, as Professor Leo observes, the equivalent of "the old High German *lóh*, and corresponds literally (allowing for the recognized modification) with the Latin *lucus*; but whilst *leáh* may enclose a thicket, or indeed an actual wood, it has a yet more general meaning, and may denote such an open field as would be rendered *campus*." Williams's Translation, Treatise on Local Nomenclature, 1852. *Lea*, the modern English word, signifies, however, meadow, pasture, or grass land. Nor must it be forgotten that the A-Sax. *leag* or *leah*, has a totally different meaning, implying a territory or district in which a particular law or custom was in force. This term, varied in different ways, as *lagu*, *leuga*, and *lowey*, was retained for centuries after the incoming of the Normans, to denote a particular liberty, franchise, or district, as the *league* of Battel Abbey, the *lowey* of Pevensey, the *lowey* of Tunbridge, &c. To some or all of these sources, we are indebted for a very large proportion of our local, and consequently of our family nomenclature in South Britain, for—

"In Ford, in Ham, in *Ley*, and Ton,
The most of English Surnames run."

To cite all the names from this source would uselessly fill a great space, but by way of sample a few may be quoted, as:—Farlee. Fairlee, Godlee, Henley, Hoadley, Penley, Walmsley, Evesleigh, Radleigh, Ridley, Woolley, Hawkesley, Horsley, Cowley, Womersley, Carley, Harley, Barley, Oxley, Colley, Tingley, Fawsley, Stanley, Shirley, Berkeley, Headley, Ashley, Bromley, Cholmondeley, Copley, Stapley, Wellesley, Pelley, Shelley, Burleigh.

LEECH. A Sax. *læce*, a physician.

"Conscience called a *leche*
To go salve tho(se) that sike ben."
Wright's P. Ploughman, p. 443.

The blood-sucking reptile (*hirudo*) is so called from its salutary properties. In the South, a village veterinary surgeon calls himself "Horse-Farrier and Cow-Leech." The ancestor of the Derbyshire Leeches

(Chatsworth), was one of the surgeons of King Edward the Third. Lysons' Derb. The name may, however, be local, as there is a place of this designation near Chester.

LEECHMAN. The same as Leech, (which see) the suffix *man* being a mere expletive. Nares gives Leachman as a physician. A Scottish family of the name give three pelicans as their arms, probably in allusion to blood-letting. An analogous instance of the unnecessary addition of 'man' to the designation of a calling is found in Tuckerman, which see.

LEEDS. The great town in Yorkshire.

LEEK. A town in Staffordshire, and parishes in cos. York and Warwick. The Leekes of Longford, co. Salop, trace to Ralph L. of Ludlow, A.D. 1334.

LEEMAN. See Lee, and the termination MAN.

LEEMING. A chapelry in Yorkshire.

LEER. See Lear.

LEES. LEESE. Places in cos. Lancaster, Stafford, Chester, and an estate at Eccles, co. Berwick.

LEESON. Perhaps a contraction from Levison.

LEET. LEETE. A meeting of cross-roads. Halliw. The origin of *leet* as applied to an assembly or convention, as in court-leet, borough-leet, is disputed. See Richardson's Dict.; but the primary idea of a 'meeting' seems to be borne out by Mr. Halliwell's definition.

LEEVES. See Levi.

LEFEVRE. O. Fr. *le fevre*, a workman, particularly a smith, like the Lat. *faber*. Modern French has rejected the word and substituted *forgeron*, though the surname is nearly as common in France as Smith is with us. Many settlements of Le Fevres have taken place in England, and at least half a dozen different coats of arms are now associated with the name in this country. The Lefevres of Heckfield came from the neighbourhood of Rouen, and established themselves in England at the Rev. of the Edict of Nantes, settling in Essex and Hampshire. B.L.G.

LEFROY. The family are of Flemish extraction, having migrated to England at the time of the Duke of Alva's persecutions. The first settler was Anthony Lefroy, A.D. 1569. B.L.G. In Petham Church, co. Kent, is the following epitaph :—

> " Sacred
> to THOS. LEFROY, of Canterbury,
> who died 3rd Nov., 1723, aged 43 ;
> of a Cambresian family
> that preferred
> Religion and Liberty
> To their Country and Property,
> In the time of the Duke of Alva's Persecutions."

LEFTWICH. A place in Cheshire.

LEGARD. LEGEARD. LEGUARD. Fr. *le garde*, the guard, keeper, or warden; one who secures or preserves.

The baronet's family are of great antiquity in Yorkshire. They are said to have become possessed of Anlaby in that shire as early as the XII century.

LEGAY. Fr. *Le Gai*, " the sprightly or cheerful." M. Pierre le Gay was driven from Rochelle by the persecution of the Protestants by Louis XIII. Though he brought little or nothing of his patrimony with him, he was so successful as a merchant, that he bought the estate of West Stoke, co. Sussex. Palmer's Nonconformists' Memorial, ii. 478.

LEGG. LEGGE. 1. See under LEE. 2. An ancient trader's sign.

> " The hosiers will dine at the *Leg*,
> The drapers at the sign of the Brush," &c.
> *London's Ordinary.*

3. An old personal name. Fil' Legg is found in H.R.

LEGGAT. Lat. *legatus*, a legate, ambassador. At the date of the Domesday survey, Hervey Legatus was a tenant in capite in co. Bucks, and Richard Legatus had the same tenure in co. Gloucester.

LEGGET. See Leggat.

LEGH. See under LEE.

LEGLESS. A corruption, probably, of some French name, prefixed by the article *le*, and not referring to any personal mutilation.

LEGROS. Fr. " the big or large."

LEGRYLE. The same as the French Le Griel, still existing in Normandy. *Grice* or *gris* is an old French and English word for a pig, and *griel* is its diminutive. In allusion to this derivation, the Norfolk family of Legryle bear boars in their arms.

LEGRYS. Fr. " the Pig." See Purcell.

LEHUNTE. The A-Sax. *hunta*, prefixed by the medieval *le*—" the hunter." The family settled in Ireland from Suffolk, temp. Oliver Cromwell. B.L.G.

LEICESTER. The chief town of Leicestershire.

LEIFCHILD. *Leffechyld* occurs in a poem of the XV. century, cited by Halliwell, in the sense of dear or beloved child ; and so early as 1222, it is found as a Christian name—Lefchild, son of Sprot. See Hale's Domesd. of St. Paul's, p. 57 ; but the family believe themselves to be of German extraction, and claim another etymology, deducing the name from *leib* and *schild*, "body-shield," from some peculiarity in the defensive armour of the original assumer. In like manner the founder of the Rothschilds is presumed to have derived his name from his using a 'red shield,' which is the literal meaning of it.

LEIGH. See under LEE.

LEIGH. LEGH. An eminent Cheshire family, who for centuries have been of High Leigh, in that co., and from whom nearly all the gentry families of the name claim descent. The Leighs are as prolific as they are ancient, if we may trust the well-known Cheshire proverb :—

"As MANY LEIGHS AS FLEAS; Massies as asses; Crewes as crows; and Davenports as dogs' tails."

The various forms of the name are Leighe, Leigh, Legh, Leghe, Ligh, Lighe, Lea, Leaye, Ley, Leye, Lee.

Mr. Shirley includes among his Noble and Gentle Men of England the following families :—

1. *Legh* of East Hall, in High Legh, co. Chester, descended from Efward de Lega, who lived at or near the period of the Conquest, and who from his name appears to have been of Saxon race. Ormerod's Cheshire, ɩ. 358.

2. *Leigh* of West Hall, in High Legh. Originally De Lymme, who married a Legh heiress in the XIII. cent.

2. *Leigh* of Adlestrop (Baron Leigh) co. Gloucester. Descended from Agnes, daughter and heiress of Richard de Legh, and of her second husband, William Venables. They had a son who took his mother's maiden name, and founded one of the great Cheshire lines of Legh or Leigh.

For many offshoots of these three main lines, see Ormerod's Cheshire, and Shirley's Noble and Gentle Men.

LEIGHTON. The family are stated to have been seated at Leighton in Shropshire prior to the Conquest. They are presumed to have sprung from *Rainald vioe-comes*, mentioned as the Domesday tenant of Lestone or Leighton. Certain it is that they were of Leighton, *eo nomine*, in the XII. century. See Shirley's Noble and Gentle Men. The principal seat of the family is now at Loton, in the above-named county.

LEITCH. See Leech.

LEITH. "The surname of Leith is of great antiquity in Scotland, and those who bore it held, in a remote era, vast possessions, including the barony of Restalrig, and others in the shire of Mid-Lothian, and territory of Leith, whence, it is presumed, the name was taken." B.L.G. The pedigree is traced only to the year 1350. The baronet's family descend from William Leith, who was provost of Aberdeen in 1350. According to Douglas there were at the latter end of the last century six distinct families of Leith, all of whom could trace their origin to that personage. Courthope's Debrett.

LEKEUX. O. Fr. "The cook." Isambert was grand *keux* of France, under St. Louis, 1250. Dixon. In England, the surname pertains to a French Protestant family settled at Canterbury before the year 1645.

LELAND. In the West, signifies a cow-pasture, but it is also probably the name of some manor or estate.

LELHOME. O. Fr. *leal homme*, a loyal man.

LE LIEVRE. A Guernsey surname, but supposed to have been adopted by a member of the English family of Hare, who settled in that island.

LELLIOT. Apparently the same as Elliott.

LEMAIRE. Fr. "The Mayor."

LEMARCHANT. Fr. "The Merchant."

LE MESURIER. O. Fr. "The Measurer."

LEMITARE. 1. A corruption of the common Fr. surname, Lemaitre, 'the master.' 2. From *limitour*, a begging friar —familiar to every reader of Chaucer.

LEMMON. See Lemon.

LEMON. O. Eng. *lemman*, paramour, sweetheart—an A-Sax. and Chaucerian word. One " Alan, the son of the Leman," occurs in the Hundred Rolls. Its primary meaning seems to be, a person much beloved, or very dear.

"And he seyde he would ben hir *Limman* or para-mour. And sche asked him zif that he were a Knyghte.—And he seyde Nay. And than sche said that he myghte not ben hir Lemman."

Maundevile's Travels, p. 24.

A tributary of the Exe, in Devonshire, is called the Leman. One family of this name, rather recently arrived from Germany, originally wrote themselves Lehman, which is doubtless a contraction of *lehnmann*, a vassal or feudal tenant. Inf. Robt. Lemon, Esq., F.S.A.

LEMOSY. From the province of Limousin, in the interior of France.

LEMOYNE. O. Fr. "The Monk."

LEMPRIERE. Said to be a corruption, or rather an ancient spelling, of *l'Empereur*. In the Chartularies of the Abbaye de la Trinité at Caen, this patronymic goes through the various gradations of Imperator, L'Empereur, Lemprere, Lempreur, to Lempriere. According to a family tradition, the name is derived from its original bearer having overturned a king, and thus become an Emperor ! It was he, not Rollo his master, who went to kiss the foot of Charles of France, and lifted it so high as to throw the monarch off his balance ! Master Wace and other vulgar historians, who make the Northman chief himself the perpetrator of this clever practical joke, are therefore quite misinformed in the matter ! Ex. inf. J. Bertrand Payne, Esq.

LEMSTER. From the observations under STER, this name might be supposed to belong to that class. It is, however, simply a curt pronunciation of Leominster, co. Hereford.

LENARD. See Leonard.

LENCH. The name of two parishes in co. Worcester.

LE NEVE. " The nephew." The

Promptorium Parvulorum has the following definitions:

"NEVE, sonys son. *Nepos.*
NEVE, broderys sone. *Neptis.*
NEVE, systerrys sonne. *Sororius.*
NEVE, neverthryfte or wastour," &c.

LENEY. A William Leny is mentioned in H.R. Perhaps the same as Lennie or as Leaney.

LENNARD. See Leonard.

LENNIE. 1. A 'nurse-name' of Leonard. 2. *L'Aîné,* Fr., corresponding with Senior, Eld, &c., has been suggested.

LENNOX. The ancient county of Dumbarton, Scotland, once much more extensive than now. The original name of the district was Leven-ach, 'the field of the Leven,' and designated not the basin only of that river, but also of Loch-Lomond, once called Loch-Leven. Levenachs came to be the name applied to the extensive possessions of the powerful Earls of the soil, and hence Levenax and Lennox. Imp. Gaz. of Scotland.

LENNY. See Lennie. An old spelling, Lany, supports the second derivation.

LENT. From the season—like Easter, Pentecost, Christmas, &c.

LENTHALL. A parish and a chapelry in co. Hereford. The family of L. of Bessels Leigh, co. Berks, are descended, through the celebrated speaker of the Long Parliament, and through the hero of Agincourt, from Lenthall of Lenthall in the reign of Edw. I. De Lenethale. H.R.

LENTON. A parish in Nottinghamshire.

LEO. The Latin form of Lion.

LEON. Spanish and Italian *leone,* a Lion.

LEONARD. The personal name. Lennie and Lankin appear to be derivatives, and Lenard and Lennard are corruptions.

LEPER. One afflicted with leprosy, a common disease in this country in Crusading times. There were many lazar-houses or hospitals for lepers in the early centuries after the Conquest. Le Lepre, Lepere. H.R.

LEPPARD. LEPARD. A leopard; either from an armorial bearing, or from a trader's sign.

LEPPER. See Leper.

LEQUESNE. Provincial Fr. for *le chêne,* the Oak.

LEREW. See Leroux.

LEROUX. Fr. "the red;" a person of florid complexion.

LESLIE. "The family of Leslie, to which belong two Scottish peerages, trace their origin to Bartholomew, a Flemish chief, who settled with his followers in the district of Garioch, in Aberdeenshire, in the reign of William the Lion. He took the

2 C

name of De Lesley from the place where he settled. The heralds, however, have an old legend representing the first man of the family as having acquired distinction and a name at once, by overcoming a knight in battle, at a spot between a *less lee* (meadow) and a greater.

BETWEEN THE LESS-LEE AND THE MAIR, HE SLEW THE KNIGHT, AND LEFT HIM THERE.
Chambers' Pop. Rhymes of Scotland, p. 26.

Another statement makes Bartholomew a *Hungarian* knight or nobleman, who came into Scotland temp. King Malcolm Canmore, in the suite of Queen Margaret, 1067. The parish of Leslie is in Aberdeenshire, and Leslie castle, the seat of the ancient barons, still exists.

The arms of the family contain three buckles, sometimes on a bend, otherwhile on a fesse, and the bearings are thus accounted for by a family tradition. Bartholomew, the personage alluded to—

"Had the good fortune to rescue from imminent danger Malcolm's Queen, Margaret, sister of Edgar Atheling and grand-daughter, maternally, of Solomon, King of Hungary, when carried away by the stream in crossing a river on horseback—dragging her to land by her belt or girdle. Hence *a belt and three buckles* were assigned to him for a coat of arms, with GRIP FAST as a motto, from the Queen calling out in these words when in danger!" B.L.G.

The Leslies of Ireland settled there from Scotland temp. James I.

LESSINGHAM. A parish in Norfolk.

LESTER. A corruption of Leicester.

LESTRANGE. See Strange.

LETBE. See Letheby.

LETHBRIDGE. Clearly a local name, though the locality is unknown. The late radical Henry Hunt, a political opponent of Sir Thos. Lethbridge, used to assert that the worthy Baronet's grandfather was a foundling, who had been exposed in a pair of '*leather breeches!*' The not altogether dissimilar name Lodbrok signifies "shaggy-breeches." See Ludbrook.

LETHEBY. The family came into England from Brittany, at the Revocation of the Edict of Nantes, under the name of Le Tebé, which was subsequently anglicized to its existing form. Inf. Dr. H. Letheby.

LETHERHOSE. From the garment. See Hosier. This name is as old as temp. Edw. I. H.R.

LETHIEULLIER. "This family of Le Thieullier appear to have been of good account in France, as well as in Germany, for some generations before they settled in England, which is supposed to have been in the reign of Elizabeth, when they fled hither to avoid the persecution in those parts on account of religion. Among the names of such French as fled to Rye in Sussex, upon the massacre of the Protestants in France in 1572, are the names of Le Tellier and Tellier ..." Hasted's Kent, II., 350. The name is a medieval spelling of Le Tuillier, the Tyler, either a maker or a placer of tiles.

LETT. A Livonian. One Let was a tenant in co. Gloucester before the Conquest. Domesday.

LETTERS. Perhaps from Letter, an estate near Loch Katrine in Scotland.

LETTS. See Lett.

LEVACHE. A corruption of Fr. *la Vache*, "the Cow." Cow also occurs as a surname—why, it would be difficult to explain, except that it was anciently a sign of a house. A London printer of the XVII. cent. adopted the sign of the "Hee-Cowe." But see under Koe.

LE VAVASOUR. See Vavasour.

LEVEN. A town in Fifeshire.

LEVENTHORPE. An estate in Yorkshire. Leventhorpe Hall, in that county, was long the residence of the family.

LEVEQUE. Fr. "the Bishop." See Ecclesiastical Surnames.

LEVER. Apparently a personal name. Hence the genitive Levers, the patronymical Leverson, and the local Leverton. But it is also local, there being three places called Lever in Lancashire.

LEVERETT. Not the young hare—but the female greyhound—Fr. *lévrette;* probably applied to a swift-footed person. In like manner Leveridge, if not local, may be the Fr. *lévriche*, which is a diminutive of *lévrette*.

LEVERIDGE. See under Leverett.

LEVERIKE. A corruption of Leofric, an A-Sax. personal name.

LEVERS. See Lever.

LEVERSON. See Lever.

LEVERTON. Parishes in cos. Nottingham and Lincoln.

LEVESON. Perhaps Louis' son, the son of Lewis or Louis. It may, however, be the son of Levi. Singularly, the H.R. have the forms De Leveson, and Le Leveson.

LEVETT. LEVIT. 1. Fr. *le Vite*, "the quick, speedy, or swift." 2. From one of the places in Normandy called Livet. The Itin. de la Normandie mentions no less than eight of these.

LEVEY. See Levi.

LEVI. This personal name seems to be the common source of Levy, Levey, Levison, Leeves, &c.

LEVIN. LEVINSON. LEVINSOHN. LEVISOHN. Levi and Levi's son. Family names of German Jews naturalized in this country.

LEVISON. See Levi.

LEWER. The same as Lower (?)

LEWES. 1. The county-town of Sussex. 2. The same as Lewis.

LEWIN. LEWINS. LEWN. 1. A corruption of the well-known A-Sax. personal name, Leofwin. 2. A contraction of the Welsh Llewellyn.

LEWIS. The Welsh personal name, the same as the Fr. Louis. Also one of the Hebrides. Many of the Welsh families conceal beneath this common, and usually plebeian name, blood and pedigree of remote antiquity. For example, LEWIS of Greenmeadow springs from Gwaethvoed, descended from the ancient princes of Britain, and a contemporary of the A-Sax. king Edgar. LEWIS of Gilfach claims from Cradoc ap Guillym, who flourished in the XIII. century. LEWIS of St. Pierre derives from Cadifor, prince or chieftain of Divet (a district which comprised Pembrokeshire and part of Caermarthen), about the time of the Norman Conquest. In these cases the name Lewis was not hereditary until temp. Henry VIII. or Elizabeth.

LEWKNOR. The first proven ancestor of this great Sussex family is Sir Roger de Lewknor, high-sheriff of the county in 1284. It is asserted, on I know not what evidence, that the name is derived from Levechenora, the ancient denomination of one of the hundreds of Lincolnshire. Pegge's Curial. Miscell. p. 208. But this is far-fetched, inasmuch as we have in Oxfordshire, a well-known parish, as also a hundred, still written Lewknor.

LEWRY. See Lowry.

LEWSEY. The same as Lucy, Luci.

LEWSON. The son of Lewis.

LEWTHWAITE. Local: see Thwaite and Lowe. The place is supposed to be in Cumberland, where the family still exist.

LEY. See under LEE.

LEYCESTER. The founder of the family was Sir Nicholas Leycester, who acquired the manor of Nether Tabley in Cheshire by marriage, and died in 1295. There his descendants of the elder line flourished till 1742. Shirley's Noble and Gentle Men. The name was probably borrowed from the chief town of Leicestershire.

LIBERTY. A franchise, or district where peculiar laws and customs are enjoyed. See under Lee. The Lond. Direct. gives us a *Jonathan Liberty*, but does not inform us whether he has any American relations. There is a village called Liberty in co. Fife.

LICKFOLD. A place near Petworth, co. Sussex.

LIDBETTER. See Leadbeater.

LIDDEL. LIDDELL. The family, in which there have been two peerages, were found among the merchants of Newcastle-upon-Tyne, some two centuries and a half since. The name seems to have been derived from the Liddel, a river of Roxburghshire.

LIDDELOW. Probably the same as Laidlaw or Ludlow.

LIDDERDALE. Probably Liddesdale, in Roxburghshire.

LIDDIARD. LIDDIAT. The two parishes of Liddiard are in Wiltshire.

LIDDINGTON. Parishes in Wiltshire and Rutland.

LIDDLE. See Liddel.

LIDGATER. Possibly a corruption of Ligator, "binder," a common surname in H.R. In the same records we find the name Stephanus Ligator-Librorum, Stephen the Bookbinder.

LIDSTON. LIDSTONE. A hamlet in Oxfordshire.

LIGHT. Probably refers to lightness of foot; or it may be the same as Lyte.

LIGHTBODY. See Body.

LIGHTFOOT. From agility in running. 'Martin with the Light Foot,' occurs in the life of Hereward the Saxon. Wright's Essays, ii. 101, &c. See Metcalfe. The synonymous Dutch surname is Ligtvoet.

LIGHTNING. This name, probably a recent sobriquet, is found in R.G., 16.

LIGO. A contraction of Linlithgow, through Lithgow.

LIGONIER. Of French extraction. The brothers Francis and John Ligonier, entered the English army, and the latter was made a knight banneret under the royal standard at the battle of Dettingen, in 1742, and was afterwards raised to the peerage as Lord Ligonier.

LILL. See Lille.

LILLE. 1. The French town. 2. The same as Lisle.

LILLY. LILLEY. LILLIE. 1. Perhaps the same as Lille or Lisle. 2. From the heraldric bearing, the fleur-de-lys. See Lys. 3. Lilley, a parish in Hertfordshire.

LILLYLOW. A Scottish phrase meaning 'bright flame.' It is not very easy to guess how it became a surname.

LILY. See Lilly.

LILYWHITE. 1. Fair, or white as a lily. 2. More probably a corruption of the local name Litelthwaite. See Thwaite; also Applewhite.

LIMBER. 1. Supple, flexible—applied perhaps to an agile person. 2. Lymbergh, two parishes in Lincolnshire.

LIMEBEER. Perhaps the same as Limber.

☞ LIN or LINN. A Celtic topographical expression, used both simply and as a prefix. It signifies a deep pool or lake, or any piece of water; but is commonly used in Scotland to designate a cascade falling into a pool. Gaz. Scotl.

LINCH. LYNCH. 1. A parish in Sussex. 2. A small hanging wood or thicket; called on the South Downs a *link*.

LINCOLN. The city.

LIND. The name of Lynne was assumed by the proprietors of the lands and barony of Lynne, in Ayrshire, as soon as surnames became hereditary in Scotland. B.L.G. Lind is Scotch for a lime tree. Jamieson. In England the name occurs in the XIV. century, as De la Lynde—"of the Linden, or lime tree." This surname is found in most of the Teutonic languages. The Fr. name Tilleul is synonymous.

LINDFIELD. A parish in Sussex, where a humble family of the name are still resident.

LINDLEY. Several places in Yorkshire are so called.

LINDO. Naturalized from Portugal. The same as Lind.

LINDSAY. This distinguished family, who boasted of twenty Earls of Crawford, extending from the year 1398 to 1808, and whose deeds have been recorded by a noble member of the house, in his "Lives of the Lindsays," were in all probability of English origin, and the name appears to have been derived from the division of the county of Lincoln still called the "Parts of Lindsey," though some genealogists deduce it from the manor of Lindsey in Essex.

LINDSEY. See Lindsay.

LINDUS. Perhaps Lindores, a village in Fifeshire.

LINEKER. Probably from A-Sax. *linece*, a linnet. Ferguson. I should prefer Linacre, a township in Lancashire, as its source.

LINFIELD. See Lindfield.

LING. Heath, in some dialects, is so called—also a fish; but a more probable derivation is from one of the two parishes of Ling in Somersetshire and in Norfolk.

LINGARD. Mr. Ferguson thinks that Lingard and Linnegar may be inversions of the O. High Germ. Girland, a name compounded of *ger*, a spear, and *lind*, the lime-tree; figuratively a shield—because shields are made of that wood.

LINGEN. Robert de Wigmore, lord of Lingen, co. Hereford, and founder of the priory of Lyngbroke, had a grandson, John, who took the name of Lingen. From him sprang the Lingens of Longner, co. Salop, &c. Shirley's Noble and Gentle Men.

LINGHAM. A known corruption of Langham.

LINK. The same as Linch.

LINKINHORNE. A parish in Cornwall.

LINLEY. See Lindley.

LINNEGAR. See Lingard.

LINNET. A Fr. name of uncertain origin.

LINNEY. Mr. Ferguson says O. Norse, *linni,* a snake.

LINSEY. See Lindsay.

LINSTEAD. Parishes in Suffolk and Kent.

LINTON. Parishes and places in cos. Roxburgh, Haddington, Cambridge, Derby, Devon, Lincoln, Hereford, Kent, York, &c.

LINTOT. A place in the department of Seine Inferieure, Normandy; another in the arrondissement of Havre. The family were in Shropshire in the XII. century.

LINWOOD. Parishes, &c., in cos. Lincoln and Hants; also a manufacturing village in Renfrewshire.

LION. By the common consent of all ages and countries, the lion has been acknowledged as one of the noblest of creatures, and there is perhaps scarcely a language under heaven in which its designation does not supply one or more personal or family names. Our Christian name Leonard means lion-hearted, and Lionel, the young Lion. Scotland had its William the Lion, as we our Richard Cœur de Lion, and this cognomen has been applied to princes and chieftains everywhere. Men of high degree of old took it from the charge of their shields; men of low degree got it from the signs of their houses; and lions of every hue now adorn the sign-post, as of yore they did the banners of the battle-field.

LIPP. See Leap.

LIPPINCOTT. The baronets (extinct 1829) traced their family into Devonshire in the XVI. century, and there is little doubt that the name was originally Luffincott, from a parish in that county so called.

LIPSCOMBE. Probably from Liscombe, a parish in Buckinghamshire.

LIPTROT. "Probably compounded with *léof,* dear; it corresponds with a German name Liebetrut." Ferguson.

LIQUORISH. *Lickorous* or *lickerish* is a medievalism retained in many dialects; it means dainty, affected, addicted to indulgence. Chaucer uses it in the form of *likerous,* to signify gluttonous, lascivious.

LISCOMBE. A hamlet in Buckinghamshire.

LISHMAN. A corruption of Leechman, or perhaps Scot. *leish,* tall and active. Jamieson.

LISLE. " Of this surname were several families, springing originally from two, which had derived the designation, one from the Isle of Ely, the other from the Isle of Wight." Burke's Ext. Peerage. Eighteen different coats of arms are ascribed to this name by Berry. The principal forms of it are Lisle, L'Isle, Lyle, Lylle, Lyell. In charters it was latinized De Insula.

LISTER. 1. A-Sax. *listre,* a person who read some portions of the church service.

2. Perhaps in some instances a corruption of Leicester. 3. A more likely derivation than either, is from the O. Eng. *litster,* a dyer, tinctor. The insurrectionary movement in Norfolk, called Lister's Rebellion, in 1381, was headed by John Lister or Littester, a dyer of Norwich, who caused himself to be proclaimed "King of the Commons." Now this worthy, being one of the persons who in that age had not yet adopted a surname, upon attaining such "bad eminence," took the designation of his trade by way of distinction, and was called John Littester, 'the dyer,' just as his forerunner and exemplar, Walter, from his having to do with tiles, had been known as Wat Tyler. For an account of the Rebellion, see Blomefield's Norfolk, and Papers of Norf. Arch. Soc. vol. v., p. 348. Litster, *tinctor.* Nominale MS.

In Lord Ribblesdale's family the name is local, as the pedigree ascends to a John de Lister, who in 6, Edward II. was resident at Derby, and transferred himself to Yorkshire, on his marriage with the daughter and heiress of John de Bolton, bow-bearer of Bolland.

LISTON. A parish in Essex, and Liston Shiels, a district in Edinburghshire.

LIT. See Lite.

LITCHFIELD. The city in co. Stafford, more properly written Lichfield.

LITE. See Lyte.

LITHERLAND. A township of Sefton, co. Lancashire.

LITHGOW. A contraction of Linlithgow, a well-known Scotch town.

LITT. O. E. *lite,* little.

LITTLE. 1. A person of diminutive stature. Like the Fr. Le Petit, the Germ. Klein, &c. 2. Perhaps the same as Liddell.

☞ LITTLE. This word enters very frequently into our local and family names; e. g. Littleford, Littlefield, Littlewood, Littleworth, Littleton.

LITTLEBOYS. See Peverel. It may however be a corruption of the French Lillebois.

LITTLECHILD. Probably a sobriquet applied by antiphrasis to a large, powerful man. Child however has a distinct meaning. See Child.

LITTLEDALE. Apparently an older and more correct form of Liddesdale, by which is intended the dale or basin of the river Liddel, in Roxburghshire. The family trace to the neighbouring county of Cumberland.

LITTLEFAIR. R.G. 16. See Littlefear.

LITTLEFEAR. A man of courage.

LITTLEFIELD. A place in Kent giving name to a hundred.

LITTLEHEAD. 1. From some *promontory* so called. 2. From the smallness of the original bearer's head—the opposite of Greathead.

LITTLEJOHN. See JOHN, a termination. As we have the surname of *Robinhood*, a sobriquet borrowed from the famous outlaw of Sherwood Forest, it is probable that this name has a similar origin from his famous compeer. It is clear, at least, that the herald who devised the family arms thought so, when he gave, "Argent, *three arrows* Gules, two in saltier and one in pale, feathered Or, between six trefoils slipped of the second." (Burke's Armory, *in nom.*) It may be remarked, however, that the French have the corresponding names of Petit-jean and Petit-pierre—Little-John and Little-Peter.

LITTLEPAGE. A personal attendant of diminutive size.

LITTLEPROUD. R.G. 16. Whether "little" and "proud," or only slightly tainted with the deadly sin, does not appear.

LITTLER. A corruption of Littleover, co. Derby. Eng. Surn. i. 141.

LITTLETON. Many places in various counties are so designated. The celebrated jurist, Sir Thomas Lyttelton, who had three sons, whose posterity were elevated to the peerage in each line, sprang maternally from Thomas de Luttelton, of co. Worcester, temp. Henry III. The surname probably originated at one of the several places called Littleton, in that county.

LITTON. Parishes, &c., in cos. Somerset, Dorset, Derby, and York.

LIVELY. From natural disposition.

LIVEMORE. The same as Livermore.

LIVENS. In early Dutch records (in the United States) are found such names as Ver—i.e. Vrouwe, Belenszoon, Ver Lievenzoon—Dame Belen's son, Dame Lieven's son. Belen and Lieven are both apparently baptismal names now obsolete. Dixon.

LIVER. Probably the same as Lever or Leaver.

LIVERMORE. Two parishes in Suffolk, more usually written Livermere.

LIVESEY. LIVESAY. A township in the parish of Blackburn, co. Lancaster.

LIVET. See Levett.

LIVICK. Probably a corruption of the Fr. *l'Evêque*, the Bishop.

LIVING. An A-Sax. personal name. There was a Living, archbishop of Canterbury, and another of the same name, bishop of Worcester.

LIVINGSTONE. A parish in Linlithgowshire.

LIZAR. LIZARS. A.-Norm. *lazar*, a leper.

LLEWELLYN. A very ancient Welsh personal name, borne by many princes and magnates of Celtic origin. Comp. Howlyn.

LLOYD. A well-known Welsh personal name—sometimes corrupted to Floyd and Flood. As an hereditary surname it does not date beyond the XVI. century, yet many of the families bearing it are of great antiquity, as, for example :—LLOYD of Bronwydd is 23rd lord of the Barony of Kemes, co. Pembroke, in hereditary descent from Martin de Tours, a companion of William the Conqueror. LLOYD of Plymog claims from Marchudd ap Cynan, who flourished in the IX. cent., and founded the eighth noble tribe of North Wales, and Powys: King Henry VII. sprang from this family. LLOYD of Aston springs from the royal house of Powys. LLOYD of Dan-yr-allt descends from Cadivor ap Dyfnwall, lord of Castle Howel, temp. Henry II., and lineally sprung from Rhodri Mawr, King of Wales. LLOYD of Coedmore claims from an ancient Prince of Ferlys. LLOYD of Clockfaen springs from the great Tudor Trevor, in the X. cent. LLOYD of Pale derives paternally from Held Molwyrogg, a chieftain of Denbighland, founder of the ninth noble tribe of N. Wales and Powys. For these and many other particulars, see B.L.G.

In proof of the numerousness of the Lloyds in the rank of Gentry, it may be mentioned that more than thirty different coats of arms are ascribed to the name.

LOADER. See Loder.

LOAKE. Probably the same as Lock.

LOAN. A township in Durham.

LOBB. A clown, a clumsy fellow. "A blunt country *lob*." Stanihurst. (Halliwell.)

LOCH. A Celtic word, implying sometimes a lake, and sometimes an arm of the sea, or æstuary.

LOCHTAY. The well-known Scottish lake.

LOCK. See Locke.

LOCKARD. Loch-Ard, a beautiful sheet of water near Ben Lomond in Scotland.

LOCKE. 1. A place where rivers meet with a partial obstruction from a wooden dam. 2. The same as Loch.

LOCKE. The Scandinavian god of mischief—the Evil Principle of the Northern mythology—was called Lók, and the name may have been afterwards a sobriquet of derision applied to a bad or injurious man.

LOCKER. A lockmaker.

LOCKETT. A corruption of Lockhart.

LOCKHART. See Lockard above—a far more probable origin than that assigned by tradition. King Robert Bruce ordered his *heart* to be conveyed to the Holy Land for burial, and the good Sir James, Lord Douglas, was deputed to carry it thither. One of his attendants took his surname of Lockhart from the circumstance of his having carried the key of the casket! Pegge's Curial. Miscell. p. 229.

LOCKINGTON. Parishes, &c., in cos. Leicester and York.

LOCKLIN. Probably Mac Laughlan, sans Mac.

LOCKMAN. 1. Perhaps the person who superintended a lock or wooden dam in a river. 2. In Scotland *lokman* means an executioner. See Henniker.

LOCKSMITH. The occupation. Locsmyth. H.R.

LOCKTON. A chapelry in Yorkshire.

LOCKWOOD. A township in Yorkshire.

LOCKYEAR. See Lockyer.

LOCKYER. A lockmaker.

LOCOCK. See Luke.

LODDIGES. "The son of Lodic or Ludwig." Talbot's Eng. Etym.

LODDON. A river in Berkshire. Also a hundred and parish in co. Norfolk.

LODER. LOADER. 1. A carter or carrier. Halliw. from Nominale MS. In the South, a man who carries out flour from a mill is called a Loader. 2. A corruption of Lowther.

LODEWICK. Ludwig, Ludovicus, Louis.

LODGE. A temporary building; sometimes a more permanent one. In many instances a manor-house of small pretensions is called a Court-Lodge. Fr. *loge*, a lodge or cabin, particularly in Forest districts.

LODGES. "Les Loges" is the name of several localities in Normandy.

LOFT. LOFFT. From residence in a loft or upper chamber. The form Ad le Loft, "at the Loft," occurs several times in H.R.

LOFTHOUSE. See Loftus.

LOFTS. A further corruption of Lofthouse. See Loftus.

LOFTUS. A contraction of Lofthouse, a parish in Yorkshire. The family "appear to have flourished in Yorkshire as early as the reign of Alfred!" B.L.G., where the archives of York Minster are given as the authority.

LOFTY. From pride or arrogance of disposition.

LOGAN. A Celtic word used in Scottish topography, both singly and as a prefix, and signifying a hollow place, or plain, or meadow surrounded by rising grounds. Gaz. of Scotl.

LOGIE. The same as Logan. Many parishes and districts of Scotland bear this name, both with and without a suffix.

LOGGIE. Probably from Logie, many parishes and places in Scotland.

LOKE. A private road or path. East. (Halliwell.) See however Locke.

LOLLARD. A Wicliffite; originally applied as a name of contempt to some dissentient from Roman Catholic views.

LOMBARD. A native of Lombardy. See Lambarde. Any banker or usurer was so called. In the Netherlands, a Lombard was an excommunicated person. He was denied the sacraments and Christian burial, and no priest would "marry him to any woman, except hee first promise to leave off being a Lumbarde, and doe make restitucion." Archæologia, xxix. 286.

LOMBE. An archaic form of Lamb.

LOMER. 1. St. Lomer, a parish in Normandy, now called Lomer-sur-Guerne, in the arrondissement of Alençon. It was anciently written *Villa Sancti Launomari.* Itin. de la Normandie. 2. A *lome* is in some dialects a tub; hence a Lomer may be a tub-maker. 3. Leomer in Domesd. is a baptismal name.

LONDE. Several places in Normandy bear the name of La Londe, particularly the great forest on the left bank of the Seine below Rouen.

LONDESBOROUGH. A parish in Yorkshire, the presumed site of the Roman station Delgovitia.

LONDON. Besides having become a local surname in the usual mode, this great city has given rise to several others, as London-bridge (E. Surn. i. 34.) Londonoys, Londonish, Londonsuch, and Londres. De London, De Londonia, De Londr. H.R.

LONDONISH. Belonging to London. So Kentish, Devenish, Cornish, &c.

LONDONOYS. Chaucer applies the word *Londenoys* to a Londoner.

LONDRES. The Fr. orthography of London. Hearne says that *Londreis* is an old expression meaning Londoners.

LONE or LUNE. A river in Lancashire.

LONG. From stature; a tall person. One of the family of Preux, an attendant on Lord Treasurer Hungerford, from his great height, acquired the sobriquet of Long Henry. On his marriage to a lady of quality he transposed this appellation to Henry Long, and became the founder of the Longs of Wiltshire. Camden. The H.R. forms of the name are Longus, Le Long, and Le Longe.

☞ **LONG.** A component syllable of many local surnames, some of which have been borrowed from places that are not found in the gazetteers; as Longbourne, "the long stream or boundary;" Longden, "the long pasture or vale;" Longdill, "the long dale;" Longhurst, "the long wood;" Longland "the long heath;" Longley, "the long meadow;" Longmire, "the long morass;" &c.

LONGBOTTOM. Local: see Bottom.

LONGCHAMP. Fr. 'long field'—a place in the arrondissement of Andeli in Normandy.

LONGDEN. Probably Longdon, parishes, &c., in cos. Salop, Stafford, Worcester, &c.

LONGE. See Long.

LONGESPEE. O. Fr. *longue espée*, "long-sword." This name was originally assigned to William Talbot, a courtier of Richard Cœur-de-Lion, on account of the length of his weapon. Dugd. Baronage.

LONGFELLOW. 1. Originally applied to a tall person. 2. An ingenious etymologist has derived it from the Fr. surname Longuevilliers. The Poet's ancestors are said to have emigrated to America from Yorkshire.

LONGHEAD. The long promontory.

LONGHURST. A township in Northumberland.

LONGMAID. See Langmead.

LONGMAN. 1. A man of great stature. 2. A village in Banffshire.

LONGMATE. Apparently not a synonym of Long*fellow*, but the same as Langmead, which see.

LONGNESSE. 1. A-Sax. *næsse*, a nose, headland, or promontory. 2. From length of nose—a personal peculiarity.

LONGRIDGE. A township in co. Durham, and a village in co. Linlithgow.

LONGSHANKS. From length of legs; the well-known sobriquet of Edward the First, and a still-existing family name.

LONGSTAFF. See Langstaffe.

LONGUEVILLE. LONGVILL. From Longueville, a small town in the department of the Lower Seine in Normandy, of which the Longuevilles, Earls of Buckingham, were anciently lords. This family gave the suffix to Overton Longueville, co. Huntingdon. Longevil, Longvile. H.R.

LONGVAL. Fr. *long*, and obs. *val*, the long vale or valley—a local surname common in France, and corrupted among us to Longvale, Longwall, Longwell, &c.

LONGVILLIERS. Long–Villers, a parish in the arrondissement of Caen, in Normandy.

LONSDALE. Considerable divisions of Westmoreland and of Lancashire are so called.

LOOKER. In the S. of Engl. a herdsman; especially, in marshy districts, a man who superintends cattle, and drives them to higher grounds in case of sudden floods, &c.

LOOSE. A parish in Kent.

LOOSELY. See Loosley.

LOOSLEY. Loseley, a hamlet and manor near Guildford, co. Surrey.

LOPES. The baronet's family, of Portuguese extraction, and long resident in the island of Jamaica, settled in England in the last century.

LOPEZ. See Lopes.

LOPPE. An uneven piece of ground, perhaps the same as *Lowe*.

LORAIGNE. LORAYNE. LORRAINE. From the well-known district of France. The Loraines are said to be a Norman family, and to have been originally settled in the county of Durham. Kirk Hall, the residence of the baronet in Northumberland, was obtained by his ancestor in marriage with the heiress of Del Strother, temp. Henry IV. Shirley's Noble and Gentle Men.

LORD. LORDE. A title given to monks and persons of superior rank; the equivalent of Dominus and Dan, which signify nothing more than *master*. In old times a sort of sobriquet, applied to the leaders of festivities, as Christmas Lords, Lords of Misrule, &c. Le Lord, is exceedingly common in H.R.

LORDAN. O. E. *lurdan*, a clown, an ill-bred person; a lazy fellow.

LORIMER. A maker of bits, spurs, &c., for horses. A Lorimers' Company for the city of London was incorporated so lately as the year 1712, though it is known to have existed in the XV. century. Those bearers of this surname who prefer a more dignified extraction, might deduce themselves from Goscelinus Loremarius, one of the Conqueror's tenants in chief, mentioned in Domesday, co. Essex; but query whether that personage's name itself, is not a mere latinization of Lorimer? Lorimar. Le Lorimer. H.R.

LORKIN. LORKING. A diminutive of Lawrence.

LORN. A district of Argyleshire.

LORRAINE. See Loraigne.

LOSCOMBE. A hamlet in Dorsetshire, parish of Netherbury.

LOSECAMP. Clearly local—though I do not find the place. In proof of the corruptibility of surnames, we may mention, that this name, probably derived from some manor or estate which was once the property of the family, would retain its phonetic identity if written *Low-scamp*.

LOSPITAL. O. Fr. *l'hospital*, "the hospital." See Spital.

LOTEMAN. 1. A-Sax. a pirate. See Lutman. 2. *Lote*, a southern provincialism for a loft. I. Atte Lote occurs in a document of 1296.

LOTHIAN. The district on the south side of the frith of Forth, which includes the counties of Haddington, Edinburgh, and Linlithgow.

LOTT. 1. A-Sax. *lote*, crafty; or A-Sax. *hlot*, a caster of lots, a fortune-teller. 2.

The Hebrew personal name.   Fil'Lote. H.R.

LOUBIER. Probably from Louviers, a considerable town in the department of Eure, in Normandy.

LOUDON. Loudoun, a great parish in Ayrshire. The progenitor of the family was James the son of Lambin, who obtained "Laudon," from Richard Morville, who died in 1189, the minister of William the Lion.

LOUDWELL. See Well.

LOUGHBOROUGH. A town in Leicestershire.

LOUIS. The personal name.

LOUNDE. See Lowndes.

LOVAINE. LOUVAINE. LOVEYNE. A celebrated city of the Netherlands.

LOVAT. A hamlet in Inverness-shire.

LOVE. This name relates not to the tender passion, but is an old modification of the Fr. *Loup*, wolf. In the same way Lupellus, the diminutive, became Loupel and Lovel. One family of this name bear wolves in their arms. Le Love. H.R.

LOVECHILD. An illegitimate person.

LOVEDAY. A day appointed for the arbitration of differences. (A-S. *lah-daeg*.) A court-leet was so called.

> " I kan holde *love-dayes*,
> And here a reves rekenyng ;
> Ac in canon nor in decretals
> I can noght rede a lyne."
> *P. Ploughman*, 3326.

But as the name occurs, with its modern spelling, and without any prefix, in Leland's Roll of Battel Abbey, and in the H.R., it probably has some other meaning.

LOVEGOD. LOVEGOOD. 'Love God.' The Germans have *Gottlieb*, the Italians *Amadio*, the French *Amadis*, in the same sense. Talbot's English Etymol.

LOVEKIN. Probably *Love*, wolf, with the termination KIN—"the little wolf." See Love.

LOVEL. LOVELL. A very common surname, since our heraldric dictionaries assign about 40 coats to it. It is a derivative of the Lat. *lupus*, wolf, thus: Lupus, Loup, Lupellus, Louvel, Lovel. The celebrated Hugh d'Abrincis, Earl of Chester, surnamed Lupus, was a nephew of the Conqueror. The barons Lovel, introduced into England at the Conquest, were lords of Yvery in Normandy. Ascelin, the son of Robert, the head of this race, who succeeded in 1083, was called Lupus on account of his violent temper. His younger son, William, Earl of Yvery, acquired the diminutive sobriquet of Lupellus, the 'little wolf,' afterwards softened to Lupel, Luvel, and Lovel. Baronage. See Wolf.

Lupus, wolf, and *Lupellus*, little wolf, were rendered French as *Lou* and *Lovel*. In the middle ages this was a common name for a dog. According to Stowe, William Collingborne was executed in the year 1484, for stigmatizing the favourites of Richard III., Catesby, Ratcliffe, and Lovel, in the following couplet:—

> THE RATTE, THE CATTE, AND LOVELL, OUR DOGGE,
> RULE ALL ENGLAND UNDER THE HOGGE.

The baronial family derived their name from William, Earl of Yvery, in Normandy, and lord of Castle Cary, co. Somerset, who acquired the sobriquet of Lupellus, "the little wolf," as his father had previously done that of Lupus. He flourished in the reign of King Stephen, and most of his descendants adopted the sobriquet as their family name. Peerage.

LOVELADY. See Lady.

LOVELOCK. Lovelocks were "pendent locks of hair, falling near or over the ears, and cut in a variety of fashions. This ridiculous appendage to the person is often alluded to by the writers previous to the Restoration." Halliw. I do not know whether any trace of this fashion is found in the middle ages, though it seems probable that the surname was first bestowed upon some fop who indulged in it. The H.R. mention one Walterus le Loveloker. Was he a cultivator of "love-locks?" I think he is more likely to have followed the sterner occupation of a *looker* after *loves*, or wolves. See Love.

LOVELUCK. See Lovelock.

LOVELY. Possibly from amiability of character; but more likely the name of some place terminating in *ley*.

LOVENEY. The ancient barony of Louvigni, near Caen, in Normandy.

LOVER. An ancient orthography of Louviers, the Norman town, is Lovver.

LOVET. LOVETT. Ricardus Lovet is said to have come hither at the Conquest, accompanied by his two sons, William and Robert. The elder held in capite, by the Conqueror's grant, lands in cos. Bedford, Berks, Leicester, and Northampton. From the XIV. century the family have been principally connected with the county of Buckingham, where as knights and gentlemen of good estate they have possessed Liscombe from generation to generation. The late Sir Jonathan Lovett was created a baronet by king George III. on the following occasion : " In the summer of 1781, the Earl of Chesterfield, having been some time absent from Court, was asked by the King, where he had been so long? 'On a visit to Mr. Lovett of Buckinghamshire,' said the Earl. '*Ah !*' said the King, '*is that Lovett of Liscombe? They are of the genuine old Norman breed ;* how happens it that they are not baronets? Would he accept the title ? Go, tell him that if he'll do so, it's much at his service; they have ever been staunch to the crown at a pinch !' "

There is a tradition that an early ancestor of the family was 'master of the wolfhounds' to one of the Norman kings. This probably arose from the peculiar arms of the family : Quarterly, three wolves' heads, and three wolves passant, and the crest, a wolf's head. These bearings are of course of the allusive kind, and relate to the name, which is a softened derivative of the Fr. *loup, louve,* a wolf. See much curious information respecting the family in Burke's Extinct Baronets. In Domesday Book a William Loveth occurs as a tenant in chief in Berks and Leicester,and a William Lovet in Bedfordshire. They were doubtless one and the same person.

LOVETOT. Two places in Normandy bear this name, which as a surname in England dates from early Norman times; viz. : Louvetot-près-Bellencombre, not far from Dieppe, and Louvetot-sur-Caudebec, in the arrondissement of Yvetot.

LOVITT. See Lovett.

☞ **LOW.** (A-Sax. *hláw*) a rising grounᴅ. Hence the names of many places which have given rise to surnames, as Ludlow, Barlow, Callow, Bedlow, Hadlow, Marlow, Winslow, Henslow, Thurlow.

LOW. See Lowe.

LOWANCE. Corresponds with the old German personal name, Leonza, of the IX. cent. Ferguson.

LOWDELL. Probably the same as Loudwell.

LOWDER. LOUDER. Corruptions of Lowther, which see.

LOWE. LOWES. 1. The same as Law —a small rising ground. See Lower. 2. Sometimes perhaps the German *lowe,* a lion. In some instances, according to tradition, the name is of Norman origin, being one of the various forms of *loup,* a wolf.

LOWELL. Probably the same as Lovell.

LOWEN. See Lewin.

LOWER. The registered pedigree of the Lowers of Cornwall carries them back to about the time of John or Henry III., and both name and family are probably from a Corno-British source. In Sussex, almost the only other county in which the name occurs, it is found as early as temp. Henry VI., but I have not yet been able to trace any connection between the two families. It is possible that the Sussex name may be equivalent to Atte-Lowe, which occurs in documents of the XIV. century. In the XV. cent. the prefix '*at*' was frequently replaced by the termination '*er*.' See the articles -LAW, -LOW, and -ER. Loherus occurs in the Domesd. of Suffolk as a baptismal name, and Lower, as an unprefixed surname, is found in the H.R. of that county.

LOWICK. Places in cos. Northumberland, Lancaster, and Northampton.

LOWMAN. See -LOW, MAN, and ER. A dweller by or upon an eminence.

LOWNDES. I can find no better etymology for this name than *launde,* O. Eng.

for a forest-glade or lawn. In 'Morte-Arthure' this word is written *loundes.* The family claim to be of Norman origin.

LOWNE. Lowland Scotch. The glossary to Burns says, "a fellow, a ragamuffin;" also a careless, half-grown lad. " The usual figure of a Skye boy is a *lown* with bare legs and feet, a ragged coat and waistcoat, a bare head, and a stick in his hand." Boswell's Tour to the Hebrides.

LOWREY. LOWRIE. See Lowry.

LOWRIE. *Lowrie* and *lawrie* are, in Scotland, designations of the fox, and the words are also applied to a person of crafty or fox-like disposition.

LOWRY. Frequently written Lewry. In Normandy there are two places called Lorei—one in the arrondissement of Evreux, the other in the Cotentin. At the making of Domesday, Hugh de Luri held lands in capite, co. Dorset. Another Norman patriarch, William Leurie, (without the territorial prefix) was a tenant in chief in cos. Oxon, Glouc., and Essex. But see Lowrie. Some Lowrys claim descent from the Scottish family of Laurie, of Maxwelton, near Dumfries, whose name was variously written Laurie, Lawrey, Lawry, Lowry, Lowrey, and Lowray. B.L.G.

LOWTH. 1. From Louth, the Lincolnshire town. 2. The Norman surname Lovet (which see) is sometimes spelt Loueth in Domesday Book.

LOWTHER. A parish in Westmoreland, the cradle of the ancient race so called. "Eminently a knightly family, traced by Brydges to Sir Gervase de Lowther, who was living in the reign of Henry III." Shirley's Noble and Gentle Men. The Earl of Lonsdale, the head of the house, is resident at Lowther Castle, in the above-named parish.

The principal variations in the spelling of this name have been Loder, Louder, Loader, Louthre, and Lowther.

LOXLEY, A parish in co. Warwick, and a liberty in co. Stafford.

LUARD. At the Revocation of the Edict of Nantes, 1685, Robert Abraham Luard came from Caen in Normandy, and settled in London; *a quo* the Luards of Lincolnshire and Essex.

LUBBOCK. Possibly from Lubeck, a city in Lower Saxony.

LUCAR. Possibly from the chapelry of Lucker, in Northumberland.

LUCAS. Gr. and Lat. Luke. Why the name of this evangelist should have become a family name in its original form, while the other three are only so in their anglicised shape, is not apparent. The Encycl. Herald. assigns eleven different coats to Lucas, but only one to Luke.

LUCCOCK. See Luke, and the termination COCK.

LUCEY. See Lucy.

LUCOCK. See Luke.

LUCOMBE. LUCKOMBE. A place in the Isle of Wight.

LUCK. LUCKE. A native either of Lucca, in Italy, or of Liege, in the Netherlands. Speaking of the latter town, Andrew Borde, in his Boke of Knowledge, says: "The lond of Lewke is a pleasaunt countre; the cheefe towne is the cytie of Lewke. The speche is base Doch." Or it may be from one of the parishes of Luc-sur-mer, or Luc-le-chateau, in Normandy.

LUCKCOCK. See Luke, and the termination COCK.

LUCKER. A chapelry in Northumberland.

LUCKETT. A diminutive of Luke.

LUCKIE. A Scottish surname; like the classical Felix, Fortunatus, &c.

LUCKIN. LUCKING. LUCKINS. See Luke.

LUCKY. 1. Fortunate. 2. A corruption of Lockey, a local name.

LUCY. Anciently De Luci. Luci is a parish in the arrondissement of Neufchâtel, in Normandy, Temp. Henry I. Richard de L. was lord of Diss, co. Norfolk. The Shaksperean Lucys claim descent from the De Charlcotes of Charlcote. Dugdale thinks they may have been maternally descended from the Norman De Luci's.

LUDBROOK. Perhaps the Norse Lodbrok. Ragnar Lodbrok, the celebrated Northman sea-king, derived his surname, signifying "shaggy-breeches," from the nether garments which he wore, made of the skins of wild beasts. Ferguson.

LUDE. An estate in Blair Athol, Perthshire, which formerly had possessors of the same name.

LUDGATE. One of the ancient gateways of the city of London, whence Ludgate Street.

LUDLOW. A town in Shropshire.

LUFF. Apparently an old personal name, whence Lufkins, and the local Luffingham, Luffincót, &c.

LUGG. A river in Herefordshire.

LUKE. The Christian name, besides standing *per se* as a family name, has given rise to several others, as Lukin, Luckins, Luckings, Luckock, Lucock, Locock, Luckett.

LUKIN. LUKYN. See Luke.

LUM. A woody valley; a deep pit. Halliwell.

LUMB. See Lum.

LUMLEY. The Lumleys are of Anglo-Saxon descent, and have been seated in the county of Durham from the time of the Conquest. Liulph, who lived before the year 1080, is the first recorded ancestor. The majestic castle of Lumley, in the

parish of Chester-le-Street, co. Durham, from which the family received their name, is still the chief abode of the Earl of Scarborough, the representative of the house.

When King James I., in 1603, visited Lumley Castle, Dr. James, Bishop of Durham, wishing to do honour to his friend John, Lord Lumley, gave his majesty a prolix account of his family; but the monarch, having little taste for such details, and growing weary, cut him short with the remark: " Oh, mon, gang na farther; let me digest the knowledge I ha' gained, for I did na ken *Adam's* name was Lumley!" Proud of their pedigree, it is not a matter of surprise that the phrase THE LOFTY LUMLEYS was applied to this family.

The Lumleys of Bradfield, baronets, (extinct 1771) descended from Dominigo Lomelin, an Italian by birth, and of the bedchamber to Henry VIII., who commanded and maintained at his own charge a troop of horse, at Boulogne, for the use of the King. His successors anglicised their name to Lumley.

LUMSDAINE. See Lumsden.

LUMSDEN. "An ancient manor in the parish of Coldingham, Berwickshire, belonging to a family of that name so early as the reign of David I. The ancient *peel* of Lumsden (see PEEL) probably occupied the site of the present farm-house of East Lumsden; but in the XIV. cent. the family removed their abode to Blanerne, on the banks of the Whitadder, where its picturesque remains still exist." Imp. Gaz. Scotl. The surname is first found in a charter between 1166 and 1182. B.L.G.

LUND. Lund is a well-known bishop's see and university in Sweden. A family of this name settled in Yorkshire from Nuremburg in the XVI. century. See Lunn.

LUNDIN. A place in Fifeshire, which in ancient times belonged to the family.

LUNDY. 1. The island in the British Channel. 2. The Fr. *Lundi,* i.e. Monday.

LUNGLEY. The same as Longley. See LONG. De Lungeley. H.R. co. Suffolk.

LUNHUNTER. One who hunts a *lun;* but what species of game that may be baffles my inquiry. See however Eng. Surn. i. 110, for some guesses on the subject.

LUNN. A corruption of Lund. There are several localities so called in Lancashire and Yorkshire.

LUNNIS. Probably a corruption of Londonoys, which see.

LUNSFORD. A manor in the parish of Echingham, co. Sussex, which, according to genealogists, belonged to the family in the reign of Edward the Confessor. The name was originally De Lundresford.

LUPTON. A township in Westmoreland.

LUSBY. A parish in Lincolnshire.

LUSCOMBE. An estate near Dawlish, co. Devon, which belonged to the family, and was their residence temp. Henry V. and probably much earlier, as the name of Hugh de Luscombe occurs in that county, 9. Edward I.

LUSTY. Stout, valorous.

LUSTYBLOOD. Shakspeare uses 'blood' in the sense of *disposition*, and we still say hot, or cold, blooded, in the same sense. A brave or valorous fellow.

LUTHER. As an English surname probably a corruption of the great northern name Lowther. It may however be identical with the Teutonic Luther, Lothaire, Lothario, &c. One of the Saxon kings of Kent was a Lothere.

LUTMAN. 1. A Sax. *lutan*, to stoop or bow; O.E. *lut* and *lout*, the same—a man who stoops in his gait. 2. A Sax. *lotman*, a pirate. 3. A pilot; see Richardson, in voc.

LUTON. A parish in Bedfordshire.

LUTTLEY. Luttley is in the parish of Enfield, in Staffordshire, and Philip de Luttley was lord thereof in the 20th year of Edward I. Hence the Luttleys of Shropshire, and those of Herefordshire, now Barneby. Shirley's Noble and Gentle Men.

LUTTMANN. See Lutman. The extinct family of this name, formerly located at Idehurst and Sparr, in the parish of Wisborough Green, co. Sussex, anciently wrote themselves *Lutemarespre* or *Lutemarespe* alias *Lotemanespe*. These spellings occur in undated deeds; but in the reign of Edw. III. the name had settled down to Lutma', i.e. Lutman. The seal attached to all the early charters of the family is ⚜ S. WILL' D'LVTHMARSPE, from which it would appear that some local name, whatever its ancient form, had become corrupted into Luttman. Inf. H. F. Napper, Esq.

LUTTRELL. A Norman family, who are found in England soon after the Conquest. In the reigns of Henry I. and Stephen, Sir John L. held in capite the manor of Hoton-Pagnel, co. York. The name is probably derived from a diminutive form of the French *loutre*, an otter.

LUTWIDGE. Ludovicus (Louis) has been suggested as the origin of this name; but the second syllable may be a corruption of *wich*, and thus it may be of local origin.

LUTWYCHE. See Lutwidge.

LUXFORD. The Luxfords of Sussex bear arms closely approximating to those of the very ancient family of *Lunsford* of the same county, of whom, according to tradition, they are a branch.

☞ **LY.** A termination—another form of Ley or Lee. See Lee. It is to this source

that we owe the *adverbial*-looking surnames which Mr. Clark has thus brought together :—

"First—Wisely, Bodily, and Barely,
Are names we only meet with rarely ;
And so with Evily, Rashly, Lightly,
Each is a name we know but slightly ;
Meanly, Softly, Slowly, Quickley,
Basely, Roughly, Loosely, Weakley,
Neatly, Cleverly, and Duly—
A curious list of Surnames truly."
Surnames Metrically Arranged, &c.

LYALL. Perhaps the same as Lisle ; perhaps O. Fr. *loyall*, loyal.

LYDDEKER. A Dutch family who settled in our American colony (Long Island) in or before 1654. At the outbreak of the American war, the representative espoused the British cause, settled in England, and founded the family here.

LYDDON. A parish in Kent—Lydden.

LYDE. An extinct parish in Herefordshire.

LYDIARD. Several parishes, &c., in co. Somerset.

LYE. See under LEE.

LYELL. A corruption of De L'Isle, through Liel and Lyle.

LYFORD. A chapelry in Berkshire.

LYGO. The same as Lithgow, Linlithgow.

LYHART. A modification of Le Hart. Walter, 29th bishop of Norwich, 1446—1472, was variously written Hart, Le Hert, and Lyhart.

LYLE. The same as Lisle.

LYMBER. See Limber.

LYMBERNER. A limeburner. Nonæ. 1341.

LYNCH. See Linch. Several gentry families of this name reside in cos. Galway and Mayo. They are descended from the settlers known as the tribes of Galway. In a document in Ulster's office, William le Petit is said to have been the ancestor of the Lynch family in Ireland. B.L.G.

LYNDE. See Lind.

LYNDON. A parish in Rutland.

LYNDSEY. See Lindsay.

LYNE. A parish in Peebles-shire ; an estate near Newdigate, co. Surrey ; and rivers in cos. Peebles, Devon, and Fife.

LYNER. H.R. Le Lyner. A maker of lines or cords ?

LYNN. See Lin. Also the town in Norfolk.

LYNNELL. Perhaps the baptismal name Lionel.

LYON. 1. Lord Strathmore's family descend from John *de* Lyon, who obtained from King David II. baronies and lands in the shires of Perth and Aberdeen. 2. See Lion.

"A whilom student at Trin. Coll., Dublin, a great fop, got the sobriquet of Dandy-Lyon, which greatly annoyed him. To his high gratification he afterwards became possessed of an estate, together with the name of Winder; but the change of name was hardly a change for the better, as he immediately became known throughout the university as *Beau-Winder!*"

LYONS. Not from the great French city, but from the small town of Lions-la-Forêt, in the department of the Eure in Normandy.

LYS. This name has a very remarkable and somewhat romantic origin. After the death of Joan of Arc, her previously humble family were ennobled, by Charles VII. in 1429, and had a grant of the following emblematical coat of arms:—" Azure between two fleurs-de-lys, Or, a sword, in pale, point upwards, supporting an open crown, fleur-de-lysé Or." In consequence of this distinction, the family assumed the name of Du Lys d'Arc. The last of the race in France is believed to have been Colombe du Lys, Prior of Coutras, who died in 1760; but the family still exist in England. At the Revocation of the Edict of Nantes in 1685, among the numerous refugees who settled in this country, was a Count Du Lys, who fixed his abode in Hampshire. "His eldest male descendant, and, as I believe," says Mr. Sneyd, in Notes and Queries, vol. vii., p. 295, " the representative of the ancient and noble family of Du Lys d'Arc, derived from a brother of the Maid of Orleans, is the Rev. J. T. Lys, Fellow of Exeter College, whose ancestors, after the period of their settlement in England, thought proper to drop the foreign title, and to curtail their name to its present form."

LYSAGHT. Presumed to be an old Irish Christian name, as Lord Lisle's family claim descent from the great house of O'Brien.

LYSLEY. The family were seated for centuries in Yorkshire. They are "a branch of the great family of Lisle, descended from Radulphus de Lisle (De Insula) at the time of the Conquest." B.L.G.

LYSONS. This family, who have been for many generations established in co. Gloucester, are said to have migrated thither from Wales. In the XVI. century the name was written Lysans, Leyson, and Lison. It was probably derived from Lison, a place in the department of Calvados, in Normandy.

LYSTER. See Lister.

LYSTOR. See Lister.

LYTE. A.-Sax. *lyt*, little—referring probably to the stature of the bearer. A good Chaucerian word. The Poor Parson is described in the Canterbury Tales (Prologue 493, &c.), as a zealous visitor of his flock:—

> "Wyd was his parisch, and houses fer asondur,
> But he ne lefte not for reyn ne thondur,
> In siknesse ne in mescheif to visite
> The ferrest in his parisshe moche and *lite.*"

i.e. the most remote members of his parish, whether great or small.

LYTEMAN. A man of diminutive stature, a little man. See Lyte.

LYTTELTON. See Littleton.

LYTTLETON. The name is derived from a place in the Vale of Evesham, co. Worcester, where the ancestors of this family, in the female line, were seated before the reign of Richard I. Shirley's Noble and Gentle Men.

LYVET. Eight places in Normandy are called Livet.

M.

MABB. A 'nurse-name' of Abraham.

MABBETT. See Mabbott.

MABBOTT. A 'nurse-name' of Abraham, through Mabb.

MABBS. See Mabb.

MABE. A parish in Cornwall.

MABERLEY. MABERLY. Probably the same as Moberley.

MABIN. Perhaps from St. Mabyn, a parish in Cornwall, or perhaps the personal name—the same as that borne by the saint to whom the parish was dedicated.

☞ **MAC-,** a well-known prefix of surnames of Celtic origin, signifying 'son of,' and therefore cognate with the *Ap-* of Welsh, the *Fitz-* of Anglo-Norman, and the *-Son* of English surnames. In England and other countries of Europe the great staple of family names is derived from a territorial source, but among the Celts of Scotland, Ireland, and Wales, the surname was almost uniformly that of the father or some ancestor, with a prefix. In Ireland *O*, (formerly *ua*) grandson or descendant, is the ordinary prefix, and the *O's* bear the proportion of ten to one to the

Macs. In Scotland the case is reversed, and while there are said to be only three indigenous surnames in *O*, there are many hundreds of *Macs.* See art. *O'* in this Dictionary.

By the kindness of correspondents who have made collections of surnames with this prefix, I am enabled to lay before the reader a nearly complete list of them—nay, it may rather be called redundant, since in many instances two or more variations of a name have been made through ignorance among the lower classes of the people. This is especially the case when the name which follows the Mac begins with a vowel, and the C is tacked on to the beginning of the same name. In this way Mac Alpine, Mac Allan, and Mac Leod have become Mac Calapine, Mac Callan, and Mac Cloud, to the total confusion of kindred and etymology. I am told that near kinsmen sometimes vary their common patronymic so much that none but themselves would imagine that they were of a common stock; thus a Mac Crie might be uncle, and a Mac Craw, cousin, to a Mac Rae. In printing these names in MAC, therefore, I am anxious to guard against their being all received as genuine surnames, and the lists, having never been subjected to any critical inquiry, must be regarded rather as a curiosity than as the veritable nomenclature of a large body of British subjects. The principal names in MAC, such as those of Clans, will receive each a separate notice in the body of the work. As before intimated, a very large proportion of those here given, *en masse*, are borne by the lowest of the Celtic people, and possess no historical interest. Some, on the other hand, have always been associated with wealth and worldly respectability; while a few are obviously English names to which *Mac* has been prefixed from mere caprice, or from a desire of assimilation to the Celtic race.

.I print the lists as I have received them; they are far from being strictly alphabetical.

The first list, collected by Lord Stair, and privately printed by his Lordship, is entitled " Seven Hundred Specimens of Celtic Aristocracy, or *Almack's* Extraordinary."

Mac Adam
Adams
Adie
Afee
Aire
Ainsh
Alaster
Alister
Allister
All
Allan
Alleney
Alley
Alpine
Alla

Mac Analty
Anaspie
Andrew
Ara
Ardel
Arly
Arthur
Art
Aranas
Asey
Askill
Aulay
Auley
Aully
Auliffe

Mac Auslan
Aughtrie
Aually
Bain
Baney
Barr
Barnet
Bay
Bayne
Bean
Beath
Beth
Binney
Blane
Brair
Braardy
Brayne
Bryde
Brain
Buchan
Burnet
Burnie
Cabe
Caffrae
Caig
Call
Callan
Calley
Callum
Calman
Camon
Cammon
Can
Cann
Cance
Caud
Cauch
Calagh
Cape
Candlish
Calmont
Carmint
Carten
Carty
Carthy
Camb
Cambridge
Carlie
Cardle
Carter
Cargill
Cartney
Carron
Carroll
Cash
Caskill
Caskie
Casland
Casse
Catan
Cay
Chie
Cheyne
Clelland
Clenachan
Clean
Cleary
Climont
Clymont
Claverty
Cleverty
Chlery
Clew

Mac Clumper
Clumpha
Cleish
Cloy
Clure
Clarens
Clarence
Clintock
Clue
Cloud
Clary
Clencham
Cluskie
Clune
Chrystle
Clung
Cavins
Carroughan
Colla
Colly
Condack
Conkey
Connechy
Conochie
Combie
Comish
Come
Collom
Coid
Coan
Coard
Colgan
Coll
Connell
Comb
Connal
Conchie
Comas
Commisky
Correl
Corkle
Corry
Cormick
Cormack
Cord
Cool
Cook
Corkindale
Corkindle
Cosh
Coul
Coughtrie
Court
Cowat
Coy
Cornick
Creery
Craw
Crea
Crie
Crorie
Criric
Crow
Crindle
Creagh
Creight
Cracken
Crossan
Creery
Croben
Crone
Crane
Creath

Mac Cririck	Mac Fayden	Mac Gregor	Mac Keon
Cready	Fadzean	Griggor	Keachie
Courtie	Faggan	Grouther	Kell
Cunn	Farlane	Grougar	Keen
Cuaig	Farlan	Groth	Kechnie
Culla	Fall	Grau	Kellar
Culloch	Farquhar	Graw	Keigh
Cullagh	Feat	Graddie	Kendrich
Cully	Fedzean	Guire	Kelekan
Cull	Fee	Gubbon	Kelvie
Culliffe	Fie	Guffog	Kenny
Curry	Figgans	Gusty	Kellan
Cutcheon	Finlay	Guirk	Kennedy
Cullich	Frederick	Guffy	Kenewaie
Cummin	Gachen	Gue	Keown
Curdy	Gane	Guiness	Kessock
Cue	Gaun	Gutcheon	Kenzie
Cubbin	Garr	Guiggan	Kengie
Curdie	Garvie	Gudzeon	Kerchar
Curtin	Gakey	Guinness	Kerrigan
Clullich	Gany	Gragh	Kerrow
Columb	Ganston	Goveny	Kersy
Conch	Gaffie	Geliatly	Kenna
Cumming	Gaw	Goldrick	Kerrell
Caw	Gavaran	Hale	Kerras
Corville	Garry	Hahan	Kerracher
Chattie	Gavily	Harg	Kergo
Cleet	Gavin	Hardie	Kerlie
Caa	Gauran	Hardy	Kersie
Crochan	Garrighan	Haffie	Kerrachee
Dannell	Garva	Hattie	Keson
Dermot	Gechie	Harrie	Kewan
Diarmaid	Geachan	Heather	Keogh
Dermid	Giehan	Henry	Kennoway
Dead	George	Hendrath	Kart
Donald	Gee	Houl	Kid
Donnell	Getterick	Houlgh	Kibbin
Donough	Geehan	Hugh	Kie
Donagh	Geachy	Hutchen	Killy
Dowale	Geoch	Ian	Killan
Douall	Genn	Ilree	Killop
Dougall	Gettigan	Ilveen	Kimm
Dowell	Gibbon	Ilquhan	Kin
Dougald	Gilchrist	Ilwraith	Kinnis
Dona	Gill	Ilroy	Kinlay
Divett	Gilliwie	Ilpheedan	Kinnon
Duff	Gilray	Ilhose	Kimmon
Dollan	Gilnary	Ilvane	Kichan
Dade	Ginn	Ildowni	Killykelly
Eagar	Gilp	Ildowie	Kinnel
Eachan	Gilligan	Ilwrac	Kinvine
Earchan	Gillicuddy	Inroy	Kintock
Eachern	Gillendrish	Innes	Kintosh
Eachirn	Ging	Indoe	Kindlay
Elmail	Gillivray	Indie	Kinstry
Elsander	Ginty	Innalty	Kinney
Elroy	Garrity	Inarty	Kinder
Elvaine	Glashan	Innish	Kinnimont
Eldery	Glashon	Intosh	Kimmie
Elrevy	Glaughn	Ilwee	Kissack
Edward	Glew	Isaac	Kirdy
English	Glinghy	Ivor	Kilterick
Enermy	Gitrick	Jannet	Koen
Enta	Ghees	Kain	Kye
Eniry	Ghie	Kane	Knight
Enau	Gowran	Kandy	Kutcheon
Evath	Goun	Kail	Kreth
Evers	Gown	Kaig	Ky
Ewan	Gough	Kardy	Kus
Ewing	Gonogil	Kay	Koskray
Evily	Gowan	Key	Kown
Ewin	Gra	Kean	Lachlan
Ewen	Grath	Keand	Lain

Mac Laine
Lane
Lagan
Laggan
Landsborgh
Lae
Lardy
Larn
Laren
Laurin
Larty
Latchie
Laws
Lay
Lauchlan
Laverty
Lawrie
Lean
Leane
Leay
Lehose
Lennan
Lerie
Leish
Leod
Lennon
Letchie
Lea
Learbuck
Levy
Lellan
Learmont
Leroy
Linty
Liver
Lintock
Loughlin
Looney
Ludock
Lullich
Lurg
Lure
Lurcan
Lurken
Luckie
Machan
Mahone
Main
Macy
Manamy
Manus
Manchan
Maran
Martin
Master
Mash
Math
Menemy
Meikan
Meiking
Meeking
Michael
Millan
Min
Mine
Minn
Millie
Monagh
Monnies
Morine
Morland
Morran
Morrissy

Mac Monzies
Menzies
Morrice
Mullin
Muldroch
Muldrochan
Munor
Murdoch
Murdie
Murtrie
Murchie
Murray
Murrich
Murrough
Murdo
Muragh
Murty
Munn
Nab
Nabe
Nair
Naghten
Nally
Nalty
Namara
Namee
Nance
Nell
Neel
Neil
Neill
Neale
Nee
Nees
Neish
Neay
Nay
Neight
Nerlie
Nerney
Neilie
Nemany
Nie
Night
Niffe
Nish
Niven
Nichol
Nielage
Noe
Noah
Nolty
Naught
Naughten
Nanbourg
Nully
Neece
Neilledge
Omie
Omish
Ohoy
Onie
Ord
Ostrich
Owan
Owat
Parlan
Parlen
Phail
Phadraig
Phadyen
Phee
Phechy

Mac Pherson
Phearson
Phie
Phiely
Philimy
Phion
Phun
Quae
Quaich
Quaker
Quater
Quaide
Quarrie
Quhae
Quillen
Quin
Queen
Quiston
Quaig
Quown
Rae
Raild
Raith
Rabbie
Reath
Reary
Redie
Rerie
Reddie
Ritchie
Robie
Robbie
Robert
Ron
Ronald
Rory
Rostie
Row
Rorie
Ruer
Shane
Sheny
Sherry
Skean

Mac Skimming
Sparran
Spirron
Sporran
Sween
Sweeny
Symon
Symond
Swiggan
Taggart
Tavish
Taverty
Tear
Togue
Toldrough
Tornish
Turk
Tyer
Ure
Veagh
Vean
Vey
Vicar
Vie
Vigors
Vitie
Viester
Voddich
Vorrich
Vurrich
Walter
Ward
Waters
Weeny
Whea
Whaunell
Wheble
What
Whirter
William
Whinnie
Whine
Whan
Wheelan

Since this list was printed, Lord Stair has collected the following additional *Macs* :—

Mac Avenny
Alexander
Almond
Angus
Adoo
Alavy
Alava
Aodh
Artley
Auck
Awee
Beolain
Breer
Brairdy
Brodie
Breny
Boyd
Brier
Culdridge
Calme
Creak
Chave
Camlay
Canelue
Combre

Mac Coggie
Crumlish
Cavill
Christian
Christie
Cardie
Coghlans
Condecky
Constantine
Conghie
Coraskin
Clenchie
Corman
Coral
Cluachan
Craghe
Condie
Caughey
Cassey
Crachan
Cray
Crailte
Crath
Crain
Crimmon

Mac Crinsau	Mac Ilhone	Mac Acy	Mac Gaver
Crochert	Ilray	Alvaney	Geary
Cual	Ilivee	Bey	Gechan
Crohon	Ilriach	Birney	Gerrand
Culinan	Ilvain	Bride	Gildowny
Cueish	Ilwhannell	Broom	Gilvray
Crorty	Ilwrich	Boyle	Ginnis
Duffie	Ilwrath	Bratney	Given
Dungal	Ilwham	Cafferty	Gladery
Duach	Ilvaine	Calder	Glasson
Dunlevy	Indoer	Calie	Glover
Dermit	Intaggart	Calla	Gorrane
Diarmid	Inatty	Callapin	Gowrlich
Elharan	Inturner	Candie	Govern
Ethelan	Indulf	Cane	Grady
Eveny	Intyre	Caysher	Gruthar
Elhalten	Ilheron	Caul	Guckin
Farren	Iver	Causland	Guigham
Favur	Ilroid	Cerran	Gnugill
Ferran	Jerrow	Chesney	Gurk
Fedris	Jan	Clarney	Gooch
Fedrees	Lurkin	Clasky	Goran
Fion	Leisle	Clauchrie	Grain
Ferchary	Lorimer	Clay	Haig
Gaan	Mouran	Clemand	Hallam
Grady	Malcolm	Clement	Hay
Gahey	Michan	Clishoe	Hutchison
Gladery	Mirref	Clive	Heffey
Garrigle	Maky	Clounan	Inalty
Gorrane	Murter	Closkie	Ilwain
Gufferty	Murtor	Clowelle	Ilway
Gaskine	Murgh	Cluney	Innany
Googan	Nain	Clurken	Intee
Gawen	Nanny	Cole	Irvine
Geraughty	Ness	Collum	Karness
Gilcolingain	Nier	Colm	Katchner
Gilcom	Orm	Combe	Keavitt
Glattery	Owen	Common	Kee
Glue	Oubrey	Commava	Keeser
Gin	Pake	Comachie	Keever
Gurk	Phadan	Coory	Keillar
Gillon	Quilton	Corrie	Kellop
Graither	Rath	Corquodale	Ken
Gildownie	Re	Coslin	Kennan
Gille	Reuric	Cowie	Kenon
Gonagh	Reynold	Crackan	Kenstry
Gillegannan	Sorlie	Creadie	Killigni
Gilriach	Starvick	Croarie	Kew
Gormigal	Sorley	Cromlish	Killiam
Gleish	Shine	Crosky	Kimmont
Gradie	Swan	Crotchart	Kindry
Gorigan	Target	Crumie	Kintry
Gowran	Tellicca	Cubbing	Kinty
Gorren	Tier	Cullum	Kniven
Gawne	Thole	Cumsky	Kippen
Grotty	Vain	Cune	Kune
Gottigan	Vane	Daniel	Kegg
Gruther	Vayne	Dorwick	Kessack
Gravie	Veal	Dymont	Kittrick
Garnet	Veall	Egan	Larnon
Gard	Vial	Elheran	Leroth
Gillipatrick	Whaney	Elhiney	Lees
Hamlan	Whinnan	Enteer	Limont
Hallan	Wyr	Entire	Lise
Hendrie	Wall	Ewney	Loug
Hir	Wren	Erlane	Lozen
Howie	Wilson	Fadon	Lue
Houston		Fare	Lugash
		Farland	Lusky
		Fedries	Mahon
		Garrock	Meeken
		Gary	Meekan
		Gavel	Michan

Patrick Boyle, Esq., of Shewalton, N.B., has kindly supplied the following :—

Mac Aldowny	Mac Avoy
Atavey	Amond

Mac Mann	Mac Quat
Mathy	Quee
Meel	Quilken
Mordie	Quillan
Mulkin	Quigan
Nellan	Quoid
Neven	Quoin
Nicholas	Quorn
Nider	Ra
Niece	Ruvie
Ninch	Seveny
Norton	Swayed
Nutty	Sliddell
Oubray	Swiney
Onehy	Taldrock
Peak	Vale
Philips	Vea
Quade	Watt

MAC ADAM. The M.'s, of Waterhead, co. Ayr, claim descent from the head of the clan Macgregor; but the name was changed, early in the XVI. century, from Macgregor to Macadam, in consequence of political troubles. B.L.G. The Macadams of Blackwater, co. Clare, who settled in Ireland temp. Jas. I., from Galloway in Scotland, were formerly called M'Cullum. Ibid.

MAC ALASTER. Traced by the MS. of 1450 to Alaster, a son of Angus Mor, Lord of the Isles, A.D. 1284. Alaster is a Gaelic form of Alexander. Skene. B.L.G.

MAC ALPINE. Said to be descended from Alpin, a Scottish king of the VIII. cent. The ancient name of the Clan Macgregor.

MACARTNEY. The ancestor was a younger son of the M'Carthy More, of co. Cork, who went to Scotland to assist King Robt.Bruce,and obtained lands in co.Argyle, and afterwards at Macartney, in Galloway. Hence the M.'s of Scotland, and of Ireland, whither a branch returned in 1630. Burke's L.G.

MAC AULAY. (*Clan Aula*). Long considered to have been derived from the *old* Earls of Lennox, and to have got their name from Aulay son of Aulay, who appears in Ragman Roll; but Skene asserts that they were of the family of De Fasselane, who at a later period succeeded to that earldom. Dr. Hume suggests quite a different origin, from Olav, the Scandinavian name, thus— Mac Olav, Mac Aulif, Macauley. Ulster Journ. of Archæology, No. 21.

MAC BETH. Gael. Mac-Beathag. The son of Rebecca.

MAC CALMAN. Gael. "The son of the Dove."

MAC CANNON. A corruption of Mackinnon.

MAC CARTHY. Those of Desmond are named from Carrthach, a warlike ancestor who flourished in the XI. cent. O'Donovan in I.P.J.

MAC CASKILL. Gael. Mac Casgeal (pron. Caskil). "The son of the White Foot!"

MAC CAUSLAND. Buey Auselan, son of O'Kyan, king of Ulster, to avoid the fury of the Danes, passed into Scotland, A.D. 1016, and joined the forces of king Malcolm II. His descendant, the baron Mac Auslane, was one of the colonists of Ulster temp. Jas. VI. and the family still flourish in Ireland as Mac Causlands. See B.L.G.

MAC CLELLAN. Gael. Mac-a-ghilledhiolan (pron. Mac-il-iolan.) "The son of the Bastard."

MAC CLINTOCK. The M.'s, originally of Scotland, have been settled in Ireland from temp. Elizabeth. B.L.G.

MAC CLOUD. A corruption of Macleod.

MAC CONKEY. A corruption of Mac Connochie.

MAC CONNOCHIE. The same as Mac Donnacha—the son of Duncan.

MAC CORKINDALE. Gael. Mac-Cork-a-daal. "The son of Corc or Cork of the Dale, or valley." Corc is an ancient Gaelic personal name.

MAC COSKER. Mac Oscar, Ossian's heroic son. In co. Wexford it is sometimes pronounced Cosgar, and thence anglicized to Cosgrave.

MAC DARBY. See Diarmuid.

MAC DERMOT. Assumed from Dermot, an ancestor, but of the family of O'Malroni. O'Donovan in I.P.J., 365. The surname was assumed in the XI. cent. B.L.G.

MAC DIARMID. See Diarmuid.

MAC DOGALL. In general derived from Dogall, eldest son of Somerled, a great Highland chief of the XII. cent. Skene.

MAC DONALD. The clan Macdonald is certainly one of the oldest and most important in Scotland, its chiefs being descended from Somerled, thane of Argyle, but sometimes styled King of the Isles, who flourished in the XII. cent.

MAC DONNELL. Descended from Donald, Lord of the Isles, a common ancestor of the Earl of Antrim. This branch has been settled in co. Clare for more than two centuries.

MAC DOUGALL. See Macdogall.

MAC DOWALL. The same as Macdougall.

MAC DUFF. Shakspeare's Macduff has a true historical basis. See under Duff.

MAC DUFFIE, (or Macphee.) The M.'s of Colonsay are of the same lineage as Macgregor and Mackinnon.

MACE. Originally Macé, a French 'nurse-name' for Matthew.

MACEFIELD. Maresfield, a parish in Sussex, is sometimes thus corruptly pronounced.

MAC EVOY. *Mac Aodh-buidhe* or the Mac Evoys are mentioned by O'Brien as

2 E

chiefs of Tuath-Fiodhbhuidhe, in Queen's co., and O'Heerin thus refers to them—

"The ancient country of Fighbrugh of the fair lands,
Is a good lordship for a chieftain.
The clan Mac Evoy are its inheritors,
The yellow-haired host of hospitality."
B.L.G.

MAC EWAN. (Clan Eoghan na Hoitreic, or clan Ewen of Otter, whose castle was on the coast of Lochfine.) Descended from a common ancestor with the Maclachlans. Skene.

MACEY. 1. From Macei near Avranches in Normandy. 2. Maci is also an old Norman form of Matthew.

MACFADZEAN. Properly Mac Fadyean. (Gael. Mac-Fad-Ian.) "The son of Long John."

MAC FARLAN. (Clan Pharlan.) Descended from Gilchrist, a younger brother of Malduin, Earl of Lennox, whose great-grandson named Pharlan, the Gaelic for Bartholomew, surnamed the clan. Skene, ii. 155.

MAC GILL or MAGILL. The son of Goll, an Ossianic name.

MAC GILLEVRAY. The son of Gille-bride. But see next article.

MAC GILLIVRAY. Mac-Gille-Bhrae (pron. Vrae) "The son of the Lad of the 'brae' or eminence." So say the Gaelic etymologists, whom it is a sin for a Southron to call in question; and it must therefore pass. A brae is the side of a hill.

MAC GILLYCUDDY. A sept of the O'Sullivans, descended from O'Sullivan-More, who gave one of his sons a third part of his chieftainry, and thereupon the latter received the name of Gillycuddie, which is interpreted to mean "the little boy of the portion." The chief alone bore this remarkable name up to the wars of 1641, when the whole sept adopted it as a surname. B.L.G.

MAC GREGOR. This clan is deduced from Gregor, or Gregorius, 3rd son of Alpin, a Scottish monarch of the VIII. cent., who was named after his godfather, Pope Gregory IV. It is often modified to Greer and Greerson.

MAC GUILLAN. Considered to be equivalent to Mac-Llewellyn. See Howlyn.

MAC HEATH. Head or Héd was a Scottish comes, temp. David I., and his son Angus was the first of the Mac Heds or Mac-heaths. Skene, ii. 163.

MACHELL. At Crakenthorpe, co. Westmoreland, temp. Norman Conquest. The name has been variously written Mauchæl, Malchael, Mauchell, and Machell, and latinized Malus Catulus,—"the good-for-nothing Puppy!" a very uncomplimentary designation, but very quietly submitted to by the bearers, as appears from many a charter in which it occurs.

MACHEN. A parish in Monmouth-shire. Perhaps the same as Machin.

MACHIN. Perhaps a corruption of Méschines.

MAC IAN. Of Ardnamurchan. From John, a son of Angus Mor. Skene, ii. 94. Mac Ian or Macdonald of Glenco. From John, son of Angus Og, Lord of the Isles. Ibid. The name means the son of John, and is sometimes anglicised to Johnson, but is of course distinct from Johnston, a local name.

MAC INNES. Gael. Mac-Aonghais (pron. Mac-Aonais.) "The son of Æneas or Angus." Skene says :—a Flemish family settled in the Highlands, XII. cent.

MAC INTAGART. Gael. 'son of a Priest.' The second recorded Earl of Ross is called Ferchard Macintagart.

MAC INTOSH. The first who appears in records is Malcolm M., steward of Lochaber in 1447. Skene, ii. 179. But afterwards, at p. 193, he speaks of Macintoshes in 1396. Burke (L.G.) deduces them from Sheagh, or Shaw, second son of Duncan Macduff, third Earl of Fife, who acquired the designation of Mac-in-tosh-ich, or "the Thane's son."

MAC INTYRE. Gael. Mac-an-taoir. "The son of the Carpenter." This Gaelic name corresponds with the Irish Mactear, which see.

MAC IVOR. Gael. Mac-Ian-Mohr. (pron. Mac-Ia-vor.) "The son of Big John."

MACK. A very ancient Scotch personal name ; also a Scottish adjective—neat, tidy.

MAC KAY. Skene observes, that "there are few clans whose true origin is more uncertain than that of the Mackays," ii. 287. Some derive them from the family of Forbes, co. Aberdeen, others from that of Mackay of Ugadale in Kintyre, and assert that they were planted in the North by William the Lion, when he took possession of Orkney and Caithness. Skene however believes them to be of Gaelic origin and indigenous to Caithness. The old form of the name is Mac Aaiodh (Aoi) 'the son of Hugh,' or, as others say, 'the son of the Guest.'

The history of this clan is fully detailed in Mackay's House and Clan of Mackay, Edinburgh, 1829.

MAC KENNAN.   MACKENNA. KENNA. Known corruptions of Mackinnon in Ulster.

MAC KENZIE. 'The son of Keneth.' The family boast of their descent from the great Anglo-Norman race of Fitz-Gerald in Ireland in the XII. cent.; but Skene says they are of unquestionably Gaelic origin.

A modern genealogist, espousing the former opinion, says that the Craig-Hall Mackenzies "were scions of the same parent stock with the house of Fitz-Gerald Earls of Desmond, and were seated on their patrimonial possessions in the district of

Kyle, on the south-western frontier of Scotland. Their relationship to the Fitz Geralds and their ownership of the lands of Craig, about A.D. 1150, are both established by a deed which I have seen in the Coulthart collection, sans date, but which from the caligraphy could not have been executed subsequently to the XII. century, wherein it appears that one David Mackenzie borrowed from his blood-relation, John, lord of Ducies and Desmond, two hundred marks, to assist in fortifying Craig Castle against the freebooters of those times." Knowles's Coulthart Genealogy. London, 1855.

MACKERELL. Walter the Deacon, a Domesday tenant-in-chief in Essex and Suffolk, left two sons, one of whom was Walter, surnamed Mascherell, a sobriquet, probably having reference to some peculiarity in his mode of eating. The omission of the S, and the hardening of CH, would form Mâcherel and Mackerell.

MAC KERRELL. Ancient in Ayrshire, and presumed to be of Norman origin. The variations are Kirriel, Kirel, and Kirrel; and the surname also exists in Sweden. B. L.G. It seems to be the same as Caryll in England, the MAC having been *appliqué*.

MACKEY. See Mackay.

MACKIE. See Mackay.

MAC KILLIGIN. Gael. Mac-Gille-Gaun. "The son of the Scrubby Fellow!" This on the authority of an excellent Gaelic scholar.

MAC KINNON. They are closely connected with the Macdonalds of the Isles, and have no history independent of that clan. Skene, ii. 259. Ultimately however they became a distinct clan. Burke (L.G.) derives them from Fingon, youngest son of Alpin, king of Scotland. The name Macfingon became afterwards Macfinden, and then Mackinnon.

MACKINTOSH. See Macintosh.

MAC KIRDY. The M'Kurerdys were the principal possessors of the Isle of Bute at a very early period. B.L.G.

MACKLIN. 1. A corruption of Mac Lean, or of Mecklin in Belgium. 2. Dutch, te Mechelen; at or of Malines.

MACKNYGHTE. From Knowles's Genealogy of Coulthart (privately printed 1855) this seems to be a local name. It is stated that the Macknyghtes of that Ilk, in the regality of Galloway, possessed the lands of Macknyghte from the time of Uchtred de Macknyghte, A.D. 1114, to 1408, when an heiress conveyed the estate to the family of Ross.

MACKRELL. MACKRILL. See Mackerell.

MACKWORTH. A parish in Derbyshire, the residence of the family at an early period.

MAC LACHLAN. The clan Lachlan or Maclachlan, possessed the barony of Strathlachlan in Argyleshire. The patriarch of the family was Lachlan Mor, who lived in the XIII. cent. B.L.G. Traced to Gilchrist, grandson of Auradan, the common ancestor of all the clans of this tribe. Skene.

MACLAINE. See Maclean.

MAC LAURIN. Gael. Mac Glorrin (pron. Mac-Lorin.) "The son of the blear-eyed, or of him who has *one white eye!*"

MAC LEAN. Originally Macgillean. From a celebrated Highland warrior, Gillean-in-Tuiodh, or Gillean of the Battleaxe. B.L.G. Gaelic etymologists say, *Mac-a-ghille-leathan*—"the son of the Broad Lad!"

MAC LENNAN. Gael. Mac-Leannan. "The son of the Concubine."

MAC LEOD. Leod, the patriarch of this Highland family, settled in Skye from the Isle of Man. Boswell's Tour. Others have strenuously argued for a Norwegian descent; but for this there is no authority. The clan Leod are of common descent with the Campbells, and, by marriage with a daughter of Macraild, one of the Norwegian nobles of the Isles, they obtained great possessions in Skye. Skene, ii. 275.

MAC LURE. Gael. *Mac Lobhair* (pron. Mac Lour.) The son of the Leper.

MAC MAHON. Mahon is the old Irish for a bear, and some genealogists, apparently on the strength of this, derive the Mac Mahons from Walter Fitz-Urse (*Ursi filius*) one of the assassins of Thomas à Becket.

MAC MANUS. The son of Manus, Magnus, 'the great or renowned.' Arthur.

MAC MATHAN. A branch of the Mackenzies formed the clan Mathan, who are descended from Mathan or Matthew, son of Keneth. The name is anglicized to Mathieson. Skene, ii. 241.

MAC MURNEY. Mac Moirne—an Ossianic hero. Ulster Journ. of Archæology, No. 2.

MAC MURROUGH. Descendants of Murrough, father of Maelmordha, king of Leinster. O'Donovan. I.P.J., 365.

MAC NAB. A branch of the Mackinnons.

MACHNACHTAN. Their traditions derive them from Lochtay; but Skene is confident of their extraction from the tribe of Moray.

MAC NAMARA. Formerly styled Mic-Conmara, as being descendants of Cu-Mara, an Irish chief of the X. cent. Cumara in Celtic means 'Hero of the Sea.' O'Donovan I.P.J. Another authority says: a great Irish family, claiming descent from Cas, king of Thomond, who flourished early in the fifth cent. The surname is derived from Con-Marra (*heros maris*) who died in 1099.

MAC NAUGHTEN. See Macnachtan.

MAC NEILL. The house of Macneill or clan Neill is one of the most ancient of the Western Highlands. Their chiefs, the M.'s of Bara, ranked amongst the ' Principes Insularum,' who formed the council of state of the Lord of the Isles. They were divided into the two great branches, Macneill of Gigha, and Macneill of Barra, the former settled in the south of Argyleshire, and the latter in Inverness-shire, places so remote from each other that they became practically two distinct clans. B.L.G.

MAC OMISH. Gael. Mac-Thomais, (pron. Omish.) The son of Thomas.

MACONOCHIE. A cadet of Campbell, from Sir Neil Campbell of Lochow (ancestor of the Duke of Argyle) whose descendant in the fourth degree assumed the name of Mac Conochie (Mac Duncan.) This name was limited to the heads of the family, the cadets being always Campbells.

MAC PHERSON. Kenneth Macpherson, who lived temp. Alex. III., was eldest son of Ewan, second son of Murdoch, *Parson* of Kingussie in Inverness-shire, and *Captain* of the clan Chattan. James Macpherson, the translator of Ossian, was born at Kingussie.

MAC QUARRIE. A clan; formerly owners of the isle of Uloa and part of Mull, [originally of the clan Alpine], but compelled to dependence on the Macdonalds, as Lords of the Isles. Their founder was the son of Guaire or Godfrey, brother of Fingo, ancestor of the Mackinnons. Skene, ii. 263.

Gaelic etymologists say—Mac-Curraidh (pron. Currai). " The son of the Giant."

MAC QUEEN. A branch of the great clan Macdonald (Lords of the Isles.) This connection was recognised so lately as the year 1778, by Alexander, Lord Macdonald. The tribe or sub-clan were known as the clan Revan. In the early part of the XV. cent., Rhoderic Dhu Revan Mac Sweene, or Mac Queen, quitted the Isles on receiving the lands of Corrybrough, &c., from which period the family have been annexed to the clan Chattan. B.L.G.

MAC RAE. This ancient Highland name, signifying the ' son of Rae,' or of *Rath,* i.e. " the fortunate one," has many orthographies, of which Macray, Macraa, Macraw, M'Crie, and M'Cree are the chief. From the prevailing characteristic of the race they were called the BLACK MACRAES. They are said to have come originally (into Scotland) from Ireland about the middle of the XIII. cent. They were allies of the Mackenzies, and a number of them fought under the Mackenzie banner at the battle of Largs. They seem never to have had a chieftain of their own. (Boswell's Tour to the Hebrides, edit. Carruthers, p. 107.) They were in considerable estimation in 1715, when there was a line of a song, "*And a' the brave M'Craas are coming ;*" but at the time of Dr. Johnson's visit to the Highlands they were but poorly off. "At Auchnasheal," says Boswell, " we

sat down on a green turf seat at the end of a house . . . . . We had a considerable circle about us, men, women, and children, all Macraes, Lord Seaforth's people. Not one of them could speak English. I observed to Dr. Johnson, it was much the same as being with a tribe of Indians."

In allusion to this want of civilization, they have sometimes been called the WILD MACRAWS. " Macrae and Macraw," observes Mr. Chambers, " are but variations of the same name. This clan is said to be the most unmixed race in the Highlands, a circumstance which seems to be attended with quite a contrary effect from what might have been expected, the Macraes and Macraws being *the handsomest and most athletic men beyond the Grampians.*" Popular Rhymes, &c., of Scotland, 1842.

MACRAY. See Macrae.

MACRIE. See Macrae.

MACREE. See Macrae.

MACRAW. See Macrae.

MAC SWEYN. A Hebridean name— "certainly Norwegian, from Sueno, king of Norway." Boswell's Tour.

MAC TEAR. A contraction of Mac Ateer or Mac Anteer (in Irish, *Mac an t'aoir,*) "the son of a Carpenter." Ulster Journ. of Archæology, No. 20.

MAC TURK. Gael. Mac Torc. " The son of the Boar."

MADDERN. A parish in Cornwall.

MADDERSON. Perhaps a translation of the Welsh patronymic Ap Madre. Fil' Madur is found in H.R. co., Huntingdon.

MADDICK. The Welsh personal name Madoc.

MADDISON. See Madison. 2. A corruption of Maddiston, a village in the parish of Muiravonside, co. Stirling.

MADDOCK. MADDOX. Madoc an ancient Welsh personal name. One Madoch was a tenant in chief in Herefordshire at the making of Domesday. He was doubtless a Welshman by birth.

MADDY. See Matthew.

MADEHURST. A parish in Sussex.

MADELY. Parishes in Staffordshire and Shropshire.

MADERSON. See Madderson.

MADGE. One of the many nicknames of Margaret.

MADISON. Probably Matty's, that is Matthew's, son. The Madisons of the county of Durham were formerly known by the uncomplimentary epithet of THE MAD MADISONS.

MADLIN. Probably Maudlin, Magdalen. See Female Christian Names.

MADOCK. Madoc, the well-known Welsh baptismal name.

MADOX. The genitive form of Madock.

MAGEOGHAN. The son of Eochagan, a celebrated chief of the O'Neile family. See Eng. Surn. ii. 69.

MAGGS. Probably one of the many nicknames of Margaret. See Female Christian Names.

MAGGOT. H.R. Apparently from Margaret.

MAGILLAPATRICK. Descended from Gillapatrick, "the servant of St. Patrick," chief of Ossory, who was slain in 995. O'Donovan in Irish Penny Journal.

MAGNAVILLE. According to De Gerville, the commune of Magneville, two leagues southward of Valognes, gave name to the ancient Earls of Essex of this surname. Mem. Soc. Antiq. Normandie, 1825.

MAGNAY. Most likely from one of the several places in Normandy called Magni.

MAGNUS. A well-known personal name, borne by many Scandinavian monarchs.

MAGOON. A corruption of Mac Gowan.

MAGOTSON. The same as Magson.

MAGSON. Apparently one of the many derivatives of Meg, or Margaret. See Female Christian Names.

MAGUIRE. 1. The co. Fermanagh was anciently the principality of the sept of Maguire, who held it for centuries after the English invasion. Lord Enniskillen was the chief of this race. B.L.G.
2. The son of Guaire, the Gaelic for Godfrey. Guaire was son of Alpin, king of Scotland. Arthur.

MAHER. A modification of O'Meagher or O'Maugher. An ancient Tipperary family.

MAHON. Descended according to tradition from the Mac Mahons, the ancient princes of Munster. At the first arrival of the English in Ireland, in the reign of Henry II., they had large possessions in that province, over which they ruled as hereditary chieftains. Courthope's Debrett. Mahon in Irish signifies a bear.

MAHONY. Anciently O'Mahony, powerful chieftains in Munster, possessing large estates on the sea coast of Kerry and Cork. B.L.G.

MAIBEN. St. Maiben is a parish in Cornwall.

MAID. MAIDMAN. I cannot arrive at any satisfactory etymology for these names, though they may perhaps have some reference to the worship of the Virgin.

MAIDEN. A parish on the borders of Wilts and Somerset, better known as Maiden-Bradley. There is also a Maiden-Newton in co. Dorset; and in Scotland various places bear this designation. But it would appear that the name was sometimes used as a sobriquet, for in the H.R. we find one Adam *le* Maiden.

MAIDMENT. The name Maidman takes this form in the parish register of Gressage All-Saints.

MAIGNY. Camden mentions this as a name introduced at the Conquest. Four places in Normandy are still called Magni.

MAILER. 1. A farmer; one who has a very small piece of ground. Jamieson. A cottager who gets some waste land for a number of years, rent-free, to improve it. Ibid. 2. Perhaps Maylor, a hundred in Flintshire.

MAIN. MAINE. MAYNE. From the French Province.

MAINWARING. In a MS. volume drawn up by Sir William Dugdale, and preserved at Over Peover, it is stated, that the name of this celebrated family has been spelt in the astonishing number of *one hundred and thirty-one* forms, in old records and more modern writings. Some of these may be cited as specimens: 1. Mesnilwarin; 2. Masnilwaren; 3. Mensilwaren; 4. Meisnilwaren; 5. Meidneilwar; 6. Meinilwarin; 7. Menilwarin; 8. Mesnilwarin; 9. Mesnilgarin; 10. Meingarin; 11. Maynwaringe; 12. Mainwayringe; 13. Manwaringe; 14. Manwairing; 15. Maynwaring: 16. Maynering; 17. Mannering: 18. Manwaring; 19. Mainwaring; 20. Manwarren. The founder of the family in England was Randulphus de Mesnilwarin, who accompanied William the Conqueror, and received from him Warmingham, Peover, and thirteen other lordships in Cheshire, together with one in Norfolk. His descendants spread into many branches in Cheshire, and other northern counties, and included many personages of eminence. For ample accounts of the family see Ormerod's Cheshire. Inf. Rev. E. H. Mainwaring Sladen.

The name Mesnil-Warin signifies the Manor of Warin.—Mesnil, now written Ménil, enters into many local names, about ninety of which are still found in the Itin. de la Normandie. Warin, Warine, or Guarine, was a common Christian name in Norman times; but the particular personage who gave name to Mesnil-Warin is lost in the mists of antiquity, and the place itself is not to be traced on the map of Normandy.

MAIR. An officer attending a sheriff for executions and arrests. Jamieson. Perhaps another form of Mayor. Mair. H.R.

MAISEY. See Macey.

MAISH. MAISHMAN. Local mispronunciations of Marsh and Marshman.

MAISTER. The Maisters of Yorkshire have a tradition of descent from the family of Le Maistre in Brittany. The name is of course the O. Fr. *le Maistre*, the Master.

MAITLAND. The Earl of Lauderdale's family were seated in the southern counties of Scotland as early at least as the XIII. century. Their chief abode was Thirlstane in Berwickshire, but the name would appear to have been derived from a place in the parish of Inveresk, co. Edinburgh, called Magdalen Pans, by corruption Maitland Pans, from a chapel dedicated to St. Mary Magdalen, which formerly stood there. This property continued in the family until 1710.

MAJENDIE. This family, of some antiquity in the province of Bearn, quitted France in 1667, in consequence of the persecution of those who professed the reformed religion. The first settler in England was the Rev. Andrew Majendie, who fixed his residence in Devonshire about the year 1700.

MAJOR. See under Mauger.

MAJORIBANKS. See Marjoribanks.

MAKEPEACE. Doubtless a mediator, or as we now commonly say, a "peacemaker." The following similar surnames, now apparently extinct, are found in medieval records: Makejoy, Makeblisse, Makeblithe, Makehayt.

MAKER. A parish of Cornwall, near to Plymouth. The fine seat of Mount Edgecombe is in this parish.

MAKINS. MAKINSON. Supposed derivatives of the personal name Mary. See Eng. Surn. i. 171.

MALACHY. From the personal name, which was not directly derived, however, from the Hebrew prophet, but from Saint Malachy, archbishop of Armagh, who is said to have died in the arms of Saint Bernard, in 1148. There are many other instances of Christian saints bearing the same names as the Worthies of the Old Testament, and we have accordingly St. Asaph, St. David, St. Sampson, &c., &c.

MALBY. Probably a corruption of Maltby.

MALCOLM. Originally a personal name, signifying Maol-Cholumb, 'the Servant of Columba,' the famous saint of Iona. So Maol-Jes, the true name of the old Earls of Strathern, means 'Servant of Jesus.' See cognate derivations under Gilchrist, Gospatrick, &c. (See Anecdotes of Olave the Black, King of Man, by Johnstone, 1780.) "Mavile means servant; therefore Malcolm (properly Mavile Columb) the servant of Columba; Malbrigd, the servant of St. Bridget ; Malpatric, the servant of St. Patrick; Malmory (Mavile Maria), the servant of St. Mary." Ecclesiologist, April, 1849. This family represent "the clan Challum or Mac Callum, settled, according to the traditions of the country, from a very early period in Argyleshire." B.L.G.

MALDEN. A parish in Surrey.

MALEMEYNS. O. Fr. "bad hands," but whether in relation to manual deformity, or to evil deeds, does not appear. The name is found temp. Edw. I. The similar name, Malebranche, "bad arm," is found at the same period.

MALIN. Probably from the town of Malines, in Belgium.

MALINES. Camden mentions this among names introduced here from the Netherlands, at the period of the Conquest. It must therefore be local, from the city of that name.

MALKIN. A common diminutive of Mary. Halliwell.

MALLAM. Malham, a township in the W.R of Yorkshire.

MALLARD. Local—and said to mean in Gaelic, "a high mound, hill, or eminence." Arthur.

MALLESON. Conjectured to be "the son of Mallet." See Mallet.

MALLET. A name remarkable from its having withstood the innovations of orthography and nation, from the period when modern history is lost in obscurity. Its origin is undoubtedly Teutonic; for we find it has arrived in England from two distinct sources, and is, strange to say, both Saxon and Norman. Of the former, the descendants are possibly extinct long ere this ; but their name appears in the Saxon Chronicle. And whilst the family tree has flourished with hardy vigour in its native Norway, from time immemorial to the present day, its Norman branch, constituting the great and distinguished house of Malet-de-Graville, which also occupies so prominent a place in the history of England, during the XI., XII., and XIII. centuries, and retaining the principle of undecayed vitality, has added lustre to the annals of France, by the greatness and honours to which it attained, and by the benefits which its services conferred on that country, from the early days of Rollo to the end of the XVI. century; and of this, a branch also established itself in the island of Jersey, in the latter part of the reign of the Conqueror, and the name is still borne by one of the most ancient families in this "isle of long lineages," where it held a seigneurie, or lordship in capite, of the Dukes of Normandy, bearing its name. It is now represented by John Mallet, Esq., Robert Philip Mallet, Esq., and William Edmund Mallet, Esq., surviving sons of the late Rev. John Mallet, rector of his original ancestral parish of Grouville, in that island. This name is derived from the word mall, the northern noun for the ponderous iron mace, in the use of which the Norse-men were such dreaded and doughty adepts, and is most properly spelt, in accordance with its derivative, with two L's, although written frequently with one only.—Contributed by W. E. Mallet, Esq.

MALLING. Parishes in Sussex and Kent.

MALMESBURY. A town in Wiltshire.

MALONE. One of the descendants of the house of O'Connor, Kings of Connaught, having received the tonsure in honour of Saint John, was called Maol Eoin, "sacred or dedicated to John," which was afterwards corrupted to Malone.

MALPAS. A town in Cheshire.

MALSTER. A corruption of Maltster.

MALTBY. Parishes and places in cos. York and Lincoln.

MALTHUS. A corruption of Malt-house.

MALTON. Two parishes in York-shire.

MALTRAVERS. The name occurs in England temp. Henry I., and it was doubt-less introduced at the Norman Conquest, though the family were not ennobled until the reign of Edward III. It may be of local origin, and allusive to some "bad passage" or traject.

MALTSTER. The occupation.

MALVERN. Two parishes in co. Wor-cester.

MALVOISON. See Mauvesyn.

MALYON. There is a parish of St. Mel-lion in Cornwall.

☞ MAN. A very usual termination of English surnames, as Workman, Long-man, Newman, Potman, Waterman—which explain themselves. There are however some, of a local origin, which require a few remarks. In the XIII. & XIV. centuries, many persons received family names, not from the designation, but from the *situation*, of their residences. A plebeian, for instance, who dwelt at a grove, would be called William at the Grove, or more curtly, Wills. atte Grove. In the succeeding centuries the awk-ward *atte*, sometimes softened to *A'* was dropped, and the name became simply Grove, Grover, or Grove*man*. In like manner were formed Beckman from beck, Castleman from castle, Crouch-man from crouch, Lakeman from lake, Parkman from park, and many others. See ER.

Man in O. Fr. signifies Norman. Kelham. And in Dutch *de Man* means 'the man,' *heros*.

MANATON. A parish in Devonshire.

MANBY. A parish in co. Lincoln.

MANDER. See Maunder.

MANDEVILLE. Goisfrid de M. was a Domesday chief-tenant in many counties. His descendants were the famous Earls of Essex, extinct in the XIII. century. From a younger branch probably sprang the famous traveller, Sir John M. in the XIV. cent. In charters, De Magna Villa and De Mandavilla. Magneville is near Valognes in Normandy, and there are two places called Mandeville, one near Louviers, and another in the arrondissement of Bayeux.

MANFRED. The old Teutonic personal name.

MANGLES. Apparently from the O. Germ. personal name Managold.

MANHOOD. A hundred in Sussex.

MANLEY. An estate in the parish of Frodsham, co. Chester, where the family were resident from the time of Roger Manley, who flourished in the reign of Henry II., till the XVI. cent. The family are assumed to have been of Norman origin, and the name is mentioned in Holinshed's list, though it was not adopted until many years after the Conquest.

MANN. This is a proper name of vast antiquity—the *Mannus* of the Teutonic mythology. Tacitus says of the Germans (cap. ii.): They celebrate in their ancient hymns, Tuisco, the earth-born, and his son Mannus, the originators and founders of their race : " Celebrant carminibus antiquis Tuistonem, terra editum, et filium *Mannum*, originem gentis conditoresque." Hence, doubtless, our word man, homo. Once adopted as a personal name, it would naturally become a surname. In some cases, however, the name is derived from *Le Man*, a native of the province of Maine, analogous to Le Breton, Le Norman, &c. Possibly also from the island in the Irish sea. See Man.

MANNAKAY. Perhaps a corruption of Manaccan, co. Cornwall.

MANNALL. Probably the same as Meynell.

MANNELL. Probably the same as Meynell.

MANNERING. A corruption of Main-waring.

MANNERS. According to Camden and other antiquaries, this noble family had their denomination from the village of Mannor, near Lanchester, co. Durham. They were certainly influential in the northern counties, and Collins traces the name to a William de Manner, who flour-ished temp. William Rufus. The pedigree is deduced by him from Sir Robert de Manners, lord of Etal in Northumberland, several generations anterior to the reign of Henry III.

MANNERSON. Probably a corruption of Manderston, a place at Dunse in Scot-land.

MANNIN. See Manning.

MANNING. An ancient personal name, still seen in Manningham, Mannington, Manningtree, &c. Mr. Ferguson derives it from the O. Norse *manningi*, a brave or valiant man.

MANNINGHAM. A township in the W.R. of Yorkshire.

MANNINGTON. A parish in Norfolk.

MANNOCK. The family pretend to be of Danish original, and to have flourished in England under the Danish monarchs ; but the pedigree is traced only to temp. Edw. III.

MANS. Probably Mantes, the Fr. city.

MANSBRIDGE. A hundred in Hamp-shire.

MANSEL. "The Mansels inhabited Le Mans in France, and came over with William the Conqueror." Taylor's Roman de Rou. Talbot's Eng. Etym. But see Mansell and Maunsell.

MANSELL. 1. The same as Maunsell. Mancel is without prefix in H.R. 2. Two parishes in Herefordshire bear this name.

MANSER or MAUNSER. A Norman Christian name, latinized Manserus.

MANSERGH. A chapelry in Westmoreland.

MANSFIELD. A parish in co. Nottingham, the ancient abode of the family, temp. Henry II. Some families derive themselves from a German source.

MANSON. From Man, an ancient personal name. See Man and Mann. In Domesd. it is written Manessuna and Mansuna.

MANT. The town of Mantes in France.

MANTELL. Turstinus Mantel occurs in the Domesd. of co. Bucks, as a tenant in chief. Probably a sobriquet, from the Fr. mantelé, a "cloak-wearer." Mauntell. H.R.

MANTON. Parishes in Lincoln and Rutlandshires.

MANUEL. An ancient personal name.

MANUS. The Celtic Mac Manus, sans Mac.

MANVELL. A corruption of Mandeville.

MANWARING. See Mainwaring.

MAPLES. An old Norman feminine name. Ma belle, "my pretty one," is corrupted in the Channel Islands to Maple and Maples.

MAPLESON. The same as Mapleston.

MAPLESTON. Probably Mappleton, parishes in cos. Derby and York.

MAPLEY. Mapperley, a township in Derbyshire.

MARCH. A town in Cambridgeshire. Le March is frequent in H.R.

MARCHAM. A parish in Berks.

MARCHANT. The old and more correct spelling of Merchant. Fr. marchand.

MARCHBANKS. A corruption of Marjoribanks, which is most vilely so pronounced.

MARCUS. The Latin form of Mark.

MARCY. Probably from Marcei, a village near Argentan in Normandy.

MARDEN. Parishes, &c., in cos. Hereford, Kent, Wilts, Sussex, &c.

MARDON. The same as Marden.

MARE. Scot. Great.

MARES. Scot. from Fr. marais. A marsh.

MARGARET. A very common XIII. century surname. See Female Christian Names.

MARGERISON. MARJORISON. See Female Christian Names. See also Gerison.

MARGERY. See Female Christian Names.

MARGESSON. Apparently a corruption of Margerison, the son of Margaret; but the Margessons of Offington, co. Sussex, are otherwise deduced, namely from Argenson, a French family. John D'Argenson, living in 1449, had two sons, one of whom fought at the battle of Pavia, in 1524, and the other, Peter D'Argenson, was founder of the English branch. So says B.L.G.; and it is added, that the Margetsons of Yorkshire sprang from that personage, which may well admit of question, for certainly D'Argenson and Margetson are not much alike.

MARGETSON. See Female Christian Names.

MARGETTS. See Female Christian Names.

MARGRAVE. Germ. markgraf, an office and title of dignity, of common origin with marquis, or lord marcher—one who had charge of the frontier of the country.

MARINER. A sailor. Le Mariner. H.R.

MARIOTT. Marietus seems to have been a personal name. In Domesd. one Alricus Marieti sune—Alric, the son of Mariet—occurs as an undertenant in many counties. See Ellis, Introd. ii. 10. De Gerville thinks it is a derivative of Mary. Eng. Surn. ii. 83. There is, however, a parish in Somerset called Merriott. See Marriott.

MARJORIBANKS. (Mis-pronounced Marchbanks.) According to the genealogy of this distinguished family, the Marjoribanks, or Majoribanks, were a branch of the Scottish Johnstones. The name is local, though I find no place now so called. The following account is from B.L.G.—"When Walter, high steward of Scotland, and ancestor of the royal house of Stuart, espoused Marjorie (Margaret) only daughter of Robert Bruce, and eventually heiress to the crown, the barony of Ratho was granted by the king as a marriage-portion to his daughter, by charter which is still extant, and these lands being subsequently denominated 'Terra de Marjorie-banks,' gave rise to the name of Marjoribanks."

MARK. MARKE. MARKES. MARKS. The Christian name.

MARKCOCK. A diminutive of Mark. See termination COCK.

MARKET. 1. From residence at a market-place. 2. A contraction of Mercator, merchant.

MARKETMAN. An attendant at markets, or perhaps the toll-taker there.

MARKHAM. A village in Nottinghamshire, which was the residence and possession of this eminent family so early as the reign of King Henry II.

MARKIN. A diminutive of Mark.

MARKLAND. 1. Local; but I find no place specifically so called. For the Anglo-Saxon system of *marks*, see Kemble's Saxons in England. 2. In Scotland, a division of land. Jamieson.

MARKWICK. Possibly local; though, as it was spelt Mar-quicke, two centuries ago, it may have been a sobriquet.

MARLAY. Perhaps from Morlaix, a town of Brittany.

MARLBOROUGH. A town in Wiltshire.

MARLER. A digger of marl—analogous to Chalker. Marl was formerly much employed as manure for land. Le Marler. H.R.

MARLEY. An estate in the parish of Battel, Sussex.

MARLOW. A town and a parish in Buckinghamshire, and a township in Herefordshire.

MARMADUKE. An early personal name.

MARMION. MARMIUN. A great feudal family sprung from Robert de Marmion, lord of Fontenay in Normandy, [which Fontenai does not appear, and there are at least eleven places so called] who came hither at the Conquest, and received from the Conqueror the castle and barony of Tamworth, co. Warwick. This personage also received the manor of Scrivelsby, co. Lincoln, in grand serjeanty, for performing the office of Champion at the coronation of the king. It is alleged that the De Marmions had held the hereditary office of champion to the Dukes of Normandy anterior to the Conquest. What is more certain is, that his successors, as long as the male issue continued, and after them the heritors of his blood, the Dymokes, held, and do hold, the fine old privilege of "riding, completely armed, on the day of the monarch's coronation, into Westminster Hall, there to challenge to combat any one who shall dare to oppose his title to the crown." The prefix *De* shows the local origin of the surname, but I find no place called Marmion, in Normandy.

MARNER. Probably a contraction of Mariner; there is, however, a place called Marnières near Evreux in Normandy.

MARNES. Possibly Mearns, a parish in co. Renfrew.

MARNEY. In 9th Edward III., Layer or Leyr-Marney, co. Essex, belonged to the family.

MARNHAM. A parish in co. Nottingham.

MARQUIS. A sobriquet, probably of recent origin.

MARR. A district of Aberdeenshire, which had its Earls as far back as the XI. century, and still gives the same title to the Erskines, although they have no possessions there. Also a parish in Yorkshire.

MARRIAN. See Maryon.

MARRINER. See Mariner.

MARRIOTT. A family tradition derives it from a town of the same name in Normandy; but no place in that province approaching the sound or orthography is to be found. The name is, however, unquestionably French, and probably one of the many derivatives of the female name Mary. Mariette and Mariotte are still found as surnames in Normandy. See De Gerville, in Mem. Soc. Ant. Norm. for 1844. See also Mariott.

MARRIS. Fr. *marais*, a marsh.

MARROT. Probably the same as Marriott.

MARRYAT. The same as Marriott.

MARS. 1. See under Morris for the possible origin of this name. There is, however, a place so called near Domfront in Normandy, from which the family may have originated. 2. The god of war. 3. The Fr. for the month of March.

MARSDEN. Chapelries, &c., in cos. Lancaster and York.

MARSH. Parishes in cos. Buckingham and Lincoln. The Kentish family appear to have been in that county from the XIV. cent. The latinization is De Marisco, and the medieval form is Ate-Mershe. The equivalent name Marais is common in France.

☞ MARSH. A termination of various local surnames, implying *palus*, low and marshy ground, as Hindmarsh, Saltmarsh, Titmarsh.

MARSHALL. This word has doubled its meaning in a very singular fashion. Cotgrave says—" a marshall of a kingdome or of a campe (an honourable place); also a black-smith; also a farrier, horse-leech, or horse-smith; also a harbinger." Richardson gives the etymon, Fr. *mares-chal*; Dutch, *maer*, a horse, and *schalck*, a servant, literally "a servant who takes care of horses." By degrees the word acquired a more dignified meaning, and was applied to the "magister equorum" or master of the cavalry, and other offices of state, some of which were not connected with horses, but with the management of great public affairs. Hence, under the *ancien régime*, the Great Marshals of France, governors of provinces, &c., as well as the Earl-Marshal of England, the Lord Marischal of Scotland, &c. Hence the verb to 'marshal' is to arrange, either soldiers on a battle-field, or armorial coats in the field of heraldry, besides other meanings. The surname though sometimes derived from the superior occupation or "honourable place," (as in the case of the old Earls of Pembroke, in whom the office of Mareschal or commander-in-chief vested hereditarily) is far too common to admit a doubt that it generally implies nothing more than farrier or shoeing-smith, in which sense it is still used in France. From a table given in Eng. Surn. ii. 163, it appears that in 1847-8 this surname stood sixtieth in the order of commonness in our family nomenclature.

MARSHAM. The Marshams of Norfolk derive their name from the town so called in that county, where John de M. resided temp. Edward I. B.L.G.

MARSHMAN. See Marsh, and the termination MAN.

MARSOM. A corruption of Marsham.

MARSON. Not *Martis filius*, but a corruption of Marston.

MARSTON. Parishes and places in cos. Chester, Hereford, Lincoln, Oxford, Stafford, Warwick, Wilts, Somerset, Derby, Buckingham, Northampton, York, Leicester, Bedford, Gloucester, &c.

MARTEL. MARTELL. A very ancient French surname, as Charles Martel, Geoffrey Martel. O. Fr. *martel,* a hammer; probably with reference to the martel-defer, the iron hammer or mace of medieval warfare. See Mallet.

MARTEN. The Martens of Sussex are stated to have come from the " province of Aquitaine, in France, and lived there Anno 1386." Kent's Grammar of Heraldry, 1716.

MARTER. See Martyr.

MARTHEWS. The same as Matthews.

MARTIN. MARTYN. From the personal name, rendered illustrious by St. Martin, the apostol of the Gauls. Many places in Normandy were dedicated to him, and from one of these sprang the great family who came hither at the Conquest under the name of De Sancto Martino. Both as a personal designation, and a surname, it is very widely spread in all the countries of western Europe. At Paris it is amongst the very commonest of all family names, answering to our own Smith for frequency. Its derivatives are Martins and Martinson. Martineau is well naturalized here, and Martinelli, Martinez, Martini, and other foreign forms are becoming so. The name of the Saint was perhaps derived from the Latin *martius,* warlike.

MARTINDALE. A chapelry of Barton, co. Westmoreland.

MARTINEAU. From the Italian Martino. Talbot's English Etymol. But this is doubtful. The family were settled at Norwich in the reign of Elizabeth.

MARTINS. See Martin.

MARTINSON. See Martin.

MARTINVAST DE. The château of Martinvast lies in the canton of Octeville, a league from Cherbourg in Normandy.

Richard, lord of this place, had lands co. Nottingham in the middle of the XII. century. Another branch held the château long after the disruption of Normandy. De Gerville in Mem. Soc. Antiq. Norm., 1825. I find the same family in Rutlandshire, temp. Edw. I. under the name of De Martivas.

MARTON. The name of many parishes, townships, manors, &c., in the northern counties, from the A-Sax. *mere,* a lake or pool, and *tún,* an enclosure or homestead. I believe that 'he only family now bearing the name are the Martons of Capernwray, co. Lancaster, who claim lineal descent from Paganus de Marton, the Norman lord of E. and W. Marton in Craven, soon after the Conquest.

MARTYN. See Martin.

MARTYR. An old personal name.

MARWOOD. Parishes, &c., in cos. Devon and Durham.

MARY. See Female Christian Names.

MARYATT. See Mariott.

MARYON. De Gerville deduces it from the personal name Mary. See Eng. Surn. ii. 83.

MASCALL. I believe that the Mascalls of Kent and Sussex were originally Marshalls. There is armorial evidence of this; and in a document of the XVI. century before me, I find the name written Marscal, which is about midway between Mareschal and Mascall.

MASCLE. See Mascall.

MASH. A provincial pronunciation of Marsh.

MASHAM. A parish in Yorkshire.

MASHMAN. The same as Marshman.

MASKELL. See Mascall.

MASON. 1. The occupation. Le Mason, Le Masson, Le Masun. H.R. 2. A township in Northumberland.

MASSENGER. Another form of Messenger.

MASSEY. See Massie.

MASSIE. A great Cheshire family, of whom, from their numerousness, the proverb, however uncomplimentary, runs—
AS MANY MASSIES AS ASSES.
The founder of the family in England was Hamon Massie, a Norman, who accompanied the Conqueror, and acquired Dunham in Cheshire, which has from that circumstance ever since borne the suffix of " Massey." From what part of Normandy that personage came is not perhaps known, but there are several places in the province from which, with about equal claims to probability, the name might be reasonably deduced; viz.: Macé-sur-Orne, near Alençon; Macei, in the arrondissement of Avranches; Marcei, in that of Argentan ; and Marcei, on the Broise, near the town of Avranches, the seat of an ancient barony.

MASSINGBERD. A very old Lincoln-shire family, dating from temp. Henry III. with the present orthography, though in the XVII. cent. the final syllable was some-times written *beard*, in order to preserve the pronunciation—that syllable clearly having reference to the appendage of the masculine chin. The meaning of the other portion of the name is not so obvious, as no word re-sembling *massing* is found in early English or Anglo-Saxon. In some Teutonic dialects, however, that or a similar form means *brass*, and hence Massingberd may signify *Brazen-beard*, with reference to the personal peculiarity. Inf. Rev. F. C. Massingberd, M.A. See Beard.

MASSINGHAM. Two parishes in Nor-folk.

MASTER. The social position; to dis-tinguish the individual from another of the same Christian name, but in servile condi-tion. The equivalent Fr. name, Lemaitre, is very common. Or perhaps the Gaelic Mac Master, sans *Mac*.

MASTERS. Apparently a Norman local name. Robt. de Mosters occurs in Domesd.

MASTERSON. A translation of the Gaelic Mac Master.

MASTERMAN. Scot. A landlord.

MATHER. MATHERS. Mathers is a village in the parish of St. Cyrus or Ec-clescraig in Kincardineshire.

MATHESON. The son of Matthew.

MATHEW. MATHEWS. See Mat-thew. The Welsh family of Mathew claim from the princes of Cardigan in the XI. cent. B.L.G. From the Welsh house sprang the Mathews of Upton-Grey, and Alton, co. Hants, and Stanstead, co. Sussex. The name is of course identical with Mat-thew.

MATHEY. A common corruption of Matthew.

MATHIAS. As Matthias.

MATTHIE. See Matthew.

MATHIESON. See Matthew.

MATIN. MATTIN. Probably corrup-tions of Martin.

MATKIN. A diminutive of Matthew.

MATSON. 1. See Matthew. 2. A parish in co. Gloucester.

MATTERFACE. A vile corruption of a distinguished Norman surname, "De Martinvast," originally from the neighbour-hood of Cherbourg. See Martinvast.

MATTHEW. This baptismal name, in-troduced here at the Conquest, has not only become a surname, but the parent of many others: to wit, Mathew, Matthews, Ma-thews, Matthewson, Matthie, Mathieson, Matson, Mayhew, Mayo, Matts, Matty, Maddy, Madison.

MATTHEWMAN. "May possibly be from the A-Sax. *mathie*, modest. Old Norse, *mœtamadr*, vir egregius." Ferguson.

MATTHEWSON. See Matthew.

MATTHIAS. The Christian name.

MATTINSON. Martin's son, or Mat-thew's son.

MATTOCK. MATTOCKS. See Mad-dock.

MATTS. A derivative of Matthew.

MATTY. See Matthew.

MAUDE. MAUD. A remarkable con-traction of De Monte Alto, De Montalt, or "of the high mountain." The first of the family in England was Eustachius de Monte Alto, who came hither at the Conquest among the followers of Hugh Lupus, Earl of Chester. From him sprang the Barons Montalt, whose elder line became extinct in the XIV. cent. Many younger branches survive under the name of Maude, and one of them, Viscount Hawarden, still enjoys the second title of Baron Montalt. Ac-cording to Burke's Commoners, the name was originally derived from a place in Italy.

MAUDLINS. The son of Maudlin or Magdalen. See Female Christian Names.

MAUDUIT. See Mawditt.

MAUFEE. La Mauffé is a place in the arrondissement of St. Lo, in Normandy. The family were in Sussex at an early period. The name still exists as Morfee and Morphew. On adjacent tombstones at Woodchurch, co. Kent, it is spelt both Morfee and Morfeet.

MAUGER. MAGOR. MAJOR. MAYOR. MAYER. Mauger, archbishop of Rouen, uncle to William the Conqueror, in consequence of great irregularities, ab-dicated his see and settled in the island of Guernsey. There he met with a lady of great beauty called Gisella or Guille, with whom, without the sanction of the Church, he formed an intimacy that resulted in a numerous progeny, some of whom took their father's, others their mother's name. "Hence," observes a correspondent, "Guilles and Maugers are as plentiful as black-berries in the Channel Islands." From one of the family sprang Sir Matthias Mayer or Mayor, a Jerseyman, and a soldier under Henry VII. who obtained a grant of arms and was lineal ancestor of R. Major, Esq., of Hurdsley, co. Hants, whose daughter Dorothy married Richard, afterwards Lord Protector Cromwell. The Maugers were very prominent in the early history of the Channel Islands.

MAUGHAN. Two parishes in Cornwall are called Mawgan.

MAUL. See Maule.

MAULE. 1. This Scottish family were "originally of French extraction; an an-cestor, Petrus de Maulia, A.D. 1076, gave large possessions to the Church." New-ton's Display of Heraldry, p. 159.
2. The family are of French origin, deriving their name from the lordship of Maule, near Paris. According to Dou-

glas's Peerage of Scotland, Guarin de Maule, a younger son of Arnold, lord of Maule, accompanied William, Duke of Normandy, to the Conquest of England. Robert de Maule, his son, accompanied David I. into Scotland, and obtained from him a grant of lands in Lothian, and so founded the family in Scotland. His great-grandson, early in the XIII. cent., married the heiress of De Valoniis, lord of Panmure, and thus the family became known as Maule of Panmure.

3. Said to be the Gælic *mal*, slow.

MAULEVERER. "*Mal-levorer*, in Latin, *Malus leporarius* or 'the Bad Hare-Hunter.' "A gentleman of this county (Yorkshire) being to slip a brace of grey-hounds to run for a great wager (Tradition is the author), so held them in the swinge, that they were more likely to strangle themselves than kill the hare; whereupon this surname was fixed on his family. I doubt not but many of this extraction are since as dexterous in the criticisms of hunting as any Nimrod whatsoever." Fuller's Worthies, iii. 453.

In Domesday Book, however, under Essex, we find—"Terra Adami filii Durandi de Malis Operibus," which Peter le Neve, Norry king of arms, considers equivalent to 'bad workman.' The truth is that the name is purely local—Maulévrier being an ancient viscounty in the arron-dissement of Yvetot in Normandy.

MAULEY. The first mention of this name occurs shortly after the death of Richard I., when John, in order to clear his way to the throne, employed his esquire Peter de Mauley, a native of Poitou, to murder his nephew, Prince Arthur, for which service De Mauley received great re-muneration in the West of England. In charters, the latinization of this name, De Malo Lacu, might be supposed to be no un-apt allusion to the "bad lake or pool" of blood thus unrighteously shed by the founder of the race.

MAULL. See Maule.

MAULOVEL. An A.-Norm. name, meaning, according to its latinization, (*Malus Lupellus*) "the bad little wolf."

MAUNDER. A beggar. O. E. *maund*, to beg.

MAUNSELL. "The curious poetical history of this family preserved in Collec-tanea Topogr. et Geneal. claims one SAHER, there written "*Sier, the syer of us all,*" as their ancestor; he appears to have been the son of Ralph Maunsel, who was living in Buckinghamshire 14. Henry II. (1167)." Shirley's Noble and Gentle Men. The name is understood to signify a native of Maine, a province of France. The Irish branch left England temp. Elizabeth.

MAURICE. The personal name Mau-ritius.

MAUREWARD. An old A.-Norm. surname, signifying "bad look," probably with reference to a squint or some other deformity of countenance.

MAUTENANT. May refer to some forgotten act of infidelity on the part of its primitive owner. Eng. Surn. An old A.-Norm. name.

MAUVESYN. O. Fr. *mal voisin*, bad neighbour. This was one of the many un-complimentary surnames borne by Norman grandees. It was introduced at the Con-quest, *Malus Vicinus* occurring in the Domesday of Suffolk. At a later period the family gave the suffix to Ridware Mau-vesyn, co. Stafford, their place of residence. It is stated in Burke's Commoners that the name may be regarded as local, and that it was derived from a tower so called in the Isle of France; but this is doubtful. See Eng. Surn., ii. 12.

MAVOR. Lat., Mavortius, Mars. A name ascribed to Welsh heroes.

MAW. MAWE. "The name Mac Coghlan is in Ireland beautified and abbre-viated into Maw; the Mac Coghlan or head of the family was called *the* Maw; and a district of King's County was known, with-in the memory of persons now living, by the appellation of the Maw's County." Southey's Doctor.

MAWBEY. The name has been written De Mauteby, Maultby, Mawteby, Maubie, Mawby, &c. It was assumed from the vil-lage of Mawtby, co. Norfolk, in or before the reign of Richard I.

MAWDESLEY. A township in Lanca-shire.

MAWDITT. Apparently a modern cor-ruption of the old baronial name Mauduit. The latinization *Male conductus*, or *De Malo Conductu*, is not complimentary to the family. The name first appears in Domesd. William Malduith, chamberlain to William the Conqueror, was a tenant in chief in Hampshire, as was a Gunfred M. in Wilt-shire.

MAWLEY. See Mauley.

MAWRICE. See Morris.

MAXEY. A parish in co. Northampton.

MAXFIELD. A shortened pronuncia-tion of Macclesfield, a town in Cheshire.

MAXON. See Maxton.

MAXTON. MAXTONE. A parish in Roxburghshire. The Maxtones of Culto-quhey in Perthshire acquired that estate by charter in 1410. B.L.G.

MAXWELL. A village in the parish of Kelso, co. Roxburgh. Herbert de Macus-well or Maxwell, the ancestor of the house, had a son, Sir John de M., who was sheriff of Roxburghshire in 1203 and 1207. B.L.G.

MAY. Has certainly no connection with the month of flowers, as it is commonly written in records Le Mai. It may be the same as the O. Scot. *maich*, A.-Sax. *mœg*, O. Eng. *mei*, son-in-law, son, or generally, any relative. Le May is common in H.R.

MAYBIN. See Maiben.

MAYCOCK. Possibly a diminutive formed from the female name Mary. Maykoc is found temp. Edw. I.

MAYDWELL. Local: "the well of the Maid," i.e. the Virgin Mary—a sacred well dedicated to that saint.

MAYER. A mayor, chief officer of a municipality. Other countries have the same surname; e.g. Germ. Meier; Du. Meyer; Fr. Lemaire, &c. But see under Mauger.

MAYFIELD. A parish in Sussex; also several places in Scotland.

MAYGER. See Major.

MAYHEW. See Matthew. There are many Fil'Maheus in H.R.

MAYLER. See Mailer.

MAYLIN. See Malin.

MAYMAN. Probably the superintendent of the sports of May-day.

MAYNARD. An ancient personal name.

MAYNE. See Maine.

MAYNEY. The Mayneys, extinct baronets, claimed probable descent from a family of Norman-Conquest origin, who numbered among their members the chivalrous Sir Walter Manny, of the time of Edward III. The head of the family was created a baronet in 1641, and spent a fair estate in the cause of the Stuarts. His son, and heir to the title, "died of actual want in 1706, his brother, broken down by indigence, having previously committed suicide." Ext. Barts. The name was probably derived from one of the places in Normandy called Magni, and it was sometimes curiously corrupted to Money.

MAYO. See Matthew and Mayow.

MAYOR. The office.

MAYOW. MAYHOW. Probably one of the many modifications of Matthew. This seems the more likely, because the Mayows of Cornwall originally wrote themselves Mayhew. See C. S. Gilbert's Cornwall.

MAYPOWDER. Mappowder, a parish in Dorsetshire.

MAYSON. A mis-spelling of Mason.

MEACHAM. Mitcham in Surrey?

MEAD. MEADE. MEADS. A-Sax. *mæd*, what is *mowed* or cut down. A Meadow. Analogous to Meadows, Du Pré, &c.

MEADE. (Ireland.) An anglicised form of the old Irish name Meagh. The family of Lord Clanwilliam have been seated for many centuries in co. Cork. At Meadestown in that county there was formerly a castle, built by the Meaghs or Meades. Smith's Hist. of Cork.

MEADER. Perhaps a maker of metheglin or mead.

MEADOWS. MEADOWES. MEADUS. See Mead.

MEADS. A pluralization of Mead.

MEADWAY. The Medway, a river of Kent.

MEAKINS. See Meekins.

MEAN. Perhaps from East or West Meon in Hampshire. At the time of the introduction of surnames the adjective *mean*, as referring to sordidness of character, was unknown. See however Mein.

MEARES. It is said that this name was originally De la Mere. B.L.G.

MEARS. A parish in Northamptonshire.

MEASAM. MEASOM. Measham, a parish in Derbyshire.

MEASOR. O. Scot. *meassour*, a macebearer—one who carries the mace before persons in authority—*hodie*, a macer. Jamieson.

MEASURE. MEASURES. O. Fr. *masure*, which means either "an old decayed house, or wall, or ruines of a building," or "a quantitie of ground containing about foure Oxe-gangs." Cotgrave. Masure, as a surname, still occurs in France.

MEATYARD. *Mete-rod, mete-wand*, and *mete-yard* are medievalisms for measuring sticks, and from the last the surname must in some way have been derived.

MECCA. A local pronunciation of Metcalfe.

MECHAM. See Meacham.

MECHANT. Fr. Bad, wicked.

MEDCALF. See Metcalfe.

MEDES. The same as Meads.

MEDHURST. Probably either Midhurst or Madehurst, both parishes in Sussex. De Medhurst. H.R. co. Kent.

MEDLAND. This name has a 'local' look; but it appears to have been a bye, or additional, name borne at an early period. The Norman grandee, Robert de Beaumont, sometimes styled Meulant or Mellent, was called by the people of Leicester, his tenants, *The Medland*. Mr. Thompson, in Winchester Vol. of Brit. Archæolog. Assoc., p. 73. That the name may still be local is shown by the occurrence in the H.R. of a Walter de Medelond, or Medeland.

MEDLAR. Mr. Ferguson thinks that this name corresponds to the Germ. family name Madler, which is probably identical with the O. Germ. Madalhari; but the occurrence in H.R. of one Nich. le Medler rather tends to shew that the name was originally applied to some medieval busybody.

MEDLEY. Undoubtedly local—but I do not find the place.

MEDLICOTT. MEDLICOTE. In all

probability local, although I have heretofore derived it from *medley-coat*, a coat of many or mixed colours, a once favourite fashion. Eng. Surn. i. 205.

MEDLOCK. Probably Matlock, co. Derby. A portion of Manchester is, however, called Chorlton-upon-Medlock.

MEDWARD. The keeper of a meadow. Le Medward. H.R. A-Sax. *mæd* and *weard*.

MEDWIN. The baptismal name is said to occur so early as the second century, in the story of King Lucius and Pope Eleutherius. In the unreformed calendar, the feast of St. Medwyn stands for January 1. The saint was buried in Scotland, in which country there is a river called Medwin, co. Lanark.

MEECHING. The old and proper name of Newhaven, co. Sussex.

MEEK. MEEKE. Of a quiet, peaceful disposition.

MEEKING. See Meekins.

MEEKINS. " De Mèschines (from Bayeux in Normandy), Meskines, Meykeynes, Meschin, Mekins, Meekins." This is Sir B. Burke's pedigree of the name as borne by the Irish family.

MEER. Mere, a lake or shallow water. It is found in composition in many names of sheets of water, as Windermere, Buttermere, Grasmere. There is, however, a Lincolnshire parish so called.

MEERES. See Mears.

MEES. A provincialism for meadows.

MEESON. A parish in Shropshire, united with Bolas. It is stated to be a corruption of the A.-Norm. name Malvoisin, or Mauvesyn. It probably bore some A-Sax. designation in older times. On the acquisition of it by the Norman family, they gave their surname as a suffix, and the suffix in course of time supplanted the former name, as in the case of Latimers in Buckinghamshire which was originally Iselhampsted, then Iselhampsted-Latimers, and finally Latimers.

MEGGS. From Margaret. See Female Christian Names.

MEGGY. A nurse-name of Margaret. See Female Christian Names.

MEGRAW. An Ulster corruption of Magrath.

MEGSON. See under Gerison.

MEIKLAM. A softening of Mac Ilquhain.

MEIKLE. O. Eng. and Scot. *mickle*, from A-Sax. *mucel*, big, stout.

MEIKLEJOHN. As Micklejohn.

MEIN. Probably A.-Norm. *mesne*: "a lord of a manour who holds of a superior lord." Bailey.

MEISON. The following inscription occurs beneath an old coat of arms. "*Meison de Com: Salop, dict. Malvosine ex antiquo.*" This statement is doubtless true, since the A-Norman family of Malvoisin varied their name to Meauvesyn, Meison, Meeson, &c. See Shaw's Staffordshire. See Mauvesyn and Meeson.

MELDRUM. A post-town and parish in Aberdeenshire.

MELLER. The family of Meller or Myller of Dorsetshire are said to descend from the *miller* of one of the abbots of Abbotsbury. After the dissolution of the monasteries, the Mellers became great purchasers " of abbey-lands in villages, and were remarkable for depopulating most of them." Hutchins's Dorset. i. 497.

MELLETT. Most likely the same as Mallet, the Norman surname.

MELLISON. See Malleson.

MELLOR. Chapelries in cos. Derby and Lancaster. The former appears to have given name to an ancient family.

MELON. Perhaps from the town of Melun, on the Seine, eleven leagues from Paris.

MELROSE. A parish in Roxburghshire, containing the town of the same name, formerly renowned for its great monastery.

MELSON. Perhaps the same as Malleson.

MELTON. Parishes, &c., in cos. Leicester, Suffolk, York, Norfolk, and Lincoln.

MELVIL. See Melville.

MELVILLE. A parish in the arrondissement of Dieppe in Normandy, hodie Melleville. The patriarch of this family, long so influential in Scotland, was a William de Malavill, a Domesd. tenant in Suffolk.

MEMBRAY. See under Mowbray.

MENDHAM. A parish on the borders of Norfolk and Suffolk.

MENZIES. The Menzies, though sometimes considered a Highland clan, are of English origin. Their name was originally Meyners, and as Skene observes, (Scot. Highl. ii. 310) "their arms, and the resemblance of their name, distinctly point them out as a branch of the English family of Manners, and consequently their Norman origin is undoubted." 2. The name, according to Mr. Arthur, has been variously written, "Maynoers, Meyners, then Menys, afterwards Meynes or Mengies, and now Menzies." It is pronounced Mengyies or Mengies. In Gaelic the family are called *Menairich*. Their *habitat* is the Perthshire Highlands, where in 1745 the clan could raise three hundred fighting men.

MEPHAM. Meopham, a parish in Kent. This is an ancient surname, being one of the few of the local class used in Saxon times. One Ælfgar æt Meâpahâm is mentioned by Mr. Kemble.

MERCATOR. The latinization of Mercer, a merchant or general dealer. This name and its English form, Le Mercer, are very common in H.R.

MERCER. I know not how this word came to be monopolized by the dealers in silk, as its true and original meaning is, a general dealer—a person who combines the trades of grocer, draper, hatter, clothier, druggist, stationer, haberdasher, undertaker, &c., &c., as many country shopkeepers do to this day. In an old song against the Friars it is said :—

> "For thai have nought to live by,
> They wandren here and there,
> And dele with divers *marcerye*
> Right as thai pedlars were."

Wright's Political Poems and Songs. vol, i. 1859.

MERCHANT. Like the Fr. Le Marchant, a general dealer.

MERCY. Perhaps applied to a person who had performed this character in some mystery or miracle-play. Or it may be the same as Marcey.

MEREDITH. An ancient Welsh personal or baptismal name.

MERES. The same as Mears.

MEREWETHER. See Merryweather.

MERIDAY. An Irish corruption of the Welsh Meredith.

MERINGTON. See Merrington.

MERLE. Perhaps the same as Murrell.

MERLIN. The old personal name.

MERRELL. Probably the same as Murrell, Morell, which see.

MERRICK. MERRICKS. MERRIX. See Meyrick.

MERRIDEW. The same as Meriday.

MERRIFIELD. The site of Salisbury Cathedral is so called in medieval documents, being a corruption of St. Mary's Field. Proceedings of Arch. Instit. at Salisbury, p. 180.

MERRIMAN. "The phrase *mery men,* applied to adherents or soldiers, may be merely expressive of their hilarity in the service of their chief.—A-Sax. *mirige,* cheerful." Jamieson. "An old term used by a chief in addressing his soldiers; *My merry men.*" Ibid. But a correspondent tells me that, from time immemorial, at Marlborough, the Merrimans have occasionally written themselves Marmion, and this is probably the true source of the surname.

MERRIOTT. A parish in Somersetshire.

MERRINGTON. A parish in Durham.

MERRITT. Probably the same as Merriott.

MERRY. Gay and cheerful in disposition.

MERRYMOWTH. From the expression of that feature. This name is found in Bury Wills., &c. Camd. Soc.

MERRYWEATHER. Formerly an idiomatic phrase for joy, pleasure, or delight. Halliw. Hence probably applied to a person of hilarious temperament. Fairweather and Fineweather are analogous surnames.

MERSH. A local pronunciation of Marsh.

MERSOM. Mersham, a parish in Kent.

MERVYN. Probably a baptismal name, as we find in Domesday Merefin, Merven, Mervinus, &c., as tenants prior to the making of that record. See Mirfin.

MERYON. This family settled at Rye, co. Sussex, in the latter part of the XVII. century, as French Protestant refugees. The original name Merignan, has passed through the several orthographies of Mirinian, Merian, and Meryon. Holloway's Rye, p. 583.

MERYWEDYR. An old spelling of Merryweather. See Eng. Surn. i. 36.

MESNILWARING. See Mainwaring.

MESSAGE. Probably from O. Fr. *messager,* a messenger.

MESSENGER. One entrusted with a message : an ancient office, as Messengers of the Exchequer, Messengers of the King, &c. It was the duty of the latter to wait upon the Secretary of State, to carry despatches, and to take state prisoners into custody. Bailey. Le Messager is common in H.R.

MESSER. Le Messor frequently occurs in medieval records for harvester, reaper, mower. In the S. it is a common corruption of the surname Mercer.

METCALFE. MEDCALF. A great Yorkshire family. In the third year of Queen Mary, Sir Christopher Metcalfe met "the judges at York, attended on with three hundred horsemen, all of his own name and kindred, well mounted and suitably attired. The Roman Fabii, the most populous tribe in that city, could hardly have made so fair an appearance, insomuch that Master Camden gives the Metcalfes this character : Quæ numerosissima totius Angliæ familia his temporibus censetur, (which at this time, viz., Anno 1607, is counted the most numerous family of England.) Here I forbear mentioning of another, which perchance might vie with them, lest casually I minister matter of contest." Fuller's Worthies, iii. p. 455. The origin of the name (probably local) is unknown. Dr. Whitaker fancifully derives it from *Mee,* a Saxon baptismal name, and *halgh,* a low, watery, flat. Others consider it a compound of the Welsh *Medd,* a mead, and *caf,* a cell or church. (Arthur.) Tradition, however, affords a much more easy explanation of it. One John Strong having seized a mad bull by the nostrils with his left hand, killed the beast with his right, and being afterwards questioned on the subject of his prowess, modestly declared that he had simply *met a calf.* From that time he acquired the surname of Metcalf! Another version of the story is that "two men being in the woods together at evening, seeing a four-footed animal coming towards them, one said, "Have you not heard of lions in these woods?" The other replied that he had, but had never seen any such thing. The animal coming near, one ran away, while the other resolved to meet it; which proving to be a *red calf*, he that met it got the name of *Metcalfe*, and he that ran away that of Lightfoot!" (Ingledew's North-Allerton.) Horace Smith is therefore clearly wrong in the assertion that—

> " Mr. Metcalf *ran off* upon meeting a cow,
> With pale Mr. Turnbull behind him !"

METEYARD See Meatyard.

METHAM. A township in Yorkshire.

METHLEY. A parish in Yorkshire.

METHUEN. The same as Methven.

METHVEN. A parish in Perthshire.

METTAM. The same as Metham.

MEUX. A township in the parish of Waghen, east riding of Yorkshire, not far from Beverley, anciently remarkable for its Cistercian Abbey.

MEW. 1. This Isle of Wight name seems to be identical with Meux and Meaux, formerly located there, and the arms correspond. 2. "An enclosure; hence *mews*, the royal stables." Jamieson. The phrase "mewed up," in the sense of confined, seems to sanction this etymology.

MEWBURN. Perhaps a corruption of Milburn, the mill-stream. There is, however, some reason to suppose that it may originally have been Medburn, "the middle stream," or "the stream of the meadows." See Nicholson and Burn's Hist. of Westmoreland and Cumberland, vol. i. p. 502.

MEWETT. Fr. *muet*. A dumb person.

MEWS. 1. The same as Meux. 2. What we now call a *mews* is a stable, or place for the reception of horses; but the word meant, in the days of falconry, a receptacle for hawks. The Fr. *muer* signifies to moult, and a cage for moulting hawks was formerly called a *mew*. Halliw. The word was afterwards extended to mean the place where hawks were kept, and this, by a not uncommon change of signification, was transferred to a stable.

MEYER. MEYERS. German *meier*, a steward, bailiff, tenant of a farm, or farmer.

MEYNIL. Norm. Fr. *mesnil*, a manorhouse. It was generally compounded with another word, as Mesnilwarin, the manor of Warin, Grentemesnil, the great manor. A great number of places in Normandy still bear the prefix of Ménil. The Meynells of Hore-Cross, co. Stafford, trace back to the reign of Hen. II., in co. Derby. The Meynells of North Kilvington, co. York, were at Hilton in Cleveland from the XII. to the XVI. century. Shirley's Noble and Gentle Men. According to Nichols' Leicestershire, the former family are supposed to be des-

cended from Hugh de Grente-Mesnil, the great Norman baron. B.L.G.

MEYRICK. A Welsh personal name formerly written Meuric, Meirric, or Meurig. It has been variously corrupted to Merrick, Merricks, Merrix, &c.

MIALL. See Mighell.

MICHAEL. The personal name.

MICHAELS. The genitive form of Michael.

MICHELBORNE. An eminent, but now extinct, Sussex family. Local: "the great stream."

MICHELL. See Mitchell. Gilbert de Aquila, otherwise called Magnus, and by the Saxons, *Mucel*, i.e., "the Great," flourished in the XI. cent. From him one of the families of Michell are illegitimately descended. Eng. Surn. ii. 190.

MICHELMORE. Local: "the great moor."

MICHERSON. The son of Michel or Michael.

MICHESON. The same as Micherson.

MICKLE. Scot. Big, large of body. A. Sax. *mucel.*

MICHIE. A nursename of Michael.

MICKLEBURGH. Local: "the great burg, or fortified place."

MICKLEFIELD. Local: "the great field.

MICKLEJOHN. See JOHN.

MICKLETHWAITE. A township in the parish of Bingley, co. York, from which county the existing families of the name have sprung.

MIDDLE. A parish in Shropshire.

MIDDLEBROOK. Local: place unknown, or perhaps now known as Milbrook. In this way, the manor and hamlet of Middleton, near Alfriston, co. Sussex, have been contracted to Milton-court and Milton-street.

MIDDLEHOPE. Local: "the middle hope." See Hope.

MIDDLEMAST. See Middlemiss.

MIDDLEMISS. A corruption of Michaelmas, which is so pronounced in some dialects. Other corrupted forms of the word, employed as surnames, are Middlemist and Middlemast. Probably from the person having been born at that festival. So Christmas, Easter, Pentecost, &c.

MIDDLEMIST. See Middlemiss.

MIDDLETON. 'The middle *tún*' or enclosure—a very common name of places. The Gazetteer mentions more than thirty parishes, chapelries, and townships, so called in S. Britain; but there are many minor localities and estates of this name (frequently several in a single county), and some of these are contracted to Milton.

MIDDLEWOOD.   Local : place un-known.

MIDGLEY.   A township in Yorkshire.

MIDLAM.   A contraction of Middle-ham, the name of many localities in various counties and shires.

MIDWINTER.   Apparently identical with Christmas, Noel, &c., (which see,) since Robert of Gloucester, speaking of the coronation of William the Conqueror, which took place on Christmas Day, 1066, says, that he was crowned "amydewynter day." *Midwinter*-day seems to have been used as the antithesis of *Midsummer*-day. See Sir H. Nicolas' Chronology of History. Midewynter. H.R.

MIERS.   See Myers.

MIGHELL.   A medieval form of Michael. The pronunciation, though not the orthography, is employed by Butler:—

" At Michæl's term had many a trial,
Worse than the Dragon and St. *Michael.*
    Hudibras. pt. 3, *canto* 2.

MILBANK. MILLBANK. The name of many trivial localities in England and Scotland.

MILBOURNE.   MILBORNE.   See Milburn for the etymology. Several places in the W. of England bear this name.

MILBURN.   Townships in Dumbar-tonshire, Northumberland, and Westmore-land. The Imp. Gazetteer of Scotl. defines *Millburn* as " any brook driving a mill, or any locality washed by such brook, and taking name from it. Brooks and localities of the name of Millburn are very numer-ous in Scotland,—many of them probably having received the name in the times of *thirlage*, when the mill of an estate or barony, together with the brook which drove it, was an object of local interest inferior only to the church and the manor house."

MILDMAY.   The family are traced to 1147, and the name to Mildmé. What the latter means, I have not been fortunate enough to guess. See however the guesses of Messrs. Ferguson and Arthur on the subject :—

Ferguson. A-Sax. *milde*, and *may*, a maiden : " The mild maiden."

Arthur. A-Sax. *milde*, soft and tender, and *dema*, a judge ; " it was owing to one of the early ancestors of the family, from his tempering the severity of the law with mercy."

MILDRED.   The personal name. See Female Christian Names.

MILEHAM.   A parish in Norfolk.

MILE.   From Milo, a not unusual per-sonal name among the Normans ; oftener, perhaps, a corruption of Michael, through Mighell. In some rural districts Michael-mas is commonly called *Mile*mas.

MILES.   See Mile.

MILESON. The son of Miles or Michael.

2 G

MILESTONE. From residence near one.

MILEY.   Perhaps a 'nursename' of Miles or Michael.

MILGROVE.   Probably the "middle grove." See Middlebrook.

MILHAM.   Millum or Millom, a parish in Cumberland.

MILICENT.   The female Christian name. The H.R. form is Fil'Milicent.

MILK.   " Certainly might be from Old Norse, *mylki*, a rustic, one who milks. But upon the whole it is more probably a diminutive of Milo, Miley, Miles." Fer-guson.

MILKER.   A milk-man or dairy-man. Le Milkar. H.R.

MILKSOP.   A common surname in many spellings in the XIII. century. See H.R.

MILL.   The old Sussex family of this name originally wrote themselves At-Milne, *i.e.* ' at the mill.' See however under Mills.

MILLAR.   The Scotch form of Miller.

MILLARD.   Mill-ward, the keeper of a mill, by the suppression of W.   So Wood-ard from Woodward.

MILLER.   The occupation ; which has also given rise to Attmill, Milner, Milne, Milnes, Mills, Milman, Millward. In H.R. Molendinarius, Le Molendinator, De Mo-lendino, &c.

MILLGATE.   Local : "the gate by the mill."

MILLICENT.   The personal designation. See Milicent.

MILLIDGE.   Milwich, a parish in Staffordshire.

MILLIGAN.   O'Milligan, an ancient Irish name.

MILLIKEN.   MILLIKIN.   Corrup-tions of Milligan.

MILLINER.   The occupation of the *man*-milliner in England, as well as the ex-istence of the word in English, is so recent, that I am disposed to consider this surname as a corruption of Milner.

MILLINGEN. A corruption of Milligan.

MILLINGTON.   A parish in Yorkshire, and a township in Cheshire.

MILLION, which occurs in 16th Re-port of Regist. Gen., is probably a corruption of St. Mellion, co. Cornwall.

MILLIS.   Probably the same as Miles.

MILMAN.   MILMAN.   One who re-sided at or near a mill—a miller.

MILLS.   Perhaps from residence near mills, in some instances. I am rather dis-posed, however, to consider it the genitive of an abbreviated form of Michael (see Miles), and the occurrence of Millson seems to favour this derivation.   But see Milson, which is ' local.'

MILLSON. See Mills.

MILLWARD. One who had custody of a manorial or monastic mill. Le Meleward, XIII. century. See Ward.

MILLWOOD. Local : "the wood by the mill."

MILNE. MILNES. O. Eng. *miln, meln,* and *mulne,* a mill. The forms in H.R. are Atte Melne, Atte Mille, De Molendino, and there is also one Alexander de Molendin' Aureo—"Alexander of the Golden Mill." There is a sept or clan of Milne in Roxburghshire.

MILNER. O. Eng. a miller.

MILO. The personal name, common in Norman times.

MILSON. A parish in Shropshire.

MILSTEAD. A parish in Kent.

MILTON. See under Middleton. Twenty-four places called Milton are given in the Eng. Gazetteer, and the Ordnance Survey shows many more in various counties.

MINCHIN. Probably an old personal name of the A-Sax. period, whence the local names Minchinton and Minchinhampton. The Irish branch went over with William III., and almost all the owners of the name are said to be located in or about Moneygall, near Menagh, co. Tipperary.

MINER. The occupation.

MINET. French Protestant refugees, after the Rev. of the Edict of Nantes.

MINN. MINNS. MINSON. MINKS. This series seems to point to Minn, (the same as Mynn) as an ancient personal name.

MINNETT. See Minnitt.

MINISTER. Lat. An attendant, servitor.

MINNITT. The family of Minnitt of Anaghbeg, co. Tipperary, are of great antiquity. The name is found in cos. York, Suffolk, and Norfolk, dating from the XIII. cent. B.L.G. It is probably the same as the modern French Minet.

MINOR. Perhaps a latinization; but more likely a mis-spelling of ' Miner.'

MINSHULL. A parish in Cheshire, and a township in the same county.

MINSTER. The O. Eng. form of *monasterium,* a monastery or great church, as York minster, Beverley minster, Westminster.

MINTER. Probably the same as moneyer, an artificer of coins. In Saxon, Norman, and more recent times, every considerable town had its mint and its moneyer or Minter.

MINTON. Perhaps from Mindton in Shropshire.

MIRFIN. An ancient personal name.

MISTER. Minster—the N being elided in rapid pronunciation.

MITCHAM. A parish in Surrey.

MITCHELHILL. Local : "the great hill "—possibly a translation of the Fr. Grammont, *grand mont.*

MITCHELL. The A-Sax. *mycel,* great, or mickle, would be a tolerably satisfactory etymon, and this may in some instances be the origin of the surname ; but I think in most cases it is derived from Michael, a very popular baptismal name in many countries, through its French form, *Michel.* This view is confirmed by the existence of the surname Mitchelson.

MITCHELSON. See Mitchell.

MITFORD. " Descended from Matthew, brother of John, who is said to have held the castle of Mitford in Northumberland, soon after the Conquest, and by whose only daughter and heiress it went to the Bertrams. The ancestors of the present family appear to have been for many ages resident at Mitford, though the castle was not in their possession till it was granted with the manor by Charles II. to Robert Mitford, Esq." Shirley's Noble and Gentle Men.

MIXWELL. Doubtless the same as Maxwell.

MIZON. Doubtless Misson, a parish in Nottinghamshire.

MOAT. MOATE. MOATES. From residence at a moated enclosure. Many places so defended acquired the specific name of The Moat. Mote, without prefix, is found in the H.R.

MOBERLEY. A parish in Cheshire, which gave name to the family in the XIII. century.

MOCKETT. Said to be a diminutive of Maurice.

MODE. Possibly connected with the A-Sax. *mód,* disposition, mood, violence, force.

MOEL. A Welsh word signifying bald.

MOFFATT. A parish partly in Lanarkshire and partly in Dumfriesshire.

MOHUN. Moyon, an ancient barony near St. Lo, in Normandy. William de Moiun, whose descendants varied their orthography to Mohun, was a great tenant in chief in the western counties. Domesd. Hence Moon, and perhaps Munn.

MOLE. A river of Surrey tributary to the Thames, and so called because in parts of its course it is subterraneous.
" And sullen Mole that runneth underneath."

MOLEHUNT. A mole-catcher. A-Sax. *molde* [*wearp*] and *hunta.* Molehunte. H.R.

MOLESWORTH. A parish in Huntingdonshire. The family can be traced in early times to that county, and to Sir Walter de Molesworth, one of Edward the First's Crusaders. B.L.G.

MOLINES. The baronial family of De Molines, who became eminent under Edw

III., are stated in the Baronages to have derived their surname from the town so called in the Bourbonnois; but there may have been an earlier settlement from one of the numerous places in Normandy called Moulines or Moulins, from the *molendina* or water-mills there existing.

MOLLEY. A corruption of Mulloy.

MOLLING. A corruption of Malling.

MOLINEUX. MOLYNEUX. This family came from Molineaux-sur-Seine, not far from Rouen, celebrated for the ruins of an ancient fortress popularly called the Castle of Robert le Diable, which was destroyed by John Sans-Terre, but re-built in 1378 by the King of Navarre. Itin. de la Normandie. The noble family trace an unbroken male descent from William de Molineux, lord of Sefton, co. Lancaster, one of the followers of William the Conqueror. Courthope's Debrett.

MOLLISON. See Female Christian Names.

MOLONY. Malaunay, a manufacturing town near Rouen in Normandy. The spelling of the name in H.R. is Maloneye.

MOLSON. The son of Moll or Mary. See Female Christian Names.

MOLTON. Two parishes in Devonshire.

MOLYNEUX. See Molineux.

MOMPESSON. Mont Pinson is a castle on the river Scie in Normandy, whence also probably the surname of Pinsent.

MONAHAN. Possibly from the Irish county, Monaghan.

MONBODDO. Domesday mentions one Manbodo as a tenant in Yorkshire.

MONCEUX. The great Norman family, who gave the suffix to Hurst-Monceux, co. Sussex, and to Compton-Monceux, co. Hants., derived their surname "from a place in the parish of Gueron, in the diocese of Bayeux, and are stated by some authorities to have come over with the Conqueror." Venables's Herstmonceux and its Lords. Lond. 1851. Fr. *monceaux*, heaps, monticuli.

MONCHENSEY. Hubert de Monte-Canisio, was a tenant in chief in Suffolk at the making of Domesday. He also possessed lands in Kent, where one of the parishes of Boughton has the suffix Monchensey, or corruptly Monchelsea, from the family. Among the numerous Monts in Normandy, I find no place approaching this name in sound, but there is a Casini in the vicinity of St. Lo.

MONCK. See Monk.

MONCKTON. See Monkton.

MONCRIEFF. Of that Ilk—a hill near Perth, renowned for its majestic panoramic view.

MONCUR. An ancient castle in the parish of Inchture, co. Perth.

MONDAY. See Times and Seasons. In H.R. Moneday.

☞ **MONEY,** *denominations of.* How such names as Farthing, Halfpenny, Penny, Twopenny, Thickpenny, Moneypenny, Manypenny, Pennymore, Grote, Tester, Ducat, &c., became hereditary surnames, or even surnames at all, it is not very easy to determine. Perhaps most of them are corruptions of other words.

Pound, Angel, Noble, Mark, and Bodle, though denominations of money, are derived with much greater probability from other sources.

MONEY. Monnay, a place in Normandy, department of Orne. Hence the De Mony of the H.R. The *Le Money* of those records is probably blundered from Le Moyne, the Monk.

MONGER. A-Sax. *mancgere*, originally a merchant of the highest class. Ælfric's mancgere is represented as trading in purple and silk, precious gems, gold, wine, oil, &c. Wright's Vocab. p. 8. The word has undergone great degradation in 'costermonger,' 'newsmonger,' &c. It stands alone as a surname, as well as in composition in Cheesemonger, Fellmonger, Woodmonger, Icemonger, Iremonger, and Ironmonger.

MONINGTON. A township in Herefordshire.

MONINS. The old Kentish family of this name (baronets 1611-1678) claimed descent from "Sir Symon de Monyn of the castle of Mayon in Normandy." I cannot find any place so called in that province.

MONK. A sobriquet of great antiquity. See ECCLESIASTICAL SURNAMES.

MONKHOUSE. From residence at a house belonging to some monastery, whence also the surname Monks.

MONKLAND. An ancient barony in Lanarkshire, and a place near Jedburgh. Also a parish in co. Hereford.

MONKS. See Monkhouse.

MONKTON. Parishes, &c., in cos. Devon, Durham, Kent, York, Wilts, Dorset, Somerset, and Ayr.

MONRO. The first of the family for whom we have distinct authority, is George Monro of Fowlis in Scotland, mentioned in documents temp. Alexander II.

MONSELL. See Maunsell or Mansell.

MONSEY. An old corrupt form of Monceaux.

MONSON. It has been stated that Monson means the son of Mon or Mun, the nickname of Edmund, but this is not probable. Lord Monson's pedigree is traced to Lincolnshire, and the year 1378. Leland spells the name Mounson, which has a French or Norman aspect.

MONTACUTE. See Montague.

MONTAGUE. "That the surname of this family," observes Collins, "was anciently written in Latin, De Monte Acuto, and in old English, Montacute, is evident from Domesday Book and other records; but the original name was Montagu, from the town of Montagu in Normandy; of which name and family there are still remaining many persons of distinction in France." The patriarch of the family in England was the great Domesday tenant, Drogo de Monteacuto, who came hither in the retinue of Robert Earl of Mortain, the Conqueror's half-brother. His descendants have been frequently ennobled in both early and modern times. There are at present three places in Normandy called Montaigu; that from which our English family sprang would appear to be Montaigu-les-Bois, in the arrondissement of Coutances, of which M. Du Bois remarks: " Ses anciens seigneurs étaient fameux dans le moyen-age." Itin. de la Normandie, 516. The parish of Montacute, co. Somerset, received its appellation from this family, who, as tenants of the Norman Earls of Mortain, had possessions there.

MONTALT. See Maude. It is asserted by some genealogists that Robert, one of the barons of Hugh Lupus, Earl of Chester, assumed the surname from his chief place of residence, an elevated spot in Flintshire, now called Mold.

MONTFICHET. Descended from Robert Gernon, a great tenant in Domesday. His son, according to Morant, took this name from the castle of Stanstead, co. Essex, from the raised mount (*mons fixus?*) which he there constructed. But there is, near Bayeux, a place called Montfiquet.

MONTEFIORE. Of recent settlement here from Italy. The name is local, from *monte*, a hill, and *fiore*, a flower or blossom —" the blooming hill."

MONTEITH. A parish in Perthshire.

MONTFORD. A parish in Shropshire.

MONTFORT. Hugh de Montfort, son of Thurstan de Bastenbergh, a Norman, accompanied the Conqueror in 1066, and obtained for his services more than one hundred lordships in Kent, Essex, Suffolk, and Norfolk. There are two places in Normandy called Mont-Fort, situated respectively near Argentan, and near Pont-Audemer. The latter, a fortified town, bore the name anterior to 1050. Itin. de la Normandie. The male line of this noble family became extinct in the XIII. cent.

The Montforts, Earls of Leicester, were of a different origin, having sprung from Almaric, natural son of Robert, king of France, from whom he received in gift the town of Montfort in France, and thence the surname. His descendant, Simon de Montfort, coming into this country, was made Earl of Leicester by King John, and his son of the same name was the great leader of the insurgent barons against Henry III.

MONTGOMERIE. Robert de Montgomery (or as the old mis-spelling genealogists had it, De Mumdegrumbie) appears to have accompanied Walter, the high stew-

ard, ancestor of the royal house of Stuart, from Wales into Scotland, where he acquired from him the manor of Eglisham, co. Renfrew, which still belongs to his lineal descendant, the Earl of Eglintoun.

The origin of Robert from the great Norman De Montgomerys cannot be doubted.

MONTGOMERY. Mont-Gomerie is near Lisieux in Normandy. Its counts, says Dubois, "jouent un rôle important dans l'histoire de Normandie." One of them, Roger de M., a kinsman of the Conqueror, accompanied him, and led the centre of his army at Hastings. In reward for his services, he was created Earl of Arundel and Shrewsbury, and received manors in many counties. From him the town and shire of Montgomery, in Wales, derive their name.

MONTMORRIS. See Morris.

MONTOLIEU. A distinguished family of Provence and Languedoc, so ancient, it is said, that St. Cyprian, who was made bishop of Marseille in 510, was a cadet of it. The present representative is the Marquis de Montolieu. The English branch descended from David M., Baron de St. Hypolite, who was driven out of France by the Revocation of the Edict of Nantes, and who entered the Dutch service, and came into England in command of the life-guards of king William III.

MONTRESOR. A family of Fr. origin and traced back to the year 1486. Two centuries later, at the Revocation of the Edict of Nantes, a branch settled in England.

MONUMENT. MONEYMENT. From residence near one.

MONYPENNY. This Scottish name is *traditionally* derived from the acquisitive habits of the first owner, which won for him the sobriquet of "mony a penny;" but that it is local is proved by the prefix De, with which it is found in early records. The family were first in possession of Pitmilly, co. Fife. About the year 1450, certain lands in Stirlingshire were erected into the barony of Monypenny, and their owner began to style himself "de eodem," or "of that Ilk." Inf. Jos. Robertson, Esq. The names Manipeni, Manypeny, and Manipenyn are found in cos. Huntingdon, Cambridge and Bedford, in H.R.

MOODIE. Gallant, courageous. Jamieson.

MOODY. See Moodie. Mody. H.R.

MOON. A corruption of Mohun. The Itin. de la Normandie, speaking of the place from whence the Mohuns derived their name (Moyon) says: "Masseville appelle ce bourg *Moon*." By a like crasis Bohun became Boon.

MOONE. See Moon.

MOORBY. A parish in Lincolnshire.

MOORE. From residence at a boggy heath or moor. The medieval forms are Atte Mor or More, De Mora, Ad Moram.

MOOREY. Local: "the moorish island."

MOORHOUSE. Places in Cumberland, Durham, Sussex, &c.

MOORMAN. See Moore, and the termination MAN.

MOORSOM. Probably Moorsham, a township in the N.R. of Yorkshire.

MOORTON. A chapelry in Gloucestershire.

MORDAN. 1. See Morden. 2. See Mordaunt.

MORDAUNT. According to the genealogy of this family, printed temp. Charles II., their patriarch was Sir Osbert le Mordaunt, who possessed Radwell, co. Bedford, by the gift of his brother, who had received it from the Conqueror, for services rendered by himself and his father. Le Mordaunt— "the Biter"—is evidently a sobriquet allusive to some feat performed with the teeth.

MORDAY. See Mordue.

MORDEN. Parishes in cos. Cambridge and Dorset.

MORDUE. "Mort-de-Dieu;" Death of God!—an oath. Morday is apparently the same name. Compare Pardew and Parday.

MORE. 1. A parish in Shropshire. 2. See Moore.

MOREFOT. Local: "the foot or termination of the moor."

MOREHOUSE. The same as Moorhouse.

MOREL. See Morell.

MORELAND. See Morland.

MORELL. "The great grandfathers of Dr. Morell [LLD., who died at Bath in 1840] both paternally and maternally were Huguenots, who resided in the province of Champagne, in France. At the memorable era of the Revocation of the Edict of Nantes, these confessors were imprisoned, their goods confiscated, and there is reason to believe that they eventually suffered martyrdom. Of one of them it is related, that during his imprisonment he was the means of confirming the faith of his fellow-prisoners by his discourses, and that he was accustomed to preach to the inhabitants of the town in which he was immured through the grating of his dungeon. Each of these admirable men left an infant son, whose respective names were Daniel Morel and Stephen Contè, and who, as it will presently appear, were the great-grandfathers of Dr. Morell. During a dreadful day of persecution, when blood was streaming in the streets, and the Protestants were fleeing from the sword, two soldiers entered a house, and after having killed some of the inmates, seeing an infant lying in the cradle, one of them, with his sword, pierced it, and the blood gushed forth.—its life, however, was saved; it was snatched up by some one, who remarked that *The babe at least was not a Protestant*, and it was taken and given to a Protestant woman, who had a little one of her own then hanging at her breast; she took the child and became a mother to it: and these two boys, both fed upon the same bosom, grew up together to be men. One of them,—that one that nearly lost his life in the cradle, was Daniel Morell, and that woman's child was Stephen Contè. Some Protestants of distinction, who were emigrants to Holland, took charge of the orphans; and they, when they arrived at manhood, attached themselves to a regiment of French refugees, which was raised about that time by the Prince of Orange, and which on his accession to the English throne, accompanied him to this country. In his service these young men passed over into Ireland, and married into Protestant families, who, like themselves, had been the victims of religious persecution. The foster brothers, who had been so nearly and wonderfully united in their infancy, saw themselves again united, in their age, in the persons of their children; for the son of Daniel Morell married the daughter of Stephen Contè, and the issue of this marriage was the late Mr. Stephen Morell, the father of Dr. Morell." Sketch of Life and Character of Rev. J. Morell, L.L.D., by the Rev. T. R. Wreford, D.D., F.S.A.. But there were other and earlier importations of this name into England, the first on record being that of one Morel, who is mentioned in the Domesday of Norfolk. The word is a diminutive of the O. Fr. More, a Moor, and refers to darkness of complexion.

MORETON. 1. Parishes and places in cos. Oxon, Bucks, Chester, Dorset, Essex, Notts, Salop, Stafford, Gloucester, Devon, Berks, &c. 2. An anglicized form of Mortain, a great baronial family founded in England by Robert, Earl of Mortain, uterine brother of William the Conqueror.

MOREY. The same as Moorey.

MORFEE. See Maufee.

MORGAN. A Welsh personal name of high antiquity. The founder of the Pelagian heresy, in the fourth century, was a true Welshman and a monk of Bangor. His name was Morgan, which signifies 'Of the Sea,' and this was correctly latinized Pelagius.

In Wales the surname often occurs with the prefix *Ap*. In England an eminent mathematician writes himself *De* Morgan. The Morgans of Golden Grove, co. Flint, descend from Marchudd ap Cynan, founder of the eighth noble tribe of North Wales and Powys; though the settled name of Morgan was not assumed until the XVI. century.

MORICE. See under Morris.

MORING. In H.R. Morin and Moryn. Perhaps from Morini, the ancient name of the district about Calais. A Deringus de Morinis founded the family of Dering, of Kent.

MORISON. The son of Maurice.

MORLAND. A parish in Westmoreland.

MORLEY. Parishes and places in cos. Derby, York, Norfolk, &c.

MORPHET. Probably a corruption of Moffatt.

MORRICE. See Morris.

MORRIS. This common surname, which is, and has been, variously written Morriss, Morres, Morice, Morrice, Maurice, Morys, Moris, Morrish, Morse; which gives rise to the patronymical forms Morrison, Morrisson, Morson; and which is found associated with various prefixes, such as Fitz, Clan, Mount, De, &c., may be traced to various sources. " Of the English families of that name," observes Burke, " there are two classes, those of native, and those of foreign, extraction. The latter came over with the Conqueror. Of the former, the most ancient are derived from Wales. One section of the foreign class had a Moorish origin, as indeed the name expresses, and crossed over from Africa to Europe by way of Spain, whence were introduced into England, and other European countries, the *Morrice* dancers, who were accustomed to perform various feats of dancing. From the same source is derived the name of Montmorency corrupted from De Monte Morisco, " of or from the Moorish Mountains," and thence abbreviated into *Moris*. (?) [The Le Moreys of H.R. somewhat favours a Moorish origin.]

" With respect to the second class of foreign origin, their name is stated to be a corruption from Mars or Mavors, the god of War. This, as well as the preceding derivation, may appertain to many continental families, but it is in Wales that it most indubitably applies to the *indigenous* families who bear the name of Morris, of which the following derivation is given by a very eminent genealogist; " Mars, Mavors, *Wallicé,* 'Mawr-rwyce,' and *Anglicé,* 'Warlike, powerful,' is a title applied to such of the ancient chieftains as were pre-eminent for valour, whose numerous descendants account for the present frequency of the name in Wales. To this, one of the mottoes borne by the family of Morris seems to have reference: *Marte et mari faventibus.*" Burke's Commoners, vol. iv. p. 488.

To these observations, which are in the main correct, I must add, that the personal name Maurice is still retained as a surname, and it may in numerous instances be the origin of Morris and similar family designations. The Roman church honours St. Maurice on the 21st of September.

It is possible also that in some cases our English Morris may be a corruption of the Fr. Du Marais, Dumaresq., latinized De Marisco, and meaning, " of the marsh."

MORRISS. See Morris.

MORRISH. See Morris.

MORRISON. MORRISSON. The son of Maurice.

MORROW. A known corruption of Mac Murrough.

MORSE. MORSS. See Morris.

MORSON. A contraction of Morison.

MORTIMER. This name was latinized *de Mortuo Mari,* and hence the notion that the name was borrowed in crusading times from the Dead Sea in Palestine. The castle and barony of Mortemer lie in the arrondissement of Neufchatel in Normandy, and of course remote from the sea; but it appears that the expression *mortua mara** was sometimes applied to stagnant waters by the Normans, and at Mortemer there was a small lake so designated. The patriarch of this family in England was Ralph de Mortemer, who came in at the Conquest, and held immense possessions in many counties, the head of his barony being Wigmore Castle, co. Hereford.

* *Mara* is the low Latin for a *mere,* or shallow lake.

MORTIMORE. See Mortimer.

MORTLAKE. A parish in Surrey.

MORTLOCK. The same as Mortlake?

MORTON. Parishes and places in cos. Derby, Lincoln, York, Warwick, Durham, Norfolk, Hereford, Northampton, &c.

MORTRAM. A corruption of Mottram.

MORVILLE. This parish, near Valognes in Normandy, gave its name, says De Gerville, to one of the Conquerors at Hastings, 1066, whose descendants were long barons of England, Scotland, and Normandy. Mem. Soc. Antiq. Norm. 1825.

MORWARD. A-Sax. *mor,* a moor, and *weard*—a guardian. A keeper of a moor; analogous to Hayward. Le Morward. H.R.

MORYS. See Morris.

MOSBERY. Perhaps Mosborough, a township in Derbyshire.

MOSE. MOASE. 1. A contraction of Moses. 2. A tributary of the Trent. 3. Moze, a parish in Kent. In H.R. there is a Le Mose, denoting some quality, nationality, or occupation.

MOSEDALE. The dale or valley of the Mose, a tributary of the river Trent?

MOSELEY. Mosley, places in cos. Stafford, Worcester, and Lancaster.

MOSES. A well-known Jewish surname.

MOSEY. A 'nurse-name' of Moses.

MOSLEY. MOCELEY. Mosley, is the name of chapelries in cos. Stafford, Worcester, and Lancaster.

MOSS. In the North a morass or bog, as Chat Moss, co. Lancaster.

The " moss-troopers " of old times were so called because they inhabited the marshy country of Liddisdale. Jamieson. In recent times many Jewish families called Moses have changed that appellation to Moss.

MOSSENDEW. Fr. *Maison-Dieu,* "An hospitall or Spittle for the poor." Cotgrave.

Several of our old cities and towns contain a 'God's House' or 'Maison-Dieu.'

"So many *masendewes*, hospytals, and spyttle howses,
As your grace hath done yet sens the worlde began.
Bale's Kynge Johan.

MOSSMAN. See Moss, and the termination MAN.

MOSTYN. The family claim descent from the patriarchal Tudor Trevor, who is said to have been Earl of Hereford in the X. century. In the reign of Henry VIII. (whose aversion to the old patronymical surnames of the Welsh is well known) the head of the family, Thomas-ap-Richard-ap-Howell, &c., who carried a long pedigree in his legal name, at the advice of Rowland Lee, bishop of Lichfield, and lord-president of Wales, adopted the local surname of Moston or Mostyn, from the chief seat of the family in Flintshire. The good bishop is said to have asked him, why he could not content himself "with one name—*like a Christian!*"

MOTE. See Moat.

MOTLEY. A parti-coloured dress probably originated this name. Domestic fools and jesters formerly wore it. It may however be local.

MOTTE. MOTT. Several localities in Normandy bear the name of La Motte, signifying a mound or hillock. La Motte and Delamotte have become naturalized in England.

MOTTRAM. A parish and a township in co. Chester.

MOUATT. See Mowatt.

MOUBRAY. See Mowbray.

MOUL. MOULE. See Mould.

MOULD. MOLD. 1. Like Maude, a corruption of Montalt. See Montalt.

MOULDER. A maker of moulds for casting metals.

MOULSON. The son of Moll or Mary.

MOULTRIE. A small river in Fifeshire, now called the Motray.

MOUNSEY. A corruption of Monceux. The parish of Herstmonceux, co. Sussex, is in rustic parlance Herst, or rather Hors-Mounseys.

MOUNT. See Mountain. Many slightly elevated spots in the South of England are known as "The Mount."

MOUNTAGUE. The same as Montague.

MOUNTAIN. 1. From residence near one. In H.R. Supra Montem. 2. Monsieur de Montaigne, probably grandson, and certainly heir to the estates, of Michael de Montaigne, the great French essayist, escaped from France at the Rev. of the Edict of Nantes, and settled in Norfolk. Jacob his son and successor anglicized the name to its present form.

MOUNTCASTLE. A locality in Scotland which I cannot identify.

MOUNTJOY. Fr. *Mont-joie*, which Cotgrave defines as "a barrow, a little hill, or heape of stones, layed in or neare a highway for the better discerning thereof, or in remembrance of some notable act performed, or accident befallen in that place; also a goale to run at; also (metaphorically) any heap." A famous French war-cry in the middle ages was "*Mont-joie St. Denis!*" and Montjoye is the title of the chief herald of France, corresponding to our Garter. Both the war-cry and the heraldic title doubtless refer to some victory which was commemorated by the casting up of a mound of earth or a great heap of stones—a practice of the highest antiquity. A district of the parish of Battel, the scene of the Norman Conquest, is still known by the name of Mountjoy. According to Sir John Maundeville an eminence near Jerusalem was formerly so called, because "it gevethe joy to pilgrymes hertes, because that there men seen first Jerusalem . . . a full fair place and a delicyous." In charters the name was written indifferently De Monte Gaudii, and De Monte Jovis.

MOUSLEY. Mowsley, a parish in co. Leicester.

MOUTH. From residence near the mouth or outlet of a river.

MOUTRIE. See Moultrie.

MOW. Of that Ilk, now called Moll, in Roxburghshire.

MOWATT. A Scottish corruption of the old baronial Montalt, or De Monte Alto.

MOWBRAY. The ancient barony of Mowbray, called by Odericus Vitalis *Molbraium*, was identical with the village of Monbrai, in the canton of Perci, an arrondissement of St. Lo in Normandy. Robert de M. was Earl of Northumberland, but his estates passing to his cousin Nigel de Albini, the latter's son Roger, at the command of Henry I., assumed the surname of Mowbray, and affixed it as a name of distinction to one of his English fiefs—now Melton-Mowbray, co. Leicester.

MOWER. The occupation. An Anglo-Saxon, soon after the Norman Conquest, acquired this name (Leofric the Mower) from his having overcome twenty men with a scythe. Wright's Essays.

MOXON. Moggie is a 'nurse-name' of Margaret. Moggie's son, would by crasis become Moxon. See Gerison.

MOYCE. MOYES. MOIST. A probable corruption of Moses, formerly written Moyses. A Moyses is found in the Domesd. of Somerset.

MOYLE. Not from *mule*, as the family appear to have imagined when they assumed for arms, 'Gules, a moyle or mule passant Argent;' but from a place in or contiguous to the parish of St. Minvor, co. Cornwall. D. Gilbert's Cornwall, ii. 67.

MOYSEY. Probably Moses, anciently written Moyses.

MOZLEY. See Mosley.

MUCH. Scot. Big of stature.

MUCHMORE. 'Much,' great, and 'more,' moor; the great moor—the name of some locality.

MUCKLE. A-Sax. *mucel*, great, big. A very ancient name. An eminent Anglo-Saxon nobleman, whose baptismal name was Æthelred, bore the additional designation of Mucel, and used the latter in legal documents, thus: "Ego Mucel, dux, consensi." See Kemble on the Surnames, &c., of the A-Saxons. *Mitchell* is the more ordinary form of the name in modern times.

MUCKLESTON. A parish in Shropshire.

MUDD. The same as Mode.

MUDDOCK. A corruption of the Welsh name Madoc.

MUDIE. *Mudy* is an old Scotticism, employed by the poet Barbour, for bold or courageous.

MUFFITT. See Moffat.

MUGGRIDGE. Evidently local, and probably from the A-Sax. *mucel*, great, and *hricg*, a ridge: "the great ridge." It is varied in orthography to Moggridge, Mockridge, Mockeridge, Muggeridge, &c. A small trader in Sussex writes *Mugridge* over his door, and announces *Muggerage's* ginger-beer in his window.

MUIR. The Scottish form of Moor. It occurs in composition with several surnames.

MULCASTER. This ancient family derive their name from the parish of Mulcaster, now corruptly written Muncaster, in Cumberland. "All the Mulcasters are descended from one David de Mulcaster, the son of Benedict Pennington, who lived in king John's time." It seems that the family of Pennington, who derived their name from the place so called in Lancashire, were possessors of Mulcaster from the earliest times, and that the surname of De Mulcaster was first assumed as here stated. See Hutchinson's Cumberland, i. 565. B.L.G. however mentions a Richard de M. as warder of the castle of Carlisle temp. William Rufus.

MULE. The animal; from stubbornness of disposition.

MULHOLLAND. The Irish Mulhollands (formerly Mulhollan) are a branch of the ancient sept of Maclallan in Argyleshire. B.L.G.

MULL. A topographical expression, as the *mull* of Cantire. In other cases it may mean *mulne*, O. E. for mill. In Lancashire it is an abbreviated form of Molineux. "Our clergyman prayed at church for Mary Mull some time ere he found out that she was a Molineux. He may well be said to have "made a *mull* of it!" From a Lancashire correspondent.

MULLENAX. A corruption of Molineux.

MULLENER. A vulgar corruption of Molineux.

MULLER. Germ. A miller. Naturalized from Germany.

MULLETT. A mullet is a fish; also a star-like charge of the heraldric shield; also a spur; but it is difficult to say how either of these things can have given rise to a surname.

MULLIN. See Mullins.

MULLINS. Moulins, a place in the department of Orne, in Normandy. See Molines.

MULLIS. Perhaps a corruption of Mullins, like Collis from Collins.

MULLNICKS. A barbarous corruption of Molineux.

MULLOY. O'MULLOY. An ancient race, in whom vests hereditarily the honour of Standard-bearer to the King in Ireland —an honour confirmed so lately as the year 1634. The present head of the family is said to be descended through more than *forty generations* from O'Niall of the Nine Hostages, King of Ireland in the fourth century. B.L.G.

MULNE. A provincialism for Mill.

MULTON. The founder of this family resided temp. Henry I. at Multon, co. Lincoln, and from thence derived his name. From him sprang the two baronial houses of this title.

MUMBY. A parish in Lincolnshire.

MUMFORD. Mundford, a parish in Norfolk.

MUMMERY. 1. A probable corruption of Montmerry, a village in the department of Orne, in Normandy. 2. It may, however, be the same as the baronial name Mowbray, which, originally Monbrai, became in the early centuries after the Conquest Munbray, Mumbray, Mombray, &c.

MUNCASTER. A chapelry in Cumberland. See Mulcaster.

MUNCEY. The same as Monceux—an ancient corruption. Muncy. H.R.

MUNCKTON. The same as Monkton.

MUNDAY. From the day of the week. See Times and Seasons.

MUNDEN. Parishes in co. Hertford.

MUNDIE. See Mundy.

MUNDY. Probably from the day of the week. The Mundys of Marheaton, co. Derby, who trace their pedigree to temp. Edward I., have a tradition of Norman descent, from a place called the abbey of Mondaye. The Itin. de la Normandie, however, shews no place so designated.

MUNGEY. A vile corruption of Mountjoy. Munjay, Munjoie. H.R.

MUNN. MUNNS. An abbreviation or nurse-name of Edmund. Camden. But more probably a corruption of the Norman Mohun. A correspondent observes that "the name is quite common in Kent, and it has only of late years spread into other counties. I have now property that went by the name of Munn's three hundred years ago."

MUNT. Possibly a corruption of the Fr. *Du Mont*, i.e. "of the hill."

MURDOCH. Robert Fil' Murdac, and 'one Meurdoch' occur in Domesday.

MURE. 1. The northern form of Moor. 2. Gael. *mohr* or *more*. Large in person. The family of Mure of Caldwell in Ayrshire trace to the reign of King David II., 1329. The name has been varied to More, Muir, Moor, &c., and there are heraldric reasons for believing the Moores of Kent and those of Ireland to have had a common origin.

MURPHY. A common Irish personal name.

MURRAY. The founder of the clan of Sutherland settled in the XII. cent. in the province of Murref, Moray, or Moravia, comprehending the modern counties of Murray or Elgin, and parts of Inverness and Banff, whence the family for several generations assumed the name of *Murref* or *De Moravia*, which they retained even after their occupation of Sudrland or Sutherland, and their elevation to that earldom. Rymer's *Fœdera*, v. 554. 20. March, 1367. They subsequently assumed the name of Sutherland. The people did the same; and the names of Murray and Sutherland still distinguish the bulk of the population near Dunrobin, although to a stranger this would scarcely appear obvious, through their sobriquets, Bain, white; Gow, smith; Roy, red, &c.

MURRELL. The same as Morell, which see.

MURTON. Townships in cos. Cumberland, Westmoreland, Northumberland, and York.

MUS. It is curious that though Mouse does not appear to be an English surname, its Latin form, Mus, is so.

MUSARD. Hascoit or Hasculfus Musard was a great Domesd. tenant in chief in the shires of Gloucester, Berks, Warwick, Derby, &c. His principal seat was *Musarden* co. Gloucester. Qu: was that place named after its proprietor, as Hardres in Kent and one or two other places have been? Cotgrave defines the word *Musard* thus: "a muser, dreamer, or dreamy fellow; one whom a little thing amuses, one that stands gazing at everything; also a pauser, lingerer, deferrer, delayer; one that's long about a businesse; a man of no dispatch."

MUSGRAVE. There is much fabulous tradition respecting the origin of this ancient family, as, that they came from Germany, where their ancestors were *musgraves* or lords-marchers—that one of them won

the daughter of an Emperor (*which*, or *when* is not specified) in the game of running at the ring, whence the *annulets* in the Musgrave shield—that the family came hither at the Norman Conquest—and that they were *moss*-graves or guardians of the *mosses* on the English border. The truth is, that the family originated at Musgrave in Westmoreland, where the name is found so early as the reign of King John, about the year 1204. A descendant acquired Edenhall in Cumberland, by marriage with a co-heiress of Stapleton in the XV. cent. See Shirley's Noble and Gentle Men.

This fine old border race, from whom have sprung a barony, and three lines of baronets, possess a curious family relic called the *Luck of Edenhall*, a painted drinking-glass, which was acquired in a singular manner. "In the garden near the house [at Edenhall] is a well of excellent spring water, called St. Cuthbert's Well. The glass is supposed to have been a sacred chalice; but the legendary tale is, that the butler, going to draw water, surprised a company of fairies who were amusing themselves upon the green near the well: he seized the glass which was standing upon its margin; they tried to recover it; but after an ineffectual struggle flew away, saying—

'If that glass either break or fall,
Farewell the luck of Edenhall.'

It is preserved with great care." Hutchinson's Cumberland, i. 269.

MUSGROVE. The same as Musgrave.

MUSKETT. The male sparrow-hawk. Analogous to Kite, Hawk, Falcon, &c.

MUSSELWHITE. A corruption of Musselthwaite. Local: see Thwaite.

MUSSENDEN. Missenden, co. Buckingham, was anciently so written. The family claim a Norman origin.

MUSSON. Muston, a parish in Yorkshire.

MUSTARD. Probably an abbreviation of Mustardmaker.

MUSTARDMAKER. A North of England surname, which reminds us of '*Durham* mustard.' In H.R. the name is Le Mustarder and Mustardman.

MUSTERS. Perhaps the same as Masters.

MUSTON. Parishes in cos. Leicester and York.

MUTRIE. See Moultrie.

MUTTER. "May perhaps be the same as the O. Germ. Muathari." Ferguson.

MUTTON. See Mytton. A family of this name are said to have possessed lands at Rusper, co. Sussex, almost from the time of the Conquest.

MYALL. See Miall.

MYCOCK. A diminutive of Michael.

MYDDLETON. See Middleton.

MYDWYF. A midwife.

2 H

MYERS. See Meyer, Meyers.

MYLNE. See Milne.

MYNORS. The name is traceable to temp. Edward II. at Treago, co. Hereford, the present residence of the family. There is a tradition of the patriarch of the race having come from Normandy with the Conqueror, and Mynors occurs in one of the lists called the Battel Abbey Roll. B.L.G.

MYRTLE. A corruption of Martel (q.v.) or of Murtle, an ancient barony in Aberdeenshire.

MYTTON. The family of M. of Halston can boast of having represented Shrewsbury in Parliament twice, thrice, or four times, every century, from the XIV. to the XIX. They originally wrote themselves De Mutton. Nimrod's Memoirs of John Mytton, Esq. Mytton is in the N.R. of co. York, and there are Mittons in the counties of Lancaster, Stafford, and Worcester. Most of the existing gentry families of this name appear to have sprung from Shropshire.

N.

NAGLE. The same as Nangle. B.L.G.

NAIL. See Nale.

NAILER. A maker of nails. The word is still in use in the iron districts. Halliwell defines it as a *seller* of nails.

NAIRN. NAIRNE. A town in Scotland, capital of Nairnshire.

NAISH. See Nash. The Naishes of Ballycullen, co. Limerick, have been seated there uninterruptedly from the time of king John, 1210. B.L.G.

NALDER. NALDERS. Qy.: Atten-Alder—"at the alder tree." See Noakes, Nash, &c.

NALE. Atten-Ale, i.e. "at the Alehouse." The tendency of the final N of the old preposition to adhere to the noun, is shown under Noakes, &c. *Nale*, in the sense of alehouse, is used by Chaucer.

☞ NAM and NUM. Common terminations, especially in America, as Wornum, Barnum, Clennam, Putnam, Varnum, Hannum—corruptions of local names in -*ham* when an N precedes that desinence.

☞ NAN. In the Celtic of Cornwall, *Nan* signifies a valley, and is found in composition with many local names which have become surnames in that peninsula, as Nancothan, Nancarrow, Nance, Nanfan, Nankivell, Nansperian, Nanphant, Nanscorus, Nanscuke, Nansladron, Nanstalon, Nants, Nanscowan, Nangarthian, Nankevil, Nanscawen.

NANCARROW. Two estates of this name, one in St. Michael Penkevil, and the other in St. Allen, co. Cornwall, formerly belonged to the family of Nancarrow. C. S. Gilbert's Cornwall.

NANCE. An estate in the parish of Illogan. co Cornwall, which was, not many generations since, in the possession of the family.

NANFAN. A Cornish family of some distinction, which produced, among other worthies, John Nanfan, Esq., the first patron of Cardinal Wolsey, who had been his chaplain. The name is evidently local (See NAN) probably from Nanfan in the parish of Cury.

NANGLE. The A. Norm. family of De Angulo, or In Angulo (whence perhaps the English Corner), took their name from their barony of Angle, situated in a nook or *angle*, close to Milford Haven, and their residence there was called Nangle's Castle. Gilbert de Angulo, who accompanied Strongbow to the Conquest of Ireland in 1172, was the progenitor of the Irish Nangles.

NANNY. I have been informed that this name is derived from Nannaw, in Wales, the original residence of the family.

NAPER. Napery is table linen, including the 'nappe' or napkin used in washing the hands, either before or after meals. In great establishments the Napier or Naper handed these napkins to the guests. One part of his duty, in the royal household, was, to hand over to the king's almoner the outworn linen of the sovereign's table for distribution to the poor. Ducange. Edinb. Rev. April, 1855.

NAPIER. An officer in the king's household—the same as Naper, which see. A Scottish legend, however, assigns a widely different origin. In a great battle between the Scots and some enemy, whose nation is not specified, the former were on the point of losing the day, when one Donald, son of the then Earl of Lennox, seized a standard, and rallied the retreating soldiers. This act of prowess changed the positions of the combatants, and resulted in the complete triumph of the Scots. The king on hearing of Donald's bravery, declared that he had NA PIER—*no equal;* commanded him to assume those words as a surname; and gave him lands in Fife, and the lands of Goffurd or Goosford. This 'mighty pretty story,' though evidently invented to explain the name, was *certified* to the heralds under the hand and seal of Sir Archibald Napier of Merchistoun, in 1625. It is proper, however, to remark, that the Napiers sprang from the house of Lennox, and that their early members wrote themselves Lenox alias Napier; and it is no derogation of the dignity of this illustrious family to suppose that an earl's son, their ancestor, should have held the office of Napier in the royal household.

NAPPER. Another form of Naper, which see. Le Naper, Le Nappere. H.R.

NARBROW. Narborough, parishes in cos. Leicester and Norfolk.

NARRAWAY. Local: "at the narrow way."

NASH. See prefix Atte or Atten. A man dwelling by an ash-tree would be called Aten Ash or Atten Ash. See H.R. Ate Nasse, Ad Nasse. On the suppression of the prefix, the N still adhered to the designation of the tree, and the name became Nash. By the same process we got Noakes, Nye, &c. It must not be forgotten, however, that there are localities called Nash, in cos. Salop, Bucks, Monmouth, &c. Yet some of these were originally called Ash. The vill of Esse or Ash, co. Oxford, was corrupted to Nashe, temp. Richard II. Dunkin's Oxfordshire i. 177.

NASMYTH. A nail-smith or nail-maker.

NASSAU. William Henry, son of Frederick de Nassau, natural son of Henry Frederick de Nassau, Prince of Orange, grandfather of King William III., accompanied the last-named personage to England in 1688, and was afterwards advanced to the peerage, as Earl of Rochford. Another Henry de Nassau also accompanied William III., and his son was created Earl of Grantham.

NAT. The nickname of Nathaniel.

NATHAN. A very common family name with the Jews, to whom it is principally restricted.

NATHANIEL. The baptismal name.

NATKINS. A diminutive of Nathaniel.

NATLAND. A chapelry in Westmoreland.

NATT. See Nat.

NAYLOR. The same as Nailer.

NEALE. NEAL. The Norman personal name Nigel was sometimes softened to this form, and some of our Neales may be of Norman blood; but I conceive that most of the families of the name have sprung from the O'Neills of Ireland.

NEAME. O. Eng. *neme*, Uncle.

NEATE. 1. A-Sax. *neát*, Cattle, or a beast. 2. The Anglo-Saxon personal name, rendered illustrious by St. Neot.

NEAVE. NEAVES. Norm.-Fr. *Le Neve,* the nephew; also spendthrift, like the Lat. *nepos.* See Le Neve, which is a very common H.R. name.

NECK. Probably a topographical term, meaning an isthmus.

NEEDHAM. 1. A market-town in Suffolk, and a parish in Norfolk. 2. Earl Kilmorey's family took their name from Needham, co. Derby, where they resided temp. Edw. III., and probably much earlier.

NEEDLE. A trader's sign—appropriate to a tailor.

"And Moses merchant-tailor at the *Needle.*"
Pasquin's Night Cap, 1612.

NEEDLER. A needle-maker. Le Nedlere. H.R. "Hugh the Nedlere." Piers Plowman.

NEELE. See Neale. Neel is unprefixed in H.R.

NEEVES. See Neave.

NEGRIS. "An Ionian named Negris, on becoming resident amongst us, anglicised his name to Black, and has left descendants who occupy a respectable position in society, without anything but their dark hair to indicate their close connection with the Veneto-Hellenic stock." Folks of Shields.

NEGUS. A probable corruption of some local name ending in *house.* According to Malone, the mixture bearing this name was invented in the reign of Queen Anne, by Colonel Negus. Richardson.

NEIGHBOUR. The social relation. The French have their Voisins, and the Germans their Nieburhs.

NEIL. NEILL. See O'Neill.

NEILSON. The son of Neil, which see.

NELME. NELMES. From Atten-Elme. "At the Elm-tree." See Noakes, Nash, &c.

NELSON. The son of Nigel. A Norman personal name.

NELTHORPE. The baronet's family is traced to Kent in the XVI. cent. The name may be a corruption of Neithorpe, a parish in co. Oxford.

NESBIT. NESBITT. Two townships in Northumberland, and another in Durham, are so called, but the lands which gave name to the Scotch and Irish Nesbitts are in Berwickshire. B.L.G.

☞ NESS. A-Sax. and Danish, *næs*, Germ. *nase*, a nose ; also a promontory, as Dengeness in Kent, and the Naze in Norway. This occurs as a termination in several names, as Longness, Thickness, Filtness, which may refer to some peculiarity in the noses of the original bearers. More probably, however, they are local.

☞ NETHER. An old English word implying 'lower' or 'under,' descriptive of many localities, and forming part of several surnames, as Nethercliffe, Nethersole, Nethershall.

NETHERCOTE. A hamlet in co. Northampton.

NETHERMILL. Several places in Scotland are so called—" the lower mill."

NETHERWOOD. Local : " the lower wood."

NETTLE. The O. Germ. *chnettili* is referred by Förstemann to the O. Germ. *kneht*, knight or child. Ferguson. See Knight.

☞ NETTLE. A-Sax. *netle*, a nettle. The growth of this weed has given names to many places. See Gazetteer. I cannot identify the localities from which are derived the surnames Nettlefield, Nettlefold, and Nettleship.

NETTLES. See Nettle.

NETTLETON. Parishes in cos. Lincoln and Wilts.

NEVE. See Neave.

NEVELL. See Neville.

NEVETT. NEVATT. The same as Knyvett.

NEVILLE. NEVELL. In Latin, *De Nova Villa*, anglicè, 'New-town.' There are two Névilles, and at least eighteen Neuvilles in Normandy, but from which of those localities this illustrious surname is derived there is no proof ; and indeed the early genealogy of the family is obscure. Dugdale, upon the authority of certain genealogists, asserts that the patriarch of the race in England was Gilbert de Neville, Admiral to the Conqueror, but there is, as the historian of the family remarks, no mention of him in Domesday. Rowland, Family of Nevill, p. 6. The great granddaughter of this Admiral, Isabel Neville, married one Robert Fitz-Maldred, who according to Roger Hoveden, was the lineal heir-male of Uchtred, Earl of Northumberland, in the days of Edmund Ironside, and a descendant in the female line from King Ethelred. The representative of the Northumbrian earls, Gospatrick, was established in his earldom by the Conqueror, but was afterwards compelled by Norman tyranny to fly into Scotland, where he became ancestor of the Earls of Dunbar, and eventually of the Nevilles of Raby. " The

Nevilles are thus a Saxon race with a Norman name." Quarterly Rev. vol. ciii. p. 32.

NEVIN. NEVINS. NEVINSON. This series points to an early but forgotten personal name.

NEW. NEWE. Norm.-Fr. A nephew.

NEWALL. NEWELL. Probably Newhall, places in cos. Chester, York, Edinburgh, Forfar, Kincardine, Ross, &c., &c.

NEWARK. A town in co. Notts, and places in the shires of Renfrew and Ayr.

NEWBALD. A parish in Yorkshire.

NEWBEGIN. See Newbiggin.

NEWBERY. NEWBERRY. Corruptions of Newbury.

NEWBIGGIN. NEWBIGGING. Bigging, a word still in use in Scotl. and the N. of Engl., signifies a building—a house, as opposed to a cottage. Isl. *bigging*, structura. Jamieson. Hence the phrase ' new biggin ' was and is applied to any considerable edifice recently constructed. In England nine, and in Scotland ten localities, are specifically so named.

NEWBOLD. 1. A name common to several places in cos. Derby, Leicester, Worcester, Cheshire, Warwick, &c. A-Sax. " the new habitation." 2. Nuboldus, a baptismal name, occurs in the Domesday of Wiltshire.

NEWBON. See Newburn.

NEWBORN. A corruption of Newburn.

NEWBURGH. According to Dugdale, the founder of this family was Henry de Newburgh, so called from the castle of that name in Normandy, a younger son of Roger de Bellomonte, Earl of Mellent. He came in with the Conqueror, and was created Earl of Warwick. Neubourg, the place probably alluded to by Dugdale, is near Louviers.

NEWBURN. Parishes and places in cos. Northumb., Fife, and Suffolk. (Newbourn).

NEWBURY. A town in Berkshire.

NEWBY. " The new habitation." Five or six places in Yorkshire, and others in Cumberland and Westmoreland, are so called.

NEWCASTLE. Besides the great town of Newcastle-on-Tyne, and the town of Newcastle-under-Lyme, there are various parishes, &c., so called in cos. Glamorgan, Radnor, Salop, Carmarthen, Pembroke, &c.

NEWCOMBE. See Newcome.

NEWCOME. *Newcomes* is defined by Halliwell, from Holinshed's Conq. of Ireland, page 55, as ' strangers newly arrived ;' but the family of this name, who trace back to Hugh Newcome, of Saltfleetby, co. Lincoln, temp. Cœur de Lion are not *parvenus* in this or any other sense. The name is doubtless the same as Newcombe, though the locality from which that is derived is not known.

NEWCOMEN. Perhaps the same as Newcome. Neucomen and Le Newecumene. H.R.

NEWDEGATE. A parish in Surrey, the habitation of the family as early as 14th King John, the first recorded ancestor being John de Niwudegate. The family were not extinct there till temp. Charles I. The Newdegates of Warwickshire are a younger branch.

NEWDIGATE. See Newdegate.

NEWELL. See Newall.

NEWENTON. See Newington.

NEWHAM. Townships in Northumberland.

NEWHOUSE. A name common to many localities.

NEWINGTON. Parishes and places in cos. Kent, Oxon, Gloucest., Surrey, Middlesex, &c. The name is common in E. Sussex, and is deduced from Sir Adam Newington of Ticehurst, 1481.

NEWLAND. Parishes and places in cos. Berks, Gloucester, Lancaster, Worcester, York, &c.

NEWLING. Probably Newlyn, a parish in Cornwall.

NEWMAN. Probably of the same origin as Newcome, as defined by Halliwell, which see. In Sussex documents of the XIII. cent. it is spelt Nieuweman, and latinized Novus Homo.

NEWMARCH. One Bernard, a companion of the Conqueror, settled near Brecknock, and founded a priory there, which became a cell to Battel Abbey. He came from the place in Normandy now called Neuf-Marché, near Neufchâtel, and formerly *Novus Mercatus*, or the "new market." Ord. Vitalis.

NEWNHAM. An estate in and near Rotherfield, co. Sussex, which had owners of its own name in the XIV. cent. Also parishes and places in cos. Gloucester, Herts, Kent, Hants, Worcester, Oxford, and Warwick.

NEWPORT. Parishes and places in cos. Cornwall, Essex, Monmouth, Salop, Bucks, York, Fife, &c.

NEWSHAM. NEWSAM. NEWSOME. Newsham; several townships in cos. Lancaster, York, &c.; Newsholme; a township in Yorkshire.

NEWSON. Qu.: Nephew's son. See New.

NEWSTEAD. Places in cos. Roxburgh, Northumberland, Lincoln, and Nottingham. The last-named is famous for its abbey, granted at the Dissolution to Sir John Byron, an ancestor of the Poet.

NEWTON. "The new enclosure, or homestead"—a widely-spread surname of many local origins, there being, besides minor localities and farms, no less than 90 parishes, townships, and chapelries in S. Britain so called, besides upwards of 50 in Scotland. The heraldric dictionaries assign nearly 40 coats to the name. The family of the great Philosopher is pretty satifactorily traced from the Newtons of Newton, co. Chester, in the XIII. cent. Sussex Arch. Coll. ix. 313.

NIALL. An extremely ancient Irish personal name, whence O'Neil, O'Neill, and many of the Neales.

NIBBS. Nib is a Fr. and O. Eng. 'nursename' for Isabel, and hence Nibbs and Niblett.

NIBLETT. See Nibbs.

NICHOL. NICHOLS. See Nicholas.

NICHOLAS. The Christian name. Hence the derivatives Nichol, Nicholls, Nicholson, Nicholay, Nix, Nicks, Nickson, Nixon, Nickels, Nicol, Nickoll, Nickerson, Nickisson, Nickinson.

NICHOLAY. See Nicholas. This name in its present spelling occurs in H.R.

NICHOLL. "The origin of the ancient family of Nicholl, written at various periods Nychol, Nicol, Nicoll, Nicholls, and Nicholl, has been by antiquaries variously and largely treated on. It is stated that in the time of Edward the Confessor, one Nicholas de Albini, *alias* Nigell or Nicholl, came over from Normandy, and was the common ancestor of the Nicholl family. In co. Chester, Robert Fitz-Nigell flourished soon after the Conquest." B.L.G.

The filial Fitz-Nichol was not unusual after the Conquest, and in some instances it became hereditary, as in the descendants of Robert Fitz-Harding, &c. See Atkins' Gloucestershire, p. 257.

Although the majority of families called Nicholl, &c., doubtlessly derive their surname from the personal name Nicholas, it is quite likely that some obtain it from the city of Lincoln, which was denominated *Nichole* by the Normans. "To the last," says Sir Fr. Palgrave, "the Normans never could learn to say *Lincoln;* they never could get nearer than *Nincol* or *Nicole.*" Hist. of Normandy and of England, vol. i., p. 703. Even the Earls of Lincoln styled themselves Contes de Nichole.

NICHOLLS. See Nicholas.

NICHOLSON. The son of Nicholas. Most families of this name trace to the counties of Northumberland and Cumberland. It is not improbable that they are descended from the great Anglo-Norman family of Fitz-Nigell or Nicholl. See Nicholl.

NICKEL. See Nichol.

NICKELS. See Nicholas.

NICKERSON. A corruption of Nicholson.

NICKINSON. The same as Nickisson.

NICKISSON. See Nicholas.

NICKS. See Nicholas.

NICKSON. See Nicholas.

NICOL. 1. The patriarch of the Nicols, Macnicols, and Nicolsons, was Mackrycul or Gregall, lord of Assint, co. Sutherland, who flourished in the XII. cent. Skene thinks the clan Nicail of Gaelic origin. ii. 298. 2. See Nicholas.

NICOLAS. The late Sir Harris Nicolas, the well-known antiquary and historian, descended from a Breton family who flourished in the XIII. and XIV. cent., one of whose members came into England at the Revocation of the Edict of Nantes, and settled at Looe in Cornwall.

NIGHT. A mis-spelling of Knight.

NIGHTINGALE. From the bird— doubtless with reference to sweetness of song in the first bearer.

NILL. The same as Knill.

NIMMO. A Scottish surname derived from lands in co. Stirling.

NISBET. NISBETT. Parishes, &c., in cos. Roxburgh, Berwick, and Haddington. See Nesbitt.

NIX. See Nicholas.

NIXON. See Nicholas.

NOAKES. NOKES. "At the Oak." See the prefix Atte, Atten. Aten Oke and Atten Oke were the original forms. When the preposition began to be dropped from this class of surnames, the final N in this instance adhered to the designation of the tree, and we obtained the form Noake, since vulgarly pluralized into Noakes. A-Noke was a transitional form. John A-Noke, who, with his constant antagonist, John Atte Style, was formerly as well known in our law courts as the redoubtable John Doe and Richard Roe of later times, was nothing more than plain John Noakes; and "Jack Noakes and Tom Styles," the phrase by which we designate the *ignobile vulgus*, are lineal descendants of those litigious 'parties.' The surname Haynoke appears to be identical with A-Noke, while Boaks is probably a crasis of "By Oaks." See the prefix By. See also the names Nye and Nash. Dean Trench has some appropriate remarks on the absorption of the article into the noun in some cases, but he does not seem to have remarked the corresponding adhesion of a part or the whole of a preposition, as in the cases above cited, as well as in Attwood, Agate, Twells, &c., &c. See Study of Works, ed. 1852, p. 118. See also Gloss. to Chaucer, edit. 1825.

NOBLE. Refers either to the physical structure, or to the rank, of the primitive bearer. There is, besides several Le Nobles, one Agnes *la* Noble in H.R.

NOCK. Probably identical with Noke or Noakes, which see. It is Noc, without prefix, in H.R.

NOCKOLD. Probably from Knockholt or Nockholt, a parish in Kent.

NOEL. Fr. Christmas. Originally a baptismal name, from the person's having been born on the day of that festival. William, the ancestor of all the English Noels, was living in the reign of Henry I., and was at that period lord of Ellenhall, co. Stafford. Shirley's Noble and Gentle Men of England. Collins says that 'Noel,' and his wife Celestria, came into England at the Conquest, and that their son Robert was called Fitz-Noel, and hence the name and family.

NOISE. See Noyes.

NOKE. A parish in Oxfordshire. See, however, Noakes.

NOLAN. See O'Nolan.

NOLLEKINS. A nurse-name of Oliver, through Noll.

NOLLEY. A nickname of Oliver.

NOLLS. Noll is one of the several nicknames of Oliver. Cromwell was commonly known among his enemies as "Old Noll."

NOLTE. A contraction of Atten Holte, i.e. "at the Holt," or grove.

NONE. "A person so called was buried at Wymondham ; and as he gave nothing to the abbey, the following epitaph was made to his memory :—

"Here lyeth None—one worse than none for ever thought ;
And because None, of none to thee, O Christ, gives nought."

Dixon, p. 53. See Nunn and Nugent.

NOON. Perhaps the same as Nunn.

NORBURY. Parishes, &c., in cos. Chester, Derby, Surrey, Salop, Stafford, &c.

NORCLIFFE. Local: "the northern cliff."

NORCOTT. NORCUTT. A township in co. Berks.

NORDEN. Evidently from 'north' and 'dean' or 'den.' I doubt not that many places in Britain are so designated, though it is remarkable that the Gazetteers, both of England and Scotland, are devoid of examples.

NORFOLK. The county.

NORGATE. A contraction of Northgate.

NORMAN. Northman or Norman was the generic name of the Norwegians. After the settlement of the *Vikingr* and their followers in various parts of England, Scotland, Neustria, &c., it was often assumed as a personal name. Many of the tenants in Domesday are called Norman and Normannus. See Normanby.

NORMANBY. There are four parishes, besides minor localities, bearing this designation, viz : three in Lincolnshire, and one in the N. Riding of Yorkshire. From

Northman, or Norwegian, and 'by,' a habitation. "That Norwegians immigrated into England even in considerable numbers, both history and the frequently occurring name of Normanby in the North of England, clearly show." Worsaae's Danes and Norwegians in England, p. 73. Mr. W. might have added that there are no less than eleven parishes called Norman*ton;* but these are chiefly in the midland counties. Normanville in Normandy, and the name of that province itself, are derived from the same source.

NORMAND. The same as Norman.

NORMANDY. From the province.

NORMANVILLE. This Norman surname corresponds to our English Normanton. The Itinéraire de la Normandie shews two places so called; one near Yvetot, and the other in the arrondissement of Evreux.

NORMANTON. Parishes, &c., in cos. Derby, Lincoln, Rutland, York, Leicester, Nottingham, &c.

NORREYS. See Norris.

NORRIS. Anciently written Le Noreis, Norres, Noreys, &c., and in Latin charters, Noricus, Norensis, &c. It is widely spread both in Normandy and England, and may imply either *North-countryman* or *the Norwegian.* Ormerod's Miscell. Palatina, p. 6. Gaimar applies the term to the Norwegians whom Harold defeated at Stamford Bridge.
"Quinte jur apres reis Harold vint,
Contre *Norreis* bataille tint."
Mon. Hist. Brit., 827.
In the Liber de Antiq. Leg. it is stated, as a peculiar circumstance, that the Barons hostile to king John, though really from different parts of England, yet were all alike called Norenses or North-countrymen. In the second sense, the word is frequently employed to denote known natives of Norway.

NORTH. SOUTH. EAST. WEST. Why surnames should have been borrowed from points of the compass, is not very readily explained; yet they do exist—all in excellent associations, and at least two of them in the Peerage. The probability is that the original bearers received their appellatives from the fact of their having migrated to particular spots from particular directions; e.g. if a Cornishman settled in Kent, he might be called West, and if a Northumbrian took up his abode in Hampshire, North would perhaps become his distinctive epithet. See Points of the Compass.

NORTHALL. A parish in co. Middlesex, and a hamlet in co. Bucks.

NORTHCOTE. A hamlet and estate in the parish of East Downe, co. Devon, which belonged to Galfridus, the lineal ancestor of this family, in the XII. cent. Shirley's Noble and Gentle Men.

NORTHCOTT. See Northcote.

NORTHCROFT. Local: see Croft.

NORTHEDGE. See Edge.

NORTHEN. A parish in Cheshire.

NORTHEY. An extinct chapelry and "deserted village," near Pevensey, co. Sussex. It was anciently a member of the Cinque Ports.

NORTHFIELD. A parish in co. Worcester.

NORTHGATE. See under Eastgate.

NORTHMAN. A native of Norway. It is found in the same orthography in H.R.

NORTHOVER. A parish in co. Somerset.

NORTHWAY. A township in co. Gloucester.

NORTHWOOD. A parish in the Isle of Wight, and a township in co. Salop.

NORTON. The Gazetteer mentions between forty and fifty parishes, townships, &c., so called, and there are hundreds of farms and minor localities. The word means simply—the northern homestead or enclosure, and corresponds to Sutton, Easton, and Weston. The original name of Lord Grantley's family was Coigniers, until temp. Edw. II., when Roger C. married the heiress of Norton, of Norton, co. York, and their son took the maternal name.

NORVALL. NORVELL. 1. Probably from Norville in the arrondissement of Havre, in Normandy. 2. Norval, a personal name.

NORWICH. From the city. The founder of the family was Geoffrey de Norwich, one of the barons in arms against King John.

NORWOOD. Places in Middlesex, Surrey, &c.

NOSWORTHY. See Worthy.

NOTBEAME. A-Sax. *hnut beám,* a hazel tree. Apud Notebem, "at the nut-tree," is a Hundred Rolls surname.

NOTCUTT. Probably a corruption of Northcote. So Breadcutt from Bradcote.

NOTLEY. Two parishes in Essex; also the site of a monastery in Buckinghamshire.

NOTMAN. *Note* is a northern provincialism for neat or black cattle, and consequently *Not*-man is identical, not with *conard,* as might appear, but with *cow-herd!* It is Noteman without prefix in H.R.

NOTON. Perhaps Notton, a township in Yorkshire.

NOTT. See Knott and Nutt.

NOTTER. An old German personal name, Nothart. Ferguson.

NOTTINGHAM. The chief town of the shire so named.

NOUGHTON. Perhaps from Nowton or Newton, co. Suffolk.

NOURSE. O. Eng. *nourice*, Nurse. See Nurse.

NOVISS. A novice, " a new beginner in any art or profession ; a raw, unskilful, and inexperienced person." Bailey.

NOWELL. 1. Probably the same as Noel. 2. The Nowels of Rede, now Netherside, co. York, deduce their pedigree from Adam *de* Nowell, who flourished there temp. Henry I. B.L.G. The presumption of a descent from the noble family of De Noailles in France, seems to have no other foundation than the similarity of sound.

NOWLAND. A corruption of Nolan.

NOX. The same as Knox.

NOYE. See Noyes.

NOYES. The family of Noyes of Wiltshire and Sussex have, time out of mind, borne the same arms as that of Noye of Cornwall, to which the celebrated attorneygeneral of Charles I. belonged. There is a tradition that three brothers of the name came over from Normandy about the time of the Conquest, and settled in the counties of Wilts, Hants, and Cornwall. The name is supposed to be derived from Noye or Noyon in Normandy, anciently called Noyon-sur-Andelle, but now Charleval, in the canton of Grainville ; but there are several localities in that province called Noyers, which may have an equal claim. The various spellings of the name are Noye, De Noye, De la Noye, Noise, Noys, Noyse. Inf. T. Herbert Noyes, Esq., junr.

NUGENT. *Gent*, according to Salverte, is the ancient French word (of which *gentil* is a diminutive form) signifying the pleasantness of a place or person ; and *no*, *noe*, *non*, or *none*, designates a low meadow which is frequently inundated. No-gent or Nugent, he adds, is the name of many towns or villages built on the banks of a river in a pleasant position, such as Nogent-sur-Seine, Nogent-sur-Marne, &c. Essai. ii. 284. The family are a branch of the great house of Belesme, being descended from Fulke de Belesme, Lord of Nogent le Rotrou, who accompanied William of Normandy and fought at the battle of Hastings. Some of his descendants assumed the surname of Nogent or Nugent, and two of them, Gilbert de Nugent and Hugh de Nugent, cousins, founded the name in Ireland temp. Henry II., they having accompanied Henry de Lacy's expedition against that country. They settled in Westmeath, on part of the estate held to this day by the representative of the family, the Marquis of Westmeath.

NUM. See NAM.

NUNN. An old A-Sax. personal name. One Nun was a kinsman of Ina, king of the West Saxons—*Nun*, *Inæ propinquus.* See Mon. Hist. Brit. 326, &c., &c. Anno 710. " Ine and *Nun*, his kinsman, fought against Gerent, king of the Welsh." Saxon Chronicle. But the surname may have originated from a lapse of a vowess, for we find in the H.R. not only one Alice la Nonne, but also " Robertus filius ejus."

NUNNES. Apparently a genitive form of Nunn.

NURSE. Probably a foster-father.

NURTON. The same as Norton.

NUTHALL. A parish in Nottinghamshire.

NUTKINS. A diminutive of Knut or Canute. Ferguson.

NUTLEY. Places in Buckinghamshire and Sussex.

NUT. NUTS. See Nutt.

NUTT. Probably Knut, the Danish personal name, which we now improperly write in two syllables—Canute. See Knott.

NUTTALL. The same as Nuthall.

NUTTER. See under Nutting.

NUTTING. Ferguson derives this name and Nutt from Knut, or Canute, the Danish personal name ; and adds that the name of Knut was derived from a wen or tumour on his head. It is however worthy of remark, that the hazel, A-Sax. *hnut-beám*, gave rise to several names of places, from some of which surnames have been derived, as Nutfield, Nuthall, Nuthurst, Nutley, Nuthampstead. The names Nutter and Nuttman are also probably connected with this tree—signifying, perhaps, dealers in its fruit.

NUTTMAN. See under Nutting.

NYAS. Nias is a young hawk, and, metaphorically, a boy. "*Niard*, a *nias* faulcon." Cotgrave.

NYE. The old form was Atten-Eye, " at the Island." See Noakes.

NYMAN. The Danish form of Newman. Ferguson.

NYTIMBER. A manor in Sussex.

O.

O. This, a very common prefix to Irish surnames, is the Celtic *ua*, grandson, descendant. In England and other European countries, the noble and wealthy generally adopted their family names from their landed possessions, but in Ireland the names of *septs* or tribes were uniformly borrowed from those of their ancient chiefs and ancestors. Many of these names are traceable up to the tenth century, and even earlier. The famous king Brian Boru, who fell at the battle of Clontarf, in 1014, "published an edict, that the descendants of the heads of tribes and families then in power, should take name from them, either from the fathers or grandfathers, and that those names should become hereditary and fixed for ever." O'Donovan in Irish Pen. Journ. p. 332. In some instances, however, families who boasted of a distinguished ancestor of earlier date, assumed his name rather than that of the grandfather or father. Ibid. p. 365. "It is obvious also," adds the same learned writer, "from the authentic Irish annals, that there are many Irish surnames now in use, which were adopted from ancestors who flourished long subsequently to the reign of Brian." 'O,' or rather ' Oy,' was used in the sense of *grandson* by the Scottish Highlanders; thus we read of a very old lady of Gaelic race, who (Argus like !) could boast of *a hundred Oyes!*

Mac, or ' son ' was, and is, also extensively used in Ireland as a prefix, though not so much as in Scotland. Hence the well-known distich :—

" Per MAC atque O, tu veros cognoscis Hibernos,
His duobus demptis, nullus Hibernus adest."

" By *Mac* and *O*, you'll always know
True Irishmen they say ;
For if they lack both *O* and *Mac*,
No Irishmen are they!"

The Galwegians who prided themselves upon not being Irishmen, issued an order in 1518, prohibiting the native septs from entering their town, declaring that "neither *O* ne *Mac* shoulde strutte ne swagger through the streetes of Galway !" Hardiman's Galway.

A vulgar error prevails in Ireland, that while the *Mac* conveys no notion of high birth, the *O'* is a mark of good family. In the province of Connaught the *O'* notifies the gentleman : the O'Connors, the O'Flahertys, and the O'Malleys are *somebodies*, while their distant kinsmen, the Connors, the Flahertys, and the Malleys are *nobodies!* Much the same notion prevails in France concerning the prefix *De.* In Ireland

the *O'* is never prefixed to any name derived from trade, with the single exception, it appears, of O'Gowan, which is similar to our Smithson.

Dr. O'Donovan's able articles in the Irish Penny Journal afford much interesting information on this subject. I must add, in conclusion, that the list of surnames in *O'* is far too long for transcription here, and therefore I must be content to give a few only. From an index to certain genealogical books at the Royal Irish Academy, it appears that there are upwards of 2000 distinct Irish surnames with this prefix, and only 200 with that of Mac. Only three Scotch surnames begin with *O'*.

OADES. Probably the same as the Odo or Eudes of Norman times.

OAK, as well as its A-Sax. parent *Ac*, (which see) enters into the composition of several local surnames, such as Oakley, Oakfield, Oakden, Oakham, Holyoake.

OAK. OAKES. From residence near a tree or trees of this species. See art. Noakes. There is however a parish called Oake in Somersetshire. Del Oke. H.R.

OAKDEN. Local : see termination Den. This was probably a swine-pasture.

OAKELY. " An ancient family, descended from Philip, who in the reign of Henry III. was lord of Oakeley, in the parish of Bishop's Castle, Shropshire, from whence he assumed his name, and which has ever since been the inheritance of his descendants." Shirley's Noble and Gentle Men.

OAKENBOTTOM. Local : "the bottom or vale where oaks grow."

OAKEY. Local: " the island where oak-trees grow." Okey without prefix is found in H.R.

OAKHAM. The county-town of Rutlandshire.

OAKLEY. Parishes, &c., in various counties. See Oakeley.

OAKSFORD. Local : "the ford by the oaks ;" or possibly a corruption of Oxford.

OARE. Perhaps a corruption of Ore, co. Sussex, or of Hoare.

OASTLER. OSTLER. The keeper of a *hostelry* or inn. How the word became degraded from master to man is not apparent.

OATES. See Oats.

OATS. "Oats," says Mr. Ferguson, "I take to be a pluralism, and class it with Ott, Otte, Otto, and the corresponding German names Otte and Otto."

OBBARD. A corruption of the corruption Hubbard.

O'BEIRNE. An ancient Irish family who have anglicized their name to Byron and Bruin!

O'BEOLAN. This was the patronymic or Gaelic name of the Earls of Ross, and we find, from the oldest Norse *saga* connected with Scotland, that a powerful chief of the North of Scotland called Beolan, married a daughter of Rollo, the founder of Normandy.

OBEY. Oby, an extinct parish, now joined with Ashby, co. Norfolk.

O'BOHILLY. The name variously written O'Bohilly, O'Bohill, O'Boyle, is of early record in Ireland, and is found in the last-mentioned form so early as the year 1099, when Canlamrach O'Boyle was bishop of Armagh. D'Alton.

O'BOLGER. An Irish sept who dwelt in Wexford and Carlow.

OBORNE. A parish in Dorsetshire.

O'BRIEN. The O'Briens of Thomond took their name from the monarch Brian Boru, who was slain at the battle of Clontarf in 1014. O'Donovan.

O'BYRNE. "The O'Byrnes were the formidable chieftains of that last subjugated district of Ireland, now the county of Wicklow; the present barony of Ballinacor and the Ranilogh were possessed exclusively by them, and they, with the O'Tooles, the territorial lords of the remainder of this county, maintained, for nearly four centuries, an unceasing war against Dublin and the English Pale." The surname first appears in 1119. D'Alton.

O'CAHAN. The O'Cahans, formerly prevalent about Coleraine, have softened their name to O'Kane, Cain, and Kane. Ulst. Journ. of Archæol., No. 20.

O'CAHANE. A family of great antiquity, claiming descent "from the renowned Niall of the Nine Hostages, King of Ireland, who brought St. Patrick a captive from France to its shores. They constituted one of the most powerful families of ancient Dalaradia in Ulster, from whence passed out the emigrants who colonized Scotland, conquered the Picts, and established a kingdom there, which, in memory of their old home, was named Dalriada. From them descended the line of Scottish Kings, the Stuarts." D'Alton. Whatever credit may attach to claims of such very high antiquity, there is no doubt that the name and family existed in the X. century, when Eogan O'Cahan was an abbot in the county of Galway, A.D. 980. The family may have been king-descended and king-producing, but their claim to the progenitorship of the royal line of Stuart is unfounded, for the latter have been satisfactorily proved to be of mingled Welsh, Saxon, and Norman blood, and their Gaelic or Irish extraction is a pure figment. See article Stuart.

O'CAIN. A Highland clan, derived, according to the ancient sennachies, from co. Fermanagh, Ireland. But Skene considers it equivalent to Cathan or Chattan, a Gaelic name.

O'CALLAGHAN. This ancient family derive their origin and their surname from Ceallachan Cathel, a famous king of Munster in the tenth century. Their territory, according to Mr. D'Alton, was partly in cos. Louth and Mayo, but especially in Cork, where 50,000 acres of land on both sides of the Blackwater, and hence called Pobble-O'Callaghan, were occupied by them.

O'CARROLL. This sept were established in Louth at an early date, and popularly styled Princes of Orgiel. They are mentioned by the annalists before the date of Strongbow's invasion. D'Alton.

O'CARY. The Four Masters record the sept of O'Cary as lords of Carbury, co. Kildare, from a very early period of Irish history. D'Alton.

OCHILTREE. A parish in Ayrshire.

OCHTERLONY. The family were ancient in co. Angus, and the name is local, though I do not observe the place.

☞ OCK, a variation of A-Sax. *ac*, an oak, occurs in such local surnames as Ockwold, Ockley, Ockenden, Baldock, Charnock, Sinnock, Coppock.

OCKENDEN. An estate at Cuckfield, co. Sussex, to which county the name seems mainly to be limited.

O'CLERY. "A name," says Mr. D'Alton, "of the deepest historic interest in genealogy. That sept had large possessions in Tyr-hugh, their chief seat being at Kilbarron, where still remain the ruins of their castle, situated on a rock over the shore of the Atlantic, near Ballyshannon. They were highly distinguished in the native literature, and became hereditary bards and historians of the O'Donnells, Princes of Tyrconnell." To this family appropriately belonged Michael O'Clery, the diligent collector of ancient manuscripts relating to Ireland, who in the early part of the XVII. century compiled the celebrated *Annals of the Four Masters*. D'Alton.

OCKMORE. A hamlet and a hundred in co. Glamorgan are called Ogmore.

O'COLEMAN. The native annalists of Ireland notice, at a very early age, the sept of O'Coleman, and sometimes of Mac Colman, the latter in the county of Louth, where the name is still of respectability. Mr. D'Alton's first mention of the surname is from the Four Masters under A.D. 1206.

The name is so purely Saxon, that it would seem probable that the sept was founded in early times by a naturalized Englishman.

O'COMHAIL. (Pronounced O'Cooil.) Comhal was the father of Finn Mac Cool, the Ossianic hero. The name is anglicized to Coyle. Ulster Journ. of Archæol. No. 2.

O'CONNELL. "From the district of Upper and Lower Connelloe, co. Limerick, the O'Connells removed to Iveragh in the western extremity of Kerry, and remained there for a considerable period, until the rebellion of 1641 transplanted them to the co. of Clare." B.L.G. In 751, say the Four Masters, died Flan O'Connell, King of the Hy Falgians. In the X. century the deaths of two O'Connells, abbots of Devenish, are commemorated; and it is singular that in that parish there are two townlands bearing the respective names of Bally-Connell and Glen-ti-Connell. At the memorable battle of Clontarf, in 1014, the chief of the O'Connells was one of the leaders. D'Alton.

O'CONNOR. The O'Connors of Connaught spring from Conor or Concovar, who died in 971. O'Donovan. The family were subdivided at an early period; and the head of one branch assumed the epithet of the O'Connor *Roe*, or the "Red-haired," while the other was known as the O'Connor *Don*, or the "Brown-haired."

O'CROWLEY. The O'Crowleys were a sept of co. Cork. Smith, in his history of that county, says that they were a cadet of the Mac Dermots of Moylurg. D'Alton.

ODAM. An estate in Lambourne, co. Berks, bestowed on the family, it is supposed, by Bourchier, Baron Fitzwarine, to whom they would appear, from armorial evidence, to have been related. Odam or, as it is sometimes written, Odeham, is synonymous with Woodham.

ODAY. See Ody.

ODBURVILE. OBURVILLA. The Domesday form of Auberville. Roger de Odburvile held eighteen lordships in the counties of Essex and Suffolk; his brother William held Berlai; and Robert de O. was a tenant in chief in co. Somerset. The Itinéraire de la Normandie shows six places called Auberville, but from which of these the family came to England is not, I believe, ascertained.

ODDY. Perhaps the same as Ody from Odo. In Oxfordshire, however, according to Halliwell, *oddy* means active, brisk— particularly in reference to old persons.

O'DEA. An ancient sept who possessed the territory in co. Clare now known as the parish of Dysart, and which of old had many castles. Nine of this name were slain at the battle of Moinmore, in 1151. D'Alton.

ODELL. A parish in Bedfordshire, the seat of an ancient barony, written Wodhull, and by Norman corruption Wahul. The great Domesday baron known as Walter Flandrensis, from his being a Fleming, held

it, and his posterity were called De Wahul Though not summoned to Parliament after Edw. I., they retained the title of Lords Wahul, until the extinction of the male line by the death of Anthony Wodehull, temp. Henry VIII.

O'DEMPSEY. The family were chiefs of Clan-Maoilughra (Glenmalira) a territory extending over part of King's and Queen's Cos. The sept O'Dymsy are mentioned at an early period in the Chancery rolls. D'Alton.

ODEN. The Odin or Wodin of the Teutonic mythology, the father of the Gods and the progenitor of ancient kings. The name was in England at the time of the Conquest or before, for Odin appears as a Domesday tenant in Cheshire, and Odinus in Wiltshire. A Ric'Odyn is found in H.R.

O'DEVLIN. A branch of the great house of O'Neill.

ODGEAR. ODGERS. Probably an old Scandinavian personal name. One Odgeir is found in the Landnamabok.

ODIARNE. Hodiernus is found in the Nonar. Inq. (Sussex, p. 396.) as a baptismal name: "Hodyern' Elys." A Hodierna Sackville also occurs temp. Wm. Conqueror. How an epithet signifying "Of this Day" came to be adopted as a name, it is hard to conjecture.

ODINGSELLS. The family came from the Netherlands, at or soon after the Conquest. Camden.

O'DIVNE. O'Duibhne is one of Ossian's heroes.

ODLING. Mr. Ferguson derives it from the O. Norse *ödlingr*, a king or noble—an *atheling*.

O'DOIN or **O'DUIN.** (Written and pronounced Dunn and Doyne.) Celt. *donn*, brown, or brown-haired; but perhaps identical with O'Duibhne, an Ossianic hero.

O'DONELAN. This sept were chiefs of Clan-Bresail, co. Galway. They claim descent from Murrough Mullethan, King of Connaught, in the VIII. century. They were accounted 'Chief-Poets' (i.e. annalists) of that province. D'Alton.

O'DONNELLY. The first recorded ancestor seems to be Giolla Mac Liag O'Dongaile, chief of Ferdroma in Donegal, who fell in a patriotic resistance of the invasion by John de Courcy, 1177. Bally-Donnelly in Tyrone has its name from this sept. D'Alton.

O'DONOHOE. From Donogh, whose father Donnell fought at Clontarf, in 1014. O'Donovan.

O'DONOGHUE. An ancient sept in co. Cork, from which district they were expelled in the twelfth century by the Mac Cartys and O'Mahonys. They then settled in Kerry, and held the country round Lough Lene and Killarney, and were divided into two lines, known as the O'Donoghue More and the O'Donoghue Ross. D'Alton.

O'DONOVAN. Some account of this family is given under Donovan, which see. The following additional particulars are from D'Alton:—

"The O'Donovans were at a very early period chiefs of Cairbre-Aodbha, the present barony of Kenry, co. Limerick, where their chief castle was at Bruree. They afterwards moved southward, over the plains of Hy Figeinte, situated in the barony of Conilloe in the same county, and extending into Kerry." When driven thence by the Baron of Offaley, they appear to have lost some of their ancient importance on their settlement in O'Driscoll's country. It appears, however, that in this, their Cork territory, they were lords of the extensive district of Clan-Cathail, and possessed the three castles of Castle Donovan, Banduff, and Rahine.

O'DORCY. In Ireland this name is sometimes gallicised to D'Arcy.

O'DOWD. From an ancestor who flourished in the VII. century. O'Donovan. The sept possessed a wide territory in cos. Mayo and Sligo. Their annals are fully displayed in Hardiman's "Hy Fiacra," the name of this district. D'Alton.

O'DOWLING. A Queen's County sept. Some Irish families change this name to Delany !

O'DRISCOLL. "The ancient sept of O'Driscoll or Hederiscoll were settled at Carberry, with Bear and Bantry, in the county of Cork. They also possessed the island of Cape Clear, the territory about the Bay of Baltimore, and part of Inveragh in Kerry. Within this ambit, they had castles in Dunashad and Dunalong near Baltimore, both of which were garrisoned by the Spaniards in the war of 1599; they had also a castle at Dunamore in Cape Clear island." D'Alton.

Mr. D'Alton relates the following anecdote illustrative of the animosity which subsisted between the native Irish and the English, in the early part of the XIV. cent., and of the tyranny to which the former were exposed. It also furnishes a weighty answer to the question, 'What's in a Name?'

"In 1310, a period when, as Sir John Davis expresses himself, 'the mere Irish were not only accounted aliens, but enemies, and altogether out of the protection of the law, so as it was no capital offence to kill them,' a very remarkable trial took place at Limerick, before John Wogan, lord-justice of Ireland; wherein a William Fitz-Roger being indicted for the murder of Roger de Cantelon, pleaded that he could not in law be guilty of murder in that instance, for that said Roger (the victim) was an Irishman, and not of free blood; that in verity *said Roger was of the cognomen of O'Hederiscoll*, and not of the name of Cantelon; and the jury found the facts to be so, *whereupon the prisoner was acquitted.*"

O'DUFF. The O'Duffs were chiefs of Hy Cruinthain, a district extending round Dunamase in the Queen's County; and the name is of record in the Irish Chancery rolls from the days of Edw. III. D'Alton.

O'DUGAN. From Dugan, an ancestor, whose son fought at Clontarf in 1014. O'Donovan.

O'DUIGENAN. The family were located at Kilronan, co. Roscommon. They were especially celebrated for their devotion to the history and literature of their country. D'Alton.

O'DUIGIN. An ancient sept in co. Clare, lords of a district in the barony of Tullagh. D'Alton.

O'DWYER. The O'Dwyers were chiefs of Kilnamanagh co. Tipperary.

ODY. The classical Otho, in its changed form of Odo, was a Norman personal name. It was afterwards corrupted to Ody, and in course of time became hereditary.

ODYEARNE. See Odiarne.

O'FAGAN. See Fagan. Mr. D'Alton's account is, however, different from that there given. He says, that "the family are by some considered of English descent." The name seems to have been well established in Meath in the XIII. century.

O'FAHY. An ancient sept of the county of Galway.

O'FALVEY. The O'Falveys were chiefs of Cork, and hereditary Admirals of Desmond. D'Alton.

O'FERRALL, Mr. D'Alton characterizes them as an "illustrious sept," whose principality covered a large portion of the present county of Longford. They were great builders of castles, and founders of abbeys. The first actual record of the name seems to occur in the year 1141, when the aged chief, Gildas O'Ferral, departed this life.

OFFER. See Offor.

OFFICER. This surname is found at Edinburgh; what particular office the founder of the family held does not appear.

OFFLEY. Parishes in cos. Hertford and Stafford.

OFFLOW. A township in Staffordshire.

OFFOR. Apparently an ancient personal name. Offers occurs in Domesday, as a tenant prior to the survey.

OFFORD. 1. Two parishes in co. Huntingdon are so called. 2. A Domesday personal name—Offerd.

O'FINN. Finn or Fionn is an old personal name implying 'fair-haired.'

O'FLAHERTY. *Flaithbheartach*, an Irish chieftain of the X. century, acquired this designation, which signifies "lordly-deeded," for his prowess, and handed it down to his posterity. O'Donovan. "This sept," says Mr. D'Alton, "were originally settled in the barony of Clare, co. Galway, whence in the XIII. century they were driven to the western side of Lough Corrib, and were there styled Lords of Iar or western Connaught. On the islands of that water they had many castles, traces of some of which still remain." D'Alton.

☞ "OF THAT ILK," literally "*of that same;*" a phrase applied in Scotland to persons whose surnames are identical with the names of their estates—a convenient substitution. It was easier to write "John of Forbes of that Ilk" the vernacular of "Johannes de Forbes, dominus ejusdem," than "John of Forbes, of Forbes." For some centuries after the first adoption of surnames the '*of*' was retained, and hence two '*ofs*' were frequently found in the designation of one person. For example, "John of Forbes of Forbes," the head of a house originally surnamed from the ancestral estate, might have brothers or sons, founders of separate families, who would be called "John of Forbes of Pitsligo," "William of Forbes of Corse," and the like; yet still "John of Forbes of Forbes" would be the only one *of that Ilk* in the genealogy.

In some cases, a spurious title "of that Ilk" was created by the vanity of upstarts, as when a man bearing a particular surname gave that name to his newly-acquired lands, and thus shuffled himself into an appearance of ancient territorial association. Such phrases as "Mac-Nab of Mac-Nab," "Mac-Intosh of Mac-Intosh," are modern and absurd *shams*, intended to indicate chief-ship at the expense of accuracy and common sense.

O'GALLAGER. The native topographers locate this sept in the baronies of Tyrhugh and Raphoe, co. Donegal, where they had castles at Lifford and Bally-shannon. D'Alton.

O'GARA. The ancient territorial lords of Moy-O'Gara and Coolavin, co. Sligo. The first recorded ancestor seems to be Roderic O'Gara, who died in 1056. D'Alton.

OGBORNE. Two parishes in Wilts are called Ogbourn.

OGDEN. See DEN.

OGER. OGERS. An ancient personal name occurring in the Domesday of Lincolnshire.

OGG. "I dare not say that Ogg—from the ancient root of *ugly*—has no connection with the King of Bashan; but its immediate progenitor is an Old Norse Oegr, who might probably be as "ugly" a customer as the giant of the iron bed." Ferguson.

OGILBY. See Ogle.

OGILVIE. OGILVY. See Ogle.

OGILWY. See Ogle.

OGLANDER. The tradition of the baronet's family is, that they came hither with the Conqueror, and settled at once in their present habitat, Nunwell in the Isle of Wight. I believe that they can *prove* residence there by authentic records from temp. Hen. III. M. de Gerville states, that the lord of Oglandres, a parish between Valognes and Pont l'Abbé, in Western Nor-

mandy, was the person referred to in this tradition. He also informs us that another branch of the family continued to reside in the parish of Oglandres, and thence passed to the château of Pertot, in the department of the Orne. The present representative in France is the Marquis d'Orglandre. Mem. Soc. Antiq. Normandie, 1825.

OGLE. The extinct peerage family (from whom springs the existing baronet), rose to eminence in the twelfth century, and derived their surname from the lordship of Oggil, co. Northumberland; but Ogle appears also to be an A-Sax. or Danish personal name, as it occurs, in composition with topographical expressions, in several family names, as Ogilvie, Ogilwy, Ogilby, and Oglesby, the residence of Ogle; Oglethorpe, the village of Ogle, &c.

OGLEBY. See Ogle.

OGLETHORPE. See Ogle.

O'GOWAN. The Celtic *gow, gowan,* is Smith; and to that form some of the Irish families have anglicized their name.

O'GRADY. In the genealogies of this family it is asserted, that they sprang from Conal-Eachluath, King of Munster in the fourth century. The sept were located first in co. Clare, and afterwards in co. Limerick.

O'GRIFFIN. Mr. D'Alton says, that "a native sept of O'Griffin is traceable in the Annals of Ireland, while it would appear that the same name, without the Milesian prefix, came early from Pembrokeshire into this country." The first O'Griffin named by Mr. D'Alton is in 1199; a Fitz-Griffin is found in 1220; and a Mac-Griffin in 1257.

O'HAGARTY. An Ulster sept, subfeudatory to the O'Neill. D'Alton.

O'HALY. The family were located in a large tract of the barony of Muskerry, co. Cork, called from them Pobble-O'Haly. The Four Masters record the death in 1309 of Dermod O'Healey, 'the most eminent of the landed gentry of his time.' D'Alton.

O'HANLON. This family were "Tanists of a large territory within the present county of Armagh, and up to the time of James I. enjoyed the honour and office of hereditary Standard-Bearer of Ulster—a privilege which Sir William Russell, when Lord Deputy, with due policy recognized; as marching against O'Neill and the northern insurgents, he committed the royal standard (which the O'Mulloy had carried through the Pale) to Hugh O'Hanlon, who had theretofore submitted to the English government." D'Alton.

O'HARA. A noble sept dating back at least to the year 1023, when the death of Donagh O'Hara is recorded by the Four Masters. Their territory comprised the present barony of Leney, with parts of those of Costello and Gallan. D'Alton.

O'HEA. An ancient family of the county of Cork, whose chief residence was Aghcinilly castle, on a territory called from them Pobble-O'Hea. D'Alton.

O'HEHIR. See Haire. Mr. D'Alton mentions that the sept of O'Hehir were territorially located at Magh-Adhair, a part of Clare lying between Ennis and Tulla. He also states that an Aulaffe O'Hehir was slain in 1094, at the battle of Fenagh, while the Four Masters notice the death in 1099, of Donogh O'Hehir, lord of Magh-Adhair.

O'HENNESY. The O'Hennesys were chiefs of Clan-Colgan in King's County, and of the territory now called the barony of Moygoish, co. Westmeath.

O'HIFFERNAN. This sept possessed a territory about Corofin, co. Clare, called from them the Muintir-Ifernain, from which stock a branch was transplanted to the barony of Owny and Arra, co. Tipperary. Their war-cry was CEART-NA-SUAS-ABOE; *The cause of right from above!* The name appears in Irish history so early as 1047. D'Alton.

O'HOGAN. The O'Hogains are an ancient sept in Tipperary, in the vicinity of Nenagh. The name occurs as early as the XIII. cent. D'Alton.

O'HORAN. A clan of Hy Maine, co. Galway. D'Alton.

O'HURLY. The sept of O'Hierlehy or Hurley are said to have sprung from the same stock as the O'Briens of Thomond. Their territory extended on the borders of Tipperary, adjoining the Limerick district of the O'Briens, afterwards called Knocklong. In the English local records the name Hurle or Hurley is found prefixed with De; but Mr. D'Alton considers the family unquestionably Milesian.

OILEY. See Doyley.

O'KANE. See O'Cahan.

O'KEARNEY. The sept of O'Kearney is placed, by O'Dugan's Topography of Ireland, in that part of Westmeath that is called Teffia; but Ortelius's map places a clan of the name in co. Cork, and they also appear to have been territorial in co. Clare. The elder family of this name adopted the sobriquet of *Sionnach*, or Fox, and by the English appellation one of the family was created Baron of Kilcoursey by Queen Elizabeth. The name occurs as O'Kerny in the XI., and as O'Cearney in the XII. cent. D'Alton.

O'KEEFE. This ancient Munster sept derive "from Art *Caemh*—the last two letters being pronounced in Irish as F, or rather as V—who was himself the son of Finguine, King of Munster, whose death in 902 the Four Masters record, as they do that of Ceallach O'Caemh in 1063." D'Alton.

O'KEELEY. This sept were located in the county of Kilkenny.

O'KELLY. By some genealogists the O'Kellys are considered as of a common

stock with the Kellys of England; but they deduce themselves from Cellach, chief of Hy-Many, and fourteenth in descent from Maine Mor. The name O'Cellaigh or O'Kelly was first assumed by the grandson of that personage in the tenth century. B.L.G.

O'KENNEDY. From a progenitor contemporary with Brian Boru. O'Donovan.

OKEOVER. This venerable and knightly family are lineal descendants of Ormus, who at the period of the Norman Conquest was lord of Okeover in Staffordshire, by grant of Nigel, abbot of Burton. During the long period of almost eight hundred years, they have flourished uninterruptedly upon that estate. See Shirley's Noble and Gentle Men.

O'KEVAN. From an ancestor who lived in the VII. century. O'Donovan.

O'KINSELLAGH. A numerous and territorial clan located in cos. Carlow and Wexford. D'Alton.

OLD. 1. See remarks under Eld. 2. A parish in co. Northampton is so called.

OLDACRE. Local: "the old acre," i.e. field.

OLDBUCK. *Cervus longævus*; perhaps originally applied to a robust, aged person.

OLDBURY. Parishes and places in cos. Salop, Warwick, Gloucester, &c.

OLDCASTLE. A township in the parish of Malpas, co. Chester, and a parish in co. Monmouth.

OLDERSHAW. Local: "the shaw of alders."

OLDFIELD. Guy de Provence, who came to this country in the suite of Eleanor, on her marriage to King Henry III. in 1236, married Alice, sister of Sir Patrick de Hartwell, and with her obtained the manor and lands of Oldfield, co. Chester. Their grandson, Richard, was the first who assumed the name De Oldfield. B.L.G.

OLDFREY. Perhaps the same as Alfrey.

OLDHAM. A town in Lancashire. The name is sometimes pluralized to Oldhams.

OLDIS. Perhaps the same as Aldous.

OLDKNOW. Local: from old, and *knowe*, Scot. for a little hill or eminence.

OLDMAN. May be equivalent to *senex*, but is more likely a corruption of Holman.

OLDMEADOW. Local: place unknown.

OLDMIXON. A Ralph de Holdmixon occurs in co. Somerset, temp. Edw. I. H.R.

OLDREY. Perhaps the A-Sax. Aldred.

OLDRIDGE. A chapelry in the parish of St. Thomas-the-Apostle, co. Devon.

OLDSON. Might be taken as a corruption of the ancient A-Sax. personal name Wulstan, sometimes written Olstan, were it not that we have the antithetical name Youngson. As it is, the two names may have been originally employed to distinguish two brothers between whom there was considerable disparity of age.

OLERENSHAW. This local name has quietly subsided into Renshaw, and it is mostly so written. It is often still further corrupted into Rench and Wrench. Inf. Rev. J. Eastwood.

OLIPHANT. Kelham and Halliwell give *olifaunt*, A.-Norm., an elephant.

> "The scarlet cloth doth make the bull to feare;
> The cullour white the *ollivant* doth shunne."
> *Deloney's Strange Histories.*

And Chaucer, in his Rime of Sire Thopas, says:—

> "There came a gret geaunt;
> His name was sire *Oliphaunt*,
> A perilous man of dede."   *Tyrwhitt.*

Tyrwhitt considers the word to mean Elephant, which he thinks a suitable name for a giant. It is remarkable, however, that in Anglo-Saxon *olfend* signifies a camel, and therefore that useful animal may, equally with the more ponderous brute, assert its claim to the honour of having surnamed this family. Some of the Oliphants bear an elephant's head as their crest; but this may be a mere blunder, like that of the Moyles, whose coat is a *mule*, whereas a 'moile' in medieval English signifies, like the Latin *jumentum*, any labouring beast, though especially a horse or mare.

OLIVE. OLLIVE. The well-known baptismal or personal name, Olaf, borne by various Norwegian, Danish, and Swedish monarchs. In Domesday, a tenant in chief called Olaf occurs in Northamptonshire.

OLIVER. Both as a baptismal name and a surname, was probably imported from France, where it was long associated with romantic literature. The Domesday of Devonshire presents us with a tenant called Oliver, in the modern orthography.

OLIVERSON. The son of Oliver.

OLIVIER. Fr. Olive-tree. The Oliviers of Potterne are of French extraction, being descended from an old family settled at Nay. B.L.G.

OLLEY. Supposed to be a 'nurse-name' of Oliver.

OLLIFF. See Olive.

OLLIVER. See Oliver.

OLNEY. A town in co. Buckingham. A Roger de Olnei occurs in the Domesday of that county, as an under-tenant.

OLORENSHAW. See Olerenshaw.

OLYFADER. A XIII. cent. surname, probably applied as a sobriquet to some one who frequently profaned the phrase "Holy Father."

O'LYNE. An ancient sept in co. Kerry. D'Alton.

O'MADDEN. This sept were chiefs of what is now styled the Barony of Longford, co. Galway, with a portion of the parish of Lusmagh in the King's County, this whole territory being in the chronicles of the country called Silanchia. The annals of Ulster record the death of *Matodhan*, lord of Silanchia, in the year 1008, and from him it would appear the sept derived their distinctive name. D'Alton.

O'MAHONY. The O'Mahonys of Desmond are named from Mahon, son of Kian, king of Desmond, who fell at Clontarf in 1014. O'Donovan. "The O'Mahonys were powerful chieftains in Munster, and had extensive estates along the seacoast of Cork and Kerry. Opposite Horse Island, off the former county, was their castle of Rosbrin, boldly erected on a rock over the sea; and its proprietor, availing himself of the natural advantage it possessed, led a life of such successful piracy that Sir George Carew, when lord president, was obliged to destroy it." D'Alton.

O'MALLEY. An ancient family formerly written O'Malie, of Morshe Castle, co. Mayo. O'Malley is foolishly gallicised to De Maillet. O'Donovan.

O'MANNING. The O'Mannings were a sept more especially located in the present barony of Tyaquin, co. Galway, where the castle of Clogher was their chief residence. D'Alton.

OMAN. The same as Homan and Holman.

OMMANEY. A place in Hampshire. Ferguson.

O'MARCACHAIN. Is translated by some families to Ryder; by others it is anglicised to Markham.

O'MEAGHER. This family were in ancient times lords of the territory now known as the barony of Ikerrin, co. Tipperary. D'Alton.

O'MEARA. "A distinguished territorial sept in the barony of Upper Ormond, co. Tipperary; and the name of their principal residence, Tuaim-ui-Meara, is still retained in that of Toomavara within that district." D'Alton.

O'MELAGHLIN. (Of Meath.) From Maelseachlainn or Malachy II. Monarch of Ireland, who died in 1022. O'Donovan.

OMER. See under Homer.

O'MOLONY. This family were chiefs of Cuiltonan, now known as the parish of Kiltonconlea, co. Clare. D'Alton.

O'MULLEN. "The O'Mullens were a Leinster sept, numerous in the counties of Dublin, Meath, and Kildare. They were also known in Ulster as O'Mullan and Mac Mullen." D'Alton.

O'MULLOY. Besides what is said under Mulloy, it may be stated, that the family were anciently lords of Fearcall, King's Co., a district extending over the existing baronies of Ballyboy, Ballycowen, and Eglish, with much of those of Geshil and Garrycastle. The first of the name mentioned by Mr. D'Alton, is Albin O'Mulloy, Bishop of Fearns, who officiated with the Archbishops of Canterbury and Dublin, and with other prelates and nobles, at the coronation of King Richard Cœur-de-Lion in Westminster Abbey in September, 1189.

O'MULMOGHERY. This ancient name is now always rendered Early, because *moch-eirghe* means ' early rising.' O'Donovan.

O'MURPHY. The name was anciently spelt O'Murroghoe. The sept extended itself widely over Ireland. Very early after the introduction of surnames into that country, the death of Flaherty O'Murroghoe, chief of Cinel Breaghain, co. Donegal, is recorded in the Annals, under A.D. 1031. D'Alton.

Among the lower orders in the South of England the word *murphy* signifies a potatoe. Does this imply that some bearer of the surname introduced that now indispensable vegetable into England from the sister island? The potatoe was cultivated in Ireland long before it was known in this country. A century ago—strange as the statement may appear to non-antiquarian readers—this esculent was scarcely known, at least in the south-eastern district. There is a tradition that potatoes were introduced into East Sussex from Devonshire, by the vicar of my native parish (Chiddingly), the Rev. John Herring, who died so recently as 1776.

O'NAUGHTON. An ancient Irish sept of co. Galway, located about the country now comprised in the baronies of Leitrim and Longford. D'Alton.

O'NEILL. Of the very great antiquity of this distinguished name and family there can be no doubt. At what period the particular ancestor from whom the surname is borrowed flourished, it is hard to say, although a definite date is assigned to him by the Irish genealogists. According to them, he lived in the fourth century of the Christian Era, and was fifty-third in descent from the founder of his race, who existed within about a century and a half of the Deluge! How or when such statements came to be invented and received, I know not. That they are honestly believed by many Irishmen I *do* know. And it is not with any desire of disturbing family prejudices and accepted traditions, much less of derogating from the high antiquity and distinguished historical associations of the O'Neills, but simply as a matter of literary and historical criticism, that I beg to demur to the following statements, set down in good faith, in a well-known publication of recent date.

" The name and origin of the house of O'Neill are traced by Irish annalists to the prince-professor of learning, *Niul*, A. M. 1800, son of Phenius Pharsa, King of Scythia, whose posterity arriving in Spain, *Milesius*, 21st in descent from Niul, became King of the northern provinces, and his widow Queen Scota, and sons, about 1200 years B.C., led a colony of 'Milesians' to Ireland, where Heremon, the youngest, became the first monarch.

" Niall the Great, 53rd in descent from Heremon, was King of Ireland, A.D. 388. He subdued the Picts and Britons, and after ravaging the coasts of Gaul, was assassinated on the banks of the Loire, *near Boulogne* (!) His army, on its return, carried off, among other captives, St. Patrick, the patron Saint of Ireland. For upwards of 600 years afterwards, Niall's descendants exclusively occupied the throne of Ireland. Three kings of his posterity were named after him, viz. : Niall II., surnamed Frassach, who died 770 ; Niall III., surnamed Caille, drowned in the river Callan, A.D. 897 ; and Niall IV., surnamed Glundubh, " black knee," killed in battle by the Danes of Dublin, A.D. 954. Daniel Ardmach O'Neill, 46th monarch of the Hy-Niall race, grandson of Niall Glundubh, died 1064, and was succeeded by Malachy, a South Hy-Niall, who died in 1048. King Mortough Mac Neill died A.D. 1168, and was the last native monarch of Ireland of the Hy Nialls." B.L.G.

Now few of the crowned heads and noblest houses of Europe trace their pedigree beyond the eighth or ninth century—many not so far by hundreds of years. Neither is a higher antiquity assumed for them, even by their most flattering genealogists. With the Celtic ex-regal and noble families, however, a love for exaggerated pedigree seems to have been always prevalent, and the Welsh, the Irish, and the Scotch, are equally addicted to it. But whoever looks dispassionately at that great gulph of darkness, the period from the fall of the Roman Empire to the epoch of Charlemagne, say the sixth, seventh, and eighth centuries, and observes the obscurity which envelopes the history even of nations, will hesitate to accept as authentic, the minute family details, and regular genealogical descents, presented to his notice by the historians of many Celtic families.

ONION. Sometimes a corruption of Unwyn, but oftener of the Welsh personal name Enion. In the register of East Grinstead, Sussex, in the first half of the XVII. century, the name is written indifferently Ennion and Onion. Benion, Bunyan, and Pinyon are also corruptions of this fine old Cambro-British designation. The force of corruption could hardly go further than this twisting of a personal appellative, not only into a graveolent vegetable, but into that which either impedes the traveller in his walk, or gives the power of flight to an eagle ! See Bunyan and Pinion.

ONLEY. Oneley a hamlet in Northamptonshire.

O'NOLAN. Of this name Mr. D'Alton remarks : " The O'Nolans were a sept of the highest antiquity, especially in co. Carlow, where they gave name to the district of Fothart O'Nolan, within which, immediately after the English invasion, Hugh de Lacy erected one of those castles which his provident care designed to sentinel the Pale. A very interesting memoir of this sept is appended to the third volume of Sir Bernard Burke's *Visitation of Seats and Arms.* The native annals commemorate their achievements from the earliest introduction of surnames, and a succession of recorded inquisitions testifies the extent of their territory."

ONSLOW. The earl of Onslow's family "were seated at Onslow in Shropshire as far back as the time of Richard I., and probably much earlier." Shirley's Noble and Gentle Men. The punning motto of this ancient house: *Festina lente*, ON SLOW! is probably one of the happiest conceits of its kind.

ONWHYN. A corruption, or an attempted refinement, of Unwyn.

O'PHELAN. From Faolan, whose son Mothea was at Clontarf battle in 1014. O'Donovan. The sept is recorded in the earliest annals of Ireland. "They were styled Princes of Desies, a territory comprising the greater part of the present county of Waterford, with a portion of Tipperary. Malachy O'Phelan was their chief at the time of the Anglo-Norman invasion, and his was the principal native force that, in co-operation with the Danes of Waterford, sought, but unsuccessfully, to hold that city against the new-comers. Malachy was taken prisoner, and condemned to die, but his life was spared at the intercession of Dermod Mac Murrough, who had on that day come down from Ferns to celebrate the marriage of his daughter with Strongbow. The sept having been afterwards expelled from their old homes, some, after a short sojourn in Western Meath, crossed the Shannon into Connaught, where they spelt the name O'Fallon; and a district in Roscommon was known as O'Fallon's country." D'Alton.

OPIE. Seems indigenous to Cornwall. Opye occurs there in the XV. cent. and Oppie at a later date.

O'QUIN. "This ancient sept is recognised in the native annals, from the earliest date of surnames; those of Ulster commemorate, among the heroes who fell at Clontarf in 1014, Neill O'Quin. Widely spreading over Ireland, this family held territory in Limerick, Clare, Longford, Westmeath, and Derry." D'Alton.

ORAM. Mr. Ferguson derives it from an old German word signifying weak, but it is more probably local. A family of De Horeham in the XIV. century took their name from an estate so called at Waldron, co. Sussex. Owram in Halifax, co. York, may possibly be the source.

ORANGE. A William de Orenge is a Domesday tenant in co. Bucks. Whence this "William of Orange" came, I cannot guess; certainly not, I should say, from the district from which his great namesake, some six hundred years later, originally had his title, that being a small town and ancient principality in the South of France, about twenty miles from Avignon, and formerly a dependency of Holland.

ORBISSON. A known Lancashire corruption of Osbaldiston.

ORCHARD. Originally meant *wyrt-yard* (A-Sax.), an enclosure for the growth of wyrts or herbs, rather than of apple-trees, as at present. The original bearers of this name must therefore have been gardeners.

ORDE. An ancient personal name. It was borne by a Somersetshire landowner before the making of Domesday. The family of Orde are of considerable antiquity, and have long held lands in the counties of Northumberland and Durham, formerly as tenants *in capite* under the Bishop. The first mentioned in the pedigree, is Simon de East Orde, who possessed Orde by the tenure alluded to in 1362. The estate is at Newbiggin, co. Northumberland.

The word *Ord* in Suffolk is topographical, and signifies a promontory.

ORDERSON. Possibly a corruption of Other's son. See Otter.

ORE. A parish near Hastings, co. Sussex, which had owners of the same name in the XIV. century, if not earlier.

OREAK. ORECK. Ferguson says, O. Norse *órikr*, weak or poor.

O'REGAN. A native sept of Meath. D'Alton.

O'REILLY. The family claim descent "from Brian, the fourth Milesian king of Connaught. The name was derived from an ancestor called Ragallagh—by softened pronunciation Reilly—who lived at the commencement of the eleventh century. His grandson Targaille, prince of East Brefny, was the first who used the name of Ua Ragallagh or O'Reilly." B.L.G.

ORFORD. A town and parish of Suffolk.

ORGAN. See under Orgles.

ORGAR. Ordgar, an A-Sax. personal name, whence doubtless Orgarswick, co. Kent.

ORGILL. From the well-known fortress of Jersey, called Mont-Orgueil?

ORGLES. The only meaning that I can attach to this word is *organs*, according to the definition of Halliwell, who cites from *MS. Douce*, 302, f. 3, the line, "He con harpe, he con syng, his *orgles* ben herd ful wyd." *Orgel*, German, an organ. Now Organ is also a well-recognised surname, and hence it would seem that the noblest of all musical instruments has lent its aid to swell our family nomenclature. In what way Orgles and Organ became family surnames it is hard to guess: perhaps the first bearers of them were medieval organists.

ORIEL. In a learned dissertation on this architectural term, by the late William Hamper, Esq., F.S.A., five different meanings are attached to it, viz:—

"I. A pent-house.
II. A porch attached to any edifice.
III. A detached gate-house.
IV. An upper story.
V. A loft.
VI. A gallery for Minstrels.
Archæologia. xxiii., 106.

The editor of the Glossary of Architecture is of opinion, that the bold *bay-windows* still called "Oriels" gave name to the various buildings, or parts of buildings, enumerated by Mr. Hamper.

Oriel College, Oxford, was first founded by King Edward II., but Edward III. bestowing on the provost and scholars "a large messuage then called La Oriole," the community removed to it, leaving their old habitation of Tackley's Inn. "This large messuage," says Mr. Hamper, "must have been distinguished by some stately porch or vestibule of sufficient importance to give an appellation to the entire edifice." The original bearer of the surname was probably a servitor in some college or great mansion. The name itself may rank with Gatehouse, Drawbridge, Kitchen, &c., which see.

ORLEBAR. In the reign of Edw. III. this name was spelt *Orlebere*. The family at Hinwick, co. Bedford, are not known to have had any possessions in the neighbouring village of Orlingbury, which, however, has been conjectured to be the origin of the surname.

ORME. A personal name not uncommon in Saxon and Norman times, and doubtless of Scandinavian origin. In the Old Norse, the generic name for serpents is *orm*. Some early landowners with this designation have impressed it upon the Ormsbys, Ormerod, Ormside, Ormes-Head, Ormskirk, in England, and upon Ormidale, the Ormistons, and Ormary, in Scotland. Domesday presents us with tenants called Orme in the counties of York and Lincoln, and in the former shire a personage so named held immediately from the crown.

ORMEROD. See the observations under Royd and Rodd. "The first syllable Orme is a common Saxon and Norman name; the second syllable Rode, (pronounced Royde in Yorkshire) is correctly explained by Dr. Whitaker (Hist. of Whalley) as the preterite of "rid,"—a ridding, clearing, or essart—*locus exsertus.* It occurs in the neighbourhood of English forests and chases from Yorkshire to Devonshire. - - - - The import of the name, then, is the *Rode* of *Orme*, the land reclaimed by him or his predecessors, from the forest. - - - The local name was assumed in or before the reign of Henry III." Ormerod is in the parish of Whalley, co. Lancaster.—*Ormerod's Parentalia.*

ORMISTON. A parish in Haddingtonshire, and a place in Roxburghshire.

ORMSBY. Parishes, &c., in cos. York, Norfolk, Lincoln, &c. The family claim a Norman origin, and the extinct baronets' ancestors were for several centuries seated in Ireland.

ORMSON. The son of Orme. See Orme.

ORMSTON. See Ormiston.

ORMSTONE. See Ormiston.

O'RONAN. The O'Ronans, or O'Ronaynes, were a sept long settled in Munster and parts of Leinster. At the time of the English invasion two of that name presided over Irish bishoprics. D'Alton.

O'ROURKE. The great antiquity of this sept is attested by the appearance of their name in the earliest Irish annalists, by whom they are styled Kings of West Brefny, a territory comprising what are now the county of Leitrim, the barony of Tullaghagh, co. Cavan, and a part of that of Carbury, co. Sligo. Some of the race seem to have been Kings of Connaught. Tiernan O'Rourke was King of Brefny and Conmachne at the time of Strongbow's invasion. D'Alton.

ORPEN. "The family of Orpen or Erpen is of remote antiquity, and is stated to be derived from Erpen, a French noble of royal descent." Such is the statement in B.L.G., though the pedigree, as there given, does not go further back than the XVI. cent.

ORR. A parish in Kirkcudbrightshire, more usually written Urr.

ORRED. Probably a corruption of some local name terminating in HEAD. According to B.L.G. the family have been for four hundred years, "and probably for a much longer period," at Wirral, in Cheshire.

ORRIN. A river in Ross-shire.

ORRIS. A known corruption of Horace.

ORROCK. A high basaltic hill in the parish of Burntisland, co. Fife.

ORSO. An early Christian name—Urso; whence Fitz-Urse.

ORSON. A Yorkshire correspondent mentions an instance of a foundling, who by popular consent received the opprobrious name of Whoreson. When the poor fellow grew up and married, the clergyman considerately registered him as Horson, and when he had a child born to him, he christened him *Valentine,* and by this association the name at length quietly subsided into *Orson.*

ORTON. A contraction of Overton. There are several places so called in cos. Northampton, Stafford, Westmoreland, Cumberland, Leicester, and Huntingdon.

O'RYAN. This family were lords of Idrone, co. Carlow. The name was not unfrequently written O'Mulryan. O'Ryan, Prince of Idrone, was slain in 1170, by Raymond le Gros, the *avant-courier* of Strongbow. D'Alton.

OSBALDISTON. A township of Blackburn, co Lancaster.

OSBERN. See Osborn.

OSBORN. OSBORNE. For a legend of the origin of this name, see Eng. Surn. ii. 3, 4. Osbernus, Osbern, Osborn, &c., are, however, variations of a very common baptismal name. Several persons bearing it occur in Domesday, as tenants in chief in different counties. Ferguson derives it from the Norse, and interprets it "the divine bear!"

OSCAR. The personal name.

OSEMAN. The same as Osmond.

OSGOOD. An A-Sax. personal name.

O'SHANLEY. The O'Shanleys or, as they were more frequently called, the Mac Shanleys, existed as a sept of Leitrim from the XIII. cent. D'Alton.

O'SHAUGHNESSY. "The O'Shaugh-nessys were lords of a mountainous district dividing Galway from Clare. The sept is traced however, in the annals of other parts of the country." The surname first appears in 1060. D'Alton.

O'SHEE. The pedigree is traced to Odanus O'Shee, lord of the cantred of Tex-nane O'Shee in Kerry, and lands in Tip-perary, in the tenth century. B.L.G.

O'SHEENAN. A sept in the counties of Limerick and Cork.

OSLER. Probably the same as Ostler.

OSMAN. OSMANT. The same as Osmond.

OSMENT. See Osmond.

OSMER. An A-Sax. personal name occurring in Domesd. as Osmer and Osmar.

OSMOND. The A-Sax. personal name.

OSMOTHERLY. This singular sur-name has long prevailed at Cliffe, in the neighbourhood of Rochester. There are two places so called; one in the parish of Ulverstone, co. Lancaster; the other in the North Riding of Yorkshire. In old docu-ments the latter is written *Osmond*erley.

OST. A host; a medieval innkeeper.

OSTELL. Norm. Fr. *ostel*, an hotel, inn, lodging, or town-residence. The old orthography is *ostayl* or *osteyl*.

OSTERMOOR. "I find,' says Mr. Ferguson, "as a Danish Christian name, Ostmer, which corresponds with our sur-name Ostermoor, and I think means "eastern gull"—a metaphorical expression for a sea-rover, from the East."

OSWALD. An A-Sax. personal name.

OSWALDKIRKE. OSWALKYRK. A parish in Yorkshire.

OSWIN. An A-Sax. personal name.

OTHER. See Otter.

OTLEY. Parishes in Yorkshire and Suffolk.

O'TOOLE. The O'Tooles, or Tuaghalls, claim an ancient Milesian descent from Cathaor More, King of Leinster, of the race of Laogaore, Monarch of Ireland, contem-porary with St. Patrick. At the time of the English invasion under Henry II., they held a great territory in co. Wicklow. From the *Telegraph*, Irish newspaper.

OTT. OTTE. See Oates.

OTTER. A Scandinavian personal name of great antiquity, and common applica-tion. It is variously spelt Otter, Ohter, Other, Othyr, Ottyr, Oter, and in Domesday book, Otre. In some one or other of these forms it occurs also in the Saxon Chronicle, the Annales Cambriæ, and the Dublin Annals. A lately-decyphered inscription on a cross in the Isle of Man reads—" *Otr* raised this cross to Fruki, his father." As a family name, it has existed from time im-memorial in the " Danish " or Northman counties of East Yorkshire, Nottingham, Lincoln and Derby, where there is almost a *clan* of Otters, though the name is rarely to be met with in other counties, and scarcely appears at all in the metropolis. Walter Fitz-Other, the celebrated castellan of Windsor, temp. William I., the reputed ancestor of the Fitzgeralds, Gerards, Wind-sors, and other great houses, was the son of Otherus, a great landowner under the Confessor, but whether the latter was of Norse descent does not appear; there is, however, something like armorial evidence of the connection of the Otters with the families alluded to. Ingram, in his trans-lation of the Saxon Chronicle, says that Otter was " originally ' *oht-here* or ' *ocht-here*,' i.e. Terror of an Army."

OTTERBOURNE. There are several localities called Otterbourne or Otterburn, in England and Scotland—" the burn fre-quented by Otters?" The most famous of these is Otterburn, co. Northumberland, the scene of the battle between Lords Percy and Douglas, commemorated in *Chevy-Chase*, the best ballad of old English minstrelsy.

OTTIWELL. An ancient personal name. Ottiwell, a natural son of the celebrated Hugh Lupus, Earl of Chester, was tutor to those unfortunate children of King Henry I., who perished at sea, in the Blanche-Nef, in 1120. This surname has been borne for several generations, as a Christian name, in a respectable northern family of Wood. Some years ago a Mr. Ottiwell Wood ap-peared as a witness in a law-suit. His name being somewhat of a puzzle to the presiding judge, he was asked to spell it, which he did distichally, to the great amusement of the court, in manner follow-ing :—

"O double T, I, double U, E,
Double L, double U, double O, D !"

OTTLEY. See Otley.

OTTO. See Oates.

OTWAY. Doubtless local, but I can-not find the place.

OUDNY. "Of that Ilk, in Scotland." Encycl. Herald. I cannot ascertain the locality.

OUGHTON. Probably the same as Houghton.

OUSELEY. Local: "the Meadow on the banks of the Ouse." The family are of considerable antiquity, and they were for-merly divided into many branches. The principal stock, or elder line, seem to have fixed themselves in Shropshire. Courthope's Debrett. The baronet springs from Nor-thamptonshire.

OUTHORN. A person sent to call subjects to arms by the sound of horn. Denham. Jamieson defines *Out-horne* as the horn blown for summoning the lieges to attend the king in *feir of were*, i.e., upon any warlike expedition.

OUTLAW. A rebel.

OUTRED. Doubtless the A-Sax. personal name Utred or Uhtred.

OUTWAITE. The same as Owthwaite.

OUVRY. The family are believed to have come into England at the Revocation of the Edict of Nantes in 1685. In the early part of the XVIII. century, they were connected with the silk trade in Spitalfields. They married into the families of De Beauvoir and Garnault, whose ancestors were also Protestant refugees. Inf. Frederic Ouvry, Esq., F.S.A.

OVEN. If the O be long, the name may be a corruption of Oving, a parish in Sussex. Mr. Ferguson, however, derives it from the O. Norse *ovanr*, inexperienced.

OVENDEN. OVENDEAN. A parish in Sussex is called Ovingdean.

OVER. Parishes and places in cos. Cambridge, Gloucester, Chester, &c.

OVERBURY. A parish in Worcestershire.

OVERMAN. Du. The master of any guild or fraternity. In the N. of England, the superintendent of a coal pit.

OVERTON. Parishes and places in cos. Hants, Chester, Lancaster, Flint, York, Wilts, Lanark, Renfrew, Edinburgh, &c.

OVERY. An extinct parish in Oxfordshire.

OVINGTON. Parishes, &c., in cos. Essex, Norfolk, Northumberland, and Southampton.

OWDEN. Probably the same as Howden, or as Oden.

OWEN. A personal name in Wales. Most of our Owens are from that principality, but it is possible that a few may be of Saxon blood, for there is an Owine in the Domesday of Yorkshire, and a still earlier Owine occurs in the Codex Diplomaticus. It is one of the most common of Welsh surnames. As I have elsewhere observed in this volume, the commonness of Welsh patronymics has tended to a great confusion of the 'gentle' and the 'simple' in Wales. There are thousands of Owens who bear that name simply because their grandfathers or perhaps their fathers bore it *as a Christian name*. In ancient families the patronymic became a stationary family name about the times of Henry VIII. and Queen Elizabeth.

The Owens of Tedsmore Hall, Denbighshire, formerly of Llunllo, are descended from Howell Dha, and the Kings of South Wales, but the first of the family who wrote himself Owen, was Roland Owen, sheriff of Montgomeryshire in 1610. B.L.G. The

Owens of Glynafon descend from Llywarch ap Bran, lord of Menai in Anglesea, founder of the second noble tribe of North Wales and Powys. B.L.G. The Owens of Orielton, co. Pembroke, Barts., spring from Hova ap Kundhelw, a nobleman of North Wales, who lived about the year 1130, and was one of the fifteen peers. Courthope's Debrett.

OWENS. From Owen.

OWLE. The bird.

OWLEGRAVE. Local: "the owl's grove."

OWLER. In some northern dialects, the alder tree; in the South, a smuggler. Kennett (quoted by Halliwell) says: "those who transport wool into France, contrary to the prohibition, are called *owlers;*" probably on account of such transactions occurring in the night, the time when owls are abroad.

OWTHWAITE. Local: see Thwaite.

OXBURGH. A parish in Norfolk.

OXCLIFFE. A sub-township in Lancashire.

OXEN. This singular (not to say *plural*) name is not easily to be accounted for. Is it Oxenham or Oxenden, deprived of its final syllable? Mr. Ferguson's explanation, if not quite satisfactory and conclusive, is at least ingenious and noteworthy. "Such a name as Oxen," says he, "must probably have been a surname. There is a Northman in the Landnamabok called Oxna-Thorir, 'Oxen-Thorir,' most probably from the number of oxen which he possessed. The surname is here a prefix, and Oxen-Thorir compares with our Apple-John—the one having been celebrated for his oxen, as the other for his apples." The comparison is faulty, for the original Mr. Apple-john did not get his name from his orchard, but was, doubtless, "a gentleman of Brutus' blood," an Apple-John of the Welsh principality.

OXENARD. Qu.: "oxen-herd?"

OXENBRIDGE. This knightly family are thus mentioned by Leland: "Oxenbridge of Southsex (Sussex) is heire by descent to this Alard [of Winchelsea] and bearith his armes." They first resided at Oxenbridge in the parish of Iden, and took their name from that estate. They rose into importance in the early part of the fourteenth century. Cooper's Winchelsea.

OXENDEN. A parish and a hamlet in co. Northampton are so called; but the gentry family originated among the *dens* of Kent. The first known ancestor of the baronets is Solomon Oxenden, who flourished in the reign of Edw. III. Shirley's Noble and Gentle Men.

OXENFORD. An old spelling of Oxford.

"In twenty manere coude he trip and dance,
After the Scole of *Oxenforde* tho,
And with his legges casten to and fro."
Chaucer, Milleres Tale.

Saulf de Oxenford is found in Domesday, among the under-tenants of Berkshire.

OXFORD. The city.

OXLAD. Perhaps literally a herd-boy, or driver of oxen; more probably, however, from a local source. See Oxlade.

OXLADE. Local; from ox, and *lade*, a water-course.

OXLEY. A manor in the parish of Bysshebury, co. Stafford. A-Sax. "a pasture for oxen"—a name given to many tri-

vial localities. The surname is found chiefly in the counties of York, Kent, and Sussex.

OXNEY. A hundred, a river-island, and a parish in Kent.

OXSPRINGE. A township in the West Riding of Yorkshire, where the family anciently resided.

OXTON. Parishes, &c., in cos. Nottingham, Chester, and York.

OYLER. I suppose a dealer in oil, and other articles of the same sort—what is now called an oil-man.

P.

PACE. A provincialism for Easter, from the Lat. *pascha*. The analogous names Christmas, Pentecost, &c., occur as family designations.

PACK. PACKE. Possibly from the Fr. *Pâque*, Easter. See Times and Seasons. But more likely from an ancient personal name Pack or Peck, from which seem to be derived the local Packington, Peckham, Paxton, Packwood, &c. Ferguson concurs in this view, and even goes so far as to derive the personal name from the A-Sax. *pæca*, a deceiver.

PACKARD. Doubtless a corruption of Picard.

PACKER. Halliwell says, a person "employed in barrelling or *packing up* herrings." In London, the occupation of the "packer-and-presser" is a well-known and lucrative one. Le Packere and Packare are in H.R. A less desirable derivation is from the A-Sax. *pæca*, a cheat or deceiver.

PACKET. 1. O. Fr. *pasquier, pasquet, paccage*, &c., signifying pastures. 2. Perhaps a hunchback. "Il porte son *pacquet*; he carries his load about with him; said of one that is huch-backt." Cotgrave. Pasket. H.R.

PACKHAM. A corruption of Peckham.

PACKMAN. In various provincial dialects, a pedlar, whose bundle is called a pack. "We do present Jane Frye to be a pickry, (pilferer) viz. for steyling of a pedler's *pac*." Town records of Seaford, Sussex, temp. Queen Elizabeth.

PACKWOOD. A parish in Warwickshire.

PACY. Either from Paci, near Evreux, (latinized in charters Paceium) or from Pacé near Alençon, both in Normandy.

PADBURY. A parish in Buckinghamshire.

PADDISON. The same as Paterson, if not from Paddy, which see.

PADDLE. Probably a corruption of either Padwell or Padhill, a local name.

PADDOCK. 1. Paddoc, without prefix, is the H.R. form. It seems to be a personal name, and to have originated, in A-Sax. times, several names of places, such as Paddockswood, Padoxhurst, &c. 2. A small park or enclosure.

PADDY. 1. Apparently an ancient personal name, whence the patronymical Paddison, the local Padwick, Paddington, Padiham, Padley, Padworth, &c. 2. Perhaps the common nickname of Patrick.

PADGETT. See Paget.

PADLEY. A township in Derbyshire.

PADMAN. A *pad* is, in several dialects, an ambling horse. A padman was therefore a man who had the care of such horses, and the name is analogous to Palfriman, Coltman, Horsman, Brockman, &c.

PAGAN. Paganus was a Norman personal name, whence the modern Payne and Paine, as well as the more ancient Paganel and Paynel. Pagan, however, exists at this day among English surnames. See 16th Report of Registr. Gen. The history of this word is not a little remarkable: I shall give it in the words of Gibbon.

"Παγη, in the Doric dialect, so familiar to the Italians, signifies a fountain; and the rural neighbourhood which frequented the same fountain derived the common appellation of *pagus* and *pagans*.   2. By an easy extension of the word, *pagan* and rural became synonymous, and the meaner rustics acquired that name, which has been corrupted into *peasant* in the modern languages of Europe.   3. The amazing increase of the military order introduced the necessity of a correlative term; and all the people who were not enlisted in the service of the prince were branded with the contemptuous epithet of Pagans.   4. The Christians were the soldiers of Christ; their adversaries, who refused his *sacrament*, or military oath of baptism, might deserve the metaphorical name of Pagans; and this popular reproach was introduced as early as the reign of Valentinian, A.D. 365, into Imperial laws and theological writings.   5. Christianity gradually filled the cities of the empire; the old religion in the time of Prudentius and Orosius retired and languished in obscure villages; and the word *pagan*, with its new signification, reverted to its primitive origin.   6. Since the worship of Jupiter and his family has expired, the vacant title of Pagans has been successively applied to all the idolaters and polytheists of the old and new world.   7. The Latin Christians bestowed it, without scruple, on their mortal enemies, the Mahometans; and the purest *unitarians* were branded with the unjust reproach of idolatry and paganism." Decline and Fall, chap. xxi. *ad finem*. The historian quotes numerous authorities. Other remarks on this word may be found in Mill's Logic; and Dean Trench, in his Study of Words, makes admirable use of the changes it has undergone.

As a personal name, and a surname, Pagan and its derivatives were probably applied by way of sobriquet. Like Boor, Le Sauvage, and Wildman, they may have had some reference to the rusticity or rudeness of the original bearers—some Northmen probably—who after the Conquest of Neustria, and the baptism of their chieftain Rollo, still declined to become Christians, and remained wedded to their old Scandinavian superstitions.

William the Conqueror was assisted in his invasion, by several persons so designated, and in Domesday Book we find among his tenants in capite, or chief holders of land, the names of Ralph Paganel and Edmund filius Pagani, i.e., Fitz-Payne. Indeed during the Norman dynasty, Paganus was one of the most common names in England; and it is to this cause that we must assign the great frequency of the name of Payne or Paine, in our family nomenclature. In times more recent than the Conquest, there have doubtless been various settlements of this widely spread name in England; for example, the Paynes who settled in Norfolk in the XV. century, claim descent from the ancient house of Paynel of Hambie, in the arrondissement of Coutances. The change from Paynel to Payne was made, it is supposed, in order to evade the vexatious laws then in force respecting aliens.

Recent research has proved the identity of the names Paganus and Paganellus, and consequently of Payne and Paynel; for in a branch of the Pagnels or Paynels of Hambie, settled in Yorkshire, both appellatives are frequently applied to the same individual.   Inf. J. Bertrand Payne, Esq.

PAGDEN. See DEN.

PAGE. Properly a young male servant —a subordinate personal attendant of great men. It is curious that the Gr. Παις, the Lat. *puer*, the Fr. *garçon*, and the Eng. *boy*, signify equally 'boy' or 'servant;' and *page*, from whatever source derived, has the same double meaning.   According to Cotgrave, a page is "a waiting or serving boy (in France, where he hath often good breeding, he ought to be a gentleman borne); thence also a tayler's boy, a ship boy."

PAGET. The family may be Norman, but the pedigree only goes back to a London civic official, temp. Henry VIII. The name seems to be a diminutive of *page*.

PAKEMAN. Qu. *packman*, a pedlar?

PAKENHAM. Lord Longford's family are traced to William de Pakenham of Pakenham, co. Suffolk, temp. Edward I.

PAKINGTON. This name was borne contemporaneously by three families, who wrote themselves De Pakington, from three several estates in the counties of Stafford, Warwick, and Leicester. It occurs as early as the reign of Henry I.

PAICE. See Pace.

PAILTHORPE. See Palethorpe.

PAIN. PAINE. See under Paganus.

PAINTER. The occupation. H.R. Pictor. See Paynter.

PAINTING. The same as Painton.

PAINTON. Paington, a parish in Devonshire.

PAIRPOINT. See Pierpoint.

PAISLEY. The Scotch town.

PALAIRET. The family came into England at the Revocation of the Edict of Nantes.

PALCOCK. A diminutive of Paul. See COCK.

PALEOLOGUS. In the Church of Landulph, co. Cornwall, is a brass plate thus inscribed:—

"Here lyeth the body of Theodore Paleologus of Pesaro in Italye, descended from ye Imperyal lyne of ye last Christian Emperors of Greece, being the sonne of Camilio, ye sonne of Prosper, the sonne of Theodoro, the sonne of John, ye sonne of Thomas, second brother of Constantine Paleologus, the 8th of that name, and last of yt lyne yt rayned in Constantinople until subdued by the Turks, who married wt Mary, ye daughter of William Balls of Hadlye in Souffolke, Gent, and had issue 5 children, Theodoro, John, Ferdinando, Maria, and Dorothy; and departed this life at Clyfton, ye 21st of Jan. 1636."

The monument is surmounted by the arms of the Eastern Empire.

From comparison of dates, &c., it appears that this descendant of the imperial line lived in the house, if not in the family, of Sir Nicholas Lower, who was then owner of the mansion of Clifton. His offspring seem to have been completely anglicised. His son Theodore simply describes himself, in his will, dated 1693, as *mariner*, and his signature is Theodore Paleologey. His sister Dorothy, who married an Arundell, is registered as " Dorothea Paleologus, de stirpe Imperatorum." Other descendants went to the West Indies, where their posterity long continued. In Cornwall the Imperial race seem to have become " small by degrees and beautifully less;" so that it requires no great stretch of the imagination to believe, with the Rev. F. V. J. Arundell, that "the imperial blood perhaps still flows in the bargemen of Cargreen!" See Archæologia. vol. xviii. p. 83.

PALETHORPE. A chapelry in Nottinghamshire.

PALEY. This was borne as a personal name, by a powerful Dane mentioned in the Saxon Chronicle as Pallig, A.D. 1101.

PALFREY. 1. A riding horse. Palefray Palfrei, Palfrey, &c. H.R. 2. Mr. Ferguson thinks it may be a baptismal name, derived from the old Germ. Baldfred, which is found so early as the VII. century.

PALFRIMAN. A keeper of *palfreys*—perhaps of those belonging to the king. The forms of the surname in H.R. are Palfreyman, Palfreur, and Palfridarius.

PALGRAVE. A parish in Suffolk. The derivation from the Germ. *pfalzgraf*, a count-palatine, as given in Eng. Surn., is therefore erroneous.

PALING. Probably Palling, a parish in Norfolk.

PALK. The family are traced to Ambrook, co. Devon, temp. Henry VII. The name is probably local. In Sussex, Pocock is sometimes corrupted to Palk. Some consider it a derivative of Paul, and the Palke of H.R. supports this opinion.

PALLANT. In Chichester and some other episcopal towns, the district surrounding the bishop's palace (*palatium* episcopi) is so called.

PALLETT. The name Hippolytus is sometimes so corrupted in medieval manuscripts.

PALLIN. The same as Palling.

PALLING. 1. A parish in Norfolk. 2. A personal name in H.R.

PALLISER. Probably a man who made palisades or park fences, or had the care of them.

PALMER. An incessant pilgrim—one who spent all his time in visiting holy shrines, whereas the ordinary pilgrim returned to his usual course of life as soon as his particular expiatory journey was finished. See Scott's Marmion, and Eng. Surn. i. 131.

" Palmers, (a baculis *palmarum*) from the staff of the palm, which they used to bear when returning from the Holy *War*," says Richardson.

" The faded palm-branch in his hand,
    Showed pilgrim from the Holy *Land*,"

says Sir Walter, which is the more correct statement; for the Palmer was rather a devotee than an ordinary Crusader. The distinction between Pilgrim and Palmer was not always strictly observed. Thus in the medieval romance of " Horn " we find the expression " Palmer-pilgrim" applied to one individual.

" En la sale est entré li paumer-pelerin."
    Wright's Essays, i. 111.

Palmarius, Palmer, Le Palmer. H.R.

PALMES. "There appears no reason to doubt the antiquity of this family, said to be descended from Manfred Palmes, who lived in the reign of Stephen, and seated at Naburn, co York, since the year 1226 by a match with the heiress of Watterville." Shirley's Noble and Gentle Men. The meaning of the name does not appear.

PALSER. A contraction of Palliser.

PAM. The name of one Ric. Pam occurs in H.R. An Austrian family of this name became naturalized here in the last century.

PAMPHILON. From *pampilion*, a coat of various colours, formerly worn by domestic servants. The word was most likely a corruption of the Fr. *papillon*, a butterfly, the gaudy hues of which were emulated by this motley costume.

PAMPLIN. The same as Pamphilon.

PAN. Corresponds with an O. Germ. name Panno. Ferguson.

PANCEFOT. This name is spelt in such varying forms, that its true orthography and its right meaning appear to be unattainable. It is written Pauncefote, Pancevolt, Pancefort, Poncefortt, Pancevot, and Pancefot. In charters it is latinized De Pede Planco, that is, " of the Splay-Foot," but for this rendering there appears to be no authority. The first of the name on record is Bernard Pancevolt, a Domesday tenant-in-chief in Hampshire. Geoffrey de Pauncevote was steward to the household of King John.

PANE. A corruption of Paine. See Pagan.

PANGBORN. A name fairly applicable to every human being; but as a surname it is doubtless derived from the parish called Pangborne, in Berkshire.

PANKHURST or **PENKHURST.** An estate in E. Sussex.

PANNACK. See Penneck.

PANNEL. See under Pagan, Paganel, of which this is an easy corruption.

PANNETT. In all probability a corruption of the French *panetier*. See under Panter.

PANNIER. Probably the same as the *pannier-man*, thus described by Bailey :

"One [in the Inns of Court] who winds a horn, or rings a bell, to call the gentlemen to dinner or supper, and provides mustard, pepper, and vinegar for the Hall."

PANT. A public fountain, cistern, or reservoir. North. A hollow declivity. West. Halliwell.

PANTER. The name of Paniter, Panter, or Panther, is derived from the office of master-baker. "In the court of France the Panitier was an officer of high consideration; and in monasteries the Paniter would seem to have been charged with the distribution of bread to the poor—no doubt in virtue of his office of chief baker." Proceedings of the Society of Antiquaries of Scotland, vol. i. p. 14.

Pantler is synonymous. Cotgrave gives "PANETIER, a *pantler*;" and Gouldm. has "*A Pantler*, panis custos, promus." R. Brunne, in his version of Langtoft's Chronicle, relates the death of King Edmund A.D. 947, by the hand of an outlaw *pantelere*, who had formerly served in the royal *panterie*. The more common form of the two is *panter*, Fr. *panetier*, Lat. *panetarius*. See more in Way's Promptorium Parv. p. 381.

PANTHER. Not from the wild beast, but the same as Panter, which see.

PANTLER. See Panter.

PANTON. A parish in Lincolnshire.

PANTRY. *Paneterie*, O. Fr., the place where bread was kept. The H.R. form is De la Paneterie; i.e., the officer, who, in great houses, dealt out the bread for the household.

PAPE. Apparently the French form of Pope. The name occurs in H.R. in the present orthography.

PAPILLON. Fr., a butterfly—probably with reference to the gaudy costume of the original bearer of the name. The surname is found in England as early as the time of the Conqueror, in the records of the church of Durham; and in subsequent reigns, it is not unfrequent. The H.R. forms are Papilion, Papilioun, Papillun, &c. But the Papillons of Kent and Sussex are of Huguenot origin, and are descendants of Anthony Papillon, the friend of Erasmus, and one of the most eminent Protestants of France. His grandson, David Papillon, settled at Lubenham, co. Leicester, and was ancestor of the Papillons of Acrise. B.L.G.

PAPPENHEIM. The family came to England with George II. The name is local.

PAPPRILL. Probably the same as Pepperell or Peverell.

PAPWORTH. Parishes in cos. Huntingdon and Cambridge.

PARADISE. Doubtless from a locality so named.

PARAGREEN. PARRAGREN. Corruptions of Peregrine.

PARAMOUR. See Parramore.

PARCEL. A probable corruption of '*Par Ciel!*' "By Heaven," an oath habitually employed by the first bearer, and so becoming his sobriquet.

PARDEE. '*Par Dieu*,' a common medieval oath. See Pardew.

"And for that licour is so presious,
That oft hath made me dronke as any mous,
Therefor I will that ther it beryd be,
My wrecchid body afore this god, *pardé*,
Mighti Bachus that is myn owen lorde,
Without variaunce to serve hym or discorde."
            MS. Rawl. c. 86. (Halliw.)

PARDEW. This is in all likelihood an oath—'*Par Dieu*'—and may have originated in a similar manner with Bigod, of which, indeed, it may be a simple translation. The habit of profane swearing, so common in the middle ages, seems to have been an importation from Normandy. See *Bigod*. William the Conqueror, Rufus, and many of their successors, set a very bad example to their subjects in this respect; and in the XII. century, Giraldus Cambrensis complains that—"there are some princes who at every word employ an enormous oath, foolishly and rashly presuming to swear by the death of God, by his eyes, his feet, his teeth,.........and irreverently strive to tear their God limb from limb." At a later period, this profanity was by no means limited to the noble, as a very slight acquaintance with Chaucer and other writers of the time will show. Profane oaths abound in the Canterbury Tales, proving that in the XIV. century it was a great national vice. How bad a character our countrymen had for it in the XV. century, is proved by the following incident at the trial of Joan of Arc. A French witness named Colette having used the name "Godon," was asked who Godon was, and replied that it was not the designation of any particular person, but a sobriquet applied generally to the English, on account of their continual use of the exclamation, "God damn it." Sharon Turner's Middle Ages, ii. 555.

PARDIE. PARDY. The same as Pardew.

PARDOE. PARDOW. See Pardew.

PARDON. Parton, a hamlet and a township in Cumberland.

PARE. Fr. *père*, father.

PARENT. Probably intended in the Fr. sense of kinsman. A very early surname. Parent. H.R.

PARFETT. PARFITT. A-Norm. *parfit*, O.E. *parfait*, perfect.

PARGETTER. PARGITER. A plasterer. The term 'pargeting' is generally applied to the more ornamental kinds of plaster work. "*Parget*, playster for wallys." Prompt. Parv.

PARHAM. Parishes in Suffolk and Sussex.

PARIS. PARRIS. The French metropolis. Many families so named must have settled in England. One Francis Parris, a

Protestant refugee from Dieppe, settled at Rye in 1572. Harl. MS. 15. 70. The surname is common in Sussex. In H.R. there are many individuals called De Paris, and De Parys.

PARISH. This rather singular name may be thus accounted for. In many parts of the South of England, in country places, the word parish is used, not so much with reference to the parochial district, as to the village immediately adjacent to the church. Hence, at the period when plebeian surnames began, two Johns or two Roberts, residing in the same ecclesiastical *parochia*, might be called respectively, John or Robert at Field, at Moor, at Hill, or what not—or John or Robert "*at the Parish.*" The family of this name formerly settled in Lincolnshire, consider it to be a modification of Paris, the Fr. metropolis.

PARK. From residence near a park. Anciently At-Parke and A Parke. See, however, Peter.

PARKE. 1. May be a derivative of Peter, and intermediate between that and Parkins; or, 2, local; either from one of the places called Parc in Normandy, situated respectively near Dieppe and Bernay; or from residence near some English park, like the De la Parocke of the H.R.

PARKEN. The same as Parkin.

PARKER. An officer who had the surveillance of a park for some royal or noble personage. Collins traces the Earl of Macclesfield's family to Thomas le Parker, temp. Edward III. The extinct baronet family, Parker of Ratton, traced their pedigree to temp. Edward I. in Sussex. Le Parkere, Le Parker, Parcarius, &c., H.R.
Anschitil Parcher is a tenant-in-chief in co. Somerset, Domesd.; and the name may therefore have another etymology.

PARKERSON. The son of a Parker: so Wrightson, Smithson, &c.; perhaps, however, a corruption of Parkinson.

PARKES. May belong to the series, Park, Parkins, Perkins, Parkinson, &c., from Peter, the Christian name; or may be local, from Parcs, near Pont-l'Evêque, or Parcs, near Alençon, both in Normandy.

PARKHOUSE. A house in or near some park.

PARKHURST. A place in the Isle of Wight.

PARKIN. PARKINS. See Peter.

PARKINSON. See Peter.

PARKMAN. The same as Parker.

PARKYN. See Peter.

PARLOUR. *Parele* is a word used by Lydgate, signifying 'to apparel;' and another medieval expression (from the Anglo-Norman) '*apparail*' means to provide, furnish, prepare, or equip. The original bearer of the name may have had something to do with military appareling or equipments.

2 L

PARMENTER. PARMITER. O.Fr. "*parmentier*, a Taylor." Cotgr. The H.R. forms are Le Parmenter, Le Parmunter, Parminter, Parmuntarius.

PARNALL. See Parnell.

PARNELL. O.Eng. Pernel, for Petronilla, a female name. In old times the word was used to designate "a lascivious woman, a confident girl." Bailey. See Female Christian Names.

PARSALL. 1. The same as Parcel. 2. a corruption of Purcell.

PARSEY. A corruption of Percy.

PARSLEY. A corruption of Passelewe or Pashley. In the South of England the R in *parsley* is dropped in pronunciation. The name was doubtless assimilated to the vegetable by an ignorant scribe.

PARSLOW. Most likely the same as Passelewe.

PARSON. PARSONS. May refer to the sacred office, in which case, see ECCLESIASTICAL SURNAMES. More probably, however, it is the same as Pearson, Pierson —the son of Peter.

PARR. In Eng. Surn. i. 169, I ventured to derive this surname from Peter, and this, through the Fr. Pierre, is probably the true origin of it in some cases; but a correspondent (the Rev. Henry Parr) says: "it is derived from the manor of Parr in Lancashire, which is also a township, and of late years has become a chapelry. There all my ancestors were settled from the XIII. century, and there is sufficient reason for concluding, that every family bearing the name has branched out from the same parent stock." B.L.G. Nichols' Topographer, iii. 353.

PARRAGREN. Peregrine, the Christian name.

PARRAMORE. If not local, may belong to the same class as Lover, Friend, Neighbour, &c.

PARRET. A river in co. Somerset is so called; but the name may be a corruption of the Fr. Pierrot, a diminutive of Peter.

PARRINGTON. Patrington, a parish in Yorkshire.

PARRIS. See Paris.

PARROCK. O. Eng. a park. De la Parocke is the form of the name in H.R.

PARROTT. May have been originally applied to a talkative person. So the classical Psittacus, from Ψιττακη. There is however equal probability of its having been derived from the river Parret, or from Pierrot, a French diminutive of Pierre, Peter. The surname has been varied to Parratt, Parrett, and Parritt.

PARRY. Welsh, Ap-Harry, the son of Henry. The surname was not fixed before the XVI. century. The Parrys of Rhydolion, co. Carnarvon, are of very ancient descent from Moreiddig o'r dyffryn aur;

while those of Noyadd Trefawr, co. Cardigan, derive their pedigree from Rhys Chwith, an esquire of the body to King Edward I., and a descendant of the ancient Lords of Cardigan. B.L.G.

PARTINGTON. A township in Cheshire.

PARTNER. An associate in any trade or labour. R.G. 16.

PARTON. A township and a hamlet in Cumberland, and a parish in Kirkcudbrightshire.

PARTRICK. A corruption of Patrick.

PARTRIDGE. Possibly from the bird; but more likely from some locality terminating in -RIDGE. Partriche is, however, a H.R. surname.

PASCALL. An Old Fr. baptismal name, Pascal, first imposed on children born at the season of *Pasche* or Easter, like Noel, Christmas, Pentecost, and others. It is commonly varied to Pascoe, Paskell, &c.

PASCOE. PASCO. See Pascall.

PASH. See Easter.

PASK. See Easter.

PASKALL. See Pascall.

PASLEY. See Passelewe.

PASMORE. Probably Peasmore, a parish in Berkshire.

PASS. A narrow entrance; an avenue. Johnson. A topographical term.

PASSAGE. From residence at one. Del Passage. H.R.

PASSELEWE. PASSELEU. Afterwards Passeley, and now Pashley. Skinner derives it "à Fr. *passe l'eau*, sc. a tranando vel transeundo aquam," but a monkish writer, in some complimentary verses upon Robert de Passeleu, the crafty ecclesiastic of Henry the Third's time, says:—

"Nec enim quia *transit*
Sed *præcellit* aquam, cognomine credo notari—
Mente quidem lenis, re dulcis, sanguine clarus;
In tribus his præcellit aquam."

The name, however, has nothing to do either with crossing, or excelling, water, but is probably derived from the manor now called Pasley or Pashley, in the parish of Ticehurst, co. Sussex.

PASSENGER. A traveller.

PASTON. Parishes in cos. Northampton and Norfolk, and a township in Northumberland. The Pastons, originally of the place so called in Norfolk, are well known through the "Paston Letters," written in the XV. century, and containing most picturesque views of society at that period.

PATCH. 1. Probably one of the modifications of Peche. 2. From the occurrence of Patcham, Patching, Patchway, &c., as names of places, it is probable that there was an early personal name Pach, or Patch. 3. A domestic fool or jester.

PATCHING. A parish in Sussex.

PATE. A badger. Halliwell.

PATEMAN. As *pate* is a northern provincialism for a badger, the original Pateman may have been a hunter of badgers, just as the patriarch of the Todmans was a catcher of foxes, and the ancestor of the Wontners, a captor of moles. See Todman, and Wontner.

PATEN. Probably the same as Paton and Peyton.

PATER. 1. The latinization of the surname Father. 2. A town in Wales, now called Pembroke Dock.

PATERNOSTER. Alice Paternoster, in the reign of Edward I., held lands in Pusey, co. Berks., by the service of saying the Lord's Prayer, *Pater noster qui es in cœlis*, &c., five times a day, for the souls of the King's ancestors; and it appears that Richard Paternoster, on succeeding to an estate in the same parish, instead of paying a sum of money as a *relief*, said the Lord's Prayer thrice, before the Barons of the Exchequer, as John, his brother, had previously done. In the same reign, another, or the same, John Paternoster held a virgate of land in East Hendred, by the service of saying one Paternoster *per diem*. The land is still called Paternoster Bank. See Blount's Tenures. Lysons' Berks.

PATERSON. See Patterson.

PATESHALL. A parish in Northamptonshire.
The family are ancient in that county, where Simon de Pateshall was sheriff, 6. Richard I.

PATEY. Perhaps from the A-Sax. *pætig, petig*, crafty.

PATIENCE. 1. A baptismal name for both sexes. A Saint Patient is honoured by the Roman church on the 11th of September. 2. The remarks under Peace apply to this name as well.

PATIENT. See Patience.

PATMAN. The same as Padman.

PATON. See Paten.

PATRICK. The personal name, borne by the patron saint of Ireland. It seems to have originated several other names which will be found below. Patric, Patrick, Patryk, &c., are the spellings in H.R., and the surname appears to have been common in the XIII. century.

PATRICKSON. The son of Patrick.

PATSON. The son of Patrick.

PATTEN. According to B L.G., Richard Patten, son and heir of Richard Patten, was of Patine, or Patten, near Chelmsford, co. Essex, in 1119. From him the Pattens of Bank Hall, co. Lancaster, claim lineal descent.

PATTENDEN. See DEN.

PATTERSON. Patrick's son.

PATTISON. The son of Patrick?

PAUL. PAULL. 1. A well-known Christian name. 2. A parish in Yorkshire, olim Paghill.

PAULET. The patriarch of this noble family was Hercules, lord of Tournon in Picardy, who coming into England. temp. Henry I., and settling on the lordship of Paulet, co. Hants, assumed his surname therefrom. Courthope's Debrett. Dugdale states, however, that the family borrowed their name from Paulet (now Pawlett) in Somersetshire, and he does not trace the pedigree beyond Sir John Paulet, who died 2. Richard II.

PAULIN. Fr. Paulin, from the Latin Paulinus.

PAULSON. The son of Paul.

PAULTON. A parish in Somersetshire.

PAUSE. Pawson is understood to be Paul's son, and it is probable that Pause is a corruption of the genitive Paul's.

PAVER. This older and more correct form of paviour, a layer of pavements, still exists as a family name.

PAVIN. An Italian gentleman named Pavini settled, two generations since, in Wales, and anglicised his surname by knocking out one of his I's. Of this fact I am as-assured by a descendant, who facetiously conjectures that the name was originally derived a non pavendo! Pavin, as a sur-name in England, dates back, however, to the XIII. century.

PAVIOUR. A paver of streets, &c.

PAVISER. A soldier armed with a pavise, or large Norman shield.

PAVYER. A paver, or, as it is now ri-diculously written, paviour.

PAW. A corruption of Paul. Hence Pawson.

PAWLE. A mis-spelling of Paul.

PAWLETT. See Paulet.

PAWSON. The son of Paul, through Paw.

PAXMAN. Probably a corruption of Packman, a hawker.

PAXON. Probably a corruption of Paxton.

PAXTON. " The family of Paxton came from the town of that name in Berwick-shire, where the ancestors were long resident as clergymen of the Presbyterian kirk." B.L.G.

PAXTON. Great and Little Paxton are parishes in co. Huntingdon.

PAYBODY. " Seems to be connected with the Danish paabyde, to command or enjoin; paabud an edict." Ferguson. See Peabody.

PAYNE. See under Pagan. One of the greatest colonies of the Paynes is at East Grinstead, co. Sussex, where for se-veral centuries they have been very abund-ant. Some of the branches, for the sake of comparative distinction, call themselves Payner!

A correspondent observes : "Note how widely spread this name is. In the Biblio-thèque Impériale at Paris, Paganellus and Paganus stand indifferently for Paynel; and other forms of the name exist in France in Payen, Paen, Payn. Italy has its Pagana, and Portugal its Payana."

PAYNTER. See Painter. According to Kelham, however, Payntier de roy meant in Norman times, serjeant of the pantry to the king. See Panter.

PAYS. Probably the same as Pace, Easter.

PEABODY. The same as Paybody. Dixon derives it from Pae-body, "one as handsome as a pae or peacock!" This is far-fetched enough for ordinary belief, but Mr. Arthur goes much further, in deducing the lineage of the name from one Boadie, a kinsman of Queen Boadicea, who escaped into Wales, and there got the name of Pea, or mountain, prefixed to his name ! !

PEACE. If not from the personification of Peace in some medieval drama, probably from a Christian name, like Faith, Charity, Honour, &c. Pax, without prefix, is found in H.R.

PEACEABLE. From the disposition of the first bearer.

PEACH. The same as Peche and Peachey.

PEACHEY. Doubtless the same as the baronial name Peche, latinized in charters De Peccato. That the latter was pronounced as a dissyllable, Peché, is shown by the painted glass in a window at Lullingstone, co. Kent, where the arms of Sir John Peche are surrounded by branches of a peach-tree, fructed, and each peach, to complete the rebus, is inscribed with the letter E— PEACH-E. See Stothard's Monumental Effigies. The modern arms of Peachey are evidently derived from those of Peche.

PEACOCK. The bird. See Pocock.

PEAK. A pointed hill, as the Peak in Derbyshire.

PEAKE. The Peakes of Llewenny, co. Denbigh, have been seated there apparently from the XIV. century, and there is little doubt of their extraction from Thomas del Peke, to whom Henry de Lacy, Earl of Lin-coln, about the year 1284, granted a burgage, &c., within the walls of Denbigh. As Llewen-nie was included within De Lacy's barony, it seems probable that it was granted at the same period. The family went into Wales in 1283, with King Edward I., doubt-less as feudatories of the De Lacys. Harl. M.S. 1933. See B.L.G. The etymology of the name is the same as that of Peak.

PEAL. The same as Peel.

PEAR. 1. Fr. Pierre, Peter. 2. Fr. père, the father. 3. One of the several places in

Normandy known as Paer and Pair. 4. The Fr. modification of the saintly name Paternus; "Sanctus Paternus, vulgò Saint-Pair." Itin. de la Normandie.

PEARCE. See Piers, from Peter.

PEARCY. See Percy.

PEARETH. This name seems to have been corrupted, in the XVI. century, from Penreth, originally De Penrith, in Cumberland. See B.L.G., Peareth of Usworth, co. Durham. Camden, speaking of Penrith in his Britannia, says: "vulgo autem *Perith* dicitur."

PEARHEAD. From a head of the shape of a pear. The late Louis-Philippe bore a sobriquet of this kind. Perheved. H.R.

PEARL. The name may have been applied metaphorically, like the baptismal Marguerite or Margaret, which signifies the same thing.

PEARMAN. A grower of pears.

PEARS. PEARSE. See Peter.

PEARSALL. An estate in co. Stafford, now written Pearshall or Pershall. The family are of Norman origin, having been founded, at the place referred to, by Robert, a follower of Robert of Stafford, early in the reign of the Conqueror. He was son of Gilbert, son of Richard, Count of Corbeil in Normandy.

PEARSON. See Pierson.

PEART. In various dialects signifies lively or brisk, and is so used by several old authors. In Sussex, "Peart and Lively" is a common appellation given to a pair of oxen.

PEARTREE. Belongs to the same class as Appletree, Plumtree, &c. At Peretre is a good H.R. surname.

PEASCOD. This name seems to belong to the same category as the old Roman Cicero, Piso, &c. Or it may have originated in the rustic customs described by Halliwell.

PEASE. Anciently Peaths, a remarkable ravine or dean in Roxburghshire.

PEAT. Is, I think, sometimes a diminutive or 'nurse-name' of Peter, and sometimes a local name, derived from the original bearer's residence on a *peat*, or moorish ground. The name in the latter sense is, therefore, analogous to Heath, Moss, Moor, &c.

PEATIE. PEATTIE. Mr. Ferguson thinks *pætig, petig*, A-Sax., crafty.

PEBODY. See Peabody.

PECHE. An ancient baronial family, called in charters, De Peccato. They appear as early as the reign of King Stephen, and they were doubtless of Norman extraction. They were of prime importance in Kent, temp. Edw. I.

PECHELL. This family were for many ages established at Montauban in Langue-doc, and held high offices of state. As Protestants, they assisted in placing Henri Quartre upon the throne, but upon the Revocation of the Edict of Nantes by Louis Quatorze, M. Samuel Pechell and his lady, la Marquise Thierry de Sabonniers, became the objects of severe persecution. M. Pechell, after having suffered extreme penalties, was at length embarked like a common felon for the French plantations in the West Indies. Ultimately, however, he escaped to Jamaica, and thence went to Ireland, where he entered the army of William III. under Marshal Schomberg. Madame Pechell fled, in the first instance, to Geneva, but afterwards succeeded in joining her husband in Ireland, with their only son, Jacob, the direct ancestor of the present baronet. See Courthope's Debrett. The name Pechel was, however, known at a much earlier period in England, as it is found in the H.R. of temp. Edward I. The meaning of it does not appear.

PECK. PECKE. As the latinization De Peccato is applied both to Peche and to Peck, the names may be identical. See Pack.

PECKHAM. The ancient family so called, derived their name from the parish of Peckham in Kent. There are armorial grounds for supposing that they sprang from the family of St. Nicholas, as the latter are presumed to have done from the Norman De Says. See Curios. of Heraldry, p. 300. Archbishop Peckham, who died in 1272, may be regarded as the founder of the fortunes of a family which ramified very widely, especially in Kent and Sussex. The member of it who made a deposition in the celebrated Scrope and Grosvenor controversy, wrote himself James du Pecham. Roll, vol. ii. p. 435. Peccam is an older, and Packham a more recent, spelling.

PEDDER. In various English dialects signifies a Pedlar; but it must not be regarded as a corruption of that word; a *ped*, in the eastern counties, means a species of hamper without a lid, for the conveyance of fish, eggs, chicken, &c.; and the person who traffics in such small articles is therefore very properly styled a Pedder. See Halliwell.

PEDDIE. Mr. Ferguson thinks that this word is a derivative of the old Norse *ped*, a mannikin or dwarf, and to the same origin he assigns Puddy, Peede, Put, Peddle, and several other not very intelligible names.

PEDDLE. See Peddie.

PEDLER. The same as Pedlar.

PEDLAR. An itinerant dealer in small wares.

PEDRO. The Spanish form of Peter.

PEEBLES. A town and parish, giving name to a Scottish shire.

PEEDE. See Peddie.

PEEK. PEEKE. See Peak.

PEEL. A fortified farm-house. "Within my recollection, almost every old house in the dales of Rede and Tyne was what is called a *peel-house*, built for securing the inhabitants and their cattle in moss-trooping times." Archæologia Æliana i. 246. Many of these border houses are moated for better defence.

"The habitations of the church-feuars [those who held lands under a monastery] were not less primitive than their agriculture. In each village or town were several small towers, having battlements projecting over the side walls, and usually an advanced angle or two, with shot-holes for flanking the door-way, which was always defended by a strong door of oak, studded with nails, and often by an exterior grated door of iron. These small *peel-houses* were ordinarily inhabited by the principal feuars and their families." Sir W. Scott. The Monastery, vol i. chap. i.

While traversing that ancient barrier, the Roman Wall, with my friend Dr. Bruce, its historian and illustrator, in 1855, I incidentally met with the name Harry o' the Peel, the bearer of which I ascertained to be Henry Wilson; but as he happened to reside in a *peel-house*, he was known to most of his neighbours by the designation referred to.

PEELING. An estate at Westham, co. Sussex.

PEERLESS. Unequalled: referring to character.

PEERS. See Piers and Peter.

PEET. See Peat.

PEGG. PEGGS. See Pegge.

PEGGE. See Female Christian Names. This, however, is doubtful, for Peg, unprefixed, is found in H.R., as well as Pegg' and Peggi.

PEGRAM. Possibly a corruption of Pilgrim.

PEIL. PEILE. PEILL. See Peel. Jamieson has, "Pele, Peyll, Peill, Peel, Paile, a place of strength, a fortification."

PEIRCE. See Piers.

PEIRCEY. See Percy.

PEIRIE. See Pirie.

PEIRSE. See Piers.

PEIRSON. The son of Peter, through Piers.

PELHAM. There are, in Hertfordshire, three parishes so denominated; namely, Pelham-Brent, Pelham-Stocking, and Pelham-Furneaux. From one of these the noble family originated, "where anciently" says Collins, "was a castle. It also appears that the pelicans, the arms of this family, were painted in the church of Pelham." The De Pelhams were possessed of the estate, in the age immediately succeeding the Norman Conquest, and there are strong probabilities of their having been descendants of one Ralph, who held the lordship in the time of Edward the Confessor.

PELL. A deep standing water, apparently another form of Pool.

PELLATT. Said to be a corruption of the baptismal name Hippolyte. The family of this name are of long standing in Sussex, occurring in the neighbourhood of Steyning in the XIII. cent.

PELLEW. Lord Exmouth's family are of Cornish origin. The name seems to be a variation of Bellew, which see.

PELLING. An old Sussex name, and probably indigenous to that county—perhaps the same as Peeling.

PELLS. See Pell.

PELTER. A dealer in *pelts, peltry*, or skins.

PELTON. Peldon, a parish in Essex.

PEMBER. Perhaps Pembury, a parish in Kent.

PEMBERTON. A chapelry in Lancashire.

PEMBRIDGE. A parish in Herefordshire.

PEMBROKE. The Welsh town.

PEN. See under CORNISH SURNAMES.

PENALMICKE. A barton and manor in the parish of Stithians, "which place gave name and original to an old family of gentlemen, from thence surnamed De Penalmicke." Hals, in D. Gilbert's Cornwall.

PENALUNA. A Cornish family. The name is local, but the place is not known.

PENCARROW. An estate at Egles-Hayle in Cornwall, which had an "old family of gentlemen" of its own name as owners, down to the reign of Henry VII. Hals, in D. Gilbert's Cornwall.

PENDAR. Seated at Trevider in Burian, co. Cornwall, for upwards of five centuries, and traditionally of the same family as Pendre. C. S. Gilbert's Cornwall.

PENDARVES. An estate in the parish of Camborne in Cornwall, the seat of the family at an early period.

PENDE. Scot. *pende*. An archway.

PENDENNIS. A castle in Cornwall.

PENDER. See Pendre.

PENDERGAST. See Prendergast.

PENDLEBURY. A township in Lancashire.

PENDLETON. Two townships in Lancashire are so called.

PENDRE. An estate in St. Burian, co. Cornwall, which continued to be the chief abode of the family until temp. Henry VI. C. S. Gilbert's Cornwall.

PENDRELL. 'Trusty Dick' and his brothers, when they saved Charles II. in Boscobel Oak, hardly thought themselves worthy of the gallows; yet their name certainly implies as much—viz., *pendereau* which old Cotgrave defines as "a little crack-rope, young slip-string," a diminutive of O. Fr. *pendard*, "a gallow-clapper, one for whom the gallowes longeth !"

PENFOLD. A pound or pen for sheep and cattle, sometimes called a pin-fold or pound-fold—a manorial prison for trespassing animals. Atte Punfald. H.R.

PENFOUND. This family, who are traced eight generations beyond the year 1620, derived their name from the estate of Penfound in Poundstock, co. Cornwall. They ruined themselves by their adherence to the Stuarts, from the time of Charles I. to "the fifteen," and Ambrose Penfound, who alienated the estate of his ancestors, died at Dartmouth about 1764. C. S. Gilbert's Cornwall.

PENGELLY. An estate in the parish of St. Neot in Cornwall, anciently the property of the family.

PENHALLOW. An estate in Philleigh, co. Cornwall, where the family dwelt from temp. Edward III. till the middle of the XVIII. cent. C. S. Gilbert's Cornwall.

PENHELLICK. An estate in the parish of St. Clement's in Cornwall, where the elder line became extinct at an early period. C. S. Gilbert's Cornwall.

PENHURST. A parish in Sussex, which belonged, in the XIV. century, to an armigerous family so called.

PENISTAN. Penniston, a town and parish in Yorkshire.

PENKEVIL. PENKIVIL. "The manor or barton of Penkevil St. Michael, co. Cornwall, belonged, in the reign of Edward I., to the family of De Wen, from whom Hals supposes it to have passed in marriage to the Penkevils; it is, however, quite as probable that the property remained in the same family, they assuming a new name from the place of their abode. They flourished, says Hals, in genteel degree, till the reign of Queen Elizabeth." D. Gilbert's Cornwall, iii. 214.

PENLEY. A chapelry in Flintshire.

PENMAN. A scribe, a "ready-writer."

PENN. Pen is a Celtic topographical word, signifying " a conical top, generally in a range of hills, as Penchrise-*pen*, Skelfhill-*pen*, &c." Jamieson. But there are several parishes, &c., to which this signification does not apply, in the counties of Buckingham and Stafford. The family of William Penn, the founder of Pennsylvania, derived their name, at an early period, from Penn, in the former county.

PENNANT. A parish and a township in Montgomeryshire. The family are traced to the celebrated Tudor-Trevor, Lord of Hereford and Whittington.

PENNECK. A Cornish name and family. Local : place unknown.

PENNELL. Pennal, a parish in Merionethshire.

PENNEY. See Penny.

PENNICK. See Penneck.

PENNIGER. Certainly *not* the Latin *penniger*, having wings ; but probably from the French and English *pennon*, a standard or banner carried in war ; a standard-bearer. Apparently another form of *penerarius*, an ensign-bearer. One John Parient was esquire of the body, and *penerarius*, to King Richard II. Jacob's Law Dict.

PENNINGTON. A parish and a township in Lancashire, and a tything in Hampshire. Gamel de Pennington, who derived his name from the first-mentioned place, is said to have been seated at Mulcaster, co. Cumberland, at the time of the Conquest. Courthope's Debrett. But Hutchinson goes much further, and finds the family there " soon after the Roman accession !" Cumberland, i. 565. In the time of King John, one branch of the family took the name of Mulcaster, from their residence. Mulcaster, now Muncaster, is still possessed by a Pennington, ennobled as Baron Muncaster.

Without according to this house the honour of a *Roman* antiquity, we may fairly claim for it a place amongst the most ancient families of these realms, as it has maintained an uninterrupted male descent for 800 years. The perpetuity of the name and family in all time to come, is guaranteed by a family relic, which may well be designated an *heir*-loom. " Sir John de Pennington was steadily attached to the unfortunate Henry VI., and gave him a secret reception at Muncaster, in his flight from his enemies. In return, the King gave him a curiously-wrought glass cup, with this blessing to the family ; that they should ever prosper, and never want a male heir, so long as they should preserve it unbroken, which the superstition of those times imagined to carry good fortune, and called it the LUCK OF MUNCASTER. Of this glass the family are still possessed." Baronetage.

PENNOCK. See Pinnock.

PENNY. Probably local. Many places in Scotland are compounded with this word (whatever it may mean), as Pennycross, Pennycuick, Pennygown, Pennimuir, &c.

PENNYFATHER. A term of reproach applied to a miser or penurious person. Nash speaks of—

" Carterly upstarts, that out-face towne and countrey in their velvets, when Sir Rowland Russet-coat, their dad, goes sagging everie day in his round gascoynes of white cotton, and hath much adoo (poor *pennie-father*) to keep his unthrift elbowes in reparations."
Pierce Pennilesse his Supplication to the Devil, 1592.

Boyer defines 'un riche faquin' as " a rich miser ; a *pennyfather*." Dict. 1783. Cotgrave englishes the O. French proverb, *Autant despend chiche que large*, (the miser matches the unthrift in expense,) by the couplet :—

" The liberall doth spend his pelfe ;
The *pennyfather* wastes himself."

The forms of the name in H.R. are Penifader and Penifadir.

PENNYMAN. In old English and Scottish, *penny* was an indefinite designation of money, without respect to its value. See Jamieson. In the North, *penny-master* was the treasurer of a town, society, or corporate body, and there are similar expressions in other languages; for instance, in Belgium, a treasurer or receiver is known as *penning-maester*. Now *master* and *man*, though antithetical in one sense, are convertible terms in another, and I am of opinion that Penny-man and Penny-master have one and the same meaning. At any rate, this appears a more rational origin for the name than that assigned in B.L.G. The family, who seem really to be traced only to the year 1599, are asserted to be of Saxon origin; and the name is said to have been anciently written "PENNA-MAN, signifying the *chief head man!*" Peniman. H.R.

PENNYSTONE. The extinct baronet family, Penestone, Peneystone, or Pennystone, of Leigh, deduced their descent from Thomas de Penyston, who is said to have flourished at Truro, co. Cornwall, in the reign of the Conqueror.

PENPONS. An estate in the parish of St. Kew, co. Cornwall, formerly the property of the family.

PENRICE. 1. A castle and manor, anciently written Pen-Rhys, in Glamorganshire, where the family resided in early times. 2. An estate in the parish of St. Austell, co. Cornwall.

PENRITH. A parish, &c., in Cumberland. The family De Penrith seem to have been resident about Newcastle-upon-Tyne, and the Scottish border, from the XII. cent. to the XVIII. In the meantime the name was changed by corruption to Peareth. See Peareth.

PENROSE. A hamlet near the Land's End in Cornwall, possessed by the family in the XV. century, and doubtless much earlier. C. S. Gilbert's Cornwall.

PENRUDDOCKE. The family first appear at Arkelby, co. Cumberland, but as there is, in the neighbourhood of that place, in the parish of Greystock, a hamlet so called, they are presumed to have originated there. The Encyc. Herald., however, assigns arms to a family of this name, in that land of *Pens*, Cornwall, and so there may be two local origins and distinct families. The surname has long been associated with Wiltshire and Hampshire.

PENRY. Welsh, Ap-Henry, the son of Henry.

PENSAM. Pensham, a hamlet of Pershore in Worcestershire.

PENSON. A corruption of Benson, or of Penston.

PENSTON. A barony and village in Haddingtonshire.

PENTECOST. See Times and Seasons. Pentecost and Pentecoste. H.R.

PENTLAND. An ancient, but now extinct, parish in Edinburghshire.

PENTON. A parish in Hampshire.

PENWARNE. An estate at Mevagissey in Cornwall, and another at Mawnan in the same county, where the family seem to have been established soon after the Conquest. C. S. Gilbert's Cornwall.

PEPLER. PEPPLER. See Peplow.

PEPLOE. See Peplow.

PEPLOR. See Peplow.

PEPLOW. Evidently a local name, from whence, apparently, the modifications Peploe, Pepler, Peplor, and Peppler.

PEPPER. Said to be a corruption of the Norman Pipard, which family gave name to Rotherfield Pipard, Clyve Pipard, and other manors in the west of England. Peper, Pepyr. H.R.

PEPPERCORNE. Doubtless from some feudal custom, connected with the holding of lands, by the nominal payment called "peppercorn-rent." Pepercorn. H.R.

PEPPERELL. See Peverel.

PEPPIN. The old French personal name Pepin.

PEPRILL. Probably from Peperellus, a latinized form of Peverel.

PEPWORTH. A corruption of Papworth.

PEPYS. Pepis in H.R. shews the name to be ancient, in nearly its present form. The etymon has not occurred to me.

PERCEVAL. See Percival.

PERCHE. A district of the south of Normandy, and extending into Orleanois.

PERCIVAL. Camden places this among baptismal names. The Earl of Egmont claims to be descended from a family who were seated at Weston-Gordeyn, in Somersetshire, in the reign of Richard Cœur de Lion. The original Percival was a cadet of the great Norman family of Yvery. See Gen. Hist. of House of Yvery, privately printed in 1742.

PERCY. William de Perci, who, with his brother Serlo, assisted in the Conquest of England, appears in Domesday as tenant in capite in many counties, especially in those of York and Lincoln. Perci is the name of a parish and canton near St. Lo, in Normandy, the ancient fief of the family. Dugdale traces the pedigree of William de Percy up to the Northman Mainfred, who settled in Neustria (Normandy) before the cession of that province to Rollo.

A popular tradition accounts otherwise for the origin of this illustrious historical surname. It asserts that Malcolm, King of Scotland, having besieged the castle of Alnwick, demanded seisin of that fortress by the surrender of the keys. The governor of the castle so managed matters, that, in delivering the keys at the end of a lance, he pierced the monarch's eye and caused his death. Hence he acquired the surname of "Pierce-Eye," which, by the omission of several useless vowels, ultimately became Percy! See Bruce's Bayeux Tapestry, p. 64.

PEREGRINE. The personal name.

PEREIRA. A Portugueze name naturalized in London.

PERFECT. Apparently refers to character.

PERIGOE. From the city of Perigueux in Guienne. The family came into England in consequence of the Revocation of the Edict of Nantes.

PERK. PERKS. PERKES. See Peter.

PERKIN. PERKINS. See Peter.

PEROWNE. A French Protestant family, who fled hither at the Revocation of the Edict of Nantes, and settled at Norwich, where some of the branches are still resident. The name is variously spelt in old registers, and it seems uncertain whether its original form was Perron, Perrone, or Peronne; if the last, it was probably derived from the French town so called. Inf. Rev. J. J. S. Perowne.

PERREN. PERRIN. A French surname of uncertain derivation.

PERRET. PERRETT. PERRATT. A French diminutive of Pierre, Peter.

PERRIER. An ancient and noble family of Brittany, traced in the archives of the Collège Héraldique at Paris, to the tenth century, and to the ancient dukes and princes of that province. The first of the name who settled in Ireland, was Mark du Perrier, who expatriated himself at the Revocation of the Edict of Nantes, 1685. B.L.G. The surname is perhaps a corruption of poirier, a pear-tree, and so analogous to Appletree, Plumtree, &c. De la Perere, Del Perer. H.R.

PERROT. Pierot, Pierre, Peter. Prince Edward used to call the favourite, Pierce or Peter de Gaveston, Perot. See N. and Q. vii. 280.

PERRY. 1. A narrowed pronunciation of Parry, Ap-Harry. 2. Amongst the tenants in capite in co. Hants, at the making of Domesday, was one "Peret forestarius." Pery. H.R.

PERRYMAN. Probably a maker of perry. The name is as old as temp. Edw. I. Peryman. H.R.

PERT. A commune in the arrondissement of Bayeux in Normandy.

PESCODD. See Peascod.

PESCOTT. See Peascod.

PESHALL. The pedigree is traced to Sir Richard de Peshall, sheriff of Staffordshire, 7. Edward III. Pershall is a township in that county.

PESKETT. A corruption of Peascod.

PESSONER. In medieval Latin, pessona signifies acorns or mast, and the original Le Pessoner was probably a collector of such food for swine.

☞ PET. A provincial corruption of pit; and hence, probably, the true forms of such surnames as Pethurst, Petford, Petley, would be Pithurst, Pitford, Pitley.

PET. Pett, a parish in Sussex.

PETCH. The same as Peche.

PETCHEY. See Peachey.

PETER. The Christian name, introduced here at the Conquest. It has become the parent of many surnames, as Peters, Peterson, Piers, Pierce, Pearse, Pearce, Pears, Peers, Pierson, Pearson, Peterken, Perkin, Perkins, Purkess and Purkis, Perk, Pyrke, Perks, Perkes, Park, Parks, Parkes, Parkin, Parkyn, Parkins, Parkinson, and perhaps Porson and Parsons.

This name was sometimes written Petre, as, anciently, by the Petres, or Peters, of Torn Newton, co. Devon. Their descendants at Harlyn, co. Cornwall, and other places in that county, wrote themselves Peter, but another branch (Lord Petre's) have always written Petre.

PETERKEN. See Peter.

PETERMAN. An eastern-counties provincialism for fisherman, probably with reference to St. Peter's original occupation. But Bailey defines it as "one who fishes in the river of Thames with an unlawful engine." The similar name Petermann is a modern introduction from Germany, and is defined as "a person with the name of Peter; also a fish—the John Dory." Noehden's Dict., where we find the English word peterman given as the equivalent of fischdieb, "fish-thief."

PETERMANN. See under Peterman.

PETERS. See Peter.

PETERSON. See Peter.

PETET. This family are known to have flourished at Ardevora, co. Cornwall, as early as the time of Henry I., and to have had a succession of six knights. The name was anciently written De Petyt, and it must therefore be local. See C. S. Gilbert's Cornwall.

PETHER. PETHERS. Probably an ancient personal name, and its genitive; whence also the local surnames Petherham, Petherbridge, and the names Petherick, Petherton, Petherwin, &c.

PETHERBRIDGE. See Pether.

PETHERHAM. See Pether.

PETHICK. A contraction of Petherick, a parish in Cornwall.

PETICOTE. See Pettycoat.

PETIFER. O. Fr. petite and fere, "the little wild beast;" doubtless an early sobriquet, analogous to Lovel, Purcell, &c. This name has been corrupted to Petipher, and, by the change of a single vowel only, it has been assimilated to Pharoah's captain of the guard, and made Potiphar.

PETIPHER. See Petifer.

PETIT. Fr. Le Petit ; from diminutive size ; a very common sobriquet in Norman and subsequent times.

> " Petit's a race, whose generous fount begun
> From Britain's first great Norman's rising sun ;
> *   *   *   *   *   *   *   *
> The long descent from such a native claim
> Worthies enrolled in that long list of fame,
> Lodged in their mouldered monuments so old,
> That they are scarce less dust than what they hold."
> *Funeral Poem for Clement Petit, Esq., of the Isle of Thanet, by E. Settle,* 1717.

Le Petit is still a common Norman surname.

PETO. From Poitou in France. Pictavensis. See Dugdale's Warwickshire, Pedigree of Peto.

PETRE. The Petres rose to eminence on the ruins of the monasteries, under Henry VIII. The name is apparently a variation of Peter, the Christian name. See Peter.

PETT. A parish in Sussex ; also a provincialism for *pit.*

PETTENGER. The same as Pottinger —an apothecary.

PETTEPHER. See Petifer.

PETTER. PETTERS. Mispronunciations of Peter and Peters.

PETTET. As Petit.

PETTIGREW. Palsgrave has *"Pety-grewe,"* genealogy ; but the name is in reality derived from the manor of Pettigrew, near Gerans, in Cornwall.

PETTINGAL. 1. Portingal is an old name for a Portuguese, or native of Portugal, and this has perhaps been corrupted from it. 2. I find in the H.R. the name *Petinicol,* which looks like " Petit Nicole," " Little Nicolas." It may therefore be a member of that very curious class to which belong Grosjean, Littlejohn, Petitpierre, &c.

PETTIT. PETTETT. See Petit.

PETTY. Fr. *petit.* Little, diminutive.

PETTYCOAT. See Peticote. It may, however, have reference to costume. In some dialects the word means a waistcoat.

PEVENSEY. A town and Cinque-port in Sussex—the site of the Roman station Anderida. The arms of the family, *an Eagle displayed,* seem to shew their derivation from the great Norman house of De Aquila, feudal lords of Pevensey in the XII. and XIII. centuries, from whom the barony received the designation of " the Honour of the Eagle."

PEVEREL. William Peverel was a natural son of William the Conqueror, who entered England at the Conquest, and re-

ceived, as his share of the subjugated country, one hundred and sixty-two manors, many of which were in the counties of Nottingham and Derby. The surname appears not to be local. I know of no place so called in Normandy ; nor do we meet with any instance of its being prefixed by *De.* In Domesday Book it is continually spelt Piperellus—" Terra Ranulphi Piperelli." Mr. Planché (Journal of Arch. Assoc. viii. 196) conjectures that it had a personal signification ; and that "it is a corruption of Puerulus, which is almost identical with Peuerellus, as we find it written in the Anglo-Norman Pipe and Plea Rolls. The *u* being pronounced *v* is now stigmatized as ' cockney.' It may, in those days, particularly by Frenchmen, have been considered correct." If this ingenious etymology be true, the old surname *Littleboys,* borne by a gentry family formerly resident at Wickham, co. Bucks, and Ashburnham, co. Sussex, may be a literal translation of this great baronial appellative.

This family ramified so extensively, that nearly forty armorial coats are assigned to the various branches of it. See Burke's Armory.

PEVERLEY. A corruption of Beverley.

PEW. A mis-spelling of Pugh.

PEWSEY. See Pusey.

PEWTER. A contraction of Pewterer, a worker in that metal—a XIV. cent. surname.

PEWTRESS. A female worker in pewter ?

PEYTON. According to Camden, the Peytons have a common descent with the Uffords, afterwards Earls of Suffolk, from the great baron William Mallet, who came hither at the Conquest. The first of the family who assumed the surname was Reginald de Peyton, lord of Peyton in the parish of Boxford, co. Suffolk, in which county, at Isleham, in later centuries, his descendants were very eminent. In medieval charters, this surname was latinized De Pavilliano and Pietonus.

PHAIRE. PHAIRS. Fare, or Phair, is a Gaelic personal name, and Mac Fare is still found in the Highlands. The family were introduced into Ireland temp. Oliver Cromwell, by Colonel Robert Phayre.

PHARE. See Phaire.

PHARAOH. This name is borne by a Gipsy tribe, who believe themselves representatives of the great Egyptian dynasty ! Mr. Ferguson remarks : " I remember meeting with it in a secluded nook of the Lake district, and wondering much how the king of Egypt had found his way into our quiet valleys. But releasing the name from the associations of the spelling, it is nothing more than the old German name *Faro."* This our ingenious author connects with the A-Sax. *fara,* and O. Norse *fari,* a traveller—not, after all, a bad name for a nomade of Gipsy blood.

PHAROAH. The same as Pharaoh.

PHARRISEE. A sobriquet applied to a sanctimonious person. R.G. 16.

PHAYER. See Phaire.

PHEASANT. The bird; unless, indeed, it may be a corruption of the Fr. *paysan*, Eng. peasant.

PHEBY. Phœbe. See Female Christian Names.

PHELIPS. A corruption of Philips.

PHELP. PHELPS. See Philip, which was often written Phelype.

PHILCOX. A diminutive of Philip.

PHILIMORE. See Filmore.

PHILIP. The baptismal name. Like other scripture designations, this was introduced at the Norman Conquest. In succeeding centuries it became the parent of several others, such as Philips, Phillips, Phillipps, Philipson, Philp, Philps, Phelp, Phelps, Phipp, Phipps, Phipson, Phippen, Phillot, Philpott, Philpotts, Philcox, Philippo, Phillopson, Filkin, Philippe, &c. It is probable, however, that some of these forms, though derived from Philip originally, have come to us in later times from continental nations.

PHILIPPE. See Philip.

PHILIPPO. See Philip.

PHILIPSON. PHILLIPSON. The son of Philip. The Philipsons of Thirlwall, co. Northumberland, were a younger branch of the family of Thirlwall, descended from *Philip* Thirlwall. Slogans of the N. of Eng. p. 26.

PHILLIMORE. See Filmore.

PHILLIPPS. See Philip.

PHILLIPS. See Philip. More than 200 traders of this name are found in the Lond. Direct.

PHILLOPSON. A corruption of Philipson.

PHILLOT. See Philip.

PHILP. PHILPS. See Philip.

PHILPOTT. PHILPOTTS. See Philip.

PHIN. A Gaelic personal name. Mac Phinn, or Mac Finn, is still found in the Highlands.

PHIPP. PHIPPS. See Philip.

PHIPPEN. See Philip.

PHIPSON. See Philip.

PHŒNIX. Most likely from Fenwick, the fine old border family. The crest of that family is "a phœnix issuant from flames."

PHYSICK. Possibly from Lefisick, a place in St. Austell, co. Cornwall, by dropping the *Le*, under the mistaken notion that it was the French particle, and then assi-milating the orthography to that of a well-known word.

PIAZZA. It appears from the baptismal registers of the parish of St. Paul, Covent Garden, during the reigns of Charles II., James II., William III., and even later, that Piazza was a favourite name for parish children. These records abound with Peter Piazza, Paul Piazza, Mary Piazza, &c. They were probably foundlings, the name indicating the place of their exposure.

PICARD. PICKARD. A native of Picardy. Pikard, Pikart. H.R. One of this name changed it, at the command of Edw. IV., to Ruddle, the place of his birth. Camden.

PICKER. An old word for a pilferer, or petty thief.

PICKERELL. A diminutive of pike, the fish. Pikerel. H.R.

PICKERING. A market town in the N. R. of Yorkshire. The name is widely spread over many counties, and there are about twenty coats assigned to it.

PICKERSGILL. Local: "the gill or rivulet inhabited by pikes or pickerell?"

PICKERT. The same as Picard.

PICKETT. A known corruption of Pigott.

PICKFORD. I do not find this local name in the Gazetteer, but it is, no doubt, the same as Pitchford in Shropshire. In the Rotuli Hundredorum of the county the possessor of that estate, spelt Picheford, is styled Sir John de Picford (Domino Johanni de Picford.)

PICKLE. PICKLES. Pikel and Pikele occur in H.R. as unprefixed surnames, with the origin of which I am unacquainted.

PICKMAN. 1. A pike-man; foot soldier. The arms contain pole-axes. 2. A man who draws up coals from a mine in 'picks' or baskets. Cheshire.

PICKNELL. PICKNOLL. Pucknoll, a parish in co. Dorset.

PICKWICK. This name is no fabrication of our great Novelist; and indeed very few of his names, however happy, however ludicrous, are so. I have noticed a large proportion of them on actual signboards in his own native county of Kent. At Folkeston there is, or at least, there recently was, a veritable Mark Tapley—one too who had been to America! Although Pickwick does not occur in our Gazetteer, it appears that a locality in Wiltshire formerly gave name to a family called De Pikewike. In the reign of Edward I., saith my record, one William de Pikewike, like his immortal namesake, found himself within the walls of a prison— I am sorry to say, for felony; but as the offence was compromised for eight shillings, we may presume that it was not a very enormous one.—Rotuli Hundredorum, vol. ii., page 273.

PICKWORTH. Parishes in cos. Rutland and Lincoln. Three distinct coats assigned to the name are allusive, containing respectively mill-picks, pick-axes, and pikes!

PICOT. See with Pigott.

PICTON. PICKTON. Townships in cos. Chester and York.

PIDCOCK. 1. Doubtless the diminutive of some Christian name—perhaps of Peter, thus :—Peter, Pete, Petecock, Pidcock. B.L.G. asserts that "the surname is derived from the armorial bearing of the family, *a pied cock*." As it happens, however, the cock is not pied, but simply parted per fesse, Or and Argent. 2. See Pidd.

PIDD. Probably the A-Sax. personal name Peada, borne by the first Christian King of Mercia. From this seems to have sprung the patronymical Pidding, with its compounds in local names, such as Piddinghoe, Piddington. I do not see the name in the form of Pid in the XIV. cent., otherwise Pidcock and Piddock might be further derivatives.

PIDDING. See Pidd.

PIDDINGTON. Parishes in cos. Oxford and Northampton.

PIDDLESDEN. A corruption of Pitlesden. It is sometime contracted to Piddle.

PIDDOCK. See Pidd.

PIERCEY. See Piercy.

PIERCY. The same as Percy.

PIERPOINT. PIERREPONT. Not from Pierrepont, in the arrondissement of Coutances, in Normandy, as stated by De Gerville, in Mem. Soc. Antiq. Norm., 1825; but from the castle of that name, on the southern borders of Picardy and diocese of Laon, which continued in the family down to the time of Richard I. That the name was introduced at the Conquest, is clear from Domesday Book, which mentions Robert and Godfrey de P. as holding of the celebrated William de Warenne, several lordships in Sussex and Suffolk. Collins. The French genealogy of the family makes Robert one of the Conqueror's lieutenant-generals. He gave the suffix to Hurst-Pierpoint, co. Sussex. The name is uniformly latinized by 'De Petro-Ponte,' and is equivalent to our indigenous Stanbridge, or Stonebridge.

A later introduction of the name occurred after the Revocation of the Edict of Nantes. In 1687, John and Henry Pierrepont arrived in London from Normandy, aged respectively 20 and 19, and joined the English army as troopers, probably as officers. Inf. J. S. Burn, Esq.

PIERS. PIERCE. Fr. *Pierre*, Peter. Piers Plowman, the well-known Dreamer of the Malvern Hills, was no other than 'Peter the Ploughman.'

> "Thom Tynker, and Betrys Belle,
> *Peyrs* Potter, and Watt at the Well."
> *Coventry Mysteries*, XV. cent.

PIERSON. The son of Piers or Peter.

PIESSE. The family came into England soon after the Revocation of the Edict of Nantes, and bore chiefly the Christian names of Louis and Charles. They have a tradition that the name was derived from the order of knighthood, created in 1560 by Pope Pius IV., and called corruptly Pies or Piesse in Brittany, from which province the Piesses of England are believed to have come.

PIG. See Pigg.

PIGEON. PIDGEON. The bird. The analogous surnames Columbus, Colombe, Dove, Taube, Dow, Doo, &c., are found in various languages.

PIGG. See under Boar and Purcell.

PIGMAN. 1. A dealer in pigs. See anecdote in Eng. Surn. i., 39. 2. A seller of crockery. Jamieson. Quasi *piggin*-man; a piggin being a small vessel of wood or earth. 3. A corruption of pike-man.

PIGGOT. See Pigot.

PIGOT. PIGOTT. O. Fr. *picote*, the small-pox; *picoté*, pock-marked or freckled. This is Camden's derivation, and I can find none that is less objectionable, for this widely diffused and very ancient name, to which our heraldric dictionaries assign above thirty different coats. The Pigotts of Edgmond, co. Salop, sprang from Prestbury, co. Chester, in the XIV. century.

Picot was, however, an ancient personal name. One Picot was a tenant in chief in Hampshire, and a Picot de Grentebrige held a similar position in Cambridgeshire.

PIGRUM. A corruption of Pilgrim.

PIKE. 1. Less likely from the fish than from the weapon, the bearer of which may have been so named. See Lance. 2. A pointed hill, as Langdale Pike.

PIKEMAN. A soldier—one who carried a pike; analogous to Spearman.

PILBEAM. A species of tree which I cannot identify, probably so named from its suitableness for the shaft of a spear; A-Sax. *pyl*. I have not met with this name out of the county of Sussex, where it is sometimes pronounced Pilbin.

PILBIN. See Pilbeam.

PILCHARD. Perhaps from the fish, upon the same principle as Herring, &c.; but more likely a corruption of Pilcher, the occupation.

PILCHER. A *pylch* was a medieval garment, made of fur (*pellis*). The word is Chaucerian, and it also occurs in Caxton's Reynard the Fox. Reynard, having turned hermit, is represented as wearing "a *pylche* and an heren sherte (a hair shirt) thereunder." Cap. V. A Pilcher was a maker of the article. Pilcher, Pilchere, Le Pilecher. H.R.

PILE. The same as Peel—a small tower. Halliwell.

PILGRIM. A frequenter of holy shrines. See Palmer. Pilegrim, Pilgrym. H.R.

PILKINGTON. A township in Lancashire, the possession of this "right ancient family, gentlemen of repute before the Conquest." Fuller's Worthies. The estate remained in their hands, until Sir Thos. Pilkington took part against Henry VII., and was killed, together with three other knights of his name and family, on the side of Richard III., at Bosworth Field. The Pilkingtons of Yorkshire, and of Westmeath in Ireland, are cadets of this ancient and knightly house. See Shirley's Noble and Gentle Men.

According to Fuller, the Saxon head of this family, at the Norman invasion, hid himself in a barn in the disguise of a thresher. "Hereupon," says our *worthy* historian, "partly alluding to the head of the flail (falling sometime on the one side, sometime on the other side); partly to himself, embracing the safest condition for the present, he gave for the motto of his arms, NOW THUS, NOW THUS." The crest of the family is a "Mower of particolours, Argent and Gules" (Shirley); but Kimber says, "a Rustick holding a Scythe, parted per fesse, Argent and Sable." This is also supposed to allude to some disguise after a decisive combat, said to be the battle of Hastings, but Mr. Shirley thinks the reference more likely to be to Bosworth Field.

PILL 1. Probably the same as Peel. 2. Pylle, a parish in Somersetshire. 3. A small creek. See Leland, Itin. iii., 29.

PILLAR. R.G., 16. H.R., Atte pilere, "at the pillar."

PILOT. The occupation.

PILSWORTH. A township in Lancashire.

PILTON. Parishes in cos. Rutland, Somerset, Devon, and Northampton.

PINCERNA. Low Latin for butler, or cup-bearer; qui vinum convivis miscet, a Græc. πινειν κιρνα, Ducange. See Butler and Botiler.

Walter Mapes, who wrote in the reign of Henry II., uses the word :—

"Mihi sapit dulcius vinum in taberna,
Quam quod aqua miscuit præsulis *pincerna*."

PINCH. PINCHES. PINCHIN. This group probably have their origin in some ancient personal name.

PINCHBECK. A parish in Lincolnshire. The surname Pincebeck is said to occur in that county in the XI. cent. See Eng. Surn. i. 27; though the document there quoted is of questionable authenticity.

PINCKNEY. See Pinkney.

PINCOMBE. See COMBE.

PINDAR. PINDER. To *pind* is to impound an animal, and a Pinder is a petty manorial officer, whose duty is to shut up strange cattle straying upon the common pasture. The Nominale M.S. has "*Inclusor*, a pynder." Halliw. Le Pinder. H.R.

PINE. From residence near a lofty tree of the species.

PINFOLD. See Penfold.

PINK. A northern provincialism signifying small.

PINKERTON. We search in vain the Gazetteers of England and of Scotland, for any locality bearing this designation; yet the surname is local, being a corruption of the Punchardon, or Pincherdon, of the so-called Battel Abbey Roll, and the Ponte-Cardon of Domesday Book, which is derived from the place now known as Pont-Chardon, near Argentan, in Normandy. The name passed early into Scotland, and in Ragman Roll, A.D. 1296, it is written Pynkerton. It is uncommon in England, but more frequently to be met with in Scotland and in the North of Ireland, to which last-named country it was introduced by Scottish colonists.

PINKNEY. The baronial family descended from Gilo de Pincheni, who lived in the reign of Henry I., and endowed the monks of St. Lucien in France with lands at Wedon, co. Northampton. The family doubtless came hither at the Conquest. The locality of Pincheni I cannot ascertain.

PINKSTONE. Doubtless Pinxton, a parish in Derbyshire.

PINN. There are places called Pin in the several arrondissements of Mortagne, Argentan, and Lisieux, in Normandy.

PINNELL. Aubrey derives it from a certain 'pine-hill,' co. Wilts; but there was a Ralph Pinel, a Domesday tenant in capite, in cos. Essex and Suffolk.

PINNER. 1. A parish in Middlesex. 2. A pin-maker; whence Pinners' Hall in London.

PINNICK. A corruption of Pinnock.

PINNIGER. See Penniger.

PINNOCK. Parishes in cos. Cornwall and Gloucester. There was a Cornish saint of this designation, who gave name to the parish of St. Pinnock. In the South of England, the little timber frameworks at the ends of an arch or drain are called 'pinnocks.' Pinnoc, *Pinoc, Pinok,* &c. H.R. See Eng. Surn. i. 80.

PINSENT. Probably a corruption of the French name Pinson. The celebrated printer, Richard Pynson, temp. Henry VIII., was a Frenchman.

PINSON. Probably the same as Mont-Pinson, (Mompesson), by the disuse of the prefix.

PINYON. From the Welsh Ap Enion, the son of Enion, a personal name. So Pritchard from Ap Richard, Richardson; Parry from Ap Harry, Harry's son. Sometimes the filial prefix is *ab* rather than *ap*, and thus Benyon and Bunyan result from the same personal name.

PIPARD. Ralph Pipard, who distinguished himself in the Welsh and Scottish wars, is said to have been a younger son of Ralph Fitz-Nicolas, temp. Henry III. Rotherfield Pipard, and Clyve Pipard derive their suffixes from this family. The name appears to be Norm. Fr., and to signify a cheat or deceiver, from the verb *piper*.

PIPE. 1. A parish in Herefordshire. 2. A personal name in Domesday.

PIPER. A player on a bag-pipe. Le Piper. H.R. Though this droning music was never so popular in England as among the Celts of Scotland and Ireland, it was much in vogue in Northumberland down to a late period. Chaucer's miller-pilgrim, though a Southron, was a piper :—

" A baggepipe cowde he blowe and sowne,
   And therewithal he brought us out of towne."

For much curious information on the archæology of bagpipes, see a paper by J. C. Fenwick, Esq., in Archæol. Æliana, N. S., vol. iii. The surname is also found in Sweden, where it was borne by a famous prime minister of Charles XII.

PIPES. See Pipe.

PIPPIN. The old illustrious French personal name, Pepin. The surname, in its present orthography, is found in H.R.

PIRIE. 1. Apparently a pear-orchard. The forms in H.R. are De la Pirie, and Ate Pyrie. 2. *Pirrie*, in Lowland Scotch, means trim; nice in dress; precise in manner; also, having a tripping manner in walking; walking with a spring. Jamieson.

PIRKISS. The same as Purkess.

PIRON. M. de Gerville, in Mem. Soc. Antiq. Norm. 1825 (vol. vii.), says, that the château of Piron, in the department of La Manche, in Normandy, gave name to a family who settled in Devon and Somerset, and called their residence Stoke Piron.

PISTOL. " A swaggering fellow. Perhaps from *pistolfo*, explained by Florio, ' a roguing begger, a cantler, an upright man that liveth by cosenage.' Hence Shakspeare's character of that name." Halliwell.

PITCAIRN. A village in the parish of Redgorton, co. Perth.

PITCAITHLY. A well-known locality in the parish of Dumbarnie, co. Perth.

PITCHER. 1. Some kind of employment—perhaps that of ' pitching,' i. e., roughly paving with boulders; or of applying pitch to ships, &c. 2. An inn sign. 3. " The man who lifts or pitches the reaped corn or hay up into the wagon." Halliwell. A person who excelled in this kind of work would readily acquire the surname.

PITCHFORD. A parish in Shropshire, which anciently belonged to the family.

PITHER. Welsh Ap-Uther, the son of Uther.

PITKIN. Peterkin. See Peter.

PITLESDEN. This family originated among the *dens* of the Kentish Weald. The elder line was extinguished in the XIV. cent., when the daughter and heir of Robert de Pitlesden of Tenterden married Vincent Herbert, ancestor of the Earl of Winchelsea. De Pytlesden. H.R.

PITMAN. PITTMAN. See Pitt, and the termination MAN. One Johannes Piteman is mentioned in H.R.

PITNEY. A parish in Somersetshire.

PITT. PIT. From residence in the vicinity of one. Hence also Pitter and Pittman.

PITTER. See Pitt, and the term. ER.

PITTLESDEN. See Pitlesden.

PITTS. See Pitt.

PIX. A shrine in which the consecrated host is placed, in the Roman ritual. It seems an unlikely source for a surname, but there are analogies in Hallowbread, Paten, Crucifix, &c.

PIXTON. Apparently local, in Oxfordshire. Picxton. H.R.

PLACE. 1. Like the Fr. *place*, a square or open space in a town. 2. More probably from a ' place,' or mansion. What is called in other shires a hall, or a court, is frequently known in the south-eastern counties as a ' place,' e.g. : Brasted Place, co. Kent, Wakehurst Place, co. Sussex, Crowhurst Place, co. Surrey.

PLACKETT. Apparently a diminutive of the Fr. *plaque*, which Cotgrave defines as " a flat lingot, or barre of mettall.........also a plate to naile against a wall." A little road-side public-house at Arlington, co. Sussex, a resort for smugglers, formerly bore the name of the " Golden Plackett,"—for what reason I could never ascertain ; neither can I see how the word can with propriety have become a family name, unless indeed it was borrowed from a sign of the same kind.

PLAFORD. See Playford.

PLAICE. See Place.

PLAIN. PLAINE. From residence at a plain, common, or level unenclosed ground.

PLAINER. See Plain, and the termination ER.

PLAISTER. A corruption of Playstow.

PLANCHÉ. Probably of Norman origin. There are three places in the province, called Planches-sur Iton, Planches-sur-Rile, and Planchez-Mellerai, situated respectively in the arrondissements of Louviers, Argentan, and Avranches.

PLANE. A corruption of Plain.

PLANT. A family in humble circumstanches at Kettering, bear the ancient royal name of Plantagenet, though now it is commonly corrupted to *Plant*. See a late number of the " Leicester Mercury."

PLANTA. A family of Swedish origin, who settled here temp. George II.

PLANTAGENET. Foulques, Count of Anjou in the twelfth century, ancestor of a long and illustrious line of English kings, extending from Henry II. to Richard III., going on pilgrimage to the Holy Land, wore in his cap a broom-plant (*Planta genesta*) in token, it is said, of humility; though why that upright, aspiring shrub should be taken in this emblematical sense, I never could ascertain. Henry II., the first of our kings to whom the surname is attributed, used the broom plant as his badge, as also did his successors, Richard Cœur de Lion, and Henry III.

PLASKETT. Plasketts, a township in the parish of Falstone, co. Northumberland.

PLASTOW. See Playstow.

PLATER. Perhaps a maker of plates for armour.

PLATT. 1. A corruption of Plott; sometimes a piece of flat ground. 2. A place, situation. North. 3. A small piece of ground. South.

PLATTS. See Platt.

PLAXTON. Perhaps a corruption of Plaxtol, co. Kent.

PLAYER. A dramatic performer.

PLAYFAIR. 1. The same as Fairplay. 2. Jamieson says, PLAY-FERE, PLAY-FAIR, a play-fellow, from *play*, and *fere*, a companion.

PLAYFORD. A parish in Suffolk.

PLAYNE. See Plain.

PLAYSTED. The same as Playstow.

PLAYSTOW. In medieval times, most large parishes had their play-stow, playsted, or *locus ludorum*, for the recreation of the inhabitants. At Selborne, co. Hants, it was corrupted to *Plestor*.

"In the midst of this spot stood, in old times, a vast oak, with a short squat body, and huge horizontal arms, extending almost to the extremity of the area. This venerable tree, surrounded with stone steps, and seats above them, was the delight of old and young, and a place of much resort in summer evenings; where the former sat in grave debate, while the latter frolicked and danced before them."

    White's Nat. Hist. of Selborne.
The forms in H.R. are Atte Pleistow, De la Pleystowe, &c.

PLEASANT. The original Mr. Pleasant was possessed, I doubt not, of the attributes by which Cotgrave defines the Fr. word *plaisant*: he was "merrie, jocond, blythe, joyfull, buxome, delightfull, gamesome, recreative, [and perhaps] also jeasting, bourding, scoffing, and flowting."

PLESSETS. The baronage traces the family to John de Plessets, or Plessis, who was of the household of King Henry III.

The name is doubtless local, and Norman, there being six places so called in the Itin. de la Normandie. The word seems to be generic, and to mean a small park. The obsolete French word *plessis*, is defined by Cotgrave as "the plashing of trees, the plaiting or foulding of their tender branches one within the other: also a hedge or walke of plashed trees." This was the earliest way of making a park, and hence the word "the *plashet*," applied in England to small enclosures for deer, &c. The modern form of this surname in France is Duplessis.

PLEYDELL. The extinct baronets sprang from Berkshire in the XV. century.

PLIMMER. Probably the same as Plummer, i.e., Plumber.

PLIMPTON. Plympton is the name of a market-town and a parish in co. Devon.

PLOMER. A corruption of Plumber. Le Plomer. H.R.

PLOT. PLOTT. A small piece of ground.

PLOUGHMAN. The occupation. R.G. See Plowman.

PLOW. PLOWE. O. Eng. A plough— probably an inn sign.

PLOWDEN. An estate in Shropshire, which had owners of the same name in the XII. century, when Roger de Plowden was a Crusader under Richard I. His descendants still possess it.

The proverb, THE CASE IS ALTERED QUOTH PLOWDEN, is thus explained by Halliwell. "[Edmund] Plowden was an eminent lawyer in Queen Mary's time, who being asked what legal remedy there was against some hogs, that trespassed on the complainant's ground, answered, he might have very good remedy; but the other telling him they were *his* hogs, NAY, THEN, THE CASE IS ALTERED, quoth Plowden!"

PLOWMAN. In Domesday we find certain under tenants described as 'Arantes homines'— ploughmen. Plouman, Le Ploghman. H.R.

PLOWRIGHT. A maker of ploughs. See under Wright. Le Plowritte. H.R.

PLUCKNETT. Plukenet is found in Holinshed's so-called Battel-Abbey Roll. The name is probably of Norman introduction. Hugh de Plugenet was made a baron by Henry II. The spelling in H.R. is a near approach to the present form, namely, Plokenet.

PLUCKROSE. Both this surname and the analogous one, Pullrose, occur in a Sussex subsidy roll, 1296. Both names probably had their origin in a feudal custom. The holding of lands by the annual rent of a rose, was very common in the middle ages, and it even exists down to the present day. A friend of mine holds a landed property on the borders of Ashdown Forest, co. Sussex, part of the Duchy of Lancaster, by one *red rose*. On the front of a farmhouse belonging to him is a large rose tree, to which the reeve of the manor periodically comes, and either *pluck*ing or *pull*ing a flower, sticks it into his button-hole, and walks off. To something of this kind the Pluckroses and the Pullroses doubtless owe their names. Pluckerose. H.R.

PLUM. PLUMB. PLUMBE. 1. A deep pool in a river or stream; the word is used in the shires of Fife and Roxburgh. Jamieson. 2. Sensible, honest. North. Halliwell. 3. A commune near Avranches in Normandy is called Plomb.

PLUMBER. A worker of lead. Lat. *plumbum.* The name is usually corrupted to Plummer.

PLUMBLY. See Plumley.

PLUMER. See Plummer.

PLUMLEY. A parish in Cheshire.

PLUMMER. A plumber, or worker in lead.

PLUMPTON. Parishes and townships in cos. Northampton, Sussex, York, Cumberland, and Lancaster.

PLUMPTRE. A parish in co. Nottingham, which was possessed by the family temp. King John.

PLUMTREE. Perhaps a corruption of Plumptre; but it may be analogous to Appletree, &c.

PLUNKET. PLUNKETT. No less than four families of this name are found in the Peerage of Ireland, where the family are considered to be of Danish extraction. They are traced in that kingdom to the reign of Henry III., and in the XIV. cent. they appear as barons of Parliament.

PLYMM. The Plym, a river of Devonshire, which gives names to Plympton, Plymstock, and Plymouth.

POCOCK. *Po* is semi-Saxon for peacock, and the last syllable has only been added, as in the cases of turkey-cock and cock-sparrow. "As proud as a *Po*," seems to have been a very ancient proverbial saying. See Wright's Political Songs, p. 159. Chaucer describes his ' Yeman ' as bearing under his belt—

"A shef of *pocock* arwes bright and kene:"

—that is arrows 'fighted' with peacock feathers; and in Bodl. M.S., 264, fol. 213, as cited by Halliwell, we read—

" A fair *pokok* of pris men paien to Juno;"

that is, "men offer to Juno (to whom the bird was sacred) a beautiful and costly peacock."

From the fancied indelicacy of this surname, it has been ridiculously modified, in pronunciation, to Poke, Palk, Polk, and Pocket!

The forms in H.R. are Pocok, Pokok, Poukoc, &c.

POCKET. See Pocock.

POCKLINGTON. A town in Yorkshire.

POER. See Power.

POET. POETT. Probably first given to some rustic rhymer.

POINDEXTER. " This name does not signify ' the right hand,' as might easily be imagined, but is an old Norman name, signifying *Spur the Steed*, and analogous to *Hotspur.* It comes from two old words, which Wace often uses in the Roman de Rou; the first meaning ' to spur,' from the Latin *pungo*; the second, 'a steed or courser,' in French *destrier*, Ital. *destriere.*" Talbot's English Etymologies.

POINT. 1. Probably a corruption of Poyntz. 2. It may signify a small promontory or headland, as Start Point, Goldstone Point, &c.

POINTING. A township in Lincolnshire.

☞ **POINTS OF THE COMPASS,** *Surnames derived from.*—When surnames were originally imposed, nothing is more natural than that individuals should have received names alluding to the situation of their actual residences, or the direction from which they had come to dwell in a particular place. Hence North, South, East, West, are well-known family names. Less common, but still acknowledged surnames, are Northern, Southerne, Eastern, Western. In like manner originated the quartettes, Norton, Sutton, Easton, Weston; and Northgate, Southgate, Eastgate, Westgate. Sometimes the group will not ' go upon all fours;' for example, we have Northcote, Southcote, and Westcote, but I do not observe an Eastcote; also Eastman, Westerman, Northman (Norman) but no Southman; again, although Eastlake and Westlake appear, I have searched in vain for a *lake* that is either boreal or meridional. It is not necessary to pursue the subject further in this place, but additional illustrations will be found under the respective heads in the Dictionary.

POINTS. See Poyntz.

POITEVIN. A native of the French province of Poitou.

POITLEVIN. See Poitevin.

☞ **POL.** See under CORNISH SURNAMES.

POLACK. A Polander.

"He smote the sledded Polacks on the ice."
Hamlet.

POLAND. From the country.

POLE. The Poles of Shute, co. Devon, baronets from 1628, claim descent from the Cheshire family of Pole, or Poole, of Poole Hall, and bear the same arms. The first settler in Devon was Arthur Pole, who temp. Richard II. married a namesake, the heiress of Pole of Honiton.

POLE, DE LA. A-Sax. *pól*, and O Eng. *pole*, a pool. A common form of it, in records, is Ate-Pole, i.e., "at the pool," afterwards softened to Pool, Poole, and Pooler. The Fr. *De la* was affected by the great merchant of Hull, who became ancestor of the De la Poles, Earls of Suffolk. He flourished in the XIV. century, and his grandson, Michael, Edward the Third's "beloved merchant," is regarded by Hume, though perhaps erroneously, as the first person of that class who rose to social greatness in England.

POLEY. A place in Hertfordshire, where the family were resident in the year 1107. They removed into Suffolk in the reign of Edward III. or Richard II.

POLHILL. See under Polwhele. In the ancient deeds of the Cornish family, the spellings Polwhele and Polhill are employed indifferently. Nichol's Top. and Geneal., i. 180. The Polhills were certainly at Detling. co. Kent, in or before the reign of Edw. III. An old spelling of the family was Polley.

POLK. 1. A contraction of Pollock, and sometimes of Pocock. 2. A pool. Halliw.

POLKINGHORNE. An estate in the parish of Gwinear, co. Cornwall, where the family were resident in the XIII. cent. C. S. Gilbert's Cornw. "From this place were denominated an old family of gentlemen surnamed Polkinhorne, who gave for their arms, Argent, three bars Sable." Hals, in D. Gilbert's Cornwall, ii. 142.

POLLARD. This name, which occurs in the H.R. as Polard, as well as in its present orthography, is probably local. Tonkin says, that the barton of Trelleigh in Redruth, co. Cornwall, was "the seat of that most ancient family of Pollard, from whence *all the others of that name* were descended." D. Gilbert's Cornwall, iii. 383. Whether this broad assertion would bear the test of genealogical investigation, I know not; certain it is, that the name is very widely spread, not alone in the West, but also in the East and North of England. In the county of Durham the owners of it acquired the family characteristic of the POLITIC POLLARDS.

POLLEN. As the name was written in the XVII. cent. *Paulyn*, there can be little doubt that it is derived from the baptismal name Paulinus.

POLLEY. A known variation of Polwhele, or Polhill, which see.

POLLINGTON. A township in the parish of Snaith, in the W. R. of Yorkshire.

POLLOCK. In Eng. Surnames, i. 169, I ventured to derive this name from Paul, of which it seemed to be a diminutive. Its true derivation, however, appears to be from a place called Pollock in Renfrewshire. The family were 'of that Ilk' in the twelfth century.

POLLOMOUNTER. See Polomonter.

POLOMONTER. This singular surname, sometimes written Pollomounter, is derived from the lands so called, in St. Newlyn, co. Cornwall, which were possessed by the family down to the XVII. cent.

POLSON. The son of Pol, i.e., Paul.

POLTER. A dealer in poultry, hodie *poulterer*.

POLWHELE. A manor in Cornwall, where, upon the authority of a distinguished member of the family, the late Rev. Rich. Polwhele, the historian of Cornwall, the family were seated before the Conquest, one Winus de Polhall having held it under the Confessor. From his descendant, Drogo de P., chamberlain to the Empress Maud, sprang the Polwheles of the West, and the Polhills of Kent and Sussex. Nichol's Top. and Geneal. i. 180.

POMEROY. The parish of S. Sauveur de la Pommeraye, in the department of La Manche, Normandy, gave name to a great family mentioned in Domesday Book, and by Brompton; and they in turn conferred it upon Berry Pomeroy, co. Devon. Mem. Soc. Antiq. Norm. vol. vii. Ralph de Pomerei held 58 lordships at the time of the Survey, in the counties of Devon and Somerset. Kelham. Pommeraye, in O. French, signifies an orchard, (Cotgrave), and De la Pomeraye is found in H.R.

POMFRET. A corruption of Pontefract in Yorkshire, which was written in the XV. cent. Powndefraite.

POND. From residence near one. Atte Pond, Ad le Pond, De Pond. H.R. It was sometimes changed to Ponder.

PONDER. See Pond. Le Pondere. H.R.

PONSONBY. The ancestors of this noble family derive their name from the parish of Ponsonby in Cumberland. Before the adoption of the surname, they are said to have been of Hale, in the same county. Still earlier, according to a family tradition, they were of noble rank in Picardy, the founder of the house in England having come over with the Conqueror, who appointed him his Barber! The *three combs* in the arms of Ponsonby are alleged in support of this story, and if further evidence can possibly be desired, the *cheveron* that separates them may adumbrate the open razor, wherewithal the dread face of the mighty Conqueror was denuded of its manly appendage!

PONT. Fr., a bridge. Herbrand de Pont-Audemer, at the time of Domesday Book, held in capite certain manors in Hampshire. Pont, with or without some suffix, and Dupont, have always been common French surnames, of which there have doubtless been several importations into this country. One of these took place on account of the Revocation of the Edict of Nantes, and, in the year 1691, we find a French refugee family of Pont resident in London. In some cases the name has been anglicised to Bridge.

PONTIFEX. Perhaps one of the XVI. century latinizations. Brückenbauer,

(Bridge-builder) is a well-known German surname. The name is derived, says Varro, "à pontem faciendo, quia sublicius pons (a bridge of piles) à pontificibus factus est primum, et restitutus sæpe." A sacred magistrate among the Romans; a pontiff or high priest. Ainsworth.

POODLE. *Pow* or *Poo* is the name given to numerous sluggish or slow-running streams in Scotland. (Gaz.) Hence Poodle may be Pow-dale, the valley of the Pow.

POOKE. Du. *pook*, a poignard or dagger. See Sword, Longespee, &c.

POOLE. POOL. See under Pole. The oldest family of this name, Poole of Poole, co. Chester, were lords of that estate from an early period. The name was variously written, in the XIV. century, Pull, Poole, and De la Poole.

POOLER. See Pole, and the termination ER.

POORE. See Poer.

POPE. A sobriquet. See ECCLESIASTICAL SURNAMES.

POPESON. Probably a sobriquet. Thomas Popeson founded 10 scholarships in Emanuel Coll., Cambridge, in 1591.

POPHAM. "The first nobilitating of the Pophams, as it is saide, was by Matilda Emperes, doughter to Henry the firste, and by Henry II., her sunne." Leland's Itinerary. The name is local, from Popham in Hampshire, where, as Mr. Shirley affirms, an ancestor, Gilbert de Popham, lived in the reign of King John; and there the elder line continued till 17 Henry VI. The Somersetshire Pophams branched out of the Hampshire family, so early as temp. Edward I. The Wiltshire branch is much lower on the tree, having sprung from the parent stock temp. Elizabeth. Noble and Gentle Men of England, p. 206.

POPJAY. An A-Norman and Chaucerian word for parrot, is *popinjay*, or *popingaye*. Medieval archers used to practice with the bow at an artificial parrot or popinjay; and shooting at the popinjay was a favourite holiday pastime. In Scotland the game itself was called *papejay* or *papinjay*. See Strutt's Sports. This was probably a complimentary sobriquet applied to a good marksman with the long bow or the cross-bow.

POPJOY. See Popjay.

POPPLETON. A parish and a chapelry in Yorkshire.

PORCH. From residence in or near the entrance of some great building. At-Porch might become Porcher in some instances. One form in H.R. is Ad Portam Ecclesiæ, "at the church-porch."

PORCHER. The family of Porcher left France at the Revocation of the Edict of Nantes, and settled in South Carolina; and a descendant established himself in England about the year 1768. Their ancestors, who were long seated at Richebourg, on the banks of the Loire, were ennobled as Counts Porcher. "They are traced," according to B.L.G., "to a very ancient date, the originator of the family being Simon le Porcher, hereditary grand huntsman to Hugh Capet, the founder of the French monarchy, from whose official duty of slaying the wounded *boar* the name is derived." *Le Porcher* signifies in O. Fr. "the swine-herd," and is a more probable origin of the name.

PORKER. Neither a young pig, nor a dealer in pork. In Domesday, the word sometime signifies a swineherd, but more usually a free occupier, who rented the privilege of feeding pigs in the woodlands, and sometimes paid his rent in kind. Ellis. Itrod. Domesd. i. 89. In the H.R. the name is written Porcarius, Porkar, and Le Porker.

PORRET. Porret is a place in the department of La Manche, in Normandy.

PORSON. Perhaps from Paul, corrupted thus: Paulson, Pawson, Porson.

PORT. Hugo de Port came into England at the Norman Conquest, and held fifty-five lordships in the counties of Hants and Dorset, as tenant in capite. One of his descendants assumed the surname of Saint-John. A Hubert de Port was also a tenant in capite in Hampshire, at the making of Domesday Book. Kelham's Domesday.

Some families of this name may be indigenous to England, ranking in the same category with Haven, Harbour, &c.; or it may be the same as the *Ad Portam*, or Atte-Gate, of medieval records.

PORTAL. The family are said to have been originally Spanish, and to have established themselves in Languedoc at the end of the XI. century. Adopting, after some centuries' residence in that province, the principles of the Huguenots, some of their members were compelled to leave France after the Revocation of the Edict of Nantes. The founder of the family in England was Henri Portal, who settled in Hampshire. B.L.G.

PORTBURY. A parish in Somersetshire.

PORTCH. The same as Porch.

PORTER. The keeper of a door. Lat. *porta*. The meaning was sometimes extended, and implied a castellan, or keeper of a castle. This was the case with the first of this name and family in Cornwall, who, in a dateless deed, of probably not later than the XIII. century, is styled *Janitor de Trematon*. He received a grant of lands from the Valletorts, then lords of Trematon, and those lands, situate just outside the venerable walls of that fine old feudal fortress, are still possessed by his descendants, who have ever since resided in the immediate vicinity. See C. S. Gilbert's Cornw. H.R. Portarius, Le Porter, &c.

2 N

PORTEUS. PORTEOUS. 1. A *porteus* is a Roman breviary, or priest's office-book. The surname may be classed with Crucifix, Pix, &c. 2. In Scotland, a *porteous* is a "list of persons indicted to appear before the Justiciary;" and *portuous roll* is a phrase still used to denote the list of criminal causes to be tried at the circuit courts. Jamieson. Hence the name may have originated from some office connected with such courts. The family of this name boast, that they have been seated at Hawkshaw, in Peebles-shire, a whole Millennium!

PORTLOCK. A parish in Somersetshire, more commonly called Porlock.

PORTMAN. A civic officer, with duties similar to those of a modern mayor. The courts of this functionary were formerly called *portmannimotes*. Portreeve is synonymous. The family of this name in Somersetshire, appear to have been eminent so early as the reign of Edward I. See Burke's Extinct Baronets.

PORTREVE. The chief magistrate of a town; apparently the synonym of mayor. Lambarde has the following account of the word, in his notice of Gravesend :—

"GRAVESENDE, in Saxon *Gerefesend*; in Latine, Limes Prætorius. The originall cause of the name of this place lieth hidd in the usuall name of the officer lately created in the town. [Gravesend was incorporated in the fourth year of Queen Elizabeth.] He is commonly called Portreve, but the woord, aunciently and truly sounded, is Portgereve, that is to say, the Ruler of the Towne. For Porte descending of the Latin woord *portus*, signifieth a Port-towne, and *gereve*, being derived of the Saxon verbe *gereccan*, to rule, was first called *gerecfa*, and then *gerefa*, and betokeneth a Ruler. So that *Portreve* is the Ruler of the Towne, and Greves-end is as much to say as the Limit, Bounde, or Precinct of such a rule or office." Perambulation of Kent, 1576. It may be observed that the city of London was governed by a Portreeve, up to the period of the Conquest. Le Portereve. H.R.

PORTSMOUTH. The great town in Hampshire.

PORTWINE. A singular corruption of Poitevin, a native of Poitou in France. So early as the time of Edward I. the corruption had proceeded as far as to Potewyne, a lady called Preciosa Potewyne occurring in H.R.

POSNET. A *posnett* is a bag into which money is put—a net used as a purse. Jamieson. The name may have been acquired by the treasurer of some fraternity.

POST. A special messenger; a courier. Halliwell quotes the following anecdote :—

"One night a drunken fellow josled against a post, but the fellow thought somebody had josled him, and fell a beating the post till his fingers were broken. Says one to him, Fie! what do you fight with a post? Is it a post? Why did he not blow his horn then?"
Oxford Jests, 1706.

POSTE. See Post.

POSTLE. POSTILL. A corruption of Apostle—analogous to Saint, Martyr, &c.

POTHECARY. An apothecary.

POTICARY. An old spelling of apothecary.

POTIPHAR. For this name—Old French turned into older Egyptian—see Petifer.

POTMAN. A potter.

POTT. POTTS. The reason for the assumption of this name is not very obvious; yet similar words have designated families of importance in other countries. For instance, there were in Flanders, in the XV. cent., a noble family of Pott, who bore a pot in their armorial coat. There was also an Italian house called the 'Little-Pots," (Pignatelli,) while a line of Spanish grandees rejoiced in the thrice-illustrious name of Padilla, or "Frying-pan!" Dixon.
In the N. of England, *potts* is a topographical term, implying deep circular hollows in the ground. This surname designates a Northumbrian clan.

POTTER. Figulus—a maker of pots.

POTTICARY. See Poticary.

POTTINGER. The old Scottish for an apothecary. Jamieson. In the Household Book of James V. of Scotland, one of the king's horses, set apart for carrying the drugs of the royal household, is jocosely known by this name :—" uno equo pharmacopile, vulgo *le Pottinger*." Archæologia, vol. xxii.

POTTMAN. A potter.

POTVINE. A Poitevin, or native of Poitou. This name is found about Dover and Canterbury.

POUCHMAKER. A maker of bags or pouches.

POULETT. This name is identical with Paulet, but Mr. Shirley's account differs considerably from what has been stated under art. Paulet. He says : " Paulet, in the hundred of North Petherton, co. Somerset, gave name to this historical family, the first on record being Sir William de Paulet, who died in 1242. He was of Leigh in Devonshire, which, with Rode, in Somersetshire, successively became the family seats. Hinton St. George, which came from the heiress of Denebaud in the reign of Henry VI., is noted by Leland as " a right goodly manor place of fre stone, with two goodly high tourres, embattled in the ynner court," which has ever since remained the seat of the elder branch of the family," now represented by Earl Poulett. Noble and Gentle Men of England.

POULSON. The son of Poule or Paul. See Eng. Surn. i.

POULTER. A dealer in poults or poultry. The last syllable of poulter*er*, is a modern vulgarism. The Poulters' Company was incorporated by Henry VIII.

POULTNEY. The same as Pulteney.

POULTON. Various parishes and places in cos. Lancaster, Cheshire, Wilts, &c.

POUNCE. A corruption of Poyntz.

POUNCEBY. POWNCEBY. Corruptions of Ponsonby.

POUND. From residence near a manorial pound: perhaps originally applied to the pinder, or pound-keeper, himself.

POUNDEN. The family were founded in Ireland by John Pounden, a native of Liege, about the year 1734. B.L.G.

POUNDER. See Pinder.

POUNTAIN. Puntain. H.R. Perhaps originally Pontianus, equivalent to Bridger.

POUNTNEY. A corruption of Poultney, or Pulteney.

POUPARD. More correctly Poupart. Fr. "An infant or young child; also a meacock or milksop." Cotgrave.

POVEY. A Gloucestershire provincialism for an owl. Halliwell mentions a Westcountry proverb—
WORSE AND WORSE, LIKE POVEY'S FOOT. As in the case of most of these rustic witticisms, we are not informed who Povey was, or where he lived.

POW. POWE. In Scotland, a generic word, meaning a sluggish stream.

POWELL. Ap-Howel — the son of Howel, a personal name common in Wales. The Powells of Nant Eos, co. Cardigan, are descended from Philip ap Howell, whose pedigree is traced to Edwin ap Grono, Lord of Tegaingl, founder of the XIII. noble tribe of North Wales and Powys. The Powells of Brandlesome, co. Lancaster, spring from Walter Powell of Bucknell in Shropshire, temp. Elizabeth, who was of the posterity of Rhys ap Tudor, King of South Wales. B.L.G. There are many other families of undoubted antiquity, derived from the best ancestry of the principality, though the name of Powell is, in all cases, of comparatively late adoption.

POWER. The surname variously written Le Poer, Power, Powre, Poore, &c., is of Norman origin. It has been illustrious in Ireland, from the time of Strongbow's invasion of that kingdom. Robert le Poer was engaged in his expedition, and received from Pembroke the territory of Waterford, excepting only "the city and the cantred of the Ostmen or Danes, whom the invaders found settled there, and in good policy encouraged as merchants." D'Alton. The family were doubtless of Norman extraction, but of their history, previously to the time of Henry II., little seems to be known. The meaning of the name is obscure.

POWIS. See Powys.

POWLE. POWLES. Corruptions either of Powell or of Paul.

POWLESLAND. Local: "land belonging to St. Paul's?" Or, perhaps, a corruption of Powys-land, a great district of Wales.

POWLETT. See Paulet. Collins says that Hercules, lord of Tournon, the ancestor of the family, came hither from Picardy, with Geoffrey Plantagenet, Earl of Anjou, third son of Henry II., and settled at Pawlet, co. Somerset.

POWNALL. A township in Cheshire.

POWNING. An ancient spelling of Poynings.

POWTER. See Porter.

POWYS. 1. A castle in the county of Montgomery. 2. *Powys* in Welsh signifies, the state of being at rest or stationary. Pughe's Dict.

POXON. A corruption of Palkson. See Palkson.

POYNDER. A bailiff; one who distrains. A Lancashire surname. Pound, to distrain. Jamieson.

POYNINGS. A parish in Sussex, which was possessed by a great family, subsequently ennobled, in the reign of Henry II. The first of the name recorded in the Baronage is Adam de Poynings, lord of Poynings, a benefactor to Lewes Priory.

POYNTER. POINTER. A *point*, in ancient costume, was a kind of tagged lace, and hence a Pointer may have been a maker of such articles.* Some of the Poynters, however, are of French origin, being descendants of Ambrose Pointier, of Arras, who settled here at the Revocation of the Edict of Nantes. The armorials of this family are *pointedly* allusive; the shield contains pointed piles; the crest is a hand holding a cross-fitchée, or pointed, to which the fore-finger points; while the motto is *Pense a pointer.*

POYNTZ. Walter filius Ponz, a tenant in chief at the time of the Norman survey, and Drogo, his brother, who held many manors in the counties of Wilts., Gloucester, Worcester, and Hereford, were sons of Walter Ponz, a noble Norman. From Drogo filius Ponz descended the family of Clifford. Kelham's Domesday.

POYZER. This name is almost peculiar to Derbyshire. To poise is to weigh, and the first of the family may have been a *weigher* of some commodity.

PRALL. Cotgrave gives *preau*, "a little medow, or medow adjoining to a house;" and Halliwell has, from the A.-Norm., *prayell*, a little meadow.

PRATER. A talkative man.

PRATT. 1. A-S. *praet*, cunning. Prat, as a surname, is very common in H.R. 2. Perhaps a contraction of Lat. *pratum*, meadow. See Pretty.

---

* "To strain a point" is a common phrase, the literal meaning of which is understood by few. The above definition serves to explain it.

PRATTMAN. See Pratt. 1. A cunning man. 2. The custodian of a meadow.

PRATY. See Pretty.

PRAY. Probably from Fr. *pré*, a meadow. De la Preye. H.R.

PREACHER. The profession. Predicator, Le Precheur. H.R.

PRECIOUS. A correspondent sends me the following anecdote. — " Walking through a town with a friend, I noticed the name of *Precious*. My friend said to me : 'You knew John Priesthouse—he was the father of this Precious': here the vulgar had corrupted the name, probably in ridicule of Priesthouse." It is remarkable how easily people in a humble condition of life will accept an *alias*, or adopt the corrupt pronunciation of their names by their illiterate neighbours ; and if these things occur in the nineteenth century, it is no wonder that we have, among the multitude of surnames handed down to us from the thirteenth and fourteenth, many that baffle even etymological guess-work, and render a rationale impossible.

PREECE. Welsh, Ap-Rhys : the same as Price.

PREEDY. See Priddy.

PREEN. A-Sax. *pren*, a priest.

PREIST. The same as Priest.

PRENDERGAST. Prendregast, a parish in Pembrokeshire, from whence went forth to the conquest of Ireland, with his neighbour, the famous Strongbow, Maurice de Prendergast, who received for his services ten knights' fees called Fernegenelan. An early Prendergast, in the first half of the XIII. century, who was accounted as one of the *Fideles* of Ireland, had summons for the French and Scottish wars. See D'Alton, p. 211.

PRENTICE. PRENTIS. An apprentice.

☞ **PRES-.** A component syllable in several local surnames, being a contraction of *Priest's* (A.S. *preostes*), as Presland, "the priest's land ;" Presley, Pressley, Presslee, "the priest's meadow ;" Preswell, "the priest's well ;" Prested, "the priest's place," &c. Preston, Prescott, Prestwick, &c., belong to the same class.

PRESCOTT. Parishes, &c., in cos. Lancaster, Oxford, and Gloucester. De Prestcot, H.R. co. Oxon.

PRESS. See Prest. The O.Fr. *prest*, ready, willing, is perhaps a likelier origin. Prest and Le Prest are common H.R. surnames. See PREST, below.

PRESSMAN. Probably 'Priest-man,' an attendant upon a priest.

PREST. 1. Mr. Ferguson says : "Prest is the Old Norse *prestr :* it is a little curious that the only man called Prest in the Directory for 1857 *is* a priest." 2. O.Fr. ready.

PRESTAGE. PRESTIGE. A corruption of Prestwich.

PRESTON. Besides the great Lancashire town, thirty-five parishes and places are named in the Gazetteer, and there are many others in various counties. The origin of the name, from *preostes-tún*, 'the priest's enclosure or homestead' is undoubted. The Prestons of Furness were traced to Richard de Preston, of Preston, co. Westmoreland, temp. Henry II.

PRESTWICH. A parish in Lancashire.

PRESTWICK. A township in Northumberland.

PRETIOUS. See Precious.

PRETTEJOHN. PRETTIJOHN. The same as Prettyjohn.

PRETTIMAN. Pretty, besides its usually recognized meanings, has in Scotland a variety of significations, as small, neat, mean or contemptible, handsome, polite and accomplished, brave and intrepid. Jamieson. The Messieurs Prettyman have, therefore, excellent scope for guessing at the true character of the founder of their name.

PRETTY. The earliest mention of this name is in the year 1192, when Engeran de Prætis attests the grant of the chapel of Hope-cum-Tideswell, by John, Earl of Moreton, to the cathedral of Lichfield. Its subsequent forms have corresponded with the changes of spelling in the adjective, thus : Praty, Pretie, Prettie, Pretty. In the XV. cent. the first of these was in use, and so Leland, born in that century, writes the adjective ; e. g. " a praty town." The name, however, has nothing to do with prettiness, but is derived from the Lat. *pratum*, a meadow. The Prettys of Scotland and Ireland are of English origin. The name is also found in Italy and in Spain. In the latter country, the family bear for arms, " a green meadow, flowered proper." Inf. Edw. Pretty, Esq., F.S.A.

PRETTYJOHN. See JOHN.

PREVOST. O.Fr., hodie *prevôt*, a Provost. The Baronet's family settled in England, from Switzerland, in the last century.

PREVO. O.Fr., a Provost.

PREW. Fr. *preux*. Brave, courageous. " Un preux chevalier"—a valiant knight.

PREWBODY. I have met with this name in one county only—that county of extraordinary surnames, Cornwall. It appears to be one of the compounds of Body, from the A-Sax. *boda*, a messenger. The first syllable may possibly be a contraction of *preost*, priest, and if so, the name may be interpreted, either as " priest's messenger," or as " priestly messenger."

PRICE. Welsh, Ap Rhys, the son of Rhys. As in the case of most other Welsh families, the settled surname is of recent adoption, even amongst the gentry, and it is hard to distinguish, by the mere name, men of family from the *ignobile vulgus*. The Prices of Castle-Madoc., co. Brecknock, spring from Bleddyn ap Maenyrch, Lord of Brecon, temp. William Rufus; and the Prices of Glangwilly, co. Carmarthen, are descended, on the female side, through the Lloyds, from Rhodri Mawr, King of Wales. B.L.G.

PRICHARD. See Pritchard.

PRICKADVANCE. Simon Prickadvance was buried at Peasmarsh, co. Sussex, 17th August, 1678. Par. Reg. This remarkable name I have nowhere else met with, though it is, probably, of good medieval origin. To *preke* or *prick* is a very common expression in Old English poetry, signifying to ride fast, to spur a horse, from prick, the ancient pointed spur, used before the introduction of rowels. " Prick ! Advance !" would therefore be a likely exclamation, employed to urge forward a body of horsemen, either in battle or the chase, and this was, in all probability, the origin of the name.

Since I wrote the above, I have noticed, in H.R., the name Prikeavant.

PRICKETT. 1. Possibly the same as Pritchard or Pritchett — the *ch* being hardened. See Ricketts. 2. From the animal. Richardson defines *pricket* as " cervus trinus, a deer two years old, so called from the state of its horns (stimuli instar)." The crest of the family is allusive, being " a pricket tripping, proper."

" If thou wilt come and dwell with me at home,
My sheepcote shall be strewed with new greene
  rushes ;
Weele haunt the trembling *prickets*, as they rome
About the fields, along the hauthorn bushes."
  Affectionate Shepheard, 1594.

" And I say beside, that 'twas a *pricket* that the princess killed."
  Love's Labour Lost, iv. 2.

In Rotuli Hundredorum, the name is written Priket.

PRIDDY. PRIDIE. PRIDDEY. PRIDAY. Priddy, a parish in co. Somerset. The name has been rather fancifully derived from *Prie-Dieu*.

PRIDE. The deadly sin ; a personation in some old ' mystery ' or miracle-play ? Pride, without any prefix, is found in H.R.

PRIDEAUX. The castle of Prideaux, according to Tonkin (D. Gilbert's Cornwall, iii., 56), was " the seat of, and gave name to, a family which hath been very eminent both in this county and in Devonshire, and still flourisheth in both." " Some would derive it," he says, "from a French original: *près d'eaux*, near the waters, for the sea formerly flowed up as high as this place." " The ancient family of Prideaux trace their descent from Paganus, lord of Prideaux Castle, in Luxilion, co. Cornwall, in the time of William I., where the family continued till the latter part of the fourteenth century." Shirley's Noble and Gentle Men.

PRIER. See Prior.

PRIEST. See Ecclesiastical Surnames.

PRIESTHOUSE. Local — from residence at a mansion belonging to some ecclesiastic. There is a dwelling called Priesthawes, originally Priesthouse, near Pevensey, co. Sussex, and there were doubtless many others in various districts. This surname has been queerly corrupted to Precious.

PRIESTLEY. From a family MS. mentioned in B.L.G. it appears that the ancient seat and inheritance of the family was in Soyland and Sowerby, in the parish of Halifax, co. York.

PRIESTLY. Not from the adjective, but probably from some locality so called : " the priest's *lee* or meadow."

PRIME. Qu. Lat. *primus*—first, best, chief, as in the old French phrase, " Le *prime* de Chevaliers," defined by Cotgrave as " a prime Knight, the paragon or flower of Knights." The French surname De la Pryme has, however, the appearance of a *local* origin.

PRIMROSE. 1. The ancestors of Lord Roseberry derived their surname from the lands of Primrose in Fifeshire. Courthope's Debrett. 2. French Protestant refugees after the Revocation of the Edict of Nantes. In 1691, a M. de Primerose was clergyman of a French church in London, but whether he was in Goldsmith's mind as the prototype of his Vicar of Wakefield, I cannot say.

PRIN. See Prynne.

PRINCE. A sobriquet, like Duke, Lord, &c.

PRINCEPS. A latinization of Prince.

PRINDLE. A small inclosure, a croft.

PRINGLE. The name of Pringle, or Hop-pringle, as it was usually written, is peculiar to the S. of Scotland. As to its etymology, antiquaries are agreed that it is a corruption of Pelerin or Pilgrim, the prefix Hop being the equivalent of the Welsh *ap*. Hop-Pringle may, therefore, mean the son of some pilgrim of distinction ; and the escallop-shells in the arms of all the families of Pringle rather favour this opinion. B.L.G. The little silver coin called a *pringle*, formerly minted in Scotland, and of about the value of an English penny, may have derived its name from one of this family, as the *bodle* did its from Bothwell.

PRINSEP. A corruption of the Lat. *princeps*, a prince.

PRIOR. See Ecclesiastical Surnames.

PRISEMAN. One who had carried off the prize in some athletic game.

PRISLEY. A corruption of Priestley.

PRITCHARD. Ap-Richard ; the son of Richard. See AP.

PRITCHETT. A corruption of Pritchard.

PRITTIE. See Pretty.

PRIZEMAN. See Priseman.

PROBERT. See Robert.

PROBUS. An ancient personal name, borne by a Cornish local saint (not in the Roman calendar), after whom the parish of St. Probus is named.

PROBYN. See Robert.

PROCTOR. PROCTER. PROCKTER. Lat. *procurator.* One who acts for another, or *takes care* of his interest. One who collected alms for lepers, or others unable to do it themselves. Halliwell. According to Kennett, beggars of any kind were called Proctors. This explains the curious inscription over Richard Watt's hospital at Rochester, founded in 1579, which declares that " six poor travellers may receive lodging, entertainment, and fourpence each, for one night, *provided they are not Rogues nor Proctors.*"

PRODGER. Ap-Roger; the son of Roger. See AP.

PROFIT. The same as Prophet.

PROPERJOHN. See JOHN.

PROPERT. See Probert.

PROPHET. Probably a sobriquet, applied to one who pretended to more than ordinary sagacity as to future events.

PROSSER. *Pross* is, according to Halliwell, a northern provincialism for ' talk, conversation.' Hence, perhaps, a *prosser* means a talkative person, or, as we commonly say, a ' proser.'

PROUD. Fuller makes it a corruption of Prude. Worthies ii. 183. It would, therefore, mean sage, rather than arrogant.

PROUDFOOT. If not a gross corruption of some other name, may relate to the gait of the original bearer. Proudfot, Prudfot, &c., H.R.

PROUDMAN. This name may possibly be taken in its literal meaning, though I am rather inclined to think it is a kind of clumsy translation of the O.Fr. Prudhomme. See that name, *infra.*

PROUT. " Id est, Proud." Hals, in D. Gilbert's Cornwall. A.Sax. *prút,* proud.

PROVIS. A corruption of Provost.

PROVOST. The mayor of a royal burgh; the dean or president of a collegiate church. Jamieson.

PROWETT. Probably a *diæresis* of Prout.

PRUDAMES. A corruption of Prudhomme.

PRUDDAH. See Prudhoe.

PRUDENCE. A personal name borne by a saint of the Roman calendar, who was bishop of Troyes, in France, and whose festival is on April 6.

PRUDHOE. Two townships in the parish of Ovingham, co. Northumberland, are so designated.

PRUDHOMME. An obsolete Fr. word, signifying " a good and true man ; a man well versed in any art or trade." Sadler. In H.R. Prodhomme, Prodomme, Prodome, Prudhomme, &c.

PRUJEAN. Fr. *preux,* and Jean ; ' Valiant John '—a sobriquet, formed like Grosjean, Prettyjohn, &c.

PRYCE. See Price.

PRYNNE. A-Sax. *pren,* a priest.

PUCKERING. The same as Pickering.

PUDDICOMBE. See COMBE.

PUDDING. A sobriquet traceable to the XIII. century. " Will. Silvestre, fil ' Silvestir Pudding de Holmstrete," occurs in 1230. N. and Q. v. 290. Pudding, Puddy'g. H.R.

PUGH. Welsh, Ap-Hugh, the son of Hugh. See AP.

PULBROOK. Perhaps a hardened pronunciation of Pulborough, a parish in Sussex. Or it may be some other locality, deriving its name from *pool* and *brook.*

PULFORD. A parish in Cheshire.

PULHAM. A town in Norfolk, and a parish in Dorset.

PULL. An archaic form of Pool or Poole.

PULLEN. I can find no better origin for this rather common surname, than the A.Norm. *pulleyn,* and Fr. *poulain,* a colt or foal ; or more generally, like the Lat. *pullus,* the young of everything. See Pulley.

PULLER. PULLAR. A Norfolk provincialism for a poultry-house. Fr. *poule,* a hen.

PULLEY. See Pullen. *Pullain* and *pullen* are found in several early plays for poultry. Halliwell. Cotgrave has " *poullailler,* a poulter, or keeper of pullaine," or chicken.

PULLEYNE. A probable corruption of the personal name Paulinus. Puleyn. H.R.

PULLIN. PULLING. See Pullen.

PULLINGER. A corruption of Fr. *boulanger,* a baker.

PULLROSE. See Pluckrose.

PULTENEY. The original name of the extinct noble family was De Clipstone, until Adam de Clipstone, acquiring the manor of Pulteney, co. Leicester, adopted the name of that place as his surname.

PULTER. A dealer in fowls *(poulets)*; what is now corruptly called a ' poulter*er.*' Le Poleter. H.R.

PUMPHREY. Welsh, Ap-Humphrey. The son of Humphrey. See AP.

PUNCH. This name is found in the Registrar General's list of oddities, and in the Rotuli Hundredorum of temp. Edward I. Its etymology has not occurred to me.

PUNCHARD. A contraction of Punchardon?

PUNCHARDON. This name is found in Holinshed's list, called the Roll of Battel Abbey, and there is no doubt that the introduction of the family into England took place at the Conquest, since Ponte-Cardon occurs in Domesday. They gave the suffix to Heanton-Punchardon, co. Devon. The name was probably derived from the place now called Pont-Chardon, in the arrondisement of Argentan, in Normandy.

PUNNETT. In Domesday we find one Ricardus Punnat, (Pugnator) the Champion. Kelham.

PUNSHON. Very probably a contraction of Punchardon, caused by rapid pronunciation.

PUNT. A corruption of *pont*, Fr., a bridge.

PUNTON. Pointon, a township in Lincolnshire.

PURBROOK. Perhaps a corruption of Purbright, a parish in Surrey.

PURCELL. A Norman name of great antiquity. As it is not found prefixed by the territorial *De*, I think it must be referred to a class of sobriquets very prevalent among the early Normans, and that it means Lat.: '*porcellus*,' O. Fr., *porcel*—a little pig. A Frenchman in our days considers '*cochon*' the most opprobrious of designations ; but it was far otherwise in ancient times, as witness the 'pigs' and 'old sows' (Porci and Scrofæ), eminent family names among the Romans ; the French Legryce, Legriel, &c. ; and our own indigenous Hogg, Pigg, Littlehog, Wildbore, &c. The arms of the various branches of the family have boars' heads, allusive to the name. Comp. Lovel from Lupus. The Purcells came into England at the Conquest, and there is a tradition of their descent from one Hugh, "the first of the followers of the Bastard Duke to set foot on the shore of Pevensey." This personage obtained some manors in Sussex, and a Geoffrey Porcellus, of Surrey, is mentioned in a Pipe Roll of 1131. The family were planted in Ireland by Sir Hugh Purcell, who took part in the subjugation of that country in the reign of Henry II., and married Beatrix, daughter of the celebrated Theobald Butler. "This name," says Mr. D'Alton, "was early introduced into Munster, where it soon became so numerous that the rolls of licenses for protection and pardon in the year 1310, (in prudence then necessitated,) included no less than thirteen adult Purcells ; while eight years previously, Hugh, Philip, Maurice, and Adam Purcell were of the Irish magnates summoned to the Scottish war. . . . In the reign of Elizabeth and James, the Purcells were seized of many castles and manors in Kilkenny."
In charters, this name is frequently, and most absurdly, latinized De Porcellis.

PURCHAS. See Purchase.

PURCHASE. Many lands and tenements throughout England bear this designation, and from some one or more of them we probably get the surname.

PURCHES. See Purchase.

PURDAY. See Pardew.

PURDEW. The same as Pardew.

PURDIE. See Pardew.

PURDOM. The same as Prudhomme.

PURDUE. See Pardew.

PURDY. See Pardew.

PURDAY. A probable corruption of Purdew.

PURE. An ancient surname, one Edric Pure having held lands before the Conquest. Domesd. A-Sax. *pure*, sound.

PUREFOY. O.Fr. *pure foy*, literally "pure faith." Originally applied to a faithful ally or follower. The family were seated at Misterton, co. Leicester, in 1277. The motto borne by one branch is "*Pure foy* est ma joie."

PURIER. Perhaps Fr. *poirier*, a pear-tree.

PURKESS. PURKISS. When William Rufus was shot in the New Forest, his body was conveyed to Winchester in the cart of a poor coal-man or charcoal burner, whose name, according to tradition, was Purkess. "He became the ancestor of a very numerous tribe, who have always lived near Stoney Cross, and some of whom may still be found at Minstead :—

> "And still—so runs our forest creed—
> Flourish that pious yeoman's seed,
> E'en in the self-same spot ;
> One horse and cart their little store,
> Like their forefather's—neither more
> Nor less the children's lot."
> W. S. Rose.

They have never become richer or poorer since the day of the king's death." Murray's Handbook of Hants.
The family may be ancient, and the tradition true, but the *name* is certainly not older than the XIII. or XIV. century, being an obvious corruption of Perkins, through Perkiss. See Peter.

PURNELL. May be the same as Burnell.

PURNEY. Probably the same as Burney.

PURSEGLOVE. See Purslow.

PURSELL. See Purcell.

PURSER. A bearer of the purse—a treasurer.

PURSEY. A corruption of Percy.

PURSLOVE. A good name for a miser ; but see Purslow.

PURSLOW. A hundred in Shropshire. The name has been modified to Purslove, and Purseglove, and this last has been matter for a little legend which may be found in Eng. Surn. ii. 17.

PURSSEY. A corruption—and how great a one !—of Percy.

PURTON. A parish in Wiltshire. "The Purtons are descended from Ranulph de

Perton, who, in the latter part of the reign of King John, and the beginning of Henry III., was settled at Perton, in the parish of Tettenhall, co. Stafford." B.L.G.

PURVES. See Purvis.

PURVIS. According to the account given in B.L.G., the Purvises of Darsham, co. Suffolk, originated from the family of Purvis "of that Ilk" in Scotland. "That Ilk," however, does not appear to be identified, although the name Purvoys, or Perves, is found in ancient records of the Lowland counties. I think the name is more likely to be derived from the A-Norm. *pervis*, or *parvise*, which Kelham defines as, "the outer court of a palace or great house. . . . Such was the place in Palace-Yard, near Westminster Hall, mentioned by Fortescue, De Laud. Leg. Ang. c. 51; and Dugdale also takes notice of the *Pervyse of Parvles*."

PUSEY. Pusey, or Pewsey, a parish in Wiltshire, which belonged to the family in very early times. Camden thus mentions the antiquity of the race :—
"From Kingston Lisle, the river Ock, just now mentioned, runs through Denchworth and Pusey, the possession of a family of that surname, and held by a *Horn*, given to their ancestors by King Canutus the Dane;" to which his editor adds: "Thus much the inscription implies; but both the character and stile thereof are modern, many hundreds of years after the Conquest; so that of what antiquity soever the Horn itself may be, the inscription must have been added long after the age of Canutus. Not but the tradition of Canutus's giving it may probably be very true, since there are so many instances of this kind in many parts of England; and Ingulphus has expressly told us, that in those days it was common to make grants of lands by horns among other things." Gibson's Camden, i. 163.

This relic is described and figured in Archæologia, iii. 13, from whence we gain the following particulars. The horn is that of an ox, of moderate size, having in the middle a ring of silver gilt, and neatly mounted on two hound's feet, which support the whole. The inscription on the ring, in Old English characters, is :—

𝔎𝔶𝔫𝔤 𝔎𝔫𝔬𝔴𝔡𝔢 𝔤𝔢𝔟𝔢 𝔚𝔶𝔩𝔩𝔶𝔞𝔪 𝔓𝔢𝔴𝔰𝔢 𝔗𝔥𝔦𝔰 𝔥𝔬𝔯𝔫𝔢 𝔱𝔬 𝔥𝔬𝔩𝔡𝔢 𝔟𝔶 𝔱𝔥𝔶 𝔩𝔬𝔫𝔡.

Dr. Hickes states, that both the horn and manor were, in his time, possessed by Charles Pusey, Esq., who had recovered them in Chancery, before Lord Chancellor Jefferies, the horn itself being produced in court, and with universal admiration received, admitted, and *proved* (!) to be the identical horn by which, as by a charter, Canute had conveyed the manor of Pusey seven hundred years before." The inscription is, doubtless, of the XV. century, but it may have replaced an older one, and the possessorship of the estate from a very early period is indisputable.

PUTLEY. A parish in Herefordshire.

PUTNAM. Puttenham, parishes in cos. Hertford and Surrey.

PUTNEY. A parish in Surrey.

PUTT. 1. See Peddie. 2. O.Fr. a pit. De la Putte. H.R.

PUTTICK. The same as Puttock.

PUTTOCK. 1. Florence of Worcester mentions an Anglo-Saxon called Puttoc. 2. A kite : "metaphorically applied," says Halliwell, "to a greedy, ravenous fellow." Puttoc. H.R.

PUZEY. See Pusey.

PYATT. See Pyott.

PYE. One of the many surnames derived from Hugh. Ap-Hugh has, in some parts of Wales, been corrupted to Pye. See anecdote in Eng. Surn. i. 180. It may, however, sometimes be derived from the bird, now called the *Mag*-pie, the first syllable of which is a puerile addition, like Tom and Robin, in 'Tom Cat' and 'Robin Redbreast.' Pye is the true O. Eng. name of the bird, as found in medieval literature ; e.g. :

> "I had wonder at whom,
> And where, the *Pye* lerned
> To leye the stikkes
> In which she layeth and bredeth.
> Ther nys wrighte, as I ween,
> Sholde wercke hir nestes to paye ;
> If any mason made a molde thereto,
> Much wonder it were."
> *Piers Plowman*, p. 223.

Let me go a little out of my way, in making use of an illustrative quotation, to remark, that this really poetical idea has been hit upon by a much more recent poet, who had probably never read the works of the Malvern Dreamer :

> "A bird's nest ; mark it well within, without,
> No tool had he that wrought, no knife to cut,
> No bodkin to insert, his little beak was all ;
> And yet how neatly finished! What nice hand,
> With every implement and means of art,
> And twenty years' apprenticeship to boot,
> Could make me such another ! "
> *Hurdis.*

PYECROFT. Local : "the croft frequented by magpies."

PYEFINCH. A provincial name of the chaffinch.

PYKE. See Pike.

PYLE. The same as Peel. There is a Northumbrian clan of this surname.

PYM. The family of John Pym, the regicide, were of respectable antiquity in Somersetshire, being traced to Philip Pym, of Brymmore, co. Somerset, 12. Edward IV. The origin of the name is doubtful.

PYMAN. A destroyer of magpies and other winged depredators? Analogous to the modern "crow tender." Comp. Todman.

PYNE. See Pine. Robt. and Jno. Pyne, Protestant refugees from Dieppe, landed at Rye, 1572. Harl. MS. 15. 70.

PYOTT. An Eng. provincialism for a magpie.

PYPARD. See Pipard.

PYRKE. See Peter.

PYWELL. Local : "the spring resorted to by magpies ?"

Q.

☞ **QUADRUPEDS,** *Names of, which have become Surnames.* The classification of my ingenious friend, Mr. Clark, runs thus:—

"Bull, Cow, Bullock, Bear and Ram,
Lyon, Tyger, Wolf, and Lamb;
Pigg, Fox, Ferrett, Buck, and Doe;
Leppard, Panther, Hind, and Roe;
Camel, Catt, Colt, Calf, and Foal,
Bruin, Badger, Beaver, Mole;
Rabbit, Squirrel, Stagg, and Hare,
Lambkin, Stoat, Fitch, Steed, and Mare;
Griffin, Galloway, and Horse,
Hunter—fleetest of the course;
Pussy, Cattle, Calver, Cony,
Palfry, too, but not a *Pony*;
Wheeler, Leader, Gelding, Trotter,
Wildbore, Nagg, Mouse, Mule, and Otter;
Roebuck, Reynard, Stallion, Hogg,
Cobb and Pointer—but no *Dog*."

As I have remarked in the article "FISHES," many of these names must not be taken *au pied de la lettre*, especially those which express varieties of the horse, as Hunter, Galloway, Cobb, Wheeler, Leader, Steed. We must also except Otter, and Reynard, which are personal, or baptismal names; and Hind, Badger, and Pointer, which are names of employments, and various others. Several seem to have been derived from Heraldry, and others were probably applied metaphorically, to denote the character, or some quality, of the original bearer. See observations on this subject in English Surn., vol. i. p. 176.

QUAE. A Gaelic name, usually prefixed by Mac.

QUAIFE. The family seem always to have been principally resident in East Sussex, and West Kent. Until within the last 150 years, the name has been spelt Coyf, and Coyfe, and tradition says, that the ancestor of the family came into England with the Conqueror, and that, at the Battle of Hastings, he wore a *hood* instead of a helmet; *unde nomen.* It is worthy of notice, that the name *Caperoun*, the Old French for a hood, is found in the Roll of Battel Abbey, and also that the family have long resided near Battel, the scene of the exploits of the presumed founder of the name.

QUAIN. O. Eng. *quaint*, neat, elegant.

QUAINT. See Quain.

QUAINTANCE. An acquaintance; analogous to Friend, Neighbour, &c.

QUAINTON. A parish in Buckinghamshire.

2 o

QUAKELY. Mr. Ferguson derives it from O. Norse *queiklegr*, excitable, inflammable.

☞ **QUALITIES.** Under this title, Mr. Clark, in his amusing list of Surnames, has arranged a goodly number of family designations, representing various passions and abstract ideas, thus:—

"Anger, Affection, and Amiss,
Bane, Anguish, Bravery, and Bliss;
Cant, Concord, Comfort, Craft, and Crime,
Hope, Joy, and Grief—subdued by time;
Faith, Fortune, Fancy, Force, and Fear,
Experience, Danger, Evil, Care;
Choice, Courage, Gallantry, and Skill,
Chance, Folly, Vigour, Want, and Will;
Grace, Honour, Justice, Worth, and Reason,
Service and Treasure (but no Treason);
Love, Truelove, Liberty, and Weal,
Guile, Mercy, Wisdom, Wit, and Zeal;
Trash, Twaddle, Tattle, Thrift, and Trust,
Height, Hatred, Hazard, Haste, and Rust;
Pride, Prudence, Patience, Pain, and Pluck,
Vice, Virtue, Villany, and Luck;
Youth, Motion, Tallent, Welfare, Need,
Wrath, Fury, Thickness, Spite, and Speed;
Fudge, Foresight, Fitness, Forecast, State,
Pomp, Service, Innocence, and Weight."

It is extremely difficult to account for this class of names. A few of them may have been borrowed from the characters who performed in the *mysteries*, miracle plays, and pageants, of the middle ages (see Eng. Surn., vol. i. p. 228); but most of them are, I suspect, either corruptions of other names, or words which are susceptible of a different interpretation. For instance, Anger, Hope, Worth, Wisdom, and others are local; Bane and Thickness relate to personal characteristics; Weight is a corruption of Wait, a minstrel, &c., &c.

QUARLES. 1. O. E. *quarel.* A stonequarry. 2. An extra-parochial district in the hundred of North Greenhoe, co. Norfolk.

QUARMAN. A quarryman.

QUARRELL. The bolt, or arrow, shot from a cross-bow was so called; but the surname is evidently derived from O. Eng. *quarel*, a stone quarry, and is thus cognate with Pitt, Hole, &c. Quarel. H.R.

QUARREOUR. A quarryman. Le Quareur. H.R.

QUARRIE. The Gaelic Mac Quarrie, deprived of its prefix.

QUARRIER. Either a quarryman, or the quarry itself. Fr. *carrière.* The Ad Quarer, and De la Quarrere of the H.R. support the latter derivation.

QUARRY. From residence near one.

QUARTERMAINE. QUARTER-MAN. See Quatremaine.

QUATREMAINE. Fr. "four hands," which form the charge of the family shield, though one would hardly venture to place the bearers of the name in the *quadrumanous* or monkey tribe! In France we find a family of Quatrebarbes, whose arms are likewise descriptive, being four beards! Quatremayns, Quatremeyns, &c. H.R.

QUAY. From residence near one.

QUAYLE. An ancient family in the Isle of Man. B.L.G.

QUEELTY. The same as Keelty.

QUEEN. The Gaelic Mac Queen, sans Mac.

QUEERAN. An old Scottish personal name—Queran. St. Queran, a Scotch Abbot, is honoured in the Roman calendar on Sept. 9.

QUELCH. A northern guttural pronunciation of Welch or Welsh.

QUENNEL. O. F. *quesnel;* an oak tree. Quesnel is a well-known Fr. surname.

QUENTIN. See St. Quentin.

QUHITELAW. "Of that Ilk," in Scotland. I cannot find the place, unless Whitelaw, on the Cheviots, is intended.

QUICK. Lively, vivacious in disposition.

QUICKE. See Quick.

QUILLAN. "The Mac Quillans were lords of the territory of the Routes, in co. Antrim, holding their chief residence in the fine old sea-girt castle of Dunluce. They are considered to have been invaders, from Wales, on earlier inhabitants of the North." D'Alton.

QUILLIAMS. A strongly aspirated form of Williams. Ferguson.

QUILLISH. Mr. Ferguson considers this an aspirated form of Willis, which is probable.

QUILLY. Quilli, a place in the arrondissement of Falaise, in Normandy.

QUILSON. As both Quill and Quilson exist as surnames, Quil or Quill would appear to be an obsolete personal name.

QUILTER. A maker of quilts.

QUILTON. The Gaelic Mac Quilton, sans Mac.

QUIN. An ancient Celtic personal name, found in Ireland as O'Quin, and in Scotland as Mac Quin. See O'Quinn.

QUINAN. An old personal name in Ireland.

QUINCE. The same as Quincy.

QUINCY, DE. The name is in Holinshed's list of the followers of William the Conqueror; but I believe the family were of no importance in England until the reign of Henry II., when Saier de Quincy had a grant from the crown, of the manor of Bushby, co. Northampton. His son, of the same name, was created Earl of Winchester by King John. Of the locality of Quincy I am ignorant. In charters, the name was latinized De Quinciato, De Quinci, De Quency.

QUINLAN. Probably an old Irish personal name.

QUINN. See Quin and O'Quinn.

QUINTEN. See St. Quintin.

QUINTIN. See St. Quintin.

QUINTON. A parish in Northamptonshire.

QUIRKE. The O'Cuirces, or Mac Quirkes, were an ancient sept in Munster. D'Alton.

QUOMMAN. The same as Quarman.

R.

RAAB. See Rabe.

RABBIT. Perhaps from some fancied resemblance to that animal. *Rabett* is, however, an archaism for a war-horse; thus in a MS. quoted by Halliwell:—

> "Then came the dewke Segwyne ryght,
> Armed on a *rabett* wyght,—"

i.e. on a strong charger. And—

> "Sir Guy bestrode a *rabyghte*,
> That was moche and lyghte."

Rabut is the form in H.R.

RABE. Germ. *rabe*, a raven or crow.

RABETT. See Rabbit. This ancient family, who have resided at Bramfield, co. Suffolk, for several centuries, claim a Norman descent. B.L.G. For the etymology see Rabbit.

RABONE. The same as Rathbone.

RABY. A township in Durham, famous for its castle; also another township in Cheshire.

RACE. In Yorkshire, a rivulet; in the South, a mill-stream; also the meeting of two tides, as Portland Race. The H.R. Race, without prefix, appears to point to some other origin.

RACHEL. See Female Christian Names.

RACINE. Fr. a root—a singular but illustrious surname in France. We have also the synonymous Radix, and Roots.

RACK. This word, in our provincial dialects, and in Old English, has so many meanings, that it is difficult to decide on the probable origin of the name. Halliwell gives no less than seventeen distinct definitions of the word, and I could, if need were, add several more.

RACKET. Camden, speaking of surnames assumed from inn and traders' signs, mentions 'Robin at the Racket' as a name so derived. I know not what *racket* may imply, except that it is the garment thus described by Jamieson: "A dress frock. Su. Gothic, *rocke*, Armorican, *roket*, Fr. *rochet*, toga."

RACKHAM. A hamlet in Sussex.

RADCLIFFE. See Radclyffe.

RADCLYFFE. A well-known family, "who trace their descent to Richard R. of Radcliffe Tower, near Bury, co. Lancaster, in the reign of Edward I." Shirley's Noble and Gentle Men.

RADFORD. Villages and hamlets in cos. Nottingham, Oxford, and Warwick.

RADIX. See Racine.

RADLEY. A parish in Berkshire.

RADMALL. See Radmell.

RADMELL. Rodmill, co. Sussex—formerly written Radmell. It had owners of its own name, called De Rademylde, in the XIV. cent.

RADNOR. A town in Radnorshire.

RADWAY. A parish in Warwickshire.

RAE. Either the Gaelic Mac Rae, deprived of its prefix; or *rae*, the Scottish form of roe, a deer. *Ra*, probably with the latter meaning, is found in A-Sax. times, as a Christian name.

RAEBURN. A stream in the parish of Eskdalemuir, co. Dumfries.

RAFFLES. A place in the parish of Mouswald, in Dumfries-shire. That parish contains five old border fortresses; the least dilapidated is that of Raffles. Gaz. Scotl.

RAFTER. A man who floats a raft of timber down a river?

RAGGETT. Reigate, in Surrey, is locally so pronounced.

RAGLAND. Raglan, a parish and castle in Monmouthshire.

RAGLESS. Qu. *reckless?*—devoid, not of rags—though Le Ragged is a H.R. surname—but of *recce* (A-Sax) care, caution.

RAGSDALE. Ragdale, a parish in Leicestershire.

RAIKE. RAIKES. In Scotl. a *rake*, or *raik*, is the extent of a course, walk, or fishing ground, as sheep-raik, cattle-raik, &c. See Jamieson.

RAILTON. Probably the same as Relton.

RAIMENT. Doubtless a corruption of Raymond.

RAINBOW. Probably from an inn or trader's sign.

RAINE. RAYNE. The northern families probably sprang from Rayne, co. Aberdeen; the southern from Raine, co. Essex.

RAINES. 1. An old spelling of the town of Rennes, in Brittany. 2. But the Raineses of Essex, Yorkshire, and Sussex, descend from Roger, a companion in arms of William the Conqueror, who rewarded him with lands at Rayne in Essex and elsewhere. Hence he and his posterity acquired the name of De Raines, or Raneis. Morant's Essex.

RAINS. See Raines.

RAINY. RAINEY. Fr. *René*, renatus, born-again, has been suggested as a probable origin. See, however, Reynolds.

RAISIN. Raisen is the name of three parishes, one of which comprises the town of Market Raisin, all in the county of Lincoln.

RAIT. The ancient family of Rait of Halgreen, co. Kincardine, derived their surname from the lands of Rate in Perthshire. B.L.G. There is a village in the last-named county called Rait.

RAKE. See Raike.

RALEIGH. An ancient Devonshire family, who, according to Fuller, derived their name from "a well-known town" in that county. I cannot discover any town, or even village, so called, though the name is indissolubly connected with the shire, in the persons of the two famous Raleighs —William, Bishop of Winchester, temp. Henry III., and the renowned, but unfortunate, Sir Walter, who were both born within its limits. In the Rotuli Hundredorum for the county of Somerset, there is a Warinus de Raleghe.

RALFS. A derivative of Ralph.

RALPH. The personal name Radulphus, introduced at the time of the Norman Conquest. It has given rise to Relfe, Realf, Ralfs, Raw, Rawes, Rawson, Rason, Rawlins, Rawlings, Rawlinson, Roaf, Rolfe, and other surnames.

RALSTON. The Ralstons "of that Ilk" are descended from the Mac Duffs, Thanes or Earls of Fife, one of whom had a son Ralph. The latter, obtaining a grant of lands in Renfrewshire, called them after his own name, Ralphs-toune. In process of time, his descendants, continuing on the same estate, wrote themselves De Ralphs-toune, or, by softened pronunciation, Ralston. See Crawfurd's Renfrewshire. See an analogous instance, in Fetherstonhaugh, of a place originally deriving its appellation from the personal name of its owner, and afterwards, with an addition, becoming the hereditary surname of his descendants.

RAM. 1. From the animal, like Bull, Hart, &c. 2. Mr. Ferguson derives it from O.-High Germ., *ram*, O.-Norse, *ramr*, strong, vigorous, which enters into the compounds Bertram, Ingram, &c. H.R. Le Ram.

RAMAGE. A.-Norm. Wild. Halliwell. Jamieson defines *rammage* as rash, thoughtless, furious.

RAME. A Cornish family. The name is doubtless derived from the manor and parish of Rame. C. S. Gilbert's Cornwall.

RAMM. See Ram.

RAMRIDGE. Local: the former syllable may be derived from the same source as the first in Ramsbotham, or Ramsbottom, which see; the latter syllable is the antithesis of -BOTTOM.

RAMSAY. This name is totally distinct from that of Ramsey. The Earl of Dalhousie's family are said to be of German extraction. They are traced from Simon de Ramsay of Dalhousie, in Lothian, temp. David I. 1140. The lands of Ramsay are in Argyleshire.

RAMSBOTHAM. RAMSBOTTOM. I am assured that this local surname is traceable to the eleventh century. The *locus in quo* appears to be in the parish of Bury, co. Lancaster, usually called *Roms*bottom. Bottom, I have already explained as a valley, or low ground, and the qualifying syllable is borrowed from the *rhoms*, *rambs*, or *ramps*, wild onions, whose botanical *habitat* is said to be localized to the place referred to, and to *Rams*den in the same vicinity.

RAMSDALE. Equivalent to Ramsbottom, which see.

RAMSDEN. A hamlet in co. Oxon, and a place near Bury, co. Lancaster. Two parishes in Essex are called Ramsdon.

RAMSEY. Parishes in Huntingdonshire and Essex.

RAND. 1. A parish near Wragby, in Lincolnshire. 2. A curt form of Randall or Randolf.

RANDALL. See Randolph. This name has been confounded with Rundle. See Rundle.

RANDOLF. RANDOLPH. The baptismal name. It has given rise to many diminutives, as Randoll, Randall, Rankin, Ranecock, Rands, Ranson, Hankin, Hanks, Hankinson, Hankey, &c.

RANDOLL. See Randolf, and Rundle.

RANDS. See Randolf.

RANECOCK. A diminutive of Randolf. See COCK.

RANFORD. Rainford, a chapelry, co. Lancaster.

RANGER. A sworn officer, whose business it was, under the old forest laws, to perform the duties mentioned in the following oath :—

"*The Oath of a Ranger.*

"You shall well and truly execute the office of a Ranger, in the purlieus of W. upon the borders of the King's Forest of W. You shall re-chase and with your hounds drive back again, the wild beasts of the Forest, as often as they shall range out of the same Forest into your purlieus. You shall truly present all unlawful hunting, & hunters of wild beasts of venery and chase, as well within the *pourallees* (perambulations), as within the Forest, and those and all other offences you shall present at the next Court of Attachments or Swainmote which shall first happen. So help you God."—*Nelson's Laws of Game.*

RANKIN. I always considered this a diminutive of Randolf (see Hankin); but there is a tradition of descent from one John, son of a knight called Jacob de Rankine, burgomaster of Ghent, who married a daughter of the head of the house of Keith, and became progenitor of the Rankines, Rankins, Rankens, Rankings, and Rangkings of Scotland, who are rather numerous in the West, and on the border. The tradition is, however, dateless and vague. Inf. M. H. Rankin, Esq.

RANSCOMB. A place near Lewes, co. Sussex.

RANSOM. RANSOME. From analogous corruptions, I should say, that this name was originally Ransham, though I find no place so called. Mr. Ferguson, with his accustomed facility, finds the etymon in the O.-Norse *ransamr*, prædabundus, piratical. "What curious changes," says he, "the whirligig of time brings round. We take our money to the descendant of the old sea-robber to take care of for us—Ransom & Co., bankers, Pall Mall. Another Ransome has turned his sword into a ploughshare, and become famed as a maker of agricultural implements at Ipswich."

RANSON. See Randolf.

RAPER. An old spelling of Roper, which see.

RAPHAEL. The designation of an archangel, which became, like Michael, a name of men. It is chiefly borne by Jews.

RAPKIN. A contraction of Ralphkin, a dimunitive of Ralph.

RAPP. Germ. *rapp*, quick, swift of foot.

RAPSON. A contraction of Ralphson, the son of Ralph.

RASHLEIGH. "Rashleigh in the parish of Wemworthy, in Devonshire, gave name to this ancient family, the elder line of which became extinct in the reign of Henry VII." Shirley's Noble and Gentle Men.

RASTRICK. A chapelry in the parish of Halifax, co. York, where the family resided in 1250. See Watson's Hist. of Halifax.

RAT. The animal : a sobriquet. Le Rat. H.R.

RATCLIFF. RATCLIFFE. Parishes and places in cos. Nottingham, Leicester, and Middlesex.

RATE. Has been explained as the Irish *raithe*, arbiter, umpire.

RATHBONE. 1. An ancient personal name? 2. A corruption of Rathbourne (A-Sax.), a quick or rapid stream.

RATHERHAM. A corruption of Rotherham.

RATLIFF. A corruption of Ratcliffe.

RATTLEBAG. I know not whether this odd surname still exists. It is common in old records, as Ratellebagg. It is probably synonymous with the O.-Fr. *claqueur*, a leper or lazar, so called because he collected alms by means of a *claquette*, clackdish, or "rattle-trap," which answered the two-fold purpose of calling the attention of the charitable, and at the same time of warning them against a too near approach to the unfortunate leper.

RATTON. An estate at Willingdon, co. Sussex, on which the family were resident in the XIV. century.

RATTRAY. Derived from a barony of the same name in Perthshire. The first of the name on record is Alan de Ratheriff, who lived in the reigns of William the Lion and Alexander II. B.L.G. The family still reside at Craighall, in the parish of Rattray.

RAVEN. A personal name derived from the bird, borne in the Danish standard. The Domesday of Leicestershire presents us with a tenant in chief called Raven—a true Scandinavian, doubtless. Rafn still exists in Denmark as a personal name, and is borne as a surname by a distinguished professor and archæologist of Copenhagen.

RAVENHILL. Local : " the Hill frequented by Ravens."

RAVENS. The genitive form of Raven.

RAVENSCROFT. A township in Cheshire.

RAVENSFIELD. A parish in Yorkshire. De Rafnesfield. H.R. of that county.

RAVENSHOLT. Local : "the *Holt* frequented by Ravens."

RAVENSTONE. Parishes in cos. Buckingham and Derby.

RAW. 1. This name, and Rawes, are diminutives of Ralph. 2. The northern form of Row, Rowe. 3. A township in Northumberland.

RAWBONE. A corruption of Rathbone.

RAWCLIFFE. Townships, &c., in cos. York and Lancaster—two in each. The ancient orthography seems to have been Rockliffe.

RAWDON. An estate in the parish of Guiseley, co. York, is " the original seat of this ancient family, which is traced to Thor de Rawdon, whose son Serlo lived in the reign of Stephen. Rawdon remained the family residence till early in the seventeenth century, when Sir George Rawdon, the then head of the house removed into the North of Ireland, and was seated at Moira, in the county of Down, where the family principally lived till the match with the heiress of Hastings in 1752." Shirley's Noble and Gentle Men.

RAWES. See Raw.

RAWLEIGH. See Raleigh.

RAWLEY. The same as Raleigh.

RAWLINGS. RAWLINS. See Ralph.

RAWLINSON. See Ralph.

RAWSON. See Raw, and Ralph.

RAWSTORNE. This family designated by Burke, " ancient and worshipful," are stated to have been settled for centuries in Lancashire, though he only traces them to 37 Henry VIII. The name would appear to be derived from Rawston in that county.

RAY. The estate of Gill, in the parish of Bromfield, co. Cumberland, belonged to the family of Reay, or Ray, from the time of William the Lion, king of Scotland, who died in 1214. Tradition says, that the original Ray was a faithful adherent of the Scottish monarch, by whom he was greatly esteemed, for his extraordinary swiftness of foot in pursuing the deer (which, like that of the Homeric hero, ποδας ωκυς Αχιλλευς, exceeded that of most horsemen and dogs) and who gave him the estate. The tenure was by a pepper-corn rent, with the stipulation, that the name of William should be perpetuated in the family. This was strictly observed from generation to generation, until the latter half of the last century, when the Mr. William Reay in possession gave to the 'hope of the house' the name of John. From these Reays have sprung most, if not all, the Rays, Wreys, and Wrays, in England. John Ray, the naturalist, originally wrote himself Wray, and his ancestors, who but a generation or two before had emigrated from Cumberland, spelt their name indifferently Wray or Wrey. The surname itself was probably borrowed from the sobriquet of William the Lion's fleet-footed vassal, *Ra*, or *raa*, being the A-Sax., and *rae* the Lowland Scottish for a roe. Hutchinson's Cumberland, 1794, vol. ii. p. 302. The fish called a *ray* was so named after the great naturalist.

There are several Le Rays in H.R.

RAYDEN. RAYDON. Raydon, or Roydon, a parish in Suffolk, and Reydon, or Roydon, a parish in Norfolk

RAYMENT. See Raiment.

RAYMOND. An ancient Christian name—Raimundus. It was introduced at the Conquest, or soon after.

The Irish Raymonds have been supposed to be descendants of Raymond le Gros, the invader of Ireland, temp. Henry II., especially as they held possessions within the ancient territory of "The Clanmaurice." It appears, however, more likely that they sprang from the family of Raymond of Essex, and settled in the sister kingdom so lately as the end of the reign of Elizabeth. See B.L.G.

RAYNE. See Raine.

RAYNER. An old personal name. Raynerus occurs as a Herefordshire tenant in capite in Domesday. Reyner and Fil' Reyner. H.R.

RAYNES. See Raines.

RAYNHAM. Rainham, a parish in Kent.

REA. See Ray, and Rae.

REACH. In the South, means a creek, and sometimes a part of a river more than usually straight. A Scottish family-name of the same orthography is pronounced as a dissyllable, with the *ch* hard, *Re-ack*, and is referred to a Celtic origin. A gentleman dining in a mixed company with one of the proprietors of this name, whom he only knew by his writings, naturally enough called him Mr. Reach (*ch* soft), and was corrected with the observation, that *ch* should be sounded like k. "I beg Mr. *Re-ack's* pardon," promptly replied the offender, "and as he is presiding over the dessert, I'll just trouble him to send me a *pe-ack!*"

READ. READE. Red. See Reed and Reid.

READER. In the archives of Norwich, *reders* and tylers occur in juxta-position; wherefore it is probable that the employment of the *reder* was that of thatching buildings with reeds. H.R. Le Reder, Le Redere.

READING. A town in Berkshire.

READMAN. 1. See Redman. 2. Possibly *réd*, A-Sax. counsel, and *man*—a counsellor or adviser. 3. The A-Sax. personal name Redmund.

READWIN. See Redwin.

READY. One of a quick or willing disposition.

REALF. See Ralph.

REARDEN. See Riordan.

REARDON. See Riordan.

REASON. Has probably no relation to that which distinguishes the man from the brute. It is perhaps a corruption of Reeve's-son—analogous to Stewardson, Cookson, &c.

REAY. See under Ray. The Reays of Scotland, however, more probably sprang from Reay, a parish in the shires of Caithness and Sutherland.

REBECK. REBBECK. A kind of ancient violin—probably a trader's sign; or perhaps local. See Beck.

RECKLESS. A man of bold and rash disposition.

RECORD. A known corruption of Rickword. A Sussex family, in the XVIII. century, wrote themselves Record, alias Rickword.

RECTOR. See ECCLESIASTICAL SURNAMES. The Fitz-Rector of H.R. induces a suspicion of broken vows. Rector has, however, other and secular applications.

REDDEN. REDDIN. 1. Corruptions of Reading, the Berkshire town. 2. A hamlet in Roxburghshire.

REDDING. 1. From Reading, co. Berks, so pronounced. 2. From Redding, a village in Stirlingshire.

REDDISH. Not *sub-rufus*, but a township in the parish of Manchester.

REDDY. The same as Ready.

REDE. 1. The same as Read, Reed, Reid, &c. 2. The Redes of Suffolk are said to be derived from Brianus de Rede, who was living in the year 1139.

REDFORD. The same as Radford.

REDGRAVE. A parish in Suffolk.

REDHEAD. Perhaps from hair and complexion; more likely local, from places so called in Forfarshire and Orkney. The Redheved of H.R., however, supports the former hypothesis. *Heved*. A-Sax., the head.

REDHOUSE. Local: place unknown.

REDLEY. The same as Ridley.

REDMAIN. A joint township with Blindcrake, co. Cumberland. The name was latinized in charters as De Rubra Manu—"of the red hand."

REDMAN. 1. Might be classed with Blackman, Whiteman, &c., in reference to complexion. 2. It is more likely identical with the *Radmannus* or *Radchenistre* of Domesday. The persons so designated held under a certain tenure, chiefly of the servile kind. According to Dr. Nash, they were freemen who served on horseback. "Radcniht—equestris homo." Ellis, Introd. Domesd., i. 74. See Roadnight. 3. The same as Redmain. 4. The same as Redmund.

REDMAYNE. See Redmain.

REDMOND. An ancient personal name. "Alexander Redmond, the first of this family who bore that surname, was of the same stock as the Earl of Pembroke, whom he accompanied to Ireland in 1170." B.L.G. Redmond of Killoughter.

REDMUND. The A-Sax. personal name.

REDPATH. A village in co. Berwick.

REDVERS. Richard de R., a Domesday tenant in capite, was eldest son of Baldwin de Brion. Ellis' Introd. Domesd.

REDWIN. An A-Sax. personal name.

REDWOOD. Local : place unknown.

REDYEAR. "Red-ear"—a sobriquet?

REECE. See Rees.

REED. 1. Red—allusive to complexion or dress, probably the former. This is a common medieval spelling. "What betokeneth it whan the sonne gothe downe *reed?*" Palsgrave. Maundevile says of the Red Sea : "that see is not more *reed* than another see." 2. Reed, a parish in Hertfordshire ; Reede, another in Suffolk. The Reeds of Cragg, co. Northumberland, probably took their name from Redesdale, in which they have been immemorially located, or rather from the river which gives name to that dale. On a mural monument in Elsdon church, erected in the year 1758, to the memory of Elrington Reed, the family are stated to have been resident in Redesdale for *more than nine hundred years.* This Sir Walter Scott calls an "incredible space " of time, and so it is ; though the high antiquity of the family is unquestionable. See notes to Rokeby. In the H.R. Le Red, and La Red, are very common, as descriptive surnames, for both sexes.

REEDING. The town of Reading, co. Berks.

REEDS. A pluralization of Reed.

REEKIE. An Edinburgh surname. It may be derived from one of the localities called Reeky Linn, or Reeking Linn ; but why not from ' Auld Reekie ' itself?

REES. A Welsh personal name, anciently Rhys, whence the modifications and derivatives, Rice, Price or Pryce, (Ap-Rhys) Apreece, Reece, Preece, &c. Sir Elidir Dhu, who flourished temp. Richard I. (a descendant, according to the Welsh genealogies, of Coel Codevog, King of Britain), was the direct ancestor of the family of Rees of Killymaenllwyd, co. Carmarthen ; and there are several other ancient families now called Rees in the Principality, although the stationary surname is of comparatively recent adoption.

REEVE. The bailiff of a franchise or manor. A-Sax. *gerefa.* One of Chaucer's Canterbury pilgrims is a Reeve, but the poet's account of his duties and pursuits reminds us more of a great man's farmbailiff than of the official reeve.

"His lordes scheep, his meet, and his dayerie,
His swyn, his hors, his stoor, and his pultrie,
Was (w)holly in this Reeve's governynge."
PROLOGUE, 599, &c.

"In auncient time," says honest old Lambarde, "almost every manor had his Reve, whose authoritie was, not only to levie the Lord's rents, to set to worke his servaunts, and to husband his demeasnes to his best profit and commoditie, but also to govern his tenants in peace, and to lead them foorth to war, when necessitie so required. And although this name, and so much of the authoritie as remained was (after the comming in of the Normanes) transferred to another, which they called Baylife; yet in sundry places of the realme (especially in copiholde manors, where olde custome prevaileth) the woord Reve is yet wel inough understood." Perambulation of Kent, 1576. H.R. Le Reve.

REEVES. A pluralization of Reeve, which see.

REGAN. See O'Regan.

REGISTER. A corruption of Rochester. *Per contra,* a Sussex peasant calls his baptismal register a *rochester.*

REID. An old northern pronunciation of *red.* See Reed. See also Jamieson's Dict.

REIGATE. A town in Surrey, where the family dwelt temp. Edward I.

REIKIE. See Reekie.

REILLY. An Irish personal name, usually prefixed with O'.

REISS. A Russian. Aberdeen Regist., quoted by Jamieson.

RELFE. See Ralph.

RELPH. See Ralph.

RELTON. A manor so called, in the hundred of Pidre, co. Cornwall, is mentioned in the Rotuli Hundredorum, temp. Edward I.

REMMINGTON. See Rimington.

RENARD. The personal name Reinardus.

RENDALL. RENDEL. RENDELL. RENDLE. Probably a mere variety of pronunciation of Rundle, which see.

RENDER. I have met with the expression *render,* applied to a man who cleaves laths. See Cleaver.

RENFREW. The Scottish town giving name to Renfrewshire.

RENN. 1. See Wren. H.R. De Rennes. 2. See Reynolds.

RENNALS. See Reynolds.

RENNER. O. E. *renne* is to run : a runner. The Promptorium Parvulorum latinizes *rennare,* as cursor ; also as fugitivus, profugus, &c.

RENNICK. See Renwick.

RENNIE. RENNY. See Reynolds.

RENNISON. See Reynolds.

RENOLDS. The same as Reynolds.

RENSHAW. 1. Renishaw, a place in co. Derby. 2. See Olerenshaw.

RENTON. A small town in Dumbartonshire.

RENWICK. Anciently Ravenwick—a parish in Cumberland.

REPINGTON. See Repton.

REPTON. A parish in Derbyshire, otherwise written Repinton. Hence the surnames Repington and Rippington, as well as Repton proper.

RERESBY. The family of Reresby, or Reversby, were seated at Thribergh, co. York, or the neighbourhood, from the time of the Conqueror. Burke's Ext. Barts.

RESKYMER. The family became extinct in the XVII. century. They had resided for fourteen generations on their estate of Reskymer, in the parish of St. Mawgan, near Helston. C. S. Gilbert's Cornwall.

RETFORD. A town in Nottinghamshire.

REVELEY. "The Reveleys, who trace their pedigree to the reign of Edward II., were originally seated at the manor-house of Reveley, on the northern bank of the river Breamish, at the south-eastern foot of Cheviot, and subsequently at Ancroft, in Northumberland." B.L.G.

REVELL. The same as Revill.

REVERE. Possibly Fr. *rivière*, a river.

REVILL. Two places in Normandy bear the name of Réville; one near Bernai, and the other in the arrondissement of Valognes. The surname still exists in Normandy.

REW. Rewe, a parish in Devonshire.

REWE. A parish in Devonshire.

REX. Possibly from one having played the part of a king in some miracle play. But more likely an abbreviated form of a familiar Christian name thus:—Richard, Rick, Ricks, Recks, Rex. In H.R. we have an Adam and a John Rex.

REYNARD. See Reynolds.

REYNARDSON. See Reynold.

REYNELL. See Reynolds. The Reynells of Ogwell, co. Devon, traced their pedigree to Sir Richard Reynell, of Pyttney, co. Somerset, who flourished in the reigns of Henry II. and Richard I., and had the custody of the castles of Launceston and Exeter. B.L.G.

REYNER. Mr. Ferguson says:—"This is the same name as that of the famous Northern sea-king, Ragnar Lodbrok, who ravaged England in the ninth century, and, being taken prisoner by Ella, king of Northumberland, was, as the legend goes, stung to death in a dungeon filled with serpents." Reinhard and Reinardus seem to be variations of the same name. H.R. Reyner and Fil' Reyner.

REYNOLDS. From Rainhold, a Teutonic personal name of great antiquity. Several tenants in chief in Domesd. are called Rainaldus.—Reynell, Reynard, Rey-

nardson, Rennals, with perhaps Renn, Rainey, Rennie, Renny, and Rennison, are modifications and diminutives.

REYNOLDSON. See Reynolds.

RHEIMS. Camden mentions this as a surname introduced about the time of the Norman Conquest. It is probably derived from the city of France so called.

RHEINLANDER. One dwelling in Rheinland, or on the borders of the Rhine. The name appears to be naturalized here from Germany.

RHIND. The name occurs in the Chartulary of Moray early in the XIII. cent., and it has been variously spelt Rhynd, Rhind, Rynd, and Rind. It is doubtless territorial, and derived either from the parish of Rhynd, co. Perth, or from the estate of Rhind, in Fifeshire. Inf. A. H. Rhind, Esq. F.S.A.

RHODES. Not from the Island, as stated in Eng. Surn.; but a corruption of Roadhouse or Rodehouse, as appears from the Par. Reg. of Eckington, co. Derby. Inf. Rev. J. Eastwood.

RHYMER. A maker of verses, who, in the middle ages, sometimes united the functions of the poet and the prophet, after the manner of the ancient bards and seers.

RHYS. The ancient Welsh personal name, now more commonly written Rees.

RIBBONS. Perhaps a corruption of Reuben, Reubens.

RICARDO. David Ricardo, the celebrated writer on political economy, born 1772, was the son of a Dutch merchant. The surname is probably synonymous with Richard.

RICE. See Rees.

RICH. More probably an abbreviation of Richard, than an epithet implying wealth. A Norman origin has been assigned to this name, I know not upon what grounds. The extinct peerage family dated from a London mercer of the XV. cent. The Hampshire family, however, are said to have written themselves Le Rich in the XIV. century, and that form is found in H.R. In Sussex this name has been in some instances corrupted from Ridge.

RICHARD. This baptismal name, besides becoming itself a surname, has given rise to many others ; viz., Richards, Richardson, Rich, Ritchie, Riches, Rick, Ricks, Rix, Rickson, Rixon, Ritson, Rickards, Ricket, Ricketts. From Dick and Hitchin, two ' nurse-names ' of Richard, we also derive Dix, Dicks, Dickson, Dixon, Digons, Dickens, Dickins, Dickinson, Dickerson, Dickison; and Hitchins, Hitchinson, Hitchcock, Hitchcox.

RICHARDS. See Richard.

RICHARDSON. See Richard.

RICHBELL. Apparently Richbold, a Teutonic personal name.

RICHER. The Norman orthography of Richard.

RICHES. The genitive of Rich, that is Richard; the son of Richard.

RICHMAN. Perhaps a corruption of Richmond. But see Rickman.

RICHMOND. A place in the arrondissement of Neufchatel in Normandy; also the famous castle of Richmond in the N. Riding of Yorkshire, built by the great Earl Alan, temp. Will. Conq., for defence against the disinherited Englishmen and Danes— "pro tuitione suorum contra infestationem Anglorum, tunc ubique exheriditatorum, similiter et Danorum; et nominavit dictum Castrum *Richemont*, suo idiomate Gallico, quod sonat Latinè *divitem montem*, in editiori ac fortiori loco sui territorii situatum." Gale, Regist. Ellis's Domesd. Richmond, in Surrey, anciently Sheen, was so called by Henry VII., on his building a palace there, after his own title of Earl of Richmond in Yorkshire.

RICHTER. Germ. A magistrate.

RICK. A common abbreviation of Richard.

RICKS. See Richard.

RICKARD. RICKARDS. See Richard.

RICKETTS. "I will, while 'tis in my mind, insert this remarque; viz., about 1620, one Ricketts of Newbury, perhaps corruptly from *Ricards*, a practitioner in physick, was excellent at the curing of children with swoln heads and small legges; and the disease being new, and without a name, he being so famous for the cure of it, they called the disease the *ricketts*; as the King's evill from the King's curing of it with his touch; and now 'tis good sport to see how they vex their lexicons, and fetch it from the Greek Ράχις, the back-bone." Aubrey's Nat. Hist. of Wilts, 4to., p. 74. Dr. Johnson says the name was given by Dr. Glisson on the first appearance of the disease. Dr. Glisson was contemporary with, and probably known to, Mr. Ricketts, and therefore Aubrey's statement may be correct. He is most likely right, too, as to Ricketts being a corruption of Rickards, which, in its turn, is a corruption of Richards.

RICKMAN. Mr. Ferguson remarks :— "We have Richman and Rickman, corresponding with a Gothic Richman, and an Old High German Ricman, quoted by Meidinger." I demur to the derivation of Richman, which is more likely a corruption of Richmond, the local name; but Rickman is doubtless of high Teutonic antiquity. It was certainly in England in Saxon times, when a Hertfordshire proprietor of this designation gave to his estate the name of Rickman's-Worth. In the Rotuli Hundredorum, Rikemund is found as a heritable name, and there is also one John fil'Rikeman.

RICKS. See Rick.

RICKSON. See Richard.

RICKWORD. Apparently an old personal name. Ricuard, Ricuardus, in Domesday.

RIDDELL. Of that Ilk, in the parish of Lilliesleaf, co. Roxburgh. There is a tradition of great antiquity, ascending to the VII. or VIII. century. See Lay of the Last Minstrel, notes—but documentary evidence goes back to the XII. only. Richard Basset, justiciar of England, temp. Hen. I., married the heiress of Riddell, and his eldest son assumed his mother's surname. Genealogists differ as to the extraction of the family. See Douglas's Baronage. Betham's Baronetage, Nisbet's Heraldry, &c.

RIDDIFORD. A probable corruption of Rutherford.

RIDDING. A hamlet in Derbyshire.

RIDDLE. See Riddell.

RIDE. Ryde, in the Isle of Wight, was formerly so written.

RIDEOUT. Possibly from *redoubt*, a military fortification. Fr. *réduit*; Ital. *ridotto*; Span. *reduto*. The H.R. Ridhut will, however, hardly bend to this etymology.

RIDER. A forest-officer, who, having a large district to supervise, was mounted, in contradistinction to the *walker*. See Walker. He was sometimes called a "riding-forester," and it was his duty to lead the King in his hunting. Nelson's Laws of Game. Rider is also local. In the Siege of Carlaverock, we are told—"William de Ridre was there, who in a blue banner bore crescents of gold." He is elsewhere called Ryther, and he probably took his name from the place so called in Yorkshire. Ryder, Lord Harrowby, claims from that source, and bears the same arms with a slight addition. H.R. Le Ridere.

RIDESDALE. Redesdale, co. Northumberland.

RIDGE. A parish in Herts. Many other minor localities are so called. The medieval form is Atte Rigge, whence Trigg. In the XVI. cent. it was commonly written A'Ridge.

RIDGER. See Ridge, and the termination ER.

RIDGEWAY. The extinct baronet family, created Lords Londonderry in Ireland, traced their pedigree to 6. Edw. IV., when Stephen Ridgeway was one of the stewards of the city of Exeter. There are two places in Devonshire called Ridgeway, one near Honiton, and the other near Plymouth, but from which of these the family sprang is unknown. In the early generations, the family wrote themselves Ridgeway alias Peacock.

RIDGMAN. See Ridge, and the termination MAN.

RIDGWAY. See Ridgeway.

RIDLER. 1. A dealer in wool is so called in Lincolnshire. 2. A maker of the peculiar kind of sieves called riddles.

RIDLEY. Places in cos. Chester, Kent, and Northumberland. The baronet's family were seated at Willimoteswick, in the last-named shire, in 1481, and there, early in the XVI. cent., was born Nicholas Ridley, the martyr-bishop. See Shirley's Noble and Gentle Men.

RIDPATH. See Redpath.

RIE. O. Fr. A bank, or elevated spot. A common medieval surname.

RIGDEN. That this name originated among the *dens* of Kent, is quite certain, though I cannot find the locality. The family have long been connected, by landed possessions, with various parishes in that county. See Hasted.

RIGG. RIGGE. RIGGS. Rigg is the medieval spelling of Ridge, which see.

RIGMAIDEN. Two gentry families, settled respectively in cos. Lincoln and Lancaster, bore this remarkable name, which at the commencement of the present century was still extant. I can give no better etymology for the name than that I have already assigned in Eng. Surn.; viz., "a romping girl." For the curious seal of *George Rygmayden*, with a rebus, see Gent. Mag. 1833, 1. 305.

RILEY. Probably derived from a place in Brittany, formerly called Rilley or Relay, the seat of an Abbey of Augustinians, in the diocese of Rennes. In the parish-registers of Newchurch, in Rossendale, co. Lancaster, the name of the Rileys was almost uniformly spelt Rilay, down to the middle of the XVIII. century. Inf. H. T. Riley, Esq.

RILL. A small stream.

RIMBAULT. The same as Rumbold?

RIMER. See Rymer.

RIMINGTON. A township in Yorkshire.

RING. Many old towns have, or have had, an open space or circus, where, in former times, bull-baiting, and such-like barbarous pastimes took place, and these are sometimes called Rings.

RINGER. A skilful ringer of church bells would readily acquire this surname. See Bellringer. The surname Ringebell, or Ringbell, is found in the H.R.

RIORDAN. An old Irish surname, variously written O'Rierdon, Reyrdon, Reardon, Rearden, &c.

RIPER. 1. A corruption of De Ripariis, or Rivers. 2. *Ripier*, a man from the sea shore, who sells fish in inland towns and villages. Cooper's Sussex Glossary. Brome calls these men *rippers*. Travels, ed. 1700, p. 274. Halliwell derives the word from *rip*, a basket, or pannier, used for carrying fish, and quotes from Havelok:—

> A stirte til him with his *rippe*
> And bigan the fish to kippe."

Le Ripier. H.R.

RIPLEY. Places in Surrey, Derby, and Yorkshire.

RIPPINGTON, See Repton.

RIPPON. RIPPIN. Ripon in Yorkshire.

RISBY. Riseby, a parish united with Roxby, co. Lincoln.

RISE. An eminence—the same as Rye or Rie.

RISELEY. A parish in Bedfordshire.

RISLEY. A chapelry in Derbyshire.

RITCHIE. See Richard.

RITH. O. Eng. *eruth*, a ford. See Eng. Surn. i. 71.

RITSON. A northern corruption of Richardson.

RIVER. From residence near one. O. Eng. Atte River; Fr. De la Rivière.

☞ **RIVERS,** SURNAMES DERIVED FROM. "Rivers," says Camden, "have imposed names to some men." He might more properly have said, to *many* men. It is unnecessary to particularize them here, as they will be found under their respective heads.

RIVINGTON. A chapelry in the parish of Bolton, co. Lancaster.

RIX. See Richard.

RIXON. See Richard.

ROACH. See Roche.

ROADNIGHT. A-Sax. *rad*, and *cnight*, a riding servitor, or attendant on horseback. In feudal times, *rodknights* were "certain servitors, who held their lands by serving their lords on horseback." Jacob's Law Dict. Spelman's Gloss. In Piers Ploughman we meet with 'redyng-kyng,' in the same sense. See Redman.

ROADS. See Rhodes.

ROAF. The personal name Ralph was sometimes so written, in the fifteenth century.

ROAKE. Probably from St. Roche, the Confessor, whose festival was anciently observed on August 16.

ROAN. A medieval spelling of Rouen, the capital of Normandy. An old poet, speaking of Richard Cœur de Lion, says:

> " Thy bowels only Carceol keeps;
> Thy corse Font Everard ;
> But *Roan* hath keeping of thy heart,
> O puissant Richard!"

The heart of this chivalrous monarch was buried in the choir of Rouen Cathedral.

ROB. A nickname of Robert.

ROBARTES. The same as Roberts.

ROBB. See Robert. A Northern pronunciation.

ROBBERDS. A coarse spelling of Roberts.

ROBBIE. See Robert.

ROBE. A contraction of Robert.

ROBERT. A Teutonic personal name of great antiquity, which was introduced into England about the time of the Conquest. As Rotbertus, it is frequently found in Domesday. Besides having itself become a surname, it has given rise to a great many others, as—Roberts, Robarts, Robertson, Robins, Robbins, Robinson, Robbie, Robison, Robeson, Robb, Robson, Roby. It has also taken the form of Fitz-Robert, and, in Wales, those of Ap-Robert and Ap-Robyn, now contracted to Probert and Probyn. Its nicknames are Dobb and Hobb, from the former of which we get Dobbs, Dobby, Dobbie, Dobson, Dabson, Dobbin, Dobbins, Dobinson ; and from the latter, Hobbs, Hobbes, Hobson, Hobbins, Hobkins, Hopkins, Hopkinson, and Hoby.

ROBERTS. ROBARTS. See Robert. The family of Roberts of Glassenbury, co. Kent, extinct baronets, according to a genealogy in Harl. MSS., are descended from a William Rookherst, a Scotchman, who settled in Kent, in the third year of Henry I., and purchased lands at Goudhurst, which he called after his own name. This name he afterwards changed to Roobertes, which finally became Roberts. The tradition of descent from a Scotchman may be true or not, but that a North Briton gave name to a place in Kent called Rookherst, is a pure figment. The termination *herst*, or *hurst*, is scarcely, if at all, known in Scotland, while the Weald of Kent, where the Robertses first appear, abounds with it. The truth, doubtless, is, that the locality called from Saxon times Rookherst, gave the name De Rookherst to its early possessors, and that one of them in later times—the son of a Robert—dropped his local surname, and assumed a patronymical one.

ROBERTSON. See Robert. A Highland clan bear this name. The Robertsons of Struan, co. Perth, are unquestionably one of the oldest families in Scotland, descending both from the Mac Donalds, Lords of the Isles, and from the ancient Earls of Athol. The surname is derived from Robert, son of Duncan (de Atholia) who arrested the murderers of James I., and for that service received a royal charter, erecting his lands into a free barony, A.D. 1451. Alexander, his son, adopted the surname Robertson, which became persistent.

ROBILLIARD. The name of a fief dependent on that of St. Ouen, in Jersey, so long the residence of the famous De Carterets.

ROBINS. ROBBINS. Robyn is a medieval diminutive, or nick-name, of Robert, as in Robin Hood, Robin Goodfellow. It generally implies something mischievous, and, in the South of England, 'What the Robin are you about?' and similar phrases, are still in use.

ROBINSON. The son of Robin, or Robert.

BEFORE YOU COULD SAY JACK ROBINSON, is a phrase implying a very brief space of time. It is "said to have originated from a very volatile gentleman of that appellation, who would call upon his neighbours, and be gone before his name could be announced." Halliwell; who shews, however, that it is not a thing of yesterday, by quoting from "an old play":—

"A warke it ys as easie to be doone,
As tys to saye, *Jacke! robys on.*"

ROBISON. ROBESON. See Robert.

ROBOTTOM. See Bottom in the Supplement.

ROBSON. See Robert.

ROBY. See Robert.

ROBYNHOD. Thomas Robynhod was a dealer in wines and charcoal at Winchelsea, in the year 1388. Cooper's Winchelsea, p. 205. Notwithstanding that the historical scepticism of our days had almost banished the great outlaw from Barnsleydale and merrie Sherwood, into the shadowy regions of Teutonic mythology, or of medieval romance, the Rev. Jos. Hunter has triumphantly asserted his existence, in real flesh and blood, under our second Edward, from documents of the greatest authenticity. See Critical and Historical Tracts, No. 4, 1852. His name occurs, not once, but several times, in 1323-4 under the orthography above given : '*Robyn Hod.*' Arguments are unnecessary to prove how popular and real a personage the freebooter was in the national mind, in the succeeding centuries. His skill as an archer was everywhere talked about and emulated, and here we have (within little more than a half-century after the date at which he flourished) a South of England tradesman assuming both his names as a surname. Whether this has descended to modern times I am unable to ascertain ; but, however this may be, it is certain that another of the Sherwood heroes has imprinted his name upon our family nomenclature in the shape of *Littlejohn*, and that at least two families so designated have taken the rank of gentry. See Burke's Armory.

ROCHE. Roache, or Roche, a parish in Cornwall ; an abbey in Yorkshire ; and a river in Lancashire. The first-named place was so called, according to Tonkin, from St. Roche, a Marsellaise saint ; but it is more likely a provincial pronunciation of *rock*, for in 1291 it is called De Rupe. D. Gilbert's Cornw., iii. 396.

The Cornish family of Roche, or De Rupe, were seated at Roch, in the reign of Richard I. C. S. Gilbert's Cornwall.

ROCHESTER. The Kentish city.

ROCHFORT. The Irish family settled in that country at, or soon after, the Anglo-Norman invasion. Their name was latinized De Rupe Forti, "of the strong rock," which is doubtless its true meaning.

ROCK. A parish in Worcestershire, a chapelry in Northumberland, and many other minor localities.

ROCKCLIFFE. See Rawcliffe. There is, however, a parish so called in Cumberland, formerly Rothcliffe. The manor was anciently the possession of Radulph de Bray, who gave it to William, the son of John de Rothcliff, in the sixth year of King John. Hutchinson's Cumberland. It is to be presumed that there was some family connection between the Brays and the Rothcliffes, and that John de R. had *resided* on the manor previously to this donation.

RODD, and RODE. A termination, the same as Royd, q.v. It is apparently an ancient particip'e of the verb to *rid*.

RODD. A place near Leominster, co. Hereford, formerly the residence of the family. C. S. Gilbert's Cornwall.

RODDAM. A township and estate in Northumberland, said to have been granted to an ancestor of the present proprietor by a charter of King Athelstan. B.L.G.

RODDEN. A parish in Somersetshire.

RODE. See Royd.

RODES. This family claim from Gerard de Rodes, a feudal baron, whose caput baroniæ was Horncastle, co. Lincoln. He lived in the reigns of Henry II., Richard I., John, and Henry III. The place from which the name was assumed does not appear.

RODGERS. See Rogers.

RODMAN. Probably the same as Redman, which see.

RODNEY. A place in co. Somerset, which was possessed by the family as early as the time of Stephen. The elder line became extinct in the XVII. century; but Lord Rodney represents a younger branch. Peerage.

RODON. The Rodons claim to be a branch of the Rowdons of Rowdon in Yorkshire. B.L.G.

RODRICK. A corruption of Roderic.

ROE. From the animal—first applied to a swift runner. See Ray.

ROEBUCK. From the animal. See Roe, and Ray.

ROELENT. The Norman mode of spelling Rhuddlan, co. Flint. A Robert de Roelent, of that place, is among the tenants in chief of Domesday.

ROFF. See Rolfe.

ROFFEY. Perhaps the same as Roffway, from Roughway, which was sometimes so pronounced.

ROFFWAY. Perhaps Roughway, a place near Horsham, co. Sussex.

ROFOOT. According to Verstegan, swift-footed as a roe. "In FOOT: there are not many surnames that herein do finish, yet such as there be have gotten such name of footmanship, as Harefoot, Rofoot, and the like, which were given for swiftness of running or going." Restitution, p. 320.

ROGER. A personal name, unknown here before the Conquest. Many persons called Roger, and Rogerus, occur as tenants in Domesday. From it are formed Rogers, Rodgers, Rogerson, &c., and from its nick-name, Hodge, we get Hodges, Hodgson, Hodgkin, Hotckin, Hotchkins, Hotchkiss, Hodgkinson, Hoskins, Hodd, Hodson, Hudson. The Norman patronymical form is Fitz-Roger, and the Welsh, Ap-Roger, now Prodger.

ROGERS. See Roger. The family of Rogers of Home, in Shropshire, are a cadet of the Norburys of Norbury in that county. In 7. Edward II., *Roger* de Norbury, son of Philip, and grandson of Roger de Norbury, had a grant of the estate of Home. His son took the name of Rogers, and his posterity under that appellation have ever since resided at Home. B.L.G.

The family of Rogers, of Wisdome, co. Devon, baronets, claim to be descended from John Rogers, prebendary of St. Paul's, the first victim of the Marian persecution.

ROGERSON. See Roger.

ROKEBY. The Rokebys of Rokeby, in Yorkshire (the scene of Sir Walter Scott's celebrated poem), held that estate uninterruptedly from the era of the Conquest till the fall of Charles I.

ROLAND. See Rowland.

ROLFE. The same as Rollo, Radulph, or Ralph. The great landholder, Goisfrid de Bec, son of Rollo, and grandson of Crispinus, baron of Bec, is styled in Domesday "Filius Rolf."

ROLLAND. The ancient personal name, variously written Rollo, Roland, Rowland, &c. In Domesday, Rolland and Rollandus.

ROLLE. The family of Lord Rolle rose upon the ruins of the monasteries in the XVI. century. The name may be local, but it seems more likely to be a modification of the Scandinavian Rollo, especially as we have the genitive form Rolles, as well as the local Rollesby, Rolleston, &c. Camden places it among Christian names.

ROLLES. See Rolle.

ROLLESTON. A parish in Staffordshire, which in very early times, and for a long series of generations, belonged to the family.

ROLLFUS. Probably a corruption of the personal name Ro(*do*)lphus, Rudolf.

ROLLINGS. The same as Rawlins or Rawlings.

ROLLISON. A corruption of Rawlinson.

ROLLO. Local, in Scotland : place unknown. Lord Rollo's lineal ancestor was John *de* Rollo, who lived in the reign of King David II. Peerage.

ROLPH. A corruption of Ralph.

ROLTE. Of Huguenot extraction. John Rolte settled at Rye, from Dieppe, in 1572. Lansd. MS. 15, 70.

ROMAINE. ROMAYNE. 1. Of or belonging to Rome. Le Romayn, H.R. The family of the Rev. William Romaine, a distinguished divine of the last century, were Huguenots, and came to England after the Revocation of the Edict of Nantes.
2. More probably, from one of the various places in France, called St. Romain. This saint, who was an early bishop of Rouen, is still honoured by the Roman church on the 9th of August.

ROMAN. 1. Probably the same as Romayne. 2. A place near Evreux, in Normandy.

ROMANE. See Romaine.

ROMARE. The first of this name on record is Gerald de Romare, feudal lord of Bolingbroke, co. Lincoln, whose son, William de Romare, was in 1118 governor of Newmarch, in Normandy, and in arms against Hugh de Gournay, then in rebellion.

ROME. A village in Ayrshire is called Old Rome.

ROMER. A roamer, a wanderer ; perhaps a pilgrim. Perhaps a corruption of Romare.

ROMILLY. The great grandfather of the late Sir Samuel Romilly "had a pretty good landed estate at Montpellier in the south of France." His son, in the year 1701, being a Protestant, visited Geneva, for the sole purpose of receiving the sacrament, and, by the advice of the celebrated theologian, Saurin, instead of returning to Montpellier, set out for London, and thus at length established the family in England. Memoirs of Sir S. Romilly, vol. i., p. 2. The name may have been borrowed from the town of Romilly, in Savoy, near Geneva.

ROMNEY. A town in Kent, anciently Romenel. A Robert de Romenel is found in the Domesday of that county.

RONALD. RONALDS. 1. A Scotch form of Reynold. 2. Gael. Ronnalt, a proper name, said to be compounded of *ronn*, foam, and *alt*, a brook or stream, and, therefore, probably local.

RONALDSON. The son of Ronald or Reynold.

ROOD. A crucifix accompanied by figures of St. John and the Virgin. Though generally placed in churches, over the chancel arch, they were doubtless occasionally placed out of doors, like ordinary way-side crosses ; and residence near one would originate the surname. Cognate surnames are Cross and Crouch.

ROOKE. The bird. I have known this sobriquet applied to a very dark complexioned person. H.R. Le Roke.

ROOKER. To rook is to cheat. Teutonic *rueken* ; Su. Gothic *rycka*. A 'rookery' is a nest of dishonest people. Hence, I am afraid the original Mr. Rooker was not remarkable for his honesty. H.R. Le Roker.

ROOM. ROOME. A place in the parish of Crail, in Fifeshire.

ROOPER. The name was originally Furneux. Richard Furneux, a lineal descendant of Robert de Fourneux, of temp. Henry I., assumed the name of Roper in 1428, on his marriage with the heiress of Roper of Turndiche, co. Derby. The name was corrupted to Rooper in the seventeenth century.

ROOTES. Probably from Routes, or Routtes, a commune in the arrondissement of Yvetot, in Normandy.

ROPER. I doubt not from the trade of making ropes, especially since we have the analogous names, Corder, Stringer, Twyner, &c., and Le Roper is common in old records. But an exception from so plebeian an origin is claimed by one family thus denominated. " There is a very ancient family of the Ropers in Cumberland, who have lived immemorially near a quarry of *red spate* there, from whence they first took the surname of Rubra Spatha." Wright's Court-Hand—where we find " Rouxcarrier, Roussir, Rooper, or Roper," latinized by De Rubra Spatha. Fuller places this family in another county. " The name of Roper in Derbyshire changed from Musard to Rubra-Spatha, Rospear, Rouspee, Rooper, Roper." Worthies i. 71. Lord Teynham's family claim from William Roper, or Rosper, who lived in the reign of Henry III., and whose descendants were of St. Dunstan's, near Canterbury, temp. Edward III. The family have ever since been connected with Kent. See Shirley's Noble and Gentle Men.

RORKE. The Irish O'Rourke.

☞ ROS. See under CORNISH SURNAMES.

ROSAGAN. A place in Cornwall, in which county the family resided temp. Edward VI.

ROSBERT. According to Camden, this family came hither from the Netherlands, at or soon after the Conquest.

ROSCARROCK. A manor in the parish of Endellion, co. Cornwall. The first of the family on record is Richard Roscarrock, who married a daughter of Giffard, and was living at Roscarrock, at an advanced age, in the year 1300. C. S. Gilbert's Cornwall.

ROSCOE. Possibly a corruption of Roscrowe. It is certainly a Cornish name.

ROSCORLA. Once a seat in the parish of St. Austell, co. Cornwall. "The seat of this ancient family has been pulled down. George Roscorla, the present representative of this decayed race, is a day-labourer at Roche." Lysons' Cornwall.

ROSCOW. See Roscoe.

ROSCROWE. An estate in the parish of Gluvias, co. Cornwall, which was possessed by the family in the XIV. century, and became extinct temp. Henry VI. or before. In the reign of Henry VIII. the name was assumed by the family of Harry, who became extinct in the XVII. century. C. S. Gilbert's Cornwall.

ROSCRUGE. An estate in the parish of St. Anthony, in Kerrier, co. Cornwall. It "gave name and original," says Hals, "to a family of gentlemen, now or lately in possession thereof." D. Gilbert's Cornwall.

ROSE. This common and very beautiful name is somewhat difficult to account for. I am inclined to think that it is often a substitution for Ross. The rose, it is true, has in all ages been regarded as the "Queen of Flowers," and as such has ever been associated with poetry and symbolism ; but how it became a surname, I can only conjecture, that it was from the device of the original bearer, whether that was displayed upon the patrician banner, or upon the ignoble sign-post. Salverte mentions a noble family of Poland, in the twelfth century, who are known to have adopted their surname of Rose from the charge of their shield ; and he adduces other instances of a similar practice. Essai, i. 240, &c. The Roses of Nairnshire, settled there from temp. Alexander III., originally wrote themselves De Roos. Hugh Rose of Geddes, by marriage with the heiress of Byset, acquired the lands of Kilravock, and had a crown charter of the barony from King John Baliol. "From that period the estate has descended lineally to the present proprietor." B.L.G.

The water-bowgets, borne by the ancient Lords De Roos of Hamlake, are found in the arms of many families of Ross and Rose, showing at least a presumed community of origin and name.

In the H.R. we find De la Rose, the meaning of which is not clear. In the same records Fil' Rose is also met with ; so that Rose must have been a personal name.

ROSEBOTTOM. Local ; "the bottom or valley where the sweet-briar rose abounds."

The fragrant dell,
Where the eglantine doth dwell.

ROSECREGG. A place in the parish of St. Anthony Meneage, co. Cornwall, in which parish the family were resident in 1820. C. S. Gilbert's Cornwall.

ROSER. Probably the Fr. *rosier*. O. Eng. *rosere*, a rose-tree. See anecdote from Maundevile, Eng. Surn. i. 185.

ROSEWARNE. An estate in Camborne, co. Cornwall, formerly the residence of the family.

ROSEWELL. See Roswell.

ROSHER. The same as Rosier ?

ROSIER. See Roser.

ROSKELLY. See Roskilly.

ROSKILLY. An estate in St. Keverne, co. Cornwall, anciently the residence of the family.

ROSKYMER. Another spelling of Reskymer.

ROSLING. A corruption of Roslyn, a village in co. Edinburgh.

ROSOMAN. A corruption of Rosamond. See Female Christian Names.

ROSS. This surname is susceptible of several explanations. 1. In some cases it is undoubtedly of foreign local origin. In Domesday we find, in Kent, a tenant called Anschitil de Ros, and, in Buckinghamshire, another named Ansgotus de Ros. These probably came from Ros, a commune in the arrondissement of Caen, in Normandy. 2. It is of British local origin. The great barons Ros, or Roos, of Hamlake, co.York, sprang from one Peter, who, in the reign of Henry I., assumed his surname from his lordship of Ros, in Holderness. Baronage. The Rosses of the South of Scotland appear to have sprung from the English family, and to have passed into Renfrewshire, as the vassals of Richard de Moreville in the XII. century, settling at Halkhead, co. Renfrew, and at Dalton, co. Dumfries. 3. There are several towns and villages in North and South Britain called Ross, and these, as well as *ross*, a heath or morass, and *ross*, a promontory, may have a claim. 4. The name seems sometimes to have had reference to the colour or complexion of the first bearer, and to have been a modification of Le Rous, Rufus, or the Red. The ancient family of Ross of Renfrew, descending from Alysandre, who flourished at Renfrew, so early as the reign of King David I., wrote themselves "*the* Ross of Renfrew," apparently down to the XV. century. See Knowles's Genealogy of Coulthart, p. 16. 5. Mr. Ferguson claims the name as Teutonic, deriving it from O. Sax., *hros*, O. Norse, *hross*, &c., a horse. 6. Mr. Skene insinuates a claim on behalf of the Gaelic. "It is well known," says he, "that the surname of Ross has always been rendered in Gaelic, *Clan Aurias*, or *Clan Gille Aurias*." Scottish Highlanders, ii. 224.

ROSSER. See Ross. A dweller upon a heath, or upon a promontory.

ROSSITER. A corrupted pronunciation of Wroxeter, a parish in Shropshire, the ancient Roman station of *Uriconium*.

ROSTHORNE. This name, which appears to be local, is now written Rawstone. B.L.G.

ROSWARNE. An estate in the parish of Camborne, co. Cornwall, which had anciently owners of the same name, who continued in possession till the reign of James I., when the De Roswarne of that day sold it to Ezekiel Grosse, gent., attorney-at-law. Concerning this lawyer, Mr. Hals tells a queer story, to the effect that a ghost pointed out to him a great treasure in the mansion (hidden there doubtless by one of the Roswarnes) which he appropriated; but the "phantasm or spectrum" so haunted him, that he was obliged to quit the place, which he sold to his clerk, John Call—probably an ancestor of the baronet of that name and county. See Davies Gilbert's Cornwall, i. 162.

ROSWELL. Said to be a corruption of the French Rosseville. It is therefore local, but I know not the place. Kent, in his Grammar of Heraldry, speaks of the Rev. Sam. Rosewell, of London, M.A., as "descended from the Rosewells, of Somersetshire, Wiltshire, and Devon, who came in with the Conqueror."

ROTHERY. Said to be a corruption of the personal name Roderic.

ROTHMAN. An old personal name, occurring in the genealogy of the East-Anglian kings, in the form of Hrothmund.

ROTHSCHILD. Whatever may have been the origin of this name, its component parts are the German for "red shield," and it is not improbable that it was originally assumed, in chivalric times, by one who chose to carry a weapon of that colour. There are several instances of some peculiarity in the weapons of ancient warriors having given rise to sobriquets, and even to transmissible or family names, such as Longespée, Strongbow, Fortescue, Brownsword. We have also an authenticated instance of an 'armiger' who chose to bear his ensigns with the single tincture Gules, or red. In the curious heraldric poem on the Siege of Carlaverock, A.D. 1300, one of the commanders is described as bearing, not indeed a shield, but a banner, *entirely red* :—

"MAIS EURMENIONS DE LA BRECTE
LA BANIERE EUT TOUTE ROUGECTE.

ROTHWELL. 1. Parishes in cos. Northampton, Lincoln, and York. 2. The family are presumed to be of Dutch extraction. The ancestor of the Rothwells of Meath accompanied William III. to Ireland. B.L.G.

ROTTEN. ROTTENHERYING. These opprobrious names occur in the archives of Hull, in the XIV. century.

ROTHERHAM. A town in Yorkshire.

ROUGH. Has probably no reference to want of polish. It is more likely to be local, and derived from residence near a *rough*, that is, a place overgrown with bushes, or a rough uneven ground.

ROUGHHEAD. An Edinburgh surname. It is possibly local, signifying "the rough or rugged promontory."

ROUGHLY. Local : "the rough lea, or pasture."

ROUGHTON. Parishes in Norfolk and Lincoln.

ROUND. In some places, the open space anciently used for the inhuman sport of bull-baiting is still called 'the Round;' and residence near such a spot would originate the surname.

ROUNDELL. See under Rundle. The Roundells of Screven, in Yorkshire, have possessed Screven ever since the early part of the XV. century, the first recorded progenitor being John Roundell, of that place, 3. Henry VI. Whitaker's Craven.

ROUNTHWAITE. Local: see THWAITE.

ROUPEL. 1. Fr. "*roupille, sorte de petite casaque*, a short coat of old." Boyer. 2. Fr. "*roupeau*, a little heron which haunteth rocks [unde nomen] and hath a peake of feathers falling backwards on the hinder part of his head." Cotgrave. The surname was doubtless a sobriquet allusive either to the dress or the gait of the first bearer of it.

ROUPELL. The family are "originally from Hesse Cassell, where they flourished in great local importance for centuries." The name still exists there as Rüppell. The first who settled in England was Captain Roupell, an officer in William III.'s guards, who accompanied that monarch from Holland in 1688. B.L.G.

ROURK. ROURKE. See O'Rourke.

ROUS. The O.Fr. *rous*, from Latin *rufus*, red, has originated the names Rous, Rouse, Rowse, and the diminutive Rowsell, whence also in many cases Russell, although the last has sometimes a local source. The name occurs in the collection of names called the Roll of Battel Abbey, and there is no doubt of its early Norman origin. The cognate Leroux is still a common surname in Normandy. The ancestor of the family is said to have been Ralph le Rufus, or Rous, who came hither with the Conqueror. From him descended the noble family (Stradbroke) settled in Suffolk from temp. Edward III., and the Rouses of Cornwall and Devon. C. S. Gilbert's Cornwall. The senior line was Rous of Modbury, co. Devon ; and the next branch, that of Edmerston, sprang from Sir Robert le Rous, a knight-banneret under Edward the Black Prince. B.L.G.

ROUSE. See Rous.

ROUSHAM. A parish in Oxfordshire.

ROUTH. A parish in the E. Riding of Yorkshire.

ROUTLEDGE. A local name, common in Cumberland. I do not find the place.

ROWAN. A place in the parish of Canonbie, co. Dumfries.

ROWBOTHAM. As Rowbottom.

ROWBOTTOM. See Bottom, in the Supplement.

ROWCLIFFE. A corruption of Rock-cliffe, a parish in Cumberland.

ROWDON. Probably the same as Raw-don

ROWE. ROW. 1. A street, or rather a series of detached houses, standing on one side only of the highway. 2. There is a parish in Dumbartonshire so called. 3. Gaelic, *rhu*, Scot. *row*, signifies a low, small, narrow peninsula. Gaz. Scotl.

Rowe, without any prefix, is found in H.R.

ROWELL. A hamlet of Hawling, co. Gloucester.

ROWLAND. 1. A common personal name, particularly in Wales. Hence Row-lands, and Rowlandson. 2. A township of Bakewell, co. Derby.

ROWLANDS. See Rowland.

ROWLANDSON. See Rowland.

ROWLES. See Rolle.

ROWLEY. The family claim to be of Saxon blood, but the name is traced only to temp. Edward II., when Randolph de Rowley was seated at Carmichan, co. Chester. Lord Langford's family settled in Ireland, temp. James I. There are parishes of Rowley in Yorkshire and Staffordshire.

ROWNTREE. The *rowan-tree* is the mountain-ash, and the name may there-fore be congenerous with Oak, Ash, &c.

ROWSE. See Rous.

ROWSELL. See Rous.

ROWTON. Townships in cos. Chester, Shropshire, &c.

ROXBERRY. Probably the same as Roxburgh.

ROXBOROUGH. ROXBROUGH. The same as Roxburgh.

ROXBURGH. The Scottish town, capital of the shire so called.

ROXBY. A parish in Lincolnshire, and a chapelry in Yorkshire. The Yorkshire surname was formerly spelt Rooksby, and occasionally Rokeby. B.L.G.

ROY. Has no relation to the Fr. *roi*. It is Gaelic, and signifies the red-haired; and, as such, it has often been used as a sobriquet, down almost to our own times, in conjunction with, or to supersede, a family name.

ROYALL. See Ryall.

☞ ROYD, a common termination of names of places in the North of England, signifying a clearing in a forest, in legal phrase, a *roda* or *assart*. "*Rode land* is used in this sense in modern German, in which the verb *roden* means to clear; hence, near the Hartz forest, Elbin-gerode, Blacherode, and Osterode. The combination of the syllable *rod*, *rode*, or *royd*, with some other term, or with the name of an original settler, has no doubt given to particular localities such de-signations as Huntroyd, Ormerod, &c., &c." [Coucher Book of Whalley Abbey; Gloss.] In Lancashire and Yorkshire, the adjunct sometimes refers to the early proprietor, as in Monkroyd, Mar-tinrode, &c.; sometimes to the trees *ridded* or cleared, as in Oakenrode, Ac-royd, Hollinrode, Holroyd, &c.; some-times to other characteristics. Notes and Queries, v., 571.

ROYELL. The same as Royle.

ROYER. This name, in its present or-thography, is found in H.R.

ROYLE. Perhaps Ryall, a township in Northumberland.

ROYSTON. Parishes in Cambridgeshire and Yorkshire.

RUBY. Probably local; see termination BY.

RUDD. Probably the same as Rodd.

RUDDER. A corruption of Rutter.

RUDDERFORTH. See Rutherfurd.

RUDDIFORD. See Rutherfurd.

RUDDIMAN. A man of ruddy com-plexion; analogous to Blackman, White-man, &c.

RUDDLE. A member of the family of Picard changed his name to Ruddle, at the instance of King Edward IV., the latter being the designation of his birth-place. Blore's Monument. Rem. I do not find the locality.

RUDDY. Of red or sanguine complex-ion.

RUDGE. An early member of this family was John de Rugge, of Seysdon, co. Stafford, who was living, 17. Edward II. Shaw's Staffordshire. Rudge and Ridge ap-pear to be identical in meaning. The sur-name is doubtless derived from a township in Shropshire so called.

RUDWICK. A Sussex name, probably derived from Rudgwick in that county.

RUE. 1. The French De la Rue, deprived of its prefix. 2. Rewe, a parish in Devon-shire.

RUEL. See Rule.

RUFF. The same as Rough.

RUFINE. This name was introduced into England by Dr. James Rufine, a student of Leyden in 1671, who came to this coun-try at the Revocation of the Edict of Nantes, and married Elizabeth, daughter of — Young, Esq., of Bradfield Hall, co. Suffolk.

RUFUS. The retained latinization of Le Rou.

RUGBY. A town in Warwickshire.

RUGELEY. A parish in Staffordshire, anciently the seat of the family.

RUGGLES. 1. This coarsely plebeian name may be from a "noble Norman source," *Rugles* being the designation of a village in the department of Eure. 2. Anciently Roggyle and Ruggle. It has been conjectured that the family sprang from the De Rugeleys of Staffordshire; but this is improbable.

RULE. Perhaps from the Roxburghshire rivulet; but more probably the A.-Norman personal name Raoul. The H.R. Ruel favours the latter derivation.

RULER. A man in command of a body of workmen.

RUM. "Rum," says Mr. Ferguson, "I take to be from O. Norse *rumr*, vir immanis, gigas—one who might truly be called a "rum customer." Hence may indeed be the origin of our word *rum* for queer, which appears indigenous to some of our northern dialects, and which I doubt, therefore, being a cant phrase." Rum is also an old personal name mentioned by Nennius : Rum map Urbgen. Mon. Hist. Brit., p. 76.

RUMBALL, RUMBELL, and perhaps **RUMBELLO.** The same as Rumbold.

RUMBLE. See Rumbold.

RUMBOLD. RUMBOL. Reinbald, a Teutonic name of great antiquity, whence Rumbolds-Wyke, co. Sussex. Reinbald, Rumbaldus, Rumoldus, &c., occur in Domesday.

RUMMENS. Rumun, an O. Norse personal name. Ferguson.

RUMMERY. A corruption of Romare ?

RUMSEY. Romsey, a town in Hampshire.

RUNCHMAN. Jamieson defines *runchie* as 'raw-boned.' Hence probably this surname, and Runciman.

RUNCIMAN. See Runchman.

RUNDELL. See Rundle.

RUNDLE. A branch of the great baronial house of Cobham, of Kent, adopted this name from their residence at a place so called, in the parish of Shorne in that county. Hasted says : "Randall, formerly called Roundall and Rundale, is a manor in this parish, which, though at present of little repute, was anciently of some note, as being one of the seats of the noble family of Cobham, where they are said to have resided before they removed to Cobham Hall." In the XIII. century, John de Cobham gave Rundale to his second son Henry, and his descendants were variously written Roundale, Rundel, Roundall, and Rundella, and so lately as 8 Henry VI. the then proprietor of the estate was styled Lord Thomas de Cobham, *alias* Rundella, Knight. The elder or Kentish line of the Cobhams terminated in an heiress, and she married Sir John Oldcastle, who was summoned to Parliament in right of his wife, as Baron

Cobham, in 1409, and who afterwards became famous as the leader of the Lollards ; but it is more than likely that the blood of that ancient race yet flows in the Rundles of the West of England. In the reigns of Edward II., Edward III., and Henry IV., the De Cobhams held lands in Devonshire, Cornwall, and Somersetshire, and some of their connections doubtless planted the family and name of Rondell or Rundle in those counties. Mr. C. S. Gilbert says : " Hole in St. Neot, the seat of John Rundle, gent., has long been the residence of the family, [seven generations]. The surname of this family, which is known to be of great antiquity in Cornwall, is supposed by some to be an abbreviation of the name of Arundell ; this, however, appears to be a matter of doubt. The name has been differently spelt, as Rundle, Randall, and Rendall. There are several branches still resident in the neighbourhood of Looe and Liskeard. A branch of Randall who resided at or near Looe, assumed the name of Morth or Murth, (so written in Talland Church) but retained the arms of Randall." Hist. Cornwall, ii. 946.

RUSBRIDGE. I find no English locality so called. The name is probably derived from the town of Rousbrugge in Belgium.

RUSBRIDGER. A native of Rousbrugge, in Belgium ; analogous to Dantziger, Hamburgher, &c. See termination ER.

RUSCOE. The same as Roscoe.

RUSH. A provincialism for 'subtle'; probably corrupted from the Fr. *rusé*.

RUSHALL. Parishes in cos. Norfolk, Stafford, and Wilts.

RUSHBROOK. A parish in Suffolk. De Russhebroc occurs in the H.R. of that county.

RUSHBURY. A parish in Shropshire.

RUSHOUT. According to a pedigree, duly certified by the French heraldic authorities in the year 1652, Lord Northwick's ancestor was Thibaut Rushaut, a noble English knight *(noble chevalier Anglois)*, who settled in France at the commencement of the fourteenth century. His posterity were Lords and Marquises of Gamaches, one of whom was of the number of the five Protestant nobles who escaped the massacre of St. Bartholomew, in consideration of being related to Catherine de Medicis. His son settled in Flanders, and his descendant, John Rushout, a native of Rousselaer in that country, settled in England, and died in 1653. His son, James Rushout, was created a baronet at the Restoration of Charles II.

RUSHTON. Parishes and places in cos. Northampton, Chester, Stafford, and Dorset.

RUSK. See Ruskin.

RUSKIN. A diminutive of some personal name, perhaps of Rusk, which is found in Lond. Directory.

RUSS. A Russian.

RUSSELL. The Duke of Bedford claims from the lords of Rosel, an ancient fief in the neighbourhood of Cherbourg in Normandy, who were a younger branch of the barons of Briquebec. Hugh de Rosel, a benefactor of the abbey of Caen, "accompanied the Conqueror to England, and was rewarded with possessions in co. Dorset, the principal of which were Kingston, afterwards called Kingston-Russell and Berwick, the latter of which is still in possession of the family." Parry's Hist. of Woburn, p. 66.

RUSTON. Parishes in Yorkshire and Norfolk.

RUTH. 1. See Female Christian Names. 2. More probably the same as Routh.

RUTHERFORD. See Rutherfurd.

RUTHERFURD. An extinct parish in co. Roxburgh. This ancient family have a tradition that their founder, a man of distinction on the Border, having conducted Ruther, King of the Scots, safely through the river Tweed, on an expedition against the South, at a place called from that event, Rutherfurd, the monarch rewarded his faithful guide with lands adjacent to the place, afterwards known as the barony of Rutherfurd. The authentic history of the family commences with Robert, Dominus de Rutherfurd, witness to a charter of David I., in 1140. The family continued to reside at Rutherfurd until the last century, and the present head of the house, though resident at Edgerston, still writes himself Rutherfurd of that Ilk.

RUTLAND. From the county.

RUTLEDGE. The same as Routledge.

RUTSON. In Cumberland and Westmoreland, this is the usual corruption of Richardson.

RUTTER. Germ. *ritter?* A rider or trooper; also a veteran soldier. According to Halliwell "the term was usually applied to a fine, dashing, boasting gallant; one so fashionable as to speak much in foreign languages;" though the application of it in that sense is not very obvious.

RUTTERFORD. See Rutherfurd.

RUVIE. RUVY. A Scottish correspondent remarks: "I was struck with the name of Ruvy or Ruvie, and on enquiring of the parish clergyman, I found that the family name had been Macgillivray! But for this assurance, one would at once think Ruthven a much likelier origin."

RYALL. A township in Stamfordham parish, co. Northumberland.

RYAN. See O'Ryan.

RYCROFT. Local : "the rye-croft," an enclosure where rye was cultivated.

RYDE. A town in the Isle of Wight.

RYDER. See Rider. Le Rydar, Le Rydere. H.R.

RYDON. The same as Roydon or Royton.

RYE. A town in Sussex. La Rie, meaning a bank, is a very common name of localities in Normandy.

RYGATE. Reigate, a town in Surrey.

RYLE. Two townships in Whittingham parish, Northumberland, are so called.

RYMAN. 1. Rye is an elevated ground. Lat. *ripa*, Fr. *rive*. The Ryman resided on such an eminence. 2. A corruption of the personal name Raymond.

RYMER. Doubtless a person skilled in making verses, like the far-famed Scotchman, Thomas the Rhymer. King Henry III. kept a court poet, or poet-laureate, called Master Henry the Versifier, and paid him one hundred shillings per annum for his poesy. Still earlier, Henry I. had a bard who wrote laudatory verses about his master, and was called Walo Versificator. Warton's Hist. of English Poetry, vol. i. p. 47. These old court-poets were called *Archipoetæ.*

RYND. See Rhynd.

RYTON. Parishes, &c., in cos. Durham, Salop, Warwick, York, &c.

RYVES. The same as Reeves.

S.

SABBAGE. A corruption of Savage.

SABBE. See Sabine.

SABINE. SABIN. Originally Sabinus, a Roman personal name, implying a descent from the Sabine nation. Sabina, its feminine, is still used as a baptismal name.

Sabbè, an old family in Norfolk, probably corrupted their name from this. H.R. Sabin, Sabyn.

SACHEVERELL. A name of uncertain meaning. It can hardly come from *sacheverel,* which, according to Halliwell, means the iron door or blower of a stove.

As it is sometimes written Sachervill, it was probably taken from some place in Normandy. The nearest approach to it I can find is Sachenvilla, now Sacquenville, near Evreux. In records it is latinized *De saltu Capellæ*, 'goat's leap' or 'goat's wood,' and the crest is a goat. In the H.R. it is written Saucheverel, without prefix, and there is one Nichs. Sans Cheverel, which, if it has any meaning, would seem to be Nicholas, *without the Little Goat*.

SACK. A loose garment—a word still in use. There was an ancient fraternity called 'fratres saccati,' or sac-friars, from the coarse sackcloth garment which they wore. "Et eodem tempore (1257) novus ordo apparuit Londini, qui, quia saccis incedebant induti, Fratres Saccati vocabantur." Matthew Paris. See Archæologia, iii. 129.

SACKER. 1. A maker of sacks or loose garments. 2. See Sack.

SACKVILLE. A place in Normandy, now called Sauqueville, near the river Scie, in the department of the Lower Seine, about seven miles from Dieppe. Collins says, that the family were lords of the town and seigniory "long before the Conquest." The name was variously written De Salchevilla, Salkavilla, Saccavilla, &c. According to genealogists, the first of the family in England was Herbrand de Salchevilla, who came in with the Conqueror, while his kinsman, Jourdain de S., was Sewer of England under the same monarch. At the commencement of the XIII. century, another Jourdain de S. founded the collegiate church of Sauqueville, which remained 'une des plus belles de la contré' until the year 1825, when it was pulled down by a neighbouring proprietor, who used its materials for building a cotton-mill. Cochet, Les Eglises de Dieppe (Egl. Rurales), p. 89, where a most interesting account of the church is given. It is added: "At the sight of a profanation so awful, the good inhabitants of Sauqueville revolted against the demolishers. There was a riot; an armed force was obliged to interfere, and these sons of the Crusaders were sent to prison for resisting a *legal order!*" This act of Vandalism deprived both Norman and English antiquaries of what might be regarded as an historical monument, since its founder, Jourdain de Sauqueville, was one of the bravest defenders of King John and his Norman dependencies against the French. A railway now traverses the desecrated churchyard of Sauqueville.

SADD. O. Eng. *sadde;* not sad, wretched, in the modern sense, but grave, serious. Two centuries ago any thing dull or heavy was so called, as sad colour, sad bread, &c.

> "A *sad* man in whom is no pride,
> Right a discrete confessor as I trow;
> His name was called Sir John Doclow."
> *M.S. Rawl. c.* 86. (Halliw).

H.R. Sad.

SADDINGTON. A parish in Leicestershire.

SADELER. The same as Sadler.

SADLEIR. The same as Sadler.

SADLER. A saddler.

SAER. See Sayer.

SAFFERY. See Savory.

SAGE. Probably a translation of *Le Sage*, still a very common French surname. It has reference to the wisdom and prudence of the original bearer. *Wise*, as an English surname, is a precise analogue. Le Sage. H.R.

SAGGERS. Probably the same as Segar, in a genitive form.

SAIL. See Sale.

SAINSBURY. Probably from Saintbury, a parish in co. Gloucester.

☞ **SAINT.** A common prefix to surnames of Norman origin, as St. Aubyn, St. Amand, St. Barbe, St. Clere, St. George, St. Germaine, St. John, St. Leger. Many places in Normandy, and elsewhere, had formerly no other name than that of the Saint to whom the Church was dedicated, and from such places these surnames have been derived.

SAINT ALBYN. The same, originally, as St. Aubyn.

SAINT AMAND. From St. Amand-des-hautes-terres, near Louviers, or St. Amand-les-Valettes, near St. Lo. in Normandy. The baronial family traced to Almaric de St. Amand, lord of Liskeard, co. Cornwall, temp. Henry III.

SAINT ANDRE, or ANDREW. St. André-la-foret is near Evreux; St. Andrê-sur-Cailli, near Rouen.

SAINT ARNOLD. Four places in Normandy bear this name (St. Arnoult).

SAINT AUBYN. According to Leland, the family of St. Albin (St. Aubyn) took their surname from a town in Brittany so called, and settled in Somersetshire soon after the Conquest. C. S. Gilbert's Cornwall. Mauger de St. Aubyn held the manor of Mattingho, co. Devon, in the reign of Henry III.; but the pedigree commences only temp. Henry IV., with Sir Guy St. Aubyn of Clowance in Cornwall, which has ever since been the seat of the family. Courthope's Debrett.

SAINT BARBE. The Norman origin of this family is undoubted, and the name occurs in Leland's rhyming and alliterative list of the Conqueror's followers :—

> " St. Barbe et Sageville
> Vernoun et Waterville."

A bourg and two villages in Normandy bear the name of St. Barbe, better known in the Roman Calendar as St. Barbara, whose coif and veil were among the relics preserved at Glastonbury, with which establishment the family were connected, holding of it the manor of Brent St. Barbe, before the reign of Edw. I. The name is thought to be peculiar to the existing family, and not to be found in Normandy, though Barbe is well-known there. Symbarbe is a corruption of this ancient name.

SAINT CLAIR. SAINT CLERE. This name, usually corrupted to Sinclair, is of French origin, and springs from the great family De Sancto Claro, in France. The noble Scottish families of this surname are descended from Sir William St. Clair, or Sinclair, who was lord of Rosslyn, &c., in Mid-Lothian, by grant of King Alexander I. Three places called St. Clair occur in the Itin. de la Normandie, in the arrondissements, severally, of St. Lo, Havre, and Yvetot. The widely-spread importance of this family is shewn by the fact that about twenty coats of arms are assigned to the name. Richard de Sent Cler occurs in the Domesday of Norfolk.

SAINT CROIX. (See De St. Croix.) 'The Holy Cross.'

> "*Olicrosse* est en Engleiz,
> Ke Saint Croix est en Franceiz."
> *Roman de Rou.*

SAINT ELOY. Ste. Eloi is in the arrondissement of Andeli in Normandy. Chaucer's Prioress used to swear by this saint :—

> "That of her smylyng was ful symple and coy ;
> Hire grettest oath was but by seynt (E) loy."
> *Canterb. Tales, Prologue*, 120.

SAINT GEORGE. This illustrious family came originally from La Marche de Limousin, in France, and derived their name from the barony of St. George, near Limoges, where, upon the authority of an old inscribed church bell, recast in 1687, they were seated in A.D. 888—though this may well be questioned. Baldwin de St. George came hither with the Conqueror and became ancestor of the St. Georges of Hatfield St. George, and of other places in England and Ireland. Other branches remained in France, and few names have been more distinguished in that country, throughout a series of ages, than that of St. George. Inf. J. Bertrand Payne, Esq.

"*St. George for England!*" would almost seem to be a mistake, since the great majority of persons so called are Irishmen.

SAINT GERMYN. St. Germain has given his name to at least twelve places in Normandy. See Itin. de la Normandie.

SAINT HILL. Berry assigns eight coats to this surname. Who the saint was, I cannot ascertain.

SAINT HILARY. One parish in Cornwall, and several in Normandy, are dedicated to this well-known French saint, and known by his name.

SAINT JERMYN. See St. Germyn.

SAINT JOHN. Several parishes in Normandy bear the name of this saint. The family were in England very soon after, if not at, the Conquest, being descended, in the male line, from the great Domesday baron, Hugh de Port. William, son of Adam de Port, took the name of St.

John in the XII. cent. on his marriage with the heiress of the powerful Norman family, so called. This surname is vilely corrupted in pronunciation to Singen. A boy, not aware of this, once read the opening lines of Pope's Essay on Man in manner following :—

> "Awake my St. *John*—leave all meaner things,
> To low ambi*tion*—and the pride of kings!"

SAINT LAWRENCE. This family (the Earl of Howth's) claim to have been barons by tenure of Howth, in Ireland, ever since the conquest of that kingdom by King Henry II., the ancestor having assisted in Strongbow's invasion. He was doubtless of Norman extraction, and he may have come either from St. Lawrent, near Bayeux, or from the place of the same name near Yvetot.

SAINT LEGER. The St. Legers came from Caen in Normandy (Chron. of Battel Abbey, p. 59), and a family tradition asserts that the patriarch, Robert, was not only present at William's invasion in 1066, but actually supported him with his hand as he quitted the ship! There are six places bearing this name mentioned in the Itin. de la Normandie. Its latinization is De Sancto Leodegario—its corruption, *Sellinger.*

SAINT LIS. The originator of this family in England was Simon de St. Lis, a participator in the Norman Conquest. William is said to have offered him in marriage to his niece Judith, widow of Waltheof, a great Saxon earl, whom he had deposed and beheaded. The lady refused him 'because he halted in one leg,' and so he courted and won her elder daughter Maud ! He was afterwards raised to the Earldoms of Huntingdon and Northampton. See the whole story in Dugdale's Baronage. The ordinary corruption of the name is Senlis or Senlez.

SAINT LO. SAINT LOE. SAINT LOW. Often corrupted to Senlow and Sentlow. There are three places called St. Loup in Normandy, situated respectively in the arrondissements of Lisieux, Bayeux, and Avranches. As the surname is latinized in charters as De Sancto Laudo, it is probably the origin of Laud.

SAINT MARTIN. St. Martin, the military saint of France (etymologically descended from Mars) was greatly honoured in Normandy, no less than twenty-five places bearing his name being given in the Itinéraire de la Norm. The family were important in England, temp. Henry II.

SAINT MAUR Camden and Dugdale agree that the noble house of Seymour (St. Maur) "entered England with William the Conqueror, or soon after," and the former says, what is doubtless true, that their name was derived from a place in Normandy ; but the Itin. Norm. furnishes no clue to the locality. Ancient forms are De Sancto Mauro, Semor, &c. See Seymour.

SAINT MICHAEL. Several places in England and Normandy bear this name. In Scotland it was sometimes written St. Michill, and St. Mitchell.

SAINT NICHOLAS. Several places both in Normandy and England are so called.

SAINT OMER. A well-known town in the Pas de Calais; also a village near Falaise in Normandy.

SAINT OWEN. The Itin. de la Normandie mentions ten localities bearing the name of this saint, with different suffixes. (St. Ouen).

SAINT PAUL. One William de St. Paul attended William the Conqueror in the invasion of England, and was rewarded with a wife, the daughter of Simon, son of Thom (a refractory Saxon) and part of his lands in Yorkshire. See Thierry's Norm. Conq. He probably came from the village of St. Paul-sur-Rile, near Pont-Audemer, in Normandy. In 1768, Robert Paul, Esq., of Ewart, in Northumberland, from a supposed descent from the Norman family, obtained an act of parliament empowering him to assume the word *Saint*, as a prefix to his former surname. This is perhaps a unique instance of *parliamentary canonization*.

SAINT PETER. See Saint Pierre.

SAINT PHILIBERT. Four parishes in Normandy bear the name of this Norman saint, but I am not aware that it is known from which of them the great Anglo-Norman baronial family sprang.

SAINT POL. See St. Paul.

SAINT PIERRE. SAINT PETER. Most likely from St. Pierre-sur-Dive, near Lisieux, the site of the great Abbey. There are, however, some ten other parishes and places in Normandy so called.

SAINT QUINTIN. St. Quintin is the chief-town of Lower Picardy, from whence Sir Hubert de St. Quintin is said to have come, at the Norman invasion. Domesday, however, mentions *Hugh* de St. Quintin, as a tenant in capite in the counties of Dorset and Essex. His grandson erected the castle of St. Quintin in Wales.

SAINT SAVER. SANZAVER. Probably St. Severus. The southern suburb of Rouen, and other places in Normandy, are so called.

SAINT SAVIOUR. Four places called St. Saveur occur in the Itin. de la Normandie.

SAINT VALORY. SAINT WALERY. From St. Valery-sur-Somme in Picardy, or St. Valery-en-Caux, in Normandy. In Domesday, Walter de St. Walerie appears as a tenant in capite in Middlesex, and he had lands in Sussex, while Ranulf de St. Walerie had several lordships in Lincolnshire.

SAKER. SACRE. The peregrine falcon; also a piece of ordnance named after it.

> "The cannon, blunderbuss, and *saker*,
> He was th' inventor of and maker."
> *Hudibras* I. ii. 335.

SALCOCK. A diminutive of Saul. See termination COCK.

SALE. SALES. A-Sax. *sel, sele*, &c. French, *salle*, a hall. "Between 1332 and 1348, the name borne by the famous knight commemorated by Froissart, and who was killed by the insurgents near Norwich, in 1381, is severally written De la Sale, De Salle, De Aula, De la Saule, De Halle, Saul, and Halle." Notes and Queries, v. 291. The North Wilts family of Hale of Bradford also wrote themselves De Aula and De la Sale. "Halle, alias De la Sale, dwellith in a pretty stone house at the east end of the town, on the right bank of Avon: a man of £100 lands by the year: an ancient gentleman since the time of Edward I." Leland's Itinerary.

SALEMAN. An attendant in a hall. See Sale, and Salmon.

SALERNE. Two places in the arrondissement of Bernai, in Normandy, bear this name. The surname is found in Sussex in the XIII. and XIV. centuries.

SALISBURY. SALUSBURY. Edward de Sarisberie, sometimes called Edward Vicecomes, was a great tenant in chief in Wiltshire and other counties, at the making of Domesday. He was a younger son of Walter de Evreux (Devereux)—one of the few instances, in those early times, of a Norman family with a Saxon name. See Hutchins' Dorset. Ellis's Introd. Domesd.

The baronet's family are descended from Adam de Salusbury, who is said to have been captain of the castle of Denbigh, at a period little subsequent to the Norman Conquest, inasmuch as his great-grandson, John Salusbury of Llewenny, co. Denbigh, died 18. Edward I. Courthope's Debrett.

SALKELD. The family so called, very influential in Cumberland in the XIV. century, probably derived their name from either Great or Little Salkeld, in that county.

SALMON. This name, though identical with the designation of a well-known fish, probably originated from another source. The manor of Salmons in Caterham, co. Surrey, is known to have belonged temp. Edw. III. to Roger Saleman. Brayley's Surrey, iv. 189. Now *sel*, A-Sax. and *salle*, Fr. signify a hall, and *saleman* would consequently be the attendant or keeper of a hall. The name under this orthography is common in the Hundred Rolls.

SALMOND. The family settled at Waterfoot, co. Cumberland, are of French origin, one of their ancestors having fled to this country during the persecutions of the Huguenots. B.L.G.

SALOMON. A well-known Jewish surname, but not confined to that race. A conspicuous personage of medieval romance is so called. Its earliest mention in England is in Domesday. A Salomonson occurs in the Lond. Direct.

SALOMONS. A Jewish family long connected with London. The name is clearly a modification of Solomon.

SALOMONSON. See Salomon.

SALT. This surname is very common in Staffordshire, in which county there is a village so called. In 1166, it is written Selte. Lib. Nig. Scacc. In the reign of Henry III. Ivo de Saut held one knight's fee in Saut, of the Barony of Stafford. Subsequently Hugh de Salt held Salt of Philip de Chetwynd. From this tenure, and from the resemblance of the arms, it is probable that Salt was a cadet of Chetwynd. In the Visitations of Staffordshire there are pedigrees of this family, from whom descend Thomas Salt, Esq., jun., M.P. for Stafford, and William Salt, Esq., F.S.A.

SALTER. A maker of salt—a business of great importance in the middle ages, when the produce of the land was almost entirely consumed on the spot, and immense quantities of victuals of all kinds had to be salted, in order that they might be kept the whole year round. Wright's Vocab. p. 9.

SALTIRE. One of the 'ordinaries' of heraldry. More probably however from the Fr. *sauteur*, a jumper.

SALTMARSHE. 1. See under Saumarez. 2. A township in co. York, the ancient possession of the family, and still their property and residence. The first of the name mentioned by Burke is William Saltmarsh, latinized De Salso Marisco, witness to a grant of Richard Strongbow in the XII. century; and Sir Peter Saltmarsh was one of the knights of the shire for co. York, 17. Edward II. B.L.G.

SALTWELL. A 'brine spring;' a local name, probably in Cheshire.

SALUSBURY. See Salisbury.

SALVAGE. An older orthography of Savage, which see.

SALVAINE. See Salvin.

SALVIN. The Durham family are descended from Sir Osbert Silvayne, of Norton Woodhouse, in the forest of Sherwood, who flourished 29. Henry III. Mr. Shirley says, that some of the name (which he supposes to be derived from that *silva*, or forest), were seated at Norton before the year 1140. Noble and Gentle Men of England. This name was latinized De Salicosa Vena.

SALWEY. About the reign of Henry III., William Salwey was lord of Leacroft, a hamlet in Staffordshire. From him descend the Shropshire family.

SAMAND. St. Amado, according to Camden. I should rather say St. Amand.

SAMBOURNE. A hamlet in co. Warwick.

SAMBROOK. Probably local, and corrupted—"the sandy brook."

SAMKIN. See Samuel.

SAMMES. See Samuel.

SAMPIERE. A corruption of St. Pierre, St. Peter. Camden.

SAMPKIN. See Samuel.

SAMPOL. A corruption of St. Pol, St. Paul. Camden.

SAMPSON. Not from the Hebrew worthy, but the son of Sam, or Samuel, the P being inserted, as in Thompson, Simpson, Jempson, &c., for strength and euphony.

SAMS. See Samuel.

SAMSON. See Sampson.

SAMUEL. A surname, pretty equally shared by Jews and Christians. It has given rise to Samuels, Sams, Samson, Sampson, Samkin, Sampkin, Sammes, and perhaps Samwell—but this last may be local.

SAMUELS. See Samuel.

SAMWELL. See Samuel.

SANCTUARY. Several monasteries had an ambit or surrounding space, where criminals might take refuge from immediate or impending danger, as the Sanctuary at Westminster. A person resident in a place so privileged, though no criminal, would readily acquire the name of Thomas, or John, at the Sanctuary.

☞ SAND. A component syllable of many local surnames, as Sandham, Sandby, Sandcroft, Sandiland. It implies a sandy district.

SANDALL. Two parishes and a township in Yorkshire are so called.

SANDALLS. See Sandall.

SANDBACH. A town in Cheshire.

SANDER. See Alexander.

SANDERCOCK. A diminutive of Sander, Alexander. See termination COCK.

SANDERS. SANDERSON. The son of Alexander—Sander being the common nickname of that appellation.

SANDFORD. "A family of acknowledged antiquity, whose ancestor 'Thomas' was certainly seated at Sandford [in the parish of Prees, co. Salop] soon after the Conquest, and which has ever since remained their principal seat." Shirley's Noble and Gentle Men. Parishes in Devon, Somerset, Oxford, &c., are likewise so called.

SANDHOE. A township in Northumberland, and a place in Yorkshire.

SANDIE. "The abbreviation of Alexander. Hence the English seem to have formed their ludicrous national designation of *Sawney* for a Scotsman." Jamieson.

SANDIESON. See Alexander, and Sandie.

SANDIFORD. An elegant suburb of Glasgow.

SANDILANDS. The surname of Lord Torpichen is traced to Sir James Sandilands, who flourished in the reign of King David II. The name is clearly local, but I do not find the place.

SANDISON. See Sanderson.

SANDS. SANDES. From residence on a sandy tract, whether near the sea or otherwise.

SANDY. A parish in Bedfordshire.

SANDYS. An archaic spelling of Sands, and pronounced like that name. Although the noble family, Barons Sandys of the Vine, did not attain that rank until the time of Henry VIII., they were amongst the most influential gentry of Hampshire in 6. Richard II.

SANFORD. See Sandford.

SANGER. Pure Anglo-Saxon for 'singer.' "Cantor, *sangere*." Wright's Vocab. p. 72.

SANGMAN. A-Sax. *sang*, a song, and *man*. A singer, or chorister.

SANGSTER. A-Sax. *sangistre*, a female singer, the feminine of Sanger. "Cantrix, *sangystre*." Wright's Vocab. For the mode in which 'songster' became applicable to the male sex, see under STER.

SANGWINE. Perhaps from disposition, but more likely the name of some saint corrupted to this form. The Scots had a St. Guinoch, and the Welsh a St. Gwenog.

SANKEY. "The Sankeys descend from a Lancashire family of considerable antiquity. The first upon record is Galfridus de Sankey, who held the lands of Sankey Magna and Sankey Parva in Lancashire, in the reign of King John." B.L.G.

SANSOM. St. Sansone, sometimes called St. Sampson, archbishop of Dol, founded a monastery near Rouen (Pentale monasterium in agro Rotomagensi) and after having performed a miracle, by ejecting a serpent from a certain cave, left his name to the place (eidem loco nomen suum reliquit). Mabillon Annal. Bened. ad ann. 655 et 831. From that place this family derived their name. The first who bore it in England was Ralph de St. Sansone, brother to Thomas, first Norman Archbishop of York, who with him had been educated at the charge of Odo, half-brother of the Conqueror. Being described by the Chroniclers as, "de nobilissima Normannorum prosapia" it has been conjectured that he was a scion of the ducal house. He was chaplain to William, and was created Baron of Dover, and, in 1099, Bishop of Worcester. In Domesday he is styled De S. Sansone, and Sanson clericus. His *son* Thomas (for the canons relating to the celibacy of the clergy were at this period very loosely observed) became Archbishop of York, and another son, Richard, was Bishop of Bayeux. From these ecclesiastics and their collateral relatives descended a numerous progeny, who varied the orthography of the name to Sansonus, Sansonius, Saunsum, Sansome, De S. Sampsone, Samson, &c., &c., and settled in many counties of England, and in Scotland. Inf. John Sansom, Esq.

SANTANDER. A corruption of St. Andrew.

SAPHIN. Probably the same as Salvine.

SAPSFORD. A corruption of Sawbridgeworth, co. Herts.

SAPWELL. A corruption of Sopewell, co. Hertford, over the convent of which Dame Juliana Berners, the well-known authoress of the Boke of St. Albans, presided.

SAPYE. A parish in co. Hereford: another in co. Worcester, now Sapey.

SARASIN. A Saracen—probably one who had embraced Christianity during the Crusades, and settled in Western Europe. It may be mentioned, that Saladin was an English surname, temp. Edward I. H.R.

SARAH. See Female Christian Names. In H.R. the forms are Sarra, Fil' Sarr, &c.

SARDINIA. This name, doubtless from the island so called, existed at Edinburgh in 1825.

SARE. See Sayers.

SAREL. SARRELL. Probably the same as Searle.

SARJEANT. SARGENT. O.Fr. from Lat. Spelman says a serjeant-at-law is so called because *serviens* ad legem. We have also serjeants-at-arms, serjeants-at-mace, &c. Cotgrave makes a *sergent*, "a footman or souldier that serves on foot." Gibbon, on the contrary, applies the word to "all horsemen who were not knights." Richardson.

SARL. The same as Searle.

SARSFIELD. The first of the family of Sarsfield who settled in Ireland, is said to have been Thomas de S., "chief banner-bearer" to King Henry II., A.D. 1172. The name is unquestionably English, and local.

SARSON. Perhaps the son of Saer. See Sayer.

SATCHELL. A small sack or bag. Probably an ancient trader's sign.

SATCHER. A maker of satchels or small bags. A.-Norm. *sachel*, Fr. *sachet*, a little bag.

SATTERLEY. A parish in Devonshire.

SATTERTHWAITE. A chapelry in Lancashire.

SAULL. SAUL. See Sale. An undertenant, Saul, is however mentioned in Domesday, and Saul is a parish in co. Gloucester.

SAUMAREZ. Lord De Saumarez is descended from a very ancient and respectable family in the island of Jersey. The original family name was De *Sausmarez*, which continues to be used by the eldest branch of the family. James, the first peer (1831) was grandson of Matthew de Saumarez, lord of the seignory of Saumarez in Guernsey, in the last century. The fiefs called Saumarez, in that island and in Jersey, are on low lands near the sea, whence the name, which signifies " saltmarsh," and is latinized in charters, De Salso Marisco.

SAUNDER. See Alexander.

SAUNDERS. 1. One of the derivatives of Alexander. 2. The family of this name in co. Wicklow, pretend that their ancestor came into England about the year 1270, and that he sprang " from Robert, Lord of Innspruck, who was second brother of Rodolph, Count of Hapsburgh, and subsequently Emperor." The founder of the family in Ireland was a follower of Cromwell. B.L.G.

SAUNDERSON. See Alexander. This seems to be one of the instances, in which a cadet of a family, bearing a territorial surname, assumed a patronymical one, so contrary to modern ideas of dignity. The Saundersons of co. Cavan are descended from Alexander de Bedick of Waslington, co. Durham, whose son, James de Bedick, used the *alias* of Saunderson, from his father's Christian name. His descendants settled in the shires of Nottingham and Lincoln, and it is from the latter county that the Saundersons just mentioned derive themselves. See B.L.G.

SAUNZ. From the well-known town of Sens, eighty-four miles S.E. of Paris.

SAVAGE. Camden says, that this surname was introduced into England by a personage in the train of Isabella of France, queen of Edward II. There were, however, earlier settlements of families so named; for a knight of this designation founded the Savages in Ireland immediately upon De Courcy's invasion, temp. Henry II. Le Sauvage was a sobriquet of early times, both in Normandy and England, which implied, perhaps, a roughness of manners, like our indigenous Wild. In ancient deeds the common latinization is Salvagius.

SAVENIE. Ralph de Savenie, or Savigni, occurs in the Domesday of Suffolk.

The Itin. de la Normandie shows three places called Savigni.

SAVERY. SAVORY. An early personal name, latinized *Savaricus*. Safrei, Saffrey. H.R.

SAVILE. One of the most illustrious families of the E. Riding of Yorkshire, where they are said to have existed in the XII. cent. In the thirteenth they were certainly flourishing in those parts. Some writers have fancifully ascribed to them an Italian origin. Shirley's Noble and Gentle Men. The name is probably Norman, and it seems to be represented in Holinshed's list by Sent Vile.

SAW. Probably Shaw.

SAWARD. An ancient Teutonic personal name. A-Sax. *sæ*, the sea, and *weard*, a keeper—the Guardian of the Sea; a fit name for a great naval commander; indeed it was an official, as well as a personal name, and was applied to the high-admiral of Saxon times. It is latinized Siwardus. The hamlets of Sewardstone, in Essex, and Sewardesley, in Northamptonshire, seem to have been so designated from ancient proprietors of this name.

SAWKINS. Perhaps a diminutive of Saul.

SAWLE. See Sale.

SAWNSEY. Perhaps from Sansei, near Criuil, in Normandy. See Chron. Battel Abbey, p. 60.

SAWYER. SAWYERS. The occupation.

SAX. A-Sax. *seax* or *sex*, a dagger or short sword.

SAXBY. Parishes in cos. Lincoln and Leicester.

SAXELBY. Parishes in cos. Lincoln and Leicester.

SAXON. This name does not denote an Anglo-Saxon, in contradistinction to a Norman origin: it was probably given to a settler from Saxony in more recent times. Or, it may possibly be a corruption of *sexton*, which is so pronounced in the West of England, or of Saxton, a local name.

SAXTON. 1. A sacristan or sexton— the lowest official in a church. 2. A parish in the West Riding of Yorkshire. H.R. De Saxton.

SAY. The first of this name mentioned by Dugdale, is Picot de Say, who, in the time of the Conqueror, was one of the principal personages in Shropshire, under Roger de Montgomery, Earl of Shrewsbury. Though the pedigree is incomplete, he was, no doubt, the progenitor of the great family of Say, which gave birth to Geoffrey de Say, one of the twenty-five barons of Magna Charta, and many other eminent persons. The barony became abeyant in 1382, and still so remains. The name appears to have been derived from the commune of Sai, near Argentan, in

Normandy. Among many *De* Says in the Hundred Rolls, are a few *Le* Says, indicating some employment, which I am unable to explain.

SAYER, whence SAYERS. An assayer of metals. Also an Anglo-Norman personal name, as Saher de Quincy, the famous Earl of Winchester. Sayer and Sayere in the Hund. Rolls, without the prefix *le*, seem to give the latter derivation the preference. With regard to the former, Kelham observes, that " when Domesday was compiled, there was always a fire ready in the Exchequer, and if they liked not the allay of the money, they burnt it, and then weighed it." Hence the expression in Domesday, ' Lib. LVI arsas et pensatas' —56lb. burnt and weighed.—Kelham's Domesday, p. 157. The Sayer would therefore be a crown officer who assayed the precious metals.

The Sayers of Essex were existing, according to B.L.G., temp. Edw. II.

SAYLOR. This surname is very rare indeed. This is not a little singular, considering the commonness of the employment. In the Hundred Rolls we have it in the forms of Le Sailliur, Le Saylliur, and Le Saler.

SAYRE. See Sayer.

SCALES. Hardwin de Scalers came in with William the Conqueror, and was ancestor of the noble family of Eschalers, or Scales, who continued in the male line till 36. Henry VI. Kelham's Domesday. The name began to be spelt De Scales about the time of Henry III. It was latinized De Scalariis.

SCAMBLER. " A bold intruder upon one's generosity or table." Such is the definition of the word by Dr. Johnson, who considers it to be Scottish.

SCAMMELL. *Scamells* is an old Scottish word for shambles. Jamieson.

SCANLAN. The Mac Scanlans were a sept of Louth, from whom the ancient locality of Bally-Mac-Scanlan took its name. The surname was sometimes written O'Scanlan. The first of the family mentioned by D'Alton is Patrick O'Scanlan, who was made Archbishop of Armagh in the year 1261.

SCARBOROUGH. A town in Yorkshire.

SCARBOROW. A corruption of Scarborough.

SCARBROW. A corruption of Scarborough.

SCARDEVILLE. Old, or Norman French possesses many words beginning with *Es*. In the process of modification, we generally drop the *E* and retain the *S*, while the modern French drop the *S* and retain the *E*. Thus, the old word *estranger* (Lat. extraneus) is on our side of the Channel ' stranger,' on the other side ' étranger.' So I suspect that this surname

is derived from Ecardenville, in the department of Eure, in Normandy—the *N* having been either dropped in the surname, or added in the local appellation. But the word has undergone still greater changes, having been anglicized to Skarfield, and *demonized* to Scare-devil ! Eng. Surn. ii. 34.

SCARISBRICK. A township in Lancashire, in early times the seat of the family. The heiress married Eccleston of Eccleston, who assumed the surname, and the estate of Scarisbrick is now in his possession. See Eccleston.

SCARLETT. Dr. Richardson observes, that scarlet was formerly used as an epithet of red ; thus Chaucer's—" Hosen of scarlet rede," and Spenser's—" Robe of scarlet red." The surname was probably applied as a sobriquet to one who affected this colour for his costume. So Blue, Purple, &c. Scarlet without prefix, in H.R. A personage of this name was elected M.P. for Lincoln in 1307, in the short parliament which sat for eighteen days at Carlisle, during the war of King Edward I. with the Scots. An ancient Tuscan family, who bore the name of Scarlatti were exiled in the thirteenth century by the Guelphs, for being Ghibellines. Their arms are different, but it is a rather curious fact, that the English Scarletts bear as their crest, a Tuscan column supported by lions' jambs. See Notes and Queries, March 17, 1860.

SCARMAN. A *scar* is a bleak, exposed situation, or a cliff. The original Scarman probably dwelt in such a locality.

SCATHLOCK. A correspondent observes, that this is a Sherwood Forest name, and that the " Robin Hood names " still linger in forest districts. Scathelock, Scatheloc. H.R.

SCATTERGOOD. 1. A corruption of some local name terminating in *wood* ? 2. A friend suggests " spendthrift." In H.R. Schatregod. The antithetical surname *Sparegood* (in H.R. Spargod), does not seem to have survived.

SCAWEN. " The name Scawen is local, and signifies a place where *skawan* or elder trees grow, and is derived from the Japhetical Greek, σκοβιεμ, sambachus, ebulus, the *elder-tree*, who suitable to his name, gives for his arms, ' Argent, a *scawen* or elder-tree, Vert.' " Hals. in D. Gilbert's Cornwall, ii. 67.

SCHARP. The same as Sharpe.

SCHNEIDER. Germ. A tailor.

SCHOLAR. This surname occurs in Encyc. Herald.

SCHOMBERG. Frederick Schomberg, a descendant of a noble family in Germany, accompanied William III. to England in 1688, and was ultimately created Duke of Schomberg.

SCHREIBER. German. A writer or clerk. The ancestor of the English family

(Schreiber of Henhurst, co. Kent) was John Charles Schreiber, son of Carl Schreiber, of an ancient family of Durlach in Suabia, who settled in London about the year 1721. B.L.G.

SCHULZE. SCHULTZ. From Germany. Germ. *schulze*, a bailiff in a village.

SCHUSTER. Germ. A shoemaker.

SCHWARS. SCHWARTZ. From Germany. Germ., black.

SCLATER. 1. The Sclaters of Hoddington, co. Hants, claim to have borrowed their name from the parish of Slaughter, or Schlauter in Gloucestershire, " where they were lords of the manor for upwards of three hundred years." B.L.G. 2. Another form of Slater. The unnecessary C has sometimes of late been resumed.

SCOBELL. According to Hals, this name, in the old Cornish language, signifies the broom-plant, and therefore takes its place, etymologically, with the illustrious Plantagenet. The family, whose original *habitat* was the counties of Cornwall and Devon, have flourished, for a long series of generations, in knightly and gentle degree, in that part of England, and have written their name Scobbahull, Scobhull, Scobbel, Scobhill, Scoble, &c. The first of the name on record is Thomas de Scobbahull, sheriff of Devonshire, in 1291. B.L.G. Scovell is not, as it might seem, a modification of this surname.

SCOBLE. See Scobell.

SCOLEMASTER. Schoolmaster. A John Scolemaster is mentioned in the Inquisitiones ad quod Damnum, temp. Henry V., and a Thomas Scolmayster in the Rotul. Orig. temp. Edw. III., but I have not met with the surname in later times.

SCOLOIGE (or Mac Scoloige). The name belongs to Fermanagh, Ireland. It is usually anglicized *Farmer,* 'scolog' being Irish for husbandman, or farmer. Notes and Queries, v. 501.

SCOON. Probably Scone in Perthshire, the ancient coronation-place of the Scottish kings, once a city, now a pitiful village of 18 houses.

" So thanks to all at once, and to each one,
Whom we invite to see us crown'd at Scone."
Macbeth.

SCOONES. A pluralized form of Scoon?

SCORE. 1. A corruption of *skawer,* which Halliwell defines as a jurat, but whose functions seem to have been more like those of "commissioners of sewers." A-Sax. *Sceawere;* a beholder, spectator, spy. Bosworth. Skawers are mentioned in connection with Pevensey Marsh in the XV. century, and Dugdale uses the word in his History of Imbanking, printed in 1662. 2. A deep, narrow, rugged indentation on the side of a hill. Isl. *skor,* fissura. Jamieson.

SCORER. A scout ; a scourer. " The kynge, beinge at Notyngham, and or he came there, sent the *scorers* all abowte the contries adjoyninge, to aspie and serche yf any gaderynges were in any place agaynst hym." Arrival of King Edward IV., quoted by Halliwell.

SCORRER. The same as Scorer.

SCOTCHER. One who levies taxes. To *scot,* or, as it is called in some dialects, to *scotch,* is to tax or amerce.

SCOTCHMAN. A native of Scotland.

SCOTLAND. Possibly from the country, but more likely from some trivial locality in the South. There are several small properties called Scotland, France, Wales, &c.

SCOTNEY. A castle and estate in East Sussex, which belonged to the family in the XIII. and XIV. centuries. The first of the name on record is Walter de Scotney, steward of the Earl of Gloucester, temp. Henry III., who was hanged on a charge of attempting the life of his master. His descendants continued at Scotney till the reign of Edward III. Blaauw's Barons' War, p. 61.

SCOTSON. The son of a Scotchman.

SCOTT. SCOT. This ranks among the most prevalent of British surnames, almost sixty coats of arms being assigned to it, while the London Directory shows about 200 traders in the metropolis so denominated. In records of early date, it is usually written *Le Scot,* implying a native of Scotland. Now, as the tendency of North Britons to ' come south ' is proverbial, we do not wonder at the commonness of the name in England ; but why many families who never lived out of Scotland should be called Scott, is not so readily explained. The Duke of Buccleuch, the head of the surname in that country, traces his pedigree to Richard le Scot, of Murdieston, co. Lanark, one of the Scottish barons, who swore fealty to our Edward I., 1296. The name exists in records of earlier date, but the claim set up by some zealous genealogists for a Norman extraction has no foundation. M. de Gerville remarks :—" It is somewhat curious that this Duke [of Buccleuch] seeks for his name in Normandy, and pretends that the original appellation was *l'Escott !*" Mem. Soc. Ant. Normandie, 1825.

The baronet's family (Scott of Ancrum, and Scott of Duninald) claim to be descended from the renowned wizard, Michael Scott, who flourished in the XII. century, and assert that the Buccleuch Scotts are from a younger branch of their house.

SCOTTS. A Scotchman.

SCOVELL. From Escoville now Ecoville, in the arrondissement of Caen, in Normandy. H.R. De Scoville, De Scovile.

SCOW. Danish *skov,* A-Sax. *scaga.* A coppice or shaw.

SCOWEN. See Scawen.

SCRAGGS. See Scroggs.

SCRASE. This Sussex family claim to have settled in the county from Denmark before the Norman Conquest, though there is no record of them earlier than the XIII. century. The name has been conjecturally derived from the great Norman appellative of Scures or D'Escures. Sussex Arch. Coll. viii. 2.

SCRIVEN. 1. O. Fr. *escrivain*, a writer, scribe. 2. A township in the parish of Knaresborough, co. York.

SCRIVENER. SCRIVENOR. O. Fr. *escrivain*, one who draws up and engrosses writings. The London Company of Scriveners was incorporated temp. James I.

SCRIVENS. See Scriven.

SCROGGS. A village in Dumfriesshire.

SCROGIE. A village in Perthshire.

SCROPE. SCROOP. "One of king Edward the Confessor's foreign attendants named Richard, to whom the Anglo-Saxons gave the derisory name of *Screope*, or ' the Scrub,' either on account of some inferior office which he held in the royal household, or perhaps as a merely satirical appellation, and who was one of the few Normans permitted to remain at court after the rest of the foreign favourites had been driven away, was enriched by his royal master with considerable possessions in this part of the border [near Ludlow] ; and, introducing there the fashion of his own countrymen, he built a strong castle between Ludlow and Leominster, which has preserved its founder's name in that of Richard's Castle. The name by which the builder was known became afterwards softened into that of Scroop." Wright's Ludlow, p. 23. The elder branch of the family afterwards became eminent in Yorkshire. The Scropes of Castle-Comb (co. Wilts,) have been there ever since the time of King Richard the Second. "The Lord Chancellor Scrope gave this mannour to his third son ; they have continued there ever since, and enjoy the old land, (about 800 li. per annum) ; and the estate is neither augmented nor diminished all this time, neither doth the family spread." Aubrey's Nat. Hist. Wiltshire, p. 119.

SCRUBY. Scrooby, a parish in Nottinghamshire.

SCRUTON. A parish in the North Riding of Yorkshire.

SCRUTTON. See Scruton.

SCRYMGEOUR. SCRIMGEOUR. "Alexander I., by special grant, appointed a member of the Carron family, to whom he gave the name of *Scrimgeour*, for his valour in a sharp fight, to the office of hereditary standard-bearer" of Scotland. Crawford's Scot. Peerage. Lord Berners employs the expression ' sore scrymmishe ' to designate a severe combat. The Hundred Rolls mention one William Eschir-

misur, who held 1½ virgate of land in Bedfordshire, temp. Edw. I. Scrymgeour, ' a skirmisher.' Talbot, Eng. Etymol. Any rough encounter is termed by Cockneys, ' a *scrimmage*.'

SCUDAMORE. Sir Alan Scudamore is said to have been a person of importance in Monmouthshire, in the reign of William Rufus, and Walter *de* Scudamore was lord of Upton, co. Wilts, in the reign of Stephen. The name is unquestionably Norman, and is said to be derived from the O. Fr. *escu d'amour*, ' the shield of love,' in allusion probably to some incident. The family motto sanctions this etymology, being " Scuto Amoris Divini"—Defended by the Shield of Divine Love.

SCURR. Jamieson has—1. " A low blackguard." Gall. Encycl, from Latin *scurra* ; and 2. *Skurr*, a small spot of fishing ground.

SCUTT. I have met with this name only in the town and neighbourhood of Brighton. It is a probable corruption of Scott. A Lancashire correspondent, however, reminds me that *scut* is a provincialism of extensive use for the tail of a hare or rabbit ; sometimes the hare itself is so called. Halliwell. A poacher near Preston went by that name, because he ordinarily wore a hare's tail, for bravado, in his hat. Such sobriquets have often superseded other names, and become hereditary surnames. H.R. Scut.

SEA. From residence near the ocean. Atte Sea, as a family name, is very common in medieval records.

SEABORN. Not ' born at sea '—but from some locality called Seabourne.

SEABRIGHT. See Sebright.

SEABROOK. I find no locality so called. It may, possibly, be a corruption of Sebright.

SEACOCK. A-Sax. *sae-cocc*, a sea gull.

SEACOMBE. A township in Cheshire.

SEAGRAVE. SEGRAVE. A parish in Leicestershire. The baronial De Segraves had possession of the lordship 12. Henry II. Baronage.

SEALE. SEAL. A parish in Kent, another in Surrey, a third in Sussex (Beeding), and a fourth in co. Leicester. Many other places were anciently so designated, from A-Sax. *sel*, a seat, hall, manorhouse, mansion.

SEALEY. See Seeley.

SEAMAN. In Sussex and Kent, and probably in other counties, this name has been corrupted into Simmons. See Simmons. In the Domesday of Surrey there is a Seman, who held lands before the making of that record. A-Sax. *Sae-mann*, a sailor.

SEAMARK. Probably from some eminence, or ' mark ' useful to mariners.

SEAMER. 1. A-Sax. *seamere*, a tailor. 2. Parishes in Yorkshire.

SEAR. See Sears.

SEARBY. A Lincolnshire parish.

SEARE. SEARES. See Sears.

SEARLE. SEARLES. Probably from Serlo, a Norman personal name, the common origin of Sarl, Sarel, Sarrell, Serrell, &c.

SEARS. 1. See Sayer. 2. Serez, a place in the arrondissement of Evreux, in Normandy. 3. "The name—which has been written Sare, Sayer, Sayers—first occurs in the reign of Edmund Ironside, A.D., 1016, and, a few centuries after, the family are found possessed of landed estates in the county of Essex, some of which remained in the name as late as the year 1770." Dixon.

SEARSON. The son of Saher or Syer.

SEATON. See Seton. Also parishes, &c., in cos. Devon, Rutland, York, Durham, Northumberland, Cumberland, &c.

SEAWARD. See Saward.

SEBEL. See Sibbald.

SEBRIGHT. William Sebright, of Sebright, in Much Baddow, co. Essex, living in the reign of Henry II., was the ancestor of this ancient family, who removed into Worcestershire at a very early period. Shirley's Noble and Gentle Men.

SECKER. Qu. the same as Segar?

SECKINGTON. A parish in Warwickshire.

SECRETAN. Probably a corruption of Sacristan. See Saxton.

SEDGER. Perhaps a corruption of Satcher.

SEDGWICK. An ancient castle and manor near Horsham, co. Sussex.

SEE. An old spelling of Sea, q. v.

SEEAR. Probably the same as Segar, by elision of the G.

SEELEY. SEELY. This word, in the forms of *sely* and *silly*, occurs in O. English writers from Chaucer to Milton, in the sense of harmless or simple. The word *silly*, the etymology of which has been debated, is much perverted from its original meaning, and the word 'simple' is now undergoing a similar degradation. 2. Ferguson derives it from A-Sax. *sél*, prosperous.

SEFFERT. A corruption of the A-Sax. personal name Sigefrid.

SEFOWL. A marine bird, sea-fowl. Sefoul. H.R.

SEGAR. SEAGER. A-Sax. *sigora*, a Conqueror, *sigor*, victorious; an ancient personal name, written in Domesday Segar, Sigar, and Sigarus. 2. A northern provincialism for sawyer, from A-Sax. *saga*, a

saw. 3. In Poitou, an eminent local surname—De Segur.

SEGRAVE. A parish in Leicestershire. The baronial family derived their descent from Gilbert de Segrave, who was lord of that place 12. Henry II. The Irish branch were settled in Ireland from temp. Edward II., their chief seat being at Killeglan, co. Meath.

SEKESTRIE. Jorden de la S. (Sextry, Sacristy.) Lewes Priory Records, XIII. cent.

SELBY. A town in Yorkshire, and a township in Northumberland. Riddleston, in the latter county, was granted in 1272, by King Edward I., to Sir Walter de Selby, and it has ever since remained in the possession of his descendants. Shirley's Noble and Gentle Men.

SELDEN. See DEN. John Selden was a native of Sussex, and it appears probable that his surname was originally borrowed from one of the many *dens* of Kent or E. Sussex.

SELDON. See Selden.

SELF. SELFE. "The name of Sewlf (sea-wolf) occurs in a charter of Canute, and it is, probably, the same as the Saulf in the Domesday of Derbyshire, where it is in the Scandinavian form." Ferguson.

SELKIRK. The county-town of Selkirkshire.

SELLEN. SELLENS. I can prove by the evidence of parish registers, &c., in Sussex, that this is a corruption of the ancient surname of Selwyn.

SELLER. SELLERS. A trader or salesman.

SELLINGER. See St. Leger.

SELLY. See Seeley.

SELMAN. See Saleman.

SELMES. Perhaps a modification of Anselmus.

SELVES. The son of Self, which see.

SELWARD. A-Sax. *sel*, a hall, and *weard*, keeper. The keeper of a hall. Bosworth.

SELWIN. SELWYN. An A-Sax. personal name of uncertain etymology.

SEMPILL. The first recorded ancestor of the noble family is Robert de Sempil, steward or chamberlain of Renfrew, in the reign of King Alexander III., whose descendant, Thomas Sempil, held the same office in 1483, and was killed at Bannockburn, as was his son John, the first lord Sempil, at Flodden. Courthope's Debrett.

SEMPLE. Camden says, a corruption of St. Paul, like Sinclair from St. Clare; but the Scottish noble family of the name seem to have a different origin. The early charters of the family are granted thus: "Thomæ dicto Sympil," "Roberto dicto Sympil," &c. In O. Scottish *sympil*, *sempill, semple,* means low-born, mean. "Gentle or 'Semple'" means, proverbially, whether high-born or low.

SENCHELL. A corruption of Seneschal.

SENDALL. The same as Sandall.

SENECAL. Seneschal, a steward.

SENESCHALL. A steward. See Sensicle and Snashall.

SENHOUSE. This family derived their surname from Sevenhouse or Senhouse, in Cumberland, parish of Cross-Canonby, and a pedigree in Hutchinson's Cumberland, ii. 268, traces them to Walter de Sevenhouse, temp. Edward III. "They were a constant family of gamesters," says a writer quoted in that work, "and the country people were wont to say, the Senhouses learn to play at cards in their mother's womb."

SENIOR. 1. An estate in co. Derby. 2. *Seigneur,* Fr. a feudal lord.

SENLOE. A corruption of Saint Lo.

SENNOCK. A contraction of Sevenoaks.

SENSICLE. The northern corruption of seneschal, steward, as Snashall is the southern. The illiterate corrupt it still further to Sensikoll.

SEPTVANS. In Eng. Surn. i. 195, I ventured a conjecture that the great Kentish family of Septvans borrowed their name from their armorial bearings, which were three (perhaps originally ' *seven*) *fans,*' or wicker winnowing baskets. It is, however, far likelier to be derived from a place in the arrondissement of Bayeux, called Sept Vents.

SERCOMBE. See COMBE.

SERGIAUX. This name was anciently written De Seriseaux or Ceresaux. The abbreviation seems to have taken place in the XIV. century. D. Gilbert's Cornwall, ii. 394.

SERGISON. Berry's Encycl. Herald. gives the name Sarjeantson (Sergeantson) and this may be the origin of Sergison.

SERJEANT. See Sarjeant.

SERJEAUX. See Sergiaux.

SERLE. See Searle.

SERRELL. See Searle.

SERVANT. Does not necessarily imply a menial attendant, for Domesday shews us several tenants-in-chief who are styled ' Servientes Regis.' In the O. Test. we find an influential person, the opponent of Nehemiah, styled Tobiah 'the Servant,' and in the same way, during the middle ages, men of large landed estates are frequently styled "servants" of particular noblemen. H.R. Serviens.

SESSIONS A possible corruption of Soissons, the Fr. town.

SETON. From a curious M.S. genealogy of this family, Sir B. Burke extracts the following passage :—" There were few surnames in Scotland before the time of King Malcolm Canmore, except that, after the manner yet used in the Highlands, they used their father's name subjoined to their own in the form of a patronymic. The said King Malcolm gave to his nobles and gentlemen particular surnames ; some by reason of their offices, and some after the names of the lands which they possessed, and some for other causes. Amongst whom the predecessor of this family got the name of Seton, as the chronicles testify, by occasion of the possession of the lands of that name, which was given to the lands by reason that the *town* thereof is situate hard upon the *sea.*"

Seaton or Seton is in Haddingtonshire. The first recorded bearer of the name is Dougal de Seton, who lived in the reign of King Alexander I.

SETTER. Probably some handicraft.

SETTLE. A market town in the parish of Giggleswick, co. York. The family, though now chiefly resident in more southern counties, have within the present century held lands at Settle, where they are known to have been *settled,* temp. Henry VII., and probably much earlier.

SEVENOKE. Sevenoaks, co. Kent, was anciently so written.

SEVERNE. From the Western river so called. De Sabrina. H.R. co. Salop.

SEWARD. See Saward.

SEWEL. SEWELL. Sewallis is a very ancient personal name, particularly in the family of Shirley, Earl Ferrers. A Sewallis, who certainly possessed Lower Eatington, co. Warwick, before the Conquest, is said to have been a "noble Saxon, issuing from the royal dukes of Saxony," (Stemmata Shirleiana, p. 5) ; but this is unsupported by any evidence. The name latinized Sewallis was doubtless Sewall or Sawald, a not uncommon baptismal appellation in Saxon times, and not improbably identical with the Ceadwal or Cedwalla of the days of the Heptarchy. Sewall is the spelling still retained in America, but in England Sewell (often modified to Shewell) is the prevailing form. It must not be forgotten, however, that in some instances the name may be local. Four places called Sewelle occur in Domesday ; and a John *de* Sewell was a follower of the Black Prince into Aquitaine. Rymer's Fœd., c. 1366.

SEWER. Anciently a great officer in royal and noble houses, whose duty was to set and remove dishes, to taste them, and to have the general management of the table. In Norman times, the office of King's sewer was one of the most important of the court. Le Sywr is the curious orthography of the H.R.

SEX. A-Sax. *seax,* a dagger. Ferguson.

SEXTON. See Saxton.

SEXTY. A corruption of *sacristy.*

SEYMOUR. A corruption of St. Maur, which see. Many of the families who write themselves Seymour, have probably little claim to a Norman origin. Some may derive from Semer, a parish in Suffolk, and others from the A.-Sax. *seamere*, a tailor. Semar is also an ancient personal name. Camden.

The great historical family derive from Roger de Sancto Mauro, or Seymour, who lived in the reign of Henry I. The ancient seats of the family were Woundy, Penhow, and Seymour Castle, all in Monmouthshire, but at a later period Wiltshire became their chief *habitat*.

SHAA. A local pronunciation of Shaw.

SHADBOLT. Ferguson derives this name from Northern roots, signifying bold in war. I think the last syllable is more likely to be a corruption of the local *bold*, a dwelling.

SHADRAKE. A corruption of the Scripture name, Shadrach.

SHADWELL. A parish in Middlesex, and a township in Yorkshire. The Sussex Shadwells probably derive from the manor of Shadwell, in the parish of Buxted, in that county, which had owners of its own name temp. Hen. VI.

SHAFTAN. A corruption of Shafto.

"Young Henry Shaftan he is hurt,
A souldier shot him with a bow."
Raid of the Reidswire.

SHAFTO. Two townships in the parish of Hartburn, co. Northumberland, are so called, and the family resided at the place named Shafto Crag. They are a known cadet of the ancient Norman house of Foliot, being descended from John Foliot, lord of Fenwick, 22. Henry II. Cuthbert Foliot married the heiress of Roger Welwick, lord of Shafto, and his son, in 10. Edward I. assumed the territorial name. The Shaftos formed a sort of Border clan, and their gathering cry was A SHAFTO! A SHAFTO!

SHAFTOE. See Shafto.

SHAILER. To shail is to walk crookedly. "I shayle with the fete, *jentretaille des piedz*." Palsgrave. Hence a Shailer is a man of awkward gait.

SHAIRP. A variation of Sharpe.

SHAKELADY. Known in Lancashire as a corruption of the ancient local surname Shackerley. The vulgar corrupt it still further by the abbreviation Shack.

SHAKESHAFT. Belongs apparently to the same class as Shakspeare, Wagstaffe, &c.

SHAKESTAFF. Analogous to Shakspeare, Shakeshaft, &c., in allusion to some feat of courage displayed by the original bearer.

SHAKSPEARE. Nomen clarum et venerabile! Much has been said and written about the true orthography of it. But since we find it spelt in documents of equal authority Chacksper, Shakespeyre, Schakespeire, Schakspere, Shakespere, Shakspere, Shakespeare, and Shaxper, it is hardly worth while to extend or re-open the discussion. Other names of comparative insignificance have been much more varied in their component letters. Concerning its etymology there can be no doubt. "The custome first πάλλειν, to *vibrate* the speare before they used it, to try the strength of it, was so constantly kept, that 'εγχἐσπαλος, a Shake-speare, came at length to be an ordinary word, both in Homer and other poets, to signifie a soldier." Francis Rous, Archæologia Attica, 1637. The Bard's contemporaries evidently understood the name in this sense. Thus Spenser:—

"Whose muse, full of high thoughts' invention,
Doth like himself heroically sound."

And Ben Johnson :—

"He seems to shake a lance,
As brandished at the eyes of ignorance."

Our family nomenclature presents us with several analogies, as Break*speare*, Win*spear*, *Shake*shaft, *Shake*launce, Hackstaff, Briselance, and Bruselance, Wagstaffe, Bickerstaffe, Hurlbat, Draweswerde (Drawsword), and Cutlemace ('Cut the club or mace'), Hackblock, &c.

The name Shakspeare is still comparatively common in South Staffordshire.

SHALLOW. A fordable place in a river. The name ranks therefore with Ford, and has no connection with what was in Shakspeare's mind when he introduced the well-known Justice that bore "the dozen white louses" in his "old coat."

SHAND. Said to be a corruption of De Champ or Deschamps. In Scotland it was anciently written Schand, and latinized Schandæus. It is of course of French origin, though of earlier importation than the Rev. of the Ed. of Nantes, 1685, as asserted in Notes & Qu., 2nd Series No. 106. Philibert de Shaunde was created Earl of Bath in 1485; but nothing is known of him except that he was a native of Brittany. Ext. Peerage. The name is common in the shires of Aberdeen and Banff. Inf. C. F. Shand, Esq.

SHANDOS. See Chandos.

SHANE. Said to be a corruption of the Fr. Duchesne, equivalent to Oakes, Noakes, &c.

SHANK. *Shank*, in Scotland, is a topographical word, meaning the projecting point of a hill. The family existed in early times in Mid-Lothian, the founder being Murdoch Schank, who is said to have discovered, and taken charge of, the body of Alexander III., King of Scotland, who met his death while hunting in 1286. For this service, Robert Bruce presented him with the lands of Castlerigg. B.L.G.

SHANNON. Probably *not* from the great Irish river, though I cannot substitute any better origin.

SHAPCOTT. Sheep-cote. The name of an estate, the locality of which I do not know.

SHARD. An opening in a wood. Yorkshire. Halliw.

SHARLAND. Shirland, a parish in co. Derby.

SHARMAN. See Sherman.

SHAROOD. See Sherwood.

SHARPE. SHARP. From natural disposition—a keen, active, acute person. H.R. Scharp.

SHARPLES. A township in Bolton, co. Lancaster, corrupted to Sharpless.

SHARRATT. See Sherwood, and Sherard.

SHARWOOD. See Sherwood.

☞ SHAW. Very common *per se*, and also as a termination. It means a small wood, from A-Sax. *scua*, a shade, a place shadowed or sheltered by trees.

"In somer when the *shawes* be sheyne,
And leves be large and long;
It is full mery in feyre foreste,
To here the foulys song."
M.S. quoted by Halliwell.

Several parishes and places bear this appellation, and to it we owe a considerable number of local surnames; e.g., Abershaw, Bagshaw, Cockshaw, Henshaw, Bradshaw, Langshaw, Eldershaw, Renshaw, &c.

SHAVEALL. A barber-ous corruption of some local name terminating in HALL.

SHAYLER. See Shailer.

SHAYLOR. See Shailer.

SHEA. See O'Shee.

SHEARER. In Scotland, a reaper; in England, one who shears sheep.

SHEARGOLD. *Shere*, or pure, gold. See remarks under Gold.

SHEARMAN. See Sherman.

SHEARS. A mis-spelt pluralization of Shire.

SHEARSMITH. See under Smith.

SHEATH. A fountain of salt water. Halliwell.

SHEATHER. A maker of sheaths or scabbards.

SHEBBEARE. A parish in Devonshire.

SHEE. See O'Shee.

SHEEHAN. The O'Sheehans were a sept in the counties of Cork and Limerick. D'Alton.

SHEEHY. Probably the same as Sheehan.

SHEEL. See Shiell.

SHEENE. SHEEN. 1. The original name of Richmond, co. Surrey. 2. A-Sax. *scinan* to shine, whence O. Eng. *shene*, bright, shining—a word frequently employed by our old poets.

SHEEPEY. Sheppey, an insulated division of Kent.

SHEEPSHANKS. Probably a sobriquet, alluding to badly-formed legs. The late Whittle Sheepshanks, Esq., was an eminent farmer; and it is related of him, that having once made a purchase at a northern fair, the seller asked him for a reference for payment, and Mr. S. replied : "Why don't you know me? I thought everybody hereabouts knew Whittle Sheepshanks." Upon which the other, fearing a hoax, rejoined : "Hoot, mon, wha ever heard o' a *sheepshank*, wi' a *whittle* (pocket-knife) to't ?"— and actually declined the transaction. The worthy gentleman soon afterwards took the name of Yorke by royal sign-manual, and

"Thus was the winter of his discontent,"
(If he had any on the subject)—
"Made glorious summer by the *name* of Yorke !"

SHEERMAN. See Sherman.

SHEFFIELD. A town in Yorkshire. The Sheffields, extinct Dukes of Buckingham, attained importance as early as the reign of Henry III. The first recorded ancestor is Sir Robert de Sheffield.

SHEIL. See Sheill.

SHEILL. The O'Sheills were an ancient clan in the county of Antrim. D'Alton.

SHELDON. A parish in Warwickshire, in ancient times the seat of the family.

SHELDRAKE. SHELDRICK. A seafowl, nearly resembling a duck. Gloss. of Heraldry. The family bear three in their arms. H.R. Le Sceldrake, Sceyldrake.

SHELF. 1. A township of Halifax, co. York. 2. Mr. Ferguson thinks from a Teutonic hero called Scelf or Scylf, the presumed founder of the Scylfingas, a Scandinavian tribe.

SHELFANGER. A parish in Norfolk, where the family had possessions temp. Edward I.

SHELFORD. Two parishes in Cambridgeshire, and another in Nottinghamshire.

SHELL. A hamlet in the parish of Himbledon, co. Worcester.

SHELLEY. Genealogists assert that the Shelleys "came out of France with William the Conqueror." Seulle, Shevele, or Sheuile, is found in the lists called the Roll of Battel Abbey. Horsfield's Lewes, ii. 176. But independently of the fact that there are several places in England called Shelley, (in Suffolk, Essex, Yorkshire, &c.) there is no authenticated, or even imaginary, pedigree which ascends beyond the XIV. century. There was formerly near Horsham, in Sussex, (the great *habitat* of this family) a park called Shelley, from which they doubtless assumed their name.

SHELTON. Parishes, &c., in cos. Bedford, Norfolk, Nottingham, and Stafford.

SHENTON. A chapelry in co. Leicester.

SHEPHERD. The occupation. As a surname it is often variously mis-spelt, as Shepard, Shephard, Shepheard, Sheppard, Shepperd. The H.R. forms of this name are Pastor and Le Pastur.

SHEPHERDSBUSH. The name of a foundling discovered at the place so called in Middlesex. See Eng. Surn. ii. 19.

SHEPHOUSE. " Sheep-house," a local name.

SHEPPERSON. The son of the Shepherd. So Wrightson, Smithson, &c.

SHERARD. SHERRARD. " Our antiquaries agree that Schirrard, who was resident in England, and held great possessions in the counties of Cheshire and Lancashire, temp. William Conq., is lineal ancestor to the present Earl of Harborough." Collins's Peerage, edit. 1768, v. 38.
Said to have been of Thornton, in Cheshire, in the XIII. cent., but the pedigree is *proved* only to William Sherard, who died in 1304. Shirley's Noble and Gentle Men.

SHERBORNE. Parishes, &c., in cos. Dorset, Gloucester, Warwick, Hants, &c. There are also Sherburnes in cos. Durham and York.

SHERER. See Shearer, and Shearman.

SHERGOLD. See Sheargold.

SHERIFF. SHERRIFF. From the office, A-Sax. *scir-geréfa*, i.e., "shire-reeve." The Domesday equivalent is *vicecomes*, which implies the deputy or substitute of a count, whose jurisdiction extended over a shire or county.

SHERIN. Sherwin, by the suppression of W.

SHERINGTON. A parish in co. Wilts, and a manor in Selmeston, co. Sussex, which had owners of the same name in the XIV. cent.

SHERLEY. See Shirley.

SHERLOCK. Having *shere*, or clear locks? The family were of importance in Ireland from the time of the Tudors. Ortelius's map locates them in the barony of Middlethird, co. Wexford. D'Alton.

SHERMAN. SHEREMAN. At Norwich, one who shears worsted, fustians, &c., an employment once known as ' shermancraft.' Eng. Surn. i. 108. The word has another distinct meaning. " Even at this day, in Norfolk, a person born out of the county is called a Shireman, i.e., born in some one of the *shires* or counties of England." Archæologia, xix, 16. But a more dignified origin may be assigned : in Domesday-book the Judge of the County-court (a very important office in Norman times) was

called a *Scirman*, i.e., Shireman. The A-Sax. *scirmann* is defined by Bosworth as " a man who superintends, shireman, provincial, an overseer, governor, provost, bailiff of a hundred." The parish of Shermanbury, in Sussex, must have taken its name, in Saxon times, from one who bore either the name or the office, or both.

SHERRELL. A corruption of Sherwell.

SHERRIN. The same as Sherin.

SHERRING. 1. The same as Sherin. 2. Shering, a parish in Essex.

SHERRY. Perhaps a corruption of Sheriff, or of Sherwin.

SHERSTON. Two parishes in Wiltshire are so called.

SHERVILL. A corruption of Sherwell.

SHERWELL. A parish in Devonshire.

SHERWIN. An ancient personal name. H.R. Scherewind, Scherewynd, &c.

SHERWOOD. A well-known forest in Nottinghamshire, the scene of the adventures of Robin Hood and his companions.

SHETHER. See Sheather.

SHEWARD. The same as Saward and Seward.

SHEWELL. See Sewell.

SHIEL. See Sheill, and Shield.

SHIELD. The primary meaning of this word is a covering or defence, whether against the weapons of an adversary, or against the inclemency of the weather. A-Sax. *scyldan*, tegere, protegere ; to cover, to protect. Richardson. As a surname, it is local, from *shiel*, a temporary hut for shepherds or labourers of any kind ; afterwards applied to more permanent habitations, and even to villages and towns.

SHIELDS. North and South Shields, cos. Northumberland and Durham.

SHIELL. See Sheill.

SHIFFNER. The baronet's family settled in London in the last century from Russia. It is probable that they were of German origin. The German *schaffner* is synonymous with the Norman-French Le Dispenser, and signifies manager or steward, (*dispensator*), from *schaffen*, to effect, procure.

SHILDRAKE. *Sheldrake*, an O.-Eng. name for a certain aquatic fowl, but of what species I cannot ascertain.

SHILDRICK. See Shildrake.

SHILL. A place near Grimsby, co. Lincoln.

SHILLCOCK. Possibly from *shrill-cock*, or *shirl-cock*, a provincial name of the throstle.

SHILLIBEER. One William Scilleber lived in Yorkshire, temp. Edward I. H.R., and was doubtless an ancestor of the Shillibeers. No probable etymology of the name has occurred to me.

SHILLING. Schelin, Schelinus, a Domesday personal name.

SHILLINGFORD. Parishes in Devonshire and Berkshire.

SHILSTONE. Perhaps Shillingstone, a parish in Dorsetshire.

SHIN. A river of Sutherlandshire.

SHINAN. Originally O'Shanahan, a sept descended from Lorcan, King of Munster, and grandfather of Brian Boru, and hence a branch of the Dalcassians. According to the Annals of the Four Masters, at the great battle of Moinmor in Desmond, fought in 1151, seven of the O'Shanahans were slain. D'Alton.

SHINGFIELD. Shinfield or Shiningfield, a parish in Berkshire.

SHINGLER. A mechanic who covered roofs with oaken tiles. Many church spires are so covered at this day; and formerly roofs, both of churches and houses, were shingled, as they are in North America at the present time. The occupation subsisted in Sussex, as a distinct trade, in the XVII. century. The name may, however, have a different origin, for *shingling* is an important process in the manufacture of iron. See Ray's Proverbs and Words, edit. 1768, app.

SHINGLETON. The same as Singleton.

SHINKFIELD. The same as Shingfield.

SHINN. See Shin.

SHINNER. "An hose, a nether stocke, a *shinner*." Nomenclator, 1585. Halliwell. See Hosier.

SHIP. Probably an inn or trader's sign.

SHIPLEY. Parishes, &c., in cos. Sussex, Derby, Northumberland, York, &c.

SHIPMAN. A mariner. This word is used in the authorized version of the Bible.

SHIPPEN. A-Sax. *scipen*, a stall or stable. A cow-house is still so called in the North. The French equivalent is Bouverie.

> "Whi is not thi table sett in the cow-stalle;
> And whi etist thou not in thi *shipun* as well as in thin halle."
>
> *M.S. Digby* 41. *(Halliwell.)*

SHIPSTER. A-Sax. *scip*, and *steóra*, a steerer. A ship-steerer, guide, pilot, or ruler. In the curious list of names given in Cocke Lorrelles Bote we read :—

> "Gogle-eyed Tomson, *shepster* of Lyn."

SHIPSTON. A parish in Worcestershire, on the river Stour.

SHIPTON. Parishes and places in cos. Salop, York, Oxford, Bucks, Gloucester, &c.

SHIPWASH. A corruption of " sheep-

2 s

wash "—a place where sheep are cleansed preparatory to shearing.

SHIPWAY. Probably from Shepway, one of the lathes, or great divisions, of the county of Kent.

SHIPWRIGHT. See under Wright. H.R. Le Schipwryte.

SHIRE. O. Eng. *shere*, clear, pure, transparent.

SHIRECLIFFE. This local surname has undergone, I am told, 55 changes and corruptions of spelling, the most common of which are Shirtliff, Shertley, and Shirtcliffe.

SHIREFF. A corruption of Sheriff.

SHIRLEY. This ancient family trace, without *hiatus*, to Sasuualo, or Sewallis, whose name, says Dugdale, " argues him to be of the old English stock," and who is mentioned in Domesday as mesne lord of Eatington, co. Warwick, under Henry de Ferrers. This, the oldest knightly family of that county, resided at Eatington until the reign of Edward III., though in the meantime, in the twelfth century, they adopted their surname from their manor of Shirley in Derbyshire. Eatington has never been alienated, and it is, at this day, one of the residences of the existing representative of the family, Evelyn Philip Shirley, Esq., M.P. See Stemmata Shirleiana, 1841 ; and Shirley's Noble and Gentle Men.

The *Sherleys* of Wiston, Preston, &c., co. Sussex (from whom sprang the remarkable " Three Brothers ") were a younger branch of the Warwickshire family. The *Shurleys* of Isfield, co. Sussex, though connected by marriage with the Sherleys, were of a different stock.

SHIREMARKS. Giles at Shiremarks lived in 1484 at Warnham, co. Sussex, a border parish to Surrey. See Cartwright's Rape of Bramber. The ' shiremarks ' were doubtless boundary stones between the two counties.

SHIRMAN. See Sherman.

SHIRREFF. A corruption of Sheriff.

SHIRRY. See Sherry.

SHIRT. May be derived from the garment, like Cloake, Mantell, &c., though this does not seem very probable.

A Mr. Shirt of Kensington, feeling himself under-valued by bearing the name of this under garment, some years ago altered it to Hirst, whereupon a punster might fairly have called him Mr. Ex-*change*. There was a Mr. Abraham Shurt in America in 1626, to whom Mr. Bowditch refers in the dedication of his humorous work, Suffolk Surnames :—

> " To the Memory
> of
> A. SHURT,
> ' the Father of American Conveyancing,'
> whose Name is associated alike
> with
> my daily Toilet, and my daily Occupation."

SHOE. Probably an ancient A-Sax. name, whence the designations of the places called Shoobrooke, Shoby, Shoebury, &c.

SHOEBOTHAM. Local: " the bottom or vale in which there is a shaw." See Shaw, and Bottom.

SHOESMITH. See Shoosmith.

SHOEWRIGHT. A-Sax. *sceo-wyrht*, a shoemaker. See Wright. This artificer also made leathern flasks, bags, and purses. Wright's Vocab, p. 9.

SHOOBRICK. SHOOBRIDGE. SHU-BRICK. Evidently a local name. See Shoe. The final *brick* is a corruption of the A-Sax. *brig*, a bridge.

SHOOLBRED. A corruption of Shul-bred in W. Sussex, formerly noted for its priory.

SHOOSMITH. A maker of horse-shoes, a farrier. Let me remark here, the impropriety of the common acceptation of the word *farrier*, which in country places is applied to a person who practices medicine for the equine race, and for domestic quadrupeds in general. In the last generation, most villages had a ' horse-farrier and cow-leech,' (See under Leech) with an oval sign-board over his door to that effect; at present such a practitioner has a brass plate with 'veterinary-surgeon' inscribed thereon. But originally, and correctly, the farrier was a man who provided horses with shoes (fers à cheval) i.e., a *shoe-smith*. In rural districts, the farrier or shoe-smith, forgetting the maxim, NE SUTOR ULTRA CREPIDAM, exceeded his function, and took care of the *health* of horses, and at length handed over the *feet* of his charge to the village blacksmith, to whom they primally and of right belonged, though meanwhile he continued to be called a farrier—the original meaning of the word being totally lost sight of.

SHOPPEE. Supposed to be a corruption of the French surname Chapuis.

SHORDITCH. Shoreditch, a part of London.

SHORE. The sea-side, or the margin of a river or lake.

SHORES. See Shore.

SHOREDICHE. See Shoreditch.

SHOREDITCH. Doubtless from the district of eastern London so designated.

SHOREHAM. A town in Sussex, and a parish in Kent.

SHORT. From diminutive stature. It bears the same orthography in H.R.

SHORTALL. This name is of record in Ireland from temp. Edward II. It is probably of English origin.

SHORTER. Possibly the same as Shotter.

SHORTHOSE. In the reign of Charles II. there were a family of this name who claimed direct descent from Prince Robert Curthose. Notes and Queries, December 5, 1857.

SHORTREED. A Selkirkshire family. The name is probably local.

SHOTBOLT. Seems to refer to archery. The last syllable may, however, be a corruption of ' bold,' a topographical term.

SHOTLANDER. German, Schotländer, a Scotchman. During the middle ages Scotchmen often fought the battles of the German princes.

SHOTLENDER. See Shotlander.

SHOTT. Perhaps a corruption of Shotts, a parish in co. Lanark.

SHOTTER. A contraction of Shotover, co. Oxford.

SHOTTON. Three places in co. Durham are so designated.

SHOUBRIDGE. See Shoobridge.

SHOULDERS. Probably a sobriquet applied to a high-shouldered man.

SHOVEL. Possibly a corruption of Fr. *cheval*, horse.

SHOVELLER. A man who used the implement in his work.

SHOWERS. Mr. Ferguson says A-Sax. *scoere*, a " shoer," or maker of shoes.

SHOWLER. The same as Shoveller—a shovel in several dialects being called a *showl*.

> " Who'll dig his grave ?
> I says the Owl;
> With my spade and *showl*,
> I'll dig his grave."
>
> *Cock Robin.*

SHREEVE. *Shrieve*, the O. Eng. spelling of Sheriff.

SHREWSBURY. The chief town of Shropshire.

SHUBRICK. See Shoobrick.

SHUCKBURGH. " William de Sucke-berge is presumed to be the first who assumed the name, from Shuckborough-Superior in Warwickshire; he was living in the third of John." The lineal descent of the earlier members of the family is, however, obscure; and the connected pedigree ascends no higher than the first year of Edward III. Shirley's Noble and Gentle Men. Baker's Northamptonshire.

SHUFFELL. SHUFFLE. See Bottom* in the Supplement. It may, however, be a corruption of Sheffield.

SHUFFLEBOTHAM. SHUFFLE-BOTTOM. My former explanation by " Shaw-field bottom " is hardly tenable. See Bottom* in the Supplement.

SHULDHAM. Shouldham Hall, co. Suffolk, was the seat of this family so early as 34 Henry III., when Sir William de Shuldham was resident there. The Shuldhams of Ireland settled in that country, in co. Cork, early in the XVIII. century.

SHURLEY. See under Shirley.

SHUTE. A parish in Devonshire, which was the residence of the family in the last century.

SHUTER. Lat. *sutor*, and O.Eng. *suter*, a shoemaker.

SHUTT. See Shute.

SIBBALD. An ancient baptismal name. In the Domesday of Northamptonshire a Sibaldus occurs as tenant in chief. As a surname it is found in Scotland in the XII. century. B.L.G.

SIBBALDSCOT. Local: "the *cote* or cottage of Sibaldus."

SIBEL. See Sibbald.

SIBSON. Apparently the son of Sibbald.

SIBTHORPE. A parish in Nottinghamshire. A Robert and a William de Sibetorp occur in the Domesday of that county, and the name is found in connection with Sibthorpe down to the XIV. century. The family of the late Colonel Sibthorpe appear to have been associated with Laneham, in the same county, from the year 1395, but there is no direct proof of their descent from the Domesday family, which is, however, probable. See B.L.G.

SICILY. An Edinburgh surname, which is derived, probably not from the Italian island, but from the female Christian name, Cicely or Cæcilia.

SICKELMORE. A corruption of sycamore, the tree. Cognate with Oak, Ash, &c.

SICKLEMORE. See Sickelmore.

☞ SIDE. A topographical expression, implying the side of a hill, stream, &c. Hence Whiteside, Silverside, &c.

SIDEBETHAM. A particularly genteel refinement of Sidebottom.

SIDEBOTTOM. A compound of Bottom, which see, in the Supplement.

SIDGWICK. The same as Sedgwick.

SIDNEY. See Sydney.

SIDWELL. An ancient personal name. A church at Exeter is dedicated to St. Sidwell.

SIEVEWRIGHT. A maker of sieves.

SIFTON. The same as Sefton.

SIGGERS. A-Sax. *sigra*; Old Norse, *sigarr*, a conqueror. Ferguson.

SIGGURS. See Segar. Possibly from the town of Segur in Poitou.

SIGMUND. An ancient German and Scandinavian name.

SIKE. See Sykes.

SIKELFOT. This name occurs in records of Lewes Priory, XIII. century. Either ' sicklefoot' from some remarkable 'splay,' or O.Eng. *siker*, that is, *sure*, foot.

SIKES. See Sykes.

SILAS. The personal name.

SILBY. Sileby, a parish in Leicestershire.

SILCOCK. A diminutive of Silas.

SILK. A parish in Lincolnshire, with the suffix of Willoughby.

SILLER. Of recent introduction from Germany. A corruption of Schiller.

SILLIFANT. This Devonshire family, originally written Sullivan, were derived from the Sullivans of Ireland, and settled in England in the year 1641.

SILLIMAN. The A-Sax. *syl*, or *sul*, a plough, is retained in the Wiltshire provincialism *sylla*. Hence Silliman is probably ploughman.

SILLY. SILLEY. John Silly, gent., of St. Wenn, altered his name from Ceely to Silly. D. Gilbert's Cornwall, iii. 237; a truly silly deed, especially for a lawyer to have executed.

SILVANUS. Sylvanus, the personal name,

SILVER. Probably an old personal name. It corresponds with the Germ. Silber. Ferguson.

SILVERLOCK. Doubtless from the hoary head of the first bearer of the name. So Blacklock, Whitelock, &c.

SILVERSIDE. A place in the Lake district is so called. Ferguson.

SILVERSPOON. Probably a trader's sign.

SILVERSTONE. A parish in co. Northampton.

SILVERTON. A parish in Devonshire.

SILVESTER. An ancient personal name. The Roman Calendar has three saints so designated. In Domesday there is a Hugo Silvestris, an epithet synonymous with the more modern Dubois and Attwood.

SIM. See Simon.

SIMBERB. A corruption of St. Barbe.

SIMCO. SIMCOE. A modern refinement of Simcock.

SIMCOCK. SIMCOX. See Simon.

SIMEON. The personal name.

SIMES. See Simon.

SIMMONS. SIMMONDS. This name is generally understood to be a derivative of Simon; but it may have come from the Domesday name Simund, which is distinct from Simon. A family of Simmons who have been resident for three centuries and a half at Seaford, co. Sussex, have evidently corrupted their appellative from Seaman; and it has gone through the following phases since the year 1553:— Seman, Seaman, Seamans, Semons, Simons, Simonds, Simmonds, Symonds, Symmonds, and Simmons. The name Seman is of very frequent occurrence in the records of the Cinque Ports, and other places on the Kent and Sussex coast, in the XIII., XIV., and subsequent centuries. It has doubtless had many distinct origins from many an " ancient mariner " of that region. In the year 1294, the ship " De la Bochere," of Winchelsea, was commanded by Benedict *Seman*, who doubtless obtained his name from his occupation. See Cooper's Winchelsea, p. 55.

SIMMS. See Simon.

SIMON. A Christian name of Norman introduction, and formerly of much more frequent use than at present. Itself a surname, it has become the parent of many others, particularly of Sim, Sims, Simes, Simson and Simpson, Simkin and Simpkin, Simpkins, Simpkinson, Simcock, Simcox, and Simcoe; also of the forms in Y, as Symonds, Symondson, Sympson, Symm, Syms, and Symes, with perhaps Sykes and Sikes, and sometimes of Simond, Simonds, Simmons, and Simmonds.

SIMOND. SIMONDS. See Simon.

SIMKIN. SIMKINS. See Simon.

SIMPKINSON. See Simon.

SIMPLE. From condition; a plebeian, as opposed to a gentleman. See Semple. H.R. Le Simple.

SIMPSON. 1. A Buckinghamshire parish. 2. The son of Simon. The Simpsons of Knaresborough deduce their lineage from the time of Edward the Confessor, and from Archil, a Saxon thane, living in that reign, and in the reign of the Conqueror. Among his other possessions was the manor of Clint in Yorkshire, where his posterity resided in the XIII. and XIV. centuries, writing themselves De Clynt. The name of Simpson (or Simon's son) was adopted from Symon, son of William de Clynt, who was living in the year 1300. See B.L.G. However contrary to our modern notions of good taste, there are several other instances of families having disused a territorial surname in favour of a patronymical one.

SIMS. See Simon.

SIMSON. The son of Sim, that is Simon. The Scottish family of Simson, Symsoun, or Symson, of Brunton, have been established in Fifeshire from the commencement of the XV. century. B.L.G.

SINCLAIR. A corruption of Saint Clair or Saint Clere.

SINCLER. A Scottish corruption of Saint Clair.

SINDEN. Perhaps a corruption of Sinjen or St. John. See however DEN.

SINDERBY. A township in Yorkshire.

SING. From an account of this family in the Bridgnorth Journal, Sept. 8, 1855, it appears that they originated from " John

Millington, commonly called Singer, alias Synge," a canon or prebendary of the church of St. Mary Magdalen, Bridgnorth, who married after the Reformation, and became progenitor of the Synges or Sings, still resident in that town.

SINGER. Doubtless from vocal skill.

SINGERMAN. The same as Singer, the final syllable being redundant, as in Tuckerman, Fisherman, &c.

SINGLEDAY. See Doubleday.

SINGLETON. A parish in Sussex, and a chapelry in Lancashire. The latter was long possessed by a very ancient family.

SINKINS. The same as Simpkins, a diminutive of Simon.

SINKLER. As vile a corruption of Sinclair, as Sinclair is of Saint Clair. Two London pork-butchers in 1852 bore the name.

SINNOCK. A corruption of Sevenoaks, co. Kent. For the story of Sir William Sennock or Sevenoke, see Lambarde's Peramb. p. 520, and Eng. Surn. ii. 119. See also Snooks in this Dictionary. The H.R. present us with a Sinoch, demanding another etymology.

SINNOT. See Synnot.

SIRED. An A-Sax. personal name.

SIRETT. See Sired.

SIRR. Mr. Ferguson deduces the curious names Sirr and Siree from the Icelandic *sìra*, a priest.

SISLEY. A mis-spelling of Cicely, the female Christian name.

SISSON. A corruption of Siston, a parish in Gloucestershire.

SISSONS. A pluralization of Sisson.

SISTERSON. Analogous to Le Neve, New, Brothers, &c.

SITTON. A corruption of Seton or Seaton.

SITWELL. 1. According to B.L.G. the Sitwells of the North of England were descended from Seawald or Seadwald, and through him from Ida, Saxon King of Northumberland. 2. See Sidwell.

SIVEWRIGHT. See Siveyer, and Wright.

SIVEYER. A maker of sieves, whence also Sivewright.

SIVIL. A mis-spelling of civil, courteous.

SIWARD. The A-Sax. personal name.

SIX. Ferguson says A-Sax. *seax*, a dagger or short sword.

SIXSMITHS. See under Smith.

SIZAR. See Sizer.

SIZER. A scholar of the lowest degree at Cambridge—a servitor. Bailey.

SKAIFE. *Scaif* is a northern provincialism for timid or fearful. H.R. Skayf.

SKARFIELD. A corruption of Scardeville.

SKEEN. See Skene.

SKEFFINGTON. The ancestors of the baronet were proprietors of Skeffington, co. Leicester, and seated there as early as the reign of Richard I.

SKEGG. As we find the genitive Skeggs, and the local names Skegby and Skegness, I think this must have been an old Scandinavian personal name.

SKEGGS. See Skegg. *Skeggi*, in Old Norse, signifies bearded.

SKELL. " A well in the Old Northern English." Camden.

SKELTON. Parishes and places in cos. Cumberland, Yorkshire, &c. The Skeltons of the former county date back to temp. Edw. II. Hutchinson's Cumberland.

SKENE. " The Skenes obtained this name for killing a very big and fierce wolf, at a hunting in company with the king, in Stocket forest in Athole ; having killed the wolf with a dagger or *skene*." Buchanan's Ancient Scottish Surnames.

A valued correspondent observes :— "This dagger story is not true. The name is local, and the lands of Skene or Schene bore that name when in possession of the Durwards, before they were possessed by the family who took their name from them. These lands are in Aberdeenshire, and now belong to the Earl of Fife, who inherits them through a female ancestor."

SKERRAT. SKERRITT. See Skerrett.

SKERRETT. Of Galway origin, and one of the thirteen tribes of that town. The name was originally Huscared. Robert Huscared or Scared held lands in Connaught under Richard de Burgo in 1242. B.L.G.

SKERRY. A sea-girt rock, or rocky islet.

SKIDMORE. A wretched corruption of Scudamore.

SKILL. Most likely the same as Skell.

SKILLER. Perhaps from Skill or Skell, as Weller from Well, &c.

SKINNER. A dealer in skins. The Skinners' Company in London received their charter of incorporation so early as the first year of Edward III. This name was commonly latinized Pelliparius.

SKIPPER. A-Sax. *scipere*, a sailor. The word is now applied to the commander of a ship.

SKIPWITH. A parish in the East Riding of Yorkshire. The first who assumed the name was Patrick de Skipwith, who flourished in the reign of Henry I. He was the second son of Robert de Estoteville, or Stuteville, baron of Cotting-ham in the reign of William the Conqueror. Shirley's Noble and Gentle Men.

SKIPWORTH. Altered from Skipwith about the year 1725. B.L.G.

SKITT. " Some time since, a man named James Kit (i.e., Christopher), took a house near mine. He was always called James Kitt—his house got the name of " Skitt's "—and the family are now all written Skitt." From a Lancashire correspondent.

SKONE. A mis-spelling of Scone, in Perthshire, once a royal city, but now a village of eighteen houses.

SKRINE. The Skrines of Warleigh, co. Somerset, have a tradition that they are descended from one Don Eskrino, a follower of Philip of Spain, when he came into England to marry Queen Mary. It is added that he remained in England, and obtained from Philip permission to bear *the arms of Spain*. This account, which does not carry much probability with it, is, however, somewhat supported by the arms borne by the family, which are : " Azure, in the dexter chief and sinister base points, a *tower* Argent ; in the sinister chief and dexter base points, a *lion-rampant* Ermine, ducally crowned Or "—certainly a remarkable resemblance to the ensigns of Castile and Leon.

SKRYMSHIRE. The same as Scrymgeour.

SKUDDER. In O. Scottish to *scud* is to quaff. Hence, probably, the first Mr. Scudder was addicted to potations.

SKULL. Mr. Ferguson fetches this name from O. Norse *skule*, signifying a protector.

SKY. 1. The Scottish island, Skye. 2. Ferguson says, Danish *sky*, shy.

SKYP. May be the A-Sax. *scip*, a ship.

SLACK. 1. A-Sax. *slaec*, slack, remiss, idle, lazy. A Norfolk correspondent says : " I knew a man whose real name was Harris, who, from his extreme laziness, always went by the name of Slack." 2. A topographical word thus variously defined by Jamieson : " i. An opening in the higher part of a hill or mountain, where it becomes less steep, and forms a sort of pass. ii. A gap or narrow pass between two hills or mountains. iii. A morass."

SLADE. This word has been variously defined as a valley, a hollow, a den, a hanging wood, a plain, a breadth of green land in fields and plantations, &c. See Eng. Surn. i. 83. The form of the surname in H.R. is De la Slade.

SLADDEN. SLADDON. See Sladen.

SLADEN. This family, seated on the coast of Kent in the early part of the XVII. century, and hardly found elsewhere until within the XIX., are presumed to have come from the town of Schleiden in the government of Aix-la-Chapelle in Rhenish Prussia. John Sleidan, the historian of the Reformation in Germany, a native of that town, was deputed to the English court by the German reformers in 1545, and it is probable that others of his name and religion afterwards sought a home in this country. Sladden, Sladdon, and Slodden, may be variations of the name; and this seems the more probable, inasmuch as the continental town is pronounced as if written with two d's. There seems, however, to be no recognized kindred between the Sladens and the Sladdens. The name of Schleiden is still well known in Germany. A Thos. de Slayden was mayor of Winchester in 1222. Milner.

SLADER. From residence at a *slade*, whatever that may be. See Slade, and the termination ER.

SLANEY. Rodolphe de Slanie or Slane, who lived in the reign of Henry I., is supposed to have come into England from Bohemia in the train of the Empress Maud. B.L.G.

SLAPE. Slippery, smooth; hence, metaphorically, crafty. Halliwell.

SLATE. An Edinburgh surname. Perhaps from Sleat, a parish of Invernessshire. 2. *Slait* or *slate*, slovenly and dirty. Jamieson.

SLATER. From the occupation, which dates in England from early times, though much increased within the last century or two. Le Sclattere, Sclatiere, &c. H.R.

SLATOR. The same as Slater.

SLATTER. SLATYER. Provincial corruptions of Slater. Slate is often pronounced *slata;* and one of the forms of the name in the H.R. is Sclatter.

SLAUGHTER. There are two parishes, as well as a hundred, so designated in Gloucestershire.

SLAYMAKER. A maker of slays, an instrument belonging to a loom.

SLEAP. Probably from Sleep, a hamlet in the parish of St. Peter, at St. Albans, co. Herts.

SLEE. The same as Sly. Hence Sleeman signifies "a sly or cunning one." Slimmon is apparently a corruption of Sleeman.

SLEEMAN. See Slee.

SLEEP. A hamlet in the parish of St. Peter, liberty of St. Albans, co. Hertford.

SLEIGH. See Sly.

SLEMMON. The same as Slimmon.

SLIMMON. See Slee.

SLIGHT. 1. Thin and tall; a personal quality. 2. Worthless; as "He's a slight lad that."—Jamieson; who derives it from *slicht*, Islandic, *slaegd*, fraus, dolus.

SLIM. Slender in person.

SLINGSBY. A parish in Yorkshire.

SLIPPER. 1. A sword-*slyper*, a cutler,

one whose principal work was to whet swords. Acts James VI. Teutonic *slippen*, acuere. Belgic *slyper*, a whetter. Jamieson. 2. One who wishes to sneak away for fear of detection. Ibid. 3. One who is tawdry and slovenly in dress. Ibid. —all under the word *slyper*.

SLIPSHOE. Perhaps *slipshod*, a sobriquet.

SLOANE. In Scotland, a *sloan* is a covetous person—"a greedy sloan." Jamieson.

SLOCOMBE. See Combe.

SLOMAN. A Jewish disguise of the personal name Soloman.

SLOPER. A *slop* is a kind of cloak or mantle, also a buskin or boot much used in the XV. cent.—hence Sloper. Eng. Surn. i. 112.

SLOSE. The family were " of that Ilk " in Scotland. I cannot discover the place.

SLOUGH. A town in Buckinghamshire, well-known to railway travellers.

SLOW. Quick being a surname, this might naturally be regarded as its antithesis; but it is not so, as it has a local meaning. Its medieval forms are De la Slo, Ad le Slow, or De la Slou. H.R. Its meaning appears to be A-Sax. *slog*, O. Eng. *sloghe*, a bog or muddy pit—a slough.

SLOWBURN. Local: " the sluggish rivulet."

SLOWMAN. 1. A man of saturnine temperament. 2. The same as Sloman. 3. More probably from Slow. See Slow and the termination MAN.

SLUCE. A sluice, or outlet for water. Several places are specifically called " the sluice."

SLY. The epithet *sly* did not primarily imply anything dishonourable; though like 'crafty' and 'cunning,' it has since come to be taken in a bad sense. Though the family did not " come in with Richard Conqueror," the Tinker is quite right in asserting that " the Slys are *no rogues*." (Taming of the Shrew. Induct.) for as Mr. C. Knight observes, " the Slys or Sleighs were *skilful* men—cunning of hand. We are informed," he adds, " that Sly was anciently a common name in Shakspeare's own town."

SLYBODY. Slytbody occurs in Sussex in the XIII. century. It has been interpreted by the tailors' phrase, " long in the fork," though it more probably means *slight*, or meagre in person. Four centuries later, it occurs in the same county as Slybody; but this form reminds us more of a moral characteristic.

SMALE. An archaic spelling of Small.

SMALL. Diminutive in person—equivalent to Little, Petit, &c.

SMALBYHYND. John Smalbyhind occurs in good company, and evidently not ashamed of his name, in deeds temp. Rich. II., 1379. It is not probable that he was of Dutch extraction.

SMALLBACK. Possibly local : "the small *beck* or stream."

SMALLBONES. This name occurs in the records of Leicester in the XIII. cent., and in the Lond. Direct. of the XIX. It probably refers to osseous slenderness.

SMALLEY. O. Norse, *smali*, a shepherd. Ferguson.

SMALLMAN. A person of diminutive stature. H.R. Smaleman.

SMALLWOOD. A township in the parish of Astbury, co. Cheshire.

SMALLWRITER. Apparently a translation of the old name Petyclerk. See Clark. The H.R. forms are Smalwriter and Smalwyritere.

SMART. Quick, active. Smert, probably a Saxon, is mentioned in Domesday, and hence it was doubtless a personal name. Smart appears without prefix in H.R., as also does Smartknave, i.e. "Quick or handy servant."

SMEATON. A parish and a township of Yorkshire.

SMEE. A mis-pronunciation of Smeeth.

SMEED. See Smeeth.

SMEETH. A parish in Kent is specifically so called. In Norfolk any flat plain bears this name. A-Sax. *smaeth.*

SMEETON. A township in Leicestershire.

SMELLIE. May be from the A-Sax. *smel,* another form of Small. Ferguson.

SMELT. A-Sax. mild, gentle. A priest mentioned in the Codex Diplomaticus bore this appropriate name. H.R. Smelt, Smelte.

SMERDON. Possibly Smarden, a parish in Kent.

SMETHURST. Local. See Smeeth, and Hurst. "The wood of the plain."

SMILES. This, I learn, is a modern invention, the original name having been Smellie.

SMIJTH. In their desire to get away from the common, plebeian, and non-descriptive Smith, many people have, within the present century, Smyth'd and Smythed themselves. One family (and that a baronet's of 1661) go farther, and *smidge* themselves into Smijth. We look into a baronetage of to-day, and we are told that one John Smijth, the founder of the house, was high sheriff of Essex and Hertford in the reign of Henry VIII.; but on turning to Kimber, published in 1771, we find no trace whatever of a Smijth, the baronet of the period being written Smyth, while by going three generations farther back we arrive at plain Smith ! It is difficult to guess how the IJ came to supplant the Y, a change offensive alike to eye and ear. A facetious friend suggests that the Mr. Smith of the 'transition' period, having substituted *y* for *i* was so much delighted, that he sought still further to decorate his name by adding a tittle to each stroke of the *y*, thus producing the *ij* of the existing *Smijth !*

SMITH. In entering upon the illustration of this surname, I feel almost overcome with the magnitude of my subject. Closely connected as it is with the personal identity of thousands upon thousands of my countrymen, enjoying as it does the proud pre-eminence of being the commonest of all English surnames, and associated as it must be with statistics, with anecdote, with archæology, with varieties of orthography, the name of Smith is a topic which requires no common handling. Why, it demands a separate essay, a dissertation, a volume, to do it anything like justice ! Nay, I am not quite sure that a new science to be designated *Smithology* would not prove quite as instructive as many existing *ologies*, while it would have the merit of being perhaps more amusing; assuredly it would come home both to "the business and bosoms" of a vast section of Englishmen. And I might go further afield and trace out the history of smith-craft from the days of Tubal-Cain—expatiate upon the labours of Vulcan, of Icarus, of Wayland Smith, and of St. Dunstan—show how mén lived in the Iron Age—bring in the classical Fabri, and Fabricii, the Schmidts of Germany, the Lefevres of France, the Fabbroni of Italy, and the Gowans of Scotland, as members of this mighty race—and deal largely in irony and " smith's-work in general." But space forbids, and I must be as brief as possible. Let us first hammer out the archæology of the subject. The word *smith*, then, is A-Sax. from *smitan*, to smite—originally, " any one who strikes or smites with a hammer, an artificer, a carpenter, smith, workman." Bosworth. So general was the application of the word, that in the Saxon Chronicle we find the expression " mighty war-smiths " applied to valorous soldiers, and the great enemy of mankind is called " hell-smith," though this phrase, being also applied to Vulcan, has probably a direct reference to " smithery " in the modern sense. One who worked in iron was called *iren-smith,* an ironsmith. In later times, Smith was applied more specifically to a worker in metals, while *wyrhta,* Wright, was the name given to artificers in wood and other materials, See Wright.

Besides Smiths simple, we have *Smithsons* (the heritors of the thrice noble name of Percy) to whom the Gaelic Mac *Gowans* correspond, as well as the *Smithmans* and *Gros-smiths,* who (if they have not corrupted their spelling) are a good set-off against the Fabrucci, or "little Smiths " of Italian celebrity. But we have many other compounds of *smith* which we shall here, for the most part, dispose of. *Black-*

smith and *Whitesmith* I have but lately discovered, and they are very rare. The *Brownsmith* was one who prepared the far-famed "brown bills," once more formidable than the "Brown Bess" of our times. *Nasmyth* is nail-smith or nailer. The *Arrowsmith* of old prepared the arrows, as the *Spearsmith* did the spears and lances, in the days of Cressy and Poictiers. The *Shoesmith* took care of horses' feet. The *Billsmith* made bills; and the *Shearsmith* shears; the *Knyfesmith*, knives; the *Locksmith*, locks and keys, in old times, as now. *Goldsmiths* have never been wanting; and the brass and copper workers of ancient days are now represented in family nomenclature by the *Arsmiths* (A-Sax. *ár*, brass), and the Copperwrights. " *Bokell-smyths* " are mentioned in the quaint poem called " Cock Lorelles Bote " in conjunction with "blackesmythes and ferrars," and hence, doubtless, our otherwise unintelligible *Bucksmith*, who thus proves himself next of kin to the Bucklers. Elsewhere I have hazarded an opinion that the odd-looking *Sucksmith* and *Sixsmiths* were ploughshare-makers, (Eng. Surn. i. 104) but further reflection induces me—though this is inverting the proper order of things—to turn them into sword-makers, *seax* being the A-Sax. for a small sword or dagger. Again, the obsolete *Hyldsmith* is a soldier, being a compound of the A-Sax. *hild*, war, battle. One William Hyldsmyth dwelt in Cambridgeshire, temp. Edward I. H.R.

More than two hundred years ago, old Verstegan asked the question—

"From whence comes Smith, all be he Knight or
    Squire,
But from the Smith that forgeth at the fire?"

yet it would appear, from the addition and alteration of a letter, that some families are anxious to avoid the imputation of so plebeian an origin. It will not do, however, for there is little doubt that all the Smithes, Smitheses, Smyths, Smythes, and Smijths, came originally from the furnace and the forge, though some of them may perhaps attack me with "hammer and tongs" for this suggestion. In France the same fastidiousness prevails on this subject, and Monsieur Lefevre (a word now supplanted by *forgeron*) often writes himself Lefebvre. I know a baron who goes still further, and is, "in any bill, warrant, quittance, or obligation," Monsieur le Baron Lefebure !

The following remarkable and happy escape from Smithdom is narrated by a correspondent: " In the last century there lived at Ellenhall, in Staffordshire, a family of small farmers called Smith. The head of the house being a stout, portly man, obtained among his neighbours the by-name of John Jolly. His sons, in the last generation, assumed this sobriquet as their surname, and by it alone are the family now recognised. They are Smiths no longer ! "

" ONE SMITH " is a not very exact description, yet it occurs in Domesday Book under Essex—" *Unus Faber* qui propter latrocinium interfectus fuit." Kelham's

theory that *faber* means either a smith or carpenter, does not hold good, for many carpentarii are specifically mentioned in the record, and, as Sir Henry Ellis has shown, in one or two instances the *fabri* were men employed in fusing or working iron-ore. Introd. i. 92.

There are many *Smithiana* in Eng. Surn. vol. i. pp. 99—104, which it is unnecessary to repeat here. But I will add one more. When the late Louis-Philippe, in 1848, found himself safe in the snug hotel at Newhaven, he enquired the name of his hostess, and being answered, that it was Mrs. Smith, his fallen majesty quietly remarked: " Smith, eh bien, I think I have heard that name before ! " He had; for it was the very *alias* which he had adopted, and " William Smith " was written upon the passport he had at that moment in his pocket !

The statistics of Smithology are given somewhat largely in the XVI. Annual Report of the Regist. Gen., from which it appears, that in the years 1838—1854, the Smiths registered for births, marriages, and deaths, amounted to 286,307 or about one in seventy of the total number of persons registered. Jones is the next name for numerosity, and it is calculated that the aggregate of Smiths and Joneses now living in England and Wales exceeds half a million, of whom more than a quarter of a million must consequently be Smiths. If to the English Smiths we add those of Scotland, Ireland, our great colonies, and America—and those of America alone, it has been jocosely stated, would more than fill Boston Common—we shall probably be correct in affirming, that since the world began no family name could ever vie in point of numbers with the immortal tribe of Smith.

Perhaps I cannot do better than give the curious results of the Registrar-General's statistical analysis of the Smiths of England and Wales, as printed in the Report above alluded to. This document shows how closely the *Joneses* are treading upon the heels of the *Smiths*, and it will be seen that, not very long ago, an alarmist might have raised the cry of " *Smith in Danger*," when, in several consecutive years, the *Joneses* were actually at the head of the poll.

" The surname of *Smith* is pre-eminently the most common in England, as that of *Jones* is in Wales; and so great is the multitude of the Welsh *Joneses*, that the latter name not only enters into competition for priority in point of numbers with the *Smiths*, but in several years shows a majority over its rival. With a view to determine the relative frequency of these two widely-spread surnames, I have ascertained the numbers of each entered in the indexes during the years 1838-54. The result is that the births, deaths, and marriages of the *Smiths* registered in this period were 286,037, and those of the *Joneses* 282,900, the excess in favour of the former being 3137 in the seventeen years. *Smith* is, therefore, unquestionably the most common surname amongst us, although the *Joneses* are little less numerous, and in six of the years actually contributed to the registers larger numbers than the *Smiths*. Together, the bearers of these two common names amounted to 568,937, or 1 in 36 of the whole number registered, during the period referred to. (See Table).

"Assuming that the persons of the surnames of *Smith* and *Jones* are born, marry, and die in the same proportions as persons of *all surnames*, it will follow that in England and Wales there are not less than *half a million* of persons bearing one or other of those two surnames. The *Smiths* amount to rather more than a quarter of a million, and the *Joneses* to little less ; together forming no inconsiderable portion of the English population. These numbers represent, on the assumption that the average number of persons in a family is the same as in the whole population at the census, viz. 4·8 persons, about 53,000 families of *Smiths*, and 51,000 families of *Joneses ;* and to give an illustration of their numerical power, it may be stated that these two great tribes are probably sufficiently numerous to people the four towns of Birmingham, Bristol, Leeds, and Hull, without any addition of persons of other surnames."

"NUMBER of PERSONS of the respective Surnames of *Smith* and *Jones* contained in the Registration Indexes of Births, Deaths, and Marriages, in each of the Years 1838—54.

			Difference.	
			More	More
	No. of the	No. of the	SMITHS	JONESES
	Surn. of	Surn. of	than	than
Yrs.	SMITH.	JONES.	JONESES.	SMITHS.
1838	14,891	14,414	477	—
1839	14,905	15,096	—	191
1840	15,483	16,256	—	773
1841	15,237	15,539	—	302
1842	15,315	15,437	—	122
1843	15,841	15,554	287	—
1844	16,203	15,932	271	—
1845	16,633	16,676	—	43
1846	17,299	17,177	122	—
1847	16,917	17,296	—	379
1848	17,313	16,958	355	—
1849	18,091	17,677	414	—
1850	17,405	17,135	270	—
1851	18,156	17,525	631	—
1852	18,564	17,649	915	—
1853	18,775	17,926	849	—
1854	19,009	18,653	356	—
Total - -	286,037	282,900	4,947	1,810
Joneses - -	282,900	- - - - -		1,810
Excess of *Smiths* 3,137	- - - - -			3,137."

In addition to the Smiths proper, there are some families passing under other names, who are in their origin, genuine members of this great tribe ; for example, *Forge*, anciently written Atte-Forge, is only a *localized* form of the word, for we may be certain that the first Mr. Atte Forge was a man of the hammer ; and it also appears pretty clear that many of our *Whites* are but Smiths in disguise. See White.

Two or three similar names may here be disposed of. *Smithett* looks like a neat diminutive; but *Smythy* and *Smythies* have decidedly the smell of the blacksmith's

shop. *Smeeth*, on the other hand, is a local surname from a parish in Kent.

" We all know *Smith*, and we have a great regard for him. A most excellent fellow is *Smith*, but such a Proteus. Think of *Smith*, and twenty individuals are presented to your mind's eye at once. Smith the soldier; Smith the sailor; Smith the country-clergyman ; Smith the engineer in the Russian service; Smith with whom you made acquaintance at Naples ; Smith that never goes out of London; Smith of Cmwrlr Castle, North Wales; and your old college friend Smith. There is something nebulous in the very name. The learned Jesuit, Matthew Wilson, who could not be concealed under the assumed name of Edward Knott, found an effectual *incognito* as Nic. Smith. Is there, then, no way in which a man bearing the name of Smith may possess individuality and identity? Surely it rests with the parents, Mr. and Mrs. Smith ; and the place where the object may best be secured is the baptismal font. If the name of Smith be no identification, at least let the sponsorial name be distinctive. Beware of John and William ; a man might as well be anonymous at once as John Smith or William Smith. Rather select such names as are of more rare occurrence. Let it be Protheroe Smith, Aquila Smith, Egerton Smith. In short, Horace, Sydney, Harry, Albert, Rowland, Herbert, Frank, Hugh, Lawrence, Caleb, Adam ; all answer the purpose of specification; each identifies Smith. Yet while securing individuality avoid peculiarity : Seth Smith is a combination which breaks the teeth." Thos. Boys in N. and Q., Aug. 20, 1859.

According to another correspondent of N. and Q., Oct. 15, 1859, there is a German society at Albany, U. S., in which the Smiths are so numerous that they are distinguished by descriptive epithets and phrases, in the following manner :—

" Big Smit.
Little Smit.
Smit from de hill.
Smit from de holler.
Smit mit de store.
Smit de blacksmit.
Smit mit de lager bier shop.
Smit without any " vrow."
Smit wot wants a " vrow."
Smit mit one leg.
Smit mit two legs.
Smit mit de pigs.
Smit mit de pig head.
Smit mit de pig feet.
Smit mit de brick-yard.
Smit mit de junk-shop.
Smit mit de bolognas.
Smit mit one eye.
Smit mit two eyes.
Smit mit de bone-picker.
Smit mit two " vrows."
Smit mit de swill-cart.
Smit mit de segar stumps.
Smit mit peach pits.
Smit mit de whiskers.
Smit mit de red hair.
Smit mit no hair.
Smit."

SMITHERS. *Smither*, from a distich in the ' Anturs of Arther' cited by Halliwell, appears to mean light, active.

" Gawan was *smyther* and smerte,
Owte of his sterroppus he sterte."

SMITHSON. The son of a smith. So Cookson, Wrightson, &c.

SMOOKER. A provincial pronunciation of Smoker. " At Preston, before the passing of the Reform Bill in 1832, every person who had a cottage with a chimney, and used the latter, had a vote, and was called a Smoker." Halliwell.

SMOOTHMAN. A flatterer.

SMYTH. An old orthography of Smith.

SMYTHE. An old form of Smith.

SNARE. 1. Possibly from the Snar, a small river of Lanarkshire. 2. A-Sax. *snear*, agile or strong.

SNASHALL. A corruption of *seneschal*, a steward.

SNEAD. 1. "A *snád* or *snæd* of land betokens a piece of ground within defined limits, but without enclosures; public woods and pasture grounds, whose boundaries are fixed by notches on trees and stakes." Leo's A-Sax. Nomenclature. The expression, a *sneath* of land, occurs in a Norfolk document dated 1699. 2. Perhaps the same as Sneyd.

SNEED. See Snead.

SNEEZUM. A corruption of Snetisham, a parish in Norfolk.

SNELGAR. Probably an old personal name from the A-Sax. *snell*, swift or brave, and *gar*, a spear.

SNELGROVE. Local : "the grove that grows quickly or strongly?" See Snell.

SNELL. A-Sax. *snell*, quick, active, bold, brave. Snelling and Snelson are its patronymics. Both were in use before the Conquest.

SNELLING. See Snell. Snellinc is found in Domesday, as a previous tenant.

SNELSON. 1. See Snell. 2. A township in Cheshire.

SNEPP. Qy. Snape, a parish in Suffolk, and a township in Yorkshire.

SNEYD. A parish in Shropshire, and a hamlet in the parish of Tunstall, co. Stafford. From the latter the family designated "the noble race of Sneyds, of great worship and account," derive their origin. They were seated there temp. Henry III. By marriage with the heiress of Tunstall they acquired other lands in that parish, and for two generations they were called Sneyd alias Tunstall. Shirley's Noble and Gentle Men.

The arms of this family are a "curiosity of heraldry," being partly of the allusive kind, and consisting of a scythe and a fleur-de-lis. The pun is in the handle of the scythe, provincially called a snead (A-Sax. *snæd*.) The fleur-de-lis is traditionally said to have been added to the coat by Richard de Tunstall, alias Sneyd, after the battle of Poictiers; but I should rather consider it to have been part of the original device, and to have an allegorical reference to the mortality of man—"the flower of the field," which "in the evening is cut down and withereth."

SNODGRASS. "Trimmed, or smooth, grass :" a local name.

SNOOKS. "This name, so generally associated with vulgarity, is only a corruption or contraction of Sevenoaks." The Kentish town is usually pronounced Se'noaks, and "the further contraction, coupled with the phonetic spelling of former days, easily passed into *S'nooks.* Messrs. Sharp and Harrison, solicitors, of Southampton, had in their possession a series of deeds in which all the modes of spelling occur from Sevenoakes down to S'nokes, in connection with a family now known as Snooks." Notes and Queries, vol. v. p. 438. A Sussex family, in the early part of the last century, bore the name of Snooke. Sevenoke, the early orthography of the town, has also been modified to Sinnock and Cennick.

SNOW. "Snow is the same name as that of an old, perhaps a mythical, king of Denmark. Some old German names are compounded with it; and perhaps Snowball may be of similar origin—*bald* or *ball*, bold." Ferguson. I am disposed, however, to refer Snowball to the same class as Peppercorn, Pluckrose, Pullrose, &c., as derived from old feudal tenures. Blount records the holding of certain lands by the payment of "one *red rose* at *Christmas*, and one *snowball* at *Midsummer*," which in the old unluxurious days, before conservatories and ice-houses were invented, must have caused the tenant many an anxious thought as to the means of "raising his rent."

SNOWBALL. See with Snow.

SNOWDON. SNOWDEN. This rather common surname is not likely to have been derived from the famous Welsh mountain. It is probably the name of some English locality.

SNOWSHILL. A parish in co. Gloucester.

SOAM. Soham, one of the three parishes in Suffolk so called.

SOAMES. A pluralization of Soam.

SOAR. A river of Leicestershire.

SOBER. Of grave and sedate character.

SOCKETT. An alias for the parish of Playden, co. Sussex.

SOCKMAN. The *socheman* or *sochemannus*, so frequently occurring in Domesday, was an inferior land-owner, who had possessions in the *soke* or franchise of a great baron. Nichols' Leicestersh. At Walcote, co. Lincoln, a Sockman held his lands by the tenure of ploughing with two oxen. Ellis, Introd. Domesd.

SODEN. See Sudden.

SOLE. 1. Two small rivers in Scotland are so called. 2. Sola and Sol were German names of the VIII. and IX. centuries. Ferguson. One Sol was a tenant in Herefordshire before the making of Domesday.

SOLOMON. SOLOMONS. The personal name. As a surname it is principally confined to the Jews.

SOLTAU. George William Soltau, Esq., who was naturalized by Act of Parliament, 17. George III., was son of Martin-William Soltau, burgomaster of Bergedorf. B.L.G.

SOMERBY. Parishes in cos. Lincoln and Leicester.

SOMERFIELD. See Somerville.

SOMERS. Appears to be the genitive form of some Teutonic personal name, from which many local names have originated; as Somerby, Somershall, Somerford, Somercoates, &c.

SOMERSET. This is one of the few instances of a surname having been borrowed from a title. Henry Beaufort, third Duke of Somerset (great-grandson of John of Gaunt), who was beheaded in 1463, for his adherence to the cause of King Henry VI., left issue a natural son, Sir Charles Somerset, Knight of the Garter. He was elevated to the peerage, and his lineal descendant, Henry Marquis of Worcester, was created Duke of Beaufort in 1682. Thus, in the same blood, the surname and the title have changed places, and instead of Beaufort, Duke of Somerset, we have Somerset, Duke of Beaufort.

SOMERSHALL. A parish in Derbyshire.

SOMERVAIL. A corruption of Somerville.

SOMERVELL. A corruption of Somerville.

SOMERVILLE. The progenitor of the noble family was Walter de Somerville, lord of Wichnor, &c., in Staffordshire, and of Aston-Somerville, in Gloucestershire, who came into England with William the Conqueror, and left two sons who became ancestors respectively of the English and of the Scottish Somervilles. Peerage. This name has been anglicized to Somerfield.

SOMMERLAT. An ancient personal name, very rarely met with as a surname. (There is one bearer of it in the London Directory for 1859.) It occurs in Domesday as Summerled, and the owner was a holder of lands prior to the Survey. Somerled, Thane of Argyle, and King of the Isles, the founder of the clan Macdonald, flourished in the XII. century.

SOMNER. A summoner, or apparitor, attached to a court of law. For a lively picture of a *sompnour*, see Chaucer, Prologue to Cant. Tales, quoted in Eng. Surn. i. 129.

☞ **SON.** An exceedingly common termination in English family nomenclature. A popular, but very erroneous, notion prevails, that it indicates a Danish extraction. I am astonished to find Worsaae in his Danes in England (page 80) asserting, that "the ending *son* or *sen* (a son) is quite peculiar to the countries of Scandinavia, whence it was brought over to England by the Scandinavian Conquests;" and further, that such endings "never appear in Saxon names." It is true that the usual practice among the Anglo-Saxons was to affix the word *ing*, implying offspring or progeny, to the proper name of the father, but it is equally true that such names as Leofwine Boudansunu (the son of Boudan), Alwinus Idessone (the son of Ida) occur among that people. Eng. Surn. i. 23, 30. Such names as Adamson, Jackson, &c., quoted by Worsaae, did not become hereditary, if they were even known at all, before the XIII. century, two or three hundred years after the importation of the Scandinavian element. I do not deny that Ericson, Hardingson, and other similar names of Danish original, existed in England in the XI. century—perhaps earlier—but they were not hereditary until long afterwards, and any attempt to shew that the hundreds of thousands of Englishmen whose names terminate in SON, are of Danish or Norwegian blood, must therefore be futile. To explain the existence of such names as those last quoted in our modern family nomenclature, I would observe: I. That personal or Christian names when once introduced into this country, were very likely to become perpetuated by the spirit of imitation among persons who were strangers in blood to the introducers, as well as among their own descendants: witness such names as Frederick, Lewis, Albert, in comparatively recent times. II. When, in process of time, hereditary surnames began to prevail throughout Christendom, many assumed the *patronymical* form, and in England SON was the affix employed. So prevalent was this fashion in the XIV. century, that there was scarcely any Christian name in use that did not become a surname by this addition, whether such name was of Saxon, French, Flemish, or Danish birth. No evidence as to race, then, can be adduced from this termination. While our ancestors were thus making the personal names of heads of families with the affix SON persistent and generic appellatives, the same process was going on in other countries. The *O's* and *Macs* in Ireland and Scotland, the *sohns* of Germany, the *sens* of Sweden, &c., may be mentioned as examples. As I have elsewhere stated, "the termination *son* is found in most languages of Gothic origin."

See the articles O', MAC, FITZ, AP.

Sometimes this termination was affixed to the title, occupation, or condition of the father, and not to his personal name; as Dukeson, Cookson, Clarkson, Smithson, Wrightson, Hindson, Stewardson.

SONGSTER. From the vocal accomplishment. See Sangster.

SOPER. A soap-boiler. A maker of this article is still called a *soaper* in Aberdeenshire. Jamieson.

SOPPET. A known corruption of Sopworth.

SOPWITH. A corruption of Sopworth, a parish in Wiltshire.

SORE. SOREL. " A stag of four years old is called a *sore*, and of three a *sorel*; and so named from their colour." It has been explained as *sub-rufus*, nearly, or approaching to, red. Richardson.

SOREL. An ancient French name, borne by the celebrated Agnes Sorel, mistress to king Charles VII. See Sore.

SORRELL. See Sorel.

SORTAIN. Soartin, or Soartinus, is found in the Domesday of Hampshire; but the few existing Englishmen of the name descend from ancestors who settled in England after the Revocation of the Edict of Nantes, 1685, and are of the same family as M. Sortin, one of the ministers of Louis XVI., who was beheaded in the French Revolution. The surname Sartain occurs in America.

SOTCHER. Lazy, effeminate. Jamieson.

SOTHCOTT. See Southcote.

SOTHEBY. Probably Sotby, a parish in Lincolnshire.

SOTHERAN. A corruption of Sotherton, a parish in Suffolk.

SOUL. SOULE. Not improbably from Soulle, a town and river in the department of La Manche in Normandy.

SOULBY. A chapelry in Westmoreland.

SOUNTING. Sompting, co. Sussex, a place remarkable for its Saxon church, is so pronounced.

SOUR. 1. Ill-tempered. 2. Camden places it among rivers. Le Sour. H.R.

SOUTER. SOUTAR. A-Sax. *sutere*, from Lat. *sutor*. A shoemaker. Still in use in Scotland.

SOUTH. See under North.

SOUTHALL. A village in Middlesex.

SOUTHAM. A town in co. Warwick, and a hamlet in co. Gloucester.

SOUTHCOMB. From records in the possession of the family, they appear to have sprung from the Combes, or De la Combes, of Somersetshire. B.L.G.

SOUTHCOTE. Southcot, a tything near Reading, co. Berks.

SOUTHDEAN. Local: " the southern valley."

SOUTHERDEN. A manor in Kent, in or near Boughton Malherbe. Hasted, v. 405.

SOUTHERWOOD. Local: the " southern wood."

SOUTHGATE. See under Eastgate. In the records of Leicester, a person is described as " Walter fil' Galf. ext. Portam de Sud"—' Walter son of Geoffrey beyond the South Gate.' XII. cent.

SOUTHWELL. The family are of great antiquity in Nottinghamshire, where they were lords of Southwell, till the reign of Henry VI. They afterwards settled in Norfolk and Suffolk, whence the ancestor of the Viscount Southwell removed to Ireland temp. James I. Peerage.

SOUTHWOOD. A parish in Norfolk.

SOWERBY. Parishes, &c., in cos. Cumberland, York, Westmoreland, &c.

SOWLE. See Soul.

SOWTER. See Souter.

SOWTON. A parish in co. Devon.

SPADER. A digger and delver.

SPAIN. SPAYNE. May have had several distinct origins, from as many early settlers. The Essex family of Hispaine, or Spayne, were descendants of Alured Hispaniensis, or De Ispania, who at the Domesday survey was a tenant in chief in various counties. Morant's Essex, ii., p. 363.

SPALDING. A parish in co. Lincoln.

SPANKIE. Sprightly; frisking; dashing; gaudy. Jamieson.

SPARHAM. A parish in Norfolk.

SPARK. SPARKE. SPARKES. SPARKS. I think the former two must represent an old personal name—the latter two its genitive form. Sparkford and Sparkenhoe, names of places, may be from the same source.

SPARLING. Germ. *sperling*, a sparrow.

SPARROW. The bird. The Sparrows of Gosfield, co. Essex, trace their pedigree to William Sparrow, of West Harling, co. Norfolk, temp. Edward III. B.L.G.

SPARROWHAWK. An ancient name of frequent occurrence in medieval records. As a personal name it was common at the epoch of the Conquest, there being several Domesday tenants so called, in the Saxon form of Sparhavoc.

SPARSHOT. Sparsholt, parishes in Berkshire and Hampshire.

SPARY. See Sperry.

SPAWFORTH. See Spofforth.

SPEAK. SPEAKE. 1. Speke, a township in Lancashire. 2. See Speke.

SPEAR. From the weapon; like Sword, Pike, &c.

SPEARMAN. A soldier; one who carried a spear—the ' lancer' of the medieval period. The word was in use at the time of the introduction of the authorized version of the Bible.

" The *spears* were heavy-armed cavalry." Halliwell.

The Spearmans of Northumberland were a petty clan, retainers of the Percys. See Bowman.

2. B.L.G. mentions "the Spearmans of Dunnington, in Salop," as "seated there since the Conquest, and said to be descended from the old Lords of *Aspramont*."

SPEARSMITH. See under Smith.

SPEECHLY. SPEECHLEY. Spetchley, a parish in Worcestershire.

SPEED. SPEEDY. Probably have reference to the swiftness of the original bearers.

SPEER. See Spear.

SPEKE. The Spekes of Somersetshire descend from Richard le Espek, who lived in the reign of Henry II. Wemworthy and Brampton, in Devonshire, were the original seats, but temp. Henry VI. Sir John Speke married the heiress of Beauchamp, and so obtained Whitelackington, co. Somerset, which continued to be the abode of his male descendants for eleven generations. Shirley's Noble and Gentle Men. I am unable to explain Le Espek.

SPELLER. Doubtless the same as Spelman.

SPELMAN. Camden says, "a learned man;" but more probably either a man who works by *spells*, or turns, with another, or a worker of spells or charms. See Eng. Surn., i. 113.

SPENCE. 1. The same as Spens. 2. A yard or enclosure.

SPENCER. In the eighteenth year of William the Conqueror lived Robertus Dispensator, otherwise called Le Despencer, because he was steward to the king. In the reign of Henry I. there were a William le Despencer and a Thurstan Dispencer, but whether these last were only successors in office, or actual descendants of Robert is not known, and the like uncertainty prevails as to subsequent bearers of the name. The unpopular Spencers of the time of Edward II. are traced by genealogists only to the reign of Henry III., though they may have been of much older date. Earl Spencer's family "claim a collateral descent from the baronial house, a claim which, without being irreconcileable perhaps with the early pedigrees of that family, admits of very grave doubts and considerable difficulties." Shirley's Noble and Gentle Men. The Earl's pedigree is, however, clearly traced to the reign of Henry VI. in Northamptonshire.

The author of the Faery Queen boasted that he belonged to this family, though "the precise link of genealogical connexion cannot now perhaps be ascertained." Baker's Northamptonshire.

SPENS. Jamieson gives the following definitions of *Spens*. 1. The place where provisions are kept. 2. The clerk of a kitchen. In the latter sense it is employed by Wyntoun. It is an ancient surname in Scotland. The Spenses of Lathallan trace continuously to the year 1296. "The Count de Spens, who ranked among the first of the Swedish nobility, and was generalissimo of their forces, sprang from this family." B.L.G.

SPENSER. A more correct orthography of Spencer.

SPERLING. Descended from Henry Sperling, a German Count of ancient family, who settled at Chigwell, co. Essex, in the last century. Germ. *sperling*, a sparrow.

SPERRY. An ancient Christian name. The Domesd. of Staffordshire has a Sperri among the tenants in chief.

SPETTIGUE. A Cornish local name; place unknown.

SPICER. O. Fr. *espicier*. What we now call a grocer, because, *inter alia*, he deals in figs (*grossi*), the French call an *épicier*, or spicer, because he sells spices, &c.

SPICKERNELL. A corruption of Spigurnell.

SPIDER. The insect; a sobriquet.

SPIGURNELL. Low Latin *spigurnellus*, "the sealer of the king's writs; from the A-Sax. *spicurran*, to inclose or shut up." Jacob. Galfridus Spigurnell took his surname from this office in the reign of Henry III.

SPILLER. The same as Spillman.

SPILLMAN. 1. May be the same as Spelman. 2. Perhaps either a maker of laths or of spindles, *spill* being a provincialism for both those articles.

SPILSBURY. Spelsbury, a parish in Oxfordshire.

SPINDLER. A maker of spindles, an implement used in making thread.

SPINK. In England the chaffinch; in Scotland the goldfinch.

SPINKE. A chaffinch; a goldfinch.

SPINKS. See Spink.

SPINNER. The occupation.

SPINNEY. A thicket; a small plantation. Halliwell. Evidently the same as the Latin *spinetum*, a bushy place, or patch of thorns. The name is probably only another form of Thorne, anciently latinized "De Spineto." In Buckinghamshire, however, *spinney* means a brook.

SPIRE. SPIRES. A city in Germany.

SPIRIT. The records of the Registrar-General show us the names of Ghost and Spirit. They were most probably sobriquets. Mr. Ferguson, however, derives the latter from the A-Sax. *sparva*, a sparrow.

SPITAL. A contraction of *hospital*, a lazar-house, or asylum for the poor, of which there were many, upon a religious basis, in the middle ages. Many hamlets both in England and Scotland are so called.

SPITTAL. See Spital.

SPITTLE. *Spital*, a contraction of hospital; a common name of localities.

SPITTLEHOUSE. See Spital.

SPOFFORD. See Spofforth.

SPOFFORTH. Gamelbar de Spofford held lands at Spofford, or Spofforth, a parish near Wetherby, co. York. Domesday. The present family of Spofforth are authentically traceable to within a few miles of that place. B.L.G.

SPOONER. A maker of spoons. A less desirable derivation is from A.-Sax. *spónere*, an enticer or seducer, from *spanan*, to allure.

SPORLE. A parish in Norfolk.

SPOTTISWOODE. The name is derived from the barony of Spottiswoode. The family were benefactors to the Abbeys of Melrose and Kelso in early times. The immediate ancestor of Spottiswoode, still " of that Ilk," was Robert de Spottiswood, who was born in the reign of King Alexander III., and died in that of Robert Bruce. B.L.G. Spottiswood is in the parish of Gordon, co. Berwick.

SPRATLEY. Probably Sproatley, a parish in Yorkshire.

SPRATT. The fish, analogous to Herring, &c.

SPRECKLEY. The same as Spratley.

SPRIGNELL. A corruption of Spigurnell, which see.

SPRING. See Times and Seasons.

SPRINGER. A sobriquet relating to the elasticity of the first bearer.

SPRINGETT. As this Kent and Sussex name is often spelt Springate, it is probably local, although I do not find any place so designated.

SPRINGLE. Perhaps Springkell, a place at Kirkpatrick-Fleming, co. Dumfries.

SPRINGTHORPE. A parish in Lincolnshire.

SPROSTON. A township in Cheshire, in which county the family still reside.

SPROTT. SPROAT. One Sprot, perhaps a Dane, was a holder of lands in cos. Derby and York before the making of Domesday. A.-Sax. *spreot*, a spear or pike; also a germ, sprout, or sprig of anything. Comp. *hastilia* in the double sense of spears and *sprouts* in Virg. Æn. iii. 37, &c.

SPROUT. Probably the same as Sprott, which see.

SPRY. " The name of Spry, Sprey, Spray, is Cornish, and signifies a sprout, branch, sprig, or slip of any matter or thing." Hals, in D. Gilbert's Cornwall, i. 29,—a very wide etymology. In the dialect of Somerset, and in the United States, ' *spry* ' means nimble, active, smart.

FROM THE PYES AND THE SPRYES, GOOD LORD DELIVER US.
According to Hals, (as above, iii. 449) these two families " turned decimators and sequestrators upon the lands and revenues of the royalist laity and clergy of this county, to that degree of hurt and damage that it occasioned the making of this short Litany, not yet forgotten in Cornwall."

SPRYNGE. See Spring.

SPURAWAY. The remarks under ' Prickadvance,' form a sufficient illustration, if indeed the name be not of *local* origin. See Spurway. Osbert *Spir-hard* occurs as the name of a person in a medieval record. N. and Q., Jan. 24, 1857.

SPURLING. Germ. *sperling*, a sparrow.

SPURR. From residence at the *spur*, or declivity, of a hill.

SPURRELL. Probably from the parish of Sporle, co. Norfolk.

SPURRETT. Probably the same as Spirit.

SPURRIER. The occupation; a maker of spurs.

SPURWAY. 1. An estate in co. Devon, long possessed by the family. 2. A-Sax. *sparwa*, a sparrow. Ferguson.

SQUIRE. SQUIRES. The attendant of a knight; also a chief servitor or messenger of an Abbey. Chron. Battel Abbey, p. 217. See Arminger.

SQUIRREL. The animal. Probably the sobriquet of an active person.

☞ **ST.** For names compounded with the word Saint, see under SAINT.

STABBACK. Probably local—the second syllable being *beck*, a stream.

STABLE. 1. A personal name mentioned in Domesday. 2. More likely to relate to stability of mind than to association with horses. 3. A corruption of Staple.

STABLEFORD. Stapleford, parishes, &c., in cos. Cambridge, Herts, Leicester, Lincoln, &c.

STABLER. One who had the care of *estables*, an O. Fr. word of extensive meaning, defined by Cotgrave, as " a stable, an osterie, an ostellerie, also a sheep-house or fould." In H.R. the word appears in the forms of Le Stabler and De Stabulo. *Stabularyus* is found in the sense of hostler in M.S. Digby, 113. Bodl. Lib., Oxon.

STACE. A corruption either of Eustace, or of Statius. It is probably of continental origin, as the final E is sometimes accented, and from Stacé we get Stacey.

STACEKYN. A diminutive of Stace.

STACEY. See Stace.

STACY. See Stace.

STACK. A precipitous rock. Jamieson.

STAFF. The Roman family of the Scipiones derived their name from the filial piety of a person who used to lead about his aged father, who was blind, and thus by metaphor became his staff *(scipio.)* Whether the English family can boast of a like honourable origin I know not.

STAFFORD. The founder of this family in England was Robert, a younger son of Roger de Toenei, standard-bearer of Normandy, whose name appears in Domesday as owner of 131 lordships in Staffordshire and other counties. The Conqueror appointed him governor of the castle of Stafford, from which he assumed a new surname. From him descended the Dukes of Buckingham and several other noble houses.

STAGG. The animal—perhaps applied to a fleet runner. See Ray.

STAGMAN. A keeper of deer; analogous to Hartman, Hindman, &c.

STAINBANK. Local: " the stony bank."

STAINBURN. Places in cos. Cumberland and York.

STAINER. One who colours or paints. The London Painters and Stainers were united into one company in 1502.

STAINES. A town in Middlesex.

STAINFORTH. Two townships in Yorkshire are so denominated.

STAINS. See Staines.

STAINTON. Parishes &c., in cos. Lincoln, Westmoreland, York, Durham, &c.

STAIR. A parish in Ayrshire, which gives title to Dalrymple, Earl of Stair.

STALKER. 1. A huntsman. 2. One who illegally kills deer. Jamieson.

STALLARD. The same as Staller.

STALLER. (A-Sax. *stalre*). Master of the horse; constable; standard-bearer. Regni vexillifer. Ellis's Domesd. i. 92.

STALLION. The animal. Hengist, the A-Saxon invader's name, doubtless meant the same thing—*hengst*, a stallion.

STALLMAN. The keeper of a stall in any fair or market, who paid the impost known, in municipal law, as stallage.

STALMAN. 1. Probably synonymous with *staller*. 2. A-Sax. *steallere*, a governor or steward of a palace. 3. See Stallman.

STAMFORD. A town in Lincolnshire, and places in cos. Northumberland, York, &c.

STAMMER. A stammerer. " Balbus, stamur." Wright's Vocab., p. 75.

STAMMERS. See Stammer.

STAMP. Probably from Estampes, now Etampes, in the department of Seine et Oise. It is sometimes written Stempe. At Boxgrove, co. Sussex, where the family have resided for three centuries, the earlier entries of the name are Stempe, and the later ones Stamp.

STAMPER. Probably some mechanical employment.

STANBOROUGH. A hundred in Devonshire.

STANBRIDGE. Places in Sussex, Bedfordshire, &c. The heiress of Stanbridge, of Stanbridge, in the former county (parish of Slinfold), married Cowper, ancestor of Earl Cowper, in the XV. century.

STANBROUGH. See Stanborough.

STANBURY. Local : " the fort or defence of stone."

STANCOMBE. See COMBE.

STANDEN. See DEN.

STANDEVEN. Of similar meaning to Standfast.

STANDERWICK. A parish in Somersetshire.

STANDFAST. Apparently refers to the possession of good feet.

STANDING. The same as Standen.

STANDISH. A parish in Lancashire, the ancient heritage of the family. The earliest recorded ancestor seems to be Thurstan de Standish, whose name appears in deeds dated 6. Henry III. This distinguished family continued to flourish on the lands from which they derived their name until the year 1807, when the last male heir died, and the estate passed to his sister's son, a Strickland, who assumed the Standish name.

STANDLEY. A corruption of Stanley.

STANES. See Staines.

STANFIELD. A parish in Norfolk.

STANFORD. Parishes and places in cos. Beds, Berks, Northampton, Worcester, Essex, Notts, Sussex, &c.

STANGER. 1. A thatcher. North. 2. From O. Fr. *èstang* (stagnum) a pond. In the same manner as Lake produced Laker, and Pond gave rise to Ponder, *stang* may have originated Stanger.

STANGMAR. An ancient Scandinavian baptismal name.

STANHOPE. The first recorded ancestor of this knightly and noble family is Walter de Stanhope, whose son Richard died in 1338, or the following year. The name is derived from Stanhope, near Darlington, co. Durham, their ancient residence. See Lord Stanhope's ' Notices of the Stanhopes.' 8vo. 1855.

STANLEY. Adam de Aldithley or Audeley, lord of Stanley, co. Chester, had two sons; 1. Liulph, ancestor of the great house of Audeley ; and 2. Adam, whose son William obtained the lands of Stanlegh from his cousin Adam de Audeley, and thence assumed the surname, in the reign of King John. Mr. Shirley remarks of the Stanleys: "As few families have acted a more prominent part in history, so few can trace a more satisfactory pedigree." Noble and Gentle Men.

STANMER. A parish in Sussex.

STANNAH. St. Anna?

STANNARD. An old baptismal name. Two tenants in chief bearing it are found in Domesday.

STANNEY. STANNICH. The manor of Stanney or Staney, in the parish of Stoke near Chester (according to Ormerod the Stanei of Domesday,) gave its name to this family, who were its owners from the reign of Richard I. to that of Edward III., when it passed with an heiress to the Bunburys. The Stanneys of the adjacent county of Salop, who were connected with the parish of Oswestry in the XV. and XVI. centuries, were doubtless of the same stock.

STANNUS. The Irish family of this name deduce their pedigree from William Stanehouse of Carbolgie, who received a patent of naturalization as a Scotch settler in Ulster in 1618. The name is identical with the English Stonehouse.

STANSFELD. A township in Yorkshire. The family are said to have "descended from a follower of the Conqueror who settled there." B.L.G.

STANSFIELD. A parish in Suffolk, and a township in Yorkshire.

STANTON. Parishes, &c., in many counties are so called.

STANVILLE. See Stanwell.

STANWAY. Parishes in cos. Essex and Gloucester.

STANVILLE. See Stanwell.

STANWELL. A parish in Middlesex.

STAPLE. Parishes, &c. in cos. Kent, Somerset, and Sussex.

STAPLER. A staple (Dutch *stapel*,) means a mart or emporium, and in old times a " merchant of the staple " signified a trader of importance. In course of time, however, the word *stapler* was monopolized by the dealer in wool, and it is now only heard in the compound "wool-stapler." Drayton, in his Polyolbion, commends Leicester—

" for her wool, whose *staple* doth excel,
And seems to overmatch the golden Phrygian fell."

STAPLES. Said to be derived from Estaples, now Etaples, a small seaport of France about eleven miles from Boulogne.

STAPLETON. This ancient family derived their name from the lordship of Stapleton on the river Tees, in the bishopric of Durham. They sprang from Nicholas de Stapleton, 17. King John, whose son, the warlike Sir Miles, was created Baron Stapleton in 1313. The Irish Sta-

pletons spring from Sir John Stapleton, a scion of the Yorkshire family, who went to Ireland temp. Henry II. and received a grant of lands from King John. Courthope's Debrett.

STAPLEY. Stapley is a township in Cheshire, where an ancient family of this name resided at an early period. The Stapleys of Sussex, extinct baronets, claimed descent from them, but it is more probable that they were indigenous to the southern county, where, in the neighbourhood of Battel (and near the hundred of Staple) a family of Staplehithe are found in the XIV. and XV. centuries.

STAR. STARR. Perhaps from the sign of an inn; but more likely from an ancient personal name written in Domesd. Ster and Sterr. It is Star without prefix in H.R.

STARBUCK. In O.Norse, *bokki* means "vir grandis, corpore et animo." Hence *storbocki* from *stór*, great, "vir imperiosus." Ferguson.

STARK. STARKE. O. Eng. Stout, strong, unyielding.

STARKIE. STARKEY. Probably the same as Stark.

STARKMAN. See Stark. The forms of the name in H.R. are Starcman and Starckeman.

STARLING. 1. An ancient baptismal name in use before the Conquest, as we have Starlinc, and Starlingus in Domesday. 2. Perhaps from the bird, like Raven, Rook, Crow, &c. 3. It may be a corruption of Stirling, the local name, or of Easterling. H.R. Starlyng, Sterlyng.

STARNE. STARNES. The same as Sterne.

START. A place in Devonshire.

STARTUP. 1. A kind of boot or leg-covering; a writer in Gent. Mag., June 1824, says, "gaiters laced down before." Gerard Legh, in his Accidence of Armory, mentions the startup as part of the habiliments of a Herald. In a compotus of the priory of Bicester, co. Oxon, dated 29. Edward III., among charges for saddlery and other horseman's gear, bought for the use of the Prior, are these entries: " One pair of *startups*, xxiid." and " in reparation of the Prior's *startups*, vid." Dunkin's Oxfordshire, ii. 221, 222. Drayton (Eclogue ix.) says:—

" When not a shepherd any thing that could,
But greaz'd his *start-ups* black as autumn sloe."

In "Thynne's Debate," as cited by Halliwell, we read :—

" A payre of *startuppes* had he on his feete,
That lased were up to the small of the legge ;
Homelie they were, and easier than meete,
And in their soles full many a wooden pegge."

This surname, which I have met with in Sussex only, was most likely applied, in the first instance, to some person who rendered himself conspicuous among his neighbours by wearing the rough high-topped boots so designated. I may remark, that the fourth line of my last quotation shows that the use of pegged soles for boots, recently introduced into this country from America, is no modern invention.

STATON. A corruption of Stainton.

STAUNDROP. A corruption of Staindrop, a parish in Durham.

STAUNTON. Parishes in cos. Nottingham, Durham, Worcester, Hereford, and Leicester, bear this name. The family of Staunton of Staunton, in the first-named shire, "can be regularly traced from the time of the Conqueror, and there is no doubt of their having been settled in Nottinghamshire, in the time of Edward the Confessor." B.L.G. In the XVIII. century the elder male line failed, and the heiress married Charlton, whose descendants have subsequently assumed the ancient name. B.L.G. "An ancient house, traced to the Conquest." Shirley's Noble and Gentle Men.

In Ireland this name dates from the earliest days after the English invasion. The names of Milo and Henry de Staunton are mentioned in A.D. 1200, as disputing concerning the patronage of the Church of Monmohenock, in Wicklow, with the Bishop of Glendaloch, Milo then being lord of the manor. D'Alton.

STAVELEY. Parishes and places in cos. Derby, Lancaster, Westmoreland, and York, are so designated.

STAVERT. Formerly written Staward, i.e. *stall-ward.* The family were old retainers of the Douglases. Folks of Shields.

STAWELL. A chapelry in Somersetshire. A family of considerable antiquity so surnamed resided in that county. B.L.G.

STAYNER. See Stainer.

STEABBEN. A corruption of Stephen.

STEAD. A-Sax. *stæde,* a stead, station, or place. Halliw. says, 'a farm house and offices.' A Steadman was therefore a farmer, or perhaps a farm-bailiff.

☞ **STEAD.** A common element in local names and surnames, as in Stedham, Binstead, Wickstead, Hampstead, Felsted, &c. See Stead, above.

STEADMAN. See Stead.

STEANE. A parish in Northamptonshire.

STEARMAN. See Sturman.

STEARN. STEARNS. See Sterne.

STEBBING. A parish in Essex.

STEDDY. May relate to steadiness of character; but is derivable with far greater probability from St. Edith, thus—Stedith, Stedi, Steddy. So Stydolph, from St. Edolph.

STEDHAM. A parish in Sussex.

STEDMAN. See Stead.

2 v

STEED. Steed and Steedman may correspond with Palfrey and Palfriman, Colt and Coltman, Brock and Brockman; but are more likely identical with Stead and Steadman.

STEEDMAN. See Steed.

STEEL. STEELE. A northern pronunciation of *stile.* In Scotl. the spur of a hill.

STEEN. See Stephen.

STEENSON. See Stephen.

STEEPLE. From residence in the vicinity of one.

STEERE. The animal. In Sussex it is pluralized to Steers. H.R. Le Ster.

STEERS. See Steere.

STEFF. See Stephen.

STEGGALL. Mr. Ferguson remarks: "As *deer* originally meant any wild animal, so *stag* seems to have meant the male of any animal, from Old Norse *steggr,* 'the male of various beasts and birds.' Hence *stag* in the North of England signifies a young horse, [in the South, a boar,] and *steg,* a gander. The terms seem to have been applied respectively to the deer and the stag *par excellence.* Steggall seems to be a diminutive of stag."

STEINMAN. This family existed at St. Gall, in Switzerland, more than four centuries ago as "Steinman, called Bingasser." The first settler in England was the great-grandfather of Mr. G. S. Steinman (a name well recognized in our antiquarian literature), who with his son came to England in 1771.

STEMBRIDGE. A corruption of Stanbridge.

STEMPE. The same as Stamp.

STEMSON. The son of Stephen.

STENHOUSE. A corruption of Stonehouse.

STENLAKE. Standlake, a parish in Oxfordshire.

STENNETT. A diminutive of Stephen.

STENNING. A surname principally confined to Sussex. All the persons bearing it, so far as my knowledge goes, trace themselves to the vicinity of Steyning in that county, which is locally pronounced like the surname.

STENSON. The son of Stephen.

STEPHEN. This scripture name, like many others, was not introduced here until the Norman Conquest, after which we find it in the form of Fitz-Stephen. It occupies a large place among our surnames in the usual genitive forms of Stephens, Stevens, Steevens, Stephenson, Stevenson, &c. A nicked or abbreviated form furnishes us with our Steen, Steenson, Stimson, Stimpson, Stinson, Stibbs; perhaps also Stubbs, Steff, Stiff, and Stennett. Tiffany and

Tiffin, from Stephanus, belong to the same category.

STEPHENS. See Stephen.

STEPHENSON. See Stephen.

STEPHYN. An old spelling of Stephen. The family of Stephens, of Tregenna, co. Cornwall, were of St. Ives in that county, temp. Edward IV., under this orthography.

STEPTOE. Probably refers to gait.

☞ **STER.** An Anglo-Saxon termination, denoting some feminine occupation, as ER does a masculine one, as spinner, spinster. Many of the surnames with this desinence shew the change of English customs in regard to the employments of women within the past few centuries : for example, brewing, baking, and weaving were formerly feminine labours, and consequently Brewster, Baxter, Webster mean the *woman* (not the man) who brews, bakes, or weaves. How these feminine words became transferred to the other gender, so as to become hereditary as surnames, is explained by Mr. Poulson, in his Beverlac, p. 128.—"When men began to invade those departments of industry by which women used to earn an honest livelihood, they retained the feminine appellation for some time, as men-midwives and men-milliners now do; but afterwards masculine words drove the feminine ones out of the language, as men had driven the women out of the employments." See more in Eng. Surn., i. 114.

STERCOCK. Perhaps a diminutive of Stephen.

STERE. See Steere.

STERLING. "Esterling, a name given to those Germans who are said to have been the first that brought the art of refining silver into England. Called Esterlings, as having come from the East." Jamieson. See also Richardson. Hence, metaphorically, *sterling* signifies anything pure or unalloyed.

STERNE. From the natural disposition of the first bearer.

STERNHOLD. May have some reference to the steering of a ship, but is more probably a corruption, by crasis, of Saint Arnold.

STERRY. 1. Sturry, a parish in Kent. 2. An old personal name—in Domesday Stari.

STEUART. The Steuarts of Allanton, co. Lanark (Barts.), are lineally descended from Alexander, sixth lord High Steward of Scotland, great grandfather of King Robert II., the first prince of the Stuart line. Courthope's Debrett.

STEVENSON. See Stephen.

STEVENS. STEEVENS. Stephen's; the son of Stephen.

STEWARD. The office. See Stewart and Stuart.

STEWARDSON. The son of the Steward. So Hindson, Cookson, &c.

STEWART. See Stuart.

STIBBS. See Stephen.

STICK. An Edinburgh surname. It may have been originally applied to a verger or staff-bearer, like 'Gold-stick,' 'Silver-stick,' &c.

STICKLAND. A corruption of Strickland.

STICKNEY. A parish in Lincolnshire.

STIFF. See Stephen.

STIGGINS. Doubtless Stigandus, Stigand, the ancient baptismal name. A dignified Archbishop, and Mrs. Weller's red-nosed pastor, then, enjoyed at least a name in common !

STIGGSON. The son of Stigand. See Stiggins.

STILE. See Style.

STILL. Stille was a tenant prior to Domesday. This must therefore have been a personal or baptismal name.

STILLINGFLEET. A parish in Yorkshire, the original abode of the family.

STILLMAN. Probably the same as Styleman.

STILWELL. See Well.

STIMSON. STIMPSON. See Stephen.

STINCHCOMBE. A parish in Gloucestershire.

STINSON. See Stephen.

STIRLING. From the town of Stirling, which gives name to the Scottish shire, anciently written Stryvelin. The family are of great antiquity, being deduced from Walter de Stryvelin, who appears as witness to a charter of Prince Henry, son of King David I., in the XII. century. Courthope's Debrett. Four baronetcies have been accorded to this family.

STIVENS. A corruption of Stephens.

STOBBS. See Stubbs.

STOCK. 1. The stock of a tree seems a very unlikely origin for a family name, yet Zouch and Curzon seem analogous, as does the Fr. Racine, not to mention the English Roots. 2. Parishes, &c., in cos. Worcester, Essex, Somerset, Dorset, and York.

STOCKBRIDGE. A parish in Hampshire.

STOCKEN. See Stocking.

STOCKER. In the West of England, to *stock* means to root up, and a *stocker* is a man employed to fell or grub up trees. Halliwell. Stocker, without prefix, is found in H.R.

STOCKHAM. A township in Cheshire.

STOCKING. Local. De Stocking. H.R. I cannot find the place.

STOCKLEY. Two parishes in Devonshire, and a parish in Durham, are so designated.

STOCKMAN. Perhaps the same as Stocker.

STOCKS. See Stock.

STOCKTON. Towns, parishes, &c., in cos. Durham, Chester, Norfolk, Warwick, Wilts, Worcester, York, and Salop.

STOCKWELL. A division of the parish of Lambeth, co. Surrey.

STODART. See Stotherd.

STODDARD. See Stotherd.

STODDART. See Stotherd.

STODHARD. STODHART. See Stotherd.

STOKER. One who has charge of a furnace.

STOKES. A pluralization of Stoke.

STOKOE. A place in Northumberland.

STOLYON. Probably a provincial form of stallion, a horse. See Stallion.

STONE. A very common local surname. There are towns, parishes, &c., so called in cos. Stafford, Buckingham, Gloucester, Kent, Worcester, &c.

STONEBRIDGE. A name applied to many minor localities.

STONECUTTER. The occupation.

STONEHAM. Two parishes in Hampshire, and a hamlet in Sussex.

STONEHEWER. A quarryman.

STONEMAN. Probably a stone-mason, or a quarryman.

STONESTREET. I know of no locality so called; but, as the name has been spelt Stanistreet, may it not be derived from the celebrated Roman road thus designated, which ran from Regnum (Chichester) to London? This seems the more probable as the Stonestreets appear to have originated in the county of Sussex, at no great distance from that road. Analogous origins for family names from Roman works, may be found under Dykes, Thirlwall, and Watling. De Stonstret. H.R. co. Kent.

STONEX. Perhaps Stanwix, co. Cumberland.

STONEY. Possibly from Loch Stoney in Forfarshire.

STONHAM. Three parishes in Suffolk are so designated.

STONOR. An estate in Oxfordshire, thus mentioned by Leland: " Stonor is a 3 miles out of Henley. Ther is a fayre parke, and a warren of connes, and fayre woods. The mansion place standithe clyminge on a hille, and hath 2 courtes buyldyd withe tymbar, brike, and flynte; Sir Walter Stonor, now pocessor of it, hathe augmentyd and strengthed the howse. The Stonors hath longe had it in possessyon." To this Mr. Shirley adds that, " the family have the reputation of being very ancient, and may certainly be traced to the twelfth century as resident at Stonor." Noble and Gentle Men.

STOOL. A provincial pronunciation of Stowell.

STORE. See Storr.

STORER. Störer is a common surname in Germany, and means " a disturber;" but our Storers are probably indigenous and conservators, rather than breakers, of the peace, for two officers of the manor of Whittlesea in the Isle of Ely, elected every year, are called Storers.

STOREY. 1. See Story. 2. Said to be the same name with Storer. B.L.G.

STORK. The bird.

STORM. Corresponds with the Old German personal name Sturm. Ferguson.

STORR. A-Sax. and O. Norse *stór*, great, vast.

STORTON. The same as Stourton.

STORY. The Scandinavian Stori. See Storr. Stori and Storius occur before the making of Domesday. They were probably of Danish blood.

STOTHARD. See Stotherd.

STOTHERD. *Stot* is a northernism for ox; and hence Stotherd is evidently " oxherd." This explains the group Stodart, Stoddart, Stoddard, Stodhart, Stothard, &c. The pronunciations *Stoth-erd, Stoth-ard*, are a ' genteel ' innovation.

STOTT. A northern provincialism for the ox.

STOUR. 1. From one of the rivers so called. 2. See Stower.

STOURTON. This family, now represented by Charles Stourton, eighteenth Baron Stourton (created 1447) were seated at Stourton, co. Wilts, soon after the Norman Conquest. The arms of the family, *Sable, a bend Or, between six fountains Proper*, are thus accounted for by Leland: " The Ryver of Stour risith ther of six fountaines or springes, whereof three be on the north side of the Parke, hard within the pale: the other three be north also, but without the Parke; *the Lord Stourton gyveth these six Fountaynes yn his armes.*" See Noble and Gentle Men.

STOUT. Valiant, courageous.

STOUTWELL. A corruption of Stuteville, as old as the XIII. century.

STOVEL. STOVELL. A likely corruption of the Norman Stuetville, or Estouteville.

STOVIN. Stoven, a parish in Suffolk.

STOW. STOWE. Parishes, &c., in cos. Selkirk, Lincoln, Salop, Huntingdon,

Suffolk, Norfolk, Essex, Oxford, Gloucester, Buckingham, Stafford, Northampton, &c.

STOWELL. Places in cos. Gloucester, Somerset, and Wilts bear the name of Stowel.

STOWER. Three parishes in Dorsetshire are so called.

STOWERS. A pluralization of Stower.

STRACEY. The baronets Strachey and Stracey both derive from the county of Essex, in the sixteenth century, and bear similar arms. The names are probably identical, and derived from a local source.

STRACHAN. A parish in Kincardineshire.

STRACHEY. See Stracey.

STRADLEY. A corruption of Stradling ?

STRADLING. This surname was latinized Easterlingus, and it seems to be a corruption of Estarling, a name given to the inhabitants of any country eastward of England, especially to those of the Hanse Towns. See Sterling.

STRAFFORD. A corruption either of one of the Stratfords, or of Strafforth, co. York.

STRAHAN. See Strachan.

STRAIGHT. Erect in person.

STRAITH. Probably the Celtic topographical word *strath*, meaning "the conjoint valley of two confluent streams," or, more loosely, any band or level of low ground between two ridges of hill or mountain. Gaz. Scotl. The word is specifically applied to a parish in Inverness-shire.

STRAITON. A parish in Ayrshire.

STRAKER. 1. One of the many meanings which the Scottish word *straik* possesses, is "engagement on the field of battle." Jamieson. Hence Straker may be equivalent to combatant or soldier. 2. A ranger of planks on a ship's side. Folks of Shields.

STRAND. The sea-shore, or the bank of a river.

STRANG. An archaic and Northern form of Strong.

STRANGE. According to some genealogists this family first appear in England at certain jousts of arms, which took place at Peverell's Castle, in the Peak of Derbyshire. There were present on the occasion Owen, Prince of Wales, a Scottish Prince, and two sons of the Duke of Brittany, one of whom, from his foreign birth, was called Guido le Strange, and became progenitor of the various baronial houses of L'Estrange and Strange. "This race of Le Strange continued for many descents in the dignity of lords barons, in Latine records called *Extranei*, for that they were strangers, brought hither by King Henry the Second,

in the year 1148." Weever's Funerall Monuments, p. 530.

STRANGEMAN. A stranger ; a settler from any other locality.

STRANGER. The same as Strangeman.

STRANGWAYES. A corruption of Strangwish, near Manchester, which was possessed by the family in the XIV. century.

STRANGWISH. See Strangwayes.

STRANGWYCH. Verstegan mentions this name as "coming belike of a *strong wyc*, hold, or fortress." Restitution, p. 329. It is doubtless the same as Strangwish or Strangways.

STRAUBENZEE. The family derive from ,Philip-William-Casimir Van Straubenzee, a captain in the Dutch Guards, who came to England about 1740, and was naturalized by Act of Parliament.

STRATFORD. Parishes, &c., in cos. Suffolk, Warwick, Wilts, Essex, Buckingham, &c.

STRATHEARN. A large district of Perthshire.

STRATTON. Parishes and places in cos. Cornwall, Dorset, Gloucester, Norfolk, Suffolk, Hants, Somerset, Wilts, &c.

STRAW. From the occupation of a thatcher. That which was a sobriquet of the well-known insurgent of temp. Richard II., has since become a settled family name.

STREATFEILD. The pedigree of the Streatfeilds of Chiddingstone, co. Kent, is traced to the early part of the XVI. century. The name has been fancifully derived from Lat. *De Strata Villa*, "the prostrate house," an ill-omened etymology, which the family do not deserve. It has also been fetched from the German *Streitfeld*, "the field of contention or of battle;" but the origin is doubtless English, and local. There may be several places of this name : I know only of one, which is a 'borough' of the manor of Robertsbridge, in East Sussex, called in a document before me, of temp. Elizabeth, Stretfelde ; and this locality is within a few miles of that which has been, for three centuries and a half, the chief *habitat* of the name.

A gentleman of this family sends me the following remarks on the orthography of the last syllable of the name :

"It is so spelt," he says, "in many names, as Hatfeild, Feilder, Feilding, Bifeild, Owldefeild. It accords with a rule of English orthography, that when the two vowels come together in a word, sound like E, and are preceded by a consonant, that the E or the I, whichever is nearest in the alphabet to this consonant, comes first. There are many exceptions to this law ; *field* is one ; but FEILD is according to the law."

STREET. 1. Parishes and places so called in cos. Sussex, Somerset, Kent, &c. 2. A public road or highway. Analogous to the Fr. De la Rue, the Italian Strada, &c. In H.R. De, De la, and Atte Strete.

In some parts of England any small hamlet is called a *street*.

STREETEN. A common pronunciation of Stretton.

STREETER. From residence by a highway. The Fr. De la Rue is an exact synonym.

STREETS. A pluralization of Street.

STRELLEY. " Strelly, anciently Strellegh, co. Nottingham, gave name and residence to the knightly family of the Strelleys, one of the oldest and most famous in the county." B.L.G.

STRICKLAND. " Descended from Walter de Stirkland, Knight, so called from the pasture ground of the young cattle called *stirks* or steers, in the parish of Morland, in the county of Westmoreland, who was living in the reign of Henry III." Shirley's Noble and Gentle Men.

STRING. Perhaps a contraction of Stringer. Mr. Bowditch informs us that *two* daughters of Mr. String, of S. Carolina, lately eloped with one person (1857.) Thus was made good the proverbial remark— " *Two Strings to one Beau.*"

STRINGER. In the days of archery, a maker of bow-strings. Nares's Glossary.

STRIPLING. This name seems to belong to the same class as Youngman, Junius, &c.

STRIVENS. Doubtless a corruption of Scrivens.

STRODE. 1. The family are said to have been descended from the ancient Dukes of Brittany, and to have been founded in England by Warinus, lord of Strode, in Dorsetshire, who adopted the surname De la Strode. B.L.G. 2. The name is derived from Strode in the parish of Ermington, co. Devon, which was in the possession of Adam de Strode, the first recorded ancestor, in the reign of Henry III. In that of Henry IV., the head of the house, married the heiress of Newenham of Newenham, which has ever since been the seat of the family. Shirley's Noble and Gentle Men.

STRONG. The physical quality; like the French Le Fort.

STRONGBOW. This illustrious sobriquet of the mighty Earl of Pembroke did not die with him, for in the next century we find one Ranulph Strongbowe living in Essex. H.R. temp. Edward I.

STRONGI'TH'ARM. " Strong-in-the Arm ;" apparently a variation of Armstrong. There is a similar French surname— Fortinbras.

STRONGMAN. One who excelled in muscular exploits.

STROOD. A town in Kent.

STROUD. A town in Gloucestershire.

STRYPE. The ancestor of the historian was Gherardt Van Strype, a member of the Dutch church in London in 1567.

STUART. The descent of the royal Stuarts from Banquo, Thane of Lochaber, the victim of King Macbeth, and their native Gaelic origin, are altogether visionary. The truth appears to be this. Alan, the son of Flaald, a man of whose paternal ancestry and nation nothing is clearly known, and who died very early in the XII. cent., was the common parent of William Fitz-Alan, ancestor of the Earls of Arundel, and of Walter Fitz-Alan, *Steward* of Scotland, whose great-grandson, Alexander, assumed Stuart as his surname, and was the ancestor of the royal race of that dynasty. From the latter of these sons springs Queen Victoria, and from the former, her Majesty's highest temporal subject, the Duke of Norfolk, premier peer of the realm. Whatever may have been the male ancestry of Flaald, it is certain that he was descended on his mother's side from the old Princes of Wales and from the ancient Saxon Earls of Mercia. See Rev. R. W. Eyton, in Arch. Journ., Dec., 1856.

STUBBS. 1. See Stephen. 2. A *stub* or *stob* is a provincial word for the stump of a tree left in forest clearings. Such a clearing would for a time acquire the appellation of " the Stubbs," and residence near it would originate the surname.

STUNT. A-Sax. Blunt, stupid, foolish. In Lincolnshire and other districts, the word has undergone a change, and means sulky, obstinate—sometimes fierce and angry. Halliw. See Eng. Surn.

STURDEE. STURDY. Stout, vigorous.

STURGEON. The fish.

STURMAN. Stirman or Stermannus occurs in Domesday as the designation of an official. Edric Stirman was, temp. Edw. Confessor, commander of the land and sea forces of the bishop of Worcester, for the king's service. (*Stermannus* navis episcopi, et ductor exercitus ejusdem episcopi, ad servicium regis). Heming Chartul. quoted in Ellis's Introd. ii. 89. There was also a king's Stirman. A-Sax. *steoran*, to steer, rule, govern.

STURT. Probably from Stert, a chapelry in the parish of Erchfont, co. Wilts.

STUTEVILLE. The founder of this family came into England with the Conqueror. His son, Robert de Stuteville, who besides this territorial surname, had the sobriquet of Fronteboef, or " bullock's face," fought against Henry I. at Tenerchebrai, and was taken prisoner. From a younger son of this personage descend the Skipwiths. The elder line failed in the XIII. century. Banks's Baronage. The name is taken from Estouteville, now Etoutteville, in the arrondissement of Yvetot, in Normandy, and formerly, in charters, Estotevilla.

STUTFIELD. A corruption of Stuteville.

STYDOLPH. A contraction of St. Edolph.

STYLE. Richardson says—" steps raised to pass over," which is perhaps as good a definition as could be given in so small a number of words; but the styles which are ' passages over a fence so contrived as that cattle cannot make use of them '—as the word might be more elaborately defined— differ nearly as much *inter se* in different districts, as do the styles of different authors. There is, however, no doubt that the surname, whether it originated in Sussex, in Cornwall, or in Northumberland, (whose *thruff-stone* styles I shall never forget) was derived from the residence of the first bearer near such a barrier. In the middle ages, the phrase " John at Style " was in common use to denote a plebeian, and it still survives in a slightly altered form in the saying, " Jack Noakes and Tom Styles." See Noakes. H.R. Ate Stile. De la Stile.

STYLEMAN. See Style, and the termination MAN.

STYLES. See Style.

SUCH. An old orthography of Zouch.

SUCKBITCH. This name, borne by more than one respectable family in the West of England, might be supposed to be derived from some legend analogous to that of Romulus and Remus. The earliest form of it, *Sokespic*, however, excludes such an origin. See Notes and Queries, v. 425.

SUCKLING. Probably local. H.R. Sucklin, and Suckling, without prefix.

SUCKSMITH. See under Smith.

SUDDEN. A known corruption of Southdean, through Soudean.

SUDLEY. SUDELEY. A parish in Gloucestershire, whose castle was the principal seat of the family, until their extinction in the elder male line in the XIV. century. They sprang from one Harold, said to have been an illegitimate son of King Harold, although Dugdale asserts that he was the son of Ralph, Earl of Hereford. He left two sons, John, who adopted the name of De Sudeley, and Robert, who settled at the castle of Ewyas, co. Hereford, and assumed that of De Ewyas.

SUETT. Suet was an under-tenant before the making of Domesday.

SUGAR. 1. A corruption of Segar, which see. 2. Mr. Ferguson thinks it is a corruption of A-Sax. *sigra*, a victor.

SUGDEN. See termination DEN.

SUGGATE. A provincial corruption of Southgate.

SULLEN. From disposition.

SULLIVAN. BY THE HAND OF SULLIVAN, is an Irish oath, which is considered

of the most obligatory character. According to an ancient rhyme, there is—

> " Nulla *manus*
> Tam liberalis
> Atque generalis
> Atque universalis
> Quam *Sullivanus*."
> —*Croker's Fairy Legends*.

So much for the generous character of the family—now for the origin of the name, as kindly communicated by a correspondent. I must premise that the surname was formerly, and is still, often prefixed by O'— shewing that Sullivan is an ancient baptismal name. " To the house of the chief who became the stock whence the present family of O'Sullivan descend, came a one-eyed Druid, who was also a bard, from Albany. He was named Levawn. Eochy, the chieftain, received him cordially as was his wont. Strange to say, he, like his guest, had but one eye. When the Druid departed from the castle, he declined all the noble gifts his host pressed upon him, but demanded from his entertainer the present of his only eye. Eochy, impelled by a generosity that had never said Nay to a request, at once tore it from its socket, and bestowed it upon his unnatural guest. There chanced, however, to be a holy man living with the outraged Eochy; who, indignant at such ingratitude, prayed fervently that the Druid's eye might depart from its place, and, together with his own, become the property of Eochy. His appeal to Heaven was heard—the Chief became miraculously possessed of two eyes, and the Druid departed for ever blind. Hence this peerless host and his posterity have carried this unparalleled instance of magnanimity to all time in their name, *Suil-Levawn*—Levawn's eye ! "

SUMMER. See Times and Seasons.

SUMMERBEE. See Somerby.

SUMPTION. This very remarkable name appears to be a contraction of " Assumption " (i.e., of the Virgin Mary), the church festival, and to be cognate with Pentecost, Christmas, Easter, &c.

SUNDAY. See Times and Seasons.

SUNNER. A Lancashire corruption of Sumner or Somner.

SURREY. See Counties, names of.

SURTEES. An ancient Durham family, Barons of the Palatinate, who took their name from residence *Super Tysam, Sur Tees*, Upon the river Tees, their chief seat being Dinsdale. The male line became extinct at an early period, and the younger branches fell into comparative decay, until within the last few generations, when by success in commercial and professional life, and by alliances, the ancient fortunes of the family were revived, and Dinsdale has been repurchased by the representative of the name.

SUSANS. 1. Suzanne-sur-Senelle, near Coutances, or Suzanne-sur-Vire, near St. Lo, in Normandy. 2. See Female Christian Names.

SUTER. See Souter.

SUTHERLAND. See Murray.

SUTOR. Lat. A shoemaker. See Souter.

SUTTABY. Sutterby, co. Lincoln.

SUTTON. In A-Sax. charters *Sud-tún* —'the southern homestead or enclosure'— a name consequently of very common application. Besides single farms and minor divisions, there are more than sixty Suttons among the parishes and other civil and ecclesiastical districts of England. Heraldry also attests the commonness of the surname by more than fifty coats assigned to it. See Norton, Easton, and Weston.

According to Dugdale the descent of the Suttons, Barons Dudley, temp. Elizabeth, was uncertain, some genealogists deducing them "from Sutton of Sutton in Holdernesse; some from the Suttons of Sutton-Madoc in Shropshire; but others from Sutton-upon-Trent, near Newark, whence the Suttons of Aram, near at hand, are descended.

The baronet (Sutton of Norwood) deduces his pedigree from Roland, son of Hervey de Sutton, of Sutton-upon-Trent, co. Nottingham, who lived in the reign of Henry III.

SWABEY. 1. The Swabeys of Buckinghamshire are descended from George Swebé or Swebey, of German extraction, who settled in St. Mary's Lambeth, about the year 1584. B.L.G. 2. Swaby, a parish in Lincolnshire.

SWAFIELD. A parish in Norfolk.

☞ SWAIN. The A-Sax. *swán*, a pastoral servant, and the Scand. *Sweyn*, a proper name originally of the same import, have impressed themselves upon many localities, which in their turn have given designations to families. Among those which do not occur in gazetteers are Swainston, Swainsland (now Swaysland), Swanston, and others.

SWAINE. SWAYNE. 1. A Scandinavian personal name of great antiquity, introduced here under the Danish rule. Domesday shows us several persons (tenants in chief and otherwise) called Svain, Suain, Suanus, Suuen, Swen or Sueno, some of whom are specifically stated to have held lands under Edward the Confessor. Suain of Essex, supposed by Morant to have been of Danish origin, was ancestor of the famous Henry de Essex, temp. Henry II. 2. The A-Sax. *swán:* see previous article. The forms in the Rotuli Hundredorum are Le Swein, Le Sweyn, and Sweyn.

SWAINSON. See under Swaine. The name of Sweynson has existed for ages in Denmark. In the XI. and XII. centuries we find it here in the forms of Filius Suani and Fitz-Swain. In Domesday the wife of Edw. filius Suani was a chief-tenant in Essex. The well-known ascendancy of the Danes in Yorkshire from the time of Ethelred, A.D. 868, downwards, accounts for that district being the principal *habitat*

of the name. The Swaynsons were located at Briggeholme, in the parish of Giggleswick, early in the XII. century, and they remained in that district until the middle of the XVIII. Early in the XII. century Adam Fitz-Swain or Swainson, was lord of Hornby Castle. "You have the advantage (says the Rev. Jos. Hunter, addressing one of the family,) of having had a line of ancestors living in a good position in the county where Sweyn, the son of Alaric, and Adam, the son of Sweyn, had such large possessions." Beatson's Polit. Index. i. 4. Inf. Rev. Edw. C. Swaynson, M.A., the existing representative of the family.

SWALE. A river of Yorkshire.

SWALLOW. 1. A parish in Lincolnshire. 2. Metaphorically applied to a person swift of foot, like the Fr. Hirondelle.

SWAN. SWANN. 1. Perhaps the same as Swaine. 2. The bird was famous in old heroic times, both as a dainty of the table, and as an heraldric badge. Edw. III. used to swear by it. See Curios. Herald. 154. One Bartholomew le Swan occurs in the archives of Battel Abbey. 3. *Swán*, A-Sax., a herdsman or pastoral servant.

SWANBOROUGH. A hundred, and an estate, near Lewes, Sussex.

SWANNELL. 1. Ferguson considers it a diminutive of Swan. The corresponding name Suanila is found in Germany so early as the VII. century. 2. Perhaps from *swan*, and *hals*, 'swan-necked,' a complimentary epithet sometimes applied to Anglo-Saxon ladies.

SWANTON. Three parishes in Norfolk are so called.

SWATTON. A parish in Lincolnshire (Swaton).

SWAYNSON. See Swainson.

SWAYSLAND. This name was written in East Sussex, in the XVI. century, Swaynesland. See Swain.

SWEAR. Scottish. Lazy, indolent. Jamieson.

SWEATMAN. SWEETMAN. Swetman occurs on A-Sax. coins as the name of a moneyer; and before and at the making of Domesday, there existed a certain Saxon freeman called Suetman and Suetmanus.

SWEDEN. From the country.

SWEDENBANK. Possibly a corruption of Swinton-Bank, an estate in the parish of Peebles, in Scotland.

SWEENY. See Mac Sweeny.

SWEET. 1. See Suett. 2. Probably an A-Sax. personal name, having reference to character. Sweeting and Sweetlove seem to belong to the same class. Ferg.

SWEETAPPLE. Doubtless either a gross corruption or a sobriquet. Near Godalming in Surrey, this delightful name is counterpoised by that of *Bitterplum*.

SWEETING. An old A-Sax. personal name; a patronymic of Sweet, which see. In Domesday, Sueting, Suetingus, &c.

SWEETLOVE. See Sweet.

SWEETMAN. See Swetman.

SWEETSER. SWEETSUR. A native of Switzerland was formerly called a Switzer; especially one of the hired guards; a mercenary soldier. The Switzers were generally fat men, and hence the distich quoted by Cotgrave:—

"A *Switzer's* bellie and a drunkard's face,
Are no true signes of penitentiall grace."

SWEPER. The man who managed the *swepe*, an engine of war for casting stones, more usually called a *balista* or *mangonel*, and much in use before the invention of gunpowder.

SWEPSTONE. Sweepstone, ¦co. Leicester.

SWETENHAM. SWETNAM. See Swettenham.

SWETMAN. An A-Sax. personal name.

SWETTENHAM. The family are said to have been seated at Swettenham, in Cheshire, before the Conquest, and there the male succession continued till 1788. The name is still borne by a descendant of the female line, who is owner of Swettenham.

SWIFT. From speed of foot. Swift and Swyft, as also Celer, are found in H.R.

SWILLINGTON. A place in the West Riding of Yorkshire. To this family belonged Adam de Swillington, who had summons to Parliament as a Baron, 3. December, 1326.

☞ **SWIN. SWINE.** A Sax. *swin*, a pig. This is the initial syllable of many names of places, and of families borrowed from them, and points to those early days when the wild boar roamed over our great forests. Among other surnames may be cited Swinburn, Swineston, Swynford, Swinnerton, Swinshead, Swindale, Swindon, Swinstead, Swinfen, Swinton.

SWINBURNE. A township in the parish of Chollerton, co. Northumberland, which was possessed by the first recorded ancestor, John, father of Sir William de Swinburne, who was living in 1278, and of Alan Swinburne, rector of Whitfield, who purchased Capheaton (the present abode of the family) from Sir Thomas Fenwick in 1274. Shirley's Noble and Gentle Men. Sir William de Swinburne, just mentioned, held Chollerton under the Umfreville family, and the arms of the Swinburnes are evidently derived from those of Umfreville.

SWINDELLS. A corruption of *swine-dale*, the valley of swine; or it may be the same as Swindle. Swindale is a chapelry in the hundred of Shap, co. Westmoreland.

SWINDLE. R.G. 16. 1. According to Halliwell, *swindle* is a provincialism used in the North for spindle. 2. Perhaps a corruption of Swindale, co. Westmoreland.

SWINDLER. R.G. 16. A maker of spindles. See Swindle.

SWINEHAM. A place near Battel Abbey, Sussex.

SWINESHEAD. Does not refer to the "pig-headedness" of the race, but to their ancient residence in Lincolnshire, famous in old times for its Abbey, and the disaster of king John.

SWINESTEAD. A parish in co. Lincoln.

SWINFEN. A hamlet in the parish of Wreford, co. Stafford, where the "very ancient family" mentioned in Boswell's Life of Johnson were seated in early times.

SWINFORD. Parishes in cos. Leicester and Stafford.

SWINGLER. Probably a flax-dresser. See Halliwell, under 'swingle.'

SWINNERTON. A parish in co. Stafford.

SWINSON. A contraction of Swainson.

SWINTON. 1. Two townships and a chapelry in Yorkshire. 2. The Swintons of Swinton Bank, co. Peebles, derive their origin from the barony of Swinton in Berwickshire, and from a Saxon proprietor called Edulphus de Swinton, who flourished in the reigns of Macbeth and Malcolm Canmore. B.L.G. The family, who continue to write themselves 'of that Ilk,' have numbered some distinguished military men, among whom stands conspicuous Sir John Swinton, who, at the battle of Beaugé in France, killed the Duke of Clarence, brother of King Henry V.

"And Swinton placed the lance in rest,
That humbled erst the sparkling crest
Of Clarence's Plantagenet."
Lay of the Last Minstrel.

SWIRE. SWYER. Swyre, co. Dorset.

SWITHIN. A well-known Anglo-Sax. personal name, rendered illustrious by St. Swithin, bishop of Winchester, who died A.D. 862.

SWONNELL. See Swannell.

SWORD. From the weapon. It has several compounds, as Brownsword, Greensword, Longsword, &c.

SWORDER. A sword-player, or a juggler with swords. For a description of this medieval pastime, see Strutt's Sports and Pastimes, Edit. 1834. p. 259.

SWYNFEN. See Swinfen.

SWYNNERTON. An ancient knightly family of Staffordshire, descended from Sir Roger de Swynnerton, who was lord of the manor of Swynnerton, 34. Edward I.

SYDENHAM. Parishes in Kent, Devon, and Oxfordshire.

SYDNEY. The founder of this family in England was Sir William Sydney, Chamberlain of King Henry II., who came from Anjou with that monarch, and was buried at Lewes Priory in 1188. Baronage. The name is said to be a corruption of St. Denis.

SYDSERF. Said to be "of that Ilk;" but the Gazetteer of Scotland mentions no such place.

SYER. 1. Perhaps the same as Sayer. 2. Possibly the O. French *sieür*, a sawyer, or sometimes a reaper. H.R. Le Syer and Fil. Syer.

SYKES. May be a nickname for Simon, like Gilkes for Gilbert, Hicks for Isaac, &c. It may, however, be local, as a *sike* in some dialects means a small rill, spring, or water-fall.

SYLVESTER. An ancient personal name.

SYLVIUS. The classical personal name.

SYMBARBE. See St. Barbe.

SYME. A nickname of Simon, whence Symes.

SYMES. See Simon.

SYMM. See Simon.

SYMONDSON. See Simon.

SYMONS. SYMONDS. See Simon.

SYMPSON. See Simon.

SYMS. See Simon.

SYNNOT. "Descended from an ancient and honourable stock, of Norman extraction. They were possessed of lands in Ireland from the time of the Invasion, and in the county where they first found footing." D'Alton. In the year 1365 the name was written Synath. The account in B.L.G. derives them from a Marquis of Lusignan, whose descendants came into England, at or soon after, the Norman Conquest.

T.

TAAFE. Lord Taafe's ancestors were a Welsh family, who settled in Ireland at the English invasion. In 1287 flourished Sir Nicholas Taafe, whose son, John Taafe, was consecrated Archbishop of Armagh. D'Alton.

TABARD. A kind of medieval coat, which still forms part of the costume of the Heralds. It was adopted for an inn sign in the fourteenth century, and was the denotement of the famous tavern in Southwark, from which Chaucer's immortal Pilgrims set forth for Canterbury.

> "Byfel that in a seasoun on a day,
> In Southwerk at the *Tabbard* as I lay,
> Redy to wenden on my pilgrimage
> To Canterbury with devout corage."

TABBERER. See under Tabor. Le Taburer. H.R.

TABBY. Supposed to be a corruption of At-Abbey, from residence near a monastery. Compare Trill, Tash, Teeth, &c.

TABER. See Tabor.

TABERNACLE. Perhaps a corruption of Tabernator, the latinized form of Taverner. See H.R.

TABOIS. See Talboys.

TABOR. A contraction of *tabourer*, one who plays on a small drum.

> "Would I could see this *tabourer*."
>   —*Shakespeare.*

> "I saw a shole of shepherds out go,
> Before them yode a lusty *tabrere*,
> That to the merry hornpipe plaid,
> Whereto they danced."
>   —*Spenser.*

TACKLEY. A parish in Oxfordshire, where the family were resident temp. Edward I. De Tackele, De Takeleye, &c. H.R.

TADLOO. Tadlow, co. Cambridge. De Tadelowe, H.R., in that shire.

TAGGART. The Gaelic Mac Taggart, sans Mac.

TAILBOYS. See Talboys.

2 w

TAILBUSH. See Talboys.

TAILOR. From the trade. It is much more frequently written Taylor. The forms in H.R. are Le Taillur, Le Tailur, Le Talyur.

TAILYOUR. An old Scotch orthography of Tailor.

TAIT. Teit was a personal name in Norway in the XI. cent. See the Heimskringla. The name is sometimes varied to Taitt, Taite and Tate.

TALBOT. This illustrious family trace, *sine hiatu*, to the great Domesday tenant, Richard Talebot. Mr. Shirley, in his Noble and Gentle Men, remarks, that " no family in England are more connected with the history of our country than this noble race; few are more highly allied. The Marches of Wales appear to have been the original seat; afterwards we find the Talbots in Shropshire, in Staffordshire, and lastly in Yorkshire."

In Ireland the settlement of a branch of the family is coeval with the English rule, Henry II. having granted Malahide to Richard Talbot, whose lineal descendant, Lord Talbot, writes himself " of Malahide" to this day.

This name is not territorial, being never prefixed with *De.* I have never seen any attempt to explain it. A *talbot* in heraldry is a hunting-dog, but of the history of the word I know nothing. Dr. Johnson defines it as " a hound," and says, though incorrectly, that " it is borne by the house of Talbot in their *arms.*" Concerning the Talbot, Legh speaks thus: " Isidore wryteth, that these houndes pursue the foote of pray, by sent of ye same, or els by ye bloud thereof, whether it be by night or daye. But I referre the judgment of that to them that love venison so well as will jeopardie a joynt for buck or doe. This hounde is enemy to the Catte." Accedens of Armory, edit. 1562. fo. 96. d.

TALBOYS. Fr. *taille-bois,* literally " cut-wood," analogous to Taillefer (cut-iron), allusive probably to some manual feat. See Bush. The surname occurs frequently in Domesday. Ivo Tailgebosch, lord of Holland, co. Lincoln, married Lucia, sister of the Saxon Earls Edwin and Morcar; and Ralph and Ivo Tailgebosc, Tallebosc, &c., were tenants in Bedfordshire. Other corruptions of this name are Tailboys, Tabois, and *Tailbush.*

TALKER. First applied, probably, to a loquacious person.

TALL. From stature, like Long, Short, &c.

TALLACK. A Cornish surname, found at Penryn and at St. Austell, and also at Norwich, where a branch settled about 1750. A place near Penryn is called Tallack's Style. The name is doubtless Celtic, and local. There is a place in Brecknockshire called Talach-Ddu.

TALLBOYS. See Talboys.

TALLIS. O. Fr. *taillis,* " a copse, grove, underwood; such wood as is felled or lopped every seven or eight years." Cotgrave. It may be regarded as the Fr. equivalent of the English Shaw.

TALLMAN. Allusive to height of stature.

TALMACHE. TALLEMACHE. See Tollemache.

TALMAGE. TALMADGE. See Tollemache.

TALVAS. Fr. " *tallevas,* a large, massive, and old-fashioned targuet (shield) having in the bottome of it a pike, whereby, when need was, it was stucke into the ground." Cotgrave.

TAME. An Oxfordshire name, probably from the river Thame. Alured de Tame occurs in Domesday. The armorials of this family, a dragon and a lion combatant, can hardly have been adopted upon the canting or allusive principle.

TAMLYN. See Thomas.

TAMMADGE. See Tollemache.

TAMPKINS. A northern form of Tompkins.

TAMPLIN. See Thomas.

TAMPSETT. A northern form of Tompsett.

TAMYS. An old spelling of Thames, from which river the name is probably derived.

TANCOCK. Possibly Dancock, a diminutive of Daniel.

TANCRED. " At a very early period, and probably not long after the Conquest, the ancestors of this family were seated at Boroughbridge (co. York), which appears to have been ever since one of the residences of the house of Tancred." Shirley's Noble and Gentle Men. The surname is clearly Norman, being derived from the personal name Tancredus.

TANFIELD. Places in cos. Durham, York, &c.

TANKARD. A vulgar corruption, as old as the XIII. cent., of the high-sounding, chivalrous, Tancred. H.R.

TANKERVILLE. An ancient barony in the arrondissement of Havre in Normandy, called in records *Tancredi villa,* " the vill of Tancred," and, at the present day, Tancarville. The ancient barons of Tancarville were hereditary chamberlains to the Dukes of Normandy. The progenitor of this noble house, so illustrious both in Normandy and England, was Ralph de Tancarville, founder of the great abbey of St. Georges de Bocherville, and chamberlain and preceptor of William the Conqueror, who in a charter, preserved by Mabillon, calls him " Radulphus, meus magister, aulæque et cameræ princeps." See Dawson Turner's Normandy, ii. 4.

TANN. A contraction of St. Anne. So Tooley from St. Olave. At Fersfield, co. Norfolk, there is a St. Anne's Well, which is vulgarly known as Tann's Well. Blomefield's Norf. i. 70.

TANNER. A well-known occupation. In H.R. Tannour, Le Tannur, Tannator, Le Tanur, &c.

TANSLEY. A township in co. Derby.

TANSWELL. The family can trace only to 1588, in the county of Dorset. From a James Tanswell born at Buckland-Newton in that shire, descend the Tanswells, the Taswells, and the Tazewells of England and of Virginia, U.S. There is a faint tradition of a French extraction, but I think the name is clearly of English origin. Tanswell appears to be a contraction of St. Anne's Well. St. Anne was a great patroness of wells, and there are many in different parts of England which bear her name. See under Tann. Other orthographies of the name are Tarzwell, Tarswell, Tasewell, &c.

TANTON. Taunton, co. Somerset.

TAPLADY. See Lady.

TAPLEY. Perhaps Taplow, co. Bucks, or Tarporley, co. Chester.

TAPLIN. See Thomas.

TAPPENDEN. An ancient Kentish family, long resident at Sittingbourne, but originally of Tappenden, otherwise Toppenden, in the parish of Smarden. Hasted's Kent, vii. 479.

TAPPER. The masculine of Tapster, which see. In the N. of England an innkeeper is still so designated. Le Tapper. H.R.

TAPSTER. Originally the woman (see *ster*)—afterwards any person, who had the care of the tap in an inn. A Shakspearean word.

TARBOTTON. (Corruptly Tarbottom.) Probably Tarbolton, a parish in Ayrshire.

TARBOX. See Torbock.

TARDY. An ancient French family, who embracing the doctrines of the Reformation, suffered much persecution, both in the XVI. and XVII. centuries. They resided for many generations at La Tremblade, in the province of Santonge. The first settler in Ireland was Monsieur Elie Tardy, who took up his residence at Dublin about 1760. B.L.G.

TARES. Analogous to Peascod. It may be regarded as the English equivalent of Cicero. Vetch is also an English surname.

TARGETT. One of the numerous surnames borrowed from Archery.

TARLETON. A chapelry in Lancashire, parish of Croston.

TARRANT. Several places in Dorsetshire are so called.

TARRING. Two parishes in Sussex are so called.

TARSWELL. The same as Tanswell.

TARZWELL. See Tanswell.

TASEWELL. See Tanswell.

TASH. Said to be a contraction of At Ash, from residence near a remarkable tree of that kind. So Trill, Teeth, &c.

TASKER. A labourer who receives his wages in kind for a certain task. Jamieson. In England, a thrasher or a reaper. In the Nominale MS. XV. cent. it is rendered *triturator*. Halliw. Tasker and Le Taskur. H.R.

TASMAN. O. Dutch, *tas*, a purse or pouch, and *man*. The great navigator of the Southern Ocean so called, gave his name to Tasmania.

TASSELL. A contraction of Tattersal?

TATE. Tata, an A-Sax. personal name. See also Tait.

TATESHALL. Now Tattershall, co. Lincoln. William the Conqueror bestowed this and other lands upon one of his followers called Eudo, from whom descended Robert de Tateshall, who built Tattershall castle, and whose son was created Baron Tateshall in 1295.

TATHAM. A parish in co. Lancaster.

TATTEN. A corruption of Tatton.

TATTERSALL. See Tateshall.

TATTERSHALL. See Tateshall.

TATNELL. Probably Tattenhall, a parish in co. Chester.

TATTON. A township in Cheshire, which was the residence of this family in the XII. century.

TATUM. See Tatham, of which it is a phonetic form.

TAUNTON. A town in Somersetshire. B.L.G. traces the Tauntons of Oxfordshire to John de Tantone, who had two sons: Richard, the progenitor of the family, and John, who was abbot of Glastonbury, 2. Edward I.

TAVERNER. TAVENER. The keeper of a tavern or inn. H.R. Le Taverner.

> "Ryght as off a *tavernere*,
> The greene busche that hangeth out,
> Is a sygne, it is no dowte,
> Outward ffolkys ffor to telle,
> That within is wyne to selle."
> *MS. Cott. Tib. A. vii.*

TAWELL. Local: "the well, or source, of the Tay?"

TAWSE. In Scotland, a whip, a schoolmaster's ferula, or any other instrument of correction—but wherefore a surname?

TAYLEURE. A 'genteel' form of Taylor. See anecdote in Eng. Surn.

TAYLOE. An American refinement upon Taylor. Folks of Shields.

TAYLOR. TAYLER. The well-known trade—*sartor*. The commonness of the occupation has led to the frequency of the surname, which, according to the XVI. Report of the Regist. Gen., 1856, stands fourth in the list of the most common family names in England and Wales, giving precedence only to Smith, Jones, and Williams. Allowing for the great preponderance of the Joneses and Williamses in Wales, where surnames are so few, Taylor may fairly challenge the right of standing next to Smith for numerosity *in England*, the state of the poll for births, deaths, and marriages, within a given short period, being—

> For Smith, 33,557.
> For Taylor, 16,775.

A really ancient and respectable family of Taylor, who apparently trace to Shadochurst, co. Kent, and the middle of the XIV. century, absurdly attempt to deduce themselves, though with more than one *hiatus valdè deflendus*, from "Baron Taillefer, who accompanied William the Conqueror in his invasion of Great Britain!" B.L.G. The H.R. forms are Le Taylir, Le Tayller, Le Tayllour, Le Tayllur, Taylour, Taylur, &c.; and there is one Alicia la Taylurese.

TEAR. The Gaelic Mac Tear, deprived of its prefix.

TEALE. 1. Possibly from the bird, like Gander, Swan, &c. 2. The Scottish *teil*, a busy-body; a mean fellow. Jamieson. The word in this sense is sometimes written *teal*. 3. *Teil*, the birch tree. Halliwell.

TEASDALE. See Teesdale.

TEBUTT. A possible corruption of Theobald. H.R. Tebbolt, Tebawd, &c.

TEDD. A nursename of Edward.

TEDNAMBURY. A corruption of St. Edmund's Bury, co. Suffolk. See Chauncey's Hertfordshire, p. 353.

TEED. Perhaps a nickname of Edward, more commonly pronounced Ted.

TEESDALE. Doubtless from the 'dale' or valley of the Tees, co. Durham. Comp. Surtees.

TEETH. May be a sobriquet, like the Roman Dentatus, but is more likely a contraction of At Heath, from residence upon one.

TEGG. A sheep in its second year. Halliwell quotes from Florio—"A *teg* or sheepe with a little head, and wooll under its belly." The word is also applied by Palsgrave to a young deer in its second year. Comp. Prickett.

TELFER. Fr. *taille-fer*. A name of great antiquity. The exploits of the noble jouglere Taillefer at the battle of Hastings are well-known. William, Count of Angoulesme, in a battle against the Northmen, engaged their king Storis, and with one stroke of his sword *Durissima*, forged by the great Wayland Smith, cut in two his body and cuirass. Hence he acquired the

sobriquet of Taillefer, or "*cut iron*." In the XVI. cent. the name in Scotland was written Tailzefer.

TELFORD. I find no locality so called. Thomas Telford, the great engineer, used to say—"When I was ignorant of Latin, I did not suspect that Telfer, my true name, might be translated, "I bear arms," [*Tela fero?*] and, thinking it unmeaning, adopted Telford." See Telfer.

TELLIER. O. Fr. *telier*, a linen-weaver. Nic. le Tellier and his family, Protestants from Dieppe, landed at Rye in 1572. Lansd. MSS. 15. 70.

TELLWRIGHT. The patriarch of this name probably followed the trade of the great Apostol. *Teld* is the A-Sax. for a tent or tabernacle, and *teldwyrhta* for a tent maker. It frequently occurs in medieval English.

> "Alle that stode on ilk a syde
> Had joye to see Clement ryde
> Byfore the Sowdan's *telde*."
> *MS. Lincoln, A. i. 17. (Halliwell).*

TEMES. An old spelling of the river Thames.

TEMPERLEY. The same as Timperley.

TEMPEST. This family, who are doubtless of Norman origin, are traced to Roger Tempest, temp. Henry I., who held three carucates and two oxgangs of land in the Shipton Fee, co. York. The name is difficult to account for: it may have reference to some storm which the first bearer encountered. Perhaps Cotgrave's definition of *tempesté* may help us to its real import: "stormed, blustered, tossed, vexed: hurried, harried, *taken or overtaken with, broken or overthrowne by, a tempest*."

TEMPLAR. See Temple.

TEMPLE. The preceptories or priories of the Knights-Templars were often called Temples, as Temple-Bruer, Temple-Newsham, &c., and even manorial residences and estates, belonging to them, obtained the same dignified appellation. The tenant or bailiff of such a property was sometimes known by the surname At-Temple, or Templeman; for example at Sompting, co. Sussex, where this order possessed lands, Peter at Temple is named in the Nona Return of 1341. In the previous century, De Temple, Du Temple, Le Templer, &c., occur in H.R.

"This family of Temple are said to be descended from Leofric, Earl of Chester, who died in 1057, leaving issue Algar, Earl of Mercia and the East Angles, and a son Henry, who, in the reign of Henry I., obtained from Robert, Earl of Leicester, a grant of the manor of Temple, co. Leicester, from whence his descendants assumed their name." Courthope's Debrett.

TEMPLEMAN. See Temple. Le Templeman. H.R.

TEMPLER. Another form of Templeman, or At Temple.

TEMPLETON. A parish in Devon, and a village in Pembrokeshire.

TEN. Ferguson considers this name identical with the O. Germ. Tenno, and the mod. Germ. Tanno.

TENDER. An attendant. In the Eastern Counties a waiter at an inn is so called.

TENISON. According to D'Alton's History of Ireland, quoted in B.L.G., the Tenysons or Tenisons are of English extraction, and the name is supposed to be the same as Tynesende in the H.R. of Oxfordshire.

TENNANT. TENNENT. A tenant—one who holds lands under another.

TENNELL. An O. Germ. personal name, Tenil. Ferguson.

TENNYSON. See Tenison.

TEPPER. See Tipper.

TERRELL. See Tyrrel.

TERN. A *tern*, or *tarn*, is a small lake.

TERREWEST. ? Fr. *terre*, and *ouest*, the western land or estate.

TERRY. Not 'the tearful one' as some etymologists have it, but a corruption of Theodoric, the personal name, like the Fr. Thierry. In H.R. Terri and Terry are without prefix.

TESTAR. See Tester.

TESTER. This word has several distinct meanings. As a surname it is probably derived from the baptismal Testard, which is found in a Pipe Roll of the year 1131. Hozier, Ann. de la France, deduces it from Guillaume "Teste-hardie," Duke of Burgundy, early in the XI. century. Testard. H.R.

TESTIMONY. A XIII. century surname. Testimonie. H.R.

TEVERSHAM. A parish in Cambridgeshire.

TEWKESBURY. A town in co. Gloucester.

THACKER. A provincialism for Thatcher. It is used in this sense by various old writers. "The original meaning of the word 'thack' is straw or rushes, our Saxon ancestors using no other covering for their houses. Afterwards it was extended to slate and tiles; and he who covered a building, either with these or the more ancient materials, was called a *thacker* or thatcher." Hallamshire Glossary, p. 162.

THACKERAY. From Thacker; so Vicary from Vicar.

THACKERY. THACKWRAY. See Thackeray.

THACKWELL. Clearly local, and may, I think, be a contraction of "At the Oak Well," (A-Sax. *ac*, oak,) from the residence of the original bearer of the surname.

THAIN. THAINE. "A *thane* was (in like manner as the earl) not probably a title of dignity, but of service, so called in the Saxon of *thenian (servire,)* and in Latin *minister*, à *ministrando*." Spelman. The A-Sax. *Thegn* is equivalent to a servant or servitor. Three London traders bear this ancient and honourable name. H.R. Le Theyn.

THAMPSETT. See Thomas.

THANKFUL. A sobriquet applied to one who made great show of gratitude? This was a common baptismal name in Puritan times.

THARP. In some districts Thorpe is so corrupted; and in Hampshire persons named Sibthorp are called Tharp.

THATCHER. The occupation. See under Thacker. In the Hundred Rolls, Le Thechare, Thacchere; also the Norm. French forms, Le Coverur, Le Covurtur, &c.

THEARLE. Perhaps a mis-spelling of Thorold.

THELWALL. A chapelry and township in Cheshire.

THELLUSSON. Lord Rendlesham's family are of noble French extraction, and traced to 1328, when Frederick de Thellusson, called Baron St. Saphorin, from his estate near Lyons, accompanied Philip VI. of France into Flanders. His descendants remained in France until the massacre of St. Bartholomew, 1572, when they took refuge at Geneva, from whence, about the middle of the last century, came Peter Thellusson, who, in 1797, made that monstrous will which has enriched the lawyers and astonished Christendom.

THEOBALD. The personal name; from which have also arisen the following surnames: Theobalds, Tibbald, Tipple, Tipkins, Tippet, Tippets, Tibbats, Tibbets, Tibbs, Tubb, Tubbs, Tubby.

THEOBALDS. See Theobald.

THEODORE. The well-known personal name.

THEROULDE. A French refugee family. The name is identical with Thorold.

THESIGER. The family came from Dresden about a century since. The orthography has been much altered.

THICK. Refers, probably, to physical structure. See Tooke.

THICKBROOM. Probably local: "a place where the broom-plant flourishes abundantly." De Tikebrom. H.R., co. Suffolk.

THICKE. See under Tooke.

THICKNESSE. *Nese*, or *nesse*, is O. Eng. for nose, from A-Sax. *nese*; and this name therefore probably refers to the *thick nose* of the original bearer.

THIERRY. This is the modern French form of Theodoric, and the immediate ancestor of the common family name Terry.

Thiery has become naturalized among us. In the chancel of Hinton-Blewett, co. Somerset, is an inscription commemorative of several generations of a family bearing it. It begins thus : " In memory of Louis Thiery, who was born in France, and (being persecuted for true religion) came over to this free and happy kingdom about the year of our Lord 1650, and was buried under this stone about the year 1680," On a tombstone in the church-yard, however, his death his fixed in the year 1665. From a communication to Notes and Queries, vol. XI., by Rev. C. W. Bingham, who adds : " In my boyhood, and probably it may still be so, there were some of the family who were farmers, and, I think, small proprietors, though their name was universally corrupted into *Carey*."

THILL. By crasis from " At the Hill."

THIMBLEBY. A parish in Lincolnshire, and a township in Yorkshire.

THIN. See Thynne.

THIRKLE. A contraction of Thurkettle.

THIRTELL. See Thurtell.

THIRLWALL. THIRLEWALL. Thirlewall Castle, now a picturesque ruin in Northumberland, near Gilsland Spa, was the residence of the family in early times. Thirlwall is on, and derives its name from, the celebrated Roman Wall, which at this point was *thirled* or bored through (A-Sax. *thyrlian*). Some have imagined that the barrier was here breached, but it seems more probable that the *thirl* was designedly and originally in the construction of the wall, for the passage of the impetuous little river Tipple. A gentleman of this family gave evidence in the celebrated Scrope and Grosvenor controversy, about the right of bearing the coat, Azure, a bend Or, he being, as he averred, the son of a Thirlewall who had attained the great age of seven score and five years! See Nicolas' Scrope and Grosvenor Cont., ii. 427.

THIRLWAY. A modification of Thirlwall.

THISTLE. Probably borrowed from heraldry, like Rose, Lis, &c.

THISELTON. Thistleton, a parish in Rutlandshire.

THISTLETHWAITE. See Thwaite.

THISTLEWOOD. Local : " the wood abounding with thistles."

THOM. See Thomas.

THOMAS. The Christian name. Though not used here prior to the Norm. Conquest, this has become one of the commonest of baptismal appellatives and surnames. It has also been a most abundant source of derivatives and nicknames, represented in our family nomenclature by Thomason, Thomerson, Thomson, Thompson, Tompson, Thom, Thoms, Toms, Thomaset,

Thomsett, Tomset, Tompsett, Tomkin, Tompkins, Tomkinson, Thompkisson, Thomlin, Tomlin, Tomlins, Thomlinson, Tomlinson. In the North, A commonly replaces O, and hence Thampsett, Tampsett, Tamlyn, Tamplin, and probably Taplin.

Some of the Welsh families of Thomas are of antiquity, though the surname is, in all cases, of comparatively recent assumption : e. g. : THOMAS of Gellywernen, co. Carmarthen, descends from Sir Hugh Treherne, one of the Welsh knights who accompanied the Black Prince to the battle of Poictiers : some members of this family have recently exchanged the name for Treherne. THOMAS of Llwyn Madoc, co. Brecknock, traces his pedigree up to that prolific source of noble and gentle blood, Elystan Glodrydd, Prince of Fferllys ; and THOMAS of Welfield, co. Radnor, springs from the same princely origin.

THOMASETT. See Thomas.

THOMASON. See Thomas.

THOMERSON. See Thomas.

THOMLIN. See Thomas.

THOMLINSON. See Thomas.

THOMPKISSON. See Thomas.

THOMPSON. See Thomas. There are, however, parishes in cos. Norfolk and Dorset so called. Almost 300 London traders bear this name, which, according to the Registrar-General, stands twenty-first in the roll of common surnames, being rarer than Edwards, and more common than White. See Prelim. Dissertation.

THOMS. See Thomas.

THOMSETT. See Thomas.

THOMSON. See Thomas.

THORBURNE. See Thurbarn.

THORESBY. North and South Thoresby are parishes in Lincolnshire. The family claim a Saxon origin, being derived from Gospatrick, lord of Thoresby, who was living at the time of the Conquest.

☞ THORNE. A component syllable of numerous local surnames, implying that thorn trees flourished in the localities ; as Silverthorne, Thorncroft, Hawthorne, Thornhill, Thornbury, Thornford, Thornwick, &c.
    Some of these may, however, be compounds of Thorne, a personal name. See next Article, 2.

THORN. THORNE. Parishes and places in cos. York, Somerset, and Northumberland. There are also many trivial localities so called, in many counties. In A-Sax. charters, thorn-trees frequently occur as boundary-marks, which from the great longevity of the tree is quite natural ; and the word enters into the composition of numerous place-names. In medieval writings the surname Thorn is latinized De Spineto, *spinetum* being equivalent to "a bushy place," or thicket of thorns and brambles, anglicè a *Spinney*, whence that surname. *

There have doubtless been several families of this name. The most important one were the Norman Thorns of Thorn-Falcon, and Thorn St. Margaret, in Somersetshire, who held under Drogo, of the castle of Dunster, and gave lands to Taunton Priory. Domesd. From them seem to have branched off the Thorns of Devon, Yorkshire, Kent, Worcestershire, Gloucestershire, Northamptonshire, &c. At Minster, in the Isle of Thanet, co. Kent, one of the ancient abodes of the family, on a tomb of one of the female members, of about the date of Edw. I., is this legend:—

" ICI GIST EDILE DE THORNE, QUE FUST D'NA DEL ESPINA."

(Here lies Edila de Thorne, who was the Lady of the Thorne.) Hasted.

In a list of persons who gave lands and *slaves* to Meaux Abbey, co. York (Cott. MS. Vitell, Cvj, and referring to *circ.* A.D. 1300) is this entry: "Walter, son of Peter de Spineto (Thorn) gave us, with his own body to be buried in our house, one ox-gang of land at Hornsburton, and Henry, the son of Simon the tenant, and all his belongings."—" Walterus filius Petri de Spineto dedit nobis, cum corpore suo apud nos sepeliendo, unam bovatam terre in Hornsburtone, et Henricum filium Symonis ipsam tenentem cum sequela sua." The last who used the latinized name was Sir Guy de Spineto, lord of Coughton, whose heiress married Throgmorton. This personage was sometimes gallicized to Sir Guy de la Spine. John Thorne, abbot of Reading, a member of this family, who became historical from the fact of Henry VIII.'s having starved him into a good appetite, and charged him a hundred pounds for the operation, used the motto—

SÆPE CREAT PULCHRAS
ASPERA SPINA ROSAS.

His kinsmen, Robert and Nicholas, benefactors to Bristol, were painted by Holbein, and the corporation, in gratitude, placed over the picture of the latter the *unscriptural* legend: EX SPINIS UVAS COLLEGIMUS—" We have gathered grapes from *Thorns !*" The motto over Sir Robert, the father, is—

" Spina vocor, superest tribuatur gloria danti
Quæ bona pauperibus Spina dat esse Deo."

Inf. William Thorn, Esq., M.D.

2. Thorne is sometimes derived from an A-Sax. personal name. An individual called Simon, the son of Thorne, was lord of the manors of North Allerton and Todwick (Elreton and Todeswick) in Yorkshire, at the time of the Conquest. These manors William seized, and gave them, together with Simon's daughters, in marriage to three of his followers—one of the young ladies being assigned to Humphrey, his

man-at-arms; another to Raoul, called Tortes-mains; and the third to an esquire, Guillaume de St. Paul. Thierry's Norm. Conq.

THORLEY. Parishes in Hertfordshire and Hampshire.

THORNBURY. Parishes and places in cos. Devon, Gloucester, Hereford, &c.

THORINGTON, THORRINGTON. Parishes in Suffolk and Essex.

THORNES. " The name is local, from Thornes in the parish of Shenstone, in the county of Stafford, where Robert, son of Roger de la Thorne, was resident early in the fourteenth century." Shirley's Noble and Gentle Men.

THORNEYCROFT. See Thornicroft.

THORNICROFT. An estate in the hundred of Macclesfield, co. Chester. Thornicroft Hall was the seat of the family for fully 500 years. See Ormerod's Cheshire.

THORNTHWAITE. Places in cos. York and Cumberland.

THORNHILL. A parish in Yorkshire. The family, who were there seated until the elder line ended in an heiress, 45. Edw. III., traced their descent from Gerneber, a noble Saxon, who possessed large tracts of land before the Conquest. B.L.G.

" Descended from the Thornhills of Thornhill, in the Peak of Derbyshire, where they were seated as early as the seventh of Edward I." Shirley's Noble and Gentle Men, (Thornhill of Stanton).

THORNTON. Parishes and places in cos. Bucks, Durham, Lancaster, Leicester, Lincoln, York, Chester, and Northumberland. Yorkshire abounds with places so called. Thorne appears to have been an old Anglo-Saxon personal name ; and hence Thornton may mean the homestead of Thorne.

THORNWELL. Thornville, a township in co. York.

THOROLD. A Teutonic personal name of great antiquity, which has given rise to a family name very widely spread, and much varied in spelling and pronunciation, the principal forms being Thorold, Turrold, Tyrell, Torel, Turrell, Tourelle, Torill, Tourle, Turl, &c., &c., &c. It comes to us from Normandy, where Turold was one of the preceptors of William the Conqueror, and his Grand-Constable at the time of the Conquest. The name of TUROLD occurs upon the Bayeux Tapestry, designating one of the ambassadors dispatched by the Norman Duke to Guy, Earl of Ponthieu, and it is supposed that the Turold there represented was the Grand-Constable. Dawson Turner's Tour in Normandy, ii. 104. This celebrated man gave his name to the town of which he was lord and founder, viz., Burgus Thoroldi, now Bourgtheroude, a few miles S.W. of Rouen. In Domesday, we find a Gilbert filius Turoldi among the tenants in chief of the counties of Wor-

---

* It appears that, in some counties, a *spinney* means any rough growth, however extensive, of underwood and bushes of whatever kind; but there can be no doubt that the word originally had the signification here attributed to it.

cester, Hereford, Cambridge, and Warwick; while an Ilbert filius Turoldi, held a like position in the second named shire. Whether these were sons of the Grand-Constable does not appear. This seems probable, though as there are many tenants called Turold in that record, it is not positively certain. Under Essex, appears one Walterus Tirelde, who is by some supposed to be the Walter Tirel who shot Rufus. Morant's Essex, i. 244.

But Thorold was also a distinguished name among the Old Norse and the Anglo-Saxons. Thorold of Buckenhale was sheriff of Lincolnshire in 1051. See Eng. Surn. i. 27. The Thorolds of Marston, in this shire, baronets, claim descent from that personage. For this Mr. Shirley thinks there is no evidence or authority, although he admits the " very great antiquity " of the family, dating to the reign of Henry I. Noble and Gentle Men.

THOROUGHGOOD. Not so good as it seems, however ; for it has no reference to moral excellence. Turgod is a Domesday baptismal appellation, and Thurgood a Danish name, which has probably been improved (?) to this orthography. See however, Thorowgood.

THOROWGOOD. From the Encyclop. Herald. it appears that a family of Thorowgood, resident at a place so called in Hertfordshire, obtained a grant of arms so recently as the last century.

THORP. See Thorpe. The Thorps of Ryton, co. Durham, are said to be descended from Robert Thorpe, of Thorpe, near Wellwyke, in Holderness, who flourished in the reign of King John. B.L.G.

☞ THORPE. THORP. A common local surname, there being numerous parishes in England so designated, besides an infinite number of smaller districts. As a *termination* it is likewise very common, as in Althorpe, Sibthorpe, Calthorpe, Westhorpe. A-Sax. and old Danish, *thorp*. Germ. *dorf*. Worsaae defines it as " a collection of houses separated from some principal estate—a village." It was in use, as an English word, in the XVI. century. An old translation of Fortescue, De Leg. Ang. speaks of England being " so filled and replenished with landed menne, that therein so small a *thorpe* cannot be found wherein dwelleth not a knight, or an esquire, or such a householder as is called a franklein." THROP is a corrupted form, whence the surnames Milthrop, Winthropp, &c.

THOUSANDPOUND. A thirteenth-century surname. The French have Centlivre (' hundred pounds ')—the Dutch Hondertmark (' hundred marks '), worth five of the Twentimarc of the H.R.; and at New York there is a Mr. Milledollar whom Dixon estimates at a thousand dollars ($1000)—but that is of course his *nominal* value only.

THRASHER. The occupation.

THREDDER. A spinner of thread. Analogous to Roper, Corder, &c.

THRELKELD. A chapelry in Greystoke parish, co. Cumberland, in which county the De Threlkelds flourished in the XIV. century, and probably earlier.

THRESHER. See Thrasher.

THREXTON. A village in Norfolk. The common people of that county have some difficulty in pronouning the *th*, and hence this local surname is frequently corrupted to Trackson and even to Traction !

THROCKMORTON. An estate in the parish of Fladbury, co. Worcester, where John de Trockemerton, the supposed ancestor of the family, was living about the year 1200. From this John descended, through many generations, another John Throkmerton, who, according to Leland, was " the first setter up of his name to any worship in Throkmerton village, the which was at that tyme neither of his inheritance or purchase, but as a thing taken of the sete (see) of Wicestre in farm; bycause [wherefore] he bore the name of the lordeship and village." He became undertreasurer of England about temp. Henry V. Shirley's Noble and Gentle Men.

☞ THROP. A termination—the same as THORPE, which see.

THROSSEL. The throstle, a bird.

THROWER. The masculine of *throwster*, a woman that throws or winds silk or thread. A-Sax. *thràwan*, to wind or twist.

THRUPP. A-Sax. *throp*. Primarily, a meeting of cross-ways, afterwards a village, because villages usually spring up in such spots. See *Thorpe*. In Wright and Halliwell's " Reliquiæ Antiquæ," vol. ii. 68, we read :

> " There stode a *thrope* of site delitable,
> In whiche that pore folke of that village
> Hadden here bestis and here herborage."

The village of Thorpe in Oxfordshire is pronounced Thrupp by the country people.

THRUSH. The bird.

THUNDER. An alias of Thor, the Jupiter-Tonans of Northern mythology, in A-Sax. *Thuner*, *Thunor*, or *Thunder;* whence our day of the week ' Thunresdaeg,' now contracted to Thursday. The name of the god became a personal name of men ; e. g. Roger of Windover, under A.D. 654, mentions an Anglo-Saxon called Thuner, whom he styles a " limb of the devil." Ferguson. On the South Downs near Brighton is a tumulus traditionally known as Thunder's Barrow, probably the grave of a Teutonic chieftain. Thunder's Hill, at Chiddingly, co. Sussex, derives its name from a family who dwelt there in the XVII. century.

THURBARN. THURBERN. Thurbernus, Thurbern, Turbernus, Turbern, and numerous other modifications, are found in Domesday, generally in association with tenants who had held prior to the Conquest. It appears to be derived from the Northern mythology, and to signify 'the son of Thor, or of the Thunderer.'

THURGAR. In Essex, the same as Thurgood, or Thoroughgood.

THURGOOD. See Thoroughgood.

THURKETTLE. An ancient Scandinavian name, which Grimm fancifully derives from the famous *kettle*, that *Thor* captured from Hymir, the giant, as a brewing-pot for the gods!

THURLBY. Parishes, &c., in co. Lincoln.

THURLOW. Great and Little Thurlow are parishes in Suffolk. Lord Thurlow's family are traced to the adjoining county of Norfolk, at the beginning of the XV. century.

THURNELL. The same as Thornhill.

THURNHAM. A township in co. Lancaster.

THURSBY. See Thoresby.

THURSDAY. See TIMES AND SEASONS.

THURSFIELD. A chapelry in Staffordshire.

THURSTON. 1. A parish in Suffolk. 2. In some cases, perhaps, from the Teutonic name Turstin, which is found in Domesday as the designation of persons both Norman and Saxon. One Turstanus is there described as ' machinator '—probably a military engineer.

THURTELL. A corruption of Thurkettle.

☞ **THWAITE.** A variety of opinions as to the meaning of this termination has been entertained. In Eng. Surn. I defined it, upon the authority of an intelligent correspondent, as " land reclaimed from a wood or forest;" while "a rough marshy ground," and "a pasture," were also suggested. According to Verstegan the pluralized variation, Thwaytes, signifies a feller of wood. A correspondent of the Gentleman's Magazine, August, 1856, makes it " a set of farm buildings." I think the origin of the word must be looked for in the A-Sax. verb *thweotan*, to cut down, and that it means an open space cleared in a forest. I find this opinion supported by Halliwell, who defines it as "land which was once covered with wood, brought into pasture or tillage." It is, therefore, nearly or quite synonymous with *Royd*, which see. The prefix seems sometimes to refer to the name of the settler who effected the clearing, as in Adamthwaite, Simonthwaite, Godderthwaite; sometimes to the trees, &c., cleared, as in Thornthwaite, Linethwaite, Hathornthwaite, Brackenthwaite, (thorns, limes, hawthorns, brakes or fern); sometimes to the size or situation of the *assart*, as in Micklethwaite, Lowthwaite, Cross-

thwaite; and sometimes to less intelligible causes. The termination prevails in the counties of Cumberland, Westmoreland, and North Lancashire. The following surnames, of which it is a component syllable, are still found in that part of England:—

Adamthwaite	Hathornthwaite
Applethwaite	Husthwaite
whence	Huthwaite
Applewhite	Lewthwaite
Brackenthwaite	Linethwaite
Brathwaite	Lowthwaite
Blathwaite	Micklethwaite
Branthwaite	Murthwaite
Brewthwaite	Orthwaite
Cornthwaite	Satterthwaite
Copperthwaite	Simonthwaite
whence	Stanthwaite
Copperwheat	Thackthwaite
Cowperthwaite	Thistlethwaite
Crossthwaite	Thornthwaite
Dowthwaite	Waberthwaite
Godderthwaite	

Some of the localities can be identified, but for the most part the surnames have survived the local designations from which they were adopted.

THWAITES. See Thwaite.

THWAYTES. See Thwaite.

THYNNE. The family of Thynne are a branch of the ancient house of Botfield or Botevile. The origin of this surname is very singular. About the reign of Edward IV. the elder branch of the Boteviles or Botfields of Stretton in Shropshire, where the family had flourished from the XIII. century, began, for some unexplained reason, to write themselves De le Inn, De la Inne, and Of the Inne; and this last form, in a generation or two, settled down into Thynne. Mr. Ralph Bigland, Somerset Herald, affirms that the alias originated with John de Botevile, who resided at one of the Inns of Court, and from thence was named John of th' Inne, otherwise Thynne. But the historian of the family remarks, that there is no evidence that the person referred to ever dwelt at any of the inns of court, though it is certain that " he lived in the family house at Church-Stretton, and that he was familiarly known as John o' th'Inne, which, abbreviated, became Thynne, though John de la Inne de Botfelde, was his usual appellation." It appears that this mansion was anciently called The Inn, and hence the name. From this elder branch of the Botfeldes sprang the Thynnes (Marquis of Bath) and from the younger branch came the family of Botfield. See Stemmata Botevilliana. By Beriah Botfield, Esq., M.P., &c. London. 4to. 1858.

The name of Thynne had, however, a much more ancient existence. The Rotul. Hund. mention one Thomas Thynne, under the hundred of Norton, co. Northampton, as living temp. Henry III. (vol. ii. p. 12.) The surname in this instance probably related to meagreness of person.

TIBBALD. See Theobald.

TIBBATS. TIBBETS. See Theobald.

TIBBS. See Theobald.

TIBETOT. The baronial family traced to the first year of Henry III. to Henry de Tibetot. They were doubtless of Norman extraction, but I do not find any place so called on the map of Normandy.

TICEHURST. A parish in Sussex, formerly Tyshurst.

TICHBORNE. Tichbourne in Hampshire, has, from a period of unknown antiquity, probably before the Conquest, been in the possession of a family who derived their name from it. They have a remarkable tradition, that a female ancestor, Mabella de Lymerston, wife of Sir Roger de T., in the XII. century, obtained from her husband as much land as she could creep round on hands and knees while a firebrand continued burning. She thus encircled several acres, with the annual value of which she founded a *dole* of 1,900 loaves. This continued to be delivered on Lady-day, till the end of the last century, when a commutation was made, and the amount is now paid in money to the poor of the parish. The land so obtained is still known by the name of the " Crawles!" An ancient prophecy affirms, that the fortunes of this venerable family will fail, should any of the lady Mabel's posterity attempt to divert the charity.

TICHBOURNE. See Tichborne.

TICKELL. TICKLE. Probably Tickhill, a town and parish in Yorkshire.

TICKLEPENNY. A place near Grimsby, co. Lincoln.

TICKNOR. TICKNER. Dutch *teekenaar*, a drawer or designer. Ferguson.

TIDCOMBE. A parish in Wiltshire.

TIDD. A Magister Thomas de Tid occurs in the H.R. of Cambridgeshire, temp. Edward I. The name is therefore local.

TIDEY. See Tidy.

TIDMARSH. A parish in Berkshire.

TIDSWELL. Tideswell, a parish in Derbyshire. A De Tideswell in that county, is found in H.R.

TIDY. In the absence of any more recondite etymology, I presume that this name, and Tidyman, refer to neatness of dress in the original bearers.

TIDYMAN. See Tidy.

TIERNEY. St. Tigernath, or Tierney, was an Irish saint of the sixth century, and third bishop of Clogher.

TIFFANY. See Stephen.

TIFFIN. See Stephen.

TIGAR. The same as Tiger.

TIGER. Probably an inn or trader's sign.

TIGHE. 1. Apparently a personal and saintly name. There is a manor of Saint Tygh, in Cuckfield, co. Sussex.
2. Sir B. Burke says, that the name was derived from a village so called in Rutlandshire, in the immediate vicinity of which, at Carlby, co. Lincoln, the ancestors of Tighe of Woodstock, co. Kilkenny, were long seated. B.L.G.

TILBURY. Three parishes in Essex bear this name.

TILDESLEY. A chapelry in Lancashire, at an early period the residence of the family. See Ormerod's Miscel. Palat. p. 26.

TILEMAN. The same as Tiler, or as Tillman. Tileman. H.R.

TILER. The occupation—a layer of tiles. Le Tilere. H.R.

TILLEY. 1. Tilly is a town or village in the department of Calvados in Normandy; and there is a second place so called in the department of Eure. Tilly, Tillé. Hund. Rolls. 2. A ' nursename ' of William.

TILLIE. See Tilley.

TILLY. See Tilley.

TILLMAN. A husbandman. " Because there were so fewe *tylmen*, the erde lay untilled." Capgrave's Chron. sub A.D. 1349.

TILLOT. TILLOTSON. See William.

TILL. See William. Sometimes perhaps a contraction of At-Hill.

TILNEY. Three parishes in Norfolk bear this name.

TILSON. See William.

TIM. A nickname of Timothy.

TIMBERLAKE. I cannot agree with Mr. Talbot (See Engl. Etym.) that this name is a mistake for " timber-leg," a man with a wooden leg ! It is clearly of the local class, and the final syllable is the same as that in Hoylake, Shiplake, &c.

TIMBS. See Timothy. I fear that my brother F.S.A., who knows so many things " not generally known," will object to this etymology, but it is the best I can do for him.

TIMBURY. Probably the same as Timsbury, parishes in cos. Somerset and Southampton.

TIMES. Probably the same as Tims, a diminutive of Timothy.

☞ TIMES AND SEASONS. Among the multifarious designations which have a place in our family nomenclature, there are few, which if taken literally, it would be so difficult to account for, as those that are identical with the names of the seasons of the year, months, and other parts of time. In this article, however, I shall attempt to explain many of these by showing their probable derivation from other sources. To begin, we have Spring, Summer, and Winter,—but no Autumn. In Eng. Surn., i. 216, I have suggested that Fall, (the name given to that season in America and in some of our provincial dialects,) may be the missing correlative; but on further reflection, I am convinced that the four surnames, Spring, Summer, Fall, Winter, have nothing to do with the periods which they seem to represent. Spring is of the same class as Wells, La Fontaine, &c.—source, *origo*. Summer is a corruption either of Somner, an officer in the ecclesiastical courts, or Sommer, a German personal name. Fall is probably the northern *fald* or *fauld*, an enclosure; while Winter is a personal A-Saxon name, rendered somewhat familiar as the designation of one of the companions of "Hereward the Saxon." Ferguson, following Grimm, supposes that Summer and Winter are derived from personifications of the two seasons in Northern mythology.

Such names as Christmas, with its kindred Yule and Noel; Easter, with its congenerous Paschall, Pask, and Pash; Pentecost; Middlemis (for Michaelmas;) and Sumption (for Assumption,) may have been conferred, in the first instance, upon infants born at those respective festivals, and may have grown afterwards, according to the practice of medieval times, into Surnames. The same origin may be attributed to surnames borrowed from the days of the week—Sunday, Monday or Munday, Thursday, Friday, Saturday—but will hardly apply to those that look like the denominations of months, as June, July, January, March, May, August, which are, in their respective places, shown to be derived from totally different sources. (See Supplement.)

A third group of surnames of similar *appearance*—Day, Weekes, Mattin and Dawn, Evening and Vesper, Noone and Morrow—may here be noticed. Day is explained in its proper place, and has no connection with *dies*. Neither has Weekes anything in common with *hebdomada*. Mattin may be either a corruption of Martin, or a derivative of Matthew; and Dawn is perhaps Daunay somewhat curtailed of its proportions, or a mispronunciation of Dorne, a Gloucestershire hamlet. Evening and Vesper are not so easily disposed of, though the former from its termination has a 'local' appearance, while the latter may possibly be the name of some forgotten trade or occupation. Noone I give up in despair; but Morrow is probably the Celtic patronymic Mac-Morough, deprived of its Mac. Upon the whole, I feel that this group of family names is the most difficult that I have had to deal with. I have doubtless fallen into misapprehensions; yet I am convinced that no amount of ingenuity or research could satisfactorily

elucidate it. See Eng. Surn., i. 216, et seq.

TIMESLOW. Timeslow occurs in the XIV. century, and in the XIX. It is probably local.

TIMM. TIMMS. See Timothy.

TIMMINGS. See Timothy.

TIMMINS. A diminutive of Timothy.

TIMOTHY. The baptismal name, whence the derivatives Timm, Tims, Timms, Timbs, Timmings, Timson, Timpson, Timpkins.

TIMPERLEY. A township in Cheshire.

TIMPKINS. See Timothy.

TIMPSON. The son of Timothy.

TIMSON. See Timothy.

TINDAL. TINDALL. See Tindale.

TINDALE. An extensive ward or district of Northumberland, which includes the Dale of the Tyne. The great Border family so called had their chief seat at Langley, near Haydon Bridge, and were styled in charters of temp. Henry II. Barons of Tynedale and Langley Castle.

TINKER. The occupation. Tincker H.R.

TINSLAY. See Tinsley.

TINSLEY. A chapelry in the parish of Rotherham, co. York.

TINSON. An abbreviated form of Stinson. Stephenson.

TINTEN. A place in the parish of St. Tudy, co. Cornwall, possessed by the family until the XIV. century, when the heiress married Carminow.

TIPKINS. Perhaps a diminutive of Theobald.

TIPLADY. See Lady.

TIPPLE. A corruption of Theobald.

TIPLER. In modern times a 'tippler' means a man who indulges freely in strong drink; and 'tipple,' as a substantive, is applied to any intoxicating beverage; thus in Poor Robin's Almanack—

"You may make pretty *tipple* if so you've a mind't,
With hops and with malt for a penny a pint;
And that's cheaper than you can buy."

Formerly however, a tippler was a seller, rather than a consumer, of such articles. In the records of the corporation of Seaford, co. Sussex, 36th Elizabeth, two townsmen are presented at the quarter sessions as common tipplers *(communes tipulatores,)* who have broken the assize of bread and beer, and are fined 2s. 6d. The same year one Symon Collingham, of Sefforde, is licensed as a Tipler, and enters into recognizances for the good governance of his house, and for abstaining from the use of unlawful games "duringe the time of his tiplinge." Similar entries occur in the records of Boston, in which town the surname of Typler was established in the earlier part of the

XVI. century. In the corporation archives of Warwick is preserved "The note of such Typlers and alehouse-kepers as the justices of peax have returned to me this Michilmas session. Thies underwriten were returnyd by Sir Thomas Lucy and Humphrey Peto, esquire." March, 15. Eliz. See Halliwell's Life of Shakspeare, p. 126. Tipeler, H.R.

TIPPER. To ' tip ' is an old word applied to the mounting of drinking-horns, cups, &c., with metals. Bailey. A *tipper* was therefore an artizan so employed. Its forms in the Hundred Rolls are Tippere and Le Tipper. The peculiar, but excellent, ale, called *tipper*, derives its name from its first brewer, Mr. Thomas Tipper, of Newhaven, co. Sussex, who flourished less than a century since. The peculiarity of this beverage arises from its being brewed from brackish water, which is obtainable from one well only ; and all attempts to imitate the flavour have hitherto failed.

TIPPET. TIPPETS. See Theobald.

TIPPING. The family of Tipping, anciently Typpynge, derived their surname from a vill or hamlet in the township of Clayton-le-Dale, co. Lancaster. The mansion called Tipping Hall was their seat temp. Edward III., and probably much earlier. B.L.G.

TIPSTAFF. " So named from the staff which they carry, tipp'd with silver. An officer who takes into custody such persons as are committed by a court of judicature." Bailey.

TIPTOFT. A corruption of Tibetot. It took place in the XV. century. Sir Paganus, a younger son of John, the second Lord Tibetot, had a son Sir John, who wrote himself Tiptoft, and was summoned to parliament as a Baron by Henry IV.

TIPTON. A parish in Staffordshire.

TIREBUCK. May relate to some feat of the chase, but is more likely a corruption of Torbock, a Lancashire local surname. See Torbock.

TIREMAN. See Tyerman.

TISDALE. See Teesdale.

TISDALL. A corruption of Teesdale, the dale or valley of the river Tees.

TITCHBOURNE. See Tichbourne.

TITCHENOR. A West Sussex family of this name reside in the neighbourhood of the village of Itchenor ; hence it is probable that the name was originally either At-Itchenor or D'Itchenor.

TITE. 1. The French orthography of Titus. 2. An Oxfordshire provincialism (now obsolete) for a spring of water. Halliwell.

TITHERIDGE. Until lately, this name, which was formerly connected with the county of Southampton, was spelt Tytheridge. From the termination *ridge* it is clearly local, but I cannot find the place.

TITLEY. A parish in Herefordshire.

TITTLE. Probably local, the last syllable being a corruption of *hill.*

TITUS. The personal name.

TOBIAS. The personal name.

TOBIN. See Tobyn.

TOBITT. The personal name.

TOBUTT. May be a corruption of Talbot. At Newdigate, co. Surrey, this name eventually became Tobit.

TOBY. The nickname of Tobias.

TOBYN. The Irish family are believed to be descended from the A. Norm. St. Aubyns—the name having formerly been spelt St. Tobin, and then Tobyn.

The name is of record in Ireland from the time of Edward the Third. It was especially established in the county of Tipperary. D'Alton. A writer in the Quarterly Review for April, 1860, speaking of the desire manifested by some of the English settlers in Ireland to be thoroughly hibernicized, mentions that the Fitz-Urses became Mac-Mahons, and the St. Aubyns Dobbin, or Tobyn."

TODD. TOD. An archaic and provincial name of the fox. The expression " wily tod " occurs in the writings of Wickliffe, and the word is made use of by B. Jonson. Before fox-hunting became a fashionable sport, and when churchwardens, acting under the Statute of 24. Hen. VIII., were accustomed to pay " xijd. for the head of every foxe," a class of men gained a precarious livelihood by hunting foxes and lesser vermin, and obtained the designations Todhunter and Todman, both of which have become well-known surnames.

TODHUNTER. See under Todd.

TODMAN. See under Todd.

☞ **TOFT.** A local termination. A. Sax. *tofte,* a little home field, or homestead. Bosworth. A piece of ground where there hath been a house. Camden. Open ground ; a plain ; a hill. Halliwell. " He hath neither *toft* nor croft," was an old proverbial saying, to signify that a man had no landed possessions.

TOKE. The Tokes of Godington, co. Kent, claim descent from Robert de Toke, who was present with Henry III. at the battle of Northampton. In the XIV. & XV. cent. the family were seated at Bere, and the Tokes of Godington, a younger branch, date from about temp. Henry VI. Shirley's Noble and Gentle Men. See Tooke.

TOKER. See under Tuckerman.

TOLCARNE. There are several places so called in Cornwall. The family are supposed to have originated at Tolcarne, in the parish of Camborne. C. S. Gilbert's Cornwall.

TOLER. See Toller.

TOLL. 1. A grove of lofty trees; a holt. 2. Toli, an A-Sax. personal name.

TOLLEMACHE. In his preface to *Orosius*, Dr. Bosworth states, that the family were among " the first Engle or Angles that settled among the Sudfolk in East Anglia." On their manor-house at Bentley, near Ipswich, there is, or was, the following distich :—

" BEFORE THE NORMANS INTO ENGLAND CAME,
BENTLEY WAS MY SEAT, AND TOLLEMACHE MY NAME."

The Etymology of the name is said to be A-Sax. "*tal*, a counting or reckoning; and *maca*, a consort, companion, fellow ; as a fellow of a college—a manager of the accounts of the realm. Hence tallies of the Exchequer." Dr. Bosworth in N. & Q., May 15, 1858. A family tradition, however, derives it from *tollmack*, "tolling of the bell," but does not tell us to what language that word belongs.

TOLLER. 1. Two parishes in Dorsetshire are so named. 2. A-Sax. *tollere*, a publican, or taker of tolls and taxes. Halliwell quotes an old poem in Harl. MS., 2260, to the effect that the—

" *Tollers* office it is ill;
For they take toll oft against skill."

that is, contrary to reason.

TOLMAN. TOLEMAN. The same as Toller.

TOLY. A contraction of Saint Olave. See Tooley.

TOM. The 'nurse-name' of Thomas.

TOMBLER. A tumbler or posture-master.

TOMBLESON. A corruption of Thomlinson. See, however, under Tombs.

TOMBS. Ferguson derives this surname, and Tombleson, from an old High German root, *tuom*, equivalent to A.-Saxon *dóm*., judgment; but as he puts them in juxtaposition with Thoms, Thomson, Tomkin, and other known derivatives of " Thomas," his etymology is not to be accepted. If this name is pronounced Tombs, it is no doubt the genitive of Tom.

TOMKIN. See Thomas.

TOMKINSON. See Thomas.

TOMLINSON. See Thomas.

TOMPKINS. See Thomas.

TOMPSETT. See Thomas.

TOMPSON. See Thomas.

TOMS. See Thomas.

TOMSETT. See Thomas.

☞ **TON.** One of the commonest terminations of names of places, and by consequence, of local surnames.

" In Ford, in Ham, in Ley, in *Ton*,
The most of English Surnames run."

Out of 1,200 names of places in the first two volumes of Kemble's A-Sax. Charters, 137 have this termination, or 11.4 per cent., but, with certain allowable deductions, Leo makes the pro-

portion 13.5 per cent., or about one-eighth ; and these occur principally in the South of England. The A-Sax. *tún* signifies an inclosed space, the area of which may be either small or large, from a cottage-homestead up to a walled *town*, which latter is indeed the same word.

TONGE. Parishes and places in cos. Kent, York, Salop, Lancaster, and Leicester.

TONGUE. 1. A parish in Sutherlandshire. 2. Tong or Tonge, parishes, &c., in Kent, Yorkshire, Salop, Lancashire, and Leicestershire.

TONI. Doubtless from Toeni, a commune in the arrondissement of Louviers, in Normandy, latinized in the XI. century Toenium. Ralph de Todeni or Toni, son of Roger de Toenio, standard-bearer of Normandy, was at the battle of Hastings. In Domesday he appears as tenant in chief in several counties, the head of his barony being Flamstead in Hertfordshire. Robert and Berenger de Todeni, doubtless near kinsmen of Ralph, are also found among the tenants in chief in the great record. The family were ennobled, and became extinct, in one person, the Lord Robert de Toni, temp. Edward I. Upon Robert de Todeni the Conqueror bestowed the lordship of Belvoir, co. Leicester, where he built the castle, afterwards so famous, and made it the head of his barony. His son and heir, William, took the name of De Albini, with the addition of Brito, " to distinguish himself," says Kelham, " from William de Albini, chief butler of the realm."

TONKIN. A diminutive of the diminutive Tony, from Anthony ?

TONSON. Tony's son, the son of Anthony.

TONSOR. 1. A latinization of Barber. The name Barbitonsor, " beard-shaver," is found in H.R. 2. One Durandus Tonsor was a Domesday tenant in chief.

TONY. See Toni.

TOOGOOD. Can hardly refer to super-excellence of character. The old spelling Towgood is almost conclusive against such derivation. The last syllable may be a corruption of *wood*.

TOOKE. A name of doubtful origin, because the several etymons which have been suggested are of nearly equal probability. I. The *De* prefixed to the name Tuke, or Touke, of the midland counties points to a local origin, and that family are said to have sprung from the Sieur de Touque, whose ancient barony in Normandy (arrondissement of Pont l'Evêque) was written in charters Touqua. I do not find Domesd. authority for this, though I do find in that ancient record (II) as landowners, prior to its compilation, persons bearing the baptismal names of Toc, Tocho, Tochi, and Toka, as well as the patronymic form, Godric *Tokeson*. III. It may be from

At-Hoke or At-Hook, implying the residence of the first bearer on an elevated spot. See Hook. IV. But this is less likely—it has been suggested that it is of O. English origin, and signifies *thick*. If it be so, Tuck was no inappropriate name for the well-known friar. Gent. Mag., June, 1846. The surname is found spelled in 17 different ways. One of the most ancient is Toke, as preserved in the Godington family for many centuries. The Tookes of Hurston Clays, co. Sussex, of London, Herts, Dorset, &c., proven descendants of that house, have employed this orthography from the XVI. century.

TOOLE. See O'Toole.

TOOLEY. A crasis of St. Olave. Tooley Street in Southwark is so called from its proximity to the church of St. Olave.

TOOMER. 1. From St. Omer. So Tooley from St. Olave; Tanswell from St. Anne's Well, &c. 2. The process of taking wool from the card is called *tooming*, and hence possibly the name may be the designation of that employment.

TOON. See Tune.

TOOT. Mr. Ferguson considers this identical with an A-Sax. personal name, Tota or Totta.

TOOTAL. Perhaps the same as Tothill.

TOOTH. This name probably has reference to some peculiarity in the teeth of the original bearer. The Romans had their Dento and Dentatus, most likely on the same account.

TOOTHACHER. Germ. *todtenacker*, field of the dead, a burying ground; analogous to our indigenous name Churchyard.

TOOVEY. See Tovey.

TOP. See Topp.

TOPCOAT. Doubtless local : see Cott or Cote.

TOPLADY. See Lady.

TOPP. An elevated spot is known in some dialects as a *top*, and is used antithetically to *bottom*, which see. Residence on such a spot would originate the surname.

TORBOCK. An estate in Lancashire, which had possessors of its own name in early times. They were of common ancestry with the distinguished house of Lathom of Lathom, being descendants of Richard, brother of Sir Robert Fitz-Henry, founder of Burscough Priory. See Latham. The name is, I think, extinct, that is, in its ancient and true orthography, though it appears to survive in plebeian life, and in the grotesque forms of Tirebuck and Tarbox.

TOREL. See Thorold. The scribes of the middle ages understood this name to signify Fr. *tourelle*, the little tower, or

turret, and accordingly latinized it by De Parva Turri. The heralds, on the other hand, read it as *taureau*, a bull, and hence the bulls' heads in the arms.

TORILL. See Thorold.

TORKINGTON. A township in Cheshire, formerly the property of the family.

TORR. In the W. of England, a craggy eminence, or more generally a hill. Places specifically so called are Tor-Abbey, Tor-Bryan, and Tor-Quay, all in Devonshire. De la Tor is the H.R. form.

TORRY. An Edinburgh surname. In some parts of Scotland *tory* is a term expressive of great indignation or contempt. Jamieson.

TOSH. A known abbreviation of Mac Intosh. " Old Molly Tosh, who long kept the Red Lion in Churchway, North Shields, became Mary Macintosh on her tombstone, where she lies sound asleep with a bundle of manuscript correspondence under her head." Folks of Shields.

TOSHACH. A chief or thane. Gael. Probably a modification of Mac Intosh.

TOTHILL. " A Tote-hill is an eminence from whence there is a good lookout." Cheshire. Archæologia, xix. 39. "Totehyll, montaignette." Palsgrave, 1530, —an evident derivative of the A-Sax. verb *totian*, to elevate or lift.

TOTTENHAM. A parish in Middlesex.

TOUCH. This name probably comes to us from the Fr. De la Touche. A *touche* is thus defined by Cotgrave—" A hoult, a little thicke grove or tuft of high trees, especially such a one as is neere a house, and serves to beautifie it, or as a marke for it."

TOUCHET. A parish in the arrondissement of Mortain in Normandy, latinized Tuschetum. From that place no doubt proceeded the great A. Norm. family, afterwards ennobled as Barons Audley. In the alliterative copy of the so-called Battel-Abbey Roll, TUCHET AND TRUCHELLE occur in association, which is *quantum valeat* evidence of the Norman origin of the name. It is stated, however, that, at a later period, one Orme, who from his musical talents acquired the cognomen of " the Harper," was the first bearer of the name, and that he was sometimes called ' Citharista ' or " *Touch-it !* " See Sir P. Leycester's Tabley MSS., quoted in Ormerod's Cheshire iii. 23.

TOUGH. Sturdy ; capable of endurance.

TOURELL. See Thorold.

TOURLE. See Thorold.

TOURNAY. A town in Artois. Gosfrid Tornai occurs in the Domesday of Lincolnshire.

TOUSSAINT. (O. Fr. *tousaintz*) a name

given to a person born on the festival of All Saints; analogous to Christmas, Noel, Pentecost, &c.

TOVEY. Tovus, otherwise Tovi, came to England with the Conqueror, and acquired several manors in Norfolk. The name is found in Domesday as Tovi or Tovius.

TOWER. TOWERS. From residence in or near a tower.

TOWES. TOWS. Said to be from St. Osyth. Comp. Toomer, Tooley, &c.

TOWGOOD. See Toogood.

TOWN. TOWNE. A-Sax. *tún*, an enclosure, homestead. At-Town would become Towner. In Cornwall a farm-yard is still called a "town-place." Your ancient *Towner* was not, therefore, what his name sounds to modern ears, but a thorough rustic.

TOWNELEY. An estate in Lancashire, which belonged to this ancient and distinguished family, whose pedigree is *said* to be traced to the time of King Alfred, and to Spartlingus, first Dean of Whalley, who flourished about the year 896. The line of this personage terminated with an heiress, Cecilia of Towneley, in the XIV. century, who married John del Legh, and conveyed the estate to his family. He died in or about 1330, and his great-grandson resumed the ancient surname of Towneley. John del Legh was a cadet of the great Cheshire family of that name. B.L.G. Towneley Hall is still the seat of this race, who may well challenge comparison in point of venerable antiquity with any family in England.

TOWNER. See Town.

TOWNSEND. TOWNSHEND. TOWNEND. "The town's end," from residence there. The forms in the Hundred Rolls, are Ate-Touneshend, Ate-Tunesend, Ate-Tunishende, &c. The analogous name Attestreteshend—"at the street's end"—is found in the same rolls, as are also Ad Caput Villæ, Ad Finem Villæ, and Bynethetoun, i.e., "beneath the town." This surname, though of essentially plebeian origin, emerged from the *ignobile vulgus* at an early period after its adoption, being traced to the year 1377, in gentle degree at Snoring Magna, co. Norfolk. In 1398, the ancestor of the Marquis Townshend was at Rainham, the present seat of the family. Leland speaking of the head of the house, in his day, says: "the grandfather of Townsende now living, was a *mean man of substance.*" Mr. Shirley calls this a 'defamatory account,' and so it may be regarded, if taken in the sense of a wealthy miser; but the old Itinerarian doubtless means a person of moderate fortune, which is no disparagement. See Noble and Gentle Men.

TOWSEY. 1. By crasis, from St. Osyth. Camden's Remains. So St. Olave became Tolye or Tooley (as Tooley Street in Southwark), St. Ebbe, Tabbe, &c. 2. Perhaps the old Fr. surname Toucey.

TOWSON. Perhaps the Fr. *Toussaints*, All-Saints' Day, or, as it was anciently called, All-Hallowtide. See Times and Seasons.

TOWZER. The occupation. To *towse*, or *tease*, is to clear the fibre of wool from entanglements.

TOZER. The same as Towzer.

TRACKSON. See Threxton.

TRACTION. A known corruption of Threxton, which see.

TRACY. This famous Norman family borrowed their surname from Traci-Boccage in the arrondissement of Caen, called in documents of the XI. cent. Traceium. They came hither at the Conquest, and were subsequently lords of Barnstaple, in Devonshire. The parishes, &c., of Woolcombe-Tracy, Bovi-Tracy, Minet-Tracy, Bradford-Tracy, &c., in Devonshire, derived their suffixes from this family. Fuller's Worthies, i., 558. The male line failed at an early period, but the heiress married John de Sudley, whose son William adopted the maternal surname. This personage has by some genealogists been considered one of the four assassins of Thomas-à-Becket, though others stoutly deny it, and assert that there were other William de Tracys living contemporaneously with him. Whoever the assassin was, a curse was said to attach to him and to his seed for ever, namely, that wherever he or they went, by land or sea, the wind should blow in a direction opposite to that of their course. Hence the well-known traditional couplet—

" ALL THE TRACYS,
HAVE THE WIND IN THEIR FACES."

In Kent, the name Tresse is considered to be identical with Tracy.

TRADER. 'John the Trader,' to distinguish him from 'John the Farmer,' or the like.

☞ **TRADES.** *Surnames derived from.* The following is Mr. Clark's list:—
" Barber, Brazier, Mason and Builder, Carrier, Carter, Carver and Gilder; Dancer, Drover, Dresser and Dyer, Cartwright, Clothier, Caner and Crier; Arrowsmith, Arkwright, Agent and Butler, Carpenter, Chandler, Cooper and Cutler; Bathmaker, Butcher, Brewer aud Broker, Cardmaker, Carman, Corder and Coker; Bellringer, Bellman, Bowman and Blacker, Paviour, Pedlar, Painter and Packer; Currier, Collier, Chanter and Cropper, Huntsman, Hosier, Hacker and Hopper; Boatwright, Baker, Binder and Brazier, Grocer, Gouger, Grinder and Glazier; Merriman, Mercer, Merchant and Miller, Banker, Chapman, Cutter and Killer; Fidler, Farmer, Joiner and Stringer, Gardener, Goldsmith, Tapper and Ringer; Horseman, Hooker, Barker and Peeler, Fryman, Fowler, Draper and Dealer; Plowright, Packman, Paver and Plater, Traveller, Tapster, Thatcher and Slater; Peddlar, Pitman, Pincher and Potter. Turner, Trimmer, Tanner and Trotter;

Shoveller, Swindler, Stainer and Smoker,
Saddler, Shearer, Salter and Stoker;
Fleshman, Foreman, Fuller and Fyler,
Taverner, Taylor, Tasker and Tyler;
Dairyman, Doctor, Drawer and Dredger,
Herdsman, Hawker, Hewer and Hedger;
Quarrier, Quilter, Rhymer and Reader,
Bowmaker, Scrivener, Presser and Pleader;
Pressman, Plumer, Poet and Pinner,
Staymaker, Sheppard, Glover and Skinner,
Tuner, Threader, Bridger and Archer,
Tirer, Thrower, Loader and Marcher;
Girdler, Stamper, Keeper and Nailer.
Rasper, Trainer, Baster and Sailer;
Warrener, Workman, Webber and Whiter,
Wheelwright, Watchman, Roper and
    Writer.
This list of names we might extend,
And fifty more at least append;
Nay—if inclined, we could recite 'em
Thus, one by one, *ad infinitum*."

TRAFFORD. An estate in the parish
of Eccles, co. Lancaster, where the ancestors of the family are said to have been established before the Norman Conquest.
The pedigree in Baines's Lancashire deduces
them from Ralph de Trafford, who died
about 1050. This Ralph may have been a
real personage, and an ancestor of the
Traffords, but he was certainly no *De*
Trafford before the Conquest. Mr. Shirley
remarks that "on the whole, it may be assumed that the antiquity of this family is
exaggerated, though the name no doubt
was derived from the locality at an early
period." Noble and Gentle Men.

TRAHERNE. See Treherne.

TRAIL. TRAILL. This N. of England family claim to be of Norse extraction,
and say that their name signifies Trolle or
Troil, the devil!

TRANGMAR. A Brighton name, apparently the same as that which existed
there as Trenchemer in 1296, (Sussex
Arch. Coll. ii. 295) the *ch* having hardened
into *g*. The original application may
have been to a mariner—one who *cuts the
sea*.

TRANT. This family, of Danish extraction, are, on Ortelius's map, located in
the Barony of Corkaguinny, co. Kerry.
D'Alton.

TRANTER. A word of uncertain
origin, signifying, according to Bailey, a
"sort of fisherman;" but Halliwell says
that it is in various dialects, a carrier.

TRAPPER. A man who takes game,
and other wild animals, by various *traps* or
contrivances. In this sense the word is
still used in America.

TRAQUAIR. A parish in Peebles-
shire.

TRASH. O. French, a bunch of grapes
—perhaps an inn sign.

TRAVELLER. A man who has visited
foreign countries.

TRAVERS. Fr. *traverse*, a cross path

or foot-road leading from one village to
another.

TRAYNOR. The Ossianic hero, Finn
Mac-Cool, was grandson of Trenmor or
Treanmhar (pron. Treanwar) whence perhaps the surnames Treanor, Traynor, and,
as Mr. Mac-Grady thinks, Mac Creanor.

☞ **TRE.** See under CORNISH SUR-
NAMES.

TREACHER. O. E. *trechoure*, a cheat.
Richardson says : " One who tricks . . .
cozens, cheats, beguiles, deceives."

TREACY. See Tracy.

TREASURER. The office. The name
is an ancient one, being found in its Latin
form of Thesaurius among the tenants in
chief of Domesday.

TREBARFOOT. An estate in the
parish of Poundstock, co. Cornwall, the
ancient seat of the family, until the extinction of the elder line in 1630. They
bore for arms three bears' feet.

TREBARTHA. A place in the parish
of Northill, co. Cornwall, where the family
flourished from the reign of Edward I. to
that of Henry VII. C. S. Gilbert's Cornwall.

TREBECK. Probably a corruption of
Troutbeck. A Dominus Thomas de Trebec
occurs in Shropshire, temp. Henry III.
H.R.

TREBLECOCK. A place in Cornwall—
Trebilcock.

TREBY. A manor in Cornwall, now
called Trebigh, in the parish of St. Eve.
It was anciently possessed by the family.
D. Gilbert's Cornwall, i. 412.

TRECARNE. The family were anciently
of Trecarne in Cornwall. The heiress
married Glynn of Glynn in that county. C.
S. Gilbert's Cornwall.

TREDCROFT. An old Sussex name.
Local : place unknown.

TREDENHAM. An ancient Cornish
family who resided at Tredenham in the
parish of Probus. There are strong reasons
for believing them to have been an offshoot
of the baronial family of Dinham of Cornwall and Devon. The prefix *Tre* in the
Cornish tongue signifies, like the Saxon
tún, an enclosure, or fenced estate. It is,
therefore, quite possible that a cadet of
Dinham or Denham (as the name was
sometimes called) may have given the
name of Tre-Denham, or "Denham's
estate " to his lands, and that afterwards
his descendants took their surname from
those lands in the ordinary way. A remarkable confirmation of this notion is,
that both families bear in their coat armour
fusils (which are far from common in
heraldry)—the noble family carrying them
in fesse, and the gentle one *in bend*. See
C. S. Gilbert's Cornwall.

TREDINNICK. An estate in the parish of St. Breock, where the family dwelt up to the extinction of the elder male line, before the year 1531. Lysons' Cornwall.

TREE. See Attree in Supplement.

TREFFRY. This name is derived from the manor of Treffry, in the parish of Lanhydrock, where it is traced to a very early period. The family afterwards removed to Fowey, where was born the gallant Sir John Treffry, who, fighting under the Black Prince at the battle of Poictiers, took the French royal standard, for which he was created a knight banneret, and had, as an *augmentation* of his arms, the Fleurs-de-lys of France. In the next century some French marauders (whether in revenge of the national disgrace or not, does not appear) attacked Place House, the residence of the family at Fowey, but met a repulse at the hands of a lady, the Mistress Treffry of the period. Leland says :—" The Frenchmen divers times assailed Fowey, and last, most notably, about Henry VI. tyme, when the wife of Thomas Trevry, with her men, repelled the French out of her house, in her husbandes absence, whereupon Thomas Trevry builded a right fair and strongly embattled tower in his house."

TREFUSIS. This ancient family have been seated from time immemorial at Trefusis, in the parish of Milor, co. Cornwall. The pedigree is traced four generations before the year 1292. Shirley's Noble and Gentle Men.

TREGAGLE. The name of this family was taken from their place of residence, Tregagle, in the parish of Probus, which that prince of etymologists, Hals, informs us signifies " the town of gagling geese, or the filthy town !" D. Gilbert's Cornwall. To this family belonged John Tregagle, an arbitrary magistrate and local tyrant, of the days of the Stuarts, whose ghost yet haunts the wilds of Cornwall. " One of this family, having become unpopular," says Mr. Davies Gilbert, " the traditions respecting a mythological personage have been applied to him. The object of these tales of unknown antiquity was, like Orestes, continually pursued by an avenging being, from whom he could find refuge only from time to time by flying to the cell or chapel on Roach Rock ; till at last his fate was changed into the performance of a task, to exhaust the water from Dozmere, with an implement less adapted, if possible, for its appropriate work, than were the colanders given to the daughter of Danaus :

Hocc' ut opinor, id est, ævo florente puellas,
Quod memorant, laticem pertusum congerere in
⸱ vas,
Quod tamen expleri nulla ratione potestur.

" Tregagle is provided simply with a limpet shell, having a hole bored through it : and with this he is said to labour without intermission ; in dry seasons flattering himself that he has made some progress towards the end of his work ; but when rain commences, and the 'omnis effusus labor'

becomes apparent, he is believed to roar so loudly, in utter despair, as to be heard from Dartmoor Forest to the Land's End."

TREGARRICK. A place in the parish of Roche, co. Cornwall, formerly the seat of the family, whereof John Tregarrick was M.P. for Truro, 7. Richard II. C. S. Gilbert's Cornwall.

TREGARTHIAN. A place in the parish of Gorran, co. Cornwall, where the family were seated temp. Edward I., or earlier. C. S. Gilbert's Cornwall.

TREGARTHYN. See Tregarthian.

TREGEARE. A place in the parish of Crowan, co. Cornwall. The family were resident there so lately as 1732. Richard Tregeare, of Tregeare, was sheriff of the county in 1704. C. S. Gilbert's Cornwall.

TREGENDER. A place in the parish of Ludgvan, co. Cornwall, which the family formerly possessed.

TREGENNA. An estate in St. Ives, co. Cornwall, where the family resided until about the reign of Charles I.

TREGERE. See Tregeare.

TREGIAN. Lands so called in the parish of St. Eue, in Cornwall, are supposed to have given name to this family. C. S. Gilbert's Cornwall.

TREGODDICK. An estate in South Petherwin, co. Cornwall, the ancient inheritance of the family, who are supposed to have become extinct temp. Charles I.

TREGONWELL. The name of this ancient family was derived from their seat so designated, in the parish of Crantock, co. Cornwall. Pollen, in his Description of Cornish Men and Manners, speaks of them as having "builded many places" and possessed "many lands and manors before the Norman Conquest." C. S. Gilbert's Cornwall. The pedigree is traced only to the latter part of the XIV. century. Shirley's Noble and Gentle Men.

TREGOTHNAN. From lands so called in Cornwall. The elder male line became extinct in the XIV. century. C. S. Gilbert's Cornwall.

TREGOYE. From an estate in Cornwall so designated. The family of Tregoye or Tregoyes ranked amongst the nobles of England, at the accession of William the Conqueror. Carew's Survey of Cornwall.

TREGOZ. A local name ; but I do not know the place from which it was taken. The first recorded ancestor of the family, who were ennobled in three branches, was William de Tregoz, who, in the fifth year of King Stephen, had the lands of William Peverell, of London, in farm. His descendants were much connected with the county of Sussex.

TREHANE. An estate in the parish of Probus, co. Cornwall, the early residence of the family.

2 Y

TREHAWKE. A place in the parish of Menheniot, co. Cornwall. The last Cornishman of the name died at Liskeard in 1790. C. S. Gilbert's Cornwall.

TREHERNE. An ancient Welsh personal name, as Trahern ap Caradoc, Prince of North Wales, 1073.

TRELAWNY. Two manors so called exist in Cornwall, and are situated respectively in the parishes of Alternon and Pelynt. "The former," says Mr. Shirley, "was the original seat of the Trelawnys, probably before the Conquest, and here they remained till the extinction of the elder branch in the reign of Henry VI. The latter was purchased from Queen Elizabeth by Sir John Trelawny, the head of a younger line of the family, in the year 1600," and it is still the seat of the baronet, who now represents the male line of this venerable house. See Noble and Gentle Men of England.

TREMAYNE. An estate in the parish of St. Martin, co. Cornwall. The pedigree is traced to Perys de Tremayne of Tremayne, in the reign of Edward III. Shirley's Noble and Gentle Men.

TREMENHEERE. "The family name of Tremenheere is derived from lands so named in the parish of Ludgvan, of which Nicholas de Tremenheere was seised before the reign of Edward I." C. S. Gilbert's Cornwall.

TREMERE. An estate in Lanivet parish, co. Cornwall. The elder line failed in the XIV. century. C. S. Gilbert's Cornwall. The surname Trimmer may be a corruption of this name.

TRENCH. From La Tranche, a town in Poitou, the possession of the family in early times. After the massacre of St. Bartholomew, Frederick de la Tranche, or Trenche, a Protestant nobleman, sought refuge from persecution on English ground, and settled in Northumberland in the year 1574. Thence his descendants passed over into Ireland, where they still flourish in the enjoyment of two peerages, the Earldom of Clancarty, and the Barony of Ashtown.

We find an indigenous family of Trench in Norfolk, temp. Edward I. H.R.

TRENCHARD. Baldwin de Ripariis, Earl of Devon, granted Hordhill, in the Isle of Wight, to the ancestor of this family, Paganus Trenchard, temp. Henry I. The name is most probably derived from the O. Fr. *trencher*, to carve; and it may refer to the occupation of the original bearer, either as a carver of viands, or as owner of a *trenchant* blade in war.

TRENCREEK. An estate at St. Creed, co. Cornwall, the residence of the family, who became extinct in the male line in 1594, when the four co-heiresses married Carminowe, Penwarne, Polwhele, and Mohun. C. S. Gilbert's Cornwall.

TRENDLE. A tything in the parish of of Pitminster, co. Somerset.

TRENGOFF. Lands in the parish of Warleggon, co. Cornwall, are so called. The family became extinct about the year 1720. A younger branch settled at Nance in the parish of Illogan, and thereupon wrote themselves Nance, alias Trengoff. C. S. Gilbert's Cornwall.

TRENGOVE. See under Goff.

TRENOWITH. An estate in the parish of Probus, co. Cornwall, where dwelt, in 12. Edward III., Michael de Trenowith, one of the knights of that shire. C. S. Gilbert's Cornwall.

TRENOWTH. See Trenowith.

TRENT. The great midland river.

TRENWITH. The original name of this family was Baillie. Thomas Baillie, the first recorded ancestor, was living 45. Edward III. His son, Henry Baillie, obtaining from the Duchy of Cornwall, a grant of the manor and barton of Trenwith, near St. Ives, began to write himself De Trenwith. The male line became extinct in 1796. C. S. Gilbert's Cornwall.

TRESCOTT. A hamlet in Staffordshire.

TRESILLIAN. Two places in Cornwall are so designated; one in the parish of Newlyn, and the other in Merther. The distinguished Sir Robert Tresillian, lord chief justice of the King's bench, who fell a victim to the resentment of the barons, at Tyburn, in 1388, was of this family. C. S. Gilbert's Cornwall.

TRESITHNEY. An estate in the parish of St. Columb, co., Cornwall, anciently the possession of the family. C. S. Gilbert's Cornwall.

TRESS. TRESSE. "The name of Tress, or Tresse, is supposed to be the same as that of Tracey, and to have been altered by vulgar corruption and the succession of time; if so, the family of Tresse, so long settled at West Malling and Offham, might very probably be a branch of the family of Tracie, possessors of the manor which still bears their name at Newington, near Sittingbourne, in the reign of Henry III." Hasted's Kent, 8vo., vol. iv., p. 535.

TRETHAKE. An ancient Cornish family, deriving the name either from Trethake in St. Clear, or Trethake in Lanteglos. "We know not how the greatness of this family ended, or when it became extinct, but a poor man of the same name died lately at East Looe, very aged." C. S. Gilbert's Cornwall.

TRETHEWY. A Cornish family. The village of Trethewy or Trethevy is in the parish of South Petherwin.

TRETHURFFE. According to tradition this family were resident at Trethurffe, in Ladock, co. Cornwall, before the Norman Conquest. The elder line ended with John Trethurffe, who was knight of that shire in the Parliament of 15. Henry VI. C. S. Gilbert's Cornwall.

TREVANION. This important and extensive family derive their name from Trevanion, in the parish of Carhayes in Cornwall, their seat in the reign of Edward II., and probably much earlier. C. S. Gilbert's Cornwall.

TREVARTHIAN. The manor of Trevarthian, in the parish of Newlyn, near Truro, " is undoubtedly the spot that gave origin to this family, who in former times ranked among the most distinguished names that have been known in the county of Cornwall." C. S. Gilbert's Cornwall.

TREVERBYN. A manor in the parish of St. Austell, which was the seat of the family as early as the Norman Conquest. Walter Treverbyn was sheriff of Cornwall in 1223. The elder male line became extinct in the XIV. century. C. S. Gilbert's Cornwall.

TREVELYAN. An estate in the parish of St. Veep near Fowey, in Cornwall, where dwelt in the reign of Edward I., Nicholas de Trevelyan, whose ancestors had possessed the property from a still earlier period. See Shirley's Noble and Gentle Men. Nettlecombe, co. Somerset, became their seat in the XV. century, and Wallington, co. Northumberland, (acquired with the heiress of Calverley of Calverley,) in the XVIII.

TREVIADOS. An estate in the parish of Constantine, co. Cornwall, where the family resided temp. Edward III. C. S. Gilbert's Cornwall.

TREVILLE. A Cornish surname derived from one of the several places so called in that peninsula. C. S. Gilbert's Cornwall.

TREVILLION. A corruption of Trevelyan.

TREVISA. A place in Cornwall, situated in St. Endor. This family, who became extinct about the end of the XVII. century, produced John Trevisa, who, at an interval of about half a century from John Wickliffe's translation, made a version of the Bible into English, and died at the age of 86, in 1470. D. Gilbert's Cornwall.

TREVISSA. See Trevisa.

TREVOR. The Welsh heralds derive the Trevors from Rourd Wiedick, father of Eignian Yothe, which Eignian held the lands of Gaercinion in Powysland, and was grandfather to Kariodoc, Earl of Hereford, early in the sixth century. The first who bore this name was the famous Tudor Trevor, Earl of Hereford, Kariodoc's grandson. Surnames were not hereditary in Wales before the reign of Henry VIII., this being the single exception that I have observed. The first person who adopted Trevor as a settled family name, was John ap Edward ap David, who died in 1494. None of his immediate ancestors had borne the baptismal name of Trevor; and it is therefore likely that he adopted it from the most illustrious of his ancestors, the renowned Earl of Hereford. The great families of Mostyn and Jenkyn are of the same family as the Trevors, and bear the same arms.

TREVRONCK. " Allan Trevronck was living in great respectability at Trevronck, in the reign of Edward III." C. S. Gilbert's Cornwall.

TREWEEK. 1. Trewick, a township in Northumberland. 2. See Treweeke.

TREWEEKE. A 'barton,' and manor in Cornwall. D. Gilbert's Cornwall.

TREWINNARD. An estate in the parish of St. Erth, co. Cornwall. The earliest recorded ancestor seems to be William de Trewinnard, a knight of the shire, 28. Edward III. C. S. Gilbert's Cornwall.

TREWOLLA. The family were of Trewolla, in Gorran parish, seven generations before 1620. C. S. Gilbert's Cornwall.

TREWOOFE. An estate in Burian, co. Cornwall, the inheritance of the family in the XV. century. C. S. Gilbert's Cornwall.

TREWREN. The family were seated at Driff in the parish of Sancreed, in the year 1340. C. S. Gilbert's Cornwall. It is doubtless a *Tre* of Cornish growth.

TREWYTHENICK. A manor in Cornelly, co. Cornwall, is so called.

TRIGG. TRIGGS. See Ridge. The Trig and Trigges of the H.R. are, however, in favour of a derivation from a personal name.

TRIGGER. 1. I knew this name, at Alfriston, co. Sussex, corrupted from the local name Trigwell. 2. A correspondent informs me that this is a rather common name at Madeley, co. Salop, where it is understood to signify an employment. A Trigger is one who cuts small watercourses, locally called *trigs*, in meadows capable of irrigation. The name is therefore analogous to Ditcher.

TRIGWELL. Probably a corruption of Tregonwell. This name is sometimes further corrupted to Trigger.

TRILL. 1. A *rill* is a small stream, a rivulet. A man whose habitation stood near one would acquire the name of Atte-Rill, which would easily shorten into Trill. 2. There must have been a locality so called, as a John de Tril occurs in H.R. co. Devon.

TRIMMER. See Tremere.

TRING. A parish in Hertfordshire.

TRIPP. The family trace by deeds to temp. Hen. VIII. in co. Somerset; but tradition derives them from the illustrious race of Howard, and accounts for the name, and the "scaling ladder" in their arms, by the following wretched little anecdote, inscribed beneath an old family ' achievement ' :—

"This atchievement was given unto my Lord Howard's 5th Son, at ye Seige of Bullogne : King Harry ye 5th being there ask'd how they took ye Town and Castle. Howard answered, I TRIPP'D up the Walls. Saith his Majesty : *Tripp shall be thy name, and no longer Howard ;* and Honrd. him with ye scaling Ladder for his Bend !" The name is found in the Rotuli Hundredorum —some century and a half before the siege alluded to—as *Trippe.*

TRIST. 1. Fr. *triste*, "sad, pensive, grieved, heavie, discontented, melancholicke, wofull, dolefull, sorrowfull : also grave, austere, sowre, harsh." Cotgrave. The name is traced in the pedigree to about the year 1370. B.L.G. 2. A nickname of Tristram.

TRISTON. Tristan, Tristram, which see.

TRISTRAM. An ancient personal name.

TRITTON. Probably from Treeton, curtly so pronounced ; a parish in co. York.

TRIVET. Trivetus, an old personal name. Trivet, H.R.

TROAKE. TROKES. Probably the same as Trocke.

TROBRIDGE. The same as Trowbridge.

TROCKE. Said to have been introduced into Ireland at the Revocation of the Edict of Nantes. A John Trocke, whose tomb bears date early in the XVIII. century, lies buried in the centre of the nave of St. Andeon's church, Dublin. The family tradition is, that the name is of German extraction ; if so, it may be derived from the Germ. *trocken*, equivalent to our indigenous surname Dry. Some branches of the family, however, spell it Troke, which almost identifies it with Troki, the Polish town and province.

TROLL. A demon or giant. O. Norse *tröll.* Ferguson. The noble family of Trolle bore a *demon* in their arms, in commemoration of an ancestor having *killed one !*

TROLLOPE. A name of uncertain derivation. A long-standing tradition in the family makes it *Trois Loups,* in consequence of some marvellous exploit performed by an early progenitor against the wolves which then infested Lincolnshire ; but as the name has been spelt Trowlop, Trolop, and Trol*hope*, I have little doubt of its belonging to the local class, although the place from which it was assumed has been forgotten. See *Hope.* The family of the baronet are ancient in Lincolnshire.

TROOP. Troup, a place in the parish of Fortingal, co. Perth.

TROTT. 1. See Trotman. 2. Mr. Ferguson deduces it from the German *traut,* dear ; Low German, *drud,* dear, beloved.

TROTMAN. A *trot* in Old Scotch means an expedition by horsemen ; a *raid.*

See Jamieson. Hence the surnames Trott, Trotter, and Trotman, probably belonging to Border warfare and pillage. Troteman. H.R.

TROTTER. See Trotman.

TROTTON. A parish in Sussex.

TROUBLEFIELD. A corruption of Turberville.

TROUT. Possibly from the fish.

TROUTBECK. A chapelry in the parish of Windermere, co. Westmoreland, anciently the estate of the family, who in later times became eminent in Cheshire. See Done.

TROW. "Trow, Troy, and Try," says Mr. Ferguson, "are different forms of *True;* as old Frieslandic, *trowe, troiwe;* German *treu.*"

TROWELL. A parish in Nottinghamshire.

TROWER. To trow, an obsolescent verb, is to believe, trust ; from the A-Sax. *treówian;* and Ferguson makes Trower synonymous with believer, religious man, or Christian.

TROY. 1. See Trow. 2. Perhaps from Troyes in France.

TRUEBODY. See under Body.

TRUELOVE. From the Scandinavian " *troe lof,*" bound in law ; a bondsman. Ulst. Journ. Arch. No. 2. Trewelove. H.R.

TRUMAN. TRUEMAN. A man of truth or integrity. Treweman H.R.

TRUGEON. An occasional spelling of Tregian.

TRULL. A parish in co. Somerset.

TRULY. Truleigh, or Truly, is a manor in the parish of Edburton, co. Sussex.

TRUMBULL. A corruption of Turnbull.

TRUNDLE. See Trendle.

TRUSSEL. An ancient Norman family, located, in the reign of Henry I., in Warwickshire. The baronage mentions, as of this family, Richard Trussel, who fell at the battle of Evesham, temp. Henry III. The O. French *troussel* signifies, says Cotgrave, "a fardle, bundle, or bunch," and this name may possibly have originated with a hunchback.

TRUSCOTT. See Trescott.

TRUSSER. 1. Probably a maker of *trusses,* padded jackets so called, which were worn under a coat of mail to prevent abraision of the skin. 2. A man who makes hay into trusses or bundles of a given weight.

TRUSTRAM. Has nothing to do with putting confidence in Aries, astrologically or otherwise, but is a simple corruption of Tristram, a name renowned in chivalrous fable.

TRUSTY. A man to be relied on; a faithful adherent.

☞ TRY. A common termination of local names, as Allstry, Oswestry, Ingestrie. A-Sax. *treow*, a tree. Most of the places so designated anciently possessed some tree, remarkable either for its age or size, or from some striking event associated with it. The veneration in which individual trees were held, in the patriarchal and Druidical ages, is well known.

TRYE. The family are of French extraction; and the name is said to be derived from a town in Normandy, so called; but I cannot find any such locality. " In the XIII. and XIV. centuries, the Tryes ranked among the highest orders of the French nobility: we find temp. Edward II. Matthew de Try, Marshal of France, rendering homage to that monarch for lands in Ponthieu, and in 3. Henry IV. Sir Jas. de Try was taken prisoner and brought to England." B.L.G. The family of Trye of Leckhampton, co. Gloucester, are traced to Rawlin Try, who lived in the reign of Richard II, and married an heiress of Berkeley, with whom he had the manor of Alkington in Berkeley. Shirley's Noble and Gentle Men. 2. See Trow.

TRYON. The founder of this family in England was Peter Tryon, who fled from the persecution of the Duke of Alva, temp. Queen Elizabeth. His family, who had long flourished in the Netherlands, were so rich, that the emigrant contrived to bring with him to England sixty thousand pounds sterling; a very large sum in those days. His second son was created a baronet in 1620.

TUBB. TUBBS. See Theobald.

TUBBY. See Theobald.

TUBMAN. In the Court of Exchequer the Tubman is, next the Postman, the senior counsel without the Bar.

TUCK. See Tooke.

TUCKER. The O. English for *fuller*. In some places fulling-mills are still called " tuck-mills." The trade was so designated in the XVII. century. " I, Nicholas Dorman, of the parrishe of Woorthe, in the countye of Sussex, *Tucker*." Will proved at Lewes, 1600.

TUCKERMAN. I cannot better elucidate this name than by giving the following account, received from a learned and well-known Transatlantic bearer of it, writing from Cambridge, U.S., in 1853 :—

" It is a Devonshire name, which I have traced in the hundreds of Coleridge and Stanborough, where it is still extant, to the reign of Henry VI., A.D. 1445. It appears to run through the same series of changes with Toke and Toker, and it was first spelled Tokerman. I have always supposed that it originated, like Toker, from the old Devonshire provincialism *toke* or *tuck*, (A-Sax. *teogan*) meaning to beat in a fulling mill. I do not well understand what is

the meaning of Tokerman, as distinct from Toker; and I have the same difficulty as to Fisherman and Fisher, Singerman and Singer, Dykerman and Dyker, and others."

TUDHOE. A place in Northumberland.

TUDOR. The Welsh form of Theodore. The surname of an English dynasty, descended from Edmund Tudor, a Welsh gentleman of ancient blood. In the Domesday of Shropshire we have, as subtenant of Roger, Earl of Shrewsbury, " Tuder, quidam Walensis "—a certain Welshman called Tudor.

TUFNELL. In the XVII. century this name was spelt Tufnaile, and I am therefore rather inclined to take it *au pied de la lettre* (or rather at the end of the finger) and to consider " tough nail " as its etymon.

TUFTON. " From Tufton, a manor in the parish of Northiam, in the county of Sussex, is deduced the name of the ancient family of the Earls of Thanet." It was originally written De Toketon. The estate remained in the possession of the family until the close of the XVIII. century. The earliest known ancestor is Elphege de Toketon, who flourished six generations prior to 1346, which would probably place him in the latter half of the XII. century. It is asserted by several genealogists, that Toketon or Tufton, the locality from which the name was borrowed, is at Rainham in Kent. Rainham was certainly the residence of the family after they forsook their Sussex abode; but the mistake seems to have arisen from the existence of a field of sixteen acres called Tufton's in that parish. For the conflicting evidence on this subject, see Pocock's Memorials of the Family of Tufton. 8vo. 1800.

The change of spelling from Toketon to Tufton took place in the XIV. century. One of the first persons who employed the latter orthography was Sir Lewis de Tufton, a commander in the second battalion of the English army at the battle of Cresci.

TUGWELL. Though borne by dentists, shoemakers, &c., this name has no connection with tugging. It is clearly local.

TUITE. This surname is local, and probably of Norman-Conquest importation into England. It was introduced into Ireland at Strongbow's invasion. Richard de Tuite, who engaged in that expedition, obtained from his leader fair possessions in Teffia, and was made a palatine peer by the title of Baron of Moyashill. He was killed in 1211, by the fall of a tower in Athlone. D'Alton.

TUKE. See Tooke.

TULLY. TULLEY. Has no connection with the Roman orator. It is probably a corruption of St. Olave. St. Olave's Well, near Lewes, is now called Tulley's Well. In like manner Tooley Street in Southwark is a corruption of St. Olave's Street.

TULLOCH. Gael. *tulach*, a hillock. There are places specifically so called in the shires of Perth, Ross, Aberdeen, &c.

TUNNARD. An ancient Lincolnshire family. In 1333 the name occurs as Tonnehyrd, and in 1381 as Tunherd. The last syllable looks like the A-Sax. *hyrd*, a keeper or herdsman, while the former may be *tún*, any enclosure, village, town, &c. In this case, the name may signify the 'town-herd,' or herdsman, one to whom was entrusted the care of the common herd of a town or village, a well-known office or employment in the middle ages.

TUNE. Has no reference to musical accomplishments. It is the A-Sax. *tún*, an inclosure. See TON.

TUNSTALL. Townstall, a parish in Devonshire.

TUPMAN. A *tup* is, in some dialects, a ram; a *tupman* may therefore mean a breeder of rams.

TUPPER. Appears in its original form as Toppfer—a name well-known in the literature of Germany and France. The family, widely scattered in the religious troubles of the XVI. cent., having "lost all" under Charles V., as obstinate Lutherans, were called *Tout-perd* in France, and, by corruption, Toupard in the Netherlands; while in Guernsey and England, and among the Puritan fathers of America, the name assumed the form so familiar to the public as the designation of the author of "Proverbial Philosophy." The principal branch went to Guernsey in 1548.

TUPPIN. TUPPEN. A corruption of the personal name Turpin. In Sussex we find a Henry Turpin, who was engaged in the Crusades; and from him the numerous Tuppens of the South-Down district probably spring. See Abbrev. Placit. temp. John. pp. 26, 30. Inf. W. S. Ellis, Esq.

TURBERVILLE. This ancient Norman surname was latinized De Turbida Villa, and oddly enough anglicized Troublefield—neither the one nor the other very complimentary to the bearers of it. The treason of Sir Thomas Turberville in attempting to betray king Edward I. into the hands of the French monarch (for which he was hanged in London) brought upon him certain condemnatory verses from a contemporary poet :—

" *Turbat tranquilla clam, Thomas Turbida villa, &c.*
Our things now in tranquillitie
Thom. Turbvill troubleth privilie."
(Lambarde's Perambulation of Kent. Wingham).

The family were eminent in Brecknockshire from the time of William Rufus. No locality in Normandy, at present, bears a name resembling Turberville.

TURBYFIELD. A monstrous corruption of Turberville.

TURBOT. See Turbutt.

TURBUTT. The family, probably of Norman origin, were in Yorkshire so early as the reign of Richard I. B.L.G. Turbert is a personal name occurring in Domesday.

TURCHETIL. A Normanized form of Thurkettle.

TURFFREY. Perhaps a corruption of Treffry.

TURKE. More probably a 'nurse-name of Turchetil, than a native of Turkey. We have, however, the analogous surname Saracen.

TURLE. See Thorold.

TURNBULL. Probably local. A tradition has, however, been made to fit the name. It seems that king Robert Bruce, being once upon a time in Stirling park, was attacked by a ferocious bull. A brave fellow, called Ruel, came to the rescue; *turned the bull;* and got not only the king's thanks, but the lands of Bedrule, and a new surname. It appears certain, however, that a champion of great stature called Turnbull fought under king David Bruce, at the battle of Halidon, and was killed there. Nisbet's Heraldry. The analogous name Chacelyon is found in Essex, temp. Hen. VI. Knatchbull may also belong to this class.

TURNER. The occupation. One of the most common of surnames—" out of all proportion," Mr. Ferguson alleges, " to the number of persons engaged in the trade " of the lathe. " We find it in fact," he continues, " as a name before the Conquest—a grant to the monastery of Croyland, in 1051, being signed, among others, by a Turnerus Capellanus. The Icelandic has *turnera*, turnamentum agere; *turnari*, a tilter—which may probably shew the origin of the name. As, however, the Turner in question was a bishop's chaplain, his " tilting " must have been only theological. But the name may probably have been baptismal, and perhaps of Norman introduction." p. 336. Le Turnur, Le Turner. H.R. See Turnour below.

TURNEY. The same as Tournay. De Turnai. H.R.

TURNOR. A 'genteel' modification of Turner, and of recent date.

TURNOUR. Those who dislike the plebeian *tournure* of Turner have contrived to turn it into Turnour. To justify this twist, they allege that they "came in with the Conqueror," leaving behind them the *Tour Noire*, or black castle, from which, as its proprietors, they had derived their surname. However this may be, both the Map and the Itinerary of Normandy fail to indicate that redoubtable fortress. A far more probable origin is *tourneour*, the Norm. French for one who took part in a tournament. In the celebrated Scrope and Grosvenor controversy respecting the right of bearing Azure, a bend Or, temp. Richard II. Sir William de Aton testifies, that Monsire le Scrope was, in his time, " le plus fort TOURNEOUR de tout notre pays "

—'*the bravest* TOURNEY-ER *of all our country ;*' he testifies, moreover, that he always wore the blue with the golden bend, as did his kinsman, Geoffry le Scrope, when he *tourned* at the tournament of Northampton.

TURRELL. See Thorold.

TURROLD. See Thorold.

TURTLE. 1. A common surname in co. Antrim, supposed to be anglicized from the old tribe Hy Tuirtre (Tuirtre). 2. The name is ancient in England. It appears to be corrupted from Thurketil or Thurkettle, thus: Thurkel, Turkil, Turtel, Turtle. See H.R.

TURTON. 1. A chapelry in co. Lancaster. 2. At Chesterfield, after many generations of Treeton, or Treton, (from Treeton, a parish between that town and Sheffield) the name turns up in the parish register as Turton.

TURVILE. The Itinéraire de la Normandie shows ten places called Tourville, but from which of these at, or soon after, the Conquest, the family came, does not appear. Early under the Norman rule the name is conspicuous among the landholders of Warwick and Leicestershire. Ralph Turvile was a benefactor to the abbey of Leicester in 1297. Their principal seat was Normanton - Turvile, co. Leicester, where the elder line became extinct in 1776. Shirley's Noble and Gentle Men.

TUSLER. To *tussle* is a provincial word for to struggle or wrestle; hence a Tusler may mean a wrestler.

TWELLS. See Wells.

TWELVETREES. From some locality trivially so denominated. So Sevenoaks in Kent, Five-Ashes in Sussex, &c. Quatrefages (four beeches) is a corresponding Fr. surname.

TWEMLOW. A township in Cheshire.

TWENTYMAN. In the XIV. century the officer who had command of twenty armed men was called a *vintenarius ;* and of this word I take Twentyman to be a translation.

TWICEADAY. Probably has reference to some habit of the original bearer.

TWINER. A spinner of twine. Analogous to Roper, Corder, Thredder, &c.

TWINING. A parish in Gloucestershire.

TWISDEN. The Twisdens, baronets of 1666, are a branch of the Twysdens, baronets of 1611. The first baronet of the younger line altered the spelling, to distinguish between the two houses. See Twysden.

TWISS. O. Scotch *twyss*, from O. Fr. *toissu*, means a girdle or sash. Jamieson. One of the many surnames borrowed from costume.

TWITTEN. In the S. of England, a narrow alley, passage, or entry. Atte Twytene occurs in Sussex in 1296.

TWOPENNY. This designation may have been given as a sobriquet to some small trader, from his usual cry, "Two a penny ;" certain it is that Fourapenny was, in the XIV. century, an orthodox family name in Norfolk. 'Simon Fourapeni.' Papers of Norfolk Archæol. Soc. iv. 253. Turnepeni is a H.R. surname. Twopenny has, however, been noticed as a corruption of Tupigny, a Flemish surname. Edinb. Rev., April, 1855.

TWOPOTTS. Probably the sobriquet of a toper.

TWYSDEN. This name is derived from Twysden, or Twysenden-Borough, an estate in the parish of Goudhurst, co. Kent, now more usually called Burr's Farm, where Adam de Twysden resided in the reign of Edward I. His descendants sold it in the reign of Henry VI. At Sandhurst, in the same county, there is another Twysden, also said to have been a seat of the family, temp. Edward I. Shirley's Noble and Gentle Men.

TYE. A topographical word of uncertain origin. It generally means a small piece of common land close to a village, as Telscombe Tye, a few miles from Brighton.

TYERMAN. TIREMAN. A dealer in dresses and all kinds of ornamental clothing. Halliwell.

TYLER. The occupation—a layer of tiles. The H.R. forms are Tegulator, Tilere, &c.

TYLOR. A 'genteel' form of Tyler.

TYNDALE. Adam de Tyndale, baron of Langley Castle, in South *Tyne-dale*, co. Northumberland, temp. Henry II., descended from a family who held Langley, temp. Henry I., by the service of a knight's fee. Few families have adhered more steadily than this to a particular estate or county. In the line of its present male representative we trace residence, successively, in the counties of Northumberland, Northampton, Norfolk, Worcester, Gloucester, Wiltshire, Somerset, and Hampshire. See B.L.G.

TYNDALL. See Tindale.

TYNE. The great northern river.

TYNKER. The occupation. One William *de* Tyneker, however, occurs in H.R. in Huntingdonshire.

TYNTE. The family are traditionally said to be an offshoot of the noble house of Arundell. In Eng. Surn. I have quoted the legendary anecdote of the founder having distinguished himself at the battle of Ascalon under Richard Cœur de Lion, and of his having had his white surcoat dyed with Saracen blood — "*tynctus* cruore Saraceno," (Burke's Commoners, vol. iv.) —whence the surname Tynte. I think this etymology must have suggested itself to some one as a *dernier ressort*. I confess that it baffles my own skill.

TYRWHITT. According to Wotton's Baronetage, the family are traced to a Sir Hercules Tyrwhitt, who flourished in the reign of Henry I. They were raised to eminence by Sir Robert Tyrwhitt, Justice of the Common Pleas and the King's Bench, in the reign of Henry IV. Their chief abode was Kettleby, co. Lincoln. Shirley's Noble and Gentle Men.

The arms of the family, *Gules, three Tyrwhits* (or lapwings), *Or,* are of course allusive, and from them, doubtless, arose the silly legend about Sir Hercules Tyrwhitt's having been rescued from impending death by the pee-wit cry of a flock of lapwings. See Eng. Surn. ii. 13. Camden cites this among curious local surnames; and according to a document quoted in Burke's Commoners, i. 583, the lands of Tyrwhitt are in Northumberland.

TYSSEN. Of Flemish origin, and resident at Ghent, and afterwards at Flushing, in Holland, about the commencement of the XVII. cent. Daniel Tyssen, of the latter town, married Apollonia Ridley, a grand-niece of Nicholas Ridley, bishop of London, who suffered in the Marian persecution. By her he had a son, who settled in London, and was naturalized by Act of Parliament in 1689.

TYSON. Gilbert Tison, a Norman of distinction, was a tenant in chief at the making of Domesday.

TYTHERIDGE. See Titheridge.

TYTLER. The Scottish family of this name are stated to be a younger branch of the noble house of Seton. The ancestor is said to have fled into France temp. James IV., in consequence of his having slain a gentleman in a sudden quarrel at a hunting match, and there to have adopted, for concealment, the name of Tytler. His two sons, bearing the same name, returned to Scotland with Queen Mary. B.L.G. The statement appears very improbable; and the etymology of the *alias,* if such it be, is unknown. Le Titteler occurs in H.R., and Jamieson, gives Titlar as a tattler, or talkative person.

TYTTERY. This family, with those of Tyzack and Henzey, were French Protestant refugees, who, towards the end of XVI. century, settled in cos. Stafford and Worcester, and introduced the broad-glass manufacture into England. N. and Q., 1856.

TYZACKE. See under Tyttery.

U.

UDALL. Local : " the dale where yew-trees grow ?"

UDELL. See Udall.

UDNY. UDNEY. A parish in Aberdeenshire, still in possession of the family.

UFFELL. Mr. Ferguson suggests that this is a diminutive of Uffa, an A-Sax. personal name.

UFFORD. " Of this family," says Sir W. Dugdale, " which afterwards arrived to great honour, I have not seen anything memorable until 53. Henry III., when Robert, a younger son of John de Peyton, of Peyton in the county of Suffolk, assuming his surname from the lordship of Ufford, in that shire, became Robert de Ufford." His son of the same name was summoned to Parliament as a baron in 1308, and his grandson, also a Robert de Ufford, was created Earl of Suffolk.

UGHTRED. An ancient personal name.

Robert Ughtred of Yorkshire flourished 28. Edward I., and was father of Thomas Ughtred, summoned to Parliament as a baron in 1343.

UGLY. Ugley, a parish in Essex, concerning which there runs a proverb :—

" UGLEY CHURCH, UGLEY STEEPLE.
UGLEY PARSON, UGLEY PEOPLE."

ULLATHORNE. Doubtless local, and, as I think, in Scotland, where places called Ulladale, Ullahouse, Ullapool, &c., are found.

ULMER. An ancient personal name, occurring in Domesday in the various forms of Ulmarus, Ulmerus, and Ulmar.

ULPH. The Scandinavian form of Wolf.

UMFRAVILLE. The founder of this noble family in England was Robert de Umfraville, otherwise called " Robert with the Beard," lord of Tour and Vian. He is named in Leland's so-called Roll of Battel Abbey.

"Marney et Maundeville,
Vipont et Umfreville."

To him the Conqueror, in the 10th year of his reign, gave the forest, valley, and lordship of Redesdale in Northumberland, to hold by the service of defending that part of the realm for ever against enemies and wolves, *with the Sword which King William had by his side when he entered Northumberland.* His descendant, Gilbert de U., was ennobled by Edward I. " This family declined from its high estate at no very distant period from its source, but it only became extinct in the male line within living memory. Its last representative but one kept a chandler's shop at Newcastle, and, ·falling into difficulties, accepted the office of keeper of St. Nicholas' Workhouse, in the same city, where he died, leaving a widow, with a son and daughter, in absolute destitution. The late Duke of Northumberland allowed the widow a pension, and procured a midshipman's appointment for the son, who obtained the rank of captain, but died without issue." Quarterly Review, April, 1860.

The name seems to be derived from one of the several places in Normandy now called Amfreville, but in some instances originally Onfreville, that is, *Hunfredi villa,* the vill or abode of Humphrey.

UMNEY. A corruption of Ommaney.

UMPELBY. UMPLEBY. See Uppleby.

UMPHRASTOUN. Stated in Encycl. Herald. To be " of that Ilk," in Scotland. That Ilk is not to be found in the Gazetteer.

UNCLE. Analogous to Father, Brother, Cousin, &c. Johannes le Uncle. H.R.

UNDERCLIFF. From residence under a cliff; or from the village of that name in the Isle of Wight. In the H.R. it is spelt Hunderclyvt.

UNDERDOWN. Nearly synonymous with Underhill.

UNDERHAY. Local : " under the hedge?" See Hay.

UNDERHILL. Local; from residence at the foot of, or *under,* a hill.

UNDERWOOD. A township in Derbyshire. In H.R. it is latinized Sub-Bosco.

UNDRELL. See Underhill.

UNETT. The family have a tradition of a Norman-Conquest origin. At an early period they branched into two lines, one of which settled in Staffordshire, and the other in Herefordshire. B.L.G.

UNIACKE. The family are traditionally descended from the Fitz-Geralds, springing from the Desmond branch of that mighty house. The following is said to be the origin of the name :—" In the skirmishes which were constantly taking place between the rival houses of Fitz-Gerald and Butler, a service attended with great danger being

necessary to be done, and the commander, hesitating whom to employ, an individual was pointed out, and recommended to him, with the remark : *Unicus est,* meaning, " He is the only person to undertake this service." These two words became not only the family motto, but also the surname of the descendants of that unique individual ! B.L.G. The family have long been connected with the counties of Cork and Waterford.

UNITE. Probably the same as Unett.

UNKETEL. UNKITTLE. Ancient forms of Anchitel.

UNTHANK. There is a township of this name in the county of Cumberland, and another in Northumberland.

UNWYN. Apparently an old personal name, the same as Onwen, a manumitted serf, mentioned in Cod. Dipl. 971. Mr. Ferguson thinks the meaning of it to be, either A-Sax. *unwine,* enemy, the reverse of *wine,* friend; or *unwinn,* unconquerable. H.R. Unwine. Unwyne.

UPCHER. Probably Upchurch, a parish in Kent.

UPCOT. Local : " the high or upper cottage." H.R. Uppecote.

UPHAM. A parish in Hampshire.

UPHILL. A parish in Somersetshire.

UPJOHN. A corruption of the Welsh Ap-John.

UPPERTON. A place near Petworth, another at Eastbourne—both in Sussex.

UPPLEBY. A Lincolnshire family. The surname has been variously written De Epulbie, Upplebaie, and Appleby, which last is supposed to be the most correct form. One of the places called Appleby is situated in Lincolnshire.

UPRICHARD. The Irish corruption of Ap Richard.

UPSALL. Two townships in Yorkshire are so called.

UPSHIRE. A hamlet in Essex. The surname is commonly spelt Upsher.

UPTHOMAS. A corruption of Ap-Thomas.

UPTON. There are many places in various counties called Upton; and there are doubtless several distinct origins for the surname. The most distinguished family, the ancestors of the Viscounts Templetown, originated at Uppeton, or Upton, an extensive manor branching into several parishes of East Cornwall, where John de Upton, grandfather of Hamelyn de Upton, who was party to a deed executed in 1218, flourished in the XII. century. See C. S. Gilbert's Cornwall, i. 462.

UPWARD. Local : " the upper ward, or district."

UPWARDS. A pluralization of Upward.

2 z

URBY. The same as Irby.

URE. 1. A Yorkshire river. 2. Eur occurs as a personal name in Domesday; and an early Scandinavian gave his name to Ureby, or Ewerby, in Lincolnshire. 3. The baronial family of Eure took their name, in the XIII. century, from the lordship of Eure or Evre, in Buckinghamshire.

A gentleman of this name having deserted a lady to whom he had been affianced, Douglas Jerrold remarked, that he could not have thought that *Ure* would have proved a *base un.*

UREN. The same as Urwyn.

URIDGE. An East Sussex name. It is found in that district temp. Edward II., in the form of De Eweregge. Sussex Arch. Coll. xii. 25.

URLING. Mr. Ferguson considers this identical with the Danish Erling, signifying industrious.

URQUHART. There are places called Urquhart in the shires of Moray, Inverness, and Ross. The family are traced to Galleroch de Urchart, who lived temp. Alexander II. His descendants were hereditary sheriffs of Cromarty.

Sir Thomas Urquhart, who flourished in the middle of the XVII. century, drew up his pedigree, which is one of the finest pieces of fictitious genealogy in existence, commencing with Adam, from whom he makes himself the *hundred and forty-third* in descent. The local origin of the surname he ignores, and derives it from Ourqhartos, "i. e., the fortunate and well-beloved," who was fifth in descent from Noah, and married the Queen of the Amazons! Another of his ancestors was the intimate friend of Nimrod, the mighty hunter; another married that daughter of Pharaoh who found Moses in the bulrushes; while another espoused a daughter of Bacchus! Dixon on Surnames, edit. 1855.

URRIE. See Urry.

URRY. 1. There is a parish called Urray on the borders of Inverness and Rossshires. 2. Mr. Ferguson derives it from the O. Norse *urri*, a dog; and asks, "Has this anything to do with our word *worry?*

Urri, a dog, would be in A-Sax. *wurri.*" This etymology appears to me preferable to Dr. Richardson's.

URSON. A translation of the A.-Norm. Fitz-Urse, rendered historical as the name borne by one of the assassins of Thomas-à-Becket. Urso and Urso Vicecomes are Domesday names.

URSWICK. A parish in Lancashire, in which county the family were resident at an early date.

URWICK. Probably the same as Urswick.

URWYN. Apparently an ancient personal name.

URYN. The same as Urwyn.

US. A termination of several surnames, being a contraction of house; for example—

Loftus   is Lofthouse
Duffus   „ Dovehouse
Bacchus „ Bakehouse
Stonnus „ Stonehouse, &c.

USBORNE. Perhaps a corruption of Ousebourne.

USHER. Fr. *huissier.* An official attendant on great persons, and in dignified courts of law, &c.

USSHER. This family, of which the celebrated Archbishop of Armagh was a member, settled in Ireland temp. King John; and the patriarch of the race is said to have adopted the surname in consequence of his having held the office of *usher* to that monarch. B.L.G.

UTLAW. An old spelling of Outlaw.

UTTERMARE. Fr. *D'outre mer,* 'from beyond the sea,' a foreigner—foreign, that is, in regard to France, from which country the name seems to have been imported. It appears to be almost entirely limited to the county of Somerset.

UTTING. A baptismal name. Utting de Cresswell was witness to a deed temp. King John. Gent. Mag. Oct. 1832. Uttyng appears as a surname in H.R.

V.

VACHER. Old Eng. *vachery*, from Fr. *vacherie*, is a cow-house, or, in a more extended sense, a dairy. There are several minor places and farms in various parts of England called, in old deeds, La Vacherie. This surname is probably either a contraction of *vachery*, or an obsolete word meaning a person who superintended one—a cowkeeper.

VACY. The same as Vesey.

VADE. Probably from the old latinization of Ford—De Vado.

VAIR. Probably the same as Vere.

VAISEY. VAIZEY. The same as Vesey.

VALANCE. VALLANCE. A place on the confines of Poitou, in France, gave name to William de Valence, who was son of Hugh le Brun, Earl of March, and Isabel, widow of King John. He came into England in 1247, by the invitation of his uterine brother, King Henry III., and was father of the renowned Aylmer de Valence, temp. Edward I.

VALE. A valley, a low ground. Johnson designates this a poetical word.

VALENTINE. The baptismal name. This surname is sometimes corrupted in the South to Follington. H.R. Valentyn.

VALET. VALLET. An attendant upon a great man. In royal households there were *valetti ad coronam*, " Valets of the Crown." See Jacob's Law Dict.

VALLENTINE. See Valentine.

VALLER. Pierre Valler, a Protestant refugee from Rouen, landed at Rye in 1572. Lansd. MS. 15. 70.

VALLETORT. In the time of William Rufus flourished Reginald de Valletort; and in 33. Henry II. Roger de Valletort was lord of Trematon Castle, co. Cornwall, from whom sprang the barons of this name. Baronage. The name is local, and signifies " the curved valley." In charters it is usually latinized De Valle Torta.

VALLINGS. The oldest traceable spelling of this name is Valeyns, which is probably identical with Valance.

VALPY. From the Italian family of Volpi, so long, and even at the present day, located at Como, whence the Norman branch came with the returning chieftains in the early Italian wars. The surname is synonymous with our Fox—*volpe*, *vulpes*. Inf. J. Bertrand Payne, Esq.

☞ VAN. A prefix to Dutch family names, many of which have become naturalized in England, as Vanburgh, Vandeput, Vansittart, Vanneck, Vanwilder, &c. Like the French DE, and the old English ATTE, it implies residence in a place; thus Hendrik Van der Veld signifies Henry at the Field; Dirk Van der Bogart, Theodore of the Orchard; Rykert Van Buren, Richard of Buren, a town in Holland, &c. So very common is this prefix in Holland, that, in speaking of a person's family name, they call it his VAN; as in the phrase: " Ik weet zyn Van niet."—I don't know his Surname.

VANACKER. The extinct baronet's family, of Dutch extraction, were London merchants, in the former half of the XVII. century.

VANDEPUT. Henry Vandeput, a member of an ancient family in the Netherlands, fled from Antwerp in 1568, to avoid the persecution of the Protestants by the Duke of Alva, and settled in England. From him descended the baronets. The name is synonymous with the English At-Well, Wells, or Weller.

VANE. Collins shews that the two peerage families of Vane and Fane are of the same origin. See Fane. The arms consist of the same tinctures and charges, viz. :— *Azure, three gauntlets, Or,* but the gauntlets of the Vanes are for the left hand, while those of the Fanes are *dexter* or right hand ones.

VANNECK. An ancient Dutch family. The founder of the English branch was Sir Joshua Vanneck, of Hevenham Hall, co. Suffolk, who was created a Baronet in 1751, and whose son was elevated to the peerage as Lord Huntingfield, in 1796.

VANSITTART. Lord Bexley is descended from an ancient German family, who traditionally derived their name from Sittart, a town in the Duchy of Juliers. The first settler in England was Peter Vansittart, who came from Dantzick about 1675, and became an eminent Russia merchant.

VARDON. VARDEN. See Verdon.

VARLEY. Verley, a parish in Essex.

VARNEY. The same as Verney.

VARNHAM. Vernham-Dean is a parish in Hampshire.

VASEY. The same as Vesey.

VASSALL. In the feudal system, a Vassal was one who held under another; more generally, one who was subject to an under-tenant or mesne lord. Hence the word became, in time, almost synonymous with slave.

VAUGHAN. Welsh *vychan*, little in stature; answering to Petit, Basset, Little, &c. A personal name of great antiquity. In the more eminent families, the Ap was disused in the XVI. and XVII. centuries. The Vaughans of Burlton Hall, co. Salop, deduce themselves from the renowned Tudor Trevor, the common patriarch of so many noble and gentle families in the principality. The Vaughans of Penmaen spring from Seissyllt, lord of Mathavarn, in the XIV. century, through Jenkin Vychan, Esquire of the body to King Henry VII., whose son John, adopted the settled name of Vychan or Vaughan. The Vaughans of Court Field, co. Monmouth, were of good antiquity before the adoption of the settled surname, in the XVI. cent. B.L.G.

VAUTORT. The same as Valletort.

VAUX. 1. It is said that the illustrious family of Vaux derived their surname from a district in Normandy; which is very probable, there being seven or eight places in that province still so designated. It is further asserted that so early as A.D. 794, a branch of the family, bearing the surname of Beaux, Baux, or Vaux, were settled in Provence; which cannot be correct, as heritable family names were not introduced until long after that date. There is, however, no doubt of the influence of the Vauxes in the South of France, and in Italy, at a remote period. A tomb erected in 1615, in the church of St. Clair at Naples, by Hieronymus de Vaux, contains the bones of divers of the females of his ancestry, namely:—

Antonia de Vaux, Queen of Sicily.
Isabella de Vaux, Queen of Naples.
Cecilia de Vaux, Countess of Savoy.
Sibella de Vaux, Princess of Piedmont.
Maria de Vaux, Dauphiness of Vienne.
Isabella de Vaux, Despotess of Servia.

The English family spring from Bertrand de Vaux, who was living in 929, and was a favourite of Robert I., Duke of Normandy, the Conqueror's grandfather. Harold de Vaux, Lord of Vaux, attended William I. at the Conquest, and was accompanied by his three sons, Hubert, Ranulph, and Robert. From Hubert sprang the great house of Vaux, or De Vallibus, of Cumberland; and from Robert came the Barons Vaux, of Harrowden, co. Northampton. The heiress of the elder line of this Robert married, in 1553, Thomas Brougham, Lord of Brougham, co. Westmoreland, and hence the title of Henry, Lord Brougham and *Vaux.*

2. The O. French form of De Vallibus, of the origin of which, as a surname, we have this account in Denton's Cumberland MSS., under the barony of Gilsland: "This great barony was given by the Earl Ranulph Meschines to one Hubertus, to be holden of him by two knights' fees and cornage: he was called De Vallibus, or Vaulx, from the dales or Vallies, whereof that country is full. The French word Vaulx (pronounced Vaux) became thence a surname to him and his posterity there, and to divers other families that took their be-

ginning from the younger brothers of this house." Hutchinson's Cumberland, i. 47.

VAVASOUR. A dignity of somewhat doubtful origin and import. Sir John Ferne regards it as the equivalent of Banneret. "These Vavasours," says he, "were called by an ancient English lawyer (Bracton), Viri magnæ dignitatis: men of great dignitye. And this worde Vavasor he interpreteth to be this: Vas sortitum ad valetudinem, a man chosen for his valour and prowesse, placinge them above the dignitye of knighthood." Blazon of Gentrie, p. 102. Vavasores Regis, who occur in Domesday Book, "are much the same with Liberi homines Regis." Selden's Titles of Honour, p. 625. Chaucer, in his description of the Frankelein, or great freeholder, says, there—

"Was no wher swiche a worthy *Vavasour.*"

See more in Halliwell, and in Eng. Surn. in voc.

The Vavasours of Yorkshire have held their estate uninterruptedly from Mauger, the founder of their race, who was one of the Conqueror's *ravasores*, except a short time in the reign of Henry III., when it is said to have been pledged to a Jew for £350. "It is observed of this family," says Fuller, "that they never married an heir, or buried their wives." Worthies of Eng. iii. 454. The male line has failed since Fuller's days, and more than once the estate has been carried to other families by a sole-heiress, whose husband has, however, adopted the ancient surname.

VAVASSEUR. See Vavasour.

VAWDREY. The name of Vaudrai, or Vaudrey, is derived from a place so called in France, where the Sieurs de Vaudrai continued to flourish until the reign of Louis XIV. Between the years 1153 and 1181, Hugh Kevelioc, Earl of Chester, granted to Sir Claud de Vaudrai lands in Altrincham, and elsewhere in that county; and from him the existing Vawdreys of Cheshire are presumed to have sprung. B.L.G.

VEAL. VEALE. 1. In old records Le Veal. O. Fr., "the calf." 2. In some cases probably from O. Fr. Le Viel, "the old," to distinguish the individual from a younger man of the same baptismal name. H.R. The form Viel is still found in Lond. Direct.

VEAR. See De Vere.

VECK. Probably the same as the Le Vecke of the H.R. Fr. L'Evêque, "the bishop."

VENABLES. The progenitor of the great Cheshire family was a tenant under Hugh Lupus, temp. William I., whom he had probably accompanied to the Conquest of England. The name is local, from Venables, a parish in the arrondissement of Louviers, in Normandy.

VENELL. Low Lat. *venella*, a passage or lane. It is still used in Scotland in that sense. H.R. En la Venele, De la Venele, In Venella, &c.

VENESS. 1. See Venus. 2. Venice, the Italian city?

VENN. Ven-Ottery is a parish in Devonshire.

VENNELL. See Venell.

VENNER. The same as Venour.

VENOUR. O. Fr. A hunter. Le Venour. Le Venur. H.R.

VENTRIS. Venturas is a not uncommon surname in Italy; and it may be found among the doctors of the canon law in England, in the middle ages. A place in the arrondissement of Montagne, in Normandy, is called La Ventrouse.

VENUS. De Venuse occurs as a surname, 31. Edw. I.—Steph. de Venuse miles. This name, by the suppression of the territorial *de*, and the final *e*, would become identical with the designation of the goddess of beauty. The locality of Venuse is unknown.

VERDON. Bertram de Verdun, the progenitor of this distinguished race, came in with the Conqueror, and was lord of Farneham-Royal, co. Bucks, which he held in chief in 1087, by the serjeanty of providing a glove for the King's right hand, on the day of his coronation, and of supporting his right hand while he held the royal sceptre. Verdun is a town in the N.E. of France, department of Meuse; and it has been suggested that the family were derived from the Counts or Viscounts of Verdun. Vide L'Art de Verifier les Dates, xiii. 444. Sussex Arch. Coll. x. 68.

The Irish Verdons are descended from Bertram Verdon, who accompanied Prince (afterwards King) John, to that country, in 1184, and was appointed Seneschal of the English Pale. D'Alton.

VERE, DE. The old pedigree of the De Veres began with a distinguished Roman, Lucius *Verus!!* (See Quarterly Review, April, 1860.)

The parish and château of Ver, in the canton of Guvray, department of La Manche in Normandy, are stated by de Gerville (Mem. Soc. Ant. Normandie, 1825) to have been the habitation of Aubrey de Vere, who was at the Conquest, and of Robert de Vere, who, in 1135, conveyed the body of King Henry I. to England. But in Clutterbuck's Hertfordshire there is an elaborate pedigree of the De Veres, which makes the first Alberic or Aubrey de Vere, son of Alphonsus surnamed *de Veer*, from a town so called, in the island of Walcheren in Holland.

In some instances, especially in Scotland, this ancient surname has been corrupted to Were and Weir.

A most eloquent lamentation over the decay of ancient families was pronounced on the judgment seat. In the year 1626, the death of Henry de Vere, Earl of Oxford, gave rise to a contest between Robert de Vere, claiming as heir male of the body of Aubrey de Vere, and Lord Willoughby of Eresby, claiming as heir-general of the last Earl. Chief Justice Crewe spoke thus:—

" This great and weighty cause, incomparable to any other that hath happened at any time, requires great deliberation, and solid and mature judgment to determine it ; and I wish that all the Judges of England had heard it (being a fit case for all) to the end we altogether might have given our humble advice to your Lordships herein. Here is represented to your Lordships *certamen honoris*, and, as I may well say, *illustris honoris*, illustrious honour. I heard a great peer of this realm, and a learned, say, when he lived, there was no king in Christendom had such a subject as Oxford. He came in with the Conqueror, Earl of Gwynes; shortly after the Conquest made Great Chamberlain of England, above five hundred years ago, by Henry I., the Conqueror's son, brother to Rufus; by Maud, the Empress, Earl of Oxford; confirmed and approved by Henry II., *Alberico comiti*, so Earl before. This great honour, this high and noble dignity, hath continued ever since in the remarkable surname of De Vere, by so many ages, descents, and generations, as no other kingdom can produce such a peer in one and the self-same name and title. I find in all this length of time but two attainders of this noble family, and those in stormy and tempestuous times, when the government was unsettled and the kingdom in competition. I have laboured to make a covenant with myself that affection may not press upon judgment, for I suppose there is no man that hath any apprehension of gentry or nobleness, but his affection stands to the continuance of so noble a name and house, and would take hold of a twig or a twine-thread to uphold it. And yet Time hath his revolutions; there must be a period and an end to all temporal things—*finis rerum*, an end of names and dignities, and whatsoever is *terrene;* and why not of De Vere? For *where is Bohun? Where is Mowbray? Where is Mortimer? Nay, which is more and most of all, where is Plantagenet?* They are entombed in the urns and sepulchres of mortality. And yet let the name and dignity of De Vere stand so long as it pleaseth God !"—*Jones's Rep.*, 101.

The decision was in favour of the male heir. On the death of his son, in 1702, without issue, the line became extinct.— *Quarterly Review*, April 1860.

VERGIL. The classical personal name —Virgilius.

VERITY. Probably a character in some old "Morality." See Vice.

VERNEY. From Vernai, a parish in the arrondissement of Bayeux, latinized in charters, temp. Hen. I., as *Vernacum.*

VERNON. William de Vernon was lord and owner of the town and district of Vernon sur Seine, in the arrondissement of Louviers in 1052. His eldest son, Richard, accompanied William the Conqueror to England in 1066, and was one of the seven barons created by the kinglet, Hugh Lupus, the Conqueror's nephew, in his county-palatine of Chester. A Walter de Vernon was also a tenant in chief in co. Bucks, at the time of the Domesday survey.

VERRALL. This name, abundant in East Sussex, and rarely found out of it, may be a corruption of Firle, a parish near Lewes — sometimes in old documents written Ferle, and usually pronounced as a dissyllable.

VERREY. See Verry.

VERRY. Said to be a 'nursename' of Everard.

VERTUE. An old spelling of Virtue.

VESEY. Robert de Veci assisted William I. at the Conquest of England, and was rewarded with great estates in the counties of Northampton, Leicester, Warwick, and Lincoln. Ivo or John de Veschi was his near kinsman, and from him, in the female line, descended Lord Vesey. Kelham's Domesday. A branch of the family, in the Irish peerage, bear the title of Viscount de Vesci.

VESK. A contraction of the Old Fr. *evesque*, a bishop.

VESPER. See TIMES and SEASONS.

VESSEY. See Vesey.

VETCH. See Tares.

VEZEY. See Vesey.

VIBERT. A Teutonic personal name— Uibert. Cod. Dipl. No. 523.

VICAR. See ECCLESIASTICAL SURNAMES.

VICARS. Descended from the family of Don Vicaro, a Spanish cavalier, who came to England in the suite of Queen Catharine of Arragon, and settled in Ireland early in the XVI. century. Mem. of Capt. Hedley Vicars, 1857.

VICARY. VICKERY. Lat. *vicarius*, a vicar, or rather a curate.

> "Quod a lewed *vicory*,
> I am a curator of holy kirke."
> *Piers Ploughman, ii. p.* 420.

> "Sire preest, quod he, art thou a *Vicary?*
> Or art thou a *Person?* say soth by thy fay,"
> *(Chaucer. Persones Prologue.)*

—In modern parlance; "Are you only a curate, or are you a rector?"
The name is sometimes local. De Vicarie. H.R.

VICE. Halliwell says—"The buffoon of our early drama." When the "Mysteries" ceased to be played for the amusement of our medieval ancestors, a kind of performances succeeded, which were known as Moralities. In these the dialogue was sustained by allegorical characters, "such as Good Doctrine, Charity, Faith, Prudence, Discretion, Death, and the like, and their discourses were of a serious cast." The foil to all these excellent personages was the Vice or Iniquity, who usually personified some evil propensity, and kept up a running fire of wit at the expense of the rest.

He was attired in comical costume and carried a wooden sword. Stubs, in his Anatomie of Abuses, 1595, asks: "Who will call him a wise man who playeth the part of a Foole or a Vice?" See Strutt's Sports and Pastimes. Ben Johnson thus alludes to this character:

> " —— But the old Vice
> Acts old Iniquity, and in the fit
> Of mimicry, gets th' opinion of a wit."

Several London traders bear this remarkable name.

VICKARE. See Vicar.

VICKERMAN. *? Homo vicarius*—a man who acts for another; a substitute.

VICKERS. See Vicars.

VICKERY. See Vicary.

VICKRESS. The same as Vickridge.

VICKRIDGE. Perhaps a corruption of *vicarage*—from residence at or near one.

VICTOR. The personal name.

VIDAL. French Protestant refugees, after the Revocation of the Edict of Nantes, 1685. The parent stock were, not many years since, resident at Montauban. The family seem to have ranged from the South of France to the North of Spain, and there are many of the name in Spanish America. The arms borne by the late Rt. Rev. O. E. Vidal, Bishop of Sierra Leone, and his immediate ancestors, indicate a Spanish rather than a French, origin.

VIDLER. A West of England pronunciation of Fiddler.

VIEL. See Veal.

VIGERS See Vigor.

VIGNOLES. At the Revocation of the Edict of Nantes, Jacques Louis Vignolles (a descendant of François la Hire, Baron of Vignoles, and seigneur of Causabon, 1550), took refuge in Holland, from whence he accompanied King William III. to England, and afterwards settled in Ireland. The name is probably a corruption, either of Fr. *vignoble*, a vineyard, or O. Fr. *vignolet*, a vine-dresser.

VIGOR. St. Vigor was a saint of considerable reputation in Normandy, and gave his name to several places in that province, from one of which the English family are conjectured to have sprung.

VIGORS. The genitive form of Vigor.

VILE. Probably a corruption of the Fr. La Ville.

VILLARS. The same as Villiers.

VILLEBOIS. This local Fr. surname, naturalized in Lincolnshire, is there pronounced Veal-Boy!

VILLERS. See Villiers.

VILLIERS. The family are said to have come into England with the Conqueror, which is probable. There are at present six places in Normandy so called, besides a larger number called Villers, one of the numerous ways in which the surname is spelled. The Earl of Jersey's family trace to Alexander de Villiers, lord of Brokesby, co. Lancaster, early in the XIII. century. Sir Richard de Villars was a Crusader under Edward I., and hence the cross and escallop shells in the coat-armour of his descendants.

VINALL. Fynagh, Fynhawe, and Vynagh, are ancient modes of spelling the name of the estate now called Vine-Hall, in the parish of Watlington, co. Sussex, which was possessed by the family in the XIV. cent. That estate gave name to the Vynehalls, afterwards of Kingston, near Lewes, who, as Vinalls, in 1657, obtained a grant of arms. Harl. MS. 1144. Sussex Arch. Coll. ix. 75.

VINCE. A 'nurse-name' of Vincent.

VINCENT. The well-known personal name. The oldest family of Vincent trace from Miles Vincent, who was owner of lands at Swinford, co. Leicester, 10. Edward II. Shirley's Noble and Gentle Men.

VINCER. Perhaps a modification of Vincent.

VINCETT. A common corruption of Vincent.

VINE. O. Eng. a vineyard—a name common to many places in the South of England. In Norman times, the culture of the vine was a considerable branch of industry, and many great houses, especially monasteries, had their vineyards. See Archæologia, vols. i. and iii., and Ellis, Introd. Domesd. i. 121.

VINES. See Vine.

VINEHALL. See Vinall.

VINER. One who had the care of a vineyard. A Walterus Vinitor, or vinedresser, occurs in Domesday, under co. Surrey. Le Vinour, Le Vynor. H.R.

VINK. A west-country form of Fink.

VINSON. VINSUN. Corruptions of Vincent.

VINTER. Probably a contraction of *vinitor*, a vine-dresser, or of *vintner*, a dealer in wine. From one of these sources it is probable that Winter is sometimes by corruption derived. Le Vineter. H.R. See Viner.

VIPON. See Vipont.

VIPONT. (Latinized 'De Veteri Ponte,' —of the Old Bridge.) There are several places in Normandy called Vieupont; and the great Anglo-Norman family so desig-

nated came from Vipont, near Lisieux. Sussex Arch. Coll. ii. 77.

VIRGIN. This name, with Virgoe (Lat. *virgo*), Verge (Fr. *vierge*), Virgint (Irish corruption), seems to relate to the *cultus* of St. Mary. A personage named Virgin is, or lately was, High-Admiral of Sweden.

VIRGINT. See Virgin.

VIRGOE. See Virgin.

VIRTUE. Perhaps from a personification in some " Morality " or drama. See Vice.

VITTY. Decent, proper, handsome. *West.* Halliwell.

VIVASH. A Devizes correspondent writes :—" Vivash, a name still of some distinction in this neighbourhood, betrays the western pronunciation of Five Ashes." I should prefer deducing it from the Fr. *vivace*, which Cotgrave defines as " livelie, lustie, strong, vigorous ; nimble, active, quicke ; full of life, mettall, spirit ; also of long life."

VIZARD. Possibly the same as Wishart.

VODDEN. Mr. Ferguson derives it from Woden, Odin, the Teutonic divinity.

VOGAN. A tything in the parish of Chippenham, co. Wilts.

VOSS. *Vos*, a Dutch and Low Germ. form of Fox.

VOWELL. Voel, an ancient personal name in Wales.

The following is related of the eccentric Dr. Barton, Warden of Merton College, Oxon. A friend told him that Dr. Vowel was dead. " *Vowel* dead !" said he ; " let us be thankful 'tis neither *U* nor *I I!*" From an Oxford newspaper.

VOWLER. A West of England pronunciation of Fowler.

VOWLES. Mr. Ferguson thinks that this name corresponds with the German and Dutch *vogel*, a fowl.

VULLIAMY. Perhaps from Villamée, a place in Brittany.

VYSE. VYZE. The rustic pronunciation of Devizes, co. Wilts. Devizes occurs as a surname about 1646.

VYVIAN. The ancient Latin personal name. The Vyvians of Truro are derived by certain genealogists from one Vivianus Annius, a Roman general, son-in-law to Domitius Corbulo ! *Quarterly Rev.* CII. p. 304. The pedigree recognized by the heralds begins only in the XIII. century, with Sir Vyel Vyvyan, knight.

W.

WACE. The vernacular form of the Latin Eustacius. It is best known as the personal name of the celebrated author of the Roman de Rou, who flourished in the XII. century, at which time it had not become a surname. Wright's Biog. Brit. Anglo-Norm. period, 206.

At a later date the name was variously written Vaice, Wasse, Wass, &c. It existed in Jersey until the XVI. century, and it is not now extinct in England. "One of the name was traditionally the perfection of a cynic—in fact an insular Diogenes; whence in Jersey-French the word signifies to snarl, as in the phrase, "Ce chien wasse." Inf. J. B. Payne, Esq.

WACEY. Perhaps the same as Vacey.

WACKETT. Probably the same as Waggett.

WADD. Wad, the name of a hero of romance. Jamieson. See Wade.

WADDEL. Perhaps a personal name. Wadel and Wadhels occur in Domesday. Also local; the same as Odell. De Wadhalle. H.R.

WADDILOVE. The personal name written in Domesday Wadel and Wadhels, is also varied to Wadelo, which may be the source of this surname.

WADDING. Perhaps the patronymical form of the A-Sax. Wade. Waddington, Waddingham, Waddingworth, &c., as names of places, seem to be derived from this source. According to Mr. D'Alton the name is of record in Ireland, from temp. Edward III.

WADDINGTON. A parish in Lincolnshire, and a chapelry in Yorkshire.

WADDY. Probably the same as Wadding.

WADE. 1. Verstegan says, "WADE, of his dwelling at a meadow;" and others make it synonymous with Ford—a water that may be waded: H.R. De Wade, and De la Wade. 2. It is also a personal name. Wade was one of the heroes of Scandinavian mythology, and became the subject of a medieval romance, often referred to in Chaucer and other writers, but now lost. "It appears," says Mr. Wright, "to have related a long series of wild adventures which Wade encountered in his boat, named Guingelot." Wright's Cant. Tales, ii. 93. A Wade or Wada, probably a Saxon, is named in Domesday, as having held lands previously to the Survey.

WADESON. The son of Wade, which see.

WADHURST. A parish in Sussex.

WADKIN. See Watkin.

WADLAND. A corruption of Woodland.

WADLAW. See Wardlaw.

WADLEY. A hamlet near Farringdon, co. Berks.

WADSWORTH. A township in Yorkshire, where the family resided in early times.

WAGEMAN. See Wager.

WAGER. *Wageoure* is used by the Scot. poet Barbour, for a mercenary soldier —one who fights for a 'wage' or hire. Hence also Wageman.

WAGG. 1. Perhaps A-Sax. *waeg*, a way. 2. Perhaps the same name as Waga, which occurs in the genealogy of the Mercian kings.

WAGGETT. A corruption of some local surname terminating in *gate*.

WAGHORN. Horn is a common termination, and the name may be local. In Scotland, a mythical person bears this appellation, and he is said to have been crowned king of liars. Hence people guilty of extravagant lying are said to be— "AS FALSE AS WAGHORN, *and he was nineteen times falser than the Deil!*" Jamieson.

WAGNER. Germ. *wagner*, a wheelwright or cartwright. Naturalized from Germany.

WAGSTAFF. Applied to one who could brandish or *wag* a staff with effect. It belongs to the same class as Shakeshaft, Longstaffe, Shakspeare, &c., and is the most common of that class. It is curious to observe, among the archives of Stratford-upon-Avon, record of proceedings between Richard *Wagstaff* and John *Shakespere*— the latter being the poet's father. See Halliwell's Life of Shakspeare, p. 41. H.R. Waggestaff, Wagestaf.

WAHULL. See Odell.

WAIGHT. The same as Wait.

WAINFLEET. A town in Lincolnshire.

WAINMAN. The driver of a wain or wagon.

WAINWRIGHT. (A - Sax. *wæn*.) *Wain* is an old, but nearly obsolete, word for wagon. In Sussex, a shed in which wagons stand is called a wain-house or 'wen-hus,' and in some parts of England a wagoner is called a wain-man, whence the surname Wenman. Nor must we forget the constellation, Charles's Wain. A Wainwright was therefore synonymous with

Cartwright and Wheelwright, also English surnames, and signified a builder of wagons.

WAISTELL. See Wastel.

WAIT. WAITE. In the Prompt. Parv. a watchman; but more generally understood to be a minstrel, especially one who performs in the night. See Halliwell, and Jamieson. Le Wayte. H.R.

WAITHMAN. A hunter. Teutoni, *weyd-man*, venator, auceps. Jamieson.

WAKE. Much discrepancy exists among genealogists as to the origin of this name and family. The baronet's family claim from Hugh Wac, lord of Wilesford, co. Lincoln, temp. Henry I., whose line ended with that Lord Wake, whose sister and heiress married Edmund of Woodstock, a younger son of Edward I. From other authorities it would appear that they spring from Hereward le Wake, who flourished under the Confessor. Archbishop Wake, who wrote a short account of his ancestry, disowns the Norman derivation, and thinks the name Le Wake, or *the Watchful*, a title given to Hereward, to describe his character as a skilful military commander. See N. and Q., 2nd S. vi. *passim*. The name Wake occurs in some copies of the so-called Battel-Abbey Roll.

WAKEFIELD. A large town in Yorkshire.

WAKELEY. See Wakley.

WAKELIN. WAKELING. 1. Walchelinus, a Domesday personal name. Walclin. H.R. 2. See Wakley.

WAKKISON. A Lancashire corruption of Watkinson.

WAKLEY. 1. Wakeley, an extra-parochial liberty, co. Hertford. 2. Mr. Ferguson classes this name with Weakley, Wakeley, Weaklin, and Wakeling, as denoting want of physical power.

WAKEMAN. A-Sax. *waec-man*, a watchman. According to Bailey's Dict. the chief officer of Ripon was anciently called the *wakeman;* but this is incorrect. The Wakeman was an inferior functionary, whose duty was to blow a cow's horn every night at nine o'clock ; and if between such blowing and sun-rise, any burglary took place, it was made good at the public charge.

WALBERTON. A parish in co. Sussex, where the family were resident temp. Edward I.

WALBY. A township in Cumberland.

WALCOT. WALCOTT. There are parishes, &c., called Walcot, in cos. Leicester, Lincoln, Somerset, and Worcester, and a Walcott in co. Norfolk. An eminent family derive their surname from Walcot, a manor in the parish of Lydbury, co. Salop. The first recorded progenitor is Roger de Walcot, 1255. His descendant, in the sixth generation, was John Walcot, of

whom the family pedigree relates, " that playing at chess with King Henry V., he gave him the check-mate with the rooke, whereupon the King changed his arms from the cross with fleur-de-lis, and gave him the rooke for a remembrance." What evidence there may be for this statement, I know not, though it certainly appears from the roll of arms of temp. Richard II. that the coat borne by John de Walcote was *Argent, on a cross patonce Azure, five fleurs-de-lis Or;* while that now borne by the family is, *Argent, a chevron between three chess-rooks Ermine.* See Shirley's Noble and Gentle Men.

According to B.L.G. the Walcots are paternally descended from an ancient Welsh tribe, one of whose members married the Walcot heiress.

WALDEGRAVE. This ancient family, who have been seated in many counties, were originally of Waldegrave, now Walgrave, in Northamptonshire The pedigree is traced to John, son of Warin de Walgrave, sheriff of London, in 1205. Leland speaks of the family thus : " As far as I can gather of young Walgreve of the Courte, the eldest house of the Walgreves cummith out of the Town of Northampton, or ther about, and there yet remaineth in Northamptonshire a man of landes of that name." See Shirley's Noble and Gentle Men.

WALDEN. Parishes, &c., in cos. Essex, Hertford, York, &c.

WALDIE. This family, long settled near Kelso, co. Roxburgh, have at different times written themselves Waitho, Watho, Waltho, and Waldie. The etymology is unknown. Mr. Ferguson makes it the same as the Scandinavian name Valdi.

WALDO. The leader of those early Protestants, the Vaudois, or Waldenses, was Peter Waldo, a merchant of Lyons, who, in the XII. century, denied transubstantiation, and translated the Gospels into French. Peter Waldo, Esq., the author of a Commentary on the Liturgy of the Church of England (1731—1803), is said to have been a lineal descendant of his illustrious namesake.

WALDRON. 1. A parish in Sussex. 2. The personal name Waleran, common in Norman times.

WALDVOGEL. German, a woodhaunting bird, a wood-fowl. This is probably a name of recent importation from Germany.

WALDY. The same as Waldie.

WALE. A local surname, traced in Irish records to the XIV. century. John de Wale was advanced, in 1348, to the see of Ardfert. D'Alton.

WALES. 1. From the country — like Ireland, Scotland, &c. 2. From a parish so called in co. York.

WALESBY. A parish in Nottingham-

3 A

shire, in which county the family resided, temp. Edward I.

WALFORD. Places in co. Hereford, &c.

WALKER. 1. A-Sax. *wealcere*, a fuller. In the N. of England, fullers' earth is called "walker's clay," and a fulling-mill a "walk-mill." In Scotland, *to walk*, or *wauk*, still means to full cloth. 2. A forest officer appointed to *walk* about a certain space of ground committed to his care. Nelson's Laws of Game. This ranks among *numerous* surnames, there being about 250 traders in London who bear it.

WALKINGTON. A parish in Yorkshire.

WALL. See Walls, to which it is ordinarily pluralized.

WALLACE. Though resembling, very closely, the Walleys and Wallis of English family nomenclature, this surname may have a distinct origin. It appears to have been anciently a personal name. Galgacus, the celebrated Caledonian chief, who opposed the arms of Agricola, has been identified by Baxter with Gwallog, a British name, and this has been suggested as the original form of the modern Wallace. See Gentleman's Mag. March, 1856, p. 218.

WALLAS. See Wallace.

WALLEN. The same as Walwyn.

WALLER. The A-Sax. *weallan* means to spring up or boil; and a *weallere* is one who boils—a boiler. At the present day the persons who rake the salt out of the leads at the salt-works at Nantwich, are called *wallers*. Halliwell. Hence the name was anciently latinized Salinator. In the North, a *Waller* is a builder of walls. The Italian surname Muratori, and the French Murier, correspond with the latter sense. H.R. Le Waller and Le Wallur.

WALLINGER. See Waller. In a document of 35. Eliz. *wallinges* are mentioned in the sense of boiling-houses for salt, at Northwich. See N. and Q. July 10, 1858. Hence a 'Wallinger' is probably a saltboiler.

WALLINGTON. Parishes and places in Hertfordshire, Norfolk, Surrey, and Northumberland.

WALLIS. Welsh—a native of Wales. Its form, in the thirteenth and fourteenth centuries, was the Norman-French Le Waleis, Le Waleys, &c., corresponding with the Le Franceis, L'Angleys, &c., of the same date. The Scottish Wallace is, perhaps, identical; but see that article. A totally different origin is, however, assigned to the name in "The Folks of Shields," where it is asserted that "the name of Walles, Wallis, Waleys, Wallase, or Wallace, is specifically derived from Valles, now Vaux, situated near Erie or Yaire, in the Beauvoisin, in France, the manor and castle of which belonged to Ralph de Valles, about the period of the Norman Conquest. The name, however (it is added) has a

generic acceptation. Philip de Valois, King of France, is termed Le Valeys in old writings; the scattered descendants of the Waldenses or Vaudois bore the same distinctive title; and the famous Scottish patriot wrote his name Walles and Wallese. One of the three judges itinerant appointed in 1176, for the northern counties, was Robert *de* Walles. The castle and vill of Valles or Walles is stated to have belonged to Sir Richard *de* Walles, in 1187............ A branch of the family settled at Burgh Wallis, between Doncaster and Pontefract, probably in the reign of Henry III." It appears to me that the writer confounds the *local* De Walles (De Vallibus, or Vaux), with the *patrial* Le Waleys, though the families and names are essentially distinct.

WALLOP. "The true and original name of this family," says Mr. Shirley, is Barton—Peter de Barton, lord of West Barton, in Hampshire, having married Alice, only daughter and heiress of Sir Robert de Wallop, who died in the eleventh year of Edward I. His great-grandson, Richard, assumed the name of Wallop, and was one of the knights of the shire in the second of Edward III. Over and Nether Wallop [co. Hants] so called, says Camden, 'from Well-hop, that is, a pretty well in the side of a hill,' continued, till the reign of Henry V., the principal seat, when Margaret de Valoynes brought into the family the manor of Farley, afterwards called Farley-Wallop, which has since been the usual residence of the Wallops." Noble and Gentle Men.

WALLS. 1. From residence hard by, or upon, a town wall. The forms in the XIII. and XIV. centuries were Atte-Wall, Super le Wal, De la Walle, &c. 2. It was also an old personal name, spelt in Domesday Walle. See also under Wallis.

WALLWORTH. Walworth, a suburb of London.

WALMESLEY. A chapelry in Lancashire.

WALPOLE. "Walpole, in Mershland, co. Norfolk, gave name to this historical family, and here Joceline de Walpole was living in the reign of Stephen. Reginald de Walpole, in the time of Henry I., seems to have been a lineal ancestor of the house. He was father of Richard, who married Emma, daughter of Walter de Howton, or Houghton, which at a very early period became the family seat." Shirley's Noble and Gentle Men.

WALROND. This ancient family were seated at Bradfield, in Uffculm, co. Devon, temp. Henry III. Noble and Gentle Men. The original deed of transfer of Bradfelde from Fulke Paynel, Lord of Bampton, to one Walerande, an ancestor, temp. King John, is still in the possession of the family. It would appear from B.L.G. that the family were resident there before the date of that grant, under the name De Bradfelle, viz., in 1154; and that of Waleran or Walrond was assumed early in the reign of King John. Waleran is an ancient personal name, which was introduced here at the Conquest.

WALSH. WALSHE. A native of Wales.

WALSHAM. Parishes in cos. Norfolk and Suffolk. The baronet's family spring from the latter county, having anciently been lords of the manor of Walsham. The name De Walsham was first assumed by a cadet of the noble house of Ufford, temp. Edward III.

WALSINGHAM. Great and Little Walsingham are parishes in Norfolk.

WALTER. A personal name of Teutonic origin, but not introduced here until the Conquest. Walterus is common among the Domesday tenants. It has become the parent of several surnames, particularly Walters, Waterson, FitzWalter, Watt, Watts, Watson, Watkins, Watkinson, Watcock.

WALTERS. See Walter.

WALTHAM. Parishes and places in Essex, Kent, Lincoln, Berks, Sussex, Hants, Leicester, &c., are so called.

WALTON. The English Gazetteer mentions more than thirty parishes and places so called; and there are one or two others in Scotland.

WALWYN. An A-Sax. personal name. In the H.R. it occurs as a surname—Walwayn.

WAMPULL. Camden mentions this among surnames derived from rivers; but I find no river so called.

WANSBROUGH. Wednesbury, co. Stafford?

WANSEY. This name is traditionally derived from a town in Normandy called Vancy, the locality of which I cannot discover. The Norman origin of the family is indisputable. Hugh de Waunci came over at, or immediately after, the Conquest, and settled at Barsham, co. Norfolk, which manor he held under William, Earl of Warenne. He seems to have been in high favour with the Earl, in many of whose charters and deeds the name of Hugh de W. stands first. The name is still retained in France; a M. Vancy was recently a member of the chamber of deputies. In England it has taken the various forms of Wauncey, Wancey, Wancie, Wanci, and Auntsey. The parish of Cleeve-Ancy, in Wiltshire, is supposed to derive its suffix from the family. The modern pronunciation is ' Waunzey ;' but formerly, in Wiltshire, it was ' Wansey.' Inf. Wm. Wansey, Esq., F.S.A.

WANT. A provincialism for the mole. Perhaps originally applied to a person of *undermining* disposition.

WANTON. A Robertus *Lascivus* occurs in Domesday, and the surname Wanton is still by no means uncommon.

WAPS. See Wasp.

WAPSHOTT. At Almner's Barns near Chertsey, co. Surrey, a yeoman family so called, resided within the last few years. They had a tradition that the farm was granted by Alfred the Great to their ancestor, Reginald Wapshott, the king's armour-bearer, and that the Wapshotts had been in uninterrupted possession from that time ! Another version of the story makes King Alfred's grantee, a *warrener*. There is no doubt of the great antiquity of this plebeian line, though it is rather more than we are compelled to believe, that surnames were hereditary in the IX. cent., and that Reginald was an English baptismal name in those early days.

The Testa de Nevil, compiled in the reign of Henry III., will probably assist in the elucidation of this name. From that record we learn that Hubert and Ralph *de Hoppeshort* held lands at Beckhampton, in Hampshire, by the serjeanty of keeping the King's harriers. Now Hoppeshort would easily corrupt itself into Wapshott, while the warrener of the tradition and the hound-keeper of the authentic record, may easily be reconciled. All we have to do, then, is to make a deduction of four centuries from the date, and to lay the *venue* in another county; and we are probably not far from the truth.

I am afraid that these Hoppeshorts were not very correct people, if we may accept the evidence of Blount's Tenures, where we read that the Hoppeshorts of Roehampton held that manor by the service " custodiendi sex damicellas (scil' meretrices) ad usum Dom. Regis" (12. Edw. I.) Perhaps, however, Blount's parenthetical gloss may be a misapprehension, and the six creatures to be kept were * * * * * * * of a more honest description—in short female dogs of the chase.

WARBOYS. As the surname War*man* seems " to mean what it says," it might appear that War*boys* has a belligerent signification ; but this is not the case, as it is a simple corruption of Verbois, a place near Rouen.

WARBURTON. A parish in Cheshire gave name to this ancient family, who are a branch of the great house of Dutton of that county. Warburton was acquired by the Duttons as early as temp. Henry II., but it was not until the reign of Edward I., or II., that this territorial surname was assumed by Sir Peter de Dutton. This worthy knight was the grandson of Sir Geoffrey de Dutton, a Crusader, to whom the Warburton crest, "a Saracen's head," alludes. " The crest which is still borne by the Warburtons refers to the Holy Land, and was probably gained by some heroic exploit in the expedition." Ormerod's Cheshire. In the Harl. MS. 139 (p. 68.) it is stated that, "This Galfrid lived in 1244. He was servynge his prynce, and vanquyshed a Sarrazin in combate—then begynnynge to seale with a Sarrazin's head." B.L.G.

WARCUP. A parish in Westmoreland.

☞ WARD. A guard or keeper. Besides standing simply, as one of our commonest surnames—187 traders bearing it occur in the Lond. Direct. of 1852—it forms the termination of several others, as Aylward, Durward, Hayward, Kenward, Milward, Woodward, &c. (which see). Comp. Warden, Warder, Gard, and Guard. The extinct Doveward was probably a keeper of the manorial pigeons—a *Columbarius.*

WARDE. See Ward.

WARDEDIEU. WARDEDU. It is asserted that the progenitor of this family " was a cadet of the family of Monceux, lords of Herst-Monceux, who becoming, in the XIII. century, a ward of the Earl of Eu (to whom the manor of Bodiam, of which he was proprietor, was feudally subject) assumed the surname of Ward d'Ou, which he transmitted to his descendants ; but as the name is usually found with the territorial prefix *De,* this statement may well be questioned." Bodiam and its Lords. p. 10. The first of the family on record is William de Wardedieu, who flourished under Henry III.

WARDEN. 1. A guardian or superintendent, as still in use in ' churchwarden,' 'way-warden,' 'Lord-warden of the Cinque Ports,' &c. 2. Parishes and places in Kent, Northumberland, Bedford, Northampton, Durham, &c. The pear known among our ancestors as the warden-pear derived its name from Warden Abbey, co. Bedford. 3. An A-Sax. personal name. One Weric Werden held lands in co. Herts before the making of Domesday.

WARDER. Custos, keeper; especially a door-keeper—still in use.

WARDEUX. Another spelling of Wardedieu.

WARDLAW. An ancient parish, merged in that of Kirk-hill, co. Inverness.

WARDLE, WARDELL, &c. Wardle or Wardhall, a township in Cheshire. One Ric. de Wardle occurs in the H.R. of Lincolnshire.

WARDLEY. A parish in co. Rutland.

WARDOU. See Wardedieu.

WARDROBE. The same as Wardroper.

WARDROPER. WARDROP. The keeper of the *wardrobe.* (O. F. *garderobe*). " Wardroper, vestiarius." Prompt. Parv. A considerable office in royal and noble households. The H.R. form is Thom' de la Warderobe.

WARDROPPER. See Wardroper.

WARE. A town in co. Herts; also an old orthography of weir, a dam in a river. See Weir and Wear.

WAREDRAPER. R. G. 16. A corruption of Wardroper, which see.

WAREHAM. A town in Dorsetshire.

WARHAM. A parish in Norfolk.

WARING. The Warings, of Waringstown, co. Devon, are descended from John Waring, who settled in Ireland temp. James I. According to B.L.G., the patriarch of the family was Miles de Guerin, who came to England with William the Conqueror.

WARK. A parish in Northumberland.

WARLEY. Parishes and places in Essex and Yorkshire.

WARLOCK. A wizard; one in compact with the Devil. The H.R. shew us a Cambridgeshire tenant bearing the ill-omened name "Nic. Warloc."

WARMAN. May mean a soldier ; but is as probably Wermund, an ancient Saxon name occurring in the genealogy of the kings of Mercia.

WARMINGTON. Parishes in cos. Warwick and Northampton are so called.

WARMOLL. Perhaps a corruption of Warmwell, co. Dorset.

WARNE. A curt pronunciation of Warren.

WARNEFORD. A parish in Hampshire.

WARNER. 1. An ancient baptismal name, written in Domesday Warnerus and Warnerius. 2. Sometimes a corruption of Warrener. "The *warner* is hardy and fell." Halliwell. H.R. Le Warner.

WARNETT. Probably the same as Garnet, or Gernet, by the substitution of W for G.

WARR. WARRE. *War* appears to be an obsolete topographical word, of uncertain meaning. It was formerly prefixed by the particles *De la,* as in the ancient family De la Warr, whose heiress married, in the XV. cent., West, the lineal ancestor of the Earl De la Warr.

WARREN. William de Warene, or Warrena, who married Gundrada, a daughter of William the Conqueror, received great possessions in Sussex, Surrey, Norfolk, Suffolk, &c., and became progenitor of the Earls of Warenne and Surrey. His chief seat, anterior to the Conquest, was at Bellencombre, a small town in the arrondissement of Dieppe, in Normandy, on the little river *Varenne.* By this name the town itself was anciently known, until upon the erection of a fortress upon an artificial mound, or *bellus cumulus,* it received, from that circumstance, the appellation of 'Bellencombrè. Arch. Journ., iii., 6. The Norman de Warennes were doubtless progenitors of many existing families of Warren; but it must not be forgotten that the surname may have a totally different source, namely, *warren*—which Bailey defines as, " a franchize or place privileged by the king for keeping conies, hares, partridges, pheasants, &c.;" though the phrase is now more commonly applied to a colony of rabbits. Thirdly, Warren, or Warinus, is an old baptismal name whence Fitz-Warine.

WARRENDER. Probably a corruption of Warrener.

WARRENER. The keeper of a warren for rabbits.

> " The *warriner* knows
> There are rabbits in breeding."
> *Cobbe's Prophecies*, 1614.   (Halliw.)

WARRIER. A warrior.

WARRINGTON. A town in Lancashire, and a hamlet in Buckinghamshire, are so denominated.

WARTER. The Warters of Shropshire, who assert a Saxon origin, derive their name from the parish of Warter, co. York. Some branches have varied the orthography to Wartyr, Watur, Water, and Walter. Burke's L.G.

WARTNABY. A chapelry in co. Leicester.

WARTON. A parish and a chapelry in co. Lancaster, and a township in Northumberland.

WARWICK. 1. Turchil de Warwick, son of Alwine, was a tenant in capite at the making of Domesday. He was of Saxon race. See Arden. 2. A parish in Cumberland, anciently written Warthwick. One Odard, owner of the estate in the XII. century, was grandfather of John de Warthwyke, who lived temp. Richard Cœur de Lion, and the descendants of the latter, in the direct male line, possessed the estate down to the XVIII. century. See Hutchinson's Cumberland, i. 154.

WARWICKER. A native of Warwick?

WASCOE. The ancient name of the province of Gascony was Vascovia, or Wascovia. This name is therefore equivalent to Gascon.

WASE. See Wace.

WASHBOURN.   WASHBURN. Washbourne, co. Worcester, gave name to this family, and was their seat until 1582. A Walter de Wasseburne occurs in the H.R. of co. Devon, temp. Edward I.

WASHER. A purifier of linen. See under Whisker.

WASHINGTON. Parishes in Durham and Sussex, and a village in Perthshire, are so called. The ancestors of George Washington, the American patriot, are presumed to have been the old gentry stock seated in Northamptonshire, and previously in Lancashire (Shirley's *Stemmata Shirleiana*, p. 136.); but the county from which the first assumer of the name sprang, is unknown. The following ingenious and almost poetical passage from Mr. Ferguson (pp. 115, 116), is worthy of quotation, though the derivation of the heritable surname Washington from an Anglo-Saxon called Wass, and his Wassings, is clearly untenable. The first De Washington—whenever and wherever he flourished—was more likely a Norman,

who had settled upon the conquered soil, than a descendant of Wass, who had colonized the spot centuries before the Conquest.

" The Anglo-Saxon name of Washington in Sussex was Wassingatún, the town of the Wass-ings, *i. e.*, sons or descendants of Wass. Thus, by two steps back, from Washington, we come to Wass, and the name of Wass still stands in the London Directory. But who was Wass? It is a little curious that the only two of that name, whom I have been able to meet with in Anglo-Saxon times, both occur in a charter of manumission (Cod. Dipl. No. 971.) to which one of them was a witness, and the other the father of a witness. Wasa and Wassing were Old German names, and Grimm refers to *wasjan*, pollere, A-Sax. *hwœs*, Old Norse, *hvass*, keen, bold. Hence probably the name of the illustrious Gustavus Wasa, king of Sweden. Thus I have connected the name of Washington with a family, probably more or less distinguished, of A-Sax. times—I have shown that one of that family, and the son of another, stood godfathers to an ancient act of freedom, both occur in a charter of manumission (Cod. Dipl. No. 971.) to which one of them was a witness, and the other the father of a witness posed a not unworthy etymon for the name—and I have suggested that it may be the same as that of another distinguished champion of his country's freedom."

WASP. A sobriquet applied to a choleric or spiteful person. Waps (A-Sax. *wœps*, a wasp), is also found as a surname.

WASS. 1. See Wace. 2. See under Washington.

WASTELL. A fine kind of bread. O. Fr. *gastel*, *gasteau*. Bread used with the wassail-bowl. Jamieson. Chaucer's Prioress fed her hounds with *Wastel brede*. Its adoption as a surname is not readily explained. See, however, Whitbread, and Simnel, in the Supplement. The name in H.R. is Wastel without prefix.

WAT. A ' nurse-name ' of Walter.

WATCOCK. See Walter.

WATER. From residence near some large pond, river, or the like. In the XIII. and XIV. centuries, the name was written Atte-Water, By-the-Water, &c.

WATERFALL. A parish in Staffordshire.

WATERHOUSE. Local, in Lincolnshire. The first recorded ancestor is Sir Gilbert Waterhouse, or Ab Aquæ Domo, who was of Kirton in that shire, temp. Henry III. B.L.G.

WATERMAN. A ferryman. See, however, Waters, and the termination MAN.

WATERS. In some dialects, the word *water* is applied to lakes and rivers, as Ullswater, Derwent-water, Black-water. Upon the adoption of surnames by the common people, a person who resided near such a place would be called William or John Atte-Water, still retained in Attwater; but on the omission of the preposition in the XV. century, the name was pluralized to Waters. The latinizations are De Aqua and Ad Aquam. See Water.

WATERSON. See Walter.

WATERTON. According to B.L.G. the family claim a Norman origin, although the first ancestor mentioned is Rayner de Waterton, lord of the manor of Waterton, co. Lincoln, temp. Henry III. In the reign of Richard II., the elder line being extinct, a younger son married Catherine Burghe, heiress to the estate of Walton, co. York, "which has since continued the residence of this ancient knightly lineage." Shirley's Noble and Gentle Men.

WATFORD. WHATFORD. A town in co. Herts, and a parish in co. Northampton.

WATKINS. See Walter.

WATKINSON. See Walter.

WATLING. This name may have been taken from the celebrated Roman Road, the Watling Street, which led from Dover to London, and thence to Chester, North Wales, and Cumberland. Comp. Dykes, Stonestreet, and Thirlwall, as surnames derived from Roman works. In the middle ages, so famous was this *via*, that the Milky Way of the heavens was sometimes known by the same designation:—

> "Lo, quod he, cast up thyne eye,
> See yonder lo, the galaxie,
> The which men clepe the milky way,
> For it is white ; and some, parfay,
> Callen it WATLING STREETE."
> *Chaucer. House of Fame.* ii. 437.

WATLINGTON. A parish in Sussex.

WATSON. See Walter.

WATT. WATTS. 1. See Walter. 2. The family of Watts of Hawkesdale Hall, co. Cumberland, deduce themselves from Sir John le Fleming, lord of Wath, on Dearn, co. York, who died 14. Edw. II. His second son Raynier assumed the territorial name De Wath, and his descendants gradually corrupted that designation to its present form. In temp. Edward III. it was De Wath or Wathes; temp. Henry VI., Wattys; temp. Henry VII., Wattes; temp. Charles I., and subsequently, Watts. See B.L.G.

WAUCHOPE. This family derive their name from the district of Wauchopedale, co. Dumfries. They were long hereditary baillies of Mid-Lothian. The first of the name mentioned by Burke is Robert Wauchope, A.D. 1387.

WAUGH. 1. A Scottish pronunciation of wall. 2. In Lancashire, *wa'* or *wau* is a well, and there are many places in that county called the "wa' (or wau) head," meaning the source of running water. 3. A corruption of Walugh, perhaps the same as the Gaelic Christian name Woloe. The Waughs of Heip, co. Roxburgh, held those lands from the XIII. to the XVII. cent.

WAWN. The provincial pronunciation of the parish of Waghen, in Yorkshire.

WAY. Way, *via*, a road, seems an unsatisfactory origin. In the Rotul. Hund. there is mention, however, of one Hugo *in Via.* (Vol. ii. p. 331.) The name is found in North Devon, temp. Henry VII.; and in that district the termination *way* is of frequent occurrence in the names of farms, homesteads, and the like, without any reference to, or connection with, roads. The

mullets hauriant in the arms of one family have been supposed to be allusive to the river Wey, co. Dorset, in which mullets are abundant. Ate-Wey is one of the forms in H.R. It may be an old baptismal designation, as Wege or Weghe is found in Domesd. as the name of a tenant anterior to the Survey.

WAYLAND. 1. *Waylande* is an archaism for valiant. 2. A hundred in Norfolk is so called. 3. Vælund, or Wayland, is a Scandinavian personal name of great antiquity. "Wayland Smith," the Vulcan of the North, is well known in the legendary history of the middle ages. All that could be collected concerning him, is found in Singer's interesting volume under this title. Lond. 1847.

WAYLEN. This name is spelt in a variety of ways in the parish register of St. James', Devizes. It is doubtless a corruption of Wayland, a name sometimes occurring in that neighbourhood in the public records. The Irish name Whelan is pronounced in the same manner as Waylen, adding the aspirate ; but it is of course totally distinct in origin. Inf. James Waylen, Esq.

WAYMAN. Dutch, *weyman*, a hunter; one who chases stags and deer (bètes fauves) with dogs. Marin's Dict.

WAYMARK. See Wymark.

WAYNFLEET. See Wainfleet.

WAYRE. See Ware, Weir, &c.

WAYT. WAYTE. See Wait.

WEAKLEY. Probably local, and not referring to want of physical robustness.

WEAKLIN. See Wakley.

WEALE. Probably a very old Teutonic personal name. Wela and Welo were Old German names of the VIII. and IX. centuries. "The etymon of it (and not an inappropriate one) may be the A.-Sax. *wela*, wealth, happiness, prosperity." Ferguson.

WEALL. See Weale.

WEALTHY. Prosperous, rich.

WEAR. An old spelling of *weir*, a fishing dam. Bailey.

WEARG. See Werge.

WEATHERALL. See Wetherell.

WEATHERBY. Wetherby, a town in Yorkshire.

WEATHERDEN. A parish in Suffolk.

WEATHERHEAD. 1. Local: "the bleak promontory?" 2. Perhaps a corruption of Wetherherd.

WEATHERHOG. "After a lamb has been weaned, until shorn of its first fleece, it is a *hogg* . . . a tup-hogg, ewe-hogg, or *wetherhogg*." N. & Q., May 29, 1856, in an article on the popular names of live stock in Scotland. Halliwell has this rather odd definition : "Wetherhog, a male or heder hog. Also a surname in the county," (i. e., Lincolnshire).

WEAVER. The occupation. H.R. Textor.

WEBB. WEBBE. A-Sax. *webba*, a weaver. H.R. Le Webbe.

> "My wife was a *webbe*,
> And wollen cloth made."
> *Piers Plowman*, i. 89.

Above 140 traders of this name occur in the Lond. Direct.

WEBBER. See Weber.

WEBER. Germ., a weaver. The indigenous Webber means the same thing.

WEBLEY. Weobley, a town in Herefordshire.

WEBSTER. A-Sax. *webbestre*, a female weaver. See the termination STER. The following lines appear to imply a difference between the Webster and the Weaver, according to the material wrought :—

> "Baksteres and brewesteres,
> And bochiers manye,
> *Wollen webbesters*,
> And *weveres of lynnen*."
> *Piers Plowman*, i. 14.

The baronet's family claim from John Webster, of Bolsover, co. Derby, whose ancestor is said to have come over from Flanders, temp. Richard II. B.L.G.

WEDDERBURN. This ancient surname is derived from the lands of Wedderburne, in Berwickshire. The head of the family in 1296 was Walter de Wedderburn, who swore fealty in that year to Edward I.

WEDGWOOD. A small hamlet in Staffordshire gave name to the ancestors of Wedgwood, the eminent potter.

WEDLAKE. Mr. Ferguson derives this name, and Wedlock, from an Old German personal name Widolaic.

WEDLOCK. The same as Wedlake.

WEEDING. The same as Weedon.

WEEDON. An estate in co. Bucks, possessed by the family temp. Hen. III. Also two parishes in Northamptonshire.

WEEKES. WEEKS. The same as Wick, which see. One of the greatest *habitats* of this name was the neighbourhood of Hastings, though the precise locality from which it was derived is unknown. Gualterus Diaconus, the ancestor of the family of De Hastings, lords of the barony of Hastings, held a knight's fee in Wikes at the making of Domesday. Ellis, Introd.. i. 421. Wikes, Wyke, Wykes, Wix, Wickes, &c., seem to be mere orthographical variations.

WEELEY. A parish in Essex.

WEEMS. A fortalice in the parish of Rescobie, in Forfarshire, called the castle of Weems, once of considerable importance, has now disappeared.

WEEMYS. See Wemyss.

WEEVER. 1. A township in Cheshire. 2. See Weaver.

WEGG. See Wagg.

WEIGHT. See Wight.

WEIGHTMAN. See Waithman, and Wightman.

WEIGHTON. A parish in Yorkshire.

WEIR. The Weirs of Lesmahago, Blackwood, &c., in Lanarkshire, claim descent from the great baronial family of De Vere, having been founded in Scotland by Baltredus de Vere, in the reign of Malcolm IV., about the middle of the twelfth century. From documents quoted in Chambers' Caledonia, it appears that the name Vere, or Weir, was by no means uncommon among the Norman settlers in Scotland, in that century.

It is, however, probable, that some families of this name derive it from residence at a *weir*, or fishing-dam, in a river. The Hundred Rolls' form, At-Were, strengthens this etymology.

WELBANK. Possibly a corruption of Welbeck, a liberty in Nottinghamshire.

WELBORN. A parish in Norfolk—Welborne.

WELBY. "Of great antiquity in the county of Lincoln, being descended from John, Lord of Castleton, who was living in the time of William the Conqueror, and is said to have assisted Robert de Todeni, Baron of Belvoir, in the defence of his castle." Courthope's Debrett. The name would appear to have been derived from the Lincolnshire parish so called; and there Sir William Welby, "who heads their well-authenticated pedigree, undoubtedly possessed property between 1307 and 1327. The manor of Frieston, with Poynton Hall, also in Lincolnshire, was held in chief by Sir Thomas Welby, a still earlier ancestor, of King Henry III., in 1216." Shirley's Noble and Gentle Men.

WELCH. WELCHMAN. A native of Wales. These names are probably of rather recent origin, the older forms being Le Waleys, Wallis, &c.

WELD. "Founded," says Mr. Shirley, "by William Weld, sheriff of London in 1352." His posterity were seated at Eaton, co. Chester, till the reign of Charles II. Lulworth, co. Dorset, was purchased in 1641. Noble and Gentle Men.

An old tradition deduces the family from one Edric Sylvaticus, or "the Wild;" but the name is far more probably derived from the residence of its first bearer in some *wald*, *weald*, or wood. He may have been properly designated 'Sylvaticus,' without any necessary inference that he was a "*wild* man of the woods."

WELDON. Great and Little Weldon are parishes in co. Northampton. The name is of record in Ireland from temp. Richard II. D'Alton.

WELFARE. Probably from Wifare, or rather Wulpher, a personal name, occurring in Domesday.

WELFORD. Parishes in cos. Northampton, Berks, and Gloucester.

WELHAM. A parish in co. Leicester, and a hamlet in co. Nottingham.

☞ WELL. The termination of numerous surnames of the local class, as Bedwell, Creswell, Faxwell, Harewell, Sitwell, Trigwell, Tugwell. In some few known instances it is a corruption of *ville*, and consequently of Norman or French origin ; thus Boswell was anciently Bosville ; Fretwell, Frescheville ; Colwell, Colville, &c. But in the great majority the termination 'means what it says'—namely, *fons, origo*. Verstegan says :—"Our ancestors, according to the different issue of waters, did differently term them. . . . . Sundry coming to possess places which were near unto Wells of especial note, having gotten thereby the name of such or such a Well, became after them so to be called; as Staniwell, of his dwelling at a well so named, of the stoniness thereof; Moswell, of a well where much moss did grow." Restit., p. 327. This is not strictly correct. Springs and Wells gave names in many instances to places, and families adopted them from those places. Sometimes when a well bore no particular name, a cottager or small proprietor resident near at hand would get the name of Atte Welle, or De la Welle, afterwards shortened and corrupted to Wells. Both Weller and Wellman, are from the same *source*. In days when pumps, to say nothing of 'water-works,' were unknown, a public well was of great importance in every village, and hence the commonness of the name of Wells and its congeners. Attwells, and its contraction Twells, with Wellspring, occur in the Lond. Direct.

Many wells, as has been already intimated, bore some characteristic epithet, as Blackwell, Whitewell, Greenwell, Coldwell, and others which are mentioned in their proper places. Three others with still more expressive epithets, which have also become surnames, I cannot identify in the Gazetteer, viz. :—Stilwell, Leapingwell, Loudwell.

Other languages have surnames of the same kind. Thus Fr. Du Puy, Dupuis, De la Fontaine ; Dutch, Van der Put ; Ital. Pozzi.

The common latinization is De Fontibus.

WELLADVICE. I found this name in the register of Charlton, near Woolwich. It is doubtless a corruption of 'well-advised,' a prudent, cautious person.

WELLAND. A parish in Worcestershire.

WELLARD. The same as Willard.

WELLBY. See Welby.

WELLBELOVED. A compliment to the excellence of the patriarch of the race. I have noticed at Dieppe, in Normandy, its synonyme in *Bienaymé*.

WELLBORN. Does not relate to good birth, but to some locality called Wellbourn—a stream running from a well.

WELLBOURNE. Welborne, a parish in Norfolk.

WELLDON. See Weldon.

WELLDONE. See Weldon.

WELLER. See Well, and the termination ER.

WELLESLEY. This great family, "terque quaterque beati"—(if having three or four titles in the peerage may be so construed)—derive their existing name from a locality called Welesley, in Somersetshire, which county, centuries later, supplied to the hero of a hundred fights the title of Duke of Wellington. But the ancient patronymic of the race is Colley, Cowley, or Colly, and their ancestor settled in Ireland in the reign of King Henry VIII. from the county of Rutland. The maternal ancestor, whose descendant took the name of Wesley, or Wellesley, in the earlier part of the XVIII. century, was standard-bearer to King Henry II. in 1172, and received large grants in the counties of Meath and Kildare. The old name of the family was Wesley, and Wellesley is only a comparatively recent resumption of the original surname. John Wesley, the founder of the Methodists, is said to have been of the same stock.

WELLING. Ferguson considers this to be the patronymic of a personal name, Well. But there is a De Wellynge in H.R. co. Norfolk.

WELLINGTON. Parishes, &c., in cos. Salop, Somerset, Hereford, and Northumberland.

WELLMAN. See Welman.

WELLOCK. See Whellock.

WELLS. 1. Towns in cos. Somerset and Norfolk. 2. A pluralization of Well, which see.

WELLSPRING. See Well.

WELMAN. Probably "well-man." See Well, and the termination MAN.

WELSH. WELSHMAN. See Welch, Welchman.

WELSTED. Local : "the place of the well."

WELTON. Parishes, &c., in cos. Northampton, York, Northumberland, and Lincoln.

WEMYSS. A parish in Fifeshire. This ancient family are still " of that Ilk," Wemyss Castle, a large and magnificent building, being the abode of the head of the family. More accounts than one are given of the origin of the family of Wemyss; but all agree as to their being derived from Macduff, Maormor of Fife, in the reign of Malcolm Canmore. They are therefore one of the very few Lowland families who, through the male line, can claim kindred with Celtic blood. The lands now forming the parish of Wemyss are said to have been part of the estate of Macduff, Shakspeare's well-known Thane of Fife. According to Sibbald, Gillimichael, the third in descent from Macduff, had a son named Hugo, who obtained these lands from his father. . . The present proprietor of the estate, J. H. E. Wemyss, Esq., is twenty-sixth in direct descent from Hugo, the son of Gillimichael." Gaz. Scotl. Another statement makes the originator of the family Michael de Wemyss, second son of Duncan, fifth Earl of Fife, who died in 1165. The Earl of Wemyss descends from a younger son.

At Wemyss Castle is preserved with great care a silver basin, which was given in 1290 by the King of Norway to Sir Michael Wemyss, on the occasion of that personage and Sir Michael Scott, of Balwearie, appearing at the Norwegian court, as ambassadors from Scotland to bring home the Princess Margaret.

WENBAN. A corruption of Wimborne, co. Dorset.

WENBORNE. A corruption of Wimborne, co. Dorset.

WENHAM. Wenham Hall, co. Suffolk, was the seat of the family at an early period. The Wenhams of Sussex settled there from the former county in the XV. century.

WENLOCK. A town in Shropshire, where the family flourished temp. Edwd. I. H.R.

WENMAN. A-Sax. wæn, wagon, and man. A wagoner. See under Wainwright.

WENSLEY. A famous dale in Yorkshire, and a township in co. Derby.

WENTWORTH. A chapelry in the parish of Wath-upon-Dearn, co. York. The estate is said to have been in the possession of the family before the Norman Conquest. The name is written in Domesday, Winterwade, and in the XIII. century it was changed to Wyntword. The male line continued at Wentworth until the extinction of the earldom of Strafford in the XVIII. century; and the existing Wentworth, of Wentworth Castle, is descended from the family on the female side.

Reginald de Wintrewade, or Wentworth, was contemporary with the compilation of Domesday.

WERE. See Weir.

WERGE. The same as Worge. It was formerly written Wearg, Wirge, &c.

WERK. Some work or building.

WESLEY. Mr. Ferguson derives this name from the Old Norse veslegr, miserable; but there can be no doubt whatever of its local origin, from one of the places called Westley, in cos. Cambridge, Suffolk, Salop, and elsewhere; though the family of John Wesley, the founder of the ism that bears his name, was of common origin with the Wellesleys. Wellesley is indeed a recent resumption of the original name.

I believe that Lord Mornington, father of the late Duke of Wellington, wrote himself Wesley in his earlier years.

WEST. See under North. The noble family (Earl Delawarr), traced by Collins to temp. Edw. II., at that period wrote themselves De West; not, it appears, from any place so called, but from their large possessions in the West of England.

Mr. Shirley observes that, "the Wests are remarkable, not so much for the antiquity of the family, as for the early period at which they attained the honour of the peerage. Sir Thomas West, the first recorded ancestor, died 17. Edward II., having married the heiress of Cantilupe, and thus become possessed of lands in Devonshire and Warwickshire. His grandson, Thomas, married the heiress of De la Warr, and thus became connected with Sussex. Few families had broader lands." Noble and Gentle Men.

WESTALL. Probably Westhall, co. Suffolk.

WESTBROOK. A tything in co. Berks.

WESTBURY. Parishes and places in cos. Wilts, Bucks, Gloucester, Salop, Hants, Somerset, &c.

WESTBY. A township in Lancashire. The family assert a Saxon descent, and say that they were settled in the hundred of Amounderness, in that county, before the Conquest; but the first member of the family mentioned in the pedigree is Gilbert de Westby, sheriff of Lancashire in 1233.

WESTCOTT. WESTCOTE. Parishes, &c., in Gloucester, Berks, Bucks, &c.

WESTENRA. Lord Rossmore's family spring from a very ancient race in Holland. They were naturalized in Ireland temp. Charles II. Peerage.

WESTERDALE. A parish in Yorkshire.

WESTERMAN. 'Western man' — a native of the West.

WESTERN. See Points of the Compass.

WESTERTON. A township in Durham.

WESTGATE. See under Eastgate. De Westgate. H.R.

WESTHORPE. A parish in Suffolk.

WESTLAKE. See Points of the Compass.

WESTLEY. Parishes, &c., in cos. Cambridge, Suffolk, and Salop.

WESTMACOTT. 1. This "was probably the A-Sax. term for a banker or money-lender, from *roestm*, interest or usury, and *scot* or *sceat*, money. For examples of the compound word, *Westmsceat*, see Bosworth's Dict." Talbot's English Etymologies. 2. Westmancoate, a hamlet in co. Worcester.

WESTMARLAND. From the county, Westmoreland.

WESTMORE. Local: "the western moor."

WESTMORELAN. From Westmoreland.

WESTON. The English gazetteers give about fifty parishes and hamlets of this name, which signifies simply 'the western enclosure,' and corresponds with Easton, Norton, and Sutton. From divers of these, some of the families of Weston have sprung; but the widely-spread Westons of Surrey and Sussex are descended from the house of De Wistoneston, or Wiston, of Wiston, co. Sussex. Weston also occurs as a personal name in the VIII. century—"Alfred, the son of Weston." Wright's Biog. Brit. A-Sax. period, p. 268.

WESTOVER. A district in the New Forest, co. Hants.

WESTPHAL. A native of Westphalia, in Germany.

WESTPHALING. The same as Westphal.

WESTRON. The same as Western.

WESTROPP. The family claim from John Westropp, son and heir of Edward Westropp, temp. King John. They settled in Ireland in the XVII. century. B.L.G. does not indicate the locality in which they originated, but the name is obviously local, and signifies, like Westhorpe, "the western village."

WESTRUPP. See Westropp.

WESTWOOD. Parishes in cos. Worcester and Wilts.

WETHERDEN. A parish in Suffolk. H.R. co. Norfolk, temp. Edward I.

WETHERELL. WETHERALL. WETHERILL. Almost all the families of this name trace to the county of Durham, and there is little doubt of their derivation from Wetheral, co. Cumberland, remarkable for its priory.

WETHERFIELD. Wethersfield, a parish in Essex.

WETHERHERD. A shepherd—one who took care of wether-sheep. This name is ancient, occurring temp. Edward I.

WETHERLEY. A hundred in Cambridgeshire.

WETTEN. See Wetton.

WETTENHALL. A township in Cheshire.

WETTON. A parish in Staffordshire.

WEVER. See Weaver.

WEY. Rivers in Surrey and Dorsetshire.

WEYLAND. An ancient Norfolk family, "whose name implies wet land," says B.L.G.; though I should call it a simple variation of Wayland. The Weylands had large possessions in Norfolk, temp. Edward I.

WEYMOUTH. A town in co. Dorset.

WHALE. 1. See Wale. 2. A sobriquet allusive to largeness of person. Whalebelly is a recognized surname.

WHALEBELLY. See Whale.

WHALEBONE. The hundred in which Brighton, co. Sussex, lies, is called Whalesbone, corruptly from Well's-bourne—from a stream which formerly traversed it, and had its source at Patcham Well.

WHALEY. See Whalley.

WHALLEY. A great parish in Yorkshire, where the ancestors of the baronet resided in the last century. Courthope's Debrett.

WHARTON. Townships in Cheshire and Westmoreland.

WHARRAM. Two parishes in Yorkshire are so designated.

WHATELEY. A chapelry in the parish of Cuddesden, co. Oxford, more usually written Wheatley.

WHATLEY. A parish in Somersetshire.

WHATMAN. An ancient baptismal name. A Wateman de London occurs in Domesday, as a previous tenant; and the name is otherwise spelt Whateman and Hwateman. In the middle ages, the family dwelt in Kent, near Romney and Hawkhurst, and left much land to monastic establishments. According to B.L.G. the Whatmans ranked "amongst the independent *yeomen* of Kent." We must bear in mind that, in old times, that phrase designated a very wealthy and influential class of persons. Hence the oft-quoted proverb:—

"A Knight of Cales, a Gentleman of Wales,
And a Laird of the North Countrée;
A *Yeoman of Kent* with his yearly rent,
Will buy them out all three."
Fuller's Worthies, ii. 121.

WHEAL. A Cornish word (*huél*) signifying a mine.

WHEATCROFT. Local: "the enclosure where wheat grows."

WHEATLEY. Parishes and places in cos. Oxon, Lancaster, Nottingham, &c.

WHEATSTONE. See Whetstone.

WHEEL. Wheal (*huél*) is the Cornish word for a mine, as Wheal Mary, Wheal

Jewell, Wheal Fortune, &c. The first bearer of the surname probably resided near some tin or lead mine.

WHEELDON. Perhaps Wheelton, a township in Lancashire.

WHEELER. In many dialects signifies wheelwright. This English surname has undergone a singular change in Normandy. M. de Gerville says : " The name of *Houelleur* which means ' charron ' [cartwright] in English, is as common, at least in the Cotentin, as that of Carron or Charron. I imagine that it was introduced into Normandy during the thirty-two years' occupation of this country by the English. The English orthography is very different from ours, namely, *Wheeler :* it literally signifies a maker of wheels." Memoires Soc. Antiq. Normandie, 1844.

WHEELTON. A township in Lancashire.

WHEELWRIGHT. Originally a maker of wheels only—afterwards, as at present, one who constructs wagons, carts, and other carriages. We have the cognate names Wainwright, Cartwright, &c.

WHELDON. See Weldon.

WHELER. See Wheeler.

WHELLOCK. A corruption of Wheelock, co. Chester.

WHELOCK. Wheelock, a township in Cheshire.

WHETSTONE. A parish in co. Leicester, and a hamlet in the parish of Tideswell, co. Derby. ·

WHETTON. See Wetton.

WHEWELL. Whewell Grange in Staffordshire, sometimes written Hewell, is known in history as the place where some of the conspirators of the Powder Plot took refuge in 1605. It has been remarked of this name, that it is *more easily whistled than spoken* ! The initial W is, however, rarely pronounced.

WHIBLEY. From Weobley, a town in Herefordshire.

WHICHCOTE. The baronet's family spring from William de Whichcote, of Whichcote in Shropshire, who was living in 1255. A marriage with the heiress of Tyrwhitt removed the family into Norfolk temp. Edward IV. Shirley's Noble and Gentle Men.

WHICKER. See Wicker.

WHIDDINGTON. Widdington, a parish in Essex, and a township in Yorkshire.

WHILE. Probably a corruption of Wild.

WHIMPER. Perhaps from Quimper, a large town in Brittany. In early names of French origin, W and Qu are sometimes convertible.

WHINES. 1. A hamlet in Forfarshire. 2. Perhaps the genitive form of Wine, an A-Sax. baptismal name.

WHIPHAM. Perhaps a contraction of Whippingham, in the Isle of Wight.

WHIPPY. The name probably of some locality.

WHIRLPENNY. One Ralph Whirlepeni occurs in H.R. Qu : was he a gambler ?

WHISHAW. An estate in the parish of Cambusnethan in Lanarkshire.

WHISKER. WHISKERS. As we have in our nomenclature a great number of names evidently referring to shape, complexion, the beard, and other personal characteristics, this name might, *prima* FACIE, appear to have originated from the facial ornaments of the gentleman who first assumed or bore it; but if we look into the history of the *word*, we shall find it very insufficient in point of antiquity to warrant such a conclusion. The fact seems to be, that until quite a recent period—long posterior to the assumption of surnames— the *whisker*, as now understood, was regarded as a mere adjunct or tributary of the beard. Indeed, there was no necessity for any distinction until the absurd and unnatural practice of shaving came into vogue. Long after that epoch—to wit, in the days of Dr. Sam. Johnson—the word *whisker* meant, not the hair of the cheek, but " the hair growing upon the upper lip; the mustachio." (Dict.) Now, the lexicographer derives *whisker* from ' whisk,' " a small besom or brush," which the facial whisker of our time sufficiently resembles, when unaccompanied by the chin-beard. But the true origin of the name has nothing to do with a face, be the same hirsute or smoot ., but refers to the honest and necessary occupation of the wash-tub; for Dr. Bosworth informs us that *wæscere* signifies, in modern English, ' a washer,' a man or woman as the case (or gender rather) might be, who cleansed dirty linen. This origin is supported by the more modern surnames Washer and Lavender; though perhaps the ante-Domesday personal name Wisgar, or Wiscar, may have a better claim.

WHISLER. See Whistler.

WHIST. Possibly from Uist, one of the Hebrides.

WHISTLER. A man much addicted to whistling would readily acquire this name.

WHISTON. Parishes and places in cos. Lancaster, Northampton, Stafford, Yorkshire, and Worcester are so called, and from one or other of them the surname is probably derived, though Mr. Ferguson considers it to be the A-Sax. personal name Wistan.

WHITAKER. 1. "The Whitakers of High Whitaker, an old-established family, were originally Whitacres of Whitacre, in the vills of Padiham and Simonstone." Folks of Shields, p. 22. 2. Two parishes in Warwickshire are so called. 3. Mr. Ferguson considers it to be the same name as Wihtgar, borne by a nephew of Cerdic, King of the West Saxons.

WHITBREAD. WHITEBREAD. The letter R is very apt to change places with the vowel preceding or following it; thus, the O. Eng. *brid* has become *bird*, and *firth*, an estuary, is, among Southrons, *frith.* In like manner, the last syllable of this word was perhaps originally *berd*, that is, beard. Thus Whitebread would be a sobriquet, like Silverlock, Redhead, &c. See, however, 'Blancpain.' *Witbred* occurs in the Hundred Rolls; and in 11. Edward I. we meet with the names Will. Milkanbred, and Walter, son of Will. Milk and bred! N. & Q., Jan. 24, 1857. The notorious murderer, Eugene Aram, heroized by a modern novelist, was usher, in 1744, to the Rev. Mr. *Painblanc*, in Piccadilly.

WHITBY. A town in Yorkshire.

WHITCHER. 1. A corruption of Whitchurch. 2. See Wicher.

WHITCHURCH. See Whitechurch.

WHITCOMBE. Parishes in cos. Dorset and Gloucester.

WHITE. Of light or fair complexion, corresponding with the Fr. Le Blond, the Gaelic Bane, the Ital. Biondi, the Dutch De Witt, the Germ. Weiss, and the old classical Candidus, Chlorus, &c. The Lond. Direct. shews almost 300 traders of this name. In the H.R. it is latinized Albus.

J. Yonge Akerman, Esq., late Sec. S. A., has suggested to me, that the name is far too common to allow of the supposition that it is derived solely from complexion, especially since the antithetical Black bears no proportion for numerousness—occurring in the above-mentioned repertory of names in the proportion of only one to ten. The Browns might be called in as allies of the Blacks, when the scale would be turned in favour of the dark complexion; yet still I think Mr. Akerman is correct in the supposition that the name White is sometimes derived, not from A-Sax. *hwit* (albus), but from *hwita*, a sharpener, swordsmith, or armourer, and one Thurcil Hwita, mentioned in a document of the time of Canute (Codex Dipl.), might be cited on that side, as well as in proof of the great antiquity of the surname. Nisbet says: "As for the antiquity of the name, Sir James Dalrymple observes one Viniet Albus, witness in a charter of King Edgar to the church of Durham, who perhaps may be the first of the surname of White."

WHITECHURCH. Parishes called Whitchurch exist in cos. Buckingham, Devon, Glamorgan, Hereford, Oxford, Pembroke, Salop, Somerset, Hants, and Warwick.

WHITEFOOT. *Wight* or *wicht* is O. Eng. and Scot. for powerful and active. Hence the name would signify a person strong and swift of foot.

WHITEFORD. "The first of this family," says Nisbet, "was Walter de Whiteford, who, for his good services done at the battle of the Largs, in the reign of King Alexander III., under the command of Alexander Seneschal, High-Steward of Scotland, got from him the lands of Whitefoord near Paisly, in the shire of Renfrew."

WHITEGIFT. See Whitgift.

WHITEHALL. This name, more anciently written Whitehaugh, appears to have been derived from a place so called in Staffordshire.

WHITEHEAD. 1. This common surname is doubtless derived from the hoary locks of its original bearer. The Annals of the Four Masters mention an Irishman of distinction who was known as "Colgan of the White Head," from this personal peculiarity. The Fr. Blancheteste is synonymous. 2. Local: "the white promontory."

WHITEHILL. Villages, &c., in cos. Edinburgh, Kincardine, Banff, and Lanark.

WHITEHORN. A town and parish in co. Wigton, now written without the E.

WHITEHORSE. Camden, speaking of surnames derived from signs of inns and houses, mentions "George at the Whitehorse" as an individual living near his own times, who had been so called from his sign. The Henry Blaunchival (Fr. *blanc cheval*) of the H.R. probably took his name from the colour of his horse.

WHITEHOUSE. A village in the parish of Tough, co. Aberdeen.

WHITELAW. One of the Cheviot hills is so called. "Several of this name are mentioned in the Ragman Roll; and in the reign of King James III. one Archibald Whitelaw was an eminent prelate, and secretary of state to that king." Nisbet.

WHITELEGG. Has no reference to crural whiteness, but is the modern form of a very ancient personal name, Wihtlæg, which is found in the genealogy of the Mercian kings.

WHITELEY. See Whitley.

WHITELOCK. WHITLOCK. From the *white locks* of the primitive bearer. Comp. Silverlock, Blacklock, &c.

WHITEMAN. Possibly the antithesis of Blackman; but more probably the same as Wightman.

WHITER. 1. One who whittles. Jamieson. 2. A bleacher?

WHITESIDES. Probably from some personal peculiarity. In the H.R. of temp. Edw. I. there is a "Ricardus Blawnc-Coste." Whitside also occurs there.

WHITFELD. See Whitfield, for localities. The Whitfelds of Kent and Sussex descend from William de Whitfeld, or Whitfield, of Whitfield Hall, in Northumberland, who flourished in the XIV. century.

WHITFIELD. WHITEFIELD. Parishes and places in cos. Derby, Kent, Northampton, and Northumberland.

WHITFORD. A parish in Flintshire.

WHITGIFT. A parish in Yorkshire.

WHITGREAVE. Whitgreave, a township in Staffordshire, gave name to this family. In the reign of Henry III., Robert Whitgreave, the first recorded ancestor, resided at Burton, near Stafford. Shirley's Noble and Gentle Men.

For a grant of arms from Humphrey, Earl of Stafford, to Robert Whitgreve, 20. Henry VI. see Camden's Remains, Edit. 1657. The arms are based on those of Stafford ; and an " augmentation " recently acquired, " a rose within a wreath of oak " refers to Thomas Whitgreave's having sheltered Chas. II. after the battle of Worcester.

WHITHAIR. From the *white hair* of the first of the name. Comp. Whitelock, Farrar, Blount, Blacklock, &c.

WHITING. The patronymical form of White. Comp. Browning.

WHITLEY. Townships, hamlets, &c., in cos. Northumberland, Berks, Somerset, Salop, Chester, and York.

WHITMILL. A corruption either of *white* mill, or of *wheat* mill.

WHITMORE. The family were seated at Whitmore, or Whittimere, in the parish of Claverley, co. Salop, in the reign of Henry III. From them sprang the Whitmores of Apley, who raised themselves to importance by commerce in the reign of Elizabeth. Shirley's Noble and Gentle Men. The Whitmores of Cheshire do not appear to have had any connection with this family, though the Heralds have assigned to them arms of a similar character, with a crest allusive to the springing of a young shoot out of an old stock. Blakeway's Sheriffs of Shropshire.

WHITNEY. A parish in Herefordshire.

WHITSTER. This name looks like the feminine of Whiter. See termination STER. If so, it should mean a bleacher ; but Halliwell says, that it is an eastern provincialism for a whitesmith.

WHITTAKER. See Whitaker.

WHITTEN. See Whitton.

WHITTEMORE. The same as Whitmore.

WHITTINGHAM. A parish in Northumberland, a township in Lancashire, and a parish in Haddingtonshire.

WHITTINGTON. Parishes and townships in cos. Stafford, Worcester, Salop, Lancaster, Gloucester, Derby, &c.

WHITTLE. There are five townships bearing this singular name, two of which are in Lancashire, two in Northumberland, and one in Derbyshire.

WHITTOCK. 1. Perhaps local, from 'white' and 'oak.' 2. Wittich, an ancient

personal name, attributed to a Teutonic mythical personage. 3. Mr. Ferguson makes it a diminutive of White.

WHITTON. There are parishes, &c., so called in cos. Lincoln, Durham, Hereford, Northumberland, Salop, Suffolk, &c.

WHITTY. Considered by Ferguson as a diminutive of White.

WHITWELL. There are places so called in cos. Derby, Norfolk, Rutland, Hants, York, and Durham.

WHITWORTH. Chapelries in Durham and Lancashire.
The Whitworths of co. Durham were descendants of the Shaftos of Northumberland. Slogans of the North of England, p. xvii.

WHOWALL. Probably the same as Whewell.

WHYATT. See Wyatt.

WHYMARK. See Wymark.

WHYTALL. See Whitehall.

WHYTE. The Scottish form of White. The Whytes, anciently free barons in the shires of Fife, Perth, &c., are said to have sprung from the noble family of Le Blanc in France. B.L.G.

WHYTEHEAD. See Whitehead.

WHYTOCK. See Whittock.

WIATT. See Wyatt.

WICH. WICHE. See Wyche.

WICHER. A *wych* is a salt spring, and a dweller near such a spring would, in the XIII. or XIV. century, readily acquire the surname De La Wyche, At Wych, or Wycher. See termination ER.

☞ **WICK.** This syllable is found in many names of places, and consequently in many local surnames ; as Inderwick, Markwick, Stredwick, Padwick, Rudwick, Wickham, Wicksteed, Wickfield. It is the A-Sax. *wic* or *wyc*, and is of a very wide signification, implying dwelling-place, mansion, village, street (Lat. *vicus*, with which it is doubtless connected), monastery, castle, camp or military station, bay, creek, &c. In local nomenclature, however, it generally implies a habitation, or a village, and sometimes, according to Prof. Leo, marshland. Several parishes in England and Scotland are designated by this word without any qualifying addition. Week and Wyke are other forms of it.

WICK. Places so called are found in cos. Worcester, Sussex, Somerset, Caithness, &c., &c.

WICKEN. Parishes in cos. Cambridge, Northampton, and Essex.

WICKENS. (Wilkins.) See William.

WICKENDEN. See termination DEN.

WICKER. 1. See Wick, and the termination ER. 2. A-Sax. *wicca*, a wizard.

WICKESON. A corruption of Wilkinson. See William.

WICKERSON. A corruption of Wilkinson. So Dickerson from Dickinson.

WICKHAM. Parishes and places in cos. Suffolk, Kent, Gloucester, Essex, Hants, Berks, Lincoln, Oxford, Cambridge, &c.

WICKING. May be the same as Wickens, i. e., Wilkins, from William. But Domesday shews us a Wikingus before the Conquest—perhaps a descendant of one of the Northman Vikingr, or sea-kings. This is rendered exceedingly probable by Bosworth's definition of *Wicing* or *wiceng*, which is "a heathen pirate," or "viking;" and the phrase "*wicing-sceatha*" was the ordinary name of a pirate or sea-robber. See also Sharon Turner's Hist. Ang.-Sax. iv. 10, note. Hence the Wickings and Wickenses may be descendants, not of some vulgar William of the fourteenth century, but of a great Northman sea-king of the eighth or ninth !

WICKLIFFE. See Wycliffe.

WICKS. See Weekes.

WICKSTED. An ancient family in Cheshire, who resided on the manor of Wicksted, and took their name from it. See B.L.G.

WICKSTEED. See Wicksted.

WICKWAR. A parish in Gloucestershire.

WIDDOWSON. WIDDERSON. WIDDESON. See Widowson.

WIDDRINGTON. An ancient Border family, said to have been settled at Widdrington Castle, co. Northumberland, before the Conquest. They figure largely in the feuds between the English and the Scots, as well as in the cause of the Stuart family from the time of Charles I. down to 1715; and this latter partizanship, though it brought them a coronet, ultimately robbed them of their lands.

What schoolboy is there who has not lamented over what may truly be called the *bootless* zeal of one of this house, who fought at the Battle of Chevy-Chace ?

"For Widdrington needs must I wayle,
    As one in doleful dumpes;
For when his legs were smitten off,
    He fought upon his stumpes !"

WIDEHOSE. A sobriquet allusive to the cut of the garment. One Ric. Wydhose is found in H.R.

WIDFORD. 1. Parishes in Essex, Gloucester, and Hertford. 2. An A-Sax. personal name.

WIDGINGTON. Perhaps the same as Widdington.

WIDICOMBE. WIDDICOMBE. Widdecombe, a parish in Devonshire.

WIDMER. A parish in Nottinghamshire.

WIDOWS. A genitive form of Wido.

WIDOWSON. Not the son of a widow, as it might seem, but the son of Guido, or Wido, a Norman personal name. At the time of the great Survey, William Filius Widonis, literally " William Wido's-son," was a tenant in chief in the counties of Wilts, Gloucester, and Somerset.

WIDVILLE. Earl Rivers in the XV. cent. was probably descended from Hugo de Widvile or Witvile, a Domesday tenant in capite.

WIGAN. A town in Lancashire.

WIGG. An old personal name. Wig occurs in the ancestry of Cerdic, king of the West Saxons, and Wiga is found in the Domesday of Yorkshire. Hence perhaps Wigson, Wigget, Wiggin, &c.

WIGGETT. See Wigg.

WIGGIN. See Wigg.

WIGGINS. See Wigg.

WIGGINGTON. Parishes, &c., in cos. Herts, Oxon, Stafford, and York.

WIGGLES. An ancient personal name, corresponding with a Frisian name still existing as Wiggele. Ferguson. Wigglesworth, in Yorkshire, means the estate of Wiggle.

WIGGLESWORTH. A township in Yorkshire.

WIGGS. The genitive form of Wigg.

WIGHT. 1. The A-Sax. *wiht* means a man, a creature, any thing; and the O. Eng. *wight*, still retained in the phrase " luckless wight," has a similar signification. Another and more usual meaning of the word, is swift or active, as in the illustrative quotation of Halliwell :—

" Y schalle gyf the two greyhowndys,
    As *wyght* as any roo"—

that is, " as swift as any roe." The Scottish form of the word is *wicht*, which Jamieson defines as, strong, powerful, active, clever; denoting strength of mind, or fertility of invention. 2. The Isle of Wight may possibly put in a claim in some cases.

WIGHTMAN. A strong, active, or clever man. See Wight.

WIGHTON. A parish in Norfolk.

WIGHTWICK. A hamlet in Staffordshire, where this ancient family resided.

WIGLEY. A hamlet in the parish of Eling, co. Hants.

WIGMORE. A parish of Herefordshire.

WIGNELL. Wiggenhall is the name of several parishes in Norfolk.

WIGRAM. Has a ' local ' appearance, and I do not find any personal name resembling it ; yet in recent times, the baronet's family, who, as Bristol merchants, can trace themselves so far back as 1712, have changed their patronymic to *Fitz-Wygram*, and obtained a grant of supporters to their arms !

WIGSELL. Wigsell, anciently Wigsale, an estate in the parish of Salehurst, co. Sussex.

WIGSON. 1. A corruption of Wilkinson, through Wickison? 2. See Wigg.

WIKES. See Weekes.

WILBAR. See Wildbore.

WILBERFORCE. Professor Pott, in his Die Familiennamen, associates this celebrated name with the Germ. *Starke*, and the Fr. *La Force;* but it is a simple corruption of Wilberfoss, a township in E. Yorkshire, where the family were settled from the early Norman reigns—traditionally from the Conquest—until the middle of the XVI. cent. Even so lately as about a century ago, the name still lingered in the parish and township. The earliest recorded individual of the name is Ilgerus de Wilberfosse, who flourished under Henry II.

WILBRAHAM. An estate in Cheshire. The earliest recorded ancestor is Richard de Wilburgham of Wilburgham, in Cheshire, who was living 43. Henry III. Shirley's Noble and Gentle Men. The family were settled there about the time of Henry II. B.L.G. Professor Pott rather absurdly deduces the name, so clearly accounted for, from a union of the English and Hebrew personal names, William and Abraham !

WILBURGHAM. See Wilbraham.

WILBURGHFOSS. An old orthography of Wilberforce.

WILBY. Parishes in Norfolk, Northampton, and Suffolk.

WILCHER. A queer corruption of Wiltshire.

WILCOCK. WILCOCKS. See William.

WILCOCKES. See William.

WILCOCKSON. See William.

WILCOX. WILCOXON. See William.

WILD. WILDE. 1. Rude, uncultivated, rustic; like the Fr. Le Sauvage. It may rank among the earliest of our surnames —one Ulric Wilde being a Domesday tenant. 2. A hamlet in Berkshire.

WILDBORE. Doubtless the animal—a wild boar. The early, or Anglo-Saxon, form of the word is preserved in the surname Wilbar (pronounced Wilebar) from *wild*, and *bár*, a boar. See art. Boar.

WILDEGOS. WILDGOOSE. See Goose.

WILDEN. A parish in Bedfordshire.

WILDISH. The Weald of Sussex is commonly called 'The Wild,' and its denizens, however harmless and civil, are known on the South Downs, and other neighbouring localities, as "*Wildish* men."

WILDMAN. 1. Equivalent to Wild. 2. See Woodhouse. 3. Perhaps a native of the Wild or Weald of Sussex.

WILDRAKE. Certainly not a "wild rake," but probably a provincial word for some species of water-fowl.

WILDS. A pluralization of Wild.

WILDSMITH. Probably a corruption of *weld*-smith. 'To weld' is defined in Bailey's Dictionary as "to forge iron."

WILEMAN. See Wildman.

WILES. Apparently an old personal name. It occurs temp. Edward I. as a surname without prefix. H.R.

WILFORD. A parish in Nottinghamshire.

WILGOS. WILLGOSS. The same as Wyldgos, or Wildgoose.

WILKERSON. A corruption of Wilkinson.

WILKIE. See William.

WILKIN. WILKINS. WILKINSON. See William.

WILKOT. From William.

WILKS. WILKES. See William.

WILL. The 'nurse-name' of William.

WILLAN. Perhaps Willen, a parish in Buckinghamshire.

WILLAMENT. See Williment.

WILLARD. This family, whose chief *habitat* is, and has been from the XIII. century, East Sussex and Kent, have a tradition of Norman descent. The name, it is said, was originally Viliard. I see no evidence of this ; and indeed the Saxon, or at least pre-Norman, origin of both name and family is indubitable. Wielard, or Wilard, was a personal name, and it is found in the names of many places, as Wylerdsley, Wyllardssey, Willardby, Willardesham, Willardestone, &c. In Domesday we find the forms Wielardus, Wilardus, Wluard, Wluuard, and Wlward. The last-mentioned occurs in Kent, the county from which the numerous Willards of America deduce themselves. For many speculations on the origin of the name and family, see *Willard Memoir*, by Joseph Willard, Esq., 8vo. Boston, U.S., 1858.

WILLBOURN. An Old German name, Wilbern.

WILLCOCK. WILLCOCKE. WILLCOCKS. See William.

WILLÉ. See William.

WILLEMENT. The tradition of the family is, that they were originally from French Flanders, and fled hither, either from the Duke of Alva's persecution, or after the Revocation of the Edict of Nantes.

The Norwich branch of the family still carry on the manufacture of crape and similar fabrics, which were first introduced into that city from the Low Countries. Inf. Thos. Willement, Esq., F.S.A. The surname appears, like Willemin, Guillemin, and other Fr. family names, to be a modification of William.

WILLER. An old personal name; O. Germ. Wilheri; Mod. Germ. Willer. Ferguson.

WILLET. WILLOTT. WILLATS. See William.

WILLIAM. I have not met with this as a surname, but it has become the *parent* of a greater number of surnames than any other baptismal appellation. The following are the chief derivatives:—Fitz-William, Mac-William, Ap-William, Williams, Williamson, Wills, Willes, Wilks, Wilkes, Wilkin, Wilkins, Wilkie, Wilkinson, Wickens, Wickeson, Wickerson, Willson and Wilson, Willcock and Wilcocke, Willcocks, Woolcock, Wilcox, Wilcockson, Wilcoxon, Willet, Willott, Willatts, Wilmot, Willmott, Willomat, Willy and Willey, Willé, Willis. Also Bill, Bilson, and Billson. An old provincial nickname of William is Till,—whence Tilson, Tillott, Tillotson, Tilly, and Tillie. Guilliam, Gilliam, Guillim, Gillett, Gillott, and Gilliat are also from this fecund source, as well as numerous continental surnames, which, though found in our directories, can hardly as yet be reckoned as naturalized amongst us.

This Christian name has produced many offshoots in France. M. de Gerville remarks: " Of Guilleaume, or Villeaume, we have formed Guillot, Guillotte, Guillard, Villot, Villard, Guillemin, Villemain, Guillemette, Guilmard, Guilmot, Guilmoto, and Guillemino." Mem. Soc. Ant. Normandie, xiii.

WILLIAMS. See William. Owing to the numerousness of this name in the Principality, it stands third in the list of common surnames in England and Wales. Within a limited period the entries of births, deaths, and marriages, in the books of the Registrar-General were, for Smith, 33,557; for Jones, 33,341: and for Williams, 21,936.

As in the case of Jones, Powell, Price, and other very common Welsh surnames, this usually plebeian patronymic is borne by several families of ancient lineage. For example, the Williamses of Llangibby Castle, co. Monmouth, although they adopted the settled surname only in the reign of Henry VIII., are of really ancient date, though their descent from the redoubtable Brychan Brecheiniog, Lord of Brecknock, in the days of King Arthur, is rather more than we are bound to accept.

WILLIAMSON. See William.

WILLIMETT. See Williment.

WILLINGDON. A parish in Sussex.

WILLINGALE. A parish in Essex.

WILLINGTON. Parishes, &c., in cos. Bedford, Chester, Derby, Durham, Flint, Northumberland, Warwick, &c. John de Willington of Willington, co. Derby, lived at, or immediately after, the time of the Conquest, and from him descended the baronial family of that name in the XIV. century. See B.L.G.

WILLIS. See William.

WILLMAN. O. Germ. Williman; mod. Germ. Willmann; a personal name. Ferguson.

WILLMER. See Willmore.

WILLMORE. Probably the same as the German personal name Wilmar, formerly written Willimar.

WILLOCK. A diminutive of William.

WILLOTT. The same as Willett.

WILLOUGHBY. Lord Middleton's family spring from Sir William de Willoughby, Lord of Willoughby, co. Lincoln, in the reign of Edward I. Shirley's Noble and Gentle Men. In a genealogy of the family drawn up temp. Elizabeth, Sir John de Willoughby, a Norman knight, is said to have held that estate by gift of William the Conqueror. In 54. Henry III. Sir William de Willoughby went to the Holy Land with Prince Edward. Ext. Peerage.

WILLOWS. From residence near trees of this kind. " In the Willows" is a XIV. century surname. The H.R. latinization is In Sallicibus.

WILLS. WILLES. See William.

WILLSON. See William.

WILLTON. See Wilton.

WILLYAMS. The same as Williams.

WILLY. WILLEY. See William.

WILMORE. See Willmore.

WILMOT. WILLMOTT. WILLOMAT. See William.

WILMSHURST. Local, and doubtless derived from some manor or estate in Kent or Sussex. (See Eng. Surn. ii. 30.) It is corrupted to Wimhurst, Wympshurst, and even (colloquially) to Wimpsutt.

WILSHER. WILSHERE. Corruptions of Wiltshire.

WILSON. See William. The Wilsons of Broomhead resided there, under this name, from temp. Edward I. till the XVIII. century. B.L.G.

WILTON. A town in Wiltshire.

WILTSHIRE. From the county.

WILYE. WILEY. A parish in Wiltshire.

WIMBLE. An A-Sax. personal name, Winebald.

WIMBOLL. See Wimble.

WIMBURN. Another spelling of Wimborne, parishes, &c., in Dorsetshire.

WIMBUSH. Wimbish, a parish in Essex.

WIMHURST. See Wilmshurst.

WIMPLER. See Wympler.

WIMPSUTT. See Wilmshurst.

WINBOLT. From Winebald, an A-Sax. personal name.

WINCH. 1. From one of the two parishes, East and West Winch, co. Norfolk. 2. A corrupt nickname of Vincent. See Finch.

WINCHELSEA. An ancient town in Sussex.

WINCKLE. WINCKLES. See Winkle. The latter form may, however, be identical with the personal name Winceslaus.

WINDER. 1. Townships in Westmoreland and Cumberland are so called. 2. Probably a winder or twister of thread. Le Windere. H.R.

WINDELL. See Windle.

WINDLE. A township in Lancashire.

WINDOW. Windo, an old German personal name.

WINDUS. The termination *us* is usually a contraction of *house*; thus Malthus stands for Malthouse, Woodus for Woodhouse, Loftus for Lofthouse, &c. By analogy, Windus would stand for Windhouse—probably a residence in an exposed situation.

WINDUST. See Windus.

WINDMILL. From residence near one.

WINDSOR. Sir Andrew Windsor, who was made a knight-banneret at the battle of the Spurs, in 1513, and who was ennobled as Lord Windsor, was a lineal descendant of Walter Fitz-Other, Castellan of Windsor, in the reign of William the Conqueror, the common ancestor of the Fitz-Geralds, Carews, Gerards, and many other distinguished families. See Fitz-Gerald.

WINFARTHING. A parish in Norfolk. Thomas de Wynneferthyn. H.R.

WINFIELD. Probably the same as Wingfield.

WING. Parishes in the shires of Buckingham and Rutland.

WINGATE. A chapelry in co. Durham.

WINGET. See Wingate.

WINGFIELD. "The Wingfields of Wingfield and Letheringham, both in Suffolk, a distinguished family of the fourteenth and fifteenth centuries, are traced nearly to the Conquest, though they do not appear to have been lords of the manor or castle of Wingfield before the reign of Edward II." Shirley's Noble and Gentle

3 c

Men. A parish in Suffolk possessed by a distinguished family temp. Edw. III. B.L.G. Latinized in charters Ala Campi.

WINGHAM. A parish in Kent.

WINGRAVE. A parish in Buckinghamshire.

WINGROVE. The same as Wingrave.

WINKLE. 1. Wincle, a township and chapelry in Cheshire. 2. Dutch, *winkel*, a shop, workshop, or laboratory. Hence perhaps Winkelman, a surname of recent introduction into England, may mean shopman or workman. Wincel, as occurring in Aldwinkle, Winchelsea, Winchelcomb, may possibly, however, be the A-Sax. for a corner.

WINKLEY. WINCKLEY. There is a parish so called in Devonshire, but the family appear to have originated at Winckley Hall, an estate in the township of Aighton, parish of Mitton, co. Lancaster. In the Coucher-Book of the neighbouring abbey of Whalley, the name of Robert de Wynkedelegh occurs in 4. Edward I., and the family continued to reside at Winckley until the XVII. century. The name appears in Lincolnshire about the middle of the XVI. century, and there is a tradition that the Winkleys of that county are descended from one of the Lancashire house, who, during some civil or religious commotion, narrowly escaped with his life, and took refuge there. The name has been variously written De Wynkedelegh, Wynkley, Winckley, and Winkley. With regard to the first orthography, it is curious to observe that, in the Coucher-Book referred to, the apparently unnecessary middle syllable *de* occurs in several local surnames. For instance Dinckley is written De Dynkedelegh, and what is now Worsley, De Workedelegh. Whether this syllable belongs etymologically to the names, or is a caprice of the scribe, I know not.

WINKSLEY. A place in Yorkshire.

WINKWORTH. Perhaps a corruption of Wentworth.

WINMEN. Winemen, an A-Sax. personal name. Cod. Dipl. No. 853.

WINMILL. See Windmill.

WINN. See Wynne.

WINNEY. Whinney, a place in Northumberland.

WINNINGTON. An ancient family of "that seed-plot of gentry," Cheshire. The paternal name was De Croxton, but in the reign of Edward I., Robert, son of Lidulfus de Croxton, marrying the heiress of Winnington of Winnington, took the surname of his wife's family. Shirley's Noble and Gentle Men.

WINPENNY. May relate to the acquisitive habits of the founder of the family. It may, however, be local. There is a parish of Win-*farthing* in Norfolk.

WINSER. A corruption of Windsor.

WINSKELL. Winskill, a township in Cumberland, united with Hunsonby.

WINSLOW. A parish in Buckinghamshire, and a township in Herefordshire.

WINSOR. See Windsor.

WINSPEAR. Belongs to the same class as Shakspeare, Breakspeare, Wagstaffe, &c.

WINSTANLEY. A township in the parish of Wigan. co. Lancaster, where the family are found temp. Henry III.

WINSTON. 1. Parishes, &c., in cos. Durham, Glouc., Pembroke, and Suffolk. 2. Winstan, an A-Sax. personal name occurring in Domesday.

WINTER. See TIMES AND SEASONS. Also see Vinter.

WINTERBORN. A corruption of one of the many places called Winterbourne, in Dorset and other western counties.

WINTERBOTTOM. WINTERBOT-HAM. See BOTTOM in Supplement. "The Winterbottoms are a time-honoured stock indigenous to Saddleworth." Folks of Shields, p. 22.

WINTERBOURNE. Properly a torrent which runs only in the rainy season of winter. Many localities in the West and other parts of England are so called.

WINTERTON. Parishes in cos. Lincoln and Norfolk.

WINTON. Townships in Yorkshire and Westmoreland. The city of Winchester is sometimes so called, from its latinization Wintonia.

WISBERRY. Probably Wisborough, a parish in Sussex.

WISDEN. See termination DEN.

WISDOM. The name of a place in the parish of Cornwood in Devonshire. See anecdote under Hele.

WISE. A man of judgment and wisdom. So the Lat. Prudens, the Fr. Le Sage, &c. Among many Le Wyses in the H.R., we have one Julia la Wyse.

WISEMAN. A conjuror. Halliwell. This was once a regular profession. Sir Francis Palgrave observes: "In parliamentary documents, we find 'Nigromauncer' attached to a man's name as an addition of lawful calling, not so frequently, indeed, as 'Smith' or 'Baker', yet evidently without any idea of concealment or absurdity. And the details preserved concerning these respectable practitioners all tend to show, that their vocation was tolerably lucrative and successful, provided the individual who tried the profession possessed the proper qualifications." Merchant and Friar, 2nd Edit. p. 217.

The occupation has subsisted until quite recent times. So lately as 1819 we are told: "Impostors who feed and live on the superstitions of the lower orders are still to be found in Yorkshire. These are called 'Wise Men,' and are believed to possess the most extraordinary power in remedying all diseases incidental to the brute creation, as well as the human race, to discover lost or stolen property, and to foretell future events. One of these wretches was a few years ago living at Stokesley, in the North Riding of Yorkshire: his name was John Wrightson, and he called himself 'the seventh son of a seventh son,' and professed ostensibly the trade of a cowdoctor. To this fellow, people whose education, it might have been expected, would have raised them above such weakness, flocked; many to ascertain the thief when they had lost any of their property; others for him to cure themselves or their cattle of some indescribable complaint. Another class visited him to know their future fortunes; and some to get him to save them from being balloted into the militia; all of which he professed himself able to accomplish. All the diseases which he was sought to remedy he invariably imputed to witchcraft, and although he gave drugs which have been known to do good, yet he always enjoined some incantation to be observed, without which he declared they could never be cured; this was sometimes an act of the most wanton barbarity, as that of roasting a game-cock alive, &c. The charges of this man were always extravagant; and such was the confidence in his skill and knowledge, that he had only to name any person as a witch, and the public indignation was sure to be directed against the poor unoffending creature, for the remainder of her life." Brand's Popular Antiq. Edit. Ellis, iii. 34.

The name may, however, have a more reputable origin, as a synonyme of *wissere*, O. English for 'teacher'—from the A-Sax. *wisian* or *wissian*, to instruct, to inform, to shew.

"Be thou our helpe, be thou our socoure,
And like a prophete to *wissen* us."
Lydgate.

The forms in the H.R. are Wisman, Wysman, and Wyseman.

WISH. Kemble and Ferguson derive this name from the Teutonic mythology—Wish being one of the names of Odin; but it is most clearly local. A *wish*, in topography, is, "a damp meadow, or marsh, or lowland in a nook formed by the sinuosity of a river or stream, and so sometimes overflowed with water." Cooper's Sussex Glossary.

WISHART. Perhaps the old personal name Guiscard. This seems likely, from the mediate form Wiscard in H.R.

WISKAR. WISKER. See Whisker.

WISTONNESTON. The ancient orthography of Wiston, co. Sussex, which had proprietors so called in very early Norman times.

WITCHER. See Wicher.

WITCHURCH. See Whitchurch.

WITFORD. Qy. Whiteford?

☞ **WITH.** A local termination occurring in such names as Sopwith, Skipwith, Beckwith. Worsaae derives it from the Danish, and says it means a forest. It is more likely identical with *worth*, which see.

WITHAM. Parishes and places in cos. Essex and Lincoln.

WITHERDEN. Probably Withernden, a manor in and near Ticehurst, co. Sussex.

WITHERICK. Probably the O. Germ. personal name Widerich.

WITHERS. Wither occurs in Domesd. as a tenant prior to that census. Widderson may be a patronymical form. H.R. Wyther.

WITHYCOMBE. Parishes in Somerset and Devon.

WITT. White, from complexion. Alwin Albus, otherwise Wit, occurs in Domesday, as also do Uuit and Uuite. A-Sax. *hwit*.

WITTINGHAM. Two parishes in Berkshire are called Wittenham.

WITTON. Parishes, &c., in cos. Chester, Huntingdon, Lancaster, Norfolk, York, Durham, and Northumberland.

WITTY. Clever, sagacious, was the meaning of this word in ancient times.

WIX. See Weekes.

WODEHOUSE. " This family is very antient, for they were Gentlemen of good rank in the time of King John, as it appeareth by many antient Grants and Evidences of theirs, which I have seene." Peacham's Compleat Gentleman, edit. 1661, p. 235. The name is derived from the lands of Woodhouse or Wodehouse, at Silfield, co. Norfolk. The first of the name mentioned in the Baronetages is Sir Constantine de Wodehouse, who married Isabel, daughter and heiress of Botetourt, at the beginning of the reign of Henry I.

WODGER. Ferguson derives it from Wudga, a personal name in the A-Sax. mythology.

WODSWORTH. A gentleman of this name being addressed as Mr. Wordsworth, it was observed that he was *non verbo dignus*—not Wordsworth! There is little doubt, however, that this name is a corruption of the other.

WOLD. An unwooded hill.

WOLF. WOLFE. WOLFF. Throughout the middle ages the wolf was regarded with a sort of mysterious awe, from his association with the unseen world—perhaps in the first instance in consequence of his constant attendance on Woden. The semimythology of those times invested this cruel beast with many remarkable attributes, some of which are still remembered in our nursery literature. Hence many of the old pagan personal names, which descended to Christian times, allude to him ; and his name is largely compounded with

our local nomenclature, a source in later times of family names. Grimm has collected a large number of Old Germ. proper names compounded with *wolf* in his 'Deutsche Grammatik,' and it would be equally easy to do the same for the English, and other languages.

In France a St. Lou, or Lupus, succeeded a St. Ursus in the see of Troyes in the V. cent., and there were several church dignitaries under Charlemagne who were called Lupus. The kinglet Hugh Lupus, Earl of Chester, is well-known as the kinsman and chief subject of the Conqueror. Lupellus, the diminutive, became softened into Lovell and Lovett, still to be found as English surnames ; and there are some curious compounds of the word. Pel-de-leu, for instance—*wolf's skin*—is an ancient family name mentioned by Ducange, and both Vis-de-Lew and Viso Lupi—*wolf's face*, occur in Domesday—the former as a tenant-in-chief in Berkshire. In the Roll of Arms of temp. Edward II., Sir William Videlou bears three wolves' heads.

Fosbroke mentions a man whose surname represents him as " worse than a wolf "—Archembaldus Pejor-Lupo. See Wolfhunt in this Dict. as a surname derived from a useful employment. See also Pott, p. 665, Eng. Surn. i. 187, and Edinb. Rev. vol. CIII. p. 369. Woolf and Woolfe are common surnames among naturalized German Jews in this country.

WOLFHONGLES. " At-Wolfhongles " occurs as a surname in H.R. Hangles is a Northern provincialism for a kind of crane for hanging a pot over the fire, from the A-Sax. *hongian*, to hang. A *wolf-hongles* was probably a place where wolves had been hung *in terrorem*. According to Saxo Grammaticus, it was the practice to hang a wolf with a parricide, and in Scandinavia and Germany wolves and dogs were frequently hung with criminals. Rorarius, a XVI. cent. writer, states, that he once saw two wolves hung from a gibbet in the forest between Cologne and Juliers, as an example to other wolves. N. and Q., April 23, 1859.

WOLFHUNT. A-Sax. *wolf* and *hunta*, wolf-hunter. A family of this name held lands in Derbyshire, by the service of keeping the Forest of the Peak clear of wolves. Archæol. Assoc. Journal, vii. 197. Nothing can be more erroneous than the popular opinion that King Edgar succeeded, by the peculiar impost of wolves' heads, which he levied upon his Welsh tributaries, in exterminating this villanous quadruped. That it existed at the time of the Norman Conquest, and even so late as the reign of Edward I., is evident from the following authorities. The Carmen de Bello Hastingensi (v. 571) states that William the Conqueror left the dead bodies of the English upon the battle-field, to be devoured " by worms, and *wolves*, and birds, and dogs "—(vermibus, atque *lupis*, avibus, canibusque voranda.) In the year 1851 many skulls of wolves were taken out of a disused medieval well at Pevensey Castle,

In the time of Edward I. John Engayne held lands in Huntingdonshire by the tenure of maintaining dogs for the King, for the purpose of hunting the *wolf*, fox, cat, badger, wild-boar, and hare, in several specified counties. See Rotuli Hundredorum, II. 627.

In the Patent Rolls of 9th of the same monarch, John Gifford of Brymmesfield is empowered to destroy the wolves in all the king's forests throughout the realm; while in the same year Peter de Corbet has a similar permission to catch wolves in the royal forests in several counties. Cal. Rot. Pat. 49. See Umfraville.

WOLLASTON. A manor in Staffordshire, of which the family were lords in early times, and which they sold to the Aston family temp. Richard II. Wollaston is in the parish of Old Swinford. Some of the Wollastons may derive their name from other places so called in cos. Gloucester and Shropshire.

WOLLEY. This family, anciently De Wolegh, or De Woley, were settled in Longdendale, co. Chester, as early as the reign of King John. B.L.G. A parish in Somersetshire is so designated.

WOLRYCHE. "This is a very ancient Shropshire family, descended from Sir Adam Wolryche, Knight, of Wenlock, living in the reign of Henry III., and who previously to his being knighted, was admitted to the Roll of Guild Merchants of the town of Shrewsbury in 1231, by the old Saxon name of Adam *Wulfric*." Shirley's Noble and Gentle Men.

WOLSEY. An ancient personal name. The great sixteenth-century Cardinal was not the first of this designation who was influential at Westminster. Half-a-dozen centuries before his time, flourished Saint Wulsy, first abbot of Westminster, " where he lived many years," says Fuller, " very exemplary for his conversation, until his death, which happened Anno Domini 960. Then was his body buried in the same monastery; and the 26th day of September was kept by the citizens of London with great veneration of his miracle-working memory." Worthies, ii. 420. A Wlsi occurs in Domesday, as an A-Sax. proprietor.

WOLSELEY. Mr. Harwood, in his notes to Erdeswick's Staffordshire, calls the Wolseleys " the most ancient amongst all the very ancient families in this county." Siward, mentioned as Lord of Wlselei in an undated deed, stands at the head of the pedigree of " this venerable house, who are said to have been resident at Wolseley (co. Stafford) even before the Norman Conquest; and it has ever since remained their seat and residence." Shirley's Noble and Gentle Men.

WOLSTON. 1. Wolstan, a parish in Warwickshire. 2. An A-Sax. personal name, Ulstan, Ulstanus. Domesday.

WOLVERTON. Parishes in cos. Warwick, Bucks, Norfolk, and Somerset.

WOMBWELL. An estate and chapelry in the W. Riding of Yorkshire, still the property of the Baronet, who claims from Robert de Wombwell, temp. King Stephen. A branch removed into Kent in the XV. century, and built Wombwell Hall, near Northfleet. Philipott Vill. Cant. It seems probable that two families in succession adopted this name from the estate; for, according to Mr. Shirley, the pedigree commences with Hugh Wombwell of Wombwell, son of Henry *Lovell* de Wombwell, temp. Edw. III., implying a change of ownership at that date. See Noble and Gentle Men.

WOMERSLEY. A parish in the W. Riding of Yorkshire.

WONTNER. *Wont* is O. Eng. and local for a mole; and a Wontner or Wonter is a mole-catcher. See Archæologia, xxxiii., 277. The H.R. form of the name is Le Wantur.

WONHAM. A manor and estate near Reigate, co. Surrey. The name is still found in the adjoining county of Sussex.

☞ **WOOD.** An initial and final syllable in numerous local surnames, as—Woodall, Woodness, Woodwell, Woodmeston, Woodnutt, Woodburn, Woodcroft, Holmwood, Garwood, Burwood, Henwood, Grimwood, Lywood, Selwood. It is, of course, the A-Sax. *wudu*, sylva, nemus.

WOOD. From residence near one. It is often pluralized to Woods; and Attwood and Bywood are other forms of the same name. Its commonest medieval spelling is Atte-Wode, afterwards softened to A'Wood. Almost every considerable wood surnamed a family, and hence the commonness of the appellation, amounting in the Lond. Direct. in its various forms to more than 300 traders. This surname is found so early as Domesday in the form of De Silva. Suffolk. The forms De la Wode, In le Wode, and Ate Wode, are found in H.R.

WOODARD. 1. Wadard, a Domesday name. 2. A corruption of Woodward by the elision of *w*; so Green'ich from Greenwich, Ber'ick from Berwick, &c.

WOODBINE. A Lincolnshire name, probably local. The heiress married Parish.

WOODBRIDGE. A town in Suffolk.

WOODCOCK. 1. The bird. 2. A term of reproach, applied to a simpleton, in many early plays. Halliwell.

WOODE. See Wood.

WOODERSON. See Widowson, and also Wither.

WOODEREVE. The bailiff or reeve entrusted with the care of timber and underwood.

WOODFALL. (Rendered famous by the printer of Junius' Letters.) A hamlet in South Wiltshire.

WOODFORD. Parishes, &c., in cos. Chester, Northampton, Wilts, Essex, &c.

WOODGATE. From residence near the gate of a wood. An ancient Kentish name, occurring in the form of Ate-Wodegate, temp. Hen. III. In documents of the XIII. century, the name is sometimes oddly written Wdegat or Wdegate.

WOODGER. See Woodyer.

WOODHALL. A parish in co Lincoln, and places in several counties.

WOODHAM. (Often pluralized to Woodhams.) Parishes, &c., in cos. Buckingham, Durham, Essex, &c.

WOODHATCH. There is a bird trivially so called; but the surname is more probably from the hatch, or gate, of a forest, which kept in the deer. Many places in woodland districts are known by such names as Mersham-Hatch, Coleman's-Hatch, Nock-Hatch, High-Hatch, &c.

WOODHEAD. A chapelry in co. Chester.

WOODHOUSE. 1. Places in cos. Leicester, Northumberland, &c. 2. The Wodehouse was a favourite character in the Christmas and other festivities of our ancestors—the "Wild Man of the Woods," usually represented as a hairy monster, wreathed about the loins and temples with holly and ivy. See more of him, with his portrait, in Eng. Surn. i. 235.

WOODIN. Doubtless Woden, the name of the great Teutonic divinity. See Oden.

WOODING. See Woodin.

WOODLAND. Many places in cos. Devon, Durham, Lancaster, Derby, &c.

WOODLEY. Parishes and places in cos. Devon, &c., &c.

WOODMAN. This name of occupation became a personal appellation long before it was adopted as a surname. A Wodeman occurs in Domesday, and at an earlier period individuals so designated gave names to Woodmancote, co. Sussex; Woodmanstone, co. Surrey; Woodmansey, co. York.

WOODMANCOTE. A parish in Sussex.

WOODMANCY. A curious corruption of Woodmansey, near Beverley, co. York.

WOODMESTON. Woodmanstone, a parish in Surrey.

WOODMONGER. A dealer in wood; a timber merchant.

WOODPECKER. The bird—a sobriquet.

WOODROFF. WOODROFFE. WOODROOF. WOODROOFFE. WOODROUGH. WOODROW. WOODRUFF. WOODROAFE. WOODRIFF. Apparently corruptions of Wood-reeve, the reeve or bailiff who has charge of woodlands.

WOODS. See Wood.

WOODSON. 1. The son of Wudda, an A-Sax. personal name, occurring as early as the VII. century. 2. See Widowson.

WOODSTOCK. A town in Oxfordshire.

WOODTHORPE. Places in cos. Leicester and Derby.

WOODUS. A local name—Woodhouse.

WOODWARD. (From wood and ward, custos: see Ward.) "An officer of the forest, whose charge is to look after the woods and vert there; his very name denotes his office; he must present all offences within his charge at the court of attachments, or swain-mote, to the chief foresters or verderers; and if he see or know any malefactors, or if he shall find any deer killed or hurt, he must acquaint a verderer thereof, and present the same at the next court of the forest. And by the law he must not walk with bow and arrows, but with a forest-bill or hatchet." Manwode, quoted in Nelson's Laws of Game. It is added that "the Woodward ought to appear at every justice-seat, and when he is called, he must present his hatchet to the Lord chief-justice in Eyre." Le Wodeward. H.R.

WOODYER. Probably 'woodman,' formed by the same rule as sawyer, collier, pavier, glazier, and brazier.

WOOF. Probably a corruption of Wolf.

WOOKEY. A parish in Somersetshire.

WOOLCOCK. See Wilcock.

WOOLCOTT. I cannot find the locality.

WOOLER. A town and parish in Northumberland.

WOOLF. WOOLFE. See Wolf.

WOOLFORD. 1. A parish in co. Warwick. 2. A-Sax. wulf, and weard. A defender against wolves. See Ferguson, p. 140.

WOOLFREYS. Probably a genitive form of Wulfred, an A-Sax. personal name.

WOOLGAR. WOOLLGAR. An exceedingly common A-Sax. personal name. Wulgar occurs on many coins and in records, and the Domesday spellings are Vlgar and Wlgar.

WOOLL. About Langport, co. Somerset, are persons of the labouring class who are commonly called Wooll; but they say that their real old name is Attwooll, probably a corruption of At-Wold. Inform. W. B. Paul, Esq. There is, however, a parish of Wool in co. Dorset.

WOOLLARD. 1. Probably the same as Willard. 2. Wulfhard, an A-Sax. personal name.

WOOLLASTON. Parishes in cos. Gloucester and Salop.

WOOLLEN. An ancient personal name, Wulfhun.

WOOLLETT. Probably the same as Willett.

WOOLLEY. WOOLEY. Anciently written Wolflege and Wolveley, i. e., Anglo-Saxonicè, 'wulfes-leag,' a district abounding in wolves—the name of many localities in Saxon times. See the force of corruption in words, which thus brings, like Phædrus, the Wolf and the Lamb together. For who would suspect, under cover of this fleecy name, the presence of the arch enemy of the fold? Truly of this surname it may be predicated, that it is a wolf in sheep's clothing!

WOOLLVEN. An under-tenant in Domesday is written Wluuen—evidently the same name.

WOOLMAN. A dealer in wool. Le Wollemongre. H.R.

WOOLMER. Wolmer Forest is near Selborne, co. Hants; but the surname is more probably from the A-Sax. personal name Wulmer.

WOOLNOTH. WOOLNOUGH. The A-Sax. personal name Ulnod, or Ulnoth. An ancient baptismal name, common in Domesday, some as tenants in capite, and others as having held lands under the Confessor.

WOOLRYCH. The A-Sax. personal name Ulrich, Ulricus.

WOOLSTAN. WOOLSTON. 1. The A-Sax. personal name Wulfstan, or Ulfstan. 2. Parishes, &c., in cos. Gloucester, Lancaster, Bucks, Chester, Berks, &c.

WOORALL. Probably a corruption of Wirral, a district of Cheshire.

WOOSTER. A corruption of Worcester.

WOOTTON. Besides parishes in many counties, there are innumerable manors, hamlets, and single houses in England so called. The word is A-Sax., and signifies the woody enclosure.

WORBOYS. This strange-looking name appears to be a corruption of Verbois, a village in the neighbourhood of Rouen, in Normandy.

WORDSWORTH. I. e., "the possession of Orde." The name of some locality which I cannot find. See Orde.

WORKMAN. A labourer. Le Worcman. H.R.

WORLD. 1. Perhaps a corruption of Worle, a parish in Somersetshire. 2. The Old Germ. name Worald, i. e., "the old man." Ferguson.

WORGE. A corruption of Worth. The name is ancient in Sussex. Robertus de Wyrche occurs in a deed of 6. Edward II. The manor of Worth or Werth, in the parishes of Brightling and Burwash, became Wercke, and the lands of which it was composed are now known as Great and Little *Worge*. See Duke's Life of Major-Gen. Worge, 1844.

WORGER. Ferguson deduces it from the Teutonic *wer* or *ver*, and *ger*, and thus it must be synonymous with Spearman.

WORMALD. Probably local, the last syllable being *wald* or *wold*. Mr. Ferguson, however, makes it a compound of two words, signifying "the old serpent."

WORMEWOOD. Mentioned by Camden as a local surname.

WORMLEIGHTON. A parish in Warwickshire.

WORMS. A city in Germany, well-known in history.

WORMSLEY. A parish in co. Hereford.

WORNUM. Warnham, a parish in Sussex.

WORRALL. Worle is a parish in Somerset; and Wirral a large district in Cheshire.

WORSLEY. A manor and township in Lancashire, formerly written Workesley, where the family are said to have resided temp. William I. Sir Elias de Workesley joined the first Crusade with Robert, Duke of Normandy. Burke's Ext. Barts.

WORSTER. A corruption of Worcester.

☞ **WORTH.** A very usual termination for family names, as Langworth, Ainsworth, Whitworth, Hepworth. It is "possibly identical with the South Germ. *wörth*; North Germ. *wuurt*; a plot of ground surrounded with water, but elevated above it, or secured with dykes or piles. . . It has probably the same meaning as the Low German *worthe*, a protected, enclosed homestead." Leo's Anglo-Saxon Local Nomenclature, p. 59. "A nook of land, generally a nook lying between two rivers." Halliwell. In some places it would seem to mean a forest, and sometimes a road or public way. "Whether originally land, closes, or farms, *worths* were acquired properties. The old expression, 'What is he worth?' in those days meant, 'Has he land? Possesses he real property?' If he had secured a Worth to himself he was called a *worthy* person, and in consequence had *worship*, i. e., due respect shewn him. A *worth* was the reward of the free; and perchance the fundamentals of English freedom were primarily connected with such apparently trivial matters, and produced such a race of *worthies* as the proud Greeks and haughty Romans might not have been ashamed of." From a lecture by Mr. J. Just, of Bury, co. Lancaster, quoted in N. & Q., vii. 584.

WORTHAM. A parish in Suffolk.

WORTHINGTON. The family are traced to Worthington, co. Lancaster, temp. Henry III.

☞ **WORTHY.** A termination of many local surnames, as Elworthy, Noseworthy, Axworthy, Langworthy. A-Sax. *weorthig*, a farm, manor, or estate.

WORTHY. May relate to worth of character, but is more probably local. See preceding article.

WORTLEY. Two chapelries in the W. Riding of Yorkshire.

WORTON. Parishes, &c., in Oxfordshire and Wilts.

WOTTON. Parishes and places in many counties, the name being interchangeable with Wootton.

WOULDHAVE. This singular name is found at Shields; but as it is sometimes spelt Woodhave, it is probably a compound of the two topographical terms Wood and Haugh, and therefore local.

WRATTEN. A Sussex name—probably the same as Ratton of Ratton, in Willingdon, XIV. cent.

WRAXALL. Parishes, &c., in cos. Dorset, Wilts, and Somerset. The baronet's family are styled " of Wraxall " in the last-named county.

WRAY. See Ray.

WREFORD. A place in Staffordshire.

WREN. WRENN. Not so likely from the bird as from the town of Rennes in Brittany. In H.R., however, it is Wrenne.

WRENCH. 1. See Olerenshaw. 2. I think it must have had another and more ancient origin, as it appears in its present orthography, and without prefix, in H.R.

WREY. An ancient Devonshire race, descended from Robert de Wrey, who flourished in 1136, and whose son was seated at Wrey, in the parish of Moreton Hampstead, from which lands the surname was doubtless borrowed. Shirley's Noble and Gentle Men.

WRIGHT. The A-Sax. *wyrhta* signifies, in its widest sense, the same as the Lat. *faber*, a workman of any kind, but more specifically an artificer in hard materials. The eminent antiquary who bears this surname observes, that "Smith was the general term for a worker in metals, and *Wright* for one who worked in wood and other materials. Hence in the later English period *smith* became the peculiar name of a blacksmith, and *wright* of a carpenter, as it is still in Scotland." Wright's Vocab. p. 10. And in this way it was understood in Chaucer's days. He says of his Reeve :—

" He was a well good *wright*—a carpenter."

(Cant. Tales. Prol. 616.) Standing singly, no doubt it generally means an artificer in wood, but its compounds, as still existing in surnames, show that workmen in other trades, and dealing with other materials, were designated by it, as Copperwright, Shoewright, Glasswright, Cheesewright.

The Boatwright, Wainwright, Cartwright, Wheelwright, Plowright, Sievewright, Arkwright, Tellwright, Shipwright, and All (or awl) wright had to do principally with wood. Goodwright was probably a maker of goads or spear-points. (A-Sax. *gád*.)

WRIGHTSMITH. A strange compound, since ' wright ' and ' smith' were originally identical. See Wright.

WRIGHTSON. The son of a Wright. See Wright. Cognate surnames are Cookson, Smithson, Stewardson, &c.

WRIOTHESLEY. See Wrottesley.

WRITTLE. A parish in Essex. De Writtle occurs in the XIII. cent.

WROTHAM. A parish in Kent, which gave name to its possessors as early as 1. King John. They are supposed to have been a branch of the great Kentish family of Dering. See Curiosities of Heraldry, p. 305.

WROTTESLEY. This family are said to have been seated at Wrottesley, co. Stafford, from the period of the Conquest. The pedigree, however, is not proved beyond Hugo de Wrottesley, lord of that manor in the reign of Henry III. Sir Hugh Wrottesley, one of the Founders of the Order of the Garter, the head of the house temp. Edward III., was a direct ancestor of the present Lord Wrottesley. Shirley's Noble and Gentle Men.

WULMER. See Woolmer.

WYAND. See Wyon.

WYATT. Has gone through the various forms of Wyat, Wiat, Wyot, and Guyot, or Guiot. The last-named three are used indifferently in the time of King John, and clearly prove the derivation of the name as a diminutive, from the Norman-French personal name Gui or Guido, which we have also received in the form of Guy. The name Guyatt is still found in West Sussex.

WYATTVILLE. The final syllable was added to the ancient and respectable name of Wyatt, by way of ornament (?) so lately as the reign of George III. for the gratification of a truly *Gothic* architect.

WYBARN. An ancient personal name. In H.R. Wyborn, Wybourn, Wyburn, &c.

WYBERGH. In 38. Edward III., William de Wybergh, of St. Bees in Cumberland, became possessed of the manor of Clifton, co. Westmoreland, by marriage with the heiress of Engayne, and there the family have ever since resided. Shirley's Noble and Gentle Men.

WYBERN. See Wybarn.

WYCH. WYCHE. A salt spring—whence the termination of Northwich, Droitwich, Nantwich, &c. The medieval form is De la Wyche, the surname of a canonized bishop of Chichester.

WYCLIFFE. A parish in the North

Riding of Yorkshire. Here John de Wycliffe, the reformer, was born in 1324.

WYE. A parish in Kent; and a picturesque western river.

WYKEHAM. Parishes, &c., in cos. Leicester, York, Lincoln, &c. It is often confounded with Wickham and Wycombe. The birthplace of the great architectural bishop, as well as his genealogy, is a disputed point.

The Wykehams of Oxfordshire are traced to the commencement of the XIV. century, when Robert de Wykeham was Lord of Swalcliffe. The male line continued till the year 1800, and the Baroness Wenman, the daughter of W. H. Wykeham, Esq., who died at that date, still possesses Swalcliffe. See Shirley's Noble and Gentle Men.

WYKES. See Weekes.

WYLD. See Wild. Le Wyld. H.R.

WYLDE. See Wild. Le Wylde. H.R.

WYLIE. A parish near Hindon, co. Wilts, now more commonly written Wily.

WYLLIE. See Wylie.

WYLY. See Wylie.

WYMAN. Wimund, an A-Sax. personal name.

WYMARK. An obsolete personal name. Wymarck Piggesteyl was an inhabitant of Winchelsea, 20. Edw. I. Cooper. It is a common Christian name in Domesday, and succeeding records down to the XIV. century.

WYMER. Probably Wymerc, or Wymark, which see.

WYMPLER. A maker of *wymples*, a kind of cape, covering the neck and shoulders—a garment much in vogue in the middle ages. Le Wimpler, Le Wymplare, Le Wimplir.

WYMPSHURST. See Wilmshurst.

WYND. A narrow passage; a word much used in Scottish towns. H.R. Wynd, and De la Wynd.

WYNDHAM. *Per crasin* from Wymondham (that is, the home or habitation of Wimund, a Saxon proprietor), co. Norfolk. The Earls of Egremont were descended from Ailwardus, a noble Saxon, who possessed Wymondham soon after the Conquest; but whether he was a descendant of Wimund does not appear. Felbrigge, in the same county, was for many ages the seat of this ancient race, who afterwards removed to Orchard, co. Somerset, which came from a coheiress of Sydenham. See Shirley's Noble and Gentle Men.

WYNEN. A correspondent observes that, "the name of Wynen is of Dutch derivation. The family date from the XIV. century, a poet standing at the head of our genealogical tree. There is, as you well know, a place called Wynen-Dale in Holland, where one of Marlborough's victories was gained. I would fain hope that our poetical ancestor had somewhat of the honour of naming the dale in question. We emigrated from Holland about 75 years ago."

WYNNE. WYNN. Welsh. The same as Gwynne—white, fair. All Welsh words commencing with G drop the initial in certain cases; thus *gwyn*, when employed as an epithet to a proper name, becomes *wyn*, as Hymel Wyn—Howel the Fair.

The noble and gentle families of Wynne, Wynn, and Winn, are derived from John Wynn Ap Hugh, standard-bearer at the battle of Norwich, A.D. 1549, in the reign of Edward VI., who traced his pedigree to Collwyn ap Tanguo, lord of Ardudwy and Eifionydd, who flourished about the beginning of the X. century, and resided at Harlech Castle.

The Wynns of Melai descended from Marchudd ap Cynan, lord of Uwch Dulas and Abergele, "who lived in the time of Rodri Mawe, King of the Britons, about the year 846." Courthope's Debrett.

WYON. From Guyon, a Norman personal name; so Wyatt from Guyot, Wasconia from Gascony, &c.

WYSE. The family of Wyse, or Wise, of cos. Cornwall, Devonshire, Waterford, &c., are said to have been of Greston, in the first-named county, in 1167. The Irish branch descend from one of the followers of Strongbow. B.L.G.

WYVILL. WYVELL. WYVILE. May be the same as Widvile, ennobled in the XV. cent. as Barons and Earls Rivers. I think, however, that it is more likely to be derived from an A-Sax. personal name which occurs as a mark of proprietorship in Wivelsfield, Wivelsden, co. Sussex, and Wiveliscombe, co. Somerset. Leo derives the prefix from the weevil (curculio granarius), which is most unlikely.

Mr. Shirley considers the Wyvills of Burton-Constable, in Yorkshire, "an ancient Norman family," and descended from Sir Humphrey de Wyvill, who lived at the time of the Conquest. They were long seated at Slingsby, co. York. See Noble and Gentle Men, p. 289. "An elder line of this family, on whom the baronetcy, created in 1611, has descended, is said to be resident in Maryland, in the United States of America." Ibid.

WYNYARD. A vineyard. In the archives of Battel Abbey, we read of lands called the Wyneyard (*de terris vocatis le Wyneyard*), and those lands are known to have been planted with the vine.

X.

Following the method of a Northern naturalist, who introduced into his work a chapter entitled " Concerning Owls in Iceland," the chapter itself consisting of the words, " There are no Owls in Iceland," I must observe, respecting surnames in X, simply that *there are no surnames in X ;* for the good and sufficient reason that this letter is initial to no English word.

Y.

YALDWYN. Probably an A.-Sax. personal name, Ealdwin.

YALE. A correspondent styles this " a genuine Cambrian name, from the family seat in Flintshire."

YALOWHAIRE. From the colour of the original bearer's locks.

YARBOROUGH. A parish in Lincolnshire, where the family were anciently resident.

YARD. YARDE. A close or enclosure. Analogous to Croft, Close, &c.

YARDLEY. 1. Parishes, &c., in cos. Hertford, Worcester, and Northampton. 2. An ancient family of the name were lords of Yardley, co. Stafford. There is an old joke of a Cockney's having broken his jawbone in an unsuccessful attempt to pronounce this name.

YARE. A river in Norfolk, whence Yarmouth.

YARNOLD. A west-country pronunciation of Arnold.

YARNTON. A parish in Oxfordshire.

YARRANTON. Probably the same as Yarnton.

YARRELL. Probably the same as Yarrow.

YARROLL. See Yarrow.

YARROW. A parish in Selkirkshire.

YARTIE. According to the Encycl. Herald. a Devonshire family—Yartie of Yartie.

YATE. See Yates.

3 D

YATES. 1. In some dialects, Y and G are convertible letters, and a gate is called a *yate* or *yat* :—

> " Therewhiles the king ate mete sat,
> The lyoun goth to play withouten the *yat.*"
> *Gy of Warwike.*

In the North of England a gate-post is called a *yate*-stoop. Halliwell. The name may therefore be considered another form of Gates. 2. Sometimes *yate* appears to signify a goat. See Archæologia, xxxii. 183.

YAXLEY. A parish in Suffolk, in which county the family were formerly resident.

YEA. An old Somersetshire family, perhaps identical with Yeo.

YEAMAN. The same as Yeoman.

YEAR. Perhaps the same as Yare.

YEARSLEY. A township in the N. Riding of Yorkshire.

YEATES. The same as Yates.

YEATHERD. *Yeat* is apparently the provincial designation of some species of domestic animal, and the surname therefore belongs to the same class as Shepherd, Wetherherd, Cowherd (Coward), &c. Qu. *goat*-herd ? See Yates 2.

YEATMAN. See Yeatherd.

YELDHAM. Two parishes in Essex are so called, and in that county an armigerous family of this name were resident in the last century.

YELL. Possibly from the Shetland isle so denominated.

YELLAND. Probably a corruption of Yealand, townships in Lancashire.

YELLOW. From peculiarity of costume in the original bearer—analogous to Blue, Scarlett, &c.

YELVERTON. A parish in Norfolk, where the family appear to have dwelt in early times. The extinct Earls of Sussex sprang from Andrew de Yelverton of that county, who flourished temp. Edward II.

YEO. An ancient Devonshire family. The Yeo is a small river of that county, a tributary of the Cready into which it falls near the town of Crediton. C. S. Gilbert derives the name from Tre-yeo, in the parish of Lancells, near Stratton, co. Cornwall. Hist. Cornw. ii. 335.

YEOMAN. A freeholder; the first degree of commoners. Some " define a *Yeoman* to be a free-born Englishman, who may lay out of his own free land in revenue to the sum of forty shillings." Bailey. Under the feudal system a knight's fee was twenty pounds, whence it would follow, that an ordinary yeoman's revenue was one-tenth part of that of the knight; though some Yeomen, for example those of Kent, were much richer. See Whatman.

YEOMANS. A pluralization of Yeoman.

YEOWELL. Perhaps the same as Whewell, or as Yule.

YERBURGH. An ancient spelling of Yarborough.

YERLE. A provincial pronunciation of Earl?

YESTER. A parish in Haddingtonshire.

YETTS. The same as Yates.

YNGLOYS. An old spelling of Inglis or English.

YOE. The same as Yeo.

YOLLAND. Perhaps a provincial pronunciation of Holland, which see.

YOOL. Yule, O.-Eng. Christmas. See TIMES AND SEASONS.

YONGE. An old spelling of Young.

YORK. YORKE. The great northern city has, at various periods, furnished surnames to several different families.

YOUDEN. *Eowthen* is one of the forms

of Odin or Woden, the Teutonic divinity, and Mr. Ferguson thinks that this name is identical.

YOUEL. The same as Yule.

YOUENS. Probably the same as Ewins or Evans.

YOULE. See Yule.

YOULTON. A township in the N. Riding of Yorkshire.

YOUNG. This very well-known surname appears to be of common origin with the classical Neander, Juvenal, &c., and to refer to the youth of the first bearer, at the time when it was adopted or imposed. The H.R. forms are Juvenis and Le Juvene, and Le Jeune was one of the most common of Fr. family names. Verstegan says : " YONG, of his fewness of years." H.R. Le Yonge, Le Yunge.

YOUNGE. See Young.

YOUNGER. A literal translation of *junior*, as applied to the distinction of persons of different ages—the antithesis of Senior.

YOUNGHUSBAND. Applied to a man who had married at an early age.

YOUNGMAN. The same as Young, the second syllable being an unnecessary addition.

YOUNGMAY. Qu : " the young maiden ?" See under Ivy. Yungemay. H.R.

YOUNGS. A pluralization of Young.

YOUNGSON. See remarks under Oldson.

YSELDON. Apparently an antique orthography of Iseldun, now Islington, co. Middlesex.

YULE. The O.-Eng. (from A-Sax.) designation of the season—now called Christmas. See Times and Seasons. In the curious old dictionary of Blount, called Glossographia, is the following passage :—

" In Yorkshire and our other northern parts, they have an old custome after sermon or service on Christmas day ; the people will, even in the churches, cry *Ule, Ule*, as a token of rejoicing, and the common sort run about the streets singing,
" Ule, Ule, Ule,
Three puddings in a pule,
Crack nuts and cry Ule."

Z.

ZACHARY. The personal name.

ZEAL. A parish in Devonshire, usually called Zeal-Monachorum.

ZIGZAG. A shoemaker at Sydenham bore this name. It was probably a sobriquet of recent application, in mockery of a crooked or shambling gait.

ZILWOOD. Local: the same as Silwood.

ZIMMERMANN. German. A carpenter. This name appears to be naturalized amongst us.

A correspondent at Philadelphia informs me, that "William Penn, in issuing patents for land in Pennsylvania, was in the habit of translating the names of Germans whenever it could be done; thus, the Carpenter family in Lancaster county are descended from a Zimmerman."

ZOUCH. The baronial family, who gave the suffix to Ashby de la Zouch, co. Leicester, were a branch of the Earls of Brittany, though genealogists differ as to the precise period and cadet. The founder of the race in England was William le Zusche, who died in the first year of King John. In a charter he calls Roger la Zusche his father, and Alan, Earl of Brittany, his grandfather. Camden mentions the latinization of this surname as " De Stipite Sicco (" of the dry trunk or log ") —for William de la Zouch, Archbishop of York, is so called in this verse, for his valour in an encounter against the Scottishmen at Bear-park, 1342—

" Est pater invictus, *Sicco de Stipite* dictus," &c.

For Zouch signifieth the stocke of a tree in the French tongue." This name has been spelt in a great variety of ways, as Souch, Such, Zoche, Zuche, Zusch, Zusche, &c.

Supplement.

SUPPLEMENT.

A.

ABERDOUR.* There is also a place so called in Fifeshire.

ABETHELL. Welsh; the son of Ethel, or Ithel.

ABEW. Welsh, Ab Hugh, the son of Hugh.

ACKHURST. One or two places in the Weald of Sussex and Kent bear this name, which signifies " the wood of oak trees," from A-Sax. *Ac* and *hurst*.

ACLAND.* " Now a farm in the parish of Landkey ; it is thus described in Westcote's Devonshire :—' Then Landkey or Londkey ; and therein Acland, or rather Aukeland, as taking name from a grove of oaks, for by such an one the house is seated, and hath given name and long habitation to the *clarous* family of the Aclands, which have many years here flourished in worshipful degree.' Hugh de Accalen is the first recorded ancestor ; he was living in 1155, from whom the present Sir Thomas Dyke Acland is twenty-second in lineal descent." Shirley's Noble and Gentle Men.

ACRE. Though now a definite quantity of land, *acre* formerly signified, like the Latin *ager*, a field, without regard to its size. This name may therefore be regarded as synonymous with Field.

ACTON.* Mr. Shirley says, that the Actons of Aldenham, baronets, spring from Engelard de Acton, of Acton Pigot and Acton Burnell, who was admitted on the roll of guild-merchants of Shrewsbury in 1209. General Acton, prime minister to the King of Naples for twenty-nine years, commencing in 1778, was of this family. Noble and Gentle Men.

ADERTON. A hamlet in the W. Riding of Yorkshire.

ADERSTON. Atherstone, co. Warwick, was anciently written Adrestone.

ADINSTOUN. " Of that Ilk—an ancient family in East Lothian, that ended in an heiress, who married Hepburn." Nisbet.

ADLINGTON. A township in Lancashire.

AFORDBY. According to the Encycl. Herald., the family formerly resided at a place so called in Lincolnshire.

AGARD. See Haggard.

AGMONDESHAM. The town now known as Amersham, co. Buckingham.

AGRICOLL. *Agricola*, the latinization of Farmer.

AIGHTON. A township in Lancashire.

AITON. Of that Ilk in Berwickshire, temp. Robert Bruce. Nisbet.

ALANBY. See Allenby.

ALBERTON. Albrighton, a township in Shropshire.

ALBERY. Albury, parishes in cos. Hertford, Oxford, and Surrey.

ALDERSEY.* The progenitor of this family was Hugh de Aldersey, of Aldersey in the parish of Coddington, co. Chester, temp. Henry III. Shirley's Noble and Gentle Men.

ALDERTON. See Aldrington in this Supplement.

ALDRINGTON. A parish near Brighton, co. Sussex, which has a ruined church, but no population. At a recent census it had but one inhabitant—the keeper of a toll-gate. It appears that that one example of the *genus homo* had lost a leg, so that the return to the Registrar-General ought to have stood thus :—

Houses............ 1
Inhabitants........ ¾ !

This place was originally of some importance, and the surname Aldrington or Alderton seems to have been adopted from it at an early period. In the latter form it still exists in Sussex.

ALEPSON. The firm of Alepson and Co., of London (Greek merchants), originally traded as " Alephloghn, Brothers, & Co." which they afterwards altered into the more portable name of Alepson.

ALFRETON. A town in Derbyshire.

ALINGTON. The Alingtons, of Swinhope in Lincolnshire, are a branch of the extinct family of the Lords Alington of Horseheath, in Cambridgeshire, who were originally of Alington in the same county, soon after the Conquest. Shirley's Noble and Gentle Men.

ALLARDYCE.* " This family," says Nisbet, " got a charter from King William, of the lands of *Albrethis* in the sheriffdom of Kincardine, ... now Allardice, which has ever since been the surname of the family."

ALLINGTON. Parishes and places in cos. Dorset, Kent, Sussex, Wilts, Suffolk, Devon, Lincoln, &c.

ALNHAM. A parish in Northumberland.

ALNWICK. A well-known castle and town in Northumberland.

ALTHAM. A chapelry in the parish of Whalley, co. Lancaster.

ALVASTON. A township in Cheshire.

ALVERTHORPE. A township in the W. Riding of Yorkshire, more commonly known as Allerthorpe.

AMBOROW. Probably a corruption of Hamborough.

ANGLE. See Nangle.

ANKITTEL. In Ireland, and written temp. Richard II., Angetale, is doubtless the same as the English Anchitel.

ANNE.* The name is local. The pedigree begins with Sir William de Anne, Constable of the castle of Tickhill, co. York, temp. Edward II. Shirley's Noble and Gentle Men.

ANNESLEY.* Ralph, surnamed Brito, of Annesley, living in 1156, is assumed to have been the son of Richard, of Annesley, mentioned in Domesday. The estate continued in the family till the extinction of the male line in 1437, when it went with the heiress to the Chaworths.

AP BRAN. Welsh—the son of Bran (Brennus).

APELDERFIELD. Local ; A-Sax., " the field of the apple-tree." See Appletree.

APOSTLES.* As a pendant to the anecdote in Eng. Surn. ii. 159, respecting a Sussex peasant desiring the clergyman to give his child the name of Acts o'Postles, I may note, that among the Registrar-General's nominal curiosities, there occurs

in 1840, as witness to a marriage, the name of *Acts Apostles* Tong !

APULDERFIELD. See Apelderfield.

ARCHBOLD.* The Archbolds of Ireland claim a Danish origin. The name occurs 1. Henry IV.

ARCHDALL. The Archdalls of Castle-Archdall, co. Fermanagh, are of English extraction. The founder of the family in Ireland, temp. Elizabeth, was John Archdall of Norton Hall, co. Norfolk. The locality of Archdall is unknown.

ARCHES. See Darke.

ARCHEVER. Perhaps a corruption of the Fr. *Archevêque*, archbishop. See anecdote under Ecclesiastical Surnames.

ARCHIE.* Nisbet says " of that Ilk;" but does not mention the locality, which I conceive it would be difficult to find. See article " Of that Ilk."

ARDBOROUGH. Probably local in Scotland.

ARDEN.* " No family in England can claim a more noble origin than the house of Arden, descended in the male line from the Saxon Earls of Warwick before the Conquest. The name was assumed from the woodlands of Arden, in the North of Warwickshire, by Siward de Arden, in the reign of Henry I., which Siward was grandson of Alwin, the sheriff, in the reign of Edward the Confessor." Shirley's Noble and Gentle Men.

ARDINGTON. A parish in Berkshire.

ARMIGILL. An ancient Teutonic personal name, formerly Hermengild. The Roman church honours a confessor called Armagill on the 16th of August.

ARMSTRANG. A provincial pronunciation of Armstrong.

ARNET. Said by Nisbet to be " of that Ilk"—perhaps identical with Arnot, a place in the parish of Stow, co. Edinburgh.

ARNWAY. Local. See Arn.

ARNWOOD. Local. See Arn.

ARSCOT. A corruption of Ascot.

ARTHINGTON. A township in the W. Riding of Yorkshire gave name to this family, at an early period. Peter de Ardington, or Arthington, about the reign of Stephen, founded a priory of Cluniac nuns there.

ARUNDELL.* According to Hoare's Wiltshire, there is no evidence whereby to affiliate the Arundells of Wardour to the Rogerius A. of Domesday ; though this is strongly probable. This ancient and influential family were formerly characterized as " THE GREAT ARUNDELLS." Shirley's Noble and Gentle Men.

ASGILL. Local. See Gill.

ASHBURY. Parishes in Berkshire and Devonshire.

ASHBORNE. Ashbourne, a town in Derbyshire.

ASHBROOK. A parish in Gloucestershire.

ASHBURNHAM.* Camden characterizes the Ashburnhams as " the most ancient family of these tracts ;" and Fuller speaks of them thus :—" My poor and plain pen is willing, though unable, to add any lustre to this family of *stupendous antiquity*—a family wherein the eminency hath equalled the antiquity thereof." Worthies, iii. 233. See also Shirley's Noble and Gentle Men.

ASHBURTON. A town in Devonshire.

ASHPITEL. The family have a tradition that their name was originally Aspinel; but I think it more probable that it is a provincialism for Hospital. See Spital.

ASHURST.* A Lancashire family of good antiquity, and, until the middle of the last century, lords of Ashurst in that county, where they appear to have been seated not long after the Conquest. Shirley's Noble and Gentle Men.

ASKERTON. A township of Lanercost, co. Cumberland.

ASSHETON. An old Lancashire family, originally seated at Assheton-under-Lyne,

unde nomen. From them proceeded two lines of baronets, and the Asshetons of Downham. Shirley's Noble and Gentle Men.

ASTLEY.* Astley Castle, co. Warwick, was the residence of the family so early as 12. Henry II., and the earliest known progenitor is Philip de Estlega, who then flourished. Noble and Gentle Men.

ASTROBY. Asterby, a parish in Lincolnshire.

ATCLIFFE. See At.

ATTERILL. See Trill.

ATTREE. " At-the-Tree." From residence near some remarkable Tree. This name is somewhat abundant in the forest districts of Sussex and the adjacent counties.

AUCHTERLONY. The same as Ochterlony.

AUBEYNE. The same as St. Aubyn.

AUDELEY. See Stanley.

AYLMER.* The Irish Aylmers claim descent from Ailmer, Earl of Cornwall, who lived in the reign of King Ethelred. They settled in Ireland at the close of the XVI. century. D'Alton.

AYDE. An occasional spelling of Ade.

B.

BACKIE. Backies is a village in the parish of Golspie in Sutherlandshire.

BACKWELL. A parish in Somersetshire.

BACONTHORP. Baconsthorpe, a parish in Norfolk.

BADBY. A parish in Northamptonshire.

BAGLEY. An extra-parochial liberty in Berkshire.

BAGWORTH. A chapelry in Leicestershire.

BAILDON. A chapelry in the W. Riding of Yorkshire.

BALCASKIE. An estate in Carnbee, co. Fife, where the family dwelt in ancient times.

BALDEN. 1. A corruption of Baldwin. 2. There are two parishes in Oxfordshire called Baldon.

BALDERSTON.* Nisbet says, " Of that Ilk," in co. Linlithgow. The name is found in the Ragman Roll as Balderstoun and Bauderston.

BALDWIN.* The Baldwins of Kinlet, co. Salop, are supposed to be of Norman origin ; but the pedigree appears to be traced only to the XIV. century. The head of the family having married a co-heiress of Childe, took that name, which his posterity now consequently bear. Shirley's Noble and Gentle Men.

BAMFYLDE. Lord Poltimore's family descend from John Baumfield, who became possessed of Poltimore, co. Devon, temp. Edward I. ; but the pedigree can be traced three generations before that period. Shirley's Noble and Gentle Men. Bampfylde (which see) is an orthographical variation.

BARBER.* The common latinization of this name in the middle ages was Barbitonsor.

BARDEN. A township in Yorkshire.

BARDWELL. A parish in Suffolk.

BARKHAM. A parish in Berkshire, and a manor in E. Sussex.

BARKSTON. Parishes, &c., in cos. Leicester and Lincoln.

BARLEYMOW. Probably from an inn sign in some rural locality.

BARNACLE.* Barnakarl or Barnakal was a surname or nickname given to a celebrated Norwegian pirate named Olver, who, setting his face against the then fashionable amusement of tossing children on spears, was nicknamed by his companions, to shew their sense of his odd scruples, *Barnakarl*, that is, " Baby's Old Man." Ferguson.

BARNARDISTON.* Mr. Shirley characterizes the B's, of the Ryes co. Suffolk, as " a very remote, but the only remaining, branch of what was in former ages the most important family in Suffolk, descended from Geoffry de Barnardiston of Barnardiston, in that county, who was living in the reign of Edward I." Noble and Gentle Men.

BARNSLEY. A parish in Gloucestershire.

BARNSTON.* I ventured, in the body of the work, to suggest that Barnston was a contraction of Barnardiston. This might seem warranted by a similarity of arms, as well as that of orthography :—

BARNARDISTON. *Azure, a fesse dancettée Ermine, between six cross-crosslets, Argent.*

BARNSTON. *Azure, a fesse indented Ermine, between six cross-crosslets fitchée, Or.*

Further, it may be observed that an ancestor of this family, Thomas de Bernaston, temp. Edw. III., bore his cross-crosslets Argent, like the Barnardistons ; and, as all heraldrists know, the difference between *dancettée* and *indented* is a modern distinction.

But, notwithstanding this great similarity, not to say identity, of arms, the families appear to be strangers in blood; for the Barnstons of Churton, co. Chester, descend from Hugh de Barnston, who was lord of a moiety of Barnston in that county, 21. Edward I. Shirley's Noble and Gentle Men.

BARON.* Baroun, or Baron, occurs in co. Tipperary, temp. Edw. II. Burke thinks that the family were a branch of the sept of FitzGerald, who " having been created palatine Barons of Burnchurch, used to distinguish themselves by adopting the title as their patronymic." D'Alton. This is, however, improbable.

BARROWMAN. The first of this name probably had his dwelling by some *barrow* or tumulus.

BARSTON. A parish in Warwickshire.

BASKERVYLE. The same as Baskerville. According to Ormerod's Cheshire, iii, 355, the Baskervyles of Old Withington,

now Glegg, are descended from Sir John Baskervyle, grantee of a moiety of Withington in 1266, and that estate has ever since remained in the family.

BASNET. O. Fr. *basunet* or bassinet, a helmet.

BATTISCOMBE. A manor near Lyme Regis, co. Dorset, in which county the family pedigree is traced to the XV. cent. See Hutchins's Dorsetshire, i. 536.

BEACHCROFT. See Beechcroft.

BEADS. Probably a genitive form of Bede, the personal name.

BECUDA. See Delanoy.

BEALE.* The Le Beale of the Hundred Rolls is probably the Fr. *le Bel,* referring to personal beauty.

BEARTUP. This strange name was formerly written Bateup ; and the last syllable is probably a corruption of *hope*, a valley.

BEATAGH. Mr. D'Alton considers the family settled in co. Meath, in the XIV. century, to have been of Danish origin.

BEAUFICE. The same as Beaufitz.

BEAUFITZ. The A-Norm. form of *beau-fils*, a son-in-law, or step-son.

BEECHCROFT. Local : " the croft where beech-trees abound."

BELCHES. Nisbet says, " of that Ilk;" but where the Ilk is, I find not.

BELFIELD. An anglicized form of Belleville.

BELLARNEYS. An O.-Fr. form of the name Beauharnois, having reference to the " beautiful armour " of the first bearer.

BELLEVILLE. A Fr. local name, signifying " the fair or beautiful town." There are several places so called in Normandy.

BELWELL. A corruption of Belleville.

BENION. BENYON. Enion, an ancient Welsh personal name, prefixed by Ab, became Benion. So Barry, Bevan, &c.

BENVILLE. Perhaps Benouville. Three places in Normandy are so called.

BENWELL. A corruption of Benville.

BEREWASHE. An old orthography of Burwash, co. Sussex.

BERINGTON. A place in the hundred of Condover, co. Salop. The Beringtons of Winsley, co. Hereford, spring from Thomas and Roger de Berington, who were living at the place indicated in the reigns of Edward I. and II.

BERKENHEAD. Birkenhead, a town in Cheshire.

BERNACK. A parish in Northamptonshire, the ancient possession of the family. The heiress of the male line was married early in the XV. cent. to Vincent. See Shirley's Noble and Gentle Men.

BERRYMAN. See BURGH, and the termination MAN.

BETTON. The ancestor of this family, Walter de Betton, had a freehold estate at Betton-Strange, near Shrewsbury, temp. Edward I. The head of the house changed his name to Bright not many years since. Shirley's Noble and Gentle Men.

BEVELL. See Beville.

BEVERCOT. Bevercoates, a parish in Nottinghamshire.

BEVERSTONE. A parish in Gloucestershire.

BEVILLE. Perhaps Beuville, near Caen, in Normandy.

BEWFICE. See Beaufitz.

BEWMARRIS. Beaumaris, a town in Anglesey.

BICKERSTAFF.* The definition is erroneous—the name being local, from Bickerstaffe, a township in the parish of Ormskirk, co. Lancaster, which in early times belonged to the family. It was sometimes written Bickerstath, whence Bickersteth.

BICKERSTATH. A corruption of Bickerstaffe.

BICKERSTETH.* See Bickerstaff above.

BICKERTON.* Nisbet says "of that Ilk," but does not indicate the locality.

BIDDULPH.* "Traced to Ormus, mentioned in the Domesday Survey. He was, it is said, of Norman descent, and is supposed to have married the Saxon heiress of Biddulph, from whence the name was afterwards assumed." Shirley's Noble and Gentle Men.

BIDLAKE. A place in Somersetshire, once in the possession of the family. Encycl. Herald.

BIGBURY. A parish in Devonshire.

BINNING. An ancient parish in co. Linlithgow, where the family were formerly resident.

☞ **BIRDS.** Mr. Clark's amusing classification had not appeared when the first sheets of this work were printed off; and I will, therefore, insert in this place the names which *prima facie* seem to have been borrowed from this part of the animal creation.

"Blackbird, Cuckoo, Duck and Drake,
Chaffinch, Chicken, Crow and Crake;
Goose and Gander, Cock and Henn,
Pheasant, Falcon, Lark and Wren;
Linnett, Eagle, Nightingale,
Gosling, Duckling, Grouse and Quail;
Partridge, Goldfinch, Pidgeon, Dove,
(Emblem of connubial love);
Heron, Reeve, Seal, Darter, Hawke,
Fowl, Woodpecker, Finch and Stork;

Robin, Raven, Rooke and Ruff,
Capon, Peacock, Coot and Chough;
Bustard, Bunting, Buzzard, too,
Throstle, Bantam, Bill and Coo;
Sparrow, Starling, Goshawk, Snipe,
Crane, Chick, Wildgoose, Creeper, Kite;
Martin, Pyefinch, Parrott, Swallow,
Titmouse, hiding in the hollow;
Birdseye, Bird, Egg, Plume and Feather,
Not inaptly brought together;
Daw, Kingfisher, Swan and Diver,
Often seen upon the river;
Hooper, Hobby, Thrush and Knott,
Gull, not easy to be caught;
Mallard, Goldhawk, Jay and Herne,
All from the tribe of Birds we learn."

BIRKEN. See Birkin.

BIRKIN. A parish in the West Riding of Yorkshire.

BIRLINGHAM. A parish in Worcestershire.

BISHOPSDALE. A township in the N. Riding of Yorkshire.

BISHOPTON. Parishes, &c., in cos. Durham and York, are so designated.

BISHTON. A parish in Monmouthshire.

BISLEY. Parishes in Gloucestershire and Surrey.

BISPHAM. Two places in Lancashire are so called.

BISSETT.* The Bissetts of Scotland were in that kingdom temp. Malcolm III. Nisbet.

BITTERPLUM. See Sweetapple.

BLABY. A parish in Leicestershire.

BLACKADAR. See Blackadder. The lands of B., where the family anciently dwelt, are in Berwickshire.

BLACKENSOP. See Blenkinsopp.

BLADEN. See Bladon.

BLADESMITH. A forger of swordblades.

BLAKENHAM. Great and Little Blakenham are parishes in co. Suffolk.

BLANCHARDEN. This name is given in Encycl. Herald. as belonging to co. Kent, and it is probably identical with Blechenden.

BLANK. Fr. *blanc.* White.

BLARE. The same as Blair.

BLATCHFORD. An estate near Cornwood, co. Devon.

BLECHENDEN. See DEN.

BLETSHO. Bletsoe, a parish in Bedfordshire.

BLEVERHASSET. A common misspelling, in old writings, of Blennerhasset.

BLITHFIELD. See Blythfield.

BLOCKLEGH. See Blockley.

3 E

BLOMER. See Bloomer.

BLOORE. A township in Staffordshire.

BLOSSOM. Possibly a corruption of Bloxham, or of Bloxholme, parishes in cos. Oxon and Lincoln.

BLOUNDELL. The same as Blundell.

BLYTHFIELD. A parish in Staffordshire.

BOBKIN. BOBKING. A diminutive of Bob, from Robert.

BOCKEN. A corruption of Bocking.

BODEHAM. An old form of Bodiam.

BODELSGATE. An old Cornwall surname, and probably local in that county.

BODENHAM. "Hugh de Bodenham, lord of Bodenham in Herefordshire, grandfather of Roger, who lived in the reign of Henry III., is the ancestor of this family, who were afterwards of Monington, and of Rotherwas, about the middle of the XV. century." Shirley's Noble and Gentle Men.

BODIAM. BODYAM. A parish and manor in Sussex. The family, who were of Norman origin, were descended from Osbern de Bodiam, otherwise FitzHugh, who held Bodiam at the making of Domesday. The elder line became éxtinct in the XIII. cent. Lower's Bodiam and its Lords. Lond. 1857.

BODYHAM. See Bodiam.

BOKELAND. The same as Buckland.

BOKENHAM. An old spelling of Buckenham, a town in Norfolk.

BOLDINGTON. Probably Bollington, the name of two townships in Cheshire.

BOND.* Mr. Shirley, speaking of the Bonds of Grange and Lutton, co. Dorset, says:—"Originally of Cornwall, and said to be a family of great antiquity, but not connected with Dorset till the middle of the XV. century." Noble and Gentle Men.

BONEFAT. A queer corruption of Bonenfant, a well-known Fr. surname, equivalent to our Goodchild.

BONEFIELD. The same as Bonfield.

BONFIELD. An anglicization of Bonville.

BONFOY. Fr. *bonne-foi*, "good faith." Analogous to Beaufoy.

BONGEY. Probably a corruption of Bungay, a town in Suffolk.

BONNINGTON. A parish in Kent.

BONNYMAN. This Scottish surname may be considered a synonym of Prettiman.

BONOVRIER. The Encycl. Herald. gives this name as of London and France. It is of course *bon ouvrier*, "the good workman."

BONSOR. Probably Fr. *bon-sieur*, "the good lord or master."

BONUS. The latinization of Good.

BONWICK. A township in Yorkshire.

BONYMAN. Possibly an anglicization of the Fr. *bonhomme*. The armorials of this family are somewhat odd, viz.: Argent, a naked man shooting an arrow out of a bow, Gules. Encycl. Herald.

BONYTON. The same as Bonithon.

BOOKE. Perhaps from the Fr. *bouc*, a he-goat, with reference, possibly, to the beard of the first owner of the name. *Barbe de bouc* is a phrase still in use to designate a small tuft of long hair under the chin.

BOORNE. See Bourne.

BORAGE. One of the numerous corruptions of the baronial Burghersh or Burwash.

BORDET. The same as Burdett.

BOREFIELD. The same as Burfield.

BOREFORD. See Burford.

BORHUNT. The Hampshire family doubtless took their name from Boarhunt, a parish in that county.

BOROUGH.* The Boroughs of Chetwynd, co. Salop, are lineally descended from Robert *Borowe*, noticed by Leland in his Itinerary, which Robert died in 1418. Shirley's Noble and Gentle Men.

BOROWDEN. Borrowden a township of Northumberland.

BORSELLE. Borezell, an estate in the parish of Ticehurst, co. Sussex.

BORTHICK. The same as Borthwick.

BORTHWICK.* The founder of this family is said to have come into Scotland from Hungary, with Queen Margaret. Thomas de Borthwick is mentioned in a charter of temp., Alexander II. Nisbet.

BOSCO. Probably retained from the latinization of At-Wood or Du-Bois, which was De Bosco.

BOSCOAN. A corruption of Boscawen.

BOSISTOW. An estate in the parish of St. Levan in Cornwall, which "in remote times" belonged to the family. D. Gilbert's Cornwall.

BOSLEY.* Bosley is a chapelry, not a parish.

BOSSOM. A corruption of Bosham, a parish in Sussex.

BOSSON. This family, formerly in Devon, Leicester, and other counties, were doubtless of French extraction. The name is probably the Norm. Fr. *boson*, a buckler or shield.

BOSTALL. See Borstall.

BOSUSTOW. See Bosistow.

BOSWELL.* Nisbet says: "The first of this name is said to have been a Norman, and to have come into Scotland in the reign of Malcolm III., and possessed lands in the Merse, called after them (his descendants) Boswell Lands."

BOTELER. See Botiler.

BOTERELL. The same as Botreux.

BOTHELL. Bothel, a township in Cumberland.

BOTHWELL. "As for the antiquity of this name, the first that I have met with is one Arthur Bothwell, of Adam, who was knighted by King James IV., whose son was likewise a knight, called Sir Francis." Nisbet. The name is derived from the parish of Bothwell, in Lanarkshire, famous for its beautiful scenery, celebrated in ancient song—

"Bothwell bank thou bloomest fair!"

BOTLESHAM. Probably Bottisham, a parish in Cambridgeshire.

☞ BOTTOM.* Mr. Ferguson says that "one half of the Directory may be said to explain the other half. Take for instance the names ending in *bottom*, which signifies a valley, or low ground. We have:—

Rowbottom,   Ramsbottom,
Rosebottom,   Tarbottam,
Shoebotham,   Winterbottom,
Sidebottom,   Higginbottom,
  and Shufflebottom.

Turn to the Directory, and we find the names :—

Rowe,   Ramm,
Rose,   Tarr,
Shew,   Winter,
Side,   Higgin,
  and Shuffil,

and all the previous list are at once explained as names of places derived from those of their owners."

This is ingenious, and may be in part correct, but I strongly doubt if the nine names cited existed as personal names in A-Sax. times.

BOUGHTON.* The family of Boughton, baronets, derive themselves from Robert de Boveton, whose grandson William de Boveton was living temp. Edw. III. The family possessed Lawford, co. Warwick, by marriage with the heiress of Allesley, temp. Henry VI., and there they resided till the year 1781, when the representative of the family, Sir Theodosius Boughton, was poisoned by his brother-in-law, John Donellan, Esq., who was executed for the offence the same year. Shirley's Noble and Gentle Men. Courthope's Debrett.

BOURDE. See Borde.

BOURDMAN. See Boardman.

BOVIS. Probably the same as Bœufs, or Bevis.

BOWLER. The Encycl. Herald. mentions this family as "of Bowler, co. Wilts."

BOXWORTH. A parish in Cambridgeshire.

BOYLE.* According to some genealogists this name was originally O'Buidhill, which would make it a Celtic patronymic rather than a Norman local name, as I have suggested. See also O'Bohilly.

BOYMAN.* A known corruption of Bowman.

BOYNTON.* Bartholomew de *Bovington*, living at the beginning of the XII. cent., stands at the head of the pedigree. Shirley's Noble and Gentle Men.

BRACE.* Sometimes a corruption of Braose.

BRACEBRIDGE. "In the time of King John, the venerable family of Bracebridge, originally of Bracebridge in Lincolnshire, acquired by marriage, in the person of Peter de B., with Amicia, daughter of Robert de Arden, and Maud, and granddaughter of Turchil de Warwick, the manor of Kingsbury, co. Warwick, an ancient seat of the Mercian Kings." Shirley's Noble and Gentle Men. In the reign of Edward II. the name was written De Brasbruge.

BRACEGIRDLE. This singular name was taken from an article of the bearer's costume, called a bracing-girdle, a kind of belt. Huloet has "*Bracynge gyrdle*, subcingulum." Halliwell.

BRACKTON. Local : "the enclosure of brakes, or fern."

BRADBRUGE. There are two places in West Sussex called Bradbridge, and from one of these no doubt the old family of Bradbruge or Broadbridge derived their name. They are traced to Roger de Bradbruge, of Town-House in Slynfold, 1355. In the XVI. cent. the heiress of the elder line married Sir Henry Hussey. The name Broadbridge is still found in West Sussex.

BRADENHAM. Parishes in cos. Norfolk and Buckingham are so called.

BRADSTONE. A hamlet in the parish of Berkeley, co. Gloucester, the ancient residence of the family.

BRADWARDEN. See Bradwardine.

BRADWARDINE. Fuller says that Archbishop Bradwardine, who died in 1349, "was descended of an ancient family at Bradwardine (now Bredwardine), in Herefordshire, who, removing thence, had settled themselves for three generations in Sussex, where this Thomas was born, in or near the city of Chichester."

BRADWELL. Parishes and places in cos. Buckingham, Chester, Derby, Essex, Suffolk, &c.

BRAILFORD. Probably Brailsford, a parish in Derbyshire.

BRAKEMAN. A soldier who superintended the great crossbow called a balista, or *brake*.

BRAMFORD. A parish in Suffolk.

BRAMHALL. See Bromhall.

BRAMSHOT. A parish in Hampshire.

BRAN. 1. See Brand. 2. The British hero, latinized Brennus, was really Bran— a Celtic personal name.

BRANSBY. A parish in Yorkshire, and a township in Lincolnshire.

BRANTINGHAM. A parish in the E. Riding of Yorkshire.

BRAUNDE. The same as Brand.

BRAY.* The Brays of Shere, co. Surrey, descend from Sir Reginald Bray, the adherent of Henry VII., who acquired the manor for his services at Bosworth Field, where he is said to have found the crown of the fallen Richard in a thorn bush. His pedigree is traced to Sir Robert Bray of Northamptonshire, father of Sir James, who lived about the period of Richard I. Shirley's Noble and Gentle Men.

BRAYFIELD. A parish in Buckinghamshire.

BRAYTOFT. A parish in Lincolnshire.

BRAYTON. A parish in Yorkshire.

BREADCAKE. If not a corruption of Bridekirk, may be a sobriquet, like Whitbread, Wastel, &c. The *inverse* Cakebread also occurs as a surname.

BRECHIN. A parish in Forfarshire.

BRECKNOCK. The Welsh town.

BREDMAN. A dealer in " the staff of life."

BREDNELL. Doubtless the same as Brudenell.

BREDWARDINE. See Bradwardine.

BREDWELL. See Bradwell.

BREEZE. Ab Rhys, Ap Rees. Welsh.

BREMBER. Bramber, an ancient town and barony in Sussex, originally written Brembre.

BREMSHETT. The same as Bramshot.

BRENCHLEY. A parish in Kent, in which county the family are still resident.

BRENDON.* One family of this name consider it as taken from the parish and barton of Brendon, on the high land near the borders of Exmoor, in North Devon, deriving the appellation from St. Brendon, or Brandon, an Irish saint, the patron of prose writers, to whom the church is dedicated.

BRENNAN.* The name is undoubtedly Irish. See Mac Brennan in this supplement.

BRENTON. Probably the same as Brinton.

BRESSINGHAM. A parish in Norfolk.

BREST. The well-known town and arsenal in Brittany.

BREWS. The same as Braose.

BREWYS. The same as Braose.

BRIANSON. The son of Bryan—the personal name.

BRICKILL. Brickhill, two parishes in Buckinghamshire.

BRID. O. Eng. *bridde*, a bird. A coat of arms was granted to Robert le Brid, alias Bird, of Brixton, co. Chester, in 1575. Encycl. Herald.

BRIDALL. Possibly from Bridell, a parish in Pembrokeshire.

BRIDDE. See Brid.

BRIDGEHOUSE. Local: "the house near the bridge." Many dwellings are so designated.

BRIDGEMORE. Probably Bridgemere, co. Chester.

BRIDPORT. A town in Dorsetshire.

BRIGHOUSE. The same as Bridgehouse. A-Sax. *brycg*, a bridge.

BRIGMAN. The same as Bridgeman. A-Sax. *brycg*, a bridge.

BRIMFIELD. A parish in Herefordshire.

BRINGHURST. A parish in Leicestershire.

BRINGLOW. Does not refer to any reduction or humiliation. It is a corruption, or rather another form, of Brinklow.

BRINKHURST. The same as Bringhurst.

BRINKLOW. A parish in Warwickshire.

BRISBANE. An estate in the parish of Largs, in Ayrshire. In 1332, William Brisbane was chancellor of Scotland. Gent. Mag., March, 1860.

BRISKOO. See Briscoe.

BRITAIGNE. BRITAIN. BRITAYNE. From the French province of Brittany.

BRIXTON. Parishes, &c., in Devonshire, Hampshire, Surrey, and Wiltshire are so called.

BROADHURST. A manor in the parish of Horsted Keynes, co. Sussex.

BROADBRIDGE. See Bradbruge.

BROADOAK. Several hamlets, farms, &c., in different counties are so called, from some spreading oak which formerly grew in them.

BROCKDON. An estate in Devonshire, the original seat of the family.

BROCKIE. "*Brocach*, mottled, speckled, freckled; Su.-Goth., *brokug*, Scotch *bruickie*. This family are of Moray descent." Folks of Shields. It seems that the earliest known mention of the name is in the Chartulary of Moray, in 1364. Two brothers of the name came from Holland and settled south of the Forth, about the beginning of the XVIII. cent. They are supposed to have been descendants of refugees in Holland from Scotland. Ibid.

BROCKTON. A township in Staffordshire.

BROKENSTAFFE. (Encycl. Herald.) This name doubtless belongs to the same class as Wagstaff, Hackstaff, &c.; though it looks more like defeat than victory.

BROKESBY. Brookesby, a parish in Leicestershire.

BROKET. An old spelling of Brockett.

BROMESTALKE. This old name looks very like an English form of Plantagenet. A strong confirmation of this derivation is, the fact that the arms assigned to the family in the Encycl. Herald. are identical with those of the Plantagenets, as Earls of Anjou ; viz.: *Gules, a chief Argent, over all an escarbuncle, Or.*

BROMHALL. A township in Cheshire.

BROMPTON. Parishes, &c., in Kent, Essex, Middlesex, Yorkshire, Shropshire, Somerset, &c., are so called.

BROOKBANK. See Brooksbank.

BROOKE.* Adam, Lord of Leighton, co. Chester, is the first recorded ancestor of the Baronet Brookes of Norton. He lived in the reign of Henry III. The elder line failed about 1632.

The Brookes of Ufford, co. Suffolk, descended from William de la Brooke, owner of the manor of Brooke, co. Somerset, who died in 1231. Noble and Gentle Men.

BROOKSBANK. Local: from residence on the bank, not of a mere streamlet, but of something much greater. "A *brook,*" says Verstegan, " we now take to be a small running water, but I find it in the Teutonick to be that which *palus* is in Latine—a waterish or moorish ground. The city of Bruxels took name of the brook land or moorish ground lying on the north side thereof." Restitution, p. 314.

BROTHERHOOD. The original bearer of this name was probably a leading member of some guild or fraternity.

BROWN.* "A name which deserves far more reverence than it generally gets. Talk of 'coming over with the Conqueror'—the first Browns came over with Hengist and Horsa—the second with Halfdene and Hastings ! I do not doubt that it is in some cases a surname derived from complexion, though in point of fact I have never met with it as an ancient Teutonic surname. As a baptismal name, on the other hand, it was very common, and both on the German and Scandinavian side of very honourable origin. As a Scandinavian name, it seems to be derived from (or at any rate to correspond with) a title of Odin. Of the men called Brúni in the Landnamabok, one is surnamed the " white," shewing clearly that it was not from complexion (unless indeed he was a 'whitey-brown'). Its meaning seems to be, "having marked or prominent eyebrows,"— which is considered to give power and dignity to a countenance.

" The German Browns are a different family. The Old Saxon and Old High German Bruno is cognate with the English

burn, and signifies fiery or impetuous. As A-Sax. names, we find Brun and Brún. In a charter of manumission occurs a *Brun bydel*—" Brown the Beadle." What a nineteenth century sound ! Mr. Turner oddly enough translates it, " the brown beadle." Ferguson, p. 297.

BROWNLOW. Local : " the brown eminence." See Low and Law.

BROWNRIGG. Local : " the brown ridge."

BROXBORNE. Broxbourne, a parish in Hertfordshire.

BRUMMELL. Probably a corruption of Bromhall.

BRUMSTEAD. A parish in Norfolk.

BUCKFIELD. Local : " a place resorted to by deer."

BUCKHAM. Local : " the home or resort of deer."

BUCKMINSTER. A parish in Leicestershire.

BUCKTHOUGHT. May be from the A-Sax. *bóc,* a beech tree, and *thwaite* which see. A clearing of beech-trees.

BUDOXHEAD. A gentry family of Devonshire formerly bore this singular name, which was derived from Budeauxhead, in the parish of St. Budeaux, near Plymouth, the church of which was built by Roger Budeokshead.

BULBECK. See Bolebeck.

BULBROOK. Perhaps Bolebrook, a manor in Hartfield, co. Sussex.

BULFACE. Probably bull-face, a translation of the Norm. Front-de-bœuf.

BULLAKER. Qu. *bullocker*—a herdsman ; one who had the care of bullocks?

BULLER.* I fear that I have done the Bullers a wrong. A *bulla* is a seal—hence the pope's *bull,* a document attested by his Holiness's leaden seal. A western correspondent observes, that "a *bullarius* is a stamper, an office in the Stannary court of Cornwall ; also in the Pope's court at Rome "—one who seals. Comp. Spigurnel.

The Bullers of Devonshire and Cornwall, are descended from Ralph Buller, who, in the fourteenth century, was seated at Woode, in the hundred of South Petherton, co. Somerset, by an heiress of Beauchamp. Shirley's Noble and Gentle Men.

BULLHEAD. See Bullface.

BULLINGHAM. A parish in Herefordshire.

BULLIVANT. Possibly the French *bel enfant,* corresponding with Fairchild, Fairbairn, &c.

BULMORE. The same as Bulmer.

BULWORK. Qu. *bulwark*—from residence near some fortification ?

BUNCKILL. Of that Ilk in Berwick-shire, where they seem to have resided in 1292. The name is probably identical with Bunkle.

BURGATE. A parish in Suffolk.

BURGHILL. Local: "the hill sur-mounted by a *burg*, tumulus, or earthwork."

BURTON.* The Marquis Conyngham is descended, in the male line, from Goiffrid de Bortona, one of the foresters of Shrop-shire in the reign of Edward I., who de-rived his name from Boreton, in the parish of Condover, in Shropshire, an estate which remained in the family till the reign of James I. Shirley's Noble and Gentle Men.

BUSKIN. The name is analagous to Startup, which see. "The Buskin," says Melmoth, "was a kind of high shoe, worn upon the stage by the actors of Tragedy, in order to give them a more heroical eleva-tion of stature." Melm. Pliny.

BUTLER.* As the name Butteler is of old standing in Ditmarsh, between the Elbe and the Eider, (see Archæologia XXXVII., p. 373, and is not likely to have been at all connected with the Fr. *bouteille*, we may conclude that the surname may sometimes be derived from the A-Sax *bótel* or *bótl*, an abode or mansion (retained in the names of Wulfenbüttel, in Germany, Newbottle in England, Bouteilles in Nor-mandy, &c.), and may signify, like the recognized *Bótel-weard*, a house steward.

BUTTERFLY. Berry mentions an armigerous family of this name, which is, of course, identical with the Fr. Papillon, now naturalized here.

BUTTOL. A corruption of Botolph, the personal name.

BYROM. A township connected with Poole, in the liberty of St. Peter, co. York, is called Byrome.

C.

CABORNE. The same as Cabburn.

CAGE. Possibly from residence near a town cage or prison.

CAHOWNE. A Scottish corruption of Colquhoun.

CAIRNCROSS. An ancient Scottish local name, met with in charters, and fun-nily latinized *Carnea Crux!*

CAIRNS. Nisbet says, "of that Ilk," but does not mention the locality.

CAITHNESS. The Scottish county.

CALCRAFT. Local: "the croft where *cale, kale*, or cabbage grows."

CALDWELL.* Of that Ilk in Renfrew-shire, where the family continued "for many years in good reputation." Nisbet. Crawfurd's Renfrewshire.

CALLADER. Probably from lands near Loch Callader, in Aberdeenshire.

CALLEYS. See Callis, below.

CALLIS. The French town, Calais, possessed by the English from temp. Ed-ward III. to Queen Mary.

CAMAYLE. One family of this name bear for their arms, three *lozenges*, and another, three *fusils*. These seem to refer to the *mascled* armour for the neck, from which the name was probably derived. See Hawberk, in this supplement.

CAMBER.* A southern provincialism for a harbour. Halliwell. Camber Castle, co. Sussex, stands near the now choked harbour of Winchelsea.

CAMBREY. See Cambray.

CAMBRIDGE. The town and university. In the Highlands of Scotland they have a Mac Cambridge. In England the 'sons of Cambridge' are innumerable.

CANDELER. See Chandler.

CAMEL. See Cammel.

CANNOCK. A parish in Staffordshire.

CANTWELL. Perhaps Canwell, a place in Staffordshire.

CAPE. From residence near, or at, a pro-montory.

CAPENHURST. Cappenhurst, a town-ship in Cheshire.

CARDIFF. CARDYFFE. A town in Glamorganshire.

CARDIGAN. The Welsh town.

CARDINGTON. Parishes in cos. Bed-ford and Salop are so denominated.

CARKETTLE. Of that Ilk in Scotland. Nisbet.

CARLIL. CARLELL. See Carlisle.

CARMARTHEN. The Welsh town.

CARNEGIE.* The lands of Carnegie are in Forfarshire.

CARRUTHERS.* The family evidently derived their name from the place indicated, though the chiefs of the house wrote themselves, from time immemorial, Carruthers of Howmain (in Annandale). The name appears in Scottish history, temp. King David II.

CARTWRIGHT.* Should any owner of this surname object to my placing him among vulgar men who make wheels and carts, he may be appeased by my assurance that two grandees named Auffroy and Maugier de *Cartrait* came hither with the Conqueror. See John Foxe, Acts and Mon. who quotes the Annals of Normandy, a Fr. manuscript in his custody. The name is very probably of original identity with Carteret.

CARUS. A latinization of Dear.

CASBORNE. The family were resident at a place so called in Kent. Encycl. Herald.

CASS. Cas, an ancient Irish personal name, found so early as the fifth century. See Macnamara.

CASTELYN. See Castelline.

CASTELLINE. Castellan, the governor of a castle.

CASTERTON. Parishes, &c., in cos. Westmoreland and Rutland.

CASTLECOMBE. A parish in Wiltshire.

CASTLEFORD. A parish in Yorkshire.

CATERYKE. Catterick, a parish in Yorkshire.

CATOR. See Cater.

CATTLE. See Cattell.

CATTYFFE. O. French *caitif*, a wretch.

CAWDREY.* An estate in the parish of Birdham, co. Sussex, is so called. It is quite distinct from Cowdray, which is a much larger estate in the same county.

CHACE. See Chase.

CHAIN. A corruption of the O. Fr. *chesne*, an oak.

CHALON. Probably from one of the French towns called Chalons.

CHALUN. See Chalon, above.

CHALTON. A parish in Hampshire.

CHAMBELYN. A corruption of Chamberlain.

CHANTECLER. Chanticleer is a trivial name for the cock, as old as the days of Chaucer, who however spells it *chaunteclere*. The arms of the family contain three cocks.

CHARTSEY. Chertsey, a town in Surrey.

CHEESEMENT. Changed by a gentleman, born in 1723, from *Cheeseman* or Cheesman! B.L.G.

CHENEVIX.* The founder of the family in England seems to have been a French Protestant minister, formerly of Mante, but a refugee in London in 1691, in consequence of the Rev. of the Edict of Nantes.

CHEQUER.* More likely a contraction of Exchequer. In the H.R. we find John, Laurence, and Roger de Scaccario—" of the Exchequer." This word originally implied any treasury. Richardson.

CHRIST. I take this name to be a shortened form of Christopher, rather than a profane use of the designation of our Saviour. Mr. Bowditch informs us that "in New York there are no less than thirteen families of Christ, including a firm of 'Spies, Christ, and Company.'"

CHRISTMASDAY See Christmas.

CLANCY. An Irish clan tributary to the O'Brian. D'Alton.

CLANCHY. "A sept of the Dal-Cassian stock, hereditary *brehons* or judges of Thomond, under the O'Bryans, its princes; while another family of the name were lords of Dartry and Rosclogher, in Leitrim." D'Alton.

CLEAN. Mac-Lean, deprived of the Celtic prefix.

CLIFTON.* The first recorded ancestor of the Cliftons, of Clifton in Lancashire, is William de Clifton, who held ten carucates of land, in the 42nd year of Henry III. Shirley's Noble and Gentle Men.
The Cliftons, of Clifton in Nottinghamshire, are derived from Gervase de Clifton, who flourished in the 5th year of King John, and the estate is still in the possession of the family. Ibíd.

CLINT. A township in the parish of Ripley, co. York, where the descendants of the Saxon thane Archil resided, and whence they took the name of De Clynt. See under Simpson.

CLIPSTONE. See Pulteney. There are parishes, &c., called Clipston and Clipstone, in cos. Northampton and Nottingham.

CLIVE.* Mr. Shirley mentions Warin de Clive, who lived temp. Henry III., as the first recorded ancestor. He also mentions that Clive, the locality from which the name is taken, is in the hundred of Northwich, co. Chester. Noble and Gentle Men.

CLUTTON.* This ancient family were of Clutton of the parish of Farndon, in Cheshire, as early as 21. Edward I., and the manor continued to be held by them temp. Henry VI. The elder line have ever remained in the county. Shirley's Noble and Gentle Men.

☞ COCK. At p. 64, I have given a copious list of names with this termination. Mr. Clark has with great industry collected the following. It is to be borne in mind that those few names which have the syllable otherwise than as a termination, principally relate to the cock, be it the *gallus* of the poultry yard, or the *gallinago* of the wood—in most instances the latter. As a rule, Cock at the beginning of a name implies a local origin, while at the end it shows that it is a diminutive of a baptismal name.

Acock, Allcock, Alecock, Adcock, Batcock, Boocock, Bidcock, Badcock ; Cockwood, Cockland, Cockshott, Deacock, Cockbill, Cockburn, Cockman, Heacock, Cockrell, Cockcroft, Cockayne, Maycock, Cockshaw, Cocksedge, Cockhead, Jaycock; Bowcock, Laycock, Salcock, Silcock, Simcock, Raincock, Grocock, Tilcock, Elcock, Ocock, Fencock, Jewcock, Jeacock, Jeffcock, Haycock, Twocock ; Pidcock, Pycock, Pullcock, Pocock, Mulcock, Mycock, Meacock, Mocock ; Johncock, Hiscock, Peacock, Purcock, Colcock, Woodcock, Glasscock, Hercock ; Handcock, Hitchcock, Highcock, Lowcock, Seacock, Shilcock, Shecock, Slowcock ; Willcock, Woolcock, Hedgecock, Hancock, Drawcock, Rancock, Thistlecock, Tancock.

COCKBURN.* A correspondent says : "The name is derived from the lands so called in Berwickshire." According to Nisbet, the pedigree is traced to the time of King Robert Bruce.

COGAN.* (The Irish family). From the termination in AN, this name might be thought indigenous to Ireland. Such, however is not the case, as Milo de Cogan, who founded the family in that country was one of those who assisted in its subjugation temp. Henry II., when, in conjunction with his uncle, Robert Fitz-Stephen, he received the whole county of Cork in reward for his services. The *De* shews the territorial origin of the name.

COLBATCH. This name appears to be local. It may have been derived from a hamlet in the parish of Herstmonceux, co. Sussex, now called Cowbeach, but anciently Coldbeche.

COLEMAN.* See also O'Coleman.

COLEPEPPER. See Culpeper.

COLLAR. See Coller and Collard.

COLVILE. See Colville.

COMBER.* This family are numerous and ancient in Sussex, though now extinct in the degree of gentry. The Combers of Shermanbury, in that county, claimed descent from "a very ancient family at Barkham [in Fletching], and that manor, according to family tradition, was bestowed upon one of the ancestors, named — de Combre, by William the Conqueror, with whom he came over from Normandy, for killing its Saxon or Danish lord in the famous battle, which placed that Duke on the throne of England." Life of Dr. Thomas Comber, Dean of Durham, 1799. This tradition seems to be unsupported by documentary evidence, and the pedigree, as re-

corded by the heralds, goes back only to Richard de Combre, temp. Henry VI., whose son, John Comber, was of Balcombe, co. Sussex, about the end of the XV. century, and in that parish the name is still to be found.

COMPIGNÉ. A refugee family who settled in London after the Rev. of the Edict of Nantes, and amassed a fortune in the silk trade. Several branches are resident in Hertfordshire and Hampshire.

COMPTON.* Mr. Shirley says : "we may conclude that the family were seated at Compton, called 'in le Windgate,' soon after the Conquest. Arnulphus and Osbertus de Compton were living in 16. Henry II., but Philip de Compton is the first of the name who certainly held the manor of Compton in the fifth of John." Noble and Gentle Men.

CONDON. The Condons were deemed so powerful a sept of old, that their territory was adopted as the name of a barony in co. Cork. D'Alton.

CONGALTON. The same as Congilton.

CONGILTON. Of that Ilk ; "which family is in East-Lothian." Nisbet.

CONRY. An Irish sept, a branch of the Southern Hy Nialls, who for centuries ruled as kings of Meath and monarchs of Ireland. They were usually called the O'Maol Conrys. Originally they were "chiefs in Teffia, in the present county of Westmeath; but in the tenth century, crossing the Shannon, they located themselves upon its western bank, and from that time were known as Connacians." This sept, who belonged to the great Bardic order, became chief Bards and hereditary Seanachies to the Kings of Connaught. It was the honourable duty of the head of the race to officiate upon the Sacred Hill at the inauguration of a new king, to present him with a white wand or sceptre, the emblem of sovereignty, to administer the coronation oath, and finally to make a record of the proceedings. D'Alton.

CONWAY.* A pedigree of the Irish Conways derives them from the Conways of Worcestershire, whose lineage was deduced from Sir William Conais, High Constable of England at the time of the Conqueror. D'Alton.

COPE.* The ancestors of the baronet appear in the character of civil servants of the crown, in the reigns of Richard II. and Henry IV. Noble and Gentle Men.

COPINGER. The Copingers of the county of Cork are said to be of Danish extraction. If this be so, the Coppingers of East Anglia are most probably from the same source.

CORBET.* See Riddell.*

CORSBIE. CORSBY. Nisbet says :— "Corsby of that Ilk, an ancient family sometime with us ;" but neither the heraldrist nor the gazetteer informs us of the *locus in quo.*

CORNS. A nickname of Cornelius.

CORSTORPHINE. A parish in Edinburghshire, from whence the gentle family so called probably originated.

COSWAY. Probably a corruption of *causeway*, as that is of *calcetum*, a road of *chalk* formed across a marsh or low ground. Such a road traversed the valley of the Arun in Sussex, and a priory which stood near one of its extremities was called De Calceto.

COTES. A manor in Staffordshire gave name to this family, who are "descended from Richard de Cotes, probably the son of Thomas de Cotes, living in 1167, when the Black Book of the Exchequer was compiled. About the reign of Henry VI. the family removed to Woodcote in Shropshire, which has since continued their principal seat, though the more ancient manor of Cotes or 'Kotes,' on the banks of the Sow, has ever remained the property of this ancient house." Shirley's Noble and Gentle Men.

COTTON. Mr. Shirley, speaking of Cotton of Landwade, Baronet, says: "It appears doubtful whether this family were denominated from Cotton, a manor in Cambridgeshire, or from a place of the same name in the parish of Stone, in Kent. There is another Cotton Hall, in Ixning, co. Suffolk, which lays claim to the same distinction." Noble and Gentle Men.

☞ COUNTIES, *Names of.** The following additional surnames derived from counties have been met with:—Anglesea, Shropshire, Warwickshire, Norfolk, Suffolk, Northumberland.

COVELL. A corruption of Colville.

COW.* This was a very common sobriquetical surname in the thirteenth century in the French forms of La Vache, Le Vache, De la Vache. The names Le Vacher, La Vacher, with the latinization Vacarius, for cow-keeper, were also of frequent occurrence. See H.R.

COWIE.* Cowie was an ancient barony.

COXWELL. Two parishes in Berwickshire are so called. The family were established for many centuries in Gloucestershire.

CRAIGY. A place called Craigy-hill, in West Lothian, gave name to this family, who are traced to the reign of David II. Nisbet.

CRAMOND.* Among the earliest bearers of this surname was William de Cramond, clerk of the wardrobe to the King of Scotland, 1278. Nisbet.

CRANSTON.* "The family took the name from the lands of Cranston, both in Teviotdale and Lothian, which they possessed of old." Nisbet. The name of Elfric de C. occurs temp. William the Lion.

CRAW. Nisbet says: "Craw of Auchencraw in the Merss, an old family, now extinct." This seems to be a northernism

3 F

for Crow, Crowe, which see. The arms contain three *raræ aves* — videlicet *white crows.*

CROKE.* The Crokes of Studley, co. Oxford, were anciently Blounts. "In 1404, Nicholas le Blount having been deeply engaged in the conspiracy to restore Richard II. to his throne, changed his name to Croke on his return to England, in order to avoid the revenge of Henry IV. The Crokes afterwards became a legal family, and seated themselves at Chilton." Shirley's Noble and Gentle Men.

CROLY.* See O'Crowley.

CROXTON. There are places so called in various counties, but the eminent family of this name spring from the township of Croxton, co. Chester, their seat in very early times. See Winnington.

CRUISE. According to D'Alton, the Irish family of this surname sprang from a Norman, who, at the Conquest, settled in Cornwall. At the invasion of Ireland under Henry II., a branch accompanied Strongbow, and obtained grants of various estates in the counties of Dublin and Meath.

CRUTCH. See Crouch.

CULPEPER. CULPEPYR. This family, who were eminent in Kent and Sussex from the XIII. to the XVIII. century, were so numerous and influential that Camden notes, in his Remaines, the remarkable fact, that, that, "at one time there were twelve Knights and Baronets alive of this house together." The Barons Colepeper, extinct in 1752, were a branch. Strange as it may appear, I believe that in the counties above mentioned the name is entirely extinct, and in other parts of England it is very rarely met with. The etymology of the word puzzles me. If it might be taken literally, (*Cull-pepper*), it was an excellent name for the celebrated herbalist, Nic. Culpeper, who was of this family.

CUNLIFFE. Local—the last syllable standing for cliffe, the same as in Hinchliffe, Shirtliffe, &c. The Encycl. Herald. has Cunliff or Concliffe of Lancashire.

CUNNINGHAM.* There is much difference of opinion as to the origin of the family, chiefly on account of the curious bifurcated heraldric bearing connected with it, called by some a *pall*, by others a *shakefork.* This is regarded by one writer as a "cross furchie" and a symbol of the Crusades; by others, as an archiepiscopal *pall*, because an early Cunningham was descended from one of the murderers of Thomas à Becket, who fled into Scotland : but this, as Nisbet remarks, would be rather an *abatement* than a *badge* of honour. "Besides," adds our zealous old heraldrist, "the matter of fact is false, for the Cunninghams were in Scotland, and so named in the reign of King David I., long before that murder, as is evident by the chartulary of the abbacy of Kelso." A third writer, Van Bassen, a Norwegian, says that the first progenitor of the family was Malcolm, son of Friskine, who assisted Prince Malcolm (Canmore) " to escape from Mac-Beth's tyranny; and being hotly pursued by the usurper's men, was forced, at a place, to hide his master, by forking hay or straw above him; and after, upon that prince's happy accession to the crown, he rewarded his preserver with the thanedom of Cunninghame, from which he and his posterity have their surname," and the *shakefork* in their arms. Sir George Mackenzie says, that the shakefork was adopted by the family because William C., an early ancestor, was Master of Horse to King William, it being "the instrument whereby hay is thrown up to horses."

CURGENVEN. This name is derived from a village in the parish of Crowan, co. Cornwall, formerly so spelt, but now commonly written Cargenwen.

CURLYON. "Cur-Lyghon in this parish [Kea] is now transnominated to Car-lyon; and here, for many descents, lived the family from thence denominated Curlyghon, and who were gentlemen of considerable fame, lands, and revenues, as appeared to me from several old Latin deeds, some bearing date 6. Henry V." Hals, in D. Gilbert's Cornwall, ii. 301. The same quaint old topographer, in another place, (St. Blazey) observes : " In this parish liveth Cur-lyon, Gent., that married Hawkins, and giveth for his arms, in a field . . . . a bezant between two castles. Now, *though the name be local*, from a place in Keye parish, so called, *yet, if I were admitted to judge or conjecture, I would say this family of Cur-Lyon, by its name and arms, were descendants of Richard Curlyon, alias King Richard I.!!*" Ibid, i. 54.

CUSTRELL. 1. O. Eng., a man who carried the arms of a knight or man-at-arms. 2. Perhaps the same as Cotterell, in its second sense, from the O. Fr. *costerau.* See Cotterell.

D.

DALEMPIT. Nisbet mentions this as an armigerous family in Scotland. The name is probably local.

DALGARNER. Probably a corruption of Dalgarnock, an extinct parish in co. Dumfries.

D'ALTON. "The tradition of the introduction of this family from France into Ireland, as preserved in the Office of Arms, records Walter D'Alton to have been its founder; that he secretly married a daughter of Louis, King of France, and having thereby incurred that monarch's displeasure, fled to England, whence he passed with Henry II. on the invasion of Ireland. He early acquired possessions in the western portion of Meath, where he and his descendants founded religious houses, and erected castles." D'Alton, p. 367. I see no reason why this Irish family should not be a branch of the English Daltons, who were of ancient standing in Lancashire.

DALY. "This family claim descent from Niall of the Nine Hostages, one of the most illustrious of the Irish kings. The sept extended itself at a very remote period over Munster and Connaught, as well as in the barony of Clonlonan, co. Westmeath; and through the long lapse of years they have been eminently distinguished as poets and annalists." In the XIV. century one of the O'Dalys of Munster "had a grant of Moynter-barry, on a customary tenure of being Rythmour or chronicler of the chief lord, and of his achievements." D'Alton.

DAUGHTERY. A corruption of Dealtry, De Alta Ripa.

DEEPROSE. The same as Diprose.

DELANOY. When Sir Cornelius Vermuyden came to England, temp. Charles I., to drain Hatfield Chase, in Yorkshire, which he had purchased of the crown, and on which he expended £400,000 in reclaiming and cultivating it, he brought with him from Holland many families as colonists. Among them were the Delanoys, Tafinders, Harnews, Becudas, Morillions, Lelieus, Beharrels, &c., some of whom survive, while others have become extinct.

DEMPSEY. See O'Dempsey.

DENHAM.* See under Tredenham.

DENNISTON.* A correspondent assures me that the lands of Daniel's-toun are so designated in early charters of the family.

DEVENISH.* The surname Le Devenys is of early introduction into Ireland. In 1302 Nicholas Deveneys had military summons for the Scottish wars. D'Alton.

DIAPER. *D'Ypre*, that is, of Ypres, or Ipres, a town of West Flanders.

DIGBY.* This family can be traced "nearly to the Conquest, and are supposed to be of Saxon origin. . . . . Tilton, in the county of Leicester, where Ælmar, the first recorded ancestor of the Digbys held lands in 1086, also gave name to the earlier generations of the family." Shirley's Noble and Gentle Men.

DIGWEED. This singular name is doubtless a corruption of that of an old Gaelic family, Dwigwid of Auchenheuf, mentioned by Nisbet.

DISHINGTON. Probably local in Scotland, in which country it occurs in 1457. Nisbet.

DOBBYN. DOBBIN. See Tobyn.

DOCWRA. DOCWRAY. A township in the parish of Penrith in Cumberland, now written Dockray.

DONALDSON.* The Donaldsons are Mac-Donalds, and bear their arms.

DONGAN. This Irish surname " appears to have been of native and Milesian origin, or, if it came over from England it was very soon naturalized." The name appears in records as O'Dongan in 1387. D'Alton.

DONNELLY. See O'Donnelly.

DORAN. An ancient Irish personal name.

DOVEWARD.* See Ward.

DOWLING. See O'Dowling.

DOYLE. I have deduced this name from the Norman Doyley, and as I think correctly, but the Irish genealogists derive it from an old Celtic patronymic, O'Dubhail.

DRAPER. Other forms in the H.R. are Le Lindraper, Le Lingedraper (Fr. *linge*, linen), and Le Lyngedraper.

DUFF.* A correspondent states that the Earl of Fife's descent from Fife Mac-Duff, in the IX. century, is unsupported by any evidence. The real descent (he adds) is that given in Douglas's Baronage.

DUKE.* A correspondent states : " A person named Duke was on the list of voters for Penryn, co. Cornwall. His original name was Rapson, but the name being very common in the neighbourhood, people long distinguished him by the name of Duke, because he kept the Duke of York's Arms !" and this has since become the recognized family name.

DULHUNTY. A corruption of the old Irish name Dallachanty.

DUMBRECK. This Scottish family, mentioned by Nisbet, probably took their name from Dumbrake castle, co. Aberdeen.

DUNMORE. DUNMURE. A local name, signifying in Gaelic " the fortified hill." Many old strongholds in Scotland are so called. The surname was probably taken from a village so designated in Stirlingshire.

DUNS. DUNSE. Mentioned by Nisbet as " of that Ilk," Dunse in Berwickshire. The celebrated schoolman, Johannes Duns Scotus, " the angelic doctor," (usually known as Duns Scotus), was of this family.

DURWARD.* The Scottish family originated from Alanus Durward, *ostiarius*, porter, or *door-ward* to King Alexander II., who created him Earl of Athol. Nisbet. See the analogous surname Porter.

DURY.* The family derived their name from Dury, in the shire of Fife, where they possessed lands in the reign of Alexander II.

E.

EARLY.* See O'Mulmoghery.

EARWIGER. Probably the same as Earwaker.

EDIE. The Scottish family of Edie appear, from armorial evidence, to be a branch of the Adamsons, and Nisbet seems to consider the names identical. See Eady.

EDINGTON.* " The chief family of this name was Edington of that Ilk, in the shire of Berwick." Nisbet.

EDNAM. According to Nisbet this is the same name as Edmiston or Edmondstoune—an extraordinary corruption.

EGAN.* The sept of Mac Egan were territorially seized of Clan-Dearmida, a district in the barony of Leitrim, co. Galway ; within which they had anciently some castles. D'Alton.

EGLINTON. The castle and lands of Eglinton are in Ayrshire. They gave name as early as the time of William the Lion, to a distinguished family. This family ended in an heiress in the XIV. century, and she married Sir John Montgomery, a lineal ancestor of the present Earl of Eglinton.

EGLINTOUN. See Eglinton.

ELLICOTT. In old Irish records this name is written indifferently Mac Elligott and *Mac Leod*. " The family originally came to Kerry in consequence of an early marriage of one of the Fitz-Maurices, Barons of Lixnaw, with an heiress of that name ; and by reason of this connection Fitz-Maurice is said to bear a tower in his coat of arms ; and a parish of Kerry, near Tralee, is called Bally-Mac-Elligott." D'Alton. The name took the form of Ellicott in the seventeenth century.

ELLIOTT.* In proof of the commonness of this surname, it may be mentioned, that during the French revolutionary war a regiment of volunteers was raised on the Border, all of whom were Elliotts. They invariably marched to the tune of—

"My name it's wee Tam Elliott,
And wha daur meddle wi' me."

See Notes and Queries, Dec. 31, 1859. "The surname of Elliot in the South, is said to have come from a village called Elliot in the North, and with that name came to the South Border in the reign of King James I. of Scotland." Nisbet.

ELME. ELLEM. A Berwickshire family, "old possessors of Elmside and Ellemford" in that county. Nisbet.

ELPHINSTONE.* "Elfyn's-toun" is the oldest designation in charters.

ENTICK. See under Enticknap.

ENTICKNAP. This unusual surname is very ancient in West Sussex, to which district it seems to be limited. Its origin is not very apparent. It may be derived from *Entick*, a supposed personal name (now a surname), and the A.-Sax. *cnæp*, an eminence—the name of some locality now undiscoverable.

ERCALL. The parish of High Ercall, co. Salop, was possessed by the De Ercalls at an early period.

ERPINGHAM. The parish so designated in Norfolk, gave name, at a very early period, to this distinguished family.

ERSKINE.* There is no doubt whatever of this name having originated from the lands of Erskine, as stated in the body of the Dictionary; but the family have a tradition of another derivation and a higher antiquity. A Scotchman, who flourished, we are told, temp. Malcolm II. (1004—1030) having killed Enric, a Danish general, at the battle of Murt-Hill, cut off his head, and with a bloody dagger in his hand, shewed it to the monarch, exclaiming in Gaelic: " I did it with my Highland sword (*Eris skyne*), and I intend to perform more such feats;" whereupon Malcolm conferred upon him the name of Erskine, and assigned him the crest of a hand holding a dagger, with the motto *Je pense plus*. A *crest*, and a *French* motto in Scotland in the tenth century are 'curiosities of heraldry' hardly surpassed by the coat-armours of Adam, Noah, King David, and Alexander the Great! See Skene, for an analogous figment.

ESMONDE. " The name," says Mr. D'Alton, " is of Norman extraction, Esmon and Sieur Esmon appearing on sundry early records." Temp. Edward I., 1303, Henry Estmund had the royal commission to provide ships in the harbours of Wexford, &c., for the use of the English then about to invade Scotland.

EUNSON. Evanson, Euanson, Eunson.

EURE. See Ure.

EUSTACE.* " De Burgo relies upon an inscription on a mounment in the church of St. Sextus, as deriving this family from the Roman martyr St. Eustachius." The founder of the name in Ireland was related to Maurice Fitz-Gerald, from whom he obtained a portion of the barony of Naas. His descendant was Baron of Castle-Martin in 1200. D'Alton.

EVERS. This name is found in co. Meath, very early after Strongbow's invasion of Ireland, in the form of De Evere. It is therefore probably of English or Anglo-Norman origin.

EWYAS. See under Sudley.

EYRE.* "The first of the name known (in Derbyshire), is William le Eyre of Hope, in the reign of Henry III." Noble and Gentle Men.

EYTON.* Another ancient family bearing this name are not at all connected with the Shropshire Eytons. The Eytons of Denbighshire deduced their pedigree from Rhys Sais, great-great-grandson of the renowned Tudor Trevor, who dwelling at Eyton, a township in that shire, about the period of the Norman Conquest, assumed the territorial prefix, and was called De Eyton. Madoc de Eyton, who died in 1331, married the heiress of David ap Grono, lord of Ruabon in the same county. At a later period, an elder son possessed Ruabon, while his younger brother continued in the old ancestral abode, and wrote himself Eyton of Eyton. Inf. Rev. E. H. M. Sladen.

EYSTON. The Eystons have been seated at East Hendred, in Berkshire, ever since the time of Henry VI. Shirley's Noble and Gentle Men. The name is doubtless an old orthography of the local Easton.

F.

FALLON. See O'Fallon.

FALLOON. Probably a Walloon, or native of what was formerly called the Spanish Netherlands. The Walloon language was said to be a relic of the ancient Gaulish, and hence the people of Artois, Hainault, Namur, Luxembourg, and part of Flanders and Brabant, who spoke it, were called Walloons or Gauls. The substitution of F or V for W is very natural. See, however, O'Fallon in this Supplement.

FANNING. The family were located in co. Limerick, and the name is of record in Ireland temp. Edward II. (D'Alton.) The latter is probably local, and identical with the English Fenning.

FEAVERYEAR. This singular surname, which is of very unusual occurrence, and apparently almost limited to the eastern counties of England, is conjectured to be a corruption of the French *Février*, the month February.

FEILDING. An old spelling of Fielding, which has been either retained or resumed by the Earl of Denbigh's family. The orthography in Collins's Peerage, edit. 1768, is uniformly Fielding. According to Lawrence's Life of Henry Fielding, the elder branch of the family have always so spelt it, a statement which I very much doubt. Mr. L. adds : " It is related of the Novelist that being once in the company of the Earl of Denbigh, his lordship was pleased to observe that they were both of the same family, and asked the reason why they spelt their names differently. ' I cannot tell, my Lord,' replied the Wit, ' unless it be that my branch of the family were the first who knew how to spell !' "

FEIRBRASS. The same as Firebrass.

☞ **FEMALE CHRISTIAN NAMES.*** Mr. Clark, speaking of Surnames adopted from feminine baptismal names, says :—

"The names thus taken up by man,
Are Betty, Polly, Constance, Anne ;
Rose, Flora, Lucy, Margery, Poll,
Goody, Catherine, Ellenor, Moll ;
Hannah, Hester, Madge, and Mattie,
Venus, Psyche, Rosa, Patty ;
Eva, Ellen, Eve, and Jane,
Virgin, Widdow, Wench, and Dame ;
Helen, Nanny, Kate, and Nell,
All surnames now are known full well."
Surnames Metrically Arranged, p. 14.

FENTON.* Of that Ilk, in Scotland temp. Alexander III. Nisbet.

FERGUSSON.* Very ancient in Ayrshire. King Robert I. granted lands in that shire to an ancestor, Fergusio Fergusii filio. Nisbet.

FIFE. " The surname Fife (but a small name now) pretends to be descended of a younger son of M'Duff, Earl of Fife. From which title they have the name, and carry the arms." Nisbet.

FITZGERALD.* In the Description of Ireland in Holinshed's Chronicle is the following passage, shewing by what mean tricks this name became so widely diffused as we now find it. " The corrupt orthographie that divers use in writing this name, doth incorporate it to houses thereto linked in no kindrede :—Some write *Gerolde* sundry *Geralde,* divers very corruptly *Gerrot,* others *Gerarde ;* but the true orthographie is *Giralde,* as may appear by Giraldus Cambrensis and others. Divers estraunge houses have also bene *shuffled in* among this familie, by sundry gentlemen christening of their children, and calling them *Giraldes,* though their surnames were of other houses ; and if after it happened that *Girald* had issue Thomas, John, Robert, or such lyke, then they would bear the surname of *Girald* as Thomas Fitz-Girald, and thus within two or three discentes *they shoove themselves among the kindrede of the Giraldines.* This is a general fault in Ireland and Wales, and a great confusion and extinguishment of houses." I fear that in another country or two, not far from Wales and Ireland, this process of " *shooving* " and " *shuffling* " into great names is not extinct, even at the present day.

FLEEMING. The O. Scotch form of Fleming, which see. The Fleemings, Earls of Wigtoun in the XIII. century were latinized Flandrensis and Flammaticus.

FORBES.* This family had become widely extended and powerful in the XV. century. " These of this name," says Nisbet, " are said by our historians to be originally from one Ochonacher, who came from Ireland, and, for killing a wild bear, took the name *Forbear* [queer act of forbearance that !] now pronounced Forbes ! " Yet he tells us, further on, that the family were lords of Forbois or Forbes in Aberdeenshire.

FORINGHAM. A corruption of Fotheringham.

FORSYTH.* Said to be " of that Ilk " in Scotland. King Robert Bruce gave lands in the sheriffdom of Stirling to Osbert, son of Robert de Forsyth. Nisbet.

FOTHERINGHAM.* The first of the family is said to have come from Hungary, with Margaret, Queen of King Malcolm Canmore. Nisbet.

FOULIS.* Nisbet says that, " the name is from the French word *feueles,* which signifies leaves ; whence these of the name are said to be of a French extract !" In the next breath he tells us that " the lands of Foulis in Angus on the borders of Perthshire belonged of old to those of this name."

FOX.* This family name has been in some instances anglicized from an Irish sept, O'Siouagh, who were possessed in Teffia, co. Westmeath, of a territory extending over the baronies of Rathcourath and Clonlonan, with parcel of the barony of Kilcoursey in King's County. The head of the sept in the time of Elizabeth was known by the title of The Fox; and he it was who obtained large grants from her Majesty in the latter county, with the title of Lord Kilcoursey. D'Alton.

FROG.* According to Mr. Clark, this name still survives. See Insects and Reptiles in this Dictionary.

FULLALOVE.* My explanation of this name, which might be accounted a piece of jocularity, is proved to be correct by the existence of the synonymous Pleynamur (that is Plein d'amour, "full of love,") in the Rotuli Hundredorum, in which valuable record several persons are so designated.

G.

GAITER. See Gater.

GARSHORE. Nisbet says, " of that Ilk " in Scotland, but fails to inform us of the place.

GAUERIGAN. In Cornish " the goat's downs "; an estate in the parish of St. Columb Major, co. Cornwall, where the family continued to reside till temp. Elizabeth.

GAY.* In some instances this name may be from the Fr. gué, a ford.

GEOGHEGAN. The sept claim descent from Fiachra, one of the sons of Nial of the Nine Hostages, monarch of Ireland in the fifth century. Their territory was called Kinel-Fiacha, and extended over the tract now called the barony of Moycashel, with parts of those of Moyashell, Rathcourath, and Fertullagh, in Westmeath, within which they erected various castles, the chief being at Castle-town-Geoghegan near Kilbeggan, whose wide site is marked on the Ordnance Survey. D'Alton.

GHOST. See Spirit.

GILCHRIST. (Referred to, but accidentally omitted in the body of the work). See under Gill in this Supplement.

☞ GILL. GIL. A prefix of many old Gaelic personal names now become surnames. Like the Lowland Scotch Gillie, it means a menial servant. In the early ages of Christianity in Scotland, it was ordinary for religious persons to devote and designate themselves as servants, either of the Saviour or of some saint. Hence among others the names—
Gillies, the servant of Jesus.

Gilchrist, the servant of Christ.
Gilleanrias, the servant of St. Andrew.
Gillebride, the servant of St. Bride or Bridget.
Gilpatric, the servant of St. Patrick.
Gillemichel, the servant of St. Michael, &c.

Analogous surnames are—
Gillespie, the servant of the Bishop.
Gilroy, the servant of the King.
Gilmour or Gillmore, the servant or henchman of a Chief.
(This article was inadvertently omitted from the body of the work.)

GILLETT. "In England there are numerous families who write their name Gillett and Gillot, all of French extraction; the former at Glastonbury, Exeter, and Banbury; the latter at Birmingham and Sheffield. It is probable that these names, as well as Jellett and Guillot, have all been originally the same, namely Gillot, the diminutive of Gilles, the French form of Giles." Ulster Journal of Archæology—szd dubito.

GLADSTANES. GLEDSTANES. Of that Ilk in Teviotdale, i. e. Roxburghshire. "This family is pretty ancient," says Nisbet, who finds the name temp. Robert III.

GLADSTONE.* The father of the Right Hon. W. E. Gladstone, now Chancellor of the Exchequer, changed the orthography of his name from Gledstanes. See Gladstanes, above.

GLEN. Of that Ilk, in Scotland. Nisbet.

GLENEAGLES. Of that Ilk, in Perthshire.

GLORIOUS. Lat. gloriosus: a boastful person.

GODLY. See Godley.

GOODHART. A Teutonic personal name of high antiquity of which Goddard is the ordinary English form. The family are of German extraction.

GOODING. Probably the same as Godin, an ancient Teutonic baptismal appellation.

GOURLAY. This name, which is probably Norman, was introduced into Scotland by William the Lion, after his captivity. Nisbet.

GOWN. A contraction of Gowan.

GRANDIDGE. A modern corruption of Grandorge.

GRANDMAIN. Fr. One who has great hands. Nisbet gives this, in his Heraldry, as the name of an English family.

GRANTHAM. From the town of Grantham, co. Lincoln. The pedigree commences with Alexander Grantham, of Grandibodium alias Grantham, in the XII. cent. See Lansdowne and Harl. MSS.

GRATWICKE. An ancient and respectable Sussex name. The locality from which it was borrowed I cannot ascertain, unless it be the manor now called Gatewyk, in Steyning.

GRAVESEND. A town in Kent. An early proprietor of the name was Sir Stephen de Gravesende. Roll of Arms, temp. Edward II.

GREENSWORD. There are several surnames borrowed from the "blade of war," such as Sword, Longsword, Brownsword, &c. Greensword seems to be of Irish origin. Dr. Doran, in his amusing article on "Names and Nicknames," mentions an ancient chieftain named Eochod, who, besides his more usual surname of "the horse-headed," bore the aliases of "the hunter" and "of the sharp green sword." Universal Review, May, 1860.

GRIGNON.* The family are of French Protestant refugee extraction from Poitou, and the form De Grignon shows a local origin.

GRINDLER. To grindle is a provincialism for to grind, and the original Mr. Grindler may therefore have been either a miller, or more probably a grinder of edge tools, a grindstone being called a grindlestone. In Scotland grintal means a granary, and grintal-man one who has the care of the same. Grintal-man and Grindler are possibly synonymous.

GRINFIELD. A modern corruption of Grenville. The connection is traceable, and the arms are those of that ancient and noble Norman race.

GRISSELL.* My conjecture is wrong. Until within the last century the name was spelt Griswold, and it is therefore local.

GUILD. May have been given to an active official in some ancient guild or brotherhood; but is more probably derived from the Danish guild or guld, gold, either with reference to the colour of the hair, or in the metaphorical sense referred to under Gold, at page 132.

GUYATT. See Wyatt.

H.

HABERSHON. Possibly from habergeon, the breast-plate—cognate with Helm, Sword, &c.

HACKETT.* "This name, Hecket, occurs on the Roll of Battel Abbey as one of the knights who attended the Conqueror from Normandy. His race early extended over Worcestershire and Yorkshire."

HAITLEY. Of that Ilk in Scotland, co. Berwick.

HALIBURTON. "The principal old family of this name was Halyburton, of that Ilk, in the shire of Berwick. The chappel of Halyburton was a pendicle of the church of Greenlaw." Nisbet. The family are mentioned so early as the reign of King Malcolm IV.

HALSEWELL. Halsewell, co. Devon, was possessed by the family surnamed from it De Halsewell, almost from the period of the Conquest, and it still belongs to their descendant, Colonel Kemeys-Tynte, whose ancestor married the heiress in the XVII. century.

HALY.* See also O'Haly.

HAMLEY. An armigerous family of considerable antiquity in Cornwall, where they are mentioned temp. Edw. III. See D. Gilbert's Cornwall, passim. The name existed contemporaneously with Hamlyn, with which it was apparently convertible in that county. Hamlyn is of course the A.-Norm. personal name Hammeline. The surname is now of rare occurrence in Cornwall, though it is found at Exeter, and since about the beginning of the present century, at Norwich.

HANDYSIDE.* That this name was derived from the personal deformity seems to be supported by the existence of the Norman sobriquet, or surname, borne by Raoul *Tortes-mains*, (literally "twisted or crooked hands,") to whom the Conqueror gave a wife and lands in Yorkshire. See under Thorn.

HANLON. See O'Hanlon.

HAREMARE. An estate in the parish of Echingham, co. Sussex, which in the XIV. century had owners of its own name.

HARNEW. See Delanoy.

HARNEY. The name of Herny or Harney is of Irish record in the rolls of Chancery from 1325. D'Alton.

HARROLD. The Irish family suppose themselves to have been introduced into that country on its invasion by the Danes, which is very probably the case.

HASLER.* The name is said to be German—a jester, from *haseliren*, to jest, play, or trifle. It occurs at Basle in Switzerland.

HAT. 1. From some peculiarity in that article of costume? 2. See Hatt.

HATHAWAY.* An ingenious ode to Anne Hathaway, the wife of Shakspeare, and attributed, without reason, to the Bard himself, plays upon her name in an agreeable pun. I shall quote but a moiety of it :—

I.
"Would ye be taught, ye feather'd throng,
With love's sweet notes to grace your song,
To pierce the heart with thrilling lay,
Listen to mine *Anne Hathaway!*
She *hath a way* to sing so clear,
Phœbus might wond'ring stop to hear.
To melt the sad, make blithe the gay,
And Nature charm, *Anne hath a way;*
  She *hath a way,*
  Anne Hathaway,
To breathe delight Anne *hath a way.*
II.
"When Envy's breath and rancorous tooth,
Do soil and bite fair worth and truth,
And merit to distress betray;
To soothe the heart Anne *hath a way.*
She *hath a way* to chase despair,
To heal all grief, to cure all care,
Turn foulest night to fairest day.
Thou know'st, fond heart, Anne *hath a way;*
  She *hath a way,*
  Anne Hathaway,
To make grief bliss, Anne *hath a way.*"

HAUTBOIS. Fr. " the elevated wood," a common local designation.

HAUTE. A great Kentish family, descended from Ivo de Haut, who flourished under Kings John and Henry III. at Ightham, co. Kent. French, *haut*, lofty ; in reference either to physical structure, or to disposition of mind.

HAWBERK. The ancient family of Hawberk of Stapleford, who became extinct in the XV. cent. were sometimes written Howbeck, which strongly suggests a local derivation. It is, however, quite as probable that the name was derived from

the A.-Norm. *hauberk*, a coat of mail. Halliwell quotes from an ancient poem :—
"Syr Mador all redy was,
With helme, and shelde, and *haubarke* shene."
The arms of the family comprise three annulets conjoined, which may possibly refer to the ringed mail of which a hauberk was composed. Sir Egerton Brydges, writing to a descendant of the family, says : " And now about *Hawberk*. I must be allowed a moment's poetical play. I have found out that the designers of their arms were bards and prophets ; that they had " a prophet's eye, a poet's fire," and that they anticipated by six centuries Gray's Welsh Bard. Have you forgot—
" Helm nor HAWBERK's twisted mail ?"
Are not the knots of rings on the shield the identical " twisted mail?" Genealogical History of the family of Brabazon. Appendix G.

HAWTE. An old spelling of Haut.

HAYMONGER. A dealer in hay. See Monger. One Hugh le Heymonger was a burgess of Great Yarmouth. See Papers of Norf. Arch. Soc. iv., 253.

HAZELGROVE.* A correspondent sends me the following curious statement about a place from which it is probable that the surname is derived.

"HAZLEGROVE, co. Chester. The rather pretty name of this place was lost for several generations, and it was only known by the uneuphonious designation of *Bullock's Smithy*. The fact which brought about so great a change was as follows:—In the early part of the XVIII. cent. there stood at the entrance to the village a blacksmith's shop or *smithy*, kept by a man named Bullock, who drove a good trade among the farmers of the neighbourhood ; and the constant use of the expression, " Go [with the horses to be shod, for example] to *Bullock's Smithy*," had at length the effect of changing the name of the hamlet. The village, now an extensive one, is partly in the parish of Stockport and partly in that of Norbury ; and, some years ago, when a district church was about to be erected in it, the good people of Bullock's Smithy felt rather ashamed of its designation, and, as there was some faint tradition of another name, the parochial records were examined, when to their delight it was discovered that the true and ancient name of the village was Hazlegrove !"
I wish that the inhabitants of a little village near Plymouth, had possessed as much good taste as the *Bullocksmithians* did, when they got a district church built for *them*. In that case their house of prayer would not have obtained the very objectionable name of *Knacker's Knowl Church*, which means something that could not be surpassed by even the wildest flights of the maddest etymologist—namely : " The-church-of-the-little-eminence—where-worn-out-horses-are-killed-for-the-food-of-dogs ! !"

HEALEY.* See also O'Haly.

HEASMAN.* Hyseman was an A-Sax. baptismal name, Hysemannes Thorn. Codex. Dipl. iii. 343.

HELDE. Germ. *held*, a hero, champion.

HENNESY. See O'Hennesy.

HERINGOD. The same as Heringaud. This name was influential in Sussex in the XIII. and XIV. centuries.

HOARE.* This family are of record in Ireland from the time of Edward II. Sir David ' le Hore ' was sheriff of co. Wexford in 1334. D'Alton.

HODD.* A-Sax. a hood. The name

may therefore have had an origin similar to that of Quaife.

HOKEDAY. See Hockday.

HOLDUP. A Hampshire surname, which, in a deed of 1725, is written Houldupp, and subsequently Houldup. Other forms of the name appear to be Holdip, Holdeep. It is probably local, the latter syllable being a corruption of *hope*, though it may belong to the same class as Standfast, Standeven, &c. See Hope.

HOLL.* Probably A-Sax. *hol*, a den or cavern.

HOLLINGWORTH. A township in the parish of Mottram, co. Chester, possessed by the family in very early times.

HOO.* The family of Thomas Hoo, created Lord Hoo and Hastings, who died in 1455, are said to have been derived from a Saxon source. It is certain that one Edrich de Ho was living contemporaneously with Archbishop Odo, the Conqueror's half-brother. The pedigree of the family, printed by W. D. Cooper, Esq., F.S.A., in Sussex Arch. Coll., vol. viii., p. 130, deduces them from Robert Hoo, of Hoo co. Kent, who died as early as the year 1000.

HOOKER.* Another meaning of the word is a shoplifter. Halliwell. "A cunning filcher, a craftie *hooker*." Florio. Only imagine the "Judicious Hooker" to be a mere synonym of an ingenious pilferer !

HOREHAM. An estate in the parish of Waldron, co. Sussex, where the family were resident in the reign of Edward III., and probably earlier.

HORNER.* The Horners, and two other families, who had greatly enriched themselves by the fall of the monasteries at the Reformation, were thus commemorated in sarcastic rhyme :—

"Popham, Horner, and Thynne ;
 When the monks popped out, they popped in."

A writer in the Quarterly Review, April, 1860, in quoting the couplet, adds : "The Horners may rely on the nursery rhyme, in which Little Jack Horner puts in his thumb and pulls out a plum, i.e., a grant of fat abbey lands !"

HORSEBURGH. "Horseburgh of that Ilk," an ancient family in the shire of Tweddale." Nisbet.

HOSEGOOD. The A-Sax. personal name Osgod.

HOSPITAL. From residence near one.

HOTOT. Two places in Normandy bear this name—one in the department of Calvados ; the other in that of the Lower Seine.

HUDDLESTONE.* In the North of England, to *huddle* means to hurl; and hence the epitaph—

On Mr. Thomas Huddlestone.

" Here lies Thomas Huddlestone ! Reader don't smile,
 But reflect while his tomb-stone you view ;
 For Death, who kill'd him, in a very short while,
 Will *huddle* a *stone* upon you !"

HUSSEY.* The Irish branch are descended from Sir Hugh Hussey, who having married the sister of Theobald Fitz-Walter, the first Butler of Ireland, obtained temp. Henry II. "large possessions in the county of Meath, including the locality of Galtrim, in the right of which the family took the palatine title of Barons of Galtrim." D'Alton.

I.

INCARNATION. Among the records of the Registrar General is the extraordinary name of *Gabriel Incarnation*. The surname appears to belong to the same class as Noel, Easter, Pentecost, Sumption, &c.

Since the above was written I have met with the following passage in an imperfect copy of a work, the title of which is unknown to me :—" Upon the entry into any religious order, it is necessary to take a new proper name ; and sometimes with the addition of some other saint, or other epithet, as Francis of St. Clare, or Thomas *of the Incarnation*, or the like."

IRBY.* The ancestors of Lord Boston were connected with co. Lincoln at a

remote period, being Lords of Ireby or Irby in that shire. The first recorded ancestor is Sir William de Ireby, 35 Henry III.

IWOOD. An estate at Warbleton, co. Sussex, which had owners of the same name in the XV. century.

IZARD.* Probably the Fr. *isard*, the chamois, or wild goat; applied in relation to swiftness of foot.

JACKET. 1. Jacquet, a diminutive of the Fr. Jacques, James. 2. The garment called a doublet. 3. Cotgrave has "Jaquet, a pilgrim to St. James of Compostella ; also a parasite, sychophant, clawbacke, pickthanke, flattering smell-feast."

JACOX. Probably a modification of James, as Simcox is of Simon, Wilcox of William, &c.

JANUARY. Not from the month, but an anglicized form of the Latin personal name Januarius.

JONES.* For the statistics of this name, and its occasional rivalry with the Smiths, see under Smith.

JULY. Not from the month, but an English form of the Latin personal name Julius.

JUNE. Not from the month, but a probable corruption of the Fr. Le Jeune, equivalent to Young.

K.

KEATING. This common Irish surname is of record from temp. Edward II. In 1302 James de Ketyng was one of the Irish magnates invited to attend King Edward in the Scottish war. D'Alton. From the local *De*, the name would appear to have been originally English.

KEELEY. See O'Keeley.

KENDELAN. The family of O'Cændelain were Tanists of Leogaire, co. Meath, of which Argus O'Cændelain died lord in 1017. D'Alton.

KILGOUR. An old Scottish family, who probably derived their name from a place so called in the parish of Falkland, co. Fife.

KINCAID.* The Kincaids were " of that Ilk," at an early date. Of the castle in the arms of the family, Nisbet remarks : " It seems the castle represents that of Edinburgh ; for these of the family were a long time constables thereof.'' An ancestor, " for his valiant service in recovering of the castle of Edinburgh from the English, in the time of King Edward I., was made constable of the said castle, and his pos-

terity enjoyed that office for many years, carrying the castle in their arms, in memory thereof, to this day. There is an old broad-sword belonging to one of the families of the name of Kincaid, upon which are the above arms, with the castle, with these words :—

" Wha will persew, I will defend
My life and honour to the end."

—Nisbet.

KINCRAIGIE. Nisbet says, " of that Ilk ;" but neither he nor the gazetteer helps us to the locality.

KINNEIR. The family had a charter of the lands so called in Fifeshire, from King Alexander II. Nisbet.

KIRKCALDIE.   KIRKCALDY.*
Nisbet designates this, " an old family, which ended in an heiress," married to Reginald Kinnaird, in or before the year 1399.

KYNNINMOND. Of that Ilk in Fifeshire. A member of this family became Bishop of Aberdeen in the year 1172. The heiress married a Murray in the XVII. cent.

L.

LACE. Probably a contraction of Lacy.

LALLY. From an old genealogy of this family it appears that Amlavus O'Maolalla, chief of Tulla-ny-Maolalla, was descended in the thirteenth generation from Maolalla, who, at the close of the tenth century, was ruler of Moen-nioge, now Clanricarde. The name was shortened first to O'Mullally, then to O'Lally, and finally to Lally. D'Alton.

LAMMIE. In Scotland, is doubtless the French *L'Ami*, " the friend."

LANDEL. Nisbet says that the family of Landel, Lord Landel of Berwickshire, " long since ended in an heiress, who was married to Sir Alexander Home, of that Ilk." It seems that the name was originally written De Landelys, Landels, &c.

LANDELLS.* It is more probable that the name is Scottish. See Landel, above.

LAST. A correspondent suggests that this refers to the trade of a cobbler—the *last* (crepida) being a not uncommon sign.

LAUDERDALE. The great district of Berwickshire, which gives title to the noble house of Maitland, in old times gave a surname to this family.

LAW.* The Laws of Lawbridge, Bogness, &c., in Scotland, are traced to the XIV. century. Nisbet.

LEECH.* This surname was latinized by *Medicus*, and it is not uncommon in medieval records. The H.R. supply an Agnes *Medica*, probably a " doctress " or she-quack of the thirteenth century.

LELIEU. Sometimes spelt Leliew and Lelew. See Delanoy.

LESLIE.* A correspondent says, that the Hungarian descent of the family is fabulous — the Bartholomew, or rather Bertholf, referred to, having received his original charter of the lands of Leslie a hundred years later than the coming of Margaret of Hungary.

LEXINGTON. LEXINTON. This name was taken from the lordship of Lexington, now Laxton in Nottinghamshire, which was possessed by Richard de Lexinton temp. King John.

LILBORNE. The same as Lilburn.

LILBURN. A parish in Northamptonshire, and two townships in Northumberland are called Lilbourne.

LILWALL. A township in Hertfordshire.

LIQUORICE. See Liquorish.

LOGAN.* The family are of record in Scotland at an early date, Dominus Robertus de Logan being mentioned in a charter of 12. Alexander II. Walter Logan of Lanarkshire swore fealty to King Edward I. in 1297. Nisbet.

LOGIE.* Of that Ilk, in Scotland. Margaret, daughter of Sir John Logie of Logie, married King David II., whose reign commenced in 1329.

LOCKERBY. A town in the parish of Dryfesdale, Annandale. The family were " of that Ilk."

LOCKHART.* A correspondent observes, that the name was spelt Loccard some generations before the time of Robert Bruce, and suggests that it is of Norman origin.

LOMAS. See Lomax.

LOMAX. This surname, and its vernacular pronunciation Lomas, have long been associated with South Lancashire. The ancient orthography appears in a MS. Rent Roll of Sir John Pilkington of Bury, Knt., dated 13. Henry VI., as Del Lumhalghes, Del Lumhalghe. To *lumhalghe*, which appears to be a topographical expression, I can attach no meaning.

In the early part of the seventeenth century the name was written Lummas : somewhat later, viz., in 1653, it first appears as Lomax. See Notes and Queries, Dec. 10, 1859. In the South of England the O in Lomas and Lomax is long.

LUKIS. A Guernsey surname. Probably another form of Lucas.

LUNDIN. Of that Ilk in Scotland. Nisbet.

LUNHUNTER.* A correspondent sends me the following satisfactory account of this name :—" A bird now known in this country as the Great Northern Diver (*Colymbus glacialis*) was formerly termed the *loon*. This name is still given to the bird by the inhabitants of the northeastern coasts of the United States of America, where it is very plentiful. Before the invention of percussion guns, it was almost impossible to shoot this bird, as it dived instantaneously on perceiving the flash of the ignited gunpowder in the pan of the old flint lock. And, in consequence, a person who entertains impracticable views is called by the Americans, a *Loonhunter*. I have frequently, in the state of Maine, heard the phrase 'going a *loon-hunting*,' applied in the same manner as we should say, ' going on a wild-goose chase.' And I have also frequently heard the epithet ' Loon-hunter,' applied to a silly ambitious person, willing to undertake what he could not by any means perform—one, in short, as we should say, likely ' to go out for wool, and come home shorn.' Many old English words and phrases, obsolete in this country, are still current in the New England States. The Americans never speak of going to shoot : what we term shooting they call gunning or *hunting*."

M.

MACARTY. " The annals of Innisfallen abound in records of the patriotism and perseverance with which the noble sept of Macarty laboured to resist the early invasions of the Danes, until they were at length induced to tolerate their settling, for commercial purposes, in the province of Desmond, of which they were kings. When Henry II. landed at Waterford, Mac Carty, King of Desmond, delivered

to him the keys of Cork, and did homage."
D'Alton. The family were divided into two
branches, Mac Carty More, and Mac Carty
Reagh.

MABSON. The son of Mab, or Abraham.

MAC BRAIR. An ancient family in
Dumfries-shire. Nisbet.

MAC BRENNAN. "The Mac Brennans were chiefs of Corcaghlan, a district
of the county of Roscommon, forming part
of that in which is the well-known mountain Slieve-Ban. So early as in the year
1150, the Four Masters record the death of
Maolisa Brannan, archdeacon of Derry."
D'Alton.

MAC CANN. The Mac Cans were
chiefs of Hy Bresail, an ancient territory
of the borders of Armagh and Tyrone, near
Lough Nea. D'Alton. The name ascends
to the XII. cent. In the year 1189 (say
the Four Masters) died Echmilidh, son of
Mac Can, "the delight and happiness of
all Tyrone."

MAC DONOUGH. "A powerful sept
in the county of Sligo, having an extensive territory in the barony of Corran;
they were also at a very early date established in co. Cork, where they held the
noble castle of Kanturk. In the former
county they are considered to have branched
from the Mac Dermots, and in the latter
from the Mac Carties." According to the
Four Masters they took their name from
one Donough, who flourished in Sligo in
1278. D'Alton.

MAC GAWLEY. A corruption of Mac
Awley. The head of the house was chief
of Calrigia on the borders of Westmeath
and King's County. The lineage is traced
from Manie, the fourth son of Niall of the
Nine Hostages; but so far as Mr. D'Alton's
account goes, the first person that occurs of
this surname is Aireachtach Mac Awley,
chief of Calrigia, who died in 1187.

Whatever may be the difference of pedigree between these Irish Mac Awleys and
the Scottish Mac Aulays, there can scarcely
be a doubt that both surnames are from a
common source, and that the root of Awley
and Aulay is the same.

MAC GUIRE. See Maguire.

MAC GUNSHENAN. A clan of this
name existed in Fermanagh about Lough
Erne. D'Alton.

MACHELL* An intelligent correspondent, who pleads for the Danish origin of the
family, reminds me that in the Domesd. of
Yorkshire the brothers Ulph and Machel
held lands in Lonsdale and Cockerham.
Other varieties of the name are Malchaen,
Mauchaell, Malchien, Catulus, and De Castro Catulino.

MAC JONNIN. A name peculiarly
located in the counties of Mayo and Galway; a branch is also traced in co. Down.
D'Alton.

MAC KETTIGAN. This sept were
anciently the territorial proprietors of
Clan-diarmada, now Clan-dermot, co.
Kerry, over which county and Donegal the
name is still extant.

MAC KINLAY. Kinlay, or Finlay, is a
Gaelic personal name; and Finlayson and
Mackinlay are therefore synonymous.

MAC MANUS.* The Mac Manus was
chief of a numerous and influential clan
of Fermanagh. According to the native
annalists, they had the command of the
shipping in Lough Erne. D'Alton.

MAC MILLAN. "The M'Millans are
said to be Buchannans by descent, and to
have changed their name upon account of
slaughter." Nisbet.

MAC NAB.* According to some authorities this name signifies "the son of the
Abbot."

MAC PHERSON.* "Strange is the
origin of the name Macpherson, though
now as common among the canny Scots
as Williams or Bowen in Wales, or as hops
or cherries in Kent. During the reign of
David I. of Scotland, it appears that a
younger brother of the chief of the then
powerful clan Chattan, espoused the
clerical life, and in due course of time
became Abbot of Kingussie. His elder
brother, whether he fell in battle or died in
his bed, somehow or other died childless,
and the chieftainship unexpectedly devolved
on the venerable abbot. Suiting the action
to the word, or rather suiting his convictions to his circumstances, the monk procured from the Pope the necessary dispensation, and the Abbot of Kingussie became
the husband of the fair daughter of the
Thane of Calder. A swarm of little
Kingussies naturally followed, and the
good people of Invernessshire as naturally
called them Macphersons—i.e., "the sons
of the parson." *Once a Week.*

MAC SHANLEY. See O'Shanley.

MAC SWEENY. A branch of the
O'Neills, who settled in Donegal, and there
established three great families. They
were also important in Munster in the
XIII. century. D'Alton.

MADDEN. See O'Madden.

MADGWICK. This name is almost
peculiar to Sussex, and it probably originated from some locality in the western
part of that county, which no longer retains its old designation. To that district
also belong Gratwicke, Padwick, Rudwick,
and other surnames terminating in WICK,
the places from which they were derived
being for the most part unknown. This
name is always pronounced as if written
Magic, and is a good example of the facility
with which a name may, by a simple
peculiarity of pronunciation, come to represent something totally different from its
real origin.

MAGRATH. "The Magraths or Craiths
are of Milesian descent. According to

O'Dugan, who wrote in the fourteenth century, they were lords of a district of Fermanagh in the twelfth and thirteenth centuries." They were a castle-building family, and erected one at Abbeyside near Dungarvan; another at Fernane, near Sledy; a third at Comragh; and a fourth at Reigh, in the barony of Glenaheiry. From the *Telegraph*, an Irish newspaper.

MANTLE. See Mantell.

MASTERTON. A village in the parish of Dunfermline, co. Fife.

MELDRUM.* The Meldrums were " of that Ilk," in the XIII. century, the first of the name mentioned by Nisbet being Alexander de Melgedrum, who flourished in 1278.

MENCE. This old Worcestershire name, which occurs in the various forms of Mayens, Mauns, Maunce, Menske, Mens, Mense, and Mence, is in all probability derived from the Rhenish city of Mayence or Mentz. Under the name of Mayens the family were owners of land in Ombersley about the year 1327. See Nash's Worcestershire, ii. 226.

MERRY.* A more likely derivation is from Merdericus, a personal name, softened by the French into Merry. The Roman church honours a Saint Merry on the 29th of August. There is also a commune in the arrondissement of Argentan called Merri.

MERTENS. Of Flemish origin. This name, or more correctly Mehrtens, is not uncommon in Belgium.

MINSTER.* There are parishes specifically called Minster in the counties of Cornwall, Kent, Essex, and Oxford.

MONCUR.* The family were " of that Ilk," temp. Robert I. and David Bruce. Nisbet.

MONCKTON. This family are of great antiquity in co. York, and derive their descent from Simon Monckton of Monckton, near Boroughbridge, which lordship his posterity enjoyed until it was made a nunnery in the year 1326, and called Nun-Monckton. Courthope's Debrett.

MONSON.* The following rather happy pun on this name is given in Willis's History of Cathedrals :—

" *Lunam* cum *Phœbo* jungito, *nomen* habes"—
Join Moon and Sun, and MONSON you will have.
                           Heraldic Anomalies.

MONTALT.* It is probable that the original name was the Norman *Mont-hault*, " the lofty hill," and that Montalt is from the latinization De Monte Alto.

MONTEITH. " The first of this name was Walter, third son to Walter, and brother to Alexander, High Steward of Scotland, who, being made Earl of Monteith,

took the surname of Monteith, which descended to all his posterity; and to show that they were originally of the stock of the Stewarts they turned the *Fesse Checqué* to a *Bend*." Nisbet.

MONYPENNY.* " Some conjecture that, upon the similitude of arms, the Monypennies are originally from the Dauphinates in France." Nisbet.

MOON.* In the Roll of Carlaverock, A.D. 1300, John de Mohun (represented as carrying a yellow banner with a black cross engrailed) is called John de *Mooun*.

    " Jaune o crois noire engreelie
    La portoit John de Mooun."
          Nicolas' Siege of Carlaverock, p. 18.

MORBROKE. An estate at Hailsham, co. Sussex, now corrupted to Mullbrooks, where the family resided in the XIV. century, the site of their residence being still marked by traces of a moat.

MORDACQUE. The family are derived from Brittany. The name is probably a modification of the Latin *mordax*, biting, sharp, cutting—a sobriquet applied to its original bearer. See Mordaunt.

A correspondent observes, that it is a singular coincidence that the first syllables of the Latin verb and the Greek verb for ' to bite '—MOR—δακ—make up the name.

MORILLION. See Délanoy.

MORTH. See Rundle.

MOUNTENEY Probably from one of the three Norman localities now called Montigni, and situated respectively near Caen, Mortain, and Rouen. In the reign of Edward I. Robert de Mounteny held lands at Sawston, co. Cambridge. The family were at a later date seated in Norfolk.

MULNE.* This word is not only a provincial, but also an archaic, form of *mill*. In the curious satirical ballad on Richard, King of the Romans, who, at the battle of Lewes, 1204, took refuge in a wind-mill, we read :—

    " The King of Alemaigne wende to do ful wel,
    He saised the *Mulne* for a Castel,
    With hare sharpe swerdes he ground the stel,
    He wende that the sayles were Mangonel."

MUMPERSON. A *mumper* is in some dialects a beggar, and it might be imagined that this family originated with a beggar's son! It is, however, a simple corruption of Mompesson, an ancient Norman name of high repute, erewhile Mont-Pinson.

MURCHISON. A corruption of Merchistoun, in Scotland, the seat of the Napiers. So, frequently, Johnson from Johnstoun.

MURTH. See Rundle.

MUSHET. A Scottish corruption of Montfichet.

N.

NAIRN.* Nairn, Lord Nairn, was " of that Ilk." Nisbet.

NAPKIN. Many years since a Sussex foundling, who had been exposed in a napkin near a brook, received the designation of *Napkin Brooker*. Whether the surname originated in some similar manner I cannot say.

NEALDS. Obviously of the same origin as Nield. The family came from Cheshire, where the latter name is prevalent.

NEELD. See Nield.

NEILD. See Nield.

NEILSON.* " Three brothers of the sirname of Oneal, came from Ireland to Scotland, in the reign of Robert the Bruce, where they got lands for their valour, and their issue changed their name a little from Oneal to Neilson; for Oneal and M'Neil are the same with Neilson." Nisbet. The first occurrence of the name noted by this author is in 1439, in Galloway.

NEVOY. Of that Ilk, in Scotland. Nisbet. Perhaps the same as Nevay, a parish now united to Essie in Forfarshire.

NIELD. This name, with its modified forms, Neild, Neeld, &c., is or has been localized to Cheshire. The origin is uncertain; it may be a corruption of Neale or Neill.

NISBET.* Of that Ilk, in Berwickshire, where Nisbet Castle was their residence. The earliest recorded ancestor is Philip de Nesbyth, whose name appears as witness to a deed of King David I. to Coldingham Priory. Nisbet's Heraldry.

NOAKES.* In the Rotuli Hundredorum, the latinization of Noakes is De Quercu.

NORVEL. NORVAL. Nisbet says, " of that Ilk." It clearly appears, then, that there have been young men who could with truth affirm—" My name is Norval ;" but whether they were sons of Grampian shepherds or not, neither the old heraldrist, nor the gazetteer informs us.

NUGENT.* Nogent le Rotrou, the ancient seat of this family, is in the province of Orleanois, just over the border of Normandy, and a few leagues to the eastward of Belesme, from whence the family were derived.

O.

O. *By* has been stated to be the shortest of English surnames ; but a correspondent points out to me one still shorter, namely, *O*. An administration to the effects of John O, of Ellesmere, co. Salop, was granted 12. June, 1585. Lichfield Act Book, fol. 150.

O'FALLON. A corruption of O'Phelan, which see. A district in Roscommon was known as O'Fallon's country. D'Alton.

O'FAY. A sept of the North of Ireland. D'Alton.

OGILVIE.* Of that Ilk, in Angus. Nisbet says—" These of this family are to be found witnesses in the charters of the Alexanders II. and III., and were very eminent in the reign of Robert the Bruce ; that King gave to Patrick Ogilvie of that Ilk the lands of Caithness, which had belonged to Malcolm de Caithness."

OLDYS. See Oldis. The following couplet, written by William Oldys the

bibliographer, exists in a MS. in the British Museum :—

"In word and *Will I am* a friend to you ;
And one friend *Old is* worth a hundred new."

OLIPHANT.* This Scottish name appears to be corrupted from the local De Oliphard, which is found in the XII. cent. In 1142 David de Oliphard accompanied King David I. in his descent upon England. It would appear that the spelling Oliphant began early in the XIV. century. Nisbet.

OMASH. This family, long connected with the Spitalfields silk-trade, were French Protestant refugees. Their name is said to have been originally D'Ormasse.

O'MULLEDY. An ancient sept in co. Galway.

ORLEBAR.* The parish of Orlingbury, co. Northampton, was spelt Orleberg, temp. Edward I., and Robert de O. held lands there. Rot. Hund. ii. 12. This is pretty conclusive evidence of the origin of the name.

OSIER. A corruption of Hosier.

P.

PAKYN. A corruption of Pagan, Paganus. There is little doubt that Pakyns Manor, in the parish of Hurst-Pierpoint, co. Sussex, takes its name from Paganus, sheriff of Sussex in the year 1157, as that personage occurs as witness to a document in association with Robert de Pierpoint and other local proprietors. W. S. Ellis, Esq., in Sussex Arch. Coll. xi. 73.

PALMER.* Sir Walter Raleigh, in the following beautiful lines, seems to regard palmer and pilgrim as synonymous terms :—

> "Give me my scallop-shell of quiet,
> My staff of truth to walk upon,
> My scrip of joy—immortal diet—
> My bottle of salvation ;
> My gown of glory, hope's true gage ;
> And thus I'll take my *pilgrimage*—
> While my soul, like a quiet *palmer*,
> Travelleth towards the land of Heaven."

PARR.* When the late Queen Caroline arrived in England after her absence on the Continent, Dr. Parr was for a short time her chaplain ; but his place was afterwards supplied by the Rev. Mr. Fellowes ; whereupon somebody penned this

EPIGRAM.
> "There's a difference between
> Dr. Parr and the Queen ;
> For the reason you need not go far—
> The Doctor is jealous
> Of certain little *Fellowes*
> Whom the Queen thinks much above *Parr*."

PAY. PAYE. See Payson, below.

PAYSON. It is asserted that this name is derived from Paine's son, Fitz Paine, Filius Pagani. If so, the more common name Pay must be a contraction of Paganus.

PEACHAM. Nisbet makes the names Pecham, or Peckham, and Peacham identical. Pecham is certainly an old orthography in the Kentish family.

PEARSON.* The following communication has been sent me by a correspondent who bears this name :—

"In the Bishop's Registers at Lichfield, at the commencement of the XIV. century, this surname is accounted for unmistakably by the following entry :— "Rogerus dictus le Person de Banquelle (*i.e.* Bakewell, co. Derby), ordained deacon in the church of the fraternity of preachers, Derby, the 3rd April, 1305, upon his patrimonial title"—and then follows a subsequent entry—"Rogerus Persone de Banquell, ordained priest in the church of the fraternity of preachers, Derby, the 23rd December, 1307, upon his patrimonial title." The same orthography is preserved in every instance—"Adam Person de Lilleshull, ordained deacon in the Conventual Church of Lilleshull (co. Salop) the 28th March, 1304." "Frater Willielmus Personn monachus de Stonleye (*i.e.* Stoneleigh, co. Warwick) ordained deacon at the parish church of Herbury (*i.e.* Harbury, co. Warwick) the 23rd September, 1335." "Frater Willielmus Person ordained priest in the parish church of the Holy Trinity, Coventry, the 21st September, 1336."—not to speak of an adherence to the same spelling in the earliest Wills of the Diocese, where in one instance

an inventory in the year 1535, occurs with the endorsement of "Persona de Morley (co. Derby)." I think sufficient grounds exist for placing the surname of Pearson amongst the number of those derived "from Occupations or Professions" already fully discussed in Mr. Lower's English Surnames."

PECKLETON. A parish in co. Leicester, where the family possessed lands at an early period. In the Testa de Nevill, compiled about the year 1240, it is written Peycelton, and in other ancient writings, Pechintone, Pekyngton, Peculden, Pygleton, Pechlington, &c. Inf. Rev. J. Peckleton Power, M.A.

PENNYCOOK. Of that Ilk, according to Nisbet—probably Penicuick, a parish near Edinburgh.

PERRIN. The Counts du Perrin held large possessions in the district of Nosière, in France, but being Huguenots, the family were compelled to quit their native land, in the earlier part of the XVIII. century, and they settled in Lisburn, in Ireland. Several members of the family have distinguished themselves at the Irish bar, and one is well known as the author of an excellent grammar of his ancestral language. Vide Ulster Journ. of Archæology, ii. 172.

PHELAN. See O'Phelan.

PIGFAT. A known corruption of Pickford.

PITBLADO. Of that Ilk. Nisbet. I cannot discover the locality.

POLWARTH. Of that Ilk, in Berwickshire. The heiress married Saint Clair, temp. James III. Nisbet.

POPHAM.* See Horner.*

POTTEN. See Potton.

POTTON. A parish in Bedfordshire.

PRINGLE.* A correspondent says: "There were unquestionably lands in Roxburghshire called Hop-pringle, meaning probably *Pilgrim's hope*, or meadow."

PRYNN. According to a statement in C. S. Gilbert's Cornwall, this family were formerly called Resprynn, and they are supposed to have originated from Resprynn, an estate in the parish of Lanhydrock.

PRYOR. PRYER. See Prior.

PUNCHEON. One Johannes Punchiun is found in H.R. without any prefix of De or Le, and the name is therefore probably a sobriquet originally applied to a person of rotund and barrel-like proportions.

PURVES.* Nisbet says that this place is in the shire of Berwick.

PUXON. Corrupted from Puxton, a parish in Somersetshire.

R.

RAIT.* Nisbet says that the family came from "the country of Rhetia," in Germany, *unde nomen*, and settling in Nairnshire temp. Malcolm IV., obtained from that monarch lands, which they designated by their own name. A most improbable statement. Sir Gervais Rait was "of that Ilk," temp. John Baliol.

RAMSBOTTOM.* I am informed that *rhoms* or *roms*, wild garlic *(allium ursinum)* abound at *Ram's* Clough, in the parish of Haslingden, co. Lancaster, a few miles from Ramsbottom. Ray considers the Island of Ramsay to have taken its name from this plant.

RATTLEBAG.* The real meaning of this word would appear, from an entry in the Hundred Rolls of temp. Edward I. to be a *usurer*. The vill of Chering, co. Essex, present that John Rattilbagg is a Christian usurer, inasmuch as Richard Alisaundre borrowed from him three quarters of wheat worth 18s., and three quarters of oats worth 3s., Rattilbagg receiving four seams of beans worth 20s., by way of usury, and yet the principal still remained due. H.R. vol. i. p. 150.

READY.* In the H.R. we find one Henry *Tutprest*, "Quite-ready."

RIDDELL.* It is remarkable that in the oldest Scottish charter extant (of the XI. century) the only surnames mentioned are Riddell and Corbet.

ROSSIE. Rossie, in Fifeshire, belonged to "Dominus Henricus Rossie, de eodem," in the reigns of David I. and Malcolm IV.

ROUPEL.* The manor of Beckenham, co. Kent, was held by a family called, in old Latin records, De Rupella; in French, De la Rochell; and in English, Rokele. They came originally from Rochelle, in France. Richard de la Rokele died possessed of the estate, 5. Edward I. Hasted Kent, I., 529.

RULE.* "The sirname of Rule they bring from St. Regulus, who brought the relicts of St. Andrew to Scotland." Nisbet.

RUNCIMAN.* May be equivalent to Palfriman, Coltman, &c., *Runcinus*, in medieval Latin, being a rowney, saddle-horse, or hackney.

RUSTAT. Perhaps from Rastatt, (or Radstadt) the great Austrian fortress.

RUTHVEN. Nisbet gives the following account :—

"The chief of this name was Ruthven, Lord Ruthven, and thereafter Earl of Gowry. They are said by some to be originally from Arragon, from the similitude of their arms; but this is no certain evidence of its self without other documents. This ancient family, as others, took their surname from their lands, called Ruthven, and were dignified with the title of Lord Ruthven by King James III."

S.

SACHEVERELL.* An intelligent correspondent (Mr. J. L. Smart) sends me the following account of the origin of the word, as applied to the blower of a stove. I cannot but imagine that the trader of Birmingham had a keen turn for satire, as well as for business and profit, in likening his fire-blower to the great "church-in-danger" divine.

"When Dr. Sacheverell was at the height of his peculiar popularity, an ironmonger at Birmingham invented the improvement to a stove, called a blower, which he, for trading purposes, to increase the sale of the article, named a *sacheverell*. I have repeatedly heard my mother, now in her ninety-first year, refer to the fact, and, as she knew Birmingham well in her youth, the point is perhaps worthy of your consideration."

SAINT CLAIR.* The following curious account is given of the establishment of this noble family in Scotland :—" William Saintclair was second son to Wildernus, Earl of Saintclair in France, whose mother was daughter to Duke Richard of Normandy, father to William the Conqueror. He was sent by his father to Scotland, to take a view of the peoples good behaviour. He was able for every game, agreeable to all company, and stiled the Seemly Saintclair. The report of his qualifications came to the Queen's ears, who desired him of her husband because of his wisdome. The King made him her cup-bearer. . . . . He got also of the King and Queen the barony of Rosline." Father Hay's Genealogie of the Sainteclaires of Rosslyn. Printed at Edinburgh, 1835.

SANDILANDS.* The barony of Sandilands is in Clydesdale.

SAURIN. See Ulst. Journ. of Arch. p. 175.

SCYTHESMITH. A maker of scythes.

SEAHORSE. A family in New Brunswick, of English descent, bear this singular name.

SIBTHORPE. The S.'s of Canwick Hall spell the name without the E final.

SICKLESMITH. This name, which is found in West Kent in the XVII. cent., means of course a maker of sickles. Sixsmiths, to which I have elsewhere attributed a different origin, is probably a corruption.

SIFLEET. Siflet, an A-Sax. personal name.

SIMNEL. " The finest sort of bread. In Shropshire, the word is still in use to designate a kind of cake. *Lambert Simnel,* the pretended Earl of Warwick, temp. Henry VII., was a baker's lad, who had been trained for the character by Simon the priest." The surname was doubtless allusive to his trade. King William the Conqueror, at the foundation of Battel Abbey, gave his monks " a memorial of his love in appointing for their daily use, bread fit for the table of a king, which is commonly called *simenel,* thirty-six ounces by weight, and one fourth more during Lent, that something might remain for charity." Chronicle of Battel Abbey, p. 27. That surnames were borrowed from such sources is evidenced by Whitbread, Wastell, &c.; and in the Hundred Rolls we find at Wroxeter a lady called *Petronilla Swetedoughe.*

SNEE. A respectable family, of French refugee extraction, settled at Edmonton, Islington, &c. The name has been corrupted.

SOULES. An ancient Scottish family dating from the reign of King David I., when Ranulphus de Soules flourished. His descendants were hereditary butlers of Scotland, under the title of *Pincerna Regis* or *Butellarius Regis.* The family seem to have conferred their name, Soulestoun, upon the lands in East Lothian, now Saltoun or Salton. Nisbet.

STANCOMB. Supposed to be a corruption of Stinchcombe, a village near Wottonunder-Edge, co. Gloucester.

STARK.* " The name of Stark with us has its rise from just such another action as that of Turnbull's (See Turnbull), but later, by saving James the IV. from a bull in the forest of Cumbernauld, by one of the name of Muirhead, who for his strength was called Stark. And to shew his descent from Muirhead he carries the armorial figures of Muirhead with a Bull's Head." Nisbet.

STARKIE.* The pedigree of this ancient family of Cheshire and Lancashire can be traced almost to the Conquest. Shirley's Noble and Gentle Men.

STARR.* It is sometimes local. H.R. De Starre, co. Lincoln.

STRACHAN.* The family are descended from Adam Strachanen, to whom Thomas, Earl of Mar, his wife's cousin, granted, temp. David II., the lands of Glenkindie, co. Aberdeen, where the family continued to reside in 1722. Nisbet.

STRAITON.* " There was an old family of this name, designed of that Ilk, from the lands of Straiton (in Ayrshire) of which King David I. gave them a charter." Nisbet.

STAVERTON. A parish in Devonshire, anciently the estate of the family.

STOVELD. The same as Stovell.

SYDSERF.* Nisbet says, that the Sideserfs were originally from France—apparently on the strength of the Fleur-de-Lys in their arms.

SYMINGTON. Parishes, &c. in cos. Ayr, Lanark, and Edinburgh.

T.

TAFINDER. See Delanoy.

TELZEPHER. Thus ingeniously do Nisbet and the Scottish genealogists misspell the old Anglo-Norman name Taillefer. See Telfer.

TENNANT.* Of that Ilk, in Scotland.

THREIPLAND. A stream bordering cos. Renfrew and Lanark is called Threipland Burn.

TORY. See Torry.

TORRY.* There are places so called in cos. Kincardine and Fife, but, according to Nisbet, the family were of that Ilk in the shire of Dumfries, till their lands were forfeited temp. James III. That monarch regranted temp. James III. the lands and church of Tory, &c., " quæ ad Georgium Tory de Eodem, *nostrum Felonem et Proditorem* pertinuerunt, ratione ejus forfeituræ."

3 H

TOWER. TOWERS.* The latinization in H.R. is De Turribus. In France, Latour and Delatour are well-known surnames.

TRANCHEMER. See Trangmar. A family of this name bear for arms " a sword plunged in a sea." Dixon.

TREADGOLD. In H.R. Tredegold.

☞ TREES, PLANTS, AND SHRUBS, *Surnames derived from.* Mr. Clark presents us with the following enumeration:—

"Ashplant, Quickset, Privet, Pine,
Thorn, Thistle, Hazel, Briars, and Vine;
Elms, Clover, Camomile, and Furze,
Ash, Nettle, Juniper, and Tares;
Heath, Linden, Beech, Box, Birch, and Broom,
Branch, Bramble, Blossom, Bough, and Bloom;
Peartree, Plumtree, Crabtree, Laurel,
Sycamore, Hay, Straw, and Sorrel;

Orchard, Appletree, and Lime,
Hickory, Maple, Musk, and Thyme;
With Lavender, Veitch, Leaf, and Ling,
And Oak, of forest-trees the king."

From this list we ought probably to eliminate a few, as belonging to other classes; and the remainder belong principally to the class denominated *local.* See the articles Atte, Ash, Noakes, &c., &c.

TROUP. Of that Ilk, in the parish of Fortingal, co. Perth. This ancient family ended in an heiress, who married a younger son of Keith, Earl Marischal. Nisbet.

TYACKE. A Cornish family of considerable antiquity, who had landed property at an early period in that county. In the Visitation of Cornwall, 1573, the name is variously written Tyacke, Tyack, and Teacke. It is conjecturally derived from the Celtic *tiak, tiac,* a ploughman.

V.

VASS. The same as Vaus, below.

VAUS. VAUSS. This surname is said by Sir James Dalrymple to be the same with De Vallibus—doubtless through Vaux, which see. In the XII. century this great Anglo-Norman family obtained a footing in Scotland, and were lords of Dirleton, co. Haddington; and from them sprang the Vauses or De Vaux, Lords Dirleton.

VIDELOU. See under Wolf.

W.

WALKINGSHAW. The lands of Walkingshaw, co. Renfrew, gave name to this family, who appear to have been possessed of them in the year 1235. They were hereditary foresters to the High Stewards of Scotland for the barony of Renfrew, and hence their armorial supporters, "Two Foresters in long gowns." See Crawfurd's Hist. Renfrew.

WALLACE.* On the whole I have very little doubt of the Welsh extraction of the Scottish patriot. Sir James Dalrymple, the eminent genealogist, deduces the family from " one Eimarus Galeius, a Welshman, so called in Scotland, upon the account of his country. He is witness in the charter of foundation of the abbacy of Selkrig, by David, younger son of King Malcolm III. From him was descended Ricardus Guallensis, as in a charter granted by him to the abbacy of Kelso, in the reign of King Alexander II." Nisbet.

WEAPONT.* A Scottish corruption of Vipont—De Veteri Ponte.

WEEMS.* This seems to be in some instances a corruption of Wemyss. Nisbet employs this orthography only. That quaint writer informs us, that "There is a strong tradition that the first of the family of Weems of that Ilk was a son of M'Duff, Thane of Fife, in the usurpation of M'Beth, who having hid himself from that tyrant's cruelty in Coves, in the east end of Fife, near his own residence, took the name Weems—the Irish word *weimh* signifying a cove."

WEIR* " The sirname of Weir is ancient with us, as Sir James Dalrymple observes in his Collections. Ranulphus de Weir is mentioned in the registers of Kelso,

Paisley, and Murray, to have lived in the time of King William (the Lyon), and Thomas de Weir in the reign of Alexander II." Nisbet.

WHITBOURN. A parish in Herefordshire.

WHITSUNDAY. Born at that festival. Wytesoneday, H.R. See Times and Seasons.

WILSON. One of the most ancient families of this name is that of the baronetage, now represented by Sir Thomas Maryon Wilson, who is sixteenth in descent from Thomas Wilson of Elton, in Yorkshire, four generations previously to 1438, and, therefore, probably born about the close of the XIII. cent. Sussex Arch. Coll., vol. xii. p. 240.

THE FAREWELL.

" My Task is past, my Care is but begun;
   My Pains must suffer Censures for reward:
   Yet hope I have, now my great pains are done,
   That gentle Spirits will 'quite them with regard.

" But if th' ungentle brood of Envy's grooms
   Misdoom my pains; no force—they do their kind;
   And I'll do mine, which is to scorn their dooms,
   That use unkindly a kind-willing mind.'

John Guillim.

ADDENDUM.

T O the courtesy of J. T. Hammack, Esq., I am indebted for the following highly curious List of Names, extracted from documents in the Office of the Registrar-General. It was compiled by a gentleman in that office (now deceased), and it may be relied upon as authentic in every particular. It serves to show (if such evidence were still necessary) the wonderful variety of our existing Family Nomenclature.

It will be found to contain numerous names not included in the body of my work, and to furnish many additional examples of the various classes. It came into my hands when most of the foregoing sheets had passed through the press; otherwise I should have taxed my ingenuity to assign a meaning to such of the designations as had previously escaped my observation. This may be a task for some future day.

The laborious collector and classifier of these surnames has, in most instances, prefixed the baptismal appellatives. Some of them are in the highest degree absurd and ridiculous, as witness *Acts* Apostles, *Portland* Duchess, *Henry Born* Noble, *Time of* Day, and *John Bottle of* Beer ! They are, however, as authentic as they are nonsensical ; though I hope for the credit and sanctity of the rite, that such names were generally imposed otherwise than at the baptismal font.

PERSONS OR THINGS RELATING TO RELIGION.

Prudence Church
Sidney Abbey
Mary Nunnery
Jane Chapel
Moses Kirk
Caroline Parsonage
Maria Vicarage
Margaret Bishoprick
Abraham Chantry
Maria Font
Thomas Sanctuary
Amelia See
John Tabernacle
Mary Pew
Ann Livings
Joseph Cardinal
Tributina Pope
Christopher Abbot
Uriah Prior
Sophia Monk
Caroline Friar
Jane Priest
Walter Martyr
Robert Prophet
Acts Apostle
Paul Saint
Arch Bishop
Stephen Dean
James Archdeacon
Archdeacon Deacon
Arthur Parson
Truth Parsons
Harry Minister

Stephen Chaplain
John Preacher
Alexander Elder
Henry Churchman
Maria Clerk
Robert Beadle
Cornelius Sexton
Sarah Chanter
Cordelia Nun
Theresa Verger
Frederick Anthem
Lydia Chant
Amelia Churchyard
Joseph Grave
Margaret Tomb
Mary Corpse
Aston Coffin
John Ghost
Isaac Hearse
Christiana Stocks
J. Waters Christ
Frances Angel
Kerenhappuch Death
Emma Heaven
David Hell
William Paradise
William Eden
William Soul
John Spirit
Susan Human
Sarah Divine
James Bible
Robert Crucifix
Edward Crosier
Mary Creed
A. Howe Gospel

Joseph Tenet
Margaret Psalms
Henry Sermon
Jane Service
Michael Pray
Walter Proverbs
Hannah Paternoster
William Worship
Gabriel Incarnation
Sarah Piety
Catherine Holy
Henry Godly
Susannah Shrive
Alfred Surplice
Thomas Papal
George Laity

THE MINERAL KINGDOM.

Charles Ore
William Gem
Joseph Jewel
Harold Stone
Jane Gold
Sarah Silver
Mary Lead
Jane Copper
Lucy Iron
Jasper Steel
Alice Pewter
Ann Brass
John Pinchbeck
Sabina Diamond
Joseph Ruby
Joseph Pearl
Sarah Agate
Joseph Coral

Thomas	Alabaster	George	Grain	James	Trussel
William	Marble	Susan	Corn	George	Forge
Ellen	Glass	Jane	Wheat	Charles	Smithy
Eustace	Delf	Richard	Oats	James	Builder
Joseph	Coal	Terry	Rye	Silas	House
Stephen	Culm	John	Barley	John	Cottage
George	Coke	William	Grass	Freedom	Lodge
Maria	Chalk	Lucy	Hay	Leigh	Grange
Samuel	Clay	Harriet	Straw	Lucy	Farm
Sophia	Shale	Emma	Clover	Amelia	Barns
Susannah	Slag	Thomas	Savin	Happy Helen	Hovel
Joseph	Slate	George	Southernwood	Nehemiah	Shed
Edith	Gravel	Joseph	Staveacre	Robinson	Stable
Monica	Flint	John	Balm	Fanny	Mews
Eli	Emery	Doretta	Rush	Frank	Manger
Lydia	Whiting	Bishop	Hemp	Jane	Brewhouse
Myra	Salts	Rowland	Cotton	Robert	Wainhouse
Sarah	Brick	Jane	Hops	Harriet	Malthouse
Emma	Whetstone	James	Malt	Eliza	Mill
John	Freestone	Advice	Reed	William	Windmill
Ruth	Silkstone	Thomas	Osier	Henry	Castle
Thomas	Ruddle	Eleanor	Bran	Sarah	Keep
Joseph	Salt	Gabriel	Chaff	William	Fort
Elizabeth	Carbon	Sarah	Woad	Emma	Garrison
Caroline	Chalklime	Ambrose	Beet	Matilda	Barrack

THE VEGETABLE KINGDOM.

Jane	Tree	James	Madder	William	Bastion
Alexander	Appletree	Eleanor	Liquorice	George	Mole
Squire	Crabtree	John	Bramble	Anna	Churches
Ellen	Figtree	William	Briars	Francis	College
Alexander	Peartree	Esther	Broom	James	Vicarage
Tom	Plumtree	James	Gorse	John	Temple
Henry	Aspen	Mary	Furze	Jane	Towers
Golding	Ash	Agnes	Heath	Esther	Pinnacle
John	Alder	George	Heather	John	Spires
Amos	Almond	Ann	Fern	Ralph	Steeple
Amplias	Birch	Emma	Cane	Ann	Porch
Josiah	Beech	Caroline	Cress	Clara	Pillar
Sally	Cork	Mark	Currant	Martha	Mart
Cooper	Cherry	Moses	Thorn	Thomas	Quay
Simon	Chesnut	Martin	Vine	Joshua	Wharf
Emily	Date	Maria	Myrtle	Isabella	Dock
Rachel	Olive	Mary	Creeper	Luke	Bridge
Alexander	Elder	Samuel	Woodbine	Mary	Arch
Caroline	Elm	Alice	Colombine	Ruth	Starling
Stephen	Hawthorn	Benjamin	Hazel	John	Buttress
William	Holly	Sarah	Eglantine	Enoch	Drawbridge
Rosa	Juniper	Hannah	Marjoram	Thomas	Ironbridge
Aaron	Lemon	John	Sage	James	Tunnel
Ann	Medlar	Augustus	Yarrow	Arthur	Fountain
Charlotte	Mulberry	Mary	Nettle	Ann	Well
Elizabeth	Maple	Ann	Orris	Amos	Conduit
Sarah	Oak	Robert	Millet	George	Hospital
Mary	Orange	Bridget	Rape	Oliver	Monument
Zacharias	Pollard	Grace	Rue	Georgina	Street
David	Pine	Mercy	Tansey	Daniel	Court
Sarah	Poplar	Winter	Moss	Job	Alley
Isaac	Sycamore	Libertine	Moss	Eliza	Bakehouse
Ann	Willows	Philip	Sorel	Amy	Taphouse
Rhoda	Bush	Susannah	Weed	Gilbert	Pantry
Banstone	Shrub	Emily	Weeds	Richard	Buttery
Zenobina	Plant	Margaret	Hemlock	Thomas	Dairy
Catherine	Herbage	Leah	Flower	Lot	Hall
Sarah	Root	Sampson	Garland	Horatio	Parlour
Thomas	Roots	Simon	Boquet	Matthew	Kitchen
Mark	Branch	Noble	Rose	Charity	Chambers
Lucy	Bough	Hannah	Tulip	John	Room
Mary	Sprout	John	Violet	Jacob	Garret
Charlotte	Twig	John	Daisy	Ellen	Loft
Edward	Leaf	Henry	Primrose	Sarah	Gallery
Hester	Leaves	Mark	Lavender	James	Office
Eleanor	Bark	Jane	Marigold	Ann	Roof
George	Gum	James	Pink	Rafter	Rafter
Andrew	Husk	Sarah	Poppy	West Hand	Larder
Edwin	Spray	Philip	Camomile	Amos	Booth
Sophia	Peel	Job	Bloom	William	Kennel
Anne	Rind	Constance	Pollen		Town
Cooper	Seed			Samuel	Village
Mark	Berry			Alice	Banister

BUILDINGS—THEIR PARTS, &c.

Webber	Pile	Alice	Window
George	Scaffold	Emma	Shutter

James	Screen
William	Stair
John	Tank
John	Oven
Fanny	Stove
James	Cowl
Sarah	Sink
Sarah	Drain
Maria	Flue
Edward	Gable
Roger	Eaves
Cecil	Wall
Walter	Tile
Ellen	Safe
Job	Doorbar
Bithia	Staple
George	Moulding

WAR, AND ITS CONCOMITANTS.

James	Warrior
Sarah	Arms
Ann	Armour
Ann	Sword
Ebenezer	Rapier
Fanny	Dagger
Judith	Pike
Michael	Battle
Charles	Lance
Rebecca	Spear
Fanny	Carbine
Jonas	Gun
Barney	Cannon
Edwin	Bullett
Industry	Ball
Thomas	Shell
Charles	Mortar
Uriah	Guard
Jemima	Staff
George	Corps
Kate	Allies
James	Private
Thomas	Troop
Sarah	Picket
Ann	Rear
Ernest	Rank
Lucy	File
John	Shield
Sarah	Gauntlet
Sarah	Standard
Joseph	Banner
John	Pillage
Quilly	Booty
Walter	Archer
James	Bow
Marian	Arrow
George	Breach
James	Trench
James	Camp
William	Campaign
Francis	Foe
Mary	Convoy
Tryphena	Conquer
Emily	Conquest
Thomas	Dirk
John	Buckler

MOODS, TEMPERAMENT, &C.

John	Eat
Jane	Eatwell
Eli	Chew
Eleanor	Cram
Thomas	Swallow
Edward	Nice
Eliza	Savory
James	Cheer
Thankfull	Joy
Solomon	Laugh
George	Jest
Anthony	Gay
Emma	Merry

Alfred	Jolly
Edith	Witty
Elizabeth	Rail
Martha	Mock
Caroline	Dance
Ann	Reel
Francis	Revel
Industry	Ball
Charles	Rout
Mary	Ride
Margaret	Riding
George	Gallop
George	Canter
Paradice	Hunt
John	Race
Rachel	Course
George	Sport
Charles	Chase
Sophia	Covey
Agnes	Cool
Selina	Colder
Rhoda	Coldman
Elizabeth	Chillman
Alfred	Chillmaid
Mary	Freeze
Lucy	Thaw
Susan	Heat
Deborah	Burn

MUSICAL INSTRUMENTS.

Walter	Buglehorn
David	Fiddle
Thomas	Fife
Juliana	Horn
Sarah	Pipe
J. Sweet	Organ
Emily	Tabor
	Drum
Catherine	Timbrel
Ellen	Harp

EPOCHS OF LIFE, &C.

Sophia	Birth
Dorcas	Death
Alfred	Marriage
Wallace	Wedlock
Julia	Born
Charles	Die
John	Life

SHAPES, &C.

Jane	Square
Lucretia	Round
Ellen	Cone
Charles	Globe
Elizabeth	Angle
James	Circus
Dinah	Circuit

RELATING TO BOOKS, &C.

James	Chart
James	Deed
Thomas	Reams
Charles	Book
Edward	Leaf
German	Page
Ann	Sheet
Robert	Press
Israel	Print
William	Quire
Timothy	Quill
Louisa	Parchment
Ursula	Pen
Ann	Ruler
Alfred	Write
Julia	Inkpen
Simon	Ledger
Larman	Register
Thomas	Record
Charles	Annals

Mary	Charter
Ralph	Riddle
Elijah	Fable
James	Letter
Hannah	Card

POINTS OF COMPASS.

Rosa	East
Reuben	West
Job	North
Alfred	South
Edward	Northeast
Emma	Northern
Jane	Southern
Jessie	Western
Joseph	Southward
Mary	Bysouth

IMPLEMENTS, TOOLS, COMMODITIES, &C.

Harriet	Bundle
Edward	Parcel
Laura	Bale
Matthew	Batch
John	Pack
George	Bunch
Thomas	Drop
Affability	Box
True	Case
Nancy	Coop
Sarah	Crate
Ann	Frame
John	Hoop
Ann	Maund
Sarah	Basket
Thomas	Barrel
James	Tub
Richard	Hoe
Mary	Roller
Terrier	Shears
Charley	Rake
Sarah	Tool
George	Awl
James	Axe
Ann	Pitchfork
Leah	Saw
John	Auger
Charles	Gimlet
John	Hammer
Thomas	Plane
John	Mallet
Llewellyn	Mattock
Emma	Shovel
Walter	Rule
Emma	Plumb
Mary	Hone
Martha	Blades
Agnes	Cleaver
Christopher	Nail
Joseph	Tack
Alfred	Hook
Rachel	Crank
Zippora	Crook
Mary	Clamp
Cornelius	Wedge
Mary	Wheel
Ann	Pulley
Keturah	Winch
William	Dredge
Bindless	Woof
Clara	Shuttle
Noah	Lever
Bernard	Scales
Sidney	Wire
Philip	Bar
Joseph	Bolt
Mary	Spike
Amelia	Hinge
Catherine	Punch
Frederick	Bellows

Harriet	Fender	Adam	Van	Sarah	Pipe
Benjamin	Irons	Anthony	Wain	Harriet	Ring
Mary	Tongs	Mary	Sleigh	Aquila	Sheath
Herbert	Candle	Kezia	Sledge	Mary	Stump
Alfred	Wick	Matilda	Spokes	Louisa	Stake
Ann	Matches	Anna	Whip	Louisa	Skates
Mary	Fuel	Abigail	Reins	Alexander	Smut
	Coke	Bridelia	Bridle	Betty	Train
	Coal	Mary	Spurs	Emily	Vizard
Mary	Pitcher	Charles	Stirrup	Sarah	Guise
Susannah	Kettle	Susan	Trace	Martin	Verge
Hannah	Pot		Strap	Sarah	Vane
Aaron	Bowl	Joseph	Timber	Job	Hartshorn
Edmund	Goblet	Edwin	Plank	John	Lye
Francis	Tankard		Beam	George	Ley
	Glass	Vile	Board	Virginia	Lees
William	Ewer	Thomas	Inchboard	Nancy	Leak
Lewis	Bason	Ann	Bench	Henry	Must
Sarah	Vase	William	Log	Ann	Mash
James	Vial	Betsy	Post		
Jasper	Bottle	Elizabeth	Rail	CHARACTERISTICS, &c.	
Edward	Pipkin	James	Veneer		
Mary	Mangle	John	Plaster	Helen	Pout
Churn	Churn	Charles	Mortar	Sarah	Regular
Sarah	Knife	Milton	Chip	Julia	Owner
Judith	Forks	Arthur	Dye	James	Wealthy
James	Clock	Ann	Furnace	John	Fatherly
Thomas	Dial	George	Link	George	Hardincat
Edgar	Bedding	Marrum	Spark	Louisa	Late
Caroline	Sheet	Jane	Rocket	Emma	Loon
Lancelot	Bolster	James	Squib	Alma	Loop
Ann	Pillow	Harriet	Rope	James	Mood
Charles	Curtain	Lewis	Ropeyarn	James	Nest
Robert	Couch	Sophia	Line	Ellen	Core
Ellen	Cushion	Ann	Cable	Eliza	Greedy
Joseph	Brush	Jane	Halter	Louisa	Kersey
George	Comb	Ann	Twist	Ann	Knocker
Eliza	Razor	Joseph	Twine	Robert	Kindly
Theresa	Sponge	Mary	Tape	Joseph	Link
Elizabeth	Towels	Martha	Cord	Clare	Mote
William	Napkin	Fanny	Tow	Peter	Open
Elisha	Lock	Bishop	Kemp	Sophia	Rant
German	Key	Rhoda	Tackle	Charles	Reason
Thomas	Keylock	James	Chain	Margaret	Summons
Zilla	Bell	John	Netting	Ann	Sweet
Elizabeth	Dumbell	Mary	Skein	Robert	Awe
Henry	Needle	Mary	Whitethread	David	Blacking
James	Bodkin	Alice	Tether	Alice	Bladder
Alfred	Hook	Edward	Shackle	Catherine	Comfort
	Eye	Ruth	Fetters	Henry	Bundle
Ann	Locket	George	Snare	William	Divan
Ann	Reel	Lucy	Hay	John	Dupe
Mary	Rag	Thomas	Straw	Samuel	Drought
	Remnant		Chaff		
	Scraps		Bran	QUALITIES, &c.	
Janet	Cage	James	Malt		
Thomas	Clout	Charles	Grist	Thomas	Carnal
Alens	Castor	John	Buckler	Elizabeth	Household
Barber	Counter	James	Bow	John	Anguish
Lovedy	Caddy	Marian	Arrow	L. Dunn	Vile
Victoria	Doll	John	Shield	Albert	Evil
Elizabeth	Toy	Fanny	Dagger	Ann	Grief
	Ladle	Peter	Dart	Anna	Fear
Ann	Tray	Thomas	Dirk	Albert	Anger
Esther	Leather	Mark	Target	Emily	Churlish
Robert	Hides	Dorothy	Corner	Esther	Base
John	Skins	Nicholas	Cranny	Faith	Cross
James	Felts	Harris	Badge	Ann	Daft
John	Cork	Louis	Ticket	Richard	Folly
Ellen	Glue	Miles	Mace	Emma	Fickle
Eve	Gas	Sarah	Club	Timothy	Fretwell
Alice	Feather	Joseph	Crutch	Emma	Frail
William	Rosin	Naomi	Cane	Mary	Silly
Hannah	Tortoiseshell	Jemima	Staff	John	Curse
Thomas	Whalebone	Hannah	Stick	William	Badman
	Hornbuckle	John	Wand	Daniel	Boast
George	Shell	Ruth	Painting	Nancy	Muff
John	Carriage	John	Picture	Mary	Bore
Jonathan	Cart	Edward	Pallet	Alice	Crimp
Arthur	Dray	Israel	Print	Timothy	Dolt
				Thomas	Drudge

Ellen	Dudgeon	Elizabeth	Stocking	Thomas	Portwine
Thomas	Dodge	Cresence	Boot	Robert	Cape
Henry	Dread	Louisa	Shoe	David	Negus
Hannah	Grim	Louisa	Gaiter	John	Spirit
George	Guile	Sidney	Stock	Elizabeth	Whiskey
Ann	Grime	Bridget	Slipper	Richard	Gin
Bridget	Hussey	Emma	Buckle	Jemima	Hollands
Mary	Idle	Philip	Brace	Maria	Shrub
Judith	Jealous	Cecilia	Belt	Catherine	Punch
Robert	Muddle	Zachariah	Button	John Bottle	of Beer
Samuel	Meddle	Thomas	Pocket	Joyce	Porter
Job	Heartless	Emily	Pouch	Dorcas	Stout
Rosanna	Flitter	Rosetta	Crutch	Elizabeth	Porterbeer
Ann	Maudlin	Anna	Silk	Susanna	Eggbeer
Sarah	Mar	Rowland	Cotton	Kezia	Wort
John	Pert	George	Tiffany	Sarah	Spruce
Longstaff	Proud	Nathaniel	Blond	Brown	Mead
James	Pry	James	Border	Joan	Perry
Charley	Rake	Eliza	Lace	John	Thirst
Rebecca	Rob	Emily	Lawn	Jacob	Tableporter
William	Sawney	Anne	Ribbons	James	Ether
Ann	Quaint	Robert	Poplin		
Fanny	Sly	Patience	Diaper	**COLOURS.**	
Sanspareil	Scamp	Robert	Braid	George	Blue
Mary	Strange	Benjamin	List	John	Red
Ellen	Shirk	John	Robes	Fanny	Orange
Catherine	Shallow	Emily	Wool	James	Yellow
Elizabeth	Wildish	Robert	Plush	Faith Hope	
Mary	Truckle	Mary	Tape	Charity	Green
Charles	Vice	Joseph	Cardinal	William	Blues
Samuel	Vague	Rhoda	Wardrobe	John	Violet
Henry	Vain			William	Purple
Frances	Wight	**DISEASES AND THEIR CON-**		James	Pink
Loveless	Wild	**COMITANTS.**		Emily	Rose
James	Lawless	John	Malady	Harriet	Scarlet
Samuel	Curt	John	Fever	Louisa	Deeprose
Harriot	Self	Phillis	Palsey	Maria	Lake
Priscilla	Rouse	Charles	Gout	Michael	Ruddy
Mary	Pride	Josiah	Fits	Florence	Greenish
Mary	Mourn	Mary	Splayfoot	Bob	Seagreen
Harriet	Care	Charlotte	Rash	Elizabeth	Roan
George	Bare	Louisa	Boils	Henry	Buff
Alfred	Denial	Henry	Hiccups	Roxanna	Gray
Mary	End	Harriet	Cramp	James	Dun
		Thomas	Flux	Belly	Brown
CLOTHING AND ORNAMENTS.		Mary	Rickets	Ann	Nutbrown
Benjamin	Garment	Croat	Stone	Simon	Chesnut
Louisa	Raiment	William	Gravel	Mark	Lavender
Reuben	Bonnet	Elizabeth	Piles	Cooper	Cherry
Edwin	Hood	Henry	Whitlow	James	Peach
Catherine	Hat	John	Corns	Aaron	Lemon
Thomas	Cap	Sam	Hurt	Charlotte	Sable
Jane	Tippet	Maria	Sore	Jessie	Black
Mark	Collar	Solomon	Pain	Lilla	White
Robert	Cape	Deborah	Burn		
Sarah	Ruffle	Frances	Gash	**TITLES, &c.**	
Rebecca	Shirt	Sarah	Wale	Mary	Title
James	Gown	Thomas	Chap	Cort	King
William	Shawl	Alexander	Glanders	Ann	Queen
Susan	Scarf	Theophilus	Spavin	Alfred	Prince
Thomas	Sash	Charles	Leper	Lydia	Nobles
Kesia	Band	Henry	Pill	Marshall	Duke
Charles	Girdle	John	Balsam	Portland	Duchess
Cloake	Spencer	Alfred	Bolus	Richard	Marquis
Harry	Mantle	Charles	Physick	Peter	Earl
Nancy	Muff	Louisa	Plaster	Henry	Count
Alfred	Cloak	George	Glister	Katurah	Baron
Elizabeth	Sandal	John	Lancet	Leah	Lord
Solomon	Curl	Frederick	Pestle	Henry Born	Noble
Elizabeth	Tress	Robert	Mortar	William	Margrave
Robert	Plume	Jonas	Kill	Ann	Dey
Elizabeth	Feather	Thomas	Cure	Eli	Knight
George	Patten			Edgar	Squire
Edward	Beads	**LIQUORS.**		Arthur	Thane
Ann	Locket	Rosina	Wines	Anna	Templar
James	Busk	Alfred	Wine	Fred	Monarch
Robert	Coat	Robert	Port	Bessie	Royal
George	Jacket	John	Sherry	Charlotte	Crown
Neesom	Vest	Hewlett	Claret	Thomas	Throne
Lydia	Hose	Jean Leon	Champagne	Albert	Rex

3 I

Sabra   State
Ernest   Rank
Daniel   Court
Elizabeth   Chancellor
Lavinia   Chamberlain
Bridget   Judge
Herbert   Law
Joseph   Justice
Bell Small   Counsellor
Sarah   Serjeant

MONEY, WEIGHTS, & MEASURES.

Margaret   Coin
Deborah   Cash
Jemima   Money
Johanna   Guinea
William   Pound
Charlotte   Crown
Thomas   Halfcrown
Charles   Shilling
Patrick   Sixpence
Joanna   Penny
George   Halfpenny
Issachar   Farthing
William   Twopenny
Martin   Mark
Capon   Noble
Elizabeth   Tester
Agnes   Ducat
Sarah   Guilder
James   Real
Edward   Weight
Matthew   Measures
Elizabeth   Anker
Selina   Butt
Joseph   Bushel
Rosa   Pipe
Jane   Gallon
William   Firkin
Louisa   Measure
Isaac   Gill
James   Pottle
Laura   Peck
Ann   Milestone
Charles   Mile
Charles   Acres
Maria   Cubit
Frederick   Furlong
Elizabeth   Yard
Richard   Ell
Josiah   Inch
Isabella   Inches
Edith   Foot
Christopher   Nail
Ann   Pole
James   Rood
Matthew   Perch
Francis   Rod
William   Pace
Mary   Weigh
Croat   Stone
Robert   Wey
William   Tod
Thomas   Load
Alpha   Last
Jemima   Truss
William   Pound
Thomas   Reams
William   Quire
Amos   Barrel
John   Boll
Eliza   Tons

THE WEATHER, &C.

Joseph   Element
Godfrey   Air
Robert   Cloud
Alice   Dew
Richard   Fog
Robert   Sky

John   Mist
Judith   Frost
J. Frost   Hoar
Mary   Freeze
Janet   Thaw
Rachel   Sleet
Ebenezer   Hail
John   Hailstorm
Ann   Hailstone
Editha   Snow
Julia   Breeze
Jonas   Gale
Margaret   Wind
Hannah   Rain
Eliza   Showers
Sarah   Storm
Thomas   Tempest
Lucy   Thunder
Ellen   Lightning
Cecily   Rainbow
Edwin   Sunshine
J. Squires   Dawn
Bridget   Morn
Overman   Day
Time of   Day
Ann   Morning
Martin   Noon
Mathews   Evening
Thirza   Night
Gallop Sampson Moon
Eliza   Star
Laurence   Stars
Sebras   Manyweathers

FIGURES, &C.

Elizabeth   Cypher
Aaron   Unit
Emma   Ace
Richard   Deuce
Ann   Tray
Caroline   Two
Martha   Twelves
Sarah   Eighteen
William   Score
Thomas   Twentyman
Ellen   Forty
David   Gross
Jabez   Million
Eliza   Billion
Rose   Even
Henry   Odd
Vincent   Pair
Abram   Double

TIMES AND SEASONS.

Mary   Season
Henry   Spring
Jane   Summer
Gilbert   Winter
John   January
Harriet   March
Rose   May
Ann   June
Richard   July
Hannah   Monday
Phillis   Friday
Samuel   Saturday
Overman   Day
Thirza   Night
Maria   Daily
Ann   Halfnight
Sophia   Morrow
Charity   Weeks
Martin   Weekly
Walter   Yearly
Alice   Halfyear
Emma   Feveryear
Emma   Longyear
Mary   Twoyearold
Daniel   Christmas

William   Christmasday
Clara   Easter
William   Lent
Philadelphia   Pentecost
William   Lammas

COMMERCE, &C.

Clementia   Trader
Tom   Buy
Charles   Sell
Joseph   Buyer
               Seller
Mary   Selling
Edgar   Price
Mary   Cost
Emma   Charge
Alice   Fare
Amos   Barter
Mary   Purchase
Rose   Pay
Matthew   Fee
Sarah   Gain
Jane   Fines
Martha   Ransom
Ellen   Bonus
Francis   Rent
Crincklay   Rate
Enos   Bond
Harriet   Check
Sarah   Bills
William   Stamps
John   Share
John   Surety
John   Thrift
Charlotte   Sale
Emily   Salvage
Thomas   Sample
George   Scrip
John   Loan
Charles   Borrow

PARTICIPLES AND VERBS.

Rebecca   Bolting
Amelia   Bending
John   Shearing
Emily   Boiling
Harriet   Buzzing
Michael   Bristling
Ann   Curling
Sarah   Cooling
Maria   Chewing
Charles   Cutting
Fanny   Dunning
James   Diving
Mary   Daring
Robert   Fanning
Jabez   Gambling
Ann   Gilding
John   Harrowing
Ann   Hooting
Emma   Hopping
Ann   Healing
Sarah   Hunting
Christiana   Lowing
George   Moulding
Hannah   Making
Maria   Nodding
Ruth   Painting
Mary   Pealing
Sarah   Panting
Henry   Pointing
Martha   Patching
Samuel   Picking
William   Pinching
Margaret   Riding
George   Rolling
Mary   Rusting
Mary   Raving
Lydia   Rowing
Hannah   Rising

James	Slaving
Mary	Selling
Enos	Standing
Mary	Scolding
Elizabeth	Swearing
Sarah	Suckling
John	Skinning
Mary	Telling
Jacob	Wailing
Lawrence	Winning
Henry	Weaving
Jane	Sings
Louisa	Pinches
Charles	Blows
William	Stamps
Eustace	Bounds
Robert	Stumbles
Emma	Swindles
William	Winks
Mary	Peeps
Ann	Squints
Richard	Shakes
Mary	Waits
Samuel	Walks
Robert	Smiles
John	Stammers
Selina	Chatters
Louisa	Skates
Ann	Wanders
Catharine	Judges
Matthew	Measures
Henry	Etches
Kate	Helps
John	Skins
Terrier	Shears
Frederick	Bellows
Alice	Bangs
Thomas	Catch
James	Caught
Fanny	Call
Charity	Came
Dorcas	Hide
Leonard	Seek
James	Gave
John	Took
John	Keep
Philip	Went
Elizabeth	Found
George	Look
Leah	Saw
Mary	See
John	Gaze
Mary	Lear
David	Ogle
James	Peer
Ann	Stare
Mahala	Wink

ADJECTIVES, &C.

Francis	Sturdy
Dinah	Hardy
Lucy	Lusty
Honor	Doughty
Charlotte	Haughty
Ann	Burley
John	Lofty
Ann	Heavy
Sarah	Dainty
Sarah	Weakly
Alfred	Jolly
Edith	Witty
Emma	Merry
John	Musty
Charles	Tidy
Gertrude	Weary
Peter	Worthy
Eleanor	Ready
Berdilia	Pretty
John	Lovely
Sarah	Lucky

James	Happy
James	Hasty
John	Handy
William	Gory
Anny	Giddy
Susan	Dowdy
Richard	Bully
Thomas	Easy
Lydia	Friendly
Maria	Busy
Dan	Bandy
Reuben	Bright
Ann	Clear
Eliza	Fair
Philip	Light
Robert	Dark
George	Darker
Michael	Fairer
Emily	Grand
Alexander	Great
William	Glorious
H. Magnus	Little
Jewson	Large
Sophia	Small
Ellen	Soar
Sabina	High
Rachel	Height
John	Lofty
Fanny	Low
Latter	Lower
Philip	Light
Ann	Heavy
Edward	Weight
James	Wide
Jonas	Broad
George	Strait
Giddy	Thick
Abraham	Long
Silas	Short
Emily	Shorter
Agnes	Tall
Ann	Loose
Caroline	Slack
William	Supple
Alfred	Stretch
Ezra	Tight
Ann	Stiff
Edward	Hard
Hannibal	Rough
John	Brittle
Charlotte	Crisp
H. Giddy	Thick
Miriam	Blunt
Tempest	Sharp
Lydia	Keen
Susannah	Sever
James	Jagged
John	Slim
Metcalf	Slight
George	Slender
Salley	Spare
Jacob	Lean
Emma	Delicate
Walter	Gaunt
Cecilia	Haggard
Walker	Faint
Zaccur	Worn
Mary	Tremble
Dinah	Meek
Zelia	Humble
Beatrice	Tame
Edith	Crouch
Lucy	Craven
Hugh	Coward
John	Fears
George	Fail
Jacob	Funk
Mary	Flee
Martha	Fright
Mary	Flight

Gertrude	Weary
George	Neat
Thomas	Smart
William	Spruce
Charles	Tidy
Julia	Trim
Elizabeth	Beau
Charles	Dandy
Judith	Trollop
Elizabeth	Tatters

SINGULAR OCCUPATIONS, &C.

Martha	Pincher
Isaac	Springer
Seth	Gamester
George	Tippler
Isabella	Sitter
Elizabeth	Swearer
Mary	Smiter
Robert	Wooer
Ann	Medler
Joseph	Smoker
Moses	Clever
Rhoda	Bragger
Elizabeth	Bouncer
Elizabeth	Croaker
Enoch	Belcher
James	Bruiser
James	Hanger
Nathan	Snapper
Thomas	Laugher
Martha	Leader
Maria	Lover
Arscott	Maker
David	Partner
Catmore	Stranger

MUCH ADO !

John	Freak
Selma	Fray
Charles	Fuss
Sarah	Pother
Ann	Row
Louisa	Rout
Peter	Scuffle
Sarah	Spree
Eliza	Fudge
Neighbour	Gammon
Ann	Mummery
Robert	Cant
Sarah	Linge
Sarah	Tattle
Robert	Twaddle
Mary	Chaff
Joseph	Scandal
John	Quirk
Eleanor	Sully
Harry	Ruse
Eliza	Gossip

THE VOICE, &C.

Joseph	Voice
Elizabeth	Tone
Francis	Melody
Nicholas	Silence
John	Music
George	Tune
Joshua	Sing
Victor	Sang
Kate	Carol
Elizabeth	Bass
Mary	Ask
Edwin	Say
Susy	Speak
Margaret	Spake
Robert	Shout
William	Yell
Miriam	Howl
Angelina	Clack
Charles	Purr

Jane	Mutter
William	Grumble
Margaret	Croak
Louisa	Screech
Franz	Hum
Catherine	Stutter
Thomas	Stammer
Betty	Titter
Husey	Heard
John	Belch
Florence	Gape
	Bark
Frank	Bray
Harriet	Ring
Benjamin	Rumble
Emma	Giggle

ACTS, MOTIONS, &c.

Jessie	Sleep
Catherine	Doze
Mary	Nap
Maria	Nodding
Mary	Wake
Reuben	Strong
Sarah	Strength
Matthew	Stout
Bridget	Bold
Thomas	Bluff
Charlotte	Bravery
William	Gallant
Priscilla	Danger
James	Courage
James	Gallantry
Ralph	Hale
Judith	Daunt
Bernard	Dare
Luke	Fearnot
David	Power
George	Rash
Eliza	Reckless
Hiram	Steady
Helen	Motion
Margaret	Hop
Sarah	Skip
Peter	Jump
George	Start
Peter	Dart
William	Sprang
Martha	Bound
Doretta	Rush
Ann	Walk
Sarah	Waddle
Susan	Dash
Elias	Glide
Jonathan	Stamp
Joseph	Step
Leonard	Stride
Harriet	Wade
Tamar	Gait
Clement	Fell
John	Trip

GAMBLING, &c.

Walter	Game
Phœbe	Gamble
Ellen	Gambling
Thomas	Swindle
Cornelia	Chance
Matilda	Hazard
Joseph	Faro
Ann	Sleight
A. Godly	Luck
Edward	Raffle
Rebecca	Billiards
Mary	Skittles
Priscilla	Cue
Emma	Chess
Charles	Die
Thomas	Dice
Elizabeth	Trick

Lucy	Trump
Peter	Wager
Mary	Winner

QUALITIES, VERBS, &c.

Clement	Rich
James	Wealthy
Harry	Richer
Jabez	Riches
Emma	Richman
Hannah	Poor
Caroline	Want
Francis	Need
Mary	Mean
Anna	Stern
William	Huff
James	Wrath
Ellen	Tiff
William	Wroth
Faith	Cross
Mary	Taunt
Martha	Cavil
Ann	Pester
Constance	Goad
Maria	Spurn
John	Quarrel
Peggy	Pinch
John	Pinchus
Thomas	Tickle
James	Tingle
Thomas	Smart
Samuel	Hurt
Charles	Pain
Elizabeth	Shove
Royall	Pull
Emma	Kick
James	Crack
David	Beat
Ann	Maul
Kate	Knock
Joseph	Blow
Mary	Batter
Susan	Crush
John	Douse
Carne	Pick
Aaron	Cleave
Harry	Clench
Charles	Hack
William	Strip
William	Wrench
Edward	Stripe
Gertrude	Strike
Honora	Burk
Hannah	Stick
Margaret	Fury
Giles	Savage
William	Strangleman
Emma	Stuck
Catherine	Stab
Susan	Duel
Ralph	Slay
James	Slain
Abram	Kill
Hannah	Slaughter
Thomas	Spite
George	Malice
Sarah	Fleet
Ralph	Swift
James	Haste
Mary	Hurry
Robert	Quick
Charlotte	Brisk
Ann	Speed
John	Slow
Sarah	Tarry
Walter	Delay
Elizabeth	Saunter
Emma	Moist
Charlotte	Dry
Eva	Damp

Harold	Damper

RIVERS.

Lydia	Rivers
Rebecca	Yare
Michael	Boyne
Noah	Cam
Caroline	Dee
Eliza	Derwent
Arthur	Dart
Eliza	Medway
Iram	Hull
Julia	Shannon
Alice	Tay
Elizabeth	Trent
Sarah	Tyne
Selina	Tweed
Emma	Humber
Hannah	Severn
Eliza	Tees
Rebecca	Thame
Charlotte	Nile
Patrick	Rhine
Jeremiah	Don
Rhodia	Jordan

MOUNTAINS.

Alfred	Mountain
Margaret	Snowdon
Arthur	Alps

NATIONALITIES, &c.

Talitha Cumi	People
Ann	Tribe
Job	English
Ellen	Irish
Trebilcock	Cornish
Thomas	Kentish
Peter	Welsh
James	Scotchman
John	Indian
Thersa	German
Master David	Norman
Jerry	Saxon
Peter	Roman
Ebenezer	French
Cornelius	Dutch
Susanna	Briton
Maria	Hollander
William	Dutchman
Jacob	Jew
Elizabeth	Jewess
Luke Potts	Pole
Phœbe	Dane
Rebecca	Turk
Ralph	Moor
Clement	Caffre
Giles	Savage
David	Wildman
Edward	Pagan
Mary	Heathen
Sarah	Christian
Martha	Morman
Catherine	Baptist

RELATIONSHIPS AND CONDITIONS IN LIFE.

Agloie	Parent
Dear	Offspring
Fanny	Kindred
Thomas	Kinsman
William	Stranger
Jeremiah	Friend
Ellen	Neighbour
Mary	Brotherhood
Hannah	Folk
Joseph	Folks
George	Fathers
Jane	Mothers
Richard	Uncle

Hannah	Uncles	Horatio	Collier	Drewry	Ostler
Phillis	Daughters	Thomas	Coalman	Samuel	Waiter
Amy	Widows	Miriam	Dyer	Mary	Boots
Sarah	Cousin	James	Stainer	Samuel	Seaman
Pilate	Cousins	Solomon	Tanner	Charles	Mariner
Lois	Brothers	Kate	Currier	Naomi	Waterman
Samuel	Sire	Peter	Skinner	Zaccheus	Ferryman
Samuel	Daddy	Caroline	Flesher	Elizabeth	Boatman
John	Husband	Moses	Butcher	Caroline	Mate
Ellen	Man	Hough N.	Baker	Isaac	Purser
Vincent	Male	Molly	Miller	Elizabeth	Skipper
William	Manhood	Joseph	Bellman	Susannah	Boatwright
Sarah	Bachelor	Robert	Ringer	Ann	Diver
Jonathan	Gent	Philip	Bellringer	Esther	Minion
Charles	Oldman	Edward	Sweeper	Henry	Miser
Martin	Newman	Sarah	Washer	Fanny	Roue
Agnes	Youngman	Elizabeth	Clothier	Joseph	Corsair
Mary	Youngson	William	Tailor	Everatt	Major
Julia	Dame	Caroline	Hatter	Lucy	Officer
James	Spouse	Joseph	Hosier	William	Commander
Thirza	Bride	Onesimus	Glover	Ebenezer	Farmer
Sarah	Virgin	Martha	Mercer	David	Gardener
Henry	Wench	Alice	Milliner	Monica	Shepherd
Mary	Maid	Rhoda	Draper	Thomas	Ploughman
Elizabeth	Maiden	Seth	Weaver	Henry	Mower
Newborn	Child	George	Carder	John	Thresher
Sarah	Children	Aaron	Thrower	Charles	Shearer
Martin	Littlechild	Anne	Trimmer	Arthur	Woodman
Henry	Boy	Herbert	Carter	Sarah	Ranger
Horace	Boys	Tom	Carrier	John	Warrener
Mary	Littleboy	Margaret	Carman	Jane	Forester
Maria	Oddboy	Luke	Driver	James	Herdsman
Kate	Stripling	Isabella	Stoker	Jacob	Hind
Abel	Bastard	Lucy	Brazier	Jesse	Swain
Thomas	Heir	Thomas	Staymaker	Martin	Grazier
Sarah	Ward	Thomas	Ploughwright	Thomas	Drover
William	Orphan	John	Brewer	Robert	Hedger
Thomas	Foundling	Eliza	Malster	Mary	Hewer
George	Godson	Lucina	Tapster	Alfred	Yeoman
Michael	Twin	Roger	Roper	Oswald	Hunter
Emma	Brat	Peter	Fisher	Ann	Huntsman
Hannah	Baby	Reuben	Pinner	Kesiah	Fowler
Susan	Girl	Eliza	Bathmaker	James	Falconer
William	Sisterson	Carter	Barber	Zadock	Barker
Laura	Masters	William	Broker	Martha	Provost
		Jabez	Cartwright	Richard	Mayor
OCCUPATIONS, EMPLOYMENTS,		Edwin	Wainwright	Elizabeth	Sheriff
AND OFFICES.		Kerenhappuch	Wheelwright	Ann	Alderman
Betty	Workman	Jeffery	Chandler	Ralph	Citizen
Amy	Foreman	Lea	Cooper	Phœbe	Freeman
Richard	Builder	James	Cryer	Leah	Burgess
Hezekiah	Mason	Dinah	Stamper	Eliza	Constable
Tom	Carpenter	Ralph	Fuller	Ann	Gailor
Benjamin	Sawyer	Luke	Sadler	Joseph	Watchman
Sarah	Joiner	Kersey	Potter	Alfred	Warder
Dolly	Slater	Joseph	Paviour	Edward	Warden
Hodges	Thatcher	Elijah	Packer	Lavinia	Chamberlain
Mary	Tiler	Jasper	Fletcher	William	Marshal
Alice	Hodman	Thomas	Moulder	Aaron	Usher
Jonas	Turner	Joseph	Fidler	John	Scrivener
Joseph	Painter	*Diehappy*	Harper	Maria	Clerk
Elizabeth	Glazier	Edward	Player	Mary	Scholar
Laban	Plumber	Thomas	Bugler	Rosanna	Herald
Sabina	Carver	Luke	Dancer	Ann	Courtier
Sarah	Gilder	Louisa	Piper	Isaac	Pothecary
Susan	Printer	Eliel	Singer	Ralph	Proctor
Joseph	Binder	Sarah	Servant	Mary	Chymist
Alfred	Goldsmith	Isabella	Steward	Amos	Cupper
Edwin	Ironmonger	Uriah	Butler	Charles	Artist
Samuel	Cutler	Emma	Coachman	Josiah	Merchant
Eli	Nailer	Peter	Footman	Sarah	Traveller
Mary	Plater		Varlet	James	Pilgrim
Comfort	Smith	Francis	Lackey	Charles	Rover
Cordelia	Shoesmith	Long	Page	Cleophas	Rider
George	Farrier	Agnes	Nurse	Fanny	Messenger
Ben	Tinker	Martha	Dresser	William	Agent
Sarah	Hawker	Bathsheba	Cook	Elizabeth	Bard
Coom	Pedlar	Ellen	Scullion	Charles	Poet
Fred	Chapman	Joyce	Porter	Anne	Reader
William	Miner	Eliza	Groom	Mary	Rhymer

Maria	Boxer
Rhoda	Witch
Amy	Wizard
Rose	Harlot
James	Gamester
Solomon	Teacher

PERSONAL NAMES.

Albert	Eden
	Paradise
Sophia	Adam
Lucy	Eve
Rose	Cain
Robert	Abel
Aaron	Moses
Mark	Aaron
Austin	Abraham
Mary	Israel
Job	Jacob
David	Absalom
James	Elisha
Emmanuel	Enoch
George	Boaz
Fanny	Ruth
Joseph	Leah
George	Hagar
Nicholas	Job
William	Japheth
Laura	Jeremiah
Coleman	Jael
William	Noah
John	Pharaoh
Charles	Potipher
Judah	Solomon
Emma	Jesse
Jenkin	David
David	Saul
John	Shadrach
Daniel	Daniel
Anne	Lot
Isaiah	Isaiah
William	Joshua
Richard	Jehu
Evelina	Elias
Maria	Sampson
Bessy	Balaam
Sarah	Goliah
Mary	Gomer
Lawrence	Dives
	Lazarus
John	Zachariah
Thomas	Zebedee
Thomas	Jude
Edward	Gabriel
Sarah	Bartholomew
Ann	Mathias
Charles	Herod
David	Matthew
Martin	Mark
Norcliffe	Luke
Happy	John
Alfred	Bobby
Emily	Tommy
John	Charley
Henry	Jackey
Elizabeth	Paddy
Roger	Harry
William	Toby
Mary	Robin
Magdalene	Jack
Tamsine	Ben
Sampson	Bill
John	Dick
Mary	Tom
Elizabeth	Will
Tom	Dan
Rebecca	Rob
William	Teddy
Elizabeth	Alfred
Mary	Josiah

Elizabeth	Joachim
Aspasia	Anthony
Jane	Arthur
Joachim	Adolphus
Richard	Albert
Amelia	Ambrose
Abraham	Amos
William	Augustus
Gracious	Abrahams
Bett	Boniface
Ann	Bardolph
Emma	Baptist
Walter	Benedict
Mary	Bertram
Benjamin	Benjamin
Jabez	Charles
Laura	Christopher
David	Clement
Emma	Colin
Louisa	Cornelius
Anthony	Constantine
Ann	Dunstan
Rebecca	Douglas
John	Edmond
Thomas	Edward
Anna	Edmund
Elizabeth	Ebenezer
Rees	Emanuel
John	Eustace
Harriet	Eugene
John	Edgar
Emma	Edwin
William	Frank
Alfred	Ferdinand
Mary	Frederick
Medium	Francis
Jane	Felix
Emanuel	Gideon
King	George
Prudence	Gerard
Uriah	Guy
David	Henry
Mary	Hugo
John	Herbert
Theodore	Jaques
Joseph	Jasper
Sarah	Jesse
George	Josiah
Job	James
Frances	Julian
Alxina	Jago
Ann	Jacks
Caroline	Jerome
Appleby	Joseph
William	Jonas
Margaret	Jonathan
Mary	Ludwig
Alma	Lewis
William	Louis
Elijah	Manuel
Mahala	Martin
Harriet	Maurice
Peter	Michael
Andrew	Oliver
Saint	Paul
John	Peter
Elsie	Philip
Evan	Robert
Rees	Roderick
Nicholas	Victor
Leveson	Randolph
Owen	Rowland
John	Ralph
John	Richard
David	Samuel
Emily	Sidney
Sarah	Simon
Peter	Stephen
Charles	Theobald
Joseph	Theodore

Timothy	Theophilus
Bezaleel	Thomas
Mary	Timothy
Cudlip	Valentine
Ann	Vincent
Ann	William
Suffolk	Walter
Catherine	Betty
Bessy	Biddy
Ann	Madge
George	Moll
Thomas	Nell
Frances	Poll
Eliza	Patty
Henry	Polly
James	Amy
Edwin	Ann
George	Annie
Sarah	Blanch
James	Caroline
Anthony	Charlotte
Stopher	Charity
Martha	Constance
Emma	Catharine
Roseanna	Columbine
Eleanor	Eleanor
Segar	Elizabeth
Ann	Ellen
Thomas	Esther
Richard	Eva
Ann	Ellinor
Emma	Florence
Selina	Frances
Kate	Fanny
Selina	Flora
Ann	Grace
Elizabeth	Helen
Margaret	Hannah
Eliza	Hester
Sugar	Jane
Martha	Janet
William	Kathleen
Mary	Lucy
Margery	Mercy
Joseph	Marie
Ann	Maud
Fanny	Margery
Victor	Nancy
Esther	Prudence
Lavinia	Rose
John	Rachel
Fanny	Sarah
Ann	Susan
Simmy	Bensusan
Maria	Phœbe
Edwin	Xerxes
Charles	Bacchus
William	Cupid
Isabella	Venus
Thomas	Mars
Amos	Charon
Richard	Daphne
John	Hector
Morgan	Ajax
William	Priam
Daniel	Cæsar
Camillus	Brutus
Maria	Plato
Alfred	Cato
Daniel	Titus
Victoria	Fabian
James	Hannibal
Samuel	Scipio
Eliza	Livy
Vincenzo	Themistocle
Anthony	Damon
Edgar	Crispin
Tom	Dominey
John	Rufus
Treasure	Tudor

Ann	Luther
John	Demetrius
Catherine	Phœnix

THINGS COMESTIBLE AND POTABLE.

James	Food
Inkerman	Dinner
Edith	Luneh
Thomas	Dine
Emma	Feast
Edwin	Meats
Fanny	Fish
Robert	Flesh
Frederick	Fowl
Benjamin	Game
Rebecca	Lamb
Polly	Mutton
Esther	Veal
Jacob Choke	Lambshead
Edmund	Roast
Simon	Fry
Pharaoh	Bacon
Jane	Brawn
Sidney	Ham
Elizabeth	Coldham
Louisa	Chicken
Joseph	Hogsflesh
Dorothy	Curry
Jonathan	Stew
Johanna	Pottage
John	Peasoop
Amelia	Marrow
Eliza	Patty
George	Parsley
James	Leek
Singular	Onion
Sophia	Garlick
David	Carrot
Lucy	Cabbage
Jane	Pease
Charlotte	Bean
Dinah	Rice
John	Sago
Jessie	Onions
John	Capers
Jacob	Girkin
Charles	Tiffin
John	Sage
Charlotte	Savory
Frederick	Spice
Horace	Pepper
Dorah	Salt
Jemima	Mustard
Miles	Mace
Thomas	Ginger
Joshua	Peppercorn
John	Tart
Thomas	Custard
John	Jelly
William	Jellies
Young	Pickles
Thomas	Cheese
Charles	Olives
Amos	Almond
William	Raisin
Elizabeth	Nut
Louisa	Chesnut
Mary	Orange
Joseph	Melon
Rodolph	Plum
James	Peach
Thomas	Pear
Cooper	Cherry
Henry	Grapes
Aaron	Lemon
Emily	Date
William	Shaddock
Charlotte	Mulberry
Arthur	Quince
William	Sweetapple
John	Codling
Harriet	Pippin
Mark	Currant
William	Gourd
Ann	Medlar
Samuel	Pears
George	Tea
Ellen	Coffee
Mary	Sugar
Job	Butter
Sally	Milk
Mary	Cream
Christian	Honey
Ruth	Candy
Ruth	Muffin
Isaac	Sop
Samuel	Rusk
Harriet	Loaf
William	Roll
Emela	Crust
Philip	Crumb
Amelia	Cake
Alfred	Cakebread
Jack	Curd
Benjamin	Whey
Esther	Caudle
Leah	Eggs
Delia	Dough
Mary	Meal
Mercy	Rolls
Arthur	Egg
Josiah	Lard

TOPOGRAPHICAL TERMS.

Ruth	Land
George	Ground
Lydia	Earth
Andrew	Mould
Sophia	Shale
Sarah	Sandy
Harry	Earthy
William	Dryland
John	Claypit
Emily	Dust
Henry	Gravel
Phineas	Peat
David	Cornfield
Susan	Hayfield
Jane	Fallowfield
Peter	Highfield
Zemira	Field
David	Fields
Charles	Mead
Kerenhappuch	Meadows
Fanny	Cowmeadow
Deborah	Downs
James	Plain
Louisa	Warren
Lister	Lea
Charity	Common
Joseph	Moat
Emily	Ditch
Herbert	Dyke
Henry	Foss
Marion	Dykes
Joseph	Furrows
William	Pit
Deborah	Burrow
Lucinda	Garden
Horatio	Orchard
Fanny	Vineyard
William	Arbour
Timothy	Bower
Edwin	Grove
Michael	Croft
William	Crop
Emmeline	Sheaf
Easter	Rick
Emmeline	Stack
Maria	Haycock
William	Valley
Uriah	Vale
Edwin	Dingle
Edward	Ravine
Sarah	Dale
Catherine	Glen
Daniel	Dell
Julia	Gully
Lystria	Hollow
Francis	Den
Peter	Hole
Sarah	Mines
Thomas	Quarry
James	Fen
Virginia	Marsh
Dancer	Moor
Ellen	Thicket
Pelina	Wood
Sidonia	Woodland
Samuel	Forest
Jael	Brake
John	Road
E. Hinder	Way
Harriet	Highway
Rosina	Lane
Conker Kooley	Alley
Lucy	Park
Emily	Lawn
Isaiah	Paddock
Sarah	Hedge
Timothy	Hill
William	Mount
Joshua	Mountain
W. Windy	Bank
Fanny	Heap
Thomas	Knoll
Michael	Cairns
Zilla	Barrow
Emma	Ridge
John	Coast
Hester	Shore
Elam	Beach
Josiah	Rock
Betty	Cliff
Leir	Sands
Harriet	Cave
Robert	Cape
Caroline	Foreland
Augustus	Bay
Francis	Beacon
Frances	Creek
James	Isle
Peggy	Eddy
Oliver	Frith
Charles	Harbour
Harriet	Havens
Clara	Rivers
Leolin	Wells
Matrona	Bourn
Patty	Ford
Mary	Wellspring
Edward	Ferry
Oldfield	Brook
Thomas	Stream
John	Pond
Ashey	Pool
Richard	Puddle
George	Horsepool
William	Lough
Maria	Lake
George	Waterfall
Jennet	Weir
Mary	Gate
Harriet	Stiles
Jane	Folds
Thomas	Hives
Thomas	Teams
Jane	Ricks
William	Sheaves

PARTS OF THE BODY, &C.

Thomas	Body
Mary	Corpse
Joseph	Carcass
John	Deadman
Cornelius	Head
Mary	Eyes
Thomas	Face
Margaret	Tear
Joseph	Temple
Charles	Tongue
John	Tooth
	Gum
David	Cheek
Elizabeth	Chin
Betsy	Brain
Jane	Brow
Charles	Pate
Miles	Skull
Hannah	Sconce
Edward	Noddle
Frances	Poll
Ann	Halfhead
Eliza	Hair
Angelina	Beard
Mary	Whisker
John	Neck
Rhoda	Bust
Alford	Arm
Harriet	Hand
Sarah	Fist
Elizabeth	Wrist
Jane	Back
Edwin	Side
John	Collarbone
Tom	Loins
Mary	Teat
Thomas	Bellies
Mary	Heart
George	Bowels
Nicholas	Gut
Susan	Liver
Aaron	Gall
John	Kidney
Jemima	Caul
John	Rump
Jane	Limb
Walter	Joint
Virtue	Bone
Rachel	Bones
Fanny	Allbones
John	Leg
Harvey	Foot
John	Toe
Caroline	Heel
Sarah	Sole
Henry	Knee
Louisa	Kneebone
Elfrida	Calf
George	Shanks
Jane	Spittle
Margaret	Urine
Jesse	Blood
James	Gore
Martha	Marrow
Benjamin	Lean
Dorcas	Hide
Mary	Halfhide
Jane	Skin
Roda	Shank
Daniel	Hough
Esther	Hoof
Job	Withers
Jonas	Whalebelly
Charles	Pluck
Martha	Beak
Mary	Wing
George	Pinion
George	Birdseye
Margaret	Ear

SHIPS AND THEIR ASSOCIATIONS.

Emma	Ship
Sarah	Fleet
Jane	Boat
John	Hulk
James	Galley
Robert	Craft
Hannah	Cutter
Josephine	Lugger
James	Punt
Mary	Tug
Thomas	Barge
Daniel	Hoy
John	Wherry
James	Sail
Herbert	Bunting
William	Log
Martha	Chart
Mary	Tug
Alice	Rope
Ann	Cable
Mary	Deck
Brian	Helm
William	Rudder
James	Tiller
Shadrach	Steer
Emily	Keel
Jacob	Hull
Anna	Stern
Cornelius	Anchor
John	Flukes
Charlotte	Boom
Alfred	Mizen
George	Locker
Melody	Luff
Edmund	Oar
Elizabeth	Paddle
Jane	Scull
Sarah	Crew
Jane	Cruise
Samuel	Seaman
Charles	Mariner
Isaac	Purser
Olive	Port
Charles	Harbour
Thomas	Quay
Emy	Wharf

BIRDS.

Maria	Fowls
Julia	Game
Albert	Birds
Royal	Bird
Enoch	Eagle
Sampson	Kite
Edward	Stork
Nicholas	Heron
Christopher	Falcon
Eliza	Goshawk
Mary	Sparrowhawk
Beghum	Crane
Jane	Buzzard
Elijah	Raven
Clara	Goldfinch
Alfred	Blackbird
Catherine	Linnet
George	Thrush
Walter	Finch
Eleanor	Pyefinch
Charlotte	Lark
Ethalinda	Nightingale
Eonoch	Woodcock
Sophia	Pheasant
Nathaniel	Partridge
Ann	Quail
Alfred	Teal
Arthur	Snipe
Mary	Marten
John	Titmouse

Ruth	Starling
Thomas	Swallow
Seth	Sparrow
Dean	Swift
Daniel	Wren
Mary	Robin
Hester	Jay
Vertue	Daw
Catherine	Rook
Emma	Gull
Ruth	Crow
Spouse	Dove
Thomas	Pigeon
Henry	Ruff
Elizabeth	Parrot
Ralph	Peacock
Richard	Cuckoo
Catherine	Crake
George	Coot
Pamela	Booby
Ruth	Swan
Maria	Wildgoose
Norman	Goose
George	Gander
J. Swallow	Gosling
Lilias	Duck
Ralph	Drake
Benjamin	Mallard
Charity	Cock
Rachael	Capon
Joseph	Bantam
Richard	Chick
John	Chicken
Joanna	Duckling

QUADRUPEDS, &C.

Joseph	Brute
Rhoda	Lion
Saint Michael	Lions
George	Panther
Edwin	Leopard
Elizabeth	Wolf
Lydia	Boar
Edward	Wildboar
Henry	Bear
Mary	Camel
Louisa	Morse
Emily	Seal
James	Turtle
Thomas	Beaver
Francis	Badger
Betty	Fox
Caroline	Fitchew
Mary	Otter
Charlotte	Sable
John	Stoat
Sophia	Musk
Pariah	Mole
Rachel	Elks
Johnson	Stag
Pamela	Roe
Malachi	Hart
Jacob	Hind
John	Roebuck
Edward	Deer
Edmund	Buck
Loftus	Doe
Thomas	Fawn
Betsy	Rabbit
Sarah	Rabbits
Emma	Coney
Asenath	Hare
Amelia	Hares
William	Leveret
Ellen	Ox
Lucy	Bull
Sampson	Bullock
Emma	Cow
Elfrida	Calf
Clement	Steer

Charlotte	Stallion	
Horatio	Mare	
Grace	Foal	
Aaron	Steed	
Joseph	Hack	
Philip	Palfrey	
James	Pony	
William	Colt	
George	Mules	
Stephen	Swine	
Phineas	Pig	
Walter	Porker	
Alma	Cur	
William	Setter	
Harry	Pointer	
John	Beagle	
Thomas	Goat	
Merelthalfcar	Lamb	
Martha	Lambkin	
Catherine	Ram	
Joanna	Cats	
Ann	Puss	
Sarah	Mouse	

INSECTS & REPTILES.

Foster	Cricket
Timothy	Beetle
Simeon	Emmet
Nancy	Blackadder
Elizabeth	Vipers
Elia	Worm
Ann	Bug
John	Flea
John	Moth
William	Wasp
Charles	Hornet
Edward	Bee
Michael	Fly
Thomas	Grub
Matthew	Mite

FISHES.

Jennett	Fish
Pamela	Shark
William	Sturgeon
George	Dolphin
Rose	Salmon
Joseph	Turbot
Uriah	Ray
Hubert	Hake
Catharine	Tunny
Emma	Ling
Frank	Herring
Lydia	Whiting
Ralph	Haddock
Penninah	Pike
Eleanor	Gudgeon
Kitty	Roach
Thomas	Dace
Edward	Tench
Eliza	Carp
Francis	Smelt
Mahala	Trout
Ellen	Bucktrout
Sarah	Sole
Harry	Flounders
Mary	Maid
Robert	Plaice
Fanny	Brill
Charles	Bream

Francis	Mullet
Samuel	Gurnet
Ann	Thornback
Joseph	Grayling
Alfred	Par
John	Lamprey
Rachel	Leech
Henry	Mussel
Philip	Oyster
Joseph	Pearl
Emma	Barnacle
Mary	Cockle
Gotobed	Crab
Joseph	Cuttle

COUNTRIES, PLACES, &C.

Ellen	World
Lydia	Earth
Charles	Globe
Robert	Nation
James	Kingdom
Florence	States
James	Albion
Minnie	Britain
Victoria	England
Brittania	Ireland
Caroline	Wales
John	Orkney
Adam	France
Edward	Gaul
James	Spain
Richard	Russia
James	Prussia
John	Norway
Daniel	Holland
Sarah	Denmark
Mary	Poland
John	Hanover
Joseph	Faro
Lucy	Greenland
William	Barbary
Amos	Cashmere
Jackson	Congo
James	Candy
John	China
Charlotte	City
Hester	Paris
Thomas	Seville
Sarah	Rome
Sarah	Canton
William	Milan
Emma	Florence
Sarah	Ghent
John	Baden
Ann	Lisle
Patrick	Rouen
Mary	Caen
Henrietta	Nantes
John	Waterloo
Edward	Nice
Mary	Marienburg
Victor	Nancy
Fanny	Cambray
Isaac	Ancona
Kate	Lima
Francis	Revel
John	Washington
Robert	Melbourne
Emily	Sydney
Johnson	Galilee
James	Calvary

Harriet	Gath
James	Troy
Henry	Shires
Maria	Shire
Bartholomew	County
Alfred	Berkshire
Rebecca	Cheshire
Colin	Derbyshire
Harriet	Devonshire
Farewell	Hampshire
Sarah	Lancashire
Martha	Shropshire
Simon	Wiltshire
Richard	Warwickshire
David	Cornwall
Philip	Essex
John	Anglesea
Sarah	Durham
Phillis	Kent
Harriot	Norfolk
Ann	Suffolk
Reuben	Rutland
Ann	Sussex
Ellen	Northumberland
John	Dorset
James	Westmorland
John	Somerset

LONDON, ITS SUBURBS, &C.

Jane	London
Lydia	Parish
Isaac	Place
Julia	Strand
Emma	Cornhill
Emma	Whitehall
Frederick	Holborn
William	Ludgate
Martha	Newington
William	Aldgate
Samuel	Paddington
Eleanor	Kennington
James	Brixton
Jane	Pancras
Elizabeth	Stepney
Thomas	Hackney
Philip	Peckham
Justina	Clapham
Henry	Lambeth
John	Battersea
James	Fulham
Hudson	Shadwell
Frederick	Kensington
Emma	Knightsbridge
Job	Stockwell
Penelope	Holloway
Sarah	Poplar
James	Hampstead
Charlotte	Haggerstone
Elias	Blackwall
Jesse	Deptford
Mary	Erith
Joseph	Kilburn
Maria	Harrow
Sarah	Norwood
Albert	Sydenham
Lodge	Richmond
Marian	Kew
Eleanor	Hornsey
Thomas	Hounslow
Anne	Kingsland

finis